www.mhhe.com/berkowitz

BUSINESS WEEK

Here you will find complete Business Week *articles which demonstrate how companies apply concepts introduced in the text.*

CURRENT EVENTS

Read about how companies apply marketing concepts. Get summarized news stories from The Wall Street Journal, Forbes, Business Week, *and many other publications. Stories are updated monthly and are categorized by subject.*

CHAPTER QUIZZES

Are you understanding the material? You'll know after taking a Practice Quiz. It either green-lights you to the next quiz or refers you to specific pages for further review.

INTERNET EXERCISES

Go online to learn how companies are using the Internet in their marketing efforts.

CAREER RESOURCES

Sooner or later students will be looking for a job. A host of Career Web sites will help them learn more about the job market and career profiles will introduce real marketing professionals.

DOWNLOADABLE SUPPLEMENTS

The key supplements are all here and can be downloaded with a click of the mouse.

The Irwin/McGraw-Hill Series in Marketing

MARKETING

EDITION 6th

Eric N. Berkowitz
University of Massachusetts

Roger A. Kerin
Southern Methodist University

Steven W. Hartley
University of Denver

William Rudelius
University of St. Thomas

Irwin McGraw-Hill

Boston   Burr Ridge, IL   Dubuque, IA   Madison, WI   New York   San Francisco   St. Louis
Bangkok   Bogotá   Caracas   Lisbon   London   Madrid
Mexico City   Milan   New Delhi   Seoul   Singapore   Sydney   Taipei   Toronto

Irwin/McGraw-Hill

A Division of The **McGraw·Hill** *Companies*

MARKETING

Copyright © 2000, 1997, 1994, 1992, 1989, 1986 by The McGraw-Hill Companies, Inc. All rights reserved. Printed in the United States of America. Except as permitted under the United States Copyright Act of 1976, no part of this publication may be reproduced or distributed in any form or by any means, or stored in a database or retrieval system, without the prior written permission of the publisher.

This book is printed on acid-free paper.

domestic   3 4 5 6 7 8 9 0 VNH/VNH 9 0 9 8 7 6 5 4 3 2 1 0
international   2 3 4 5 6 7 8 9 0 VNH/VNH 9 0 9 8 7 6 5 4 3 2 1 0

ISBN 0-07-365645-3

Vice president/Editor-in-chief: *Michael W. Junior*
Publisher: *David Kendric Brake*
Sponsoring editor: *Karen Westover Black*
Senior developmental editor: *Diane E. Beausoleil*
Senior marketing manager: *Colleen J. Suljic*
Senior project manager: *Susan Trentacosti*
Senior production supervisor: *Heather D. Burbridge*
Freelance design coordinator: *Laurie J. Entringer*
Senior photo research coordinator: *Keri Johnson*
Photo research: *Michael J. Hruby & Associates*
Supplement coordinator: *Marc Mattson*
Compositor: *Precision Graphics, Inc.*
Typeface: *10.5/12 Times Roman*
Printer: *Von Hoffmann Press, Inc.*

Library of Congress Cataloging-in-Publication Data
Marketing / Eric N. Berkowitz . . . [et al.]. -- 6th ed.
     p.   cm. -- (The Irwin/McGraw-Hill series in marketing)
   Includes bibliographical references and index.
   ISBN 0-07-365645-3
   1. Marketing.   I. Berkowitz, Eric N.   II. Series.
 HF5415.M29474   2000
 658.8--dc21   99-30269

INTERNATIONAL EDITION   ISBN 0-07-116830-3
Copyright © 2000. Exclusive rights by The McGraw-Hill Companies, Inc. for manufacture and export.
This book cannot be re-exported from the country to which it is consigned by McGraw-Hill.
The International Edition is not available in North America.

http://www.mhhe.com

PREFACE

The Millennium. While *Marketing,* Sixth Edition, appears at the dynamic dawn of the 21st century, this text also represents our long-standing commitment to a creative, active, and engaging approach to the study of marketing that has been the foundation of our success. The interest in our approach has grown dramatically through the first five editions, putting *Marketing* in the position of the market leader in the introductory textbook market. Hundreds of instructors have become regular users of our materials as students have expressed enthusiasm for the writing style and demonstrated positive learning outcomes. The success of the approach in the United States has led to adaptations in Canada and Poland, and likely future versions in Latin America and Russia. To continue the use and growth of *Marketing* and its features, we are pleased to offer the Sixth Edition as the most comprehensive, up-to-date, and innovative marketing textbook available to you today, and we appreciate the opportunity to explore the exciting field of marketing with you!

DISTINCTIVE FEATURES OF OUR APPROACH

The innovative pedagogical approach we developed through our own classroom experiences was introduced in the first edition in 1986. While each new edition has offered new content, cases, and examples to reflect changes in the marketing discipline and the marketplace, the distinctive features of our approach have remained as the foundation of the text and the supporting supplements. The features which you may recognize from previous editions and which are prominent in this edition include:

- An easy-to-read, high-involvement, interactive writing style that engages students through active learning techniques, timely and interesting examples, and challenging applications.
- A vivid and accurate description of businesses and marketing professionals—through cases, exercises, and testimonials—that allows students to "personalize" marketing and identify possible career interests and role models.
- The use of extended examples, involving people making marketing decisions, that students can easily relate to text concepts and that emphasize a decision-making orientation.
- Comprehensive and integrated coverage of traditional and contemporary scholarly concepts illustrated through relevant practitioner-related literature.
- A rigorous pedagogical framework based on the use of learning objectives, concept checks, key words, chapter summaries, and supportive student supplements such as the Student CD-ROM and the Study Guide.
- A package of support materials to accommodate a wide variety of instructor teaching styles and student learning styles.

Feedback from many of the 2,200 instructors and 400,000 students who have used our text and package in the past has encouraged us to build on these strengths as we developed the sixth edition of *Marketing.*

NEW FEATURES IN THIS EDITION

The new millennium promises exciting, challenging, and unpredictable changes for all of us. The beginning of the 21st century, however, may be particularly dramatic for marketing students, managers, and instructors. The emergence of digital technology and electronic commerce is literally changing everything. Traditional topics such as marketing research, advertising, and distribution are suddenly in the middle of this extraordinary transition. In addition, many new topics and concepts such as disintermediation and rich media are emerging as important additions to the field of marketing.

To build on the strengths of *Marketing* and to incorporate the most recent developments in the field, we expanded the product development process used so successfully in past editions. In addition to focus group discussions about the use of each component of the text and supplement package, and formal marketing research which solicited detailed evaluations from users and nonusers, we engaged a product development task force that continually provided qualitative feedback about content and design issues. The result has been the addition of many new topics and content areas, the revision and retention of important and enduring concepts, and the development of several new design and pedagogical features. Changes in the organization of this edition include:

- A new chapter entitled Interactive Marketing and Electronic Commerce has been added as Chapter 8 to provide coverage of the many new aspects of the digital revolution. The chapter discusses how the new marketspace creates customer value and provides a learning mechanism—the six Cs—to facilitate discussion of online consumer purchasing behavior.
- Relationship marketing and information technology topics previously covered in Chapter 10 (fifth edition) have been integrated into the relevant sections of the sixth edition. Sales forecasting topics are now covered in Chapter 9. Collecting and Using Marketing Information (previously Chapter 8) has become Chapter 9 and the five-step marketing research approach has been revised based on feedback from students and instructors. Market Segmentation, Targeting, and Positioning (previously Chapter 9) has become Chapter 10.
- Chapter 17 has been revised and updated to reflect the new concepts and techniques now prevalent in Supply Chain and Logistics Management.
- Direct Marketing has been added to Chapter 19, now titled Integrated Marketing Communications and Direct Marketing. This change is consistent with the growing interest in direct marketing and its importance as an element of the promotional mix.
- Chapter 20 now covers advertising, sales promotion, and public relations as the three elements of the promotion mix that focus primarily on mass communication.

The content of *Marketing* has also been revised to provide complete and current coverage of emerging issues, new marketing terms, trends, and changes in business practices. Examples include:

- brand personality
- banner ads
- bots
- commercial online services
- computer-mediated buying
- corporate Web sites
- disintermediation
- the Economic Espionage Act
- electronic commerce
- emotional intelligence
- extranets
- exurbs and penturbia
- interactive marketing
- intranets
- ISO 14000
- marketspace
- mass customization
- portals

- reverse logistics
- rich media
- supply chain management
- sustainable development

- vendor-managed inventory
- webcasting
- yield management pricing

In addition, new sections have been added to several chapters. For example, Chapter 1 now contains expanded material on building customer relationships, details of Rollerblade's strategy to reach narrower market segments, and the increasing importance of mass customization. The supply chain and logistics management chapter now includes a section relating marketing channels, logistics, and supply chain management. Chapter 16, Marketing Channels and Wholesaling, contains a new section on Internet marketing channels and Chapter 18, Retailing, now includes a section about online retailing.

Marketplace examples have been updated to reflect the most recent activities of large and small organizations, and to provide relevant, logical illustration of the concepts discussed in the text. Some of these include:

- Rollerblade's introduction of several new products—the Outback™ and the Coyote™—for the rough-road skater and terrain skater segments.
- Schwab's transition to an "e-corporation" and the success of its online stock brokerage service.
- 3M's creative adhesive pull-apart advertising campaign to overcome engineers' reluctance to adopt new technologies.
- The integrated marketing communications campaigns used by Taco Bell and the Olympics.
- P&G's efforts to improve Web advertising through its own advertising investments and by encouraging useful measurement procedures for the industry.
- Using nontraditional marketing research like "cool hunters" to identify key trends likely to sweep popular culture.

Finally, the package of support materials has been expanded to provide more flexibility for instructors as they "customize" their course for the particular need of their students. New features of the package include:

- A student CD-ROM that contains video clips, chapter quizzes, Internet links, and a marketing plan template.
- An expanded Instructor Survival Kit that contains new sample products and the Internet In-Class Activities.
- New videos and cases including America Online, Palm Computing, BMW, LearningByte, Airwalk, and Reebok. Updated videos include Rollerblade and Fallon McElligott.
- A completely redesigned text Web site (www.mhhe.com/berkowitz) and software (called PageOut) to allow instructors to easily design a course Web site.
- An optional reduced-rate, 16-week subscription to *Business Week.*

In addition, we have completely revised and updated the instructor's manual, test bank, instructor's CD-ROM, transparencies, PowerPoint™ slides, and the study guide.

NEW INTERNET PEDAGOGY

In addition to a new chapter (Chapter 8) on interactive marketing and electronic commerce, we have developed a three-level pedagogy for Internet coverage in *Marketing* and its supplements. The first level is designed to generate student interest and demonstrate a marketing application through short activities described in a Web Link (see the example on the next page) in each chapter.

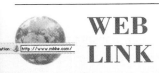

WEB LINK   How Typical Is Your Home Town?

Marketers collect and use environmental information to better understand consumers. One way to begin an environmental scan is to compare economic data about a particular segment of the population to what is "typical" or "average" for the entire population. Do you think your home town is typical? To find out visit CACI Marketing System's Web site at http://demographics.caci.com, select "free sample," and type in the zip code of your home town. CACI provides a comparison of your zip code's population with the averages for the nation.

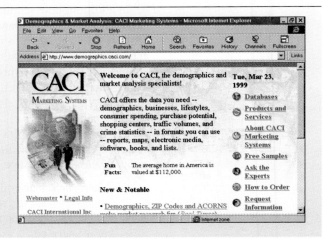

The second level is designed to challenge students with an issue or problem or question that can be answered using the Internet as a resource. These Internet Exercises (see example below) are located at the end of each chapter and are designed to allow instructors to evaluate students' performance if the exercises are used as assignments.

INTERNET EXERCISE

Most Web pages accept some form of advertising. If you were to advise your college or university to advertise on the Web, what three Web pages would you recommend? You can use the information at www.adhome.com to help make your recommendation.

1 What is the monthly rate for a full banner ad at each of the Web sites?
2 Describe the profile of the audience for each of the Web sites.
3 Calculate the CPM for each Web site.

WEB SITE	MONTHLY RATE	AUDIENCE PROFILE	CPM
1.			
2.			
3.			

The third level of our approach to integrate Internet-related marketing topics into a marketing course is through the design of Internet In-Class Activities. These activities are contained in the In-Class Activity Manual, which is part of the Instructor's Survival Kit. The Internet In-Class Activities can be used by instructors to encourage classroom discussions and student interaction. Examples, some tied to the text, include:

- Comparison Shopping for Personal Digital Assistants
- Testing Your Consultants's Aptitude: The Boston Consulting Group Case
- Checking Your Roots . . . If You Really Want to Know!

HELPFUL PEDAGOGICAL FEATURES

Several features facilitate student involvement in the study of marketing. Whenever possible, students are encouraged to take the role of a marketing decision maker or to question the reason for particular marketing actions. Initial inquiries are often posed to students in captions in the margins of the text. In addition, examples of contemporary people and organizations, and their marketing decisions, appear in the chapter opening vignettes, the Marketing NewsNet boxes, and the end-of-chapter cases.

The book alerts the reader to special topics with corresponding icons. These include: customer value, global topics, technology, cross-functional topics, and ethics and social responsibility issues.

Each chapter uses three reinforcement tools. Learning objectives are presented at the beginning of each chapter to provide readers with a general "map" of the material to follow. At the end of each major section of a chapter, Concept Checks pose two or three questions to test recall and understanding. Finally the Summary and Key Terms and Concepts at the end of each chapter provide further reinforcement of the chapter material.

We believe that the use of these unique learning aids lets students learn about, understand, and integrate the many marketing topics covered in our textbook, and provides an approach that increases the likelihood of an enjoyable and successful experience for students.

THE ORGANIZATION OF THE BOOK

The sixth edition of *Marketing* is divided into five parts. Part I, Initiating the Marketing Process, looks first at what marketing is and how it creates customer value and customer relationships (Chapter 1). Then Chapter 2 provides an overview of the strategic marketing process that occurs in an organization—which provides a framework for the text. Appendix A provides a sample marketing plan as a reference for students. Chapter 3 analyzes the five major environmental factors in our changing marketing environment, while Chapter 4 discusses the significance of ethics and social responsibility in marketing decisions.

Part II, Understanding Buyers and Markets, first describes, in Chapter 5, the nature and scope of world trade and the influence of cultural differences on global marketing practices. Next, Chapter 6 describes how individual consumers reach buying decisions. Finally, because of their important differences from individual consumers, industrial and organizational buyers and how they make purchase decisions are covered in Chapter 7.

In Part III, Targeting Marketing Opportunities, the growing importance of interactive marketing and electronic commerce is discussed in Chapter 8. This chapter emphasizes the key role of the Internet as a means of identifying, understanding, and communicating with target markets. The marketing research function is discussed in Chapter 9, and the process of segmentation and targeting markets and positioning products appears in Chapter 10.

Part IV, Satisfying Marketing Opportunities, covers the four Ps—the marketing mix elements. The product element is divided into the natural chronological sequence of first developing new products and services (Chapter 11) and then managing the existing products (Chapter 12) and services (Chapter 13). Pricing is covered in terms of underlying pricing analysis (Chapter 14), followed by actual price setting (Chapter 15), and Appendix B, Financial Aspects of Marketing. Three chapters address the place (distribution) aspects of marketing: Marketing Channels and Wholesaling (Chapter 16), Supply Chain and Logistics Management (Chapter 17), and Retailing (Chapter 18). Retailing is a separate chapter because of its importance and interest as a career for many of today's students. Promotion is also covered in three chapters. Chapter 19 discusses integrated marketing communications and direct marketing, topics that have grown in importance in the marketing discipline recently. The primary forms of mass market communication—advertising, sales promotion, and public relations—are covered in Chapter 20. Personal selling and sales management is covered in Chapter 21.

Part V, Managing the Marketing Process, expands on Chapter 2 to describe specific techniques and issues related to blending the four marketing mix elements to plan, implement, and control marketing programs (Chapter 22).

The book closes with several useful supplemental sections. Appendix C, Career Planning in Marketing, discusses marketing jobs and how to get them, and Appendix D, provides 22 Alternate Cases. In addition, a detailed glossary and three indexes (name, company/product, and subject) complete the book.

EXTENSIVE SUPPLEMENTAL RESOURCES

The variety of students, instructors, programs, institutions, and teaching environments who use our text necessitates our providing a comprehensive, integrated, and flexible package of innovative instructional supplements. We assure the quality of the supplements by being involved, as authors or supervisors, in the production of all of the supplements that now accompany our text. To ensure flexibility, we and our publisher have invested extraordinary amounts of time and financial resources to offer every possible instructional aid. These supplements, and several of their unique features, are described below.

Instructor's Manual   The Instructor's Manual includes lecture notes, discussions of the Marketing NewsNet boxes, the Web Link boxes, the Ethics and Social Responsibility Alerts, and the Internet Exercises, and answers to the Applying Marketing Concepts and Perspectives questions. Supplemental Lecture Notes are also provided. The sixth edition of the Instructor's Manual also includes teaching suggestions and detailed information about integrating the other supplements.

Transparency Masters   Available on our Web site for downloading and printing are over 100 masters. Please contact your Irwin/McGraw-Hill representative if you desire a printed copy.

Transparency Acetates   A set of 200 four-color overhead transparency acetates is available free to adopters. More than 50 percent of these have been developed from information outside the text. In addition, the acetates now include a greater ratio of print advertisements that demonstrate key marketing theories. Several of the ads correspond with the companies that are featured in the video cases, making it possible to teach a more integrated lecture. Each of the transparency acetates from outside of the text is accompanied by lecture notes to assist instructors in integrating the material into their lectures.

PowerPoint® Presentation Slides   New to this edition, this software includes a PowerPoint viewer and a set of over 500 PowerPoint slides, and was prepared by Dr. Joseph Cangelosi at the University of Central Arkansas. The slides include topics not covered in the acetate package and other key concepts covered in the text. Those instructors who have PowerPoint can customize and add to this valuable presentation tool.

Video Case Studies   A unique series of 22 contemporary marketing cases is available on videotape cassettes. Each video case corresponds with chapter specific topics and an end-of-chapter case in the text. Over 40 percent of the video cases have been updated or are new. The video cases feature a variety of organizations and provide balanced coverage of services consumer products, small businesses, Fortune 500 firms, and business-to-business examples. America Online, Palm Computing, BMW, Reebok, and Rollerblade are just a few of the exciting video cases that are available with the sixth edition.

Video Case and Appendix D Case Teaching Notes   This supplement includes teaching notes for the video cases and alternate cases.

Instructor's CD-ROM   Irwin/McGraw-Hill's new Instructor CD-ROM for Marketing will contain video clips, PowerPoint® slides, and acetates for the text. Great for enhancing class presentations, CD-ROM enables the instructor to show video segments as they pertain to lectures or access the software or electronic slides instantly. The CD-ROM will also include the print supplements and electronic supplements so that the instructor has access to all of the supplements on one disk.

Instructor's Survival Kit and In-Class Activities   Today's students are more likely to learn and be motivated by active, participative experiences than by classic classroom lecture and discussion. While our many other supplements like video cases and transparencies enhance classroom instruction, the Instructor's "Survival Kit" contains three specific elements of special value to today's instructors:

- In-class activities. What we term "in-class" activities have received such extremely positive feedback from our customers—both instructors and students— that we have expanded the number and variety included in the package. These in-class activities may relate to a specific video case or example from the text or may be totally new. For example, some popular activities from our past editions include the Mountain Dew versus Surge taste test, and the "Ethics Quiz." These not only elicit classroom discussion, but also have a learning value in helping students understand marketing.
- "Props" to help run the in-class activities. With the time pressures on today's instructors, our goal is to make their lives simpler. So included in the survival kit are the props to run the activities, such as brochures for BMW's Z3 Roadster, ads for CNS's Breathe Right® Nasal Strips, and samples of 3M's VHB™ tape.
- Sample products. *Marketing,* in both the text and supplements, utilizes examples of offerings from both large and small firms that will interest today's students. A number of these are included in the survival kit when they may be new or unusual to students, items such as Breathe Right® Nasal Strips. Also, when appropriate, sample ads are included among our transparencies.

Test Bank   Our test bank has been developed and class tested to provide an accurate and exhaustive source of test items for a wide variety of examination styles. It contains more than 3,000 questions, categorized by topic and level of learning (definitional, conceptual, or application). The test questions for the sixth edition are more application oriented and include questions for each end-of-chapter video case. A Test Item Table allows instructors to select questions from any section of a chapter at any of the three levels of learning. The Test Bank includes approximately 10 essay questions, and over 100 multiple-choice questions per chapter, making it one of the most comprehensive test packages on the market. The Test Bank also includes questions for Appendixes A, B, and D.

Computest   In addition to the printed format, an electronic version of the test bank is available free to adopters. The Computest program allows instructors to select any of the questions, make changes if desired, or add new questions—and quickly print out a finished set customized to the instructor's course. The program also allows instructors to conduct online testing.

Study Guide   Authored by William Carner of The University of Texas, the Study Guide enables the students to learn and apply marketing principles instead of simply memorizing facts for an examination. The Study Guide includes chapter outlines for student note-taking, sample tests, critical thinking questions, and flash cards. The new format is based on the results of student focus groups.

Marketing Planning Software   Revised for Windows®, the marketing plan software is designed to help students use the strategic marketing process introduced in Chapter 2 and Appendix A and discussed in detail in Chapter 22. The software provides a personal and computer-based tool for involving students in the planning process, and is available on the Student CD-ROM, Instructor's CD-ROM, and the *Marketing*, sixth edition, Web site.

Business Week Edition   For an additional $8.25, students will receive a 16-week subscription to *Business Week*. This is a great opportunity to bring real business news into your classroom all semester long.

Student CD-ROM   This exciting and free resource will encourage students to think critically and require students to be active learners. The Student CD-ROM will include the entire text for quick and easy reference, chapter quizzes with immediate feedback and the page where the answer can be found, video clips for each chapter which present examples of how real companies are applying marketing concepts and theory, Web links to the companies referenced in the text so the student can stay on top of current developments, a narrated walk-through of a real company marketing plan, and a narrated guide through creating a new marketing plan. Finally, it will include the concept checks from the text and the answers so the students can test their knowledge of key concepts, terms, and topics.

Marketing Web site   Visit our exciting new Web site at www.mhhe.com/berkowitz to find an array of features and resources for both instructors and students. The site includes helpful information about the sixth edition of *Marketing*, as well as a link to the Irwin/McGraw-Hill Marketplace, where students and instructors can obtain up-to-the-minute marketing news and information.

PageOut: The Course Web Site Development Center and PageOut Lite
This Web page generation software, free to adopters, is designed for professors just beginning to explore Web site options. In just a few minutes, even the most novice computer user can have a course Web site.

Simply type your material into the template provided and PageOut Lite instantly converts it to HTML—a universal Web language. Next, choose your favorite of three easy-to-navigate designs and your Web homepage is created; complete with online syllabus, lecture notes, and bookmarks. You can even include a separate instructor page and an assignment page.

PageOut offers enhanced point-and-click features including a Syllabus Page that applies real-world links to original text material, an automated grade book, and a discussion board where instructors and your students can exchange questions and post announcements.

Online Learning Center   McGraw-Hill content and the power of the Web combine to offer you Online Learning Centers—pedagogical features and supplements for McGraw-Hill books on the Internet. Students can simply point-and-click their way to key terms, learning objectives, chapter overviews, PowerPoint slides, exercises, and Web links. And professors profit from the instant access to lecture materials, Instructor's Manuals, test banks, PowerPoint slides, and answers to all exercises in one place.

McGraw-Hill Learning Architecture   This unique new Web-based learning system gives instructors ownership over online course administration, study aids and activities, and Internet links to featured companies in many of the McGraw-Hill texts. You can now place course materials online, facilitating the assignment of quizzes and homework—even the tracking of student progress—all from the comfort of your own computer. The system also works to break down traditional instructor/student communication barriers by providing students with an e-mail forum for course topics in addition to auto-graded tests and lecture slide reviews.

DEVELOPMENT OF THIS BOOK

To ensure continuous improvement of our product we have utilized an extensive review and development process for each of our past editions. Building on that history, the sixth edition developmental process included several phases of evaluation and a variety of stakeholder audiences (e.g., students, instructors, etc.). The first phase of the review process asked adopters to suggest improvements to the organization of the text and possible changes to the supplements. The second phase encompassed a more detailed review of each chapter, as the text was used by adopters in the classroom. We also surveyed students to find out what they liked about the book and what changes they would suggest. Finally a group of instructors who do not use the text gave us feedback on the fifth edition.

Reviewers who were vital in the changes that were made to this edition include:

Kerri Acheson
St. Cloud State University

Roy Adler
Pepperdine University

Thom J. Belich
Metropolitan State University

Kevin Bittle
Johnson & Wales University

William J. Carner
University of Texas, Austin

Kay Chomic
City University, Bellevue, WA

Clare Comm
University of Massachusetts, Lowell

Steven Engel
University of Colorado

Richard Hansen
Ferris State University

Robert Jones
California State University—Fullerton

Terrence Kroeten
Concordia College

Debra Laverie
Texas Tech

Patricia Manninen
Northshore Community College

Peter McClure
University of Massachusetts, Boston

Linda Morable
Richland College

William Motz
Lansing Community College

Vonda Powell
University of Virginia

Barbara Ribbens
University of Evansville

Larry Rottmeyer
Dallas Baptist University

Doris M. Shaw
Kent State University

James V. Spiers
Arizona State University

Scott Swan
College of William and Mary

Ruth Taylor
Southwest Texas State University

Blaise Waguespack, Jr.
Embry-Riddle Aeronautical University

Jerry W. Wilson
Georgia Southern University

PRODUCT DEVELOPMENT TEAM

A special acknowledgment is due to the following people who were members of our Product Development Team. This group of gifted instructors gave us input during every stage of development of the text and supplements package. Specifically, they critiqued the new design of the text, gave recommendations for the topic selection and editing of the video cases, and reviewed several supplements.

Nadia J. Abgrab
Johnson & Wales University

Kevin Bittle
Johnson & Wales University

William Carner
University of Texas, Austin

Eddie V. Easley
Wake Forest University

Jacqueline Karen
University of Illinois, Urbana-Champaign

Douglas Kornemann
Milwaukee Area Technical College

Priscilla LaBarbera
New York University

Mike Luchett
University of Central Florida

Debra Laverie
Texas Tech

Ronald Michaels
University of Central Florida

William G. Mitchell
University of Texas at San Antonio

Maria Sanella
Boston College

Charles Schewe
University of Massachusetts, Boston

Eric Shaw
Florida Atlantic University

Ruth Ann Smith
Virginia Polytechnic Institute and State University

James Spiers
Arizona State University

Ruth Taylor
Southwest Texas State University

Robert Williams
Northern Arizona University

ACKNOWLEDGMENTS

The preceding section demonstrates the amount of feedback and developmental input that went into this project, and we are deeply grateful to the numerous people who have shared their ideas with us. Reviewing a book or supplement takes an incredible amount of energy and attention, and we are glad so many of our colleagues took the time to do it. Their comments have inspired us to do our best.

Reviewers who contributed to the first five editions of this book include:

Linda Anglin
Mankato State University

William D. Ash
California State University, Long Beach

Patricia Baconride
Fort Hays State University

Siva Balasubramanian
University of Iowa

A. Diane Barlar
University of West Florida

James H. Barnes
University of Mississippi

Frederick J. Beier
University of Minnesota

Thomas M. Bertsch
James Madison University

Kevin W. Bittle
Johnson & Wales University

Nancy Bloom
Nassau Community College

William Brown
University of Nebraska, Omaha

William G. Browne
Oregon State University

Stephen Calcich
Norfolk State University

William Carner
University of Texas at Austin

Gerald O. Cavallo
Fairfield University

S. Tamer Cavusgil
Michigan State University

Sang Choe
University of Southern Indiana

Clark Compton
University of Missouri, St. Louis

Ken Crocker
Bowling Green State University

Joe Cronin
University of Kentucky

James Cross
University of Nevada, Las Vegas

Lowell E. Crow
Western Michigan University

John H. Cunningham
University of Oregon

Bill Curtis
University of Nebraska, Lincoln

Dan Darrow
Ferris State University

Martin Decatur
Suffolk County Community College

Francis DeFea
El Camino College

Linda M. Delene
Western Michigan University

Paul Dion
Bryant College

William B. Dodds
Fort Lewis College

James H. Donnelly
University of Kentucky

Roget W. Egerton
Southwestern Oklahoma State University

Barbara Evans
University of Melbourne (Australia)

Charles Ford
Arkansas State University

Donald Fuller
University of Central Florida

Marc Goldberg
Portland State University

Leslie A. Goldgehn
California State, Hayward

Kenneth Goodenday
University of Toledo

James Gould
Pace University—White Plains Campus

James L. Grimm
Illinois State University

Pola B. Gupta
University of Northern Iowa

Donald V. Harper
University of Minnesota

Robert C. Harris
University of Northern Colorado

James A. Henley, Jr.
University of Tennessee at Chattanooga

Richard M. Hill
University of Illinois

Al Holden
St. John's University

Kristine Hovsepian
Ashland University

Jarrett Hudnal
Stephen F. Austin State University

Mike Hyman
University of North Texas

Donald R. Jackson
Ferris State University

Kenneth Jameson
California State University, Dominguez Hills

James C. Johnson
St. Cloud State University

Mary Joyce
Bryant College

Herbert Katzenstein
St. John's University

Ram Kesaran
University of Detroit

Roy Klages
State University of New York at Albany

Terry Kroeten
North Dakota State University

Priscilla LaBarbera
New York University

Duncan G. LaBay
University of Massachusetts at Lowell

Richard Lapidus
University of Nevada–Las Vegas

Irene Lange
California State University, Fullerton

Ed Laube
Macomb Community College

Gary Law
Cuyahoga Community College

Wilton Lelund
Southwest Texas State University

Karen LeMasters
University of Pennsylvania

Richard C. Leventhal
Metropolital State College

Leonard Lindenmuth
State University of New York–Binghamton

Lynn Loudenback
New Mexico State University

Robert Luke
Southwest Missouri State University

Michael R. Luthy
Drake University

Richard J. Lutz
University of Florida

Marton L. Macchiete
Plymouth State University

Kenneth Maricle
Virginia Commonwealth University

Elena Martinez
University of Puerto Rico

James McAlexander
Iowa State University

Peter J. McClure
University of Massachusetts, Boston

Jim McHugh
St. Louis Community College at Forest Park

Gary F. McKinnon
Brigham Young University

Lee Meadow
Northern Illinois University

James Meszaros
County College of Morris

Ron Michaels
Indiana University

Stephen W. Miller
St. Louis University

Fred Morgan
University of Oklahoma

Donald F. Mulvihill
Virginia Commonwealth University

Janet Murray
Cleveland State University

Keith Murray
Bryant University

Joseph Myslivec
Central Michigan University

Donald G. Norris
Miami University (OH)

Carl Obermiller
University of Washington

Dave Olson
North Hennepin Community College

James Olver
College of William & Mary

Philip Parron
Northwestern College

Allan Palmer
University of North Carolina, Charlotte

Dennis Pappas
Columbus Technical Institute

Richard Penn
University of Northern Iowa

June E. Parr
Eastern Washington University

John Penrose
University of Texas, Austin

William Pertula
San Francisco State University

Michael Peters
Boston College

William S. Piper
The University of Southern Mississippi, Gulf Park

Gary Poorman
Normandale Community College

Joe Puzi
Florida Atlantic University

James P. Rakowski
Memphis State University

Heikki Rinne
Brigham Young University

Jean Romeo
Boston College

Robert W. Ruekert
University of Minnesota

Eberhard Seheuling
St. John's University

Starr F. Schlobohm
University of New Hampshire

Stan Scott
University of Alaska

Harold S. Sekiguchi
University of Nevada

Bob E. Smiley
Indiana State University

Allen Smith
Florida Atlantic University

Craig Stacey
Northeastern University

Miriam B. Stamps
University of South Florida

Robert Swerdlow
Lamar University

Vincent P. Taiani
Indiana University of Pennsylvania

Clint Tankersaley
Syracuse University

Andrew Thacker
California State Polytechnic University, Pomona

Fred Trawick
University of Alabama at Birmingham

Thomas L. Trittipo
Central State University, Oklahoma

Sue Umashankar
University of Arizona

Ottilia Voegtli
University of Arizona

Gerald Waddle
Clemson University

Randall E. Wade
Rogue Community College

Harlan Wallingford
Pace University

Robert S. Welsh
Central Michigan University

Ron Weston
Contra Costa College

Max White
Southwestern Oklahoma State University

James Wilkins
University of Southwestern Louisiana

Kaylene Williams
University of Delaware

Robert Witherspoon
Triton College

Van R. Wood
Texas Tech University

William R. Wynd
Eastern Washington University

Thanks are also due to David H. Gobeli of Oregon State University, Ruth Ann Smith of Virginia Polytechnic Institute, and James Cross of the University of Nevada–Las Vegas who assisted in the revision of Chapters 2, 8, and 17, respectively; Michael Blumfield for his assistance on Appendix A; Joann Peck for revising the Test Bank; Linda Rochford and Rajiv Vaidyanathan of the University of Minnesota–Duluth, Giana Eckhardt, Susan Rosen, and Mark Weber of the University of Minnesota, John Mullins and Christina L. Grippi of the University of Denver, and Jay Kraznow, Tom Davies, and Patrick Hetzel who wrote or contributed significantly to the cases; Michael J. Vessey who provided research assistance on the text and who coordinated our efforts on the In-Class Activities; Stanley V. Scott of Columbia College who coordinated the revision of the Instructor's Manual; and Rick Armstrong, Robert Vaaler, Paul Fagan, Bruce MacLean, and Nick Kaufman who produced our new videos.

Many businesspeople also provided great help in making available information that appears in the text and supplements—much of it for the first time in college materials. Thanks are due to Gary Null of Honeywell, Barbara Jo Davis of Ken Davis Products, L. David Ostlie of Energy Performance Systems, and Jane Westerlund of the Caplow Co. We also acknowledge the help of David Samuels and Nick Skally of Rollerblade, Randall F. Peters and Leah Peters of Paradise Kitchens, and James Watkins (formerly CEO), John McKeon, and Dr. Sarah Risch of Golden Valley Microwave Foods. Finally, we thank Dr. Daniel Cohen, Kirk Hodgden, and Gary Tschautscher of CNS (Breath Right®); Julie Thompson, Fred Senn, and Kathy Spraitz of Fallon McElligott; David Reynolds-Gooch and Todd DiMartini of 3M; Rajiv Tandon and Kay Christianson of Learning Byte International; and Larry Miller and Howard Singer of AT&T's a2b music.

Staff support from the University of Massachusetts, Southern Methodist University, the University of Denver, and the University of St. Thomas was essential. We gratefully acknowledge the help of Louise Holt, Lori Sterrett, and Lucy Toton for their many contributions.

Finally, we acknowledge the professional efforts of the Irwin/McGraw-Hill staff. Completion of our book and its many supplements required the attention and commitment of many editorial, production, marketing, and research personnel. Our Burr Ridge–based team included David Brake, Diane Beausoleil, Susan Trentacosti, Colleen Suljic, Laurie Entringer, Heather Burbridge, Keri Johnson, Marc Mattson, Greg Gulledge, Michael Hruby, David Anthony, Greg Bowman, Carol Preston, and many others! Handling the countless details of a text and teaching package sometimes causes patience to be challenged. We thank all these people for their efforts and—in the end—their good humor!

Eric N. Berkowitz
Roger A. Kerin
Steven W. Hartley
William Rudelius

BRIEF CONTENTS

CONTENTS

PART V

MARKETING

PART ONE

INITIATING THE MARKETING PROCESS

CHAPTER 1
Marketing: A Focus on Customer Relationships and Value

CHAPTER 2
Linking Marketing and Corporate Strategies
Appendix A: A Sample Marketing Plan

CHAPTER 3
The Changing Marketing Environment

CHAPTER 4
Ethics and Social Responsibility in Marketing

Creating customer value and developing customer relationships. This is the essence of the marketing process described in Part One. Chapter 1 introduces the marketing process by describing the actions of David Samuels as he and Rollerblade, Inc. expand the market for the product and industry created by the company barely a decade ago. Chapter 2 describes how organizations such as Ben & Jerry's utilize the strategic marketing process to serve their customers. Following Chapter 2 is a sample marketing plan (Appendix A) that illustrates the outcome of the strategic marketing process and provides a reference for students to study and use. In Chapter 3 the dimensions of the business environment and how it has and will change are presented. These changes are described in terms of social, economic, technological, competitive, and regulatory forces. Finally, Chapter 4 provides a framework for including ethical and social responsibility considerations in marketing decisions.

CHAPTER ONE

MARKETING: A FOCUS ON CUSTOMER RELATIONSHIPS AND VALUE

1

AFTER READING THIS CHAPTER YOU SHOULD BE ABLE TO:

● Define marketing and explain the importance of (1) discovering and (2) satisfying consumer needs and wants.

● Distinguish between marketing mix elements and environmental factors.

● Understand how organizations build strong customer relationships using current thinking about customer value and relationship marketing.

● Describe how today's market orientation era differs from prior eras oriented to production and selling.

● Understand the meaning of ethics and social responsibility and how they relate to the individual, organizations, and society.

● Know what is required for marketing to occur and how it creates customer value and utilities for consumers.

NATURE, OUTBACK, AND COYOTES! NATURAL SCIENCE 101?

Well, . . . not quite!

David Samuels and his colleagues have the classic marketing problem of any mind-bending company that has created an entire industry! What do they do for an encore? What do they do to innovate, to provide products that prospective buyers want . . . that build continuing, loyal customer relationships? A big part of the answer *is* nature, outback, and coyotes or—more properly—Nature™, Outback X™, and Coyote™.[1] But that puts us ahead of the Rollerblade® story.

The Three-Century Old Innovation　In the early 1700s a Dutch inventor trying to simulate ice skating in the summer created the first roller skates by attaching spools to his shoes. His in-line arrangement was the standard design until 1863 when the first skates with rollers set as two pairs appeared. This design became the standard, and in-line skates virtually disappeared from the market.

In 1980, two Minnesota hockey-playing brothers found an old pair of in-line skates while browsing through a sporting goods store. Working in their garage, they modified the design to add polyurethane wheels, a molded boot shell, and a toe brake. They sold their product, which they dubbed "Rollerblade skates," out of the back of their truck to hockey players and skiers as a means of staying in shape during the summer. In the mid-1980s an entrepreneur bought the company from the brothers and then hired marketing executive Mary Horwath to figure out how to market Rollerblade skates.

Understanding the Consumer　"When I came here," remembers Horwath, "I knew there had to be a change." By focusing only on serious athletes who used in-line skates to train for other sports, Rollerblade had developed an image as a training product. Conversations with in-line skaters, however, convinced Horwath that using Rollerblade skates:

- Was incredible fun.
- Was a great aerobic workout and made the skater stronger and healthier.
- Was quite different from traditional roller skating, which was practiced alone, mostly inside, and by young girls.
- Would have great appeal to people other than just off-season ice hockey skaters and skiers.

Horwath saw her task as changing the image in people's minds—or "repositioning"— Rollerblade skates to highlight the benefits people saw in in-line skating. Using what she called "guerrilla marketing," Horwath used her tiny $200,000 annual marketing budget to gain national exposure for Rollerblade skates using inexpensive, nontraditional promotional methods such as "demo vans" loaded with skates that people could try for free.

What a Difference a Decade Makes   Fast-forward from the late 1980s to the late 1990s. The marketing problems of David Samuels, senior director of Sports Innovation for Rollerblade, Inc are a far cry from those faced by Mary Horwath in the late 1980s. As shown in Figure 1–1, she and the company succeeded in popularizing

FIGURE 1–1
Number of in-line skaters in the United States. What led to this skyrocketing growth? For some answers, see the text.

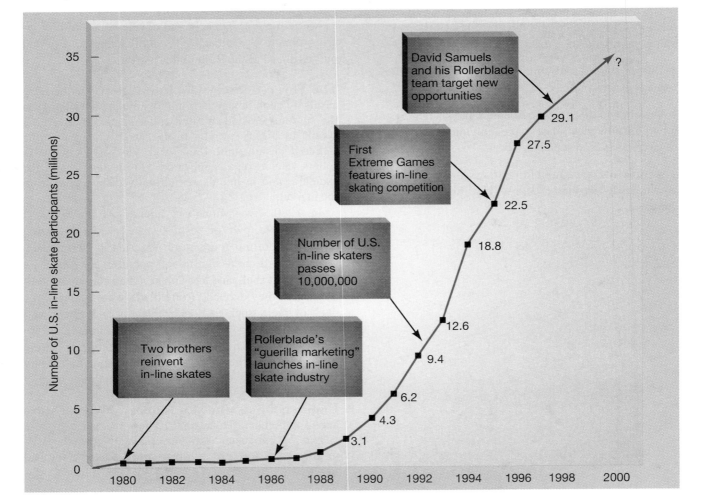

in-line skating—and actually succeeded in launching an entirely new industry, as evidenced by the 29.1 million U.S. in-line skaters in 1997 (the latest data available). One measure of the success of in-line skating is that it appeared in the first Extreme Games competition in 1995.

But Rollerblade, Inc.'s success in launching an industry carries its own dangers: competitors. There are more than 30 of them facing off with David Samuels and Rollerblade, Inc. as the twenty-first century starts. Rollerblade, Inc. has 35 percent of the annual industry sales, no other competitor having more than 10 percent. Thus, Samuel's goal is to develop new skating products for current and new segments of buyers, forging strong, loyal customer relationships in the process. This is where breakthrough innovations on Rollerblade, Inc.'s in-line skates such as Nature™, Outback X™, and Coyote™ come in. This situation presents a huge marketing lesson: Changing consumer tastes and changing competitive offerings require that organizations search continuoulsy for ways to provide genuine value to customers, or the organizations will die. Thus, the future of organizations such as Rollerblade, Inc. rely on the in-depth understanding of their customers' wants and needs by employees such as David Samuels.

Rollerblade Skates, Marketing, and You   What marketing strategy are David Samuels and his Rollerblade marketing team using to try to maintain the skyrocketing growth of in-line skating shown in Figure 1–1? By the time you reach the end of this chapter, you will know the answer to this question.

One key to how well Samuels succeeds lies in the subject of this book: marketing. In this chapter and in the rest of the book we'll introduce you to many of the people, organizations, ideas, activities, and jobs in marketing that have spawned the products and services that have been towering successes, shattering failures, or something in between.

Marketing affects all individuals, all organizations, all industries, and all countries. This text seeks not only to teach you marketing concepts, but also to demonstrate its many applications and how it affects our lives. This knowledge should make you a better consumer, help you in your career, and enable you to be a more informed citizen.

In this chapter and those that follow, you will feel the excitement of marketing. You will be introduced to the dynamic changes that will affect all of us in the future. You will also meet many men and women—like David Samuels and Mary Horwath—whose marketing creativity sometimes achieved brilliant, extraordinary results. And who knows? Somewhere in these pages you may find a career.

WHAT IS MARKETING?

Being a Marketing Expert: Good News–Bad News

In many respects you are a marketing expert already. But just to test your expertise, try the "marketing expert" questions in Figure 1–2. These questions—some of them easy, others mind boggling—show the diverse problems marketing executives grapple with every day. You'll find the answers in the next few pages.

The Good News: You Already Have Marketing Experience   You are somewhat of an expert because you do many marketing activities every day. You already know many marketing terms, concepts, and principles. For example, would you sell more Sony Walkmans at $500 or $50 each? The answer is $50, of course, so your experience in shopping for products—and maybe even selling them—already gives you great insights into the world of marketing. As a consumer, you've already been involved in thousands of marketing decisions—but mainly on the buying, not the marketing, side.

FIGURE 1–2
The see-if-you're-really-a-
marketing-expert test

ANSWER THE QUESTIONS BELOW. THE CORRECT ANSWERS ARE GIVEN LATER IN THE CHAPTER.

1. In a magazine article, a well-known actress said she often "rollerbladed" for fun and exercise. What was Rollerblade, Inc.'s reaction? (*a*) delighted, (*b*) upset, or (*c*) somewhere in between. Why?
2. What is "Polavision"? (*a*) a new breathable contact lens, (*b*) a TV network that competes with Home Box Office, (*c*) special bifocal glasses, (*d*) instant movies, or (*e*) a political newspaper.
3. Right after World War II, International Business Machines Corporation (IBM) commissioned a study to estimate the total market for electronic computers. The study's results were (*a*) less than 10, (*b*) 1,000, (*c*) 10,000, (*d*) 100,000, or (*e*) 1 million or more.
4. True or false: Building good customer relationships is a critical marketing issue today, as illustrated by having a loyal Kleenex customer spending more than $1,000 during his or her lifetime, in today's dollars.
5. True or false: "Grinding" done by city kids today uses a skateboard with bad wheels or bearings.

The Bad News: Surprises about the Obvious   Unfortunately, common sense doesn't always explain some marketing decisions and actions. An actress's saying in a national magazine that she "often rollerbladed" (question 1, Figure 1–2) sounds like great publicity, right? But Rollerblade, Inc. was upset. Legally, Rollerblade® is a trademark registered at the U.S. Patent and Trademark Office (USPTO)—as shown by the ®—and, as a brand name, should be used only to identify that firm's products and services. With letters to offenders and advertisements like the one below, Rollerblade, Inc. is trying to protect a precious asset: its brand identity. The ™ after the Coyote™ brand shows that Rollerblade claims trademark rights to the name at the USPTO but that it has not received official registration.[2]

Under American trademark law, if consumers generally start using a brand name as the generic term to describe the product rather than the source of the product, then the company loses its exclusive rights to the name. "Rollerblade" skates would become "rollerblade"— just another English word to describe all kinds of in-line skating. That fate has already befallen some famous American products such as linoleum, aspirin, cellophane, escalator, yo-yo, corn flakes, and trampoline.[3]

Rollerblade, Inc. ran this ad to communicate a specific message. It's also part of a "reminder" letter sent to people who *slip*. What is the message? For the answer and why it is important, see the text.

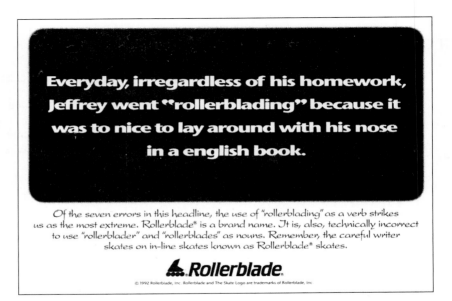

Everyday, irregardless of his homework, Jeffrey went "rollerblading" because it was to nice to lay around with his nose in a english book.

Of the seven errors in this headline, the use of "rollerblading" as a verb strikes us as the most extreme. Rollerblade® is a brand name. It is, also, technically incorrect to use "rollerblader" and "rollerblades" as nouns. Remember, the careful writer skates on in-line skates known as Rollerblade® skates.

Rollerblade.
© 1992 Rollerblade, Inc. Rollerblade and The Skate Logo are trademarks of Rollerblade, Inc.

Today American firms are spending millions of dollars in both advertising and court cases to protect their important brand names. Examples are Kimberly-Clark's Kleenex tissues and towels and 3M's Scotch tape. Coca-Cola takes dozens of restaurants to court every year for serving another cola drink when the patron asks for a Coca-Cola or even a Coke. Because legal and ethical issues such as the Rollerblade skates trademark problem are so central to many marketing decisions, they are addressed throughout the book.

The point here is that although your common sense usually helps you in analyzing marketing problems, sometimes it can mislead you. This book's in-depth study of marketing augments your common sense with an understanding of marketing concepts to help you assess and make marketing decisions more effectively.

Marketing: Using Exchanges to Satisfy Needs

The American Marketing Association, representing marketing professionals in the United States and Canada, states that "**marketing** is the process of planning and executing the conception, pricing, promotion, and distribution of ideas, goods, and services to create exchanges that satisfy individual and organizational objectives."[4] Many people incorrectly believe that marketing is the same thing as advertising or personal selling; this definition shows marketing to be a far broader activity. Further, this definition stresses the importance of beneficial exchanges that satisfy the objectives of both those who buy and those who sell ideas, goods, and services—whether they be individuals or organizations.

To serve both buyers and sellers, marketing seeks (1) to discover the needs and wants of prospective customers and (2) to satisfy them. These prospective customers include both individuals buying for themselves and their households and organizations that buy for their own use (such as manufacturers) or for resale (such as wholesalers and retailers). The key to achieving these two objectives is the idea of **exchange,** which is the trade of things of value between buyer and seller so that each is better off after the trade. This vital concept of exchange in marketing is covered below in more detail.

The Diverse Factors Influencing Marketing Activities

Although an organization's marketing activity focuses on assessing and satisfying consumer needs, countless other people, groups, and forces interact to shape the nature of its activities (Figure 1–3). Foremost is the organization itself, whose mission and objectives determine what business it is in and what goals it seeks. Within the organization, management is responsible for establishing these goals. The marketing department works closely with a network of other departments and employees to help provide the customer-satisfying products required for the organization to survive and prosper.[5]

Figure 1–3 also shows the key people, groups, and forces outside the organization that influence marketing activities. The marketing department is responsible for facilitating relationships, partnerships, and alliances with the organization's customers, its shareholders (or often representatives of groups served by a nonprofit organization), its suppliers, and other organizations. Environmental forces such as social, technological, economic, competitive, and regulatory factors also shape an organization's marketing activities. Finally, an organization's marketing decisions are affected by and, in turn, often have an important impact on society as a whole.

The organization must strike a continual balance among the sometimes differing interests of these individuals and groups. For example, it is not possible to simultaneously provide the lowest-priced and highest-quality products to customers and pay the highest prices to suppliers, highest wages to employees, and maximum dividends to shareholders.

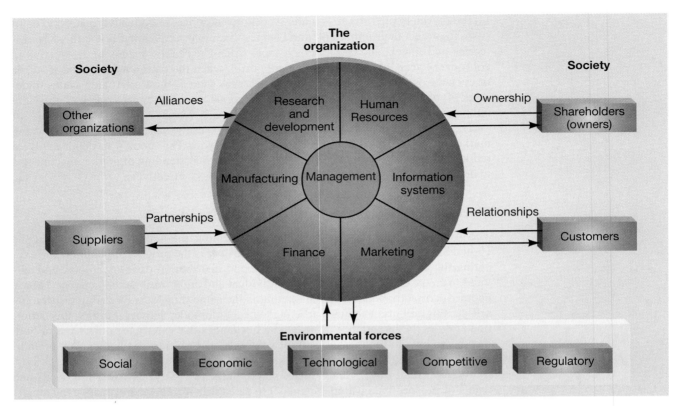

FIGURE 1–3
An organization's marketing department relates to many people, groups, and forces

Requirements for Marketing to Occur

For marketing to occur, at least four factors are required: (1) two or more parties (individuals or organizations) with unsatisfied needs, (2) a desire and ability on their part to be satisfied, (3) a way for the parties to communicate, and (4) something to exchange.

Two or More Parties with Unsatisfied Needs   Suppose you've developed an unmet need—a desire for information about how technology is reshaping the workplace and the personal lives of consumers—but you didn't yet know that *Time Digital* magazine existed. Also unknown to you was that several copies of *Time Digital* were sitting on the magazine rack at your nearest supermarket, waiting to be purchased. This is an example of two parties with unmet needs: you, with a need for technology-related information, and your supermarket owner, needing someone to buy a copy of *Time Digital*.

Desire and Ability to Satisfy These Needs   Both you and the supermarket owner want to satisfy these unmet needs. Furthermore, you have the money to buy the item and the time to get to the supermarket. The store's owner has not only the desire to sell *Time Digital* but also the ability to do so since it's stocked on the shelves.

A Way for the Parties to Communicate   The marketing transaction of buying a copy of *Time Digital* will never occur unless you know the product exists and its location. Similarly, the store owner won't stock the magazine unless there's a market of potential consumers near the supermarket who are likely to buy. When you receive a free sample in the mail or see the magazine on display at the checkout lane, this communications barrier between you (the buyer) and your supermarket (the seller) is overcome.

Something to Exchange   Marketing occurs when the transaction takes place and both the buyer and seller exchange something of value. In this case, you exchange your money for the supermarket's *Time Digital*. Both of you have gained something and also given up something, but you are both better off because you have each satisfied your unmet needs. You have the opportunity to read *Time Digital,* but you gave up some money; the store gave up the *Time Digital* but received money, which enables it to remain in business. This exchange process and, of course, the ethical and legal foundations of exchange are central to marketing.[6]

CONCEPT CHECK

1. What is marketing?

2. Marketing focuses on _____ and _____ consumer needs.

3. What four factors are needed for marketing to occur?

HOW MARKETING DISCOVERS AND SATISFIES CONSUMER NEEDS

The importance of discovering and satisfying consumer needs is so critical to understanding marketing that we look at each of these two steps in detail next.

Discovering Consumer Needs

The first objective in marketing is discovering the needs of prospective consumers. Sound simple? Well, it's not. In the abstract, discovering needs looks easy, but when you get down to the specifics of marketing, problems crop up.

New Coke was not a successful new product.

Some Product Disasters   With much fanfare, a decade ago, Coca-Cola replaced its 98-year-old Coke with a better-tasting cola called New Coke. Polaroid, flushed with the success of its instant still-photography business, introduced Polavision (question 2, Figure 1–2) as the first instant home movie camera. While Coca-Cola reintroduced its original formula only 79 days after New Coke's launch, Polaroid withdrew its consumer product and tried to redirect it to industrial application. Both firms lost millions in their failed attempts to introduce new products.

These are two of the best-known product disasters in recent U.S. history, but thousands of lesser-known products fail in the marketplace every year. One major reason is that, in each case, the firm miscalculated consumers' wants and needs for these products. In the case of New Coke, Coca-Cola provoked a nationwide uproar from old formula loyalists by failing to understand their bond with the existing product. Polaroid did not anticipate that consumers would prefer the convenience of videotape technology over Polavision.

The solution to preventing such product failures seems embarrassingly obvious. First, find out what consumers need and want. Second, produce what they do need and want and don't produce what they don't need and want. This is much more difficult than it sounds.

It is frequently very difficult to get a precise reading on what consumers want and need when they are confronted with revolutionary ideas for new products. Right after World War II, IBM asked one of the most prestigious management consulting firms in the United States to estimate the total future market for all electronic computers for all business, scientific, engineering, and government uses (question 3, Figure 1–2). The answer was less than 10! Fortunately, key IBM executives disagreed, so IBM started building electronic computers anyway. Where would IBM be today if it had assumed the market estimate was correct? Most of the firms that bought computers five years after the market study had not actually recognized they were prospective buyers because they had no understanding of what computers could do for them—they didn't recognize their own need for faster information processing.

Consumer Needs and Consumer Wants   Should marketing try to satisfy consumer needs or consumer wants? The answer is both! Heated debates rage over this question, and a person's position in the debate usually depends on the definitions of needs and wants and the amount of freedom given to prospective customers to make their own buying decisions.

A *need* occurs when a person feels physiologically deprived of basic necessities such as food, clothing, and shelter. A *want* is a felt need that is shaped by a person's knowledge, culture, and personality. So if you feel hungry, you have developed a basic need and desire to eat something. Let's say you then want to eat an apple or a candy bar because, based on your past experience and personality, you know these will satisfy your hunger need. Effective marketing, in the form of creating an awareness of good products at convenient locations, can clearly shape a person's wants. Rollerblade in-line skates are an example.

At issue is whether marketing persuades prospective customers to buy the "wrong" things—say, a candy bar rather than an apple to satisfy hunger pangs. Certainly, marketing tries to influence what we buy. A question then arises—at what point do we want government and society to step in to protect consumers? Most consumers would say they want government to protect us from harmful drugs and unsafe cars but not from candy bars and soft drinks. The issue is not clear-cut, which is why legal and social issues are central to marketing. Because even psychologists and economists still debate the exact meanings of *need* and *want,* we shall avoid the semantic arguments and use the terms interchangeably in the rest of the book.

As shown in Figure 1–4, discovering needs involves looking carefully at prospective customers, whether they are children buying M&M's candy, college students buying Rollerblade in-line skates, or firms buying Xerox photocopying machines. A principal activity of a firm's marketing department is to carefully scrutinize its consumers to understand what they need, to study industry trends, to examine competitors' products, and to even analyze the needs of a customer's customer.

What a Market Is   Potential consumers make up a **market,** which is (1) people (2) with the desire and (3) with the ability to buy a specific product. All markets ultimately are people. Even when we say a firm bought a Xerox copier, we mean one or several people in the firm decided to buy it. People who are aware of their unmet needs may have the desire to buy the product, but that alone isn't sufficient. People must also have the ability to buy, such as the authority, time, and money. As we saw earlier in the definition of marketing, people may buy, or accept, more than just goods or services. For example, they may buy an idea that results in an action, such as having their blood pressure checked annually or turning down their thermostat to save energy.

FIGURE 1–4
Marketing's first task:
discovering consumer needs

Satisfying Consumer Needs

Marketing doesn't stop with the discovery of consumer needs. Because the organization obviously can't satisfy all consumer needs, it must concentrate its efforts on certain needs of a specific group of potential consumers. This is the **target market**—one or more specific groups of potential consumers toward which an organization directs its marketing program.

The Four Ps: Controllable Marketing Mix Factors   Having selected the target market consumers, the firm must take steps to satisfy their needs. Someone in the organization's marketing department, often the marketing manager, must take action and develop a complete marketing program to reach consumers by using a combination of four tools, often called the four Ps—a useful shorthand reference to them first published by Professor E. Jerome McCarthy:[7]

- *Product.* A good, service, or idea to satisfy the consumer's needs.
- *Price.* What is exchanged for the product.
- *Promotion.* A means of communication between the seller and buyer.
- *Place.* A means of getting the product into the consumer's hands.

We'll define each of the four Ps more carefully later in the book, but for now it's important to remember that they are the elements of the marketing mix, or simply the **marketing mix.** These are the marketing manager's controllable factors, the marketing actions of product, price, promotion, and place that he or she can take to solve a marketing problem. The marketing mix elements are called controllable factors because they are under the control of the marketing department in an organization.

The Uncontrollable, Environmental Factors   There are a host of factors largely beyond the control of the marketing department and its organization. These factors can be placed into five groups (as shown in Figure 1–3): social, technological, economic, competitive, and regulatory forces. Examples are what consumers themselves want and need, changing technology, the state of the economy in terms of whether it is expanding or contracting, actions that competitors take, and government restrictions. These are the **environmental factors** in a marketing decision, the uncontrollable factors involving social, economic, technological, competitive, and regulatory forces.

Wal-Mart and Lands' End provide customer value using two very different approaches. For their strategies, see the text.

Wal-Mart
www.wal-mart.com

Lands' End Direct Merchants
www.landsend.com

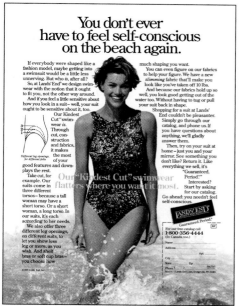

These five forces may serve as accelerators or brakes on marketing, sometimes expanding an organization's marketing opportunities and other times restricting them. These five environmental factors are covered in Chapter 3.

Traditionally, many marketing executives have treated these environmental factors as rigid, absolute constraints that are entirely outside their influence. However, recent studies and marketing successes have shown that a forward-looking, action-oriented firm can often affect some environmental factors. IBM's technical breakthroughs gave birth to the entire digital electronic computer industry, even though initial estimates of demand were low. Cable TV companies have redefined their competition to include telephone companies and vice versa. These technological, competitive, and regulatory factors might have forestalled productive marketing actions had they been seen as completely uncontrollable.

THE MARKETING PROGRAM: HOW CUSTOMER RELATIONSHIPS ARE BUILT

A firm's marketing program connects the firm to its customers. To clarify this link, we shall first discuss the critically important concepts of customer value, customer relationships, and relationship marketing and then illustrate these concepts with the marketing program at Rollerblade.

New Standards in Customer Value and Customer Relationships

Intense competition in today's fast-paced domestic and global markets has caused massive restructuring of many American industries and businesses. American managers are seeking ways to achieve success in this new, more intense level of global competition.[8]

This has prompted many successful U.S. firms to focus on "customer value," which has become a critical marketing issue for both sellers and buyers. That firms gain loyal customers by providing unique value is the essence of successful marketing. What is new, however, is a more careful attempt at understanding how a firm's customers perceive value. For our purposes, **customer value** is the unique combination of benefits received by targeted buyers that includes quality, price, convenience, on-time delivery, and both before-sale and after-sale service. The Marketing NewsNet explains how firms actually try to place a dollar value on a loyal, satisfied customer.[9]

Research suggests that firms cannot succeed by being all things to all people.[10] Instead, firms must find ways to build long-term customer relationships to provide unique value that they alone can deliver to targeted markets. Many successful firms have chosen to deliver outstanding customer value with one of three value strategies—best price, best product, or best service.

Companies such as Wal-Mart, Southwest Airlines, Price/Costco, and Dell Computer have all been successful offering consumers the best price. Other companies such as Nike, Starbucks, Microsoft, and Johnson & Johnson claim to provide the best products on the market. Finally, companies such as Lands' End and Home Depot deliver value by providing exceptional service.

But changing tastes can devastate once-successful marketing strategies. Levi Strauss has discovered today's teens aren't buying its Levi's jeans but prefer the trendier offerings of Old Navy, the Gap, Tommy Hilfiger, MUDD, and JNCO. So in 1999 it closed half of its 22 North American plants and laid off 5,900 employees.[11]

Relationship Marketing and the Marketing Program

Meaningful customer relationships are achieved by the firm's identifying creative ways to connect closely to its customers through specific marketing mix actions implemented in its marketing program.

MARKETING NEWSNET

Customer Relationships: Valuing the Retained Customer!

CUSTOMER VALUE

How can a firm put a financial dollar value on good customer relationships with a satisfied customer? The answer: Try to put a dollar value on what a satisfied, loyal, repeat customer spends on the firm's products during a year or a lifetime. Sophisticated firms have learned another marketing lesson: It's a lot cheaper and easier to keep existing customers than try to find new ones!

Frito-Lay, for example, estimates that the average loyal consumer in the southwestern United States eats 21 pounds of salty snack chips a year, about $52.50 annually on its snacks such as Lay's and Ruffles potato chips and Doritos and Tostitos tortilla chips. Exxon estimates that a loyal customer will spend $500 annually for its branded gasoline, not including candy, snacks, oil, or repair services purchased at its gasoline stations. Kimberly-Clark reports that loyal customers will buy 6.7 boxes of its Kleenex tissues each year and will spend more than $1,000 on facial tissue over their lifetime, in today's dollars (question 4, Figure 1–2).

These calculations have focused marketer attention on customer retention. Ford Motor Company has set a target of increasing customer retention—the percentage of Ford owners whose next car is also a Ford—from 60 percent to 80 percent. Why? Ford executives say that each additional percentage point is worth $100 million in profit—a staggering $2 billion per year in increased profits if Ford can reach its target!

Relationship Marketing: Easy to Understand   The hallmark of developing and maintaining effective customer relationships is today called **relationship marketing,** linking the organization to its individual customers, employees, suppliers, and other partners for their mutual long-term benefits. Note that these mutual long-term benefits between the organization and its customers require links to other vital stakeholders—including suppliers, employees, and "partners" such as wholesalers or retailers in a manufacturer's channel of distribution. In an ideal setting, relationship marketing involves a personal, ongoing relationship between the organization and an individual customer. This is the kind of relationship a rural nineteenth century family in the United States probably had with its general store.

Relationship Marketing: Difficult to Implement   Huge manufacturers find this rigorous standard of relationship marketing difficult to achieve. Today's information technology, along with cutting-edge manufacturing and marketing processes, have led to **mass customization,** tailoring goods or services to the tastes of individual customers in high volumes at a relatively low cost. Thus, you can place an Internet order for all the components of a Dell or Apple computer and have it delivered in four or five days—a configuration tailored to your unique wants. This combines the best features of both mass production and tailoring the firm's product to a single customer's unique wants—what some marketers call strategies to reach "segments of one."

But there are other forces working against these kinds of personal relationships between company and customer. Researchers Fournier, Dobscha, and Mick observe that "the number of one-on-one relationships that companies ask consumers to maintain is untenable,"[12] as evidenced by the dozens of credit card and financing offers a typical consumer gets in a year. A decade ago you might have gone to a small store to buy a book or music record, being helped in your buying decision by a salesclerk or the store owner. Today's marketplace, through Internet purchases, often involves bringing the seller and buyer more closely together through eliminating one or more resellers in the channel of distribution. The effect today is that you can use the Internet to buy books directly from amazon.com or download music to your computer from AT&T's a2b

(Case 22 in Appendix D). In the process, you may lose the personal, tender-loving-care connection that you once had with your own special book or music store, making it very difficult for stores such as these to really practice relationship marketing.

The Marketing Program

Effective relationship marketing strategies help marketing managers discover what prospective customers need. They must translate this information into some concepts for products the firm might develop (Figure 1–5). These concepts must then be converted into a tangible **marketing program**—a plan that integrates the marketing mix to provide a good, service, or idea to prospective buyers. These prospects then react to the offering favorably (by buying) or unfavorably (by not buying), and the process is repeated. As shown in Figure 1–5, in an effective organization this process is continuous: Consumer needs trigger product concepts that are translated into actual products that stimulate further discovery of consumer needs.

A Marketing Program for Rollerblade

To see some specifics of an actual marketing programs, let's return to the earlier example of David Samuels, Rollerblade, Inc., and their in-line skates. Looking at the in-line skating horizon, David Samuels notes that Rollerblade's long-run strategy is to focus on three areas: (1) expand the market, (2) use the company's strengths in technology, and (3) "stay ahead of the trends." These three areas of focus are intertwined, but each deserves careful scrutiny.

Expanding the Market for Rollerblade Skates   In terms of expanding the market, Samuels comments, "Our challenges are to find new venues, new reasons for people to skate." The foundation on which to build marketing programs reaching these new settings rests on two key elements:

- Finding the right benefits—or competitive points of difference (discussed in detail in Chapter 11)—to stress in reaching potential buyers. Three key benefits and points of difference for customers underlie all of Rollerblade's marketing efforts: (1) fun, (2) fitness and health, and (3) excitement.
- Targeting key segments of prospective customers and satisfying them with the specific kinds of Rollerblade brands of skates that they want. In the 1980s this target was 18- to 35-year-old men and women who were active, health and sports conscious, and had money to spend on a new sport.

FIGURE 1–5
Marketing's second task: satisfying consumer needs

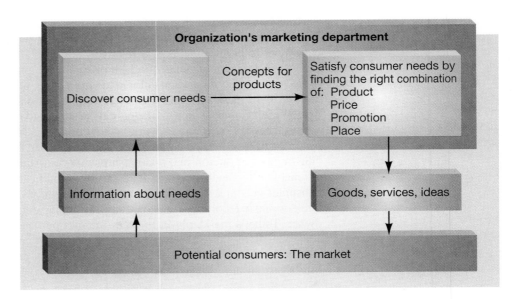

Today, while the fundamental customer benefits remain the same, David Samuels is now trying to reach narrower, more focused segments of customers than in the past. These now vary from children and recreation segments to fitness/performance, in-line hockey, and "aggressive" segments. Let's look at several of these market segments and the products that Samuels and Rollerblade have developed to provide key benefits to satisfy their needs:[13]

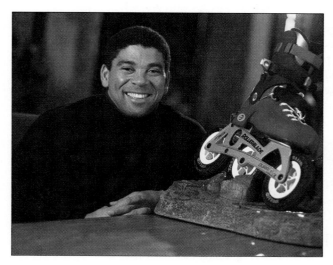

David Samuels and the Coyote™

- *Children segment.* Most parents can't afford to buy a new set of in-line skates each season as their children's feet grow. No problem now! With the Xten-plus™ line, the skate "grows" in four extensions to provide a skate for four sizes of a child's feet.
- *Rough-road skater segment.* Do you skate on country or city roads with bumpy and cracked pavement? Yes? Then try the Outback X™ line, whose air-filled wheels and full-suspension frame can give you a smooth ride over rough roads.
- *Student/transportation segment.* Need an in-line skate to get you from the dorm to your second-hour Econ 101 class but need something to wear in the classroom? The Nature™ line is for you because you can snap the frame/wheels off your skates and sit in class in the hiking boots that are part of the skate.
- *Terrain/"aggressive" segment.* Like to skate down snowless ski hills in the summer? The Coyote™ fills the bill. Its six-inch, pneumatic tires provide a full inch of shock absorption plus good traction on slick surfaces—an in-line skate for aggressive, all-terrain skating.

Rollerblade has more than 20 lines of skates targeted to different market segments. As illustrated in Figure 1–6 for the Xten-plus™ and Outback X™ brands, most

| | **MARKETING PROGRAM ACTIVITY TO REACH** | | |
MARKETING MIX ELEMENT	**FAST-GROWING KIDS SEGMENT**	**"ROUGH-ROAD" SEGMENT**	**RATIONALE FOR MARKETING PROGRAM ACTIVITY**
Product	Offer the Xten-plus™, a skate for children that "extends" so that it changes four shoe sizes as the children grow	Offer the Outback X™, a skate with trapped air filled wheels and a full-suspension frame that cushions the ride on rough roads and cracked pavement	Use new-product research, the latest technology, and extensive testing to offer high-quality skates that satisfy the wants and needs of carefully identified customer segments
Price	Price at $99 a pair	Price at $199 a pair	Attempt to set prices that provide genuine value to the customer segment that is targeted
Promotion	Use demo vans and blade-mobiles to introduce children to in-line skating while working with Rollerblade dealers to place ads in local newspapers	Feature Rollerblade brand in ESPN in-line sports competitions and magazines such as *Shape, Fitness, Mademoiselle,* and *Inline* and local newspapers	Continue to increase awareness of in-line skating to those new to the sport while offering specific skate designs for more advanced segments wanting them
Place	Distribute the Xten-plus™ through sporting goods stores	Distribute the Outback X™ through specialty in-line sporting goods stores	Make it easy for buyers in the segment to buy at an outlet that is convenient and where they feel comfortable

FIGURE 1–6

Marketing programs for two of Rollerblade, Inc's. skates, targeted at two distinctly different customer segments: fast-growing kids and rough-road skaters

Rollerblade brands require a slightly different marketing program to reach their targeted segments of potential customers.

Exploiting Strengths in Technology   In 1995 Rollerblade, Inc. was sold to Nordica, an Italian ski company owned by the Benetton organization. This provided huge technology synergies for the two firms. Examples of exploiting tomorrow's technology—some with Nordica, some on Rollerblade's own—include:

- *TriForce™ Technology.* Using Nordica's experience in designing ski boots, Rollerblade used this technology in its skates to support key parts of the foot that generate skating power and then reduce the shock by redistributing the energy out through the toes and heel.
- *Active Brake Technology® (ABT®) system.* Until ABT® brakes arrived, in-line skaters had to lift the toe of their braking foot to force the heel brake onto the

Rollerblade's various product lines meet the needs of distinctly different segments of users.

WEB LINK

What Are the Latest Models in Rollerblade's Product Line?

As described in the text, a key focus of marketing efforts by David Samuels and Rollerblade is to introduce new products that meet the needs of increasingly diverse segments of in-line skaters, such as off-road, rough road, and transportation segments. These skates and accessories for these segments in-

corporate many of the more than 200 patents held by Rollerblade.

Visit Rollerblade's Web site at www.rollerblade.com. What are the differences in the key features of the Coyote™ and the Outback X™? What are the advantages of the ABT®2 braking system?

road. The ABT® system enables skater to simply slide their braking skate forward, causing the braking device to lower automatically—enabling them to keep all eight wheels on the ground and making skating safer.

Rollerblade's stress on the technology is reflected in the more than 200 patents it holds on key elements of its in-line skate line. The Web Link touches on Rollerblade's strategy on in-line skate products, its technology, and its line of accessories.

Staying Ahead of the Trends   Consumer tastes change—and quickly! This is the reason for David Samuel's concerns that Rollerblade stay ahead of trends in the marketplace. Some examples:

- *The Bladerunner® line.* In the 1980s Rollerblade brands of skates were sold through sporting goods stores. But as dozens of new competitors emerged. Rollerblade found that their skates were being sold through mass-merchant chains such as Target and Wal-Mart. Thus, Rollerblade introduced a line of lower-priced skates targeted at customers new to the sport—Bladerunner® by Rollerblade®—to be sold through these outlets.
- *Skates for women in-line skaters.* Half of all in-line skaters today are women. Because the physiology of a woman's foot is different than a man's, this difference can cause problems for women who are serious in-line skaters but skate in a shoe designed mainly for men. Solution: a line of women's in-line skates with a higher arch, narrower heel, and lower cuff to add comfort and protection.
- *Shoes for grinders.* Today's kids love to "grind"—to slide along handrails, curbs, and ledges. To reach this segment Samuels and Rollerblade designed and introduced the RB Grind Shoe™, which features a patented Twin Bar Roller System™ that makes grinding easier and longer lasting on curbs[14] (question 5, Figure 1–2).

Having created a new sport and an entirely new industry, Rollerblade's problems are over, right? Not at all! In a free-market system, success encourages competition and imitations. The Rollerblade case at the end of the chapter lets us look at the marketing strategies that David Samuels and Rollerblade are developing for the next century.

CONCEPT CHECK

1. An organization can't satisfy the needs of all consumers, so it must focus on one or more subgroups, which are its _____ .

2. What are the four marketing mix elements that make up the organization's marketing program?

3. What are uncontrollable variables?

HOW MARKETING BECAME SO IMPORTANT

Marketing is a driving force in the modern global economy. To understand why this is so and some related ethical aspects, let us look at (1) the evolution of the market orientation, (2) ethics and social responsibility in marketing, and (3) the breadth and depth of marketing activities.

Evolution of the Market Orientation

Many market-oriented manufacturing organizations have experienced four distinct stages in the life of their firms. We can use the Pillsbury Company as an example.

Production Era   Goods were scarce in the early years of the United States, so buyers were willing to accept virtually any goods that were produced and make do with them as best they could. French economist J. B. Say described the prevailing business theory of the period: "Production creates its own demand." The central notion was that products would sell themselves, so the major concern of business firms was production, not marketing.

In 1869, Charles Pillsbury founded his company on the basis of high-quality wheat and the accessibility of cheap water power. Robert Keith, a Pillsbury president, described his company at this stage: "We are professional flour millers. Blessed with a supply of the finest North American wheat, plenty of water power, and excellent milling machinery, we produce flour of the highest quality. Our basic function is to mill quality flour."[15] As shown in Figure 1–7, this production era generally continued in America through the 1920s.

Sales Era   About that time, many firms discovered that they could produce more goods than their regular buyers could consume. Competition became more significant, and the problems of reaching the market became more complex. The usual solution was to hire more salespeople to find new markets and consumers. Pillsbury's philosophy at this stage was summed up simply by Keith: "We must hire salespersons to sell it [the flour] just as we hire accountants to keep our books." The role of the Pillsbury salesforce, in simplified terms, was to find consumers for the goods that the firm found it could produce best, given its existing resources. This sales era continued into the 1950s for Pillsbury and into the 1960s for many other American firms (see Figure 1–7).

The Marketing Concept Era   In the 1960s, marketing became the motivating force in Pillsbury. Since then its policy can be stated as, "We are in the business of satisfying needs and wants of consumers." This is really a brief statement of what has

FIGURE 1–7
Four different orientations in the history of American business

come to be known as the **marketing concept;** the idea is that an organization should (1) strive to satisfy the needs of consumers (2) while also trying to achieve the organization's goals.

The statement of a firm's commitment to satisfying consumer wants and needs that probably launched the marketing concept appeared in a 1952 annual report of General Electric Company:[16] "The concept introduces . . . marketing . . . at the beginning rather than the end of the production cycle and integrates marketing into each phase of the business." This statement had two important points. First, it recognized that sales is just one element of marketing—that marketing includes a much broader range of activities. Second, it changed the point at which marketing ideas are fed into the production cycle from *after* an item is produced to *before* it is designed. Clearly the marketing concept is a focus on the consumer. Unfortunately, although many companies endorsed the marketing concept and defined the purpose of their business as the creation and retention of satisfied customers, implementation of the concept proved to be very difficult.

The Market Orientation Era   Many of the implementation issues are now being addressed by the total quality management movement. Firms such as DuPont, Marriott, and Toyota have achieved great success in the marketplace by putting huge effort into implementing the marketing concept, giving their firms what has been called a *market orientation.* An organization that has a **market orientation** focuses its efforts on (1) continuously collecting information about customers' needs and competitors' capabilities, (2) sharing this information across departments, and (3) using the information to create customer value.

A key aspect of this market orientation is that understanding consumers and competitors requires involvement of managers and employees throughout the firm. DuPont, for example, encourages employees to learn about customers' needs by participating in their "Adopt a Customer" program. Similarly, Marriott sends employees to stay in competitors' hotels and assess their facilities and services.[17]

Ethics and Social Responsibility: Balancing the Interests of Different Groups

As organizations have changed their orientation, society's expectations of marketers have also changed. Today, the standards of marketing practice have shifted from an emphasis on producers' interests to consumers' interests. In addition, organizations are increasingly encouraged to consider the social and environmental consequences of their actions. Because the interests of consumers, organizations, and society may differ, marketing managers must often find solutions acceptable to all parties. Guidelines for ethical and socially responsible behavior can help managers with the complex decisions involved in balancing consumer, organizational, and societal interests.

Ethics   Many marketing issues are not specifically addressed by existing laws and regulations. Should information about a firm's customers be sold to other organizations? Should advertising by professional service providers, such as accountants and attorneys, be restricted? Should consumers be responsible for assessing the safety of a product in "normal-use" situations? These, and many other questions, relate to **ethics,** which are the moral principles and values that govern the actions and decisions of an individual or group. Many companies, industries, and professional associations have developed codes of ethics to assist managers.

Social Responsibility   While many difficult ethical issues involve only the buyer and seller, others involve society as a whole. For example, suppose you change the oil in your old Chevy yourself and dump the used oil in a corner of your backyard. Is this just a transaction between you and the oil manufacturer? Not quite! The used oil may

ETHICS AND SOCIAL RESPONSIBILITY ALERT

ETHICS

Socially Responsible, Environmentally Friendly, *and* Competitive?

Many organizations today are trying to incorporate social responsibility into their marketing activities. One reason is that socially responsible decisions are likely to have a significant positive impact on society by improving the marketplace and the environment. Another reason is that most of the organization's constituents are taking interest in the issue. Investors now evaluate environmental track records, consumers express interest in environmental issues, and employees often encourage socially responsible behavior.

Unfortunately, many environmentally friendly products have been costly to produce, and consumers have not been willing to pay a premium for them. As a result, companies often question if they can be socially responsible and competitive.

In the past, policy makers protected the environment through strict environmental regulations even if it eroded competitiveness, while companies tried to appeal to consumers with the often intangible environmental benefits of their products. More recently, some experts have suggested that the solution is innovation that either offsets the cost of improving environmental impact or increases customer value. For example, Scotchbrite Never Rust Wool Soap Pads from 3M—which are made from recycled plastic bottles—are more expensive than competitors (S.O.S and Brillo) but superior because they don't rust or scratch.

Should companies consider social responsibility in their decision? Must environmentally friendly products be competitively priced?

contaminate the soil, so society will bear a portion of the cost of your behavior. This example illustrates the issue of **social responsibility,** the idea that organizations are part of a larger society and are accountable to society for their actions. The well-being of society at large should also be recognized in an organization's marketing decisions. In fact, some marketing experts stress the **societal marketing concept,** the view that an organization should discover and satisfy the needs of its consumers in a way that also provides for society's well-being. The difficulty firms face as they attempt to be socially responsible and competitive is discussed in the Ethics and Social Responsibility Alert.[18]

The societal marketing concept is directly related to **macromarketing,** which looks at the aggregate flow of a nation's goods and services to benefit society.[19] Macromarketing addresses broad issues such as whether marketing costs too much, whether advertising is wasteful, and what resource scarcities and pollution side effects result from the marketing system. While macromarketing issues are addressed briefly in this book, the book's main focus is on how an individual organization directs its marketing activities and allocates its resources to benefit its customers, or **micromarketing.** An overview of this approach appears in Chapter 2. Because of the importance of ethical and social responsibility issues in marketing today, they—and related legal and regulatory actions—are discussed throughout this book. In addition, Chapter 4 focuses specifically on issues of ethics and social responsibility.

The Breadth and Depth of Marketing

Marketing today affects every person and organization. To understand this, let's analyze (1) who markets, (2) what they market, (3) who buys and uses what is marketed, (4) who benefits from these marketing activities, and (5) how they benefit.

Who Markets?   Every organization markets! It's obvious that business firms involved in manufacturing (Tommy Hilfiger, Heinz, Nike), retailing (Abercrombie & Fitch, Toys "Я" Us, Nordstrom), and providing services (Merrill Lynch, America On-

Marketing is used by businesses and nonprofit organizations, causes, and places.

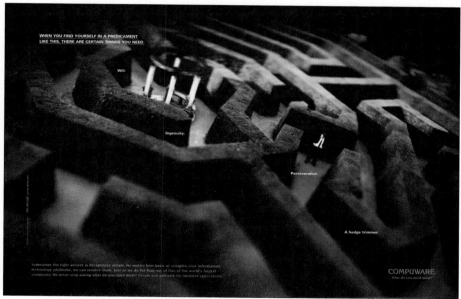

line, Chicago Cubs) market their offerings. Today many other types of marketing are also popular. Nonprofit organizations (San Francisco Opera, American Museum of Natural History, your local hospital) also engage in marketing.[20] Your college or university, for example, probably has a marketing program to attract students, faculty members, and donations. Places (cities, states, countries) often use marketing efforts to attract tourists, conventions, or businesses. Chile's "Make the Move" campaign is designed to attract businesses interested in a South American location. Organizations associated with special events or causes use marketing to inform and influence a target audience. These marketing activities range from announcements regarding the Olympics to government agencies discouraging smoking to private groups promoting a social cause such as literacy. Finally, individuals such as political candidates often use marketing to gain attention and preference.

What Is Marketed?   Goods, services, and ideas are marketed. Goods are physical objects, such as toothpaste, cameras, or computers, that satisfy consumer needs.

Services are intangible items such as airline trips, financial advice, or telephone calls. Ideas are intangibles such as thoughts about actions or causes. Some of these—such as lawn mowers, dry cleaning, and annual physical examinations—may be bought or accepted by individuals for their own use. Others, such as high-volume office copiers and vending machine repair services, are bought by organizations. Finally, the products marketed in today's global marketplace are increasingly likely to cross a nation's boundaries and involve exports, imports, multinational teams of employees, and international marketing (covered in Chapter 5).[21]

Who Buys and Uses What Is Marketed?   Both individuals and organizations buy and use goods and services that are marketed. **Ultimate consumers** are the people—whether 80 years or 8 months old—who use the goods and services purchased for a household. A household may consist of 1 person or 10. (The way one or more of the people in the household buys for it is the topic of consumer behavior in Chapter 6.) In contrast, **organizational buyers** are units such as manufacturers, retailers, or government agencies that buy goods and services for their own use or for resale. (Industrial and organizational buyer behavior is covered in Chapter 7.) Although the terms *consumers, buyers,* and *customers* are sometimes used for both ultimate consumers and organizations, there is no consistency on this. In this book you will be able to tell from the example whether the buyers are ultimate consumers, organizations, or both.

Who Benefits?   In our free-enterprise society there are three specific groups that benefit from effective marketing: consumers who buy, organizations that sell, and society as a whole. True competition between products and services in the marketplace ensures that we consumers can find value from the best products, the lowest prices, or exceptional service. Providing choices leads to the consumer satisfaction and quality of life that we have come to expect from our economic system.

Organizations that provide need-satisfying products with effective marketing programs—for example, McDonald's, IBM, Avon, and Merrill Lynch—have blossomed, but competition creates problems for ineffective competitors. For example, Wang Computers, DeLorean cars, and W. T. Grant retail stores were well-known names a while back but may now be unknown to you. Effective marketing actions result in rewards for organizations that serve consumers and in millions of marketing jobs such as those described in Appendix C.

Finally, effective marketing benefits society. It enhances competition, which, in turn, improves both the quality of products and services and lowers their prices. This makes the countries more competitive in world markets and provides jobs and a higher standard of living for their citizens.

How Do Consumers Benefit?   Marketing creates **utility,** the benefits or customer value received by users of the product. This utility is the result of the marketing exchange process. There are four different utilities: form, place, time, and possession. The production of the good or service constitutes *form utility. Place utility* means having the offering available where consumers need it, whereas *time utility* means having it available when needed. *Possession utility* is getting the product to consumers so they can use it.

Thus, marketing provides consumers with place, time, and possession utilities by making the good or service available at the right place and right time for the right consumer. Although form utility usually arises in manufacturing activity and could be seen as outside the scope of marketing, an organization's marketing activities influence the product features and packaging. Marketing creates its utilities by bridging space (place utility) and hours (time utility) to provide products (form utility) for consumers to own and use (possession utility).

CONCEPT CHECK   **1.** Like Pillsbury, many firms have gone through four distinct orientations for their business: starting with the _____ era and ending with today's _____ era.

2. What are the two key characteristics of the marketing concept?

3. In this book the term *product* refers to what three things?

SUMMARY

1 Combining personal experience with more formal marketing knowledge will enable us to identify and solve important marketing problems.

2 Marketing is the process of planning and executing the conception, pricing, promotion, and distribution of ideas, goods, and services to create exchanges that satisfy individual and organizational objectives. This definition relates to two primary goals of marketing: (*a*) assessing the needs of consumers and (*b*) satisfying them.

3 For marketing to occur, it is necessary to have (*a*) two or more parties with unmet needs, (*b*) a desire and ability to satisfy them, (*c*) communication between the parties, and (d) something to exchange.

4 Because an organization doesn't have the resources to satisfy the needs of all consumers, it selects a target market of potential customers—a subset of the entire market—on which to focus its marketing program.

5 Four elements in a marketing program designed to satisfy customer needs are product, price, promotion, and place. These elements are called the *marketing mix,* the *four Ps,* or

the *controllable variables* because they are under the general control of the marketing department.

6 Environmental factors, also called *uncontrollable variables,* are largely beyond the organization's control. These include social, technological, economic, competitive, and regulatory forces.

7 Building on customer value and relationship marketing concepts, successful firms develop mutually beneficial long-term relationships with their customers.

8 In marketing terms, U.S. business history is divided into four periods: the production era, the sales era, the marketing concept era, and the current market orientation era.

9 Marketing managers must balance consumer, organizational, and societal interests. This involves issues of ethics and social responsibility.

10 Both profit-making and nonprofit organizations perform marketing activities. They market products, services, and ideas that benefit consumers, organizations, and countries. Marketing creates utilities that give benefits, or customer value, to users.

KEY TERMS AND CONCEPTS

marketing p. 9
exchange p. 9
market p. 12
target market p. 13
marketing mix p. 13
environmental factors p. 14
customer value p. 15
relationship marketing p. 15
mass customization p. 15
marketing program p. 16

marketing concept p. 21
market orientation p. 21
ethics p. 21
social responsibility p. 22
societal marketing concept p. 22
macromarketing p. 22
micromarketing p. 22
ultimate consumers p. 24
organizational buyers p. 24
utility p. 24

 INTERNET EXERCISE

Welcome to the opportunity to buy CD-quality music over the Internet! AT&T's a2b music uses revolutionary technology to provide digital downloading of songs and albums from some of the music industry's top artists. Go to the a2b music Web site: www.a2bmusic.com.

1 What do you think of the selection of artists a2b music has?

2 What are the strengths and weaknesses of the online music industry? Is it the future of music retailing?

3 Would *you* buy a CD from your favorite artists over the Internet? Why or why not?

Case 22 in Appendix D describes a2b music's marketing strategy and asks you to download and assess the quality of its Internet music.

APPLYING MARKETING CONCEPTS AND PERSPECTIVES

1 What consumer wants (or benefits) are met by the following products or services? (*a*) Carnation Instant Breakfast, (*b*) Adidas running shoes, (*c*) Hertz Rent-A-Car, and (*d*) television home shopping programs.

2 Each of the four products or stores in question 1 has substitutes. Respective examples are (*a*) a ham and egg breakfast, (*b*) regular tennis shoes, (*c*) taking a bus, and (*d*) a department store. What consumer benefits might these substitutes have in each case that some consumers might value more highly than those products mentioned in question 1?

3 What are the characteristics (e.g., age, income, education) of the target market customers for the following products or services? (*a*) *National Geographic* magazine, (*b*) *Wired* magazine, (*c*) New York Giants football team, and (*d*) the U.S. Open tennis tournament.

4 A college in a metropolitan area wishes to increase its evening-school offerings of business-related courses such as marketing, accounting, finance, and management. Who are the target market customers (students) for these courses?

5 What actions involving the four marketing mix elements might be used to reach the target market in question 4?

6 What environmental factors (uncontrollable variables) must the college in question 4 consider in designing its marketing program?

7 Polaroid introduced instant still photography, which proved to be a tremendous success. Yet Polavision, its instant movie system, was a total disaster. (*a*) What benefits does each provide to users? (*b*) Which of these do you think contributed to Polavision's failure? (*c*) What research could have been undertaken that might have revealed Polavision's drawbacks?

8 David Samuels and Rollerblade, Inc. are now trying to grow in-line skating—and the company—globally, just as they succeeded in doing in the United States. What are the advantages and disadvantages of trying to reach new global markets?

9 Does a firm have the right to "create" wants and try to persuade consumers to buy goods and services they didn't know about earlier? What are examples of "good" and "bad" want creation? Who should decide what is good and bad?

 CASE 1-1   ROLLERBLADE, INC.

In the fiercely competitive in-line skate marketplace, what does the future hold for Rollerblade?

As David Samuels, senior director for Sports Innovation at Rollerblade, Inc., explains, innovative technology—in the form of new and better skates—will continue to be key for Rollerblade to stay ahead of the competition. Rollerblade must also find ways to expand the market for in-line skates. "Our challenge is to provide new venues, new reasons for people to skate. There's a lot of growth for us to catch up on in terms of household penetration," says Samuels.

THE SITUATION TODAY

When Rollerblade was founded, it was the only manufacturer of in-line skates in the world. Today the industry has more than 30 competitors, many that sell lower-priced skates than Rollerblade through mass-merchandising chains. Some of the large sporting goods manufacturers, like Nike, that have not traditionally sold in-line skates are now looking for ways to grow and are exploring the in-line skate market. Further, as shown earlier in Figure 1–1, Samuels is concerned that the exploding growth of the in-line skate market seen in the early 1990s is slowing.

THE MARKETING PROGRAM

Expanding the market and continuing to be the leader in product innovation gives Rollerblade a strategic advantage in the marketplace. Yet it is a solid and creative marketing mix that will enable Rollerblade to pass these advantages along to the customer.

The product is the most important "P" in Rollerblade's marketing mix. From introducing the premier braking technology on the market today—ABT brakes—to adding products for new market segments—RB Grind Shoes for the aggressive segment—Rollerblade is always trying to anticipate customer needs and wants. The Grind Shoe, for instance, is a regular athletic shoe with twin roller bars on the instep of the sole enabling the wearer to slide across railings, curbs, etc.—to "grind." Samuels notes, "Our aggressive segment was doing these tricks on rails with snowboards, skateboards, in-line skates, and bicycles, why not do it while you're walking to school? That's how we came up with the idea." Similarly, the Nature was introduced when Rollerblade discovered students needed something they could skate to class in, and then be able to wear into class. Rollerblade also came out with new product offerings for its kids (Dazzle and Zoom), women (Burner and Viablade, specially contoured to a woman's foot and leg structure), and fitness segments (eSeries) within the last year. Not to mention the far-out Coyote™ and Outback X for the off-road segment.

Rollerblade's promotional strategy continues to set it apart from the competitors, too. Its new print campaign features the ABT braking technology and the tagline "Exercise your soul." The Rollerblade Web site (www.rollerblade.com) is one of the most popular promotional tools with Rollerblade's loyal customers, as it provides chat rooms for aggressive skaters, racers, and fitness skaters.

Since Rollerblade does not have the resources of an industry giant like Nike, it finds ways to communicate with the customer that do not entail huge cash outlays. For example, Rollerblade provides information or product samples to media that, in turn, do in-line-skating features for articles or broadcast programs. It also develops promotional partnerships through sponsoring events and creating sweepstakes with other companies. Recently Rollerblade teamed up with Taco Bell, Curad, Wise Snacks, and Honeywell for joint advertising that benefits the partners but is less expensive for Rollerblade than purchasing nationwide television or radio ads by itself.

Rollerblade also promotes its brands by creating special promotions. Examples are Blade Cross™ competitions at ski hills during the summer to promote the Coyote line and the Blade Fitness™ "workout program on wheels" with a specific curriculum to be used for health club workouts. In addition, Rollerblade receives publicity from its charitable efforts and contributions to silent auctions.

Finally, Rollerblade sponsors a competitive team of aggressive skaters and racers that competes around the world and regularly wins such events as ESPN's X-Games, and has one of the premiere female in-line skate racers as its fitness spokesperson. It is creative and unorthodox approaches such as these that Samuels believes will keep Rollerblade ahead of the competition in the twenty-first century.

Rollerblade practices an across-the-board strategy when it comes to distribution and price. Samuels says, "Our distribution channels run the gamut. We are everywhere from the large mass market stores to specialty in-line dealers. Additionally, Rollerblade has chosen to hit every single price point possible. We have skates that are at the very high end, as well as skates as low as $79 under the Rollerblade brand. We also take a different brand name called Blade Runner and bring those products to the large mass markets of the world." Giving the lower-priced skates an alternate brand name allows Rollerblade to uphold its high-quality image in the marketplace while still providing an opportunity for beginners to test out the sport.

ISSUES FOR THE FUTURE

Some of the pressing issues in the future are global expansion, creating new segments of skaters, and expanding the product line. As Samuels explains, "Currently, the U.S. makes up over 50 percent of the marketplace worldwide. But Europe has been significant also. Germany is definitely one of the strongest countries for in-line skating." Other areas of growth include Australia and New Zealand, Japan, Mexico, and Korea. Rollerblade hopes to widen its global reach as the company continues to grow.

The youth segment should prove to be one of the most important segments in the future. "One of the biggest changes that's happened to us, and to the world really, is the power of youth. Kids who are anywhere from 10 to 12 years old on up into their twenties have been able to make a significant impact with so little money," explains Samuels. Rollerblade expects young people to continue to shape the recreational sports markets well into the future. Finally, Rollerblade has begun to offer products that are not in-line skates, such as the RB Grind Shoe and accessories like helmets, wrist, elbow, and knee pads, skate bags, and skate tools. Rollerblade will continue to introduce products that respond to consumer needs and desires—constantly working to improve skate comfort, durability, and technologies.

Questions

1   What trends in the environmental forces (social, economic, technological, competitive, and regulatory) identified in Figure 1–3 in the chapter (*a*) work for and (*b*) work against Rollerblade, Inc.'s potential growth in the twenty-first century?

2   What are the differences in marketing goals for Rollerblade, Inc. (*a*) in 1986 when Rollerblade was launched and (*b*) today?

3   How should David Samuels and Rollerblade, Inc. translate the broad goals identified in Question 2 into a specific marketing program for the Nature skate—to integrate product, price, promotion, and place actions? Refer to Figure 1–6 and the text.

4   What are the (*a*) advantages and (*b*) disadvantages of having Rollerblade, Inc. become part of the Benetton sport group? Refer to the text as well as the videocase.

5   In searching for global markets to enter, (*a*) what are some criteria that Rollerblade, Inc. should use to select countries to enter and (*b*) what three or four countries meet these criteria best and are the most likely candidates?

LINKING MARKETING AND CORPORATE STRATEGIES

2

AFTER READING THIS CHAPTER YOU SHOULD BE ABLE TO:

• Describe the three organizational levels of strategy and their components.

• Describe how the three organizational levels of strategy relate to each other and how they influence the marketing function.

• Describe the strategic marketing process and its three key phases: planning, implementation, and control.

• Understand how organizations search for new marketing opportunities and select target markets.

• Explain how the marketing mix elements are blended into a cohesive marketing program.

• Describe how marketing control compares actual results with planned objectives and acts on deviations from the plan.

DOZENS OF ICE CREAM FLAVORS AND 7.5 PERCENT TO PHILANTHROPY: WHO IS THIS, ANYWAY?

These two entrepreneurs aren't just your typical Tom, Dick, or Harry! Consider some facts about their company:

• It introduces in 1999 the first unbleached paperboard pint container for the ice cream flavor World's Best Vanilla.
• It contributes 7.5 percent of its pretax profits to philanthropic efforts.
• Its franchised PartnerShops are available to non-profit organizations to provide training and job opportunities for people such as at-risk youth.
• It buys all of its milk and cream from one dairy cooperative whose members guarantee a bovine-growth-hormone free supply.
• Its Waterbury Factory tour is Vermont's leading tourist attraction with more than 250,000 visits annually.

By now you know the company: Ben & Jerry's, or more formally, Ben & Jerry's Homemade, Inc.![1]

Ben & Jerry's is proof that the American Dream is still alive and well. Ben Cohen and Jerry Greenfield (the Ben & Jerry's guys at left and right on the opposite page) were grade school classmates on Long Island. In 1978 they headed north to Vermont and started an ice cream parlor in a renovated gas station.[2] Buoyed with enthusiasm, $12,000 they had borrowed and saved, and ideas from the $5 they spent on a Penn State correspondence course in ice cream making (with perfect scores on their open-book tests!) they were off and running.[3]

By the late 1990s, Ben & Jerry's Homemade had more than $170 million in sales—mainly from selling its incredibly rich ice cream. It had franchised more than 150 of its "Scoop Shop" retail outlets. The characteristics sought in ideal franchise sites and characteristics of ideal franchise owners are suggested in the Ben & Jerry's Web site given in the end-of-chapter Internet

Exercise. The company has international sales in Europe, the Mideast, and Asia. Not bad for two guys that started with a single ice cream parlor two decades ago.

In terms of its social mission, Ben & Jerry's in its own workplace has (1) instituted a companywide worklife survey, (2) committed to paying a "liveable wage," (3) improved its employee benefits, and (4) sought to purchase its supplies from socially responsible suppliers. Outside its internal operations, Ben & Jerry's is a leader in protecting the environment, peaceful conflict resolution, and corporate philanthropy.[4]

So where's the problem? In the late 1990s Ben & Jerry concluded the company's sales were flattening and it needed more professional managers to help stimulate growth—a potential challenge in light of American consumers' concerns about fat and cholesterol. At the same time the two founders want to preserve the company's legendary concern for the environment and social responsibility.

Chapter 2 describes how organizations set their overall direction and link these activities to marketing strategies—the very tasks Ben & Jerry now face. In essence, this chapter describes how organizations try to implement the marketing concept to provide genuine value to their customers.

LEVELS OF STRATEGY IN ORGANIZATIONS

This chapter first distinguishes among different kinds of organizations and the different levels within them. We then compare strategies at three different levels in an organization.

Today's Organizations: Kinds, Levels, and Building Blocks

Large organizations in existence today are often extremely complex. While this is not true for your corner deli or for some of the small businesses highlighted in our textbook cases, all of us deal in some way with huge organizations every day, so it is useful to understand (1) the two basic kinds of organizations, (2) the levels that exist in them, and (3) the four building blocks that are vital to an organization's success.

Kinds of Organizations   Today's organizations can be broadly divided into business firms and nonprofit organizations. A *business firm* is a privately owned organization that serves its customers in order to earn a profit. Business firms must earn profits to survive. **Profit** is the reward to a business firm for the risk it undertakes in offering a product for sale; the money left over after a firm's total expenses are subtracted from its total revenues. In contrast to business firms, a *nonprofit organization* is a nongovernmental organization that serves its customers but does not have profit as an organizational goal. For simplicity in the rest of the book, however, the terms *firm, company, corporation,* and *organization* are used to cover both business and nonprofit operations.

Levels in Organizations and How Marketing Links to Them   Whether explicit or implicit, organizations such as Ben & Jerry's have a strategic direction. Marketing not only helps shape this direction but must also help implement it. Figure 2–1 summarizes the focus of this direction at each of the three levels in an organization.

The **corporate level** is where top management directs overall strategy for the entire organization. Multimarket, multiproduct firms such as Hewlett-Packard or Johnson & Johnson really manage a portfolio of businesses, variously termed strategic business units (SBUs), strategic business segments, and product-market units (PMUs).[5]

The term **business unit** refers to an organization that markets a set of related products to a clearly defined group of customers. The **business unit level** is the level at which business unit managers set the direction for their products and markets. The strategic direction is more specific at the business level of an organization. For

FIGURE 2–1

The three levels of strategy in organizations

less complex firms with a single business focus, such as Ben & Jerry's, the corporate and business unit levels may merge.

Each business unit has marketing and other specialized activities (e.g., finance, research and development, or human resource management) at the **functional level,** which is where groups of specialists create value for the organization. The term *department* generally refers to these specialized functions, such as the marketing department or information systems department. At the functional level, the strategic direction becomes more specific and focused. So, just as there is a hierarchy of levels within organizations, there is also a hierarchy of strategic direction set by management at that level.

Marketing has a role at each of these organizational levels. In a larger corporation with multiple business units, the marketing department may be called upon to build a broad corporate image and to provide comparative analyses of market strengths and opportunities. At the business level, the marketing department provides leadership for the other functional activities when applying the marketing concept. But it also must serve as part of a team of functional specialists that develops and implements actual programs at the functional level, which is why cross-functional teams are so vital in today's competitive world. Armed with an understanding of the marketplace, the marketing department then identifies key target markets and develops specific programs to serve them.

Building Blocks for an Organization's Success   Management theorists have attempted to identify key factors that are essential to a firm's success. One such structure appears in Figure 2–2, which identifies four critical factors: (1) customer relationships, to ensure genuine value for customers; (2) innovation, to ensure customers' access to the latest technologies; (3) quality, to ensure an excellence and consistency in what is sold; and (4) efficiency, to lower costs and, hence, the price paid by customers. Note that improving each of these factors at a particular time might cause other factors to decline. Thus, it is a continuing challenge for an organization to strike

FIGURE 2–2
A combination of customer relationships, innovation, quality, and efficiency are the building blocks for an organization's success

the right balance among these four "building blocks" that are the foundation for an organization's success.[6]

Strategy at the Corporate Level

Complex organizations such as Coca-Cola, the railroads, and Sears, Roebuck & Co. must ask themselves not just what *business* they are in but what *portfolio of businesses* they are in. As shown in Figure 2–1, this portfolio of businesses is often coordinated with a corporate strategy consisting of a common corporate vision, common goals, and a common philosophy that unites them. We will define these terms carefully, but, in actual practice, the terms are not used rigorously and often overlap.

Developing the Corporate Vision   A **corporate vision** is a clear word picture of the organization's future, often with an inspirational theme. It sets the overall direction for the organization, describing what it strives to be—stretching the organization, but not beyond the imagination. Even though the terms are often used interchangeably, a vision is something to be pursued, while a mission (discussed later) is something to be accomplished. Ideally, this vision is a short sentence that can inspire employees, investors, and customers.

Coca-Cola's worldwide vision is simple but effective: "to put a Coke within arm's reach of every consumer in the world."[7] In fact, in 1996 Coca-Cola set a policy that was a "first" for a U.S. consumer products firm: It downgraded its U.S. business unit to make it just one of six international business units, thereby eliminating the very concept of "domestic" and "international" units. Participants at conferences in Bulgaria have this Coke-within-an-arm's-reach-of-every-consumer vision delivered in an unusual way: They typically drink *both* a cup of expresso coffee and a bottle of Coke at morning and afternoon breaks!

Railroads have not been so successful. They have let other forms of transportation take business away from them, possibly because their vision included only competitors and market share within the railroad business itself. The railroads have not actively sought to compete within the broader vision of transportation as a whole.[8] This narrow definition hurt railroads because they failed to design effective strategies to compete with a broad range of competitors, including airlines, trucks, bus lines, and cars. So U.S. railroads, like the U.S. auto firms described in the Marketing NewsNet box that follows, have had to reassess ways of delivering "quality" to their customers. Studies of organizations that have experienced decades of success show they translate their vision from words to pictures using a vivid description of what it will be like to achieve their audacious 10- to 30-year goals.[9]

Setting Corporate Goals   Broadly speaking, a **goal** is a targeted level of performance set in advance of work. Therefore, **corporate goals** provide strategic performance targets that the entire organization must reach to pursue its vision. Several different types of goals have been identified that business firms can pursue, each of which has some strengths and limitations:

- *Profit.* Classic economic theory assumes a firm seeks to maximize long-run profit, achieving as high a financial return on its investment as possible. One difficulty with this is what is meant by *long run.* A year? Five years? Twenty years?
- *Sales revenue.* If profits are acceptable, a firm may elect to maintain or increase its sales level even though profitability may not be maximized. Increased sales revenue may gain promotions for key executives.
- *Market share.* A firm may choose to maintain or increase its market share, sometimes at the expense of greater profits if industry status or prestige is at stake. **Market share** is the ratio of sales revenue of the firm to the total sales revenue of all firms in the industry, including the firm itself.
- *Unit sales.* Sales revenue may be deceiving because of the effects of inflation, so a firm may choose to maintain or increase the number of units it sells, such as cars, cases of breakfast cereal, or TV sets.
- *Quality.* A firm may emphasize the need to maintain or improve the quality of its products and services, especially if quality has been poor in the past. The Marketing NewsNet box on the next page describes W. Edwards Deming's "quality chain" that revolutionized global thinking about quality.[11]
- *Employee welfare.* A firm may recognize the critical importance of its employees by having an explicit goal stating its commitment to good employment opportunities and working conditions for them.

MARKETING NEWSNET

Adding Customer Value through the Quality Chain Reaction

When W. Edwards Deming went to Japan in 1950 to help rebuild postwar Japan, he shared a very profound model with Japanese industry. This model helped launch the quality revolution that has contributed to dramatic global change in the automobile industry. For example, the market share of U.S. automobile firms in the United States has dropped from more than 99 percent in 1950 to about 40 percent today. Although many other factors contributed to this decline, the U.S. automobile industry has had to improve its product and process quality to compete effectively.

The model is shown below. It has become a mantra for the quality movement. Assuming an organization has an otherwise effective strategy and management structure in place, the model shows the additional benefits from improving the quality of products, services, and processes. The first benefit is a decrease in costs as a direct result of less waste. A consequence of less waste is greater process productivity. This allows lower prices, which combines with the improved products and services to allow the organization to compete more effectively. The ultimate payoff is that the firm stays in business and provides jobs because it provides greater value to the customers.

The amount of benefit can be quantified by looking at the cost of poor quality. Experts claim that 10 percent to 20 percent of sales revenues are needed to cover the cost of poor quality in the form of production waste and rework, complaints and warranty costs, and defective products. Through well-designed marketing programs, marketers can help reduce the cost of poor quality and contribute directly to a firm's performance.

- *Social responsibility.* A firm may respond to advocates of corporate responsibility and seek to balance conflicting goals of consumers, employees, and stockholders to promote overall welfare of all these groups, even at the expense of profits. Ben & Jerry's is an example of such a firm.

Many private organizations that do not seek profits also exist in the United States. Examples are museums, symphony orchestras, operas, private hospitals, and research institutes. These organizations strive to provide goods or services to consumers with the greatest efficiency and the least cost. The nonprofit organization's survival depends on its meeting the needs of the consumers it serves. Although technically not falling under the definition of "nonprofit organization," government agencies also perform marketing activities in trying to achieve their goal of serving the public good.

Developing a Corporate Philosophy and Culture   An organization may also have a **corporate philosophy** that establishes the values and "rules of conduct" for running it.[12] Statements such as "respecting the dignity of all employees" or "being a good citizen of the local community" are examples of corporate philosophies. The Ethics and Social Responsibility Alert describes a critical global corporate citizenship issue. An organization's **corporate culture** refers to a system of shared attitudes and behaviors held by the employees that distinguish it from other organizations. Firms around the world are frantically trying to change their corporate cultures in response to increased global competition. Both Hewlett-Packard (HP) and Apple

ETHICS AND SOCIAL RESPONSIBILITY ALERT

The Global Dilemma: How to Achieve Sustainable Development

ETHICS

Corporate executives and world leaders are increasingly asked to address the issue of "sustainable development," a term that involves having each country find an ideal balance between meeting the needs of the present generation at the expense of future ones.[10] This often involves adding jobs today in highly polluting industries, thereby pushing cleanup actions into the future.

Eastern Europe and the nations of the former Soviet Union provide an example. Tragically, poisoned air and dead rivers are the legacies of seven decades of communist rule. With more than half of the households of many of these nations below the poverty level, should the immediate goal be a cleaner environment or more food, clothing, housing, and consumer goods? What should the heads of these governments do? What should Western firms trying to enter these new, growing markets do? What will be the impact on future generations?

Should the environment or economic growth come first? What are the societal trade-offs?

Computer are well-known for their corporate cultures that stimulate innovation and new-product development, but the cultures are implemented very differently. An engineering manager at HP achieved both success and job satisfaction in a culture that stressed collaboration, consensus seeking, and rock-solid engineering ability. Recruited to Apple two miles down the road, she encountered a culture that exalted heroes, slick user interfaces, and "evangelists" who could sell their products to the outside world. After 14 months, she returned to Hewlett-Packard whose culture was more in sync with her own.[13]

CONCEPT CHECK

1. What are the three levels in today's large organizations?
2. What is the difference between corporate vision and corporate goals?

Strategy at the Business Unit Level

The strategic direction for each business unit spells out how it will help the organization accomplish its vision. This business unit strategy has three major components: mission, business unit goals, and competencies. Each component is critical and must be understood if marketing activities are to be relevant.

Defining the Business Unit's Mission   This is probably the best-known mission statement anywhere:

> To explore strange new worlds, to seek out new life and new civilizations, to boldly go where no one has gone before.

This is the continuing mission for the Starship Enterprise, as Gene Roddenberry wrote it for the "Star Trek" adventure series. The "business unit goals" of the Starship Enterprise vary with each trip, but the competencies center on advanced technology, strong leadership, and a skilled crew. All these contribute to pursuing the vision of the Starship Enterprise's larger organization, the Starfleet and the Federation of Planets.

The **business mission** (or **business unit mission**) is a statement that specifies the markets and product lines in which a business will compete. It communicates—ideally in one sentence—the scope of a business unit. A mission statement can

How does this Sears ad reflect
its search for a new mission
and focus? The text describes
its recent success story.

Sears, Roebuck and Co.
www.sears.com

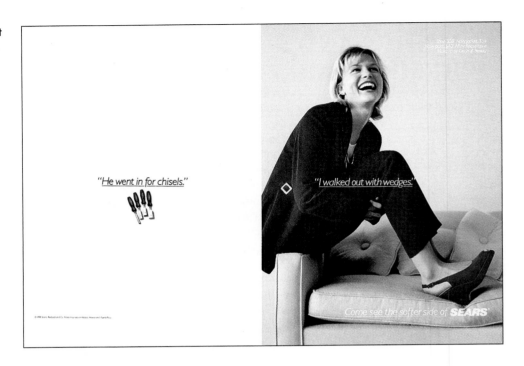

"He went in for chisels."

"I walked out with wedges."

Come see the softer side of **SEARS**

dramatically affect the range of a firm's marketing activities by narrowing or broadening the competitive playing field.[14]

The case of the Domestic Merchandising Group at Sears, Roebuck & Co. shows the tortuous path a business unit can follow as its searches for its mission in today's competitive environment. For Sears, narrower and clearer mission and business unit statements were necessary for the corporation to accomplish a very fundamental vision—to survive.

In the 1980s, Sears discovered that discounters and specialty stores such as Home Depot and Toys "Я" Us were winning over more and more of Sears's traditional middle-class customers. This left Sears scrambling to find a market niche. First, it tried promoting itself as a fashion-oriented department store for higher income customers. Failing at that, Sears then experimented with budget products and finally with "everyday low prices," without success. Besides offering insurance, real estate, finance, and services, it also continued its century-old catalog business.

In the process of running all these different business units, Sears executives discovered that the company had lost focus—it no longer had a clear vision of what businesses it was in, who its customers really were, and how it could provide value to them. So in a series of traumatic decisions in the early 1990s, Sears sold or spun off its real estate, insurance, and financial services businesses and completely shut down its $3-billion-a-year catalog operations—much to the delight of its Lands' End, JCPenney, Spiegel, and Fingerhut catalog competitors.

Today, the Domestic Merchandising Group at Sears believes it has rediscovered itself by redefining its mission and leveraging its reputation for trust, integrity, and fair value.[15] Its new mission, summarized in Figure 2–3, is "to be a compelling place to shop, work, and invest."[16] This is further refined by focusing on women and their families as its core customers, expanding its clothing lines, and increasing its emphasis on convenient home repair services while retaining its strengths in appliances and tools. By clearly defining the business mission, marketing activities can be more focused and effective.

Specifying the Business Unit's Goals   A **business unit goal** is a performance target the business unit seeks to reach in an effort to achieve its mission. Goals measure how well the mission is being accomplished. These goals must be balanced to

FIGURE 2–3
Mission and goals of Domestic Merchandising Group, Sears, Roebuck & Co.

BUSINESS UNIT MISSION

To be a compelling place to shop, work, and invest.

BUSINESS UNIT GOALS (STRATEGIC INITIATIVES)

- Focus on core businesses.
- Serve the target customer.
- Be market driven.
- Achieve consistent productivity improvement.
- Drive organizational transformation.

form a consistent, achievable pattern and should address fundamental issues such as customer satisfaction, innovation, internal processes, and, of course, financial performance.[17] In fact, the pattern of goals provides strategic direction since organizations often get what they measure.

Figure 2–3 shows that the business goals for Sears's Domestic Merchandising Group are in the form of five strategic initiatives to complement the group's mission of being a compelling place to shop, work, and invest. At the business unit level, many firms try, where possible, to construct goals that are more specific and measurable. These are often called **objectives,** which are specific, measurable performance targets and deadlines. Because there is no consistency in the use of the terms "goals" and "objectives," the terms are used interchangeably throughout this book.

The use of quantified performance measures and targets can be illustrated by an approach developed by the Boston Consulting Group (BCG), *business portfolio analysis,* that analyzes a firm's business units (called strategic business units, or SBUs, in the BCG analysis) as though they were a collection of separate investments.[18] While used at the business unit level here, this BCG analysis has also been applied at the product line or individual product or brand level. The popularity of this kind of portfolio analysis is shown by the fact that more than 75 percent of the largest U.S. firms have used it in some form. BCG, a nationally known management consulting firm, advises its clients to locate the position of each of its SBUs on a growth-share matrix (Figure 2–4). The vertical axis is the *market growth rate,* which is the annual rate of

FIGURE 2–4
Boston Consulting Group growth-share matrix for a strong, diversified firm showing some strategic plans

Boston Consulting Group
www.bcg.com

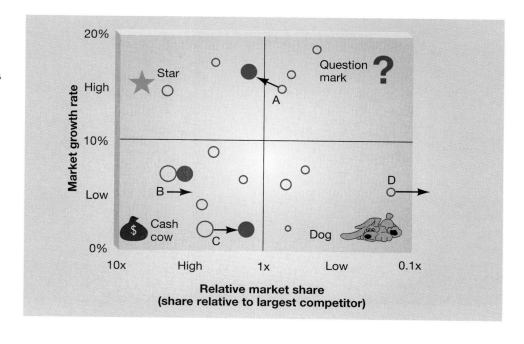

growth of the specific market or industry in which a given SBU is competing. This axis in the figure runs from 0 to 20 percent, although in practice it might run even higher. The axis has arbitrarily been divided at 10 percent into high-growth and low-growth areas.

The horizontal axis is the *relative market share*, defined as the sales of the SBU divided by the sales of the largest firm in the industry. A relative market share of 10× (at the left end of the scale) means that the SBU has 10 times the share of its largest competitor, whereas a share 0.1× (at the right end of the scale) means it has only 10 percent of the sales of its largest competitor. The scale is logarithmic and is arbitrarily divided into high and low relative market shares at a value of 1×.

BCG has given specific names and descriptions to the four resulting quadrants in its growth-share matrix based on the amount of cash they generate for or require from the firm:

- Cash cows (lower-left quadrant) are SBUs that typically generate large amounts of cash, far more than they can invest profitably in their own product line. They have a dominant share of a slow-growth market and provide cash to pay large amounts of company overhead and to invest in other SBUs.
- Stars (upper-left quadrant) are SBUs with a high share of high-growth markets that may not generate enough cash to support their own demanding needs for future growth. When their growth slows, they are likely to become cash cows.
- Question marks or problem children (upper-right quadrant) are SBUs with a low share of high-growth markets. They require large injections of cash just to maintain their market share, much less increase it. Their name implies management's dilemma for these SBUs: choosing the right ones to invest in and phasing out the rest.
- Dogs (lower-right quadrant) are SBUs with a low share of low-growth markets. Although they may generate enough cash to sustain themselves, they do not hold the promise of ever becoming real winners for the firm. Dropping SBUs in this quadrant from a business portfolio is generally advocated except when relationships with other SBUs, competitive considerations, or potential strategic alliances exist.[19]

Strategies emerging from a business portfolio analysis: Intel "builds" its chip business while Procter & Gamble "divests" its Duncan Hines cake mix line to Aurora Foods.

What firm that had won the prestigious Malcolm Baldrige Quality Award did this little-known Finnish Firm leap-frog? How? For the answers, and some key reasons, see the text.

Nokia
nokia.com

The 14 circles in Figure 2–4 show the current SBUs in a strong, diversified firm. The area of each circle is proportional to the corresponding SBU's annual sales revenue.

The portfolio in Figure 2–4 is a mixed one. On the favorable side, one half of its SBUs are large and have high market shares, but, unfortunately, the other half are small with low market shares. Because most firms have limited influence on the market growth rate (the factor shown on the vertical axis), their main alternative in a growth-share matrix framework is to try to change the relative market share (the factor on the horizontal axis).

To accomplish this, management makes conscious decisions on what role each SBU should have in the future and either injects or removes cash from it. Four alternative strategies are available for each SBU. The firm can invest more in the SBU to *build* its share (SBU A in Figure 2–4), as Intel has done with its computer chip product lines. Or it can invest just enough to *hold* the SBU's share at about its current level (SBU B in the figure). Or it can *harvest* the SBU (SBU C in the figure), trying to milk its short-term cash flow even though it may lose share and become a dog in the longer run. Finally, the firm can *divest* the SBU (SBU D) by phasing it out or actually selling it to gain cash, as Procter & Gamble did by selling its Duncan Hines cake mix line to Aurora Foods.

The primary strengths of business portfolio analysis include (1) forcing a firm to assess each of its SBUs in terms of its relative market share and industry market growth rate, which, in turn, (2) requires the firm to forecast which SBUs will be cash producers and cash users in the future. Weaknesses are that (1) it is often difficult to get the information needed to locate each SBU on the growth-share matrix, (2) there are other important factors missing from the analysis such as possible synergies among the SBUs when they use the same salesforce or research and development facilities, and (3) there are problems in motivating people in an SBU that has been labeled a dog or even a cash cow and is unlikely to get new resources from the firm to grow and provide opportunities for promotion.[20] In addition, planners have had difficulty incorporating competitive information into portfolio analysis,[21] and formal experiments show the technique may not provide as effective an allocation of resources as more traditional methods of financial analysis.[22]

Specifying the Business Unit's Competencies   Whereas the mission defines the scope of the business or business unit and the goals define its strategic performance dimensions, its **business unit competencies**—special capabilities resulting from its personnel, resources, or functional units—determine the means for achieving success.[23] These competencies should be distinctive enough to provide a **competitive advantage,** a unique strength relative to competitors, often based on quality, time, cost, or innovation.[24]

For example, if a firm such as 3M or Hewlett-Packard has a goal of generating a specific portion of its sales from new products, it must have a supporting competency in research and development. It must also have a supportive competency to manufacture and market its new products in a timely and effective way. Hewlett-Packard has a truly competitive advantage with its fast cycle time, which allows it to bring innovative products to markets in large volume rapidly.[25]

Another strategy is to develop a competency in total quality management (TQM). **Quality** here means those features and characteristics of a product that influence its ability to satisfy customer needs. Firms often try to improve quality or reduce new product cycles through **benchmarking**—discovering how others do something better than your own firm so you can imitate or leapfrog competition. Benchmarking often involves studying operations in completely different businesses. When General Mills sought ideas on how to reduce the time to convert its production lines from one cereal to another, it sent a team to observe the pit crews at the Indianapolis 500 race. The result: General Mills cut its plant change-over time by more than half.

If properly done, product quality can lead to a competitive advantage, or at least help a firm remain competitive with other firms that have focused on quality improvement.[26] In the case of Motorola, however, winning the Malcolm Baldrige Quality Award after years of quality improvement efforts did not protect it from a more responsive and innovative digital cellular phone by Nokia, a Finnish firm. While Motorola focused on incremental improvements to its analog cellular phone, Nokia developed superior digital products, matching and exceeding Motorola's quality, but with lower prices than Motorola. The result: Motorola's share of the U.S. cellular phone market in two years fell from 54 percent to 41 percent.[27]

Understanding and responding to new market opportunities with new products is the driving force for industry change and is one of marketing's more critical challenges. Thus, specific TQM practices of quality training, process improvement, and benchmarking may not produce competitive advantage by themselves. Rather, as described in the Marketing NewsNet box and earlier in Figure 2–2, quality is only one weapon in a firm's arsenal of strategy initiatives.

Strategy at the Functional Level

The functional departments, such as marketing, respond to the corporate and business strategic directions by creating functional goals, which are simply extensions of the corporate and business goals. For marketing, an example of a functional goal is "to create a new image that emphasizes the soft side of merchandising," as Sears has actually done. To accomplish the functional goals requires program plans that spell out very specific marketing objectives with associated actions, responsibilities, and dates.

MARKETING NEWSNET

Quality as One Element of Competitive Advantage

CUSTOMER VALUE

Some quality consultants see a quality strategy as the one solution for all organizations that want to become more competitive; some even claim that quality is just as important as financial results or that it will lead to improved financial performance. A focus on quality has helped make Ford Motor Company ("Quality is Job One") more profitable and has helped propel the Ford Taurus to a best seller. But a focus on quality has not had the same effect for General Motors' Saturn business unit. Why?

A study of 150 successful organizational turnarounds found that total quality management is not a cure-all and that typical TQM approaches have limited impact. It also noted that poor quality is behind other important causes of business downturn or failure, such as high costs and strategic errors. Indeed, as described earlier in Figure 2–2, high quality must be tied judiciously to customer relationships, innovation, and efficiency to achieve success.

Nonetheless, poor product and service quality can be competitive disadvantages, especially since customers today often demand quality on a par with competition. This is a lesson the American automobile industry has learned the hard way, and it explains why many organizations with past quality problems are inclined to pursue a quality strategy.

The experience with General Motors' Saturn business illustrates this. Saturn has focused on providing top value to the customers through low defects and excellent, low-pressure service. Unfortunately, Saturn has yet to make reasonable profits after several years of operation, at least in part because of a high cost structure and a product that offers few benefits beyond the competitors' offerings. Successful organizations must emphasize quality—but not as a way to solve more fundamental strategic problems.

An objective of the new Sears promotional program was to increase customer awareness about its new marketing efforts.

However, marketing does not operate by itself in an organization. Successful marketing efforts today are really cross-functional team efforts involving specialists from all the functional units to analyze, implement, and control programs to accomplish the corporate and business strategic directions. The strategic marketing process described in the next section provides the framework for making this happen.

CONCEPT CHECK

1. "Make Sears a compelling place to shop, work, and invest" is an example of what kind of business unit statement?

2. What is business portfolio analysis?

3. What is a competitive advantage, and why is it important?

THE STRATEGIC MARKETING PROCESS

All approaches to planning try to find answers to these key questions:

1. Where are we now?
2. Where do we want to go?
3. How do we allocate our resources to get to where we want to go?
4. How do we convert our plans into actions?
5. How do our results compare with our plans, and do deviations require new plans and actions?

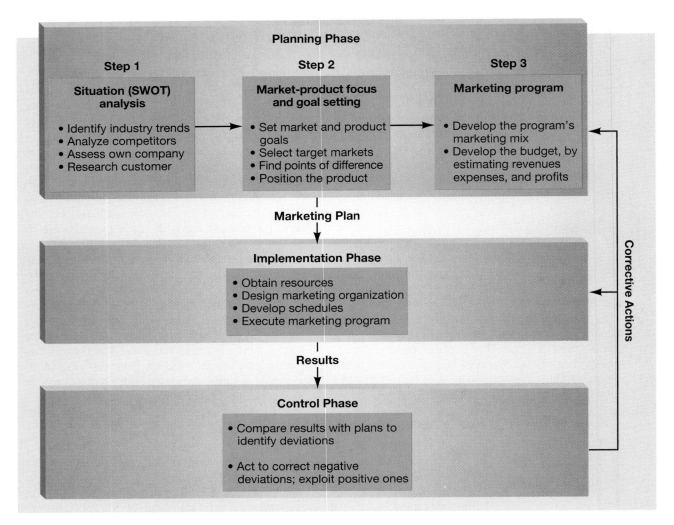

Planning Phase

Step 1	Step 2	Step 3
Situation (SWOT) analysis	**Market-product focus and goal setting**	**Marketing program**
• Identify industry trends • Analyze competitors • Assess own company • Research customer	• Set market and product goals • Select target markets • Find points of difference • Position the product	• Develop the program's marketing mix • Develop the budget, by estimating revenues expenses, and profits

Marketing Plan

Implementation Phase

• Obtain resources
• Design marketing organization
• Develop schedules
• Execute marketing program

Results

Control Phase

• Compare results with plans to identify deviations

• Act to correct negative deviations; exploit positive ones

Corrective Actions

FIGURE 2–5
The strategic marketing process

This same approach is used in the **strategic marketing process,** whereby an organization allocates its marketing mix resources to reach its target markets. This process is divided into three phases: planning, implementation, and control (Figure 2–5).

The strategic marketing process is so central to the activities of most organizations that they formalize it as a **marketing plan,** which is a road map for the marketing activities of an organization for a specified future period of time, such as one year or five years. Appendix A at the end of this chapter provides guidelines for writing a marketing plan and also presents a sample marketing plan for Paradise Kitchens,® Inc., a firm that produces and distributes a line of spicy chilies under the Howlin' Coyote® brand name. The sequence of activities that follow parallels the elements of the marketing plan that appears in Appendix A.

The following section gives an overview of the strategic marketing process that places Chapters 3 through 21 in perspective. In Chapter 22 we examine the strategic marketing process again in more depth.

Strategic Marketing Process: The Planning Phase

As shown in Figure 2–5, the planning phase of the strategic marketing process consists of the three steps shown at the top of the figure: (1) situation analysis, (2) market-product focus and goal setting, and (3) the marketing program. Let's use the recent marketing planning experiences of several companies to look at each of these steps.

A SWOT analysis can suggest ways for Ben & Jerry's to leverage these well-known products and flavors. To see if any of these flavors are buried in Ben & Jerry's "Flavor Graveyard," check their Web site in the Web Link box.

Ben & Jerry's, Inc.

www.benjerry.com

Step 1: Situation (SWOT) Analysis   The essence of the **situation analysis** is taking stock of where the firm or product has been recently, where it is now, and where it is headed in light of the organization's plans and the external factors and trends affecting it. The situation analysis box in Figure 2–5 is the first of the three steps in the planning phase.

An effective short-hand summary of the situation analysis is a **SWOT analysis**, an acronym describing an organization's appraisal of its internal **s**trengths and **w**eaknesses and its external **o**pportunities and **t**hreats. Both the situation and SWOT analyses can be done at the level of the entire organization, the business unit, the product line, or the specific product. As an analysis moves from the level of the entire organization to the specific product, it, of course, gets far more detailed. For small firms or those with basically a single product line, an analysis at the firm or product level is really the same thing.

Let's assume you are the consultant for Ben & Jerry's who provides the SWOT analysis shown in Figure 2–6. Note that your SWOT table has four cells formed by the

FIGURE 2–6
Ben & Jerry's: a "SWOT" to get it growing again

LOCATION OF FACTOR	TYPE OF FACTOR	
	FAVORABLE	**UNFAVORABLE**
Internal	**STRENGTHS** • Prestigious, well-known brand name among U.S. consumers • 40% share of the U.S. super premium ice cream market • Strong position among customers built on reputation for pure ingredients and social responsibility	**WEAKNESSES** • Danger that B&J's social responsibility actions may add costs, reduce focus on core business • Need for experienced managers to help growth • Flat sales and profits in recent years
External	**OPPORTUNITIES** • Growing demand for quality ice cream in overseas markets • Increasing U.S. demand for frozen yogurt and other low-fat desserts • Success of many U.S. firms in extending successful brand in one product category to others	**THREATS** • Consumer concern with fatty desserts; B&J's customers are the type who read new government-ordered nutritional labels • Competes with giant Pillsbury and its Haagen-Dazs brand • International downturns increase the risks for B&J in European and Asian markets

combination of internal versus external factors (the rows) and favorable versus unfavorable factors (the columns) that summarize Ben & Jerry's strengths, weaknesses, opportunities, and threats. A more in-depth SWOT analysis might use more detailed checklists of internal and external factors, as shown in the Paradise Kitchens SWOT in Appendix A. For simplicity, the Ben & Jerry's SWOT does not contain this level of detail.

A SWOT analysis helps a firm identify the strategy-related factors in these four cells that can have a major effect on the firm. The ultimate goal is to identify the *critical* factors affecting the firm and then build on vital strengths, correct glaring weaknesses, exploit significant opportunities, and avoid disaster-laden threats. That is a big order. This ultimate goal is not simply to develop the SWOT analysis but to translate the results of the analysis into specific actions to help the firm grow and succeed.

Although the SWOT analysis is a shorthand look at the situation analysis, it is based on an exhaustive study of the four areas shown in step 1 of the planning phase of the strategic marketing process in Figure 2–5 that are the foundation on which the firm builds its marketing program:

- Identifying trends in the firm's industry.
- Analyzing the firm's competitors.
- Assessing the firm itself.
- Researching the firm's present and prospective customers.

Examples of more in-depth analyses in these four areas appear in the marketing plan in Appendix A and the chapters in this textbook cited in that plan.

One way for firms to utilize the SWOT results is to assess market-product strategies. Four such strategies representing the four combinations of (1) current and new markets and (2) current and new products appear in Figure 2–7.

As Ben & Jerry attempt to increase the sales revenue of their firm, they must consider all four of the alternative market-product strategies shown in Figure 2–7. For example, they can try to use a strategy of *market penetration*—increasing sales of present products in their existing markets, in this case by increasing sales of Ben & Jerry's present ice cream products to U.S. consumers. There is no change in either the basic product line or the market served, but increased sales are possible through actions such as better advertising, more retail outlets, lower prices, or new flavors. As described in the Web Link box, Ben & Jerry's flavors that don't meet customer tastes wind up in its "Flavor Graveyard."

Market development, which here means selling existing Ben & Jerry's products to new markets, is a reasonable alternative. Asian and European consumers are good candidates as possible new markets. There is good news and bad news for this strategy: increasing incomes of households in those markets present great opportunities, but the Ben & Jerry's brand is relatively unknown.

An expansion strategy using *product development* involves selling a new product to existing markets. Figure 2–7 shows that the firm could try leveraging the Ben &

FIGURE 2–7
Four market-product strategies: alternative ways to expand sales revenues for Ben & Jerry's

MARKETS	PRODUCTS	
	CURRENT	**NEW**
Current	**MARKET PENETRATION** Selling more Ben & Jerry's super premium ice cream to Americans	**PRODUCT DEVELOPMENT** Selling a new product such as children's clothing under the Ben & Jerry's brand to Americans
New	**MARKET DEVELOPMENT** Selling Ben & Jerry's super premium ice cream in Asian markets for the first time	**DIVERSIFICATION** Selling a new product such as children's clothing in Asian markets for the first time

WEB LINK

Ben & Jerry's Flavors: From Chocolate Fudge Brownie and Phish Food to . . . The Flavor Graveyard!

Ben & Jerry's develops and introduces its flavors of ice cream, yogurts, and sherbets in response to both consumer . . . ahem! . . . tastes and important social causes it supports. For more than a decade, the brownies for the Ben & Jerry's very popular Chocolate Fudge Brownie ice cream and low-fat frozen yogurt have been supplied by Greystone Bakery in Yonkers, New York—a nonprofit organization that trains and employs homeless and low-income people for self-sufficiency. As for Phish Food, the Vermont-based rock band Phish do-

nates all the royalties it received from the sales of Phish Food ice cream to support efforts toward environmental preservation of Lake Champlain, on the border between New York and Vermont.

But not all flavors last. The ones that don't wind up in Ben & Jerry's "Flavor Graveyard." To see Ben & Jerry's current flavors and those in the Flavor Graveyard, visit www.euphoria.benjerry.com/graveyard/graveyard.html

Jerry's brand, as mentioned earlier, by selling its own Ben & Jerry's brand of children's clothing in the United States. This, of course, has dangers because Americans may not be able to see a clear connection between the company's expertise in ice cream and, say, children's clothing.

Diversification involves developing new products and selling them in new markets. This is a potentially high-risk strategy for Ben & Jerry's—and for most firms—because the company has neither previous production experience nor marketing experience on which to draw. For example, in trying to sell a Ben & Jerry's brand of children's clothing in Asia, the company has expertise neither in producing children's clothing nor in marketing to Asian consumers.

Which strategies will Ben and Jerry follow? Keep your eyes, ears, and taste buds working to discover their marketing answers in the twenty-first century.

Step 2: Market-Product Focus and Goal Setting   Finding a focus on what product offerings will be directed toward which customers (step 2 of the planning phase in Figure 2–5) is essential for developing an effective marketing program (step 3). This focus often comes from the firm's using **market segmentation,** which involves aggregating prospective buyers into groups, or segments, that (1) have common needs and (2) will respond similarly to a marketing action. Ideally a firm can use market segmentation to identify the segments on which it will focus its efforts—its target market segments—and develop one or more marketing programs to reach them.

Goal setting here involves setting measurable marketing objectives to be achieved—possibly for a specific market, a specific product or brand, or an entire marketing program. As mentioned earlier, there is a hierarchy of goals and objectives flowing from the corporate strategy set by top management on down to the levels of the marketing managers.

We can illustrate steps 2 and 3 in the planning phase of the strategic marketing process by using the Paradise Kitchens® marketing plan from Appendix A. This firm is trying to expand its line of Howlin' Coyote® spicy chilies from 3 to 20 U.S. metropolitan markets. Stated simply, the five-year marketing plan for Paradise Kitchens specifies these step 2 activities:

- *Set marketing and product goals.* As mentioned later in Chapter 11, the chances of new-product success are increased by specifying both market and product goals. Paradise Kitchens® will grow its present markets by expanding brands and flavors, add 17 new metropolitan markets in the next five years, enter the food-service market, and add new products.

A small business such as Paradise Kitchens has a carefully developed focus for its marketing program.

- *Select target markets.* Howlin' Coyote® chilies will be targeted at one- to three-person households with annual incomes above $30,000 in which both adults are likely to work outside the home—adventurous consumers wanting premium-quality Southwestern/Mexican food products.
- *Find points of difference.* **Points of difference** are those characteristics of a product that make it superior to competitive substitutes. (Chapter 11 points out that this is the single most important factor in the success or failure of a new product.) For Howlin' Coyote® chilies these are unique spicy taste; quality, convenience, and a range of flavors; and premium packaging.
- *Position the product.* Howlin' Coyote® chilies will be "positioned" in consumers' minds as "very high-quality, authentic Southwestern/Mexican tasting chilies that can be prepared easily and quickly."

Details in these four elements of step 2 provide a solid foundation to use in developing the marketing program—the next step in the planning phase of the strategic marketing process.

Step 3: Marketing Program   Activities in step 2 tell the marketing manager which customers to target and which customer needs the firm's product offerings can satisfy—the *who* and *what* aspects of the strategic marketing process. The *how* aspect—step 3 in the planning phase—involves developing the program's marketing mix and its budget.

Figure 2–8 shows components of each marketing mix element that are combined to provide a cohesive marketing program. For the five-year marketing plan of Paradise Kitchens, these marketing mix activities include the following:

- *Product strategy.* Offer a current line of five Howlin' Coyote® chilies with proprietary flavoring, high-quality ingredients without preservatives, and packaging with a Southwestern motif that communicates the brand's uniqueness.

FIGURE 2–8
Elements of the marketing mix that compose a cohesive marketing program

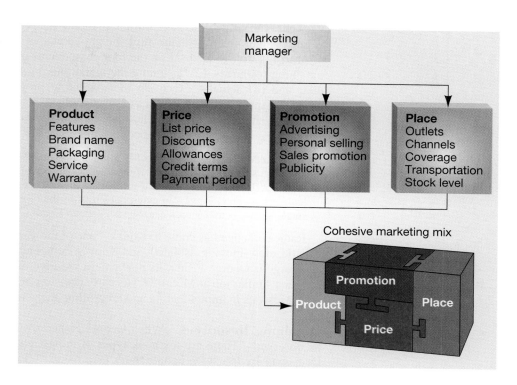

- *Price strategy.* Price Howlin' Coyote® chili at $2.99 for a 10- to 11.5-ounce package, comparable to other frozen offerings and higher than the canned and dried chili varieties.
- *Promotion strategy.* Feature in-store demonstrations to highlight the product's unique qualities, recipes using the brand to stimulate use, and various kinds of cents-off coupons to generate trial and repeat-purchase of the brand.
- *Place (distribution) strategy.* Use food distributors with current sales volumes, shifting to brokers as increased sales volumes justify them.

Putting this marketing program into effect requires that the firm commit time and money to it in the form of a budget. The budgeting process starts with a sales forecast based on estimates of units expected to be sold—probably by month, quarter, and year. Estimated expenses for the marketing mix activities comprising the marketing program are estimated and balanced against expected revenues to estimate the program's profitability. This budget is really the "sales" document presented to top management to gain approval for the budgeted resources to implement the marketing program.

CONCEPT CHECK

1. What is the difference between a strength and an opportunity in a SWOT analysis?

2. What is market segmentation?

3. If Ben & Jerry's attempts to enter Asian markets with its super premium ice cream, which market-product strategy would it be using?

Strategic Marketing Process: The Implementation Phase

As shown in Figure 2–5, the result of the tens or hundreds of hours spent in the planning phase of the strategic marketing process is the firm's marketing plan. Implementation, the second phase of the strategic marketing process, involves carrying out the marketing plan that emerges from the planning phase. If the firm cannot put the marketing plan into effect—in the implementation phase—the planning phase was a waste of time. Figure 2–5 also shows the four components of the implementation phase: (1) obtaining resources, (2) designing the marketing organization, (3) developing schedules, and (4) actually executing the marketing program designed in the planning phase. Eastman Kodak provides a case example.

Fortune magazine provides the stage on which we can study an American firm facing both the implementation and control phases of the strategic marketing process:

> The DRAMATIC restructuring of U.S. industry won't be over, as the saying goes, until the fat lady sings. Hundreds of companies have performed massive renovations—Ford, Chrysler, Texaco, Xerox, IBM. But now the diva enters. She is the last of the great, corpulent, 20th-century American enterprises to sing the rejuvenation aria. She walks to center stage. She turns to the audience. She is Eastman Kodak.[28]

Radical change has come to Kodak, "one of the most bureaucratic, wasteful, paternalistic, slow-moving, isolated, and beloved companies in America."[29] And the agent of change is George Fisher, its new chief executive officer, who had spectacular success in a similar job at Motorola. His early decisions are classic management and marketing lessons in implementing and controlling the activities of a corporate giant.

Obtaining Resources   When George Fisher arrived at Kodak in the mid 1990s, he observed, "There are textbook types of things that are wrong with this company. Decisions are too slow. People don't take risks."[30] So he pushed some revolutionary decisions that seemed obvious to him:

- Focus on Kodak's core business: imaging.
- Serve customer needs better, and stress quality.
- Shorten product-development cycles.
- Encourage a more dynamic, risk taking, fast-decision culture.

Fisher needed money to implement these ideas, however, so he obtained $8 billion by selling off divisions not related to Kodak's core imaging business.

Designing the Marketing Organization   A marketing program needs a marketing organization to implement it. This is especially true for firms such as Kodak facing constantly changing global markets. Figure 2–9 shows the organization chart of a typical manufacturing firm, giving some details of the marketing department's structure. Four managers of marketing activities are shown to report to the vice president of marketing: the managers of product planning, marketing research, sales, and advertising and promotion. Depending on the size of the organization, there may be several product planning managers—each responsible for a separate product line. Also, several regional sales managers and an international sales manager may report to the manager of sales. This marketing organization is responsible for converting marketing plans to reality.

Developing Schedules   One key to effective implementation is setting deadlines, which are supported by schedules of important milestones that make the deadlines achievable. "Half the people in the world have yet to take their first picture," says Fisher. So he sees huge opportunities for Kodak in global, developing markets and in digital imaging technologies that may replace film in many applications. Some of the deadlines Fisher set shortly after his arrival:

- Have 50,000 Kodak Enhance Stations in operation by 2001. Benefiting from Kodak's digital imaging technology, you can blow up your tiny 20-year-old snapshot (not the negative, which you've lost!) into a surprisingly clear 4×6 or 8×10 enlargement.[31]

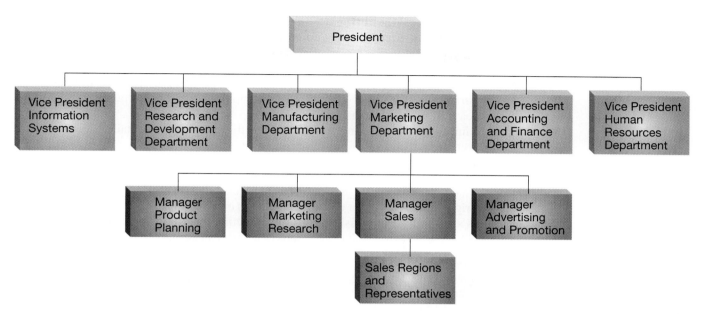

FIGURE 2-9
Organization of a typical manufacturing firm, showing a breakdown of the marketing department

- Launch PhotoNet—a service that lets you see your photos online—by 1998.[32] This is shown in the ads below.
- Introduce a high-quality film (the E200) for professional photogaphers—by 1998.[33]
- Introduce by 1996 the "Advantix" Advanced Photographic System (APS), a "smart" film and camera, that lets users get three different picture sizes from the same roll of film.[34]
- Invest $1.1 billion in China by 2002 with three Chinese manufacturers to produce and distribute film and cameras.[35]

Want *both* your prints and your pictures online to send them to your family? The solution: Kodak PhotoNet or Picture Disk! This is one of Kodak's steps to fill in its planning gap.

Eastman Kodak Company
www.kodak.com

Executing the Marketing Program   Marketing plans are meaningless pieces of paper without effective execution of those plans. This effective execution requires attention to detail for both marketing strategies and marketing tactics. A **marketing strategy** is the means by which a marketing goal is to be achieved, usually characterized by a specified target market and a marketing program to reach it. Although the term *strategy* is often used loosely, it implies both the end sought (target market) and the means to achieve it (marketing program).

To implement a marketing program successfully, hundreds of detailed decisions are often required, such as writing advertising copy or selecting the amount for temporary price reductions. These decisions, called **marketing tactics,** are detailed day-to-day operational decisions essential to the overall success of marketing strategies. Compared with marketing strategies, marketing tactics generally involve actions that must be taken right away. We cannot cover many aspects of marketing tactics in detail in a book of this size, and the emphasis here is on marketing strategy—the strategic marketing process. Here are examples of both kinds of decisions Fisher made at Kodak:

- Marketing strategy decision: develop a strategic partnership with five Japanese companies (including Fuji, Canon, and Nikon) to develop its smart film and camera—the Advanced Photographic System, Advantix.
- Marketing tactics decision: assign 10 newly formed teams the responsibility of studying issues such as cycle-time improvement to squeeze excessive time and costs out of Kodak's bloated, slow-moving, new product development process.

Issues that surface at the marketing tactics level can become marketing strategy or corporate strategy issues. There are no precise lines between marketing strategies and marketing tactics because one shades into the other, but effective marketing program implementation requires excruciating concern for details in both areas.

Strategic Marketing Process: The Control Phase

The control phase of the strategic marketing process seeks to keep the marketing program moving in the direction set for it (see Figure 2–5). Accomplishing this requires the marketing manager (1) to compare the results of the marketing program with the goals in the written plans to identify deviations and (2) to act on these deviations— correcting negative deviations and exploiting positive ones.

Comparing Results with Plans to Identify Deviations   In 1998, as George Fisher looked at the company's sales revenues (from continuing operations) from 1993 through 1997, he didn't like what he saw: the very flat trend, or AB in Figure 2–10. Technological innovations such as digital cameras were redefining the entire amateur photographic market. Also, Fuji started a price war in 1997, cutting some film pack prices by 50 percent and reducing Kodak film sales drastically. This and other factors were inhibiting Kodak's growth opportunities.

Extending the 1993–1997 trend to 2003 (BC in Figure 2–10) showed flat sales revenues, a totally unacceptable, no-growth strategy. Fisher announced that his goal for Kodak was to increase sales and profits a minimum of 13 percent annually. Applying this annual growth rate gives the target sales revenue line through the year 2003, shown as BD in Figure 2–10. This reveals a huge wedge-shaped shaded gap in the figure. Planners call this the *planning gap,* the difference between the projection of the path to reach a new goal (line BD) and the projection of the path of the results of a plan already in place (line BC).

The ultimate purpose of the firm's marketing program is to "fill in" this planning gap—in Kodak's case, to move its future sales revenue line from the essentially no-growth line BC up to the challenging high-growth target of line BD. Having a challenging series of quantified annual sales revenue targets is not enough. Poor

FIGURE 2–10
Evaluation and control of
Kodak's marketing program

performance could result in actual sales revenues being far less than the targeted levels. This is the essence of evaluation—comparing actual results with planned objectives.

Acting on Deviations   When the evaluation shows that actual performance is not up to expectations, a corrective action is usually needed to adjust and improve the program and help it achieve the planned objective. In contrast, comparing results with plans may sometimes reveal that actual performance is far better than the plan called for. In this case the marketing manager wants to uncover the reason for the good performance and act to exploit it.

Effective control at Kodak—and all organizations—requires that deviations not only be identified but that positive deviations be exploited and negative ones be corrected. Two recent Kodak "mid-course corrections" to act on deviations from targets illustrate these principles:

- *Exploiting a positive deviation.* The Kodak Enhance Stations found spectacular consumer acceptance in enlarging small prints quickly and easily. Kodak exploited this success not only by installing several thousand of these machines around the world but by quickly introducing even more sophisticated do-it-yourself machines that let consumers crop, fix up, and reprint old pictures in their local photo shops.
- *Correcting a negative deviation.* In 1997 Kodak blew $100 million launching its Advanced Photographic System (APS) camera and film only to discover it could not stock store shelves and could not process film at enough locations during the launch. After fixing these problems it relaunched APS successfully in 1998.

The strategic marketing process is discussed in greater detail again in Chapter 22.

CONCEPT CHECK

1. What is the control phase of the strategic marketing process?

2. How do the objectives set for a marketing program in the planning phase relate to the control phase of the strategic marketing process?

SUMMARY

1 Today's large organizations, both business firms and non-profit organizations, are often divided into three levels. These levels are, from highest to lowest, the corporate, business unit, and functional levels.

2 At the highest level, corporate strategy involves setting the strategic direction for the entire organization, using statements of corporate vision, corporate goals, and corporate philosophy and culture. Four keys to a firm's success are customer relationships, innovation, quality, and efficiency.

3 At the business unit level, direction comes from the business unit's mission, goals, and competencies. Concepts such as portfolio analysis, competitive advantage, total quality management, and benchmarking help the business unit achieve its mission and goals.

4 Strategy and direction at the functional level come from having the marketing department work closely with other functional units, such as manufacturing and finance, to achieve the vision, mission, and goals coming from all three organizational levels.

5 The strategic marketing process involves an organization allocating its marketing mix resources to reach its target markets. It has three phases: planning, implementation, and control.

6 The planning phase of the strategic marketing process has three steps, each with more specific elements: situation (SWOT) analysis, market-product focus and goal setting, and marketing program.

7 The implementation phase of the strategic marketing process has four key elements: obtaining resources, designing the marketing organization, developing schedules, and executing the marketing program.

8 The control phase of the strategic marketing process involves comparing results with the planned targets to identify deviations and taking actions to correct negative deviations and exploit positive ones.

KEY TERMS AND CONCEPTS

profit p. 30
corporate level p. 30
business unit p. 30
business unit level p. 30
functional level p. 31
corporate vision p. 32
goal p. 33
corporate goals p. 33
market share p. 33
corporate philosophy p. 34
corporate culture p. 34
business (unit) mission p. 35
business unit goal p. 36

objectives p. 37
business unit competencies p. 40
competitive advantage p. 40
quality p. 40
benchmarking p. 40
strategic marketing process p. 42
marketing plan p. 42
situation analysis p. 43
SWOT analysis p. 43
market segmentation p. 45
points of difference p. 46
marketing strategy p. 50
marketing tactics p. 50

 Location: http://www.mhhe.com/

INTERNET EXERCISE

Want to own a Ben & Jerry's Franchised Scoop Shop? Every day Ben & Jerry's lovers call the company with great ideas and places for the next perfect Scoop Shop. But the company is very selective in screening locations and qualifying applicants. To see these criteria, visit: www.benjerry.com/scoop/franchise

APPLYING MARKETING CONCEPTS AND PERSPECTIVES

1 (*a*) Explain what a vision statement is. (*b*) Using Coca-Cola as an example from the chapter, explain how it gives a strategic direction to its organization. (*c*) Create a vision statement for your own career.

2 (*a*) How might top management try to change the "corporate culture" of its organization? (*b*) What has George Fisher done at Kodak to change its corporate culture?

3 Using the business unit mission statement for the Domestic Merchandising Group at Sears shown in Figure 2–3, write a comparable, plausible mission statement for its two other major groups: (*a*) the Allstate Insurance Group (selling property and liability insurance) and (*b*) the Homart Development Company (which develops and manages shopping centers and community centers).

4 Why does a product often start as a question mark and then move counterclockwise around BCG's growth-share matrix shown in Figure 2–4?

5 What organizational or business unit competencies best describe (*a*) your college or university, (*b*) your favorite restaurant, and (*c*) the company that manufactures the computer you own or use most often?

6 What is the main result of each of the three phases of the strategic marketing process? (*a*) planning, (*b*) implementation, and (*c*) control.

7 Select one strength, one weakness, one opportunity, and one threat from the SWOT analysis for Ben & Jerry's shown in Figure 2–6, and suggest a specific possible action that might result.

8 Many American liberal arts colleges have traditionally offered an undergraduate degree in liberal arts (the product) to full-time 18- to 22-year-old students (the market). How might such a college use the four market-product expansion strategies shown in Figure 2–7 to compete in the 1990s?

9 The goal-setting step in the planning phase of the strategic marketing process sets quantified objectives for use in the control phase. What actions are suggested for a marketing manager if measured results are below objectives? Above objectives?

10 Read Appendix A, "A Sample Marketing Plan." Then write a 600-word executive summary for the marketing plan using the numbered headings shown in the plan.

 CASE 2–1   SPECIALIZED BICYCLE COMPONENTS, INC.

The speaker leans forward with both intensity and pride in his voice. "We're in the business of creating a bike that delivers the customer their best possible ride," he explains. "When the customer sees our red 'S,' they say this is the company that understands the cyclist. It's a company of riders. The products they make are the rider's products." The speaker is Chris Murphy, Director of Marketing for Specialized Bicycle Components, Inc.—or just "Specialized" to serious riders.

THE COMPANY

Specialized was founded in 1974 by Mike Sinyard, a cycling enthusiast who sold his VW van for the $1,500 startup capital. Mike started out importing hard-to-find "specialized" bike components, but the company began to produce its own bike parts by 1976. Specialized introduced the first major production mountain bike in the world in 1980, revolutionizing the bike industry, and since then has maintained a reputation as the technological leader in the bike and bike accessory market. In fact, since the company's founding, its formal mission statement has remained unchanged: "To give everyone the best ride of their life!"

You probably recognize the Stumpjumper and the Rockhopper as two of the most popular mountain bikes today, both made by Specialized. The company continues to innovate, with its introduction of a European-style city bike, the Globe. It also sells road bikes and an extensive line of bike accessories, including helmets, water bottles, jerseys, and shoes. As Chris says, "The customer is buying the ride from us, not just the bike."

The first professional mountain bike racing team was created by Specialized in 1983, and Ned Overland, the

Team Specialized captain, became a six-time national champion and the first-ever world champion. Specialized also counts Ned as one of its design consultants. The company banks on the perception, and reality, that this race-proven technology trickles down to the entire line of Specialized bikes and products.

THE ENVIRONMENT

The bike market is driven by innovation and technology, and with the market becoming more crowded and competitive, the fight for the consumer is intense. Specialized divides the bike market into two categories: (1) the independent retailer, and (2) the end-user consumer. While its focus in designing the product is on the end-user consumer, it only sells directly to the retailer, and realizes a strong relationship with the dealers is a key factor for success. Steve Meineke, president of Specialized USA (the domestic unit of Specialized), refers to the on-floor salesperson as "our most important partner."

The end-user consumer is broken down into two target age-groups: the 18–25-year-old college students and the 30- to 40-year-old professional "techies." To differentiate itself from the rest of the market, Specialized positions itself as the innovator in mountain bikes—its models are what the rest of the industry imitates.

Mountain bikes account for approximately two thirds of total industry bike sales, with road bikes accounting for the other third. The sport of mountain biking experienced a huge surge from 1989 to 1993, but in the mid-1990s sales began to flatten. Does Chris believe this trend will hurt Specialized? "We believe we will see growth in the next six or seven years as the entry level participants trade up—trade their lower end bikes for higher end bikes," he explains.

Specialized began cultivating what was to become an extensive global distribution network as early as 1982. It now boasts subsidiaries in 25 countries in Asia, North America, South America, Europe, and Australia, enabling the red "S" to become a symbol of performance-driven products around the world.

THE ISSUES

How can Specialized stay at the forefront of an industry that now includes more than 20 manufacturers? Strategic placement in the marketplace is one way. Specialized recently designed its own server, the World Ride Web, on the Internet (www.specialized.com/bikes). The Web site offers international mountain bike trail and road bike trail directories, e-mail access to Specialized engineers, a trail preservation network, and a dealer directory that connects users directly to dealer homepages, in addition to the standard product information. Specialized's new bike, the Globe, recently appeared on *Seinfeld* and was on display in Gap clothing stores. Specialized believes these nontraditional promotional strategies are helping

to keep the Specialized name on the cutting edge and in front of the end-user consumer.

Targeting its other market segment, the dealers, Specialized launched a "Best Ride Tour." It loaded up trailers full of the new models and visited 30 cities nationwide, enabling retailers and shop employees to test ride the bikes they will be ordering for the coming year—"Ride Before You Buy."

Specialized is also eager to become involved in joint ventures to keep its technological edge. In 1989 it released the Composite wheel, which was a joint venture between Specialized and Du Pont. The wheel is so aerodynamic it actually saves a rider more than 10 minutes over a 100 mile ride. Specialized also entered into a distribution relationship with GripShift in 1994, allowing the high-end gear manufacturer access to its extensive dealer network. Why is this beneficial to Specialized? It's another way to support the dealers by providing a top-notch product for its customers that Specialized can support in its marketing efforts.

Specialized sponsors races, provides racer support teams, initiates mountain biking safety programs, and is involved in trail-access advocacy groups all over the world. But, as it was in Specialized's early years, Mike sees a commitment to top quality and design as the most important factor for future success: "Even though we've been around for 20 years, this company still feels like it has something to prove. I expect it will always be that way."

Questions

These questions focus on the three steps of the planning phase of the strategic marketing process.

1 Do a SWOT analysis for Specialized. Use Figure 2–6 in Chapter 2 and Figure 1 in Appendix A as guides. In assessing internal factors (strengths and weaknesses), use the material provided in the case. In assessing external factors (opportunities and threats) augment the case material with what you see happening in the bicycle industry.

2 As part of step 2 of the planning phase, and using your SWOT analysis, select target markets on which you might focus for present and potential bikers.

3 As part of step 3 of the planning phase and using your answers in questions 1 and 2 above, outline Specialized's marketing programs for the target market segments you chose.

A SAMPLE MARKETING PLAN

"We get 200 to 300 marketing and business plans a year describing some inventor's or entrepreneur's new idea, but we provide startup financing for only two or three," observes Arthur R. Kydd, the chief executive officer of St. Croix Venture Partners.

His firm, St. Croix, has provided the seed money and venture capital to launch more than 60 firms in the past 30 years that today employ more than 5,000 people. Kydd continues:

> But new ideas are a dime a dozen and so are new products and new technologies. What sets a potentially successful idea, product, or technology apart from all the rest is markets and marketing. If you have a real product with a distinctive point of difference that satisfies the needs of customers, you may have a winner. And you get a real feel for this in a well-written marketing or business plan.[1]

This appendix (1) describes what marketing and business plans are—including their purposes and guidelines in writing effective plans—and (2) provides a sample marketing plan.

MARKETING PLANS AND BUSINESS PLANS

After explaining the meanings, purposes, and audiences of marketing plans and business plans, this section describes some writing guidelines for them and what external funders often look for in successful plans.

Marketing and Business Plans: Meanings, Purposes, and Audiences

A *marketing plan* is a road map for the marketing activities of an organization for a specified future period of time, such as one year or five years.[2] It is important to note that no single "generic" marketing plan applies to all organizations and all situations. Rather, the specific format for a marketing plan for an organization depends on the following:

- *The target audience and purpose.* Elements included in a particular marketing plan depend heavily on (1) who the audience is and (2) what its

purpose is. A marketing plan for an internal audience seeks to point the direction for future marketing activities and is sent to all individuals in the organization who must implement the plan or who will be affected by it. If the plan is directed to an external audience—such as friends, banks, venture capitalists, or potential investors—for the purpose of raising capital, it has the additional function of being an important sales document. In this case it contains elements such as the strategic plan/focus, organization, structure, and biographies of key personnel that would rarely appear in an internal marketing plan. Also, the financial information is far more detailed when the plan is used to raise outside capital. The elements of a marketing plan for each of these two audiences are compared in Figure A–1.

- *The kind and complexity of the organization.* A small neighborhood restaurant has a somewhat different marketing plan than Nestlé, which serves international markets. The restaurant's plan would be relatively simple and directed at serving customers in a local market. In Nestlé's case, because there is a hierarchy of marketing plans, various levels of detail would be used—such as the entire organization, the business unit, or the product/product line.

- *The industry.* Both the restaurant serving a local market and Medtronic, selling heart pacemakers globally, analyze competition. Not only are their geographic thrusts far different, but the complexities of their offerings and, hence, the time periods likely to be covered by their plans also differ. A one-year marketing plan may be adequate for the restaurant, but Medtronic may need a five-year planning horizon because product-development cycles for complex, new medical devices may be three or four years.

In contrast to a marketing plan, a *business plan* is a road map for the entire organization for a specified future period of time, such as one year or five years.[3] A key difference between a marketing plan and a business plan is that the business plan contains details on the research and development (R&D)/operations/manufacturing activities of the organization. Even for a manufacturing business, the marketing plan is probably 60 or 70 percent of the entire business plan. For businesses like a small restaurant or auto repair shop, their marketing and business plans are virtually identical. The elements of a business plan typically targeted at internal and external audiences appear in the two right-hand columns in Figure A–1.

The Most-Asked Questions by Outside Audiences

Lenders and prospective investors reading a business or marketing plan that is used to seek new capital are probably the toughest audiences to satisfy. Their most-asked questions include the following:

1. Is the business or marketing idea valid?
2. Is there something unique or distinctive about the product or service that separates it from substitutes and competitors?
3. Is there a clear market for the product or service?
4. Are the financial projections realistic and healthy?
5. Are the key management and technical personnel capable, and do they have a track record in the industry in which they must compete?
6. Does the plan clearly describe how those providing capital will get their money back and make a profit?

Rhonda M. Abrahms, author of *The Successful Business Plan,* observes that "within the first five minutes of reading your . . . plan, readers, must perceive that the answers to these questions are favorable."[4] While her comments apply to plans seeking to raise capital, the first five questions just listed apply equally well to plans for internal audiences.

Writing and Style Suggestions

There are no magic one-size-fits-all guidelines for writing successful marketing and business plans. Still, the following writing and style guidelines generally apply[5]:

- Use a direct, professional writing style. Use appropriate business terms without jargon. Present and future tenses with active voice are generally better than past tense and passive voice.

FIGURE A–1
Elements in typical marketing and business plans targeted at different audiences

Element of the Plan	Marketing Plan		Business Plan	
	For Internal Audience (to Direct Firm)	For External Audience (to Raise Capital)	For Internal Audience (to Direct Firm)	For External Audience (to Raise Capital)
1. Executive summary	✓	✓	✓	✓
2. Description of company		✓		✓
3. Strategic plan/focus		✓		✓
4. Situation analysis	✓	✓	✓	✓
5. Market-product focus	✓	✓	✓	✓
6. Marketing program strategy and tactics	✓	✓	✓	✓
7. R&D and operations program			✓	✓
8. Financial projections	✓	✓	✓	✓
9. Organization structure		✓		✓
10. Implementation plan	✓	✓	✓	✓
11. Evaluation and control	✓		✓	
Appendix A: Biographies of key personnel		✓		✓
Appendix B, etc.: Details on other topics	✓	✓	✓	✓

- Be positive and specific to convey potential success. At the same time, avoid superlatives ("terrific," "wonderful,"). Specifics are better than glittering generalities. Use numbers for impact, justifying projections with reasonable quantitative assumptions, where possible.
- Use bullet points for succinctness and emphasis. As with the list you are reading, bullets enable key points to be highlighted effectively.
- Use "A-level" (the first level) and "B-level" (the second level) headings under the numbered section headings to help readers make easy transitions from one topic to another. This also forces the writer to organize the plan more carefully. Use these headings liberally, at least one every 200 to 300 words.
- Use visuals where appropriate. Photos, illustrations, graphs, and charts enable massive amounts of information to be presented succinctly.
- Shoot for a plan 15 to 35 pages in length, not including financial projections and appendixes. But an uncomplicated small business may require only 15 pages, while a high-technology startup may require more than 35 pages.
- Use care in layout, design, and presentation. Laser or ink-jet printers give a more professional look than do dot matrix printers or typewriters. Use 11 or 12 point type (you are now reading 10.5 point type) in the text. Use a serif type (with "feet," like that you are reading now) in the text because it is easier to read, and sans serif (without "feet") in graphs and charts. A bound report with a nice cover and clear title page adds professionalism.

These guidelines are used, where possible, in the sample marketing plan that follows.

SAMPLE FIVE-YEAR MARKETING PLAN FOR PARADISE KITCHENS,® INC.

To help interpret the marketing plan for Paradise Kitchens,® Inc. that follows, we will describe the company and suggest some guidelines in interpreting the plan.

Background on Paradise Kitchens,® Inc.

With a degree in chemical engineering, Randall F. Peters spent 15 years working for General Foods and Pillsbury with a number of diverse responsibilities: plant operations, R&D, restaurant operations, and new business development. His wife Leah, with degrees in both molecular cellular biology and food science, held various Pillsbury executive positions in new category development and packaged goods and restaurants R&D. In the company's startup years, it survived on the savings of Randy and Leah—the cofounders of Paradise Kitchens. Today Randy serves as president and CEO of Paradise Kitchens, and Leah focuses on R&D and corporate strategy. The first products entered distribution in 1990.

Interpreting the Marketing Plan

The marketing plan that follows for Paradise Kitchens, Inc. is based on an actual plan developed by the company.[6] To protect proprietary information about the company, a number of details have been altered, but the basic logic of the plan has been kept.

Notes in the margins next to the Paradise Kitchens plan fall into two categories:

1. *Substantive notes* are shaded blue and elaborate on the significance of an element in the marketing plan and are keyed to chapter references in this textbook.
2. *Writing style, format, and layout notes* are shaded red and explain the editorial or visual rationale for the element.

A closing word of encouragement! Writing an effective marketing plan is hard—but challenging and satisfying—work. However, dozens of the authors' students have used effective marketing plans they wrote for class in their interviewing portfolio to show prospective employers what they could do and to help them get their first job.

The Table of Contents provides quick access to the topics in the plan, usually organized by section and subsection headings.

Seen by many experts as the single most important element in the plan, the Executive Summary, with a maximum of two pages, "sells" the documents to readers through its clarity and brevity. See question 10 at the end of Chapter 2.

The Company Description highlights the recent history and recent successes of the organization.

The Strategic Focus and Plan sets the strategic direction for the entire organization, a direction with which proposed actions of the marketing plan must be consistent. This section is not included in all marketing plans. See Chapter 2.

The qualitative Mission/ Vision statement focuses the activities of Paradise Kitchens for the stakeholder groups to be served. See Chapter 2.

Box explains significance of Marketing Plan element

Box gives writing style, format, and layout guidelines

FIVE-YEAR MARKETING PLAN
Paradise Kitchens,® Inc.

Table of Contents

1. Executive Summary

2. Company Description

Paradise Kitchens®, Inc. was started in 1989 by cofounders Randall F. Peters and Leah E. Peters to develop and market Howlin' Coyote® Chili, a unique line of single serve and microwaveable Southwestern/Mexican style frozen chili products. The Howlin' Coyote® line of chili was introduced into the Minneapolis–St. Paul market in 1990. The line was subsequently expanded to Denver in 1992 and Phoenix in 1994.

To the Company's knowledge, Howlin' Coyote® is the only premium-quality, authentic Southwestern/Mexican style, frozen chili sold in U.S. grocery stores. Its high quality has gained fast, widespread acceptance in these markets. In fact, same-store sales doubled in the last year for which data are available. The Company believes the Howlin' Coyote® brand can be extended to other categories of Southwestern/ Mexican food products.

Paradise Kitchens believes its high-quality, high-price strategy has proven successful. This marketing plan outlines how the Company will extend its geographic coverage from 3 markets to 20 markets by the year 2003.

3. Strategic Focus and Plan

This section covers three aspects of corporate strategy that influence the marketing plan: (1) the mission/vision, (2) goals, and (3) core competence/sustainable competitive advantage of Paradise Kitchens.

Mission/Vision

The mission and vision of Paradise Kitchens is to market lines of high-quality Southwestern/Mexican food products at premium prices that satisfy consumers in this fast-growing food segment while providing challenging career opportunities for employees and above-average returns to stockholders.

<u>Goals</u>

For the coming five years Paradise Kitchens seeks to achieve the following goals:

- Nonfinancial goals
    1. To retain its present image as the highest-quality line of Southwestern/ Mexican products in the food categories in which it competes.
    2. To enter 17 new metropolitan markets.
    3. To achieve national distribution in two convenience store or supermar- ket chains by 2001 and five by 2003.
    4. To add a new product line every third year.
    5. To be among the top three chili lines—regardless of packaging (frozen, canned) in one third of the metro markets in which it competes by 2001 and two thirds by 2003.
- Financial goals
    1. To obtain a real (inflation-adjusted) growth in earnings per share of 8 percent per year over time.
    2. To obtain a return on equity of at least 20 percent.
    3. To have a public stock offering by the year 2001.

> In keeping with the goal of achieving national distribution through chains, Paradise Kitchens recently obtained distribution through a convenience store chain where it uses this point-of-purchase ad that adheres statically to the freezer case.

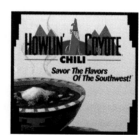

<u>Core Competency and Sustainable Competitive Advantage</u>

In terms of core competency, Paradise Kitchens seeks to achieve a unique ability (1) to provide distinctive, high-quality chilies and related products using Southwestern/ Mexican recipes that appeal to and excite contemporary tastes for these products and (2) to deliver these products to the customer's table using effective manufacturing and distribution systems that maintain the Company's quality standards.

To translate these core competencies into a sustainable competitive advantage, the Company will work closely with key suppliers and distributors to build the rela- tionships and alliances necessary to satisfy the high taste standards of our customers.

The Goals section sets both the financial and non- financial targets—where possible in quantitative terms—against which the company's performance will be measured. See Chapter 2.

Lists use parallel construc- tion to improve readability—in this case a series of infinitives starting with "To . . .".

To improve readability, each numbered section usually starts on a new page. (This is not done in this plan to save space.)

The Situation Analysis is a snapshot to answer the question, "Where are we now?" See Chapter 2.

The SWOT Analysis identifies strengths, weaknesses, opportunities, and threats to provide a solid foundation as a springboard to identify subsequent *actions* in the marketing plan. See Chapter 2.

Each long table, graph, or photo is given a figure number and title. It then appears as soon as possible after the first reference in the text, accommodating necessary page breaks. This also avoids breaking long tables like this one in the middle. Short tables or graphs that are less than 1 ½ inches are often inserted in the text without figure numbers because they don't cause serious problems with page breaks.

Effective tables seek to summarize a large amount of information in a short amount of space.

4. Situation Analysis

This situation analysis starts with a snapshot of the current environment in which Paradise Kitchens finds itself by providing a brief SWOT (strengths, weaknesses, opportunities, threats) analysis. After this overview, the analysis probes ever-finer levels of detail: industry, competitors, company, and consumers.

SWOT Analysis

Figure 1 shows the internal and external factors affecting the market opportunities for Paradise Kitchens. Stated briefly, this SWOT analysis highlights the great strides taken by the company in the eight years since its products first appeared on grocers'

Figure 1. SWOT Analysis for Paradise Kitchens

Internal Factors	Strengths	Weaknesses
Management	Experienced and entrepreneurial management and board	Small size can restrict options
Offerings	Unique, high-quality, high-price products	Many lower-quality, lower price competitors
Marketing	Distribution in 3 markets with excellent acceptance	No national awareness or distribution
Personnel	Good work force, though small; little turnover	Big gap if key employee leaves
Finance	Excellent growth in sales revenues	Limited resources may restrict growth opportunities when compared to giant competitors
Manufacturing	Sole supplier ensures high quality	Lack economies of scale of huge competitors
R&D	Continuing efforts to ensure quality in delivered products	
External Factors	**Opportunities**	**Threats**
Consumer/Social	Upscale market, likely to be stable; Southwestern/Mexican food category is fast-growing segment	Premium price may limit access to mass markets.
Competitive	Distinctive name and packaging in its markets.	Not patentable; competitors can attempt to duplicate product
Technological	Technical breakthroughs enable smaller food producers to achieve many economies available to large competitors	
Economic	Consumer income is high; convenience important to U.S. households	More households "eating out," and bringing prepared take-out into home
Legal/Regulatory	High U.S. Food & Drug Admin. standards eliminate fly-by-night competitors	

The text discussion of Figure 1 (the SWOT Analysis table) elaborates on its more important elements. This "walks" the reader through the information from the vantage of the plan's writer. (In terse plans this accompanying discussion is sometimes omitted, but is generally desirable to give the reader an understanding of what the company sees as the critical SWOT elements.)

The Industry Analysis section provides the backdrop for the subsequent, more detailed analysis of competition, the company, and the company's customers. Without an in-depth understanding of the industry, the remaining analysis may be misdirected. See Chapter 2.

Even though relatively brief, this in-depth treatment of the Spicy Southwestern/Mexican food industry in the United States demonstrates to the plan's readers the company's understanding of the industry in which it competes. It gives both external and internal readers confidence that the company thoroughly understands its own industry.

shelves. In the Company's favor internally are its strengths of an experienced management team and board of directors, excellent acceptance of its lines in the three metropolitan markets in which it competes, and a strong manufacturing and distribution system to serve these limited markets. Favorable external factors (opportunities) include the increasing appeal of Southwestern/Mexican foods, the strength of the upscale market for the Company's products, and food-processing technological breakthroughs that make is easier for smaller food producers to compete.

Among unfavorable factors, the main weakness is the limited size of Paradise Kitchens relative to its competitors in terms of the depth of the management team, available financial resources, and national awareness and distribution of product lines. Threats include the danger that the Company's premium prices may limit access to mass markets and competition from the "eating-out" and "take-out" markets.

Industry Analysis: Trends in Spicy and Mexican Foods

Total spice consumption increased 50 percent from 1985 to 1995, and consumption of spices jumped from an annual average of 2 pounds per American in 1988 to 2.7 pounds in 1994. Currently, Mexican food and ingredients are used in 64 percent of American households. Burritos, enchiladas, and taco dinner kits, which had insignificant numbers in 1981, reached between 4 percent and 11 percent of American households in 1996. Age Wave, Inc.'s *1998 Boomer Report* also stated that Baby Boomers consumed 84 percent more Mexican food in 1995 than they did in 1986.

According to *Grocery Marketing,* as the general population becomes more accustomed to different ethnic cuisines and styles of eating, spicy foods and unusual flavors are turning up on the dinner tables of middle America and the aisles of supermarkets, as well. As Baby Boomers grow older, their taste buds will become less sensitive, and they will want stronger-tasting foods. In addition to age, growth in population, incomes, and tastes in the American diet should continue to fuel the trend for spicy foods in the United States. Retail sales of fiery food could top $1.8 billion in the year 2000, according to *Packaged Facts,* up from $1 billion in 1994.

These trends reflect a generally more favorable attitude toward spicy foods on the part of Americans. The Southwestern/Mexican market includes the foods shown in Figure 2.

This summary of sales in the Southwestern/Mexican product category shows it is significant and provides a variety of future opportunities for Paradise Kitchens.

Figure 2. Some Foods Included in the Southwestern/Mexican Product Category, 1996

Item	Percent of Sales	Sales in Millions
Salsa	39%	$624
Cheese/bean dips	13	208
Refried beans	9	144
Seasoning mix	8	128
Chilies	7	112
Taco shells	7	112
Dinner kits	5	80
Taco sauce	3	48
Enchilada sauce	2	32
Other	7	112
Total	100%	$1,600

As with the Industry Analysis, the Competitors Analysis demonstrates that the company has a realistic understanding of who its major competitors are and what their marketing strategies are. Again, a realistic assessment gives confidence to both internal and external readers that subsequent marketing actions in the plan rest on a solid foundation. See Chapters 2, 3, 8, 9, and 10.

Competitors in Southwestern/Mexican Market

The chili market represents $495 million in annual sales. The products fall primarily into two groups: canned chili (62 percent of sales) and dry chili (16 percent of sales). The remaining 22 percent of sales go to frozen chili products. Besides Howlin' Coyote,® Stouffers and Marie Callender's offer frozen chilies as part of their broad line of frozen dinners and entrees. Major canned chili brands include Hormel, Wolf, Dennison, Stagg, Chili Man, Chili Magic, and Castleberry's. Their retail prices range from $0.99 to $1.79.

This page uses a "block" style and does *not* indent each paragraph, although an extra space separates each paragraph. Compare this page with page 61, which has indented paragraphs. Most readers find indented paragraphs in marketing plans and long reports are easier to follow.

Bluntly put, the major disadvantage of the segment's dominant product, canned chili, is that it does not taste very good. A taste test described in the October 1990 issue of *Consumer Reports* magazine ranked 26 canned chili products "poor" to "fair" in overall sensory quality. The study concluded, "Chili doesn't have to be hot to be good. But really good chili, hot or mild, doesn't come out of a can."

Dry mix brands include such familiar spice brands as Lawry's, McCormick, French's, and Durkee, along with smaller offerings such as Wick Fowler's and Carroll Shelby's. Their retail prices range from $0.99 to $1.99. The *Consumer Reports* study was more favorable about dry chili mixes, ranking them from "fair" to "very good." The magazine recommended, "If you want good chili, make it with fresh ingredients and one of the seasoning mixes we tested." A major drawback of dry mixes is that they require the preparers to add their own meat, beans, and tomatoes and take more preparation time than canned or frozen chilies.

The *Consumer Reports* study did not include the frozen chili entrees from Stouffer's or Marie Callender's (Howlin' Coyote® was not yet on the market at the time of the test). However, it is fair to say that these products—consisting of ground beef, chili beans, and tomato sauce—are of average quality. Furthermore, they are not singled out for special marketing or promotional programs by their manufacturers. Marie Callender's (including cornbread) retails for $3.09, and Stouffer's retails for $2.99.

The Company Analysis provides details of the company's strengths and marketing strategies that will enable it to achieve the mission, vision, and goals identified earlier. See Chapters 2, 9, and 22.

Company Analysis

The husband-and-wife team that cofounded Paradise Kitchens, Inc. in 1989 has 44 years of experience between them in the food-processing business. Both have played key roles in the management of the Pillsbury Company. They are being advised by a highly seasoned group of business professionals, who have extensive understanding of the requirements for new product development.

Currently, Howlin' Coyote® products compete in the chili and Mexican frozen entree segments of the Southwestern/Mexican food market. While the chili obviously competes as a stand-alone product, its exceptional quality means it can complement such dishes as burritos, nachos, and enchiladas and can be readily used as a smothering sauce for pasta, rice, or potatoes. This flexibility of use is relatively rare in the prepared food marketplace. With Howlin' Coyote® Paradise Kitchens is broadening the position of frozen chili in a way that can lead to impressive market share for the new product category.

The Company now uses a single outside producer with which it works closely to maintain the consistently high quality required in its products. The greater volume has increased production efficiencies, resulting in a steady decrease in the cost of goods sold.

Customer Analysis

In terms of customer analysis, this section describes (1) the characteristics of customers expected to buy Howlin' Coyote® products and (2) health and nutrition concerns of Americans today.

The higher-level "A heading" of Customer Analysis has a more dominant typeface and position than the lower-level "B heading" of Customer Characteristics. These headings introduce the reader to the sequence and level of topics covered. The organization of this textbook uses this kind of structure and headings.

Customer Characteristics. Demographically, chili products in general are purchased by consumers representing a broad range of socioeconomic backgrounds. Howlin' Coyote® chili is purchased chiefly by consumers who have achieved higher levels of education and whose income is $30,000 and higher. These consumers represent 57 percent of canned and dry mix chili users.

The five Howlin' Coyote® entrees offer a quick, tasty meal with high-quality ingredients.

Satisfying customers and providing genuine value to them is why organizations exist in a market economy. This section addresses the question of "Who are the customers for Paradise Kitchens's products?" See Chapters 5, 6, 7, and 9.

The household buying Howlin' Coyote® has one to three people in it. Among married couples, Howlin' Coyote® is predominantly bought by households in which both spouses work. While women are a majority of the buyers, single men represent a significant segment. Anecdotally, Howlin' Coyote® has heard from fathers of teenaged boys who say they keep a freezer stocked with the chili because the boys devour it.

Because the chili offers a quick way to make a tasty meal, the product's biggest users tend to be those most pressed for time. Howlin' Coyote®'s premium pricing also means that its purchasers are skewed toward the higher end of the income range. Buyers range in age from 25 to 55. Because consumers in the western United States have adopted spicy foods more readily than the rest of the country, Howlin' Coyote®'s initial marketing expansion efforts will be concentrated in that region.

Health and Nutrition Concerns. Coverage of food issues in the U.S. media is often erratic and occasionally alarmist. Because Americans are concerned about their diets, studies from organizations of widely varying credibility frequently receive significant attention from the major news organizations. For instance, a study of fat levels of movie popcorn was reported in all the major media. Similarly, studies on the healthfulness of Mexican food have received prominent "play" in print and broadcast reports. The high caloric levels of much Mexican and Southwestern-style food has been widely reported and often exaggerated.

Less certain is the link between these reports and consumer buying behavior. Most indications are that while Americans are well-versed in dietary matters, they are not significantly changing their eating patterns. The experience of other food manufacturers is that Americans expect certain foods to be high in calories and are not drawn to those that claim to be low-calorie versions. Low-fat frozen pizza was a flop. Therefore, while Howlin' Coyote® is already lower in calories, fat, and sodium than its competitors, those qualities are not being stressed in its promotions. Instead, in the space and time available for promotions, Howlin' Coyote®'s taste, convenience, and flexibility are stressed.

5. Market-Product Focus

This section describes the five-year marketing and product objectives for Paradise Kitchens and the target markets, points of difference, and positioning of its lines of Howlin' Coyote® chilies.

Marketing and Product Objectives

Howlin' Coyote®'s marketing intent is to take full advantage of its brand potential

---

This section demonstrates the company's insights into a major trend that has a potentially large impact.

Size of headings should give a professional look to the report and not overwhelm the reader. These two headings are too large.

As noted in Chapter 11, the chances of success for a new product are significantly increased if objectives are set for the product itself and if target market segments are identified for it. This section makes these explicit for Paradise Kitchens. The objectives also serve as the planned targets against which marketing activities are measured in program implementation and control.

A heading should be spaced closer to the text that follows (and that it describes) than the preceding section to avoid confusion for the reader. This rule is *not* followed for the "Target Markets" heading, which now unfortunately appears to "float" between the preceding and following paragraphs.

This section identifies the specific niches or target markets toward which the company's products are directed. When appropriate and when space permits, this section often includes a market-product grid. See Chapter 10.

---

while building a base from which other revenues sources can be mined—both in and out of the retail grocery business. These are detailed in four areas below:

- Current markets. Current markets will be grown by expanding brand and flavor distribution at the retail level. In addition, same-store sales will be grown by increasing consumer awareness and repeat purchases. With this increase in same-store sales, the more desirable broker/warehouse distribution channel will become available, increasing efficiency and saving costs.

- New markets. By the end of Year 5, the chili and salsa business will be expanded to a total of 20 metropolitan areas. This will represent 72 percent of U.S. food store sales.

- Food service. Food service sales will include chili products and smothering sauces. Sales are expected to reach $693,000 by the end of Year 3 and $1.5 million by the end of Year 5.

- New products. Howlin' Coyote®'s brand presence will be expanded at the retail level through the addition of new products in the frozen-foods section. This will be accomplished through new product concept screening in Year 1 to identify new potential products. These products will be brought to market in Years 2 and 3. Additionally, the brand may be licensed in select categories.

Target Markets

The primary target market for Howlin' Coyote® products is households with one to three people, where often both adults work, with individual income typically above $30,000 per year. These households contain more experienced, adventurous consumers of Southwestern/Mexican food and want premium quality products.

To help buyers see the many different uses for Howlin' Coyote® chili, recipes are even printed on the *inside* of the packages.

An organization cannot grow by offering only "me-too products." The greatest single factor in a new product's failure is the lack of significant "points of difference" that sets it apart from competitors' substitutes. This section makes these points of difference explicit. See Chapter 11.

A positioning strategy helps communicate the company's unique points of difference of its products to prospective customers in a simple, clear way. This section describes this positioning. See Chapters 10 and 11.

Everything that has gone before in the marketing plan sets the stage for the marketing mix actions—the 4 Ps—covered in the marketing program. See Chapters 11 through 21.

The section describes in detail three key elements of the company's product strategy: the product line, its quality and how this is achieved, and its "cutting edge" packaging. See Chapters 11, 12, and 13.

Points of Difference

The "points of difference"—characteristics that make Howlin' Coyote® chilies unique relative to competitors—fall into three important areas:

- Unique taste and convenience. No known competitor offers a high-quality, "authentic" frozen chili in a range of flavors. And no existing chili has the same combination of quick preparation and home-style taste.

- Taste trends. The American palate is increasingly intrigued by hot spices, and Howlin' Coyote® brands offer more "kick" than most other prepared chilies.

- Premium packaging. Howlin' Coyote®'s high-value packaging graphics convey the unique, high-quality product contained inside and the product's nontraditional positioning.

Positioning

In the past chili products have been either convenient or tasty, but not both. Howlin' Coyote® pairs these two desirable characteristics to obtain a positioning in consumers' minds as very high-quality "authentic Southwestern/Mexican tasting" chilies that can be prepared easily and quickly.

6. Marketing Program

The four marketing mix elements of the Howlin' Coyote® chili marketing program are detailed below. Note that "chile" is the vegetable and "chili" is the dish.

Product Strategy

After first summarizing the product line, the approach to product quality and packaging are covered.

Product Line. Howlin' Coyote® chili, retailing for $2.99 for a 10- or 11.5-ounce serving, is available in five flavors. The five are:

- Green Chile Chili: braised extra-lean pork with fire-roasted green chilies, onions, tomato chunks, bold spices, and jalapeno peppers, based on a Southwestern favorite.

- Red Chile Chili: extra-lean cubed pork, deep-red acho chilies, and sweet onions; known as the "Texas Bowl of Red."

- Beef and Black Bean Chili: lean braised beef with black beans, tomato chunks, and Howlin' Coyote®'s own blend of red chilies and authentic spicing.

- Chicken Chunk Chili: hearty chunks of tender chicken, fire-roasted green chilies, black beans, pinto beans, diced onions, and zesty spices.
- Mean Bean Chili: vegetarian, with nine distinctive bean varieties and fire-roasted green chilies, tomato chunks, onion, and a robust blend of spices and rich red chilies.

Unique Product Quality. The flavoring systems of the Howlin' Coyote® chilies are proprietary. The products' tastiness is due to extra care lavished upon the ingredients during production. The ingredients used are of unusually high quality. Meats are low-fat cuts and are fresh, not frozen, to preserve cell structure and moistness. Chilies are fire-roasted for fresher taste, not the canned variety used by more mainstream products. Tomatoes and vegetables are select quality. No preservatives or artificial flavors are used.

Packaging. Reflecting the "cutting edge" marketing strategy of its producers, Howlin' Coyote® bucks conventional wisdom in packaging. It avoids placing predictable photographs of the product on its containers. (Head to any grocer's freezer and you will be hardpressed to find a product that does not feature a heavily stylized photograph of the contents.) Instead, Howlin' Coyote®'s package shows a Southwestern motif that communicates the product's out-of-the-ordinary positioning. This approach signals the product's nontraditional qualities: "adventurous" eating with minimal fuss—a frozen meal for people who do not normally enjoy frozen meals.

The Southwestern motif makes Howlin' Coyote®'s packages stand out in a supermarket's freezer case.

Price Strategy

Howlin' Coyote® Chili is, at $2.99 for a 10- to 11.5-ounce package, priced comparably to the other frozen offerings and higher than the canned and dried chili varieties. However, the significant taste advantages it has over canned chilies and the convenience advantages over dried chilies justify this pricing strategy.

This "introductory overview" sentence tells the reader the topics covered in the section—in this case in-store demonstrations, recipes, and cents-off coupons. While this sentence may be omitted in short memos or plans, it helps readers see where the text is leading. These sentences are used throughout this plan. This textbook also generally utilizes these introductory overview sentences to aid your comprehension.

Elements of the Promotion Strategy are highlighted here with B-headings in terms of the three key promotional activities the company is emphasizing for its product line: in-store demonstrations, recipes featuring its Howlin' Coyote® chilies, and cents-off coupons. See Chapters 19, 20, and 21.

Photos or sample ads can illustrate key points effectively, even if they are not in color as they appear here.

Promotion Strategy

Key promotion programs feature in-store demonstrations, recipes, and cents-off coupons.

In-Store Demonstrations. In-store demonstrations will be conducted to give consumers a chance to try Howlin' Coyote® products and learn about their unique qualities. Demos will be conducted regularly in all markets to increase awareness and trial purchases.

Recipes. Because the products' flexibility of use is a key selling point, recipes will be offered to consumers to stimulate use. The recipes will be given at all in-store demonstrations, on the back of packages, and through a mail-in recipe book offer. In addition, recipes will be included in coupons sent by direct-mail or free-standing inserts. For new markets, recipes will be included on in-pack coupon inserts.

Cents-Off Coupons. To generate trial and repeat-purchase of Howlin' Coyote® products, coupons will be distributed in four ways:

- In Sunday newspaper inserts. Inserts are highly read and will help generate awareness. Coupled with in-store demonstrations, this has been a very successful technique so far.

 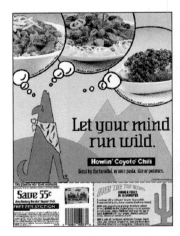

Sunday newspaper inserts encourage consumer trial and provide recipes to show how Howlin' Coyote® chili can be used in summer meals.

Another bulleted list adds many details for the reader, including methods of gaining customer awareness, trial, and repeat purchases as Howlin' Coyote® enters new metropolitan areas. The lack of a space between bulleted items makes it more difficult reading for some readers compared to, say, the bulleted list on page 00.

The Place Strategy is described here in terms of both (1) the present method and (2) the new one to be used when the increased sales volume makes it feasible. See Chapters 16, 17, and 18.

All the marketing mix decisions covered in the just-described marketing program have both revenue and expense effects. These are summarized in this section of the marketing plan. See Appendix B.

Note that this section contains no introductory overview sentence. While the sentence is not essential, many readers prefer to see it to avoid the abrupt start with Past Sales Revenues.

The graph shows more clearly the dramatic growth of sales revenue than data in a table would do.

- In-pack coupons. Inside each box of Howlin' Coyote® chili will be coupons for $1 off two more packages of the chili. These coupons will be included for the first three months the product is shipped to a new market. Doing so encourages repeat purchases by new users.
- Direct-mail chili coupons. Those households that fit the Howlin' Coyote® demographics described above will be mailed coupons. This is likely to be an efficient promotion due to its greater audience selectivity.
- In-store demonstrations. Coupons will be passed out at in-store demonstrations to give an additional incentive to purchase.

Place (Distribution) Strategy

Howlin' Coyote® is distributed in its present markets through a food distributor. The distributor buys the product, warehouses it, and then resells and delivers it to grocery retailers on a store-by-store basis. This is typical for products that have moderate sales—compared with, say, staples like milk or bread. As sales grow, we will shift to a more efficient system using a broker who sells the products to retail chains and grocery wholesalers.

7. Financial Data and Projections

Past Sales Revenues

Historically, Howlin' Coyote® has had a steady increase in sales revenues since its introduction in 1990. In 1994, sales jumped spectacularly, due largely to new promotion strategies. Sales have continued to rise during the last four years, but at a less dramatic rate. The trend in sales revenues appears in Figure 3.

Figure 3.   Sales Revenues for Paradise Kitchens, Inc.

One key indicator of what future sales will be is to look at what past sales have been. Paradise Kitchens is justifiably proud of the dramatic growth in its past sales revenues and highlights this information. For simplicity, this sample marketing plan omits revenues from the salsa line.

Because this table is very short, it is woven into the text, rather than given a figure number and title.

Because the plan proposes to enter 17 new metropolitan markets in the coming five years (for a total of 20), it is not possible to simply extrapolate the trend in Figure 3. Instead, management's judgment must be used. Methods of making sales forecasts—including the "lost horse technique used here—are discussed in Chapter 8.

The Five-Year Financial Projections section starts with the judgment forecast of cases sold and the resulting net sales. Gross profit and then operating profit—critical for the company's survival—are projected and show the company passes break-even and becomes profitable in Year 2. An actual plan often contains many pages of computer-generated spreadsheet projections, usually shown in an appendix to the plan.

Five-Year Projections

Five-year financial projections for Paradise Kitchens appear below:

			Projections				
		Actual	Year 1	Year 2	Year 3	Year 4	Year 5
Financial Element	Units	1998	1999	2000	2001	2002	2003
Cases sold	1,000	353	684	889	1,249	1,499	1,799
Net sales	$1,000	5,123	9,913	12,884	18,111	21,733	26,080
Gross profit	$1,000	2,545	4,820	6,527	8,831	10,597	12,717
Operating profit (loss)	$1,000	339	985	2,906	2,805	3,366	4,039

These projections reflect the continuing growth in number of cases sold (with 8 packages of Howlin' Coyote® chili per case) and increasing production and distribution economies of scale as sales volume increases.

8. Organization

Paradise Kitchens's present organization appears in Figure 4. It shows the four people reporting to the President. Below this level are both the full-time and part-time employees of the Company.

At present Paradise Kitchens operates with full-time employees in only essential positions. It now augments its full-time staff with key advisors, consultants, and subcontractors. As the firm grows, people with special expertise will be added to the staff.

Figure 4. The Paradise Kitchens Organization

The Organization of Paradise Kitchens appears here. It reflects the bare-bones organizational structure of successful small businesses. Often a more elaborate marketing plan will show the new positions expected to be added as the firm grows. See Chapter 22. Biographical sketches of key personnel often appear as an appendix of a marketing plan targeted at external audiences and used to try to help obtain funding.

The Implementation Plan shows how the company will turn plans into results. Gantt charts are often used to set deadlines and assign responsibilities for the many tactical marketing decisions needed to enter a new market. See Chapter 22.

The essence of Evaluation and Control is comparing actual sales with the targeted values set in the plan and taking appropriate actions. Note that the section briefly describes a contingency plan for alternative actions, depending on how successful the entry into a new market turns out to be. See Chapter 22.

Various appendixes may appear at the end of the plan, depending on the purpose and audience for them. For example, resumes of key personnel or detailed financial spreadsheets often appear in appendixes, such as those shown here.

9. Implementation Plan

Introducing Howlin' Coyote® chilies to new metropolitan areas is a complex task and requires that creative promotional activities gain consumer awareness and initial trial among the target market households identified earlier. The anticipated rollout schedule to enter these metropolitan markets appears in Figure 5.

Figure 5.   Rollout Schedule to Enter New U.S. Markets

Year	New Markets Added	Cumulative Markets	Cumulative Percentage of U.S. Market
Today (1998)	2	5	16
Year 1 (1999)	3	8	21
Year 2 (2000)	4	12	29
Year 3 (2001)	2	14	37
Year 4 (2002)	3	17	45
Year 5 (2003)	3	20	53

The diverse regional tastes in chili will be monitored carefully to assess whether minor modifications may be required in the chili recipes. For example, what is seen as "hot" in Boston may not be seen as "hot" in Dallas. As the rollout to new metropolitan areas continues, Paradise Kitchens will assess manufacturing and distribution trade-offs. This is important in determining whether to start new production with selected high-quality regional contract packers.

10. Evaluation and Control

Monthly sales targets in cases have been set for Howlin' Coyote® chili for each metropolitan area. Actual case sales will be compared with these targets and tactical marketing programs modified to reflect the unique sets of factors in each metropolitan area. The speed of the roll-out program will increase or decrease, depending on the Paradise Kitchens's performance in the successive metropolitan markets it enters. Similarly, as described above in the section on the implementation plan, Paradise Kitchens may elect to respond to variations in regional tastes by using contract packers, which will reduce transportation and warehousing costs but will require special efforts to monitor production quality.

Appendix A. Biographical Sketches of Key Personnel

Appendix B. Detailed Financial Projections

value through entertainment, education, or integration with other transactions. Pepsi follows this approach by offering an interactive experience consisting of games, contests, screen savers, and movie previews at its Web page. Future changes are likely to include a decline in the use of intermediaries such as travel agents, stockbrokers, and real estate agents because the Net Generation relies on the Internet, and Web sites such as Netscape's Netcenter, as a source of information and a means of interacting with sellers.[1]

The Net Generation is clearly changing the marketing environment. It represents a demographic shift, an economic influence, and a force likely to increase the use of digital technologies. Anticipating changes such as these and responding to them often means the difference between marketing success and failure. This chapter describes how the marketing environment has changed in the past and is likely to change in the future.

ENVIRONMENTAL SCANNING IN THE NEW MILLENNIUM

Changes in the marketing environment are a source of opportunities and threats to be managed. The process of continually acquiring information on events occurring outside the organization to identify and interpret potential trends is called **environmental scanning.**

Tracking Environmental Trends

Environmental trends typically arise from five sources: social, economic, technological, competitive, and regulatory forces. As shown in Figure 3–1 and described later in this chapter, these forces affect the marketing activities of a firm in numerous ways.

To illustrate how environmental scanning is used, consider the following trend:[2]

> Coffee industry marketers have observed that the percentage of adults who drink coffee has declined from 75 percent in 1962 to 47 percent in 1998. Age-specific analysis indicates that coffee consumption declined among all age groups, including 18 to 24 year olds, despite the perception that young adults are leading a revival in coffee drinking.

FIGURE 3–1
Environmental forces affecting the organization, as well as its suppliers and customers

What types of businesses are likely to be influenced by this trend? What future would you predict for coffee?

You may have concluded that this trend is likely to influence coffee manufacturers and supermarkets. If so, you are absolutely correct—manufacturers have responded by offering new flavors, and supermarkets have added coffee boutiques and gourmet brands such as Starbucks to try to reverse the trend.[3] Predicting the future of coffee requires assumptions about the number of years the declining trend will continue and the rate of decline in various age groups. Did you consider these issues in your analysis? Because experts make different assumptions, their forecasts range from a 30 percent decline to a 13 percent increase by 2005—a range that probably includes your forecast!

Environmental scanning also involves explaining trends. Why has coffee consumption been declining? One explanation is that consumers are switching from coffee to other beverages such as soft drinks, juices, or water. Another explanation is that preferences have shifted to better-tasting but more expensive types of coffee, and consumers have reduced their use to maintain the same level of expenditure. Identifying and interpreting trends, such as the decline in coffee consumption, and developing explanations, such as those offered in this paragraph, are essential to successful environmental scanning.

An Environmental Scan of the United States

What other trends might affect marketing in the future? A firm conducting an environmental scan of the United States might uncover key trends such as those listed in Figure 3–2 for each of the five environmental factors.[4] Although the list of trends is far from complete, it reveals the breadth of an environmental scan—from population shifts to remote suburbs and small towns, to the growth of electronic commerce, to the emergence of "network corporations." These trends affect consumers and the businesses and nonprofit organizations that serve them. Trends such as these are covered as the five environmental forces are described in the following pages.

FIGURE 3–2
An environmental scan of the United States

ENVIRONMENTAL FORCE	TREND IDENTIFIED BY AN ENVIRONMENTAL SCAN
Social	• Movement toward "natural" and healthful products and lifestyles • Growing number and importance of older Americans • Population shifts to remote suburbs and small towns • Greater desire for product simplicity and honesty in advertising
Economic	• Dramatic growth of electronic commerce • Increase in per-capita income and standard of living • U.S. firms adjust to crises in international markets • Economic growth reduces concern about inflation and budget deficit
Technological	• Increased use of information and communication technology • Growing focus on the Internet as consumers and businesses go online • Expanded computer power and growth of "smart" products • Growing use of electronic money or "e-cash"
Competitive	• New flexible employment agreements and growth of telecommuting • The emergence of fast, responsive "network corporations" • Mergers reduce costs through economies of scale • More international competition from emerging countries
Regulatory	• Increasing emphasis on free trade and deregulation • Greater concern for pollution and global warming • New legislation related to information collection and privacy • New legislation to encourage consumer savings

ture of the American family. Thirty years ago 40 percent of all households consisted of married couples with children. Today, that type of household is just 25 percent of the

Regional Marketing   A new trend within marketing focuses not only on the shifting of consumers geographically but also on the differences in their product preferences based on where they live. This concept has been referred to as **regional marketing,** which is developing marketing plans to reflect specific area differences in taste preferences, perceived needs, or interests. For example, Procter & Gamble observed that vacuum brick-packs of coffee were relatively more popular than cans in the South. The company repackaged their Folgers brand coffee for those markets and developed a new advertising campaign. Sales of Folgers coffee increased 32 percent in the targeted markets.[19] In Chapter 10, you will learn more about this approach to the market referred to as *geographical segmentation.*

Technology has aided marketers to begin to understand the variations of regional preferences. Computerized cash registers have allowed companies to collect and analyze large amounts of sales data for geographical units as small as neighborhoods. Scott Paper found that their paper towels had a 47.7 percent share in Chicago yet only a 2.5 percent share in Los Angeles.[20] And, with advances in direct marketing approaches (described in Chapter 19), this focus on regional marketing allows a better targeting of ads and products. Ideally, Scott Paper can now create a specific campaign for their heavy users in Chicago and develop a marketing strategy to encourage new purchases in Los Angeles.

Because several ethnic groups are geographically concentrated, ethnic marketing is an increasingly important part of regional marketing. Consider, for example, that 43 percent of U.S. Asians live in Los Angeles, New York City, and San Francisco and that two thirds of Hispanics live in Florida, Texas, and California. Saturn combined ethnic and regional marketing by running a Spanish-language advertising campaign, using a testimonial from San Antonio, Texas, firefighter Ernest Imperial, in Texas and California. The ads were not used in Florida, where more than 55 percent of the Hispanic population is Cuban—a group for which a different Hispanic dialect was needed.[21]

Culture

A second social force, **culture,** incorporates the set of values, ideas, and attitudes of a homogeneous group of people that are transmitted from one generation to the next. Culture includes both material and abstract elements, so monitoring cultural trends in the United States is difficult but important for marketing. Cross-cultural analysis needed for global marketing is discussed in Chapter 5.

The Changing Roles of Women and Men   One of the most notable changes in the United States in the past 25 years has been in the roles of women and men. These changes have had a significant impact on marketing practices.

Today some 138 million people work, nearly twice the number of 25 years ago. One reason is that people are staying in the work force longer now that mandatory retirement has been outlawed and financial penalties for working past 65 have been reduced. Another reason is the growing number of women entering the work force. From 1975 through 1998 the percentage of all labor-force-age women who were working rose from 46 percent to 60 percent, and the percentage of women in the work force with school-age children rose to more than 77 percent. The growing numbers of women in the work force are reflected in their representation in many occupations. For example, women account for more than half of all financial managers, accountants and auditors, technical writers, economists, public relations specialists, and authors.[22] *Fortune* magazine recently reported that 11 percent of the officers and directors of the 500 largest corporations in the United States are women and suggested that women are "at last achieving profound power in the most important and influential industries."[23]

The increasing number of women in the work force has increased the number of dual-income households. To cope with the demands of managing careers and a household, men and women have learned new roles as consumers and household decision

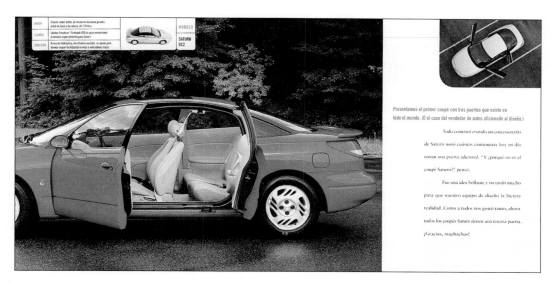

Saturn combined ethnic and regional marketing by using Spanish-language promotions in some states.

Saturn
www.saturncars.com

makers. For example, a recent survey indicated that 24 percent of men consider themselves the primary shopper for their household's groceries. Similarly, women now purchase 50 percent of all new cars sold in the United States. As the roles of men and women change, marketers must adjust their marketing programs and their assumptions about how men and women shop. *Cigar Aficionado* magazine recently acknowledged a growing women's market for cigars, and *Parents* magazine has revised its coverage to reflect a growing male readership.[24]

Changing Attitudes and Values   Culture also includes attitudes and values. In recent years some major attitudinal changes have occurred toward work, lifestyles, and consumption. Recent study has shown a change in the work ethic. There is a growing sense that the Puritan ethic of "I live to work" may be redefined as "I work to live." Work is seen as a means to an end—recreation, leisure, and entertainment—which has contributed to a growth in sales of products such as sports equipment, vacations, and electronic stereo equipment. As attitudes toward work change, U.S. consumers are placing increased importance on quality of life.

There is greater concern for health and well-being as evidenced by the level of sports participation in the United States and increased interest in health and diet. Sears fitness products, Nike workout clothes, and Lean Cuisine dinners are but a few products developed in response to and profiting from this trend.

A change in consumption orientation is also apparent. Today, and for the foreseeable future, **value consciousness**—or the concern for obtaining the best quality, features, and performance of a product or service for a given price—will drive consumption behavior. Innovative marketers have responded to this new orientation in numerous ways. Holiday Inn Worldwide has opened Holiday Express hotels, designed to offer comfortable accommodations with room rates lower than Holiday Inns. Revlon's Charles of the Ritz, known for its upscale and expensive cosmetics, has introduced the Express Bar, a collection of modified, medium-priced cosmetics. Even American Express is adding low-fee credit cards to its line of well-known, high-priced, and exclusive green, gold, and platinum charge cards.[25]

CONCEPT CHECK

1. Explain the term *regional marketing.*

2. What are the marketing implications of blended families?

3. The work ethic of today may best be stated as "I work _____."

ECONOMIC FORCES

The third component of the environmental scan, the **economy,** pertains to the income, expenditures, and resources that affect the cost of running a business and household. We'll consider two aspects of these economic forces: a macroeconomic view of the marketplace and a microeconomic perspective of consumer income.

Macroeconomic Conditions

Of particular concern at the macroeconomic level is the inflationary or recessionary state of the economy, whether actual or perceived by consumers or businesses. In an inflationary economy, the cost to produce and buy products and services escalates as prices increase. From a marketing standpoint, if prices rise faster than consumer incomes, the number of items consumers can buy decreases. This relationship is evident in the cost of a college education. Today, average annual tuition is the equivalent of 250 hours of pay for an average worker, up from 110 hours of pay in 1960.[26]

Whereas inflation is a period of price increases, recession is a time of slow economic activity. Businesses decrease production, unemployment rises, and many consumers have less money to spend. The U.S. economy experienced recessions in the early 1970s, early 1980s, and early 1990s. While the U.S. economy has been growing in recent years, observers watch for events such as drop in the stock market, dramatic increases in oil prices, or a war, which might trigger a recession.[27]

Consumer expectations of an inflationary and recessionary U.S. economy is an important element of environmental scanning. Consumer spending, which accounts for two thirds of U.S. economic activity, is affected by expectations of the future. Surveys of consumer expectations are tracked over time by research organizations, who ask questions such as "Do you expect to be better or worse off financially a year from now?" Surveyors record the share of positive and negative responses to these and related questions and construct an index. The higher the index, the more favorable are consumer expectations. Figure 3–5 shows the fluctuations in the Consumer Sentiment Index and annual vehicle sales. As can be seen, sales are closely related to expectations. This relationship has helped Chrysler plan its automobile production and avoid producing too many or too few cars. Levitz, the largest U.S. furniture retailer, also tracks consumer economic expectations since furniture sales reflect perceptions of the future economic environment.[28]

FIGURE 3–5
University of Michigan consumer sentiment index and automobile sales: 1970–1998

www.athena.sca.isr.umich.edu/scripts/mine/mine.asp

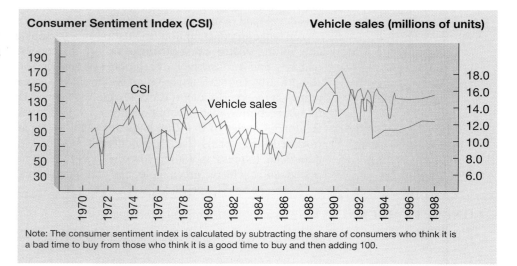

Note: The consumer sentiment index is calculated by subtracting the share of consumers who think it is a bad time to buy from those who think it is a good time to buy and then adding 100.

WEB LINK   How Typical Is Your Home Town?

Marketers collect and use environmental information to better understand consumers. One way to begin an environmental scan is to compare economic data about a particular segment of the population to what is "typical" or "average" for the entire population. Do you think your home town is typical? To find out visit CACI Marketing System's web site at http://demographics.caci.com, select "free sample," and type in the zip code of your home town. CACI provides a comparison of your zip code's population with the averages for the nation.

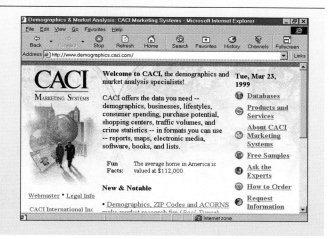

Consumer Income

The microeconomic trends in terms of consumer income are also important issues for marketers. Having a product that meets the needs of consumers may be of little value if they are unable to purchase it. A consumer's ability to buy is related to income, which consists of gross, disposable, and discretionary components.

Gross Income   The total amount of money made in one year by a person, household, or family unit is referred to as **gross income.** While the typical U.S. household earned only about $10,000 of income in 1970, it earned about $37,000 in 1997. When gross income is adjusted for inflation, however, income of that typical U.S. household was relatively stable from 1970 to 1997. Figure 3–6 shows the distribution of annual income among U.S. households.[29] Are you from a typical household? Read the accompanying Web Link to learn how you can determine the median household income in your home town.

FIGURE 3–6
Income distribution of U.S. households

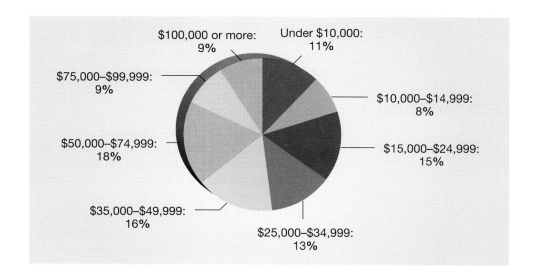

As consumers' discretionary income increases, so does the enjoyment of pleasure travel.

Westin Hotels & Resorts
www.westin.com

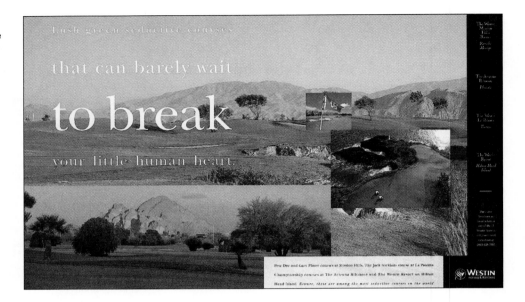

Disposable Income   The second income component, **disposable income,** is the money a consumer has left after paying taxes to use for food, shelter, and clothing. Thus, if taxes rise at a faster rate than does income, consumers must economize. In recent years consumers' allocation of income has shifted. As the economy and the stock market has grown, people have decreased their allocation for personal savings to record lows and increased their disposable incomes to record highs. Much of the money is being spent on new categories of "necessities" such as vitamins and supplements; antibacterial bodywashes, lotions, and deodorants; anti-wrinkle creams; and children's shampoos, toothpaste, and bath products.[30]

Discretionary Income   The third component of income is **discretionary income,** the money that remains after paying for taxes and necessities. Discretionary income is used for luxury items such as vacations at a Westin resort. An obvious problem in defining discretionary versus disposable income is determining what is a luxury and what is a necessity.

The Department of Labor has calculated a budget for a household of four persons. Using these budget amounts, the Census Bureau defines a household as having discretionary income if its spendable income exceeds that of an average, similarly sized family by 30 percent or more. Recent studies suggest that two thirds of all American households have some discretionary income. Two-person households have the highest average discretionary income at $15,500, compared with an average of $13,480 for all households with discretionary income.[31]

TECHNOLOGICAL FORCES

Our society is in a period of technological dramatic change. **Technology,** a major environmental force, refers to inventions or innovations from applied science or engineering research. Each new wave of technological innovation can replace existing products and companies. Do you recognize the items pictured on page 85 and what they may replace?

Technology of Tomorrow

Technological change is the result of research, so it is difficult to predict. Some of the most dramatic technological changes occurring now, however, include the following:

1. The declining cost and size, and increasing power, of microprocessors.
2. The convergence of television, personal computer, and telephone technologies.

3. The pervasive trend toward "connectedness" through the World Wide Web.

4. The emergence of biotechnology as a key component of the economy.

These trends in technology are seen in today's marketplace. The power of microprocessors has doubled every 18 months for the past 25 years—suggesting that microprocessors at least 10 times more powerful than today's Pentium will be available in just five years (for about $25!). The Internet already offers electronic magazines, shopping, and advertising, and between 20,000 and 25,000 new Web sites are being added each month. Other technologies such as satellite disks, DVD, MP3, HDTV, and voice recognition software are likely to replace or substitute for existing technologies such as cable TV, video tapes, CDs, low-resolution TV, and manual operations such as typing.[32]

Technology's Impact on Customer Value

Advances in technology are having important effects on marketing. First, the cost of technology is plummeting—causing the customer value assessment of technology-based products to focus on other dimensions such as quality, service, and relationships. When Computer Associates International introduced its software program Simply Money, it gave away the first million copies. Computer Associates reasoned that satisfied customers would later buy upgrades and related products. A similar approach is now used by many cellular telephone vendors, who charge little for the telephone if the purchase leads to a telephone service contract.[33]

Technology also provides value through the development of new products. Oldsmobile now offers customers an auto-navigation system that uses satellite signals to help the driver reach any destination. Under development are radarlike collision avoidance systems that disengage cruise control, reduce the engine speed, and even apply the brakes.[34] Other new products likely to be available soon include a "smart ski" with an embedded microprocessor that will adjust the flexibility of the ski to snow conditions; injectable health monitors that well send glucose, oxygen, and other clinical information to a wrist-watch-like monitor; and electronic books that will allow you to download any volume and view it on pages coated with electronic "ink" and embedded electrodes.[35]

Technology can also change existing products and the ways they are produced. Many companies are using technological developments to allow *recycling* products through the manufacturing cycle several times. The National Association for Plastic Container Recovery, for example, estimates that 50 percent of all plastic bottles are now recycled—usually to make polyester fibers that are spun into everything from

Technological change leads to new products. What products might be replaced by these innovations?

Examples of a recycling program by Ford and a precycling program by Lever.

sweaters to upholstery. In Germany, Ford emphasizes that its cars are assembled with parts that can be recycled. The ad above showing a child's toy, exclaims "I was a car" in the headline. Another approach is *precycling*—efforts by manufacturers to reduce waste by decreasing the amount of packaging they use. The development of new packaging materials, for example, has allowed DuPont to introduce a "minisip" collapsible pouch as an alternative to milk cartons in school lunch programs.[36]

Information Technology

Ultimately, the most important developments for marketers may be those related to information technology. Improved methods of collecting, storing, analyzing, and distributing information about consumers will allow marketers to better understand and serve customers. To provide customized service it is important to know who customers are, their product or service preferences, their individual approach to interacting with the company, and how they make a purchase. MCI has developed a sophisticated customer service system that electronically identifies callers, assesses their account history, and routes priority customers to get first-class treatment within three rings! In the future, smart software may interview customers via E-mail and automatically respond to simple questions, problems, or orders or make connections with a real person to deal with more difficult topics.[37]

Another recent development has been the use of electronic maps for a host of marketing applications. Labeled **geographic information systems** (GIS), this technology records different layers of data on the same map.[38] For example, a company can now develop a map of a city with additional information, such as demographics or sales, included in the layout. The fast-food chain Arby's, Inc. uses a GIS map to select store locations. Coca-Cola uses GIS to determine the best routing for its delivery trucks. And the Census Bureau now markets its TIGER (Topologically Integrated Geographic Encoding and Reference) file, a landmark project in demography. This software will provide a minutely detailed, computerized map of the entire United States, which can be combined with a company's own database to analyze customer sales. Do you want to drive somewhere during spring break? The American Automobile Association can provide you with a GIS map. The challenge for marketers in the new millennium will be to keep pace with the possibilities of digital technology.

Maps generated by geographic information systems, such as the map at right created with ESRI software, allow companies to make sophisticated marketing decisions.

ESRI

www.esri.com

COMPETITIVE FORCES

The fourth component of the environmental scan, **competition,** refers to the alternative firms that could provide a product to satisfy a specific market's needs. There are various forms of competition, and each company must consider its present and potential competitors in designing its marketing strategy.

Alternative Forms of Competition

There are four basic forms of competition that form a continuum from pure competition to monopolistic competition to oligopoly to monopoly. Chapter 14 contains further discussions on pricing practices under these four forms of competition.

At one end of the continuum is *pure competition,* in which every company has a similar product. Companies that deal in commodities common to agribusiness (for example, wheat, rice, and grain) often are in a pure competition position in which distribution (in the sense of shipping products) is important but other elements of marketing have little impact.

In the second point on the continuum, *monopolistic competition,* the many sellers compete with their products on a substitutable basis. For example, if the price of coffee rises too much, consumers may switch to tea. Coupons or sales are frequently used marketing tactics.

Oligopoly, a common industry structure, occurs when a few companies control the majority of industry sales. For example, AT&T, MCI, and Sprint control approximately 80 percent of the $16 billion international long-distance telephone service market. Similarly, the entertainment industry in the United States is dominated by Viacom, Disney, and Time Warner, and the U.S. defense contractor industry consists of Boeing, Raytheon, and Lockheed Martin. Critics of oligopolies suggest that because there are few sellers, price competition among firms is not desirable because it leads to reduced profits for all producers.[39]

The final point on the continuum, *monopoly,* occurs when only one firm sells the product. It has been common for producers of goods considered essential to a community: water, electricity, and telephone service. Typically, marketing plays a small role in a monopolistic setting because it is regulated by the state or federal government. Government control usually seeks to ensure price protection for the buyer, although deregulation in recent years has encouraged price competition in the electricity market.[40] The U.S. Justice Department recently filed an antitrust suit against Microsoft, claiming that its 86 percent share of the PC operating system market has given the company excessive control of the computer and software industries.[41]

Components of Competition

In developing a marketing program, companies must consider the factors that drive competition: entry, bargaining power of buyers and suppliers, existing rivalries, and substitution possibilities.[42] Scanning the environment requires a look at all of them. These factors relate to a firm's marketing mix decisions and may be used to create a barrier to entry, increase brand awareness, or intensify a fight for market share.

Entry   In considering the competition, a firm must assess the likelihood of new entrants. Additional producers increase industry capacity and tend to lower prices. A company scanning its environment must consider the possible **barriers to entry** for other firms, which are business practices or conditions that make it difficult for new firms to enter the market. Barriers to entry can be in the form of capital requirements, advertising expenditures, product identity, distribution access, or switching costs. The higher the expense of the barrier, the more likely it will deter new entrants. For example, Lucent Technologies is the largest supplier of phone network equipment in the world, and its past customers find it less expensive to upgrade their equipment than switch to another supplier.[43]

Power of Buyers and Suppliers   A competitive analysis must consider the power of buyers and suppliers. Powerful buyers exist when they are few in number, there are low switching costs, or the product represents a significant share of the buyer's total costs. This last factor leads the buyer to exert significant pressure for price competition. A supplier gains power when the product is critical to the buyer and when it has built up the switching costs.

Existing Competitors and Substitutes   Competitive pressures among existing firms depend on the rate of industry growth. In slow-growth settings, competition is more heated for any possible gains in market share. High fixed costs also create competitive pressures for firms to fill production capacity. For example, airlines offer discounts for making early reservations and charge penalties for changes or cancellations in an effort to fill seats, which represent a high fixed cost.

The New Look in American Corporations

Competition has had two other important effects on corporate America: (1) the use of the Internet as a way of doing business and (2) the restructuring of corporations.

Competing on the Internet   The Internet is changing customers' expectations about convenience, price, quality, and service. As a result, traditional bureaucratic, hierarchical organizations are learning that a new model—the "network organization" or "e-corporation"—is evolving as a new form of competition. These firms combine computer, the Web, and software to change everything about the way they operate. One of the most visible examples of the change is the brokerage firm Charles Schwab. In 1995 the company had no sales on the Web. Today more than $4 billion worth of securities are traded through the Schwab Web page every week. Customers access their account through an Internet connection, obtain research and information, place buy and sell orders, and receive confirmation in real time. Of Schwab's 5.5 million customers, 2 million are active electronic investors who account for one third of Schwab's assets.

The Internet is creating a new form of competition that will have an impact on every industry and business. Already 400,000 companies have created a presence on the Web, and while customers are changing the way they buy, workers and managers are changing too. Sales and service people are becoming consultants accessible by any customer. Managers are becoming coordinators of information, and businesses are beginning to operate with teams specializing in a narrow group of customer's needs. Industries to watch for rapid change include vacation travel, books, music, entertainment, computer hardware, and computer software.[44]

Restructuring Corporations   Although the process is known by various names—reengineering, streamlining, or **restructuring**—the result is the same: striving for more efficient corporations that can compete globally. For many firms, restructuring means reducing duplicate efforts in multiple company locations, closing or changing unprofitable plants and offices, and often laying off hundreds or thousands of employees. For example, Ford Motor Company recently merged its U.S. and European product development operations, refurbished seven plants, and reduced the number of managers by 20 percent. The result has been an improvement in efficiency—Ford has reduced the amount of time needed to get an engine from design to testing from 24 months to 100 days. Another result, however, has been a huge reduction in the number of middle managers in the work force. Employers are shifting from a philosophy of unconditional lifetime employment to one of "lifelong employability." This view is based on the idea that employers have an obligation to provide an opportunity of self-improvement and employees have an obligation to take charge of their own careers.[45]

Another approach to restructuring has been through mergers, acquisitions, and takeovers. In 1998 there were more than 12,000 mergers, including the seven largest of all time: Exxon and Mobil, Travelers Group and Citicorp, SBC Communications and Ameritech, Bell Atlantic and GTE, AT&T and Tele-Communications, NationsBank and Bank America, and British Petroleum and Amoco.[46] What is the explanation? In general, firms are striving for market dominance by ensuring control of distribution channels, access to markets, and cost reduction through economies of scale. Businesses are also discovering that information technology will allow effective management of large and complex organizations. Experts debate whether these mergers are good for the economy. While firms that dominate a market might command higher prices, they may also be vulnerable to faster, customer-focused entrepreneurs.[47]

CONCEPT CHECK

1. What is the difference between a consumer's disposable and discretionary income?

2. In pure competition there are _____ number of sellers.

3. What is a network organization?

REGULATORY FORCES

For any organization, the marketing and broader business decisions are constrained, directed, and influenced by regulatory forces. **Regulation** consists of restrictions state and federal laws place on business with regard to the conduct of its activities. Regulation exists to protect companies as well as consumers. Much of the regulation from the federal and state levels has been passed to ensure competition and fair business practices. For consumers, the focus of legislation is to protect them from unfair trade practices and ensure their safety.

Protecting Competition

Major federal legislation has been passed to encourage competition, which is deemed desirable because it permits the consumer to determine which competitor will succeed and which will fail. The first such law was the *Sherman Antitrust Act* (1890). Lobbying by farmers in the Midwest against fixed railroad shipping prices led to the passage of this act, which forbids (1) contracts, combinations, or conspiracies in restraint of trade and (2) actual monopolies or attempts to monopolize any part of trade or commerce. Because of vague wording and government inactivity, however, there was only one successful case against a company in the nine years after the act became law, and the Sherman Act was supplemented with the *Clayton Act* (1914). This act forbids certain actions that are likely to lessen competition, although no actual harm has yet occurred.

In the 1930s the federal government had to act again to ensure fair competition. During that time, large chain stores appeared, such as the Great Atlantic & Pacific Tea Company (A&P). Small businesses were threatened, and they lobbied for the *Robinson-Patman Act* (1936). This act makes it unlawful to discriminate in prices charged to different purchasers of the same product, where the effect may substantially lessen competition or help to create a monopoly.

Product-Related Legislation

Various federal laws in existence specifically address the product component of the marketing mix. Some are aimed at protecting the company, some at protecting the consumer, and at least one at protecting both.

Company Protection   A company can protect its competitive position in new and novel products under the patent law, which gives inventors the right to exclude others from making, using, or selling products that infringe the patented invention. The federal copyright law is another way for a company to protect its competitive position in a product. The copyright law gives the author of a literary, dramatic, musical, or artistic work the exclusive right to print, perform, or otherwise copy that work. Copyright is secured automatically when the work is created. However, the published work should bear an appropriate copyright notice, including the copyright symbol, the first year of publication, and the name of the copyright owner, and it must be registered under the federal copyright law. Digital technology has necessitated new copyright legislation to improve protection of copyrighted digital products. Producers of DVD movies, music recordings, and software want protection from devices designed to circumvent anti-piracy elements of their products.[48]

Consumer Protection   There are many consumer-oriented federal laws regarding products. One of the oldest is the *Meat Inspection Act* (1906), which provides for meat products to be wholesome, unadulterated, and properly labeled. The *Food, Drug and Cosmetics Act* (1938) is one of the most important of the federal regulatory laws. This act is aimed principally at preventing the adulteration or misbranding of the three categories of products. The various federal consumer protection laws include more than 30 amendments and separate laws relating to food, drugs, and cosmetics, such as the *Poison Prevention Packaging Act* (1970), the *Infant Formula Act* (1980) and the *Nutritional Labeling and Education Act* (1990). Various other consumer protection laws have a broader scope, such as the *Fair Packaging and Labeling Act* (1966), the *Child Protection Act* (1966), and the *Consumer Product Safety Act* (1972), which established the Consumer Product Safety Commission to monitor product safety and establish uniform product safety standards. Many of these recent laws came about because of **consumerism,** a grassroots movement started in the 1960s to increase the influence, power, and rights of consumers in dealing with institutions. The *Clean Air Act* (1990), designed to curb acid rain and air pollution, the *Telephone Consumer Protection Act* (1991), focusing on telemarketing abuses, and the *Children's Online*

ETHICS AND SOCIAL RESPONSIBILITY ALERT

Should Corporate Executives Be Personally Liable for Environmental Offenses?

ETHICS

Public concern over air, water, and ground pollution has sparked a debate over whether corporate executives should be personally liable for their company's environmental offenses. Opinion polls indicate that 75 percent of the general public believe they should; 51 percent of large-company executives believe they should not. The U.S. Justice Department has been criticized for not aggressively pursuing executive convictions and fines. In an average year, about 100 executive convictions or guilty pleas have been made

for environmental offenses, with fines ranging from several hundred thousand to millions of dollars and jail terms averaging one year. Exxon Corporation was fined $100 million for fouling Alaskan waters with oil; the president of a Burlington, Massachusetts, company was sentenced to two years in jail for ordering his employees to dump toxic waste down a sewer; and several judges have ordered executives to join the Sierra Club as part of their sentences.

Should corporate executives be personally liable for environmental offenses? If yes, should the penalty include both fines and prison terms? If no, who is liable?

Privacy Protection Act (1998), requiring parental permission before collecting personal information from minors,[49] are recent responses to consumer interests. This movement continues and is reflected in growing consumer demands for ecologically safe products and ethical and socially responsible business practices. One hotly debated issue concerns liability for environmental abuse. Read the Ethics and Social Responsibility Alert and ask yourself: Should corporate executives be personally liable for environmental offenses?[50]

Both Company and Consumer Protection   Trademarks are intended to protect both the firm selling a trademarked product and the consumer buying it. A Senate report states that:

> The purposes underlying any trademark statute [are] twofold. One is to protect the public so that it may be confident that, in purchasing a product bearing a particular trademark which it favorably knows, it will get the product which it asks for and wants to get. Secondly, where the owner of a trademark has spent energy, time, and money in presenting to the public the product, he is protected in this investment from misappropriation in pirates and cheats.

This statement was made in connection with another product-related law, the *Lanham Act* (1946), which provides for registration of a company's trademarks. Historically, the first user of a trademark in commerce had the exclusive right to use that particular word, name, or symbol in its business. Registration under the Lanham Act provides important advantages to a trademark owner that has used the trademark in interstate or foreign commerce, but it does not confer ownership. A company can lose its trademark if it becomes generic, which means that it has primarily come to be merely a common descriptive word for the product. Coca-Cola, Whopper, and Xerox are registered trademarks, and competitors cannot use these names. Aspirin and escalator are former trademarks that are now generic terms in the United States and can be used by anyone. In 1988, the *Trademark Law Revision Act* resulted in a major change to the Lanham Act—allowing a company to secure rights to a name before actual use by declaring an intent to use the name.[51]

One of the most recent changes in trademark law is the U.S. Supreme Court's ruling that companies may obtain trademarks for colors associated with their products. The reason is that, over time, consumers may begin to associate a particular color with a specific brand. Examples of products that may benefit from the new law include NutraSweet's sugar substitute in pastel blue packages and Owens-Corning Fiberglas

These products are identified by protected trademarks. Are any of these trademarks in danger of becoming generic?

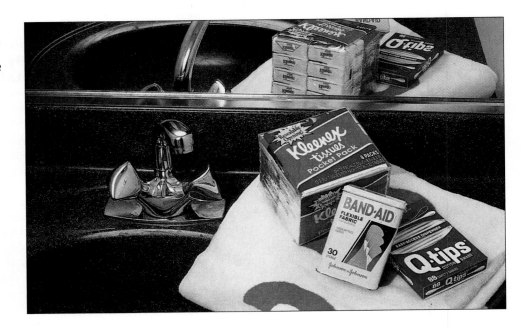

Corporation's pink insulation.[52] Another area of growing interest is the registration of Internet addresses, or domain names, as trademarks. Microsoft Corp., for example, recently learned that another company claims to have the rights to the name "Internet Explorer"—the name Microsoft uses for its browser software.[53]

Regulatory Controls on Pricing

The pricing component of the marketing mix is the focus of regulation from two perspectives: price fixing and price discounting. Although the Sherman Act did not outlaw price fixing, the courts view this behavior as *per se illegal* (*per se* means "through or of itself"), which means the courts see price fixing itself as illegal.

Certain forms of price discounting are allowed. Quantity discounts are acceptable; that is, buyers can be charged different prices for a product provided there are differences in manufacturing or delivery costs. Promotional allowances or services may be given to buyers on an equal basis proportionate to volume purchased. Also, a firm can meet a competitor's price "in good faith." Legal aspects of pricing are covered in more detail in Chapter 15.

Distribution and the Law

The government has four concerns with regard to distribution—earlier referred to as "place" actions in the marketing mix—and the maintenance of competition. The first, *exclusive dealing,* is an arrangement with a buyer to handle only the products of one manufacturer and not those of competitors. This practice is only illegal under the Clayton Act when it substantially lessens competition.

Requirement contracts require a buyer to purchase all or part of its needs for a product from one seller for a period of time. These contracts are not always illegal but depend on the court's interpretation of their impact on distribution.

Exclusive territorial distributorships are a third distribution issue often under regulatory scrutiny. In this situation, a manufacturer grants a distributor the sole rights to sell a product in a specific geographical area. The courts have found few violations with these arrangements.

The fourth distribution strategy is a *tying arrangement,* whereby a seller requires the purchaser of one product to also buy another item in the line. These contracts may be illegal when the seller has such economic power in the tying product that the seller can restrain trade in the tied product. Legal aspects of distribution are reviewed in greater detail in Chapter 16.

Advertising and Promotion Controls

Promotion and advertising are aspects of marketing closely monitored by the Federal Trade Commission (FTC), which was established by the *FTC Act of 1914.* The FTC has been concerned with deceptive or misleading advertising and unfair business practices and has the power to (1) issue cease and desist orders and (2) order corrective advertising. In issuing a *cease and desist order,* the FTC orders a company to stop practices it considers unfair. With *corrective advertising,* the FTC can require a company to spend money on advertising to correct previous misleading ads. The enforcement powers of the FTC are so significant that often just an indication of concern from the commission can cause companies to revise their promotion.

A landmark legal battle regarding deceptive advertising involved the Federal Trade Commission and Campbell Soup Co. It had been Campbell's practice to insert clear glass marbles into the bottom of soup containers used in print advertisements to bring the soup ingredients (for example, noodles or chicken) to the surface. The FTC ruled that the advertising was deceptive because it misrepresented the amount of solid ingredients in the soup, and it issued a cease and desist order. Campbell and its advertising agency agreed to discontinue the practice. Future ads used a ladle to show the ingredients.[54]

Other laws designed to regulate advertising practices include the *Federal Cigarette Labeling and Advertising Act* (1967), which requires health warnings on cigarette ads and packages, the *Public Health Cigarette Smoking Act* (1971), which prohibits advertising tobacco products on radio and television, and the *Children's Television Act* (1990), which limits the maximum amount of advertising during children's television programs to 10.5 minutes per hour on weekends and 12 minutes per hour on weekdays.

Control through Self-Regulation

The government has provided much legislation to create a competitive business climate and protect the consumer. An alternative to government control is **self-regulation,** where an industry attempts to police itself. The major television networks, for example, have used self-regulation to set their own guidelines for TV ads for children's toys. These guidelines have generally worked well. There are two problems with self-regulation, however: noncompliance by members and enforcement. In addition, if attempts at self-regulation are too strong, they may violate the Robinson-Patman Act. The best-known self-regulatory group is the Better Business Bureau (BBB). This agency is a voluntary alliance of companies whose goal is to help maintain fair practices. Although the BBB has no legal power, it does try to use "moral suasion" to get members to comply with its ruling. The BBB recently developed a new service, BBB Online, to provide objective consumer protection for Internet shoppers. Participating companies must agree to follow the Bureau's standards for commerce before they display the BBB Online logo on their Web site.[55]

CONCEPT CHECK

1. The _____ Act was punitive toward monopolies, whereas the _____ Act was preventive.

2. Describe some of the recent changes in trademark law.

3. How does the Better Business Bureau encourage companies to follow its standards for commerce?

SUMMARY

1 The population of the United States is aging as the over-65 population grows. Baby boomers, Generation X, and the Net Generation are important target markets with very different interests as consumers. The structure of American families is changing as blended families become more common. The population is shifting to Western and Sunbelt states and to remote suburbs and small towns.

2 Recognition of racial, ethnic, and geographical differences in product preferences has given rise to companies developing tailored marketing plans.

3 Culture incorporates material and abstract elements. Values are changing toward the roles of women and men, work, quality of life, and consumption.

4 Disposable income is the number of dollars left after taxes. Discretionary income is the money consumers have after purchasing their necessities. The median gross income (dollars before taxes) of U.S. households has been stable since 1970 in real income terms.

5 Technology increases customer value by reducing the cost of products, providing new products, and improving existing products. The most important new development for marketers may be advances in information technology that allow increasingly customized service.

6 Competition has had two major effects on U.S. corporations: (*a*) the use of the Internet as a way of doing business and (*b*) restructuring through mergers to improve efficiency.

7 The Sherman Antitrust Act of 1890 made monopolies illegal, whereas the Clayton Act tried to outlaw actions believed to lead to monopolies.

8 A company's brand name or symbol can be protected under the Lanham Act, but if the name becomes generic, the company no longer has sole right to the trademark.

9 Price fixing has been viewed as illegal by the courts. However, price discounting is allowed to meet competition or to account for differences in the cost of manufacture or distribution.

10 There are four aspects of distribution reviewed by courts: exclusive dealing arrangements, requirements contracts, exclusive territorial distributorships, and tying arrangements.

11 The Federal Trade Commission monitors unfair business practices and deceptive advertising. Two methods used in enforcement are (*a*) cease and desist orders and (*b*) corrective advertising.

12 Self-regulation attempts are common to some industries and are facilitated by organizations such as the Better Business Bureau. However, the effectiveness of self-regulation is coming under greater scrutiny by the courts.

KEY TERMS AND CONCEPTS

environmental scanning p. 74
social forces p. 76
demographics p. 76
mature household p. 76
baby boomers p. 77
Generation X p. 77
baby boomlet p. 77
blended family p. 78
regional marketing p. 80
culture p. 80
value consciousness p. 81
economy p. 82

gross income p. 83
disposable income p. 84
discretionary income p. 84
technology p. 84
geographic information systems p. 86
competition p. 87
barriers to entry p. 88
restructuring p. 89
regulation p. 89
consumerism p. 90
self-regulation p. 93

INTERNET EXERCISE

There are many sources of information that might be useful in an environmental scan. Two particularly useful Web sites include FEDSTATS (www.fedstats.gov) and *American Demographics* (www.demographics.com). The FEDSTATS page links 70 federal agencies including the U.S. Census Bureau, the Department of Commerce, and the Bureau of Labor Statistics. The *American Demographics* page provides text, tables, and graphics, and a search tool for articles describing consumer trends. Use the sites to help answer the following questions:

1 What is the current (to the minute) population of the United States? The world? What is the projected population of the United States in 2050?

2 What social or consumer trends are described in a recent edition of *American Demographics?*

APPLYING MARKETING CONCEPTS AND PERSPECTIVES

1 For many years Gerber's has manufactured baby food in small, single-sized containers. In conducting an environmental scan, identify three trends or factors that might significantly affect this company's future business, and then propose how Gerber's might respond to these changes.

2 Describe the new features you would add to an automobile designed for the mature household. In what magazines would you advertise to appeal to this target market?

3 The population shift from suburbs to exurbs and penturbia was discussed in this chapter. What businesses and industries are likely to benefit from this trend? How will retailers need to change to accommodate these consumers?

4 New technologies are continuously improving and replacing existing products. Although technological change is often difficult to predict, suggest how the following companies and products might be effected by the Internet and digital technologies: (*a*) Kodak cameras and film, (*b*) American Airlines, and (*c*) the Metropolitan Museum of Art.

5 In recent years in the brewing industry, a couple of large firms that have historically had most of the beer sales (Anheuser-Busch and Miller) have faced competition from many small regional brands. In terms of the continuum of competition, how would you explain this change?

6 When the airline industry became deregulated, how do you think the role of marketing changed? What elements of the marketing mix are more or less important since the deregulation?

7 The Johnson Company manufactures buttons and pins with slogans and designs. These pins are inexpensive to produce and are sold in retail outlets such as discount stores, hobby shops, and bookstores. Little equipment is needed for a new competitor to enter the market. What strategies should Johnson consider to create effective barriers to entry?

8 Why would Xerox be concerned about its name becoming generic?

 ## CASE 3–1   IMAGINATION PILOTS ENTERTAINMENT

What develops critical thinking, problem solving, and math skills; has an original musical score and sound effects; utilizes full-color graphics; and involves an adventure with the circus? The answer is one of the newest forms of edutainment—a CD-ROM game developed for children called "Where's Waldo?" The game is part of a growing number of offerings from an industry that is rapidly adapting to a wide variety of changes in the business environment. According to the *Hollywood Reporter,* which follows the new developments, "interactive start-ups face new challenges as they stake a claim in a rapidly changing market."

THE COMPANY

The developer of the "Where's Waldo?" game is a fast-growing, entrepreneurial company called Imagination Pilots Entertainment (www.ipilots.com). The founder of the company, Howard Tullman, has focused on developing multimedia entertainment, educational software, and interactive "cinematic" adventures with strong game content. One of the company's first products was the interactive CD-ROM game called *Blown Away,* which was developed as part of a joint venture with MGM/United Artists and released after the movie by the same name. Imagination Pilot's *Blown Away* won the "Game of the Year" award from *Computer Life* magazine, the Gold Medal Invision Award for Best Graphic Design from

New Media magazine, and the Innovators Software Showcase Award. Other Imagination Pilots products include *Panic in the Park* starring Erika Eleniak; *Virtual Erector Set,* which allows children to build 3-D, real-time models of vehicles; and an adventure game sequel to Arnold Schwarzenegger's movie, *Eraser.*

THE CHANGING ENVIRONMENT

Managers at Imagination Pilots are constantly monitoring social, economic, technological, competitive, and regulatory trends that may influence their business or the CD-ROM game industry. The most obvious trend, for example, is the rapid growth of the software market. Revenues for the packaged software market are expected to grow at an annual rate of 13 percent reaching $153 billion by 2000. In addition, while many industries are laying off employees, the software industry is a net creator of jobs—employing more than 435,000 workers in the United States alone, according to the Bureau of Labor Statistics. A niche within the overall software market is the multimedia software market. Multimedia products combine video, animation, still pictures, voice, music, graphics, and text into a single system, usually on CD-ROM and very often for education or entertainment applications. Sales of CD-ROM titles have doubled each year for the past several years and now exceed $1.2 billion.

Related trends are the increasing penetration of computers into homes due to declining PC prices, and the increasing number of installed CD-ROM drives. According to Tullman, "There are only now becoming enough PC CD-ROM computers in the marketplace, in terms of total units, to permit a number of products to be successful." Although the number has been increasing at an annual rate of 25 percent, the number of worldwide CD-ROM computers was still only a portion of all computers in use. The price of software is also declining while consumer expectations are increasing. Tullman observes that "the price of children's software is decreasing, and continues to decrease even while there is a greater demand for quality . . . the consumer and parents want to pay less for individual games, but they want them to be of high quality."

Increasing competition also represents a challenge for Imagination Pilots. In the children's entertainment category software developers include Electronic Arts, Acclaim Entertainment, Sierra On-Line, Broderbund, Xiphias, and a very large number of relatively small firms. In addition, as growth of computer sales slows in the corporate market, many large firms, including Microsoft, IBM, Compaq, and Apple Computer, are expected to try to develop children's software as a way into the home market. Many new titles are being introduced by both past developers and new entrants—creating a very competitive market.

A final factor Imagination Pilots and other developers must consider is the possibility of regulation. Concern about the content of some games had led to a discussion about the potential need for a rating system, much like the system used for movies.

THE ISSUES

Imagination Pilots is faced with several key challenges. First, it must attempt to ensure the success of new titles planned for development. Second, it must obtain distribution for existing and future products. Although the two are related, they require attention to very different issues.

Establishing a new title in a cluttered marketplace is likely to be difficult for any software developer. Estimates suggest that from $800,000 to $1.5 million is required to develop a competitive CD-ROM product. As a result, many firms seek partnerships or alliances to spread costs and reduce risk. Recovering the investment may be difficult, however, if sales volume is low or the profit margin of each unit sold is low. Part of Imagination Pilots' strategy is to license rights to existing stories, such as "Where's Waldo?", or movies, such as *Blown Away* and *Eraser*. Tullman believes that the name recognition of licensed titles is important to ensure adequate

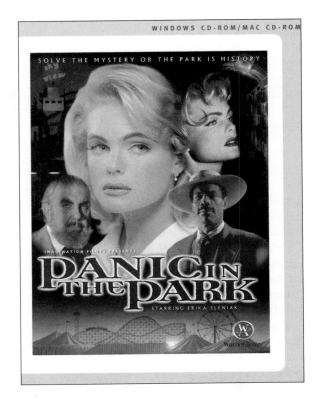

consumer interest. Some developers of children's software have used product line extensions to extend the life of existing titles. Sierra On-Line's *Quest,* for example, is now in its sixth release. New titles will need much more, though, to gain a foothold in the market.

Daniel P. Di Caro, chief operating officer at Imagination Pilots, argues that "distribution is increasingly becoming the most important factor in the success of a product, assuming you have a good product to start with." In the past the traditional channel of distribution was through software specialty stores such as Egghead Software, Babbages, and Software Etc. More recently, sales have increased in computer superstores such as CompUSA, department stores such as Sears and Wal-Mart, consumer electronic stores such as Best Buy and Circuit City, and warehouse stores such as Sam's and Office Depot. Their relationship with Warner Music Group provides Imagination Pilots with a strong distribution partner with access to many of these channels. In

the future additional channels such as catalogs, interactive television channels, and kiosks may offer the company new distribution opportunities. Imagination Pilots is already testing an online service which makes its games available to the Internet and World Wide Web community!

Questions

1 Conduct an environmental scan for Imagination Pilots Entertainment. How are each of the five environmental forces (social, economic, technological, competitive, and regulatory) likely to influence their multimedia game business?

2 What are the key challenges facing Imagination Pilots? Describe the actions taken by Imagination Pilots to (*a*) ensure the success of, and (*b*) obtain distribution for its games.

3 What are the advantages of making Imagination Pilot's games available online?

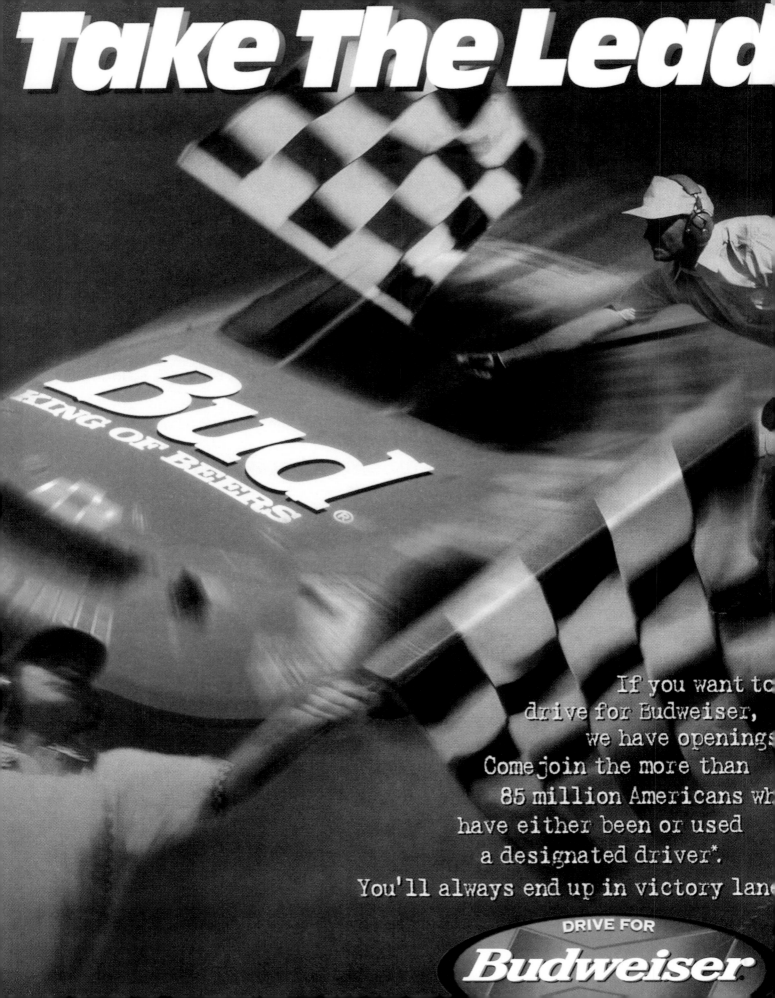

CHAPTER FOUR

ETHICS AND SOCIAL RESPONSIBILITY IN MARKETING

4

AFTER READING THIS CHAPTER YOU SHOULD BE ABLE TO:

• Appreciate the nature and significance of ethics in marketing.

• Understand the differences between legal and ethical behavior in marketing.

• Identify factors that influence ethical and unethical marketing decisions.

• Distinguish among the different concepts of ethics and social responsibility.

• Recognize the importance of ethical and socially responsible consumer behavior.

THERE IS MORE BREWING AT ANHEUSER-BUSCH THAN BEER

Why would a company spend more than $200 million since 1982 trying to convince people not to abuse its products and millions more to decrease litter and solid waste? Ask Anheuser-Busch, the world's largest brewer.

Anheuser-Busch has been a leader in the campaign for responsible drinking and environment-conscious disposition of its packaging. The company's "Know When to Say When" campaign began in 1982 and consists of a variety of programs and activities designed to fight alcohol abuse. The campaign's most visible element is a national advertising effort that includes television, radio, print, and outdoor ads. In 1989, the brewery made beer history by creating a Department of Consumer Awareness and Education to encourage safe driving and responsible drinking habits. Such efforts have contributed to a sizeable decline in fatal drunk-driving accidents and a 40 percent drop in teenage drunk-driving deaths since 1990.

Anheuser-Busch furthers these efforts with English- and Spanish-language versions of its "Family Talk about Drinking" program aimed at parents. This program consists of a free guidebook and video designed to help parents discuss the topic of underage drinking with their children. More than 2 million guidebooks have been distributed to parents and educators since 1990.

Responsibility at Anheuser-Busch is broader than the successful "Know When to Say When" campaign. The company is an advocate and sponsor of numerous efforts to preserve the environment. A notable example is its massive recycling effort through Anheuser-Busch Recycling Corporation (ABRC). ABRC is the world's largest recycler of aluminum cans. ABRC recycles more than

600 million pounds of aluminum annually—the equivalent of more than 110 percent of the beer cans sold by Anheuser-Busch. The rationale for founding ABRC was simple: Voluntary recycling reduces litter and solid waste while conserving natural resources.

Anheuser-Busch acts on what it views as an ethical obligation to its customers with the "Know When to Say When" campaign. At the same time, the company's multifaceted efforts to protect the environment reflect its social responsibility to the general public.[1]

NATURE AND SIGNIFICANCE OF MARKETING ETHICS

Ethics are the moral principles and values that govern the actions and decisions of an individual or group.[2] They serve as guidelines on how to act rightly and justly when faced with moral dilemmas.

Ethical/Legal Framework in Marketing

A good starting point for understanding the nature and significance of ethics is the distinction between legality and ethicality of marketing decisions. Figure 4–1 helps to visualize the relationship between laws and ethics.[3] While ethics deal with personal moral principles and values, **laws** are society's values and standards that are enforceable in the courts. This distinction can sometimes lead to the rationalization that if a behavior is within reasonable ethical and legal limits, then it is not really illegal or unethical. When a recent survey asked the question, "Is it OK to get around the law if you don't actually break it?" 61 percent of businesspeople who took part responded "Yes."[4] How would you answer this question?

There are numerous situations in which judgment plays a large role in defining ethical and legal boundaries. Consider the following situations. After reading each, assign it to the cell in Figure 4–1 that you think best fits the situation along the ethical–legal continuum.[5]

1. More than 70 percent of the physicians in the Maricopa County (Arizona) Medical Society agreed to establish a maximum fee schedule for health services to curb rising medical costs. All physicians were required to adhere to this schedule as a condition for membership in the society. The U.S. Supreme Court ruled that this agreement to set prices violated the Sherman Act and represented price fixing, which is illegal.
2. A company in California sells a computer program to auto dealers showing that car buyers should finance their purchase rather than paying cash. The program omits the effect of income taxes and misstates the interest earned on savings over the loan period. The finance option always provides a net benefit over the cash option. Company employees agree that the program does mislead buyers, but say the company will "provide what [car dealers] want as long as it is not against the law."
3. China is the world's largest tobacco-producing country and has 300 million smokers. Approximately 700,000 Chinese die annually from smoking-related illnesses. This figure is expected to rise to more than 2 million by 2025. China restricts tobacco imports. U.S. trade negotiators advocate free trade, thus allowing U.S. tobacco companies to market their products in China. Critics say that the U.S. government should not assist in the promotion of smoking in China.

Did these situations fit neatly into Figure 4–1 as clearly ethical and legal or unethical and illegal? Probably not. As you read further in this chapter, you will be asked to consider other ethical dilemmas.

FIGURE 4–1
Classifying marketing
decisions according to ethical
and legal relationships

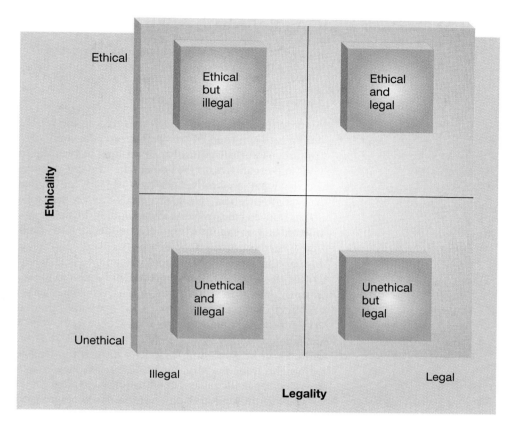

Current Perceptions of Ethical Behavior

There has been a public outcry about the ethical practices of businesspeople.[6] Public opinion surveys show that 58 percent of U.S. adults rate the ethical standards of business executives as only "fair" or "poor"; 90 percent think white-collar crime is "very common" or "somewhat common"; 76 percent say the lack of ethics in businesspeople contributes to tumbling societal moral standards; only the U.S. government is viewed as less trustworthy than corporations among institutions in the United States; and advertising practitioners and car salespeople are thought to be among the least ethical occupations. A recent survey of 1,694 corporate employees generally confirms this public perception. When asked if they were aware of ethical problems in their companies, 41 percent answered yes.

There are at least four possible reasons the state of perceived ethical business conduct is at its present level. First, there is increased pressure on businesspeople to make decisions in a society characterized by diverse value systems. Second, there is a growing tendency for business decisions to be judged publicly by groups with different values and interests. Third, the public's expectations of ethical business behavior has increased. Finally, and most disturbing, ethical business conduct may have declined.

CONCEPT CHECK

1. What are ethics?

2. What are four possible reasons for the present state of ethical conduct in the United States?

UNDERSTANDING ETHICAL MARKETING BEHAVIOR

Researchers have identified numerous factors that influence ethical marketing behavior.[7] Figure 4–2 presents a framework that shows these factors and their relationships.

Societal Culture and Norms

As described in Chapter 3, *culture* refers to the set of values, ideas, and attitudes of a homogeneous group of people that are transmitted from one generation to the next. Culture also affects ethical relationships between individuals, groups, and the institutions and organizations they create. In this way, culture serves as a socializing force that dictates what is morally right and just. This means that moral standards are relative to particular societies.[8] These standards often reflect the laws and regulations that affect social and economic behavior, including business practices, which can create moral dilemmas. For example, Levi Strauss decided to end much of its business dealings in China because of what the company called "pervasive human rights abuses." According to its vice president for corporate marketing: "There are wonderful commercial opportunities in China. But when ethical issues collide with commercial appeal, we try to ensure ethics as the trump card. For us, ethical issues precede all others."[9]

Many of the laws affecting U.S. marketing practices were outlined in Chapter 3. Actions that restrain trade, fix prices, deceive buyers, and result in unsafe products are considered morally wrong in the United States and other countries. However, different cultures view marketing practices differently. Consider the use of another's ideas, copyright, trademark, or patent. These are viewed as intellectual property, and unauthorized use is illegal and unethical in the United States.

Outside the United States, however, is another story.[10] U.S. companies estimate that unauthorized use of their copyrights, trademarks, and patents in countries such as China, Mexico, and Korea costs about $63 billion annually. In Korea, for instance, copying is partly rooted in its society's culture. According to a U.S. trade official, many Koreans "have the idea that the thoughts of one man should benefit all," and the Korean government rarely prosecutes infringements.

Read the accompanying Marketing NewsNet,[11] keeping in mind the ethical–legal framework in Figure 4–1. Would the unauthorized use of copyrighted computer software be considered unethical despite its prevalence?

Business Culture and Industry Practices

Societal culture provides a foundation for understanding moral behavior in business activities. *Business cultures* "comprise the effective rules of the game, the boundaries be-

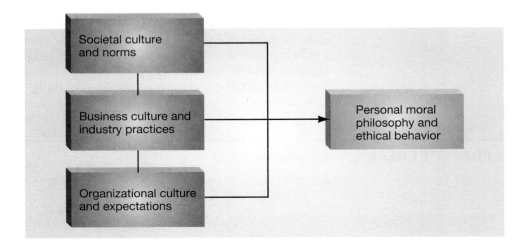

FIGURE 4–2
A framework for understanding ethical behavior

MARKETING NEWSNET

Software Piracy and Pirates at Home and Abroad

TECHNOLOGY

Have you copied a friend's software? If yes, you are among 33 percent of college students who acquire software by copying it. And yes, you are a software pirate because unauthorized copying of software is illegal.

The incidence and implications of software piracy are enormous. The U.S. Software Publishers Association (SPA) estimates that 4 in every 10 new business software applications installed globally are pirated, that is, copied illegally. The unauthorized copying of business software costs their producers the equivalent of $12.4 billion in worldwide sales annually.

Software piracy has become widespread in many countries and regions of the world. According to SPA, 77 percent of software in Eastern Europe is pirated, 65 percent in the Middle East and Africa, 62 percent in Latin America, and 39 percent in Western Europe. Countries with the highest piracy rates are Vietnam (98 percent), China (96 percent), Bulgaria (93 percent), and Russia (89 percent). About 28 percent of the software used in the United States has been copied illegally.

Software programs are intellectual property, and their unauthorized use is illegal in many countries. But, for some, their reproduction and distribution is not considered unethical. Indeed, 42 percent of U.S. college students consider the practice acceptable behavior!

tween competitive and unethical behavior, [and] the codes of conduct in business dealings."[12] Consumers have witnessed numerous instances where business cultures in the brokerage (inside trading), insurance (deceptive sales practices), and defense (bribery) industries went awry. Business culture affects ethical conduct both in the exchange relationship between sellers and buyers and in the competitive behavior among sellers.

Ethics of Exchange   The exchange process is central to the marketing concept. Ethical exchanges between sellers and buyers should result in both parties being better off after a transaction.

Prior to the 1960s, the legal concept of **caveat emptor**—let the buyer beware—was pervasive in the American business culture. In 1962 President John F. Kennedy outlined a **Consumer Bill of Rights** that codified the ethics of exchange between buyers and sellers. These were the right (1) to safety, (2) to be informed, (3) to choose, and (4) to be heard. Consumers expect and often demand that these rights be protected, as have American businesses.

The right to safety manifests itself in industry and federal safety standards for most products sold in the United States. In fact, the U.S. Consumer Product Safety Commission routinely monitors the safety of 15,000 consumer products. However, even the most vigilant efforts to ensure safe products cannot foresee every possibility. Mattel's experience with its Cabbage Patch Snacktime Kids doll is a case in point.[13] The doll was designed to "eat" plastic french fries, celery, and other tidbits by drawing them into its motorized mouth. Despite exhaustive laboratory and in-home testing, Mattel executives did not consider that a child's hair might get caught in the doll's mouth and cause harm.

It did! Mattel immediately informed buyers of the safety issue, pulled the dolls from store shelves, refunded buyers, and discontinued the product.

The right to be informed means that marketers have an obligation to give consumers complete and accurate information about products and services, but this is not always the case. For example, three U.S. advertising agencies recently agreed to settle Federal Trade Commission (FTC) claims that they failed to disclose the actual costs of car leases and credit transactions in their advertising for three Japanese car makers.[14] This right also applies to the solicitation of personal information over the Internet and its subsequent use by marketers.[15] A recent FTC survey of Web sites indicated that 92 percent collect personal information such as consumer e-mail addresses, telephone numbers, shopping habits, and financial data. Yet only 14 percent of Web sites inform consumers of what is done with this information once obtained. Because consumers often assume that personal information is confidential, it was therefore understandable that subscribers to America Online (AOL) balked when AOL proposed giving member information to partners who could then telemarket to them. AOL backed down. The consumer right to be informed has spawned numerous federal legislation and self-regulation initiatives restricting disclosure of subscriber information by online services.

Relating to the third right, today many supermarket chains demand "slotting allowances" from manufacturers, in the form of cash or free goods, to stock new products. This practice could limit the number of new products available to consumers and interfere with their right to choose. One critic of this practice remarked: "If we had had slotting allowances a few years ago, we might not have had granola, herbal tea, or yogurt."[16]

Finally, the right to be heard means that consumers should have access to public-policy makers regarding complaints about products and services. This right is illustrated in limitations put on telemarketing practices. Consumer complaints about late-night and repeated calls resulted in the Telephone Consumer Protection Act of 1991. Additional curbs on misrepresentation have been enacted by the FTC as a result of continued consumer complaints.[17]

Mattel recognized consumer rights to safety and to be informed in its recall of the popular Cabbage Patch Snacktime Kids doll.

Mattel
www.mattel.com

Ethics of Competition   Business culture also affects ethical behavior in competition. Two kinds of unethical behavior are most common: (1) industrial espionage and (2) bribery.

Industrial espionage is the clandestine collection of trade secrets or proprietary information about a company's competitors. About 50 percent of large U.S. and Canadian firms have uncovered espionage in some form, costing them more than $100 billion a year.[18] This practice is most prevalent in high-technology industries such as electronics, specialty chemicals, industrial equipment, aerospace, and pharmaceuticals, where technical know-how and trade secrets separate industry leaders from followers. But espionage can occur anywhere—even in the ready-to-eat cookie industry! Procter & Gamble charged that competitors photographed its plants and production lines, stole a sample of its cookie dough, and infiltrated a confidential sales presentation to learn about its technology, recipe, and marketing plan. The competitors paid Procter & Gamble $120 million in damages after a lengthy dispute.[19] The **Economic Espionage Act** makes the theft of trade secrets a federal crime in the United States. It prescribes prison sentences of up to 15 years and fines up to $500,000 for individuals. Agents of foreign governments found guilty of industrial espionage face a 25-year prison sentence and a $10 million fine.[20]

The second form of unethical competitive behavior is giving and receiving bribes and kickbacks. Bribes and kickbacks are often disguised as gifts, consultant fees, and favors. This practice is more common in business-to-business and government marketing than in consumer marketing. For example, two American Honda Motor Company executives were recently fined and sentenced to prison for extracting $15 million in kickbacks from Honda dealers and advertising agencies, and a series of highly pub-

WEB LINK

The Commercial Corruption Perception Index

Commercial corruption in the global marketplace varies widely by country. Transparency International, based in Berlin, Germany, polls employees of multinational firms and institutions and political analysts and annually ranks countries based on the perceived level of corruption.

To obtain the most recent ranking, visit the Transparency International Web site at www.transparency. de/documents/press-releases/index.html/.

Scroll to the Corruption Perception Index, and see where the United States stands in the rankings as well as its neighbors, Canada and Mexico. Which country listed in the most recent ranking has the best ranking, and which has the worst ranking?

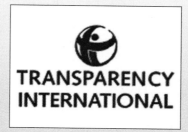

licized trials uncovered widespread bribery in the U.S. Defense Department's awarding of $160 billion in military contracts.[21]

The prevalence of bribery in international marketing prompted legislation to curb this practice. The **Foreign Corrupt Practices Act** makes it a crime for U.S. corporations to bribe an official of a foreign government or political party to obtain or retain business in a foreign country. In the past 20 years, at least 25 individuals and corporations have been convicted or have pleaded guilty to bribery or related offenses. Bribery is looked upon differently in other business cultures, however. In France and Greece, bribes paid to foreign companies are a tax-deductible expense![22]

In general, ethical standards are more likely to be compromised in industries experiencing intense competition and in countries in earlier stages of economic development. A recent poll of executives employed by multinational firms revealed that Nigeria, Russia, and Columbia evidenced the least ethical business cultures. Denmark, Finland, and Sweden were viewed as having the most ethical business cultures among industrialized countries.[23] Commercial corruption on a worldwide scale is monitored by Transparency International. Visit their Web site described in the accompanying Web Link box, and view the most recent country corruption rankings.

Corporate Culture and Expectations

A third influence on ethical practices is corporate culture. *Corporate culture* reflects the shared values, beliefs, and purpose of employees that affect individual and group behavior. The culture of a company demonstrates itself in the dress ("We don't wear ties"), sayings ("The IBM Way"), and manner of work (team efforts) of employees. Culture is also apparent in the expectations for ethical behavior present in formal codes of ethics and the ethical actions of top management and co-workers.

Codes of Ethics   A **code of ethics** is a formal statement of ethical principles and rules of conduct. It is estimated that 60 percent of U.S. companies and one half of European companies have some sort of ethics code, and 1 of every 10 corporate boards of directors now has a separate ethics committee to monitor company practices.[24] Ethics codes and committees typically address contributions to government officials and political parties, relations with customers and suppliers, conflicts of interest, and accurate recordkeeping. For example, General Mills provides guidelines for dealing with suppliers, competitors, and customers and recruits new employees who share these views. However, an ethics code is rarely enough to ensure ethical behavior. Johnson & Johnson

CODE OF ETHICS

Members of the American Marketing Association (AMA) are committed to ethical professional conduct. They have joined together in subscribing to this Code of Ethics embracing the following topics:

Responsibilities of the Marketer

Marketers must accept responsibility for the consequence of their activities and make every effort to ensure that their decisions, recommendations, and actions function to identify, serve, and satisfy all relevant publics: customers, organizations, and society.

Marketers' professional conduct must be guided by:

1. The basic rule of professional ethics: not knowingly to do harm.
2. The adherence to all applicable laws and regulations.
3. The accurate representation of their education, training and experience.
4. The active support, practice, and promotion of this Code of Ethics.

Honesty and Fairness

Marketers shall uphold and advance the integrity, honor, and dignity of the marketing profession by:

1. Being honest in serving consumers, clients, employees, suppliers, distributors, and the public.

2. Not knowingly participating in conflict of interest without prior notice to all parties involved.
3. Establishing equitable fee schedules including the payment or receipt of usual, customary, and/or legal compensation or marketing exchanges.

Rights and Duties of Parties in the Marketing Exchange Process

Participants in the marketing exchange process should be able to expect that:

1. Products and services offered are safe and fit for their intended uses.
2. Communications about offered products and services are not deceptive.
3. All parties intend to discharge their obligations, financial and otherwise, in good faith.
4. Appropriate internal methods exist for equitable adjustment and/or redress of grievances concerning purchases.

It is understood that the above would include, *but is not limited to*, the following responsibilities of the marketer:

In the area of product development and management

- Disclosure of all substantial risks associated with product or service usage.

FIGURE 4–3
American Marketing
Association Code of Ethics

American Marketing Association
www.ama.org

has an ethics code and emphasizes that its employees be just and ethical in their behavior. But neither prohibited some of its employees from shredding papers to hinder a recent government probe into the firm's marketing of an acne cream, Retin-A.[25]

The lack of specificity is one of the major reasons for the violation of ethics codes. Employees must often judge whether a specific behavior is really unethical. The American Marketing Association has addressed this issue by providing a detailed code of ethics, which all members agree to follow. This code is shown in Figure 4–3.

Ethical Behavior of Management and Co-Workers   A second reason for violating ethics codes rests in the perceived behavior of top management and co-workers.[26] Observing peers and top management and gauging responses to unethical behavior play an important role in individual actions. A recent study of business executives reported that 40 percent had been implicitly or explicitly rewarded for engaging in ethically troubling behavior. Moreover, 31 percent of those who refused to engage in unethical behavior were penalized, either through outright punishment or a diminished status in the company.[27] Clearly, ethical dilemmas often bring personal and professional conflict. For this reason, 35 states have laws protecting **whistle-blowers,** employees who report unethical or illegal actions of their employers. Some firms, such as General Dynamics and Dun & Bradstreet, have appointed ethics officers responsible for safeguarding these individuals from recrimination.

Personal Moral Philosophy and Ethical Behavior

Ultimately, ethical choices are based on the personal moral philosophy of the decision maker. Moral philosophy is learned through the process of socialization with friends and family and by formal education. It is also influenced by the societal, business, and

FIGURE 4–3 *(CONCLUDED)*

- Identification of any product component substitution that might materially change the product or impact on the buyer's purchase decision.
- Identification of extra-cost added features.

In the area of promotions

- Avoidance of false and misleading advertising.
- Rejection of high-pressure manipulation, or misleading sales tactics.
- Avoidance of sales promotions that use deception or manipulation.

In the area of distribution

- Not manipulating the availability of a product for purpose of exploitation.
- Not using coercion in the marketing channel.
- Not exerting undue influence over the reseller's choice to handle the product.

In the area of pricing

- Not engaging in price fixing.
- Not practicing predatory pricing.
- Disclosing the full price associated with any purchase.

In the area of marketing research

- Prohibiting selling or fund raising under the guise of conducting research.

- Maintaining research integrity by avoiding misrepresentation and omission of pertinent research data.
- Treating outside clients and suppliers fairly.

Organizational Relationships

Marketers should be aware of how their behavior may influence or impact on the behavior of others in organizational relationships. They should not demand, encourage, or apply coercion to obtain unethical behavior in their relationships with others, such as employees, suppliers, or customers.

1. Apply confidentiality and anonymity in professional relationships with regard to privileged information.
2. Meet their obligations and responsiblities in contracts and mutual agreements in a timely manner.
3. Avoid taking the work of others, in whole or in part, and represent this work as their own or directly benefit from it without compensation or consent of the originator or owner.
4. Avoid manipulation to take advantage of situations to maximize personal welfare in a way that unfairly deprives or damages the organization or others.

Any AMA members found to be in violation of any provision of this Code of Ethics may have his or her Association membership suspended or revoked.

Source: Reprinted by permission of the American Marketing Association.

corporate culture in which a person finds him- or herself. Moral philosophies are of two types: (1) moral idealism and (2) utilitarianism.[28]

Moral Idealism   **Moral idealism** is a personal moral philosophy that considers certain individual rights or duties as universal, regardless of the outcome. This philosophy exists in the Consumer Bill of Rights and is favored by moral philosophers and consumer interest groups. For example, the right to know applies to probable defects in an automobile that relate to safety.

This philosophy also applies to ethical duties. For example, Jerome LiCari, director of research for the Beech-Nut Nutrition Corporation, advised the Food and Drug Administration that Beech-Nut was selling a blend of synthetic ingredients labeled as 100 percent apple juice. He did so only after his superiors ignored his internal memos. Beech-Nut was subsequently fined $2 million, the company's market share dropped 3 percent, and two executives were indicted. When asked why he acted as he did, LiCari said: "I thought apple juice should be made from apples."[29] LiCari later resigned from Beech-Nut.

Utilitarianism   An alternative perspective on moral philosophy is **utilitarianism,** which is a personal moral philosophy that focuses on "the greatest good for the greatest number," by assessing the costs and benefits of the consequences of ethical behavior. If the benefits exceed the costs, then the behavior is ethical. If not, then the behavior is unethical. This philosophy underlies the economic tenets of capitalism and, not surprisingly, is embraced by many business executives and students.[30]

Utilitarian reasoning was apparent in Nestlé Food Corporation's marketing of Good Start infant formula, sold by Nestlé's Carnation Company. The formula, promoted as hypoallergenic, was designed to prevent or reduce colic caused by an infant's allergic reaction to cow's milk—a condition suffered by 2 percent of babies. However, some severely milk-allergic infants experienced serious side effects after using Good Start, including convulsive vomiting. Physicians and parents charged that the hypoallergenic claim was misleading, and the Food and Drug Administration investigated the matter. A Nestlé vice president defended the claim and product, saying, "I don't understand why our product should work in 100 percent of cases. If we wanted to say it was fool-proof, we would have called it allergy-free. We call it hypo-, or less, allergenic."[31] Nestlé officials seemingly believed that most allergic infants would benefit from Good Start—"the greatest good for the greatest number." However, other views prevailed, and the claim was dropped from the product label.

An appreciation for the nature of ethics, coupled with a basic understanding of why unethical behavior arises, alerts a person to when and how ethical issues exist in marketing decisions. Ultimately, ethical behavior rests with the individual, but the consequences affect many.

CONCEPT CHECK

1. What rights are included in the Consumer Bill of Rights?

2. What ethical practice is addressed in the Foreign Corrupt Practices Act?

3. What is meant by moral idealism?

UNDERSTANDING SOCIAL RESPONSIBILITY IN MARKETING

As we saw in Chapter 1, the societal marketing concept stresses marketing's social responsibility by not only satisfying the needs of consumers but also providing for society's welfare. **Social responsibility** means that organizations are part of a larger society and are accountable to that society for their actions. Like ethics, agreement on the nature and scope of social responsibility is often difficult to come by, given the diversity of values present in different societal, business, and organizational cultures.[32]

Concepts of Social Responsibility

Figure 4–4 shows three concepts of social responsibility: (1) profit responsibility, (2) stakeholder responsibility, and (3) societal responsibility.

Profit Responsibility   *Profit responsibility* holds that companies have a simple duty—to maximize profits for their owners or stockholders. This view is expressed by Nobel Laureate Milton Friedman, who said, "There is one and only one social responsibility of business—to use its resources and engage in activities designed to increase its profits so long as it stays within the rules of the game, which is to say, engages in open and free competition without deception or fraud."[33] Genzyme, the maker of Ceredase, a drug that treats a genetic illness called Gaucher's disease that affects 20,000 people worldwide, has been criticized for apparently adopting this view in its pricing practices. Genzyme charges up to $200,000 for a year's worth of Ceredese. Critics claim this practice takes advantage of the federal "orphan drug" law, which grants companies a seven-year monopoly on drugs for rare diseases, and is engaged in profiteering. A Genzyme spokesperson responded by saying that Ceredase profits are below industry standards and that the company freely gives the drug to patients without insurance.[34]

Stakeholder Responsibility   Frequent criticism of the profit view has led to a broader concept of social responsibility. *Stakeholder responsibility* focuses on the obligations an organization has to those who can affect achievement of its objectives.

FIGURE 4–4
Three concepts of social
responsibility

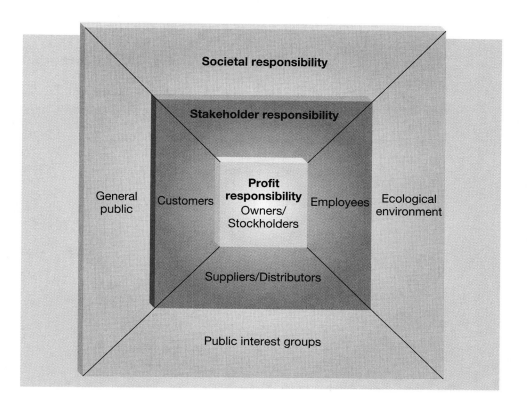

FIGURE 4–4
Three concepts of social responsibility

These constituencies include customers, employees, suppliers, and distributors. Source Perrier S.A., the supplier of Perrier bottled water, exercised this responsibility when it recalled 160 million bottles of water in 120 countries after traces of a toxic chemical were found in 13 bottles. The recall cost the company $35 million, and $40 million more was lost in sales. Even though the chemical level was not harmful to humans, Source Perrier's president believed he acted in the best interests of the firm's consumers, distributors, and employees by removing "the least doubt, as minimal as it might be, to weigh on the image of the quality and purity of our product."[35]

Societal Responsibility   An even broader concept of social responsibility has emerged in recent years. *Societal responsibility* refers to obligations that organizations have to the (1) preservation of the ecological environment and (2) general public. Concerns about the environment and public welfare are represented by interest and advocacy groups such as Greenpeace, an international environmental organization.

Chapter 3 detailed the growing importance of ecological issues in marketing. Companies have responded to this concern through what is termed **green marketing**— marketing efforts to produce, promote, and reclaim environmentally sensitive products. Green marketing takes many forms.[36]

At 3M, product development opportunities emanate both from consumer research and its "Pollution Prevention Pays" program. This program solicits employee suggestions on how to reduce pollution and recycle materials. During the past 20 years, this program has generated 4,000 ideas that eliminated more than 1.5 billion pounds of air, water, and solid waste pollutants from the environment. Mercedes-Benz designed its S-class sedans and 500/600 SEC luxury coupes to be entirely recyclable. Levi Strauss markets cotton clothing lines that are organically grown and naturally colored, thus reducing the need for dyes, a source of water pollution. The aluminum industry recycles two thirds of aluminum cans for reuse and pays consumers more than $1 billion annually for used cans. These voluntary responses to environmental issues have been implemented with little or no additional cost to consumers.

MARKETING NEWSNET

Will Consumers Switch Brands for a Cause? Yes, If . . .

American Express Company pioneered cause-related marketing (CRM) when it sponsored the renovation of the Statue of Liberty. This effort raised $1.7 million for the renovation, increased card usage among cardholders, and attracted new cardholders. In 1998, U.S. companies raised more than $2.5 billion for causes they champion. It is estimated that CRM will raise $5 billion in 2001.

CRM benefits companies as well as causes. Research indicates that 60 percent of U.S. consumers say they have a more favorable opinion of companies that support causes. Also, 76 percent of consumers say they will switch to a brand or retailer that supports a good cause if the price and quality of brands or retailers are equal. In short, CRM may be a valued point of difference for brands and companies, all other things being equal.

Almost 8,500 companies around the world have met ISO 14000 standards for environmental quality and green marketing. Japan has the most ISO 14000 certified companies.

ISO 14000
www.iso14000.com

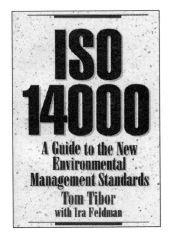

A global undertaking to further green marketing efforts is the ISO 14000 initiative developed by the International Standards Organization (ISO) in Geneva, Switzerland. **ISO 14000** consists of worldwide standards for environmental quality and green marketing practices. These standards have been embraced by 38 countries, including the United States, members of the European Union, and most Pacific Rim nations.[37]

Socially responsible efforts on behalf of the general public are becoming more common. A formal practice is **cause-related marketing** (CRM), which occurs when the charitable contributions of a firm are tied directly to the customer revenues produced through the promotion of one of its products.[38] This definition distinguishes CRM from a firm's standard charitable contributions, which are outright donations. For example, Procter & Gamble raises funds for the Special Olympics when consumers purchase selected company products, and MasterCard International links usage of its card with fund raising for institutions that combat cancer, heart disease, child abuse, drug abuse, and muscular dystrophy. Barnes & Noble promotes literacy, and Coca-Cola sponsors local Boys and Girls Clubs. Avon Products, Inc., focuses on different issues in different countries: breast cancer in the United States, Canada, Philippines, Mexico, Venezuela, Malaysia, and Spain; programs for women who care for senior citizens in Japan; emotional and financial support for mothers in Germany; and AIDS in Thailand. CRM programs incorporate all three concepts of social responsibility by addressing public concerns and satisfying customer needs. They can also enhance corporate sales and profits as described in the accompanying Marketing NewsNet.[39]

Marketing and social responsibility programs are often integrated, as is the case with McDonald's. Its concern for ill children is apparent in the opening of another Ronald McDonald House for children and their families.

McDonald's
www.mcdonalds.com

The Social Audit

Converting socially responsible ideas into actions involves careful planning and monitoring of programs. Many companies develop, implement, and evaluate their social responsibility efforts by means of a **social audit,** which is a systematic assessment of a firm's objectives, strategies, and performance in the domain of social responsibility. Frequently, marketing and social responsibility programs are integrated, as is the case with McDonald's. The company's concern for the needs of families with children who are chronically or terminally ill was converted into some 130 Ronald McDonald Houses. These facilities, located near treatment centers, enable families to stay together during the child's care. In this case, McDonald's is contributing to the welfare of a portion of its target market.

A social audit consists of five steps:[40]

1. Recognition of a firm's social expectations and the rationale for engaging in social responsibility endeavors.
2. Identification of social responsibility causes or programs consistent with the company's mission.
3. Determination of organizational objectives and priorities for programs and activities it will undertake.
4. Specification of the type and amount of resources necessary to achieve social responsibility objectives.
5. Evaluation of social responsibility programs and activities undertaken and assessment of future involvement.

Corporate attention to social audits will increase in the twenty-first century as companies seek to achieve sustainable development and improve the quality of life in a global economy.[41] **Sustainable development** involves conducting business in a

Reebok has been a leader
in improving workplace
conditions in factories that
produce its sporting apparel
and equipment.

Reebok
www.reebok.com

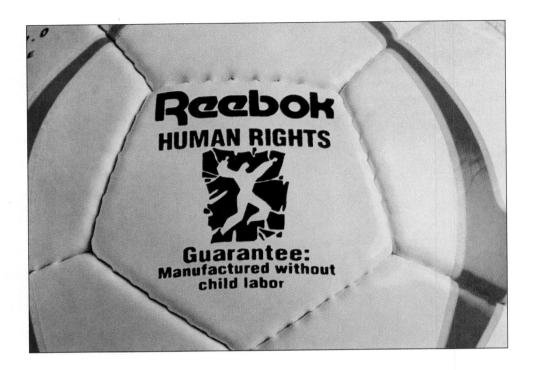

way that protects the natural environment while making economic progress. Ecologically responsible initiatives such as green marketing represent one such initiative. Recent initiatives related to working conditions at offshore manufacturing sites that produce goods for U.S. companies focus on quality-of-life issues. Public opinion surveys show that 90 percent of U.S. citizens are concerned about working conditions under which products are made in Asia and Latin America.[42] Companies have responded by imposing closer supervision of offshore manufacturing activities. Reebok, for example, now monitors production of its sporting apparel and equipment to ensure that no child labor is used in making its products.[43]

Turning the Table: Consumer Ethics and Social Responsibility

Consumers also have an obligation to act ethically and responsibly in the exchange process and in the use and disposition of products. Unfortunately, consumer behavior is spotty on both counts.

Unethical practices of consumers are a serious concern to marketers. These practices include filing warranty claims after the claim period, misredeeming coupons, making fraudulent returns of merchandise, providing inaccurate information on credit applications, tampering with utility meters, tapping cable TV lines, recording copyrighted music and videocassettes, and submitting phony insurance claims. The cost to marketers in lost sales revenue and prevention expenses is huge.[44] For example, consumers who redeem coupons for unpurchased products or use coupons destined for other products cost manufacturers $1 billion each year. The record industry alone loses $1 billion annually as a result of illegal recording, and about 12 percent of VCR owners make illegal copies of videotapes, costing producers millions of dollars in lost revenue. Electrical utilities lose between 1 percent and 3 percent of yearly revenues because of meter tampering.

Consumer purchase, use, and disposition of environmentally sensitive products relate to consumer social responsibility. Research indicates that consumers are sensitive to ecological issues.[45] However, research also shows that consumers (1) may be unwilling to sacrifice convenience and pay potentially higher prices to protect the environment and (2) lack the knowledge to make informed decisions dealing with the purchase, use, and disposition of products.[46]

Consumer confusion over which products are environmentally safe is also apparent, given marketers' rush to produce "green products." For example, few consumers realize that nonaerosol "pump" hairsprays are the second-largest cause of air pollution, after drying paint. In California alone, 27 tons of noxious hairspray fumes are expelled every day. And "biodegradable" claims on a variety of products, including trash bags, have not proven to be accurate, thus leading to buyer confusion. The FTC recently drafted guidelines that describe the circumstances when environmental claims can be made and would not constitute misleading information. For example, an advertisement or product label touting a package as "50 percent more recycled content than before" could be misleading if the recycled content has increased from 2 percent to 3 percent.[47]

Ultimately, marketers and consumers are accountable for ethical and socially responsible behavior. The twenty-first century will prove to be a testing period for both.

CONCEPT CHECK

1. What is meant by social responsibility?

2. Marketing efforts to produce, promote, and reclaim environmentally sensitive products are called _____ .

3. What is a social audit?

SUMMARY

1 Ethics are the moral principles and values that govern the actions and decisions of an individual or group. Laws are society's values and standards that are enforceable in the courts. Operating according to the law does not necessarily mean that a practice is ethical.

2 Ethical behavior of businesspeople has come under severe criticism by the public. There are four possible reasons for this criticism: (*a*) increased pressure on businesspeople to make decisions in a society characterized by diverse value systems, (*b*) a growing tendency to have business decisions judged publicly by groups with different values and interests, (*c*) an increase in the public's expectations for ethical behavior, and (*d*) a possible decline in business ethics.

3 Numerous external factors influence ethical behavior of businesspeople. These include the following: (*a*) societal culture and norms, (*b*) business culture and industry practices, and (*c*) organizational culture and expectations. Each factor influences the opportunity to engage in ethical or unethical behavior.

4 Ultimately, ethical choices are based on the personal moral philosophy of the decision maker. Two moral philosophies are most prominent: (*a*) moral idealism and (*b*) utilitarianism.

5 Social responsibility means that organizations are part of a larger society and are accountable to that society for their actions.

6 There are three concepts of social responsibility: (*a*) profit responsibility, (*b*) stakeholder responsibility, and (*c*) societal responsibility.

7 Growing interest in societal responsibility has resulted in systematic efforts to assess a firm's objectives, strategies, and performance in the domain of social responsibility. This practice is called a social audit.

8 Consumer ethics and social responsibility are as important as business ethics and social responsibility.

KEY TERMS AND CONCEPTS

ethics p. 100
laws p. 100
caveat emptor p. 103
Consumer Bill of Rights p. 103
Economic Espionage Act p. 104
Foreign Corrupt Practices Act p. 105
code of ethics p. 105
whistleblowers p. 106

moral idealism p. 107
utilitarianism p. 107
social responsibility p. 108
green marketing p. 109
ISO 14000 p. 110
cause-related marketing p. 110
social audit p. 111
sustainable development p. 111

INTERNET EXERCISE

Corporate Watch is an online magazine and resource center committed to monitoring the social, political, economic, and environmental impact of actions taken by global corporations around the world. A wide variety of topics are covered, many of which are also discussed in Chapter 4.

Visit the Corporate Watch Web site at www.corp watch.com. Choose a topic from Chapter 4 pertaining to social responsibility that interests you, such as sustainable development or green marketing and answer the following questions:

1   Which companies are highlighted from the "Green-wash Awards?"

2   Visit the "Headlines" or "Archives" link. Can you update at least one example in the text related to socially responsible behavior?

APPLYING MARKETING CONCEPTS AND PERSPECTIVES

1   What concepts of moral philosophy and social responsibility are applicable to the practices of Anheuser-Busch described in the introduction to this chapter? Why?

2   Five ethical situations were presented in this chapter: (*a*) a medical society's decision to set fee schedules, (*b*) the use of a computer program by auto dealers to arrange financing, (*c*) smoking in China, (*d*) the copying of trademarks and patents in Korea, and (*e*) the pricing of Ceredase for the treatment of a rare genetic illness. Where would each of these situations fit in Figure 4–1?

3   The American Marketing Association Code of Ethics shown in Figure 4–3 details the rights and duties of parties in the marketing exchange process. How do these rights and duties compare with the Consumer Bill of Rights?

4   Compare and contrast moral idealism and utilitarianism as alternative personal moral philosophies.

5   How would you evaluate Milton Friedman's view of the social responsibility of a firm?

6   The text lists several unethical practices of consumers. Can you name others? Why do you think consumers engage in unethical conduct?

7   Cause-related marketing programs have become popular. Describe two such programs that you are familiar with.

CASE 4–1   PRICING IN THE PHARMACEUTICAL INDUSTRY

In 1999, U.S. consumers were projected to spend more than $110 billion for prescription drugs used to treat acute and chronic ailments. In the past five years, prescription drug prices rose 85 percent, which was four times the rate of health care spending overall for the same period.

These statistics have prompted severe criticism of pharmaceutical firms by public health officials, government agencies, and consumer advocacy groups. Pharmaceutical firm executives in the United States have responded, citing the large research and development costs for drugs, federal regulations, and extensive testing required to obtain Food and Drug Administration (FDA) approval, and marketplace uncertainties as valid reasons for high drug prices.

FAIR AND REASONABLE PRICING

A central issue in the debate concerning prescription drug pricing relates to what is a "fair and reasonable price." Critics of drug pricing spotlight instances where they believe the prices charged are excessive. For instance, drugs to treat ulcers sell in the range of $1,300 to $1,400 annually per patient. Drugs that control cholesterol costs patients $1,015 to $1,265 per year per patient. Persons suffering from high blood pressure pay almost $850 annually to treat this condition. People over the age of 65, many with fixed incomes, bear these costs. For example, 49 percent of the sales of high blood pressure medication are accounted for by the elderly.

Pharmaceutical firms counter critics' charges of excessive pricing using a variety of arguments. They note that the research and development cost of a new medication can be more than $150 million and span a decade of development and testing. Moreover, the risk is very high since the majority of new drugs are never successfully commercialized. In addition, the U.S. pharmaceutical industry spends about $11 billion annually for marketing the newest drugs to doctors and consumers. Finally, pharmaceutical firms note that the loss of patent protection for their brand-name drugs and the growing popularity of generic (no-name) drugs have to be considered when judging price levels for brand-name medications.

Debate over what is a "fair and reasonable" price for drugs typically focuses on economic versus societal factors, and the relative importance of a firm's stakeholders in setting prices. Often the final pricing decision depends on the individual judgment and moral sensitivity of the managers making the decision.

PROLIFE: PRICING ADL

Issues in the pricing of ADL, a treatment for Alzheimer's disease which affects the elderly, were recently faced by Prolife, a small pharmaceutical company. A task force of company executives was considering the pricing strategy for ADL. Two points of view were expressed: (1) pursuing a high-price strategy designed to recoup the costs of the drug quickly and getting a jump on the competition and (2) pursuing a lower-price strategy to increase the drug's availability to victims of the disease.

Steve Vaughn, an Assistant Product Manager at Prolife, was the principal proponent of a lower-price strategy. He argued that a less aggressive price strategy made sense even though it would take slightly longer to recoup the initial investment in ADL. Having a family member afflicted with Alzheimer's disease, Mr. Vaughn felt that the ability of victims and their families to pay for the drug should be considered when setting the price for ADL. He was overruled, however, by the task force members. Believing that his views deserved attention and action, and that "bottom line" considerations did not negate his position, he lobbied other task force members and has thought about expressing his opinion to senior executives at Prolife. He was cautioned by Bill Compton, a Prolife Senior Product Manager and his mentor, to reconsider his position noting that Prolife is a business and that "rocking the boat" might not be an advantage to his career at Prolife.

Questions

1 Who are the primary stakeholders who must be considered when setting prices for prescription drugs?

2 How might the personal moral philosophies of moral idealism and utilitarianism be applied to prescription drug pricing in general and in the specific case of ADL?

3 How might the three concepts of social responsibility described in Chapter 4 be applied to prescription pricing in general and in the specific case of ADL?

4 If you were Steve Vaughn, what would you do in this situation?

PART TWO

2

UNDERSTANDING
BUYERS AND
MARKETS

CHAPTER 5
Global Marketing and World Trade

CHAPTER 6
Consumer Behavior

CHAPTER 7
Organizational Markets and Buyer Behavior

Using local and global perspectives to understand people as individual consumers and as members of companies that become organizational buyers is the focus of Part Two. Chapter 5 describes the nature and scope of world trade and examines the global marketing activities of such companies as 3M, Coca-Cola, Colgate-Palmolive, Ericsson, IKEA, Kodak, L'Oreal, and Volvo. Chapter 6 examines the actions buyers take in purchasing and using products, and explains how and why one product or brand is chosen over another. In Chapter 7 Gary Null, the international business director for a laser-based communication system at Honeywell, helps explain how organizational buyers purchase laser technology and products for their own use or resale. Together these chapters help marketing students understand individual, family, and organizational purchases in a variety of cultural environments.

CHAPTER FIVE

GLOBAL MARKETING AND WORLD TRADE

5

AFTER READING THIS CHAPTER YOU SHOULD BE ABLE TO:

• Describe the nature and scope of world trade from a global perspective and its implications for the United States.

• Explain the effects of economic protectionism and the implications of economic integration for global marketing practices.

• Understand the importance of environmental factors (cultural, economic, and political) in shaping global marketing efforts.

• Describe alternative approaches firms use to enter and compete in global markets.

• Identify specific challenges marketers face when crafting worldwide marketing programs.

TARGETING GLOBAL SNEEZERS, WHEEZERS, SNORERS . . . AND MORE!

"I knew instantly *it* would be huge when I talked to *him*," says Dr. Dan Cohen, chief executive officer of CNS, Inc. The "it" was a rudimentary spring-loaded adhesive device to stick to your nose to open up the nasal passages and improve breathing. The "him" was Bruce Johnson, the device's inventor, whose breathing and snoring problems had even driven him to put straws or paper clips up his nose at night to breathe better.

After millions of dollars of additional research and development, the meeting resulted in the spectacularly successful Breathe Right® nasal strips targeted at athletes, those with allergies, those who snore, . . . and those who *sleep* with those who snore.

Breathe Right® strips were an immediate marketing success in the United States, so Dr. Cohen counted the world's noses and sought to enter the global marketplace. Too small to "go global" on its own, CNS partnered with 3M to distribute the Breathe Right® strips internationally including Korea, shown on the opposite page. The result? Breathe Right® strips are marketed in more than 40 countries today.[1]

American marketers cannot ignore the vast potential of global markets. About 95 percent of the world's population having two-thirds of the world's purchasing power live outside the United States. In fact, many global markets are growing faster than comparable markets in the United States.

Pursuit of global markets by American and foreign marketers ultimately results in world trade. This chapter describes the nature and scope of world trade and highlights challenges firms such as CNS and 3M face when they undertake global marketing.

DYNAMICS OF WORLD TRADE

The dollar value of world trade has more than doubled in the past decade and will exceed $8 trillion in 2002. Manufactured goods and commodities account for 75 percent of world trade. Service industries, including telecommunications, transportation, insurance, education, banking, and tourism, represent the other 25 percent of world trade.

World Trade Flows

All nations and regions of the world do not participate equally in world trade. World trade flows reflect interdependencies among industries, countries, and regions and manifest themselves in country, company, industry, and regional exports and imports.

Global Perspective   Figure 5–1 shows the estimated dollar value of exports and imports among North American countries, Western Europe, Asian/Pacific Rim countries, and the rest of the world, including intraregional trade flows.[2] The United States, Western Europe, Canada, and Japan together account for two thirds of world trade.[3]

Not all trade involves the exchange of money for goods or services. In a world where 70 percent of all countries do not have convertible currencies or where government-owned enterprises lack sufficient cash or credit for imports, other means of payment are used. An estimated 20 percent of world trade involves **countertrade,** the practice of using barter rather than money for making global sales.

Countertrade is popular with many Eastern European nations, Russia, and Asian countries. For example, the Malaysian government recently exchanged 20,000 tons of

FIGURE 5–1
Illustrative world trade flows
(billions of dollars)

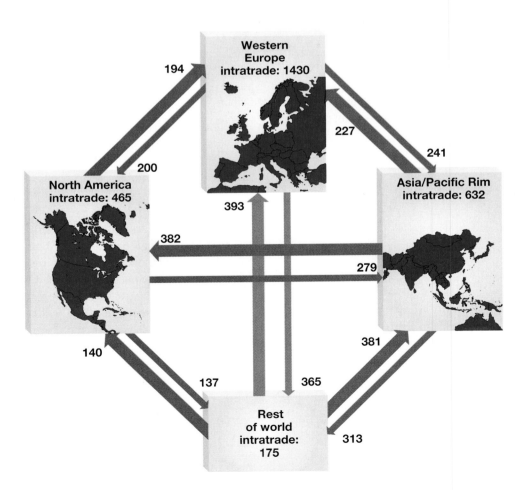

rice for an equivalent amount of Philippine corn. Volvo of North America delivered automobiles to the Siberian police force when Siberia had no cash to pay for them. It accepted payment in oil, which it then sold for cash to pay for media advertising in the United States.[4]

A global perspective on world trade views exports and imports as complementary economic flows: A country's imports affect its exports and exports affect its imports. Every nation's imports arise from the exports of other nations. As the exports of one country increase, its national output and income rise, which, in turn, leads to an increase in the demand for imports. This nation's greater demand for imports stimulates the exports of other countries. Increased demand for exports of other nations energizes their economic activity, resulting in higher national income, which stimulates their demand for imports. In short, imports affect exports and vice versa. This phenomenon is called the **trade feedback effect** and is one argument for free trade among nations.

United States Perspective   The United States is the world's perennial leader in terms of **gross domestic product** (GDP), which is the monetary value of all goods and services produced in a country during one year. The United States is also among the world's leaders in exports due in large part to its global prominence in the aircraft, chemical, office equipment, pharmaceutical, telecommunications, and professional service industries. However, the U.S. percentage share of world exports has shifted downward over the past 25 years, while its percentage share of world imports has increased. Therefore, the relative position of the United States as a supplier to the world has diminished despite an absolute growth in exports. At the same time, its relative role as a marketplace for the world has increased, particularly for automobile, textile, apparel, and consumer electronics products.

The difference between the monetary value of a nation's exports and imports is called the **balance of trade.** When a country's exports exceed its imports, it incurs a surplus in its balance of trade. When imports exceed exports, a deficit has occurred. World trade trends in U.S. exports and imports are reflected in the U.S. balance of trade. Since 1975 two important things have happened in U.S. exports and imports. First, with a few exceptions, imports have significantly exceeded exports each year, indicating that the United States has a continuing balance of trade deficit. Second, the volume of both exports and imports is about 15 to 20 times what it was in the 1970s—showing why almost every American is significantly affected. The effect varies from the products they buy (Samsung VCRs from Korea, Waterford crystal from Ireland, Louis Vuitton luggage from France) to those they sell (General Motors's cars to Europe, Du Pont's chemicals to the Far East) and the additional jobs and improved standard of living that result.

World trade flows to and from the United States reflect demand and supply interdependencies for goods and services among nations and industries. The three largest importers of U.S. goods and services are Canada, Japan, and Mexico. These countries purchase approximately 40 percent of U.S. exports. The three largest exporters to the United States are Japan, Canada, and Mexico.[5]

The United States is Asia's largest export market, buying about one third of the exports of Japan, Taiwan, South Korea, and China, a quarter of Hong Kong's exports, and 40 percent of the Philippines's exports. The trade imbalance between the United States and Asia is illustrated by the fact that Japan and China combine for about half of the total U.S. balance of trade deficit in the late 1990s.[6]

Competitive Advantage of Nations

As companies in many industries find themselves competing against foreign competitors at home and abroad, government policy makers around the world are increasingly asking why some companies and industries in a country succeed globally while

FIGURE 5–2
Porter's "diamond" of national
competitive advantage

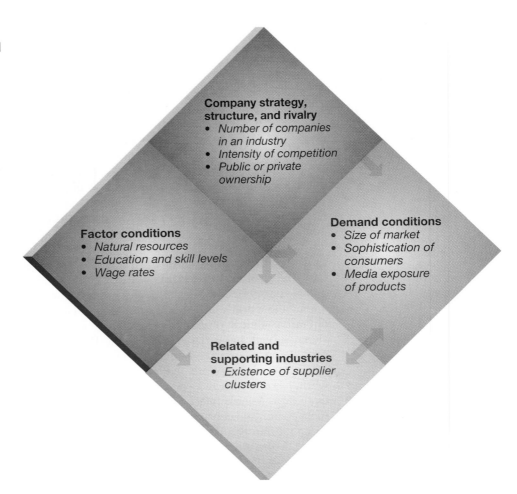

others lose ground or fail. Harvard Business School Professor Michael Porter suggests a "diamond" to explain a nation's competitive advantage and why some industries and firms become world leaders.[7] He identified four key elements, which appear in Figure 5–2:

1. *Factor conditions.* These reflect a nation's ability to turn its natural resources, education, and infrastructure into a competitive advantage. Consider Holland, which exports 59 percent of the world's cut flowers. The Dutch lead the world in the cut-flower industry because of their research in flower cultivation, packaging, and shipping—not because of their weather.

2. *Demand conditions.* These include both the number and sophistication of domestic customers for an industry's product. Japan's sophisticated consumers demand quality in their TVs and radios, thereby making Japan's producers such as Sony, Sanyo, Matsushita, and Hitachi among the world leaders in the electronics industry.

3. *Related and supporting industries.* Firms and industries seeking leadership in global markets need clusters of world-class suppliers that accelerate innovation. The German leadership in scientific and industrial instrumentation relates directly to the cluster of supporting German precision engineering suppliers.

4. *Company strategy, structure, and rivalry.* These factors include the conditions governing the way a nation's businesses are organized and managed, along with the intensity of domestic competition. The Italian shoe industry has become a world leader because of intense domestic competition among firms such as

Sony and Bruno Magli have succeeded in the global marketplace as well as in their domestic markets.

Sony
www.sony.com

Bruno Magli
www.brunomagli.it

MAB, Bruno Magli, and Rossimoda, which has made shoes for Christian Dior and Anne Klein Couture.

In Porter's study, case histories of firms in more than 100 industries were analyzed. While the strategies employed by the most successful global competitors were different in many respects, a common theme emerged—a firm that succeeds in global markets has first succeeded in intense domestic competition. Hence competitive advantage for global firms grows out of relentless, continuing improvement, innovation, and change.

It is important to note, however, that it is not essential to be a giant company to gain benefits in global markets. Numerous small firms succeed in foreign niche markets or by utilizing unique information, licenses, or technology. In fact, in one unusual respect a small regional American firm has an advantage over its huge rivals in the international arena. That is when it can trade product technology and marketing ideas with foreign firms with whom it does not compete directly. McKay Envelopes is a small firm that produces a variety of specialized packaging for photo finishers. By exchanging information with regional European printers, it is able to obtain information on new printing equipment, inks, running speeds, and printing plates that give high-quality printing—thereby gaining an advantage over its American competitors. It, in turn, provides ideas to the European printers, so the exchange benefits both parties.

CONCEPT CHECK

1. What is the trade feedback effect?

2. What variables influence why some companies and industries in a country succeed globally while others lose ground or fail?

FIGURE 5–3
How protectionism affects
world trade

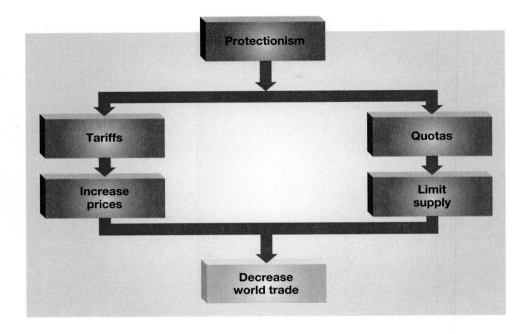

FIGURE 5–3
How protectionism affects
world trade

EMERGENCE OF A BORDERLESS ECONOMIC WORLD

Three trends in the late twentieth century have significantly affected world trade. One trend has been a gradual decline of economic protectionism exercised by individual countries. The second trend is apparent in the formal economic integration and free trade among nations. A third trend is evident in global competition among global companies for global consumers.

Decline of Economic Protectionism

Protectionism is the practice of shielding one or more sectors of a country's economy from foreign competition through the use of tariffs or quotas. The principal economic argument for protectionism is that it preserves jobs, protects a nation's political security, discourages economic dependency on other countries, and encourages the development of domestic industries. Read the accompanying Ethics and Social Responsibility Alert and ask yourself if protectionism has an ethical and social responsibility dimension.[8]

Tariffs and quotas discourage world trade as depicted in Figure 5–3. **Tariffs,** which are a government tax on goods or services entering a country, primarily serve to raise prices on imports. For example, the average tariff on manufactured goods in industrialized countries is 4 percent.[9]

The effect of tariffs on world trade and consumer prices is substantial. Consider U.S. rice exports to Japan. The U.S. Rice Millers' Association claims that if the Japanese rice market were opened to imports by lowering tariffs, lower prices would save Japanese consumers $6 billion annually, and the United States would gain a $300 million share of the Japanese rice market. Similarly, tariffs imposed on bananas by Western European countries cost consumers $2 billion a year. Ecuador (the world's largest banana exporter), Mexico, Guatemala, and Honduras are seeking to end this levy.[10]

A **quota** is a restriction placed on the amount of a product allowed to enter or leave a country. Quotas can be mandated or voluntary and may be legislated or negotiated by governments. Import quotas seek to guarantee domestic industries access to a certain percentage of their domestic market. The best-known quota concerns the mandatory or voluntary limits of foreign automobile sales in many countries. Quotas imposed by Eu-

ETHICS AND SOCIAL RESPONSIBILITY ALERT

Global Ethics and Global Economics: The Case of Protectionism

World trade benefits from free and fair trade among nations. Nevertheless, governments of many countries continue to use tariffs and quotas to protect their various domestic industries. Why? Protectionism earns profits for domestic producers and tariff revenue for the government. There is a cost, however. For example, protectionist policies cost Japanese consumers somewhere between $75 billion and $110 billion annually. U.S. consumers pay about $70 billion each year in higher prices because of tariffs and other protective restrictions.

Sugar import quotas in the United States, automobile import quotas in many European countries, beer import tariffs in Canada, and rice import tariffs in Japan protect domestic industries but also interfere with world trade for these products. Regional trade agreements, such as those found in the provisions of the European Union and the North American Free Trade Agreement, may also pose a situation whereby member nations can obtain preferential treatment in quotas and tariffs whereas nonmember nations do not.

Protectionism, in its many forms, raises an interesting global ethical question. Is protectionism, no matter how applied, an ethical practice?

ropean countries make European cars 25 percent more expensive than similar models in the United States or Japan, costing European customers $40 billion per year. Less visible quotas apply to the importation of mushrooms, heavy motorcycles, color TVs, and sugar. For example, U.S. sugar import quotas have existed for over 50 years and preserve about half of the U.S. sugar market for domestic producers. American consumers pay an estimated $1.6 billion annually in extra food costs because of this quota.[11]

Every country engages in some form of protectionism. However, protectionism has declined over the past 50 years due in large part to the *General Agreement on Tariffs and Trade (GATT)*. This international treaty was intended to limit trade barriers and promote world trade through the reduction of tariffs, which it did. However, GATT did not explicitly address nontariff trade barriers, such as quotas and world trade in services, which often sparked heated trade disputes between nations.

World Trade Organization
www.wto.org

As a consequence, the major industrialized nations of the world formed the **World Trade Organization** (WTO) in 1995 to address a broad array of world trade issues. There are 132 WTO member countries, including the United States, which account for more than 90 percent of world trade. The WTO is a permanent institution that sets rules governing trade between its members through panels of trade experts who (1) decide on trade disputes between members and (2) issue binding decisions. The WTO reviews more than 100 disputes annually. For instance, the WTO denied Eastman Kodak's multimillion-dollar damage claim that the Japanese government protected Fuji Photo from import competition. In another decision, the WTO allowed Britain, Ireland, and the European Union to reclassify U.S.-produced local area network (LAN) computer equipment as telecommunications gear. The new classification effectively doubled the import tariff on these U.S. goods.[12]

Rise of Economic Integration

In recent years a number of countries with similar economic goals have formed transnational trade groups or signed trade agreements for the purpose of promoting free trade among member nations and enhancing their individual economies. Three of the best-known examples are the European Union (or simply EU), the North American Free Trade Agreement, and Asian Free Trade Areas.

FIGURE 5–4
The countries of the European
Union in 1999

European Union
www.eurunion.org

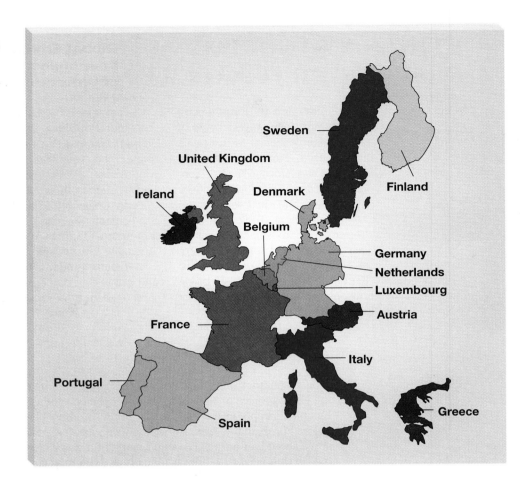

European Union In 1993, 12 European countries effectively eliminated most of the barriers to the free flow of goods, services, capital, and labor across their borders. This event, after decades of negotiation, formed a single market composed of 390 million consumers with a combined gross domestic product only slightly less than that of the United States. Original members of the European Union were Great Britain, Ireland, Denmark, Belgium, the Netherlands, Luxembourg, Germany, France, Italy, Greece, Portugal, and Spain. Austria, Finland, and Sweden joined the European Union in 1995, bringing its membership to 15 countries (see Figure 5–4). The Swiss have elected not to join the European Union.

The European Union creates abundant marketing opportunities because firms no longer find it necessary to market their products and services on a nation-by-nation basis. Rather, Pan-European marketing strategies are possible due to greater uniformity in product and packaging standards; fewer regulatory restriction on transportation, advertising, and promotion imposed by countries; and removal of most tariffs that affect pricing practices.[13] For example, Colgate-Palmolive Company now markets its Colgate toothpaste with one formula and package across EU countries at one price. This practice was previously impossible because of different government regulations and tariffs. Europeanwide distribution from fewer locations is also feasible given open borders. French tire maker Michelin recently closed 180 of its European distribution centers and now uses just 20 to serve all EU countries. Pan-European marketing opportunities will benefit further from the issuance of a common currency called the "euro," which will replace national currencies in 2002 in 11 EU countries. Great Britain, Denmark, Sweden, and Greece will retain their own currencies.[14]

NAFTA
http://iepnt1.itaiep.doc.gov/
nafta/nafta2.htm

North American Free Trade Agreement The North American Free Trade Agreement (NAFTA) became effective in 1994 and lifted many trade barriers between the United States and Mexico. This agreement, when coupled with the 1988 U.S.–Canada Fair Trade Agreement, established a North American trade arrangement similar to that of the European Union. The reduction of tariffs and other provisions of NAFTA promoted relatively free trade among the United States, Canada, and Mexico and created a marketplace with about 380 million consumers. Negotiations are under way to expand NAFTA to create a 34-country Free Trade Area of the Americas by 2005. This agreement would include the United States, Canada, Mexico, and Latin American and Caribbean countries.[15]

NAFTA has stimulated trade flows among member nations as well as cross-border manufacturing and investment. For example, Whirlpool Corporation's Canadian subsidiary stopped making washing machines in Canada and moved that operation to Ohio. Whirlpool then shifted the production of household trash compactors, kitchen ranges, and compact dryers to Canada. Ford invested $60 million in its Mexico City manufacturing plant to produce smaller cars and light trucks for global sales.

Asian Free Trade Agreements   Efforts to liberalize trade in East Asia—from Japan and the four "Little Dragons" (Hong Kong, Singapore, South Korea, and Taiwan) through Thailand, Malaysia, and Indonesia—are also growing despite an economic downturn in the late 1990s. While the trade agreements are less formal than those underlying the European Union and NAFTA, they have reduced tariffs among countries and promoted trade.[16]

A New Reality: Global Competition among Global Companies for Global Consumers

The emergence of a largely borderless economic world has created a new reality for marketers of all shapes and sizes. Today, world trade is driven by global competition among global companies for global consumers.

Global Competition   **Global competition** exists when firms originate, produce, and market their products and services worldwide. The automobile, pharmaceutical, apparel, electronics, aerospace, and telecommunication fields represent well-known industries with sellers and buyers on every continent. Other industries that are increasingly global in scope include soft drinks, cosmetics, ready-to-eat cereals, snack chips, and retailing.

Global competition broadens the competitive landscape for marketers. The familiar "Pepsi Challenge" taste comparison waged by Pepsi-Cola against Coca-Cola in the United States has been repeated around the world, including India and Argentina. Procter & Gamble's Pampers and Kimberly-Clark's Huggies have taken their disposable diaper rivalry from the United States to Western Europe. Boeing and Europe's Airbus Industries can be found vying for lucrative commercial aircraft contracts on virtually every continent.

Collaborative relationships also are becoming a common way to meet the demands of global competition. Global **strategic alliances** are agreements among two or more independent firms to cooperate for the purpose of achieving common goals such as a competitive advantage or customer value creation. For instance, several of the world's largest telecommunication equipment makers, including Ericsson (Sweden), Northern Telecom (Canada), Siemens (Germany), and 3Com and Worldcom (two U.S. firms), have formed Juniper Networks, Inc., an alliance created to build devices to speed global Internet communications. General Mills and Nestlé of Switzerland created Cereal Partners Worldwide for the purpose of fine-tuning Nestlé's European cereal marketing and distributing General Mills cereals worldwide. This global alliance is expected to produce worldwide sales of $1 billion by 2000.[17]

Pepsi-Cola is available in more than 190 countries and territories and accounts for a quarter of all soft drinks sold internationally. This Brazilian ad—"How to make jeans last 10 years"—features the popular Diet Pepsi brand targeted at weight-conscious consumers.

PepsiCo, Inc.
www.pepsico.com

Global Companies   Three types of companies populate and compete in the global marketplace: (1) international firms, (2) multinational firms, and (3) transnational firms.[18] All three employ people in different countries, and many have administrative, marketing, and manufacturing operations (often called divisions or subsidiaries) around the world. However, a firm's orientation toward and strategy for global markets and marketing defines the type of company it is or attempts to be.

An *international firm* engages in trade and marketing in different countries as an extension of the marketing strategy in its home country. Generally speaking, these firms market their existing products and services in other countries the same way they do in their home country. Avon, for example, successfully distributes its product line through direct selling in Asia, Europe, and South America, employing virtually the same marketing strategy used in the United States.

A *multinational firm* views the world as consisting of unique parts and markets to each part differently. Multinationals use a **multidomestic marketing strategy,** which means that they have as many different product variations, brand names, and advertising programs as countries in which they do business. For example, Lever Europe—a division of Unilever—markets its fabric softener known as Snuggle in the United States in 10 different European countries under seven brand names, including Kuschelweich in Germany, Coccolino in Italy, and Mimosin in France. These products have different packages, different advertising programs, and occasionally different formulas.[19]

A *transnational firm* views the world as one market and emphasizes cultural similarities across countries or universal consumer needs and wants more than differences. Transnational marketers employ a **global marketing strategy**—the practice of standardizing marketing activities when there are cultural similarities and adapting them when cultures differ. This approach benefits marketers by allowing them to realize economies of scale from their production and marketing activities.

Global marketing strategies are popular among many business-to-business marketers such as Caterpillar and Komatsu (heavy construction equipment) and Texas Instruments, Intel, Hitachi, and Motorola (semiconductors). Consumer goods marketers such as Timex, Seiko, and Citizen (watches), Coca-Cola and Pepsi-Cola (cola soft drinks), Gillette (personal care products), and McDonald's (fast foods) successfully execute this strategy.

MARKETING NEWSNET

The Global Teenager: A Market of 240 Million Consumers

The "global teenager" market consists of 240 million 13- to 19-year-olds in Europe, North and South America, and industrialized nation of Asia who have experienced intense exposure to television (MTV broadcasts in more than 75 countries), movies, travel, and global advertising by companies such as Bennetton, Sony, Nike, and Coca-Cola. The similarities among teens in these countries are greater than their differences. For example, a global study of teenagers' rooms in 25 countries indicated it was difficult, if not impossible, to tell whether the rooms were in Los Angeles, Mexico City, Tokyo, or Paris. Why? Teens buy a common gallery of products: Nintendo video games, Tommy Hilfiger apparel, Levi's blue jeans, Nike athletic shoes, Procter & Gamble Cover Girl makeup, and Clearasil facial medicine.

Teenagers around the world appreciate fashion and music and desire novelty and trendier designs and images. They also acknowledge an "Americanization" of fashion and culture based on a study of 6,500 teens in 26 countries. When asked what country had the most influence on their attitudes and purchase behavior, the United States was named by 54 percent of teens from the United States, 87 percent of those from Latin America, 80 percent of the Europeans, and 80 percent of those from the Far East.

Global Consumers   Global competition among global companies often focuses on the identification and pursuit of global consumers. **Global consumers** consist of customer groups living in many countries or regions of the world who have similar needs or seek similar features and benefits from products or services.[20] Evidence suggests the emergence of a global middle-income class, a youth market, and an elite segment, each consuming or using a common assortment of products and services regardless of geographic location. A variety of companies have capitalized on the global consumer. Whirlpool, Sony, and IKEA have benefited from the growing global middle-income class desire for kitchen appliances, consumer electronics, and home furnishings, respectively. Levi's, Nike, and Nintendo have tapped the global youth market, as described in the accompanying Marketing NewsNet.[21] DeBeers, Chanel, Gucci, and Rolls Royce successfully cater to the elite segment for luxury goods worldwide.

CONCEPT CHECK

1. What is protectionism?

2. The North American Free Trade Agreement was designed to promote free trade among which countries?

3. What is the difference between a multidomestic marketing strategy and a global marketing strategy?

A GLOBAL ENVIRONMENTAL SCAN

Global companies conduct continuing environmental scans of the five sets of environmental factors described earlier in Figure 3–1 (social, economic, technological, competitive, and regulatory forces). This section focuses on three kinds of uncontrollable environmental variables—cultural, economic, and political-regulatory variables—that affect global marketing practices in strikingly different ways than those in domestic markets.

Cultural Diversity

Marketers must be sensitive to the cultural underpinnings of different societies if they are to initiate and consummate mutually beneficial exchange relationships with global consumers. A necessary step in this process is **cross-cultural analysis,** which involves the study of similarities and differences among consumers in two or more nations or societies.[22] A thorough cross-cultural analysis involves an understanding of and an appreciation for the values, customs, symbols, and language of other societies.

Values   A society's **values** represent personally or socially preferable modes of conduct or states of existence that are enduring. Understanding and working with these aspects of a society are important factors in successful global marketing. For example,[23]

- McDonald's does not sell hamburgers in its restaurants in India because the cow is considered sacred by almost 85 percent of the population. Instead, McDonald's sells the McMaharajah: two all-mutton patties, special sauce, lettuce, cheese, pickles, onions on a sesame-seed bun.
- Germans have not been overly receptive to the use of credit cards such as Visa or MasterCard and installment debt to purchase goods and services. Indeed, the German word for debt, *Schuld,* is the same as the German word for guilt.

These examples illustrate how cultural values can influence behavior in different societies. Cultural values become apparent in the personal values of individuals that affect their attitudes and beliefs and the importance assigned to specific behaviors and attributes of goods and services. These personal values affect consumption-specific values, such as the use of installment debt by Germans, and product-specific values, such as the importance assigned to credit card interest rates.

Customs   **Customs** are the norms and expectation about the way people do things in a specific country. Clearly customs can vary significantly from country to country. For example, 3M Company executives were perplexed when the company's Scotch-Brite floor-cleaning product initially produced lukewarm sales in the Philippines. When a Filipino employee explained that consumers there customarily clean floors by pushing coconut shells around with their feet, 3M changed the shape of the pad to a foot and sales soared! Some other customs are unusual to Americans. Consider, for example, that in France, men wear more than twice the number of cosmetics than women do and that Japanese women give Japanese men chocolates on Valentine's Day.

Customs also relate to nonverbal behavior of individuals in different cultural settings. The story is told of U.S. executives negotiating a purchase agreement with their Japanese counterparts. The chief American negotiator made a proposal that was met with silence by the Japanese head negotiator. The American assumed the offer was not acceptable and raised the offer, which again was met with silence. A third offer was made, and an agreement was struck. Unknown to the American, the silence of the Japanese head negotiator meant that the offer was being considered, not rejected. The Japanese negotiator obtained several concessions from the American because of a misreading of silence! Unlike U.S. businesspeople, who tend to express opinions early in meetings and negotiations, Japanese executives prefer to wait and listen. The higher their position, such as chief negotiator, the more they listen.[24]

Cultural Symbols   **Cultural symbols** are things that represent ideas and concepts. Symbols or symbolism play an important role in cross-cultural analysis because different cultures ascribe different meanings to things. So important is the role of symbols that a field of study, called **semiotics,** has emerged that examines the correspondence between symbols and their role in the assignment of meaning for people. By adroitly using cultural symbols, global marketers can tie positive symbolism to their products and services to enhance their attractiveness to consumers. However, improper use of symbols can spell disaster. A culturally sensitive global marketer will know that[25]

- North Americans are superstitious about the number 13, and Japanese feel the same way about the number 4. *Shi,* the Japanese word for four, is also the word for death. Knowing this, Tiffany & Company sells its fine glassware and china in sets of five, not four, in Japan.
- "Thumbs-up" is a positive sign in the United States. However, in Russia and Poland, this gesture has an offensive meaning when the palm of the hand is shown, as AT&T learned. The company reversed the gesture depicted in ads, showing the back of the hand, not the palm.

Cultural symbols evoke deep feelings. Just ask executives at Coca-Cola Company's Italian office. In a series of advertisements directed at Italian vacationers, the Eiffel

Tower, Empire State Building, and the Tower of Pisa were turned into the familiar Coca-Cola bottle. However, when the white marble columns in the Parthenon that crowns Athens's Acropolis were turned into Coca-Cola bottles, the Greeks were outraged. Greeks refer to the Acropolis as the "holy rock," and a government official said the Parthenon is an "international symbol of excellence" and that "whoever insults the Parthenon insults international culture." Coca-Cola apologized for the ad.[26]

Global markets are also sensitive to the fact that the "country of origin or manufacture" of products and services can symbolize superior or poor quality in some countries. For example, Russian consumers believe products made in Japan and Germany are superior in quality to products from the United States and the United Kingdom. Japanese consumers believe Japanese products are superior to those made in Europe and the United States. About 48 percent of Americans say the quality of products from Asia is not as good as products made in the United States.[27]

Language   Global marketers should not only know the native tongues of countries in which they market their products and services but also the nuances and idioms of a language. Even though about 100 official languages exist in the world, anthropologists estimate that at least 3,000 different languages are spoken. There are 11 official languages spoken in the European Union, and Canada has two official languages (English and French). Seventeen major languages are spoken in India alone.

English, French, and Spanish are the principal languages used in global diplomacy and commerce. However, the best language to communicate with consumers is their own, as any seasoned global marketer will attest to. Unintended meanings of brand names and messages have ranged from the absurd to the obscene[28]:

- When the advertising agency responsible for launching Procter & Gamble's successful Pert shampoo in Canada realized that the name means "lost" in French, it substituted the brand name Pret, which means "ready."
- In Italy, Cadbury Schweppes, the world's third-largest soft drink manufacturer, realized that its Schweppes Tonic Water brand had to be renamed Schweppes Tonica because "il water" turned out to be the idiom for a bathroom.

- The Vicks brand name common in the United States is German slang for sexual intimacy; therefore, Vicks is called Wicks in Germany.

Experienced global marketers use **back translation,** where a translated word or phrase is retranslated into the original language by a different interpreter to catch errors.[29] For example, IBM's first Japanese translation of its "Solution for a small planet" advertising message yielded "Answers that make people smaller." The error was caught and corrected. Nevertheless, unintended meanings still occur in the most unlikely situations. A Japanese tire manufacturer found it necessary to publicly apologize in Brunei (a British-protected sultanate on the coast of Borneo) for the tread grooves on one of its tire brands. Some critics claimed the tread resembled a verse from the Koran, the sacred book of the Muslims written in Arabic.

Cultural Ethnocentricity   The tendency for people to view their own values, customs, symbols, and language favorably is well-known. However, the belief that aspects of one's culture are superior to another's is called *cultural ethnocentricity* and is a sure impediment to successful global marketing.

An outgrowth of cultural ethnocentricity exists in the purchase and use of goods and services produced outside of a country. Global marketers are acutely aware that certain groups within countries disfavor imported products, not on the basis of price, features, or performance, but purely because of their foreign origin. **Consumer ethnocentrism** is the tendency to believe that it is inappropriate, indeed immoral, to purchase foreign-made products.[30] Ethnocentric consumers believe that buying imported products is wrong because such purchases are unpatriotic, harm domestic industries, and cause domestic unemployment. Are you an ethnocentric consumer? The accompanying Marketing NewsNet might help you answer this question.[31]

In Japan, principally a tea-drinking country, Nestlé has converted the market not just to coffee but to instant coffee.

Nestlé

www.nestle.com

Cultural Change   Cultures change slowly. Nevertheless, fewer impediments to world trade are likely to accelerate the rate of cultural change in societies around the world. A challenge facing global marketers is to anticipate how cultures are changing, particularly with respect to the purchase and use of goods and services.

An acknowledged master of anticipating cultural change and responding quickly is Nestlé, the world's largest packaged food manufacturer, coffee roaster, and chocolate maker. Nestlé derives 98 percent of its sales outside of its home country, Switzerland, because the company is always among the first to identify changing consumption patterns in diverse cultures. Consider Great Britain and Japan, with two very different cultures but a common passion—tea. Nestlé pioneered coffee marketing in both countries with its Nescafé instant coffee. The cultural preference for tea was changing, and Nestlé capitalized on this change. Today, Britons consume one cup of coffee for every two cups of tea. Thirty years ago, the ratio was one cup of coffee for every six cups of tea. The Japanese are now among the world's heaviest consumers of instant coffee on a per capita basis. Nestlé is a dominant coffee marketer in both countries.[32]

Economic Considerations

Global marketing is also affected by economic considerations. Therefore, a scan of the global marketplace should include (1) a comparative analysis of the economic development in different countries, (2) an assessment of the economic infrastructure in these countries, (3) measurement of consumer income in different countries, and (4) recognition of a country's currency exchange rates.

Stage of Economic Development

There are more than 200 countries in the world today, each of which is at a slightly different point in terms of its stage of economic development. However, they can be clas-

MARKETING NEWSNET

Are You an Ethnocentric Consumer?

Would you tend to agree or disagree with the following statements?

1. Buy American-made products. Keep America working.
2. It is always best to purchase American products.
3. It may cost me in the long run, but I prefer to support American products.
4. Curbs should be put on all imports.

If you tended to agree with these 4 and 13 other similar statements, you can call yourself an ethnocentric consumer.

Professors Terrence Shimp and Subhash Sharma at the University of South Carolina developed a 17-statement consumer ethnocentrism scale designed to identify the tendency of American consumers to purchase foreign- versus American-made products. Frequent agreement with statements such as those above means that a consumer would have a tendency to accentuate the positive aspects of domestic products and discount the virtues of foreign-made items.

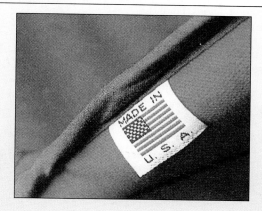

It is important to note that consumer ethnocentrism has been observed in France, Japan, Korea, and Germany as well. In these countries, it was also found that the more ethnocentric a consumer was, the less likely he or she was to rate the quality of foreign-made products highly. Similar conclusions have been suggested in national surveys in other parts of Europe and Asia.

The prevalence of consumer ethnocentrism in a country has important marketing implications. Specifically, consumer resistance to foreign-made products will make the task of global marketers more difficult.

sified into two major groupings that will help the global marketer better understand their needs:

- *Developed* countries have somewhat mixed economies. Private enterprise dominates, although they have substantial public sectors as well. The United States, Canada, Japan, and most of Western Europe can be considered developed.
- *Developing* countries are in the process of moving from an agricultural to an industrial economy. There are two subgroups within the developing category: (1) those that have already made the move and (2) those that remain locked in a preindustrial economy. Countries such as Poland, Hungary, Australia, Israel, Venezuela, and South Africa fall into the first group. In the second group are Pakistan, Sri Lanka, Tanzania, and Chad, where living standards are low and improvement will be slow. The economies of developing countries are expected to average 5 percent annual growth compared with 2 percent annual growth for developed countries through 2000.

A country's stage of economic development affects and is affected by other economic factors, as described next.

Economic Infrastructure The **economic infrastructure**—a country's communications, transportation, financial, and distribution systems—is a critical consideration in determining whether to try to market to a country's consumers and organizations. Parts of the infrastructure that North Americans or Western Europeans take for granted can be huge problems elsewhere—not only in developing nations but even in countries of Eastern Europe and the former Soviet Union where such an infrastructure is assumed to be in place. Consider, for instance, transportation and distribution systems in these countries. Two-lane roads with horse-drawn carts that limit average speeds to 35 or 40 miles per hour are commonplace—and a nightmare for firms requiring prompt truck delivery. Wholesale and retail institutions tend to be small, and a majority are operated by new owner-managers still learning the ways of a free market system. These conditions have prompted firms such as Danone, a French food company, to establish their own wholesale, retail, and delivery systems. Danone delivers its products to 700 shops in Russia and has set up 60 shops-in-shops, where it has its own retail sales associates and cash registers.[33]

The communication infrastructure in these countries, including telecommunication and postal systems, also differ. About one in ten people have a telephone. As for postal systems, *Reader's Digest* learned to send its magazine by registered mail in brown envelopes—or by private delivery services—because attractive packages tend to get "lost" frequently. These problems have led to several billion dollar investments to upgrade telecommunication and postal systems in these countries.

Even the financial and legal system can cause problems. Formal operating procedures among financial institutions and private properties did not exist under communism and are still limited. As a consequence, it is estimated that two thirds of the commercial transactions in Russia involve nonmonetary forms of payment.[34] The legal red tape involved in obtaining title to buildings and land for manufacturing, wholesaling, and retailing operations also has been a huge problem. Nevertheless, the Coca-Cola Company has invested $750 million from 1991 through 1998 to build bottling and distribution facilities in Russia, Allied Lyons has spent $30 million to build a plant to make Baskin-Robbins ice cream, and Mars recently opened a $200 million candy factory outside Moscow.[35]

Consumer Income and Purchasing Power   A global marketer selling consumer goods must also consider what the average per capita or household income is among a country's consumers and how the income is distributed to determine a nation's purchasing power. Per capita income varies greatly between nations. Average yearly per capita income in EU countries is $20,000 and is less than $200 in some developing countries such as Vietnam. A country's income distribution is important because it gives a more reliable picture of a country's purchasing power. Generally

The Coca-Cola Company has made a huge financial investment in bottling and distribution facilities in Russia.

The Coca-Cola Company
www.thecoca-colacompany.com

speaking, as the proportion of middle-income class households in a country increases, the greater a nation's purchasing power tends to be. Figure 5–5 shows the worldwide disparity in the percentage distribution of households by level of purchasing power.[36] In established market economies such as those in North America and Western Europe, 65 percent of households have an annual purchasing capability of $20,000 or more. In comparison, 75 percent of households in the developing countries of South Asia have an annual purchasing power of less than $5,000.

Seasoned global marketers recognize that people in developing countries often have government subsidies for food, housing, and health care that supplement their income. Accordingly, people with seemingly low incomes are actually promising customers for a variety of products. For example, a consumer in South Asia earning the equivalent of $250 per year can afford Gillette razors. When that consumer's income rises to $1,000, a Sony television becomes affordable, and a new Volkswagen or Nissan can be bought with an annual income of $10,000. In developing countries of Eastern Europe, a $1,000 annual income makes a refrigerator affordable, and $2,000 brings an automatic washer within reach. These facts have not gone unnoticed by Whirlpool, which now aggressively markets these products in Eastern Europe.

Income growth in developing countries of Asia, Latin America, and Central and Eastern Europe is expected to stimulate world trade well into the next century. The number of consumers in these countries earning the equivalent of $10,000 per year is expected to surpass the number of consumers in the United States, Japan, and Western Europe combined by 2005.[37]

Currency Exchange Rates   Fluctuations in exchange rates among the world's currencies are of critical importance in global marketing. Such fluctuations affect everyone—from international tourists to global companies.

A **currency exchange rate** is the price of one country's currency expressed in terms of another country's currency, such as the U.S. dollar expressed in Japanese yen or Swiss francs. Failure to consider exchange rates when pricing products for global markets can have dire consequences. Mattel learned this lesson in 1998. The company was unable to sell its popular Holiday Barbie doll and accessories in many international markets because they were too expensive. Why? Barbie prices, expressed in U.S. dollars, were set without regard for how they would translate into foreign currencies and were too high for many buyers.[38]

FIGURE 5–5
How purchasing power differs
around the world

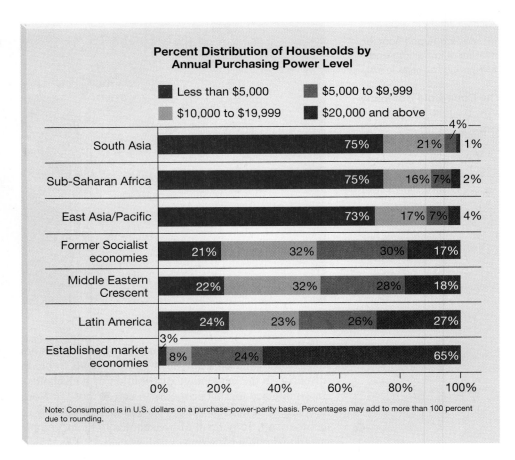

**Percent Distribution of Households by
Annual Purchasing Power Level**

Note: Consumption is in U.S. dollars on a purchase-power-parity basis. Percentages may add to more than 100 percent due to rounding.

Exchange rate fluctuations have a direct impact on the sales and profits made by global companies. When foreign currencies can buy more U.S. dollars, for example, U.S. products are less expensive for the foreign customer. This was the case during the 1990s, and U.S. exports grew accordingly. Short-term fluctuations, however, can have a significant effect on the profits of global companies. Hewlett-Packard recently gained nearly a half million dollars of additional profit through exchange rate fluctuation in one year. On the other hand, Nestlé has lost as much as a million dollars in six months due to fluctuations in the Swiss franc compared with other currencies.[39]

Political-Regulatory Climate

The political and regulatory climate for marketing in a country or region of the world lies not only in identifying the current climate but in determining how long a favorable or unfavorable climate will last. An assessment of a country or regional political-regulatory climate includes an analysis of its political stability and trade regulations.

Political Stability   Trade among nations or regions depends on political stability. Billions of dollars have been lost in the Middle East and the former Federal Republic of Yugoslavia as a result of internal political strife and war. Losses such as these encourage careful selection of politically stable countries and regions of the world for trade.

Political stability in a country is affected by numerous factors, including a government's orientation toward foreign companies and trade with other countries. These factors combine to create a political climate that is favorable or unfavorable for marketing and financial investment in a country or region of the world. Marketing man-

WEB LINK

Checking a Country's Political Risk

The political climate in every country is regularly changing. Governments can make new laws or enforce existing policies differently. Numerous consulting firms prepare political risk analyses that incorporate a variety of variables such as the risk of internal turmoil, external conflict, government restrictions on company operations, and tariff and nontariff trade barriers.

The PRS Group maintains multiple databases of country-specific information and projections, including country political risk ratings. These ratings can be ac-

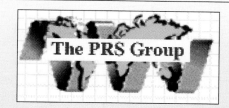

cessed at http://www.prsgroup.com/gptop.html. What country has the most favorable business climate and the least favorable business climate?

agers monitor political stability using a variety of measures and often track country risk ratings supplied by agencies such as the PRS Group. Visit the PRS Group Web site shown in the accompanying Web Link and see the most recent political risk ratings for countries.

Trade Regulations Countries have a variety of rules that govern business practices within their borders. These rules can often serve as trade barriers.[40] For example, Japan has some 11,000 trade regulations. Japanese car safety rules effectively require all automobile replacement parts to be Japanese and not American or European; public health rules make it illegal to sell aspirin or cold medicine without a pharmacist present. The Malaysian government instituted advertising regulations stating that "advertisements must not project or promote an excessively aspirational lifestyle," and Sweden outlaws all advertisements to children.

Trade regulations also appear in free trade agreements among countries. European Union nations abide by some 10,000 rules that specify how goods are to be made and marketed. For instance, the rules for a washing machine's electrical system are detailed on more than 100 typed pages. Regulations related to contacting consumers via telephone, fax, and E-mail without their prior consent and toy advertising to children also exist. The European Union's ISO 9000 quality standards, though not a trade regulation, have the same effect on business practice. **ISO 9000** standards, developed by the International Standards Organization (ISO) in Geneva, Switzerland, refer to standards for registration and certification of a manufacturer's quality management and quality assurance system. Many European companies require suppliers to be ISO 9000 certified as a condition of doing business with them. Certified companies have undergone an on-site audit that includes an inspection of its facilities to ensure that documented quality control procedures are in place and that all employees understand and follow them. More than 100 countries have adopted ISO 9000 standards, and 60,000 certificates have been issued worldwide with about 17,000 going to U.S. firms.[41]

CONCEPT CHECK

1. Semiotics involves the study of _____ .

2. When foreign currencies can buy more U.S. dollars, are U.S. products more or less expensive for a foreign consumer?

FIGURE 5–6
Alternative global market-entry
strategies

GLOBAL MARKET-ENTRY STRATEGIES

Once a company has decided to enter the global marketplace, it must select a means of market entry. Four general options exist: (1) exporting, (2) licensing, (3) joint venture, and (4) direct investment.[42] As Figure 5–6 demonstrates, the amount of financial commitment, risk, marketing control, and profit potential increases as the firm moves from exporting to direct investment.

Exporting

Exporting is producing goods in one country and selling them in another country. This entry option allows a company to make the least number of changes in terms of its product, its organization, and even its corporate goals. Host countries usually do not like this practice because it provides less local employment than under alternative means of entry.

Indirect exporting is when a firm sells its domestically produced goods in a foreign country through an intermediary. It involves the least amount of commitment and risk but will probably return the least profit. This kind of exporting is ideal for the company that has no overseas contacts but wants to market abroad. The intermediary is often a broker or agent that has the international marketing know-how and the resources necessary for the effort to succeed.

Direct exporting is when a firm sells its domestically produced goods in a foreign country without intermediaries. Most companies become involved in direct exporting when they believe their volume of sales will be sufficiently large and easy to obtain that they do not require intermediaries. For example, the exporter may be approached by foreign buyers that are willing to contract for a large volume of purchases. Direct exporting involves more risk than indirect exporting for the company but also opens the door to increased profits.

Harley-Davidson is one company that uses an exporting strategy. It exports about one fourth of its annual production of heavyweight motorcycles. Japan, Germany, and Canada, in that order, represent the company's largest markets. Exporting is often used by smaller U.S. businesses.[43] Sixty percent of American firms exporting products in 1998 had fewer than 100 employees. These firms accounted for an estimated 40 percent of total U.S. merchandise exports in 1998.[44]

Harley-Davidson, Inc. exports about one fourth of its annual production of heavyweight motorcycles. The company is represented internationally by 577 independent dealers in 55 countries.

Harley-Davidson, Inc.
www.harley-davidson.com

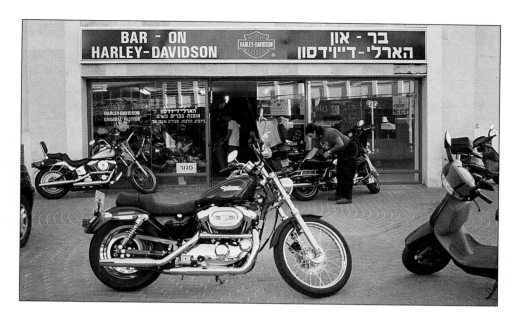

Licensing

Under licensing, a company offers the right to a trademark, patent, trade secret, or other similarly valued items of intellectual property in return for a royalty or a fee. In international marketing the advantages to the company granting the license are low risk and a capital-free entry into a foreign country. The licensee gains information that allows it to start with a competitive advantage, and the foreign country gains employment by having the product manufactured locally. Yoplait yogurt is licensed from Sodima, a French cooperative, by General Mills for sales in the United States.

There are some serious drawbacks to this mode of entry, however. The licensor forgoes control of its product and reduces the potential profits gained from it. In addition, while the relationship lasts, the licensor may be creating its own competition. Some licensees are able to modify the product somehow and enter the market with product and marketing knowledge gained at the expense of the company that got them started. To offset this disadvantage, many companies strive to stay innovative so that the licensee remains dependent on them for improvements and successful operation. Finally, should the licensee prove to be a poor choice, the name or reputation of the company may be harmed.

Two variations of licensing, local manufacturing and local assembly, represent alternative ways to produce a product within the foreign country. With local manufacturing, a U.S. company may contract with a foreign firm to manufacture products according to stated specifications. The product is then sold in the foreign country or exported back to the United States. With local assembly, the U.S. company may contract with a foreign firm to assemble (not manufacture) parts and components that have been shipped to that country. In both cases, the advantage to the foreign country is the employment of its people, and the U.S. firm benefits from the lower wage rates in the foreign country.

A third variation of licensing is franchising. Franchising is one of the fastest-growing market-entry strategies. By the late 1990s, more than 35,000 franchises of U.S. firms were located in countries throughout the world. Franchises include soft-drink, motel, retailing, fast-food, and car rental operation and a variety of business services. McDonald's is a premier global franchiser: more than 70 percent of the company's stores are franchised, and 70 percent of the company's operating income is projected to come from non-U.S. operations in 2001.[45]

McDonald's uses franchising as a market-entry strategy and 70 percent of the company's projected operating income will come from non-U.S. operations in 2001.

McDonald's
www.mcdonalds.com

Joint Venture

When a foreign country and a local firm invest together to create a local business, it is called a **joint venture.** These two companies share ownership, control, and profits of the new company. Investment may be made by having either of the companies buy shares in the other or by creating a third and separate entity. This was done by Caterpillar, Inc., the world's largest manufacturer of earth-moving and construction equipment. It recently created NEVAMASH with its joint venture partner, Kirovsky Zvod, a large Russian manufacturer of heavy equipment.[46]

The advantages of this option are twofold. First, one company may not have the necessary financial, physical, or managerial resources to enter a foreign market alone. The joint venture between Ericsson, a Swedish telecommunications firm, and CGCT, a French switch maker, enabled them together to beat out AT&T for a $100 million French contract. Ericsson's money and technology combined with CGCT's knowledge of the French market helped them to win the contract that neither of them could have won alone. Similarly, Ford and Volkswagen formed a joint venture to make four-wheel-drive vehicles in Portugal. Second, a government may require or strongly encourage a joint venture before it allows a foreign company to enter its market. This is the case in China. Today, more than 50,000 Chinese–foreign joint ventures operate in China.[47]

The disadvantages arise when the two companies disagree about policies or courses of action for their joint venture or when governmental bureaucracy bogs down the effort. For example, U.S. firms often prefer to reinvest earnings gained, whereas some foreign companies may want to spend those earnings. Or a U.S. firm may want to return profits earned to the United States, while the local firm or its government may oppose this—the problem now faced by many potential joint ventures in Eastern Europe, Russia, Latin America, and South Asia.

Direct Investment

The biggest commitment a company can make when entering the global market is **direct investment,** which entails a domestic firm actually investing in and owning a foreign subsidiary or division.[48] Examples of direct investment are Nissan's Smyrna, Tennessee, plant that produces pickup trucks and the Mercedes-Benz factory in Vance, Alabama, that makes the company's M-class sports utility vehicle. Many U.S.-based global companies also use this mode of entry. Reebok entered Russia by creating a subsidiary known as Reebok Russia, Motorola established a wholly owned Chinese subsidiary that manufactures mobile phones and other telecommunication equipment, and Ford has plans to build an $800 million automobile plant in Brazil.

For many firms, direct investment often follows one of the other three market-entry strategies.[49] For example, Ernst & Young, an international accounting and management consulting firm, entered Hungary first by establishing a joint venture with a local company. Ernst & Young later acquired the company, making it a subsidiary with headquarters in Budapest.

The advantages to direct investment include cost savings, better understanding of local market conditions, and fewer local restrictions. Firms entering foreign markets using direct investment believe that these advantages outweigh the financial commitments and risks involved.

CONCEPT CHECK

1. What mode of entry could a company follow if it has no previous experience in global marketing?

2. How does licensing differ from a joint venture?

CRAFTING A WORLDWIDE MARKETING EFFORT

The choice of a market-entry strategy is a necessary first step for a marketer when joining the community of global companies. The next step involves the challenging task of designing, implementing, and controlling marketing programs worldwide.

Product and Promotion Strategies

Global companies have five strategies for matching products and their promotion efforts to global markets. As Figure 5–7 shows, the strategies focus on whether a company extends or adapts its product and promotion message for consumers in different countries.

A product may be sold globally in one of three ways: (1) in the same form as in its home market, (2) with some adaptations, or (3) as a totally new product[50]:

1. *Product extension.* Selling virtually the same product in other countries is a product extension strategy. It works well for products such as Coca-Cola, Gillette razors, Breathe Right nasal strips, Wrigley's gum, and Levi's jeans. However, it didn't work for Jell-O (a more solid gelatin was preferred to the powder in England) or Duncan Hines cakes (which were seen as too moist and crumbly to eat with tea in England).

2. *Product adaptation.* Changing a product in some way to make it more appropriate for a country's climate or preferences is a product adaptation strategy. Exxon

FIGURE 5–7

Five product and promotion strategies for global marketing

Gillette delivers the same global message whenever possible, as shown in the Sensor for Women ads from France, Norway, and the United States.

The Gillette Company
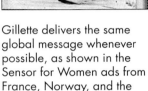
www.gillette.com

sells different gasoline blends based on each country's climate. Gerber baby food comes in different varieties in different countries. Vegetable and Rabbit Meat is a favorite food in Poland. Freeze-Dried Sardines and Rice is popular in Japan.

3. *Product invention.* Alternatively, companies can invent totally new products designed to satisfy common needs across countries. Black & Decker did this with its Snake Light Flexible Flashlight. Created to address a global need for portable lighting, the product became a best seller in North America, Europe, Latin America, and Australia and is the most successful new product developed by Black & Decker.

An identical promotion message is used for the product extension and product adaptation strategies around the world. Gillette uses the same global message for its men's toiletries: 'Gillette, the Best a Man Can Get." Even though Exxon adapts its gasoline for different countries, the promotion message is unchanged: 'Put a Tiger in Your Tank."

Global companies may also adapt their promotion message. For instance, the same product may be sold in many countries but advertised differently. As an example, L'Oreal, a French health and beauty products marketer, introduced its Golden Beauty brand of sun care products through its Helena Rubenstein subsidiary in Western Europe with a communication adaptation strategy. Recognizing that cultural and buying motive differences related to skin care and tanning exist, Golden Beauty advertising features dark tanning for Northern Europeans, skin protection to avoid wrinkles among Latin Europeans, and beautiful skin for Europeans living along the Mediterranean Sea, even though the products are the same. Other companies use a dual adaptation strategy by modifying both their products and promotion messages. Nestlé does this with Nescafé coffee. Nescafé is marketed using different coffee blends and promotional campaigns to match consumer preferences in different countries.

Distribution Strategy

Distribution is of critical importance in global marketing. The availability and quality of retailers and wholesalers as well as transportation, communication, and warehousing facilities are often determined by a country's stage of economic development. Figure 5–8 outlines the channel through which a product manufactured in one country must travel to reach its destination in another country. The first step involves the seller; its headquarters is the starting point and is responsible for the successful distribution to the ultimate consumer.

The next step is the channel between two nations, moving the product from one country to another. Intermediaries that can handle this responsibility include resident

FIGURE 5–8
Channels of distribution in
global marketing

buyers in a foreign country, independent merchant wholesalers who buy and sell the product, or agents who bring buyers and sellers together.

Once the product is in the foreign nation, that country's distribution channels take over.[51] These channels can be very long or surprisingly short, depending on the product line. In Japan fresh fish go through three intermediaries before getting to a retail outlet. Conversely, shoes only go through one intermediary. In other cases, the channel does not even involve the host country. Procter & Gamble sells its soap door to door in the Philippines because there are no other alternatives in many parts of that country. The sophistication of a country's distribution channels increase as its economic infrastructure develops. Supermarkets facilitate selling products in many nations, but they are not popular or available in many others where culture and lack of refrigeration dictate shopping on a daily rather than a weekly basis. For example, when Coke and Pepsi entered China, both had to create direct-distribution channels, investing in trucks and refrigerator units for small retailers.[52]

Pricing Strategy

Global companies also face many challenges in determining a pricing strategy as part of their worldwide marketing effort. Individual countries, even those with free trade agreements, may impose considerable competitive, political, and legal constraints on the pricing latitude of global companies. Of course, economic factors such as the costs of production, selling, and tariffs, plus transportation and storage costs, also affect global pricing decisions.

Pricing too low or too high can have dire consequences. When prices appear too low in one country, companies can be charged with dumping, a practice subject to severe penalties and fines. **Dumping** is when a firm sells a product in a foreign country below its domestic price or below its actual cost. This is often done to build a company's share of the market by pricing at a competitive level. Another reason is that the products being sold may be surplus or cannot be sold domestically and, therefore, are already a burden to the company. The firm may be glad to sell them at almost any price. A recent trade dispute involving U.S. apple growers and Mexico is a case in point. Mexican trade officials claimed that U.S. growers were selling their red and golden delicious apples in Mexico below the actual cost of production. They imposed a 101 percent tariff on U.S. apples, and a severe drop in U.S. apple exports to Mexico resulted. Subsequent negotiations set a price floor on the price of U.S. apples sold to Mexico.[53]

When companies price their products very high in some countries but competitively in others, they face a gray market problem. A **gray market,** also called parallel importing, is a situation where products are sold through unauthorized channels of distribution. A gray market comes about when individuals buy products in a lower-priced country from a manufacturer's authorized retailer, ship them to higher-priced countries, and then sell them below the manufacturer's suggested retail price through unauthorized retailers. Many well-known products have been sold through gray markets, including Olympus cameras, Seiko watches, IBM personal computers, and Mercedes-Benz cars. Parallel importing is legal in the United States. It is illegal in the European Union.[54]

CONCEPT CHECK   **1.** Products may be sold globally in three ways. What are they?

2. What is dumping?

SUMMARY

1 The dollar value of world trade has more than doubled in the past decade and will exceed $8 trillion in 2002. Manufactured goods and commodities account for 75 percent of world trade, while services account for 25 percent.

2 Not all world trade involves the exchange of money for goods or services. About 20 percent of world trade involves countertrade, the practice of using barter rather than money for making global sales.

3 A global perspective on world trade views exports and imports as complementary economic flows. A country's exports affect its imports and vice versa. This phenomenon is called the *trade feedback effect.*

4 The United States is the world's perennial leader in terms of gross domestic product and among the world's leaders in exports. Nevertheless, the United States has incurred a continuing balance of trade deficit since 1975.

5 The reason some companies and some industries in a country succeed globally while others do not lies in their nation's competitive advantage. A nation's competitive advantage arises from specific conditions in a nation that foster success.

6 Three trends in the late twentieth century have significantly affected world trade: (*a*) a gradual decline of economic protec-tionism, (*b*) an increase in formal economic integration and free trade among nations, and (*c*) global competition among global companies for global consumers.

7 Although global and domestic marketing are based on the same marketing principles, many underlying assumptions must be reevaluated when a firm pursues global opportunities. A global environmental scan typically considers three kinds of uncontrollable environmental variables. These include cultural diversity, economic conditions, and political-regulatory climate.

8 Four global market-entry strategies are exporting, licensing, joint venture, and direct investment. The relative difficulty of global marketing, as well as the amount of financial commitment, risk, marketing control, and profit potential, increase in moving from exporting to direct investment.

9 Crafting a worldwide marketing effort involves designing, implementing, and controlling a marketing program that standardizes marketing mix elements when there are cultural similarities and adapting them when cultures differ.

KEY TERMS AND CONCEPTS

countertrade p. 20
trade feedback effect p. 121
gross domestic product p. 121
balance of trade p. 121
protectionism p. 124
tariffs p. 124
quota p. 124
World Trade Organization p. 125
global competition p. 127
strategic alliances p. 127
multidomestic marketing strategy p. 128
global marketing strategy p. 128
global consumers p. 129
cross-cultural analysis p. 130

values p. 130
customs p. 130
cultural symbols p. 131
semiotics p. 131
back translation p. 132
consumer ethnocentrism p. 132
economic infrastructure p. 133
currency exchange rate p. 135
ISO 9000 p. 137
exporting p. 138
joint venture p. 140
direct investment p. 140
dumping p. 143
gray market p. 143

INTERNET EXERCISE

Global marketers interested in evaluating opportunities in developing countries can obtain valuable information at a Web site maintained by the International Trade Administration at www.stat-usa.gov/itabems.html. The International Trade Administration labels these developing countries Big Emerging Markets (BEMs) and provides a concise background on each country.

Use the International Trade Administration (ITA) Web site for big emerging markets to answer the following questions:

1 Which countries has the ITA identified as big emerging markets?

2 Examine three countries of your choice and identify
  a. The major business sectors in each country.
  b. The leading U.S. exports to and the leading U.S. imports from each country.
  c. The tariffs and import barriers imposed by each country.

APPLYING MARKETING CONCEPTS AND PERSPECTIVES

1 What is meant by this statement: "Quotas are a hidden tax on consumers, whereas tariffs are a more obvious one"?

2 Is the trade feedback effect described in the text a long-run or short-run view on world trade flows? Explain your answer.

3 The United States is considered to be a global leader in the development and marketing of pharmaceutical products, and Merck & Co. of New Jersey is a world leader in prescription drug sales. What explanation can you give for this situation based on the text discussion concerning the competitive advantage of nations?

4 How successful would a television commercial in Japan be if it featured a husband surprising his wife in her dressing area on Valentine's Day with a small box of chocolates containing four candies? Why?

5 As a novice in global marketing, which alternative for global market-entry strategy would you be likely to start with? Why? What other alternatives do you have for a global market entry?

6 Coca-Cola is sold worldwide. In some countries, Coca-Cola owns the bottling facilities; in others, it has signed contracts with licensees or relies on joint ventures. When selecting a licensee in each country, what factors should Coca-Cola consider?

CASE 5–1   CNS, INC., AND 3M: BREATHE RIGHT® NASAL STRIP

"When we first began marketing this product, what was so gratifying, particularly as a physician, were the literally thousands of letters and phone calls we would receive talking about how much better people slept at night. Almost all the letters began with 'thank you, thank you, thank you!' Just three thank you's. It was, 'I haven't gotten a good night's sleep like this in 10 years.'"

What is Dr. Dan Cohen, CEO OF CNS, Inc., talking about? It's Breathe Right® nasal strips, the innovative adhesive pad with a small spring inside that, when attached to the nose, pulls the nasal passages open and makes it easier to breathe. Since its introduction in the United States, Breathe Right strips have been coveted by athletes hoping to improve their performance through increased oxygen flow, snorers (and, more often, snorers' spouses) hoping for a sound night's sleep, and allergy and cold sufferers looking for relief for their stuffed noses.

HOW THIS WEIRD-LOOKING STRIP CAME ABOUT

The Breathe Right® strip was invented by Bruce Johnson, who suffered from chronic nasal congestion. At times he would put straws or paper clips up his nose at night to keep his nasal passages open. After tinkering in his workshop for years, he came up with a prototype design for the Breathe Right® strip. He brought the prototype to CNS, which was in the sleep disorders diagnostic equipment business at the time. Dr. Cohen knew instantly the market for the strips would be huge. After the products received Food and Drug Administration (FDA) approval and became successful in the market,

CNS divested its other interests and went to work marketing the strips full time.

Being a small company, CNS did not have the budget to launch a large-scale marketing campaign. But it got the break it needed when Jerry Rice, the wide receiver for the San Francisco 49ers, wore one of the strips on national TV when the 49ers won the 1995 Superbowl. The entire nation became aware of the product overnight, and demand for the strips increased dramatically. An indication of this national awareness was discussion on TV talk shows and even appearances of the strip in cartoons.

EVERYBODY HAS A NOSE: THE DECISION TO GO INTERNATIONAL

The problems that the Breathe Right® strips solve—snoring, congestion—are not unique to the U.S. population. Also, with the media being so global today, people around the world were seeing U.S. athletes wearing the strip and wondering how they could get their noses on some. CNS decided to take Breathe Right® international. But because it was still a relatively small company and had no experience in the global marketplace, it opted to take on a distribution partner that had extensive global outlets already in place as well as the ability to market the product abroad. 3M, makers of such products as Post-It™ notes and the leader in stick-to-skin products around the world, became the international distributor for Breathe Right® strips.

David Reynolds-Gooch, International Business Manager at 3M, explains that the strips fit in well with 3M's existing adhesive line of first-aid products and are sold in channels with which 3M has extensive leverage:

pharmacies, hypermarkets, and food markets. 3M agreed to take control of all the marketing and communication responsibilities in addition to the distribution in return for a percentage of the sales revenue of the strips. The strips are "co-branded" in the international markets: The packages say both Breathe Right® and 3M.

BREATHING RIGHT AROUND THE WORLD

3M introduced the Breathe Right® strip in Japan, then it was rolled out in Europe, and now can be found in more than 40 countries from Australia to South America. 3M used a similar approach to that used by CNS in the United States: Create awareness during the introduction phase through public relations—sports related and otherwise. "The first year we had incredible PR success," remembers Reynolds-Gooch. "We believe we got about $14 million worth of free TV, radio, and print time around the world." This was done through such tactics as having the South African rugby team wear the strips while it won the World Cup of rugby and having pulmonologists and breathing experts describe the benefits of the product on talk shows in Japan, Australia, Europe, and Latin America.

CNS quickly discovered some major differences in marketing the product here and abroad. For instance, as Gary Tschautscher, Vice President of International Marketing at CNS explains, "In the United States, we positioned and distributed the strips as part of the cough/cold category of products. As we rolled it out internationally, suddenly we realized in some countries that section in the store doesn't even exist. So where do you position your product?" Additionally, says Reynolds-Gooch, "There really aren't many large drug chains or pharmacy chains. The stores are independent in most countries by

law. So what that means is you have to go through multiple layers of distribution, and ultimately we were able to influence the pharmacists because of the other products 3M distributes in the stores." Finally, there is no couponing in most countries in the world. That vehicle for inducing trial of a new product is not available, and hence a lot more in-store sampling is needed.

BREATHE RIGHT® IN THE TWENTY-FIRST CENTURY

Both CNS and 3M face some issues for the future as Breathe Right strips gain in popularity around the globe. While the athletic segment of the market gets most of the publicity, the snorers are the bulk of the market for the strips internationally. Reynolds-Gooch has identified creating heavy users—those who use the strip every night—as the most important marketing point for the future, ahead of people with seasonal colds or allergies.

Also, many of the markets that have been identified as "hot" new markets throughout the business community may not be appropriate for the Breathe Right strips. For example, Latin America and Asia (especially China) are emerging markets with steadily increasing income levels and large populations, but the average age in these countries is under 30, and people under 30 typically do not have snoring problems with the frequency that older people do.

Questions

1 What are the advantages and disadvantages of CNS taking its Breathe Right® strip into international markets?
2 What advantages does CNS gain by having 3M as its international licensing partner? What are the advantages for 3M?
3 What criteria might CNS and 3M use in selecting countries to enter? Using these criteria, which five or six countries would you enter?
4 Which market segment would you target in entering the international markets—snorers, athletes, people with chronic congestion and allergies, or a new segment?
5 Which marketing mix variables do you think CNS should concentrate on the most to succeed in a global arena? Why?

New Engine Gets
Better Acceleration And Higher MPG.*

Smart New Exterior Design.
(New Colors, Too!)

A *Consumers Digest* Best Buy
Five Years In A Row!†

Around-The-Clock
Roadside Assistance.**

97% Of Owners Would
Recommend Prizm To A Friend!††

Call 1-888-99PRIZM
Or Visit www.chevrolet.com

A Constant Reminder Of Your
Superior Intelligence.

Relax.
This Is One Great Car.

introducing

CHEVROLET PRIZM

CHAPTER SIX

CONSUMER BEHAVIOR

6

AFTER READING THIS CHAPTER YOU SHOULD BE ABLE TO:

- Outline the stages in the consumer decision process.

- Distinguish among three variations of the consumer decision process: routine, limited, and extended problem solving.

- Explain how psychological influences affect consumer behavior, particularly purchase decision processes.

- Identify major sociocultural influences on consumer behavior and their effects on purchase decisions.

- Recognize how marketers can use knowledge of consumer behavior to better understand and influence individual and family purchases.

GETTING TO KNOW THE AUTOMOBILE CUSTOM(H)ER

Who will buy more than 60 percent of all new cars in 2001? Who already spends more than $81 billion on new and used cars and trucks and automotive accessories? Who influences 80 percent of all automotive-buying decisions? Women—yes, women.

Women are a driving force in the U.S. automotive industry. Enlightened automakers have hired women design engineers and marketing executives to help them understand this valuable custom(h)er. What have they learned? First, women prefer "sporty" vehicles that are relatively inexpensive and fun to drive rather than "sports" cars, luxury cars, and full-sized trucks with bigger engines and higher price tags. Second, a vehicle's "feel" is important to women. Sleek exteriors and interior designs that fit proportions of smaller drivers as well as opening ease for doors, trunks, and hoods are equally important. What are women buying? About 75 percent buy American-made vehicles.

Third, women approach car buying in a deliberate manner. They approach car buying, usage, and maintenance from a woman's point of view. They often visit auto-buying Web sites to gather information and will shop an average of three dealerships before making a purchase decision. Fourth, while men and women look for the same car features, their priorities differ. Both sexes value dependability most, but more women consider it a higher priority. Women also rank low price, ease of maintenance, and safety higher than men. Men view horsepower and acceleration as being more important than women. Finally, automakers have learned that 66 percent of women dislike the car-buying process.

Recognition of women as purchasers and influencers in car and truck buying has also altered the behavior of dealers. Many dealers now use a one-price policy and have stopped negotiating a vehicle's price. Industry research indicates that 68 percent of new-car buyers dread the price negotiation process involved in buying a car, and women often refuse to do it at all![1]

This chapter examines **consumer behavior,** the actions a person takes in purchasing and using products and services, including the mental and social processes that precede and follow these actions. This chapter shows how the behavioral sciences help answer questions such as why people choose one product or brand over another, how they make these choices, and how companies use this knowledge to provide value to consumers.

CONSUMER PURCHASE DECISION PROCESS

Behind the visible act of making a purchase lies an important decision process that must be investigated. The stages a buyer passes through in making choices about which products and services to buy is the **purchase decision process.** This process has the five stages shown in Figure 6–1: (1) problem recognition, (2) information search, (3) alternative evaluation, (4) purchase decision, and (5) postpurchase behavior.

Problem Recognition: Perceiving a Need

Problem recognition, the initial step in the purchase decision, is perceiving a difference between a person's ideal and actual situations big enough to trigger a decision.[2] This can be as simple as finding an empty milk carton in the refrigerator; noting, as a first-year college student, that your high school clothes are not in the style that other students are wearing; or realizing that your laptop computer may not be working properly.

In marketing, advertisements or salespeople can activate a consumer's decision process by showing the shortcomings of competing (or currently owned) products. For instance, an advertisement for a compact disc (CD) player could stimulate problem recognition because it emphasizes the sound quality of CD players over that of the conventional stereo system you may now own.

Information Search: Seeking Value

After recognizing a problem, a consumer begins to search for information, the next stage in the purchase decision process. First, you may scan your memory for previous experiences with products or brands.[3] This action is called *internal search.* For frequently purchased products such as shampoo, this may be enough. Or a consumer may undertake an *external search* for information.[4] This is especially needed when past experience or knowledge is insufficient, the risk of making a wrong purchase decision is high, and the cost of gathering information is low. The primary sources of external information are: (1) *personal sources,* such as relatives and friends whom the consumer trusts; (2) *public sources,* including various product-rating organizations such as *Consumer Reports,* government agencies, and TV "consumer programs"; and (3) *marketer-dominated sources,* such as information from sellers that include advertising, salespeople, and point-of-purchase displays in stores.

FIGURE 6–1
Purchase decision process

| Problem recognition: Perceiving a need | Information search: Seeking value | Evaluation of alternatives: Assessing value | Purchase decision: Buying value | Postpurchase behavior: Value in consumption or use |

Brand	Model	Price	Headphones	Error Correction	Bumps	Locate Speed
Panasonic	SL-SX500	$150	Very Good	Excellent	Very Good	Excellent
Phillips (A CR best buy)	AZ7383	100	Good	Excellent	Excellent	Very Good
Phillips	AZ7583	120	Good	Very Good	Excellent	Very Good
Sony	D-E409CK	140	Good	Good	Excellent	Good
Aiwa	XP-SP1200	145	Very Good	Fair	Good	Good
Sony	D-E401	100	Good	Good	Very Good	Good
Panasonic	SL-SW505	150	Fair	Excellent	Excellent	Excellent
JVC	XL-P34	80	Good	Excellent	Good	Excellent
Sony	D-ES55	200	Good	Very Good	Good	Fair
Panasonic	SL-S230	80	Good	Good	Very Good	Excellent
Aiwa	XP-570	75	Good	Good	Good	Fair

Rating:
Excellent
Very Good
Good
Fair
Poor

FIGURE 6–2
Consumer Reports' evaluation of portable compact disc players (abridged)

Consumer Reports
www.consumerreports.org

Suppose you consider buying a portable CD player. You will probably tap several of these information sources: friends and relatives, portable CD-player advertisements, and several stores carrying CD players (for demonstrations). You might study the comparative evaluation of portable CD players that appeared in *Consumer Reports,* published by a product-testing organization, a portion of which appears in Figure 6–2.

Alternative Evaluation: Assessing Value

The information search stage clarifies the problem for the consumer by (1) suggesting criteria to use for the purchase, (2) yielding brand names that might meet the criteria, and (3) developing consumer value perceptions. Based only on the information shown in Figure 6–2, what selection criteria would you use in buying a portable CD player? Would you use price, ease of use, the quality of headphones, or some combination of these and other criteria?

For some of you, the information provided may be inadequate because it does not contain all the factors you might consider when evaluating portable CD players. These factors are a consumer's **evaluative criteria,** which represent both the objective attributes of a brand (such as the locate speed) and the subjective ones (such as prestige) you use to compare different products and brands.[5] Firms try to identify and capitalize on both types of criteria to create the best value for the money sought by you and other consumers. These criteria are often displayed in advertisements.

Consumers often have several criteria for evaluating brands. (Didn't you in the preceding exercise?) Knowing this, companies seek to identify the most important evaluative criteria that consumers use when judging brands. For example, among the evaluative criteria shown in the columns of Figure 6–2, suppose that you use three in considering brands of portable CD players: (1) a list price no more than $100, (2) error correction, and the (3) locate speed. These criteria establish the brands in your

evoked set—the group of brands that a consumer would consider acceptable from among all the brands in the product class of which he or she is aware.[6] Your three evaluative criteria result in five models in your evoked set. If these brands don't satisfy you, you can change your evaluation criteria to create a different evoked set of models.

Purchase Decision: Buying Value

Having examined the alternatives in the evoked set, you are almost ready to make a purchase decision. Two choices remain: (1) from whom to buy and (2) when to buy.

For a product like a portable CD player, the information search process probably involved visiting retail stores, seeing different brands in catalogs, viewing portable CD-player promotions on a home shopping television channel, or visiting a seller's Web site. The choice of which seller to buy from will depend on such considerations as the terms of sale, your past experience buying from the seller, and the return policy. Often a purchase decision involves a simultaneous evaluation of both product attributes and seller characteristics. For example, you might choose the second-most preferred portable CD player brand at a store with a liberal refund and return policy versus the most preferred brand at a store with more conservative policies.

Deciding when to buy is frequently determined by a number of factors. For instance, you might buy sooner if one of your preferred brands is on sale or its manufacturer offers a rebate. Other factors such as the store atmosphere, pleasantness of the shopping experience, salesperson persuasiveness, time pressure, and financial circumstances could also affect whether a purchase decision is made or postponed.[7]

Information technology is expected to revolutionize the consumer purchase decision process in the next decade. Consumer **computer-mediated buying,** or online buying, is the use of Internet technology to seek information, evaluate alternatives, and make purchase decisions.[8] This technology also allows marketers to customize their offering to the specific needs of individuals thereby increasing customer value and satisfaction, as described in the accompanying Marketing NewsNet.[9] The growth of consumer computer-mediated buying and its implications for marketing is detailed in Chapter 8.

Postpurchase Behavior: Value in Consumption or Use

After buying a product, the consumer compares it with his or her expectations and is either satisfied or dissatisfied. If the consumer is dissatisfied, marketers must decide whether the product was deficient or consumer expectations too high. Product deficiency may require a design change; if expectations are too high, perhaps the company's advertising or the salesperson oversold the product's features.

Sensitivity to a customer's consumption or use experience is extremely important in a consumer's value perception. For example, research on long-distance telephone services provided by MCI, Sprint, and AT&T indicates that satisfaction or dissatisfaction affects consumer value perceptions.[10] Studies show that satisfaction or dissatisfaction affects consumer communications and repeat-purchase behavior. Satisfied

MARKETING NEWSNET

Computer-Mediated Buying: Creating Customer Value in Cyberspace

Information technology has changed the way many consumers seek information, evaluate alternatives, and make purchase decisions. Consider just a few ways that inventive marketers use the Internet to create customer value by easing the consumer decision process. The Gap (www.gap.com) provides a virtual dressing room that allows visitors to mix and match outfits. Eddie Bauer Home (www.eddiebauer.com) allows visitors to enter the dimensions of a room, rearrange furniture, and even turn pieces upside down for inspection. Music Boulevard (www.musicblvd.com) lets you listen to featured albums before making a selection.

Not interested in clothing, furniture, or music? Then how about car buying? General Motors (www.gm.com) and Chrysler (www.chrysler.com) allow shoppers to choose options, compare prices, and obtain a price quote via phone or e-mail without ever visiting a dealership. Industry surveys show that a quarter of all new-car buyers use the Internet for "virtual shopping." By

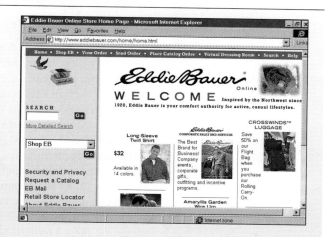

2001, half of all new-car buyers will visit a Web site to gather car information, evaluate choices, and make purchase decisions.

These examples illustrate just a few of the ways computer-mediated buying is creating a more informed consumer. Information technology can create customer value by easing the decision process.

buyers tell three other people about their experience. Dissatisfied buyers complain to nine people![11] Satisfied buyers also tend to buy from the same seller each time a purchase occasion arises. The financial impact of repeat-purchase behavior is significant. For example, Ford Motor Company estimates that each time the company increases its number of repeat buyers by 1 percent, Ford increases its profit by $100 million. Accordingly, firms such as General Electric (GE), Johnson & Johnson, Coca-Cola, and British Airways focus attention on postpurchase behavior to maximize customer satisfaction and retention.[12] These firms, among many others, now provide toll-free telephone numbers, offer liberalized return and refund policies, and engage in staff training to handle complaints, answer questions, and record suggestions. For example, GE operates a database that stores 750,000 answers about 8,500 of its models in 120 product lines to handle 3 million calls annually.[13] Research has shown that such efforts produce positive postpurchase communications among consumers and contribute to relationship building between sellers and buyers.

Often a consumer is faced with two or more highly attractive alternatives, such as a Panasonic or Sony portable CD player. If you choose the Panasonic, you may think, "Should I have purchased the Sony?" This feeling of postpurchase psychological tension or anxiety is called **cognitive dissonance.** To alleviate it, consumers often attempt to applaud themselves for making the right choice. So after your purchase, you may seek information to confirm your choice by asking friends questions like, "Don't you like my portable CD player?" or by reading ads of the brand you chose. You might even look for negative information about the brand you didn't buy and decide that Sony's error correction, which was rated "good" in Figure 6–2, was actually a deficiency. Firms often use ads or follow-up calls from salespeople in this postpurchase stage to try to convince buyers that they made the right decision. For many years, Buick ran an advertising campaign with the message, "Aren't you really glad you bought a Buick?"

Involvement and Problem-Solving Variations

Sometimes consumers don't engage in the five-step purchase decision process. Instead, they skip or minimize one or more steps depending on the level of **involvement,** the personal, social, and economic significance of the purchase to the consumer.[14] High-involvement purchase occasions typically have at least one of three characteristics—the item to be purchased (1) is expensive, (2) can have serious personal consequences, or (3) could reflect on one's social image. For these occasions, consumers engage in extensive information search, consider many product attributes and brands, form attitudes, and participate in word-of-mouth communication. Low-involvement purchases, such as toothpaste and soap, barely involve most of us, whereas stereo systems and automobiles are very involving. Researchers have identified three general variations in the consumer purchase process based on consumer involvement and product knowledge. Figure 6–3 summarizes some of the important differences between the three problem-solving variations.[15]

Routine Problem Solving   For products such as toothpaste and milk, consumers recognize a problem, make a decision, and spend little effort seeking external information and evaluating alternatives. The purchase process for such items is virtually a habit and typifies low-involvement decision making. Routine problem solving is typically the case for low-priced, frequently purchased products. It is estimated that about 50 percent of all purchase occasions are of this kind.

Limited Problem Solving   In limited problem solving, consumers typically seek some information or rely on a friend to help them evaluate alternatives. In general, several brands might be evaluated using a moderate number of different attributes. You might use limited problem solving in choosing a toaster, a restaurant for dinner, and other purchase situations in which you have little time or effort to spend. Limited problem solving accounts for about 38 percent of purchase occasions.

Extended Problem Solving   In extended problem solving, each of the five stages of the consumer purchase decision process is used in the purchase, including considerable time and effort on external information search and in identifying and evaluating alternatives. Several brands usually are in the evoked set, and these are evaluated on many attributes. Extended problem solving exists in high-involvement purchase situations for items such as automobiles and investments in stocks and

FIGURE 6–3
Comparison of problem-solving variations

CHARACTERISTICS OF PURCHASE DECISION PROCESS	EXTENDED PROBLEM SOLVING	LIMITED PROBLEM SOLVING	ROUTINE PROBLEM SOLVING
Number of brands examined	Many	Several	One
Number of sellers considered	Many	Several	Few
Number of product attributes evaluated	Many	Moderate	One
Number of external information sources used	Many	Few	None
Time spent searching	Considerable	Little	Minimal

CONSUMER INVOLVEMENT — HIGH ← → LOW

bonds. Firms marketing these products put significant effort into informing and educating these consumers. Twelve percent of purchase occasions fall into this category.

Situational Influences

Often the purchase situation will affect the purchase decision process. Five **situational influences** have an impact on your purchase decision process: (1) the purchase task, (2) social surroundings, (3) physical surroundings, (4) temporal effects, and (5) antecedent states.[16] The purchase task is the reason for engaging in the decision in the first place. Information searching and evaluating alternatives may differ depending on whether the purchase is a gift, which often involves the social visibility, or for the buyer's own use. Social surroundings, including the other people present when a purchase decision is made, may also affect what is purchased. Physical surroundings such as decor, music, and crowding in retail stores may alter how purchase decisions are made. Temporal effects such as time of day or the amount of time available will influence where consumers have breakfast and lunch and what is ordered. Finally, antecedent states, which include the consumer's mood or the amount of cash on hand, can influence purchase behavior and choice.

Figure 6–4 shows the many influences that affect the consumer purchase decision process. The decision to buy a product also involves important psychological and sociocultural influences, the two important topics discussed during the remainder of this chapter. Marketing mix influences are described in Chapters 11 through 21.

FIGURE 6–4

Influences on the consumer purchase decision process

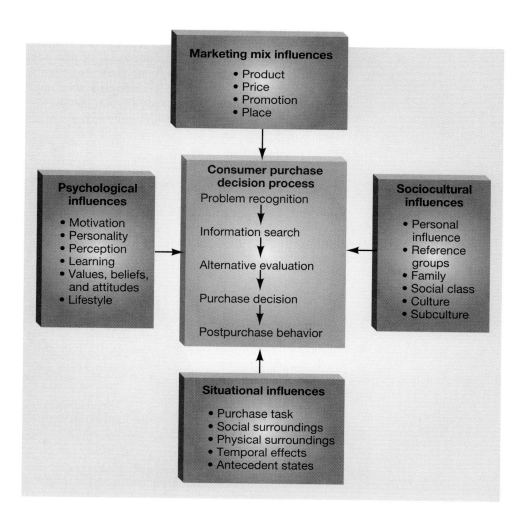

PSYCHOLOGICAL INFLUENCES ON CONSUMER BEHAVIOR

Psychology helps marketers understand why and how consumers behave as they do. In particular, concepts such as motivation and personality; perception; learning; values, beliefs, and attitudes; and lifestyle are useful for interpreting buying processes and directing marketing efforts.

Motivation and Personality

Motivation and personality are two familiar psychological concepts that have specific meanings and marketing implications. They are both used frequently to describe why people do some things and not others.

Motivation   **Motivation** is the energizing force that causes behavior that satisfies a need. Because consumer needs are the focus of the marketing concept, marketers try to arouse these needs.

An individual's needs are boundless. People possess physiological needs for basics such as water, sex, and food. They also have learned needs, including esteem, achievement, and affection. Psychologists point out that these needs are hierarchical; that is, once physiological needs are met, people seek to satisfy their learned needs. Figure 6–5 shows one need hierarchy and classification scheme that contains five

FIGURE 6–5
Hierarchy of needs

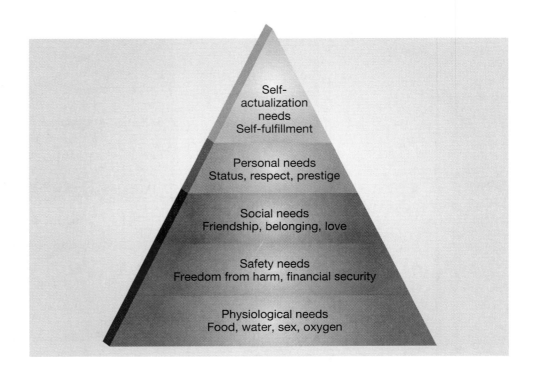

need classes.[17] *Physiological needs* are basic to survival and must be satisfied first. A Burger King advertisement featuring a juicy hamburger attempts to activate the need for food. *Safety needs* involve self-preservation and physical well-being. Smoke detector and burglar alarm manufacturers focus on these needs. *Social needs* are concerned with love and friendship. Dating services and fragrance companies try to arouse these needs. *Personal needs* are represented by the need for achievement, status, prestige, and self-respect. The American Express Gold Card and Brooks Brothers Clothiers appeal to these needs. Sometimes firms try to arouse multiple needs to stimulate problem recognition. Michelin combined security with parental love to promote tire replacement for automobiles. *Self-actualization needs* involve personal fulfillment. For example, the U.S. Army recruiting program invites you to "Be all you can be."

Personality   **Personality** refers to a person's consistent behaviors or responses to recurring situations. Although numerous personality theories exist, most identify key traits—enduring characteristics within a person or in his or her relationship with others. Such traits include assertiveness, extroversion, compliance, dominance, and aggression, among others. Research suggests that compliant people prefer known brand names and use more mouthwash and toilet soaps. In contrast, aggressive types use razors, not electric shavers, apply more cologne and after-shave lotions, and purchase signature goods such as Gucci, Yves St. Laurent, and Donna Karan as an indicator of status.[18] Cross-cultural analysis also suggests that residents of different countries have a **national character,** or a distinct set of personality characteristics common among people of a country or society.[19] For example, Americans and Germans are relatively more assertive than Russians and the English.

These personality characteristics are often revealed in a person's **self-concept,** which is the way people see themselves and the way they believe others see them.[20] Marketers recognize that people have an actual self-concept and an ideal self-concept. The actual self refers to how people actually see themselves. The ideal self describes how people would like to see themselves. These two self "images" are reflected in the products and brands a person buys including automobiles, home appliances and furnishings, magazines, clothing, grooming and leisure products, and frequently, the stores a person shops. The importance of self-concept is summed up by a senior executive at Barnes & Noble: "People buy books for what the purchase says about them—their taste, their cultivation, their trendiness."[21]

Perception

One person sees a Cadillac as a mark of achievement; another sees it as ostentatious. This is the result of **perception**—the process by which an individual selects, organizes, and interprets information to create a meaningful picture of the world.

Selective Perception   Because the average consumer operates in a complex environment, the human brain attempts to organize and interpret information with a process called *selective perception,* a filtering of exposure, comprehension, and retention. *Selective exposure* occurs when people pay attention to messages that are consistent with their attitudes and beliefs and ignore messages that are inconsistent. Selective exposure often occurs in the postpurchase stage of the consumer decision process, when consumers read advertisements for the brand they just bought. It also occurs when a need exists—you are more likely to "see" a McDonald's advertisement or the Golden Arches by the road when you are hungry rather than after you have eaten a pizza.

Selective comprehension involves interpreting information so that it is consistent with your attitudes and beliefs. A marketer's failure to understand this can have disastrous results. For example, Toro introduced a small, lightweight snowblower called the

ETHICS AND SOCIAL RESPONSIBILITY ALERT

The Ethics of Subliminal Messages

For almost 50 years, the topic of subliminal perception and the presence of subliminal messages embedded in commercial communications has sparked debate. Although there is no substantive scientific support for the concept of subliminal perception, the Federal Communications Commission has denounced subliminal messages as deceptive. Still, consumers spend $50 million a year for audiotapes with subliminal messages designed to help them raise their self-esteem, quit smoking, or lose weight.

Subliminal messages are not illegal in the United States, however, and marketers occasionally pursue opportunities to create these messages. For example, Time Warner Interactive's Endorfun, a CD-ROM puzzle game, has a music soundtrack with more than 100 subliminal messages meant to make players feel good about themselves, even if they can't solve the puzzle. One message says, "I am a winner." Puzzle players are informed that subliminal messages exist and instructions on how to turn off the soundtrack are provided.

Do you believe that attempts to implant subliminal messages are a deceptive practice and unethical, regardless of their intent?

Snow Pup. Even though the product worked, sales failed to meet expectations. Why? Toro later found out that consumers perceived the name to mean that Snow Pup was a toy or too light to do any serious snow removal. When the product was renamed "Snow Master," sales increased sharply.[22]

Selective retention means that consumers do not remember all the information they see, read, or hear, even minutes after exposure to it. This affects the internal and external information search stage of the purchase decision process. This is why furniture and automobile retailers often give consumers product brochures to take home after they leave the showroom.

Because perception plays such an important role in consumer behavior, it is not surprising that the topic of subliminal perception is a popular item for discussion. **Subliminal perception** means that you see or hear messages without being aware of them. The presence and effect of subliminal perception on behavior is a hotly debated issue, with more popular appeal than scientific support. Indeed, evidence suggests that such messages have limited effects on behavior.[23] If these messages did influence behavior, would their use be an ethical practice? (See the accompanying Ethics and Social Responsibility Alert.[24])

Perceived Risk   Perception plays a major role in the perceived risk in purchasing a product or service. **Perceived risk** represents the anxieties felt because the consumer cannot anticipate the outcomes of a purchase but believes that there may be

Companies use a variety
of strategies to reduce
consumer-perceived risk.

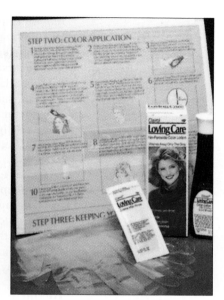

negative consequences. Examples of possible negative consequences are the size of
the financial outlay required to buy the product (Can I afford $200 for those skis?),
the risk of physical harm (Is bungee jumping safe?), and the performance of the product (Will the hair coloring work?). A more abstract form is psychosocial (What will
my friends say if I wear that sweater?). Perceived risk affects information search because the greater the perceived risk, the more extensive the external search phase is
likely to be.

Recognizing the importance of perceived risk, companies develop strategies to reduce the consumer's risk and encourage purchases. These strategies and examples of
firms using them include the following:

- Obtaining seals of approval: the Good Housekeeping seal or Underwriter's Lab-
  oratory seal.
- Securing endorsements from influential people: The National Fluid Milk Proces-
  sor Promotion Board.
- Providing free trials of the product: sample packages of Duncan Hines Peanut
  Butter Cookies.
- Giving extensive usage instructions: Clairol haircoloring.
- Providing warranties and guarantees: Cadillac's four-year, 50,000-mile, Gold
  Key Bumper-to-Bumper warranty.

Learning

Much consumer behavior is learned. Consumers learn which information sources to
use for information about products and services, which evaluative criteria to use when
assessing alternatives, and, more generally, how to make purchase decisions. **Learning** refers to those behaviors that result from (1) repeated experience and (2) thinking.

Behavioral Learning *Behavioral learning* is the process of developing automatic responses to a situation built up through repeated exposure to it. Four variables
are central to how consumers learn from repeated experience: drive, cue, response,
and reinforcement. A *drive* is a need that moves an individual to action. Drives, such
as hunger, might be represented by motives. A *cue* is a stimulus or symbol perceived
by consumers. A *response* is the action taken by a consumer to satisfy the drive, and a

reinforcement is the reward. Being hungry (drive), a consumer sees a cue (a billboard), takes action (buys a hamburger), and receives a reward (it tastes great!).

Marketers use two concepts from behavioral learning theory. *Stimulus generalization* occurs when a response elicited by one stimulus (cue) is generalized to another stimulus. Using the same brand name for different products is an application of this concept, such as Tylenol Cold & Flu and Tylenol P.M. *Stimulus discrimination* refers to a person's ability to perceive differences in stimuli. Consumers' tendency to perceive all light beers as being alike led to Budweiser Light commercials that distinguished between many types of "lights" and Bud Light.

Cognitive Learning   Consumers also learn through thinking, reasoning, and mental problem solving without direct experience. This type of learning, called *cognitive learning,* involves making connections between two or more ideas or simply observing the outcomes of others' behaviors and adjusting your own accordingly. Firms also influence this type of learning. Through repetition in advertising, messages such as "Advil is a headache remedy" attempt to link a brand (Advil) and an idea (headache remedy) by showing someone using the brand and finding relief.

Brand Loyalty   Learning is also important because it relates to habit formation—the basis of routine problem solving. Furthermore, there is a close link between habits and **brand loyalty,** which is a favorable attitude toward and consistent purchase of a single brand over time. Brand loyalty results from the positive reinforcement of previous actions. So a consumer reduces risk and saves time by consistently purchasing the same brand of shampoo and has favorable results—healthy, shining hair. There is evidence of brand loyalty in many commonly purchased products in the United States and the global marketplace. However, the incidence of brand loyalty appears to be declining in North America, Mexico, European Union nations, and Japan.[25]

Values, Beliefs, and Attitudes

Values, beliefs, and attitudes play a central role in consumer decision making and related marketing actions.

Attitude Formation   An **attitude** is a "learned predisposition to respond to an object or class of objects in a consistently favorable or unfavorable way."[26] Attitudes are shaped by our values and beliefs, which are learned. Values vary by level of specificity. We speak of American core values, including material well-being and humanitarianism. We also have personal values, such as thriftiness and ambition. Marketers are concerned with both, but focus mostly on personal values. Personal values affect attitudes by influencing the importance assigned to specific product attributes. Suppose thriftiness is one of your personal values. When you evaluate cars, fuel economy (a product attribute) becomes important. If you believe a specific car has this attribute, you are likely to have a favorable attitude toward it.

Beliefs also play a part in attitude formation. **Beliefs** are a consumer's subjective perception of *how well* a product or brand performs on different attributes. Beliefs are based on personal experience, advertising, and discussions with other people. Beliefs about product attributes are important because, along with personal values, they create the favorable or unfavorable attitude the consumer has toward certain products and services.

Attitude Change   Marketers use three approaches to try to change consumer attitudes toward products and brands, as shown in the following examples.[27]

1. *Changing beliefs about the extent to which a brand has certain attributes.* To allay consumer concern that aspirin use causes an upset stomach, The Bayer Company successfully promoted the gentleness of its Extra Strength Bayer Plus aspirin.

Attitudes toward Colgate toothpaste and Extra Strength Bayer aspirin were successfully changed by these ads. How? Read the text to find out how marketers can change consumer attitudes toward products and brands.

2. *Changing the perceived importance of attributes.* Pepsi-Cola made freshness an important product attribute when it stamped freshness dates on its cans. Prior to doing so, few consumers considered cola freshness an issue. After Pepsi spent about $25 million on advertising and promotion, a consumer survey found that 61 percent of cola drinkers believed freshness dating was an important attribute![28]

3. *Adding new attributes to the product.* Colgate-Palmolive included a new antibacterial ingredient, tricloson, in its Colgate Total toothpaste and spent $100 million marketing the brand. The result? Colgate replaced Crest as the market leader for the first time in 25 years.[29]

Lifestyle

Lifestyle is a mode of living that is identified by how people spend their time and resources (activities), what they consider important in their environment (interests), and what they think of themselves and the world around them (opinions). The analysis of consumer lifestyles (also called *psychographics*) has produced many insights into consumers' behavior. For example, lifestyle analysis has proven useful in segmenting and targeting consumers for new and existing products (see Chapter 9).

Lifestyle analysis typically focuses on identifying consumer profiles. The most prominent example of this type of analysis is the Values and Lifestyles (VALS) Program developed by SRI International.[30] The VALS Program has identified eight interconnected categories of adult lifestyles based on a person's self-orientation and resources. Self-orientation describes the patterns of attitudes and activities that help people reinforce their social self-image. Three patterns have been uncovered; they are oriented toward principles, status, and action. A person's resources encompass income, education, self-confidence, health, eagerness to buy, intelligence, and energy level. This dimension is a continuum ranging from minimal to abundant. Figure 6–6 shows the eight lifestyle types and their relationships and highlights selected

FIGURE 6–6
VALS 2 psychographic segments

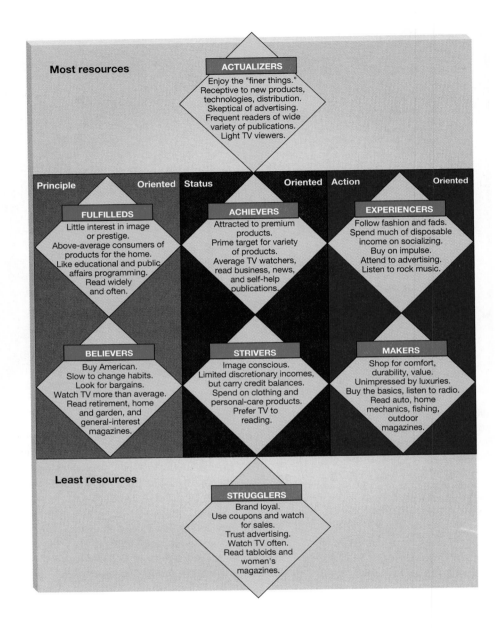

Most resources

ACTUALIZERS
Enjoy the "finer things."
Receptive to new products,
technologies, distribution.
Skeptical of advertising.
Frequent readers of wide
variety of publications.
Light TV viewers.

Principle   Oriented   Status   Oriented   Action   Oriented

FULFILLEDS
Little interest in image
or prestige.
Above-average consumers of
products for the home.
Like educational and public
affairs programming.
Read widely
and often.

ACHIEVERS
Attracted to premium
products.
Prime target for variety
of products.
Average TV watchers,
read business, news,
and self-help
publications.

EXPERIENCERS
Follow fashion and fads.
Spend much of disposable
income on socializing.
Buy on impulse.
Attend to advertising.
Listen to rock music.

BELIEVERS
Buy American.
Slow to change habits.
Look for bargains.
Watch TV more than average.
Read retirement, home
and garden, and
general-interest
magazines.

STRIVERS
Image conscious.
Limited discretionary incomes,
but carry credit balances.
Spend on clothing and
personal-care products.
Prefer TV to
reading.

MAKERS
Shop for comfort,
durability, value.
Unimpressed by luxuries.
Buy the basics, listen to radio.
Read auto, home
mechanics, fishing,
outdoor
magazines.

Least resources

STRUGGLERS
Brand loyal.
Use coupons and watch
for sales.
Trust advertising.
Watch TV often.
Read tabloids and
women's
magazines.

behavioral characteristics of each. Before reading further, visit the VALS Program Web site shown in the accompanying Web Link. Complete the short survey and find out your lifestyle category within seconds. Does it describe you?

The VALS Program seeks to explain why and how consumers make purchase decisions. For example, *principle-oriented consumers* try to match their behavior with their views of how the world is or should be. These older consumers divide into two categories. Fulfilleds are mature, satisfied, and reflective people who value order, knowledge, and responsibility. Most are well-educated and employed in a profession. Believers, with fewer resources to draw on, are conservative, conventional people with concrete beliefs and strong attachments to family, church, and community. *Status-oriented consumers* are motivated by the actions and opinions of others. These consumers include Achievers, who are successful and career-oriented; value duty, structure, prestige and material rewards; and have abundant resources at their disposal. Strivers, with fewer resources, seek motivation, self-definition, and social approval, and define success in purely financial terms. *Action-oriented consumers* are intensely

WEB LINK

Identify Your VALS Profile

The Values and Lifestyles (VALS) Program developed by SRI International has identified eight interconnected adult lifestyle categories based on a person's self-orientation and resources. The text provides a brief description of each category.

Do you wish to know your VALS profile? If you do, simply respond to the questions on the VALS™2 questionnaire (http://future.sri.com). In addition to obtaining your profile in real time, you can examine the characteristics of your and other profiles in greater detail.

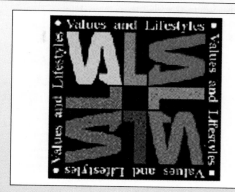

involved in social and physical activity, enjoy variety, and are risk-takers. Experiencers are young, enthusiastic, impulsive, and rebellious consumers who are still formulating life values and behavior patterns. Makers too are energetic but focus their attention on practical matters related to family, work, and physical recreation. While Experiencers maintain a vicarious relationship with their surroundings, Makers experience life by working on it—building a house and raising children.

Two consumer types stand apart. Actualizers are successful, sophisticated, active, take-charge people with high self-esteem and abundant resources of all kinds. Image is important to them, not as evidence of power or status, but as an expression of taste, independence, and character. By comparison, Strugglers are poor, often uneducated, and frequently concerned about their well-being. They are the oldest of the VALS consumer types.

Each of these categories exhibits different buying behavior and media preferences. For example, Believers and Makers typically own pickup trucks and fishing gear; Actualizers are likely to own a foreign luxury car or a home computer. Actualizers, Fulfilleds, and Achievers are most likely to read business magazines such as *Fortune*. Experiencers read sports magazines, Makers read automotive magazines, and Believers are the heaviest readers of *Reader's Digest*.

CONCEPT CHECK

1. The problem with the Toro Snow Pup was an example of selective _____.

2. What three attitude-change approaches are most common?

3. What does *lifestyle* mean?

SOCIOCULTURAL INFLUENCES ON CONSUMER BEHAVIOR

Sociocultural influences, which evolve from a consumer's formal and informal relationships with other people, also exert a significant impact on consumer behavior. These involve personal influence, reference groups, the family, social class, culture, and subculture.

Firms use sports figures or celebrities as spokespersons to represent their products, such as Brett Favre for Right Guard Sport and Cindy Crawford for Omega watches, in the hope that they are opinion leaders.

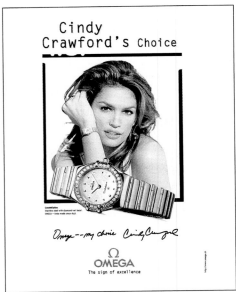

Personal Influence

A consumer's purchases are often influenced by the views, opinions, or behaviors of others. Two aspects of personal influence are important to marketing: opinion leadership and word-of-mouth activity.

Opinion Leadership   Individuals who exert direct or indirect social influence over others are called **opinion leaders.** Opinion leaders are more likely to be important for products that provide a form of self-expression. Automobiles, clothing, club membership, home video equipment, and PCs are products affected by opinion leaders, but appliances are not.[31] A recent study by *Popular Mechanics* magazine identified 18 million men who influence the purchases of some 85 million consumers for "do-it-yourself" products.[32]

About 10 percent of U.S. adults are opinion leaders.[33] Identifying, reaching, and influencing opinion leaders is a major challenge for companies. Some firms use sports figures or celebrities as spokespersons to represent their products, such as Brett Favre for Right Guard Sport and Cindy Crawford for Omega watches, in the hope that they are opinion leaders. Others promote their products in media believed to reach opinion leaders. Still others use more direct approaches. For example, Chrysler Corporation recently invited influential community leaders and business executives to test drive its Dodge Intrepid, Chrysler Concorde, and Eagle Vision models. Some 6,000 accepted the offer, and 98 percent said they would recommend their tested car. Chrysler estimated that the number of favorable recommendations totaled 32,000.[34]

Word of Mouth   People influencing each other during their face-to-face conversations is called **word of mouth.** Word of mouth is perhaps the most powerful information source for consumers because it typically involves friends viewed as trustworthy. When consumers were asked in a recent survey what most influences their buying decisions, 37 percent mentioned a friend's recommendation, and 20 percent said advertising. When a similar question was posed to Russian consumers, 72 percent said advice from friends, and 24 percent said advertising.[35]

The power of personal influence has prompted firms to promote positive and retard negative word of mouth.[36] For instance, "teaser" advertising campaigns are run in advance of new product introductions to stimulate conversations. Other techniques such as

MARKETING NEWSNET

Psst. Have You Heard . . . ? The Nemesis of Negative Word of Mouth in Global Marketing

Global marketers have learned painfully that word of mouth is a powerful information source in developing countries. Rumors that result in negative word of mouth are particularly common. For example, several food products in Indonesia, including some sold by Nestlé, were rumored to contain pork, which is prohibited to the 160 million Muslim consumers in that country. Nestlé spent $250,000 in advertising to counteract the rumor.

In Russia, Mars, Inc. had to confront the untrue claim that 200,000 Moscow children acquired diabetes from Snickers candy bars. Pabst Blue Ribbon beer was hit by a rumor in China that its beer was poisoned. Actually, a home-brewed beer had been poured into an empty Pabst bottle and resold.

Negative word of mouth has been shown to reduce the credibility of a company's advertising and con-

sumers' intention to buy products. Its effect can be particularly damaging for companies that have recently entered a new country.

advertising slogans, music, and humor also heighten positive word of mouth. On the other hand, rumors about Kmart (snake eggs in clothing), McDonald's (worms in hamburgers), and Corona Extra beer (contaminated beer) have resulted in negative word of mouth, none of which was based on fact. Overcoming or neutralizing negative word of mouth is difficult and costly. Firms have found that supplying factual information, providing toll-free numbers for consumers to call the company, and giving appropriate product demonstrations also have been helpful. Negative word of mouth is particularly challenging for global marketers as described in the accompanying Marketing NewsNet.[37]

Reference Groups

Reference groups are people to whom an individual looks as a basis for self-appraisal or as a source of personal standards. Reference groups affect consumer purchases because they influence the information, attitudes, and aspiration levels that help set a consumer's standards. For example, one of the first questions one asks others when planning to attend a social occasion is, "What are you going to wear?" Reference groups have an important influence on the purchase of luxury products but not of necessities—reference groups exert a strong influence on the brand chosen when its use or consumption is highly visible to others.[38]

Consumers have many reference groups, but three groups have clear marketing implications. A *membership group* is one to which a person actually belongs, including fraternities, social clubs, and the family. Such groups are easily identifiable and are targeted by firms selling insurance, insignia products, and charter vacations. An *aspiration group* is one that a person wishes to be a member of or wishes to be identified with, such as a professional society. Firms frequently rely on spokespeople or settings associated with their target market's aspiration group in their advertising. A *dissocia-*

tive group is one that a person wishes to maintain a distance from because of differences in values or behaviors.

Family Influence

Family influences on consumer behavior result from three sources: consumer socialization, passage through the family life cycle, and decision making within the family.

Consumer Socialization The process by which people acquire the skills, knowledge, and attitudes necessary to function as consumers is **consumer socialization**.[39] Children learn how to purchase (1) by interacting with adults in purchase situations and (2) through their own purchasing and product usage experiences. Research shows that children evidence brand preferences at age two, and these preferences often last a lifetime.[40] This knowledge has prompted Sony to introduce "My First Sony," a line of portable audio equipment for children; Time, Inc. to launch *Sports Illustrated for Kids;* Polaroid to develop the Cool Cam camcorder for children between ages 9 and 14; and Yahoo! and America Online to create special areas where young audiences can view their children's menu—Yahooligans! and Kids Only, respectively.

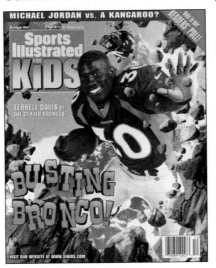

Family Life Cycle Consumers act and purchase differently as they go through life. The **family life cycle** concept describes the distinct phases that a family progresses through from formation to retirement, each phase bringing with it identifiable purchasing behaviors.[41] Figure 6–7 illustrates the traditional progression as well as contemporary variations of the family life cycle, including the prevalence of single-person households with and without children who will account for about one third of U.S. households in 2002. Young singles' buying preferences are for nondurable items, including prepared foods, clothing, personal care products, and entertainment. They comprise about 9 percent of households and represent a target market for recreational travel, automobile, and consumer electronics firms. Young married couples without children are typically more affluent than young singles because usually both spouses are employed. These couples account for about 10 percent of households and exhibit preferences for furniture, housewares, and gift items for each other. Young marrieds with children represent about 17 percent of households and are driven by the needs of their children. They make up a sizeable market for life insurance, various children's products, and home furnishings. Single parents with children (8 percent of households) are the least financially secure of households with children. Their buying preferences are affected by a limited economic status and tend toward convenience foods, child care services, and personal care items.

Middle-aged married couples with children comprise about 23 percent of households and are typically better off financially than their younger counterparts. They are a significant market for leisure products and home improvement items and represented the fastest-growing family life cycle stage in the late 1990s. Middle-aged couples without children account for 20 percent of households and typically have a large amount of discretionary income. These couples buy better home furnishings, status automobiles, and financial services.

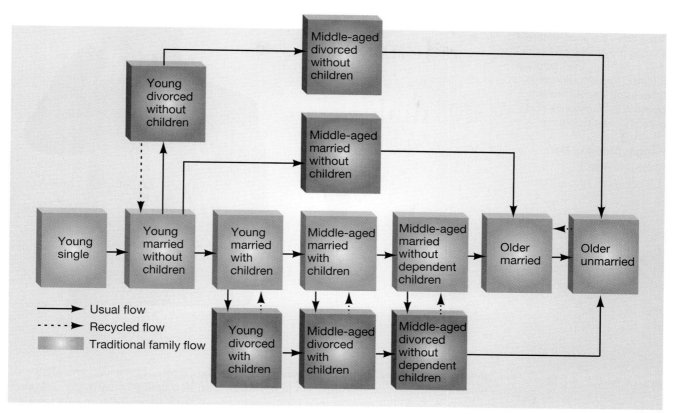

FIGURE 6–7
Modern family life cycle

Persons in the last two phases—older married and older unmarried—make up 13 percent of households. They are a sizeable market for prescription drugs, medical services, vacation trips, and gifts for younger relatives. These consumers represented the second-fastest-growing family life cycle stage in the late 1990s.

Family Decision Making   A third influence in the decision-making process occurs within the family. Two decision-making styles exist: spouse-dominant and joint decision making. With a joint decision-making style, most decisions are made by both husband and wife. Spouse-dominant decisions are those for which either the husband or the wife is responsible. Research indicates that wives tend to have the most say when purchasing groceries, children's toys, clothing, and medicines. Husbands tend to be more influential in home and car maintenance purchases. Joint decision making is common for cars, vacations, houses, home appliances and electronics, medical care, and long-distance telephone services. As a rule, joint decision making increases with the education of the spouses.[42]

Roles of individual family members in the purchase process are another element of family decision making. Five roles exist: (1) information gatherer, (2) influencer, (3) decision maker, (4) purchaser, and (5) user. Family members assume different roles for different products and services. This knowledge is important to firms.[43] For example, 89 percent of wives either influence or make outright purchases of men's clothing. Knowing this, Haggar Clothing, a menswear marketer, now advertises in women's magazines such as *Vanity Fair, Mademoiselle,* and *Redbook.* Even though women are often the grocery decision maker, they are not necessarily the purchaser. More than 40 percent of all food-shopping dollars are spent by male customers. Increasingly, preteens and teenagers are the information gatherers, influencers, decision makers, and

The Haggar Clothing Co. recognizes the important role women play in the choice of men's clothing. The company directs a large portion of its advertising toward women because they influence and purchase men's clothing.

Haggar Clothing Co.
www.haggar.com

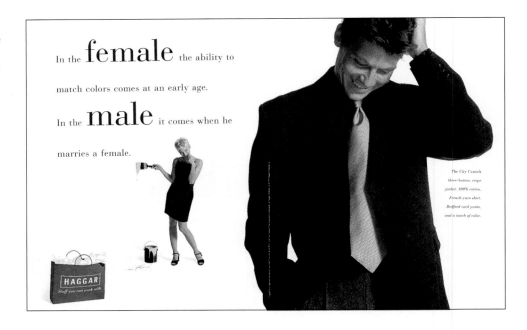

In the **female** the ability to match colors comes at an early age. In the **male** it comes when he marries a female.

The City Canada three-button, crepe jacket. 100% cotton, French-yarn shirt, Bedford cord pants, and a touch of color.

HAGGAR
Stuff you can work with.

purchasers of products and services items for the family, given the prevalence of working parents and single-parent households. Children under 18 currently influence more than $500 billion in annual family purchases.[44] This figure helps to explain why, for example, Nabisco, Johnson & Johnson, Apple Computer, Kellogg, P&G, and Oscar Mayer, among countless other companies, spend more than $1.5 billion annually in media that reach preteens and teens.

Social Class

A more subtle influence on consumer behavior than direct contact with others is the social class to which people belong. **Social class** may be defined as the relatively permanent, homogeneous divisions in a society into which people sharing similar values, interests, and behavior can be grouped. A person's occupation, source of income (not level of income), and education determine his or her social class. Generally speaking, three major social class categories exist—upper, middle, and lower—with subcategories within each. This structure has been observed in the United States, Great Britain, Western Europe, and Latin America.[45]

To some degree, persons within social classes exhibit common attitudes, lifestyles, and buying behaviors. Compared with the middle classes, people in the lower classes have a more short-term time orientation, are more emotional than rational in their reasoning, think in concrete rather than abstract terms, and see fewer personal opportunities. Members of the upper classes focus on achievements and the future and think in abstract or symbolic terms.

Companies use social class as a basis for identifying and reaching particularly good prospects for their products and services. For instance, AT&T has used social class for identifying preferences for different styles of telephones, JCPenney has historically appealed to the middle classes, and *New Yorker* magazine reaches the upper classes. In general, people in the upper classes are targeted by companies for items such as financial investments, expensive cars, and evening wear. The middle classes represent a target market for home improvement centers, automobile parts stores, and personal hygiene products. Firms also recognize differences in media preferences among classes: lower and working classes prefer sports and scandal magazines, middle classes read fashion, romance, and celebrity (*People*) magazines, and upper classes tend to read literary, travel, and news magazines.

Culture and Subculture

As described in Chapter 3, culture refers to the set of values, ideas, and attitudes that are accepted by a homogeneous group of people and transmitted to the next generation. Thus we often refer to the American culture, the Latin American culture, or the Japanese culture. Cultural underpinnings of American buying patterns were described in Chapter 3; Chapter 5 explored the role of culture in global marketing.

Subgroups within the larger, or national, culture with unique values, ideas, and attitudes are referred to as **subcultures.** Various subcultures exist within the American culture. The three largest racial/ethnic subcultures in the United States are African-Americans, Hispanics, and Asians. These three groups will account for 33 percent of the U.S. population in 2005. They spend more than $950 billion annually for goods and services.[46] Each of these groups exhibit sophisticated social and cultural behaviors that affect their buying patterns.

African-American Buying Patterns   African-Americans represent the largest racial/ethnic subculture in the United States in terms of population and purchasing power. Consumer research on African-American buying patterns have focused on similarities and differences with whites. When socioeconomic status differences between African-Americans and whites are removed, there are more similarities than points of

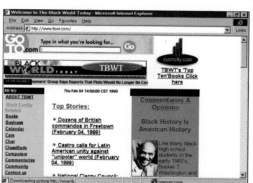

difference. Differences in buying patterns are greater within the African-American subculture, due to levels of socioeconomic status, than between African-Americans and whites of similar status.

Even though similarities outweigh differences, there are consumption patterns that do differ between African-Americans and whites.[47] For example, African-Americans spend far more than whites on boy's clothing, rental goods, and radios. Adult African-Americans are twice as likely to own a pager and spend twice as much for online services, on a per capita basis, than whites. African-American women spend three times more on health and beauty products than white women. Furthermore, the typical African-American family is five years younger than the typical white family. This factor alone accounts for some of the observed differences in preferences for clothing, music, shelter, cars, and many other products, services, and activities.[48] Finally, it must be emphasized that, historically, African-Americans have been deprived of employment and educational opportunities in the United States. Both factors have resulted in income disparities between African-Americans and whites, which influence purchase behavior.

Recent research indicates that while African-Americans are price conscious, they are strongly motivated by quality and choice. They respond more to products such as apparel and cosmetics and advertising that appeal to their African-American pride and heritage as well as address their ethnic features and needs regardless of socioeconomic status.

Appreciation for the context in which African-Americans make purchase decisions is a necessary first step in understanding their buying patterns. Current research on African-American purchase behavior reveals that stereotypes are often misleading, as they also are for the Hispanic and Asian subcultures.

Hispanic Buying Patterns   About 50 percent of Hispanics in the United States are immigrants, and the majority are under the age of 25. Hispanics will surpass African-Americans as the largest ethnic/racial subculture in the United States by 2010, due in part to migration patterns.

Research on Hispanic buying practices has uncovered several consistent patterns:[49]

1. Hispanics are quality and brand conscious. They are willing to pay a premium price for premium quality and are often brand loyal.
2. Hispanics prefer buying American-made products, especially those offered by firms that cater to Hispanic needs.
3. Hispanic buying preferences are strongly influenced by family and peers.
4. Hispanics consider advertising a credible product information source, and about $1.4 billion is spent annually on Spanish-language advertising by firms in the United States.
5. Convenience of use is not an important product attribute to Hispanic homemakers with respect to food preparation or consumption, nor is low caffeine in coffee and soft drinks, low fat in dairy products, and low cholesterol in packaged foods.

Despite some consistent buying patterns, marketing to Hispanics has proven to be a challenge for two reasons.[50] First, the Hispanic subculture is diverse and composed of Mexicans, Puerto Ricans, Cubans, and others of Central and South American ancestry. Cultural differences among these nationalities often affect product preferences. For example, Campbell Soup Company sells its Casera line of soups, beans, and sauces using different recipes to appeal to Puerto Ricans on the East Coast and Mexicans in the Southwest. Second, a language barrier exists, and commercial messages are frequently misinterpreted when translated into Spanish. A U.S. airline painfully learned this lesson when the Spanish translation of its "We Earn Our Wings Daily" message implied that passengers often ended up dead. Campbell Soup has overcome the language issue. It provides Spanish and English labels on its soups in parts of the western and southwestern United States.

Sensitivity to the unique needs of Hispanics by firms has paid huge dividends. For example, Metropolitan Life Insurance is the largest insurer of Hispanics. Goya Foods dominates the market for ethnic food products sold to Hispanics. Best Foods' Mazola

PepsiCo often uses Spanish language advertising to promote its soft drinks to the Hispanic community in the United States.

PepsiCo, Inc.
www.pepsico.com

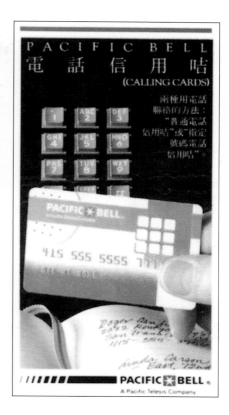

Companies such as Pacific Bell often must address subcultural differences in language and custom.

Pacific Bell
www.pacbell.com

Corn Oil captures two thirds of the Hispanic market for this product category. Time, Inc. has more than 200,000 subscribers to its *People en Espanol.*.

Asian Buying Patterns   About 70 percent of Asians in the United States are immigrants, and most are under the age of 30. Recent U.S. census figures indicate that Asian-Americans are the fastest-growing racial/ethnic subculture in the United States.

The Asian subculture is composed of Chinese, Japanese, Filipinos, Koreans, Asian-Indians, people from Southeast Asia, and Pacific Islanders. The diversity of the Asian subculture is so great that generalizations about buying patterns of this group are difficult to make.[51] Consumer research on Asian-Americans suggests that individuals and families divide into two groups. "Assimilated" Asian-Americans are conversant in English, highly educated, hold professional and managerial positions, and exhibit buying patterns very much like the typical American consumer. This group buys 15 percent of the 2,500 pianos Steinway makes every year in North America. "Nonassimilated" Asian-Americans are recent immigrants and still cling to their native languages and customs. The diversity of Asian-Americans evident in language, customs, and tastes requires marketers to be sensitive to different Asian nationalities. For example, Anheuser-Busch's agricultural products division sells eight different varieties of California-grown rice, each with a different Asian label to cover a range of nationalities and tastes. The company's advertising also addresses the preferences of Chinese, Japanese, and Koreans for different kinds of rice bowls.

Studies also show that the Asian-American subculture as a whole is characterized by hard work, strong family ties, appreciation for education, and median family incomes exceeding those of white families. Moreover, this subculture is the most entrepreneurial in the United States, as evidenced by the number of Asian-owned businesses. These qualities led Metropolitan Life Insurance to identify Asians as a target for insurance following the company's success in marketing to Hispanics.

CONCEPT CHECK

1. What are the two primary forms of personal influence?

2. Marketers are concerned with which types of reference groups?

3. What two challenges must marketers overcome when marketing to Hispanics?

SUMMARY

1 When a consumer buys a product, it is not an act but a process. There are five steps in the purchase decision process: problem recognition, information search, alternative evaluation, purchase decision, and postpurchase behavior.

2 Consumers evaluate alternatives on the basis of attributes. Identifying which attributes are most important to consumers, along with understanding consumer beliefs about how a brand performs on those attributes, can make the difference between successful and unsuccessful products.

3 Consumer involvement with what is bought affects whether the purchase decision process involves routine, limited, or extended problem solving. Situational influences also affect the process.

4 Perception is important to marketers because of the selectivity of what a consumer sees or hears, comprehends, and retains.

5 Much of the behavior that consumers exhibit is learned. Consumers learn from repeated experience and reasoning. Brand loyalty is a result of learning.

6 Attitudes are learned predispositions to respond to an object or class of objects in a consistently favorable or unfavorable way. Attitudes are based on a person's values and beliefs concerning the attributes of objects.

7 Lifestyle is a mode of living reflected in a person's activities, interests, and opinions of himself or herself and the world.

8 Personal influence takes two forms: opinion leadership and word-of-mouth activity. A specific type of personal influence exists in the form of reference groups.

9 Family influences on consumer behavior result from three sources: consumer socialization, family life cycle, and decision making within the household.

10 Within the United States there are social classes and subcultures that affect a consumer's values and behavior. Marketers must be sensitive to these sociocultural influences when developing a marketing mix.

KEY TERMS AND CONCEPTS

consumer behavior p. 150
purchase decision process p. 150
evaluative criteria p. 151
evoked set p. 152
computer-mediated buying p. 152
cognitive dissonance p. 153
involvement p. 154
situational influences p. 155
motivation p. 156
personality p. 157
national character p. 157
self-concept p. 157
perception p. 157
subliminal perception p. 158

perceived risk p. 158
learning p. 159
brand loyalty p. 160
attitude p. 160
beliefs p. 160
lifestyle p. 161
opinion leaders p. 164
word of mouth p. 164
reference groups p. 165
consumer socialization p. 166
family life cycle p. 166
social class p. 168
subcultures p. 169

INTERNET EXERCISE

Location: http://www.mhhe.com/

A customer's consumption or use experience with products and services is extremely important in determining value perceptions. Furthermore, postpurchase experiences can lead to positive or negative word of mouth and influence the likelihood of repeat-purchase behavior.

Service Intelligence, Inc. maintains a Web site (www.serviceintelligence.com) that catalogs customer stories of unpleasant and pleasant experiences with air-lines, banks, retailers, and other businesses. Visit their Web site, click Customer Service Heroes & Horror Stories, and answer the following questions:

1 Are there more "horror" stories than "hero" stories?
2 Choose two particular businesses, such as airlines and banks. What is the most frequently mentioned complaint customers have for each business?

APPLYING MARKETING CONCEPTS AND PERSPECTIVES

1 Review Figure 6–2 in the text, which shows the CD-player attributes identified by *Consumer Reports.* Which attributes are important to you? What other attributes might you consider? Which brand would you prefer?
2 Suppose research at Apple Computer reveals that prospective buyers are anxious about buying PCs for home use. What strategies might you recommend to the company to reduce consumer anxiety?
3 A Porsche salesperson was taking orders on new cars because he was unable to satisfy the demand with the limited number of cars in the showroom and lot. Several persons had backed out of the contract within two weeks of signing the order. What explanation can you give for this behavior, and what remedies would you recommend?
4 Which social class would you associate with each of the following items or actions: (*a*) tennis club membership, (*b*) an arrangement of plastic flowers in the kitchen, (*c*) *True Romance* magazine, (*d*) Smithsonian magazine, (*e*) formally dressing for dinner frequently, and (*f*) being a member of a bowling team.
5 Assign one or more levels of the hierarchy of needs and the motives described in Figure 6–5 to the following products: (*a*) life insurance, (*b*) cosmetics, (*c*) *The Wall Street Journal,* and (*d*) hamburgers.
6 With which stage in the family life cycle would the purchase of the following products and services be most closely identified: (*a*) bedroom furniture, (*b*) life insurance, (*c*) a Caribbean cruise, (*d*) a house mortgage, and (*e*) children's toys?
7 "The greater the perceived risk in a purchase situation, the more likely that cognitive dissonance will result." Does this statement have any basis given the discussion in the text? Why?

 CASE 6–1   KEN DAVIS PRODUCTS, INC.

"Cooking is a lot like music," explains Barbara Jo Davis. "There are musicians who are excellent musicians and they can play any of the classical music to perfection, but they don't know how to improvise. And then there are the jazz musicians who can do both of these things."

"The same thing is true of cooks," continues Barbara. "There are the cooks who can follow a recipe . . . and will be the best cooks in the world as long as they have a recipe. But if they have to improvise, then they're lost. So what we want to do is help those who aren't the improvisers."

THE COMPANY

Barbara Jo Davis is president of Ken Davis Products, Inc., a small regional business that develops and markets barbecue sauces. The company was founded by Barbara Davis's late spouse Ken Davis. Ken owned a restaurant where he served his grandmother's recipe for barbecue sauce, and he received such positive feedback from his customers he decided to write the recipe down to ensure it would taste the same every time he made it. He called in Barbara, then a home economist for a large consumer foods corporation, to help him do it. Shortly afterwards

Ken closed the restaurant, married Barbara, and began marketing his barbecue sauce full time. Barbara Davis stayed with the consumer foods corporation, becoming a manager for the test kitchens and for the cookbooks, until 1988 when she left to work for Ken Davis Products full time.

While Ken Davis Products is a market leader in its region, it has not expanded nationwide. Barbara Davis explains, "What I hear consumers say again and again is the reason they buy Ken Davis barbecue sauces is because it's a local company. I think the reason we're the market leaders is because it's a personal product. People know who the person is. They can see me driving around in my car."

PRODUCTS, CUSTOMERS, AND ENVIRONMENT

In addition to the Original Ken Davis Barbecue Sauce, the company also sells Smooth and Spicy Barbecue Sauce, with jalepeno peppers added to it, and a line of marinade sauces called Jazz It Up. Through consumer testing and focus groups, Barbara Davis discovered the real problem consumers are facing when they cook is how to add flavor to the meats they are eating. Hence the Jazz It Up line of marinade sauces was born. Ken Davis Products now offers four varieties of cooking sauces—Orange Citrus, Lemon Lime, Southwestern, and Mesquite. "They're really a hybrid between marinades and cooking sauces because you can use them as an ingredient, a marinade, or even as a dipping sauce," explains Barbara Davis. This was a natural product line extension for Ken Davis Products based on its reputation in the barbecue sauce market.

The company does not target specific consumer segments because it seems the consumers are just about everybody. Barbara Davis has discovered through consumer focus groups that the barbecue sauce buying decision is still made by the female head of the household, but everybody in the family seems to participate in the deci-

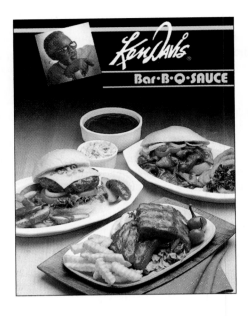

sion. "Kids especially like our sauce a lot," explains Barbara Davis, "and elderly people like the Original Recipe because it's got a lot of flavor but it's not hot or spicy."

The Food and Drug Administration (FDA) recently passed legislation requiring all consumer food products to nutrition label their products in a standardized way. For small companies such as Ken Davis Products, this meant the added expense of finding an independent laboratory to analyze the products and redesigning the labels. Barbara Davis thinks this new legislation works to the advantage of Ken Davis Products, though. "New people can compare and see Ken Davis is indeed lower in sodium than most of the other barbecue sauces on the market."

THE ISSUES

Ken Davis Products prides itself on staying abreast of changing consumer tastes and trends. In addition to conducting focus groups, Barbara Davis solicits informal feedback from current and potential Ken Davis customers. She will talk to testers at an in-store sampling or even walk up to shoppers in the barbecue sauce aisle and ask them about their purchases. Barbara Davis believes, "You have to listen to your consumer because you're not in this business to please yourself. You're in business to please your consumer." In addition to discovering the latest tastes, she has learned from her customers that the primary promotional vehicle used to spread the word about Ken Davis Products is word-of-mouth.

To make the most of this strategy, Ken Davis Products participates in event marketing and in-store sampling. Ken Davis used to always say, "The best way to sell a food product is to get people to taste it, because it's ultimately the taste that will keep them as customers." Bar-

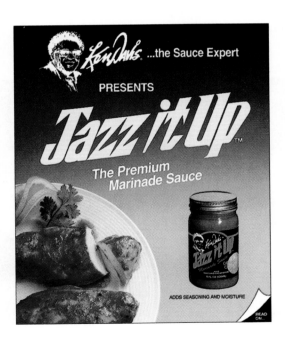

bara Davis has found another successful strategy to get people talking about Ken Davis Products is to become involved in the community. She regularly talks to groups of young entrepreneurs or invites school children to her test kitchen to learn how to cook. "You do all of these little things just to get people thinking Ken Davis. And they don't even know they're thinking Ken Davis half the time. But it's so ingrained that when they go to the grocery store, why would they look at those other brands?" Barbara Davis also sends out a newsletter twice a year to Ken Davis Products users with new recipe ideas and stories about the company. Today's busy family is always on the look-out for quick and easy recipes.

Ken Davis Products also uses some more traditional promotional vehicles, such as Free Standing Inserts (FSIs) in the Sunday paper and radio advertising. The FSIs include a coupon to induce new customers to try the product. The radio ads reflect the local, homegrown differentiation strategy used by Ken Davis Products. Barbara Davis does the commercials herself, which are completely unrehearsed. "That way I don't have to pay talent," she chuckles.

THE MULTIPLE ROLES OF A SMALL BUSINESSPERSON

After working for a large corporation and then becoming a small business entrepreneur, Barbara Davis is in a unique position to comment on the satisfactions and hardships of owning your own business. She stresses that you have to know everything about your business—you can't specialize like in a large corporation. You also get to make all the decisions and have the satisfaction of being a part of the process every step of the way. "But," Barbara adds, "you have to work harder than you have ever worked in your life. You have to always be working. When I was working for a corporation, I resented working all those hours because it wasn't for me. But now when I'm working all these hours I live it because I am doing if for myself. That's the reward—it's all for you."

Questions

1 In what ways have American eating habits changed over the past decade that affect a barbecue sauce manufacturer?

2 What are the two or three main (*a*) objective evaluative criteria and (*b*) subjective evaluative criteria consumers of Ken Davis barbecue sauces might use?

3 How can Ken Davis Products do marketing research on consumers to find out what they eat, to learn how they use barbecue sauces, and to get ideas for new products?

4 (*a*) Do you think a small, local company such as Ken Davis Products should have entered the market as a premium-priced product or a low-priced product? (*b*) What should its pricing strategy be today?

5 What do you see the (*a*) satisfactions and (*b*) concerns of being in business for yourself?

CHAPTER SEVEN

ORGANIZATIONAL MARKETS AND BUYER BEHAVIOR

7

AFTER READING THIS CHAPTER YOU SHOULD BE ABLE TO:

• Distinguish among industrial, reseller, and government markets.

• Recognize key characteristics of organizational buying that make it different from consumer buying.

• Understand how types of buying situations influence organizational purchasing.

• Recognize similarities and differences in industrial and reseller purchase behavior.

LASER TECHNOLOGY IS BRIGHT AT HONEYWELL

Gary Null views light very differently from most people. He pictures a world where information is processed at the speed of light and electricity is converted to light with unprecedented efficiency.

As the International Business Development Director at Honeywell, MICRO SWITCH Division, Null shares responsibility for the global launch of Honeywell's newest innovation, the *Vertical Cavity Surface Emitting Laser* or VCSEL (pronounced "Vik-Sel"). VCSEL is emerging as the light source of choice for high-speed short-wavelength communication systems. Numerous other potential applications exist in computer networks and consumer, industrial, and office products.

Successful commercialization of this innovative laser technology depends on a coordinated worldwide team effort that draws on the talents of MICRO SWITCH design and application engineers and marketing and sales professionals. Their efforts focus on demonstrating the performance, cost, and reliability advantages of the VCSEL over existing technology to a diverse set of organizational buyers around the world. It also requires knowing which people influence the purchasing decision; what factors they consider when choosing suppliers, technology, and products; and when, where, and how buying decisions are made in Asian, European, and Latin American business cultures.

Null believes Honeywell, MICRO SWITCH Division, is poised to capture a significant share of the multibillion dollar global market for laser technology and products. Ultimate success will depend on continued product development that creates customer value and effective marketing to an ever-increasing number of industrial buyers of laser technology in a worldwide marketplace.[1]

The challenge facing Null of marketing to organizations is often encountered by both small, startup corporations and large, well-established companies such as Honeywell. Important issues in marketing to organizations are examined in this chapter, which analyzes the types of organizational buyers, key characteristics of organizational buying, and some typical buying decisions.

THE NATURE AND SIZE OF ORGANIZATIONAL MARKETS

Gary Null and Honeywell's MICRO SWITCH Division engage in business marketing. **Business marketing** is the marketing of goods and services to commercial enterprises, governments, and other profit and not-for-profit organizations for use in the creation of goods and services that they then produce and market to other business customers, as well as individuals and ultimate consumers.[2] Because more than half of all U.S. business school graduates take jobs in firms that engage in business marketing, it is important to understand the fundamental characteristics of organizational buyers and their buying behavior.

Organizational buyers are those manufacturers, wholesalers and retailers, and government agencies that buy goods and services for their own use or for resale. For example, all these organizations buy computers and telephone services for their own use. However, manufacturers buy raw materials and parts that they reprocess into the finished goods they sell, whereas wholesalers and retailers resell the goods they buy without reprocessing them. Organizational buyers include all the buyers in a nation except the ultimate consumers. These organizational buyers purchase and lease tremendous volumes of capital equipment, raw materials, manufactured parts, supplies, and business services. In fact, because they often buy raw materials and parts, process them, and sell the upgraded product several times before it is purchased by the final organizational buyer or ultimate consumer, the aggregate purchases of organizational buyers in a year are far greater than those of ultimate consumers.

Organizational buyers are divided into three different markets: (1) industrial, (2) reseller, and (3) government markets.

Industrial Markets

There are more than 13.7 million firms in the industrial, or business, market (Figure 7–1).[3] These **industrial firms** in some way reprocess a product or service they buy before selling it again to the next buyer. This is certainly true of a steel mill that converts iron ore into steel. It is also true (if you stretch your imagination) of a firm selling

FIGURE 7–1
Type and number of organizational customers

TYPE OF ORGANIZATION	NUMBER	KIND OF MARKET
Manufacturers	387,000	Industrial (business) markets—11,552,000
Mining	28,000	
Construction	672,000	
Farms, forestry, and fisheries	955,000	
Service	8,594,000	
Finance, insurance, and real estate	617,000	
Transportation and public utilities	276,000	
Not-for-profit associations	23,000	
Wholesalers	512,000	Reseller markets—2,076,000
Retailers	1,564,000	
Government units	85,000	Government markets—85,000

Printed in English, the Moscow Yellow Pages lists more than 22,000 industrial, trade, joint venture, and government office telephone numbers and addresses. Read the text to find out how firms in Germany, Russia, and the United States work together to produce, promote, and distribute this directory.

Moscow Yellow Pages

www.russia.net/country/
moscow-yellow-pages.html

services, such as a bank that takes money from its depositors, reprocesses it, and "sells" it as loans to its borrowers.

The importance of services in the United States today is emphasized by the composition of the industrial markets shown in Figure 7–1. The first four types of industrial firms (manufacturers; mining; construction; and farms, forestry, and fisheries) sell physical products and represent one sixth of all the industrial firms, or about 2 million. The services market sells diverse services such as legal advice, auto repair, and dry cleaning. Along with finance, insurance, and real estate businesses and transportation and public utility firms, these service firms represent about 82 percent of all industrial firms, or about 9.5 million. Because of the size and importance of service firms and some 23,000 not-for-profit organizations (such as the American Red Cross), service marketing is discussed in detail in Chapter 13.

Reseller Markets

Wholesalers and retailers who buy physical products and resell them again without any reprocessing are **resellers.** In the United States there are almost 1.6 million retailers and 512,000 wholesalers. In Chapters 16 through 18 we shall see how manufacturers use wholesalers and retailers in their distribution ("place") strategies as channels through which their products reach ultimate consumers. In this chapter we look at these resellers mainly as organizational buyers in terms of (1) how they make their own buying decisions and (2) which products they choose to carry.

Government Markets

Government units are the federal, state, and local agencies that buy goods and services for the constituents they serve. There are about 85,000 of these government units in the United States. Their annual purchases vary in size from the $898 million the Federal Aviation Administration intends to spend for 3,000 computerized workstations for 22 major air traffic control centers in the United States to lesser amounts spent by local school or sanitation districts.[4]

Global Organizational Markets

Industrial, reseller, and government markets also exist on a global scale. International trade statistics indicate that the largest exporting industries in the United States focus on organizational customers, not ultimate consumers.

The majority of world trade involves manufacturers, resellers, and government agencies buying goods and services for their own use or for resale to others. The exchange relationships often involve numerous transactions spanning the globe as described in Chapter 5. For example, U.S.-based Pratt & Whitney sells aircraft engine components to Europe's Airbus Industrie, the world's second-largest aircraft manufacturer. Airbus then sells its passenger airplanes to Japan Airlines, which flies U.S. businesspeople to the Orient. A New York City firm solicits advertising for and a publisher in Germany prints the Moscow Yellow Pages on behalf of the Moscow city government and telephone system for resale to businesses through Moscow stores, hotels, and international trade centers such as the Armand Hammer Center in Red Square. Honeywell, MICRO SWITCH Division, sells its technology and products to manufacturers of data communication systems worldwide through electronic component resellers in more than 20 countries and directly to national governments around the world.

MEASURING DOMESTIC AND GLOBAL INDUSTRIAL, RESELLER, AND GOVERNMENT MARKETS

The measurement of industrial, reseller, and government markets is an important first step for a firm interested in gauging the size of one, two, or all three of these markets

in the United States and around the world. This task has been made easier with the **North American Industry Classification System (NAICS).**[5] NAICS provides common industry definitions for Canada, Mexico, and the United States, which facilitate the measurement of economic activity in the three member countries of the North American Free Trade Agreement (NAFTA). NAICS replaced the Standard Industrial Classification (SIC) system, a version of which has been in place for more than 50 years in the three NAFTA member countries. The SIC neither permitted comparability across countries nor accurately measured new or emerging industries. Furthermore, NAICS is consistent with the International Standard Industrial Classification of All Economic Activities, published by the United Nations, to facilitate measurement of global economic activity.

The NAICS groups economic activity to permit studies of market share, demand for goods and services, import competition in domestic markets, and similar studies. NAICS designates industries with a numerical code in a defined structure. A six-digit coding system is used. The first two digits designate a sector of the economy, the third

FIGURE 7-2
NAICS breakdown for information industries sector: NAICS code 51 (abbreviated)

digit designates a subsector, and the fourth digit represents an industry group. The fifth digit designates a specific industry and is the most detailed level at which comparable data is available for Canada, Mexico, and the United States. The sixth digit designates individual country-level national industries. Figure 7–2 presents an abbreviated breakdown within the Information Industries Sector (code 51) to illustrate the classification scheme.

The NAICS permits a firm to find the NAICS codes of its present customers and then obtain NAICS-coded lists for similar firms. Also, it is possible to monitor NAICS categories to determine the growth in various sectors and industries to identify promising marketing opportunities. However, NAICS codes, like the earlier SIC codes, have important limitations. The NAICS assigns one code to each organization based on its major economic activity, so large firms that engage in many different activities are still given only one NAICS code. A second limitation is that five-digit National industry codes are not available for all three countries because the respective governments will not reveal data when too few organizations exist in a category. Despite these limitations, development of NAICS represents yet another effort toward economic integration in North America and the world.

CONCEPT CHECK   **1.** What are the three main types of organizational buyers?

2. What is the North American Industry Classification System (NAICS)?

CHARACTERISTICS OF ORGANIZATIONAL BUYING

Organizations are different from individuals, so buying for an organization is different from buying for yourself or your family.[6] True, in both cases the objective in making the purchase is to solve the buyer's problem—to satisfy a need or want. But unique objectives and policies of an organization put special constraints on how it makes buying decisions. Understanding the characteristics of organizational buying is essential in designing effective marketing programs to reach these buyers.

Organizational buying behavior is the decision-making process that organizations use to establish the need for products and services and identify, evaluate, and choose among alternative brands and suppliers. Key characteristics of organizational buying behavior are listed in Figure 7–3 and discussed next.[7]

FIGURE 7–3
Key characteristics of
organizational buying
behavior

MARKET CHARACTERISTICS
- Demand for industrial products and services is derived.
- Few customers typically exist, and their purchase orders are large.

PRODUCT OR SERVICE CHARACTERISTICS
- Products or services are technical in nature and purchased on the basis of specifications.
- There is a predominance of raw and semifinished goods purchased.
- Heavy emphasis is placed on delivery time, technical assistance, postsale service, and financing assistance.

BUYING PROCESS CHARACTERISTICS
- Technically qualified and professional buyers exist and follow established purchasing policies and procedures.
- Buying objectives and criteria are typically spelled out, as are procedures for evaluating sellers and products (services).
- Multiple buying influences exist, and multiple parties participate in purchase decisions.
- Reciprocal arrangements exist, and negotiation between buyers and sellers is commonplace.
- Online buying over the Internet is widespread.

OTHER MARKETING MIX CHARACTERISTICS
- Direct selling to organizational buyers is the rule, and physical distribution is very important.
- Advertising and other forms of promotion are technical in nature.
- Price is often negotiated, evaluated as part of broader seller and product (service) qualities, typically inelastic owing to derived demand, and frequently affected by trade and quantity discounts.

Demand Characteristics

Consumer demand for products and services is affected by their price and availability and by consumers' personal tastes and discretionary income. By comparison, industrial demand is derived. **Derived demand** means that the demand for industrial products and services is driven by, or derived from, demand for consumer products and services. For example, the demand for Weyerhaeuser's pulp and paper products is based on consumer demand for newspapers, Domino's "keep warm" pizza-to-go boxes, Federal Express packages, and disposable diapers. Derived demand is often based on expectations of future consumer demand. For instance, Whirlpool purchases parts for its washers and dryers in anticipation of consumer demand, which is affected by the replacement cycle for these products and by consumer income.

As demand for the products that comprise the Information Superhighway grows, so too will the demand for the technology that makes them possible. Read the accompanying Marketing NewsNet to see how companies that produce microchips and microprocessors will benefit from the merging of telecommunications, information, and data networks on the Information Superhighway.[8]

Size of the Order or Purchase

The size of the purchase involved in organizational buying is typically much larger than that in consumer buying. The dollar value of a single purchase made by an organization often runs into the thousands or millions of dollars. For example, Motorola was recently awarded a $63 million contract to install a cellular phone system in Brazil.[9] With so much money at stake, most organizations place constraints on their

MARKETING NEWSNET

The Global Information Superhighway Is Paved with Silicon Chips

The twenty-first century will witness the merging of telecommunications, information, and data networks into what has been labeled the "Information Superhighway." As new products and applications emerge for use by businesses and consumers alike, demand for microchips (the small piece of silicon that holds a complex electronic circuit) and demand for microprocessors (a miniature computer consisting of one or more microchips) will expand dramatically.

Companies that produce microchips and microprocessors will benefit from the demand derived from the sale of a multitude of products and technologies that comprise the Information Superhighway. Powerful microprocessors and multimedia graphics software will boost demand for DRAMS (dynamic random-access memory chips), a business dominated by Korean and Japanese firms. Demand for digital-signal-processing chips that speed up video and graphics will boost the fortunes of U.S.-based Texas Instruments and Europe's SGS-Thomson. Demand for multimedia chips will grow as telephone and cable TV companies begin buying video ser-

vices and set-top boxes to deliver movies and interactive games to homes.

"The Information Highway will be paved with silicon," says an executive at Texas Instruments, and microchip demand will be driven by the telecommunication, information, and data networks that travel the highway.

---

buyers in the form of purchasing policies or procedures. Buyers must often get competitive bids from at least three prospective suppliers when the order is above a specific amount, such as $5,000. When the order is above an even higher amount, such as $50,000, it may require the review and approval of a vice president or even the president of the company. Knowing how the size of the order affects buying practices is important in determining who participates in the purchase decision and makes the final decision, and also the length of time required to arrive at a purchase agreement.

Number of Potential Buyers

Firms selling consumer products or services often try to reach thousands or millions of individuals or households. For example, your local supermarket or bank probably serves thousands of people, and Quaker Oats tries to reach 80 million American households with its breakfast cereals and probably succeeds in selling to a third or half of these in any given year. In contrast, firms selling to organizations are often restricted to far fewer buyers. Gulfstream Aerospace Corporation can sell its business jets to a few thousand organizations throughout the world, and B. F. Goodrich sells its original equipment tires to fewer than 10 car manufacturers.

Sylvania focuses on buyers' objective of reducing costs to improve profits.

Sylvania
www.sylvania.com

Organizational Buying Objectives

Organizations buy products and services for one main reason: to help them achieve their objectives. For business firms the buying objective is usually to increase profits through reducing costs or increasing revenues. Southland Corporation buys automated inventory systems to increase the number of products that can be sold through its 7-Eleven outlets and to keep them fresh. Nissan Motor Company switched its advertising agency because it expects the new agency to devise a more effective ad campaign to help it sell more cars and increase revenues. To improve executive decision making, many firms buy advanced computer systems to process data. The objectives of nonprofit firms and government agencies are usually to meet the needs of the groups they serve. Thus, a hospital buys a high-technology diagnostic device to serve its patients better. Understanding buying objectives is a necessary first step in marketing to organizations. Recognizing the high costs of energy, Sylvania promotes to prospective buyers cost savings and increased profits made possible by its fluorescent lights.

Many companies today have broadened their buying objectives to include an emphasis on buying from minority- and women-owned suppliers and vendors. Companies such as Chrysler, Coca-Cola, Coors, and JCPenney report that sales, profits, and customer satisfaction have increased due to their minority- and women-owned supplier and vendor initiatives.[10] The successful efforts of Sears Roebuck are described in the accompanying Marketing NewsNet.[11]

Organizational Buying Criteria

In making a purchase the buying organization must weigh key buying criteria that apply to the potential supplier and what it wants to sell. **Organizational buying**

MARKETING NEWSNET

Minority- and Women-Owned Suppliers Create Customer Value at Sears, Roebuck and Co.

Sears is a leader in forging innovative links with minority- and women-owned suppliers and vendors. According to Sears chairman of the board and CEO, Arthur C. Martinez, "Minority- and women-owned suppliers have helped transform our apparel and merchandising strategies."

A visible and successful result of Sears' efforts is the Anthony Mark Hankins Signature Line of clothing for women introduced into Sears in 1996. Anthony Mark Hankins is an award-winning African-American designer. Pictured here are two of his designs from his Fall 1998 Signature Collection for Sears.

The Sears commitment to furthering its involvement with minority- and women-owned suppliers and vendors is consistent with the diversity of customers that the retailer serves. "We want African-Americans, Hispanic-Americans, and Asian-Americans to know Sears is their store," says Gilbert Davila, the company's director of ethnic marketing. He added: "Sears knows how important the ethnic customer is—and Sears is out front developing product lines and mar-

keting approaches that tell these customers in no uncertain terms: You are welcome here."

criteria are the objective attributes of the supplier's products and services and the capabilities of the supplier itself. These criteria serve the same purpose as the evaluative criteria used by consumers and described in Chapter 6. Seven of the most commonly used criteria are (1) price, (2) ability to meet the quality specifications required for the item, (3) ability to meet required delivery schedules, (4) technical capability, (5) warranties and claim policies in the event of poor performance, (6) past performance on previous contracts, and (7) production facilities and capacity.[12] Suppliers that meet or exceed these criteria create customer value.

Organizational buyers who purchase products and services in a global marketplace often supplement their buying criteria with supplier ISO 9000 certification. As described in Chapter 5, ISO 9000 certification means that a supplier has undergone an on-site audit to ensure that a quality management and quality assurance system is in place. 3M, which buys and markets its products globally, has 80 percent of its manufacturing and service facilities ISO 9000 certified. According to the company's director of quality control, certification also gives 3M confidence in the consistent quality of its suppliers' manufacturing systems and products.[13]

Many organizational buyers today are transforming their buying criteria into specific requirements that are communicated to prospective suppliers. This practice, called **reverse marketing,** involves the deliberate effort by organizational buyers to build relationships that shape suppliers' products, services, and capabilities to fit a buyer's needs and those of its customers.[14] For example, consider the case of Johnson

**Plymouth Neon.
Now Available In Original.**

Hi.

And New Faster Acting.

[neon] Say hello to the new Plymouth Neon Sport Coupe. As friendly as the original but now in a more potent formula. An all-new adrenaline-producing performance suspension. Ever so eager performance-tuned steering. Dual air bags.* ABS. And 150 very, very frisky horses.* Not to mention rear spoiler in back and power bulge hood up front. Warning: Daily use exceeds recommended levels of fun. Neon models start at $10,000 (4-Door), $11,740 (2-Door), $14,100 (Sport Coupe), including destination fee.*

PLYMOUTH NEON ⊛

Read the text to learn how Johnson Controls, Inc., the seat supplier for Neon, played an important role in making the Neon a success.

Johnson Controls, Inc.
www.jci.com

Controls, Inc., the supplier of seats for Chrysler's small car, the Plymouth Neon.[15] Johnson was able to meet Chrysler's cost target but not its safety, weight, and comfort requirements. After five 11-hour days, Johnson and Chrysler engineering and marketing staffs jointly worked out the technical details to satisfy Chrysler's performance requirements at a price acceptable to both parties. Ongoing reverse marketing efforts also exist. Harley-Davidson expects even its long-term suppliers to provide written plans of their efforts to improve quality, and it monitors the progress of these suppliers toward achieving these goals.

With many U.S. manufacturers adopting a "just-in-time" (JIT) inventory system that reduces the inventory of production parts to those to be used within hours or days, on-time delivery is becoming an even more important buying criterion and, in some instances, a requirement.[16] Caterpillar trains its key suppliers at its Quality Institute in JIT inventory systems and conducts supplier seminars on how to diagnose, correct, and implement continuous quality improvement programs. The just-in-time inventory system is discussed further in Chapter 17.

Buyer-Seller Relationships and Supply Partnerships

Another distinction between organizational and consumer buying behavior lies in the nature of the relationship between organizational buyers and suppliers. Specifically, organizational buying is more likely to involve complex and lengthy negotiations concerning delivery schedules, price, technical specifications, warranties, and claim policies. These negotiations can last for more than a year. This was the case when Los Alamos National Laboratory recently purchased a $35 million Cray Research T90 supercomputer that performs up to 60 million calculations per second.[17]

Reciprocal arrangements also exist in organizational buying. **Reciprocity** is an industrial buying practice in which two organizations agree to purchase each other's products and services. The U.S. Justice Department frowns on reciprocal buying because it restricts the normal operation of the free market. However, the practice exists and can limit the flexibility of organizational buyers in choosing alternative suppliers.

ETHICS AND SOCIAL RESPONSIBILITY ALERT

Scratching Each Other's Back: The Ethics of Reciprocity in Organizational Buying

ETHICS

Reciprocity, the buying practice in which two organizations agree to purchase each other's products and services, is frowned upon by the U.S. Justice Department because it restricts the normal operation of the free market. Reciprocal buying practices do exist, however, in a variety of forms, including certain types of countertrade arrangements in international marketing. Furthermore, the extent to which reciprocity is viewed as an ethical issue varies across cultures. In many Asian countries, for instance, reciprocity is often a positive and widespread practice.

Reciprocity is occasionally addressed in the ethics code of companies. For instance, the Quaker Oats Company's code of ethics states:

In many instances, Quaker may purchase goods and/or services from a supplier who buys products or services from us. This practice is normal and acceptable, but suppliers may not be asked to buy our products and services in order to become or continue to be a supplier.

Do you think reciprocal buying is unethical?

Regardless of the legality of reciprocal buying, do you believe this practice is ethical? (See the accompanying Ethics and Social Responsibility Alert.)[18]

Long-term relationships are also prevalent.[19] As an example, Scandinavian Airlines System recently announced the purchase of 35 Boeing 737–600 airliners with an option to buy another 35 in the future for a total expenditure of $2.4 billion. With aircraft deliveries beginning in late 1998 and continuing into the twenty-first century, Scandinavian Airlines cited its desire for a long-term relationship with "a professional and solid supplier" such as Boeing.[20] Dana Corporation is presently engaged in a 10-year, $2 billion contract to supply Mack Trucks with axles, clutches, and frame assemblies.

In some cases, buyer-seller relationships develop into supply partnerships.[21] A **supply partnership** exists when a buyer and its supplier adopt mutually beneficial objectives, policies, and procedures for the purpose of lowering the cost and/or increasing the value of products and services delivered to the ultimate consumer. Intel, the world's largest manufacturer of microprocessors and the "computer inside" most personal computers, is a case in point. Intel supports its suppliers by offering them quality management programs and by investing in supplier equipment that produces fewer product defects and boosts supplier productivity. Suppliers, in turn, provide Intel with consistent high-quality products at a lower cost for its customers, the makers of personal computers, and finally you, the ultimate customer. Retailers, too, are forging partnerships with their suppliers. Wal-Mart and Kmart have such a relationship with Procter & Gamble for ordering and replenishing P&G's products in their stores. By using computerized cash register scanning equipment and direct electronic linkages to P&G, these retailers can tell P&G what merchandise is needed, along with how much, when, and to which store to deliver it on a daily basis. Because supply partnerships also involve the physical distribution of goods, they are again discussed in Chapter 17 in the context of supply chains.

Online Buying in Organizational Markets

A final distinction between organizational and consumer buyer behavior resides in the use of Internet/World Wide Web technology in the purchase process. Although lacking the visibility of consumer online shopping, business-to-business electronic commerce is huge. In fact, organizational buyers account for 80 percent of the total

Supply partnerships are an important reason for Intel's success in the computer industry.

Intel Corporation
www.intel.com

dollar value of all online transactions. It is expected that U.S. and European organizational buyers alone will purchase about $400 billion worth of products and services online by 2002.[22]

The popularity of online buying will grow in the twenty-first century for two reasons. First, organizational buyers depend heavily on timely supplier information that describes product availability, technical specifications, application uses, price, and delivery schedules. This information can be conveyed quickly via Internet/World Wide Web technology. Second, business marketers have found that this technology can reduce marketing costs, particularly sales and advertising expense, for many types of products and services. For these reasons, online buying is prominent in all three kinds of organizational markets.[23] For example, airlines order $100 million in spare parts from the Boeing Company Web site each year. Customers of W. W. Grainger, a large U.S. wholesaler of maintenance, repair, and operating supplies, buy about $41 million worth of these products annually online. Supply and service purchases totaling $650 million each year are made online by the Los Angeles County government.

An ambitious online buying initiative is the Trading Process Network (TPN) operated by General Electric (GE) Information Services. TPN is a service that enables GE buyers to post requests for quotes, negotiate, and place orders with global suppliers. GE expects to buy more than $5 billion in products and services in 2000 and estimates that the cost of purchasing and supplies has declined by 20 percent because of TPN. GE's success prompted a number of other large firms—such as Hewlett-Packard, 3M, Consolidated Edison, and Textron Automotive—and some 1,400 small and medium-sized manufacturers to join TPN for the purpose of improving and expanding online buying with their suppliers and customers.[24] Visit the TPN Web site shown in the accompanying Web Link to appreciate the process and benefits of online buying and selling in organizational markets. Chapter 8 expands on the role of electronic commerce in marketing and its importance for business and consumer marketers.

WEB LINK

The GE Trading Process Network Demonstrates the Process and Benefits of Online Buying and Selling in Organizational Markets

You only have to visit the General Electric Information Services Trading Process Network Web site (www.tpn.geis.com) to appreciate how online buying and selling for organizations actually works. General Electric Information Services has created a virtual marketplace where buyers and sellers can exchange information, products, and services effectively and efficiently.

To learn about the process and benefits of online buying and selling, go to the GE TPN™ Web site and click Getting Started. You will see the buying and selling process and benefits prominently listed. How does the buying process compare with the description in your text? What are the benefits of online buying?

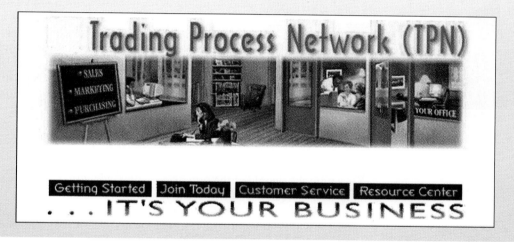

The Buying Center: A Cross-Functional Group

For routine purchases with a small dollar value, a single buyer or purchasing manager often makes the purchase decision alone. In many instances, however, several people in the organization participate in the buying process. The individuals in this group, called a **buying center,** share common goals, risks, and knowledge important to a purchase decision. For most large multistore chain resellers, such as Sears, 7-Eleven convenience stores, Kmart, or Safeway, the buying center is highly formalized and is called a *buying committee.* However, most industrial firms or government units use informal groups of people or call meetings to arrive at buying decisions.

The importance of the buying center requires that a firm marketing to many industrial firms and government units understand the structure, technical and business functions represented, and behavior of these groups. One researcher has suggested four questions to provide guidance in understanding the buying center in these organizations:[25] Which individuals are in the buying center for the product or service? What is the relative influence of each member of the group? What are the buying criteria of each member? How does each member of the group perceive our firm, our products and services, and our salespeople?

Answers to these questions are difficult to come by, particularly when dealing with industrial firms, resellers, and governments outside the United States.[26] For example, U.S. firms are often frustrated by the fact that Japanese buyers "ask a thousand questions" but give few answers, sometimes rely on third-party individuals to convey views on proposals, are prone to not "talk business," and often say yes to be courteous when they mean no. U.S. firms in the global chemical industry recognize that production engineering personnel have a great deal of influence in Hungarian buying groups, while purchasing agents in the Canadian chemical industry have relatively more influence in buying decisions.

People in the Buying Center   The composition of the buying center in a given organization depends on the specific item being bought. Although a buyer or purchasing manager is almost always a member of the buying center, individuals from other functional areas are included depending on what is to be purchased. In buying a million-dollar machine tool, the president (because of the size of the purchase) and the production vice president or manager would probably be members. For key components to be incorporated in a final manufactured product, a cross-functional group of individuals from research and development (R&D), engineering, and quality control are likely to be added. For new word-processing equipment, experienced secretaries who will use the equipment would be members. Still, a major question in penetrating the buying center is finding and reaching the people who will initiate, influence, and actually make the buying decision.[27]

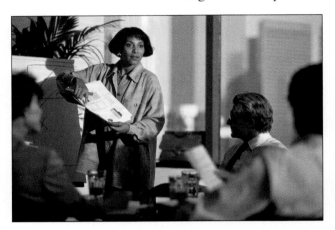

Roles in the Buying Center   Researchers have identified five specific roles that an individual in a buying center can play.[28] In some purchases the same person may perform two or more of these roles.

- *Users* are the people in the organization who actually use the product or service, such as a secretary who will use a new word processor.
- *Influencers* affect the buying decision, usually by helping define the specifications for what is bought. The information systems manager would be a key influencer in the purchase of a new mainframe computer.
- *Buyers* have formal authority and responsibility to select the supplier and negotiate the terms of the contract. The purchasing manager probably would perform this role in the purchase of a mainframe computer.
- *Deciders* have the formal or informal power to select or approve the supplier that receives the contract. Whereas in routine orders the decider is usually the buyer or purchasing manager, in important technical purchases it is more likely to be someone from R&D, engineering, or quality control. The decider for a key component being incorporated in a final manufactured product might be any of these three people.
- *Gatekeepers* control the flow of information in the buying center. Purchasing personnel, technical experts, and secretaries can all keep salespeople or information from reaching people performing the other four roles.

Stages in an Organizational Buying Decision

As shown in Figure 7–4 (and covered in Chapter 6), the five stages a student might use in buying a portable compact disk (CD) player also apply to organizational purchases. However, comparing the two right-hand columns in Figure 7–4 reveals some key differences. For example, when a portable CD player manufacturer buys headphones for its units from a supplier, more individuals are involved, supplier capability becomes more important, and the postpurchase evaluation behavior is more formalized. The headphone-buying decision illustrated is typical of the steps in a purchase made by an organization.[29] Later in the chapter we will analyze more complex purchases made by industrial and reseller organizations.

STAGE IN THE BUYING DECISION PROCESS	CONSUMER PURCHASE: PORTABLE CD PLAYER FOR A STUDENT	ORGANIZATIONAL PURCHASE: HEADPHONES FOR A CD PLAYER
Problem recognition	Student doesn't like the sound of the stereo system now owned and desires a portable CD player.	Marketing research and sales departments observe that competitors are including headphones on their models. The firm decides to include headphones on their own new models, which will be purchased from an outside supplier.
Information search	Student uses past experience, that of friends, ads, and *Consumer Reports* to collect information and uncover alternatives.	Design and production engineers draft specifications for headphones. The purchasing department identifies suppliers of CD player headphones.
Alternative evaluation	Alternative portable CD players are evaluated on the basis of important attributes desired in a CD player and several stores are visited.	Purchasing and engineering personnel visit with suppliers and assess (1) facilities, (2) capacity, (3) quality control, and (4) financial status. They drop any suppliers not satisfactory on these factors.
Purchase decision	A specific brand of portable CD player is selected, the price is paid, and the student leaves the store.	They use (1) quality, (2) price, (3) delivery, and (4) technical capability as key buying criteria to select a supplier. Then they negotiate terms and award a contract.
Postpurchase behavior	Student reevaluates the purchase decision, may return the portable CD player to the store if it is unsatisfactory, and looks for supportive information to justify the purchase.	They evaluate suppliers using a formal vendor rating system and notify supplier if phones do not meet its quality standard. If problem is not corrected, they drop the firm as a future supplier.

FIGURE 7–4
Comparing the stages in consumer and organizational purchases

Types of Buying Situations

The number of people in the buying center and the length and complexity of the steps in the buying process largely depend on the specific buying situation. Researchers who have studied organizational buying identify three types of buying situations, which they have termed **buy classes.**[30] These buy classes vary from the routine reorder, or **straight rebuy,** to the completely new purchase, termed **new buy.** In between these extremes is the **modified rebuy.** Some examples will clarify the differences:

- *Straight rebuy.* Here the buyer or purchasing manager reorders an existing product or service from the list of acceptable suppliers, probably without even checking with users or influencers from the engineering, production, or quality control departments. Office supplies and maintenance services are usually obtained as straight rebuys. Online buying is often used for straight rebuys.
- *Modified rebuy.* In this buying situation the users, influencers, or deciders in the buying center want to change the product specifications, price, delivery schedule, or supplier. Although the item purchased is largely the same as with the straight rebuy, the changes usually necessitate enlarging the buying center to include people outside the purchasing department.
- *New buy.* Here the organization is a first-time buyer of the product or service. This involves greater potential risks in the purchase, so the buying center is enlarged to include all those who have a stake in the new buy. The purchase of laser technology and products from Honeywell, MICRO SWITCH Division, represents a new buy for many companies.

	BUY-CLASS SITUATION	
BUYING CENTER DIMENSION	**NEW BUY**	**STRAIGHT/MODIFIED REBUY**
People involved	Many	Few
Decision time	Long	Short
Problem definition	Uncertain	Well-defined
Buying objective	Good solution	Low-price supplier
Suppliers considered	New/present	Present
Buying influence	Technical/operating personnel	Purchasing agent

FIGURE 7–5

How the buying situation affects buying center behavior

Figure 7–5 summarizes how buy classes affect buying center tendencies in different ways.[31]

The marketing strategies of sellers facing each of these three buying situations can vary greatly because the importance of personnel from functional areas such as purchasing, engineering, production, and R&D often varies with (1) the type of buying situation and (2) the stage of the purchasing process.[32] If it is a new buy for the manufacturer, you should be prepared to act as a consultant to the buyer, work with technical personnel, and expect a long time for a buying decision to be reached. However, if the manufacturer has bought the component part from you before (a straight or modified rebuy), you might emphasize a competitive price and a reliable supply in meetings with the purchasing agent.

CONCEPT CHECK

1. What one department is almost always represented by a person in the buying center?

2. What are the three types of buying situations or buy classes?

TWO ORGANIZATIONAL NEW BUY DECISIONS

New buy purchase decisions are ones where the most purchasing expertise is needed and where both the benefits of good decisions and penalties of bad ones are likely to be greatest. This means that effective communication among people in the buying center is especially important. Tracing the stages in the buying decisions made by a manufacturer and a reseller highlights some of the similarities and differences of organizational buying. They also illustrate the challenges involved in marketing to organizations.

An Industrial Purchase: Machine Vision Systems

Machine vision is becoming widely regarded as one of the keys to the factory of the future. The chief elements of a machine vision system are its optics, light source, camera, video processor, and computer software. Vision systems are mainly used for product inspection. They are also becoming important as one of the chief elements in the information feedback loop of systems that control manufacturing processes. Vision systems, selling in the price range of $5,000, are mostly sold to original equipment manufacturers (OEMs) who incorporate them in still larger industrial automation systems, which sell for $50,000 to $100,000.

Finding productive applications for machine vision involves the constant search for technology and designs that satisfy user needs. The buying process for machine vision components and assemblies is frequently a new buy because many machine vision

The purchase of machine vision systems involves a lengthy organizational buying process.

systems contain elements that require some custom design. Let's track five purchasing stages that a company such as the Industrial Automation Division of Siemens, a large German industrial firm, would follow when purchasing components and assemblies for the machine vision systems it produces and installs.

Problem Recognition   Sales engineers constantly canvass industrial automation equipment users and manufacturers such as American National Can, Ford Motor Company, Grumman Aircraft, and many Asian and European firms for leads on upcoming industrial automation projects. They also keep these firms current on Siemens' technology, products, and services. When a firm needing a machine vision capability identifies a project that would benefit from Siemens' expertise, company engineers typically work with the firm to determine the kind of system required to meet the customer's need.

After a contract is won, project personnel must often make a **make-buy decision**—an evaluation of whether components and assemblies will be purchased from outside suppliers or built by the company itself. (Siemens' produces many components and assemblies.) When these items are to be purchased from outside suppliers, the company engages in a thorough supplier search and evaluation process.

Information Search   Companies such as Siemens employ a sophisticated process for identifying outside suppliers of components and assemblies. For standard items such as connectors, printed circuit boards, and components such as resistors and capacitors, the purchasing agent consults the company's purchasing databank, which contains information on hundreds of suppliers and thousands of products. All products in the databank have been prenegotiated as to price, quality, and delivery time, and many have been assessed using **value analysis**—a systematic appraisal of the design, quality, and performance of a product to reduce purchasing costs.

For one-of-a-kind components or assemblies such as new optics, cameras, and light sources, the company relies on its engineers to keep current on new developments in product technology. This information is often found in technical journals and industry magazines or at international trade shows where suppliers display their most recent innovations. In some instances, supplier representatives might be asked to make presentations to the buying center at Siemens. Such a group often consists of a project engineer; several design, system, and manufacturing engineers; and a purchasing agent.

Alternative Evaluation   Three main buying criteria are used to select suppliers: price, performance, and delivery. Other important criteria include assurance that a supplier will not go out of business during the contractual period, assurance that the supplier will meet product quality and performance specifications, and service during the contractual period. Typically, two or three suppliers for each standard component and assembly are identified from a **bidders list**—a list of firms believed to be qualified to supply a given item. This list is generated from the company's purchasing databank as well as from engineering inputs. Specific items that are unique or one-of-a-kind may be obtained from a single supplier after careful evaluation by the buying center.

Firms selected from the bidders list are sent a quotation request from the purchasing agent, describing the desired quantity, delivery date(s), and specifications of the components or assemblies. Suppliers are expected to respond to bid requests within 30 days.

Purchase Decision   Unlike the short purchase stage in a consumer purchase, the period from supplier selection to order placement to product delivery can take several weeks or even months. Even after bids for components and assemblies are submitted, further negotiation concerning price, performance, and delivery terms is likely. Sometimes conditions related to warranties, indemnities, and payment schedules have to be agreed on.

The purchase decision is further complicated by the fact that two or more suppliers of the same item might be awarded contracts. This practice can occur when large orders are requested. Furthermore, suppliers who are not chosen are informed why their bids were not selected.

Postpurchase Behavior   As in the consumer purchase decision process, postpurchase evaluation occurs in the industrial purchase decision process, but it is formalized and often more sophisticated. All items purchased are examined in a formal product acceptance process. The performance of the supplier is also monitored and recorded. Performance on past contracts determines a supplier's chances of being asked to bid on future purchases, and poor performance may result in a supplier's name being dropped from the bidders list.

The Nesco American Harvest food dehydrator first successfully sold by Montgomery Ward and now by other retailers.

Nesco/American Harvest Corp.

www.nesco.com

A Reseller Purchase: A Home Food Dehydrator

Resellers—wholesalers and retailers—resell the products they purchase without physically changing them. As a result, the stages in their buying decision process differ from those of manufacturers. As an example, let's look at Montgomery Ward's decision to stock a home food dehydrator.

Problem Recognition Members of Ward's buying committee for electric appliances continually look for appealing new items to stock in its stores and sell through its catalogs. Open to new ideas, the buying committee considered a home food dehydrator, an electric device that dries fresh fruit and vegetables and competes with canning and freezing in home food preservation.

Information Search Ward's committee assessed the market size to see if a genuine consumer demand exists for food dehydrators. It analyzed how the dehydrators work, their quality, and the chances that unhappy consumers would return these purchased appliances to the store for a refund.

Alternative Evaluation The buying committee found no home food dehydrators of satisfactory quality that they wanted to sell. Then Montgomery Ward was approached by a new, startup firm—American Harvest—which sells its home food dehydrator under the American Harvest brand name. Initial quality-control tests showed that it met Ward's high standards for electric appliances.

A senior buyer on Ward's buying committee checked on the firm itself. He found two young entrepreneurs who had manufactured 500 such dehydrators—a number Montgomery Ward could sell in a day or two if the product "hit." These entrepreneurs were currently financed on a shoestring through bank loans obtained by using their cars as collateral. The two men had several patents on their device, and it had received the Underwriter's Laboratory approval. The Ward's buyer persuaded the two men to (1) seek better financing and (2) contract out the production of their dehydrators to a larger manufacturer that could produce them in the quantities and with the quality Montgomery Ward required.

Purchase Decision The Ward's buyer signed a contract with American Harvest for its home food dehydrator. At that time no other major chain or catalog store (for example, Sears, Target, JCPenney, or Kmart) was selling such an appliance. But although Montgomery Ward had no competition from its major rivals, there was no assurance the dehydrator would sell. On a big gamble, Montgomery Ward advertised the American Harvest dehydrator on the inside front cover of its fall catalog—an extremely valuable advertising space.

Postpurchase Behavior Ward's buyer and buying committee hit paydirt. The company sold more than 20,000 dehydrators in October and November—the peak period for using the appliance—at a retail price of $89. Montgomery Ward concluded that its decision was a good one and contracted for an expanded American Harvest line for the following fall. Today other chains such as Sears and Wal-Mart carry the line.

The two preceding examples of organizational purchases suggest four lessons for marketers to increase their chances of selling products and services to organizations. Firms selling to organizations must (1) understand the organization's needs, (2) get on the right bidders list, (3) find the right people in the buying center, and (4) provide value to organizational buyers.

CONCEPT CHECK

1. What is a make-buy decision?

2. What is a bidders list?

SUMMARY

1 Organizational buyers are divided into three different markets: industrial, reseller, and government. There are about 13.7 million industrial firms, 2 million resellers, and 85,000 government units.

2 Measuring industrial, reseller, and government markets is an important first step for firms interested in gauging the size of one, two, or all three markets. The North American Industry Classification System (NAICS) is a convenient starting point to begin this process.

3 Many aspects of organizational buying behavior are different from consumer buying behavior. Some key differences between the two include demand characteristics, number of potential buyers, buying objectives, buying criteria, size of the order or purchase, buyer-seller relationships and partnerships, online buying, and multiple buying influences within companies.

4 The buying center concept is central to understanding organizational buying behavior. Knowing who composes the buying center and the roles they play in making purchase decisions is important in marketing to organizations. The buying center usually includes a person from the purchasing department and possibly representatives from R&D, engineering, and production, depending on what is being purchased. These people can play one or more of five roles in a purchase decision: user, influencer, buyer, decider, or gatekeeper.

5 The three types of buying situations, or buy classes, are the straight rebuy, the modified rebuy, and the new buy. These form a scale ranging from a routine reorder to a totally new purchase.

6 The stages in an organizational buying decision are the same as those for consumer buying decisions: problem recognition, information search, alternative evaluation, purchase decision, and postpurchase behavior. Examples of organizational purchases described are the purchase of machine vision technology components by an electronics manufacturer and a home food dehydrator by a reseller.

7 To market more effectively to organizations, a firm must try to understand the organization's needs, get on the right bidders list, reach the right people in the buying center, and provide value to organizational buyers.

KEY TERMS AND CONCEPTS

business marketing p. 178
organizational buyers p. 178
industrial firms p. 178
resellers p. 179
government units p. 179
North American Industry Classification System (NAICS) p. 180
organizational buying behavior p. 181
derived demand p. 182
organizational buying criteria p. 184
reverse marketing p. 185

reciprocity p. 186
supply partnership p. 187
buying center p. 189
buy classes p. 191
straight rebuy p. 191
new buy p. 191
modified rebuy p. 191
make-buy decision p. 193
value analysis p. 193
bidders list p. 194

INTERNET EXERCISE

The North American Industry Classification System (NAICS) structures 24 industrial sectors into their component industries. The NAICS can be accessed at www.census.gov/eped/www/naics.html. A person only has to click NAICS codes to obtain industry breakdowns.

You have been hired by a large industrial firm as a market analyst. Your first assignment is to identify the kinds of companies and services that fall into the Arts, Entertainment, and Recreation industry sector (code 71) and make a presentation to senior management. Your immediate supervisor advises you that senior management would be interested in the following information:

1 How many three-, four-, five-, and six-digit industries exist in the Arts, Entertainment, and Recreation industry sector?

2 How is the performing arts, spectator sports, and related industries subsector (code 711) structured? That is, how would you display this subsector using the framework shown in Figure 7–2?

APPLYING MARKETING CONCEPTS AND PERSPECTIVES

1 Describe the major differences among industrial firms, resellers, and government units in the United States.

2 Explain how the North American Industry Classification System (NAICS) might be helpful in understanding industrial, reseller, and government markets, and discuss the limitations inherent in this system.

3 List and discuss the key characteristics of organizational buying that make it different from consumer buying.

4 What is a buying center? Describe the roles assumed by people in a buying center and what useful questions should be raised to guide any analysis of the structure and behavior of a buying center.

5 Effective marketing is of increasing importance in today's competitive environment. How can firms more effectively market to organizations?

6 A firm that is marketing multimillion-dollar wastewater treatment systems to cities has been unable to sell a new type of system. This setback has occurred even though the firm's systems are cheaper than competitive systems and meet U.S. Environmental Protection Agency (EPA) specifications. To date, the firm's marketing efforts have been directed to city purchasing departments and the various state EPAs to get on approved bidders lists. Talks with city-employed personnel have indicated that the new system is very different from current systems and therefore city sanitary and sewer department engineers, directors of these two departments, and city council members are unfamiliar with the workings of the system. Consulting engineers, hired by cities to work on the engineering and design features of these systems and paid on a percentage of system cost, are also reluctant to favor the new system. (*a*) What roles do the various individuals play in the purchase process for a wastewater treatment system? (*b*) How could the firm improve the marketing effort behind the new system?

 ## CASE 7–1   ENERGY PERFORMANCE SYSTEMS, INC.

"What we need," says David Ostlie matter-of-factly, "is just one electric utility to say 'yes'—to try our technology. Then the Whole-Tree Energy™ technology will speak for itself." David Ostlie is president of Energy Performance Systems, Inc. (EPS), a firm he founded in 1988 to produce environmentally-clean, cheap electricity by growing, harvesting, transporting, drying, burning *whole* hardwood trees (trunks, branches, and all) in either (1) old retrofitted coal and oil (fossil fuel) power plants or (2) new power plants.

THE IDEA

Dave Ostlie points to three key features that make the EPS-owned and patented Whole-Tree Energy™ (WTE) technology unique:

1 Using *whole* hardwood trees. The use of whole trees saves a tremendous amount of time and energy over using wood chips—a common form for wood burned to produce electricity. "Hardwood trees" here means all broadleaf trees—mainly species such as cottonwood, aspen, birch, maple, and poplar (essentially all trees but conifers).

2 Drying the whole trees. Moisture is the culprit that leads to incomplete wood combustion and reduced energy output, resulting in emissions that lead to air pollution and acid rain. So the WTE process dries the trees to remove about 70 percent of the moisture prior to combustion, using waste heat from the combustion process itself.

3 Three-stage combustion. The whole trees burn at three levels in the furnace: (*a*) as trees in a 12-foot deep, mid-level pile, (*b*) as wood char that falls and is burned on a grate below the pile, and (*c*) as volatile gases (gasified wood) above the pile that burns cleanly like natural gas. The result is an incredibly *environmentally-clean,* efficient combustion process.

The simplicity of the technology is a big plus compared to many of the current alternative energy technologies being studied around the world.

THE COMPANY

EPS is based on the Whole-Tree Energy™ technology and owns U.S., Canadian, European, and Japanese patents. The WTE™ technology has been scaled up in four successive tests that have demonstrated the feasibility of large-scale power production from sustained burning of whole trees. The mission of EPS: To commercialize the Whole-Tree Energy™ technology.

THE ISSUES

In assessing the Whole-Tree Energy™ technology, three critical issues soon emerge: (1) the environment and pollution, (2) jobs and economic development, and (3) buying interest of utilities.

The Environment and Pollution

Conventional coal-fired power plants, the staple for utilities, produce large volumes of SO_2, NO_x, ash, and extra CO_2 that contribute to air pollution, acid rain, and global warming. Based on test results, a WTE™ plant produces far less pollution than comparable fossil-fuel plants. Compared to a coal plant, the following levels of pollution have been demonstrated for a WTE™ plant:

- SO_2—less than $1/400$ of that for coal (on a fuel comparison basis) because wood contains virtually no sulfur.
- NOx—approximately $1/10$ of that for coal due to the naturally low nitrogen content of wood fuel and the multistage WTE™ combustion process.
- Ash—less than $1/10$ of that for coal. The ash produced can be returned to the forest or sold as a fertilizer. Coal ash is considered a hazardous waste and must be stored indefinitely in specially-designed storage ponds.
- Extra CO_2—Coal plants release enormous amounts of CO_2 to the atmosphere by burning the remnants of prehistoric plant life—coal—in large quantities. The rapidly increasing level of atmospheric CO_2 due to the burning of fossil fuels is a significant cause of global climate change. In contrast, using biomass—including trees—as a fuel results in no net addition of CO_2 to the atmosphere because the amount of CO_2 removed over the life of the tree is equal to that released by the tree, regardless of the tree's end use.

The net effect of burning a renewable biomass—trees—instead of fossil fuels will be a reduction in air pollution, acid rain, and global warming.

Jobs and Economic Development

WTE™ plants will burn (1) hardwoods that are unsalable (not wanted by other forest product firms), (2) fast-growing energy trees raised on plantations that can be harvested as often as every five to six years and add agricultural jobs, and (3) waste wood left over by other forest product firms. Harvesting overage hardwoods actually stimulates forest regeneration and often provides better habitat for wildlife. The U.S. Forest Service reports that much of the 20 billion tons of U.S. hardwoods are overage, not wanted by the logging, paper, and pulp industries and should be harvested.

A 100 megawatt WTE™ plant—providing enough electricity for a city of 100,000 people—will provide over 600 jobs in growing, harvesting, and transporting whole trees and in the plant producing electricity. In the search for local jobs, this is a huge benefit for economic development organizations trying to increase local employment.

Buying Interest of Utilities

To avoid more electrical blackouts, U.S. utilities must add new electrical generating capacity. For EPS, this provides an opportunity, either (1) by retrofitting to use in WTE™ some of the hundreds of coal and oil-fired plants throughout the United States that are operated infrequently because of their pollution problems or (2) by building new plants to use the WTE™ technology.

In an electric utility, capacity planners project the demand for electricity by industrial, commercial, and residential users and assess the utility's ability to supply the demand. The chief executive officer makes the recommendation to add new capacity, a decision reviewed by the board of directors. The vice president of power supply probably recommends the technology to be used and the site for the new power plant.

As Ostlie talks to prospective utility customers about the WTE™ technology, six concerns emerge that are covered below.

1 Can enough heat be generated by burning wood to produce electricity? "All the skeptics said we couldn't get a high enough temperature by burning wood," says Ostlie. "But in

Cost of producing electricity using four different fuels, cents/kilowatt-hour

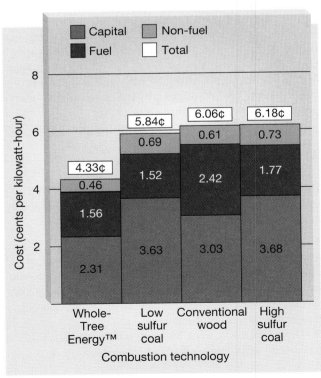

Source: Research Triangle Institute, Electric Power Research Institute and Energy Performance Systems, Inc.

one recent heat-release test we produced values higher than those of state-of-the-art coal plants."

2 Can whole trees be loaded, transported, and dried? Forestry experts told Ostlie he couldn't load and transport whole trees on a truck because the branches wouldn't compress. So he hired a logger and did it. The WTE™ technology calls for large-scale drying of whole trees in an air-supported dome like those used in a sports stadium.

3 Are there enough trees available at reasonable cost to support commercial-size power plants? In about 75 percent of the United States enough biomass in the form of trees exists within a 50-mile radius to support a 100 megawatt power plant using the WTE™ technology. To support such a power plant, only about 0.1 percent of the land in a 50-mile radius of the plant would be harvested each year. Residential biomass and waste wood from pulp and timber mill operations are potential fuel sources, as are natural stands. Ultimately, much of the tree resource may come from short-rotation, hybrid tree plantations that provide farmers with an alternative cash crop.

4 What are the environmental benefits of WTE™ for utilities? Besides being increasingly sensitive to environmental concerns, a utility retrofitting a polluting electric power plant with Whole-Tree Energy™ can gain over a million dollars a year in SO_2 credits"—an incentive for a utility to offset power produced by its high-pollution plants with electricity produced by nonpolluting plants.

5 What will it cost to build a retrofitted or new WTE™ power plant? A major appeal of the WTE™ process is its simplicity relative to say, coal-fired power plants. To retrofit an existing 100 megawatt coal plant, it will cost about $25 million—thereby putting back into production an existing plant that is of little value. To build a new 100-megawatt WTE™ plant would take about $100 million, about 25 to 30 percent less than a new fossil fuel plant.

6 What will the cost be of electricity produced by a WTE™ plant? A recent feasibility study evaluating the WTE™ technology estimated that a WTE™ power plant could produce a kilowatt-hour of electricity for 20 to 40 percent less than today's fossil fuel plants (see figure).

"It's not far away, but we've still got to make that first sale," adds Dave Ostlie.

Questions

1 In a utility's decision whether to buy and use the WTE™ technology (*a*) who comprises the buying center and (*b*) what aspects of the buying decision does each look at?

2 What are some of the key elements EPS should have in developing its strategy to market WTE™ to prospective utility buyers?

3 As a concerned citizen, (*a*) what do you see as the key benefits of the WTE™ technology and (*b*) what do you personally see as the potential "show stoppers" for WTE™—the critical things that can prevent it from being commercialized and becoming a reality.

4 A new product or technology like WTE™ requires educating a number of key groups, or "influencers", about the technology. Excluding the electric utilities themselves, (*a*) what groups, or market segments, should EPS try to reach, (*b*) what key benefits should be emphasized to each, and (*c*) what promotional methods or media should EPS use to reach each segment?

PART THREE

3

TARGETING MARKETING OPPORTUNITIES

CHAPTER 8
Interactive Marketing and Electronic Commerce

CHAPTER 9
Turning Marketing Information into Action

CHAPTER 10
Market Segmentation, Targeting, and Positioning

Part Three focuses on targeting marketing opportunities. Chapter 8 illuminates the revolutionary change in marketing opportunities made possible through electronic commerce. Developments in interactive marketing and electronic commerce have captured the eye and imagination of marketers because of the innovative ways value can be created for consumers in this new exchange environment. Chapter 9 describes how people with similar wants and needs become the target of marketing opportunities. This chapter details how information about prospective consumers is linked to marketing strategy and decisive actions and how information technology improves this process. Finally, Chapter 10 describes how Reebok International, New Balance, and Vans design shoes to satisfy different customers and covers the steps a firm uses in segmenting and targeting a market and then positioning its offering in the marketplace. The chapter also shows how the application of segmentation, targeting, and positioning were used by Apple Computer in the launch of its iMac line of personal computers.

File   Edit   View   Go   Favorites   Help

Address http://www.aol.com/

AOL.COM

| AOL NetFind | Web Centers | My News |

So, You Want to Buy a House... Read home listings and mortgage info.

Tuesday, April 6, 1999

NATO Bombing, Week Two: Get full coverage of the Kosovo crisis.

High Tech, Low Price: Save on top name electronics in Shopping.

Daily Essentials
- Top News
- Stocks
- Scores
- Weather
- Comics
- Horoscopes
- AOL NetMail

My News: Yugoslavia Declares Kosovo Truce

Search the Web Here:

AOL NetFind
- Web Search
- Yellow Pages
- White Pages
- E-mail Lookup
- Newsgroups
- Kids Only
- Personal Home Page Search
- Maps &

Web Centers
- Autos
- Business & Careers
- Computing
- Entertainment
- Health & Fitness
- Home & Garden
- International
- Local

Shortcuts
- Try AOL Now
- Get Tax Help
- Star Wars Qui
- Fantasy Sport
- Travel Bargains
- Buy a New Ca
- Buy a Used C

INTERACTIVE MARKETING AND ELECTRONIC COMMERCE

8

AFTER READING THIS CHAPTER YOU SHOULD BE ABLE TO:

• Understand what electronic commerce and interactive marketing are and how they create customer value.

• Distinguish among the different types of electronic networks that make electronic commerce and interactive marketing possible.

• Identify online consumers and their purchasing behaviors.

• Recognize why certain types of products and services are particularly suited for electronic commerce.

• Explain how companies create a presence in the electronic marketspace through different kinds of Web sites and different forms of online advertising.

• Describe how companies benefit from electronic commerce and interactive marketing.

BUILDING THE WORLD'S LARGEST SHOPPING MALL WITHOUT LAYING A BRICK

"Our strong retail partnerships allow us to offer exclusive merchandise and some of the best values...," observes Wendy L. Brown. Is Brown describing the stores at your nearest shopping mall? Not at all, because Wendy Brown is vice president of commerce strategy for America Online (AOL) and the power behind AOL's powerhouse Shopping Channel, the world's largest virtual shopping mall. Merchants in AOL's Shopping Channel include mainstream "brick and mortar" retailers, such as Barnes & Noble, Eddie Bauer, FAO Schwartz, Godiva, J. Crew, JCPenney, Macy's, the Gap, and Toys "Я" Us, and most of the top electronic retailers, such as amazon.com, Music Boulevard, eToys, Video Now, Digital Chef, and 1-800-Flowers. AOL's Shopping Channel is one reason almost 75 percent of Web surfers visit the AOL.com Web site at least once a month and is also why the average visitor spends 246 minutes a month interacting with its many services.

"AOL and AOL.com provide the prime real estate that is critical to the establishment of any retail brand—online and offline," says Brown. She adds, "In addition, savvy retailers today also recognize that a strong presence online is increasingly influencing consumer buying offline by reaching a key customer base, providing increased convenience and up-to-the-minute information, and prompting purchases."[1]

America Online is a great success story. Its success is due in part to a revolutionary change in technology that has made possible electronic commerce and interactive marketing. The purpose of this chapter is to describe the nature and scope of electronic commerce, online consumer and purchasing behaviors, and interactive marketing practice.

THE NEW MARKETSPACE AND ELECTRONIC COMMERCE

Consumers and businesses populate two parallel and complementary markets today. One is the traditional marketplace, where buyers and sellers engage in exchange relationships in a material environment mostly inhabited by people, facilities (stores and offices), and physical objects. The other is the **marketspace,** an information- and communication-based electronic exchange environment mostly occupied by sophisticated computer and telecommunication technologies and digitized offerings. You enter the marketspace whenever you access the World Wide Web or log onto a commercial online service such as America Online. But the marketspace is broader than "the Web." It is electronic commerce in its many forms. **Electronic commerce** is "any activity that uses some form of electronic communication in the inventory, exchange, advertisement, distribution, and payment of goods and services."[2]

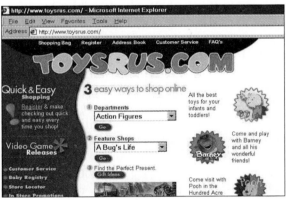

Toys "Я" Us has a significant presence in both the traditional marketplace and the new marketspace.

Toys "Я" Us
www.tru.com

Electronic commerce has existed for many years, and consumers benefit from it every day. Consider the familiar chore of grocery shopping. Each time a checkout clerk at the local supermarket scans your grocery items, precise data on what was purchased are electronically transmitted to the store's warehouse and to suppliers who replenish the store's stocks. Suppose you pay for your purchase with an ATM or debit card. You swipe the card through a transaction terminal, which reads the information on the card's magnetic strip. Enter your personal identification number (PIN), and the terminal routes the transaction through an ATM network back to your bank for authorization against your checking account. Funds are then electronically transferred from your bank to the supermarket's bank. The transaction is completed in a few seconds. Now comes the hard part—preparing a meal!

Your grocery transaction, eased by electronic point-of-sale scanning and payment equipment and systems, was made possible by proprietary computer and telecommunication networks devised and managed solely for companies that owned and used them. These networks dominated electronic commerce until 1996—a year etched in ancient history. The World Wide Web burst upon the scene that year, and a new era of electronic commerce and interactive marketing was born.

Interactive marketing involves buyer–seller electronic communications in a computer-mediated environment in which the buyer controls the kind and amount of information received from the seller. Interactive marketing, made possible by the Internet, the World Wide Web, and commercial online services, has numerous applications and presents new opportunities for customer value creation.

The Nature and Scope of Electronic Commerce

Electronic commerce today consists of a family of electronic networks, each with a different application. These applications illustrate the varied nature and broad scope of electronic commerce and interactive marketing.

Business-to-Consumer Electronic Commerce   The most widely visible application of electronic commerce exists in business-to-consumer interactive marketing, involving the Internet, the World Wide Web, and commercial online services. Many people view these three as being the same. They are not.[3]

The **Internet** is an integrated global network of computers that gives users access to information and documents. Anyone with a personal computer, a modem, and proper software can access the Internet free and can obtain and share information with others via e-mail, electronic messages transmitted to and from Internet host computers. More than 250 million people are projected to have access to the Internet in 2005, with 29 percent residing in the United States. The Internet is a network upon which the system known as the World Wide Web runs.

The **World Wide Web** (WWW) is a part of the Internet that supports a retrieval system that formats information and documents into Web pages. The "Web" uses hypertext markup language (html) to format documents to be viewed by users with a browser program, such as Netscape's Navigator or Microsoft's Internet Explorer. A hypertext transfer protocol (http) is the means by which documents are actually delivered from a Web site to a user's computer. A Uniform Resource Locator (URL) identifies each site, a location in the marketspace akin to the traditional marketplace street address. The typical URL for a business might be http://www.yourcompany.com; for an organization, http://www.yourorganization.org; and a government agency, http://www.youragency.gov. If you haven't already done so, visit the Web site for this book at http://www.mhhe.com/berkowitz.

Systems with much of the popular appeal of the World Wide Web, but not dependent on the Internet, are commercial online services. **Commercial online services** offer electronic information and marketing services to subscribers who are charged a monthly fee. America Online, CompuServe, and Prodigy are well-known commercial online services. For example, America Online provides some 17 million subscribers globally with news, entertainment, e-mail, Internet access, and online shopping opportunities. Its subscribers can order thousands of products and services from more than 400 companies. They can buy and sell investments through distant brokerage services; do their banking with a local bank; make airline, hotel, and car-rental reservations; and inspect product ratings from *Consumer Reports*.

Business-to-consumer electronic commerce activity has skyrocketed since 1996, due in large part to the World Wide Web and commercial online services. Figure 8–1 charts the actual and projected growth of online consumers and expenditures.[4] It is expected that the number of U.S. households buying online will quadruple between 1998 and 2002, with more than one-half of all U.S. households buying something online in 2002. Online U.S. consumer expenditures for products and services are also expected to quadruple between 1998 and 2002.

Business Support Functions   Many companies have adapted Internet-based technology internally to support their external electronic commerce initiatives. An

FIGURE 8–1
Growth of U.S. business-to-consumer electronic commerce: 1996–2002

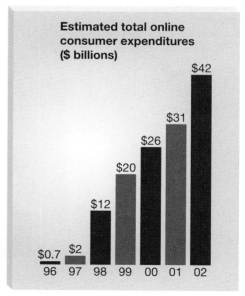

Intranet is an Internet/Web-based network used within the boundaries of an organization. It is essentially a private Internet that may or may not be connected to the public Internet. Those that are connected are protected by "firewalls" from outside intrusion ("hacking") by millions of Internet users.

Intranets serve primarily as a business support function network and facilitate the internal, electronic exchange of corporate data and files. By 2001, an estimated 133 million companies in the United States and Europe will have Intranets.[5] The pharmaceutical giant Eli Lilly & Co. operates an extensive Intranet known as ELVIS (Eli Lilly Virtual Information System). Employees can access internal job postings, corporate policies and handbooks, and a daily news summary on scientific and competitive developments in the global pharmaceutical industry. Marketing and sales information is also transmitted to field offices and employees in more than 120 countries instantaneously and electronically to better serve Eli Lilly customers.[6] The use of Intranets for selling and sales management is discussed further in Chapter 21.

Business-to-Business Electronic Commerce   The largest application of electronic commerce exists in the realm of business-to-business interactive marketing. As described in Chapter 7, online buying between businesses accounts for a great majority of the dollar value of all online transactions in the United States.

Business-to-business electronic commerce comes in two forms. **Electronic data interchanges** (EDI) combine proprietary computer and telecommunication technologies to exchange electronic invoices, payments, and information between businesses, such as suppliers, manufacturers, and retailers. When linked with store scanning equipment and systems, EDI provides a seamless electronic link from a retail checkout counter to suppliers and manufacturers. Wal-Mart and Procter & Gamble pioneered the use of EDI in the 1980s. Today, EDI is commonly used in retail, apparel, transportation, pharmaceutical, grocery, health care, and insurance industries, as well as by local, state, and federal government agencies. About 95 percent of the companies listed in the Fortune 1000 use EDI, which is an indispensable electronic network for supply chain and logistics management as described in Chapter 17. At Hewlett-Packard, for example, one million EDI transactions are made every month.[7]

A second form of business-to-business electronic commerce is an Extranet, an extension of a company's Intranet. An **Extranet** is an Internet/Web-based network that permits private business-to-business communication between a company and its sup-

FIGURE 8–2
Growth of U.S. business-to-business electronic commerce: 1996–2002

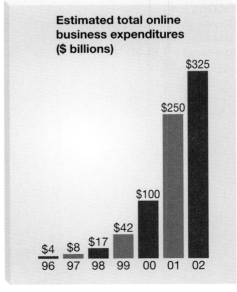

MARKETING NEWSNET

The Twenty-First Century E-Corporation Is Virtually Here

TECHNOLOGY

Electronic commerce and e-corporations continue to evolve with new Internet, Intranet, and Extranet applications. Increasingly, companies are focusing on creating seamless streams of information between corporate functions (manufacturing, sales, marketing, finance, human resources); suppliers, partners, and distributors; and the ultimate customer. Computer software for the different forms of electronic commerce, called e-ware, that makes it easier for businesses to market products and services via the Web (Internet), to get the most out of customer and competitive data (Intranet), and to manage relationships with suppliers and customers (Extranet) represents the next evolutionary phase of electronic commerce and the e-corporation.

VF Corporation, the maker of Lee, Wrangler, Britannia, and Rustler jeans; Timber Creek khakis; Healthtex clothes for kids; Jantzen bathing suits; and JanSport backpacks, has taken the lead in stitching together an e-corporation with e-ware. The company has invested

more than $70 million in computer software alone to link functions, people, and companies for the purpose of getting the right information, in the right form, to the right place, at the right time. According to a senior VF executive, "If we pull this off, no one else will be close" in integrating data across operations. Another executive replied, "Knock on wood."

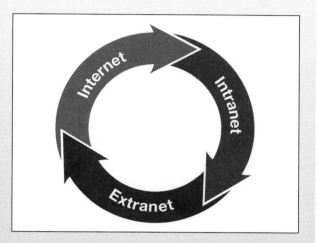

pliers, distributors, and other partners (such as advertising agencies). Extranets are less expensive and more flexible to operate than EDI because of their connection with the public Internet. General Electric's Trading Process Network (TPN) highlighted in Chapter 7 is an example of an Extranet. Another is the Automotive Network Exchange (ANX), a collaborative effort among General Motors, Ford, and Daimler Chrysler, which is described later in Chapter 17. TPN and AMX represent virtual business communities populated by an array of companies sharing information and doing business with each other electronically in the new marketspace.

EDI and Extranets will account for the bulk of U.S. electronic commerce expenditures for goods and services into the twenty-first century. Figure 8–2 shows that the dollar value of online U.S. business-to-business expenditures is projected to increase 19-fold between 1998 and 2002, reaching $325 billion in 2002.[8] This figure is almost eight times larger than projected online U.S. consumer expenditures in 2002!

The fusion of Internet, Intranet, and Extranet Web-based technologies common in electronic commerce will create the "e-corporation or virtual organization" of the next decade. Apparel maker VF Corporation is already on its way toward becoming an e-corporation, as described in the accompanying Marketing NewsNet.[9]

Marketing.com: Electronic Commerce and Customer Value Creation

Despite the widespread attention given the new marketspace and electronic commerce, its economic significance is small compared with the traditional marketplace. Electronic commerce is expected to represent less than 8 percent of total U.S. consumer and industrial goods and services expenditures in 2001, and less than 1 percent of global expenditures. Why then has electronic commerce and interactive marketing captured the eye and imagination of marketers?

Marketers believe that the possibilities for customer value creation are greater in marketspace than the traditional marketplace.[10] Remember from Chapter 1 that marketing creates time, place, form, and possession utilities for customers, thereby providing value. In marketspace, the provision of direct, on-demand information is possible from marketers *anywhere* to customers *anywhere* at *any time*. Why? Geographical constraints and operating hours do not exist in marketspace. For example, Recreational Equipment (www.rei.com), an outdoor gear marketer, reports that 35 percent of its orders are placed between 10:00 P.M. and 7:00 A.M., long after and before retail stores are open for business. Twenty percent of amazon.com book sales are from buyers who live outside the United States. Possession utility—getting a product or service to consumers so they can own or use it—is accelerated. Airline, car rental, and lodging electronic reservation systems such as Travelocity (www.travelocity.com) allow comparison shopping for the lowest fares, rents, and rates and almost immediate access to and confirmation of travel arrangements and accommodations.

The greatest marketspace opportunity for marketers, however, lies in its potential for creating form utility. Interactive two-way Internet/Web-based communication capabilities in marketspace invite consumers to tell marketers exactly what their requirements are, making customization of a product or service to fit the buyer's exact needs possible. For instance, Bluefly.com, an apparel company, encourages customers to develop their own catalog free of unwanted items. Consumers can specify the brands, clothing category, and sizes right for their needs. Bluefly.com will instantaneously create a personalized catalog just for them.

CONCEPT CHECK

1. What is electronic commerce?

2. Online U.S. consumer expenditures for products and services are expected to increase ___ percent between 1998 and 2002, while online U.S. business-to-business expenditure for goods and services is projected to increase ___-fold between 1998 and 2002.

3. How can electronic commerce create customer value?

ONLINE CONSUMERS AND BUYING BEHAVIOR IN THE NEW MARKETSPACE

Who are online consumers, and what do they buy? Why do they choose to purchase products and services in the new marketspace rather than or in addition to the traditional marketplace? Answers to these questions are important to marketers today and offer clues to the future growth of electronic commerce and interactive marketing.

The Online Consumer

Many labels are given online consumers—cybershoppers, Netizens, and e-shoppers—suggesting they are a homogeneous segment of the population. They are not, but as a group, they do differ demographically from the general population.

Online Consumer Profile   Online consumers differ from the general population in one important respect. They own or have access to a computer. Slightly less than 40 percent of U.S. households have a computer in their home with Internet/Web access, although access is often possible at work or school. Figure 8–3 profiles Internet/World Wide Web users.[11]

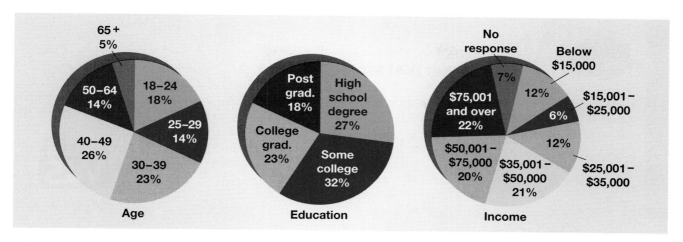

FIGURE 8–3
Demographics of Internet/
World Wide Web users

Online consumers are a subsegment of all Internet/Web users.[12] Research indicates that about 55 percent of Internet/Web users have sought product or service information online before making a purchase. For example, it is expected that 50 percent of new car buyers will visit Web sites such as Auto-By-Tel, Microsoft Carpoint, and Autoweb.com to car shop in 2001. Still by mid-1999, only about 25 percent of Internet/Web users actually purchased a product or service online. This figure is projected to exceed 50 percent in 2002.

As a group, online consumers tend to be better educated, younger, and more affluent than the general population, which makes them an attractive market. The majority are married (59 percent) and male (60 percent), although the number of online women consumers is increasing rapidly. Specially developed Web sites for women such as women.com have capitalized on this trend.

Online Consumer Psychographics   Not all Internet/Web users use the technology the same way, nor are they all likely to be online buyers. SRI International, the same research firm that developed the Values and Lifestyles (VALS) Program described in Chapter 5, has identified 10 distinct Internet/Web user profiles, called iVALS segments, which illustrate how diverse Internet/Web users can be (Figure 8–4).[13]

FIGURE 8–4
iVALS Internet user segments

WEB LINK

What iVALS Type Are You?

Are you curious about how you stack up as an Internet user? If you are, complete the short iVALS questionnaire developed by SRI International at http://www.future.sri.com:80/vals/ivals/segs.html, and find out.

In addition to obtaining your profile, you can examine the characteristics of your and other profiles in greater detail. You may also wish to compare your iVALS profile with your VALS profile identified in the Chapter 5 Web Link.

Internet/Web users differ along two dimensions: (1) how heavily and enthusiastically they use the Internet and (2) the reason for usage.[14] Wizards are the most active and skilled Internet users and possess sophisticated technical skills. Mostly male and relatively young, Wizards are likely to be active online consumers, especially for products such as computers, software, and technical information. At the other extreme are Immigrants. They are skeptical of the Internet and do not use it willingly, often only if forced to do so at school or at work. Immigrants have limited technical skills and are among the least promising online consumers.

The remaining eight segments fall between these extremes. Pioneers and Surfers are attracted to the Internet because of its recreational possibilities. They visit Web sites for the enjoyment of seeing what's there and, like recreational shoppers, are good prospects for online buying. Socialites and Sociables are among the youngest Internet users and value the social aspects of the Internet. They are heavy users of chat rooms and online communities where they can meet new people.

Workers and Seekers use the Internet mostly as a professional tool. Workers are mainly upscale, professional males who use the Internet as a source for research and industry information. Seekers are also professionally oriented and seek to improve their productivity through Internet use. College professors, students, and consultants populate these categories because of their information-intensive needs and visit Web sites that provide news, information summaries, and directories. Finally, Upstreamers and Mainstreamers are generalists. They use the Internet for a combination of personal and professional reasons. Like Workers and Seekers, they rely on the Internet to help them in their careers. And like Pioneers and Surfers, they enjoy browsing the Internet and use it for personal tasks such as online banking, investing, and shopping.

Do any of these iVALS consumer profiles fit you? Take a break and visit the SRI International Web site listed in the accompanying Web Link. Complete the short questionnaire, and find out which iVALS segment best describes your Internet/Web activity and usage.

Online Consumer Purchasing Behavior

Much still needs to be learned about online consumer purchase behavior in the new marketspace. While research has documented the most frequently purchased products and services bought online, marketers also need to know why these items are popular and why consumers prefer to shop and buy in the new marketspace.

What Online Consumers Buy   There are six general product and service categories that appear to be particularly suited for electronic commerce.[15] One category consists of items for which product information is an important part of the purchase decision, but prepurchase trial is not necessarily critical. Items such as computers, computer accessories, and consumer electronics sold by dell.com and egghead.com fall into this category. So do books, which accounts for the sales growth of amazon.com and Barnes & Noble (www.barnesandnoble.com). Both booksellers publish short reviews of new books that visitors to their Web sites can read before making a purchase decision. According to an authority on electronic commerce, "You've read the reviews, you want it, you don't need to try it on."[16] A second category includes items for which audio or video demonstration is important. This category consists of CDs and videos sold by columbiahouse.com, cdnow.com, and towerrecords.com. The third category contains items that can be delivered digitally, including computer software, travel reservations and confirmations, brokerage services, and electronic ticketing. Popular Web sites for these items include travelocity.com, ticketmaster.com, and schwab.com.

Unique items, such as collectibles, specialty goods, and foods and gifts, represent a fourth category. Collectible auction houses (www.auctions-on-line.com and www.eworldauction.com), wine merchant Virtual Vineyards (www.virtualvin.com), and flower and gift marketer 1-800-Flowers (www.1800flowers.com) sell these products. A fifth category includes items that are regularly purchased and where convenience is very important. Many consumer-packaged goods, such as grocery products, fall into this category, which has benefited peapod.com and netgrocer.com, two online grocers. A final category of items consists of highly standardized products and services for which information about price is important. Certain kinds of insurance (auto and homeowners), home improvement products, casual apparel, and toys make up this category. These categories dominate online consumer shopping today and for the foreseeable future, as shown in Figure 8–5.[17]

Why Consumers Buy Online: The Six Cs   Marketers emphasize the customer value creation possibilities in the new marketspace. However, consumers typically refer to six reasons why they prefer to buy online (also called the six Cs): convenience, cost, choice, customization, communication, and control (Figure 8–6).

Online buying is *convenient*. Consumers can visit Wal-Mart at www.wal-mart.com to scan and order from among 80,000 displayed products without fighting traffic, finding a parking space, walking through long aisles, and standing in store check-out lines. Alternatively, online consumers can use **bots,** electronic shopping agents or robots

FIGURE 8–5
Online consumer sales by product/service category: 1999 and 2002

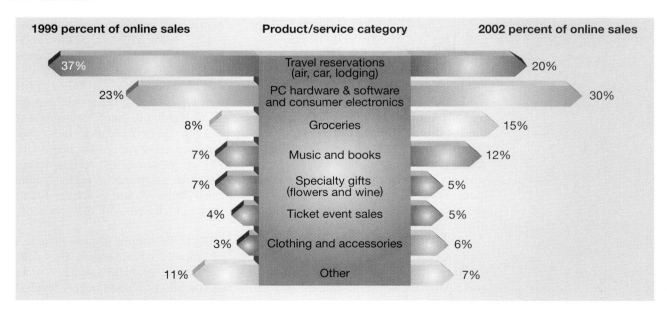

FIGURE 8–6

Why consumers buy online

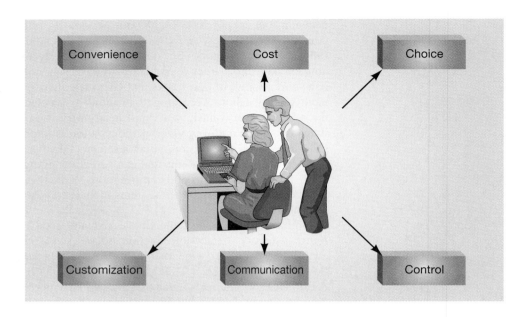

that comb Web sites, to compare prices and product or service features. In either instance, an online consumer has never ventured from his or her PC monitor. Consumer *cost* is a second reason for buying online. Recent research indicates that almost 90 percent of the 30 most popular items bought online can be purchased at the same price or cheaper than in retail stores.[18] A consumer's cost of external search, including time spent and often the hassle of shopping, is also reduced. Shopping convenience and external search costs are two major reasons for the growth of online buying among women, particularly for those who work outside the home.[19]

Choice and *customization* opportunities are two additional reasons consumers buy online. Consumers desiring selection can avail themselves of numerous Web sites for almost any product or service they want. For instance, online buyers of consumer electronics can shop individual manufacturers such as Bose (www.bose.com) or Sony (www.sony.com) or visit iqvc.com, a general merchant with more than 100,000 products. Even with a broad selection, some consumers prefer one-of-a-kind items that fit their specific needs. Consider, for instance, buying a Barbie doll for a child. Online buyers can shop etoys.com and choose a Barbie doll from 117 versions available. On the other hand, a visit to Mattel at www.barbie.com allows buyers to design their own doll. They can specify the doll's skin tone, eye and hair color, hairstyle, clothes, accessories, and give her a name. Fill out a questionnaire, and a computer-generated personality profile for Barbie is prepared.[20]

Online consumers also welcome the interactive *communication* capabilities of Internet/Web-based technologies that allow them to engage in an electronic dialogue with marketers. These "push" technologies send information to online consumers automatically according to their expressed preferences. Garden Escapes, Inc. (www.garden.com), which provides visitors with a computer-aided design for home landscaping, is a case in point.[21] Through state-of-the-art garden design techniques and working with plants and shrubs appropriate to particular geographical regions, online gardeners can create and then see what their finished landscape will look like instantaneously. If it meets with their approval, items can be purchased, with delivery scheduled in time for the best planting.

The sixth reason consumers prefer to buy online is the *control* it gives them over their purchase decision process. Online buyers are empowered consumers. They deftly use Internet/Web-based technology to seek information, evaluate alternatives, and make purchase decisions on their own terms and conditions. Online buyers regularly

ETHICS AND SOCIAL RESPONSIBILITY ALERT

Sweet and Sour Cookies in the New Marketspace

Privacy and security are two key reasons consumers are leery of online shopping. A recent *Business Week*/Harris poll reported that of those yet to buy online, 61 percent said they would be more likely to do so if the privacy of their personal information and communications could be protected. Even 56 percent of online buyers have doubts that their personal information will be used properly.

The privacy and security concerns of online buyers are related to the "cookies" described in the text and how those cookies can be used or misused. A percolating issue in electronic commerce is whether the U.S. government should pass Internet/Web privacy laws. A majority of consumers (53 percent) appear to favor such action. Companies have adopted initiatives to develop their own privacy standards without government action. The Online Privacy Alliance (www. privacyalliance.org) is a consortium of businesses and associations that aims to promote electronic commerce through online privacy policies and self-regulation. TRUSTe (www.etrust.org) awards its trademark to Web sites that comply with standards of privacy protection and disclosure.

Do you think that governmental or self-regulation is the best way to deal with issues of privacy and security in the new marketspace?

engage **portals** and "search engines," which are electronic gateways to the World Wide Web that supply a broad array of news and entertainment, information resources, and shopping services.[22] Well-known portals include Yahoo!, Infoseek, Snap, Excite, Lycos, Microsoft's Internet Start, and Netscape's Netcenter. To evaluate alternatives, consumers visit comparison-shopping Web sites such as comparenet.com and price.com or employ bots such as Yahoo! Shopping and Excite's Product Finder, which provide product descriptions and prices for a wide variety of brands and models. The result of these activities is a more informed consumer and discerning shopper. In the words of one marketing consultant, "In the marketspace, the customer is in charge."[23]

Even though consumers have many reasons for buying online, a segment of Internet/Web users refrain from making purchases for privacy and security reasons as described in the accompanying Ethics and Social Responsibility Alert.[24] Those consumers are concerned about a rarely mentioned seventh "C"—cookies. **Cookies** are computer files that a marketer can download onto the computer of an online shopper who visits the marketer's Web site.[25] Cookies allow the marketer's Web site to record a user's visit, track visits to other Web sites, and store and retrieve this information in the future. Cookies also contain information provided by visitors, such as expressed product preferences, personal data, and financial information, including credit card numbers. Clearly, cookies make possible customized and personalized content for online shoppers. The controversy surrounding cookies is summed up by an authority on the technology: "At best a cookie makes for a user-friendly Web world: like a doorman or salesclerk who knows who you are. At worst, cookies represent a potential loss of privacy."[26]

CONCEPT CHECK

1. Which iVALS segment is the least promising group for online buying? Why?

2. Why is it that travel reservations account for such a large percentage of online buying?

3. What are the six reasons consumers prefer to buy online?

INTERACTIVE MARKETING IN THE NEW MARKETSPACE

Interactive communication between buyers and sellers and consumer control over what, where, when, and how information is exchanged in the new marketspace have significant implications for marketing practice. Even though the fundamental tasks of marketing refined in the traditional marketplace still apply—creating customer value by providing the right product, at the right time, at the right place, at the right price—the setting is very different.[27] A challenge for marketers in the new marketplace is to have an electronic presence that attracts the attention and interaction of the online consumer and makes a profit.

Creating a Presence in the New Marketspace

Marketers create a presence in the new marketspace through their Web sites and online advertising.

Corporate and Marketing Web Sites   Companies employ two major types of Web sites, each with a different purpose.[28] A **corporate Web site** is designed to accommodate interactive communication initiated by a company's employees, investors, suppliers, and customers. These sites provide information about the company such as its history, mission and corporate values, products and services, and annual report. Many contain recent news releases and offer opportunities for visitors to ask questions and make comments through e-mail. More advanced Web sites provide interactive entertainment features such as games to keep a visitor's attention. Corporate Web sites are not specifically designed to promote and sell a company's products or services; however, some do. Rather, they serve to build relationships with customers and other important constituencies. Visit the Gillette Company (www.gillette.com) and Gulfstream Aerospace Corporation, a leading manufacturer of business jets (www.gulfstreamaircraft.com), to see the similarity of corporate Web sites across different industries.

A **marketing Web site** is designed to engage consumers in interactive communication or dialogue that will result in the sale of a company's product or service or move the consumer closer to a purchase. In contrast to corporate Web sites, marketing Web sites initiate interactive communication with prospective buyers. These sites outnumber corporate Web sites by a wide margin.

Marketing Web sites come in two general forms: (1) transactional sites and (2) promotional sites. Transactional Web sites are essentially electronic storefronts, such as those operated by amazon.com and cdnow. They focus principally on converting an online browser into an online buyer. Many provide access to human service representatives to assist in making purchases. For example, two thirds of the sales through Dell Computer's Web site (www.dell.com) involve human sales representatives.[29] These

MARKETING NEWSNET

Cisco Systems Makes Its Living on the Net

When it comes to electronic commerce, no one understands it better than Cisco Systems. The reason? Cisco's business is electronic commerce. The San Jose, California-based company sells 80 percent of the networking products that make the Internet, and most corporate Intranets and Extranets, work.

Cisco generates almost 60 percent of its sales, or about $10 million per day, through its Web site, Cisco Connection Online (www.cisco.com). At last count, Cisco accounted for roughly one third of all U.S. revenues generated by electronic commerce. Cisco's Web site blends technical support with every step in selling and servicing its products, all of which are custom-built to a customer's specifications. For example, Cisco's Configuration Agent software walks customers through the dozens of components that typically go into one of its products. Its Status Agent software lets customers track the progress of their orders online. Overall, 7 out of 10 customer requests for technical support are filled electronically—at satisfaction rates that eclipse those involving human interaction.

sites also can be used for customer research and feedback. Cathay Pacific Airlines is a case in point. Its Web site (www.cathay-usa.com) is used to interview frequent fliers to determine their travel preferences and buying habits in addition to performing other functions. A truly multifunctional transactional Web site is operated by Cisco Systems, the company that sells 80 percent of the networking products that make the Internet, and corporate Intranets and Extranets, work. Read the accompanying Marketing News-Net to see how its Web site—Cisco Connection Online—blends technical support with every step in selling and servicing its products before and after a transaction.[30]

Promotional Web sites have a very different purpose than transactional sites. They promote a company's products and services and provide information on how items can be used and where they can be purchased. They often engage the visitor in an interactive experience involving games, contests, and quizzes with electronic coupons and other gifts as prizes. Procter & Gamble maintains separate Web sites for 24 of its leading brands, including Pringles potato chips (www.pringles.com), Vidal Sasson hair products (www.vidalsasson.com), Scope mouthwash (www.scope-mouthwash.com), and Pampers diapers (www.pampers.com).[31] Promotional sites can be effective in generating interest in and trial of a company's products and services.[32] General Motors reports that 80 percent of the people visiting a Saturn store first visited the brand's Web site (www.saturn.com). The Metropolitan Life Insurance Web site (www.metlife.com) is a proven vehicle for qualifying prospective buyers of its insurance and financial services.

Marketing Web sites can be expensive to develop and maintain, particularly with the growing use of sophisticated interactive and experiential activities and eye-catching animation and three-dimensional graphics. The average marketing Web site costs $1 million to develop and takes one year to launch. The cost of creating a transaction-based Web site is about 10 times that of a promotional Web site.[33]

Having a corporate or marketing Web site does not, by itself, guarantee that online consumers will ever visit it. While a Web site can be invaluable in conveying information,

Print advertisements are frequently used to create awareness of and interest in corporate and marketing Web sites.

creating product involvement, and even making sales, online consumers must first be attracted to the site. Attracting online consumers is difficult in an increasingly cluttered marketspace where 100,000 Web sites are added to the World Wide Web and commercial online services each week. Advertising plays an important role in the new marketspace just as it does in the traditional marketspace. In fact, companies prominently advertise their Web sites using conventional print and broadcast media and direct mail, in addition to using online advertising.

Online Advertising   A primary objective of online advertising is to generate sales directly and quickly through a marketer's transactional Web site.[34] However, because most companies operate both in the new marketspace and the traditional marketplace, other objectives for online advertising exist. Creating awareness and a favorable image of a company and its products and services are frequently stated objectives for corporate Web sites. Online advertising is also used to support a company's traditional sales channel, including retail stores and building customer relationships. This is the objective of the Clinique division of Estee Lauder Companies, which markets cosmetics through department stores. Clinique reports that 80 percent of current customers who visit its Web site (www.clinique.com) later purchase a product at a retail store; 37 percent of non-Clinique buyers make a Clinique purchase after visiting the site.[35]

Companies have adopted two approaches for placing online advertising. One approach focuses on buying space on a heavily trafficked Web portal, such as Yahoo!, or a commercial online service. The second involves buying space on commercially sponsored **Web communities**—Web sites that cater to a particular group of individuals who share a common interest. Members of the Web communities are prime targets for advertisements linked with the topic of the site. For instance, iVillage.com, the Women's Network, is a Web community for women and includes topics such as

Banner ads are a popular form of online advertising. This sequence of banners from <u>usa.net</u> is typical.

career management, personal finances, parenting, relationships, beauty, and health. Avon and Charles Schwab Investments are among the many companies that advertise on iVillage.com.

Companies have several options when deciding which type of advertisement to use. The most common form of advertisement are *banner ads*—strip ads that usually contain a company or product name or some kind of promotional offer. Online consumers merely need to click on the ad to visit either a company's corporate or marketing Web site. About 50 percent of online advertising consisted of banner ads in 1998.[36] The typical monthly space cost for a banner ad is $10,000. The second most common form of online advertising consists of *sponsorships*.[37] These ads are typically integrated with a Web community site. For example, Schering-Plough's allergy remedy, Claritin, is a sponsor of the OnHealth Network's Web site (<u>www.onhealth.com</u>). This site provides health and fitness information for adults and families. Sponsorships accounted for 30 percent of online advertising in 1998.

Two other types of ads account for most of the remaining kinds of online advertising. *Key word ads* are linked to Web portals or search engines such as Yahoo! or Excite. Whenever a customer initiates a search using a certain key word, an ad for a product related to that word will appear. Miller Brewing Company, for instance, purchased the key word "beer" on Yahoo!. Every online consumer who searches Yahoo! using that word sees an advertisement for Miller Genuine Draft Beer. *Interstitials* or *intermercials* are similar to television ads because they often incorporate video and audio features. An interstitial appears automatically on the computer screen in the time interval after the user clicks on a Web site and before it appears on the screen just as television ads appear in the time interval between programs. Recent research suggests that interstitial ads are twice as effective at generating brand awareness than banner ads.[38] Industry analysts project that by 2002, 50 percent of ads will be banners, 25 percent will be sponsorships, and 25 will be interstitials.[39]

Many companies today have supplemented their online advertising with **webcasting**—the practice of pushing out corporate and marketing Web site information to online consumers rather than waiting for them to find the site on their own.[40] Webcasting services, such as Pointcast (<u>www.pointcast.com</u>), automatically deliver customized information to an online consumer's computer, including news, entertainment, and company product and service information, based on their preferences.[41] Webcasting is likely to improve the effectiveness of online advertising. Why? According to one authority on electronic commerce: "Now instead of waiting for Web surfers to stumble onto their sites and banner ads, marketers can send animated ads directly to the desktops of target customers. . . . Merchants can now approach live sales prospects and not just couch potatoes."[42]

The Gap has found its Web site to be an important source of incremental sales.

Gap
www.gap.com

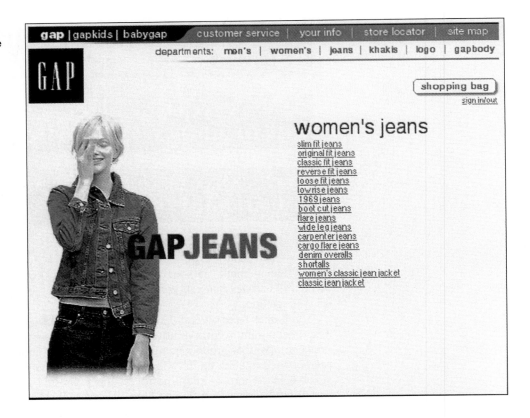

How Companies Benefit from Electronic Commerce and Interactive Marketing

Interactive marketing and electronic commerce have profoundly changed the exchange relationship between customers and companies. Continual advances in interactive digital technology and development of new marketing applications promise even more change in the future.

Marketers recognize the customer value creation potential in the new marketspace. However, electronic commerce and interactive marketing can provide numerous other benefits to companies. Notably, electronic commerce has been already shown to lower costs. Cost savings in inventory handling, order processing, and communications made possible by corporate Intranets, Extranets, and electronic data interchanges are huge. For example, the cost to process an order using an Extranet is $1.50. The same order using paper, including administrative costs, is $40.00—a savings of 96 percent![43] Similarly, online marketers are not burdened by the cost of building and operating retail stores. This fact has led many retailers to set up Web sites. The Gap, for instance, generates more sales volume from its Web site at (www.gap.com) than any one of its stores save one.[44]

The technology of electronic commerce and interactive marketing allows for greater flexibility in managing elements of the marketing mix. For example, online marketers routinely adjust prices in response to changing environmental conditions, purchase situations, and purchase behaviors of online buyers.[45] For example, Virtual Vineyards offers different prices and deals to its customers depending on how and what they purchased in the past. Other online marketers monitor an online shopper's "clickstream"—the way that person navigates through the World Wide Web. If the visitor behaves like a price-sensitive shopper—perhaps by comparing many different products—that person may be offered a lower price. The life of an advertisement is also shortened in marketspace. Many advertisements in marketspace have a life of 4 hours in any 24-hour period and are adjusted to a particular online buyer's purchase behavior. In short, customization can apply to price and promotion elements of the marketing mix, not just products and services described earlier.

Finally, because the new marketspace has no geographical boundaries, marketers can benefit from its global reach. An online U.S. consumer from Chicago can access Marks & Spencer, the well-known British department store at (www.marks-and-spencer.co.uk) to shop for clothing as easily as a person living near London's Picadilly Square. Large and small consumer and business-to-business marketers alike have found that this benefit has broadened their customer base.

Despite these benefits, few companies have mastered electronic commerce and interactive marketing.[46] More often than not, marketers have found the pathway to profit in marketspace to be more illusionary than real because of higher costs and lower profit margins than they anticipated.[47]

CONCEPT CHECK	**1.** What is the difference between a corporate Web site and a marketing Web site?
	2. Why is webcasting expected to improve the effectiveness of online advertising?
	3. How do companies benefit from electronic commerce and interactive marketing?

SUMMARY

1 Consumers and businesses populate two parallel and complementary markets today—the traditional marketplace and the new marketspace characterized by electronic commerce networks and interactive marketing.

2 Electronic commerce consists of a family of electronic networks, each with a different application. Business-to-consumer electronic commerce is the most visible application, involving the Internet, the World Wide Web, and commercial online services. Corporate electronic networks such as the Intranet are used to perform internal company functions, while electronic data interchanges (EDI) and Extranets are used for business-to-business electronic commerce.

3 Electronic commerce creates time, place, possession, and form utility in novel ways, resulting in customer value.

4 Online consumers represent a subsegment of all Internet/Web users and differ demographically from the general population. They tend to be better educated, younger, and more affluent than the general population. The majority are married and male. They also exhibit distinct psychographic profiles.

5 Six general product and service categories appear to be particularly suited for electronic commerce. However, travel reservations, PC hardware and software, and consumer electronics account for the majority of online consumer purchases.

6 Consumers typically refer to six reasons they prefer to buy online: convenience, cost, choice, customization, communication, and control over the purchase process. However, consumers are concerned about privacy and security when making online purchases.

7 Marketers create a presence in the new marketspace through Web sites and online advertising. Web sites come in two forms, corporate Web sites and marketing Web sites. Marketing Web sites are of two types: (*a*) transactional sites and (*b*) promotional sites. The principal form of online advertising is banner ads.

8 Electronic commerce and interactive marketing not only provide novel opportunities for customer value creation but also result in cost savings, marketing mix flexibility, and global exposure.

KEY TERMS AND CONCEPTS

marketspace p. 204
electronic commerce p. 204
interactive marketing p. 204
Internet p. 204
World Wide Web (WWW) p. 205
commercial online services p. 205
Intranet p. 206
electronic data interchange (EDI) p. 206

Extranet p. 206
bots p. 211
portals p. 213
cookies p. 213
corporate Web site p. 214
marketing Web site p. 214
Web communities p. 216
webcasting p. 217

INTERNET EXERCISE

What are the most recent statistics and trends in interactive marketing and electronic commerce? Look no further than Nua Internet Surveys (Nua), an online service that abstracts up-to-date research on Internet/Web usage and applications from around the world. Nua conveniently organizes research by business, social, technical, demographic, and geographic categories for easy inspection.

Visit the Nua Web site at www.nua.ie/surveys. Your assignment is as follows:

1 Choose a topic covered in the chapter that interests you, such as the demographics of Internet/Web users. Compare and contrast the most recent research published in Nua with information contained in the chapter. Don't be surprised if you find differences!

2 Choose two regions of the world, such as North America and Europe. How does Internet/Web usage and electronic commerce differ between the two regions based on the most recent research?

APPLYING MARKETING CONCEPTS AND PERSPECTIVES

1 How do marketers use the Internet, Intranets, electronic data interchanges (EDI), and Extranets to create customer value through electronic commerce?

2 By mid-1999, only about 25 percent of Internet/Web users had actually purchased something online. Have you made an online purchase? If so, why do you think so many people who have access to the Internet and the World Wide Web are not also online buyers? If not, why are you reluctant to do so? Do you think that electronic commerce benefits consumers even if they don't make a purchase?

3 Compared to the marketplace, the marketspace offers marketers opportunities to create greater time, place, form, and possession utility. How do you think electronic commerce rates in terms of creating these values? Take a shopping trip at a virtual retailer of your choice (don't buy anything unless you really want to), or choose from one of the companies listed below. Then compare the time, place, form, and possession utility provided by the virtual retailer with that you enjoyed during a nonelectronic experience shopping for the same product category. Here are some sites you might like to visit: www.usairways.com; www.jango.com; www.dell.com.

4 Visit each of the following Web sites: www.singles.com; www.wsnbc.com; www.schwab.com; www.virualemporium.com; www.gateway.com. Which of the iVALS segments would be most attracted to each of these sites? Why?

5 Suppose you are planning to open an electronic store on the World Wide Web. How likely would a Web site featuring each of the following product categories be to succeed? Why?

a High-priced, high-fashion women's shoe salon.

b An energy comparison shopping service where consumers can shop for the best gas and electricity rates.

c Video rental service.

6 Visit Internet bookseller www.amazon.com or www.barnesandnoble.com. As you tour the company's Web site, think about how shopping for books online compares with a trip to your university bookstore to buy books. Specifically, compare your shopping experiences with respect to each of the six Cs of electronic commerce.

7 Suppose you are planning to buy a new car so you decide to visit www.autobytel. Based on your experience visiting that site, do you feel you would enjoy more or less control in negotiating with the dealer when you actually purchase your vehicle?

8 Visit the Web site for your university or college. Based on your visit, would you conclude that the site is a corporate or a marketing site? Why? If it is a marketing Web site, is it a transactional site or a promotional site? Why?

9 Visit a Web community such as www.women.com or www.parents.com. What companies/products advertise on the community's Web site? Why do you think those companies/products chose the Web community as an advertising venue? Do you think the choice was a good one? Why?

10 One of the benefits that electronic commerce and interactive marketing provides for companies is the ability to obtain consumer information that can be used to more effectively manage the marketing mix. Catalina Marketing Corporation, for example, creates profiles of its online customers' product category and brand preferences and use this information to generate personalized coupons. Some consumers, however, worry about their privacy as companies like Catalina create highly detailed customer databases. Visit Catalina's Web site at www.valuepage.com to determine what information you must provide to obtain your own customized coupons. Is the added value of the coupons worth the price of the information you must reveal to get it? Why or why not?

CASE 8–1   AMERICA ONLINE, INC.

"America Online started as a vision of Steve Case to provide basic e-mail and bulletin board communication services," says Wendy Brown, vice president of commerce strategy at America Online (AOL). This, of course, was several years before the commercialization of the World Wide Web (WWW) and the Internet. Over the years, AOL has added a variety of communication services, information "channels," shopping opportunities, and personalization features. Today, AOL has become the convenient tool that, according to Brown, "people use to be able to manage their lives, stay in touch with others, buy things, and learn."

THE COMPANY

Myer Berlow, senior vice president of interactive marketing, says, "the important thing to understand about our business model is that we have a dual income stream. We have subscriber revenues and we have other revenues, namely advertising and e-commerce." To maintain its revenue growth, AOL has had to address several key challenges—including attracting new members and managing its network "access" capabilities.

The essence of AOL's growth strategy is to be the easiest and most convenient Internet online service. To increase the number of members, AOL has developed several programs to get its software in the hands of potential customers. For example, AOL has mailed disks to computer users, shrinkwrapped copies with computer magazines, and placed freestanding displays in selected retailers. In addition, AOL has offered up to 250 free hours to potential customers to encourage them to explore the service during a one trial-month period. To ensure that installation is easy, the software is designed so that trial users of AOL's service only need to "point and click" and the software installs itself. To make the access and navigation of its online service easy, AOL designed a well-organized, graphical user interface to allow users to quickly and easily navigate the service. These and other design features have been important elements in converting trial users to paying members.

AOL has also grown through key acquisitions and alliances. In 1997, AOL purchased Internet pioneer CompuServe, which had approximately 2 million members worldwide. In 1998, AOL's acquisition of the leading Internet browser, Netscape, brought an additional 15 million members to the company. "Our merger with Netscape provides us with another world-class brand, a fast-growing portal, innovative talent, and cutting-edge

technologies," said Steve Case. AOL also entered into strategic alliances with Sun Microsystems to provide software for e-commerce, Bell Atlantic to provide convenient and affordable high-speed online access to millions of AOL members across the United States, and DirectTV, Philips Electronics, and others to add interactivity to the television viewing experience.

To manage growth, AOL has had to revise how to predict and deal with unexpected demand for its service. When AOL switched from usage (time spent) to flat-rate (monthly fee) pricing a few years ago, it created an "access crisis" that made the nightly news. Demand temporarily surged beyond AOL's capacity and caused members to receive unwanted busy signals. AOL failed "to estimate what kind of pent-up demand there was among our members," Brown said. That challenge has since been resolved, as AOL spent millions of dollars to add connectivity capacity.

AOL has now become the largest online service in the world with over 18 million "members" or paid subscribers who connect to the service an average of 55 minutes per day. Millions more access its Web site, www.aol.com. In 1998, about 16 percent of AOL's $2.6 billion in revenues came from advertising and e-commerce, a substantial increase from 9 percent in 1996.

E-COMMERCE AT AOL

Nearly 9 million U.S. households had shopped via the Internet in 1998, generating $7.8 billion in online retail sales, according to a report from Forrester Research, Inc. By 2003, more than 40 million U.S. households will shop online, producing $108 billion in revenues, and accounting for 6 percent of U.S. consumer retail spending. "The Internet is the first medium that really solves the marketers dilemma. It lets consumers seek information about a particular brand and enables them to buy it quickly, thereby simplifying the entire purchase process," says Berlow.

The potential of e-commerce became clear during the 1998 holiday season when AOL members spent $1.2 billion online. During this period, almost 1.25 million AOL members made their first purchase online. AOL estimates that 84% of its present members "window-shopped" and 44% bought merchandise through AOL or aol.com. Members who shopped online were very satisfied with the experience. They said they appreciated AOL's ease-of-use, convenience, and security of their online transactions, not to mention the great values offered by many of its retail partners. Moreover, research indicates that once members shop online, they develop an e-commerce habit, purchasing one to three items during the first three months alone.

This success was largely due to the 110 merchants and "e-tailers" (such as Eddie Bauer, J. Crew, Toys "Я" Us, Macy's, Barnes and Noble, Digital Chef, etc.) AOL partnered with to enhance AOL's Shopping Channel. AOL's e-commerce goal is to offer consumers "one-stop shopping" convenience, branded products and services, and value. What are AOL shoppers buying? Based on traffic averages to AOL Shopping Channel departments, the Toys, Kids, and Babies category held the number-one spot, followed closely by apparel. The average AOL holiday shopper purchased two items online every week during the holiday shopping season and spent about $54. Since interactive marketing and e-commerce are growing rapidly, AOL continues to attract e-tailers, other mass merchandisers, and service providers to sell their wares through AOL. Recent agreements with Unilever, First USA (credit cards), Citibank, AmeriTrade and e-trade (brokerage), eBay (online auctions), and *The Financial Times* (news) are among many companies partnering with AOL in long-term relationships.

ENSURING THE FUTURE OF E-COMMERCE

While the future of e-commerce looks bright, AOL faces several important issues. According to a Boston Consulting Group study, retailers must continue to offer consumers compelling reasons to shop online. Further

advances in convenience, cost, choice, customization, communication, and control must be made for more consumers to change their shopping behavior. With respect to *convenience,* "portals" are expected to be the primary means consumers will use to access and browse the Internet. While AOL is the world's leading Internet online service, it will need to promote and defend its leadership position against the efforts made by Disney, Microsoft, Yahoo!, and other formidable competitors.

In terms of *cost,* consumers should benefit by reduced costs for products and services purchased online because they can order directly from the manufacturers, retailers, or service providers. Moreover, they can search the Internet for the best price for the products and services they desire. However, retailers often must resolve channel conflicts that arise as a result of selling online directly to consumers. Specifically, some potential online retailers may hesitate or choose not to sell online because it might cannibalize sales through existing channels, alienate existing distribution partners, and, more important, lower margins for all in the channel. Retailers who choose to sell online may be able to charge a premium if they provide superior service, enhanced features, and a strong brand presence not found on other online portals' or retailers' Web sites.

Giving consumers *choice* in their Internet experience will continue to be critical. AOL must continue to expand the choices available to its subscribers, both in terms of the types (shopping, e-mail, messaging, news, etc.) and depth (number of retail partners for each shopping category) of the services offered. These retail partners must provide AOL members with a broad array of goods and services available for browsing or purchasing online. To date, AOL has offered the most comprehensive array of top brand names and it must continue to do so.

As Dell Computer, Mattel, and other companies have demonstrated, "build-to-order" systems allow customers to *customize* their product and service purchases with the feature set they want and at a price they can afford. For AOL and its partners, the continued integration of manufacturing, database, customer service, and fulfillment or service delivery systems must provide consumers with the customization they desire. In addition, *communications* issues must be resolved. Cable modems, digital subscriber lines (DSL), fiber optics, and other technologies need to become more readily available to consumers. AOL's alliances with telecommunication companies and acquisitions of Personalogic and When.com are a start but more needs to be done.

Finally, online consumers want to *control* the personal and financial data that is gathered during an online visit or transaction. Specifically, they want to know whether their data is safeguarded, how it is used by e-tailers, and if it is disclosed to other organizations for marketing purposes. Consumers also want the ability to restrict access to morally objectionable Web sites and "chat rooms" and to protect their computers from "viruses." International Data Corporation estimates the market for Internet security software to reach $7.4 billion by 2002. While AOL has taken the lead in developing its "Parental Controls" as well as an extensive privacy policy, additional efforts may be required as international e-commerce grows and demands for a "safer" Internet increase. Overall, con-

sumers seem to be—as was the case with ATM machines—becoming more and more comfortable with shopping online, which is—at least on AOL—safer than handing over your credit card at a restaurant.

Questions

1   How has the vision or mission of AOL changed from the early 1980s to the present?

2   How does AOL facilitate online shopping or e-commerce? What are the advantages and disadvantages of using AOL for online shopping versus the more traditional method you may use?

3   What challenges has AOL overcome to attract both consumers and retailer partners to engage in e-commerce? What challenges do they still need to overcome?

4   What are the six "C's" of e-commerce and what is AOL's marketing strategy in each of these areas?

CHAPTER NINE

TURNING MARKETING INFORMATION INTO ACTION

9

AFTER READING THIS CHAPTER YOU SHOULD BE ABLE TO:

- Identify a five-step marketing research approach leading to marketing actions.

- Describe how secondary and primary data are used in marketing, including the uses of questionnaires, observations, experiments, and panels.

- Understand how information technology enables information systems to be used that link massive amounts of marketing information to meaningful marketing actions.

- Recognize alternative methods to forecast sales and use the lost-horse and linear trend extrapolation methods to make a simple forecast.

LISTENING TO CONSUMERS EARLY: TRYING TO REDUCE MOVIE RISKS!

"Blockbuster movies" are essential for today's fiercely competitive world of filmmaking—examples being movies such as *Titanic* (opposite page), *Shoeless Joe*, *Teenie Weenies*, and *3000!*

What's in a Movie Name?   Can't remember those last three movies—even after scratching your head? Well, it turns out marketing research on moviegoers in test screenings discovered they had problems with those names, too. Here's the title these three movies started with, where they wound up, and the reason:

- *Shoeless Joe* became *Field of Dreams* because audiences thought Kevin Costner might be playing a homeless person.
- *Teenie Weenies* became *Honey, I Shrunk the Kids* when moviegoers couldn't relate the original title to what they saw in the movie.
- *3000* became *Pretty Woman* when audiences didn't have a clue what the number meant. Hint: It was the number of dollars to spend an evening with Julia Roberts.[1]

Filmmakers want movie titles that are concise, attention-getting, capture the essence of the film, and have no legal restrictions—basically the same factors that make a good brand name.

How Filmmakers Try to Reduce Risk   Is research on movie titles expensive? Very! But the greater expense is selecting a bad title that can kill a movie and cost the studio millions of dollars. So with today's big budget films costing almost $70 million to produce and market,[2] how can movie studios reduce their risk of losses? One part of reducing risk: Use marketing research to recruit people to attend sneak previews (test screenings) of a forthcoming movie and then ask them questions that might bring about improvements in the final edit of the movie.

Without reading ahead, think about answers to these questions:

- Whom would you recruit for these test screenings?
- What questions would you ask them to help you in editing or modifying the title or parts of the film?

While *Field of Dreams* and *Star Wars Episode I: The Phantom Menace* have little else in common, they—like virtually every major U.S. movie produced today—use test screenings to obtain the key reactions of consumers likely to be in the target market. Figure 9–1 summarizes some of the key questions that are used in these test screenings, both to select the people for the screenings and to obtain key reactions of those sitting in the screenings.

Here are some examples of changes to movies that have resulted from this kind of marketing research:

- *Making the plot move faster.* Disney cut a duet by Pocahontas and John Smith in *Pocahontas* because it got in the way of the action and confused test audiences.[3]
- *Reaching a market segment more effectively.* More action footage was added for Kevin Costner when preview screening showed young males were less enthusiastic about *The Bodyguard* than young females.[4]
- *Changing an ending.* *Fatal Attraction* had probably the most commercially successful "ending-switch" of all time. In its sneak previews, audiences liked everything but the ending, which had Alex (Glenn Close) committing suicide and managing to frame Dan (Michael Douglas) as her murderer by leaving his fingerprints on the knife she used. The studio shot $1.3 million of new scenes for the ending that regular audiences eventually saw.[5]

Sometimes studios get the pleasant news in test screenings that a movie or plot "works" with an audience. This was the case when James Cameron, writer-director of *Titanic,* sat in on the first test screening of his $200 million epic and watched the audience go wild, a huge relief after months of bad vibes.[6] Because the first two weeks of

FIGURE 9–1
Marketing research questions asked in test screenings of movies, and how they are used

POINT WHEN ASKED	KEY QUESTIONS	USE OF QUESTION(S)
Before the test screening	• How old are you? • How frequently do you pay to see movies? • What movies have you seen in the last three months?	Decide if person fits profile of target audience for movie. If yes, invite to test screening. If not, don't invite.
After the test screening	• What do you think of the title? What title would you suggest?	Change movie title.
	• Were any characters too distasteful? Who? How?	Change aspects of some characters.
	• Did any scenes offend you? Which ones? How?	Change scenes.
	• How did you like the ending? If you didn't like it, how would you change it?	Change or clarify ending.
	• Would you recommend the movie to a friend?	Overall indicator of liking and/or satisfaction with movie.

attendance after a movie's release often determine its success or failure today, marketing research on names and plots are even more important than in the past.[7]

Besides test screenings, motion picture firms also use marketing research to do concept tests of proposed plots and to design and test the $17 million marketing campaigns that support a typical movie's launch.[8] These examples show how marketing research is linked to marketing strategy and decisive actions, the main topic of this chapter. Marketing research is often used to help a firm develop sales forecasts, the final topic in the chapter.

THE ROLE OF MARKETING RESEARCH

To place marketing research in perspective, we can describe (1) what it is, (2) some of the difficulties in conducting it, and (3) the process marketing executives can use to make effective decisions.

What Marketing Research Is and Does

Marketing research is the process of defining a marketing problem and opportunity, systematically collecting and analyzing information, and recommending actions to improve an organization's marketing activities.[9]

A Means of Reducing Risk and Uncertainty   Marketing research attempts to identify and define both marketing problems and opportunities and to generate and evaluate marketing actions. Although marketing research can provide few answers with complete assurance, it can reduce risk and uncertainty to increase the likelihood of the success of decisions made by marketing managers.

How can Fisher-Price do marketing research on young children who can't even fill out a questionnaire? For the answer, see the text.

Fisher-Price
www.fisherprice.com

FIGURE 9–2

Five-step marketing research approach leading to marketing actions

Why Good Marketing Research Is Difficult

The dilemmas faced by marketing researchers when trying to assess consumers' willingness to buy products or services they are not familiar with illustrate why good marketing research requires great care—especially because of the inherent difficulties in asking consumers questions. For example,

- Do consumers really know whether they are likely to buy a particular product that they probably have never thought about before?
- Even if they know the answer, will they reveal it? When personal or status questions are involved, will people give honest answers?
- Will their actual purchase behavior be the same as their stated interest or intentions? Will they buy the same brand they say they will?

A task of marketing research is to overcome these difficulties to provide useful information on which marketing executives can act.

Steps in Making Effective Decisions

A **decision** is a conscious choice from among two or more alternatives. All of us make many such decisions daily. At work we choose from alternative ways to accomplish an assigned task. At college we choose from alternative courses. As consumers we choose from alternative brands. No magic formula guarantees correct decisions all the time.

Managers and researchers have tried to improve the outcomes of decisions by using more formal, systematic approaches to *decision making,* the act of consciously choosing from alternatives. People who do not use some kind of system—and many do not—may make poor decisions. The systematic approach to making marketing decisions described in this chapter uses five steps and is shown in Figure 9–2. Although this five-step approach is used here to focus on marketing decisions, it provides a mental checklist for making any decision—either business or personal. These five steps are covered in the next sections.

CONCEPT CHECK

  1. What is marketing research?

  2. What are the five steps marketing research uses to help lead to marketing actions?

STEP 1: DEFINE THE PROBLEM

Toy designers at Fisher-Price Toys, the nation's top marketer of infant and preschool toys, had a problem some years back: They developed toys they thought kids would

like, but how could they be certain? To research the problem, Fisher-Price gets children to play at its state-licensed nursery school in East Aurora, New York. Behind one-way mirrors Fisher-Price designers and marketing researchers watch the children use—and abuse—the toys to develop better products.

Fisher-Price's toy testing shows how to define the problem and its two key elements: setting the research objectives and identifying resulting marketing actions suggested by the research. For example, the original model of a classic Fisher-Price toy, the chatter telephone, was simply a wooden phone with a dial that rang a bell. Observers noted, however, that the children kept grabbing the receiver like a handle to pull the phone along behind them, so a designer added wheels, a noisemaker, and eyes that bobbed up and down on an experimental version of the toy.

Set the Research Objectives

Objectives are the goals the decision maker seeks to achieve in solving a problem. Typical marketing objectives are increasing revenues and profits, discovering what consumers are aware of and want, and finding out why a product isn't selling well. For Fisher-Price the immediate research objective was to decide whether to market the old or new chatter telephone.

Identify Possible Marketing Actions

Effective decision makers specify **measures of success,** which are criteria or standards used in evaluating proposed solutions to the problem. Different research outcomes—on the measure of success—lead to different marketing actions. For the Fisher-Price problem, if a measure of success were the total time children spent playing with each of the two chatter telephone designs, the results of observing them would lead to clear-cut actions as follows:

PLAYTIME WITH DESIGN	POSSIBLE MARKETING ACTION
• Children spent more time playing with old design.	Continue with old design; don't introduce new design.
• Children spent more time playing with new design.	Introduce new design; drop old design.

One test of whether marketing research should be undertaken is if different outcomes will lead to different marketing actions. If all the research outcomes lead to the same action—such as top management sticking with the older design regardless of what the observed children liked—the research is useless and a waste of money. In this case research results showed that kids liked the new design, so Fisher-Price introduced its noise-making pull-toy telephone, which has become a toy classic and has sold millions.

Toy marketing research goes beyond manufacturers such as Fisher-Price. Every summer Digital Research, Inc., a marketing research firm, evaluates hundreds of toys to select *Family Fun* magazine's "Toy of the Year" award. More than 600 children "toy testers" are involved. And they've been right on the money in selecting Barney the TV dinosaur, Tickle Me Elmo, and Sing & Snore Ernie as hot toys—ones that jumped off retailer shelves later—but they missed Furby, which arrived too late to be judged.[10]

Most marketing researchers would agree with philosopher John Dewey's observation that "a problem well-defined is half-solved," but they know that defining a problem is an incredibly difficult, although essential, task. For example, if the objectives are too broad, the problem may not be researchable. If they are too narrow, the value of the research results may be seriously lessened. This is why marketing researchers spend so much time in defining a marketing problem precisely and writing a formal proposal describing the research to be done.[11]

STEP 2: DEVELOP THE RESEARCH PLAN

The second step in the marketing research process involves (1) specifying the constraints on the research activity, (2) identifying the data needed for marketing actions, and (3) determining how to collect the data.

Specify Constraints

The **constraints** in a decision are the restrictions placed on potential solutions by the nature and importance of the problem. Common constraints in marketing problems are limitations on the time and money available to solve the problem. Thus, Fisher-Price might set two constraints on its decision to select either the old or new version of the chatter telephone: the decision must be made in 10 weeks, and no research budget is available beyond that needed for collecting data in its nursery school.

Identify Data Needed for Marketing Actions

Often marketing research studies wind up collecting a lot of data that are interesting but are irrelevant for the marketing decisions that result in marketing actions. In the Fisher-Price chatter telephone case, it might be nice to know the children's favorite colors, whether they like wood or plastic toys better, and so on. In fact, knowing answers to these questions might result in later modifications of the toy, but right now the problem is to select one of two toy designs. So this study must focus on collecting data that help managers make a clear choice between the two chatter telephone designs.

Determine How to Collect Data

Determining how to collect useful marketing research data is often as important as actually collecting the data—Step 3 in the process, which is discussed later. Two key elements in deciding how to collect the data are (1) concepts and (2) methods.

Concepts   One valuable type of concept, a *hypothesis,* is a conjecture or idea about the relationship of two or more factors or what might happen in the future. Hypotheses that lead to marketing actions can come from many sources: theoretical reasoning, marketing studies, technical breakthroughs, informal conversations, educated guesses, and even suggestions from customers.

For example, with the chatter telephone, Fisher-Price managers have the hypothesis that adding a noisemaker, wheels, and eyes to the basic design will make the toy more fun for children and increase sales. The proposed design is really a *new-product concept,* a tentative description of a product or service the firm might offer for sale.

Marketing research turned up these "toys of the year," except Furby—who was late to the starting gate.

Methods   *Methods* are the approaches that can be used to collect data to solve all or part of a problem. For example, if you are the marketing researcher at Fisher-Price responsible for the chatter telephone, you face a number of methods issues in developing your research plan, including the following:

- Can we actually ask three- or four-year-olds meaningful questions they can answer about their liking or disliking of the two designs?
- Are we better off not asking them questions but simply observing their behavior?
- If we simply observe the children's behavior, how can we do this in a way to get the best information without biasing the results?

Millions of other people have asked similar questions about millions of other products and services. In the case of the chatter telephone, let's assume you decide that actual questioning of the children is unreliable, that you want to use a method that involves actually watching them play with the toys, and that to avoid biasing the children's behavior you make your observation from behind a one-way glass.

How can you find and use the methodologies that other marketing researchers have found successful? Information on useful methods is available in tradebooks, textbooks, and handbooks that relate to marketing and marketing research. Some periodicals and technical journals such as the *Journal of Marketing* and the *Journal of Marketing Research,* published by the American Marketing Association, summarize methods and techniques valuable in addressing marketing problems. Of course, a Fisher-Price marketing executive must apply the methods that have worked for others to the particular problems that Fisher-Price faces. Special methods vital to marketing are (1) sampling and (2) statistical inference.

Marketing researchers often select a group of distributors, customers, or prospects, ask them questions, and treat their answers as typical of all those in whom they are interested. There are two ways of sampling, or selecting representative elements from a population: probability and nonprobability sampling. **Probability sampling** involves using precise rules to select the sample such that each element of the population has a specific known chance of being selected. For example, if a college wants to know how last year's 1,000 graduates are doing, it can put their names in a bowl and randomly select 50 names of graduates to contact. The chance of being selected—50/1,000 or 0.05—is known in advance, and all graduates have an equal chance of being contacted. This procedure helps select a sample (the 50 graduates) that is representative of the entire population (the 1,000 graduates) and allows conclusions to be drawn about the entire population.

When time and budget are limited, researchers may opt for **nonprobability sampling** and use arbitrary judgments to select the sample so that the chance of selecting a particular element may be unknown or 0. If the college decides arbitrarily to select the 50 graduates from last year's class who live closest to the college, many members of the class have been arbitrarily eliminated. This has introduced a bias that makes it dangerous to draw conclusions about the population from this geographically restricted sample.

The method of **statistical inference** involves drawing conclusions about a *population* (the "universe" of all people, stores, or salespeople about which they wish to generalize) from a *sample* (some elements of the universe) taken from that population. To draw accurate inferences about the population, the sample elements should be representative of that universe. If the sample is not typical, bias can be introduced, resulting in bad marketing decisions.

CONCEPT CHECK

1. How do research objectives relate to marketing actions?

2. What does *constraints* mean?

3. What is the difference between concepts and methods?

STEP 3: COLLECT RELEVANT INFORMATION

Collecting enough relevant information to make a rational, informed marketing decision sometimes simply means using your knowledge to decide immediately. At other times it entails collecting an enormous amount of information at great expense.

Figure 9–3 shows how the different kinds of marketing information fit together. **Data,** the facts and figures pertinent to the problem, are divided into two main parts: secondary data and primary data. **Secondary data** are facts and figures that have already been recorded before the project at hand, whereas **primary data** are facts and figures that are newly collected for the project.

Secondary Data

Secondary data divide into two parts—internal and external secondary data—depending on whether the data come from inside or outside the organization needing the research.

Internal Secondary Data   Data that have already been collected and exist inside the business firm or other organization are internal secondary data. These include financial statements (such as the firm's balance sheet and income statement), research reports, customer letters, sales reports on customer calls, and customer lists.

External Secondary Data   Published data from outside the firm are external secondary data. Probably the best known are U.S. Census Bureau reports. The *U.S. Census of Population* is published every 10 years and provides detailed information on American households, such as number of people per household, their ages, their sex, household income, and education of the head of the household. These are basic sources of information used by manufacturers and retailers to identify characteristics and trends of ultimate consumers.

Other census reports are vital to business firms selling products and services to organizations. The *U.S. Census of Manufacturers,* published about every five years, lists

FIGURE 9–3
Types of marketing
information

the number and size of manufacturing firms by industry group (the North American Industry Classification System described in Chapter 7). The *U.S. Census of Retail Trade,* also published about every five years, provides comparable detailed information on retailers. In addition, trade associations, universities, and business periodicals provide detailed data of value to marketing researchers. Useful marketing information from online databases from these kinds of organizations has skyrocketed in recent years. The Web Link box provides examples.

A number of different kinds of marketing research organizations serve the needs of their clients. These range from specialized syndicated services that provide a standard set of data on a regular basis such as the Nielsen Media Research's TV ratings to suppliers that contract with clients to conduct a complete marketing research project.

New marketing data services have now emerged that offer *single-source data,* information provided by a single firm on household demographics and lifestyle, purchases, TV viewing behavior, and responses to promotions such as coupons and free samples.[12] The significant advantage of single-source data is the ability of one service to collect, analyze, and interrelate all this information. BehaviorScan, offered by Information Resources, Inc., tracks about 60,000 households in 26 U.S. market areas. Campbell Soup's Swanson frozen dinners used the information from a single-source data service to shift a TV ad campaign from a serious to light theme and increase sales of Swanson dinners 14 percent.[13]

Advantages and Disadvantages of Secondary Data   A general rule among marketing people is to use secondary data first and then collect primary data. Two important advantages of secondary data are (1) the tremendous time savings if the data have already been collected and published and (2) the low cost (e.g., most census reports are available for only a few dollars each). Furthermore, a greater level of detail is often available through secondary data. Because the U.S. Census Bureau can require business establishments to report information about themselves, its industry data usually are more complete than if a private organization attempted to collect them.

WEB LINK   **Online Databases Useful in Marketing**

Information in online databases available through the Internet divide into two categories: (1) indexes to articles in publications, which are accessed through keyword searches, and (2) statistical and directory data on households, products, and companies.

Online databases of indexes, abstracts, and full-text information from journals and periodicals include:

- Lexis-Nexis' Academic Universe, which gives full-text information from more than 650 U.S. periodicals and abstracts from more than 1000 sources. (www.lexis-nexis.com)
- ProQuest databases from UMI, Inc., which contain academic articles from more than 800 management, marketing, and business periodicals and journals. (www.umi.com)
- General BusinessFile ASAP from Information Access Company, which contains references, abstracts, and full-text articles from more than 1,000 U.S. and international business and industry publications. (www.library.iacnet.com)

Statistical and directory information about households, products, and companies through online databases include:

- Moody's Business and Financial Information, which gives data on more than 23,000 domestic and international public companies that are traded on the NYSE, AMEX, and NASDAQ stock exchanges. (www.fisonline.com)
- Dow Jones Interactive from Dow Jones & Company (publisher of *The Wall Street Journal*), which provides up-to-the-minute business news; secondary research reports on companies, industries, and countries; and up to 25 years of historical pricing on thousands of securities. (www.dowjones.com)
- STAT-USA from the Department of Commerce, which provides domestic and international business, trade, and economic information from more than 50 U.S. government agencies. (www.stat-usa.gov)

Some of these sites are accessible only if a subscription fee has been paid by an organization. To check out these sites, access your college or university Web site, click on the icon for your library, and then click on these or other useful databases to which your institution subscribes.

However, these advantages must be weighed against some significant disadvantages. First, the secondary data may be out of date, especially if they are U.S. Census data collected only every 5 or 10 years. Second, the definitions or categories might not be quite right for your project. For example, suppose you are interested in the age group from 13 to 16, but many census data age statistics appear only from the 10 to 14 and 15 to 19 age groupings. Finally, because the data are collected for another purpose, they may not be specific enough for your needs as a marketing researcher. In such cases it may be necessary to collect primary data.

CONCEPT CHECK

1. What are methods?

2. What is the difference between secondary and primary data?

3. What are some advantages and disadvantages of secondary data?

Primary Data

There are really only two ways to collect primary data, the original data for a marketing study: (1) by observing people and (2) by asking them questions.

Observational Data   Facts and figures obtained by watching, either mechanically or in person, how people actually behave is the way marketing researchers collect **observational data.** National TV ratings, such as those of the Nielsen Media Re-

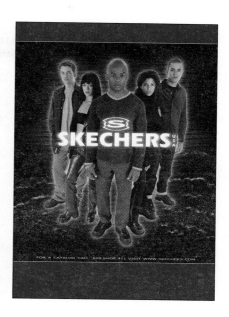

How do you do marketing research on things as diverse as toothbrushes, soap pads, and fashion products for teenagers? For some creative answers, see the text.

Oral-B Laboratories
www.oralb.com

search shown in Figure 9–4, are an example of mechanical observational data collected by a "people meter," which is attached to TV sets in 5,000 homes across the country. The people meter is supposed to measure who in the household is watching what program on every TV set owned. The Nielsen TV ratings in Figure 9–4 are the percentage of people-meter households whose TV sets were tuned to the program. Because there are an estimated 99.4 million TV households in the U.S., a single Nielsen rating point represents 1 percent, or 994,000 households.

Precision in Nielsen ratings is critical because a change of 1 percentage point can mean gaining or losing up to $50 million during the main viewing season since advertisers pay rates based on the size of audience for a TV program. Programs that have consistently low ratings—less than 9 percent or 10 percent—often can't get advertisers and are dropped from the air.

The people meter's limitations—as with all observational data collected mechanically—relate to how its measurements are taken. Critics of people meters aren't so sure the devices are measuring large segments of the population, such as young people at bars or parties. Competitive services have started that hope to do a better job of measuring these hard-to-reach groups in an unbiased way.[14]

Watching consumers in person or by videotaping them are other observational approaches. For example, Aurora Foods observes how consumers bake cakes in its Duncan Hines test kitchens to see if the baking instructions on the cake mix box are understood and followed correctly. Gillette marketing researchers actually videotaped consumers brushing their teeth in their own bathrooms to see how they really brush—not just how they *say* they brush. The result: Gillette's new Oral-B Cross Action toothbrush that's supposed to do a better job—at $4.99 each![15]

Personal observation is both useful and flexible, but it can be costly and unreliable when different observers report different conclusions in watching the same event. Also, although observation can reveal *what* people do, it cannot easily determine *why* they do it, such as why they are buying or not buying a product. This is a principal reason for using questionnaires.

FIGURE 9–4
Nielsen ratings of the top 10 national television programs from February 2, 1999 through February 7, 1999

RANK	PROGRAM	NETWORK	NIELSEN RATING
1	ER	NBC	20.3
2	Frasier	NBC	17.0
3	Friends	NBC	16.9
4	NBC Sunday Night Movie (The '60's Pt. 1)	NBC	15.1
5	60 Minutes	CBS	14.8
6	Touched by an Angel	CBS	14.7
7	Veronica's Closet	NBC	14.1
8	Jesse	NBC	13.5
9	Dateline NBC—Monday	NBC	13.0
10	CBS Sunday Movie (Night Ride Home)	CBS	12.3

Questionnaire Data **Questionnaire data** are facts and figures obtained by asking people about their attitudes, awareness, intentions, and behaviors. Because so many questions might be asked in questionnaires, it is essential that the researcher concentrate on those directly related to the marketing problem at hand. Many marketing researchers divide questionnaire data used for hypothesis generation from those used for hypothesis evaluation.

Marketing studies for *hypothesis generation* involve a search for ideas that can be evaluated in later research. Hamburger Helper didn't fare too well with consumers when General Mills introduced it. Initial instructions called for cooking a half pound of hamburger separately from the noodles or potatoes, which were later mixed with the hamburger. *Individual interviews* (a single researcher asking questions of one respondent) showed that consumers (1) didn't think it contained enough meat and (2) didn't want the hassle of cooking in two different pots. So the Hamburger Helper product manager changed the recipe to call for a full pound of meat and to allow users to prepare it in one dish; this converted a potential failure into a success.[16]

Focus groups are informal sessions in which 6 to 10 past, present, or prospective customers are directed by a discussion leader, or moderator, to identify what they do and don't like about the firm's products and its competitors' products, how they use the products, and special needs they have that the products don't address. Often tape recorded and conducted in special interviewing rooms with a one-way mirror, these groups enable marketing researchers and managers to hear and watch consumer reactions. The informality and peer support in an effective focus group uncover ideas that are often difficult to obtain with individual interviews.

In the mid-1990s 3M sought ways to push further into the home-care business and decided to target the wool soap pads niche, which was dominated by giants SOS and Brillo. 3M ran eight focus groups around the United States and heard consumers complain that standard wool pads scratched their expensive cookware. These interviews led to 3M's internationally successful Scotch-Brite® Never Scratch soap pad.[17]

Finding "the next big thing" for consumers has become the obsession not only for food companies but also for firms in many other industries.[18] The result is that in the 1990s many marketing researchers have come to rely on techniques that are far more basic—many would say bizarre—than more traditional individual or focus group interviews. These "fuzzy front end" methods attempt to identify elusive consumer tastes or trends far before typical consumers have recognized them themselves. Examples of unusual ways to collect consumer data and their results include the following:

• Having consumers take a photo of themselves every time they snack resulted in General Mills' Homestyle "Pop Secret" popcorn, which delivers the real butter and bursts of salt in microwave popcorn that consumers thought they could only get from the stovetop variety.[19]

- Having children and teenagers compete in a contest to submit designs for a new catsup label resulted in 60,000 designs from which Heinz picked three to test on 10 million bottles of catsup.[20]

Unusual techniques are also being used to try to spot trends early. Some examples include:

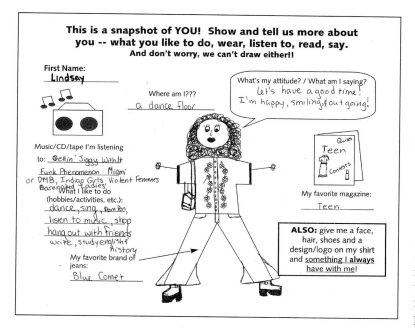

- Having teenagers complete a drawing was used by researchers at Teenage Research Unlimited to help discover what teenagers like, wear, listen to, and read.[21]
- Hiring "cool hunters," people with tastes far ahead of the curve, to identify the "next big things" likely to sweep popular culture. Wet Seal uses this method to anticipate teenage girls' fashion picks such as slip dresses, fitted angora sweaters, and hooded sweaters with zippers.[22] Skechers spots footwear trends using this method.

In *hypothesis evaluation* the marketing researcher tests ideas discovered in the hypothesis generation stage to help the marketing manager recommend marketing actions. This test usually is a mail, telephone, personal, fax, or Internet survey of a large sample of past, present, or prospective consumers. In choosing between these alternatives, the marketing researcher has to make important trade-offs to balance cost against the expected quality of information obtained. Personal interview surveys have a major advantage of enabling the interviewer to be flexible in asking probing questions or getting reactions to visual materials, but are very costly to conduct. Mail surveys are usually biased because those most likely to respond have had especially positive or negative experiences with the product or brand. While telephone interviews allow flexibility, they are increasingly difficult to complete because respondents may hang up on the interviewer, who they believe may be a telemarketer. Fax and Internet surveys are restricted to respondents having the technologies.

The high cost of reaching respondents in their homes using personal interviews has led to a dramatic increase in the use of *mall intercept interviews,* personal interviews of consumers while on visits to shopping centers. These face-to-face interviews reduce the cost of personal visits to consumers in their homes while providing the flexibility to show respondents visual cues such as ads or actual product samples. Technology has even made possible "virtual shopping trip" simulations by enabling a mall intercept respondent to "walk" through store aisles and "buy" products while sitting in front of a computer screen.

Figure 9–5 shows typical problems to guard against in wording questions to obtain meaningful answers from respondents. For example, in a question of whether you eat at fast-food restaurants regularly, the word *regularly* is ambiguous. Two people might answer "yes" to the question, but one might mean "once a day" while the other means "once or twice a year." Both answers appear as "yes" to the researcher who tabulates them, but they suggest that dramatically different marketing actions be directed to each of these two prospective consumers. Therefore, it is essential that marketing research questions be worded precisely so that all respondents interpret the same question similarly.

FIGURE 9–5
Typical problems in wording
questions

PROBLEM	SAMPLE QUESTION	EXPLANATION
Leading question	Why do you like Wendy's fresh meat hamburgers better than those of competitors made with frozen meat?	Consumer is led to make statement favoring Wendy's hamburgers.
Ambiguous question	Do you eat at fast-food restaurants regularly? ☐ Yes ☐ No	What is meant by word *regularly*—once a day, once a month, or what?
Unanswerable question	What was the occasion for your eating your first hamburger?	Who can remember the answer? Does it matter?
Two questions in one	Do you eat Wendy's hamburgers and chili? ☐ Yes ☐ No	How do you answer if you eat Wendy's hamburgers but not chili?
Nonexhaustive question	Where do you live? ☐ At home ☐ In dormitory	What do you check if you live in an apartment?
Nonmutually exclusive answers	What is your age? ☐ Under 20 ☐ 20–40 ☐ 40 and over	What answer does a 40-year-old check?

Suppose tonight after school you open a letter from your state legislator and see a questionnaire that includes the two questions shown here:

QUESTION	YES	NO
Environment 1 Do you think that our state should enact Gestapo-type laws that would reward citizens for spying on and reporting on other citizens for such offenses as air or water pollution?	☐	☐
University autonomy 2 Would you agree that administrators of state-supported educational institutions should be discharged for pampering revolutionaries?	☐	☐

He is looking for a "no" answer to the first question and a "yes" to the second. He is "stacking the deck," using leading questions. Reporting statistical results of such biased questions would give a very distorted picture of the constituents' actual opinions. (Unfortunately these are real questions from a legislator's survey!) Hence the proper phrasing of a question is vital in uncovering useful marketing information.

Figure 9–6 shows a number of different formats for questions taken from a Wendy's survey that assessed fast-food restaurant preferences among present and prospective consumers. Question 1 is an example of an *open-end question,* which the respondent can answer in his or her own words. In contrast, questions in which the respondent simply checks an answer are *closed-end* or *fixed alternative questions.* Question 2 is an example of the simplest fixed alternative question, a *dichotomous question* that allows only a "yes" or "no" answer.

A fixed alternative question with three or more choices uses a *scale.* Question 5 is an example of a question that uses a *semantic differential scale,* a seven-point scale in which the opposite ends have one- or two-word adjectives that have opposite meanings. For example, depending on how clean the respondent feels that Wendy's is, he or she would check the left-hand space on the scale, the right-hand space, or one of the five intervening points. Question 6 uses a *Likert scale,* in which the respondent is asked to indicate the extent to which he or she agrees or disagrees with a statement.

Wendy's changes continuously in response to changing customer wants, while keeping its "Fresh Ingredients, Quality Choices" image.

Wendy's Restaurant

www.wendys.com

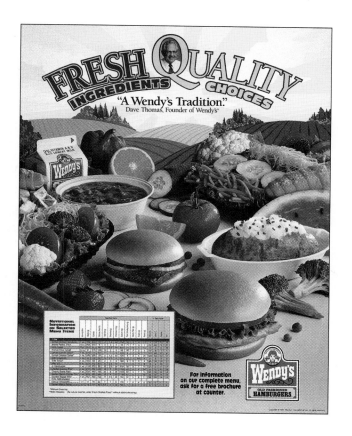

The questionnaire in Figure 9–6 is an excerpt of a precisely worded survey that provides valuable information to the marketing researcher at Wendy's. Questions 1 to 8 inform him or her about the likes and dislikes in eating out, frequency of eating out at fast-food restaurants generally and at Wendy's specifically, and sources of information used in making decisions about fast-food restaurants. Question 9 gives details about the personal characteristics of the respondent or the respondent's household, which can be used in trying to segment the fast-food market, a topic discussed in Chapter 10.

Electronic technology has revolutionized traditional concepts of "interviews" or "surveys." Today, respondents can walk up to a kiosk in a shopping center, read questions off a screen, and key their answers into a computer on a touch screen. Even fully automated telephone interviews exist: an automated voice questions respondents over the telephone, who key their replies on a touch-tone telephone.

Panels and Experiments   Two special ways that observations and questionnaires are sometimes used are panels and experiments.

Marketing researchers often want to know if consumers are changing their behavior over time, and so they take successive measurements of the same people. A *panel* is a sample of consumers or stores from which researchers take a series of measurements. For example, in this way a consumer's switching from one brand of breakfast cereal to another can be measured. Nielsen's national TV ratings are developed from its people-meter households that make up a panel and are measured repeatedly through time.

An *experiment* involves obtaining data by manipulating factors under tightly controlled conditions to test cause and effect. The interest is in whether changing one of the independent variables (a cause) will change the behavior of the dependent variable that is studied (the result).

FIGURE 9–6
Sample questions from
Wendy's survey

1 What things are most important to you when you decide to eat out and go to a
  restaurant?

  _____

  _____

  _____

  _____

  _____

2 Have you eaten fast-food restaurant food in the past three months?
  ☐ Yes   ☐ No
3 If you answered "yes" to Question 2, how often do you eat fast food?
  ☐ Once a week or more ☐ Two or three times a month ☐ Once a month or less
4 How important is it to you that a fast-food restaurant satisfy you on the following
  characteristics? Check the box that describes your feelings.

CHARACTERISTIC	VERY IMPORTANT	SOMEWHAT IMPORTANT	IMPORTANT	UNIMPORTANT	SOMEWHAT UNIMPORTANT	VERY UNIMPORTANT
Taste of food	☐	☐	☐	☐	☐	☐
Cleanliness	☐	☐	☐	☐	☐	☐
Price	☐	☐	☐	☐	☐	☐
Variety on menu	☐	☐	☐	☐	☐	☐

5 Check the space on the scale below that describes how you feel about Wendy's on
  the characteristics shown.

CHARACTERISTIC	CHECK THE SPACE DESCRIBING HOW WENDY'S IS		
Taste of food	Tasty	_ _ _ _ _ _	Not tasty
Cleanliness	Clean	_ _ _ _ _ _	Dirty
Price	Inexpensive	_ _ _ _ _ _	Expensive
Variety on menu	Wide	_ _ _ _ _ _	Narrow

In marketing experiments, the independent variables of interest are often one or
more of the marketing mix variables, such as the product features, price, or advertising
used. The ideal dependent variable usually is a change in purchases of an individual,
household, or entire organization. For example, food companies often use "test markets," a kind of marketing experiment discussed in Chapter 11, to determine if consumers will buy a new brand or product. And in late 1998 Wal-Mart opened three
"experimental" stand-alone supermarkets to gauge consumer acceptance before deciding to open others.[23]

A potential difficulty with experiments is that outside factors (such as actions of
competitors) can distort the results of an experiment and affect the dependent variable
(such as sales). A researcher's task is to identify the effect of the marketing variable of
interest on the dependent variable when the effects of outside factors in an experiment
might hide it.

Advantages and Disadvantages of Primary Data   Compared with secondary data, primary data have the advantage of being more timely and specific to the
problem being studied. The main disadvantages are that primary data are usually far
more costly and time consuming to collect than secondary data.

FIGURE 9–6
(*concluded*)

6 Check the box that describes your agreement with the statement.

STATEMENT	STRONGLY AGREE	AGREE	DON'T KNOW	DISAGREE	STRONGLY DISAGREE
Adults like to take their families to fast-food restaurants.	☐	☐	☐	☐	☐
Our children have a say in where the family eats.	☐	☐	☐	☐	☐

7 How important is this information about fast-food restaurants?

SOURCE OF INFORMATION	VERY IMPORTANT SOURCE	SOMEWHAT IMPORTANT SOURCE	NOT AN IMPORTANT SOURCE
Television	☐	☐	☐
Newspapers	☐	☐	☐
Billboards	☐	☐	☐
Mail	☐	☐	☐

8 In the past three months, how often have you eaten at each of these three fast-food restaurants?

RESTAURANT	ONCE A WEEK OR MORE	TWO OR THREE TIMES A MONTH	ONCE A MONTH OR LESS
Burger King	☐	☐	☐
McDonald's	☐	☐	☐
Wendy's	☐	☐	☐

9 Please answer the following questions about you and your household.
  a Are you ☐ Male ☐ Female
  b Are you ☐ Single ☐ Married ☐ Other (widowed, divorced)
  c How many children under age 18 live in your home?
    ☐ 0 ☐ 1 ☐ 2 ☐ 3 ☐ 4 ☐ 5 or more
  d What is your age?
    ☐ 24 or under ☐ 25–39 ☐ 40 or over
  e What is your approximate total annual household income?
    ☐ Less than $15,000 ☐ $15,000–$30,000 ☐ More than $30,000

CONCEPT CHECK

1. A mail questionnaire asks you, "Do you eat pizza?" What kind of question is this?

2. Does a mail, telephone, or personal interview survey provide the greatest flexibility for asking probing questions?

3. What is the difference between a panel and an experiment?

Information Technology and Marketing Actions

Today's marketing managers can be drowned in such a flood of information that they have difficulty making effective, timely decisions. The solution: Find ways to manage the information properly. While a decade ago managers talked about "manufacturing information systems" or "marketing information systems," the lines of separation of information among the various departments in a firm are now disappearing. So today, all generally fall under the broader term of **information technology,** which involves designing and managing computer and communication networks to provide an information system to satisfy an organization's needs for data storage, processing, and access.

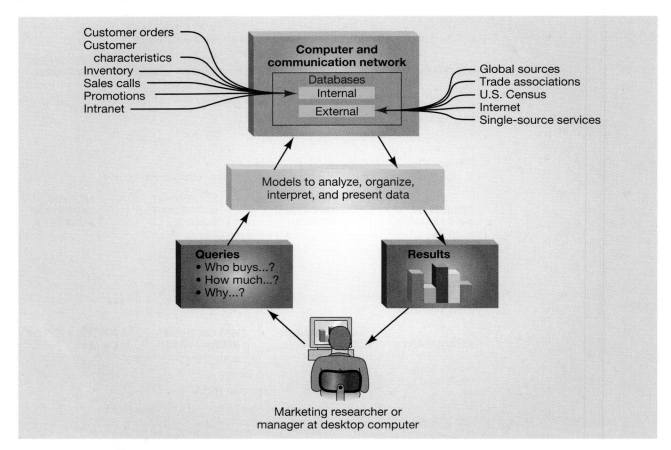

FIGURE 9–7
How marketing researchers
and managers use information
technology to turn information
into action

Key Elements of an Information System   Figure 9–7 shows how marketing researchers and managers use information technology to frame questions that provide answers that enable them to take marketing actions. At the bottom of Figure 9–7 the marketer queries the databases in the information system with marketing questions needing answers. These questions go through models of the relationships among the data contained in the databases to be able to access the key bits of information needed. The databases form the core of the computer and communication networks that collect and store millions of bits of information. These databases range from internal sources like customer orders and characteristics to external ones that are available from the Internet, U.S. Census, and trade associations. After the search of the databases, the models select the pertinent data—often summarizing them in tables and graphics for easy interpretation.

Querying the Information System   What kind of questions might the marketer ask the information system? Here are some examples:

1. What are the demographic characteristics of our present customers?
2. How do these demographic characteristics vary by kind of product purchased from our line?
3. What kinds of TV programs and magazines do these customers watch or read?
4. If we advertise on a specific TV program, how many of our existing customers and prospective new ones are we likely to reach?
5. What incremental sales revenue can we expect from this TV ad?

Note that these questions are progressively more complex and move subtly from asking questions about known facts to making sophisticated "what if" projections. For example, the first two questions have exact answers that are available from the firm's internal records. The third question may require calculating the relationship between data in different databases. The last two questions require making assumptions to build hypothetical models about the relationships between different marketing variables—models that are self-correcting as new data become available.

An information system such as this permits a marketing manager to reach decisions using *sensitivity analysis*, asking what if questions to determine how changes in a factor such as price or advertising affect marketing results such as sales revenues or profits.[24]

Peopleless Marketing Actions   With today's information systems, some marketing actions require a lot of people input. Other actions require almost none. Catalog companies such as Lands' End, Fingerhut, and Spiegel use sophisticated "data mining"—hunting through the computer databases for tiny nuggets of information about customers—to reach them more efficiently. For example, Fingerhut studies about 3,500 variables over the lifetime of a consumer's relationship; it found that customers who had changed residences are three times as likely as regular customers to buy tables, fax machines, and decorative products but no more likely to buy jewelry or footwear. So Fingerhut has created a catalog targeted at consumers who have recently moved—a somewhat people-intensive marketing action.[25]

Today's information technology and systems have also made some marketing actions possible with almost no people involved. For example, "mass customization" has enabled Levi's retail clerks to ask a customer a few questions, take computer measurements, and deliver a personal pair of jeans in about three weeks. Custom Foot retail outlets do the same for shoes—requiring a lot of computer power and only a little people power.[26] And you can place an Internet order for your preferred configuration of a Dell computer that goes directly to its production line, resulting in the delivery of this computer within a week—all with few Dell marketers involved.

STEP 4: DEVELOP FINDINGS AND RECOMMENDATIONS

Mark Twain once observed, "Collecting data is like collecting garbage. You've got to know what you're going to do with the stuff before you collect it." Thus, marketing data and information have little more value than garbage unless they are analyzed carefully and translated into findings and recommendations for the marketing managers responsible for action. Let's illustrate this process of converting marketing information to action—not garbage—with a case example.

Assume you are doing marketing research for cranberry juice for Ocean Spray's product manager, whose immediate task is to take it into Asian and European markets.[27] You have some special challenges. Because the word "cranberry" isn't a part of any foreign language, you have to (1) find a name for the juice, (2) design a package, and (3) develop ads that will encourage foreign consumers to try the new product and acquire a liking for its bittersweet taste. Your marketing research plan involves looking at Ocean Spray's internal secondary data to learn lessons from the past and collecting primary data on reactions of target market consumers in three Asian and three European countries to a series of proposed brand names, packages, and ads. Let's look at how the three components of Step 4 in our marketing research approach—developing findings and recommendations—applies to your Ocean Spray decisions.

Analyze the Data

In analyzing the primary data from Taiwan, one Asian country you are studying, you discover Ocean Spray—*Hoshien Pei*—sounds a bit like the U.S. name and translates

How can Ocean Spray do marketing research to introduce cranberry juice to Asian (left) and European (right) markets—when consumers there have never heard of cranberries? The text outlines its approach.

Ocean Spray Cranberries
www.oceanspray.com

as "healthy refreshment." Seems like a good start, perhaps justifying testing the name on a larger sample of prospective consumers. But you also learn from studying internal secondary data that uncontrollable factors can also affect your chances of success. When Ocean Spray previously tried to sell its cranberry juice to the British in bottles, belated marketing research showed that those consumers like their juice in boxes. This is a pretty clear indication that testing various designs of boxes makes sense in Great Britain, one of the European countries in your study.

Present the Findings

An important task of market researchers is to present their findings clearly to those responsible for actions. This involves getting to the heart of the matter while avoiding trivial issues, and delivering the results in clear English—without unnecessary obfuscation, a word illustrating exactly what *not* to do in presenting results to busy managers![28] Generally, effective presentations of marketing research results require organizing the data into meaningful tables, figures, and graphs. Let's assume that you and your product manager present findings to top management that show consumer reactions in three Asian and three European countries to samples of proposed (1) brand names, (2) packaging concepts, and (3) mock-ups of possible ads.

Make Recommendations

Findings aren't the same as recommendations for actions! For example, assume your findings in the previous element of Step 4 stated that two of the three Asian countries clearly preferred bottles to boxes and the third country was split about evenly. In contrast, all three European countries preferred their cranberry juice in boxes. These are the findings from your marketing research, but are not yet recommendations.

However, effective marketing research must move from simply making findings to the final stage of developing specific recommendations. Suppose that in considering a variety of production, distribution, and promotional factors you and your product manager conclude that a single packaging design must be used throughout Asia, the same logic applying to Europe. As a result your action recommendations on packaging to top management are: use bottles in Asia and boxes in Europe—the packaging shown in the Ocean Spray ads on the opposite page.

STEP 5: TAKE MARKETING ACTIONS

Effective marketing research doesn't stop with findings and recommendations—someone has to put the recommendations into effect and monitor how the decisions turned out, which is the essence of Step 5.

Implement the Recommendations

"Making something happen" with the research results—putting them into action—is critical, or the research was a waste of time. In Ocean Spray's case let's assume that as product manager you decide on the ads shown on the opposite page and on the packaging shown in these ads. These actions are the whole point of the research: You have increased the chance of success of your cranberry juice in international markets and reduced your risk by undertaking systematic marketing research.

Evaluate the Results

Evaluating results is a continuing way of life for effective marketing managers. There are really two aspects of this evaluation process:

- *Evaluating the decision itself.* This involves comparing actual results with plans. If results don't achieve what is targeted, the manager must take corrective actions. Wearing your product manager's hat, if sales of bottled cranberry juices in Asia aren't up to plans, you must discover the reasons and correct the problem.
- *Evaluating the decision process used.* Perhaps the marketing research that was done on Ocean Spray's international markets was flawed. The task is to learn lessons that can improve future marketing research studies done by Ocean Spray.

Again, systematic marketing research cannot guarantee success. But it can improve a firm's success rate for its marketing decisions.

CONCEPT CHECK

1. In querying an information system, give an example of a question that might be answered directly from the data in the system versus a question that would need some kind of a model to obtain an answer.

2. In marketing research, what is the difference between developing findings and recommendations and taking marketing actions?

MARKET AND SALES FORECASTING

Forecasting or estimating the actual size of a market is often a key goal in a marketing research study. Good sales forecasts are important for a firm as it schedules production.[29] We will discuss (1) some basic forecasting terms, (2) two major approaches to forecasting, and (3) specific forecasting techniques.

Basic Forecasting Terms

Unfortunately, there are no standard definitions for some forecasting concepts, so it's necessary to take care in defining the terms used.

Market or Industry Potential The term **market potential,** or **industry potential,** refers to the maximum total sales of a product by all firms to a segment under specified environmental conditions and marketing efforts of the firms. For example, the market potential for cake mix sales to U.S. consumers in 2003 might be 12 million cases—what Pillsbury, Betty Crocker, Duncan Hines, and other cake mix producers would sell to American consumers under the assumptions that (1) past patterns of dessert consumption continue and (2) the same level of promotional effort continues relative to other desserts. If one of these assumptions proves false, the estimate of market potential will be wrong. For example, if American consumers suddenly become more concerned about eating refined sugar and shift their dessert preferences from cakes to fresh fruits, the estimate of market potential will be too high.

Sales or Company Forecast What one firm expects to sell under specified conditions for the uncontrollable and controllable factors that affect the forecast is the **sales forecast,** or **company forecast.** For example, Duncan Hines might develop its sales forecast of 4 million cases of cake mix for U.S. consumers in 2003, assuming past dessert preferences continue and the same relative level of advertising expenditures among it, Pillsbury, and Betty Crocker. If Betty Crocker suddenly cuts its advertising in half, Duncan Hines's old sales forecast will probably be too low.

With both market potential estimates and sales forecasts, it is necessary to specify some significant details: the product involved (all cake mixes, only white cake mixes, or only Bundt cake mixes); the time period involved (month, quarter, or year); the segment involved (United States, Southwest region, upper-income buyer, or single-person households); controllable marketing mix factors (price and level of advertising support); uncontrollable factors (consumer tastes and actions of competitors); and the units of measurement (number of cases sold or total sales revenues).

Two Basic Approaches to Forecasting

A marketing manager rarely wants a single number for an annual forecast, such as 5,000 units or $75 million in sales revenue. Rather, the manager wants this total subdivided into elements the manager works with, such as sales by product line or sales by market segment. The two basic approaches to sales forecasting are (1) subdividing the total sales forecast (top-down forecast) or (2) building the total sales forecast by summing up the components (buildup forecast).

Top-Down Forecast A **top-down forecast** involves subdividing an aggregate forecast into its principal components. A shoe manufacturer can use a top-down forecast to estimate the percentage of its total shoe sales in a state and develop state-by-state forecasts for shoe sales for the coming year. The "Survey of Buying Power"

	1998 Regional State Summaries of. . .					
Region/State	**Population**		**Effective Buying Income**		**Retail Sales**	
	Total Population (Thousands)	Percentage of U.S.	Total EBI ($000)	Percentage of U.S.	Total Retail Sales ($000)	Percentage of U.S.
Middle Atlantic	38,320.3	14.1793	684,011,632	15.5457	337,080,731	13.2381
New Jersey	8,078.3	2.9892	160,134,925	3.6394	78,290,968	3.0747
New York	18,197.6	6.7335	315,102,328	7.1614	142,486,171	5.5958
Pennsylvania	12,044.2	4.4566	208,774,378	4.7449	116,303,502	4.5676

FIGURE 9–8

U.S. population, effective buying income, and retail sales for selected states, 1998

published annually by *Sales and Marketing Management* magazine is a widely used source of such top-down forecasting information.

For example, as shown in Figure 9–8, the state of New York has 6.73 percent of the U.S. population, 7.16 percent of the U.S. effective buying income, and 5.60 percent of the U.S. retail sales. If the shoe manufacturer wanted to use a single factor related to expected shoe sales, it would choose the factor that has been most closely related to shoe sales historically, in this case the percentage of U.S. retail sales. The top-down forecast would then be that 5.60 percent of the firm's sales would be made in the state of New York.

Sometimes multiple factors are considered, such as the *buying power index* (BPI) developed by *Sales and Marketing Management* magazine that gives weights of 0.2, 0.5, and 0.3, respectively, to the three previously mentioned factors, as follows:

$$BPI = (0.2 \times \text{Percentage of population}) + (0.5 \times \text{Percentage of effective buying income}) + (0.3 \times \text{Percentage of retail sales})$$

$$= (0.2 \times 6.7335) + (0.5 \times 7.1614) + (0.3 \times 5.5958)$$

$$= 1.3467 + 3.5807 + 1.6787$$

$$= 6.606 = 6.6\%$$

Thus the BPI forecasts that 6.6 percent of the firm's shoe sales will occur in New York—significantly higher than if retail sales alone were used for the forecast. The forecast can be customized by using subclassifications of the "Survey of Buying Power" statistics. Population is reported by age group, effective buying income is reported in categories, and retail sales are reported by line of merchandise.

Buildup Forecast   A **buildup forecast** involves summing the sales forecasts of each of the components to arrive at the total forecast. It is a widely used method when there are identifiable components such as products, product lines, or market segments in the forecasting problem.

Figure 9–9 shows how Boeing's aerospace department uses the buildup approach to develop a sales forecast involving three broad categories of projects or products: (1) work currently under contract that can be forecast precisely, (2) follow-up work that is likely to result from current contracts, and (3) new business that results from Boeing's proposals for new business, which is difficult to forecast. Each of these three forecasts is the sum of a number of individual products or projects, which for simplicity are not

FIGURE 9-9
Buildup approach to a
two-year sales forecast for
Boeing's aerospace
department

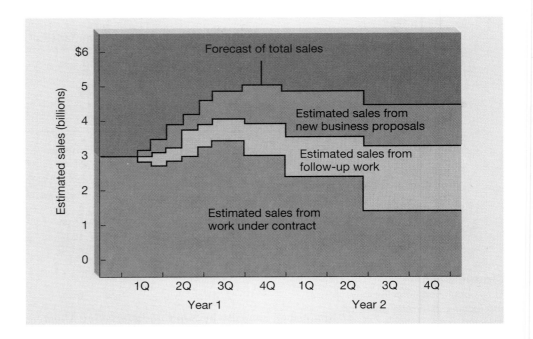

shown. In turn, forecasts for each of the three kinds of business can be summed to give the total sales forecast for the entire department.

Specific Sales Forecasting Techniques

Broadly speaking, three main sales forecasting techniques are available that can lead to the forecasts used in the top-down or buildup approaches. Ordered from least costly in terms of both time and money to most costly, these are (1) judgments of the decision maker, (2) surveys of knowledgeable groups, and (3) statistical methods.

Judgments of the Decision Maker   Probably 99.9 percent of all sales forecasts are judgments of the person who must act on the results of the forecast—the individual decision maker. An example is the forecasts of likely sales, and hence the quantity to order, for the thousands of items stocked in a typical supermarket that must be forecast by the stock clerk or manager. A **direct forecast** involves estimating the value to be forecast without any intervening steps. Examples appear in your daily life: How many quarts of milk should I buy? How much time should I allow to drive to the game? How much money should I get out of the automated teller machine? Your mind may go through some intervening steps but so quickly you're unaware of it.

Thus, in estimating the amount of money to get from the automated teller machine, you probably made some unconscious (or conscious) intervening estimates (such as counting the cash in your pocket or the special events you need cash for) to obtain your direct estimate. Lost-horse forecasting does this in a more structured way. A **lost-horse forecast** involves starting with the last known value of the item being forecast, listing the factors that could affect the forecast, assessing whether they have a positive or negative impact, and making the final forecast. The technique gets its name from how you'd find a lost horse: go to where it was last seen, put yourself in its shoes, consider those factors that could affect where you might go (to the pond if you're thirsty, the hayfield if you're hungry, and so on), and go there. For example, a product manager for Wilson's tennis rackets in 1999 who needed to make a sales forecast through 2003 would start with the known value of 1999 sales and list the positive factors (more tennis courts, more TV publicity) and the negative ones (competition from other sports, high prices of graphite and ceramic rackets) to arrive at the final series of annual sales forecasts.

Surveys of Knowledgeable Groups   If you wonder what your firm's sales will be next year, ask people who are likely to know something about future sales. Four common groups that are surveyed to develop sales forecasts are prospective buyers, the firm's salesforce, its executives, and experts.

A **survey of buyers' intentions forecast** involves asking prospective customers whether they are likely to buy the product during some future time period. For industrial products with few prospective buyers who are able and willing to predict their future buying behavior, this can be effective. For example, there are probably only a few hundred customers in the entire world for Boeing's largest airplanes, so Boeing carefully surveys these prospects to develop its sales forecasts and production schedules.

A **salesforce survey forecast** involves asking the firm's salespeople to estimate sales during a coming period. Because these people are in contact with customers and are likely to know what customers like and dislike, there is logic to this approach. However, salespeople can be unreliable forecasters—painting too rosy a picture if they are enthusiastic about a new product and too grim a forecast if their sales quota and future compensation are based on it.

A **jury of executive opinion forecast** involves asking knowledgeable executives inside the firm—such as vice presidents of marketing, research and development, finance, and production—about likely sales during a coming period. Although this approach is fast and includes judgments from diverse functional areas, it can be biased by a dominant executive whose judgments are deferred to by the others. Also, the technique raises questions about how valuable judgments are from executives who rarely come in contact with customers—such as vice presidents of finance and production.

A **survey of experts forecast** involves asking experts on a topic to make a judgment about some future event. For example, 20 electronics and TV experts might be asked when a 25-inch high-definition television (HDTV) set might sell to consumers for less than $1,000. One form of a survey of experts forecast is a *technological forecast,* which involves estimating when breakthroughs in basic science will occur. In 1963, experts used a technological forecast to estimate the year by which a limited degree of weather control would occur. Their estimate: 1990! While this technological forecast looks silly today, the technique is valuable in helping managers make new product development decisions.

Statistical Methods   The best-known statistical method of forecasting is **trend extrapolation,** which involves extending a pattern observed in past data into the future. When the pattern is described with a straight line, it is *linear trend extrapolation.* Suppose that in early 1995 you were a sales forecaster for the Xerox Corporation and had actual sales revenues running from 1984 to 1994 (Figure 9–10). Using linear trend extrapolation, you draw a line to fit the past data and project it into the future to give the forecast values shown for 1995 to 2004.

If in 1997 you want to compare your forecasts with actual results, you are in for a surprise—illustrating the strength and weakness of trend extrapolation. Trend extrapolation assumes that the underlying relationships in the past will continue into the future, which is the basis of the method's key strength: simplicity. If this assumption proves correct, you have an accurate forecast. However, if this proves wrong, the forecast is likely to be wrong. In this case your forecasts from 1995 through 1997 were too high, largely because of fierce competition in the photocopying industry.

In practice, marketing managers often use several of the forecasting techniques to estimate the size of markets important to them. Also, they often do three separate forecasts based on different sets of assumptions: (1) "best case" with optimistic assumptions,

FIGURE 9–10
Linear trend extrapolation of sales revenues of Xerox, made at the start of 1995

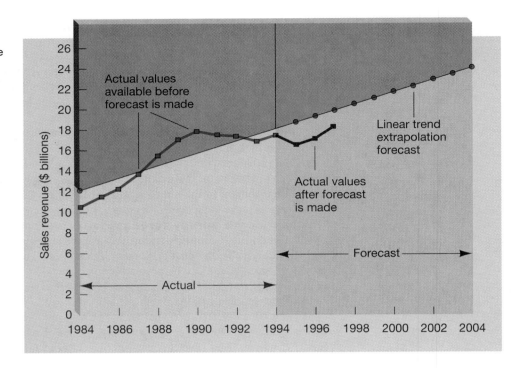

(2) "worst case" with pessimistic ones, and (3) "most likely case" with most reasonable assumptions.

CONCEPT CHECK

1. What is the difference between the top-down and buildup approaches to forecasting sales?

2. How do you make a lost-horse forecast?

3. What is linear trend extrapolation?

SUMMARY

1 Marketing research is the process of defining a marketing problem and opportunity, systematically collecting and analyzing information, and recommending actions to improve an organization's marketing activities. The chapter uses a five-step marketing research sequence that can lead to better decisions.
2 Defining the problem, step 1 in the sequence, involves setting the research objectives and identifying possible marketing actions.
3 Developing the research plan, step 2, requires specifying constraints on the problem, identifying data needed, and determining how to collect it.
4 Collecting relevant information, step 3, includes considering pertinent secondary and primary data. Secondary data have been recorded prior to the project and include those pieces of information internal and external to the organization. Primary data are collected specifically for the project and are obtained by either observing or questioning people.
5 Information technology enables massive amounts of marketing data to be stored, processed, and accessed. Today's in-

formation systems can be queried to guide decisions and even programmed to make ordering decisions.
6 Developing findings and recommendations is step 4. It involves analyzing data, presenting findings, and making recommendations to decision makers.
7 Step 5 in the sequence involves taking marketing actions by implementing the recommendations and evaluating results.
8 Two basic approaches to forecasting sales are the top-down and buildup methods. Three forecasting techniques are judgments of individuals, surveys of groups, and statistical methods.
9 Individual judgments are the most widely used forecasting methods. Two common examples are direct and lost-horse forecasts.
10 Asking questions of groups of people who are knowledgeable about likely future sales is another frequently used method of forecasting. Four such groups are prospective buyers, the salesforce, executives, and experts.
11 Statistical forecasting methods, such as trend extrapolation, extend a pattern observed in past data into the future.

KEY TERMS AND CONCEPTS

marketing research p. 227
decision p. 228
objectives p. 229
measures of success p. 229
constraints p. 230
probability sampling p. 231
nonprobability sampling p. 232
statistical inference p. 232
data p. 232
secondary data p. 232
primary data p. 232
observational data p. 234
questionnaire data p. 236

information technology p. 241
market or industry potential p. 246
sales or company forecast p. 246
top-down forecast p. 246
buildup forecast p. 247
direct forecast p. 248
lost-horse forecast p. 248
survey of buyers' intentions forecast p. 249
salesforce survey forecast p. 249
jury of executive opinion forecast p. 249
survey of experts forecast p. 249
trend extrapolation p. 249

INTERNET EXERCISE

WorldOpinion calls its Web site "the world's market research Web site." To check out the latest marketing research news, jobs that are available, and details of more than 8,500 research locations in 99 countries, go to www.worldopinion.com and do the following:

1   Click on the "Latest research news" banner on WorldOpinion's home page to read about the current news and issues facing the market research industry. Then, click on a topic of interest under "This week's news."

2   Click the "News Stand" button in the left-side menu of WorldOpinion's home page. Scroll down to the "Census and You" Web link and then click to go to the site. On the Census Web page, locate the "People" option on the menu bar and click. As of today, what is the total estimated population of the United States?

3   Under the "Research resources" banner, click on the "Links to major researchers' sites" link. Scroll down the Web page to obtain information on the following market research firms:

a. Click on the "Gallup" link to go to its home page. Then, click on the link that is specified to find out how The Gallup Organization conducts its polls.

b. Click on the "Abt Associates, Inc." and "Market Facts, Inc." links (or other firms of interest) to identify the market research positions currently available.

APPLYING MARKETING CONCEPTS AND PERSPECTIVES

1   Nielsen obtains ratings of local TV stations by having households fill out diary questionnaires. These give information on (*a*) who is watching TV and (*b*) what program. What are the limitations of this questionnaire method?

2   For the two questions in the legislator's questionnaire shown in the chapter, (*a*) what is the factual issue for which opinions are sought, and (*b*) how has the legislator managed to bias the question to get the answer he wants?

3   Rework question 1 in the legislator's questionnaire to make it an unbiased question in the form of (*a*) an open-end question and (*b*) a Likert scale question.

4   A rich aunt has decided to set you up in a business of your own choosing. To her delight, you decide on a service business—giving flying lessons in ultralight planes to your fellow college students. Some questions from the first draft of a mail questionnaire you plan to use are shown below. In terms of Figure 9–5, (*a*) identify the problem with each question and (*b*) correct it. NOTE: Some questions may have more than one problem.

a. Have you ever flown in commercial airliners and in ultralight planes?   ☐ Yes   ☐ No

b. Why do you think ultralights are so much safer than hang gliders? _____

c. At what age did you first know you like to fly?
☐ Under 10   ☐ 10 to 20   ☐ 21 to 30   ☐ Over 30

d. How much did you spend on recreational activities last year?
☐ $100 or less   ☐ $401 to $800   ☐ $1,201 to $1,600
☐ $101 to $400   ☐ $801 to $1,201   ☐ $1,600 or more

e. How much would you pay for ultralight flying lessons?

_____

f. Would you sign up for a class that met regularly?

☐ Yes   ☐ No

5 Aim toothpaste runs an in-store experiment evaluating a coupon along with (*a*) in-store ads in half the stores and (*b*) no in-store ads in the other half of the stores. The results of the Aim experiment are as follows, where a sales index of 100 indicates average store sales in the weeks before the experiment.

(*a*) What measures of success are appropriate? (*b*) What are your conclusions and recommendations? (*c*) How can marketers use experiments such as this?

6 Another field experiment with coupons and in-store advertising for Wisk detergent is run. The index of sales is as follows:

	WEEKS BEFORE COUPON	WEEK OF COUPON	WEEK AFTER COUPON
Without in-store ads	100	144	108
With in-store ads	100	268	203

What are your conclusions and recommendations?

7 The format in which information is presented to a harried marketing manager is often vital. (*a*) If you were a marketing manager and interrogated your information system, would you rather see the results as they are shown in question 5 or question 6? (*b*) What are one or two strengths and weaknesses of each format?

8 Suppose Fisher-Price wants to run an experimental and control group experiment to evaluate a proposed chatter telephone design. It has two different groups of children on which to run an experiment for one week each. The control group has the old toy telephone, whereas the experimental group is exposed to the newly designed pull toy with wheels, a noisemaker, and bobbing eyes. The dependent variable is the average number of minutes during the two-hour play period that one of the children is playing with the toy, and the results are as follows:

ELEMENT IN EXPERIMENT	EXPERIMENTAL GROUP	CONTROL GROUP
Experimental variable	New design	Old design
After measurement	62 minutes	13 minutes

Should Fisher-Price introduce the new design? Why?

9 Suppose you are to make a sales forecast using a top-down approach to estimate the percentage of a manufacturer's total U.S. sales going to each of the 50 states. You plan to use only a single factor—percentage of U.S. population, percentage of effective buying income, or percentage of retail sales. Which of the three factors would you use if your sales forecast were for each of the following manufacturers, and why? (*a*) Morton salt, (*b*) Christian Dior dresses, and (*c*) Columbia records.

10 Which of the following variables would linear trend extrapolation be more accurate for? (*a*) Annual population of the United States or (*b*) annual sales of cars produced in the United States by General Motors. Why?

CASE 9–1   ENVIROSELL

You probably take those security cameras in stores for granted. You've assumed that you are being watched by store employees to prevent 'shrinkage,' a euphemistic expression for shoplifting. Would it surprise you to know that some of those video cameras, which you may or may not be aware of, are there conducting marketing research?

THE COMPANY

Envirosell is a New York–based consumer behavior research company that studies the relationships between consumers, products, and commercial spaces. If a company wants to know whether a point-of-purchase (P-O-P) display is effective or how the effectiveness of an in-store promotion can be improved, Envirosell can tell them through analysis of how consumers relate to the retail environment and the products within it.

Many prominent consumer products companies including General Mills, Apple Computer, Fisher-Price, Hallmark Cards, and Warner-Lambert use Envirosell to help them understand how to better reach customers. U.S. and international banking institutions such as Citibank, Banca di Roma, Credit du Nord-France, Master-Card International; food service providers such as Burger King and Starbucks Coffee; retailers such as Waldenbooks/Brentano's and Blockbuster Entertainment; advertising and promotional agencies; and even the U.S. Postal Service, can be counted among Envirosell's customers.

THE SERVICE

Envirosell gathers data on consumer behaviors primarily through observational techniques. Trackers can be assigned to follow shoppers in stores to observe and record their behavior. Real-time video cameras and film cameras are used to record customer behavior for later analysis. A third source of information on customers is Envirosell's databases.

Paco Underhill, President of Envirosell, explains that a typical study may generate from 150 to 300 hours of videotape. What is unique about Envirosell, according to Underhill, is not how the data are collected but how they are analyzed. Envirosell takes the tape to their studios in New York where a spreadsheet is designed, and from 30,000 to 50,000 data points are collected about how customers buy for a given product-service category. This information is then presented to the client with graphs, maps, and short video clips to allow the client to watch how customers shop and purchase not just the client's product/service but how customers shop and purchase in that category. For example, Fisher-Price would learn how consumers purchase toys—how easily can the child or parent see and reach the toy; how many other alternatives are examined before making a decision; are certain Fisher-Price or competitive toys examined, considered,

selected, or ignored more than others; and how does the retail environment contribute to the way that the customer relates to the product?

Underhill feels that the Envirosell service complements other types of research that are commonly used. Attitudinal data, often collected with consumer surveys or focus groups, can provide insight into how consumers think. Scanning data utilizing the UPC (universal product code) information at point of sale tell companies what people are buying. Envirosell's observational techniques provides information on *how* customers buy. Envirosell will collect information on consumer attitudes as well but more as an addition to their observational techniques. Interviewers may intercept shoppers as they leave the store to ask them questions. This allows Envirosell to compare what customers say about what they did in the store with what they actually did based on observational data.

Underhill feels that the Envirosell service is particularly important for marketers as the retail environment grows more competitive. Increasingly, consumer decisions are made at point of sale, which means understanding how consumers buy a category is critical to successful marketing programs. In addition, the increasing emphasis on relationship marketing—with a goal towards long-term, cost-effective individual relationships with customers—means that organizations need database marketing. Database marketing or micromarketing provides the organization with continuously updated demographic and consumption information on the consumer. And that includes more than just the traditional attitudinal and sales data used in the past.

Questions

1 What are the advantages and disadvantages of Envirosell's observation techniques compared with consumer surveys?
2 Discuss how Envirosell's techniques might be combined with an in-store experiment. Give an example of a research project that could utilize such an approach.
3 What reliability issues are raised with video observational techniques? How can Envirosell attempt to control for these?

CHAPTER TEN

MARKET SEGMENTATION, TARGETING, AND POSITIONING

10

AFTER READING THIS CHAPTER YOU SHOULD BE ABLE TO:

- Explain what market segmentation is, when to use it, and the five steps involved in segmentation.

- Recognize the different factors used to segment consumer and organizational markets.

- Understand the significance of heavy, medium, and light users and nonusers in targeting markets.

- Develop a market-product grid to use in segmenting and targeting a market.

- Interpret a cross tabulation to analyze market segments.

- Understand how marketing managers position products in the marketplace.

SNEAKERS STORY: FROM LITTLE SKIRMISHES TO ALL-OUT WAR

What do you need in the sneaker business to stand out from the pack when consumers are faced—literally—with a "wall" of athletic shoes, like that shown on the opposite page?

This is the $12 billion dollar question for sneaker manufacturers around the world. The $12 billion is the estimated size of the global market for "sneakers," a term that includes all kinds of athletic shoes. To answer this question, sneaker manufacturers are searching for new market segments of consumers and ways to differentiate their products from everyone else's! This search for market segments applies to all sneaker manufacturers from the giants such as Nike and Reebok to smaller competitors such as New Balance and Vans.

Quick Quiz   Vans? Without peeking at the answers in the Marketing NewsNet[1] box on page 257, try to connect the age of the average consumer of the brand in the right column below to the appropriate brand (in alphabetical order) in the left column:

SNEAKER BRAND	CONSUMER'S AVERAGE AGE
New Balance	15
Nike	25
Reebok	33
Vans	42

Hint: "Shredders" are a key target market for one of the brands. Using age to segment markets is just one alternative available to sneaker manufacturers, as discussed later in the chapter.

The Sneaker Turmoil   The "walls" of sneakers in sporting goods and mass merchandiser stores across the United States are just one symptom of the turmoil in the industry. And times are gone when sneaker manufacturers give superstars such as Michael and Shaq—if you need last names, you're not a basketball fan—$15 million or

$30 million to use their name as a brand. Here are some other elements in the sneaker turmoil:

- Sales of men's sneakers are flat—not growing—and sales of high-tech basketball shoes are languishing.
- In 1994, sales of athletic footwear (sneakers) to American women 12 and older passed those of men in that age group for the first time.
- U.S. kids are turning from buying 10 to 15 pairs of sneakers a year to "wearing brown"—wearing brown boots or casual shoes, a trend that may accelerate when Michael Jordan's signature brands are less fashionable now that he has retired from basketball.[2]
- Pressed by public outcry, firms such as Nike and Reebok joined together to approve a monitoring system and code of conduct to curtail use of sweatshop labor abroad.[3]

Reebok's marketing research shows that while only 1 out of every 27 American girls were involved in sports in 1971, the ratio today is 1 in 3! Thus, Reebok has given special emphasis to the female segment. Reebok's strategy, designing shoes to satisfy needs of different customers, illustrates successful market segmentation, the main topic of this chapter. The intense competition in sneakers also explains why Reebok's segmentation strategy includes nonsneaker products, as discussed in detail in the next few pages. The Marketing NewsNet box also describes how small firms such as Vans and New Balance have succeeded using segmentation strategies to reach special groups of customers.

After discussing why markets need to be segmented, this chapter covers the steps a firm uses in segmenting and targeting a market and then positioning its offering to the marketplace.

WHY SEGMENT MARKETS?

A business firm segments its markets so it can respond more effectively to the wants of groups of prospective buyers and thus increase its sales and profits. Nonprofit organizations also segment the clients they serve to satisfy client needs more effectively while achieving the organization's goals. Let's use the dilemma of sneaker buyers finding their ideal Reebok shoes to describe (1) what market segmentation is and (2) when it is necessary to segment markets.

What Market Segmentation Means

People have different needs and wants, even though it would be easier for marketers if they didn't. **Market segmentation** involves aggregating prospective buyers into groups that (1) have common needs and (2) will respond similarly to a marketing action. The groups that result from this process are **market segments,** a relatively homogeneous collection of prospective buyers.

The existence of different market segments has caused firms to use a marketing strategy of **product differentiation,** a strategy that has come to have two different but related meanings. In its broadest sense, product differentiation involves a firm's using different marketing mix activities, such as product features and advertising, to help consumers perceive the product as being different and better than competing products. The perceived differences may involve physical features or nonphysical ones, such as image or price.

In a narrower sense, product differentiation involves a firm's selling two or more products with different features targeted to different market segments. A firm can get into trouble when its different products blend together in consumers' minds and don't reach distinct market segments successfully. The Reebok example discussed below

MARKETING NEWSNET

Shoe Segments for the Little Guys: Shredders versus Boomers

CUSTOMER VALUE

"It's not a lot of bucks," comments Lee Dansi, "considering one small mistake . . ." You can complete his sentence when you hear what he does for a living.

A top racer in the sport of street luge, Dansi earns less than $25,000 a year in endorsements and prizes lying on an eight-foot-long skateboard racing down hills at more than 70 miles an hour while dragging his feet on the concrete for control. But life has changed for Dansi: Vans, Inc., a California sneaker manufacturer, now pays him a salary, supplies his Vans shoes, and sponsors him in competitions.

Never heard of Vans shoes? Well, maybe you're a bit too old, as suggested by the answers to the quiz questions from the first page of the chapter:

SNEAKER BRAND	CONSUMER'S AVERAGE AGE
Vans	15
Nike	25
Reebok	33
New Balance	42

The recent successes of Vans and New Balance brands in their niche market segments are indicators of the revolutionary competition that has emerged in the sneaker market going into the twenty-first century. A look at their strategies also provides road maps for how small companies can succeed against giant competitors by responding effectively to needs of smaller segments of consumers.

Vans

Vans has targeted the rising wave of young athletes, often in the perilous world of board-riding sports. "Shredders," "riders," or simply "skaters" to their peers, the youth who wear Vans ride their skateboards down handrails, their snowboards down mountain trails, and their stunt bikes down slippery, muddy hills. In the next three years, these markets are expected to double. With $180 million in sales in 1998, Vans encourages its athletes—most of whom frown on Nike and Reebok shoes—to help it design its shoes and low-key ads. Selling for about $25 less than a pair of Nikes at retail, Vans had a breakthrough when the Footlocker chain started featuring the Vans line in its more than 1,000 outlets.

New Balance

Talk about boring: How about using a marketing strategy that includes moderate prices, extra-wide shoe widths available, links with podiatrists who insert foot supports in the extra-wide shoes—all actions targeted at serving the weightier (!) baby boomers. This is New Balance, whose $700 million of 1998 sales included customers such as Steve Jobs and Dustin Hoffman. Its $4 million advertising budget was less than 1 percent of Nike's $750 million and Reebok's $425 million. And you don't see well-known athletes in New Balance ads because, as its president says, "We'd just as soon pass the $10 to $15 a pair we need in a superstar endorsement to the customer."

Stay tuned for the future for Vans and New Balance! Now that they have demonstrated the importance of the shredder and boomer segments, Nike and Reebok are moving more aggressively to reach those customers.

shows how the company is using both market segmentation and product differentiation strategies.

Segmentation: Linking Needs to Actions   The definition of market segmentation first stresses the importance of aggregating—or grouping—people or organizations in a market according to the similarity of their needs and the benefits they are looking for in making a purchase. Second, such needs and benefits must be related to specific, tangible marketing actions the firm can take. These actions may involve separate products or other aspects of the marketing mix such as price, advertising or personal selling activities, or distribution strategies—the four Ps (product, price, promotion, place).

The process of segmenting a market and selecting specific segments as targets is the link between the various buyers' needs and the organization's marketing program

FIGURE 10–1
Market segmentation links market needs to an organization's marketing program

(Figure 10–1). Market segmentation is only a means to an end: In an economist's terms, it relates supply (the organization's actions) to demand (customer needs). A basic test of the usefulness of the segmentation process is whether it leads to tangible marketing actions to increase sales and profitability.

How Reebok's Segmentation Strategy Developed   In 1979 Paul Fireman, who had dropped out of college to run his family's business, wandered through an international trade fair and saw Reebok's custom track shoes. He bought the U.S. license from the British manufacturer and started producing top-of-the-line running shoes at about the time the running boom had peaked.

In a brilliant marketing decision, Fireman introduced the first soft-leather aerobic-dance shoe—the Reebok "Freestyle"—in 1982. The flamboyant colors of these Reebok designer sneakers captured the attention of aerobic-dance instructors and students alike. Figure 10–2 shows Reebok introduced a variety of shoes, from tennis shoes, children's shoes ("Weeboks"), and basketball shoes in 1984 to Step Trainers in 1991.[4]

A $3-billion-a-year sneaker business has a huge appetite and need for revenues. So in 1993 Reebok introduced its athletic clothing lines—including the Greg Norman Collection, and in 1997 it launched a line of Greg Norman golf shoes.[5] Choosing a product differentiation strategy stressing technology, in 1997 Reebok launched a line of "DMX-enhanced" running shoes that its ads said was "the best running shoe in the

FIGURE 10–2
Market-product grid showing how 10 different styles of Reebok shoes reach segments of customers with different needs

MARKET SEGMENT		PRODUCT									
GENERAL	GROUP WITH NEED	RUNNING SHOES (1981)	AEROBIC SHOES (1982)	TENNIS SHOES (1984)	BASKETBALL SHOES (1984)	CHILDREN'S SHOES (1984)	WALKING SHOES (1986)	CROSS-TRAINERS SHOES (1988)	STEP-TRAINERS SHOES (1991)	ATHLETIC CLOTHING (1993)	GOLF SHOES (1997)
Performance-conscious consumers (athletes)	Runners	P						P			
	Aerobic dancers		P					P			
	Tennis players			P				P			
	Basketball players				P			P			
	Step exercisers							S	P		
	Golfers									P	P
Fashion-conscious consumers (nonathletes)	Comfort- and style-conscious	S	S	S	S		S	S		S	
	Walkers	S	S	S	S		P	P		S	
	Children					P					

Key: P = Primary market; S = Secondary market

history of the world" and gave extra cushioning by distributing air through six chambers in the shoe to create extra cushioning.[6]

What segmentation strategy will Reebok use to take it into the twenty-first century? Only Reebok knows, but it will certainly involve trying to differentiate its products more clearly from its global competitors and perhaps target segments such as shredders, baby boomers, and global consumers.

Using Market-Product Grids   A **market-product grid** is a framework to relate the segments of a market to products offered or potential marketing actions by the firm. The grid in Figure 10–2 shows different markets of sneaker users as rows in the grid, while the columns show the different shoe products (or marketing actions) chosen by Reebok, so each cell in a market-product grid can show the estimated market size of a given product sold to a specific market segment.

The lightly shaded cells in Figure 10–2, labeled P, represent the primary market segment that Reebok targeted when it introduced each shoe. The darker shaded cells, labeled S, represent the secondary market segments that also started buying the shoe. In some cases, Reebok discovered that large numbers of people in a segment not originally targeted for a style of shoe bought it anyway. In fact, as many as 75 to 80 percent of the running shoes and aerobic-dance shoes are bought by nonathletes represented by the (1) comfort- and style-conscious and (2) walker segments shown in Figure 10–2—although walkers may object to being labeled "nonathletes." When this trend became apparent to Reebok in 1986, it introduced its walking shoes targeted directly at the walker segment.

Figure 10–2 also suggests one of the potential dangers of a firm's using market segmentation: subdividing an entire market into two or more segments, thereby increasing the competition from other firms that focus their efforts on a single segment. Notice that Reebok's strategy is to reach both the performance (athletes) and fashion (nonathletes) segments. To reach each segment more effectively, in the 1990s Reebok divided its U.S. operations into two separate units: "Technology," targeted at athletes, performance-oriented consumers, and children, and "Lifestyle," targeted at style-conscious consumers.

When to Segment Markets

A business firm goes to the trouble and expense of segmenting its markets when this increases its sales revenue, profit, and ROI. When its expenses more than offset the potentially increased revenues from segmentation, it should not attempt to segment its market. The specific situations that illustrate this point are the cases of (1) one product and multiple market segments, (2) multiple products and multiple market segments, and (3) "segments of one," or mass customization.

One Product and Multiple Market Segments   When a firm produces only a single product or service and attempts to sell it to two or more market segments, it avoids the extra costs of developing and producing additional versions of the product, which often entail extremely high research, engineering, and manufacturing expenses. In this case, the incremental costs of taking the product into new product segments are typically those of a separate promotional campaign or a new channel of distribution. Although these expenses can be high, they are rarely as large as those for developing an entirely new product.

Movies and magazines are single products frequently directed to two or more distinct market segments. Movie companies often run different TV commercials or magazine ads featuring different aspects of a newly released film (love, or drama, or spectacular scenery) that are targeted to different market segments. *Time* magazine now publishes more than 200 different U.S. editions and more than 100 international editions, each targeted at its own geographic and demographic segments and its own mix of advertisements. As shown above, Street and Smith's spring *Baseball* issue uses different covers in different regions of the United States, featuring a baseball star from that region. Although multiple TV commercials for movies and separate covers or advertisements for magazines are expensive, they are minor compared with the costs of producing an entirely new movie or magazine for another market segment.

Multiple Products and Multiple Market Segments   Reebok's different styles of shoes, each targeted at a different type of user, are an example of multiple products aimed at multiple markets. Manufacturing these different styles of shoes is clearly more expensive than producing one but seems worthwhile if it serves customers' needs better, doesn't reduce quality or increase price, and adds to the sales revenues and profits.

Marketing experts increasingly stress the two-tier marketing strategies—what some call "Tiffany/Wal-Mart strategies"—that will be necessary for the United States in the twenty-first century.[7] Since 1980 the U.S. middle class has declined in size; the wealthiest fifth has seen its income grow by 21 percent, and the bottom three-fifths have seen their incomes stagnate or even decline. The result is that many firms are now offering different products or services to high-end and low-end segments:

- Gap's Banana Republic chain sells blue jeans for $58, while its Old Navy stores sell a slightly different version for $22.
- General Motors' Saturn unit not only sells its no-haggling-on-price new cars but is aggressively marketing its "pre-owned" cars to reduce customer fears about buying a used car.
- The Walt Disney Company is carefully marketing two distinct Winnie-the-Poohs—such as the original line-drawn figures on fine china sold at Nordstroms and a cartoon-like Pooh on polyester bedsheets sold at Wal-Mart—and these Poohs don't play together on the shelves of the same retailer.

The lines between customer segments often blur, however, as shown by the Cadillacs and Mercedes in Wal-Mart parking lots.

The key to successful product differentiation and market segmentation strategies is to assess how they provide the organization with **synergy,** the increased customer value achieved through performing organizational functions more efficiently. The "increased customer value" can take many forms: more products, improved quality on existing products, lower prices, easier access to product through improved distribution, and so on. But the ultimate criterion is that customers should be better off as a result of the increased synergy.

Some car manufacturers have failed to achieve expected synergies as they offered many models and options to try to reach diverse market segments. They have concluded that the costs of developing, producing, marketing, and servicing dozens of slightly different models probably outweigh the higher prices that consumers are willing to pay for the wider array of choices. This is why General Motors recently reduced the number of basic car platforms from 12 to 5—a "car platform" being small front-wheel drive cars or large rear-wheel drive cars.

Segments of One: Mass Customization   American marketers are rediscovering today what their ancestors running the corner butcher shop or general store knew a century ago: Every customer is unique and has unique wants and needs. Economies of scale in manufacturing and marketing during the past century made mass-produced goods so affordable that most customers were willing to compromise their individual tastes and settle for standardized products. Today's information technology and flexible manufacturing and marketing processes have made mass customization possible, tailoring goods or services to the tastes of individual customers in high volumes and at a relatively low cost.

Paris Miki, the Japanese eyewear retailer with the most outlets in the world, is a case study of effective mass customization that enables customers to help design their own eyeglasses. Paris Miki spent five years developing a system—called the Eye Tailor in the United States—that eliminates the need for the customer to try on countless pairs of eyeglasses to find the right one. The system takes a digital photo of the customer's face, analyzes its key features, and collects statements from the customer about the kind of look desired. Working with the optician on details, customers receive a photo-quality picture of themselves with the proposed eyeglass design. A technician in the store grinds the lenses and assembles them to the frames within an hour.[8]

In the Paris Miki system, customers gain the benefits from information technology, flexible production, and personal choice to satisfy an individual customer's wants and needs.

CONCEPT CHECK

1. Market segmentation involves aggregating prospective buyers into groups that have two key characteristics. What are they?

2. What is product differentiation?

3. The process of segmenting and targeting markets is a bridge between what two marketing activities?

STEPS IN SEGMENTING AND TARGETING MARKETS

The process of segmenting a market and then selecting and reaching the target segments is divided into the five steps discussed in this section, as shown in Figure 10–3 on the next page. Segmenting a market is not a science—it requires large doses of common sense and managerial judgment.

FIGURE 10–3

The process of segmenting and targeting markets involves five key steps

	Steps in segmenting and targeting markets	
Identify market needs	• Form prospective buyers into segments • Form products to be sold into groups • Develop a market-product grid and estimate size of markets • Select target markets • Take marketing actions to reach target markets	Execute marketing program

Market segmentation and target markets can be abstract topics, so put on your entrepreneur's hat to experience the process. Suppose you own a Wendy's fast-food restaurant next to a large urban university that offers both day and evening classes. Your restaurant specializes in the Wendy's basics: hamburgers, french fries, Frosty milkshakes, and chili. Even though you are part of a chain and have some restrictions on menu and decor, you are free to set your hours of business and to undertake local advertising. How can market segmentation help?

Form Prospective Buyers into Segments

Grouping prospective buyers into meaningful segments involves meeting some specific criteria for segmentation and finding specific variables to segment the consumer or industrial market being analyzed.[9]

Criteria to Use in Forming the Segments   A marketing manager should develop segments for a market that meet five principal criteria:

* *Potential for increased profit and ROI.* The best segmentation approach is the one that maximizes the opportunity for future profit and ROI. If this potential is maximized through no segmentation, don't segment. For nonprofit organizations, the analogous criterion is the potential for serving client users more effectively.
* *Similarity of needs of potential buyers within a segment.* Potential buyers within a segment should be similar in terms of a marketing activity, such as product features sought or advertising media used.
* *Difference of needs of buyers among segments.* If the needs of the various segments aren't appreciably different, combine them into fewer segments. A different segment usually requires a different marketing action that, in turn, means greater costs. If increased revenues don't offset extra costs, combine segments and reduce the number of marketing actions.
* *Feasibility of a marketing action to reach a segment.* Reaching a segment requires a simple but effective marketing action. If no such action exists, don't segment.
* *Simplicity and cost of assigning potential buyers to segments.* A marketing manager must be able to put a market segmentation plan into effect. This means being able to recognize the characteristics of potential buyers and then assigning them to a segment without encountering excessive costs.

The Russians' love of the dark meat on a chicken—like legs and thighs—is an example of using these five criteria in global market segmentation. Americans prefer the white chicken meat. The result is that in 1997 about one in every four legs of U.S. chickens were eaten by Russians, a large part of $793 million of U.S. poultry exports there.[10]

DILBERT   **by Scott Adams**

MAIN DIMENSION	SEGMENTATION VARIABLES	TYPICAL BREAKDOWNS
CUSTOMER CHARACTERISTICS		
Geographic	Region	Northeast; Midwest; South; West
	City size	Under 10,000; 10,000–24,999; 25,000–49,999; 50,000–99,999; 100,000–249,999; 250,000–499,999; 500,000–999,999; 1,000,000 or more
	Metropolitan area	Metropolitan statistical areas (MSAs); consolidated metropolitan statistical areas (CMSAs); primary metropolitan statistical areas (PMSAs)
	Density	Urban; suburban; small town; rural
Demographic	Gender	Male; female
	Age	Under 6; 6–11; 12–17; 18–24; 25–34; 35–44; 45–54; 55–64; 65–74; 75 and over
	Race	African-American; Asian; Hispanic; White/Caucasian; other
	Life stage	Infant; preschool; child; youth; collegiate; adult; senior
	Birth era	Baby boomer (1946–1964); generation X (1965–1976); baby boomlet/generation Y (1977–present)
	Household size	1; 2; 3–4; 5 or more
	Residence tenure	Own home; rent home
	Marital status	Never married; married; separated; divorced; widowed
Socioeconomic	Income	Under $15,000; $15,000–$24,999; $25,000–34,999; $35,000–$49,999; $50,000–$74,999; $75,000 and over
	Education	Some high school or less; high school graduate (or GED); some college or vocational/associate degree; college graduate; post-graduate
Psychographic	Personality	Gregarious; compulsive; extroverted; aggressive; ambitious; etc.
	Values (VALS2)	Actualizers; fulfilleds; achievers; experiencers; believers; strivers; makers; strugglers
	Lifestyle	Use of one's time; values and importance; beliefs
BUYING SITUATIONS		
Outlet type	In-store	Department; specialty; outlet; convenience; supermarket; superstore/mass merchandiser; catalog
	Direct	Mail order/catalog; door-to-door; direct response; Internet
Benefits sought	Product features	Situation specific; general
	Needs	Quality; service; price/value; financing; warranty, etc.
Usage	Usage rate	Light user; medium user; heavy user
	User status	Nonuser; ex-user; prospect; first-time user; regular user
Awareness and intentions	Product knowledge	Unaware; aware; informed; interested; intending to buy; purchaser; rejection
Behavior	Involvement	Minimum effort; comparison; special effort

FIGURE 10–4

Segmentation variables and breakdowns for U.S. consumer markets

Ways to Segment Consumer Markets   Figure 10–4 shows a number of variables that can be used to segment U.S. consumer markets, many based on those planned for the 2000 U.S. Census. They are divided into two general categories: customer characteristics and buying situations. Some examples of how certain characteristics can be used to segment specific markets:

- *Region* (a geographical customer characteristic). Campbell's found that its canned nacho cheese sauce, which could be heated and poured directly onto nacho chips, was too hot for Americans in the East and not hot enough for those in the West and Southwest. The result: Today Campbell's plants in Texas and California produce a hotter nacho cheese sauce to serve their regions than that produced in the other plants.
- *Household size* (a demographic customer characteristic). More than half of all U.S. households are made up of only one or two persons, so Campbell's packages

What special benefit does a MicroFridge offer, and to which market segment might this appeal? The answer appears in the text.

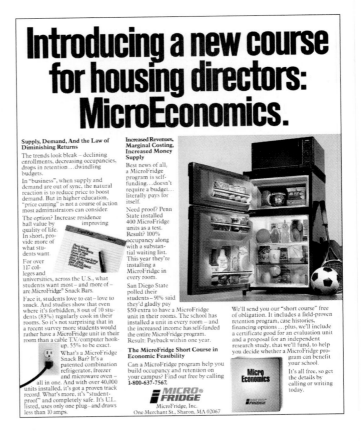

meals with only one or two servings—from Great Starts breakfasts to L'Orient dinners.

- *Lifestyle* (a psychographic customer characteristic). Psychographic variables are consumer activities, interests, and opinions. With 70 percent of women working outside the home, millions of men are performing shopping chores their fathers didn't. Because men buy 32 percent of frozen foods and 24 percent of baby food, more firms are targeting men with their ads.[11]
- *Benefits sought* (a buying situations characteristic). Important benefits offered to different customers are often a useful way to segment markets because they can lead directly to specific marketing actions, such as a new product, ad campaign, or distribution system. For example, MicroFridge targets its combination microwave/refrigerator/freezer at college dorm residents, who are often woefully short of space. Busy, time-short consumers are making computer teleshopping for groceries a reality for 10,000 households in Chicago and San Francisco; the online grocery-shopping service, called "Peapod," receives the computer order and then uses its own employees to fill the orders and its own drivers to deliver them.[12]
- **Usage rate** (quantity consumed or patronage—store visits—during a specific period; varies significantly among different customer groups). Airlines have developed frequent-flyer programs to encourage passengers to use the same airline repeatedly—a technique sometimes called "frequency marketing," which focuses on usage rate.

To obtain usage rate data, the Simmons Market Research Bureau periodically surveys about 20,000 adults 18 years of age and older to discover how the products and services they buy and the media they watch relate to their demographic characteristics. Figure 10–5 shows the results of a question Simmons asks about the respondent's frequency of use (or patronage) of "fast-food restaurants."[13]

Welcome to online grocery shopping! (1) With her son looking on, Patti Landry picks out what she wants at a nearby Jewel store, where (2) one Peapod employee selects the items. Another Peapod employee delivers it, so that she and her family can eat some of these items at dinner.

Peapod
www.peapod.com

 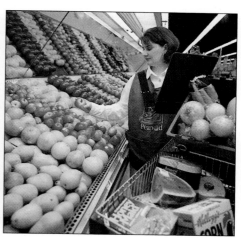

As shown in the right column of Figure 10–5, the importance of the segment increases as we move up the table. Among nonusers of these restaurants, prospects (who *might become* users) are more important than nonprospects (who are *never likely* to become users). Moving up the rows to the users, it seems logical that light users of these restaurants (1 to 5 times per month) are important but less so than medium users (6 to 13 times per month), who, in turn, are a less important segment than the critical group—the heavy users (14 or more times per month). The "Actual Consumption" column in Figure 10–5 shows how much of the total monthly usage of these restaurants are accounted for by the heavy, medium, and light users.

Usage rate is sometimes referred to in terms of the **80/20 rule,** a concept that suggests 80 percent of a firm's sales are obtained from 20 percent of its customers. The percentages in the 80/20 rule are not really fixed at exactly 80 percent and 20 percent, but suggest that a small fraction of customers provide a large fraction of a firm's sales. For example, Figure 10–5 shows that the 24.3 percent of the U.S. population who are heavy users of fast-food restaurants provide 46.9 percent of the consumption volume.

The "Usage Index per Person" column in Figure 10–5 emphasizes the importance of the heavy-user group even more. Giving the light users (1 to 5 restaurant visits per month) an index of 100, the heavy users have an index of 465. In other words, for every $1.00 spent by a light user in one of these restaurants in a month, each heavy user spends $4.65. This is the reason for the emphasis in almost all marketing strategies on effective ways to reach these heavy users. Thus, as a Wendy's restaurant owner you want to keep the heavy-user segment constantly in mind.

FIGURE 10–5
Patronage of fast-food restaurants by adults 18 years and older: Simmons Market Research Bureau Spring 1998 Survey

USER OR NONUSER	SPECIFIC SEGMENT	NUMBER (1,000S)	PERCENTAGE	ACTUAL CONSUMPTION (%)	USAGE INDEX PER PERSON	IMPORTANCE OF SEGMENT
Users	Heavy users (14+ per month)	46,565	24.3%	46.9%	465	High
	Medium users (6–13 per month)	57,303	29.8	39.2	317	
	Light users (1–5 per month)	64,294	33.5	13.9	100	
Total users		168,162	87.6	100.0	275	
Nonusers	Prospects	?	?	0	0	
	Nonprospects	?	?	0	0	
Total nonusers		23,861	12.4	0	0	Low
Total	Users and nonusers	192,023	100.0%	100.0%	—	

FIGURE 10–6
Comparison of various kinds
of users and nonusers for
Wendy's, Burger King, and
McDonald's restaurants

**Simmons Market Research
Bureau**

www.smrb.com

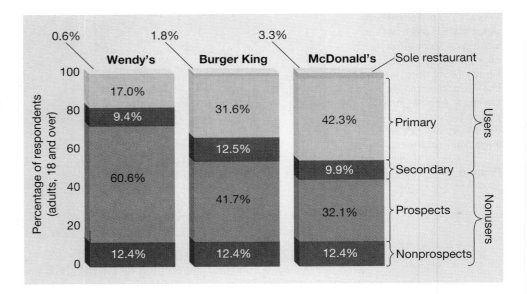

As part of the Simmons fast-food survey, restaurant patrons were asked if each restaurant was (1) the sole restaurant they went to, (2) the primary one, or (3) one of several secondary ones. This national information, shown in Figure 10–6, might give you, as a Wendy's owner, some ideas in developing your local strategy.[14] The Wendy's bar in Figure 10–6 shows that your sole (0.6 percent), primary (17.0 percent), and secondary (9.4 percent) user segments are somewhat behind Burger King and far behind McDonald's, so a natural strategy is to look at these two competitors and devise a marketing program to win customers from them.

The "nonusers" part of your own bar in Figure 10–6 also provides ideas. It shows that 12.4 percent of adult Americans don't go to fast-food restaurants in a typical month (also shown in Figure 10–5) and are really nonprospects—unlikely to ever patronize your restaurant. But the 60.6 percent of the Wendy's bar shown as prospects may be worth detailed thought. These adults use the product category (fast-food restaurants) but *do not* go to Wendy's. New menu items or new promotional strategies might succeed in converting these "prospects" to "users." One key conclusion emerges about usage: in market segmentation studies, some measure of usage or revenues derived from various segments is central to the analysis.

In determining one or two variables to segment the market for your Wendy's restaurant, very broadly we find two main markets: students and nonstudents. To segment the students, we could try a variety of demographic variables, such as age, sex, year in school, or college major, or psychographic variables, such as personality characteristics, attitudes, or interests. But none of these variables really meets the five criteria listed previously—particularly the fourth criterion about leading to a feasible marketing action to reach the various segments. Four student segments that *do* meet these criteria include the following:

- Students living in dormitories (college residence halls, sororities, fraternities).
- Students living near the college in apartments.
- Day commuter students living outside the area.
- Night commuter students living outside the area.

These segmentation variables are really a combination of where the student lives and the time he or she is on campus (and near your restaurant). For nonstudents who might be customers, similar variables might be used:

- Faculty and staff members at the university.
- People who live in the area but aren't connected with the university.
- People who work in the area but aren't connected with the university.

What variables might Savin use to segment the organizational markets for its answer to "digital document handling" problems? For the possible answer and related marketing actions, see the text.

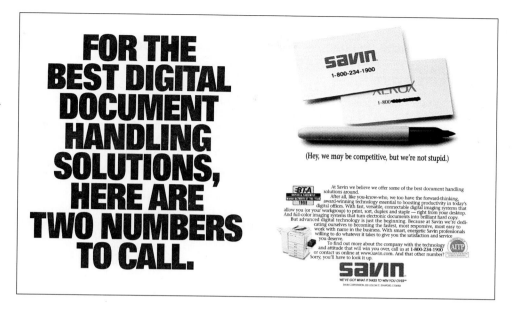

People in each of these segments aren't quite as similar as those in the student segments, which makes them harder to reach with a marketing program or action. Think about (1) whether the needs of all these segments are different and (2) how various advertising media can be used to reach these groups effectively.

Ways to Segment Organizational Markets   Variables for segmenting organizational markets are shown in Figure 10–7. A product manager at Savin responsible for its new digital document handling systems might use a number of these segmentation variables, as follows:

- *Location.* Firms located in a metropolitan statistical area (MSA) might receive a personal sales call, whereas those outside the MSA might be contacted by telephone.
- *NAICS code.* Firms categorized by the North American Industry Classification System (NAICS) code as manufacturers that deal with customers throughout the world might have different fax and document handling needs than do retailers or lawyers serving local customers.
- *Number of employees.* The size of the firm is related to the volume of digital documents produced for a given industry or NAICS, so firms with varying numbers of employees might be a specific target market for different Savin systems.

Form Products to Be Sold into Groups

As important as grouping customers into segments is finding a means of grouping the products you're selling into meaningful categories. If the firm has only one product or service, this isn't a problem, but when it has dozens or hundreds, these must be grouped in some way so buyers can relate to them. This is why department stores and supermarkets are organized into product groups, with the departments or aisles containing related merchandise. Likewise, manufacturers have product lines that are the groupings they use in the catalogs sent to customers.

What are the groupings for your restaurant? It could be the item purchased, such as a Frosty, chili, hamburgers, and french fries, but this is where judgment—the qualitative aspect of marketing—comes in. Students really buy an eating experience, or a meal that satisfies a need at a particular time of day, so the product grouping can be defined by meal or time of day as breakfast, lunch, between-meal snack, dinner, and

MAIN DIMENSION	SEGMENTATION VARIABLES	TYPICAL BREAKDOWNS
CUSTOMER CHARACTERISTICS		
Geographic	Global region	Domestic; international (Europe; South America; Asia; etc.)
	U.S. region	Northeast; Midwest; South; West
	Metropolitan area	Metropolitan statistical areas (MSAs); consolidated metropolitan statistical areas (CMSAs); primary metropolitan statistical areas (PMSAs)
	Density	Urban; surburban; small town; rural
Demographic	NAICS code	2-digit: sector; 3-digit: subsector; 4-digit: industry group; 5-digit: industry; 6-digit: U.S. industry
	NAICS sector	Agriculture, forestry, fishing, and hunting (11); mining (21); utilities (22); construction (23); manufacturing 31–33; etc.
	Number of employees	1–99; 100–499; 500–999; 1,000–4,999; 5,000 and over
	Annual sales	Under $1 million; $1 million–$9.9 million; $10 million–$49.9 million; $50 million–$99.9 million; $100 million–$499.9 million; $500 million–$999.9 million; $1 billion–$4.9 billion; $5 billion and over
	Number of stores or locations	1–9; 10–49; 50–99; 100–499; 500–999; 1,000 and over
BUYING SITUATIONS		
Nature of good	Kind	Product; service
	Where used	Installation; component; supplies
	Application	Office use; limited production use; heavy production use
Buying condition	Purchase location	Centralized; decentralized
	Who buys	Individual buyer; group of buyers
	Type of buy	New buy; modified rebuy; straight rebuy

FIGURE 10–7

Segmentation variables and breakdowns for U.S. organizational markets

after-dinner snack. These groupings are more closely related to the way purchases are actually made and permit you to market the entire meal, not just your french fries or Frosties.

Develop a Market-Product Grid and Estimate Size of Markets

Developing a market-product grid means labeling the markets (or horizontal rows) and products (or vertical columns), as shown in Figure 10–8. In addition, the size of the market in each cell, or the market-product combination, must be estimated. For your restaurant this involves estimating the number of, or sales revenue obtained from, each kind of meal that can reasonably be expected to be sold to each market segment. This is a form of the usage rate analysis discussed earlier in the chapter.

The market sizes in Figure 10–8 may be simple "guesstimates" if you don't have time for formal marketing research (as discussed in Chapter 9). But even such crude estimates of the size of specific markets using a market-product grid are far better than the usual estimates of the entire market.

Select Target Markets

A firm must take care to choose its target market segments carefully. If it picks too narrow a group of segments, it may fail to reach the volume of sales and profits it needs. If it selects too broad a group of segments, it may spread its marketing efforts so thin that the extra expenses more than offset the increased sales and profits.

Criteria to Use in Picking the Target Segments   There are two different kinds of criteria present in the market segmentation process: (1) those to use in divid-

FIGURE 10–8
Selecting a target market for
your fast-food restaurant next
to an urban university (target
market is shaded)

		PRODUCTS: MEALS			
MARKETS	**BREAK-FAST**	**LUNCH**	**BETWEEN-MEAL SNACK**	**DINNER**	**AFTER-DINNER SNACK**
STUDENT					
Dormitory	0	1	3	0	3
Apartment	1	3	3	1	1
Day commuter	0	3	2	1	0
Night commuter	0	0	1	3	2
NONSTUDENT					
Faculty or staff	0	3	1	1	0
Live in area	0	1	2	2	1
Work in area	1	3	0	1	0

Key: 3 = Large market; 2 = Medium market; 1 = Small market; 0 = No market.

ing the market into segments (discussed earlier) and (2) those to use in actually picking the target segments. Even experienced marketing executives often confuse these two different sets of criteria. The five criteria to use in actually selecting the target segments apply to your Wendy's restaurant this way:

- *Size.* The estimated size of the market in the segment is an important factor in deciding whether it's worth going after. There is really no market for breakfasts among dormitory students (Figure 10–8), so why devote any marketing effort toward reaching a small or nonexistent market?
- *Expected growth.* Although the size of the market in the segment may be small now, perhaps it is growing significantly or is expected to grow in the future. Night commuters may not look important now, but with the decline in traditional day students in many colleges, the evening adult education programs are expected to expand in the future. Thus, the future market among night commuters is probably more encouraging than the current picture shown in Figure 10–8.
- *Competitive position.* Is there a lot of competition in the segment now or is there likely to be in the future? The less the competition, the more attractive the segment is. For example, if the college dormitories announce a new policy of "no meals on weekends," this segment is suddenly more promising for your restaurant.
- *Cost of reaching the segment.* A segment that is inaccessible to a firm's marketing actions should not be pursued. For example, the few nonstudents who live in the area may not be economically reachable with ads in newspapers or other media. As a result, do not waste money trying to advertise to them.
- *Compatibility with the organization's objectives and resources.* If your restaurant doesn't have the cooking equipment to make breakfasts and has a policy against spending more money on restaurant equipment, then don't try to reach the breakfast segment.

As is often the case in marketing decisions, a particular segment may appear attractive according to some criteria and very unattractive according to others.

Choose the Segments   Ultimately, a marketing executive has to use these criteria to choose the segments for special marketing efforts. As shown in Figure 10–8, let's assume you've written off the breakfast market for two reasons: too small market size and incompatibility with your objectives and resources. In terms of competitive position and cost of reaching the segment, you choose to focus on the four student segments and not the three nonstudent segments (although you're certainly not going to turn away business from the nonstudent segments). This combination of market-product segments—your target market—is shaded in Figure 10–8.

Take Marketing Actions to Reach Target Markets

The purpose of developing a market-product grid is to trigger marketing actions to increase revenues and profits. This means that someone must develop and execute an action plan.

Your Wendy's Segmentation Strategy   With your Wendy's restaurant you've already reached one significant decision: There is a limited market for breakfast, so you won't open for business until 10:30 A.M. In fact, Wendy's first attempt at a breakfast menu was a disaster and was discontinued in 1986. Wendy's evaluates possible new menu items continuously, not only to compete with McDonald's and Burger King but with a complex array of supermarkets, convenience stores, and gas stations that sell reheatable packaged foods as well as new "easy-lunch" products.

Another essential decision is where and what meals to advertise to reach specific market segments. An ad in the student newspaper could reach all the student segments, but you might consider this "shotgun approach" too expensive and want a more focused "rifle approach" to reach smaller segments. If you choose three segments for special actions (Figure 10–9), advertising actions to reach them might include:

- *Day commuters* (an entire market segment). Run ads inside commuter buses and put flyers under the windshield wipers of cars in parking lots used by day commuters. These ads and flyers promote all the meals at your restaurant to a single segment of students—a horizontal cut through the market-product grid.
- *Between-meals snacks* (directed to all four student markets). To promote eating during this downtime for your restaurant, offer "Ten percent off all purchases between 2:00 and 4:30 P.M. during winter quarter." This ad promotes a single meal to all four student segments—a vertical cut through the market-product grid.
- *Dinners to night commuters.* The most focused of all three campaigns, this ad promotes a single meal to a single student segment. The campaign might consist of a windshield flyer offering a free Frosty with the coupon when the person buys a hamburger and french fries.

Depending on how your advertising actions work, you can repeat, modify, or drop them and design new campaigns for other segments you feel warrant the effort. This example of advertising your Wendy's restaurant is just a small piece of a complete marketing program using all the elements of the marketing mix.

Wendy's can target different market segments with different advertising programs.

FIGURE 10–9
Advertising actions to reach
specific student segments

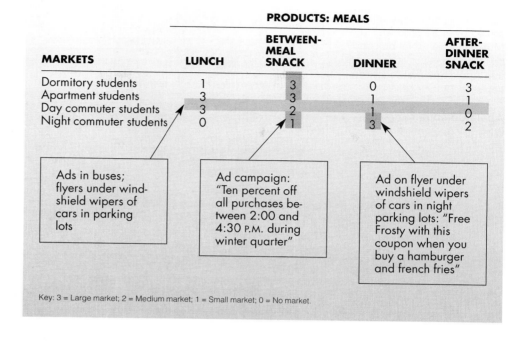

Key: 3 = Large market; 2 = Medium market; 1 = Small market; 0 = No market.

Apple's Ever-Changing Segmentation Strategy   Steven Jobs, John Scully, Michael Spindler, Gilbert Amelio, and—deja vu!—Steven Jobs! Apple Computer came full circle in 1997 with the return of Steve Jobs. Each of these Apple CEOs presided over some of the most innovative and questionable market-product decisions during their tenure.[15]

Steven Jobs and Stephen Wozniak didn't realize they were developing today's multibillion-dollar PC industry when they invented the Apple I in a garage on April Fool's Day, 1976. Typical of young companies, Apple focused on its products and had little concern for its markets. When IBM—"Big Blue"—entered the PC market in 1981, Apple was forced to become a "real company," much to the chagrin of its creative young engineers who were likened to "Boy Scouts without adult supervision."

With the introduction of the IBM PC, Big Blue quickly dominated the market, having licensed its operating system from Microsoft. Apple lost significant market share, and many experts predicted it wouldn't survive. Jobs realized that Apple needed to "grow up" and therefore sought professional marketing expertise. Enter John Scully, who concluded that Apple needed to update its market-product strategies. His solution was to differentiate Apple's line of computers more clearly and to target them at important market niches.

The succession of Apple CEOs after Scully also sought to formalize and give cohesiveness to Apple's market segmentation strategy and to target specific Apple machines to particular market segments. With varying degrees of success, the core product strategy continued to be the innovation of Apple's line of Macintosh computers.

Upon Steve Jobs's return to Apple in 1997, he detailed his vision for a reincarnated Apple. He announced the controversial "Think Different" advertising campaign and described upcoming new Macs. He deleted many models from Apple's existing line and announced Apple would also sell computers direct via The Apple Store over the Internet and the phone, patterning the site after Dell Computer.

In 1998 Apple re-targeted the consumer and education markets by introducing the iMac—the most innovative PC ever created according to many PC and business analysts. The iMac, initially priced at $1,299, was fast, Internet-ready, easy-to-use, and the first PC to eliminate the 3.5-inch floppy drive for storage. Instead, other storage options were developed by Imation, Iomega, and other third-party vendors. By the end

What market segments for Apple's computers are represented by these products? The Marketing NewsNet box and text discussion provide insights into Apple's market segmentation strategy.

Apple Computer
www.apple.com

of 1998, more than 800,000 units had been sold, making the iMac the greatest PC product launch ever.[16] In early 1999, Apple introduced iMacs in five "fruit" flavors: blueberry, strawberry, tangerine, grape, and lime.

As in most segmentation situations, a single Apple product does not fit into an exclusive market niche. Rather, there is overlap among products in the product line and also among the markets to which they are directed. But a market segmentation strategy enables Apple to offer different products to meet the needs of the different market segments, as shown in the Marketing NewsNet box on the opposite page. What does Steve Jobs have in store for Apple? Here are some of his plans for 2000 and beyond:

- Presenting its new, faster, value-priced Power Macintosh G4s.
- Increasing its market share by adding new retail outlets and selling through its own Apple Store.
- Positioning the Mac as the best game platform—a growing market segment—due to its superior graphics compared to its PC rivals.

Market-product challenges for Apple to overcome in the new millennium include:

- Maintaining the sales momentum of its consumer iMacs.
- Reducing the price differential between Apple's Power Macs and PowerBooks and their PC counterparts.
- Marketing its new wireless portable PC—the iBook.

MARKETING NEWSNET

Apple's Segmentation Strategy: Search for the Right Niches

"Camp Runamok" was the nickname some computer industry wags gave to Apple Computer in the early 1980s because the entrepreneurial company had no coherent series of product lines directed at identifiable market segments. And as Apple's history indicates, this moniker was well deserved!

Today, Apple has targeted its various lines of Macintosh computers at specific market segments, as shown below. Because the market-product grid shifts as a firm's strategy changes, the one shown here is based on Apple's product line in early 1999. This market-product grid is a simplification because each "product" is really a series of Macintosh computers in that line. Each series has computers specifically configured to the desires of the customer, such as PowerPC processor speed, amount of memory, an add-on graphics card, drive type and speed/size, and kind of connection for Internet and intranet access. There is also an overlap of likely market segments from one product line to another.

Nevertheless, the grid suggests a market-product strategy for Apple's product lines: iMacs (*Business Week*'s 1998 Product of the Year) for the consumer and educational market segments, Power Mac G4s for users who need more speed, PowerBooks and iBooks for those who need portability; and servers for Internet developers and network users. And coming for the 21st century: a new Mac OS X operating system.

MARKETS			PRODUCTS (PERSONAL COMPUTERS)				
SECTOR		**SEGMENT**	**POWER MAC-INTOSH G4**	**POWER-BOOK G4**	**IMAC**	**IBOOK**	**POWER MAC-INTOSH G4 SERVER**
Consumer/household		Family/games			✓	✓	
Education	Kindergarten through 12th grade	Students			✓	✓	
		Faculty/administration	✓	✓		✓	✓
	College and university	Students	✓	✓	✓	✓	
		Faculty/administration	✓	✓		✓	✓
Commercial	Small business	Owners/employees	✓	✓	✓	✓	✓
	Large business	Administration/technical	✓	✓			✓
	Design and publishing	Media/graphics/Internet	✓	✓			✓
		Desktop publishing	✓	✓			✓

Stay tuned to see if Steve Jobs and these market-product strategies will continue Apple's "phoenix-like" rise from its own ashes!

CONCEPT CHECK

1. What are some of the variables used to segment consumer markets?

2. What are some criteria used to decide which segments to choose for targets?

3. Why is usage rate important in segmentation studies?

ANALYZING MARKET SEGMENTS USING CROSS TABULATIONS

To do a more precise market segmentation analysis of your Wendy's restaurant, suppose you survey fast-food patrons throughout the metropolitan area where your restaurant is located, using the questionnaire shown in Figure 9–6. You want to use this information as best you can to study the market's segments and develop your strategy. Probably the most widely used approach today in marketing is to develop and interpret cross tabulations of data obtained by questionnaires.

Developing Cross Tabulations

A **cross tabulation,** or "cross tab," is a method of presenting and relating data having two or more variables. It is used to analyze and discover relationships in the data. Two important aspects of cross tabulations are deciding which of two variables to pair together to help understand the situation and forming the resulting cross tabulations.

Pairing the Questions   Marketers pair two questions to understand marketing relationships and to find effective marketing actions. The Wendy's questionnaire in Figure 9–6 gives many questions that might be paired to understand the fast-food business better and help reach a decision about marketing actions to increase revenues. For example, if you want to study your hypothesis that as the age of the head of household increases, patronage of fast-food restaurants declines, you can cross tabulate questions 9*d* and 3.

Forming Cross Tabulations   Using the answers to question 3 as the column headings and the answers to question 9*d* as the row headings gives a cross tabulation, as shown in Figure 10–10, using the answers 586 respondents gave to both questions. The figure shows two forms of the cross tabulation:

- The raw data or answers to the specific questions are shown in Figure 10–10A. For example, this cross tab shows that 144 households whose head was 24 years or younger ate at fast-food restaurants once a week or more.

FIGURE 10–10
Two forms of a cross tabulation relating age of head of household to fast-food restaurant patronage

A. ABSOLUTE FREQUENCIES

AGE OF HEAD OF HOUSEHOLD (YEARS)	FREQUENCY			
	ONCE A WEEK OR MORE	2 OR 3 TIMES A MONTH	ONCE A MONTH OR LESS	TOTAL
24 or less	144	52	19	215
25 to 39	46	58	29	133
40 or over	82	69	87	238
Total	272	179	135	586

B. ROW PERCENTAGES: RUNNING PERCENTAGES HORIZONTALLY

AGE OF HEAD OF HOUSEHOLD (YEARS)	FREQUENCY			
	ONCE A WEEK OR MORE	2 OR 3 TIMES A MONTH	ONCE A MONTH OR LESS	TOTAL
24 or less	67.0%	24.2%	8.8%	100.0%
25 to 39	34.6	43.6	21.8	100.0
40 or over	34.4	29.0	36.6	100.0
Total	46.4%	30.6%	23.0%	100.0%

- Answers on a percentage basis, with the percentages running horizontally, are shown in Figure 10–10B. Of the 215 households headed by someone 24 years or younger, 67.0 percent ate at a fast-food restaurant at least once a week and only 8.8 percent ate there once a month or less.

Two other forms of cross tabulation using the raw data shown in Figure 10–10A are as described in problem 7 at the end of the chapter.

Interpreting Cross Tabulations

A careful analysis of Figure 10–10 shows that patronage of fast-food restaurants is related to the age of the head of the household. Note that as the age of the head of the household increases, fast-food restaurant patronage declines, as shown by the boxed percentages on the diagonal in Figure 10–10B. This means that if you want to reach the heavy-user segment, you should direct your marketing efforts to the segment that is 24 years old or younger.

As discussed earlier in the chapter, there are various ways to segment a consumer market besides according to age. For example, you could make subsequent cross tabulations to analyze patronage related to where students live and the meals they eat to obtain more precise information for the market-product grid in Figure 10–8.

Value of Cross Tabulations

Probably the most widely used technique for organizing and presenting marketing data, cross tabulations have some important advantages. The simple format permits direct interpretation and an easy means of communicating data to management. They have great flexibility and can be used to summarize experimental, observational, and questionnaire data. Also, cross tabulations may be easily generated by today's personal computers.

Cross tabulations also have some disadvantages. For example, they can be misleading if the percentages are based on too small a number of observations. Also, cross tabulations can hide some relations because each typically only shows two or three variables. Balancing both advantages and disadvantages, more marketing decisions are probably made using cross tabulations than any other method of analyzing data.

The ultimate value of cross tabulations to a marketing manager lies in obtaining a better understanding of the wants and needs of buyers and targeting key segments. This enables a marketing manager to "position" the offering in the minds of buyers, the topic discussed next.

POSITIONING THE PRODUCT

When a company offers a product commercially, a decision critical to its long-term success is how to position it in the market on introduction. **Product positioning** refers to the place an offering occupies in consumers' minds on important attributes relative to competitive offerings.

Two Approaches to Product Positioning

There are several approaches to positioning a new product in the market. Head-to-head positioning involves competing directly with competitors on similar product attributes in the same target market. Using this strategy, Dollar competes directly with Avis and Hertz, and Volvo pits its turbo-charged cars against Porsche.

Differentiation positioning involves seeking a less competitive, smaller market niche in which to locate a brand. As shown in the Web Link box, Buy.com is positioning itself

WEB LINK

"The Lowest Prices on Earth": The Most Precise Positioning Statement Ever?

Here's an idea for a new business: Sell dollar bills for 85 cents!

The only problem is Scott Blum, CEO of Buy.com, is pretty much doing it already by selling consumer products at or below cost. He is trying to position the company as being synonymous with low price—as shown by Buy.com's tag line: "the lowest prices on Earth." Blum's strategy is described in more detail at the start of Chapter 18.

As discussed in the text, product positioning refers to the place an offering occupies in a consumer's mind. In Buy.com's case, this means the *absolute* lowest prices. Sound crazy? Visit the www.Buy.com Web site, and see for yourself. Compare its prices with those of other Internet sellers. Are they the lowest?

If Buy.com isn't an active Web site when you read this, it probably *was* a crazy idea!

as having the "lowest prices on Earth" to buyers on the Internet. McDonald's, trying to appeal to the health-conscious segment, introduced its low-fat McLean Deluxe hamburger to avoid direct competition with Wendy's and Burger King. Companies also follow a differentiation positioning strategy among brands within their own product line to try to minimize cannibalization of a brand's sales or shares.

Product Positioning Using Perceptual Maps

A key to positioning a product effectively is the perceptions of consumers. In determining a brand's position and the preferences of consumers, companies obtain three types of data from consumers:

1. Evaluations of the important attributes for a product class.
2. Judgments of existing brands with the important attributes.
3. Ratings of an "ideal" brand's attributes.

From these data, it is possible to develop a **perceptual map,** a means of displaying or graphing in two dimensions the location of products or brands in the minds of consumers. The example illustrates how a manager can use perceptual maps to see how consumers perceive competing products or brands and then take actions to try to change the product offering and the image it projects to consumers.

GM's Positioning for 1990   By the 1980s General Motors (GM) was concerned that the image of its five main models of U.S. cars—Chevrolet, Pontiac, Oldsmobile, Buick, and Cadillac—had so blurred in the minds of American consumers that they could not distinguish one brand from another. So in 1982 GM interviewed consumers and developed the perceptual map shown in Figure 10–11A. Note that the two dimensions on the perceptual map are (1) low price versus high price and (2) family/conservative versus personal/expressive appeal. Figure 10–11A shows that GM indeed had a problem. Although there was some variation in the vertical dimension (consumers' perception of price), there was little difference in the horizontal dimension (family/conservative appeal versus personal/expressive appeal). Then GM set new goals for where it wanted its models to be when its small car Saturn would be introduced (which turned out to be 1990). This involves **repositioning** the models, or changing the place an offering occupies in a consumer's mind relative to competitive offerings.

Figure 10–11A highlights the special 1980s problem GM faced in having its divisions sell nearly identical cars to nearly identical market segments: Pontiac went head-to-head with Chevrolet for younger buyers and Buick and Oldsmobile did the same for

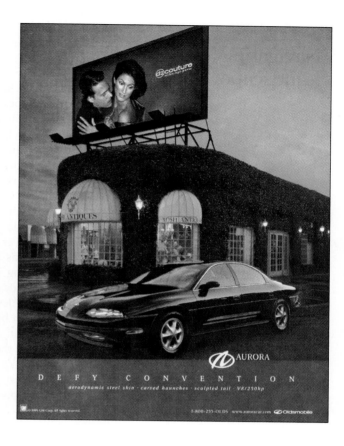

To which market segments are these General Motors cars targeted? Do potential buyers see them as the same or different? For the company's position dilemma and strategy, see the text and Figure 10–11.

the sixtyish segment. So divisions were cannibalizing each others' sales. The figure shows that its 1990 goals included the following:

- Position Saturn as a low-priced, stylish import-fighter.
- Try to reposition Pontiac as a more personal/expressive (stylish) car and Chevrolet as a more family/conservative car.
- Try to reposition Buick as a higher priced, family/conservative car and Oldsmobile as a more stylish car.

FIGURE 10–11
GM's strategy to reposition its major car brands from 1982 to 1990 to . . . 2002(?)

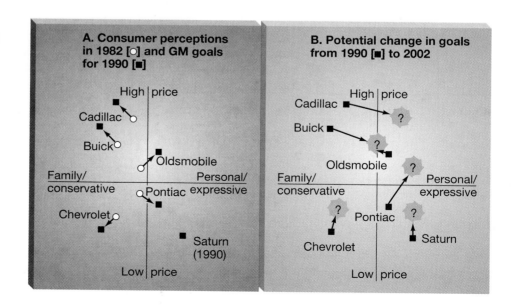

Things didn't work out quite the way GM expected. One problem was the sudden 1990s love affair Americans had with minivans, pickup trucks, and sports utility vehicles.

GM's Positioning for 2002   In the late 1990s GM embarked on several strategies that accentuated the importance of making some difficult product repositioning decisions. It invested about $3 billion in its "four-country strategy" that involved building virtually identical new car production plants in Argentina, Poland, China, and Thailand—plus a fifth and newer plant in Brazil.[17] GM also announced major reorganizations to combine its five marketing divisions into one and to consolidate engineering operations—all directed at reducing the development time for GM cars and trucks and to improve their marketing.[18] The problem: All these actions didn't directly address the fact that from 1992 to 1997 GM's market share was falling in all car and truck categories except for small cars—where profits are lowest.

Cadillac is an example of GM's positioning dilemma. Cadillac's basic problem: The average Cadillac buyer is 63! So it's clear that Cadillac must find ways to compete with foreign rivals such as Lexus, Mercedes, and BMW to attract younger luxury-car buyers without destroying its classic image and losing its present buyers. One strategy: The Cadillac Escalade sport-utility vehicle, introduced in 1998.[19]

We can look at GM's designs and advertising for its current lines and assess where GM wants the models to be positioned in, say, the year 2002. Figure 10–11B is just such a projection. One thing is certain. Americans of all ages want more stylish cars and are moving to the right in the positioning matrix in Figure 10–11B—especially as minivans and pickup trucks take over more of the "family/conservative" end of the scale.

Gazing into our own crystal ball and those of reporters close to GM, Figure 10–11B suggests possible GM repositioning strategies for 2002:

- Cadillac—move in the direction of more personal/expressiveness to attract younger buyers.
- Buick and Oldsmobile—GM-watchers are betting these two divisions will merge, with a positioning between their 1990 locations.[20]
- Pontiac—add price, power, and sportiness to reach younger buyers now driving foreign cars.
- Chevrolet—keep it conservative and a bit more pricey to distinguish the brand from Pontiac and Saturn.
- Saturn—GM's "orphan"; Saturn achieved huge customer acceptance and loyalty when launched, but billions of dollars in the early 1990s were pumped into new models intended to revive the stodgy images of Oldsmobile and Buick, leaving Saturn with an empty new-model cupboard; watch for pricier Saturn models— perhaps a compact sedan and larger sports utility vehicle.[21]

Are these positioning projections correct? Read today's GM ads and see for yourself. Your personal car-buying decisions will affect the outcome as well.

CONCEPT CHECK

1. What is cross tabulation?

2. What are some advantages of cross tabulations?

3. Why do marketers use perceptual maps in product positioning decisions?

SUMMARY

1 Market segmentation is aggregating prospective buyers into groups that have common needs and will respond similarly to a marketing action.

2 A straightforward approach to segmenting, targeting, and reaching a market involves five steps: (*a*) form prospective buyers into segments by characteristics such as their needs, (*b*) form products to be sold into groups, (*c*) develop a market-product grid and estimate size of markets, (*d*) select target markets, and (*e*) take marketing actions to reach the target markets.

3 Marketing variables are often used to represent customer needs in the market segmentation process. For consumer markets, typical customer variables are region, metropolitan statistical area, age, income, benefits sought, and usage rate. For industrial markets, comparable variables are geographical location, size of firm, and North American Industry Classification (NAICS) code.

4 Usage rate is an important factor in a market segmentation study. Users are often divided into heavy, medium, and light users.

5 Nonusers are often divided into prospects and nonprospects. Nonusers of a firm's brand may be important because they are prospects—users of some other brand in the product class that may be convinced to change brands.

6 Criteria used (*a*) to segment markets and (*b*) to choose target segments are related but different. The former includes potential to increase profits, similarity of needs of buyers within a segment, difference of needs among segments, and feasibility of a resulting marketing action. The latter includes market size, expected growth, the competitive position of the firm's offering in the segment, and the cost of reaching the segment.

7 A market-product grid is a useful way to display what products can be directed at which market segments, but the grid must lead to marketing actions for the segmentation process to be worthwhile.

8 Cross tabulations are widely used today in market segmentation studies to identify needs of various customer segments and the actions to reach them.

9 A company can position a product head-to-head against the competition or seek a differentiated position. A concern with positioning is often to avoid cannibalization of the existing product line. In positioning, a firm often uses consumer judgments in the form of perceptual maps to locate its product relative to competing ones.

KEY TERMS AND CONCEPTS

market segmentation p. 256
market segments p. 256
product differentiation p. 256
market-product grid p. 259
synergy p. 260
usage rate p. 264

80/20 rule p. 265
cross tabulation p. 274
product positioning p. 275
perceptual map p. 276
repositioning p. 276

INTERNET EXERCISE

In its two-decade history, Apple computer has initiated a series of creative market segmentation strategies, with new product lines targeted at specific market segments. For a continuing update of Apple's strategies, go to www.apple-history.com and click on the "Intro" and "History" menu options. As you read the narrative, identify the various market-product strategies Apple has employed, compared to those described in the text and the Marketing NewsNet box. Given Apple's recent turnaround, do you think Apple can continue its comeback in the twenty-first century? Do you believe Apple can survive as a "niche" PC marketer? Why or why not?

APPLYING MARKETING CONCEPTS AND PERSPECTIVES

1 What variables might be used to segment these consumer markets? (*a*) lawnmowers, (*b*) frozen dinners, (*c*) dry breakfast cereals, and (*d*) soft drinks.

2 What variables might be used to segment these industrial markets? (*a*) industrial sweepers, (*b*) photocopiers, (*c*) computerized production control systems, and (*d*) car rental agencies.

3 In Figure 10–9 the dormitory market segment includes students living in college-owned residence halls, sororities, and fraternities. What market needs are common to these students that justify combining them into a single segment in studying the market for your Wendy's restaurant?

4 You may disagree with the estimates of market size given for the rows in the market-product grid in Figure 10–9. Estimate the market size, and give a brief justification for these market segments: (*a*) dormitory students, (*b*) day commuters, and (*c*) people who work in the area.

5 Suppose you want to increase revenues from your fast-food restaurant shown in Figure 10–9 even further. What advertising actions might you take to increase revenues from (*a*) dormitory students, (*b*) dinners, and (*c*) after-dinner snacks from night commuters?

6 Look back at Figure 9–6. Which questions would you pair to form a cross tabulation to uncover the following relationships?

(*a*) frequency of fast-food restaurant patronage and restaurant characteristics important to the customer, (*b*) age of the head of household and source of information used about fast-food restaurants, (*c*) frequency of patronage of Wendy's and source of information used about fast-food restaurants, or (*d*) how much children have to say about where the family eats and number of children in the household.

7 Look back at Figure 10–10A. (*a*) Run the percentages vertically and tell what they mean. (*b*) Express all numbers in the table as a percentage of the total number of people sampled (586) and tell what the percentages mean.

8 In Figure 10–10, (*a*) what might be other names for the three patronage levels shown in the columns? (*b*) Which is likely to be of special interest to Wendy's and why?

 ## CASE 10–1   PAISLEY PARK RECORDS

How do you market—and perhaps "reposition"—George Clinton, a legendary musician/songwriter? That is the marketing task facing Paisley Park Records, the record label of The Artist Formerly Known as Prince. It is also an important issue for Alan Leeds, vice president in charge of Paisley Park Records, and—of course—George Clinton, whose recording opportunities are under study.

THE ARTIST

George Clinton is one of the most respected and influential musician/songwriters in the popular music industry. Since the early 1970s, he has been instrumental in the ongoing development and refinement of what is now called Urban Contemporary music. He is considered the Father of Funk, the dance-oriented rhythm and blues that has dominated African-American popular music in the last 15 years. He has also inspired musical genres from hip hop to rap.

Clinton's best known work was in the late 1970s and 1980s, with the groups Parliament and Funkadelic and their amalgam P-Funk. All of the major songwriter/producers (the people who dominate Urban Contemporary music in the 1990s) claim Clinton as a mentor and an influence—this includes The Artist, Jimmy Jam and Terry Lewis, Teddy Riley, L.A. and Babyface, etc.

Clinton is probably the second most sampled songwriter, behind only James Brown. "Sampling" is a term unique to the late 1980s and 1990s and is the result of the increasing use of computers in the creation of music. A "sample" is a small piece of a previously recorded song that is used in a new song or composition. Samples vary in length but generally involve a few bars of a song—sometimes only a single instrument (a guitar solo, a bass line) or all the elements (rhythm, vocals, solos). Clinton's music is sampled primarily by rappers.

Clinton's persona is, to some extent, better known than his music. A frequent guest on David Letterman and MTV, BET, and other video-oriented programs, Clinton's long, rainbow-colored hair is a familiar trademark. His irreverent humor pokes fun at the normal image of the rock'n'roll or Rhythm and Blues (R&B) star. And, although he has not had a "hit" record (sales of more than half a million units) in years, he still has a large, highly loyal following.

THE COMPANY

Paisley Park Records is a small record label associated with and distributed and marketed by Warner Bros. Records. Paisley Park chooses its acts and then oversees the recording, marketing, and packaging. Warner Bros. then manufactures the records themselves, distributes them to retailers, and takes the primary responsibility for marketing the records—advertising, contacts with radio stations, television video, etc.

Make no mistake about it: Paisley Park is The Artist's record label. Although run by Alan Leeds, The Artist himself is the final decision maker on who the label signs and records. In that sense, Paisley Park is different from most other record companies. Most companies have large A&R (artists and repertoire) staffs; these are people who weed out the many artists seeking to be signed to the labels. At Paisley Park Records, the decisions on whom to sign are more likely to be personal than at other labels.

THE ISSUES

The marketing problem is that George Clinton has *not* had a hit record in years. In 1990, he signed a new recording contract with Paisley Park Records. And the addition of George Clinton to that label's short roster probably was more a personal decision by The Artist—a sincere fan of Clinton—than a purely business decision. Upon signing, Clinton received a small part in the moderately successful film, *Graffitti Bridge*.

A significant part of Clinton's problem is that he doesn't seem to fit into any of the many market segments within the music industry—particularly the two key conduits for marketing in the industry, radio and music

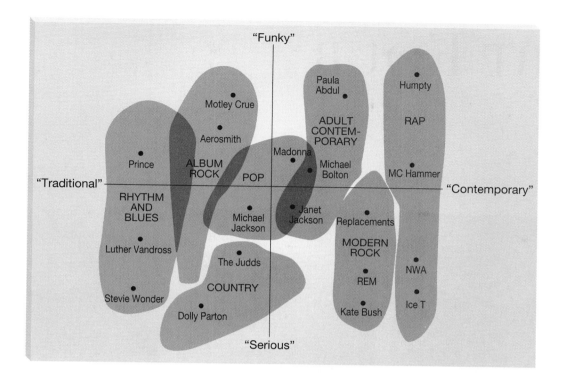

video television. Although he is clearly a legend in the Urban Contemporary market, Urban Contemporary program directors and DJs are not interested in his new music—they perceive Clinton as an "oldie" performer and are less likely to play his new material. Pop or CHR radio (Contemporary Hits Radio, the modern equivalent of Top 40 radio formats) see Clinton as too much an Urban Contemporary artist for their formats. And, though MTV will interview Clinton at almost any opportunity, they are very slow to play his videos. The results are that Clinton's records generally sell about 100,000 units each, based on the loyalty of his core audience.

Alan Leeds, Clinton, and his advisors want to develop a long-term strategy to reposition George Clinton. When Clinton signed with Paisley Park, he had already completed an album, "Cinderella Theory," that was to be released on that label. The Paisley Park strategy is to use the marketing of "Cinderella Theory" to prepare the way for the release of Clinton's future albums.

As they look at Clinton's past music and marketing, several features emerge:

- Clinton's irreverent humor that viewers see on MTV and the David Letterman show is carried through on Clinton's longstanding use of "cartoon" graphics on his albums.
- Clinton's lyrics for his music have great depth and sophistication, a fact often lost on listeners and viewers.
- Traditionally George Clinton has been almost the only artist featured in his music—seldom using important backup support.

As they analyze the opportunities for repositioning George Clinton, they see two key dimensions to the music segments relative to Clinton's opportunities: (1) a traditional-to-contemporary dimension and (2) a serious-to-funky dimension. They reach two big decisions: (1) make Clinton more "contemporary" on the first dimension and (2) make Clinton more "serious" on the second dimension. Given these marketing strategy decisions, what actions should George Clinton, Alan Leeds, and Paisley Park Records take to implement these plans?

Questions

1 What are some of the key reasons an artist of the stature of George Clinton has problems getting a hit record at this stage of his career?

2 What specific market segments would you target to give new life to George Clinton's career?

3 Suppose we develop the perceptual map as shown above by plotting the two dimensions described in the case along the two axes. Suppose that some key *Billboard* magazine charts are positioned about as shown. (There is actually more overlap among the charts that, for simplicity, has not been shown.) What are some of the potential advantages and disadvantages of trying to reposition George Clinton to make him (*a*) more "contemporary" and (*b*) more "serious"? Locate George Clinton's (*c*) present position on the perceptual map and (*d*) the new position he is moving toward.

4 What marketing actions would you recommend to achieve the repositioning of George Clinton?

PART FOUR

4

SATISFYING MARKETING OPPORTUNITIES

Part Four covers the unique combination of products, price, place, and
promotion that results in an offering for potential customers. How products
and services are developed and managed is the focus of Chapters 11, 12,
and 13. Pricing is covered in Chapters 14 and 15 and Appendix B. Three
chapters address the place (distribution) element, which includes retailing
innovations. Finally, three promotion chapters cover topics ranging from
Taco Bell's integrated marketing communication program, to Claritin's interactive Web advertising, to Joan Rothman's efforts to sell Dun & Bradstreet's
database products and services.

CHAPTER ELEVEN

DEVELOPING NEW PRODUCTS AND SERVICES

11

AFTER READING THIS CHAPTER YOU SHOULD BE ABLE TO:

• Understand the ways in which consumer and industrial products can be classified and marketed.

• Explain the implications of alternative ways of viewing "newness" in new products.

• Analyze the factors contributing to a product's success or failure.

• Recognize and understand the purposes of each step of the new-product process.

A NEW-PRODUCT LESSON FROM 3M: A BETTER PRODUCT *AND* A CREATIVE WAY TO GET THAT MESSAGE TO TARGET BUYERS

3M's Todd DiMartini knows that "having a better mousetrap"—or in his case a better industrial adhesive—isn't enough! He knows he also has to get prospective buyers to make the effort to learn about the adhesive, understand its benefits, and think about ways to actually apply it. Here's a quick-take on the marketing issues he faced recently:

• *The product?* A revolutionary 3M VHB™ (for "very high bonding") tape made with high-strength structural adhesives that can make a continuous bond on cars and airplanes stronger than spot welds or rivets.
• *The target market?* Mechanical engineers responsible for the designs of everything from trucks and cars to ceilings in buildings.
• *The marketing task?* To get the target mechanical engineers to seriously consider the 3M VHB tape adhesive and actually use it in applications where they normally use screws or rivets.

Todd DiMartini and his marketing staff developed the advertisement shown on the opposite page that ran in design engineering magazines.[1] Note the detailed text, which stresses the VHB tape's points of difference to prospective users. How can DiMartini and his team rework the ad to make it even more effective in getting design engineers to consider VHB tape and actually specify it in their designs? The answer appears later in Chapter 11 and illustrates the team creativity needed for new-product success.

A brief look at 3M's adhesives technologies provides us with insights into how its new products enable 3M to find synergies to design multiple products for multiple markets (discussed in Chapters 10 and 22). In the 1950s,

3M developed an acrylate adhesive, for example, that made possible the introduction of its Scotch™ Magic™ Tape that you can write on with a pen or pencil. 3M's search for creative products led it into the research that makes it a world leader today in adhesives technology.

3M's research has led to dozens of revolutionary 3M adhesive products, including the following:

- 3M™ Post-It® Notes. The adhesive enables you to stick and unstick that note to your friend over and over again.
- 3M™ Nexcare™ Waterproof Bandages with Tattoo Designs. This is a bandage that combines superior, waterproof wound protection with popular designs that children want to wear.
- Scotch™ Pop-up Tape. This is the latest version of the tape everyone uses to wrap gifts and mend well-worn pages in textbooks.
- 3M™ Latitude™ Drug-in-Adhesive technology. This has led to breakthrough advances in delivery of pharmaceuticals, including the Minitran™ (nitroglycerin) transdermal delivery system, which is the smallest daily nitroglycerin patch in the world.[2]

Note the technology common to all these new products: 3M's ability to coat a variety of adhesives with strikingly different characteristics onto a continuous surface.

The essence of marketing is in developing products such as a new, technologically advanced adhesive to meet buyer needs. A **product** is a good, service, or idea consisting of a bundle of tangible and intangible attributes that satisfies consumers and is received in exchange for money or some other unit of value. Tangible attributes include physical characteristics such as color or sweetness, and intangible attributes include becoming healthier or wealthier. Hence, a product includes the breakfast cereal you eat, the accountant who fills out your tax return, or the American Red Cross, which provides you self-satisfaction when you donate your blood. In many instances we exchange money to obtain the product, whereas in other instances we exchange our time and other valuables, such as our blood.

The life of a company often depends on how it conceives, produces, and markets new products. This is the exact reason that 3M encourages its researchers to spend up to 15 percent of their time on projects of their own choosing—"bootlegging time" they call it. This strategy contributes to more than 500 3M patents a year.[3] In this chapter we discuss the decisions involved in developing and marketing new products and services. Chapters 12 and 13 cover the process of managing existing products and services, respectively.

THE VARIATIONS OF PRODUCTS

A product varies in terms of whether it is a consumer or industrial good. For most organizations the product decision is not made in isolation because companies often offer a range of products. To better appreciate the product decision, let's first define some terms pertaining to products.

Product Line and Product Mix

A **product line** is a group of products that are closely related because they satisfy a class of needs, are used together, are sold to the same customer group, are distributed through the same type of outlets, or fall within a given price range.[4] Polaroid has two major product lines consisting of cameras and film; Nike's product lines are shoes and

Nike's striking ads gain attention for its product lines of shoes and clothing.

Nike, Inc.
www.nike.com

clothing; the Mayo Clinic's product lines consist of inpatient hospital care, outpatient physician services, and medical research. Each product line has its own marketing strategy.

Within each product line is the *product item,* a specific product as noted by a unique brand, size, or price. For example, Downy softener for clothes comes in 12-ounce and 22-ounce sizes; each size is considered a separate item and assigned a distinct ordering code, or *stock keeping unit* (*SKU*).

The third way to look at products is by the **product mix,** or the number of product lines offered by a company. The Cray Research division of Silicon Graphics has a single product line consisting of supercomputers, which are sold mostly to governments and large businesses. American Brands, Inc., however, has many product lines consisting of cigarettes (Pall Mall), sporting equipment (Titleist golf balls), distilled beverages (Jim Beam liquors), and even services (Pinkerton security).

Classifying Products

Both the federal government and companies classify products, but for different purposes. The government's classification method helps it collect information on industrial activity. Companies classify products to help develop similar marketing strategies for the wide range of products offered. Two major ways to classify products are by degree of product tangibility and type of user.

Degree of Tangibility   Classification by degree of tangibility divides products into one of three categories. First is a *nondurable good,* an item consumed in one or a few uses, such as food products and fuel. A *durable good* is one that usually lasts over an extended number of uses, such as appliances, automobiles, and stereo equipment. *Services* are defined as activities, benefits, or satisfactions offered for sale, such as marketing research, health care, and education. According to this classification, government data indicate that the United States is becoming a service economy, the reason for a separate chapter (Chapter 13) on the topic.

This classification method also provides direction for marketing actions. Nondurable products such as Wrigley's gum are purchased frequently and at relatively low cost. Advertising is important to remind consumers of the item's existence, and wide distribution in retail outlets is essential. A consumer wanting Wrigley's Spearmint Gum would most likely purchase another brand of spearmint gum if Wrigley's were not available. Durable products, however, generally cost more than nondurable goods and last longer, so consumers usually deliberate longer before purchasing them. Therefore, personal selling is an important component in durable-product marketing because it assists in answering consumer questions and concerns.

Marketing is increasingly being used with services. Services are intangibles, so a major goal in marketing is to make the benefits of purchasing the product real to consumers. Thus, Northwest Airlines shows the fun of a Florida vacation or the joy of seeing grandparents. People who provide the service are often the key to its success in the market because consumers often evaluate the product by the service provider they meet—the Hertz reservation clerk, the receptionist at the university admissions office, or the nurse in the doctor's office.

Type of User   The second major type of product classification is according to the user. **Consumer goods** are products purchased by the ultimate consumer, whereas **industrial goods** are products used in the production of other products for ultimate consumers. In many instances the differences are distinct: Oil of Olay face moisturizer and Bass shoes are clearly consumer products, whereas Cray computers and high-tension steel springs are industrial goods used in producing other products or services.

There are difficulties, however, with this classification because some products can be considered both consumer and industrial items. A Compaq computer can be sold to consumers as a final product or to industrial firms for office use. Each classification results in

The Rolex brand of watch is an example of a specialty good.

Rolex
www.rolex.com

PICABO STREET
ATTACKS THE MOUNTAIN WITH
A HEADLONG STYLE THAT IS AN
ELECTRIFYING COMBINATION OF
STRENGTH AND GRACE.

IT'S ALSO A PRETTY FAIR
DESCRIPTION OF HER ROLEX.

No woman skier flies down a mountain like Picabo Street. At the 1994 Olympics in Lillehammer, her daring and skill made her the toast of international skiing and won her a silver medal in the Downhill, and four years later in Nagano, she topped herself by capturing an Olympic gold medal in the Super G. Picabo's chosen timepiece has long demonstrated the same combination of style and substance. In addition to being strikingly attractive, its legendary Oyster case, along with its Triplock winding crown and crystal, protects the complex mechanical movement under the most rigorous conditions. And in Picabo's case, those conditions can be very rigorous indeed.

ROLEX

Lady Yacht Master
Officially Certified Swiss Chronometer

For the name and location of an Official Rolex Jeweler near you, please call 1-800-36ROLEX. Rolex ● Oyster Perpetual, Triplock and Lady Yacht Master are trademarks.

different marketing actions. Viewed as a consumer product, the Compaq would be sold through computer stores. As an industrial product, the Dell might be sold by a salesperson offering discounts for multiple purchases. Classifying by the type of user focuses on the market and the user's purchase behavior, which determine the marketing mix strategy.

CLASSIFYING CONSUMER AND INDUSTRIAL GOODS

Because the buyer is the key to marketing, consumer and industrial product classifications are discussed in greater detail.

Classification of Consumer Goods

Convenience, shopping, specialty, and unsought products are the four types of consumer goods. They differ in terms of (1) effort the consumer spends on the decision, (2) attributes used in purchase, and (3) frequency of purchase.

   Convenience goods are items that the consumer purchases frequently, conveniently, and with a minimum of shopping effort. **Shopping goods** are items for which the consumer compares several alternatives on criteria, such as price, quality, or style. **Specialty goods** are items, such as Tiffany sterling silver, that a consumer makes a special effort to search out and buy. **Unsought goods** are items that the consumer either does not know about or knows about but does not initially want. Figure 11–1 shows how the classification of a consumer product into one of these four types results in different aspects of the marketing mix being stressed. Different degrees of brand loyalty and amounts of shopping effort are displayed by the consumer for a product in each of the four classes.

   The manner in which a consumer good is classified depends on the individual. One person may view a camera as a shopping good and visit several stores before deciding on a brand, whereas a friend may view cameras as a specialty good and will only buy a Nikon.

   The product classification of a consumer good can change the longer a product is on the market. When first introduced, the Litton microwave oven was unique, a specialty

FIGURE 11–1
Classification of consumer goods

TYPE OF CONSUMER GOOD

BASIS OF COMPARISON	CONVENIENCE	SHOPPING	SPECIALTY	UNSOUGHT
Product	Toothpaste, cake mix, hand soap, laundry detergent	Cameras, TVs, briefcases, clothing	Rolls Royce cars, Rolex watches	Burial insurance, thesaurus
Price	Relatively inexpensive	Fairly expensive	Usually very expensive	Varies
Place (distribution)	Widespread; many outlets	Large number of selective outlets	Very limited	Often limited
Promotion	Price, availability, and awareness stressed	Differentiation from competitors stressed	Uniqueness of brand and status stressed	Awareness is essential
Brand loyalty of consumers	Aware of brand, but will accept substitutes	Prefer specific brands, but will accept substitutes	Very brand loyal; will not accept substitutes	Will accept substitutes
Purchase behavior of consumers	Frequent purchases; little time and effort spent shopping; routine decision	Infrequent purchases; comparison shopping; uses decision time	Infrequent purchases; extensive time spent to decide and get the item	Very infrequent purchases, some comparison shopping

good. Now there are competing brands on the market, and microwaves are a shopping good for many consumers.

Classification of Industrial Goods

A major characteristic of industrial goods is that their sales are often the result of *derived demand;* that is, sales of industrial products frequently result (or are derived) from the sale of consumer goods. For example, if consumer demand for Fords (a consumer product) increases, the company may increase its demand for paint spraying equipment (an industrial product). Industrial goods are classified not only on the attributes the consumer uses but also on how the item is to be used. Thus, industrial products may be classified as production or support goods.

Production Goods   Items used in the manufacturing process that become part of the final product are **production goods.** These include raw materials such as grain or lumber, as well as component parts. For example, a company that manufactures door hinges used by GM in its car doors is producing a component part. As noted in Chapter 7, the marketing of production goods is based on factors such as price, quality, delivery, and service. Marketers of these products tend to sell directly to industrial users.

Support Goods   The second class of industrial goods is **support goods,** which are items used to assist in producing other goods and services. Support goods include installations, accessory equipment, supplies, and services.

- *Installations* consist of buildings and fixed equipment. Because a significant amount of capital is required to purchase installations, the industrial buyer deals directly with construction companies and manufacturers through sales representatives. The pricing of installations is often by competitive bidding.
- *Accessory equipment* includes tools and office equipment and is usually purchased in small-order sizes by buyers. As a result, instead of dealing directly with buyers, sellers of industrial accessories use distributors to contact a large number of buyers.
- *Supplies* are similar to consumer convenience goods and consist of products such as stationery, paper clips, and brooms. These are purchased with little effort, using the straight rebuy decision sequence discussed in Chapter 7. Price and delivery are key factors considered by the buyers of supplies.
- *Services* are intangible activities to assist the industrial buyer. This category can include maintenance and repair services and advisory services such as tax or legal counsel. The reputation of the seller of services is a major factor in marketing these industrial goods.

CONCEPT CHECK

1. Explain the difference between product mix and product line.

2. What are the four main types of consumer goods?

3. To which type of good (industrial or consumer) does the term *derived demand* generally apply?

NEW PRODUCTS AND WHY THEY FAIL

New products are the lifeblood of a company and keep it growing, but the financial risks are large. Before discussing how new products reach the stage of commercialization when they are available to the consumer, we'll begin by looking at *what* a new product is.

When Nintendo cancelled Sony's contract to provide parts, Sony got even—big time! The retaliation: Sony's new product, PlayStation.

Sony Corporation
www.sony.com

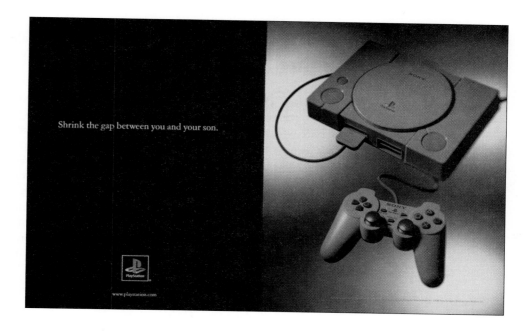

What Is a New Product?

The term *new* is difficult to define. Does changing the color of a laundry detergent mean it is a new product, as a new hot-air appliance that cooks like a regular oven but with the speed of a microwave would be considered new? There are several ways to view the newness of a product.

Newness Compared with Existing Products   If a product is functionally different from existing offerings, it can be defined as new. The microwave oven and automobile were once functionally new, but for most products the innovation is more a modification of an old product than a dramatic functional change.

Breathe Right® strips: What kind of innovation are they and what does this mean for marketing strategy? For the answers see the text and Figure 11–2.

Breathe Right®
www.breatheright.com

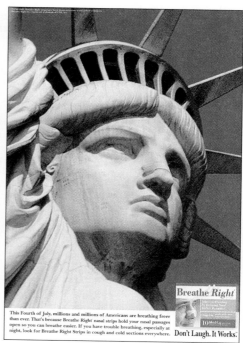

Newness in Legal Terms The Federal Trade Commission (FTC) advised that the term *new* be limited to use with a product up to six months after it enters regular distribution. The difficulty with this suggestion is in the interpretation of the term *regular distribution.*

Newness from the Company's Perspective Successful companies are starting to view newness and innovation in their products at three levels. At the lowest level, which usually involves the least risk, is a product line extension. This is an incremental improvement of an exciting or important product for the company, such as Frosted Cheerios or Diet Cherry Coke or Sensor for Women—extensions of the basic Cheerios or Diet Coke or men's Sensor product lines, respectively. At the next level is a significant jump in the innovation or technology, such as Sony's leap from the micro tape recorder to the Walkman. The third level is true innovation, a truly revolutionary new product, like the first Apple computer in 1976. Sometimes strange circumstances cause a company to introduce a new product; Sony developed its widely successful PlayStation video game system because Nintendo cancelled a parts contract with Sony—suddenly putting Sony into a new line of products.[5] Effective new product programs in large firms deal at all three levels.

Newness from the Consumer's Perspective A fourth way to define new products is in terms of their effects on consumption. This approach classifies new products according to the degree of learning required by the consumer, as shown in Figure 11–2.

With *continuous innovation,* no new behaviors must be learned. Breathe Right® nasal strips mentioned at the start of Chapter 5 are an example. In the 1994 Super Bowl San Francisco wide receiver Jerry Rice had what looked like a piece of adhesive tape across his nose. In fact, it was actually a Breathe Right® strip that helped hold his nasal passages open and let him breathe. Partly as a result of the free Super Bowl publicity, sales of Breathe Right® strips skyrocketed—and not just for athletes. The main target market: everyday people who snore. In November 1995, the U.S. Food and Drug Administration allowed the manufacturer to market the device as a snoring treatment when tests showed that 75 percent of people snored less often and less loudly when using the strip than when they didn't. The beauty of this innovation is that neither Jerry Rice nor typical people have to change their behaviors to adopt the product. With consumer products requiring minimal consumer education, such as Breathe

FIGURE 11–2
Consumption effects define newness

	LOW DEGREE OF CHANGE BEHAVIOR AND LEARNING NEEDED BY CONSUMER HIGH		
BASIS OF COMPARISON	**CONTINUOUS INNOVATION**	**DYNAMICALLY CONTINUOUS INNOVATION**	**DISCONTINUOUS INNOVATION**
Definition	Requires no new learning by consumers	Disrupts consumer's normal routine but does not require totally new learning	Establishes new consumption patterns among consumers
Examples	Sensor and New Improved Tide	Electric toothbrush, compact disc player, and automatic flash unit for cameras	VCR, Jet Stream Oven, and home computer
Marketing emphasis	Generate awareness among consumers and obtain widespread distribution	Advertise benefits to consumers, stressing point of differentiation and consumer advantage	Educate consumers through product trial and personal selling

Right® strips, effective marketing depends on generating awareness and having strong distribution in appropriate outlets.

With *dynamically continuous innovation,* only minor changes in behavior are required for use. An example is built-in, fold-down child seats such as those available in Chrysler minivans. Built-in car seats for children require only minor bits of education and changes in behavior, so the marketing strategy is to *educate* prospective buyers on their benefits, advantages, and proper use.

A *discontinuous innovation* involves making the consumer learn entirely new consumption patterns in order to use the product. After decades of voice-recognition research, IBM introduced its ViaVoice Gold in 1998. If you are using ViaVoice Gold early in the twenty-first century, you will be able to speak to your computer and watch your own words appear on your computer screen and, you will also be able to open Windows programs with your voice. The risk that IBM faces in introducing this discontinuous innovation is that you will have to learn new behaviors in producing your word-processed memos and reports, which—along with potential technical glitches in the computer's ability to recognize your unique voice sounds—may restrict acceptance and sales of this new product.[6] Hence, marketing efforts for discontinuous innovations involve not only gaining consumer awareness but also educating consumers on both the benefits and proper use of the innovative product. Personal selling and creative advertising are often needed to achieve this consumer education—activities that can cost millions of dollars for some discontinuous innovations.

Why Products Fail

The thousands of product failures that occur every year cost American businesses billions of dollars. Recent research summarized in Figure 11–3 suggests that it takes about 3,000 raw unwritten ideas to produce a single commercially successful new product.[7] To learn marketing lessons and convert potential failures to successes, we can analyze why new products fail and then study several failures in detail. As we go through the new-product process later in the chapter, we can identify ways such failures might have been avoided—admitting that hindsight is clearer than foresight.

FIGURE 11–3

What it takes to launch one commercially successful new product

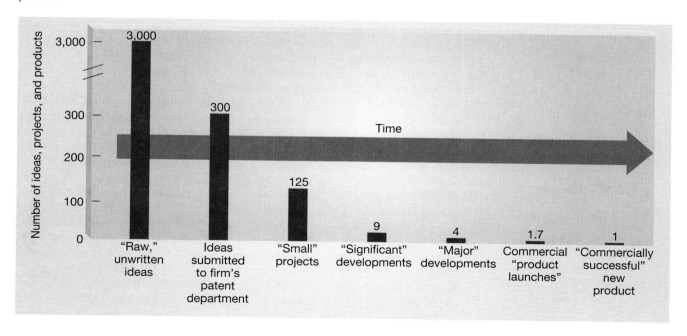

New product success or
failure? For the special
problems these products
face, see the text.

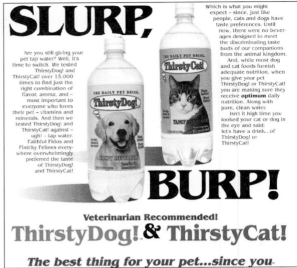

Marketing Reasons for New-Product Failures   Both marketing and non-marketing factors contribute to new-product failures, as shown in the accompanying Marketing NewsNet box.[8] Using the research results from several studies[9] on new-product success and failure and also those described in the Marketing NewsNet box, we can identify seven critical marketing factors—sometimes overlapping—that often separate new product winners and losers:

1. *Insignificant "point of difference."* Shown as the most important factor in the Marketing NewsNet box, a distinctive "point of difference" is essential for a new product to defeat competitive ones—through having superior characteristics that deliver unique benefits to the user. In the mid-1990s General Mills introduced "Fingos," a sweetened cereal flake about the size of a corn chip. Consumers were supposed to snack on them dry, but they didn't.[10] The point of difference was not important enough to get consumers to give up competing snacks such as popcorn, potato chips, or Cheerios from the box late at night.

2. *Incomplete market and product definition before product development starts.* Ideally, a new product needs a precise **protocol,** a statement that, before product development begins, identifies (1) a well-defined target market; (2) specific customers' needs, wants, and preferences; and (3) what the product will be and do. Without this precision, loads of money disappear as research and development (R&D) tries to design a vague product for a phantom market. This combines factors 2 and 5 in the Marketing NewsNet box. Apple Computer's hand-sized Newton computer that intended to help keep the user organized fizzled badly because no clear protocol existed. In contrast, US Robotics' Palm Pilot is wildly successful because it was designed from the outset to link to desktop computers.[11]

3. *Too little market attractiveness.* Shown as factor 8 in the Marketing NewsNet, market attractiveness refers to the ideal situation every new product manager looks for: a large target market with high growth and real buyer need. But often, when looking for ideal market niches, the target market is too small and competitive to warrant the R&D, production, and marketing expenses necessary to reach it. In the early 1990s Kodak discontinued its Ultralife lithium battery. Seen as a major breakthrough because of its 10-year shelf life, the battery was touted as lasting twice as long as an alkaline battery. Yet the product was only available in the 9-volt size, which accounts for less than 10 percent of the batteries sold in the United States.

MARKETING NEWSNET

What Separates New-Product Winners and Losers

What makes some products winners and others losers? Knowing this answer is a key to a new-product strategy. R. G. Cooper and E. J. Kleinschmidt studied 203 new industrial products to find the answers shown below.

The researchers defined the "product success rate" of new products as the percentage of products that reached the company's own profitability criteria. Product "winners" are the best 20 percent of performers and "losers" are the worst 20 percent. For example, for the first factor in the table below, 98 percent of the winners had a major point of difference compared with only 18 percent of the losers.

Note that the table below includes both marketing and nonmarketing factors. Most of the marketing factors below tie directly to the reasons cited in the text for new-product failures that are taken from a number of research studies. These include having a point of difference and a well-defined product before actual development starts (a product protocol).

FACTOR AFFECTING PRODUCT SUCCESS RATE	PRODUCT "WINNERS" (BEST 20%)	PRODUCT "LOSERS" (WORST 20%)	% DIFFERENCE (WINNERS–LOSERS)
1. Point of difference, or uniquely superior product	98%	18%	80%
2. Well-defined product before actual development starts	85	26	59
3. Synergy, or fit, with firm's R&D, engineering, and manufacturing capabilities	80	29	51
4. Quality of execution of technological activities	76	30	46
5. Quality of execution of activities before actual development starts	75	31	44
6. Synergy, or fit, with marketing mix activities	71	31	40
7. Quality of execution of marketing mix activities	71	32	39
8. Market attractiveness, ones with large markets, high growth, significant buyer need	74	43	31

4. *Poor execution of the marketing mix.* Coca-Cola thought its Minute Maid Squeeze-Fresh frozen orange juice concentrate in a squeeze bottle was a hit. The idea was that consumers could make one glass of juice at a time, and the concentrate stayed fresh in the refrigerator for over a month. After two test markets, the product was finished. Consumers loved the idea, but the product was messy to use, and the advertising and packaging didn't educate them effectively on how much concentrate to mix.

5. *Poor product quality on critical factors.* Overlapping somewhat with point 1, this factor stresses that poor quality on one or two critical factors can kill the product, even though the general quality is high. For example, the Japanese, like the British, drive on the left side of the road. Until 1996 U.S. carmakers sent Japan few right-drive cars—unlike German carmakers who exported right-drive models in a number of their brands.[12]

6. *Bad timing.* The product is introduced too soon, too late, or at a time when consumer tastes are shifting dramatically. Coaches of college baseball teams are

FIGURE 11–4
Why did these new products
fail?

As explained in detail in the text, new products often fail because of one or a combination of seven reasons. Look at the two products described below, and try to identify which reason explains why they failed in the marketplace:

- Del Monte's Barbecue Ketchup that contained finely chopped onions and was aimed at the heavy ketchup-eating segment.
- Mennen's Real deodorant, a cream-like antiperspirant developed for women, that was applied like a roll-on.

Compare your insights with those in the text.

increasingly concerned about the use of aluminum baseball bats that can rocket a baseball at a pitcher's head. Small wonder that Worth's "Copperhead ACX" bat is causing concern among these coaches. The ACX enlarges the bat's "sweet spot" using a piezoelectric circuit that automatically dampens vibrations and lengthens a batter's hits.[13]

7. *No economical access to buyers.* Grocery products provide an example. Today's mega-supermarkets carry 30,000 different products (meaning they carry 30,000 different SKUs). With about 34 new food products introduced each day, the fight for shelf space is tremendous in terms of costs for advertising, distribution, and shelf space.[14] Because shelf space is judged in terms of sales per square foot, Thirsty Dog! (a zesty beef-flavored, vitamin-enriched, mineral-loaded, lightly carbonated bottled water for your dog) must displace an existing product on the supermarket shelves. Many small manufacturers simply do not have the money to gain effective exposure for their products.

A Look at Some Failures   Before reading further, study the product failures described in Figure 11–4, and try to identify which of the eight reasons is the most likely explanation for their failure. The two examples are discussed in greater detail below.

Del Monte aimed its Barbecue Ketchup to the heavy ketchup-using segment—children and teenagers. The problem is that most consumers in this segment hate onions, so the product's difference—onions mixed with regular ketchup—worked against it. As a result, the target market was too small. The product was subsequently reintroduced as a gourmet sauce for meat cooked on outdoor grills.

Poor execution of the marketing mix hurt Real, Mennen's deodorant. The product was introduced with a $14 million advertising campaign. One problem, though, was that customers found that if they twisted the dispenser too hard, too much cream came out, creating an instant mess. Also, the name Real gave little indication of the product or its benefits.

Developing successful new products may sometimes involve luck, but more often it involves having a product that really meets a need and has significant points of difference over competitive products. The likelihood of success is improved by paying attention to the early steps of the new-product process described in the next section of the text.

1. From a consumer's viewpoint, what kind of innovation would an improved electric toothbrush be?

2. What does "insignificant point of difference" mean as a reason for new-product failure?

THE NEW-PRODUCT PROCESS

Companies such as General Electric, Sony, or Procter & Gamble take a sequence of steps before their products are ready for market. Figure 11–5 shows the seven stages of the **new-product process,** the sequence of activities a firm uses to identify business opportunities and convert them to a saleable good or service. This sequence begins with new-product strategy development and ends with commercialization.

New-Product Strategy Development

For companies, **new-product strategy development** involves defining the role for a new product in terms of the firm's overall corporate objectives. This step in the new-product process has been added by many companies recently to provide a needed focus for ideas and concepts developed in later stages.

Objectives of the Stage: Identify Markets and Strategic Roles   During this new-product strategy development stage the company uses the environmental scanning process described in Chapter 3 to identify trends that pose either opportunities or threats. Relevant company strengths and weaknesses are also identified. The outcome of new-product strategy development is not only new-product ideas but identifying markets for which new products will be developed and strategic roles new products might serve—the vital protocol activity explained earlier in the discussion of the Marketing NewsNet on new-product winners and losers.

Booz, Allen & Hamilton, Inc., a national consulting firm, asked firms what strategic role was served by their most successful recent product. These roles, shown in Figure 11–6, help define the direction of new-product development and divide into externally and internally driven factors.

Henry C. Yuen is an example of using an externally driven action to preempt a market segment (Figure 11–6). Not your typical TV couch potato, Yuen tried to tape a baseball game and got only snow. Unlike the rest of us who might just have mumbled, Yuen took his PhD degree in mathematics and co-invented "VCR Plus"—the device millions of TV fans use to set their VCRs by punching in numbers from newspaper listings.[15]

FIGURE 11–5
Stages in the new-product process

FIGURE 11–6
Strategic roles of most
successful new products

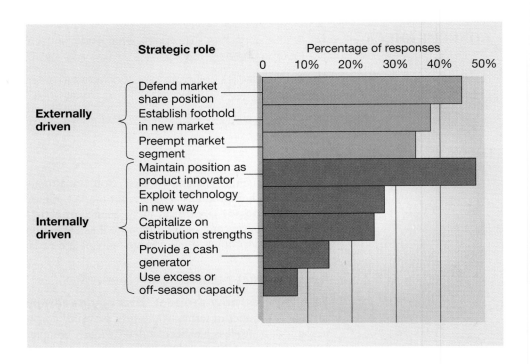

Cross-Functional Teams   Another key to 3M's success in new-product development is its use of *cross-functional teams,* a small number of people from different departments in an organization who are mutually accountable to a common set of performance goals. Teams are especially important in new-product development so that individuals from R&D, marketing, manufacturing, finance, and so forth can simultaneously search together in a constructive environment for new product and market opportunities. In the past 3M and other firms often utilized these department people in sequence—possibly resulting in R&D designing new products that the manufacturing department couldn't produce economically and that the marketing department couldn't sell.[16]

One 3M cross-functional team studied creative ways to get the attention of design engineers to find uses for its VHB tape—the example that started the chapter. The team came up with the idea of putting an actual piece of VHB tape between two pieces of film in the ad itself. The resulting ad (shown at left) then challenged engineers reading it to pull the film apart—and also to note their design problem on another part of the ad and to fax it to 3M.

3M's experiences suggest some conclusions about today's style of teamwork:

- Teams are ongoing, not just a one-shot effort.
- Teamwork takes time because the members have to learn about each other and find a comfort level.
- Team members can—and do—disagree, and that's okay.
- Teams can be informal or formal, depending on the task that needs doing.
- Teams need "champions," individuals willing and able to carry messages and requests to management and to move the project forward.

The VHB pull-apart challenge for design engineers; note the actual pull-apart films in the bottom of the ad

Because program and product champions are so important in marketing, they are discussed again in Chapter 22.

Customer ideas on new products appear in many settings. What geographic area in the United States might you go to for consumer ideas on (1) an Infiniti luxury sports utility vehicle and (2) a Mazda Miata? The text provides the answers.

Infiniti

www.infiniti-usa.com/docs/QX4/index

Mazda

www.mazdausa.com/mia

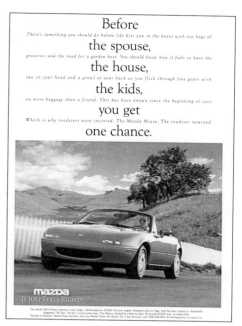

Idea Generation

Developing a pool of concepts as candidates for new products, or **idea generation,** must build on the previous stage's results. New-product ideas are generated by consumers, employees, basic R&D, and competitors.

Customer Suggestions   Companies often analyze consumer complaints or problems to discover new-product opportunities. They also pose complaints to a sample of consumers, who are asked to suggest products with such deficiencies in order to identify new product opportunities. Listening to growing concerns about cholesterol and fat in its food, McDonald's reformulated its shakes with a low-fat mixture and introduced a low-fat hamburger.

Five years after Infiniti's audacious QK4 luxury car was a smash with consumers, the company started searching for a luxury sport utility add-on to its line. So researchers flew from Infiniti's California headquarters to affluent Westchester County, New York, to conduct one-on-one interviews with Infiniti owners living in the area. Soon the picture of the new sport utility vehicle emerged: 4-wheel drive, priced under $40,000, drives more like a car than a truck, low step for easy boarding, etc. Monthly sales of the vehicle exceeded projections by 60 percent.[17]

Employee and Co-Worker Suggestions   Employees may be encouraged to suggest new product ideas through suggestion boxes or contests. The idea for General Mills's $350 million-a-year Nature Valley Granola Bars came when one of its marketing managers observed co-workers bringing granola to work in plastic bags.

Research and Development Breakthroughs   Another source of new products is a firm's basic research, but the costs can be huge. As described in the Marketing NewsNet box,[18] Sony is the acknowledged world leader in new-product development in electronics. Its scientists and engineers produce an average of four new products each business day. Sony's research and development breakthroughs have led to innovative products, and its ability to manufacture and market those products has made it a legend in the electronics industry, popularizing VCRs, the Walkman, and—coming into your future?—digital video disks (DVDs)?

MARKETING NEWSNET

TECHNOLOGY

The World Consumer Electronics Champ: And Its Name Is . . .?

The "battle for the living room" begins this company's twenty-first century. To win, it will have to keep linking technology and entertainment, content and hardware, digital insides and perfectly cool plastic outsides, in a new new new digital dance, daily. Late in the twentieth century, it was already a nearly $50 billion concern polled as America's "most respected brand" and known—along with Coke, Nike, and MTV—as one of the four most creative companies in the world. Yet its army of engineers work in an "eel's bedroom." Heard enough to know? It is Sony.

This Japan-based company with tentacles around the world made transistor history early on, launched the likes of Walkman and PlayStation, and came up with designs that said "wow" and wormed their way into consumers' hearts. But in a society that has gone from abacus to analog to digital in about one generation, you have to re-invent and re-integrate yourself regularly. Walkman, Handycam, Discman—keep running!

Under the new CEO, Nobuyuki Idei, who came out of marketing, Sony is attempting just that. Under way now: perfecting product to win the DVD (digital video disk) war, launching satellite broadcast service, making management more American and more international at the same time, taking risks that can't always be market-researched, creating products that are lifestyle-exciting, computerizing mixes of video and audio, whatever!

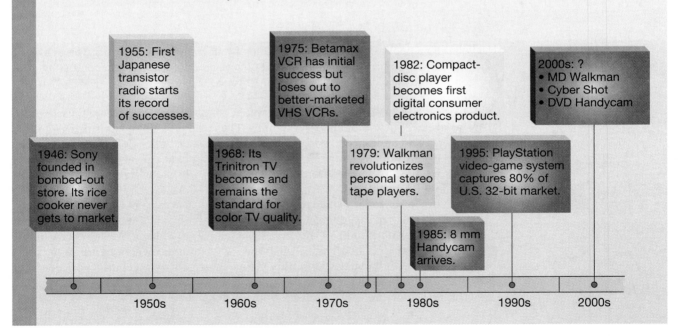

1946: Sony founded in bombed-out store. Its rice cooker never gets to market.

1955: First Japanese transistor radio starts its record of successes.

1968: Its Trinitron TV becomes and remains the standard for color TV quality.

1975: Betamax VCR has initial success but loses out to better-marketed VHS VCRs.

1979: Walkman revolutionizes personal stereo tape players.

1982: Compact-disc player becomes first digital consumer electronics product.

1985: 8 mm Handycam arrives.

1995: PlayStation video-game system captures 80% of U.S. 32-bit market.

2000s: ?
• MD Walkman
• Cyber Shot
• DVD Handycam

1950s   1960s   1970s   1980s   1990s   2000s

Not all R&D labs have Sony's genius for moving electronic breakthroughs into the marketplace. Take Xerox Corporation's Palo Alto Research Center (PARC). In maybe the greatest electronic fumble of all time, by 1979 PARC had what's in your computer system now—graphical user interfaces, mice, windows and pull-down menus, laser printers, and distributed computing. Concerned with aggressive competition from Japan in its core photocopier business, Xerox didn't even bother to patent these breakthroughs. Apple Computer's Steven Jobs visited PARC in 1979, adapted many of the ideas for the Macintosh, and the rest is history.[19]

Even getting R&D breakthroughs into the marketplace—which PARC never did— doesn't guarantee success. Eye-popping high-definition television (HDTV) is making

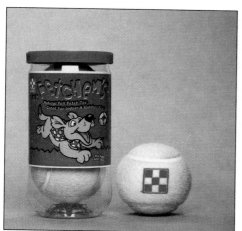

"R.P. Fetchem" dog toy

its grand entrance on the stage of U.S. consumer electronics—at initial prices of $5,000 to $12,000.[20] While the TV picture is far better than on your analog TV set, is HDTV worth the improvement? As you read this, hundreds of manufacturers and retailers are also wondering. You, and millions of consumers like you, hold the answer.

Professional R&D laboratories also provide new-product ideas. Labs at Arthur D. Little helped put the crunch in Cap'n Crunch cereal and the flavor in Carnation Instant Breakfast. Because broccoli is increasingly felt to contain cancer-fighting properties, Little's labs are trying to find ways to make the vegetable more appealing to today's consumers. Some ideas now in test: sweetened broccoli-based vegetable juices and a chocolate-flavored powdered broccoli-juice drink mix. An idea sent back to the drawing boards: broccoli cereal.[21]

Competitive Products   New-product ideas can also be found by analyzing the competition. A six-person intelligence team from the Marriott Corporation spent six months traveling around the country staying at economy hotels. The team assessed the competition's strengths and weaknesses on everything from the soundproof qualities of the rooms to the softness of the towels. Marriott then budgeted $500 million for a new economy hotel chain, Fairfield Inns.

Screening and Evaluation

The third stage of the new product process is **screening and evaluation,** which involves internal and external evaluations of the new-product ideas to eliminate those that warrant no further effort.

Internal Approach   Internally, the firm evaluates the technical feasibility of the proposal and whether the idea meets the objectives defined in the new-product strategy development step. In the 1990s Penn Racquet Sports, the largest U.S. producer of tennis balls, faced flat sales because of a decade-long lull in recreational tennis. What to do? Penn Racquet employees observed that many used tennis balls are given as a toy to the family dog. So in 1998 the company designed and introduced R.P. Fetchem—a dye-free "natural felt fetch toy" that looks remarkably like . . . a tennis ball! One difference: The balls carry the Ralston Purina logo because of a licensing agreement with the giant dog-food producer.[22]

Tiny Magnetic Poetry, Inc. has a limited budget for customer research. But, as shown in the Web Link box, that has not restricted employees from extending the product line from magnetic words for refrigerator doors to electronic ones for the Internet.[23]

A year's worth of consumer interviews went into the development of Sun Chips.

External Approach   Concept tests are external evaluations that consist of preliminary testing of the new-product idea (rather than the actual product) with consumers. Concept tests usually rely on written descriptions of the product but may be augmented with sketches, mockups, or promotional literature. Several key questions are asked during concept testing: How does the customer perceive the product? Who would use it? How would it be used?

Frito-Lay spent a year interviewing 10,000 consumers about the concept of a multigrain snack chip. The company experimented with 50 different shapes before settling on a thin, rectangular chip with ridges and a slightly salty, nutty flavor. The product, Sun Chips, is highly successful.

WEB LINK

ElectroMagnetic Poetry: From Fridge . . . to . . . Cyberspace

Brand and product line extensions, like adding Diet Coke to the Coke line or Frosted Cheerios to the Cheerios line, are well-established marketing strategies. But if you start with Magnetic Poetry—the words on a strip with magnetic backing mainly found on refrigerators—where do you go next?

It turns out the company has taken Magnetic Poetry into more than 50 items. The "Original Edition" has given birth to the Flip Series (words on both sides of the tiles), Kids Edition, Gardener Edition, and Really Big Words Edition. Pretty tame? Then consider Accessory Editions for car bumpers (Bumper Poet), your coffee mug (Magnetic Poetry), or your lunch box (Poetry

Case). Or World Series will let you do foreign language sentences. Or you can paint your walls with Poetry Paint that makes any surface hold magnets, a surface than can be painted or papered over if you want.

For the computer segment, there's ElectroMagnetic Poetry, an application that can also be used as a screen saver. Word tiles will float by on your computer screen that your mouse clicks can grab and arrange. If your newly created poem is too good to lose, you can save it, print it, or paste it into an e-mail note to a friend.

To see these new product line extensions, check out: www.magneticpoetry.com

---

CONCEPT CHECK

1. What step in the new-product process has been added in recent years?

2. What are four sources of new-product ideas?

3. What is the difference between internal and external screening and evaluation approaches used by a firm in the new-product process?

Business Analysis

Business analysis involves specifying the features of the product and the marketing strategy needed to commercialize it and making necessary financial projections. This is the last checkpoint before significant capital is invested in creating a prototype of the product. Economic analysis, marketing strategy review, and legal examination of the proposed product are conducted at this stage. It is at this point that the product is analyzed relative to the firm's marketing and technological synergies, two criteria noted in the Marketing NewsNet shown earlier in the chapter.

The marketing strategy review studies the new-product idea in relation to the marketing program to support it. The proposed product is assessed to determine whether it will help or hurt sales of existing products. Likewise, the product is examined to assess whether it can be sold through existing channels or if new outlets will be needed. Profit projections involve estimating the number of units expected to be sold but also the costs of R&D, production, and marketing.

As an important aspect of the business analysis, the proposed new product is studied to determine whether it can be protected with a patent or copyright. An attractive new-product proposal is one in which the technology, product, or brand cannot easily be copied.

Development

Product ideas that survive the business analysis proceed to actual **development,** turning the idea on paper into a prototype. This results in a demonstrable, producible

Mattel's laboratory testing subjects its toys and dolls, like Barbie here, to extreme tests to ensure quality and protect children.

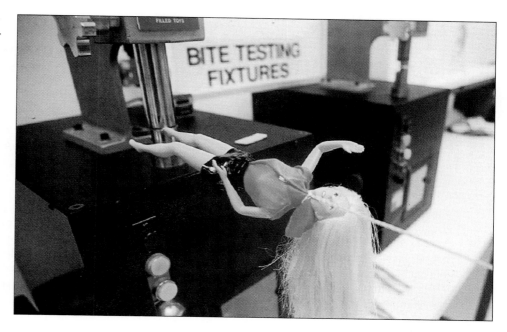

product in hand. Outsiders seldom understand the technical complexities of the development stage, which involves not only manufacturing the product but also performing laboratory and consumer tests to ensure that it meets the standards set. Design of the product becomes an important element.

Liquid Tide, introduced by P&G, looks like a simple modification of its original Tide detergent. However, P&G sees this product as a technological breakthrough: the first detergent without phosphates that cleans as well as existing phosphate detergents. To achieve this breakthrough, P&G spent 400,000 hours and combined technologies from its laboratories in three countries. The new ingredient in Liquid Tide that helps

Why do you want General Electric to pass the "bird strike test" on its new GE90 jet engine? For the answer, see the text.

ETHICS AND SOCIAL RESPONSIBILITY ALERT

Sports Utilities versus Cars: Godzilla Meets a Chimp?

Make car wrecks safe. This sounds sort of stupid. But . . . the problem is death! The high and heavy pickups, vans, and sport utility vehicles (SUVs) are now involved in nearly 20 percent of all U.S. highway deaths. When one huge vehicle meets a bitty car, the larger, higher one smashes the smaller one's passenger compartment, instead of going head-to-head at bumper level. The people in the car become 81 percent of the deaths in these accidents.

The problem is also money. These mega-vehicles now account for nearly 50 percent of Detroit's sales and most of its profits. Improving the cars—with side air bags and steel supports—is cheaper than lowering the frame or adding a crumple zone for the frame of the bigger vehicle. Nothing is easy. And consumers love the power of these hefty rides, about 2,000 pounds heavier than a compact car.

Change may have to come from National Highway & Transportation Safety Administration mandates. Its chief, Ricardo Martinez, points to the complete redesign of Mercedes Benz's M-class SUV as the model for what should be done. Mercedes engineers addressed compatibility of their SUV with smaller cars, so the Mercedes SUV frame and bumper is as much as nine inches lower than Detroit's SUVs. This makes the bumpers of Mercedes SUVs and those of small cars more likely to meet in a crash, dramatically increasing the safety for small-car passengers.

Who should crush the crashes here? Is it up to the National Highway & Transportation Safety Administration? The insurance companies? The vehicle manufacturers? Consumers?

---

suspend the dirt in wash water came out of the P&G research lab in Cincinnati. The cleaning agents in the product came from P&G scientists in Japan. Water-softening technology came from P&G's lab in Belgium. In a blind test consumers preferred Liquid Tide nine to one over the detergent of their choice.

The prototype product is tested in the laboratory to see if it achieves the physical standards set for it if used the way it is intended. But safety tests are also critical for when the product isn't used as planned. To make sure seven-year olds can't bite Barbie's head off and choke, Mattel clamps her foot in steel jaws in a test stand and then pulls on her head with a wire. Similarly, car manufacturers have done extensive safety tests by crashing their cars into concrete walls. As mentioned in the Ethics and Social Responsibility Alert box, consumer groups are increasingly concerned about what happens when a pickup truck or sport utility vehicle hits a small car when their bumpers don't line up.[24] Auto industry tests are identifying some feasible, but costly, solutions.

Industrial products often have special, exacting test requirements. For example, jet engines for commercial aircraft have to pass a "bird strike test" and have minimal engine damage when a carcasses of ducks or gulls are fired into the whirling jet engine operating on a test stand. Why this weird field test? To simulate the conditions that might occur when your plane ingests an unfortunate seagull or duck standing around on the runway at takeoff. General Electric's huge new GE90 is used to power Boeing 777 commercial jets. As a result of tests like these, GE engineers redesigned the GE 90's jet engine blades, and it passed its next bird strike test with flying colors.[25]

Market Testing

The **market testing** stage of the new-product process involves exposing actual products to prospective consumers under realistic purchase conditions to see if they will buy. Often a product is developed, tested, refined, and then tested again to get consumer reactions through either test marketing or purchase laboratories.

FIGURE 11–7
The most popular test markets

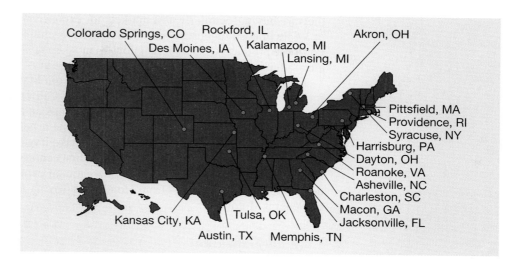

Test Marketing   Test marketing involves offering a product for sale on a limited basis in a defined area. This test is done to determine whether consumers will actually buy the product and to try different ways of marketing it. Only about a third of the products test marketed do well enough to go on to the next phase. These market tests are usually conducted in cities that are viewed as being representative of U.S. consumers. Figure 11–7 shows the cities commonly used for market tests.

In examining the commercial viability of the new product, companies measure sales in the test area, often with *store audits* that measure the sales in grocery stores and the number of cases ordered by a store from the wholesaler. This gives the company an indication of potential sales volume and market share in the test area. Market tests are also used to check other elements of the marketing mix besides the product itself such as price, level of advertising support, and distribution. Representativeness of the test market to the target market for the product is very important so that results can be projected. Market tests also are time consuming and expensive because production lines as well as promotion and sales programs must be set up. Costs can run over a million dollars. Market tests also reveal plans to competitors, sometimes enabling them to get a product into national distribution first. Although Hunt-Wesson got its Prima Salsa Tomato Sauce into the test market first, Chesebrough-Pond's Ragu Extra Thick & Zesty beat it into national introduction. Competitors can also try to sabotage test markets. With such problems, some firms skip test markets completely or use simulated test markets.

Simulated Test Markets   Because of the time, cost, and confidentiality problems of test markets, manufacturers often turn to *simulated* (or *laboratory*) *test markets* (*STM*), a technique that simulates a full-scale test market but in a limited fashion. STMs are often run in shopping malls, where consumers are questioned to identify who uses the product class being tested. Willing participants are questioned on usage, reasons for purchase, and important product attributes. Qualified persons are then shown TV commercials or print ads for the test product along with competitors' advertising and are given money to make a decision to buy or not buy a package of the product (or the competitors') from a real or simulated store environment. If the test product is not purchased, the consumer may receive it as a free sample and be interviewed later for reactions.

When Test Markets Don't Work   Test marketing is a valuable step in the new-product process, but not all products can use it. Testing a service beyond the concept level is very difficult because the service is intangible and consumers can't see what they are buying. Similarly, test markets for expensive consumer products such as cars or VCRs or costly industrial products such as jet engines or computers are impractical. For these products consumer reactions to mockup designs or one-of-a-kind prototypes are all that is feasible.

An extreme example: In 1984 car designer Tom Matano took his marketing director for a spin in his new roadster prototype near a California beach. "People in Porsches were chasing us and a guy was running next to us on the sidewalk, asking questions," Matano recalls. The marketing director became a believer and helped introduce the Mazda Miata, whose half-million cars sold make it one of the most popular sports cars ever—and a launching pad into the twenty-first century. Because of California's sensitivity to car styles and trends, many international carmakers now have marketing and design headquarters there—from Honda and Toyota to the Lincoln-Mercury division of General Motors.[26]

Commercialization

Finally, the product is brought to the point of **commercialization**—positioning and launching it in full-scale production and sales. Companies proceed very carefully at the commercialization stage because this is the most expensive stage for most new products, especially consumer products.

Increasing the Success Rate of New Products   In recent years, companies have begun to recognize that speed is important in bringing a new product to market. Recent studies have shown that high-tech products coming to market on time are far more profitable than those arriving late. As a result, some companies—such as Sony, NEC, Honda, AT&T, and Hewlett-Packard—have overlapped the sequence of stages described in this chapter. With this approach, termed *parallel development* (the simultaneous development by cross-functional teams of both the product and the production process), marketing, manufacturing, and R&D personnel stay with the product from conception to production. The results are a significant reduction in new-product development times. Honda has cut car development from five years to three, while Hewlett-Packard has reduced the development time for computer printers from 54 months to 22.

Space on supermarket shelves is so limited that retailers often charge manufacturers slotting fees and failure fees.

Effective cross-functional teams at Hewlett-Packard have reduced new-product development times significantly.

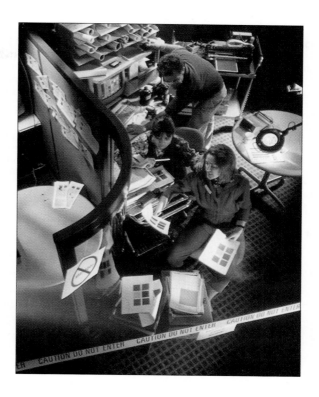

The Risks and Uncertainties of the Commercialization Stage   The job is far from over when the new product gets to the commercialization stage. In fact, disasters still often occur. Some examples include the following:

- The high quality of the 5 or 50 prototypes that were handcrafted in the R&D lab with lots of tender loving care can't be replicated on the mass-production lines.
- Costs have gotten so far beyond original budgets that customers won't buy the product at the new price point that must be set to make a profit.
- Buyers can't understand the benefits of the new product without extensive, costly education activities—necessitating new training of the sales force and distributors, along with new videos and infomercials.
- Competitors introduce their new product a few weeks before the firm's own product hits the market, making the product obsolete before potential customers ever see it.

The last point in the list—bad timing—gives new-product managers nightmares. IBM, for example, killed several laptop computer prototypes because competitors introduced better, more advanced machines to the market before IBM.

Grocery products have special problems at the commercialization stage. Because space is so limited on supermarket shelves, many require manufacturers to pay a **slotting fee,** a payment a manufacturer makes to place a new item on a retailer's shelf. This can run to several million dollars for a single product. But there's even another potential expense. If a new grocery product does not achieve a predetermined sales target, some retailers require a **failure fee,** a penalty payment by a manufacturer to compensate the retailer for sales its valuable shelf space never made. To minimize the financial risk of a new product failure, many grocery product manufacturers use *regional rollouts,* introducing the product sequentially into geographical areas of the United States to allow production levels and marketing activities to build up gradually.

Figure 11–8 identifies the purpose of each stage of the new-product process and the kinds of marketing information and methods used. The figure also suggests information

STAGE OF PROCESS	PURPOSE OF STAGE	MARKETING INFORMATION AND METHODS USED
New-product strategy development	Identify new-product niches to reach in light of company objectives	Company objectives; assessment of firm's current strengths and weaknesses in terms of market and product
Idea generation	Develop concepts for possible products	Ideas from employees and co-workers, consumers, R&D, and competitors; methods of brainstorming and focus groups
Screening and evaluation	Separates good product ideas from bad ones inexpensively	Screening criteria, concept tests, and weighted point systems
Business analysis	Identify the product's features and its marketing strategy, and make financial projections	Product's key features, anticipated marketing mix strategy; economic, marketing, production, legal, and profitability analyses
Development	Create the prototype product, and test it in the laboratory and on consumers	Laboratory and consumer tests on product prototypes
Market testing	Test product and marketing strategy in the marketplace on a limited scale	Test markets, simulated test markets (STMs)
Commercialization	Position and offer product in the marketplace	Perceptual maps, product positioning, regional rollouts

FIGURE 11–8
Marketing information and methods used in the new-product process

that might help avoid some new product failures. Although using the new-product process does not guarantee successful products, it does increase a firm's success rate.

CONCEPT CHECK

1. How does the development stage of the new-product process involve testing the product inside and outside the firm?

2. What is a test market?

3. What is commercialization of a new product?

SUMMARY

1 A product is a good, service, or idea consisting of a bundle of tangible and intangible attributes that satisfies consumers and is received in exchange for money or some other unit of value. A company's product decisions involve the product item, product line, and range of its product mix.

2 Products can be classified by tangibility and by user. By degree of tangibility, products divide into nondurable goods, durable goods, and services. By user, the major distinctions are consumer or industrial goods. Consumer goods consist of convenience, shopping, and specialty products. Industrial goods are for either production or support.

3 There are several ways to define a new product, such as the degree of distinction from existing products, a time base specified by the FTC, a company perspective, or effect on a consumer's usage pattern.

4 In terms of its effect on a consumer's use of a product, a discontinuous innovation represents the greatest change and a

continuous innovation the least. A dynamically continuous innovation is disruptive but not totally new.

5 The failure of a new product is usually attributable to one of seven marketing reasons: insignificant point of difference, incomplete market and product definition before product development begins, too little market attractiveness, poor execution of the marketing mix, poor product quality on critical factors, bad timing, and no economical access to buyers.

6 The new-product process consists of seven stages. Objectives for new products are determined in the first stage, new-product strategy development; this is followed by idea generation, screening and evaluation, business analysis, development, market testing, and commercialization.

7 Ideas for new products come from several sources, including consumers, employees, R&D laboratories, and competitors.

8 Screening and evaluation can be done internally or externally.

9 Business analysis involves defining the features of the new product, a marketing strategy to introduce it, and a financial forecast.
10 Development involves not only producing a prototype product but also testing it in the lab and on consumers to see that it meets the standards set for it.

11 In market testing new products, companies often rely on market tests to see that consumers will actually buy the product when it's offered for sale and that other marketing mix factors are working. Products surviving this stage are commercialized—taken to market.

KEY TERMS AND CONCEPTS

product p. 286
product line p. 286
product mix p. 287
consumer goods p. 288
industrial goods p. 288
convenience goods p. 289
shopping goods p. 289
specialty goods p. 289
unsought goods p. 289
production goods p. 290
support goods p. 290

protocol p. 294
new-product process p. 297
new-product strategy development p. 297
idea generation p. 299
screening and evaluation p. 301
business analysis p. 302
development p. 302
market testing p. 304
commercialization p. 306
slotting fee p. 307
failure fee p. 307

 INTERNET EXERCISE

Jalepeno soda? Aerosol mustard? These are just two of the more than 60,000 failed consumer products on the shelves of the New Product Showcase and Learning Center in Ithaca, New York. You probably can't visit the Showcase personally to learn important new-product lessons like executives from firms such as Procter & Gamble and Kraft do, but you can visit its Web site (www.showlearn.com). Study several of the failed products on the Web site and try to identify which of the reasons discussed earlier in the chapter explain the failures—shown as "Bob's Favorite Flops" (www.showlearn.com/favflops). Or check out "Rising Stars" (www.showlearn.com/risingstar)—products seen as about to take off into fame and fortune.

APPLYING MARKETING CONCEPTS AND PERSPECTIVES

1 Products can be classified as either consumer or industrial goods. How would you classify the following products: (*a*) Johnson's baby shampoo, (*b*) a Black & Decker two-speed drill, and (*c*) an arc welder?
2 Are products such as Nature Valley Granola bars and Eddie Bauer hiking boots convenience, shopping, specialty, or unsought goods?
3 Based on your answer to problem 2, how would the marketing actions differ for each product and the classification to which you assigned it?
4 In terms of the behavioral effect on consumers, how would a PC, such as a Macintosh PowerBook or an IBM ThinkPad, be classified? In light of this classification, what actions would you suggest to the manufacturers of these products to increase their sales in the market?
5 Several alternative definitions were presented for a new product. How would a company's marketing strategy be affected if it used (*a*) the legal definition or (*b*) a behavioral definition?
6 What methods would you suggest to assess the potential commercial success for the following new products: (*a*) a new, improved ketchup, (*b*) a three-dimensional television system that took the company 10 years to develop, and (*c*) a new children's toy on which the company holds a patent?
7 Look back at Figure 11–6, which outlines the roles for new products. If a company followed the role of defending market share position, what type of positioning strategy might be implemented?
8 Concept testing is an important step in the new-product process. Outline the concept tests for (*a*) an electrically powered car and (*b*) a new loan payment system for automobiles that is based on a variable rate interest. What are the differences in developing concept tests for products as opposed to services?

CASE 11–1　PALM COMPUTING, INC.

Developing new products often requires a complicated and challenging sequence of activities. "It's not as simple as taking what the customer wants and creating a product," says Joe Sipher, director—Wireless Products at Palm Computing, Inc., a subsidiary of 3Com Corp. "If we did that, we would have ended up with something like Apple Computer's Newton, which was a failure because it incorporated too many features into the product." While this perspective seems counter-intuitive, it has proven highly successful for Palm Computing, the market leader for personal digital assistants (PDA).

THE COMPANY

The original PalmPilot inventors, Jeff Hawkins and Donna Dubinsky, started out developing personal computing connectivity and shorthand software for other PDA manufacturers in the spring of 1994. According to Dubinsky, "We started out as an applications software company. We worked with Casio, Sharp, Hewlett-Packard, Apple, and others—everybody who was working in the field at that time. But none of the platforms were compelling. Most thought a PDA should be a smaller version of a laptop computer." Although Palm Computing was the leading software developer for these PDA entrants, sales were too low to keep the company running. "The reasons why early handheld computers failed were because they had too many features, making

them too big, too slow, too heavy, and too expensive," explains Andrea Butter, vice president of marketing.

Palm Computing managers saw a dismal future in being the leading applications provider for a nonexistent market. However, as Butter states, "We felt we knew what customers wanted to do in handheld computing and one day an investor challenged us and said, 'If you know how to do it, why don't you do it?'" They accepted the challenge and today Palm Computing is the market share leader in the PDA industry. To provide additional funding and technology for the PalmPilot, U.S. Robotics, a leading modem manufacturer, acquired Palm Computing in 1995, which in turn was acquired in 1997 by 3Com Corp., a leading manufacturer of information access products and network system solutions.

During 1998, Palm Computing sold 1.3 million units in the total U.S. handheld market. By 2000, Palm Computing's sales are expected to reach 1.8 million units in a total PDA market of 2.7 million units.

THE POSITIONING DILEMMA

Defining this type of product has been a challenge. These products have been referred to as information appliances, smart handheld computers, personal information managers, and personal digital assistants (PDA). Physically, these products have a thin, panel-like body (like the "communicator" from the original Star Trek series) measuring about 5" × 3" × 0.5". They typically do not have keyboards or keypads; instead, they use a pen or stylus and handwriting recognition software to allow users to store addresses and telephone numbers, enter appointments on a calendar, make notes and to-do lists, and interface with personal computers to transfer e-mail and other data. Hawkins and Dubinsky viewed PDAs as digital replacements for paper-based systems, such as DayTimers, Rolodexes, and Post-it® Notes.

PALM COMPUTING'S NEW PRODUCT PROCESS

Hawkins used his own experience with the "GRiDPad," the first handheld computer developed in the mid-1980s, and "Graffiti," a shorthand-type of handwriting recognition software developed for other entrants in the PDA market, to design the original PalmPilot. Hawkins' R&D consisted of carrying a rectangular block of wood in his shirt pocket with "function buttons" glued to it. When people asked him if he was free for lunch, he would take out his "connected organizer," tap on a "button," and observe their reactions. Hawkins tried several variations before settling on a final design: the PalmPilot would only have four function buttons (calendar, addresses and phone numbers, to-do lists, and memos) because those were the most frequently used applications. In addition, Palm Computing conducted a survey among customers of Casio's "Zoomer" PDA. The most important finding was that 90 percent used a personal computer. As a result, the new PalmPilot would also include PC connectivity. Finally, the PalmPilot would only be sold in computer and office supply stores because their salespersons were perceived to have greater skills in selling technology-based products.

The original PalmPilot was launched in 1996 at Demo'96, a trade show whose attendees were technology opinion leaders. The PalmPilot was the "media darling of the show" and sales took off from there. The original PalmPilot has since been retired. The PalmPilot Connected Organizer product line has included the PalmPilot Professional ($149), the Palm III ($249), the Palm IIIx ($369), the Palm V ($449), and the Palm VII ($599). Each of these models has the same minimalist design as the original.

COMPETITION AND THE PDA MARKET

When Windows CE 1.0 came out in 1997, Dubinsky recalls, "We said, 'Oh-oh, it's all over for us now.'" But it turned out that consumers weren't interested in devices that were positioned between PDAs and personal computers. In 1998, International Data Corp. reported that Windows CE devices held only a 15 percent market share, but may garner a 55 percent share by 2002. Hardware manufacturers, such as Hewlett-Packard, Casio, Philips, etc., have partnered with Microsoft and are enthusiastic about newer versions of this OS software and other innovations in battery and memory technology that allow them to offer more features such as color touch-screens for graphics, charts, and other presentations, slimmed down versions of Microsoft's popular Word and Excel programs, the familiar Windows-like interface, and Internet searching and paging via a PC card interface in their products. However, these products are still pricey, sluggish, and consume more power than those from Palm Computing. At the low end of the market, companies such as Casio and Royal have introduced single-function PDA devices at $99 or less. Finally, Palm Computing faces competition from Web-based personal information managers (PIM), which perform identical functions as the PalmPilot. These organizers are stored at one's Internet service provider and accessed via browsers, such as Netscape or Internet Explorer, or portals, such as Yahoo! or America Online (AOL).

THE FUTURE OF PALM COMPUTING

Palm Computing has responded by introducing two new products: the Palm IIIe and Palm Vx. Both compete with Windows CE-based systems. Both products offer better screen contrast and faster processors, but no changes in the Palm OS, the "operating system" software that gives these PDAs their handwriting recognition, time management, database (address and telephone number), and note-taking functionality. The Palm IIIe offers twice the memory as previous models while the Palm Vx has a sleeker, slimmer design, recessed buttons, and lithium instead of AAA batteries for 10 hours of life. Palm Computing also encouraged third-party software developers to extend the Palm OS's functionality to include e-mail, Internet search, expense recording, and even e-commerce applications. To further expand its share of the PDA market, Palm Computing has licensed its OS to Handspring for use in its "Visor" and to other original equipment manufacturers (OEM) for their private label brands, such as IBM's "WorkPad" PDA and Qualcomm's "pdQ," a combination PDA organizer and cellular telephone. Finally, Palm Computing has encouraged others to develop accessories for the Palm Connected Organizer product line.

Palm Computing's Palm VII, introduced in mid-1999, could revolutionize the PDA marketplace. The Palm VII is targeted at the rapidly growing wireless and mobile market, which has an estimated potential market of 21 million subscribers by 2002. The $599 Palm VII is positioned between a two-way pager and a laptop computer with wireless Internet access, and is virtually identical to the Palm III except for the wireless antenna that connects users to the proprietary Palm.net "Web clipping" service. E-Trade, Ticketmaster, The Wall Street Journal Interactive Edition, The Weather Channel, USA Today, Yahoo!, and other Palm.net content partners optimized content for the memory and small screen of Palm VII. In addition, users can send and receive short e-mail messages through Palm.net's iMessenger service. Future Palm Computing PDAs may include full Internet Web site access and e-mail messaging.

Questions

1 Which of the steps in the new product process discussed in Chapter 11 did Palm Computing use to develop the PalmPilot? What activities did Palm Computing use in each step?
2 What are the characteristics of the PalmPilot target market?
3 What kinds of learning or behavioral changes were required by consumers who purchased the PalmPilot?
4 What are the key "points of difference" of the PalmPilot when compared to substitute products?
5 How would you rate the PalmPilot on the following reasons for success or failure: significant points of difference; size of market; product quality; market timing; and access to consumers?

ROAD NEVER ENDS

RUN AFTER RUN, MILE AFTER NEVER-ENDING MILE, NOTHING KEEPS YOU GOING BETTER THAN GATORADE. LIFE IS A SPORT.

CHAPTER TWELVE

MANAGING PRODUCTS AND BRANDS

12

AFTER READING THIS CHAPTER YOU SHOULD BE ABLE TO:

- Explain the product life-cycle concept and relate a marketing strategy to each stage.

- Recognize the differences in product life cycles for various products and their implications for marketing decisions.

- Understand alternative approaches to managing a product's life cycle.

- Describe elements of brand personality and brand equity and the criteria for the good brand name.

- Explain the rationale for alternative branding strategies employed by companies.

- Understand the benefits of packaging and warranties in the marketing of a product.

GATORADE: THE ACTIVE THIRST-QUENCHER FOR INTENSE SWEATY SITUATIONS AND PARCHED PALATES

The thirst for Gatorade is unquenchable as far as Sue Wellington is concerned. She should know. Wellington is president of Gatorade's U.S. operations and has forged a successful marketing career nurturing the Gatorade brand into a beverage powerhouse that commands more than 80 percent of the $1.5 billion U.S. sports drink market.

Like Kleenex in the tissue market and Jello among gelatin desserts, Gatorade has become synonymous with sports drinks. Concocted in 1965 at the University of Florida as a rehydration beverage for the school's football team, the drink was called "Gatorade" by an opposing team's coach after watching his team lose to the Florida Gators in the Orange Bowl. The name stuck, and a new beverage product class was born. Today, Gatorade is the official sports drink of Major League Baseball, the National Football League, the National Basketball Association, and the National Hockey League.

The Stokely-Van Camp Co. bought the Gatorade formula in 1967 and commercialized the product. The original Gatorade was a liquid with a lemon-lime flavor. An orange flavor was added in 1971 and a fruit-punch flavor in 1983. Instant Gatorade was introduced in 1979. Quaker Oats purchased Stokely-Van Camp in 1983, at which time Gatorade sales were $97 million. Quaker Oats executives immediately began to build sales through a variety of means. More flavors were added and multiple package sizes were offered using different containers—glass and plastic bottles and aluminum cans. Distribution expanded first to include convenience stores and supermarkets followed by vending machines and fountain service. Consistent advertising and promotion effectively conveyed the product's benefits and links to athletic competition using popular athletes such as

Michael Jordan as spokespersons. International opportunities were vigorously pursued. Gatorade is sold in more than 20 major countries throughout Europe, Latin America, and Asia. The result? Gatorade sales have grown at a 21 percent annual rate since 1984. Gatorage marketing has deflected the efforts of 50 to 60 competing sports drink brands since 1967, including Coca-Cola's PowerAde and PepsiCo's All Sport. But Wellington notes, "Remember, our main competitor is tap water." Under her guidance, Quaker Oats introduced Gatorade Frost in 1997, with a "lighter, crisper" taste aimed at expanding the brand's reach beyond participants in organized sports to other usage occasions that she terms "intense sweaty situations." "We're a brand for the active thirst market, anytime anybody is hot and parched." Gatorade Frost proved to be a welcome relief for parched palates, racking up first-year sales of $150 million. Gatorade Fierce, with a "bolder" taste, was introduced in early 1999 and is expected to repeat the success of Gatorade Frost. Today, Gatorade is the largest-selling brand sold by Quaker Oats.[1]

The marketing of Gatorade illustrates the effective management of a product in a dynamic marketplace. This chapter shows how the actions taken by Gatorade executives are typical of those made by successful marketers in managing products and brands.

PRODUCT LIFE CYCLE

Products, like people, have been viewed as having a life cycle. The concept of the **product life cycle** describes the stages a new product goes through in the marketplace: introduction, growth, maturity, and decline (Figure 12–1).[2] There are two curves shown in this figure, total industry sales revenue and total industry profit, which represent the sum of sales revenue and profit of all firms producing the product. The reasons for the changes in each curve and the marketing decisions involved are discussed in the following pages.

Introduction Stage

The introduction stage of the product life cycle occurs when a product is first introduced to its intended target market. During this period, sales grow slowly, and profit is minimal. The lack of profit is often the result of large investment costs in product development, such as the $1 billion spent by Gillette to develop and launch the MACH 3 razor shaving system. The marketing objective for the company at this stage is to create consumer awareness and stimulate trial—the initial purchase of a product by a consumer.

Companies often spend heavily on advertising and other promotion tools to build awareness among consumers in the introduction stage. For example, Frito-Lay spent $30 million to promote its SunChips multigrain snacks to consumers and retailers, and Gillette budgeted $300 million in advertising alone to introduce the MACH 3 razor to consumers.[3] These expenditures are often made to stimulate *primary demand,* or desire for the product class (such as multigrain snack chips), rather than for a specific brand since there are no competitors with the same product. As competitors introduce their own products and the product progresses along its life cycle, company attention is focused on creating *selective demand,* or demand for a specific brand.

Other marketing mix variables also are important at this stage. Gaining distribution is often a challenge because channel intermediaries may be hesitant to carry a new product. Moreover, in this stage a company often restricts the number of variations of the product to ensure control of product quality. For example, SunChips originally came in only two flavors and Gatorade in only one. Gillette offered only a single version of the MACH 3 razor.

FIGURE 12-1
How stages of the product life cycle relate to a firm's marketing objectives and marketing mix actions

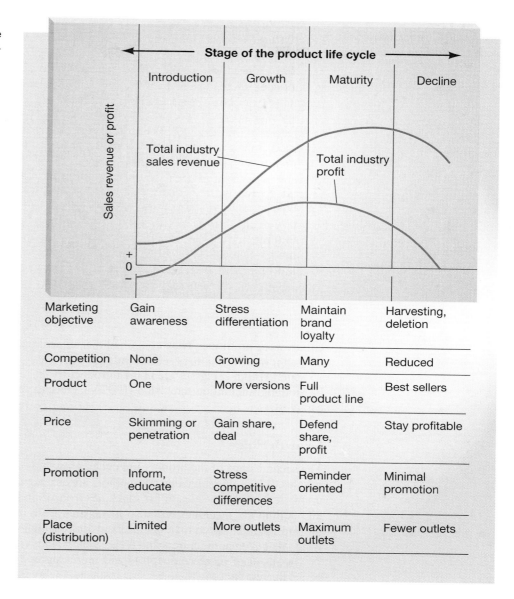

	Introduction	Growth	Maturity	Decline
Marketing objective	Gain awareness	Stress differentiation	Maintain brand loyalty	Harvesting, deletion
Competition	None	Growing	Many	Reduced
Product	One	More versions	Full product line	Best sellers
Price	Skimming or penetration	Gain share, deal	Defend share, profit	Stay profitable
Promotion	Inform, educate	Stress competitive differences	Reminder oriented	Minimal promotion
Place (distribution)	Limited	More outlets	Maximum outlets	Fewer outlets

During introduction, pricing can be either high or low. A high initial price may be used as part of a *skimming* strategy to help the company recover the costs of development as well as capitalize on the price insensitivity of early buyers. 3M is a master of this strategy. According to a 3M manager, "We hit fast, price high, and get the heck out when the me-too products pour in."[4] High prices also tend to attract competitors more eager to enter the market because they see the opportunity for profit. To discourage competitive entry, a company can price low, referred to as *penetration pricing*. This pricing strategy also helps build unit volume, but a company must closely monitor costs. These and other pricing techniques are covered in depth in Chapter 15.

Figure 12–2 charts the stand-alone fax machine product life cycle for business use in the United States from the early 1970s through 1999.[5] As shown, sales grew slowly in the 1970s and early 1980s after Xerox pioneered the first lightweight portable fax machine that sent and received documents. Fax machines were originally sold direct to businesses through company salespeople and were premium priced. The average price for a fax machine in 1980 was $12,700. By today's standards, those fax ma-

FIGURE 12–2
Product life cycle for the stand-alone fax machine for business use: 1970–1999

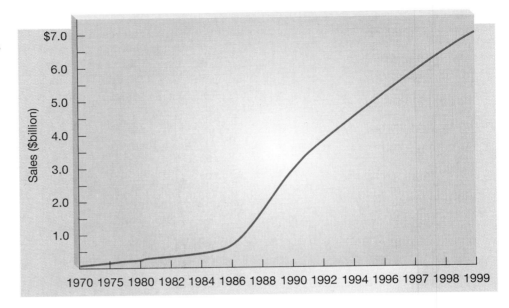

chines were primitive. They contained mechanical parts, not electronic circuitry, and offered few of the features seen in today's models.

Several product classes are in the introductory stage of the product life cycle. These include high-definition television (HDTV), electric vehicles, and digital cameras and camcorders.

Growth Stage

The second stage of the product life cycle, growth, is characterized by rapid increases in sales. It is in this stage that competitors appear. For example, Figure 12–2 shows the dramatic increase in sales of fax machines from 1986 to 1990. The number of companies selling fax machines was also increasing, from one in the early 1970s to four in the late 1970s to seven manufacturers in 1983, which sold nine brands. By 1990 there were some 25 manufacturers and 60 possible brands from which to choose.

The result of more competitors and more aggressive pricing is that profit usually peaks during the growth stage. For instance, the average price for a fax machine declined from $3,300 in 1985 to $1,500 in 1990. At this point the emphasis of advertising shifts to stimulating selective demand, in which product benefits are compared with those of competitors' offerings.

Product sales in the growth stage grow at an increasing rate because of new people trying or using the product and a growing proportion of *repeat purchasers*—people who tried the product, were satisfied, and bought again. As a product moves through the life cycle, the ratio of repeat to trial purchasers grows. Failure to achieve substantial repeat purchasers usually means an early death for a product. Alberto-Culver introduced Mr. Culver's Sparklers, which were solid air fresheners that looked like stained glass. The product moved quickly from the introduction to the growth stage, but then sales plummeted. The problem was there were almost no repeat purchasers because buyers treated the product like cheap window decorations, left them there, and didn't buy new ones. Durable fax machines meant that replacement purchases were rare; however, it was common for more than one machine to populate a business as their use became more widespread. In 1995, there was one fax machine for every eight people in a business in the United States.

Changes start to appear in the product during the growth stage. To help differentiate a company's brand from those of its competitors, an improved version or new features are added to the original design, and product proliferation occurs. Changes in fax machines included (1) models with built-in telephones; (2) models that used plain, rather than thermal, paper for copies; (3) models that integrated telex for electronic mail purposes; and (4) models that allowed for secure (confidential) transmissions. For SunChips and Gatorade, new flavors and package sizes were added during the growth stage.

In the growth stage it is important to gain as much distribution for the product as possible. In the retail store, for example, this often means that competing companies fight for display and shelf space. Expanded distribution in the fax industry is an example. In 1986, early in the growth stage, only 11 percent of office machine dealers carried this equipment. By the mid-1990s, more than 70 percent of these dealers carried fax equipment, distribution was expanded to other stores selling electronic equipment, and the fight continues for which brands will be displayed.

Numerous product classes or industries are in the growth stage of the product life cycle. Examples include disposable 35-mm cameras, cellular telephones, and laptop computers.

Maturity Stage

Electric vehicles and digital cameras and camcorders are in the introductory stage of the product life cycle. Honda and Canon are two early marketers of these products.

Honda
www.honda.com
Canon
www.canondv.com

The third stage, maturity, is characterized by a slowing of total industry sales or product class revenue. Also, marginal competitors begin to leave the market. Most consumers who would buy the product are either repeat purchasers of the item or have tried and abandoned it. Sales increase at a decreasing rate in the maturity stage as fewer new buyers enter the market. Profit declines because there is fierce price competition among many sellers and the cost of gaining new buyers at this stage increases.

Marketing attention in the maturity stage is often directed toward holding market share through further product differentiation and finding new buyers. For example, fax machine manufacturers developed models suitable for small and home businesses,

MARKETING NEWSNET

Will the Upstart Internet Bury the Familiar Fax?

Technological substitution often causes the decline stage in the product life cycle. Will the Internet and e-mail replace fax machines?

This question has caused heated debates. Even though sales of Internet host computers are in the growth stage of the product life cycle (see the graph), fax machine sales continue to grow as well. Industry analysts estimate that there are more than 125 million e-mail user accounts worldwide. However, the growth of e-mail has not affected faxing because the two technologies do not directly compete for the same messaging applications.

E-mail is used for text messages and faxing is predominately used for communicating formatted documents by business users. Fax usage is expected to increase through 2000, and sales of stand-alone fax

machines are expected to increase into the twenty-first century. Internet technology may eventually replace facsimile technology, but not in the foreseeable future.

which today represent a substantial portion of industry sales. Still, a major factor in a company's strategy in this stage is to reduce overall marketing cost by improving promotional and distribution efficiency.

Stand-alone fax machines for business use approached the maturity stage in the early 1990s. By 1998, more than 80 percent of industry sales were captured by six producers (Brother, Canon, Hewlett-Packard, Muratec, Panasonic, and Sharp), reflecting the departure of many marginal competitors. Industry sales had slowed in the late 1990s compared with triple-digit average annual dollar sales increases in the late 1980s. By 1999, there were an estimated 30 million stand-alone fax machines for business use installed throughout the world.

Numerous product classes and industries are in the maturity stage of their product life cycle. These include carbonated soft drinks, automobiles, and TVs.

Decline Stage

The decline stage occurs when sales and profits begin to drop. Frequently, a product enters this stage not because of any wrong strategy on the part of the company but because of environmental changes. Technological innovation often precedes the decline stage as newer technologies replace older technologies. The word-processing capability of personal computers pushed typewriters into decline. Compact discs did the same to cassette tapes in the prerecorded music industry. Will Internet technology and e-mail spell doom for fax machines? The accompanying Marketing NewsNet offers one perspective on this question.[6]

Products in the decline stage tend to consume a disproportionate share of management time and financial resources relative to their potential future worth. A company will follow one of two strategies to handle a declining product: deletion or harvesting.

Deletion   Product *deletion,* or dropping the product from the company's product line, is the most drastic strategy. Because a residual core of consumers still consume or use a product even in the decline stage, product elimination decisions are not taken lightly. When Coca-Cola decided to drop what is now known as Classic Coke, consumer objection was so intense that the company brought the product back.

Harvesting   A second strategy, *harvesting,* is when a company retains the product but reduces marketing support costs. The product continues to be offered, but salespeople do not allocate time in selling nor are advertising dollars spent. The purpose of harvesting is to maintain the ability to meet customer requests. For example, Gillette continues to sell its Liquid Paper correction fluid for use with typewriters in the era of word-processing equipment.

Some Dimensions of the Product Life Cycle

Some important aspects of product life cycles are (1) their length, (2) the shape of their curves, and (3) how they vary with different levels of the products.

Length of the Product Life Cycle   There is no exact time that a product takes to move through its life cycle. As a rule, consumer products have shorter life cycles than industrial products. For example, many new consumer food products such as SunChips move from the introduction stage to maturity in 18 months. The availability of mass communication vehicles informs consumers faster and shortens life cycles. Also, the rate of technological change tends to shorten product life cycles as new product innovation replaces existing products.

The Shape of the Product Life Cycle   The product life-cycle curve shown in Figure 12–1 is the *generalized life cycle,* but not all products have the same shape to their curve. In fact, there are several different life-cycle curves, each type suggesting different marketing strategies. Figure 12–3 shows the shape of life-cycle curves for four different types of products: high learning, low learning, fashion, and fad products.

FIGURE 12–3
Alternative product life cycles

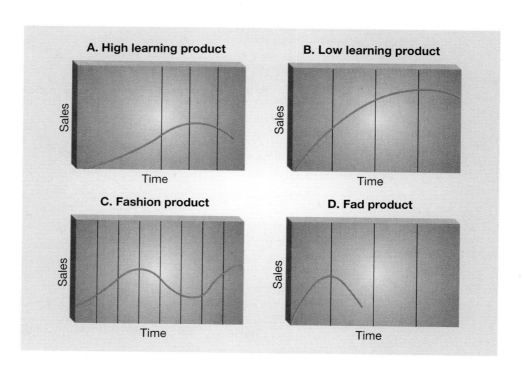

A. High learning product
B. Low learning product
C. Fashion product
D. Fad product

A *high learning product* is one for which significant education of the customer is required and there is an extended introductory period (Figure 12–3A). Products such as home computers had this type of life-cycle curve because consumers have to understand the benefits of purchasing the product or be educated in a new way of performing a familiar task. Convection ovens, for example, necessitate that the consumer learn a new way of cooking and alter familiar recipes.

In contrast, for a *low learning product* sales begin immediately because little learning is required by the consumer, and the benefits of purchase are readily understood (Figure 12–3B). This product often can be easily imitated by competitors, so the marketing strategy is to broaden distribution quickly. In this way, as competitors rapidly enter, most retail outlets already have the innovator's product. It is also important to have the manufacturing capacity to meet demand. A recent example of a successful low learning product is Gillette's MACH 3 razor. Introduced in mid-1998, MACH 3 is projected to record $1 billion in sales before 2001.[7]

FIGURE 12–4
Video game life cycles by product class, product form, and brand

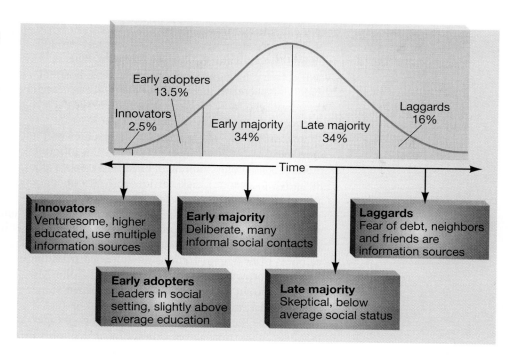

A *fashion product* (Figure 12–3C), such as hemline lengths on skirts or lapel widths on sports jackets, is introduced, declines, and then seems to return. Life cycles for fashion products most often appear in women's and men's clothing styles. The length of the cycles may be years or decades.

A *fad,* such as wall walkers or toe socks, experiences rapid sales on introduction and then an equally rapid decline (Figure 12–3D). These products are typically novelties. They include car tatoos sold in southern California and described as the first removable and reusable graphics for automobiles and vinyl dresses, fleece bikinis, and an Astro-Turf miniskirt made by Thump, Inc., a Minnesota clothing company.[8]

The Product Level: Class, Form, and Brand   The product life shown in Figure 12–1 is a total industry or product class curve. Yet, in managing a product it is important to often distinguish among the multiple life cycles (class, form, and brand) that may exist. **Product class** refers to the entire product category or industry, such as video games shown in Figure 12–4A.[9] **Product form** pertains to variations within the class. For video games, product form exists in the computing capability of game players such as 8-, 16- and 32/64-bit machines. Game players have a life cycle of their own and typically move from the introduction stage to maturity in five years. A final type of life-cycle curve can represent a video-game brand, apparent in the U.S. sales of Nintendo, Sony, and Sega advanced video games charted in Figure 12–4B. Sales of these brands are driven by the purchase of their game players and the number and quality of their games. Expect the video-game product class, product form, and brand life cycles to change again in 2000 following Sega's introduction of its Dreamcast 128-bit machine and Sony's new PlayStation.[10]

The Life Cycle and Consumers   The life cycle of a product depends on sales to consumers. Not all consumers rush to buy a product in the introductory stage, and the shapes of the life-cycle curves indicate that most sales occur after the product has been on the market for some time. In essence, a product diffuses, or spreads, through the population, a concept called the *diffusion of innovation.*[11]

Some people are attracted to a product early, while others buy it only after they see their friends with the item. Figure 12–5 shows the consumer population divided into five categories of product adopters based on when they adopt a new product. Brief profiles accompany each category. For any product to be successful, it must be purchased by innovators and early adopters. This is why manufacturers of new pharmaceuticals try to gain adoption by leading hospitals, clinics, and physicians that are widely respected in the medical field. Once accepted by innovators and early adopters, the adoption of new products moves on to the early majority, late majority, and laggard categories.

Several factors affect whether a consumer will adopt a new product or not. Common reasons for resisting a product in the introduction stage are usage barriers (the product is not compatible with existing habits), value barriers (the product provides no incentive to change), risk barriers (physical, economic, or social), and psychological barriers (cultural differences or image).[12]

Companies attempt to overcome these barriers in numerous ways. They provide warrantees, money-back guarantees, extensive usage instructions, demonstrations, and free samples to stimulate initial trial of new products. For example, software developers offer demonstrations downloaded from the Internet. Maybelline allows consumers to browse through the Cover Girl Color Match system on its Web site to find out how certain makeup products will look. In-store and mailed samples are one of the most popular means to gain consumer trial. In fact, 71 percent of consumers consider a sample to be the best way to evaluate a new product. When Lever Brothers introduced its Lever 2000 triple-threat skin soap bar that moisturizes, deodorizes, and kills bacteria, it had to give consumers an incentive to change from their current soap. How? The company sent samples of the new product to half of all U.S households and recorded sales of $27.6 million.[13]

CONCEPT CHECK

1. Advertising plays a major role in the _____ stage of the product life cycle, and _____ plays a major role in maturity.

2. How do high learning and low learning products differ?

3. What does the life cycle for a fashion product look like?

MANAGING THE PRODUCT LIFE CYCLE

An important task for a firm is to manage its products through the successive stages of their life cycles. This section discusses the role of the product manager, who is usually responsible for this, and analyzes three ways to manage a product through its life cycle: modifying the product, modifying the market, and repositioning the product.

Role of a Product Manager

The product manager (sometimes called *brand manager*) manages the marketing efforts for a close-knit family of products or brands.[14] Introduced by P&G in 1928, the product manager style of marketing organization is used by consumer goods firms such as General Mills and Frito-Lay and by industrial firms such as Intel and Hewlett-Packard. The U.S. Postal Service and General Motors recently began using product managers as well. All product managers are responsible for managing existing products through the stages of the life cycle, and some are also responsible for developing new products. Product managers' marketing responsibilities include developing and executing a marketing program for the product line described in an annual marketing plan and approving ad copy, media selection, and package design. The role of product managers in planning, implementing, and controlling marketing strategy is covered in depth in Chapter 22.

Modifying the Product

Product modification involves altering a product's characteristic, such as its quality, performance, or appearance, to try to increase and extend the product's sales. Wrinkle-free cotton slacks sold by Levi Strauss, Haggar, and Farah revitalized sales of men's casual pants and now account for 60 percent of the men's cotton pants product class sales. A modest modification of Black & Decker's Phillips screwdriver, which prevents the tip from slipping out of the screw, expanded sales substantially.[15]

New features, packages, or scents can be used to change a product's characteristics and give the sense of a revised product. Procter & Gamble revamped Pantene shampoo and conditioner with a new vitamin formula and relaunched the brand with a multimillion dollar advertising and promotion campaign. The result? Pantene, a brand first introduced in the 1940s, became the top-selling shampoo and conditioner in the United States in an industry with more than 1,000 competitors.

Modifying the Market

With **market modification** strategies, a company tries to increase a product's use among existing customers, create new use situations, or find new customers.

Increasing Use   Promoting more frequent usage has been a strategy of Campbell Soup Company. Because soup consumption rises in the winter and declines during the summer, the company now advertises more heavily in warm months to encourage consumers to think of soup as more than a cold-weather food. Similarly, The Florida Orange Growers Association advocates drinking orange juice throughout the day rather than for breakfast only.

Creating New Use Situation   Finding new uses for an existing product has been the strategy behind Woolite, a laundry soap. Originally intended for the hand washing of woolen material, Woolite now promotes itself for use with all fine clothing items. The Milk Processor Education Program suggests a new use situation by substituting milk for water or other ingredients in preparing food.

The Milk Processor Education Program (MilkPEP) promotes the use of milk rather than water or other ingredients in preparing food. According to a MilkPEP executive, "If every household one day a week added milk rather than water to instant coffee and made a caffe latte, it would add [up to] $100 million to the bottom line of the milk industry."

The Milk Processor Education Program
www.whymilk.com

Finding New Users   Harley-Davidson has successfully marketed its cruiser motorcycle to women. Women now represent 9 percent of its customers compared with only 2 percent in 1985. Sony and Nintendo have expanded their user base by developing video games specially designed for children under 13 years old.[16]

Repositioning the Product

Often a company decides to reposition its product or product line in an attempt to bolster sales. *Product repositioning* is changing the place a product occupies in a consumer's mind relative to competitive products. A firm can reposition a product by changing one or more of the four marketing mix elements. Four factors that trigger a repositioning action are discussed next.

Reacting to a Competitor's Position   One reason to reposition a product is because a competitor's entrenched position is adversely affecting sales and market share. Procter & Gamble repositioned its venerable Ivory soap bar in response to the success of Lever 2000, sold by Lever Brothers. Lever 2000, a bar soap that moisturizes, deodorizes, and kills bacteria, eroded P&G's dominance of the bar soap market. P&G responded with its own triple-threat soap called New Ivory Ultra Safe Skin Care Soap. The problem? The new Ivory doesn't float![17]

Reaching a New Market   When Unilever introduced iced tea in Britain in the mid-1990s, sales were disappointing. British consumers viewed it as leftover hot tea, not suitable for drinking. The company made its tea carbonated and repositioned it as a cold soft drink to compete as a carbonated beverage and sales improved. New Balance, Inc. has repositioned its athletic shoes for aging baby boomers. Instead of competing head-on against Nike, Reebok, and Fila, the company offers an expansive range of widths tailored for an older consumer's higher weight and networks with podiatrists who use the wide models to insert foot-support devices.[18]

Catching a Rising Trend   Changing consumer trends can also lead to repositioning. Consumer interest in "functional foods" is an example.[19] These foods offer health and dietary benefits beyond nutrition and represent an $85 billion market today that is expected to grow to $250 million by 2002. A number of products have capitalized on this trend. Quaker Oats now makes the FDA-approved claim that oatmeal, as part of a low saturated fat, low cholesterol diet, may reduce the risk of heart disease. Calcium-enriched products, such as Nutri-Grain bars, Tropicana juice, and Uncle Ben's Calcium Plus rice, focus on healthy bone structure for children and adults.

Changing the Value Offered   In repositioning a product, a company can decide to change the value it offers buyers and trade up or down. **Trading up** involves adding value to the product (or line) through additional features or higher quality materials. Michelin has done this with its "run-flat" tire that can travel up to 50 miles at 55 miles-per-hour after suffering total air loss. Dog food manufacturers, such as Ralston Purina, also have traded up by offering super premium foods based on "life-stage nutrition." Mass merchandisers, such as Sears and JCPenney, can trade up by adding a designer clothes section to their store.

　　Trading down involves reducing the number of features, quality, or price. For example, airlines have added more seats, thus reducing leg room, and eliminated extras, such as snack service and food portions. Trading down often exists when companies engage in **downsizing**—reducing the content of packages without changing package size and maintaining or increasing the package price. Firms have been criticized for this practice, as described in the accompanying Ethics and Social Responsibility Alert.[20]

ETHICS AND SOCIAL RESPONSIBILITY ALERT

Consumers Are Paying More for Less in Downsized Packages

ETHICS

For more than 30 years, Starkist put 6.5 ounces of tuna into its regular-sized can. Today, Starkist puts 6.125 ounces of tuna into its can but charges the same price. Colgate-Palmolive's Ajax king-size laundry detergent package has remained the same size, but the contents have been cut from 61 ounces to 55 ounces, and the package price increased from $2.59 to $2.79. Procter & Gamble cut the number of Pampers disposable diapers in its packages while leaving the price the same. The price of Mennen Speed Stick deodorant has not changed, but it now comes in a larger package with 2.25 ounces of deodorant versus 2.5 ounces in the previous, smaller package.

Consumer advocates charge that "downsizing" packages while maintaining or increasing prices is a subtle and unannounced way of taking advantage of consumer's buying habits. Manufacturers argue that this practice is a way of keeping prices from rising beyond psychological barriers for their products.

Is downsizing an unethical practice if manufacturers do not inform consumers that the package contents are less than they were previously?

CONCEPT CHECK

1. How does a product manager help manage a product's life cycle?

2. What does "creating new use situations" mean in managing a product's life cycle?

3. Explain the difference between trading up and trading down in repositioning.

BRANDING

A basic decision in marketing products is **branding,** in which an organization uses a name, phrase, design, symbols, or combination of these to identify its products and distinguish them from those of competitors. A **brand name** is any word, "device" (design, sound, shape, or color), or combination of these used to distinguish a seller's goods or services. Some brand names can be spoken, such as a Gatorade or Rollerblade. Other brand names cannot be spoken, such as the rainbow-colored apple (the *logotype* or *logo*) that Apple Computer puts on its machines and in its ads. A **trade name** is a commercial, legal name under which a company does business. The Campbell Soup Company is the trade name of that firm.

A **trademark** identifies that a firm has legally registered its brand name or trade name so the firm has its exclusive use, thereby preventing others from using it. In the United States, more than 700,000 trademarks are registered with the U.S. Patent and Trademark Office, and these trademarks are protected under the Lanham Act. A well-known trademark can help a company advertise its offerings to customers and develop their brand loyalty. Figure 12–6 shows examples of well-known trademarks.

Because a good trademark can help sell a product, *product counterfeiting,* which involves low-cost copies of popular brands not manufactured by the original producer, has been a growing problem. Counterfeit products can steal sales from the original manufacturer or hurt the company's reputation. Counterfeiting losses to U.S. companies exceed $50 billion in every year. To protect against counterfeiting, the U.S. government passed the Trademark Counterfeiting Act, which makes counterfeiting a federal offense with offenders subject to prison sentences, damage payments, and seizure of counterfeit merchandise.

FIGURE 12–6
Examples of well-known trademarks, brand names, and trade names

Brand name that can be spoken
Big Mac hamburger
Levi's jeans
Teflon plastic
Betty Crocker cake mix
Macintosh computer

Brand name that cannot be spoken

Trade name/ legal name of organization
Campbell Soup Company
Compaq Corporation
Ford Motor Company
Kellogg Company
Ralston Purina Company

Trademark, brand name, or trade name registered with the U.S. Patent and Trademark Office

Trademark protection is a significant issue in global marketing. For instance, the transformation of the Soviet Union into individual countries has meant that many U.S. firms, such as Xerox, have had to reregister trademarks in each of the republics to prohibit misuse and generic use ("xeroxing") of their trademarks by competitors and consumers.

Consumers may benefit most from branding. Recognizing competing products by distinct trademarks allows them to be more efficient shoppers. Consumers can recognize and avoid products with which they are dissatisfied, while becoming loyal to other, more satisfying brands. As discussed in Chapter 6, brand loyalty often eases consumers' decision making by eliminating the need for an external search.

Brand Personality and Brand Equity

Product managers recognize that brands offer more than product identification and a means to distinguish their products from competitors. Successful and established brands take on a **brand personality,** a set of human characteristics associated with a brand name.[21] Research shows that consumers often assign personality qualities to products—traditional, romantic, rugged, sophisticated, rebellious—and choose brands that are consistent with their own or desired self-image. Marketers can and do imbue a brand with a personality through advertising that depicts a certain user or usage situation and conveys certain emotions or feelings to be associated with the brand. For example, the personality traits associated with Coca-Cola are all-American, real, and cool; with Pepsi, young, exciting, and hip; and with Dr Pepper, nonconforming, unique, and fun.

A good brand name is of such importance to a company that it has led to a concept called **brand equity,** the added value a given brand name gives to a product beyond the functional benefits provided.[22] This value has two distinct advantages. First, brand equity provides a competitive advantage, such as the Sunkist label that implies quality fruit and the Gatorade name that defines sport drinks. A second advantage is that consumers are often willing to pay a higher price for a product with brand equity. Brand equity, in this instance, is represented by the premium a consumer will pay for one brand over another when the functional benefits provided are identical. Intel microchips, Bose audio systems, Duracell batteries, Microsoft computer software, and Louis Vuitton luggage all enjoy a price premium arising from brand equity.

Licensing

The value of brand equity is evident in the strategy of licensing. **Licensing** is a contractual agreement whereby a company allows another firm to use its brand name, patent, trade secret, or other property for a royalty or a fee. Licensing can be very prof-

Ruffles and Chee-tos are in Israel now, and more Frito-Lay snack items may follow. Entry into Israel was made possible through a licensing agreement with Elite Foods in Israel.

Elite Company
www.elite.co.il

itable to a licensor and a licensee as annual worldwide retail sales of licensed products exceed $110 billion.[23] Playboy has earned more than $260 million licensing its name for merchandise ranging from shoes in the United States to wallpaper in Europe and cooking classes in Brazil. Murjani has sold more than $500 million of clothing worldwide bearing the Coca-Cola logo.

Licensing also assists companies in entering global markets with minimal risk. Frito-Lay licensed Elite Foods in Israel to produce and market Frito-Lay's Ruffles potato chips and Chee-tos cheese-flavored corn puffs. These brands capture a significant percent of the salty snack market in Israel.

Picking a Good Brand Name

We take brand names such as Dial, Sanyo, Porsche, and Adidas for granted, but it is often a difficult and expensive process to pick a good name. Companies will spend between $25,000 and $100,000 to identify and test a new brand name.[24] For instance, Intel spent $45,000 for the Pentium name given its family of microchips.[25] There are five criteria mentioned most often when selecting a good brand name.[26]

- The name should suggest the product benefits. For example, Accutron (watches), Easy Off (oven cleaner), Glass Plus (glass cleaner), Cling-Free (antistatic cloth for drying clothes), Powerbook (laptop computer), and Tidy Bowl (toilet bowl cleaner) all clearly describe the benefits of purchasing the product.
- The name should be memorable, distinctive, and positive. In the auto industry, when a competitor has a memorable name, others quickly imitate. When Ford

named a car the Mustang, Pintos, Colts, and Broncos soon followed. The Thunderbird name led to the Phoenix, Eagle, Sunbird, and Firebird.

- The name should fit the company or product image. Sharp is a name that can apply to audio and video equipment. Excedrin, Anacin, and Nuprin are scientific-sounding names, good for an analgesic. However, naming a personal computer PCjr, as IBM did with its first computer for home use, neither fit the company nor the product. PCjr, sounded like a toy and stalled IBM's initial entry into the home-use market.

- The name should have no legal or regulatory restrictions. Legal restrictions produce trademark infringement suits, and regulatory restrictions arise through improper use of words. For example, the U.S. Food and Drug Administration discourages the use of the word *heart* in food brand names. This restriction led to changing the name of Kellogg's Heartwise cereal to Fiberwise, and Clorox's Hidden Valley Ranch Take Heart Salad Dressing had to be modified to Hidden Valley Ranch Low-Fat Salad Dressing.[27] Increasingly, brand names need a corresponding address on the Internet. This further complicates name selection because more than 2 million domains are already registered.

- Finally, the name should be simple (such as Bold laundry detergent, Sure deodorant, and Bic pens) and should be emotional (such as Joy and Obsession perfumes). In the development of names for international use, having a nonmeaningful brand name has been considered a benefit. A name such as Exxon does not have any prior impressions or undesirable images among a diverse world population of different languages and cultures. The 7Up name is another matter. In Shanghai, China, the phrase means "death through drinking" in the local dialect, and sales have suffered as a result.[28]

Do you have an idea for a brand name? If you do, check to see if the name has been already registered with the U.S. Patent and Trademark Office by visiting its Web site described in the accompanying Web Link.

Branding Strategies

In deciding to brand a product, companies have several possible strategies, including manufacturer branding, reseller branding, or mixed branding approaches.

Manufacturer Branding With **manufacturer branding,** the producer dictates the brand name using either a multiproduct or multibrand approach. **Multiproduct branding** is when a company uses one name for all its products. This approach is often referred to as a *blanket* or *family* branding strategy (Figure 12–7).

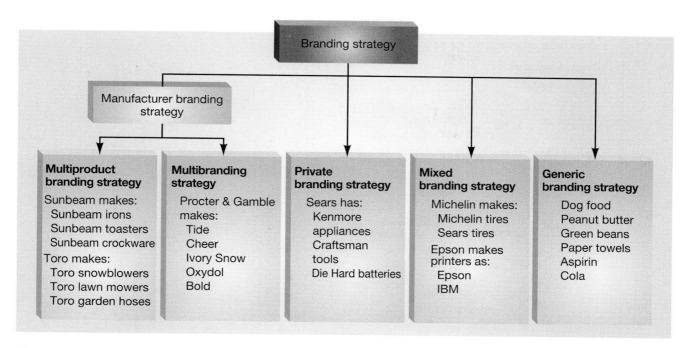

FIGURE 12–7
Alternative branding strategies

There are several advantages to multiproduct branding. Capitalizing again on brand equity, consumers who have a good experience with the product will transfer this favorable attitude to other items in the product class with the same name. Therefore, this brand strategy makes possible *line extensions,* the practice of using a current brand name to enter a new market segment in its product class. Campbell Soup Company effectively employs a multiproduct branding strategy with soup line extensions. It offers regular Campbell soup, home-cooking style, and chunky varieties and more than 100 soup flavors. This strategy can also result in lower advertising and promotion costs because the same name is used on all products, thus raising the level of brand awareness.

Some companies employ *subbranding,* which combines a family brand with a new brand. For example, ThinkPad is a subbrand to the IBM name. Quaker Oats has successfully used subbranding for Gatorade with the introduction of Gatorade Frost and Gatorade Fierce, with unique flavors developed for each.

A strong brand equity also allows for *brand extension,* the practice of using a current brand name to enter a completely different product class.[29] For instance, the equity in the Tylenol name as a trusted pain reliever allowed Johnson & Johnson to successfully extend this name to Tylenol Cold & Flu and Tylenol PM, a sleep aid. Fisher-Price, an established name in children's toys, was able to extend this name to children's shampoo and conditioners and baby bath and lotion products.

However, there is a risk with brand extensions. Too many uses for one brand name can dilute the meaning of a brand for consumers. Marketing experts claim this has happened to the Arm & Hammer brand given its use for toothpaste, laundry detergent, gum, cat litter, air freshener, carpet deodorizer, and anti-perspirant.[30]

A recent variation on brand extensions is the practice of **co-branding,** the pairing of two brand names of two manufacturers on a single product.[31] For example, Hershey Foods has teamed with General Mills to offer a co-branded breakfast cereal called Reese's Peanut Butter Puffs and with Nabisco to provide Chips Ahoy cookies using Hershey's chocolate morsels. Citibank co-brands MasterCard and Visa with American Airlines and Ford. Co-branding benefits firms by allowing them to enter new product classes and capitalize on an already established brand name in that product class.

An alternative manufacturer's branding strategy, **multibranding,** involves giving each product a distinct name. Multibranding is a useful strategy when each brand

The strong brand equity of Louis Vuitton makes possible successful brand extensions, including fashion writing instruments.

Louis Vuitton
www.louisvuitton.com

is intended for a different market segment. P&G makes Camay soap for those concerned with soft skin and Safeguard for those who want deodorant protection. Black & Decker markets its line of tools for the household do-it-yourselfer segment with the Black & Decker name, but uses the DeWalt name for its professional tool line. Disney uses the Miramax and Touchstone Pictures names for films directed at adults and its Disney name for children's films.

Multibranding strategies become more complex in the global marketplace. As an example, P&G uses multiple brand names for the same product when competing internationally. For instance, PertPlus shampoo is sold as Rejoice in Hong Kong, PertPlus in the Middle East, and Vidal Sassoon in the United Kingdom. However, international branding strategies do differ. In Japan, where corporate names are important, P&G markets the company's name prominently with the brand name of the product.

Compared with the multiproduct approach, promotional costs tend to be higher with multibranding. The company must generate awareness among consumers and retailers for each new brand name without the benefit of any previous impressions. The advantages of this approach are that each brand is unique to each market segment and there is no risk that a product failure will affect other products in the line.

The multibranding approach in Europe is slowly being replaced by **euro-branding,** the strategy of using the same brand name for the same product across all countries in the European Union. This strategy has many of the benefits linked with multiproduct branding in addition to making Pan-European advertising and promotion programs possible.

Private Branding   A company uses **private branding,** often called *private labeling* or *reseller branding,* when it manufactures products but sells them under the brand name of a wholesaler or retailer. Radio Shack, Sears, and Kmart are large retailers that have their own brand names. Food products are often private labeled for supermarkets. Private brands account for 14 percent of U.S. food sales, 36 percent of British food sales, and about 18 percent of food sales in France and Germany.[32]

Black & Decker uses a multibranding strategy to reach different market segments. Black & Decker markets its line of tools for the do-it-yourselfer market with the Black & Decker name, but uses the DeWalt name for its professional tool line.

Black & Decker
www.blackanddecker.com

Matsushita of Japan manufactures VCRs for Magnavox, GE, Sylvania, JCPenney, and Curtis Mathes. The advantage to the manufacturer is that promotional costs are shifted to the retailer or other company, and the manufacturer can often sell more units through others than by itself. There is a risk, though, because the manufacturer's sales depend heavily on the efforts of others.

Mixed Branding   A compromise between manufacturer and private branding is **mixed branding,** where a firm markets products under its own name and that of a reseller because the segment attracted to the reseller is different from their own market. Sanyo and Toshiba manufacture television sets for Sears as well as for themselves. This process is similar to Michelin's, which manufactures tires for Sears as well as under its own name. Kodak uses a mixed branding approach in Japan to increase its sales of 35-mm film. In addition to selling its Kodak brand, the company now makes "COOP" private label film for the Japanese Consumer Cooperative Union, which is a group of 2,500 stores. Priced significantly below its Kodak brand, the private label seeks to attract the price-sensitive Japanese consumer.[33]

Generic Branding   An alternative branding approach is the **generic brand,** which is a no-brand product such as dog food, peanut butter, or green beans. There is no identification other than a description of the contents. The major appeal is that the price is up to one third less than that of branded items. Generic brands account for less than 1 percent of total grocery sales. The limited appeal of generics has been attributed to the popularity of private brands and greater promotional efforts for manufacturer brand-name items. Consumers who use generics see these products as being as good as brand-name items, and, in light of what they expect, users of these products are relatively pleased with their purchases.

MARKETING NEWSNET

Creating Customer Value through Packaging: Pez Heads Dispense More Than Candy

CUSTOMER VALUE

Customer value can assume numerous forms. For Pez Candy, Inc., customer value manifests itself in some 250 Pez character candy dispensers. Each 99 cent refillable dispenser ejects tasty candy tablets in a variety of flavors that delight preteen and teens alike.

Pez was formulated in 1927 by Austrian food mogul Edward Haas III and successfully sold in Europe as an adult breath mint. Pez, which comes from the German word for peppermint, *pfefferminz,* was originally packaged in a hygienic, headless plastic dispenser. Pez first appeared in the United States in 1953 with a headless dispenser, marketed to adults. After conducting extensive marketing research, Pez was repositioned with fruit flavors, repackaged with licensed character heads on top of the dispenser, and remarketed as a children's product in the mid-1950s. Since then, most top-level licensed characters and hundreds of other characters have become Pez heads. Consumers eat more than 1 billion Pez tablets annually, and company sales growth exceeds that of the candy industry as a whole.

The unique Pez package dispenses a "use experience" for its customers beyond the candy itself, namely, fun. And fun translates into a 98 percent awareness level for Pez among teenagers and 89 percent among mothers with children. Pez has not advertised its product for years. With that kind of awareness, who needs advertising?

PACKAGING

The **packaging** component of a product refers to any container in which it is offered for sale and on which information is communicated. To a great extent, the customer's first exposure to a product is the package, and it is an expensive and important part of the marketing strategy. For Pez Candy, Inc., the character head-on-a-stick plastic container that dispenses a miniature brick candy, is the central element of its marketing strategy as described in the accompanying Marketing NewsNet.[34]

Creating Customer Value through Packaging

Today's packaging costs exceed $75 billion, and an estimated 12 cents of every dollar spent by a consumer goes to packaging. Despite the cost, packaging is essential because packages provide important benefits for the manufacturer, retailer, and ultimate consumer.

Communication Benefits　A major benefit of packaging is the information on it conveyed to the consumer, such as directions on how to use the product and the composition of the product, which is needed to satisfy legal requirements of product disclosure. For example, a new labeling system for packaged and processed foods, which created a uniform format for nutritional and dietary information, became effective in the mid-1990s at a cost of $2 billion to food companies. Other information consists of

Can you name this soft drink brand?

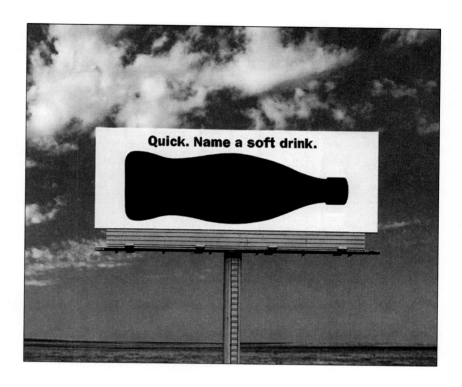

seals and symbols, either government required or commercial seals of approval (such as the Good Housekeeping seal).

Functional Benefits   Packaging often plays an important functional role, such as convenience, protection, or storage. Quaker State has changed its oil containers to eliminate the need for a separate spout, and Borden has changed the shape of its Elmer's Wonder Bond adhesive to prevent clogging of the spout.

The convenience dimension of packaging is becoming increasingly important. Kraft Miracle Whip salad dressing and Del Monte ketchup are sold in squeeze bottles, microwave popcorn has been a major market success, and Folgers coffee is now packaged in single-serving portions.

Consumer protection has become an important function of packaging, including the development of tamper-resistant containers. Today, companies commonly use safety seals or pop-tops that reveal previous opening. Nevertheless, no package is truly tamper resistant. U.S. law now provides for maximum penalties of life imprisonment and $250,000 fines for package tampering.

Perceptual Benefits   A third component of packaging is the perception created in the consumer's mind. Just Born Inc., a candy manufacturer of such brands as Jolly Joes and Mike and Ike Treats, discovered the importance of this component of packaging. For many years the brands were sold in old-fashioned black and white packages, but when the packaging was changed to four color, with animated grape and cherry characters, sales increased 25 percent. Coca-Cola brought back its famous pale-green, contoured 8-ounce bottle to attract consumers who remember drinking soft drinks from glass bottles, not from aluminum cans and large plastic bottles. A worldwide sales increase of 8 percent was linked to the new-old bottle.[35]

A package can connote status, economy, and product quality. Procter & Gamble's Original Pringles, with its unique cylindrical packaging, offers uniform chips, minimal breakage, freshness, and better value for the money than flex-bag packages for chips.

In the past, the color of packages was selected subjectively. For example, the famous Campbell's soup can was the inspiration of a company executive who liked Cornell

The unique cylindrical packaging for Pringles provides both functional and perceptual benefits and serves as a major point of difference for the snack chip.

Pringles
www.pringles.com

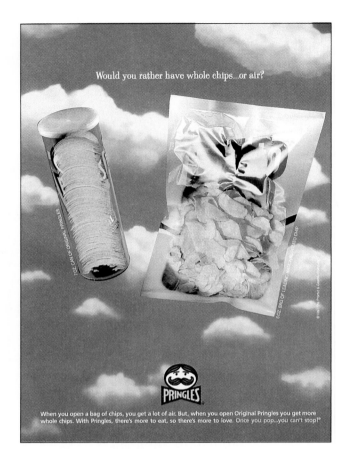

University's red and white football uniforms. Today, there is greater recognition that color affects consumers' perceptions.[36] When the color of the can of Barrelhead Sugar-Free Root Beer changed to beige from blue, consumers said it tasted more like old-fashioned root beer. And Owens-Corning judged the pink color of its fiber insulation to be so important that the color was given trademark status by the courts.

Global Trends in Packaging

Two global trends in packaging originating in the mid-1990s will continue into the twenty-first century. One trend involves the environmental effects of packaging, the other focuses on packaging health and safety concerns.

Environmental Sensitivity Because of widespread worldwide concern about the growth of solid waste and the shortage of viable landfill sites, the amount, composition, and disposal of packaging material continues to receive much attention.[37] Recycling packaging material is a major thrust. Procter & Gamble now uses recycled cardboard in 70 percent of its paper packaging and is packaging Tide, Cheer, Era, and Dash detergents in jugs that contain 25 percent recycled plastic. Spic and Span liquid cleaner is packaged in 100 percent recycled material. Other firms, such as the large U.K. retailer Sainsbury, emphasize the use of less packaging material. Sainsbury examines every product it sells to ensure that each uses only the minimum material necessary for shipping and display. Not surprisingly, when ARCO, one of the world's largest petrochemical firms, announced that its new packaging material would reduce packaging volume by 40 percent compared with corrugated paper shipping containers, the news was favorably received by manufacturers and retailers alike.

European countries have been trendsetters concerning packaging guidelines and environmental sensitivity. Many of these guidelines now exist in provisions governing trade to and within the European Union. In Germany, for instance, 80 percent of packaging material must be collected, and 80 percent of this amount must be recycled or reused to reduce solid waste in landfills. U.S. firms marketing in Europe have responded to these guidelines, and ultimately benefitted U.S. consumers.

Increasingly, firms are using life-cycle analysis (LCA) to examine the environmental effect of their packaging at every stage from raw material sources and production through distribution and disposal. A classic use of LCA was the decision by McDonald's to abandon the polystyrene clam-shells it used to package its hamburger. LCA indicated that the environment would be better served if the amount of solid waste packaging was reduced than if the polystyrene shells were recycled. McDonald's elected to package its hamburgers in a light wrap made of paper and polyethylene and eliminate the polystyrene package altogether.

Health and Safety Concerns   A second trend involves the growing health and safety concerns of packaging materials. Today, a majority of U.S. and European consumers believe companies should make sure products and their packages are safe, regardless of the cost, and companies are responding to this view in numerous ways.[38] Most butane lighters sold today, such as those made by BIC, contain a child-resistant safety latch to prevent misuse and accidental fire. Child-proof caps on pharmaceutical products and household cleaners and sealed lids on food packages are now common. New packaging technology and materials that extends a product's *shelf life* (the time a product can be stored) and prevent spoilage continue to be developed with special applications for less-developed countries.

PRODUCT WARRANTY

A final component for product consideration is the **warranty,** which is a statement indicating the liability of the manufacturer for product deficiencies. There are various degrees of product warranties with different implications for manufacturers and customers.[39]

The Variations of a Warranty

Some companies offer *express warranties,* which are written statements of liabilities. In recent years the government has required greater disclosure on express warranties to indicate whether the warranty is a limited-coverage or full-coverage alternative. A *limited-coverage warranty* specifically states the bounds of coverage and, more important, areas of noncoverage, whereas a *full warranty* has no limits of noncoverage. Cadillac is a company that boldly touts its warranty coverage. The Magnuson-Moss Warranty/FTC Improvement Act (1975) regulates the content of consumer warranties and so has strengthened consumer rights with regard to warranties.

With greater frequency, manufacturers are being held to *implied warranties,* which assign responsibility for product deficiencies to the manufacturer. Studies show that warranties are important and affect a consumer's product evaluation. Brands that have limited warranties tend to receive less positive evaluations compared with full-warranty items.

The Growing Importance of Warranties

Warranties are important in light of increasing product liability claims. In the early part of this century the courts protected companies, but the trend now is toward "strict liability" rulings, where a manufacturer is liable for any product defect, whether it followed reasonable research standards or not. This issue is hotly contested by companies and consumer advocates.

Warranties represent much more to the buyer than just protection from negative consequences—they can hold a significant marketing advantage for the producer. Sears has built a strong reputation for its Craftsman tool line with a simple warranty: if you break a tool, it's replaced with no questions asked. Zippo has an equally simple guarantee: "If it ever fails, we'll fix it free."

CONCEPT CHECK

1. How does a generic brand differ from a private brand?

2. Explain the role of packaging in terms of perception.

3. What is the difference between an expressed and an implied warranty?

SUMMARY

1 Products have a finite life cycle consisting of four stages: introduction, growth, maturity, and decline. The marketing objectives for each stage differ.

2 In the introductory stage the need is to establish primary demand, whereas the growth stage requires selective demand strategies. In the maturity stage the need is to maintain market share; the decline stage necessitates a deletion or harvesting strategy.

3 There are various shapes to the product life cycle. High learning products have a long introductory period, and low learning products rapidly enter the growth stage. There are also different curves for fashions and fads. Different product life-cycle curves can exist for the product class, product form, and brand.

4 In managing a product's life cycle, changes can be made in the product itself or in the target market. Product modification approaches include changes in the quality, performance, or appearance. Market modification approaches entail increasing a product's use among existing customers, creating new use situations, or finding new users.

5 Product repositioning can come about by reacting to a competitor's position, reaching a new market, capitalizing on a rising trend, or changing the value offered in a product.

6 Branding enables a firm to distinguish its product in the marketplace from those of its competitors. Successful and established brands take on a brand personality, a set of human characteristics associated with a brand name. A good brand name should suggest the product benefits, be memorable, fit

the company or product image, be free of legal restrictions, and be simple and emotional. A good brand name is of such importance that is has led to a concept of brand equity, the added value a given brand name gives to a product beyond the functional benefits provided.

7 Licensing of a brand name is being used by many companies. The company allows the name to be used without having to manufacture the product.

8 Manufacturers can follow one of three branding strategies: a manufacturer's brand, a reseller brand, or a mixed brand approach. With a manufacturer's branding approach, the company can use the same brand name for all products in the line (multiproduct, or family, branding) or can give products different brands (multibranding).

9 A reseller, or private, brand is used when a firm manufactures a product but sells it under the brand name of a wholesaler or retailer. A generic brand is a product with no identification of manufacturer or reseller that is offered on the basis of price appeal.

10 Packaging provides communication, functional, and perceptual benefits. The two global emerging trends in packaging are greater concerns regarding the environmental impact and the health and safety of packaging materials.

11 The warranty, a statement of a manufacturer's liability for product deficiencies, is an important aspect of a manufacturer's product strategy.

KEY TERMS AND CONCEPTS

product life cycle p. 314
product class p. 321
product form p. 321
product modification p. 323
market modification p. 323
trading up p. 324
trading down p. 324
downsizing p. 324
branding p. 325
brand name p. 325
trade name p. 325
trademark p. 325
brand personality p. 326

brand equity p. 326
licensing p. 326
manufacturer branding p. 328
multiproduct branding p. 328
co-branding p. 329
multibranding p. 329
euro-branding p. 330
private branding p. 330
mixed branding p. 331
generic brand p. 331
packaging p. 332
warranty p. 335

INTERNET EXERCISE

New Product News provides a central Internet location on the latest new products. It provides a forum for companies to present their most recent new products. New Product News is updated daily with company press releases from the entire world. Some 30 product categories with one or more new products are typically listed by New Product News each day. A unique feature of New Product News is that a company Web site address that can be accessed immediately follows each new product description.

Visit the New Product News Web site at www.new productnews.com and go to "new items this week." Your assignment is outlined below:

1   Identify and describe how a new product listed promotes more frequent usage, creates a new use situation, reaches a new market or new users, or changes the value offered to consumers.

2   Identify and describe a new product that is branded using a family branding strategy, a subbranding strategy, or a brand extension strategy.

APPLYING MARKETING CONCEPTS AND PERSPECTIVES

1   Listed here are three different products in various stages of the product life cycle. What marketing strategies would you suggest to these companies? (*a*) GTE cellular telephone company—growth stage, (*b*) Mountain Stream tap-water purifying systems—introductory stage, and (*c*) hand-held manual can openers—decline stage.

2   It has often been suggested that products are intentionally made to break down or wear out. Is this strategy a planned product modification approach?

3   The product manager of GE is reviewing the penetration of trash compactors in American homes. After more than two decades in existence, this product is in relatively few homes.

What problems can account for this poor acceptance? What is the shape of the trash compactor life cycle?

4   For several years Ferrari has been known as the manufacturer of expensive luxury automobiles. The company plans to attract the major segment of the car-buying market who purchase medium-priced automobiles. As Ferrari considers this trading-down strategy, what branding strategy would you recommend? What are the trade-offs to consider with your strategy?

5   The nature of product warranties has changed as the federal court system reassesses the meaning of warranties. How does the regulatory trend toward warranties affect product development?

CASE 12–1   BMW

"We're fortunate right now at BMW in that all of our products are new and competitive," says Jim McDowell, vice president of marketing at BMW, as he explains BMW's product life cycle. "Now, how do you do that? You have to introduce new models over time. You have to logically plan out the introductions over time, so you're not changing a whole model range at the same time you're changing another model range."

BMW's strategy is to keep its products in the introduction and growth stages by periodically introducing new models in each of its product lines. In fact, BMW does not like to have any products in the maturity or decline stage of the product life cycle. Explains McDowell, "If a product is declining, we would prefer to withdraw it from the market, as opposed to having a strategy for dealing with the declining product. We're kind of a progressive, go get 'em company, and we don't think it does

our brand image any good to have any declining products out there. So that's why we work so hard at managing the growth aspect."

BMW—THE COMPANY AND ITS PRODUCTS

BMW is one of the preeminent luxury car manufacturers in Europe, North America, and the world today. BMW produces several lines of cars, including the 3 series, the 5 series, the 7 series, the Z line (driven by Pierce Brosnan as James Bond in *Goldeneye*), and the new X line, BMW's "sport activity" vehicle line. In addition, BMW is now selling Rovers, a British car line anchored by the internationally popular Land Rover sport utility vehicle, and will begin selling Rolls Royce vehicles in 2003.

Sales of all the BMW, Rover, and Land Rover vehicles have been on the rise globally. High-profile image campaigns (such as the James Bond promotion) and the award-winning BMW Web site (where users can design their own car) continue to increase the popularity of BMW's products.

PRODUCT LIFE CYCLE

BMW cars typically have a product life cycle of seven years. To keep products in the introductory and growth stages, BMW regularly introduces new models for each of its series to keep the entire series "new." For instance, with the 3 series, it will introduce the new sedan model one year, the new coupe the next year, then the convertible, then the station wagon, and then the sport hatchback. That's a new product introduction for five of the seven years of the product life cycle. McDowell explains, "So, even though we have seven-year life cycles, we constantly try and make the cars meaningfully different and new about every three years. And that involves adding features and other capabilities to the cars as well." How well does this strategy work? BMW often sees its best sales numbers in either the sixth or seventh year after the product introduction.

As global sales have increased, BMW has become aware of some international product life cycle differences. For example, it has discovered that some competitive products have life cycles that are shorter or longer than seven years. In Sweden and Britain automotive product life cycles are eight years, while in Japan they are typically only four years long.

BRANDING

"BMW is fortunate—we don't have too much of a dilemma as to what we're going to call our cars." McDowell is referring to BMW's trademark naming system that consists of the product line number and the motor type. For example, the designation "328" tells you the car is in the 3 series and the engine is 2.8-liters in size. BMW has found this naming system to be clear and logical and can be easily understood around the world. The Z and X series don't quite fit in with this system. BMW had a tradition of building experimental, open-air cars and calling them Z's, and hence when the prototype for the Z3 was built, BMW decided to continue with the Z name. For the sport activity vehicle, BMW also used a letter name—the X series—since the four-wheel drive vehicle didn't fit with the sedan-oriented 3, 5, and 7 series. Other than the Z3 (the third in the Z series) and the X5 (named 5 to symbolize its mid-sized status within that series), the BMW branding strategy is quite simple,

Do you have a favorite road?

You will.

In a BMW, the highway suddenly becomes more inviting. The curves more exhilarating. You'll realize there are so many roads to choose from... and there is one car waiting to help you make the most of them all.

The Ultimate Driving Machine®

unlike the evocative names many car manufacturers choose to garner excitement for their new models.

MANAGING THE PRODUCT THROUGH THE WEB—THE WAVE OF THE FUTURE

One of the ways BMW is improving its product offerings even further is through its innovative Web site (www.bmwusa.com). At the site, customers can learn about the particular models, e-mail questions, and request literature or test-drives from their local BMW dealership. What really sets BMW's Web site apart from other car manufacturers, though, is the ability for customers to configure a car to their own specifications (interior choices, exterior choices, engine, packages, and options) and then transfer that information to their local dealer. As Carol Burrows, product communications manager for BMW, explains, "The BMW Web site is an integrated part of the overall marketing strategy for BMW. The full range of products can be seen and interacted with online. We offer pricing options online. Customers can go to their local dealership via the Web site to further discuss costs for purchase of a car. And it is a distribution channel for information that allows people access to the information 24 hours a day at their convenience."

Questions

1 Compare the product life cycle described by BMW for its cars to the product life cycle shown in Figure 12–1. How are they (*a*) similar and (*b*) dissimilar?

2 Based on BMW's typical product life cycle, what marketing strategies are appropriate for the 3 series? The X5?

3 Which of the three ways to manage the product life cycle does BMW utilize with its products—modifying the product, modifying the market, or repositioning the product?

4 How would you describe BMW's branding strategy (manufacturer branding, private branding, or mixed branding)? Why?

5 Go to the BMW Web site (www.bmwusa.com) and design a car to your own specifications. How does this enable you as a customer to evaluate the product differently than would be otherwise possible?

CHAPTER THIRTEEN

MANAGING SERVICES

13

AFTER READING THIS CHAPTER YOU SHOULD BE ABLE TO:

- Describe four unique elements of services.

- Recognize how services differ and how they can be classified.

- Understand the way in which consumers purchase and evaluate services.

- Develop a customer contact audit to identify service advantages.

- Understand the important role of internal marketing in service organizations.

- Explain the role of the four Ps in the services marketing mix.

SNOWBOARDING IS COMING TO A MOUNTAIN NEAR YOU!

When aging baby boomers decided to ski less, ski resorts began looking for new ways to increase sales. Like many businesses, the resorts investigated marketing actions ranging from pursuing new products (in this case, new services) and new markets to changing their pricing and promotion practices. The changes have excited many consumers. Carol Brownson, an avid skier, says, "If this is as close to heaven as I can get, that's OK. It's pretty close."

The variety of new services offered by ski resorts has increased dramatically in recent years. Colorado's Vail Ski Resort opened the nation's first mountaintop business communications center equipped with a video conferencing room, a stock-quote terminal, and digital phone lines for computer and Internet connections. Sugarbush in Vermont added guided tours that they call "woods skiing." Alpine Meadows near Lake Tahoe, California, created a Family Ski Zone for a relaxed environment for skiers with children. Many resorts have also opened new terrain left in its natural state and added snow shoeing, dogsledding, snowmobiling, and cross-country skiing to their offerings.

The biggest change, however, may be snowboarding. While the number of skiers has grown at an annual rate of only 2 percent, the number of snowboarders has soared 270 percent since 1987. In the United States alone there are currently more than 4.5 million snowboarders. And worldwide interest is reflected in snowboarding's debut as a medal event in the Winter Olympics. Resorts that once forbid snowboarding now welcome the diverse group of snowboard enthusiasts. Many ski areas have developed "terrain parks" and obstacle courses for snowboarders, and they even offer loyalty programs to encourage repeat visits. By most measures snowboarding has become the fastest growing sport in the United States, and one you probably can't miss if you happen to be near a mountain with snow on it!

Ski resorts—and all service organizations—face another special challenge: matching demand and capacity. Historically, ski areas could attract consumers only during the winter months, leaving their resorts idle the rest of the year. Ski areas across the United States, however, are now learning how to attract visitors with horseback riding, music and art festivals, fly-fishing, and mountain biking. The International Mountain Bicycling Association estimates that the number of ski resorts open to bikes has recently grown to 200. Mammoth Mountain in California, for example, reported that 50,000 visitors paid to ride on its 60 miles of trails during the summer.[1]

As the actions of the U.S. ski industry illustrate, the marketing of services is unique and challenging. In this chapter we discuss how services differ from traditional products (goods), how service consumers make purchase decisions, and the ways in which the marketing mix is used.

THE UNIQUENESS OF SERVICES

As noted in Chapter 1, **services** are intangible items such as airline trips, financial advice, or automobile repair that an organization provides to consumers. To obtain these services, consumers exchange money or something else of value, such as their own time.

Services have become one of the most important components of the U.S. economy. About 90 percent of the 2.7 million new jobs created each year are in the services sector. In addition, more than 50 percent of the gross domestic product now comes from services. As shown in Figure 13–1, services accounted for $4.679 trillion in 1998, which was an increase of more than 300 percent since 1980. Services also represent a large export business—the $280 billion of services exports in 1998 is one of the few areas in which the United States has a trade surplus.[2]

The growth in this sector is the result of increased demand for services that have been available in the past and the increasing interest in new services. At Your Service, for example, is a Cincinnati-based personal and business concierge company designed for time-strapped executives and dual-career couples. If a customer has a wish, from finding gifts for corporate guests to picking up dry cleaning, CEO Dave Lima and his 60 employees make it come true. Other new services include the following: Mo-

FIGURE 13–1

Importance of services in the U.S. gross domestic product (GDP)

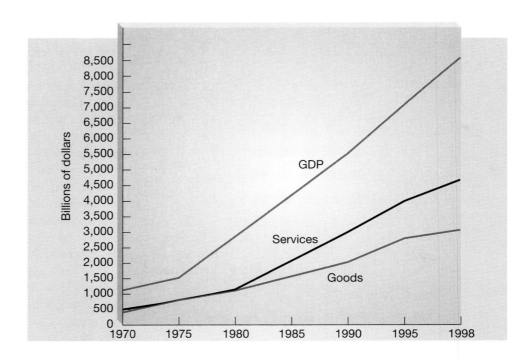

Why do many services emphasize their tangible benefits? The answer appears in the text.

British Airways
www.us.british-airways.com

Korean Air
www.koreanair.com

torola's pager-like system for automobiles allows owners to remotely lock or unlock their car or to disable their engine if the car has been stolen; Broadcast.com provides access to hundreds of radio and TV stations and offers a convenient means of broadcasting business meetings; and many banks now offer mobile banks to serve low- and middle-income neighborhoods and elderly customers who cannot easily leave their homes. These firms and many others like them are examples of the groundbreaking and imaginative services that will play a role in our economy in the future.[3]

The Four I's of Services

There are four unique elements to services: intangibility, inconsistency, inseparability, and inventory. These four elements are referred to as the **four I's of services.**

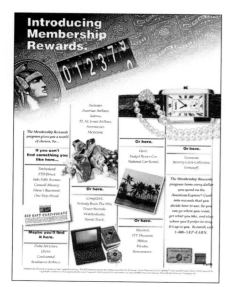

American Express Co.
www.americanexpress.com

Intangibility   Services are intangible; that is, they can't be held, touched, or seen before the purchase decision. In contrast, before purchasing a traditional product, a consumer can touch a box of laundry detergent, kick the tire of an automobile, or sample a new breakfast cereal. Because services tend to be a performance rather than an object, they are much more difficult for consumers to evaluate. To help consumers assess and compare services marketers try to make them tangible or show the benefits of using the service. A British Airways advertisement shows a traveler enjoying a "private cabin" furnished with an armchair that transforms into a bed; Korean Air emphasizes its sleeper seats, in-seat phones, and personal TVs; and American Express emphasizes the gifts available to cardholders through its Membership Rewards program.

Inconsistency   Developing, pricing, promoting, and delivering services is challenging because the quality of a service is often inconsistent. Because services depend on the people who provide them, their quality varies with each person's capabilities and day-to-day job performance. Inconsistency is much more of a problem in services than it is with tangible goods. Tangible products can be good or bad in terms of quality, but with modern production lines the quality will at least be consistent. On the other hand, one day the Philadelphia

People play an important role in the delivery of many services.

Hyatt Hotels Corporation
www.hyatt.com

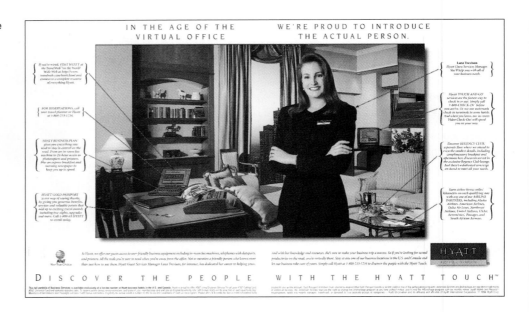

Phillies baseball team may have great hitting and pitching and look like a pennant winner and the next day lose by 10 runs. Or a soprano at New York's Metropolitan Opera may have a bad cold and give a less-than-perfect performance. Whether the service involves tax assistance at Arthur Andersen or guest relations at the Ritz-Carlton, organizations attempt to reduce inconsistency through standardization and training.[4]

Inseparability   A third difference between services and goods, and related to problems of consistency, is inseparability. In most cases, the consumer cannot (and does not) separate the deliverer of the service from the service itself. For example, to receive an education, a person may attend a university. The quality of the education may be high, but if the student has difficulty interacting with instructors, finds counseling services poor, or does not receive adequate library or computer assistance, he or she may not be satisfied with the educational experience. Students' evaluations of their education will be influenced primarily by their perceptions of instructors, counselors, librarians, and other people at the university.

The amount of interaction between the consumer and the service provider depends on the extent to which the consumer must be physically present to receive the service. Some services such as haircuts, golf lessons, medical diagnoses, and food service require the customer to participate in the delivery of the services. Other services such as car repair, dry cleaning, and waste disposal process tangible objects with less involvement from the customer. Finally, services such as banking, consulting, education, and insurance can now be delivered electronically, often requiring no face-to-face customer interaction.[5]

Inventory   Inventory of services is different from that of goods. Inventory problems exist with goods because many items are perishable and because there are costs associated with handling inventory. With services, inventory carrying costs are more subjective and are related to **idle production capacity,** which is when the service provider is available but there is no demand. The inventory cost of a service is the cost of paying the person used to provide the service along with any needed equipment. If a physician is paid to see patients but no one schedules an appointment, the fixed cost of the idle physician's salary is a high inventory carrying cost. In some service businesses, however, the provider of the service is on commission (the Merrill Lynch stockbroker) or is a part-time employee (a clerk at Sears). In these businesses, inventory carrying costs can be significantly lower or nonexistent because the idle produc-

FIGURE 13–2
Inventory carrying costs of
services

tion capacity can be cut back by reducing hours or having no salary to pay because of
the commission compensation system. Figure 13–2 shows a scale of inventory carrying costs represented on the high side by airlines and hospitals and on the low end by
real estate agencies and hair salons. The inventory carrying costs of airlines is high because of high-salaried pilots and very expensive equipment. In contrast, real estate
agencies and hair salons have employees who work on commission and need little expensive equipment to conduct business. One reason service providers must maintain
production capacity is because of the importance of time to service customers people
don't want to wait long at the emergency room!

The Service Continuum

The four I's differentiate services from goods in most cases, but many companies are
not clearly service-based or good-based organizations. Is IBM a computer company or
service business? Does Dow Jones provide only goods in the sense of publishing *The
Wall Street Journal,* or does it consider itself a service in terms of up-to-date business
information? As companies look at what they bring to the market, there is a range from
the tangible to the intangible or good-dominant to service-dominant offerings referred
to as the **service continuum** (Figure 13–3).

FIGURE 13–3
Service continuum

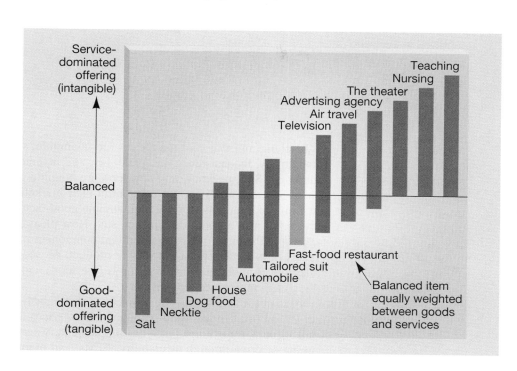

MARKETING NEWSNET

The Competition Is Tough . . . and That's Before the Game Starts!

Like most services, professional sports teams know that inconsistency can reduce consumer interest. How well a team will play from game to game or year to year is difficult to control and predict. So in addition to providing a core service such as major league baseball, many teams have invested in marketing programs that build an image and increase the entertainment value for fans. Advertising, promotional events, merchandise licensing, endorsements, new facilities with corporate sponsors and luxury boxes (or skyboxes), and logos have all become important marketing activities for sports teams.

While individual teams compete with each other, they also compete with other sports. The big four—baseball, football, basketball, and hockey—have seen significant shifts in popularity in recent years. Baseball, for example, has seen attendance and TV ratings steadily decline, particularly since the World Series was cancelled in 1994. Football has become the most popular sport in the United States through strong promotion of Monday Night Football and Sunday afternoon programs. Hockey has improved through expansion into southern states and experiments with new technology to make the puck more visible on television. Finally, basketball has been the fastest-growing sport in the world (after soccer). Michael Jordan's retirement and the 1998–99 NBA strike, however, are certain to reduce the popularity of the sport among casual fans.

The competition isn't limited to major sports though. Marketing efforts by many other familiar sports such as golf, tennis, gymnastics, soccer, and figure skating have been increasing. In addition, women's leagues are vying for fans' attention. And finally, many new and unfamiliar sports such as skysurfing, parachuting, hang-gliding, ice-climbing, bull-riding, in-line skating, skateboarding, and bicycle racing are developing growing fan interest. Sports marketers face an exciting challenge as they attempt to match the many entertainment aspects of sports to the evolving interests of sports fans. And, of course, everyone wants to know which sport might offer the next Michael Jordan!

Teaching, nursing, and the theater are intangible, service-dominant activities, and intangibility, inconsistency, inseparability, and inventory are major concerns in their marketing. Salt, neckties, and dog food are tangible goods, and the problems represented by the four I's are not relevant in their marketing. However, some businesses are a mix of intangible service and tangible good factors. A clothing tailor provides a service but also a good, the finished suit. How pleasant, courteous, and attentive the tailor is to the customer is an important component of the service, and how well the clothes fit is an important part of the product. As shown in Figure 13–3, a fast-food restaurant is about half tangible goods (the food) and half intangible services (courtesy, cleanliness, speed, convenience).

For many businesses today it is useful to distinguish between their core product—either a good or a service—and supplementary services. A core service offering such as a bank account, for example, also has supplementary services such as deposit assistance, parking or drive-through availability, ATMs, and monthly statements. Supplementary services often allow service providers to differentiate their offering from competitors, and they may add value for consumers. While there are many potential supplementary services, key categories of supplementary services include information delivery, consultation, order taking, billing procedures, and payment options.[6] See the accompanying Marketing NewsNet to learn why sports teams try to augment their core offering.[7]

Classifying Services

Throughout this book, marketing organizations, techniques, and concepts are classified to show the differences and similarities in an organized framework. Services can also be classified in several ways, according to (1) whether they are delivered by people or equipment, (2) whether they are profit or nonprofit, or (3) whether or not they are government sponsored.

Delivery by People or Equipment   As seen in Figure 13–4, companies offering services provided by professionals include management consulting firms such as Booz, Allen & Hamilton. Skilled labor is required to offer services such as Sears appliance repair or Sheraton catering service. Unskilled labor such as that used by Brinks store-security forces is also a service provided by people.

Equipment-based services do not have the marketing concerns of inconsistency because people are removed from provision of the service. Electric utilities, for example, can provide service without frequent personal contact with customers. To keep in touch with their customers, many utilities such as the Public Service Company of New Mexico now conduct frequent marketing research efforts.[8]

Profit or Nonprofit Organizations   Many organizations involved in services also distinguish themselves by their tax status as profit or nonprofit organizations. In contrast to *profit organizations, nonprofit organizations'* excesses in revenue over expenses are not taxed or distributed to shareholders. When excess revenue exists, the money goes back into the organization's treasury to allow continuation of the service. Based on the corporate structure of the nonprofit organization, it may pay tax on revenue-generating holdings not directly related to its core mission. The 600,000 nonprofit organizations in the United States now generate 10 percent of the gross domestic product.[9]

The American Red Cross, United Way, Greenpeace, Outward Bound, the Salvation Army, and the University of Florida are nonprofit organizations. Such organizations historically have not used marketing practices in the belief that they were inappropriate. In recent years, however, nonprofit organizations such as hospitals, universities, and museums have turned to marketing to increase their revenues. The

FIGURE 13–4
Service classifications

Nonprofit services often advertise.

The Salvation Army
www.salvationarmyusa.org

Outward Bound
www.outwardbound.com

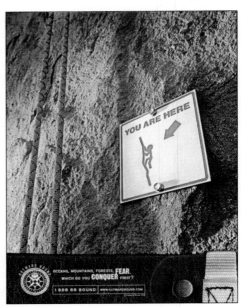

United States Postal Service
ww.usps.gov

Girl Scouts of the U.S.A. is a good example. Faced with eight years of falling membership, they adopted a marketing orientation that reversed its membership trend and attracted more than 2 million young girls to become Girl Scouts.[10]

Government Sponsored or Not   A third way to classify services is based on whether they are government sponsored. Although there is no direct ownership and they are nonprofit organizations, governments at the federal, state, and local levels provide a broad range of services. The United States Postal Service, for example, has adopted many marketing activities. Their "We Deliver" campaigns are designed to change its image of a huge bureaucracy and to focus the organization's efforts on customer satisfaction. Because faxes and E-mail have reduced first-class postage revenue by $6 billion, the Postal Service now tries to attract FedEx and UPS customers to its two-day package delivery service. Another marketing program has converted 700 postal offices to retail outlets that sell collector stamps, Pony Express sweatshirts, and even neckties! Government sponsorship does not limit competition, however. Britain's Royal Mail recently opened an office in Manhattan to compete with the U.S. Postal Service for international direct mail business.[11]

CONCEPT CHECK

1. What are the four I's of services?

2. Would inventory carrying costs for an accounting firm with certified public accountants be (*a*) high, (*b*) low, or (*c*) nonexistent?

3. To eliminate service inconsistencies, companies rely on _____ and _____.

HOW CONSUMERS PURCHASE SERVICES

Colleges, hospitals, hotels, and even charities are facing an increasingly competitive environment. Successful service organizations, like successful product-oriented firms, must understand how the consumer makes a service purchase decision and quality evaluation and in what ways a company can present a differential advantage relative to competing offerings.

The Purchase Process

Many aspects of services affect the consumer's evaluation of the purchase. Because services cannot be displayed, demonstrated, or illustrated, consumers cannot make a prepurchase evaluation of all the characteristics of services.[12] Similarly, because service providers may vary in their delivery of a service, an evaluation of a service may change with each purchase. Figure 13–5 portrays how different types of goods and services are evaluated by consumers. Tangible goods such as clothing, jewelry, and furniture have *search* properties, such as color, size, and style, which can be determined before purchase. Services such as restaurants and child care have *experience* properties, which can only be discerned after purchase or during consumption. Finally, services provided by specialized professionals such as medical diagnoses and legal services have *credence* properties, or characteristics that the consumer may find impossible to evaluate even after purchase and consumption.[13] To reduce the uncertainty created by these properties, service consumers turn to personal sources of information such as early adopters, opinion leaders, and reference group members during the purchase decision process.[14]

Assessing Service Quality

Once a consumer tries a service, how is it evaluated? Primarily by comparing expectations about a service offering to the actual experience a consumer has with the service.[15] Differences between the consumer's expectations and experience are identified through **gap analysis.** This type of analysis asks consumers to assess their expectations and experiences on dimensions of service quality such as those described in Figure 13–6.[16] Expectations are influenced by word-of-mouth communications, personal needs, past experiences, and promotional activities, while actual experiences are determined by the way an organization delivers its service.[17] The relative importance of the various dimensions of service quality varies by the type of service.[18] In the fast-food industry, Burger King is an example of a firm trying to implement gap analysis. What if someone is dissatisfied and complains? See the Marketing NewsNet on page 351 for four steps that can help.[19]

FIGURE 13–5
How consumers evaluate
goods and services

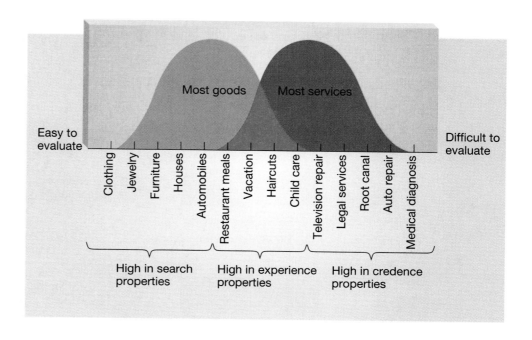

FIGURE 13–6
Dimensions of service quality

DIMENSION AND DEFINITION	EXAMPLES OF QUESTIONS STOCK BROKERAGE CUSTOMERS MIGHT ASK
Reliability: Ability to perform the promised service dependably and accurately	Does my stockbroker follow exact instructions to buy or sell?
Tangibles: Appearance of physical facilities, equipment, personnel, and communication materials	Is the monthly report easy to read and understand?
Responsiveness: Willingness to help customers and provide prompt service	Is my stockbroker willing to answer my questions?
Assurance: Knowledge and courtesy of employees and their ability to convey trust and confidence	Does my broker refrain from acting busy or being rude when I ask questions?
Empathy: Caring, individualized attention provided customers	Does my broker try to determine what my specific financial objectives are?

Customer Contact and Relationship Marketing

Consumers judge services on the entire sequence of steps that make up the service process. To focus on these steps or "service encounters," a firm can develop a **customer contact audit**—a flowchart of the points of interaction between consumer and service provider.[20] This is particularly important in high-contact services such as hotels, educational institutions, and automobile rental agencies. Figure 13–7 is a consumer contact audit for renting a car from Hertz. The interactions identified in a customer contact audit often serve as the basis for developing relationships with customers.

FIGURE 13–7
Customer contact in car rental (green shaded boxes indicate customer activity)

The Hertz Corporation
www.hertz.com

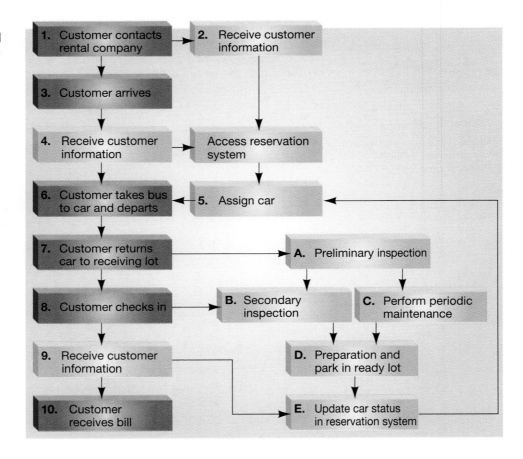

MARKETING NEWSNET

What if Someone Complains? How Services Can Recover from Failure to Satisfy a Customer

Many service companies have developed strategies to encourage customer satisfaction and loyalty. Despite these efforts, however, every company has some service failures that lead to customer complaints. How can services recover from these situations? Professors Stephen Tax and Stephen Brown suggest four steps:

Step 1: Identify service failures. Only 5 to 10 percent of dissatisfied customers choose to complain—the rest simply switch companies or make negative comments to other people. One way companies encourage customers to express concerns is through 800 numbers.

Step 2: Resolve customer problems. Once customers complain, they want fair procedures, interactions, and outcomes. Because most complaints are first expressed to "front-line" employees, a key to resolving complaints is training employees to handle likely situations and giving them the authority to resolve problems. Federal Express, for example, gives new customer service representatives five weeks of training before assigning them to a location.

Step 3: Communicate and classify service failures. This step reflects the concept of organizational learning, or the capacity to improve performance based on experience. Service providers need complaint processing forms and a culture that encourages employees to respond to complaints. Nordstrom, for example, celebrates extraordinary efforts by employees to deal with complaints at company meetings.

Step 4: Integrate data and improve overall service. Because only a small percentage of customers complain, other sources of relevant, timely information are needed. Information from surveys, focus groups, advisory panels, and other sources must be integrated with the complaint information to identify areas for service quality improvement.

Many firms are improving their methods of dealing with complaints. Holiday Inn displays the guest relations 800 number in each of its rooms. At Hampton Inn any employee, including janitors and maids, can provide a customer with a complete refund. Xerox uses a "Customer Action Request Form" to collect detailed information about complaints. United Airlines discovered that frequent business travelers represent 6 percent of their passengers and 37 percent of their revenue and were most likely to complain. And Sears decided to guarantee its appliance repair service. In every case, the goal is to obtain customer satisfaction, maintain loyalty, and learn from failure!

A Customer's Car Rental Activities A customer decides to rent a car and (1) contacts the rental company (see Figure 13–7). A customer service representative receives the information (2) and checks the availability of the car at the desired location. When the customer arrives at the rental site (3), the reservation system is again accessed, and the customer provides information regarding payment, address, and driver's license (4). A car is assigned to the customer (5), who proceeds by bus to the car pickup (6). On return to the rental location (7), the car is parked and the customer checks in (8), providing information on mileage, gas consumption, and damages (9). A bill is subsequently prepared (10).

Each of the steps numbered 1 to 10 is a customer contact point where the tangible aspects of Hertz service are seen by the customer. Figure 13–7, however, also shows a series of steps lettered A to E that involve two levels of inspections on the automobile. These steps are essential in providing a car that runs, but they are not points of customer interaction. To create a service advantage, Hertz must create a competitive advantage in the sequence of interactions with the customer. For example, Hertz has attempted to eliminate step 4 for some customers.

Relationship Marketing   The contact between a service provider and a customer represents a service encounter that is likely to influence the customer's assessment of the purchase. The number of encounters in a service experience may vary. Disney, for example, estimates that a park visitor will have 74 encounters with Disney employees in a single visit. These encounters represent opportunities to develop social bonds, or relationships, with customers. The relationship may also be developed through loyalty incentives such as airline frequent flyer programs and through service delivery systems such as the computer terminals given to high-volume customers by Federal Express. These elements are the basis for relationship marketing, which provides several benefits for service customers including the continuity of a single provider, customized service delivery, reduced stress due to a repetitive purchase process, and an absence of switching costs. Recent surveys of consumers have indicated that while customers of many services are interested in being "relationship customers," they also require that the relationship be balanced in terms of loyalty, benefits, and respect for privacy.[21]

CONCEPT CHECK

1. What are the differences between search, experience, and credence properties?

2. Hertz created its differential advantage at the points of _____ in their customer contact audit.

MANAGING THE MARKETING OF SERVICES

Just as the unique aspects of services necessitate changes in the consumer's purchase process, the marketing management process requires special adaptation.[22] As emphasized earlier in the chapter, in services marketing the employee plays a central role in attracting, building, and maintaining relationships with customers.[23] This aspect of services marketing has led to a concept called internal marketing.[24]

Internal marketing is based on the notion that a service organization must focus on its employees, or internal market, before successful programs can be directed at customers.[25] The internal marketing concept holds that an organization's employees (its "internal market") will be influenced to develop a market orientation if marketing-like activities are directed at them. This idea suggests that employees and employee development through recruitment, training, communication, and administration are critical to the success of service organizations.[26]

Let's use the four Ps framework of the text for discussing the marketing mix for services.

Product (Service)

To a large extent, the concepts of the product component of the marketing mix discussed in Chapters 11 and 12 apply equally well to Cheerios (a good) and to American Express (a service). Yet there are three aspects of the product/service element of the mix that warrant special attention: exclusivity, brand name, and capacity management.

WEB LINK

All the Marketing Information a Banker Needs!

The financial services industry is fortunate to have a Web site that provides information about many relevant topics, including marketing. To see for yourself, go to http://www.bankinfo.com, and click on "Marketing Magic." There is a lot to choose from, but you might find it interesting to learn how to choose and register a Web site domain name (click on "Naming Names"). Use http://www.bankweb.com to check on the domain names currently in use in the state in which you reside.

Exclusivity   Chapter 11 pointed out that one favorable dimension in a new product is its ability to be patented. Remember that a patent gives the manufacturer of a product exclusive rights to its production for 17 years. A major difference between products and services is that services cannot be patented. Hence the creator of a successful fast-food hamburger chain could quickly discover the concept being copied by others. Domino's Pizza, for example, has seen competitors copy the quick delivery advantage that propelled the company to success.

Branding   An important aspect in marketing goods is the branding strategy used. However, because services are intangible and, therefore, more difficult to describe, the brand name or identifying logo of the service organization is particularly important in consumer decisions.[27] The financial services industry, for example, has failed to use branding to distinguish what consumers perceive to be similar offerings by banks, mutual fund companies, brokerage firms, and insurance companies. Federal Express, however, is a strong service brand name because it suggests the possibility that it is government sanctioned, and it describes the nature and benefit (speed) of the service.[28] Take a look at the figures at the top of this page to determine how successful some companies have been in branding their service by name, logo, or symbol. Use the Web Link to learn about another form of branding—Web domain names!

Capacity Management   Most services have a limited capacity due to the inseparability of the service from the service provider and the perishable nature of the service. For example, a patient must be in the hospital at the same time as the surgeon to "buy" an appendectomy, and only one patient can be helped at that time. Similarly, no additional surgery can be conducted tomorrow because of an unused operating room or an available surgeon today—the service capacity is lost if it is not used. So the service component of the mix must be integrated with efforts to influence consumer demand.[29] This is referred to as **capacity management.**

Service organizations must manage the availability of the offering so that (1) demand matches capacity over the duration of the demand cycle (for example, one day, week, month, year), and (2) the organization's assets are used in ways that will maximize the

Logos create service identities.

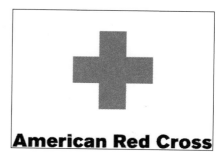

FIGURE 13–8
Managing capacity in a hotel

* Employees of corporations called upon by salesforce (book rooms through special reservations line).
† Customers reserving rooms via public telephone number or by just "walking in."

return on investment (ROI).[30] Figure 13–8 shows how a hotel tries to manage its capacity during the high and low seasons. Differing price structures are assigned to each segment of consumers to help moderate or adjust demand for the service. Airline contracts fill a fixed number of rooms throughout the year. In the slow season, when more rooms are available, tour packages at appealing prices are used to attract groups or conventions, such as an offer for seven nights in Orlando at a reduced price. Weekend packages are also offered to buyers. In the high-demand season, groups are less desirable because guests who will pay high prices travel to Florida on their own.

Pricing

In the service industries, *price* is referred to in various ways. Hospitals refer to charges; consultants, lawyers, physicians, and accountants to fees; airlines to fares; and hotels to rates. Regardless of the term used, price plays two essential roles: (1) to affect consumer perceptions and (2) to be used in capacity management. Because of the intangible nature of services, price can indicate the quality of the service. Would you wonder about the quality of a $100 surgery? Studies have shown that when there are few well-known cues by which to judge a product, consumers use price.[31] Look at the accompanying ad for dental services. Would you have concerns about the offer or think it's a good value for the money?

The capacity management role of price is also important to movie theaters, airlines, restaurants, and hotels. Many service businesses use **off-peak pricing,** which consists of charging different prices during different times of the day or days of the week to reflect variations in demand for the service. Airlines offer discounts for weekend travel, and movie theaters offer matinee prices. The New York State Thruway Authority has been testing different toll amounts for different times of the day to try to reduce traffic during rush hour.[32]

Place (Distribution)

Place or distribution is a major factor in developing a service marketing strategy because of the inseparability of services from the producer. Historically in services marketing, little attention has been paid to distribution. But as competition grows, the value of conve-

Price influences perceptions of services.

nient distribution is being recognized. Hairstyling chains such as Fantastic Sam's Family Haircutters, legal firms such as the Hyatt chain, and accounting firms such as Deloitte and Touche all use multiple locations for the distribution of services. In the banking industry, customers of participating banks using the Cirrus system can access any one of thousands of automatic teller systems throughout the United States. The availability of electronic distribution through the World Wide Web now provides global coverage for travel services, banking, entertainment, and many other information-based services.

Promotion

The value of promotion, specifically advertising, for many services is to show the benefits of purchasing the service. It is valuable to stress availability, location, consistent quality, and efficient, courteous service.[33] The Kelly Services ad below, for example, describes the many services, resources, and benefits available to its customers. In addition, services must be concerned with their image. Promotional efforts, such as Andersen Consulting's "Who says you can't be big and nimble?" campaign or Merrill Lynch's use of the bull in its ads, contribute to image and positioning strategies.[34] In most cases promotional concerns of services are similar to those of products.

   In the past, advertising has been viewed negatively by many nonprofit and professional service organizations. In fact, professional groups such as law, dentistry, and

Services need promotional programs.

Andersen Consulting
www.ac.com

Kelly Services
www.kellyservices.com

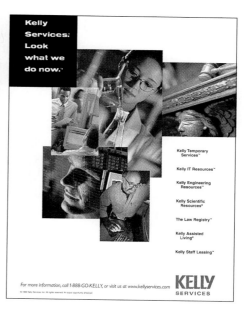

medicine had previously barred their members from advertising by their respective professional codes of conduct. A Supreme Court case in 1976, however, struck down this constraint on professional services advertising.[35] Although opposition to advertising remains strong in some professional groups, the barriers to promotion are being broken down. In recent years, advertising has been used by religious groups; legal, medical, and dental services; educational institutions; and many other service organizations. Attorney Rosalie Osias of Long Island, New York, more than doubled the number of cases at her real estate and banking law practice by running ads in two trade newspapers covering the mortgage banking industry in New York.[36]

Another form of promotion, publicity, has played a major role in the promotional strategy of nonprofit services and some professional organizations. Nonprofit organizations such as public school districts, the Chicago Symphony Orchestra, religious organizations, and hospitals have used publicity to disseminate their messages. Because of the heavy reliance on publicity, many services use public service announcements (PSAs), and because PSAs are free, nonprofit groups have tended to rely on them as the foundation of their media plan.[37] However, as discussed in Chapter 20, the timing and location of a PSA are under the control of the medium, not the organization. So the nonprofit service group cannot control who sees the message or when the message is given.

SERVICES IN THE FUTURE

What can we expect from the services industry in the future? New and better services, of course, and an unprecedented variety of suppliers. Many of the changes will be driven by two factors—deregulation and technological development.

One by one, transportation, telecommunications, financial services, professional services, and other services have gone through some kind of regulatory changes. The changes have generally led to a greater variety of services and, most recently, to a convergence of many of the suppliers of services. Banks, brokerages, and insurance companies, for example, all want to offer one-stop shopping for financial services. Other businesses we traditionally think of as manufacturers are adding services. Ford, General Electric, and General Motors, for example, now offer consumer loans, credit cards, mortgages, commercial loans, and insurance. In recognition of the growing importance of services to most businesses, *Fortune* magazine's ranking of the 500 largest companies in the United States now includes industrial and service firms.

Technological changes are also likely to change the service industry. Perhaps the most dramatic is the trend toward Internet-based services such as banking, travel and vacation planning, and personalized shopping. For example, egift offers to wrap and ship "great gifts for everyone" at a discount! The Internet will also soon make it possible to obtain movies, software programs, video games, photographs, and virtually all digital information electronically for a fee. Other businesses are using technology to change the way they operate. Many airlines, for example, are replacing traditional paper tickets with electronic versions called E-tickets. And new technology-driven services such as Delphi, a satellite communications service for automobiles, are quickly becoming available to a large number of consumers. Future readers of this book may simply use their computer and a cable, telephone, or satellite connection to read assigned pages or to download a copy of the book![38]

CONCEPT CHECK

    1.   Matching demand with capacity is the focus of _____ management.

    2.   How does a movie theater use off-peak pricing?

    3.   What factors will influence future changes in services?

SUMMARY

1 Services have four unique elements: intangibility, inconsistency, inseparability, and inventory.

2 Intangibility refers to the difficulty of communicating the service benefits. Inconsistency refers to the difficulty of providing the same level of quality each time a service is purchased. Inseparability means that consumers cannot separate the deliverer of the service from the service itself. Inventory costs for services are related to the cost of maintaining production capacity.

3 Services can be classified in several ways. The primary distinction is whether they are provided by people or equipment. Other distinctions of services are in terms of tax status (profit versus nonprofit) or whether the service is provided by a government agency.

4 Consumers can evaluate three aspects of goods or services: search properties, experience properties, and credence properties.

5 A gap analysis determines if consumers' expectations are different from their actual experiences.

6 A customer contact audit is a flowchart of the points of interaction between a service provider and its customers. Interactions are opportunities for relationship marketing.

7 Internal marketing, which focuses on an organization's employees, is critical to the success of a service organization.

8 Because services cannot be patented, unique offerings are difficult to protect. In addition, because services are intangible, brands and logos (which can be protected) are particularly important to help distinguish among competing service providers.

9 The inseparability of production and consumption of services means that capacity management is important in the service element of the mix. This process involves smoothing demand to meet capacity.

10 The intangible nature of services makes price an important cue to indicate service quality to the consumer.

11 Distribution has become an important marketing tool for services, and electronic distribution allows some services to provide global coverage.

12 Historically, promotion has not been viewed favorably by many nonprofit and professional service organizations. In recent years this attitude has changed, and service organizations have increased their promotional activities.

KEY TERMS AND CONCEPTS

services p. 342
four I's of services p. 343
idle production capacity p. 344
service continuum p. 345
gap analysis p. 349

customer contact audit p. 350
internal marketing p. 352
capacity management p. 353
off-peak pricing p. 354

 INTERNET EXERCISE

The *Journal of Services Marketing* is a comprehensive source of information for anyone interested in the latest services marketing concepts, cases, trends, application, and strategies. Go to the *Journal*'s home page (http://www.mcb.co.uk/jsm.htm), click on "click here to view current and previous contents pages," and use the search function to investigate one of the following topics: relationship marketing, implications of the Internet for services marketing, or the advertising of services.

1 How many articles are available regarding the topic you selected?

2 Describe three insights you obtained from the summaries of the articles.

APPLYING MARKETING CONCEPTS AND PERSPECTIVES

1 Explain how the four I's of services would apply to a Marriott Hotel.

2 Idle production capacity may be related to inventory or capacity management. How would the pricing component of the marketing mix reduce idle production capacity for (*a*) a car wash, (*b*) a stage theater group, and (*c*) a university?

3 What are the search, experience, and credence properties of an airline for the business traveler and pleasure traveler? What properties are most important to each group?

4 Outline the customer contact audit for the typical deposit you make at your neighborhood bank.

5 The text suggests that internal marketing is necessary before a successful marketing program can be directed at consumers. Why is this particularly true for service organizations?

6 Outline the capacity management strategies that an airline must consider.

7 Draw the channel of distribution for the following services: (*a*) a restaurant, (*b*) a hospital, and (*c*) a hotel.

8 How does off-peak pricing influence demand for services?

9 In recent years, many service businesses have begun to provide their employees with uniforms. Explain the rationale behind this strategy in terms of the concepts discussed in this chapter.

10 Look back at the service continuum in Figure 13–3. Explain how the following points in the continuum differ in terms of consistency: (*a*) salt, (*b*) automobile, (*c*) advertising agency, and (*d*) teaching.

 ## CASE 13–1   LEARNINGBYTE INTERNATIONAL

"Here at LearningByte International (LBI) we're at the leading edge of changing a well-entrenched paradigm. That brings all the joys and frustrations that can come with it," explains Dr. Rajiv Tandon, president of LBI. "Anytime you bring a paradigm change you face resistance. So the biggest joy of my job is to be able to slowly break down those barriers and prevail," Tandon continues.

Tandon and his colleagues at LBI, a startup firm that has gone from 4 to 120 employees in a few years, are at the forefront of a quiet revolution in training and education. The "well-entrenched paradigm" he refers to is traditional classroom-based training—probably much like you're experiencing in your own college courses. What LBI proposes is an innovative technology-based instruction (TBI) system. Rajiv Tandon gets pleasure out of showing clients how much more effective TBI is than classroom-based training in many applications, causing many firms to rethink their methods of providing training services to employees.

MARKET OPPORTUNITIES

Large companies with many locations, such as car-rental agencies, hotels, airlines, real-estate agencies, banks, and cruise lines, need to train hundreds of new employees frequently throughout the year. In the past, new hires would be instructed by professionals in training courses in central locations that could last up to one month. Many companies still employ this training model, but it is often very costly and can provide poor results because of the diverse skill levels of the employees to be trained. Using personalized, technology-based instruction puts the learner, not the presenter, in charge of the learning process, lets the learner go at his/her own pace, and saves the company time and money. LBI is at the forefront of this movement, and its methods have been shown to compress training time by 46 percent; increase learning retention by 50 percent; and reduce the cost of development, maintenance, and delivery by 64 percent.

HOW DOES LBI ACHIEVE THESE MIRACULOUS RESULTS?

The LBI learning system consists of its trademark three-step LearningByte™: Preview, Show Me, and Try It. Trainees sit at their own computers, and at their own pace go through each three-step learning module:

- Preview step—provides a conceptual and motivational overview of the topic.
- Show Me step—demonstrates and explains the procedures required to complete the skill.
- Try It step—allows the learner to perform the skill and provides corrective feedback to help the learner master the skill.

As Kay Christianson, vice president of sales and marketing for LBI notes, the learner needn't go through the steps in a sequential order. "They can go directly to Try It and experiment for themselves and, if they get stuck, they can always go back to Show Me to see what the learning is supposed to be like. So it allows for a high level of interactivity in the training and for flexibility in the way the student learns the information."

The LearningBytes can be delivered to the learner through different media: on a CD, on a wide-area network, on a local-area network, through a browser on the Internet, or through the Internet itself. The Web-based versions of LBI's training courses are the most popular—these allow companies to update and maintain the training program very easily and cost effectively, as well as to reach all their employees smoothly and quickly. LBI has developed the Web-based versions of its training modules using Java, the highly advanced multimedia development platform introduced by Sun Microsystems, which allows the programs to be as fast and interactive as possible.

THE MARKET

LBI sees its target market as the Fortune 1000 companies, the largest corporations in the United States. These companies have the critical mass needed to justify large training programs, as well as a continued need for training and re-training. Within these companies, LBI's customers come primarily from the people who are directly affected by the training, such as the director of a call center, the vice president of sales, or the chief information officer. The travel/leisure industry, the hardware and software manufacturing industries, and organizations that deliver traditional instructor-led courses that know they need to diversify are key markets where LBI has had success selling its product.

TWO RECENT EXAMPLES

LBI recently developed a customized training program for an international airline's baggage and reservations departments. This airline is very geographically dispersed, so it did not make sense for it to have to constantly transport new employees to a central location for training. Also, with the large number or people performing these jobs, the training needs are almost constant. The content of the training is very process oriented, which lends itself very easily to TBI. So far, the airline has been pleased with its strategic decision to transition its training regimen to a technology-based system, and the partnership between it and LBI remains profitable for both parties.

National Car Rental is another of LBI's prominent clients. "The course we designed for National's agent new-hire training is centered around customer service, listening skills, products that they will sell, and sales skills. So it's a complete course that provides rental agents with all the skills they need to learn in order to be on the job quickly," explains Christianson. LBI's training system enabled National to reduce agent new-hire training from three weeks to three days.

Check out LBI's Web site (www.learningbyte.com/case studies) to see examples of the three-step LearningBytes developed for two other clients of LBI.

Questions

1   What are (*a*) the advantages and (*b*) the disadvantages of LearningByte International's technology-based instruction over conventional classroom methods?

2   Given your answer to question 1 above, (*a*) what are the key criteria LBI should use in identifying prospective customers for its service, (*b*) what market segments meet your criteria, and (*c*) what are possible sales objections these segments might have that you have to address?

3   Suppose a large international hotel chain asks LBI to make a proposal to train its thousands of front-desk clerks and receptionists. (*a*) How would you design a three-step LearningByte to train them how to check in a customer? (*b*) How can LBI demonstrate the points of difference or benefits to the hotel chain of its technology-based instruction to obtain a contract to design a training module?

CHAPTER FOURTEEN

PRICING: RELATING OBJECTIVES TO REVENUES AND COSTS

14

AFTER READING THIS CHAPTER YOU SHOULD BE ABLE TO:

• Identify the elements that make up a price.

• Recognize the constraints on a firm's pricing latitude and the objectives a firm has in setting prices.

• Explain what a demand curve is and how it affects a firm's total and marginal revenue.

• Recognize what price elasticity of demand means to a manager facing a pricing decision.

• Explain the role of costs in pricing decisions.

• Calculate a break-even point for various combinations of price, fixed cost, and unit variable cost.

WHEN THAT "LITTLE PRICE CUT" IS A BIG DEAL . . . AND RUNS INTO BILLIONS OF DOLLARS!

Wal-Mart uses periodic price cuts as part of its marketing strategy. So do other retailers such as Home Depot and manufacturers such as Pillsbury, IBM, and . . . Boeing!

So what's the big deal about price cutting if almost all business firms do it? In Boeing's case recent price cuts are humongously big deals—and ones that Boeing must live with for years to come.

The Setting   In 1997 Boeing merged with McDonnell Douglas, the other remaining major U.S. manufacturer of large commercial jet aircraft. This left Boeing in a duopoly setting, with Europe's Airbus Industrie being the only other major commercial aircraft producer in the world. Boeing became obsessed with the need to maintain its traditional 60 percent share of the world's commercial jet aircraft market.

The Tragedy: Prices, Revenues, and Costs
Boeing's obsession with market share underlies some disastrous results. In fact, Boeing:

- Embarked on a price war with Airbus Industrie, cutting prices big time—sometimes 25 percent off list price![1]
- Is likely to lose money on the first 400 of the nearly 900 next-generation Boeing 737s it produces, half the company's backlog—largely because of its cut-rate prices.[2]
- Agreed to rebates on past sales to some airlines, such as Southwest, to match the discount price Boeing offered to other airlines.
- Spent billions of dollars to try to untangle a huge production bottleneck it found in trying to increase deliveries from 200 planes in 1995 to more than 500 planes in 1998.[3]
- Shut down two aircraft assembly lines temporarily because of parts and labor shortages and paid millions of dollars to some airlines for late-delivery penalties.

MARKETING NEWSNET

Jetliner Cross-Functional Teams and Customer Value: Addressing Sleeplessness in Seattle

CROSS FUNCTIONAL

The new economics of jetliner pricing, production, and use has reawakened Boeing, the Seattle giant. Boeing now utilizes a variety of cross-functional teams to add genuine value for its customers—both the airlines that buy Boeing jetliners and the passengers that ride in them.

Boeing's cross-functional teams blend not only employees from different functional areas within the firm but also its suppliers and customers as well. Here are some actions triggered by these teams:

- Introduction of a new 737-800 model. This upgrade of the 737 series—the best-selling jetliner in aviation history—offers the airline customers more range, more speed, and better operating economics.
- Boeing 777 customer-value innovations. Listening to passengers like you, the Boeing Triple-7 provides 6'4" of center aisle headroom, a 5.7-inch TV screen in the seatback in front of each passenger, and most seats that are 18.5 inches wide—1.5 inches wider than most economy jetliner seats.

Boeing Company
www.boeing.com

But the airlines wanted customer value, too, in the form of the flexibility to reconfigure seats to handle different uses for the plane, which generates a conflict between the customer value of the airlines and that of passengers. Until things change, in flying on Boeing 777s you might avoid seats in rows 16, 31, 40, and 43. They're still only 17 inches wide! So delivering customer value for all of a firm's customers often requires some difficult trade-offs.

- Has watched the mix of products shift from its huge 400-passenger widebody 747 line to its updated, much smaller 737 line, which lists for $33 million to $57 million—and is far less than half the list price of 747s.[4]

The Net Result   Boeing lost billions of dollars in revenue because of its price cuts, and those price cuts plus production costs spiraling upward led to $4.45 billion of write-down losses over an 18-month period. These cash flow problems plus the Asian recession caused Boeing to announce layoffs of 48,000 employees through 2001.[5]

As Boeing discovered, cutting price isn't always the solution. As we'll see in this chapter, a firm can go bankrupt if, in the long run, the prices customers pay don't cover its production and marketing expenses and also provide some profit. Innovative companies now recognize that value for their customers is more than simply a low price. As shown in the Marketing NewsNet,[6] Boeing has utilized cross-functional teams to improve jetliner designs as well as to speed up jetliner and spare parts delivery to customers. But as the box shows, sometimes what is seen as greater customer value for one group (reconfiguration flexibility for airlines) can conflict with that for another (wider seats for all the passengers).

Welcome to the fascinating—and intense—world of pricing, where myriad forces come together in the specific price prospective buyers are asked to pay. This chapter and Chapter 15 cover important factors used in setting prices.

NATURE AND IMPORTANCE OF PRICE

The price paid for goods and services goes by many names. You pay *tuition* for your education, *rent* for an apartment, *interest* on a bank credit card, and a *premium* for car insurance. Your dentist or physician charges you a *fee*, a professional or social organization charges *dues*, and airlines flying their Boeing—or other—jetliners charge a *fare*. In business, a consultant may require a *retainer* for services rendered, an executive is given a *salary*, a salesperson receives a *commission*, and a worker is paid a *wage*. Of course, what you pay for clothes or a haircut is termed a *price*.

What Is a Price?

These examples highlight the many varied ways that price plays a part in our daily lives. From a marketing viewpoint, **price** is the money or other considerations (including other goods and services) exchanged for the ownership or use of a good or service. For example, Shell Oil recently exchanged 1 million pest control devices for sugar from a Caribbean country, and Wilkinson Sword exchanged some of its knives for advertising used to promote its razor blades. This practice of exchanging goods and services for other goods and services rather than for money is called **barter.** These transactions account for billions of dollars annually in domestic and international trade.

For most products and services, money is exchanged, although the amount is not always the same as the list or quoted price, because of the discounts, allowances, and extra fees shown in Figure 14–1. Suppose you decide to buy a Lamborghini Diablo SV because its 510-horsepower engine moves you from 0 to 62 mph in 3.9 seconds. The list price is $255,000. As a vehicle incentive for buying within the year you receive $20,000 off the list price. You agree to pay half down and the other half when the car is delivered, which results in a financing fee of $19,000. To ship the car from Italy you will pay a $6,000 destination charge. You are given a trade-in allowance of $1,000 for your 1990 Honda Civic DX, which is the *Kelley Blue Book* (www.kbb.com) value of your car.[7]

FIGURE 14–1
The price of four different purchases

PRICE EQUATION

ITEM PURCHASED	PRICE	= LIST PRICE	INCENTIVES AND – ALLOWANCES	+ EXTRA FEES
New car bought by an individual	Final price	= List price	– Vehicle incentive Cash discount Trade-ins	+ Financing charges Special accessories Destination charges
Term in college bought by a student	Tuition	= Published tuition	– Scholarship Other financial aid Discounts for number of credits taken	+ Special activity fees
Bank loan obtained by a small business	Principal and interest	= Amount of loan sought	– Allowance for collateral	+ Premium for uncertain creditworthiness
Merchandise bought from a wholesaler by a retailer	Invoice price	= List price	– Quantity discount Cash discount Seasonal discount Functional or trade discount	+ Penalty for late payment

are sensitive to matching production capacity with unit volume. Using unit volume as an objective, however, can sometimes be misleading from a profit standpoint. Volume can be increased by employing sales incentives (such as lowering prices, giving rebates, or offering lower interest rates). By doing this the company chooses to lower profits in the short run to quickly sell its product. This happened when Fiat offered $1,600 rebates and zero-interest financing in Italy on its $10,000 Uno compact car.[18]

Survival   In some instances, profits, sales, and market share are less important objectives of the firm than mere survival. Continental Airlines has struggled to attract passengers with low fares, no-penalty advance-booking policies, and aggressive promotions to improve the firm's cash flow. This pricing objective has helped Continental to stay alive in the competitive airline industry.

Social Responsibility   A firm may forgo higher profit on sales and follow a pricing objective that recognizes its obligations to customers and society in general. Medtronics followed this pricing policy when it introduced the world's first heart pacemaker. Gerber supplies a specially formulated product free of charge to children who cannot tolerate foods based on cow's milk. Government agencies, which set many prices for services they offer, use social responsibility as a primary pricing objective.

CONCEPT CHECK

1. What factors impact the list price to determine the final price?

2. How does the type of competitive market a firm is in affect its latitude in setting price?

STEP 2: ESTIMATING DEMAND AND REVENUE

Basic to setting a product's price is the extent of customer demand for it. Marketing executives must also translate this estimate of customer demand into estimates of revenues the firm expects to receive.

Fundamentals of Estimating Demand

Newsweek decided to conduct a pricing experiment at newsstands in 11 cities throughout the United States.[19] At that time, Houston newsstand buyers paid $2.25. In Fort Worth, New York, Los Angeles, San Francisco, and Atlanta, newsstand buyers paid the regular $2.00 price. In San Diego, the price was $1.50. The price in Minneapolis–St. Paul, New Orleans, and Detroit was only $1.00. By comparison, the regular newsstand price for *Time* and *U.S. News & World Report,* *Newsweek*'s competitors, was $1.95. Why did *Newsweek* conduct the experiment? According to a Newsweek executive, at that time, "We want to figure out what the demand curve for our magazine at the newsstand is." And you thought that demand curves only existed to confuse you on a test in basic economics!

The Demand Curve   A **demand curve** shows a maximum number of products consumers will buy at a given price. Demand curve D_1 in Figure 14–5 shows the newsstand demand for *Newsweek* under conditions existing. Note that as price falls, people buy more. But price is not the complete story in estimating demand. Economists stress three other key factors:

1. *Consumer tastes.* As we saw in Chapter 3, these depend on many factors such as demographics, culture, and technology. Because consumer tastes can change quickly, up-to-date marketing research is essential.
2. *Price and availability of other products.* As the price of close substitute products falls (the price of *Time*) and their availability increases, the demand for a product declines (the demand for *Newsweek*).
3. *Consumer income.* In general, as real consumer income (allowing for inflation) increases, demand for a product also increases.

The first of these two factors influences what consumers *want* to buy, and the third affects what they *can* buy. Along with price, these are often called **demand factors,** or factors that determine consumers' willingness and ability to pay for goods and services. As discussed earlier in Chapters 9 and 11, it is often very difficult to estimate demand for new products, especially because consumer likes and dislikes are often so difficult to read clearly. For example, Campbell Soup spent seven years and $55 million on a supersecret project to produce a line of Intelligent Quisine (IQ) food products. The company expected that its line of 41 breakfasts, lunches, dinners, and snacks would be the first foods "scientifically proven to lower high levels of cholesterol, blood sugar, and blood pressure."[20] After 15 months in a Ohio test market, Campbell Soup yanked the entire IQ line when it fell far short of expectations because customers found the line too pricey and lacking in variety.

Movement Along versus Shift of a Demand Curve   Demand curve D_1 in Figure 14–5 shows that as the price is lowered from $2 to $1.50, the quantity demanded increases from 3 million (Q_1) to 4.5 million (Q_2) units per year. This is an example of a

Newsweek

FIGURE 14–5
Illustrative demand curves for *Newsweek* magazine

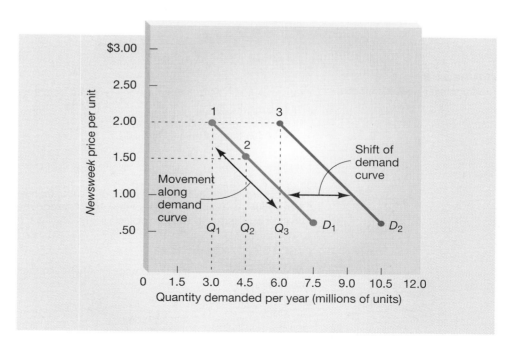

movement along a demand curve and assumes that other factors (consumer tastes, price and availability of substitutes, and consumer income) remain unchanged.

What if some of these factors change? For example, if advertising causes more people to want *Newsweek,* newsstand distribution is increased, and consumer incomes double, then the demand increases. This is shown in Figure 14–5 as a shift of the demand curve to the right, from D_1 to D_2. This increased demand means that more *Newsweek* magazines are wanted for a given price: At a price of $2, the demand is 6 million units per year (Q_3) on D_2 rather than 3 million units per year (Q_1) on D_1.

Fundamentals of Estimating Revenue

While economists may talk about "demand curves," marketing executives are more likely to speak in terms of "revenues generated." Demand curves lead directly to three related revenue concepts critical to pricing decisions: **total revenue, average revenue,** and **marginal revenue** (Figure 14–6).

Demand Curves and Revenue   Figure 14–7A again shows the demand curve for *Newsweek,* but it is now extended to intersect both the price and quantity axes. The demand curve shows that as price is changed, the quantity of *Newsweek* magazines sold throughout the United States changes. This relationship holds whether the price is increased from $2.50 to $3.00 on the demand curve or is reduced from $1 to $0 on the curve. In the former case the market demands no *Newsweek* magazines, whereas in the latter case 9 million could be given away at $0 per unit.

It is likely that if *Newsweek* was given away, more than 9 million would be demanded. This fact illustrates two important points. First, it can be dangerous to extend a demand curve beyond the range of prices for which it really applies. Second, most demand curves are rounded (or convex) to the origin, thereby avoiding an unrealistic picture of what demand looks like when a straight-line curve intersects either the price axis or the quantity axis.

Figure 14–7B shows the total revenue curve for *Newsweek* calculated from the demand curve shown in Figure 14–7A. The total revenue curve is developed by simply multiplying the unit price times the quantity for each of the points on the demand curve. Total revenue starts at $0 (point *A*), reaches a maximum of $6,750,000 at point *D,* and returns to $0 at point *G.* This shows that as price is reduced in the *A*-to-*D* segment of the

FIGURE 14–6
Fundamental revenue concepts

Total revenue (*TR*) is the total money received from the sale of a product. If:

    TR = Total revenue
     P = Unit price of the product
    Q = Quantity of the product sold

then:

    $TR = P \times Q$

Average revenue (*AR*) is the average amount of money received for selling one unit of the product, or simply the price of that unit. Average revenue is the total revenue divided by the quantity sold:

$$AR = \frac{TR}{Q} = P$$

Marginal revenue (*MR*) is the change in total revenue obtained by selling one additional unit:

$$MR = \frac{\text{Change in TR}}{\text{1 unit increase in Q}} = \frac{\Delta TR}{\Delta Q} = \text{slope of TR curve}$$

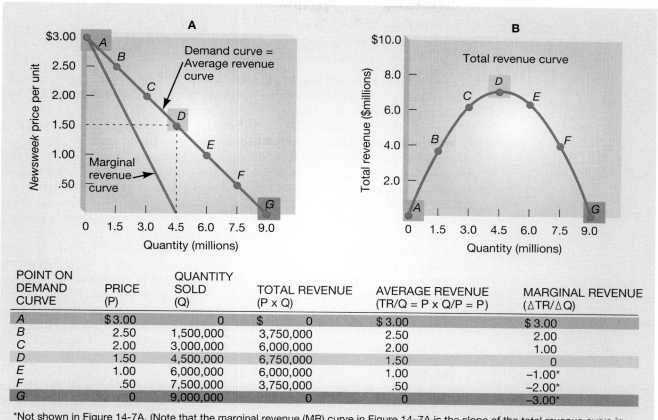

POINT ON DEMAND CURVE	PRICE (P)	QUANTITY SOLD (Q)	TOTAL REVENUE (P x Q)	AVERAGE REVENUE (TR/Q = P x Q/P = P)	MARGINAL REVENUE (ΔTR/ΔQ)
A	$3.00	0	$ 0	$3.00	$3.00
B	2.50	1,500,000	3,750,000	2.50	2.00
C	2.00	3,000,000	6,000,000	2.00	1.00
D	1.50	4,500,000	6,750,000	1.50	0
E	1.00	6,000,000	6,000,000	1.00	−1.00*
F	.50	7,500,000	3,750,000	.50	−2.00*
G	0	9,000,000	0	0	−3.00*

*Not shown in Figure 14-7A. (Note that the marginal revenue (MR) curve in Figure 14–7A is the slope of the total revenue curve in Figure 14–7B.)

FIGURE 14–7
How a downward-sloping demand curve affects total, average, and marginal revenue.

curve, total revenues are increased. However, cutting price in the *D*-to-*G* segment results in a decline in total revenue.

Marginal revenue, which is the slope of the total revenue curve, is positive but decreasing when the price lies in the range from $3 to above $1.50 per unit. Below $1.50 per unit, though, marginal revenue is actually negative, so the extra quantity of magazines sold is more than offset by the decrease in the price per unit.

For any downward-sloping, straight-line demand curve, the marginal revenue curve always falls at a rate twice as fast as the demand curve. As shown in Figure 14–7A, the marginal revenue becomes $0 per unit at a quantity sold of 4.5 million units—the very point at which total revenue is maximum (see Figure 14–7B). A rational marketing manager would never operate in the region of the demand curve in which marginal revenue is negative. This means that in Figure 14–7A this manager would set prices only in the *A*-to-*D* segment of the demand curve.

What price did *Newsweek* select after conducting its experiment? It kept the price at $2.00. However, through expanded newsstand distribution and more aggressive advertising, *Newsweek* was later able to shift its demand curve to the right and charge a price of $2.50 without affecting its newsstand volume.

Price Elasticity of Demand   With a downward-sloping demand curve, we have been concerned with the responsiveness of demand to price changes. This can be conveniently measured by **price elasticity of demand,** or the percentage change in quantity demanded relative to a percentage change in price. Price elasticity of demand (E) is expressed as follows:

$$E = \frac{\text{Percentage change in quantity demanded}}{\text{Percentage change in price}}$$

Because quantity demanded usually decreases as price increases, price elasticity of demand is usually a negative number. However, for the sake of simplicity and by convention, elasticity figures are shown as positive numbers.

Price elasticity of demand assumes three forms: elastic demand, inelastic demand, and unitary demand elasticity. *Elastic demand* exists when a small percentage decrease in price produces a larger percentage increase in quantity demanded. Price elasticity is greater than 1 with elastic demand. *Inelastic demand* exists when a small percentage decrease in price produces a smaller percentage increase in quantity demanded. With inelastic demand, price elasticity is less than 1. *Unitary demand* exists when the percentage change in price is identical to the percentage change in quantity demanded. In this instance, price elasticity is equal to 1.

Price elasticity of demand is determined by a number of factors. First, the more substitutes a product or service has, the more likely it is to be price elastic. For example, butter has many possible substitutes in a meal and is price elastic, but gasoline has almost no substitutes and is price inelastic. Second, products and services considered to be necessities are price inelastic. For example, open-heart surgery is price inelastic, whereas airline tickets for a vacation are price elastic. Third, items that require a large cash outlay compared with a person's disposable income are price elastic. Accordingly, cars and yachts are price elastic; books and movie tickets tend to be price inelastic.

Price elasticity is important to marketing managers because of its relationship to total revenue. For example, with elastic demand, total revenue increases when price decreases, but decreases when price increases. With inelastic demand, total revenue increases when price increases and decreases when price decreases. Finally, with unitary demand total revenue is unaffected by a slight price change.

Because of this relationship between price elasticity and a firm's total revenue, it is important that marketing managers recognize that price elasticity of demand is not the same over all possible prices of a product. Figure 14–7B illustrates this point using the *Newsweek* demand curve shown in Figure 14–7A. As the price decreases from $2.50 to $2, total revenue increases, indicating an elastic demand. However, when the price decreases from $1 to 50 cents, total revenue declines, indicating an inelastic demand. Unitary demand elasticity exists at a price of $1.50.

Price Elasticities for Brands and Product Classes   Marketing executives also recognize that the price elasticity of demand is not always the same for product classes (such as stereo receivers) and brands within a product class (such as Sony and Marantz). For example, marketing experiments on brands of cola, coffee, and snack and specialty foods generally show elasticities of 1.5 to 2.5, indicating they are price elastic. By comparison, entire product classes of fruits and vegetables have elasticities of about 0.8—they are price inelastic.[21]

Recently, the price elasticity of demand for cigarettes has become a hotly debated public health issue and a matter of corporate ethics and social responsibility. Research generally shows that cigarettes are price inelastic.[22] However, price elasticity differs by the age of the smoker. Because 12 to 17 year olds often have limited "spending money," this group is very price elastic in its demand for cigarettes. As a result, many legislators recommend far higher excise taxes on cigarettes to increase their prices significantly with the goal of reducing teen-age smoking. Thus, price elasticity is not only a relevant concept for marketing managers, it is also important for public policy affecting pricing practices.

What are the marketing secrets of the entrepreneur who entered the frozen-entree fray, against the advice of experts? For the answer, see the text and the Marketing NewsNet box.

Michelina's Frozen Foods
www.michelinas.com

CONCEPT CHECK

1. What is the difference between a movement along and a shift of a demand curve?

2. What does it mean if a product has a price elasticity of demand that is greater than 1?

STEP 3: ESTIMATING COST, VOLUME, AND PROFIT RELATIONSHIPS

While revenues are the moneys received by the firm from selling its products or services to customers, costs or expenses are the moneys the firm pays out to its employees and suppliers. Marketing managers often use marginal analysis and break-even analysis to relate revenues and costs at various levels of units sold, topics covered in this section.

The Importance of Controlling Costs

The profit equation described at the beginning of the chapter showed that Profit = Total revenue − Total cost. Therefore, understanding the role and behavior of costs is critical for all marketing decisions, particularly pricing decisions. Four cost concepts are important in pricing decisions: **total cost, fixed cost, variable cost,** and **marginal cost** (Figure 14–8).

Many firms go bankrupt because their costs get out of control, causing their total costs to exceed their total revenues over an extended period of time. This is why sophisticated marketing managers make pricing decisions that balance both their revenues and costs. An example, described in the Marketing NewsNet box, is that of an entrepreneur who has achieved spectacular success in three different food businesses by controlling costs and attending to critical details that ensure that his products provide

MARKETING NEWSNET

The Secrets of a Food Entrepreneur: Pay Attention to Detail and Control Costs

"I think I'm well liked by my employees," he says, "but I'm a [soft expletive] on quality. If the pasta is a little mushy, I get a lot of upset." The speaker is Jeno Paulucci, chief executive officer of Lugino's foods and called the "nation's most accomplished food entrepreneur in recent times" by *Fortune* magazine. Across five decades and through three huge new-food businesses, Paulucci's secrets have remained consistent: (1) a passion for detail and (2) low, low overhead to control costs. The effect has been to provide genuine value to customers that, in turn, has resulted in huge success for his three separate businesses, described here.

Chun King Foods. In 1945 Paulucci became a local legend—the son of Italian immigrant parents selling Chinese food to mostly Scandinavian customers on Minnesota's Iron Range. But Chun King took off when GIs returning from World War II sought the convenience—and customer value—of easy-to-prepare dinners. In 1966 Paulucci sold Chun King to what was then R. J. Reynolds for $63 million.

Jenos. He took the cash and started producing pizzas and pizza rolls. How did Paulucci get the idea for pizza rolls? His response: "I had to do something with my egg roll machines"—a low-cost way of utilizing his leftover Chun King equipment. By 1972 Jeno's was the U.S. leader in frozen pizza and frozen hot snacks. But Paulucci got bored with the business and sold it to Pillsbury for $150 million in 1985. Paulucci's quality concern: "The pies got smaller, with more artificial ingredients. I didn't like making food that way."

Luginos. In 1990, against the judgment of experts, Paulucci entered the overcrowded frozen-entree fray, competing with giant brands such as Stouffer, Healthy Choice, and Weight Watchers. Paulucci was unfazed and observes, "All those big companies with all their overhead—I knew if we paid attention to the little things our plan would work." Two examples: (1) Paulucci packs the pasta in his Michelina's Italian dinners separately from the sauce to improve flavor, and (2) he sells his Italian dinners for about half the price of competitors—by controlling his costs.

His credo: "Gold is in the details"—which applies to customer value, costs, and prices.

genuine value to customers. Controlling costs carefully has enabled him to sell his Michelina's Italian dinners at prices well below those of his competitors.[23]

Marginal Analysis and Profit Maximization

A basic idea in business, economics, and indeed everyday life is marginal analysis. In personal terms, marginal analysis means that people will continue to do something as long as the incremental return exceeds the incremental cost. This same idea holds true in marketing and pricing decisions. In this setting, **marginal analysis** means that as long as revenue received from the sale of an additional product (marginal revenue) is greater than the additional cost of production and selling it (marginal cost), a firm will expand its output of that product.[24]

Marginal analysis is central to the concept of maximizing profits. In Figure 14–9A, marginal revenue and marginal cost are graphed. Marginal cost starts out high at lower quantity levels, decreases to a minimum through production and marketing efficiencies, and then rises again due to the inefficiencies of overworked labor and equipment. Marginal revenue follows a downward slope. In Figure 14–9B, total cost and total revenue curves corresponding to the marginal cost and marginal revenue curves are graphed. Total cost initially rises as quantity increases but increases at the slowest rate at the quantity where marginal cost is lowest. The total revenue curve increases to a maximum and then starts to decline, as shown in Figure 14–7B.

The message of marginal analysis, then, is to operate up to the quantity and price level where marginal revenue equals marginal cost (MR = MC). Up to the output

KEY TERMS AND CONCEPTS

price p. 363
barter p. 363
value p. 364
value-pricing p. 364
profit equation p. 365
pricing constraints p. 366
pricing objectives p. 369
demand curve p. 371
demand factors p. 371
total revenue p. 372
average revenue p. 372

marginal revenue p. 372
price elasticity of demand p. 373
total cost p. 375
fixed cost p. 375
variable cost p. 375
marginal cost p. 375
marginal analysis p. 376
break-even analysis p. 377
break-even point p. 378
break-even chart p. 379

INTERNET EXERCISE

Want to check out the options and prices on your next car? First, write down the features you want in a car. Then, check out these three Web sites:

- General Motors: www.gmbuypower.com
- Ford: www.buyerconnection.com
- An independent car buying service: www.autobytel.com

After you have printed the price quotes for the cars you desire from the above Web sites, call or visit a local dealer and get a quote for the cars with the same featuers. Compare the prices and experiences of buying a car from the Internet and the traditional car dealer. What are the similarities and differences, if any, in negotiating the list prices, vehicle incentives, trade-in allowances, financing, warranties, accessories (or option packages), destination charges, etc. of the cars you want?[25]

APPLYING MARKETING CONCEPTS AND PERSPECTIVES

1 How would the price equation apply to the purchase price of (*a*) gasoline, (*b*) an airline ticket, and (*c*) a checking account?

2 What would be your response to the statement, "Profit maximization is the only legitimate pricing objective for the firm"?

3 How is a downward-sloping demand curve related to total revenue and marginal revenue?

4 A marketing executive once said, "If the price elasticity of demand for your product is inelastic, then your price is probably too low." What is this executive saying in terms of the economic principles discussed in this chapter?

5 A marketing manager reduced the price on a brand of cereal by 10 percent and observed a 25 percent increase in quantity sold. The manager then thought that if the price were reduced by another 20 percent, a 50 percent increase in quantity sold would occur. What would be your response to the marketing manager's reasoning?

6 A student theater group at a university has developed a demand schedule that shows the relationship between ticket prices and demand based on a student survey, as follows:

TICKET PRICE	NUMBER OF STUDENTS WHO WOULD BUY
$1	300
2	250
3	200
4	150
5	100

(*a*) Graph the demand curve and the total revenue curve based on these data. What ticket price might be set based on this analysis? (*b*) What other factors should be considered before the final price is set?

7 Touché Toiletries, Inc. has developed an addition to its Lizardman Cologne line tentatively branded Ode d'Toade Cologne. Unit variable costs are 45 cents for a 3-ounce bottle, and heavy advertising expenditures in the first year would result in total fixed costs of $900,000. Ode d'Toade Cologne is priced at $7.50 for a 3-ounce bottle. How many bottles of Ode d'Toade must be sold to break even?

8 Suppose that marketing executives for Touché Toiletries reduced the price to $6.50 for a 3-ounce bottle of Ode d'Toade and the fixed costs were $1,100,000. Suppose further that the unit variable cost remained at 45 cents for a 3-ounce bottle. (*a*) How many bottles must be sold to break even? (*b*) What dollar profit level would Ode d'Toade achieve if 200,000 bottles were sold?

9 Executives of Random Recordings, Inc. produced an album entitled *Sunshine/Moonshine* by the Starshine Sisters Band. The cost and price information was as follows:

Album cover	$	1.00 per album
Songwriter's royalties		0.30 per album
Recording artists' royalties		0.70 per album
Direct material and labor costs to produce the album		1.00 per album
Fixed cost of producing an album (advertising, studio fee, etc.)	100,000.00	
Selling price		7.00 per album

(*a*) Prepare a chart like that in Figure 14–11 showing total cost, fixed cost, and total revenue for album quantity sold levels starting at 10,000 albums through 100,000 albums at 10,000 album intervals, that is, 10,000, 20,000, 30,000, and so on. (*b*) What is the break-even point for the album?

 CASE 14–1   WASHBURN INTERNATIONAL, INC.

"The relationship between musicians and their guitars is something really extraordinary—and is a fairly strange one," says Brady Breen in a carefully understated tone of voice. Breen has the experience to know. He's production manager of Washburn International, one of the most prestigious guitar manufacturers in the world. Washburn's instruments range from one-of-a-kind, custom-made acoustic and electric guitars and basses to less-expensive, mass-produced ones.

THE COMPANY AND ITS HISTORY

The modern Washburn International started in 1977 when a small Chicago firm bought the century-old Washburn brand name and a small inventory of guitars, parts, and promotional supplies. At that time annual revenues of the company were $300,000 for the sale of about 2,500 guitars. Washburn's first catalog, appearing in 1978, told a frightening truth:

> Our designs are translated by Japan's most experienced craftsmen, assuring the consistent quality and craftmanship for which they are known.

At that time the American guitar-making craft was at an all-time low. Guitars made by Japanese firms such as Ibane and Yamaha were in use by an increasing number of professionals.

Times have changed for Washburn. Today the company sells about 250,000 guitars a year. Annual sales exceed $50 million. All this resulted from Washburn's aggressive marketing strategies to develop product lines with different price points targeted at musicians in distinctly different market segments.

THE PRODUCTS AND MARKET SEGMENTS

Arguably the most trendsetting guitar developed by the modern Washburn company appeared in 1980. This was the Festival Series of cutaway, thin-bodied flattops, with built-in bridge pickups and controls, which went on to become the virtual standard for live performances. John Lodge of the Moody Blues endorsed the 12-string version—his gleaming white guitar appearing in both concerts and ads for years. In the time since the Festival Series appeared, countless rock and country stars have used these instruments including Bob Dylan, Dolly Parton, Greg Allman, John Jorgenson, and George Harrison.

Until 1991 all Washburn guitars were manufactured in Asia. That year Washburn started building its high-end guitars in the United States. Today Washburn marketing executives divide its product line into four levels. From high-end to low-end these are:

- One-of-a-kind, custom units.
- Batch-custom units.
- Mass-customized units.
- Mass-produced units.

The one-of-a-kind custom units are for the many stars that use Washburn instruments. The mass-produced units targeted at first-time buyers are still manufactured in Asian factories.

PRICING ISSUES

Setting prices for its various lines presents a continuing challenge for Washburn. Not only do the prices have to reflect the changing tastes of its various segments of musicians, but the prices must also be competitive with the prices set for guitars manufactured and marketed globally. In fact, Washburn and other well-known guitar manufacturers have a prestige-niche strategy. For Washburn this involves endorsements by internationally known musicians who play its instruments and lend their names to lines of Washburn signature guitars. This has the effect of reducing the price elasticity or price sensitivity for these guitars. Stars playing Washburn guitars like Nuno Bettencourt, David Gilmour of Pink Floyd, Joe Perry of Aerosmith, and Darryl Jones of the Rolling Stones have their own lines of signature guitars—the "batch-custom" units mentioned earlier.

Joe Baksha, Washburn's executive vice president, is responsible for reviewing and approving prices for the company's lines of guitars. Setting a sales target of 2,000 units for a new line of guitars, he is considering a suggested retail price of $329 per unit for customers at one of the hundreds of retail outlets carrying the Washburn line. For planning purposes, Baksha estimates half of the final retail price will be the price Washburn nets when it sells its guitar to the wholesalers and dealers in its channel of distribution.

Looking at Washburn's financial data for its present Chicago plant, Baksha estimates that this line of guitars must bear these fixed costs:

Rent and taxes	= $12,000
Depreciation of equipment	= $ 4,000
Management and quality control program	= $20,000

In addition, he estimates the variable costs for each unit to be:

Direct materials =	$25/unit
Direct labor =	8 hours/unit @ $14/hour

Carefully kept production records at Washburn's Chicago plant make Baksha believe that these are reasonable estimates. He explains, "Before we begin a production run, we have a good feel for what our costs will be. The U.S.-built N-4, for example, simply costs more than one of our foreign-produced Mercury or Wing series electrics."

Caught in the global competition for guitar sales, Washburn searches for ways to reduce and control costs. After much agonizing, the company decided to move to Nashville, Tennessee. In this home of country music, Washburn expects to lower its manufacturing costs because there are many skilled workers in the region, and its fixed costs will be reduced by avoiding some of the expenses of having a big city, Chicago, location. Specifically, Washburn projects that it will reduce its rent and taxes expense by 40 percent and the wage rate it pays by 15 percent in relocating from Chicago to Nashville.

Questions

1 What factors are most likely to affect the demand for the lines of Washburn guitars (*a*) bought by a first-time guitar buyer and (*b*) bought by a sophisticated musician who wants a signature model signed by David Gilmour or Joe Perry?

2 For Washburn what are examples of (*a*) shifting the demand curve to the right to get a higher price for a guitar line (movement *of* the demand curve) and (*b*) pricing decisions involving moving *along* a demand curve?

3 In Washburn's Chicago plant what is the break-even point for the new line of guitars if the retail price is (*a*) $329, (*b*) $359, and (*c*) $299? Also, (*d*) if Washburn achieves the sales target of 2,000 units at the $329 retail price, what will its profit be?

4 Assume that Washburn moves its production to Nashville and that the costs are reduced as projected in the case. Then, what will be the (*a*) new break-even point at a $329 retail price for this line of guitars and (*b*) the new profit if it sells 2,000 units?

5 If for competitive reasons, Washburn eventually has to move all its production back to Asia, (*a*) which specific costs might be lowered and (*b*) what additional costs might it expect to incur?

CHAPTER FIFTEEN

PRICING: ARRIVING AT THE FINAL PRICE

15

AFTER READING THIS CHAPTER YOU SHOULD BE ABLE TO:

- Understand how to establish the initial "approximate price level" using demand-oriented, cost-oriented, profit-oriented, and competition-oriented approaches.

- Identify the major factors considered in deriving a final list or quoted price from the approximate price level.

- Describe adjustments made to the approximate price level based on geography, discounts, and allowances.

- Prepare basic financial analyses useful in evaluating alternative prices and arriving at the final sales price.

- Describe the principal laws and regulations affecting pricing practices.

GILLETTE KNOWS THE VALUE OF A GREAT SHAVE

How much is a close and comfortable shave worth? Ask The Gillette Company, the world leader in shaving technology and marketing. Gillette commands 71 percent of the North American and European markets for shaving razors and blades and captures 91 percent of the market for blades in Latin America and 69 percent in India.

Product innovation that benefits the customer is a critical ingredient in Gillette's success. Gillette's breakthrough MACH 3 shaving system is an example. MACH 3 is the first and only shaving system with three progressively aligned blades that provides men with a closer shave in fewer strokes with less irritation. According to Gillette's consumer tests, men preferred MACH 3 nearly two-to-one over the company's hugely successful SensorExcel shaving system introduced in 1994, and by a still larger margin over rival products.

Such innovation naturally translates into the price customers are willing to pay. Gillette's pricing research indicated men would pay 45 percent more for the MACH 3 than they paid for the SensorExcel given the shaving benefit provided. Gillette ultimately chose a 35 percent price premium over SensorExcel and supported the 1998 launch of MACH 3 with a first-year marketing support budget of $300 million—the largest marketing effort in the company's history. MACH 3 is scheduled to be marketed in 100 countries by 2000 and expected to log $1.8 billion in annual worldwide sales.[1]

The marketing success of MACH 3 illustrates the imaginative commercialization of shaving technology at a price point that creates value for the consumer. In addition to understanding consumer demand, cost, competition, and profit considerations played a role in Gillette's pricing decisions as will be discussed later.

This chapter describes how companies such as Gillette select an approximate price level, highlights important

385

FIGURE 15–1
Steps in setting price

considerations in setting a list or quoted price, and identifies various price adjustments that can be made to prices set by the firm—the last three steps an organization uses in setting price (Figure 15–1). In addition, an overview of legal and regulatory aspects of pricing is provided.

STEP 4: SELECT AN APPROXIMATE PRICE LEVEL

A key to a marketing manager's setting a final price for a product is to find an "approximate price level" to use as a reasonable starting point. Four common approaches to helping find this approximate price level are (1) demand-oriented, (2) cost-oriented, (3) profit-oriented, and (4) competition-oriented approaches (Figure 15–2). Although these approaches are discussed separately below, some of them overlap, and an effective marketing manager will consider several in searching for an approximate price level.

Demand-Oriented Approaches

Demand-oriented approaches weigh factors underlying expected customer tastes and preferences more heavily than such factors as cost, profit, and competition when selecting a price level.

Skimming Pricing   A firm introducing a new or innovative product can use **skimming pricing,** setting the highest initial price that customers really desiring the product are willing to pay. These customers are not very price sensitive because they weigh the new product's price, quality, and ability to satisfy their needs against the same characteristics of substitutes. As the demand of these customers is satisfied, the firm lowers the price to attract another, more price-sensitive segment. Thus, skimming pricing gets its name from skimming successive layers of "cream," or customer segments, as prices are lowered in a series of steps.

Skimming pricing is an effective strategy when (1) enough prospective customers are willing to buy the product immediately at the high initial price to make these sales profitable, (2) the high initial price will not attract competitors, (3) lowering price has only a minor effect on increasing the sales volume and reducing the unit costs, and (4) customers interpret the high price as signifying high quality. These four conditions are most likely to exist when the new product is protected by patents or copyrights or its uniqueness is understood and valued by customers. Gillette adopted a skimming strategy for the MACH 3 shaving system since many of these conditions applied, including

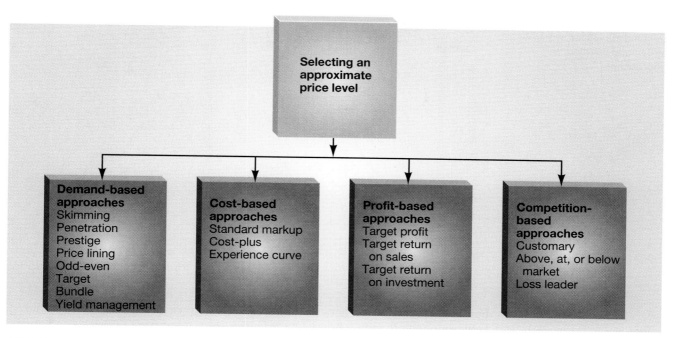

FIGURE 15–2
Four approaches for selecting
an approximate price level

patent protection. The MACH 3 shaving system has some 35 patents that protect its product and manufacturing process technology.[2]

Penetration Pricing   Setting a low initial price on a new product to appeal immediately to the mass market is **penetration pricing,** the exact opposite of skimming pricing. Sony Corporation consciously chose a penetration strategy when it introduced its PlayStation video-game player first in Japan and later in the United States in 1995. Sony's penetration strategy was designed to quickly gain market share, attract price-sensitive consumers, discourage competitors from entering the market, and according to a company executive, "achieve a massive mass market," which it did.[3]

The conditions favoring penetration pricing are the reverse of those supporting skimming pricing: (1) many segments of the market are price sensitive, (2) a low initial price discourages competitors from entering the market, and (3) unit production and marketing costs fall dramatically as production volumes increase. A firm using penetration pricing may (1) maintain the initial price for a time to gain profit lost from its low introductory level or (2) lower the price further, counting on the new volume to generate the necessary profit. Sony chose the second approach for its video-game player. Sony slashed the price of PlayStation to half of its original price 18 months after its introduction.[4]

In some situations penetration pricing may follow skimming pricing. A company might initially price a product high to attract price-insensitive consumers and recoup initial research and development costs and introductory promotional expenditures. Once this is done, penetration pricing is used to appeal to a broader segment of the population and increase market share.[5]

Prestige Pricing   As noted in Chapter 14, consumers may use price as a measure of the quality or prestige of an item so that as price is lowered beyond some point, demand for the item actually falls. **Prestige pricing** involves setting a high price so that status-conscious consumers will be attracted to the product and buy it (Figure 15–3A). The demand curve slopes downward and to the right between points *A* and *B*

FIGURE 15–3
Demand curves for two types of demand-oriented approaches

but turns back to the left between points B and C because demand is actually reduced between points B and C. From A to B buyers see the lowering of price as a bargain and buy more; from B to C they become dubious about the quality and prestige and buy less. A marketing manager's pricing strategy here is to stay above price P_o (the initial price).

Rolls-Royce cars, Chanel perfume, Cartier jewelry, Lalique crystal, and Swiss watches have an element of pricing appeal in them and may sell worse at lower prices than at higher ones.[6] The recent success of Swiss watchmaker TAG Heuer is an example. The company raised the average price of its watches from $250 to $1,000, and its sales volume increased sevenfold![7]

Price Lining   Often a firm that is selling not just a single product but a line of products may price them at a number of different specific pricing points, which is called **price lining.** For example, a discount department store manager may price a line of women's dresses at $59, $79, and $99. As shown in Figure 15–3B, this assumes that demand is elastic at each of these price points but inelastic between these price points. In some instances all the items might be purchased for the same cost and then marked up at different percentages to achieve these price points based on color, style, and expected demand. In other instances manufacturers design products for different price points, and retailers apply approximately the same markup percentages to achieve the three or four different price points offered to consumers. Sellers often feel that a limited number (such as three or four) of price points is preferable to 8 or 10 different ones, which may only confuse prospective buyers.[8]

Odd-Even Pricing   Sears offers a Craftsman radial saw for $499.99, the suggested retail price for a MACH 3 razor set (razor and two blades) is $6.99, and Kmart sells Windex glass cleaner on sale for 99 cents. Why not simply price these items at $500, $7, and $1, respectively? These firms are using **odd-even pricing,** which involves setting prices a few dollars or cents under an even number. The presumption is that consumers see the Sears radial saw as priced at "something over $400" rather than "about $500." In theory, demand increases if the price drops from $500 to $499.99. There is some evidence to suggest this does happen. However, consumers may interpret these odd-ending prices as meaning lower quality.[9]

Target Pricing   Manufacturers will sometimes estimate the price that the ultimate consumer would be willing to pay for a product. They then work backward through

MARKETING NEWSNET

Achieving a Target Price: Cross-Functional Planning Pays a Customer Value Dividend to Compaq Computer

CROSS FUNCTIONAL

Personal computer buyers today demand better hardware and more software and expect to pay less for computer power and reliability. It is therefore understandable that creating and sustaining customer value in the PC industry is a constant challenge. Compaq Computer Corporation has met the customer value challenge and sells more personal computers than any other firm in the United States. One reason for Compaq's success has been its focus on target pricing.

Target pricing at Compaq involves cross-functional planning and integration. It begins by first determining what the final retail list price to the buyer should be, followed by the subtraction of retailer markup and the company's desired profit margin. Managers of the materials, engineering, manufacturing, and marketing functions resolve among themselves how to allocate the remaining costs to make a product that provides the desired features at the desired retail price point.

Target pricing at Compaq demands discipline, teamwork, originality, and a collective commitment to develop products at prices that PC buyers are willing to pay. Does it work? With target pricing, Compaq built a $3 billion business in home computers from scratch in two years.

---

markups taken by retailers and wholesalers to determine what price they can charge wholesalers for the product. This practice, called **target pricing,** results in the manufacturer deliberately adjusting the composition and features of a product to achieve the target price to consumers. Canon uses this practice for pricing its cameras, and Heinz adopted target pricing for its complete line of pet foods. Compaq Computer Corporation successfully employed target pricing when it entered the home computer market, as described in the accompanying Marketing NewsNet.[10]

Bundle Pricing   A frequently used demand-oriented pricing practice is **bundle pricing**—the marketing of two or more products in a single "package" price. For example, Delta Air Lines offers vacation packages that include airfare, car rental, and lodging. Bundle pricing is based on the idea that consumers value the package more than the individual items. This is due to benefits received from not having to make separate purchases and enhanced satisfaction from one item given the presence of another. Moreover, bundle pricing often provides a lower total cost to buyers and lower marketing costs to sellers.[11]

Yield Management Pricing   Have you noticed seats on airline flights are priced differently within coach class? What you observed is **yield management pricing**—the charging of different prices to maximize revenue for a set amount of capacity at any given time.[12] As described in Chapter 13, service businesses engage in capacity management, and an effective way to do this is by varying prices by time, day, week, or season. Yield management pricing is a complex approach that continually matches demand and supply to customize the price for a service. Airlines, hotels, cruise ships, and car rental companies frequently use it. American Airlines estimates that yield management pricing produces an annual revenue that exceeds $500 million.[13]

CONCEPT CHECK

1. What are the circumstances in pricing a new product that might support skimming or penetration pricing?

2. What is odd-even pricing?

Cost-Oriented Approaches

With cost-oriented approaches the price setter stresses the supply or cost side of the pricing problem, not the demand side. Price is set by looking at the production and marketing costs and then adding enough to cover direct expenses, overhead, and profit.

Standard Markup Pricing Managers of supermarkets and other retail stores have such a large number of products that estimating the demand for each product as a means of setting price is impossible. Therefore, they use **standard markup pricing,** which entails adding a fixed percentage to the cost of all items in a specific product class. This percentage markup varies depending on the type of retail store (such as furniture, clothing, or grocery) and on the product involved. High-volume products usually have smaller markups than do low-volume products. Supermarkets such as Kroger, Safeway, and Jewel have different markups for staple items and discretionary items. The markup on staple items like sugar, flour, and dairy products varies from 10 percent to 23 percent, whereas markups on discretionary items like snack foods and candy ranges from 27 percent to 47 percent. These markups must cover all expenses of the store, pay for overhead costs, and contribute something to profits. For supermarkets these markups, which may appear very large, result in only a 1 percent profit on sales revenue if the store is operating efficiently. By comparison, consider the markups on snacks and beverages purchased at your local movie theater. The markup on soft drinks is 87 percent, 65 percent on candy bars, and a whopping 90 percent on popcorn! An explanation of how to compute a markup, along with operating statement data and other ratios, is given in Appendix B to this chapter.

Cost-Plus Pricing Many manufacturing, professional services, and construction firms use a variation of standard markup pricing. **Cost-plus pricing** involves summing

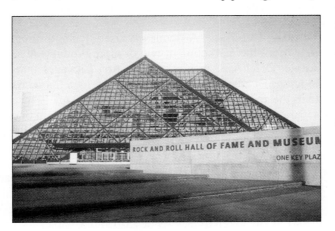

the total unit cost of providing a product or service and adding a specific amount to the cost to arrive at a price. Cost-plus pricing generally assumes two forms. With *cost-plus percentage-of-cost pricing,* a fixed percentage is added to the total unit cost. This is often used to price one- or few-of-a-kind items, as when an architectural firm charges a percentage of the construction costs of, say, the $92 million Rock and Roll Hall of Fame and Museum in Cleveland, Ohio. In buying highly technical, few-of-a-kind products such as hydro-electric power plants or space satellites, country governments have found that general contractors are reluctant to specify a formal, fixed price for the procurement. Therefore, they use *cost-plus fixed-fee pricing,* which means that a supplier is reimbursed for all costs, regardless of what they turn out to be, but is allowed only a fixed fee as profit that is independent of the final cost of the project. For example, suppose that the National Aeronautics and Space Administration agreed to pay Boeing $1.2 billion as the cost of a space shuttle and agreed to a $100 million fee for providing that space shuttle. Even if Boeing's cost increased to $2 billion for the space shuttle, its fee would remain $100 million.

The rising cost of legal fees has prompted some law firms to adopt a cost-plus pricing approach. Rather than billing clients on an hourly basis, lawyers and their clients agree on a fixed fee based on expected costs plus a profit for the law firm.[14] Many advertising agencies also use this approach. Here, the client agrees to pay the agency a fee based on the cost of its work plus some agreed-on profit, which is often a percentage of total cost.[15]

Experience Curve Pricing   The method of **experience curve pricing** is based on the learning effect, which holds that the unit cost of many products and services declines by 10 percent to 30 percent each time a firm's experience at producing and selling them doubles.[16] This reduction is regular or predictable enough that the average cost per unit can be mathematically estimated. For example, if the firm estimates that costs will fall by 15 percent each time volume doubles, then the cost of the 100th unit produced and sold will be about 85 percent of the cost of the 50th unit, and the 200th unit will be 85 percent of the 100th unit. Therefore, if the cost of the 50th unit is $100, the 100th unit would cost $85, the 200th unit would be $72.25, and so on. Because prices often follow costs with experience curve pricing, a rapid decline in price is possible. Japanese and U.S firms in the electronics industry often adopt this pricing approach. This cost-based pricing approach complements the demand-based pricing strategy of skimming followed by penetration pricing. For example, CD player prices have decreased from $900 to less than $200, fax machine prices have declined from $1,000 to under $300, and cellular telephones that sold for $4,000 are now priced below $99. Panasonic, Sony, Samsung, Zenith, and other television manufacturers will use experience curve pricing for HDTV sets. Consumers will benefit because prices will decline as cumulative sales volume grows.[17]

Panasonic expects to be a leader in the successful commercialization of HDTV.

Panasonic
www.panasonic.com

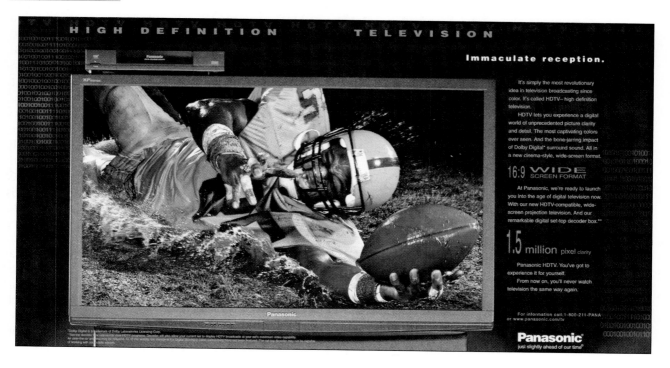

Profit-Oriented Approaches

A price setter may choose to balance both revenues and costs to set price using profit-oriented approaches. These might either involve a target of a specific dollar volume of profit or express this target profit as a percentage of sales or investment.

Target Profit Pricing   A firm may set an annual target of a specific dollar volume of profit, which is called **target profit pricing.** Suppose a picture framing store owner wishes to use target profit pricing to establish a price for a typical framed picture and assumes the following:

- Variable cost is a constant $22 per unit.
- Fixed cost is a constant $26,000.
- Demand is insensitive to price up to $60 per unit.
- A target profit of $7,000 is sought at an annual volume of 1,000 units (framed pictures).

The price can be calculated as follows:

$$\text{Profit} = \text{Total revenue} - \text{Total cost}$$

$$\text{Profit} = (P \times Q) - [FC + (UVC \times Q)]$$

$$\$7,000 = (P \times 1,000) - [\$26,000 + (\$22 \times 1,000)]$$

$$\$7,000 = 1,000P - (\$26,000 + \$22,000)$$

$$1,000P = \$7,000 + \$48,000$$

$$P = \$55$$

Note that a critical assumption is that this higher average price of a framed picture will not cause the demand to fall.

Target Return-on-Sales Pricing   A difficulty with target profit pricing is that although it is simple and the target involves only a specific dollar volume, there is no benchmark of sales or investment used to show how much of the firm's effort is needed to achieve the target. Firms such as supermarket chains often use **target return-on-sales pricing** to set typical prices that will give the firm a profit that is a specified percentage, say, 1 percent, of the sales volume. Suppose the owner decides to use target return-on-sales pricing for the frame shop and makes the same first three assumptions shown previously. The owner now sets a target of 20 percent return on sales at an annual volume of 1,250 units. This gives

$$\text{Target return on sales} = \frac{\text{Target profit}}{\text{Total revenue}}$$

$$20\% = \frac{TR - TC}{TR}$$

$$0.20 = \frac{P \times Q - [FC + (UVC \times Q)]}{TR}$$

$$0.20 = \frac{P \times 1,250 - [\$26,000 + (\$22 \times 1,250)]}{P \times 1,250}$$

$$P = \$53.50$$

So at a price of $53.50 per unit and an annual quantity of 1,250 frames,

$$TR = P \times Q = \$53.50 \times 1,250 = \$66,875$$

$$TC = FC + (UVC \times Q) = \$26,000 + (\$22 \times 1,250) = \$53,500$$

$$\text{Profit} = TR - TC = \$66,875 - \$53,500 = \$13,375$$

WEB LINK   Tracking the Success of MACH 3

The innovative MACH 3 shaving system is very likely to bolster the sales and operating profit for Gillette's blades and razors business. You can track the suc-

World-Class Brands, Products, People

cess of MACH 3 by visiting The Gillette Company Web site at http://www.gillette.com. Go to the Investors page, click business and investment profiles, and review the performance chart entitled Blades and Razors Sales and Profit from Operations.

How have sales, dollar operating profit, and operating profit margin for blades and razors changed since Gillette introduced the MACH 3 shaving system in mid-1998?

As a check,

$$\text{Target return on sales} = \frac{\text{Target profit}}{\text{Total revenue}} = \frac{\$13,375}{\$66,875} = 20\%$$

The Gillette Company expects that its MACH 3 shaving system will increase both the dollar volume of profit and the return-on-sales for its blades and razor business. Why? The MACH 3 gross profit is three time higher than that for Gillette's Sensor-Excel shaving system![18] Visit the Web site described in the accompanying Web Link to see the effect of the MACH 3 on Gillette's blade and razor sales, dollar operating profit, and operating profit margins.

Target Return-on-Investment Pricing   Firms such as General Motors and many public utilities set annual return-on-investment (ROI) targets such as ROI of 20 percent. **Target return-on-investment pricing** is a method of setting prices to achieve this target.

Suppose the store owner sets a target ROI of 10 percent, which is twice that achieved the previous year. She considers raising the average price of a framed picture to $54 or $58—up from last year's average of $50. To do this, she might improve product quality by offering better frames and higher-quality matting, which will increase the cost but will probably offset the decreased revenue from the lower number of units that can be sold next year.

To handle this wide variety of assumptions, today's managers use computerized spreadsheets to project operating statements based on a diverse set of assumptions. Figure 15–4 shows the results of computerized spreadsheet simulation, with assumptions shown at the top and the projected results at the bottom. A previous year's operating statement results are shown in the column headed "Last Year," and the assumptions and spreadsheet results for four different sets of assumptions are shown in columns A, B, C, and D.

In choosing a price or another action using spreadsheet results, the decision maker must (1) study the results of the computer simulation projections and (2) assess the realism of the assumptions underlying each set of projections. For example, the store owner sees from the bottom row of Figure 15–4 that all four spreadsheet simulations exceed the after-tax target ROI of 10 percent. But, after more thought, she judges it to be more realistic to set an average price of $58 per unit, allow the unit variable cost to increase by 20 percent to account for more expensive framing and matting, and settle for the same unit sales as the 1,000 units sold last year. She selects simulation D in this computerized spreadsheet approach to target ROI pricing and has a goal of 14 percent after-tax ROI. Of course, these same calculations can be done by hand, but this is far more time consuming.

ASSUMPTIONS OR RESULTS	FINANCIAL ELEMENT	LAST YEAR	SIMULATION			
			A	B	C	D
Assumptions	Price per unit (P)	$50	$54	$54	$58	$58
	Units sold (Q)	1,000	1,200	1,100	1,100	1,000
	Change in unit variable cost (UVC)	0%	+10%	+10%	+20%	+20%
	Unit variable cost	$ 22.00	$ 24.20	$ 24.20	$ 26.40	$ 26.40
	Total expenses	$ 8,000	Same	Same	Same	Same
	Owner's salary	$18,000	Same	Same	Same	Same
	Investment	$20,000	Same	Same	Same	Same
	State and federal taxes	50%	Same	Same	Same	Same
Spreadsheet simulation results	Net sales (P × Q)	$50,000	$64,800	$59,400	$63,800	$58,000
	Less: COGS (Q × UVC)	22,000	29,040	26,620	29,040	26,400
	Gross margin	$28,000	$35,760	$32,780	$34,760	$31,600
	Less: total expenses	8,000	8,000	8,000	8,000	8,000
	Less: owner's salary	18,000	18,000	18,000	18,000	18,000
	Net profit before taxes	$ 2,000	$ 9,760	$ 6,780	$8,760	$ 5,600
	Less: taxes	1,000	4,880	3,390	4,380	2,800
	Net profit after taxes	$ 1,000	$ 4,880	$ 3,390	$ 4,380	$ 2,800
	Investment	$20,000	$20,000	$20,000	$20,000	$20,000
	Return on investment	5.0%	24.4%	17.0%	21.9%	14.0%

FIGURE 15–4
Results of computer spreadsheet simulation to select price to achieve a target return on investment

Competition-Oriented Approaches

Rather than emphasize demand, cost, or profit factors, a price setter can stress what competitors or "the market" is doing.

Customary Pricing For some products where tradition, a standardized channel of distribution, or other competitive factors dictate the price, **customary pricing** is used. Tradition prevails in the pricing of Swatch watches. The $40 customary price for the basic model has not changed in 10 years.[19] Candy bars offered through standard vending machines have a customary price of 60 cents, and a significant departure from this price may result in a loss of sales for the manufacturer. Hershey typically has changed the amount of chocolate in its candy bars depending on the price of raw chocolate rather than vary its customary retail price so that it can continue selling through vending machines.

Above-, At-, or Below-Market Pricing For most products it is difficult to identify a specific market price for a product or product class. Still, marketing managers often have a subjective feel for the competitors' price or market price. Using this benchmark, they then may deliberately choose a strategy of **above-, at-, or below-market pricing.**

Among watch manufacturers, Rolex takes pride in emphasizing that it makes one of the most expensive watches you can buy—a clear example of above-market pricing. Manufacturers of national brands of clothing such as Hart Schaffner & Marx and Christian Dior and retailers such as Neiman-Marcus deliberately set premium prices for their products.

Large mass-merchandise chains such as Sears and Montgomery Ward generally use at-market pricing. These chains often establish the going market price in the minds of their competitors. Similarly, Revlon and Cluett Peabody & Company (the maker of Arrow shirts) generally price their products "at market." They also provide a reference price for competitors that use above- and below-market pricing.

In contrast, a number of firms use a strategy of below-market pricing. Manufacturers of all generic products and retailers who offer their own private brands of products ranging from peanut butter to shampoo deliberately set prices for these products about 8 percent to 10 percent below the prices of nationally branded competitive products such as Skippy peanut butter, Vidal Sassoon shampoo, or Crest toothpaste. Below-market pricing also exists in business-to-business marketing. Hewlett-Packard, for instance, consciously priced its line of office personal computers below Compaq and IBM to promote a value image among corporate buyers.[20]

Loss-Leader Pricing   For a special promotion many retail stores deliberately sell a product below its customary price to attract attention to it. The purpose of this **loss-leader pricing** is not to increase sales but to attract customers in hopes they will buy other products as well, particularly the discretionary items carrying large markups. Mass merchandisers such as Target have sold home videos at half their customary price to attract customers to their stores. According to an industry observer, "Video is one of the mass merchandisers' favorite traffic-building devices."[21]

CONCEPT CHECK

1. What is standard markup pricing?

2. What profit-based pricing approach should a manager use if he or she wants to reflect the percentage of the firm's resources used in obtaining the profit?

3. What is the purpose of loss-leader pricing when used by a retail firm?

STEP 5: SET THE LIST OR QUOTED PRICE

The first four steps in setting price covered in Chapter 14 and this chapter result in an approximate price level for the product that appears reasonable. But it still remains for the manager to set a specific list or quoted price in light of all relevant factors.

One-Price versus Flexible-Price Policy

A seller must decide whether to follow a one-price or flexible-price policy. A **one-price policy** is setting the same price for similar customers who buy the same product and quantities under the same conditions. Saturn Corporation uses this approach in its "no haggle, one-price" price for both new and used Saturn cars. Some retailers such as Dollar General and Family Dollar have married this policy with a below-market approach to include all merchandise in their stores. At Dollar Tree, everything in the store costs no more than $1![22] In contrast, a **flexible-price policy** is offering the same product and quantities to similar customers but at different prices. As noted at the end of this chapter, there are legal

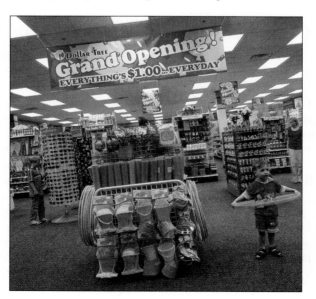

ETHICS AND SOCIAL RESPONSIBILITY ALERT

Flexible Pricing: Is There Race and Gender Discrimination in Bargaining for a New Car?

What do 60 percent of perspective buyers dread when looking for a new car? That's right! They dread negotiating the price. Price bargaining, however, has a more serious side and demonstrates shortcomings of flexible pricing when purchasing a new car: the potential for price discrimination by race and gender. Recent research among 153 car dealers in a large midwestern city suggests that car dealers offer male and female African-Americans and white females higher prices than white males even though all buyers used identical bargaining strategies

when negotiating the price of a new car. African-American males were typically offered the highest price, followed by African-American females, white females, and white males.

New car price bargaining has been eliminated by an increasing number of car dealers, most notably Saturn dealers. Saturn's no haggle, one-price policy for new cars has been recently expanded to preowned or used Saturns. According to a Saturn executive, "People don't want to dicker on price, period, whether it's a house, suit of clothes, or a car. When you have to dicker, you feel uncomfortable because you always feel you paid too much." In certain instances, some consumers do.

constraints under the Robinson-Patman Act to prevent carrying a flexible-price policy to the extreme of price discrimination.

Prices paid by an ultimate consumer illustrate the differences in these two policies, although the same principles apply to manufacturers and wholesalers as well. When you buy a Wilson Sting tennis racket from a discount store, you are offered the product at a single price. You can buy it or not, but there is no variation in the price under the seller's one-price policy. But with a house, the seller generally uses a flexible-price policy, and you might negotiate a purchase at a price that lies within a range of prices. Flexible prices give sellers greater discretion in setting the final price in light of demand, cost, and competitive factors.

Car dealers have traditionally used flexible pricing based on buyer–seller negotiations to agree on a final sale price. However, as detailed in the Ethics and Social Responsibility Alert, flexible pricing may result in race and gender discrimination.[23]

Company, Customer, and Competitive Effects

As the final list or quoted price is set, the effects on the company, customers, and competitors must be assessed.

Company Effects   For a firm with more than one product, a decision on the price of a single product must consider the price of other items in its product line or related product lines in its product mix. Within a product line or mix there are usually some products that are substitutes for one another and some that complement each other. Frito-Lay recognizes that its tortilla chip product line consisting of Baked Tostitos, Tostitos, and Doritos brands are partial substitutes for one another and its bean and cheese chip dip line and salsa sauces complement the tortilla chip line.

A manager's challenge when marketing multiple products is **product-line pricing,** the setting of prices for all items in a product line. When setting prices, the manager seeks to cover the total cost and produce a profit for the complete line, not necessarily for each item. For example, the penetration price for Sony's PlayStation video-game player was likely below its cost, but the price of its video games (comple-

Frito-Lay recognizes that its tortilla chip products are partial substitutes for one another and its bean and cheese dips and salsa sauces complement tortilla chips. This knowledge is used for Frito-Lay product-line pricing.

Frito-Lay, Inc.

www.frito-lay.com

mentary products) was set high enough to cover the loss and deliver a handsome profit for the PlayStation product line.[24]

Product-line pricing involves determining (1) the lowest priced product and price, (2) the highest priced product and price, and (3) price differentials for all other products in the line.[25] The lowest and highest priced items in the product line play important roles. The highest priced item is typically positioned as the premium item in quality and features. The lowest priced item is the traffic builder designed to capture the attention of the hesitant or first-time buyer. Price differentials between items in the line should make sense to customers and reflect differences in their perceived value of the products offered. Behavioral research also suggests that the price differentials should get larger as one moves up the product line.

Customer Effects   In setting price, retailers weigh factors heavily that satisfy the perceptions or expectations of ultimate consumers, such as the customary prices for a variety of consumer products. Retailers have found that they should not price their store brands 20 to 25 percent below manufacturers' brands. When they do, consumers often view the lower price as signaling lower quality and don't buy. Manufacturers and wholesalers must choose prices that result in profit for resellers in the channel to gain their cooperation and support. Toro failed to do this on its lines of lawn mowers and snow throwers. It decided to augment its traditional hardware outlet distribution by also selling through big discounters such as Kmart and Target. To do so, it set prices for the discounters substantially below those for its traditional hardware outlets. Many unhappy hardware stores abandoned Toro products in favor of mowers and snow throwers from other manufacturers.

Competitive Effects   A manager's pricing decision is immediately apparent to most competitors, who may retaliate with price changes of their own. Therefore, a manager who sets a final list or quoted price must anticipate potential price responses from competitors. Regardless of whether a firm is a price leader or follower, it wants to avoid cutthroat price wars in which no firm in the industry makes a satisfactory profit. As an example, price wars in the U.S. airline industry in the early 1990s resulted in carrier losses exceeding $12 billion, the collapse of three airlines (Eastern, Pan Am, and Midway), and the bankruptcy of three others. Price reductions as little as 1 cent can have a significant effect in a highly competitive environment. This is the case in the residential long-distance telephone industry, where AT&T, MCI, and Sprint compete head-to-head for customers. Each time a competitor lowers its per-minute charge by a penny and AT&T matches the price, it gives up $1 billion in revenues.[26]

Balancing Incremental Costs and Revenues

When a price is changed or new advertising or selling programs are planned, their effect on the quantity sold must be considered. This assessment, called *marginal analysis* (Chapter 14), involves a continuing, concise trade-off of incremental costs against incremental revenues.

Do marketing and business managers really use marginal analysis? Yes, they do, but they often don't use phrases such as *marginal revenue, marginal cost,* and *elasticity of demand.*

Think about these managerial questions:

- How many extra units do we have to sell to pay for that $1,000 advertisement?
- How much savings on unit variable cost do we have to get to keep the break-even point the same if we invest in a $10,000 labor-saving machine?
- Should we hire three more salespeople or not?

All these questions are a form of marginal or incremental analysis, even though these exact words are not used.

Figure 15–5 shows the power—and some limitations—of marginal analysis applied to a marketing decision. Note that the frame store owner must either conclude that a simple advertising campaign will more than pay for itself in additional sales or not undertake the campaign. The decision could also have been made to increase the average price of a framed picture to cover the cost of the campaign, but the principle still applies: Expected incremental revenues from pricing and other marketing actions must more than offset incremental costs.

The example in Figure 15–5 shows both the main advantage and difficulty of marginal analysis. The advantage is its common-sense usefulness, and the difficulty is ob-

FIGURE 15–5
The power of marginal analysis in real-world decisions

Suppose the owner of a picture framing store is considering buying a series of magazine ads to reach her up-scale target market. The cost of the ads is $1,000, the average price of a framed picture is $50, and the unit variable cost (materials plus labor) is $30.

This is a direct application of marginal analysis that an astute manager uses to estimate the incremental revenue or incremental number of units that must be obtained to at least cover the incremental cost. In this example, the number of extra picture frames that must be sold is obtained as follows:

$$\text{Incremental number of frames} = \frac{\text{Extra fixed cost}}{\text{Price} - \text{Unit variable cost}}$$

$$= \frac{\$1,000 \text{ of advertising}}{\$50 - \$30}$$

$$= 50 \text{ frames}$$

So unless there are some other benefits of the ads, such as long-term goodwill, she should only buy the ads if she expects they will increase picture frame sales by at least 50 units.

taining the necessary data to make decisions. The owner can measure the cost quite easily, but the incremental revenue generated by the ads is difficult to measure. She could partly solve this problem by offering $2 off the purchase price with use of a coupon printed in the ad to see which sales resulted from the ad.

STEP 6: MAKE SPECIAL ADJUSTMENTS TO THE LIST OR QUOTED PRICE

When you pay 60 cents for a bag of M&Ms in a vending machine or receive a quoted price of $10,000 from a contractor to build a new kitchen, the pricing sequence ends with the last step just described: setting the list or quoted price. But when you are a manufacturer of M&M candies or gas grills and sell your product to dozens or hundreds of wholesalers and retailers in your channel of distribution, you may need to make a variety of special adjustments to the list or quoted price. Wholesalers also must adjust list or quoted prices they set for retailers. Three special adjustments to the list or quoted price are (1) discounts, (2) allowances, and (3) geographical adjustments (Figure 15–6).

Discounts

Discounts are reductions from list price that a seller gives a buyer as a reward for some activity of the buyer that is favorable to the seller. Four kinds of discounts are especially important in marketing strategy: (1) quantity, (2) seasonal, (3) trade (functional), and (4) cash discounts.[27]

Quantity Discounts   To encourage customers to buy larger quantities of a product, firms at all levels in the channel of distribution offer **quantity discounts,** which are reductions in unit costs for a larger order. For example, an instant photocopying service might set a price of 10 cents a copy for 1 to 25 copies, 9 cents a copy for 26 to 100, and 8 cents a copy for 101 or more. Because the photocopying service gets more of the buyer's business and has longer production runs that reduce its order-handling costs, it is willing to pass on some of the cost savings in the form of quantity discounts to the buyer.

Quantity discounts are of two general kinds: noncumulative and cumulative. *Noncumulative quantity discounts* are based on the size of an individual purchase order. They

FIGURE 15–6
Three special adjustments to list or quoted price

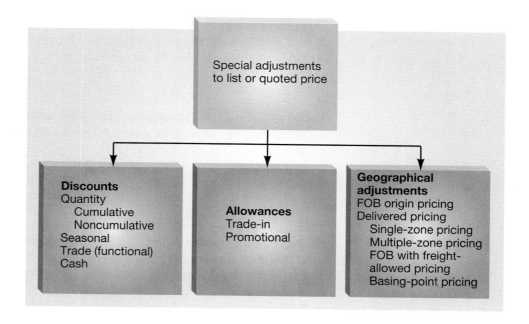

Toro uses seasonal discounts to stimulate consumer demand and smooth out seasonal manufacturing peaks and troughs.

The Toro Company
www.toro.com

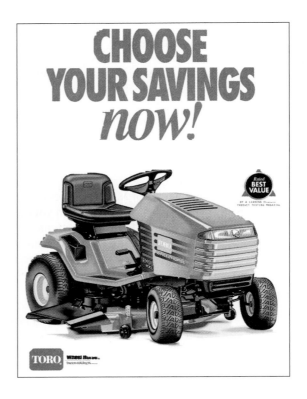

encourage large individual purchase orders, not a series of orders. This discount is used by Federal Express to encourage companies to ship a large number of packages at one time. *Cumulative quantity discounts* apply to the accumulation of purchases of a product over a given time period, typically a year. Cumulative quantity discounts encourage repeat buying by a single customer to a far greater degree than do noncumulative quantity discounts.

Seasonal Discounts   To encourage buyers to stock inventory earlier than their normal demand would require, manufacturers often use seasonal discounts. A firm such as Toro that manufactures lawn mowers and snow throwers offers seasonal discounts to encourage wholesalers and retailers to stock up on lawn mowers in January and February and on snow throwers in July and August—five or six months before the seasonal demand by ultimate consumers. This enables Toro to smooth out seasonal manufacturing peaks and troughs, thereby contributing to more efficient production. It also rewards wholesalers and retailers for the risk they accept in assuming increased inventory carrying costs and having supplies in stock at the time they are wanted by customers.

Trade (Functional) Discounts   To reward wholesalers and retailers for marketing functions they will perform in the future, a manufacturer often gives trade, or functional, discounts. These reductions off the list or base price are offered to resellers in the channel of distribution on the basis of (1) where they are in the channel and (2) the marketing activities they are expected to perform in the future.

Suppose a manufacturer quotes price in the following form: list price—$100 less 30/10/5. The first number in the percentage sequence always refers to the retail end of the channel, and the last number always refers to the wholesaler or jobber closest to the manufacturer in the channel. The trade discounts are simply subtracted one at a time. This price quote shows $100 is the manufacturer's suggested retail price; 30 percent of the suggested retail price is available to the retailer to cover costs and provide a profit of $30 ($100 × 0.3 = $30); wholesalers closest to the retailer in the channel get 10 percent of their selling price ($70 × 0.1 = $7); and the final group of wholesalers in

FIGURE 15–7
The structure of trade discounts

the channel (probably jobbers) that are closest to the manufacturer get 5 percent of their selling price ($63 × 0.05 = $3.15). Thus, starting with the manufacturer's retail price and subtracting the three trade discounts shows that the manufacturer's selling price to the wholesaler or jobber closest to it is $59.85 (Figure 15–7).

Traditional trade discounts have been established in various product lines such as hardware, food, and pharmaceutical items. Although the manufacturer may suggest the trade discounts shown in the example just cited, the sellers are free to alter the discount schedule depending on their competitive situation.

Cash Discounts   To encourage retailers to pay their bills quickly, manufacturers offer them cash discounts. Suppose a retailer receives a bill quoted at $1,000, 2/10 net 30. This means that the bill for the product is $1,000, but the retailer can take a 2 percent discount ($1,000 × 0.02 = $20) if payment is made within 10 days and send a check for $980. If the payment cannot be made within 10 days, the total amount of $1,000 is due within 30 days. It is usually understood by the buyer that an interest charge will be added after the first 30 days of free credit.

Naive buyers may think that the 2 percent discount offered is not substantial. What this means is that the buyer pays 2 percent on the total amount to be able to use that amount an extra 20 days—from day 11 to day 30. In a 360-day business year, this is an effective annual interest rate of 36 percent (2% × 360/20 = 36%). Because the effective interest rate is so high, firms that cannot take advantage of a 2/10 net 30 cash discount often try to borrow money from their local banks at rates far lower than the 36 percent they must pay by not taking advantage of the cash discount.

Retailers provide cash discounts to consumers as well to eliminate the cost of credit granted to consumers. These discounts take the form of discount-for-cash policies.

Allowances

Allowances—like discounts—are reductions from list or quoted prices to buyers for performing some activity.

Trade-in Allowances   A new car dealer can offer a substantial reduction in the list price of that new Ford Taurus by offering you a trade-in allowance of $500 for your Chevrolet. A trade-in allowance is a price reduction given when a used product is part of the payment on a new product. Trade-ins are an effective way to lower the price a buyer has to pay without formally reducing the list price.

MARKETING NEWSNET

Everyday Low Prices at the Supermarket = Everyday Low Profits: Creating Customer Value at a Cost

Who wouldn't welcome low retail prices everyday? The answer is supermarket chains—76 percent of U.S. grocery stores have not adopted this practice. Supermarkets prefer Hi-Lo pricing based on frequent specials where prices are temporarily lowered then raised again. Hi-Lo pricing reflects allowances that manufacturers give supermarkets to push their product. Consider a New York City supermarket whose advertisement is shown here. It regularly pays $1.15 for a can of Bumble Bee white tuna ($55.43 ÷ 48 = $1.15), but the allowances reduces the cost to 96 cents. A price special of 99 cents still provides a 3 cent retail markup ($0.99 retail price in ad—$0.96 cost). When the price on tuna returns to its regular level, the store's gross margin on tuna increases substantially on those cans that were bought with the allowance but not sold during the price special promotion.

Everyday low pricing (EDLP) eliminates manufacturer allowances and can reduce average retail prices by up to 10 percent. While EDLP provides lower average prices than Hi-Lo pricing, EDLP does not allow for deeply discounted price specials. EDLP can create

everyday customer value and modestly increase supermarket sales—but at a cost. Already slim supermarket chain profits can slip by 18 percent with EDLP without the benefit of allowances as described earlier. Also, some argue that EDLP without price specials is boring for many grocery shoppers who welcome price specials. EDLP has been hailed as "value pricing" by manufacturers, but supermarkets view it differently. For them, EDLP means "Everyday Low Profits!"

Promotional Allowances   Sellers in the channel of distribution can qualify for **promotional allowances** for undertaking certain advertising or selling activities to promote a product. Various types of allowances include an actual cash payment or an extra amount of "free goods" (as with a free case of pizzas to a retailer for every dozen cases purchased). Frequently, a portion of these savings is passed on to the consumer by retailers.

Some companies, such as Procter & Gamble, have chosen to reduce promotional allowances for retailers by using everyday low pricing. **Everyday low pricing** (EDLP) is the practice of replacing promotional allowances with lower manufacturer list prices. EDLP promises to reduce the average price to consumers while minimizing promotional allowances that cost manufacturers billions of dollars every year. However, EDLP does not necessarily benefit supermarkets as described in the accompanying Marketing NewsNet.[28]

Geographical Adjustments

Geographical adjustments are made by manufacturers or even wholesalers to list or quoted prices to reflect the cost of transportation of the products from seller to buyer. The two general methods for quoting prices related to transportation costs are (1) FOB origin pricing and (2) uniform delivered pricing.

FOB Origin Pricing FOB means "free on board" some vehicle at some location, which means the seller pays the cost of loading the product onto the vehicle that is used (such as a barge, railroad car, or truck). **FOB origin pricing** usually involves the seller's naming the location of this loading as the seller's factory or warehouse (such as "FOB Detroit" or "FOB factory"). The title to the goods passes to the buyer at the point of loading, so the buyer becomes responsible for picking the specific mode of transportation, for all the transportation costs, and for subsequent handling of the product. Buyers farthest from the seller face the big disadvantage of paying the higher transportation costs.

Uniform Delivered Pricing When a **uniform delivered pricing** method is used, the price the seller quotes includes all transportation costs. It is quoted in a contract as "FOB buyer's location," and the seller selects the mode of transportation, pays the freight charges, and is responsible for any damage that may occur because the seller retains title to the goods until delivered to the buyer. Although they go by various names, four kinds of delivered pricing methods are (1) single-zone pricing, (2) multiple-zone pricing, (3) FOB with freight-allowed pricing, and (4) basing-point pricing.

In *single-zone pricing* all buyers pay the same delivered price for the products, regardless of their distance from the seller. This method is also called *postage stamp pricing* because it is the way that U.S. postal rates are set for first-class mail. So although a store offering free delivery in a metropolitan area has lower transportation costs for goods shipped to customers nearer the store than for those shipped to distant ones, customers pay the same delivered price.

In *multiple-zone pricing* a firm divides its selling territory into geographic areas or zones. The delivered price to all buyers within any one zone is the same, but prices across zones vary depending on the transportation cost to the zone and the level of competition and demand within the zone. The U.S postal system uses multiple-zone pricing for mailing certain packages. This system is also used in setting prices on long distance phone calls.

With *FOB with freight-allowed pricing,* also called *freight absorption pricing,* the price is quoted by the seller as "FOB plant—freight allowed." The buyer is allowed to deduct freight expenses from the list price of the goods, so the seller agrees to pay, or "absorbs," the transportation costs.

Basing-point pricing involves selecting one or more geographical locations (basing point) from which the list price for products plus freight expenses are charged to the buyer. For example, a company might designate St. Louis as the basing point and charge all buyers a list price of $100 plus freight from St. Louis to their location. Basing-point pricing methods have been used in the steel, cement, and lumber industries where freight expenses are a significant part of the total cost to the buyer and products are largely undifferentiated.

Legal and Regulatory Aspects of Pricing

Arriving at a final price is clearly a complex process. The task is further complicated by legal and regulatory restrictions. Chapter 3 described the regulatory environment of companies. Here we elaborate on the specific laws and regulations affecting pricing decisions. Five pricing practices have received the most scrutiny: (1) price fixing, (2) price discrimination, (3) deceptive pricing, (4) geographical pricing, and (5) predatory pricing[29] (Figure 15–8).

Price Fixing A conspiracy among firms to set prices for a product is termed **price fixing.** Price fixing is illegal per se under the Sherman Act (*per se* means in and of itself). When two or more competitors explicitly or implicitly set prices, this practice is called *horizontal price fixing.* For example, Hoffman-LaRoche and BASF recently pled guilty to price fixing in the human and animal vitamin industry and paid the largest fine in U.S. history, $725 million.[30]

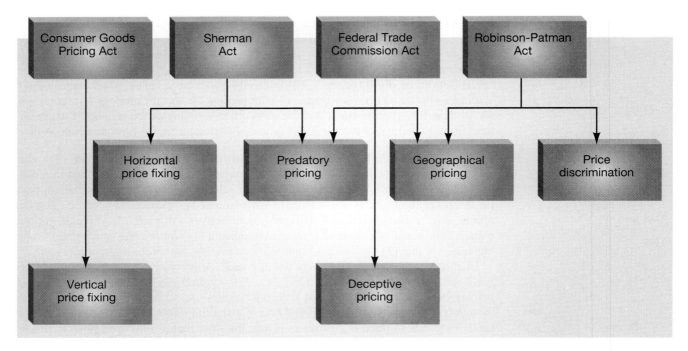

FIGURE 15–8
Pricing practices affected by
legal restrictions

Vertical price fixing involves controlling agreements between independent buyers and sellers (a manufacturer and a retailer) whereby sellers are required to not sell products below a minimum retail price. This practice, called *resale price maintenance,* was declared illegal per se in 1975 under provisions of the Consumer Goods Pricing Act. Nevertheless, in 1995, Reebok International and its Rockport Company subsidiary agreed to settle government charges that they tried to fix the prices of their footwear with retailers. The companies agreed to pay $9.5 million in the settlement.[31] However, manufacturers and wholesalers can fix the maximum retail price for their products provided the price agreement does not create an "unreasonable restraint of trade" or is anticompetitive.[32]

It is important to recognize that a manufacturer's "suggested retail price" is not illegal per se. The issue of legality only arises when manufacturers enforce such a practice by coercion. Furthermore, there appears to be a movement toward a "rule of reason" in pricing cases. This rule holds that circumstances surrounding a practice must be considered before making a judgment about its legality. The rule of reason perspective is the direct opposite of the per se rule, which holds that a practice is illegal in and of itself.

Price Discrimination   The Clayton Act as amended by the Robinson-Patman Act prohibits **price discrimination**—the practice of charging different prices to different buyers for goods of like grade and quality. However, not all price differences are illegal; only those that substantially lessen competition or create a monopoly are deemed unlawful. Moreover, "goods" is narrowly defined and does not include discrimination in services.

A unique feature of the Robinson-Patman Act is that it allows for price differentials to different customers under the following conditions:

1. When price differences charged to different customers do not exceed the differences in the cost of manufacture, sale, or delivery resulting from differing methods or quantities in which such goods are sold or delivered to buyers. This condition is called the *cost justification defense.*

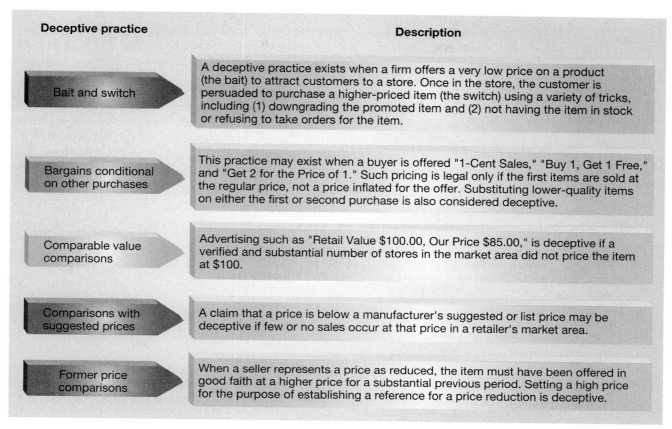

Deceptive practice	Description
Bait and switch	A deceptive practice exists when a firm offers a very low price on a product (the bait) to attract customers to a store. Once in the store, the customer is persuaded to purchase a higher-priced item (the switch) using a variety of tricks, including (1) downgrading the promoted item and (2) not having the item in stock or refusing to take orders for the item.
Bargains conditional on other purchases	This practice may exist when a buyer is offered "1-Cent Sales," "Buy 1, Get 1 Free," and "Get 2 for the Price of 1." Such pricing is legal only if the first items are sold at the regular price, not a price inflated for the offer. Substituting lower-quality items on either the first or second purchase is also considered deceptive.
Comparable value comparisons	Advertising such as "Retail Value $100.00, Our Price $85.00," is deceptive if a verified and substantial number of stores in the market area did not price the item at $100.
Comparisons with suggested prices	A claim that a price is below a manufacturer's suggested or list price may be deceptive if few or no sales occur at that price in a retailer's market area.
Former price comparisons	When a seller represents a price as reduced, the item must have been offered in good faith at a higher price for a substantial previous period. Setting a high price for the purpose of establishing a reference for a price reduction is deceptive.

FIGURE 15–9
Five most common deceptive pricing practices

2. Price differences resulting from meeting changing market conditions, avoiding obsolescence of seasonal merchandise including perishables or closing out sales.

3. When price differences are quoted to selected buyers in good faith to meet competitors' prices and are not intended to injure competition. This condition is called the *meet the competition defense.*

The Robinson-Patman Act also covers promotional allowances. To legally offer promotional allowances to buyers, the seller must do so on a proportionally equal basis to all buyers distributing the seller's products. In general, the rule of reason applies frequently in price discrimination cases and is often applied to cases involving flexible pricing practices of firms.

Deceptive Pricing   Price deals that mislead consumers fall into the category of deceptive pricing. Deceptive pricing is outlawed by the Federal Trade Commission Act. The FTC monitors such practices and has published a regulation titled "Guides against Deceptive Pricing" designed to help businesspeople avoid a charge of deception. The five most common deceptive pricing practices are described in Figure 15–9. As you read about these practices it should be clear that laws cannot be passed and enforced to protect consumers and competitors against all of these practices, so it is essential to rely on the ethical standards of those making and publicizing pricing decisions.

Geographical Pricing   FOB origin pricing is legal, as are FOB freight-allowed pricing practices, providing no conspiracy to set prices exists. Basing-point pricing can be viewed as illegal under the Robinson-Patman Act and the Federal Trade Commission

Act if there is clear-cut evidence of a conspiracy to set prices. In general, geographical pricing practices have been immune from legal and regulatory restrictions, except in those instances in which a conspiracy to lessen competition exists under the Sherman Act or price discrimination exists under the Robinson-Patman Act.

Predatory Pricing   **Predatory pricing** is the practice of charging a very low price for a product with the intent of driving competitors out of business. Once competitors have been driven out, the firm raises its prices. This practice is illegal under the Sherman Act and the Federal Trade Commission Act. Proving the presence of this practice has been difficult and expensive because it must be shown that the predator explicitly attempted to destroy a competitor and the predatory price was below the defendant's average cost.[33]

CONCEPT CHECK

1. Why would a seller choose a flexible-price policy over a one-price policy?

2. If a firm wished to encourage repeat purchases by a buyer throughout a year, would a cumulative or noncumulative quantity discount be a better strategy?

3. Which pricing practices are covered by the Sherman Act?

SUMMARY

1 Four general approaches for finding an approximate price level for a product or service are demand-oriented, cost-oriented, profit-oriented, and competition-oriented pricing.

2 Demand-oriented pricing approaches stress consumer demand and revenue implications of pricing and include eight types: skimming, penetration, prestige, price lining, odd-even, target, bundle, and yield management.

3 Cost-oriented pricing approaches emphasize the cost aspects of pricing and include three types: standard markup, cost-plus, and experience curve pricing.

4 Profit-oriented pricing approaches focus on a balance between revenues and costs to set a price and include three types: target profit, target return-on-sales, and target return-on-investment pricing.

5 Competition-oriented pricing approaches stress what competitors or the marketplace are doing and include three types: customary; above-, at-, or below-market; and loss-leader pricing.

6 Given an approximate price level for a product, a manager must set a list or quoted price by considering factors such as one-price versus a flexible-price policy; the effects of the proposed price on the company, customer, and competitors; and balancing incremental costs and revenues.

7 List or quoted price is often modified through discounts, allowances, and geographical adjustments.

8 Legal and regulatory issues in pricing focus on price fixing, price discrimination, deceptive pricing, geographical pricing, and predatory pricing.

KEY TERMS AND CONCEPTS

skimming pricing p. 386
penetration pricing p. 387
prestige pricing p. 387
price lining p. 388
odd-even pricing p. 388
target pricing p. 389
bundle pricing p. 389
yield management pricing p. 389
standard markup pricing p. 390
cost-plus pricing p. 390
experience curve pricing p. 391
target profit pricing p. 392
target return-on-sales pricing p. 392
target return-on-investment pricing p. 393
customary pricing p. 394

above-, at-, or below-market pricing p. 394
loss-leader pricing p. 395
one-price policy p. 395
flexible-price policy p. 395
product-line pricing p. 396
quantity discounts p. 399
promotional allowances p. 402
everyday low pricing p. 402
FOB origin pricing p. 403
uniform delivered pricing p. 403
basing-point pricing p. 403
price fixing p. 403
price discrimination p. 404
predatory pricing p. 406

INTERNET EXERCISE

Price discrimination, as defined by the Robinson-Patman Act, has been the subject of an enormous amount of litigation between buyers and sellers since its enactment in 1936. A unique Web site (www.lawmall.com/rpa) provides an up-to-date summary of price discrimination issues that is targeted toward businesspeople.

Visit the LawMall Web site to find answers to three frequently asked questions concerning Robinson-Patman Act lawsuits:

1   What are the litigation stages and estimated length of a Robinson-Patman Act lawsuit?
2   What are the estimated expenses of a Robinson-Patman Act price discrimination lawsuit?
3   What remedies are afforded plaintiffs in a Robinson-Patman Act price discrimination lawsuit?

APPLYING MARKETING CONCEPTS AND PERSPECTIVES

1   Under what conditions would a camera manufacturer adopt a skimming price approach for a new product? A penetration approach?

2   What are some similarities and differences between skimming pricing, prestige pricing, and above-market pricing?

3   A producer of microwave ovens has adopted an experience curve pricing approach for its new model. The firm believes it can reduce the cost of producing the model by 20 percent each time volume doubles. The cost to produce the first unit was $1,000. What would be the approximate cost of the 4,096th unit?

4   The Hesper Corporation is a leading manufacturer of high-quality upholstered sofas. Current plans call for an increase of $600,000 in the advertising budget. If the firm sells its sofas for an average price of $850 and the unit variable costs are $550, then what dollar sales increase will be necessary to cover the additional advertising?

5   Suppose executives estimate that the unit variable cost for their VCR is $100, the fixed cost related to the product is $10 million annually, and the target volume for next year is 100,000 recorders. What sales price will be necessary to achieve a target profit of $1 million?

6   A manufacturer of motor oil has a trade discount policy whereby the manufacturer's suggested retail price is $30 per case with the terms of 40/20/10. The manufacturer sells its products through jobbers, who sell to wholesalers, who sell to gasoline stations. What will the manufacturer's sale price be?

7   What are the effective annual interest rates for the following cash discount terms? (*a*) 1/10 net 30, (*b*) 2/10 net 30, and (*c*) 2/10 net 60.

8   Suppose a manufacturer of exercise equipment sets a suggested price to the consumer of $395 for a particular piece of equipment to be competitive with similar equipment. The manufacturer sells its equipment to a sporting goods wholesaler who receives a 25 percent markup and a retailer who receives a 50 percent markup. What demand-oriented pricing approach is being used, and at what price will the manufacturer sell the equipment to the wholesaler?

9   Is there any truth in the statement, "Geographical pricing schemes will always be unfair to some buyers?" Why or why not?

CASE 15–1 MY OWN MEALS

"The kids generally like the fast-food meals. I tend to not like them because I try to stay away from the high fat," says Angela Harmon, mother of three young girls. "I have to have something that is nutritious and fast," remarks Mary Champlain, mother of two. Comments like these and her own experiences led Mary Anne Jackson to conclude that there was an opportunity to provide parents with better children's food options. As Mary explains, "being a busy working mother, I knew that there was a need for this type of product in the marketplace."

THE IDEA

Mary's insight about the marketplace was supported by several socioeconomic trends. For example:

- More than 65 percent of working mothers now have school-age children, the highest percentage ever.
- About 90 percent of children under the age of 7 eat at McDonald's at least 4 times per month.
- More than 90 percent of homes in the United States now have microwave ovens.
- Women already represent almost half of the total workforce. By the year 2000, two out of three new entrants into the labor force will be women.

With this evidence, some food industry experience and business education, and a lot of entrepreneurial spirit, Mary Anne Jackson set out to satisfy the need for nutritious, convenient children's meals. Her idea: develop a line of healthy, microwaveable meals for children 2 to 10 years old.

THE COMPANY

Ms. Jackson started by founding a company, My Own Meals, Inc., with a line of five healthy microwaveable meals. The meals were offered in shelf-stable "retort" packages, which are like flexible cans. This created a whole new category of prepared foods, and raised more than a few eyebrows among the major food companies. Mary observed that "The need for children's meals was not being addressed in the past, and I think this was because most major food companies are run by men." Eventually, however, the big companies challenged My Own Meals with their own entries into the new category. Tyson, Banquet (Con Agra), and Hormel each intro-

duced new children's meals, although Tyson and Banquet launched frozen meals. The competition reinforced Mary's efforts, "Having competitors come into the marketplace justified the existence of the category," she explains.

The product line was developed using a lot of marketing research—hundreds of busy mothers provided input about product quality, usage rates, and price. The results indicated that customers would serve their children high-quality meals between three and four times each month and that they would be willing to pay approximately $2.30 for each meal. Based on this information Mary estimated that the potential retail market was $500 million!

THE ISSUE: SETTING RETAIL PRICES

"We were trying to decide if we were priced appropriately and competitively for the marketplace, and we decided that we would look at the price elasticity for our product line," observes Mary Anne Jackson. "We found that the closer we came to $3.00 a unit, the lower the volume was, and overall we were losing revenues and profits," said Jackson.

To arrive at final retail prices for her company's products Mary Anne Jackson considered factors related to demand, cost, profit, and competition. For example, because lower-quality brands had entered the market, My Own Meals needed a retail price that reflected the superior quality of its products. "We're premium priced because we're a higher quality product than any of our competitors. If we weren't, our quality image would be lowered to the image that they have," explains Jackson. At some stores, however, prices approached $3.00 and consumer demand decreased.

To estimate the prices consumers would see on their shelves, Jackson needed to estimate the cost of producing the meals and add My Own Meal's markup. Then she determined the markup of each of the distribution channels—retail grocery stores, mass merchants, day care centers, and military commissaries—would add to reach the retail price. The grocery stores were very concerned about profitability and used a concept called direct product profitability (DPP) to determine prices and shelf space. "They want to know how much money they make on each square foot of the shelf dedicated to each product line. I had to do a DPP analysis to show them why they were making more on our products for our space than the competition," remarks Mary Anne Jackson. Finally, Mary considered competitors' prices which were:

- Looney Toons (Tyson) $2.49
- Kid Cuisine (Banquet) $1.89
- Kid's Kitchen (Hormel) $1.19

Mary knew that it was important to consider all of these factors in her pricing decisions. The price would influence the interest of consumers and retailers, the reactions of competitors, and ultimately the success of My Own Meals!

Questions

1 In what ways are the demand factors of (*a*) consumer tastes, (*b*) price and availability of substitute products, and (*c*) consumer income important in influencing consumer demand for My Own Meals products?

2 How can (*a*) demand-based, (*b*) cost-based, (*c*) profit-based, and (*d*) competition-based approaches be used to help My Own Meals arrive at an approximate price level?

3 Why might the retail price of My Own Meal's products be different in grocery stores, mass merchants, day care centers, and military commissaries?

FINANCIAL ASPECTS OF MARKETING

Basic concepts from accounting and finance provide valuable tools for marketing executives. This appendix describes an actual company's use of accounting and financial concepts and illustrates how they assist the owner in making marketing decisions.

THE CAPLOW COMPANY

An accomplished artist and calligrapher, Jane Westerlund, decided to apply some of her experience to the picture framing business in Minneapolis. She bought an existing retail frame store, The Caplow Company, from a friend who owned the business and wanted to retire. She avoided the do-it-yourself end of the framing business and chose three kinds of business activities: (1) cutting the frame, mats, and glass for customers who brought in their own pictures or prints to be framed; (2) selling prints and posters that she had purchased from wholesalers; and (3) restoring high-quality frames and paintings.

To understand how accounting, finance, and marketing relate to each other, let's analyze (1) the operating statement for her frame shop, (2) some general ratios of interest that are derived from the operating statement, and (3) some ratios that pertain specifically to her pricing decisions.

The Operating Statement

The operating statement (also called an *income statement* or *profit-and-loss statement*) summarizes the profitability of a business firm for a specific time period, usually a month, quarter, or year. The title of the operating statement for The Caplow Company shows it is for a one-year period (Figure B–1). The purpose of an operating statement is to show the profit of the firm and the revenues and expenses that led to that profit. This information tells the owner or manager what has happened in the past and suggests actions to improve future profitability.

The left side of Figure B–1 shows that there are three key elements to all operating statements: (1) sales of the firm's goods and services, (2) costs incurred in making and selling the goods and services, and (3) profit or loss, which is the difference between sales and costs.

Sales Elements   The sales element of Figure B–1 has four terms that need explanation:

- *Gross sales* are the total amount billed to customers. Dissatisfied customers or errors may reduce the gross sales through returns or allowances.
- *Returns* occur when a customer gives the item purchased back to the seller, who either refunds the purchase price or allows the customer a credit on subsequent purchases. In any event, the seller now owns the item again.
- *Allowances* are given when a customer is dissatisfied with the item purchased and the seller reduces the original purchase price. Unlike returns, in the case of allowances the buyer owns the item.
- *Net sales* are simply gross sales minus returns and allowances.

The operating statement for The Caplow Company shows that

Gross sales	$80,500
Less: Returns and allowances	500
Net sales	$80,000

The low level of returns and allowances shows the shop generally has done a good job in satisfying customers, which is essential in building the repeat business necessary for success.

Cost Elements   The *cost of goods sold* is the total cost of the products sold during the period. This item varies according to the kind of business. A retail store purchases finished goods and resells them to customers without reworking them in any way. In contrast, a manufacturing firm combines raw and semifinished materials and parts, uses labor and overhead to rework these into finished goods, and then sells them to customers. All these activities are reflected in the cost of goods sold item on a manufacturer's operating statement. Note that the frame shop has some features of a pure retailer (prints and posters it buys that are resold without alteration) and a pure manufacturer (assembling the raw materials of molding, matting, and glass to form a completed frame).

FIGURE B–1
Examples of an operating
statement

THE CAPLOW COMPANY
Operating Statement
For the Year Ending December 31, 1998

Sales	Gross sales			$80,500
	Less: Returns and allowances			500
	Net sales			$80,000
Costs	Cost of goods sold:			
	Beginning inventory at cost		$ 6,000	
	Purchases at billed cost	$21,000		
	Less: Purchase discounts	300		
	Purchases at net cost	20,700		
	Plus freight-in	100		
	Net cost of delivered purchases		20,800	
	Direct labor (framing)		14,200	
	Cost of goods available for sale		41,000	
	Less: Ending inventory at cost		5,000	
	Cost of goods sold			36,000
	Gross margin (gross profit)			$44,000
	Expenses:			
	Selling expenses:			
	Sales salaries	2,000		
	Advertising expense	3,000		
	Total selling expense		5,000	
	Administrative expenses:			
	Owner's salary	18,000		
	Bookkeeper's salary	1,200		
	Office supplies	300		
	Total administrative expense		19,500	
	General expenses:			
	Depreciation expense	1,000		
	Interest expense	500		
	Rent expense	2,100		
	Utility expenses (heat, electricity)	3,000		
	Repairs and maintenance	2,300		
	Insurance	2,000		
	Social security taxes	2,200		
	Total general expense		13,100	
	Total expenses			37,600
Profit or loss	Profit before taxes			$ 6,400

Some terms that relate to cost of goods sold need clarification:

- *Inventory* is the physical material that is purchased from suppliers, may or may not be reworked, and is available for sale to customers. In the frame shop inventory includes molding, matting, glass, prints, and posters.
- *Purchase discounts* are reductions in the original billed price for reasons such as prompt payment of the bill or the quantity bought.
- *Direct labor* is the cost of the labor used in producing the finished product. For the frame shop this is the cost of producing the completed frames from the molding, matting, and glass.
- *Gross margin (gross profit)* is the money remaining to manage the business, sell the products or services, and give some profit. Gross margin is net sales minus cost of goods sold.

The two right-hand columns in Figure B–1 between "Net sales" and "Gross margin" calculate the cost of goods sold:

Net sales		$80,000
Cost of goods sold		
Beginning inventory at cost	$ 6,000	
Net cost of delivered purchases	20,800	
Direct labor (framing)	14,200	
Cost of goods available for sale	41,000	
Less: ending inventory at cost	5,000	
Cost of goods sold		36,000
Gross margin (gross profit)		$44,000

This section considers the beginning and ending inventories, the net cost of purchases delivered during the year, and the cost of the direct labor going into making the frames. Subtracting the $36,000 cost of goods sold from the $80,000 net sales gives the $44,000 gross margin.

Three major categories of expenses are shown in Figure B–1 below the gross margin:

- *Selling expenses* are the costs of selling the product or service produced by the firm. For The Caplow Company there are two such selling expenses: sales salaries of part-time employees waiting on customers and the advertising expense of simple newspaper ads and direct-mail ads sent to customers.
- *Administrative expenses* are the costs of managing the business, and, for The Caplow Company, include three expenses: the owner's salary, a part-time bookkeeper's salary, and office supplies expense.
- *General expenses* are miscellaneous costs not covered elsewhere; for the frame shop these include seven items: depreciation expense (on her equipment), interest expense, rent expense, utility expenses, repairs and maintenance expense, insurance expense, and social security taxes.

As shown in Figure B–1, selling, administrative, and general expenses total $37,600 for The Caplow Company.

Profit Element　What the company has earned, the *profit before taxes,* is found by subtracting cost of goods sold and expenses from net sales. For The Caplow Company, Figure B–1 shows that profit before taxes is $6,400.

General Operating Ratios to Analyze Operations

Looking only at the elements of Caplow's operating statement that extend to the right-hand column highlights the firm's performance on some important dimensions. Using operating ratios such as *expense-to-sales ratios* for expressing basic expense or profit elements as a percentage of net sales gives further insights:

ELEMENT IN OPERATING STATEMENT	DOLLAR VALUE	PERCENTAGE OF NET SALES
Gross sales	$80,500	
Less: Returns and allowances	500	
Net sales	80,000	100%
Less: Cost of goods sold	36,000	45
Gross margin	44,000	55
Less: Total expenses	37,600	47
Profit (or loss) before taxes	$ 6,400	8%

Westerlund can use this information to compare her firm's performance from one time period to the next. To do so, it is especially important that she keep the same definitions for each element of her operating statement, also a significant factor in using

Jane Westerlund (left) and an assistant assess the restoration of a gold frame for regilding.

the electronic spreadsheets discussed in Chapter 15. Performance comparisons between periods are more difficult if she changes definitions for the accounting elements in the operating statement.

She can use either the dollar values or the operating ratios (the value of the element of the operating statement divided by net sales) to analyze the firm's performance. However, the operating ratios are more valuable than the dollar values for two reasons: (1) the simplicity of working with percentages rather than dollars and (2) the availability of operating ratios of typical firms in the same industry, which are published by Dun & Bradstreet and trade associations. Thus, Westerlund can compare her firm's performance not only with that of *other* frame shops but also with that of *small* frame shops that have annual net sales, for example, of under $100,000. In this way she can identify where her operations are better or worse than other similar firms. For example, if trade association data showed a typical frame shop of her size had a ratio of cost of goods sold to net sales of 37 percent, compared with her 45 percent, she might consider steps to reduce this cost through purchase discounts, reducing inbound freight charges, finding lower-cost suppliers, and so on.

Ratios to Use in Setting and Evaluating Price

Using The Caplow Company as an example, we can study four ratios that relate closely to setting a price: (1) markup, (2) markdown, (3) stockturns, and (4) return on investment. These terms are defined in Figure B–2 and explained below.

Markup   Both markup and gross margin refer to the amount added to the cost of goods sold to arrive at the selling price, and they may be expressed either in dollar or percentage terms. However, the term *markup* is more commonly used in setting retail prices. Suppose the average price Westerlund charges for a framed picture is $80. Then in terms of the first two definitions in Figure B–2 and the earlier information from the operating statement,

NAME OF FINANCIAL ELEMENT OR RATIO	WHAT IT MEASURES	EQUATION
Selling price ($)	Price customer sees	Cost of goods sold (COGS) + Markup
Markup ($)	Dollars added to COGS to arrive at selling price	Selling price – COGS
Markup on selling price (%)	Relates markup to selling price	$\dfrac{\text{Markup}}{\text{Selling price}} \times 100 = \dfrac{\text{Selling price} - \text{COGS}}{\text{Selling price}} \times 100$
Markup on cost (%)	Relates markup to cost	$\dfrac{\text{Markup}}{\text{COGS}} \times 100 = \dfrac{\text{Selling price} - \text{COGS}}{\text{COGS}} \times 100$
Markdown (%)	Ability of firm to sell its products at initial selling price	$\dfrac{\text{Markdowns}}{\text{Net sales}} \times 100$
Stockturn rate	Ability of firm to move its inventory quickly	$\dfrac{\text{COGS}}{\text{Average inventory at cost}}$ or $\dfrac{\text{Net sales}}{\text{Average inventory at selling price}}$
Return on investment (%)	Profit performance of firm compared with money invested in it	$\dfrac{\text{Net profit after taxes}}{\text{Investment}} \times 100$

FIGURE B–2

How to calculate selling price, markup, markdown, stockturn, and return on investment

ELEMENT OF PRICE	DOLLAR VALUE
Cost of goods sold	$36
Markup (or gross margin)	44
Selling price	$80

The third definition in Figure B–2 gives the percentage markup on selling price:

$$\text{Markup on selling price (\%)} = \frac{\text{Markup}}{\text{Selling price}} \times 100$$

$$= \frac{44}{80} \times 100 = 55\%$$

And the percentage markup on cost is obtained as follows:

$$\text{Markup on cost (\%)} = \frac{\text{Markup}}{\text{Cost of goods sold}} \times 100$$

$$= \frac{44}{36} \times 100 = 122.2\%$$

Inexperienced retail clerks sometimes fail to distinguish between the two definitions of markup, which (as the preceding calculations show) can represent a tremendous difference, so it is essential to know whether the base is cost or selling price. Marketers generally use selling price as the base for talking about "markups" unless they specifically state that they are using cost as a base.

Retailers and wholesalers that rely heavily on markup pricing (discussed in Chapter 15) often use standardized tables that convert markup on selling price to markup on cost, and vice versa. The two equations below show how to convert one to the other:

$$\text{Markup on selling price (\%)} = \frac{\text{Markup on cost (\%)}}{100\% + \text{Markup on cost (\%)}} \times 100$$

$$\text{Markup on cost (\%)} = \frac{\text{Markup on selling price (\%)}}{100\% - \text{Markup on selling price (\%)}}$$

Using the data from The Caplow Company gives

$$\text{Markup on selling price (\%)} = \frac{\text{Markup on cost (\%)}}{100\% + \text{Markup on cost (\%)}} \times 100$$

$$= \frac{122.2}{100 + 122.2} \times 100 = 55\%$$

$$\text{Markup on cost (\%)} = \frac{\text{Markup on selling price (\%)}}{100\% - \text{Markup on selling price (\%)}} \times 100$$

$$= \frac{55}{100 - 55} \times 100 = 122.2\%$$

The use of an incorrect markup base is shown in Westerlund's business. A markup of 122.2 percent on her cost of goods sold for a typical frame she sells gives 122.2% × $36 = $44 of markup. Added to the $36 cost of goods sold, this gives her selling price of $80 for the framed picture. However, a new clerk working for her who erroneously priced the framed picture at 55 percent of cost of goods sold set the final price at $55.80 ($36 of cost of goods sold plus 55% × $36 = $19.80). The error, if repeated, can be disastrous: frames would be accidentally sold at $55.80, or $24.20 below the intended selling price of $80.

Markdown   A markdown is a reduction in a retail price that is necessary if the item will not sell at the full selling price to which it has been marked up. The item might not sell for a variety of reasons: the selling price was set too high or the item is out of style or has become soiled or damaged. The seller "takes a markdown" by lowering the price to sell it, thereby converting it to cash to buy future inventory that will sell faster.

The markdown percentage cannot be calculated directly from the operating statement. As shown in the fifth item of Figure B–2, the numerator of the markdown percentage is the total dollar markdowns. Markdowns are reductions in the prices of goods that are purchased by customers. The denominator is net sales.

Suppose The Caplow Company had a total of $700 in markdowns on the prints and posters that are stocked and available for sale. Since the frames are custom made for individual customers, there is little reason for a markdown there. Caplow's markdown percent is then

$$\text{Markdown(\%)} = \frac{\text{Markdowns}}{\text{Net sales}} \times 100$$

$$= \frac{\$700}{\$80,000} \times 100$$

$$= 0.875\%$$

Other kinds of retailers often have markdown ratios several times this amount. For example, women's dress stores have markdowns of about 25 percent, and menswear stores have markdowns of about 2 percent.

Stockturn Rate   A business firm is anxious to have its inventory move quickly, or "turn over." Stockturn rate, or simply stockturns, measures this inventory movement. For a retailer a slow stockturn rate may show it is buying merchandise customers don't want, so this is a critical measure of performance. When a firm sells only a single product, one convenient way to measure stockturn rate is simply to divide its cost of goods sold by average inventory at cost. The sixth item in Figure B–2 shows how to calculate stockturn rate using information in the following operating statement:

A customer discusses choices of framing and matting for her print with Jane Westerlund.

$$\text{Stockturn rate} = \frac{\text{Cost of goods sold}}{\text{Average inventory at cost}}$$

The dollar amount of average inventory at cost is calculated by adding the beginning and ending inventories for the year and dividing by 2 to get the average. From Caplow's operating statement, we have

$$\text{Stockturn rate} = \frac{\text{Cost of goods sold}}{\text{Average inventory at cost}}$$

$$= \frac{\text{Cost of goods sold}}{\frac{\text{Beginning inventory} + \text{Ending inventory}}{2}}$$

$$= \frac{\$36,000}{\frac{\$6,000 + \$5,000}{2}}$$

$$= \frac{\$36,000}{\$5,500}$$

$$= 6.5 \text{ stockturns per year}$$

What is considered a "good stockturn" varies by the kind of industry. For example, supermarkets have limited shelf space for thousands of new products from manufacturers each year, so they watch stockturn carefully by product line. The stockturn rate in supermarkets for breakfast foods is about 17 times per year, for pet food about 22 times, and for paper products about 25 times per year.

Return on Investment   A better measure of the performance of a firm than the amount of profit it makes in a year is its ROI, which is the ratio of net income to the investment used to earn that net income. To calculate ROI, it is necessary to subtract income taxes from profit before taxes to obtain net income, then divide this figure by the investment that can be found on a firm's balance sheet (another accounting statement that shows the firm's assets, liabilities, and net worth). While financial and accounting experts have many definitions for "investment," an often-used definition is "total assets."

For our purposes, let's assume that Westerlund has total assets (investment) of $20,000 in The Caplow Company, which covers inventory, store fixtures, and framing equipment. If she pays $1,000 in income taxes, her store's net income is $5,400, so her ROI is given by the seventh item in Figure B–2:

$$\text{Return on investment} = \text{Net income/investment} \times 100$$

$$= \$5,400/\$20,000 \times 100$$

$$= 27\%$$

If Westerlund wants to improve her ROI next year, the strategies she might take are found in this alternative equation for ROI:

$$\text{ROI} = \text{Net sales/investment} \times \text{Net income/net sales}$$

$$= \text{Investment turnover} \times \text{Profit margin}$$

This equation suggests that The Caplow Company's ROI can be improved by raising turnover or increasing profit margin. Increasing stockturns will accomplish the former, whereas lowering cost of goods sold to net sales will cause the latter.

CHAPTER SIXTEEN

MARKETING CHANNELS AND WHOLESALING

16

AFTER READING THIS CHAPTER YOU SHOULD BE ABLE TO:

• Explain what is meant by a marketing channel of distribution and why intermediaries are needed.

• Recognize differences between marketing channels for consumer and industrial products and services in domestic and global markets.

• Describe the types and functions of firms that perform wholesaling activities.

• Distinguish among traditional marketing channels, electronic marketing channels, and different types of vertical marketing systems.

• Describe factors considered by marketing executives when selecting and managing a marketing channel, including channel conflict and legal restrictions.

GATEWAY: ADDING HIGH TOUCH TO HIGH-TECH MARKETING CHANNELS

Just when conventional wisdom says that virtual stores will replace the brick-and-mortar kind, the world's second largest direct marketer of personal computers is investing in real, not electronic storefronts! Gateway, which began selling personal computers directly to consumers in 1985, operates 58 Gateway Country showrooms in the United States and 125 worldwide. Following a successful debut in Europe and Japan, the company plans to open a total of 400 showrooms. Why? Gateway has found that many personal computer buyers still prefer browsing in a store and talking with a salesperson.

The showrooms blend high tech with high touch. At Gateway Country showrooms, customers can see, touch, test, and custom configure a computer system to meet their needs with the help of highly trained representatives. Customers are encouraged to surf the Internet, watch movie clips using a DVD drive, or visit with Gateway personnel or other customers in a comfortable setting. Showrooms reflect Gateway's Midwestern roots in North Sioux City, South Dakota. The décor includes tractor seats, mock silos, and grain bins.

However, Gateway does not stock personal computers at its showrooms. Customers who want to buy a computer must still order one from Gateway, which will custom build the system to the customer's specifications at its factories and ship it directly to a customer's home or business. In this way, Gateway retains the economic benefits of direct selling. The rapid expansion of Gateway Country showrooms attests to the success of this venture. In the final analysis, "The stores will be measured largely by whether they help Gateway build relationships with its customers," says Joseph J. Burke, the company's senior vice president for global business development.[1]

The novel approach to marketing channels evidenced by Gateway Country showrooms has already paid a handsome sales dividend to the company. Computer industry analysts estimate that 80 percent of Gateway's sales growth can be attributed to its showrooms.

This chapter focuses on marketing channels of distribution and why they are an important component in the marketing mix. It then shows how such channels benefit consumers and the sequence of firms that make up a marketing channel. Finally, it describes factors that influence the choice and management of marketing channels, including channel conflict and legal restrictions.

NATURE AND IMPORTANCE OF MARKETING CHANNELS

Reaching prospective buyers, either directly or indirectly, is a prerequisite for successful marketing. At the same time, buyers benefit from distribution systems used by firms.

Defining Marketing Channels of Distribution

You see the results of distribution every day. You may have purchased Lay's Potato Chips at the 7-Eleven store, a book through Amazon.com, and Levi's jeans at Sears. Each of these items was brought to you by a marketing channel of distribution, or simply a **marketing channel,** which consists of individuals and firms involved in the process of making a product or service available for use or consumption by consumers or industrial users.

Marketing channels can be compared with a pipeline through which water flows from a source to terminus. Marketing channels make possible the flow of goods from a producer, through intermediaries, to a buyer. Intermediaries go by various names (Figure 16–1) and perform various functions.[2] Some intermediaries actually purchase items from the seller, store them, and resell them to buyers. For example, Sunshine Biscuits produces cookies and sells them to food wholesalers. The wholesalers then sell the cookies to supermarkets and grocery stores, which, in turn, sell them to consumers. Other intermediaries such as brokers and agents represent sellers but do not actually take title to products—their role is to bring a seller and buyer together. Century 21 real estate agents are examples of this type of intermediary. The importance of intermediaries is made even clearer when we consider the functions they perform and the value they create for buyers.

FIGURE 16–1
Terms used for marketing intermediaries

TERM	DESCRIPTION
Middleman	Any intermediary between manufacturer and end-user markets
Agent or broker	Any intermediary with legal authority to act on behalf of the manufacturer
Wholesaler	An intermediary who sells to other intermediaries, usually to retailers; usually applies to consumer markets
Retailer	An intermediary who sells to consumers
Distributor	An imprecise term, usually used to describe intermediaries who perform a variety of distribution functions, including selling, maintaining inventories, extending credit, and so on; a more common term in industrial markets but may also be used to refer to wholesalers
Dealer	An even more imprecise term that can mean the same as distributor, retailer, wholesaler, and so forth

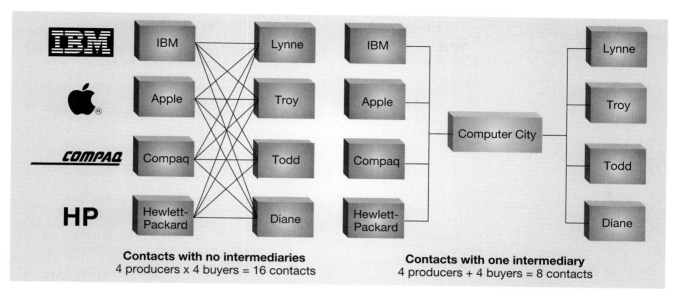

FIGURE 16–2
How intermediaries minimize transactions

Value Created by Intermediaries

Few consumers appreciate the value created by intermediaries; however, producers recognize that intermediaries make selling goods and services more efficient because they minimize the number of sales contacts necessary to reach a target market. Figure 16–2 shows a simple example of how this comes about in the personal computer industry. Without a retail intermediary (such as Computer City), IBM, Apple, Compaq, and Hewlett-Packard would each have to make four contacts to reach the four buyers shown who are in the target market. However, each producer has to make only one contact when Computer City acts as an intermediary. Equally important from a macromarketing perspective, the total number of industry transactions is reduced from 16 to 8, which reduces producer cost and hence benefits the consumer. This simple example also illustrates why computer manufacturers constantly compete with each other to gain access to computer retailers such as Computer City, Circuit City, and CompUSA.

Functions Performed by Intermediaries   Intermediaries make possible the flow of products from producers to buyers by performing three basic functions (Figure 16–3).[3] Most prominently, intermediaries perform a transactional function that involves buying, selling, and risk taking because they stock merchandise in anticipation of sales. Intermediaries perform a logistical function evident in the gathering, storing, and dispersing of products (see Chapter 17 on supply chain and logistics management). Finally, intermediaries perform facilitating functions, which assist producers in making goods and services more attractive to buyers.

All three groups of functions must be performed in a marketing channel, even though each channel member may not participate in all three. Channel members often negotiate about which specific functions they will perform. Sometimes disagreements result, and a breakdown in relationships among channel members occurs. This happened recently when PepsiCo's bottler in Venezuela switched to Coca-Cola. Because all marketing channel functions had to be performed, PepsiCo either had to set up its own bottling operation to perform the marketing channel functions, or find another bottler, which it did.[4]

Consumer Benefits from Intermediaries   Consumers also benefit from intermediaries. Having the goods and services you want, when you want them, where you want them, and in the form you want them is the ideal result of marketing channels. In

FIGURE 16–3
Marketing channel functions
performed by intermediaries

more specific terms, marketing channels help create value for consumers through the four utilities described in Chapter 1: time, place, form, and possession. Time utility refers to having a product or service when you want it. For example, FedEx provides next-morning delivery. Place utility means having a product or service available where consumers want it, such as having an Exxon gas station located on a long stretch of lonely highway. Form utility involves enhancing a product or service to make it more appealing to buyers. For example, Compaq Computer delivers unfinished PCs to dealers, which then add memory, chips, modems, and other parts, based on consumer specifications.[5] Possession utility entails efforts by intermediaries to help buyers take possession of a product or service, such as having airline tickets delivered by a travel agency.

CONCEPT CHECK   **1.** What is meant by a marketing channel?

2. What are the three basic functions performed by intermediaries?

CHANNEL STRUCTURE AND ORGANIZATION

A product can take many routes on its journey from a producer to buyers, and marketers search for the most efficient route from the many alternatives available.

Marketing Channels for Consumer Goods and Services

Figure 16–4 shows the four most common marketing channels for consumer goods and services. It also shows the number of levels in each marketing channel, as evi-

FIGURE 16–4
Common marketing channels
for consumer goods and
services

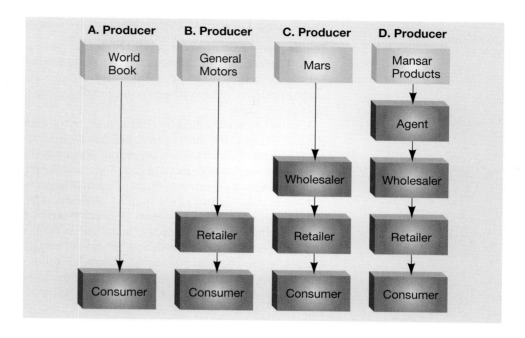

denced by the number of intermediaries between a producer and ultimate buyers. As the number of intermediaries between a producer and buyer increases, the channel is viewed as increasing in length. Thus the producer → wholesaler → retailer → consumer channel is longer than the producer → consumer channel.

Channel A represents a **direct channel** because a producer and ultimate consumers deal directly with each other. Many products and services are distributed this way. A number of insurance companies sell their financial services using a direct channel and branch sales offices, and World Book Educational Products sells its encyclopedias direct to consumers. Schwan's Sales Enterprises of Marshall, Minnesota, markets a full line of frozen foods in 49 states and parts of Canada using door-to-door salespeople who sell from refrigerated trucks. Because there are no intermediaries with a direct channel, the producer must perform all channel functions.

The remaining three channel forms are **indirect channels** because intermediaries are inserted between the producer and consumers and perform numerous channel functions. Channel B, with a retailer added, is most common when a retailer is large and can buy in large quantities from a producer or when the cost of inventory makes it too expensive to use a wholesaler. Manufacturers such as General Motors, Ford, and Chrysler use this channel, and a local car dealer acts as a retailer. Why is there no wholesaler? So many variations exist in the product that it would be impossible for a wholesaler to stock all the models required to satisfy buyers; in addition, the cost of maintaining an inventory would be too high. However, large retailers such as Sears, 7-Eleven, Safeway, and JCPenney buy in sufficient quantities to make it cost effective for a producer to deal with only a retail intermediary.

Adding a wholesaler in Channel C is most common for low-cost, low-unit value items that are frequently purchased by consumers, such as candy, confectionary items, and magazines. For example, Mars sells its line of candies to wholesalers in case quantities; then they can break down (sort) the cases so that individual retailers can order in boxes or much smaller quantities.

Channel D, the most indirect channel, is employed when there are many small manufacturers and many small retailers and an agent is used to help coordinate a large supply of the product. Mansar Products, Ltd. is a Belgian producer of specialty jewelry that uses agents to sell to wholesalers in the United States, which then sell to many small retailers.

Marketing Channels for Industrial Goods and Services

The four most common channels for industrial goods and services are shown in Figure 16–5. In contrast with channels for consumer products, industrial channels typically are shorter and rely on one intermediary or none at all because industrial users are fewer in number, tend to be more concentrated geographically, and buy in larger quantities (see Chapter 7).

Channel A, represented by IBM's large, mainframe computer business, is a direct channel. Firms using this channel maintain their own salesforce and perform all channel functions. This channel is employed when buyers are large and well defined, the sales effort requires extensive negotiations, and the products are of high unit value and require hands-on expertise in terms of installation or use.

Channels B, C, and D are indirect channels with one or more intermediaries to reach industrial users. In Channel B an **industrial distributor** performs a variety of marketing channel functions, including selling, stocking, and delivering a full product assortment and financing. In many ways, industrial distributors are like wholesalers in consumer channels. Caterpillar relies on industrial distributors to sell its construction and mining equipment in almost 200 countries. In addition to selling, Caterpillar distributors stock 40,000 to 50,000 parts and service equipment using highly trained technicians.[6]

Channel C introduces a second intermediary, an *agent,* who serves primarily as the independent selling arm of producers and represents a producer to industrial users. For example, Stake Fastener Company, a California-based producer of industrial fasteners, has an agent call on industrial users rather than employing its own salesforce.

Channel D is the longest channel and includes both agents and distributors. For instance, Harkman Electric, a small Texas-based producer of electric products, uses agents to call on distributors who sell to industrial users.

Electronic Marketing Channels

These common marketing channels for consumer and industrial goods and services are not the only routes to the marketplace. Advances in electronic commerce have opened new avenues for reaching buyers and creating customer value as described in Chapter 8.

Interactive electronic technology has made possible **electronic marketing channels** which employ the Internet to make goods and services available for consumption or use by consumers or industrial buyers. A unique feature of these channels

FIGURE 16–5
Common marketing channels for industrial goods and services

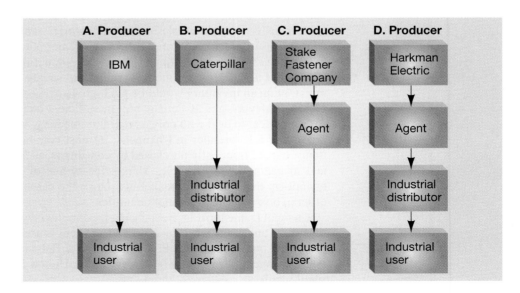

FIGURE 16–6
Representative electronic marketing channels

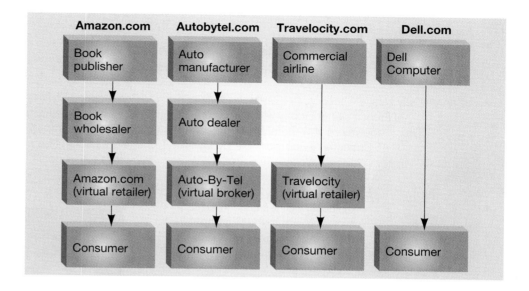

is that they combine electronic and traditional intermediaries to create time, place, form, and possession utility for buyers.[7]

Figure 16–6 shows the electronic marketing channels for books (Amazon.com), automobiles (Auto-By-Tel.com), reservation services (Travelocity.com), and personal computers (Dell.com). Are you surprised that they look a lot like common marketing channels? An important reason for the similarity resides in channel functions detailed in Figure 16–3. Electronic intermediaries can and do perform transactional and facilitating functions effectively and at a relatively lower cost than traditional intermediaries because of efficiencies made possible by information technology. However, electronic intermediaries are incapable of performing elements of the logistical function, particularly for products such as books and automobiles. This function remains with traditional intermediaries or with the producer, as evident with Dell Computer Corporation and its direct channel.

Many services can be distributed through electronic marketing channels, such as travel reservation marketed by Travelocity.com, financial securities by Schwab.com, and insurance by MetLife.com. Software too can be marketed this way. However, many other services such as health care and auto repair still involve traditional intermediaries.

Direct Marketing Channels

Many firms also use direct marketing channels to reach buyers. **Direct marketing channels** allow consumers to buy products by interacting with various advertising media without a face-to-face meeting with a salesperson. Direct marketing channels includes mail-order selling, direct-mail sales, catalog sales, telemarketing, interactive media, and televised home shopping (for example, the Home Shopping Network). U.S. sales revenue attributed to direct marketing channels exceeds $1.4 trillion.[8]

Some firms sell products almost entirely through direct marketing channels. These firms include L.L. Bean (apparel), Sharper Image (expensive gifts and novelties), and Egghead.com (personal computers). Manufacturers such as Nestlé and Sunkist, in addition to using traditional channels composed of wholesalers and retailers, employ direct marketing through catalogs and telemarketing to reach more buyers. At the same time, retailers such as JCPenney use direct marketing techniques to augment conventional store merchandising activities. Some experts believe that direct marketing will account for 20 percent of all retail transactions in the United States and 10 percent of retail transactions in Europe by 2002. Direct marketing is covered in greater depth in Chapter 19.

MARKETING NEWSNET

Nestlé and General Mills: Cereal Partners Worldwide

Can you say Nestlé Cheerios *miel amandes?* Millions of French start their day with this European equivalent of General Mill's Honey Nut Cheerios, made possible by Cereal Partners Worldwide (CPW). CPW is the food industry's first strategic alliance designed to be a global business; it joined the cereal manufacturing and marketing capability of U.S.-based General Mills with the worldwide distribution clout of Swiss-based Nestlé.

From its headquarters near Lake Geneva, Switzerland, CPW first launched General Mills cereals under the Nestlé label in France, the United Kingdom, Spain, and Portugal in 1991. Today, CPW competes in 70 markets worldwide and expects to achieve its goal of $1 billion in profitable sales by 2000.

The General Mills–Nestlé strategic alliance is also likely to increase the ready-to-eat worldwide market share of these companies, which are already rated as the two best-managed firms in the world. CPW is on track to reach its goal of a 20 percent worldwide share by 2000.

Multiple Channels and Strategic Alliances

In some situations producers use **dual distribution,** an arrangement whereby a firm reaches different buyers by employing two or more different types of channels for the same basic product. For example, GE sells its large appliances directly to home and apartment builders but uses retail stores to sell to consumers. In some instances, firms use multiple channels when a multibrand strategy is employed (see Chapter 12). Hallmark sells its Hallmark greeting cards through Hallmark stores and select department stores, and its Ambassador brand of cards through discount and drugstore chains. In other instances, a firm will distribute modified products through different channels. Zoecon Corporation sells its insect control chemicals to professional pest-control operators such as Orkin and Terminex. A modified compound is sold to the Boyle-Midway Division of American Home Products for use in its Black-Flag Roach Ender brand.

A recent innovation in marketing channels is the use of **strategic channel alliances,** whereby one firm's marketing channel is used to sell another firm's products.[9] An alliance between Kraft Foods and Starbucks is a case in point. Kraft distributes Starbucks coffee in U.S. supermarkets and internationally. Strategic alliances are popular in global marketing, where the creation of marketing channel relationships is expensive and time consuming. For example, General Motors distributes the Swedish Saab through its Saturn dealers in Canada. General Mills and Nestlé have an extensive alliance that spans 70 international markets. Read the accompanying Marketing NewsNet so you won't be surprised when you are served Nestlé (not General Mills) Cheerios in Europe, Mexico, and parts of Asia.[10]

A Closer Look at Channel Intermediaries

Channel structures for consumer and industrial products assume various forms based on the number and type of intermediaries. Knowledge of the roles played by these intermediaries is important for understanding how channels operate in practice.

The terms *wholesaler, agent,* and *retailer* have been used in a general fashion consistent with the meanings given in Figure 16–1. However, on closer inspection, a variety of

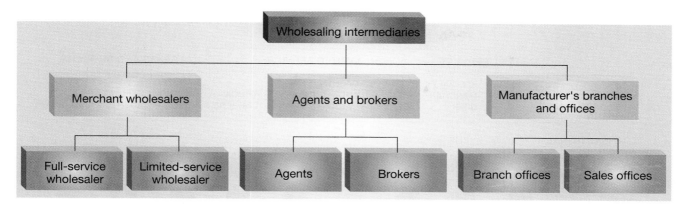

FIGURE 16–7
Types of wholesaling
intermediaries

specific types of intermediaries emerges. Figure 16–7 shows a common classification of intermediaries that engage in wholesaling activities—those activities involved in selling products and services to those who are buying for the purposes of resale or business use. Intermediaries engaged in retailing activities are discussed in detail in Chapter 18. Figure 16–8 describes the functions performed by major types of independent wholesalers.[11]

Merchant Wholesalers   Merchant wholesalers are independently owned firms that take title to the merchandise they handle. They go by various names, including industrial distributor (described earlier). About 83 percent of the firms engaged in wholesaling activities are merchant wholesalers.

Merchant wholesalers are classified as either full-service or limited-service wholesalers, depending on the number of functions performed. Two major types of full-service wholesalers exist. **General merchandise** (or *full-line*) **wholesalers** carry a broad assortment of merchandise and perform all channel functions. This type of wholesaler is most prevalent in the hardware, drug, and clothing industries. However, these wholesalers do not maintain much depth of assortment within specific product lines. **Specialty merchandise** (or *limited-line*) **wholesalers** offer a relatively narrow range of products but have an extensive assortment within the product lines carried. They perform all channel functions and are found in the health foods, automotive parts, and seafood industries.

Four major types of limited-service wholesalers exist. **Rack jobbers** furnish the racks or shelves that display merchandise in retail stores, perform all channel functions, and sell on consignment to retailers, which means they retain the title to the products displayed and bill retailers only for the merchandise sold. Familiar products such as hosiery, toys, housewares, and health and beauty aids are sold by rack jobbers. **Cash and carry wholesalers** take title to merchandise but sell only to buyers who call on them, pay cash for merchandise, and furnish their own transportation for merchandise. They carry a limited product assortment and do not make deliveries, extend credit, or supply market information. This wholesaler is common in electric supplies, office supplies, hardware products, and groceries. **Drop shippers,** or *desk jobbers,* are wholesalers who own the merchandise they sell but do not physically handle, stock, or deliver it. They simply solicit orders from retailers and other wholesalers and have the merchandise shipped directly from a producer to a buyer. Drop shippers are used for bulky products such as coal, lumber, and chemicals, which are sold in extremely large quantities. **Truck jobbers** are small wholesalers who have a small warehouse from which they stock their trucks for distribution to retailers. They usually handle limited assortments of fast-moving or perishable items that are sold for cash directly from trucks in their original packages. Truck jobbers handle products such as bakery items, dairy products, and meat.

Agents and Brokers   Unlike merchant wholesalers, agents and brokers do not take title to merchandise and typically provide fewer channel functions. They make

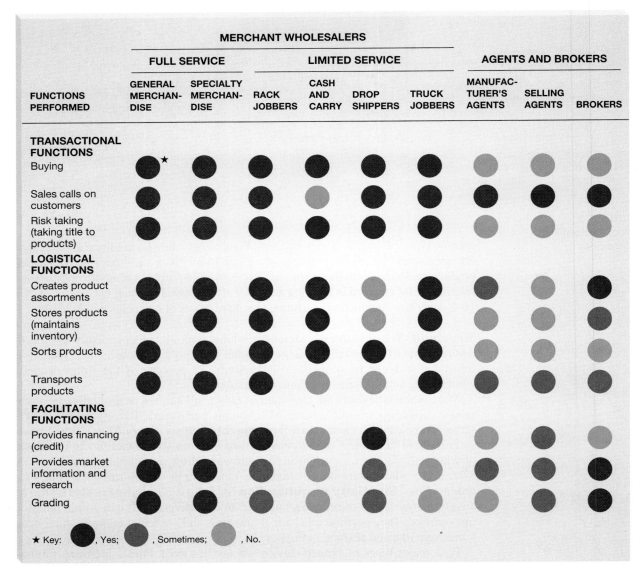

FUNCTIONS PERFORMED	MERCHANT WHOLESALERS						AGENTS AND BROKERS		
	FULL SERVICE		LIMITED SERVICE						
	GENERAL MERCHAN-DISE	SPECIALTY MERCHAN-DISE	RACK JOBBERS	CASH AND CARRY	DROP SHIPPERS	TRUCK JOBBERS	MANUFAC-TURER'S AGENTS	SELLING AGENTS	BROKERS

TRANSACTIONAL FUNCTIONS

Buying

Sales calls on customers

Risk taking (taking title to products)

LOGISTICAL FUNCTIONS

Creates product assortments

Stores products (maintains inventory)

Sorts products

Transports products

FACILITATING FUNCTIONS

Provides financing (credit)

Provides market information and research

Grading

★ Key: ⬤, Yes; ⬤, Sometimes; ⬤, No.

FIGURE 16–8
Functions performed by
independent wholesaler types

their profit from commissions or fees paid for their services, whereas merchant whole-salers make their profit from the sale of the merchandise they own.

Manufacturer's agents and selling agents are the two major types of agents used by producers. **Manufacturer's agents,** or *manufacturer's representatives,* work for several producers and carry noncompetitive, complementary merchandise in an exclusive territory. Manufacturer's agents act as a producer's sales arm in a territory and are principally responsible for the transactional channel functions, primarily selling. They are used extensively in the automotive supply, footwear, and fabricated steel industries. However, Swank Jewelry, Japanese computer firms, and Apple have used manufacturer's agents as well. By comparison, **selling agents** represent a single producer and are responsible for the entire marketing function of that producer. They design promotional plans, set prices, determine distribution policies, and make recommendations on product strategy. Selling agents are used by small producers in the textile, apparel, food, and home furnishing industries.

Brokers are independent firms or individuals whose principal function is to bring buyers and sellers together to make sales. Brokers, unlike agents, usually have no continuous relationship with the buyer or seller but negotiate a contract between two parties and then move on to another task. Brokers are used extensively by producers of seasonal products (such as fruits and vegetables) and in the real estate industry.

A unique broker that acts in many ways like a manufacturer's agent is a food broker, representing buyers and sellers in the grocery industry. Food brokers differ from conventional brokers because they act on behalf of producers on a permanent basis and receive a commission for their services. For example, Nabisco uses food brokers to sell its candies, margarine, and Planters peanuts, but it sells its line of cookies and crackers directly to retail stores. Manufacturer's agents sell Mr. Coffee coffee makers to appliance and mass merchandisers and food brokers sell its replacement coffee filters to supermarkets.

Manufacturer's Branches and Offices   Unlike merchant wholesalers, agents, and brokers, manufacturer's branches and sales offices are wholly owned extensions of the producer that perform wholesaling activities. Producers assume wholesaling functions when there are no intermediaries to perform these activities, customers are few in number and geographically concentrated, or orders are large or require significant attention. A *manufacturer's branch office* carries a producer's inventory and performs the functions of a full-service wholesaler. A *manufacturer's sales office* does not carry inventory, typically performs only a sales function, and serves as an alternative to agents and brokers.

Vertical Marketing Systems and Channel Partnerships

The traditional marketing channels described so far represent a loosely knit network of independent producers and intermediaries brought together to distribute goods and services. However, new channel arrangements have emerged for the purpose of improving efficiency in performing channel functions and achieving greater marketing effectiveness. These new arrangements are called vertical marketing systems and channel partnerships. **Vertical marketing systems** are professionally managed and centrally coordinated marketing channels designed to achieve channel economies and maximum marketing impact.[12] Figure 16–9 depicts the major types of vertical marketing systems: corporate, contractual, and administered.

FIGURE 16–9
Types of vertical marketing systems

Corporate Systems   The combination of successive stages of production and distribution under a single ownership is a *corporate vertical marketing system.* For example, a producer might own the intermediary at the next level down in the channel. This practice, called *forward integration,* is exemplified by Polo/Ralph Lauren, which manufactures clothing and also owns apparel shops. Other examples of forward integration include Goodyear, Singer, Sherwin Williams, and the building materials division of Boise Cascade. Alternatively, a retailer might own a manufacturing operation, a practice called *backward integration.* For example, Kroger supermarkets operate manufacturing facilities that produce everything from aspirin to cottage cheese, for sale under the Kroger label.

Contractual Systems   Under a *contractual vertical marketing system,* independent production and distribution firms integrate their efforts on a contractual basis to obtain greater functional economies and marketing impact than they could achieve alone. Contractual systems are the most popular among the three types of vertical marketing systems. They account for about 40 percent of all retail sales.

Three variations of contractual systems exist. *Wholesaler-sponsored voluntary chains* involve a wholesaler that develops a contractual relationship with small, independent retailers to standardize and coordinate buying practices, merchandising programs, and inventory management efforts. With the organization of a large number of independent retailers, economies of scale and volume discounts can be achieved to compete with chain stores. IGA and Ben Franklin variety and craft stores represent wholesaler-sponsored voluntary chains. *Retailer-sponsored cooperatives* exist when small, independent retailers form an organization that operates a wholesale facility cooperatively. Member retailers then concentrate their buying power through the wholesaler and plan collaborative promotional and pricing activities. Examples of retailer-sponsored cooperatives include Associated Grocers, Ace Hardware, and Certified Grocers.

The most visible variation of contractual systems is **franchising,** a contractual arrangement between a parent company (a franchisor) and an individual or firm (a franchisee) that allows the franchise to operate a certain type of business under an established name and according to specific rules. Franchises generate about $1 trillion in sales through about 700,000 outlets annually in the United States.[13] Four types of franchise arrangements are most popular. Manufacturer-sponsored retail franchise systems are prominent in the automobile industry, where a manufacturer such as Ford licenses dealers to sell its cars subject to various sales and service conditions. Manufacturer-sponsored wholesale systems are evident in the soft-drink industry, where Pepsi-Cola licenses wholesalers (bottlers) who purchase concentrate from Pepsi-Cola and then carbonate, bottle, promote, and distribute its products to supermarkets and restaurants. Service-sponsored retail franchise systems are provided by firms that have designed a unique approach for performing a service and wish to profit by selling the franchise to others. Holiday Inn, Avis, and McDonald's represent this franchising approach. Service-sponsored franchise systems exist when franchisors license individuals or firms to dispense a service under a trade name and specific guidelines. Examples include Snelling and Snelling, Inc. employment services, and H&R Block tax services. Service-sponsored franchise arrangements are the fastest-growing type of franchise. Franchising is discussed further in Chapter 18.

Administered Systems   In comparison, *administered vertical marketing systems* achieve coordination at successive stages of production and distribution by the size and influence of one channel member rather than through ownership. Procter & Gamble, given its broad product assortment ranging from disposable diapers to detergents, is able to obtain cooperation from supermarkets in displaying, promoting, and pricing its products. Wal-Mart can obtain cooperation from manufacturers in terms of product specifications, price levels, and promotional support, given its position as the world's largest retailer.

Channel Partnerships   Increasingly, channel members are forging channel partnerships akin to supply partnerships described in Chapter 7. A **channel partnership** consists of agreements and procedures among channel members for ordering and physically distributing a producer's products through the channel to the ultimate consumer.[14] A central feature of channel partnerships is the collaborative use of modern information and communication technology to better serve customers and reduce the time and cost of performing channel functions.

The partnership Levi Strauss & Company has with Modell's Sporting Goods in New York is a case in point.[15] By using point-of-sale scanning equipment and direct electronic linkage to Levi Strauss in San Francisco, Modell's can instantaneously inform Levi Strauss what styles and sizes of jeans are needed, create purchase orders, and convey shipping instructions without any human involvement. The result? The costs of performing transaction, logistic, and facilitating functions are substantially reduced, and the customer is virtually assured of having his or her preferred 501 Levi jeans in stock. The role of information and communication technology in supply chain and logistics management is discussed further in Chapter 17.

CONCEPT CHECK

1. What is the difference between a direct and an indirect channel?

2. Why are channels for industrial products typically shorter than channels for consumer products?

3. What is the principal distinction between a corporate vertical marketing system and an administered vertical marketing system?

CHANNEL CHOICE AND MANAGEMENT

Read the text to find out how technology helped Kroger become one of the nation's largest flower retailers.

The Kroger Company
www.kroger.com

Marketing channels not only link a producer to its buyers but also provide the means through which a firm implements various elements of its marketing strategy. Therefore, choosing a marketing channel is a critical decision.

Factors Affecting Channel Choice and Management

The final choice of a marketing channel by a producer depends on a number of factors that often interact with each other.

Environmental Factors   The changing environment described in Chapter 3 has an important effect on the choice and management of a marketing channel. For example, the Fuller Brush Company, which is a name synonymous with door-to-door selling, now uses catalogs and has opened retail stores in some cities. Rising employment among women, resulting in fewer being at home during working hours, prompted this action. Advances in the technology of growing, transporting, and storing perishable cut flowers has allowed Kroger to eliminate flower wholesalers and buy direct from flower growers around the world. Kroger's annual cut-flower sales exceed $100 million, making it one of the largest flower retailers in the United States.[16] The Internet has created new marketing channel opportunities for children's toys, sporting goods and equipment, and music and video products.[17]

Consumer Factors   Consumer characteristics have a direct bearing on the choice and management of a marketing channel. Determining which channel is most appropriate is based on answers to fundamental questions such as: Who are potential customers? Where do they buy? When do they buy? How do they buy? What do they buy? These answers also indicate the type of intermediary best suited to reaching target buyers. For

The Internet has created new marketing channel opportunities for the distribution of children's toys.

FAO Schwarz

www.faoschwarz.com

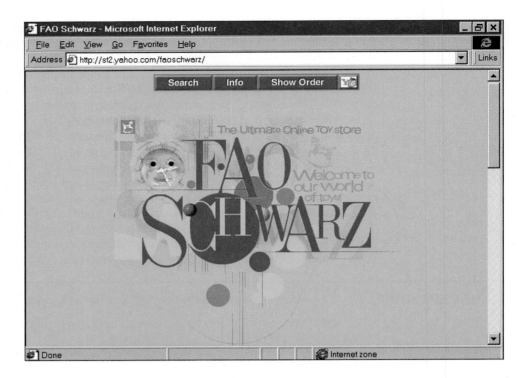

example, Ricoh Company, Ltd. studied the serious (as opposed to recreational) camera user and concluded that a change in marketing channels was necessary. The company terminated its contract with a wholesaler who sold to mass merchandise stores and began using manufacturer's agents who sold to photo specialty stores. These stores agreed to stock and display Ricoh's full line and promote it prominently. Sales volume tripled within 18 months. Recognizing that car buyers now comparison shop on the Internet, Ford, General Motors, Chrysler, and Mercedes Benz now have their own Web sites to provide price and model information.[18]

Product Factors   In general, highly sophisticated products such as large, scientific computers, unstandardized products such as custom-built machinery, and products of high unit value are distributed directly to buyers. Unsophisticated, standardized products with low unit value, such as table salt, are typically distributed through indirect channels. A product's stage in the life cycle also affects marketing channels. This was shown in the description of the fax machine product life cycle in Chapter 12.

Company Factors   A firm's financial, human, or technological capabilities affect channel choice. For example, firms that are unable to employ a salesforce might use manufacturer's agents or selling agents to reach wholesalers or buyers. If a firm has multiple products for a particular target market, it might use a direct channel, whereas firms with a limited product line might use intermediaries of various types to reach buyers.

Company factors also apply to intermediaries. For example, personal computer hardware and software producers wishing to reach business users might look to value-added resellers such as Micro Age, which has its own salesforce and service staff that calls on businesses.

Channel Design Considerations

Recognizing that numerous routes to buyers exist and also recognizing the factors just described, marketing executives typically consider three questions when choosing a marketing channel and intermediaries:

WEB LINK   Check the VISA ATM Locator

VISA offers a valuable Web resource in its ATM Locator that can be accessed at www.visa.com. VISA has some 460,000 automatic teller machines in 120 countries. One is probably in your neighborhood, wherever that is in the world! To find the nearest VISA ATM, follow the easy ATM Locator directions and request a site map. You'll be in the money in no time. Here's the map for McGraw-Hill Higher Education's neighborhood.

1. Which channel and intermediaries will provide the best coverage of the target market?
2. Which channel and intermediaries will best satisfy the buying requirements of the target market?
3. Which channel and intermediaries will be the most profitable?

Target Market Coverage   Achieving the best coverage of the target market requires attention to the density and type of intermediaries to be used at the retail level of distribution. Three degrees of distribution density exist: intensive, exclusive, and selective. **Intensive distribution** means that a firm tries to place its products and services in as many outlets as possible. Intensive distribution is usually chosen for convenience products or services; for example, candy, fast food, newspapers, and soft drinks. Increasingly, medical services are distributed in this fashion. Cash, yes cash, is also distributed intensively by VISA. Visit VISA's Web site described in the Web Link, to locate the nearest VISA automatic teller machine.

Exclusive distribution is the extreme opposite of intensive distribution because only one retail outlet in a specified geographical area carries the firm's product. Exclusive distribution is typically chosen for specialty products or services; for example, automobiles, some women's fragrances, men's suits, and yachts. Sometimes retailers sign exclusive distribution agreements with manufacturers. For instance, Radio Shack now sells only Compaq's Presario home computers in its 7,000 stores.[19]

Selective distribution lies between these two extremes and means that a firm selects a few retail outlets in a specific area to carry its products. This is the most common form of distribution intensity and is usually associated with shopping goods or services such as Rolex watches, Ben Hogan golf clubs, and Henredon furniture.

The type or availability of a retail outlet will also influence whether a target market is reached. For example, the L'eggs division of the Hanes Corporation distributes fashionable white pantyhose to nurses through catalogs because supermarkets and department stores do not typically carry these items.

Satisfying Buyer Requirements   A second consideration in channel design is gaining access to channels and intermediaries that satisfy at least some of the interests buyers might want fulfilled when they purchase a firm's products or services. These interests fall into four categories: (1) information, (2) convenience, (3) variety, and (4) attendant services.

Information is an important requirement when buyers have limited knowledge or desire specific data about a product or service. Properly chosen intermediaries communicate with buyers through in-store displays, demonstrations, and personal selling. Computer stores originally grew in popularity as a source for small computers because they provided such information. Similarly, direct sales firms such as Amway, Avon, and Tupperware have been able to identify the unique information needs of Japanese women and successfully communicate the benefits of their products and method of selling. Amway is one of the fastest-growing firms in Japan, and Avon records millions of dollars in Japanese sales each year through direct selling.

Convenience has multiple meanings for buyers, such as proximity or driving time to a retail outlet. For example, 7-Eleven stores with more than 5,000 outlets nationwide satisfy this interest for buyers, and candy and snack food firms benefit by gaining display space in these stores. For other consumers, convenience means a minimum of time and hassle. Jiffy Lube and Q-Lube, which promise to change engine oil and filters quickly, appeal to this aspect of convenience.

Variety reflects buyers' interest in having numerous competing and complementary items from which to choose. Variety is evident in both the breadth and depth of products and brands carried by intermediaries, which enhances their attraction to buyers. Thus, manufacturers of pet food and supplies seek distribution through pet superstores such as Petco and PetsMart, which offer a wide array of pet products.

Attendant services provided by intermediaries are an important buying requirement for products such as appliances that require delivery, installation, and credit. Therefore, Whirlpool seeks dealers that provide such services.

Profitability The third consideration in designing a channel is profitability, which is determined by the margins earned (revenues minus cost) for each channel member and for the channel as a whole. Channel cost is the critical dimension of profitability. These costs include distribution, advertising, and selling expenses associated with different types of marketing channels. The extent to which channel members share these costs determines the margins received by each member and by the channel as a whole.

Global Dimensions of Marketing Channels

Marketing channels around the world reflect traditions, customs, geography, and the economic history of individual countries and societies. Even so, the basic marketing channel functions must be performed. But differences do exist and are illustrated by highlighting marketing channels in Japan—the world's second-largest economy and the second-largest U.S.–world trade partner.

Intermediaries outside Western Europe and North America tend to be small, numerous, and often owner operated. Japan, for example, has less than one half of the population and a land mass less than 5 percent of the United States. However, Japan and the United States have about the same number of wholesalers and retailers. Why? Japanese marketing channels tend to include many intermediaries based on tradition and lack of storage space. As many as five intermediaries are involved in the distribution of soap in Japan compared with one or two in the United States.

Understanding marketing channels in global markets is often a prerequisite to successful marketing. For example, Gillette attempted to sell its razors and blades through company salespeople in Japan as it does in the United States, thus eliminating wholesalers traditionally involved in marketing toiletries. Warner-Lambert Company sold its Schick razors and blades through the traditional Japanese channel involving wholesalers. The result? Schick achieved a commanding lead over Gillette in the Japanese razor and blade market.[20]

Channel relationships also must be considered. In Japan, the distribution *keiretsu* (translated as "alignments") bonds producers and intermediaries together.[21] The bond, through vertical integration and social and economic ties, ensures that each channel member benefits from the distribution alignment. The dominant member of the distribution *keiretsu*, which is typically a producer, has considerable influence over channel

MARKETING NEWSNET

Creative Cosmetics and Creative Marketing in Japan

How does a small U.S. cosmetics firm sell 1.5 million tubes of its lipstick in Japan annually? Fran Wilson Creative Cosmetics attribute their success to a top-quality product, an effective advertising program, and distribution. The firm's Moodmatcher lip coloring comes in green, orange, silver, black, and six other funky hues that change to a shade of pink, coral, or red, depending on a woman's chemistry when it's applied.

The company does not sell to department stores. According to a company spokesperson, "Shiseido and Kanebo keep all the other Japanese or import brands out of the major department stores." Rather, the company sells its Moodmatcher lipstick through a Japanese distributor and marketing channel that reaches Japan's 40,000 beauty salons. The result? The company captures 20 percent of the $4.3 million of lipsticks exported annually to Japan by U.S. companies.

member behavior, including which competing products are sold by other channel members. Well-known Japanese companies such as Matsushita (electronics), Nissan and Toyota (automotive products), Nippon Gakki (musical instruments), and Kirin (and other brewers and distillers) employ the distribution *keiretsu* extensively. Shiseido and Kanebo, for instance, influence the distribution of cosmetics through Japanese department stores. Nevertheless, Fran Wilson Creative Cosmetics of New York City has been able to capture 20 percent of the lipsticks exported to Japan by U.S. companies. Read the accompanying Marketing NewsNet to find out how this creative marketer did it.[22]

Channel Relationships: Conflict, Cooperation, and Law

Unfortunately, because channels consist of independent individuals and firms, there is always potential for disagreements concerning who performs which channel functions, how profits are allocated, which products and services will be provided by whom, and who makes critical channel-related decisions. These channel conflicts necessitate measures for dealing with them. Sometimes they result in legal action.

Conflict in Marketing Channels   Channel conflict arises when one channel member believes another channel member is engaged in behavior that prevents it from achieving its goals. Two types of conflict occur in marketing channels: vertical conflict and horizontal conflict.

Vertical conflict occurs between different levels in a marketing channel; for example, between a manufacturer and a wholesaler or retailer or between a wholesaler and a retailer. Three sources of vertical conflict are most common. First, conflict arises when

---

ETHICS AND SOCIAL RESPONSIBILITY ALERT

The Ethics of Slotting Allowances

How firms acquire and use influence in marketing channels has often prompted legal restrictions. Nevertheless, influence gained through the economic strength, expertise, identification with others, and legitimate rights of channel members can be used in numerous ways.

Some supermarket chains demand slotting allowances from manufacturers, paid in the form of money or free goods, to stock and display products. The allowances, which can range from $100 for a single store to upwards of $25,000 for a supermarket chain, have been labeled "ransom" and "extortional allowances" by manufacturers. Supermarket operators see these allowances as a reasonable cost of handling business for manufacturers.

Is the practice of charging slotting allowances unethical behavior?

---

a channel member bypasses another member and sells or buys products direct, a practice called **disintermediation.** This conflict emerged when Jenn-Air, a producer of kitchen appliances, decided to terminate its distributors and sell direct to retailers. Second, disagreements over how profit margins are distributed among channel members produce conflict. This happened when Compaq Computer Corporation and one of its dealers disagreed over how price discounts were applied in the sale of Compaq's products. Compaq Computer stopped selling to the dealer for 13 months until the issue was resolved. A third conflict situation arises when manufacturers believe wholesalers or retailers are not giving their products adequate attention. For example, H. J. Heinz Company found itself in a conflict situation with its supermarkets in Great Britain when the supermarkets promoted and displayed private brands at the expense of Heinz brands.

Horizontal conflict occurs between intermediaries at the same level in a marketing channel, such as between two or more retailers (Target and Kmart) or two or more wholesalers that handle the same manufacturer's brands. Two sources of horizontal conflict are common. First, horizontal conflict arises when a manufacturer increases its distribution coverage in a geographical area. For example, a franchised Cadillac dealer in Chicago might complain to General Motors that another franchised Cadillac dealer has located too close to its dealership. Second, dual distribution causes conflict when different types of retailers carry the same brands. For instance, the launch of Elizabeth Taylor's Black Pearls fragrance by Elizabeth Arden was put on hold when department store chains such as May and Dillard refused to stock the item once they learned that mass merchants Sears and JCPenney would also carry the brand. Elizabeth Arden subsequently introduced the brand only through department stores.[23]

Cooperation in Marketing Channels   Conflict can have destructive effects on the workings of a marketing channel, so it is necessary to secure cooperation among channel members. One means is through a **channel captain,** a channel member that coordinates, directs, and supports other channel members. Channel captains can be producers, wholesalers, or retailers. P&G assumes this role because it has a strong consumer following in brands such as Crest, Tide, and Pampers. Therefore, it can set policies or terms that supermarkets will follow. McKesson, a pharmaceutical drug wholesaler, is a channel captain because it coordinates and supports the product flow from numerous small drug manufacturers to more than 20,000 drugstores and some 6,000 hospitals nationwide. Wal-Mart and Home Depot are retail channel captains because of their strong consumer image, number of outlets, and purchasing volume.

A firm becomes a channel captain because it is typically the channel member with the ability to influence the behavior of other members.[24] Influence can take four forms. First, economic influence arises from the ability of a firm to reward other members given its strong financial position or customer franchise. Microsoft Corporation and Toys "Я" Us have such influence. Expertise is a second source of influence over other channel members. For example, American Hospital Supply helps its customers (hospitals) manage inventory and streamline order processing for hundreds of medical supplies. Third, identification with a particular channel member may also create influence for that channel member. For instance, retailers may compete to carry the Ralph Lauren line, or clothing manufacturers may compete to be carried by Neiman-Marcus, Nordstrom's, or Bloomingdale's. In both instances the desire to be associated with a channel member gives that firm influence over others. Finally, influence can arise from the legitimate right of one channel member to direct the behavior of other members. This situation would occur under contractual vertical marketing systems where a franchisor could legitimately direct how a franchisee behaves. Other means for securing cooperation in marketing channels rest in the different variations of vertical marketing systems.

Channel influence can be used to gain concessions from other channel members. For instance, some large supermarket chains expect manufacturers to pay allowances, in the form of cash or free goods, to stock and display their products. Some manufacturers call these allowances "extortion" as described in the Ethics and Social Responsibility Alert.[25]

Legal Considerations   Conflict in marketing channels is typically resolved through negotiation or the exercise of influence by channel members. Sometimes conflict produces legal action. Therefore, knowledge of legal restrictions affecting channel strategies and practices is important. Some restrictions were described in Chapter 15, namely vertical price-fixing and price discrimination. However, other legal considerations unique to marketing channels warrant attention.[26]

In general, suppliers can select whomever they want as channel intermediaries and may refuse to deal with whomever they choose. However, the Federal Trade Commission and the Justice Department monitor channel practices that restrain competition, create monopolies, or otherwise represent unfair methods of competition under the Sherman Act (1890) and the Clayton Act (1914). Six practices have received the most attention (Figure 16–10).

Dual distribution, although not illegal, can be viewed as anticompetitive in some situations. The most common situation arises when a manufacturer distributes through its own vertically integrated channel in competition with independent wholesalers and retailers that also sell its products. If the manufacturer's behavior is viewed as an attempt to lessen competition by eliminating wholesalers or retailers, then such action would violate both the Sherman and Clayton Acts.

FIGURE 16–10
Channel strategies and practices affected by legal restrictions

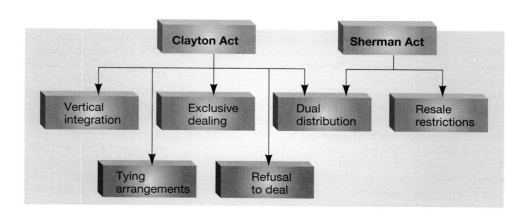

Vertical integration is viewed in a similar light. Although not illegal, this practice is sometimes subject to legal action under the Clayton Act if it has the potential to lessen competition or foster monopoly.

The Clayton Act specifically prohibits exclusive dealing and tying arrangements when they lessen competition or create monopolies. *Exclusive dealing* exists when a supplier requires channel members to sell only its products or restricts distributors from selling directly competitive products. *Tying arrangements* occur when a supplier requires a distributor purchasing some products to buy others from the supplier. These arrangements often arise in franchising. They are illegal if the tied products could be purchased at fair market values from other suppliers at desired quality standards of the franchiser. Full-line forcing is a special kind of tying arrangement. This practice involves a supplier requiring that a channel member carry its full line of products in order to sell a specific item in the supplier's line.

Even though a supplier has a legal right to choose intermediaries to carry and represent its products, a *refusal to deal* with existing channel members may be illegal under the Clayton Act. *Resale restrictions* refer to a supplier's attempt to stipulate to whom distributors may resell the supplier's products and in what specific geographical areas or territories they may be sold. These practices have been prosecuted under the Sherman Act. Today, however, the courts apply the "rule of reason" in such cases and consider whether such restrictions have a "demonstrable economic effect."

CONCEPT CHECK	**1.** What are the three degrees of distribution density?
	2. What are the three questions marketing executives consider when choosing a marketing channel and intermediaries?
	3. What is meant by "exclusive dealing?"

SUMMARY

1 A marketing channel consists of individuals and firms involved in the process of making a product or service available for use by consumers or industrial users.

2 Intermediaries make possible the flow of products and services from producers to buyers by performing transactional, logistical, and facilitating functions. At the same time, intermediaries create time, place, form, and possession utility.

3 Channel structure describes the route taken by products and services from producers to buyers. Direct channels represent the shortest route because producers interact directly with buyers. Indirect channels include intermediaries between producers and buyers.

4 In general, marketing channels for consumer products and services contain more intermediaries than do channels for industrial products and services. In some situations, producers use Internet, direct marketing, multiple channels and strategic channel alliances to reach buyers.

5 Numerous types of wholesalers can exist within a marketing channel. The principal distinction between the various types of wholesalers lies in whether they take title to the items they sell and the channel functions they perform.

6 Vertical marketing systems are channels designed to achieve channel function economies and marketing impact. A vertical marketing system may be one of three types: corporate, administered, or contractual.

7 Marketing managers consider environmental, consumer, product, and company factors when choosing and managing marketing channels.

8 Channel design considerations are based on the target market coverage sought by producers, the buyer requirements to be satisfied, and the profitability of the channel. Target market coverage comes about through one of three levels of distribution density: intensive, exclusive, and selective distribution. Buyer requirements are evident in the amount of information, convenience, variety, and service sought by consumers. Profitability relates to the margins obtained by each channel member and the channel as a whole.

9 Marketing channels in the global marketplace reflect traditions, customs, geography, and the economic history of individual countries and societies. These factors influence channel structure and relationships among channel members.

10 Conflicts in marketing channels are inevitable. Vertical conflict occurs between different levels in a channel. Horizontal conflict occurs between intermediaries at the same level in the channel.

11 Legal issues in the management of marketing channels typically arise from six practices: dual distribution, vertical integration, exclusive dealing, tying arrangements, refusal to deal, and resale restrictions.

KEY TERMS AND CONCEPTS

marketing channel p. 420
direct channel p. 423
indirect channels p. 423
industrial distributor p. 424
electronic marketing channels p. 424
direct marketing channels p. 425
dual distribution p. 426
strategic channel alliances p. 426
general merchandise wholesalers p. 427
specialty merchandise wholesalers p. 427
rack jobbers p. 427
cash and carry wholesalers p. 427
drop shippers p. 427

truck jobbers p. 427
manufacturer's agents p. 428
selling agents p. 428
brokers p. 428
vertical marketing systems p. 429
franchising p. 430
channel partnership p. 431
intensive distribution p. 433
exclusive distribution p. 433
selective distribution p. 433
disintermediation p. 436
channel captain p. 436

INTERNET EXERCISE

Franchising is a large and growing industry both inside and outside the United States. For many individuals, franchising offers an opportunity to operate one's own business.

The Internet provides a number of Web sites that feature franchising opportunities. The International Franchise Association (www.franchise.org) features an extensive array of information, including answers to questions about franchising. The Franchise Opportunity Story (www.franchise.com) lists franchise opportunities for the aspiring franchisee.

1 Visit the Franchise Opportunity Store Web site, and go to How Much Franchises Cost. In what category of business is the franchise investment the highest and the lowest?

2 Visit the International Franchise Association Web site, and go to Frequently Asked Questions About Franchising. What is the business failure rate among franchises? Is the business failure rate better or worse than the failure rate for new businesses in general?

APPLYING MARKETING CONCEPTS AND PERSPECTIVES

1 A distributor for Celanese Chemical Company stores large quantities of chemicals, blends these chemicals to satisfy requests of customers, and delivers the blends to a customer's warehouse within 24 hours of receiving an order. What utilities does this distributor provide?

2 Suppose the president of a carpet manufacturing firm has asked you to look into the possibility of bypassing the firm's wholesalers (who sell to carpet, department, and furniture stores) and selling direct to these stores. What caution would you voice on this matter, and what type of information would you gather before making this decision?

3 What type of channel conflict is likely to be caused by dual distribution, and what type of conflict can be reduced by direct distribution? Why?

4 How does the channel captain idea differ among corporate, administered, and contractual vertical marketing systems with particular reference to the use of the different forms of influence available to firms?

5 Comment on this statement: "The only distinction among merchant wholesalers and agents and brokers is that merchant wholesalers take title to the products they sell."

6 How do specialty, shopping, and convenience goods generally relate to intensive, selective, and exclusive distribution? Give a brand name that is an example of each goods-distribution matchup.

CASE 16–1   CRESTON VINEYARDS

Larry Rosenbloom's customers include individuals, retail stores, restaurants, hotels, and even the White House! Because of the many types and large numbers of customers, distribution is as important as production at Creston Vineyards. As Larry explains, "We need distributors in our business . . . as most other [businesses] do, to get the product to the end user, to the consumer."

THE COMPANY

In 1772 Franciscan Padres introduced wine to the La Panza Mountains of California when they founded Mission San Luis Obispo south of what is now San Francisco. The potential of the region for growing grapes remained a secret, however, until 1980 when Stephanie and Larry Rosenbloom purchased an abandoned ranch and started Creston Vineyards. Because it takes several years for vines to grow and produce grapes, Creston did not sell its first wine until 1982. Today, the 569-acre ranch has 155 acres of planted vineyards and produces more than 55,000 cases of eight varieties of wines. The production facilities include a 15,000-square-foot winery and 2,000 square feet of laboratory and office space.

Since 1982 Creston wines have won more than 500 awards in wine tasting events and competitions. In addition, the Rosenblooms are particularly proud of the fact that their wine was served at the inaugurations of Presidents Reagan, Bush, and Clinton. It was at the inaugurations that Creston conceived the concept of an "Artist Collection" of labels—painted by James Paul Brown, who also painted the presidents' portraits. The artistic labels added another dimension of distinctiveness to the Creston products. In fact, Creston's success has attracted the attention of Mondavi, Beringer, Kendall-Jackson, J. Lohr, and several other large Northern California wineries, which have recently purchased land and started vineyards near the Creston location.

THE INDUSTRY AND DISTRIBUTION CHANNELS

The wine industry is undergoing several very interesting changes. First, sales have increased in recent years after a general decline since 1984. The decline was attributed to changing consumer demographics, shifting buying habits, and concerns about the economy. At least some of the recent interest in wine is related to the press reports suggesting the possible health benefits of red wine. A second change is the significant increase in the price of wine due to a low supply of good international wines and changing exchange rates, and an infestation of vine-eating insects (phylloxera) on over 20 percent of California's vineyards. Finally, many wine producers are trying to change the image of wine from a beverage only for special occasions and gourmet foods to a beverage for any occasion.

The industry also faces several distribution challenges. The large number of wine producers and the variety of consumers requires a sophisticated system of distribution channels. By combining different types of intermediaries, the industry is able to meet the requirements of many customers. In addition, because the sale of wine is regulated, the use of multiple distribution channels facilitates the sale of wine in many locations.

One of the most common channels of distribution involves a distributor buying wine directly from the vineyard and reselling it to retail stores and restaurants within a geographic area. Some distributors, however, may not need quantities large enough to warrant purchasing directly from the vineyard. They usually purchase several brands at the same time from a warehouse. A broker may facilitate sales by providing information to distributors, training the distributor's salesforce, and even assisting in sales calls to retailers. John Drady, 1 of 12 brokers for Creston Vineyards explains: "It's very important that we translate our knowledge and our selling skills to the distributor's salespeople so they can, in turn, go out and [sell] more readily on their own."

Other channels are also used by Creston. In California, for example, Creston can sell directly to any customer. The vineyard also sells directly to some large retailers, such as Trader Joe's. Another channel of distribution is through wine clubs, which provide club members with information about wines and an average of six wines per year. The popularity of wine clubs has been increasing and they now account for 15 percent of Creston's sales. The newest type of distribution channel is through online services. Creston now has a page on the World Wide Web that provides information about its wines and allows orders to be shipped directly to consumers in 12 states where direct sales are legal.

THE ISSUES

In an industry with thousands of products and hundreds of producers, Creston is relatively new and small. Selecting and managing its distribution channels to best meet the needs of many constituents is a key task. Providing marketing assistance, product information, and appropriate assortment, transportation, storage, and credit are just a few of the functions the warehouse, brokers, distributors, and retailers may provide as the product moves from the vineyard to the end-user.

Creston also faces a situation where new, and possibly more efficient, channels are becoming available. Direct sales, wine clubs, and online services have generated substantial sales for Creston. Other channels, or new variations of existing channels, may also be available in the future. Overall, Creston must continue to utilize distribution channels to provide value to customers ranging from large retailers, to hotels and restaurants, to individuals, to the White House!

Questions

1 What functions must be performed by intermediaries in the wine industry?

2 What intermediaries and distribution channels are currently used by Creston vineyards?

Supply Chain:
Managing Logistics
For the 21st Century

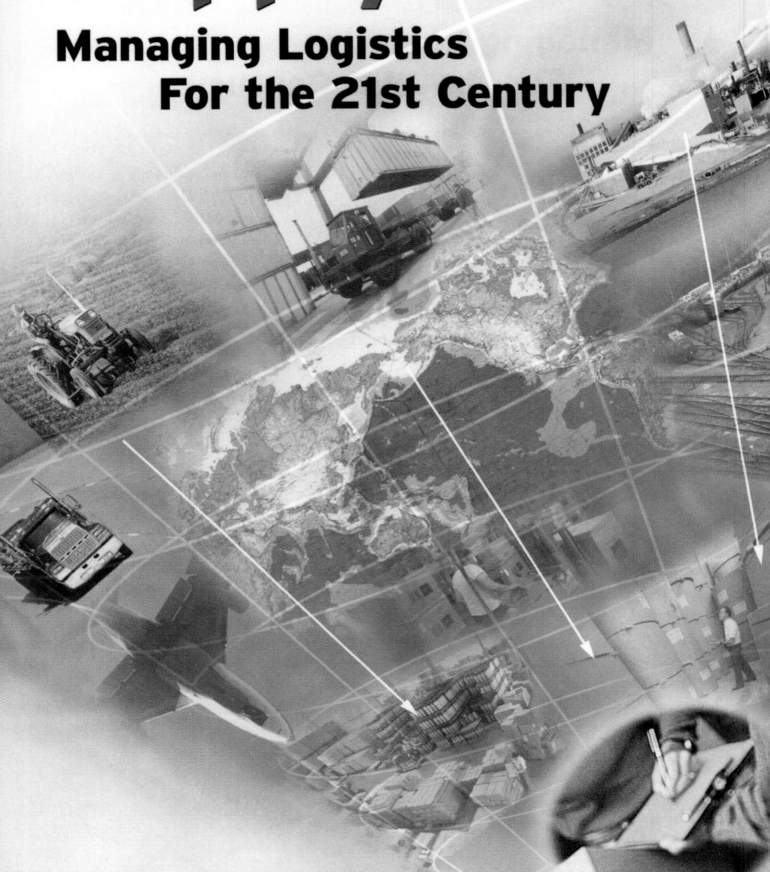

CHAPTER SEVENTEEN

SUPPLY CHAIN AND LOGISTICS MANAGEMENT

17

AFTER READING THIS CHAPTER YOU SHOULD BE ABLE TO:

- Explain what supply chain and logistics management are and how they relate to the marketing mix.

- Understand the nature of logistics trade-offs among transportation, inventory, and other logistics functions.

- Explain how managers trade off different "logistics costs" relative to customer service in order to reach a logistics decision.

- Recognize how customer service in logistics decisions contributes to customer value and successful marketing programs.

- Describe the key logistics functions of transportation, warehousing and materials handling, order processing, and inventory management and the emerging role of third-party logistics providers.

OUCH! EVEN THE BEST COMPANIES CAN FEEL THE STING OF THE BULLWHIP

Bad things can happen to great companies. Just ask Boeing, Hewlett-Packard, Bristol-Myers Squibb, and Procter & Gamble. Each of these industry leaders have experienced the bullwhip's sting at one time or another for one or more of their products.

What is the bullwhip, and why does its sting hurt so bad? Companies define the bullwhip as too much or too little inventory to satisfy customer needs, missed production schedules, and ineffective transportation or delivery caused by miscommunication among material suppliers, manufacturers, and resellers of consumer and industrial goods. Its sting is poor customer service and lost revenue and profit opportunities.

Suppliers, manufacturers, and resellers know that to get a handle on the bullwhip, attention needs to focus on the technology and coordinated activities that make possible the physical flow and transformation of goods from the raw materials stage to the final consumer or industrial user. They also recognize that accurate, timely, and shared information can soften the bullwhip's sting, thereby benefiting customers and companies alike.[1]

Welcome to the unglamorous—but critical—world of supply chain and logistics management. The essence of the problem is simple: It makes no sense to have brilliant marketing programs to sell world-class products if the products aren't available at the right time, at the right place, and in the right form and condition that customers want them. It's finding the continuing solutions through time that's always the problem. This chapter describes the role of supply chains and logistics management in marketing and how a firm balances distribution costs against the need for effective customer service.

SIGNIFICANCE OF SUPPLY CHAIN AND LOGISTICS MANAGEMENT

We often use the term *physical distribution,* but rarely consider its significance in marketing. U.S. companies spend about $500 billion transporting raw materials and finished goods each year and another $375 billion on material handling, warehousing, storage, and holding inventory. Worldwide, these activities cost companies $2 trillion.[2] In this section, we describe contemporary approaches to physical distribution, including supply chains and logistics management and illustrate how each affect elements of the marketing mix.

Relating Marketing Channels, Logistics, and Supply Chain Management

A marketing channel relies on logistics to actually make products available to consumers and industrial users—a point emphasized in the previous chapter. **Logistics** involves those activities that focus on getting the right amount of the right products to the right place at the right time at the lowest possible cost. The performance of these activities is **logistics management,** the practice of organizing the *cost-effective flow* of raw materials, in-process inventory, finished goods, and related information from point of origin to point of consumption to satisfy *customer requirements.*[3]

Three elements of this definition deserve emphasis. First, logistics deals with decisions needed to move a product from the source of raw materials to consumption, or the *flow* of the product. Second, those decisions have to be made in a *cost-effective* manner. While it is important to drive down logistics costs, there is a limit—the third point of emphasis. A firm needs to drive down logistics costs as long as it can deliver expected *customer service,* which mean satisfying customer requirements. The role of management is to see that customer needs are satisfied in the most cost-effective manner. When properly done, the results can be spectacular. Procter & Gamble is a case in point. Beginning in the early 1990s, the company set out to meet the needs of consumers more effectively by collaborating and partnering with its suppliers and retailers to ensure that the right products reached store shelves at the right time and at a lower cost. The effort was judged a success when, during an 18-month period in the late 1990s, P&G's retail customers recorded a $65 million savings in logistics costs while customer service increased.[4]

The Procter & Gamble experience is not an isolated incident. Today, logistics management is embedded in a broader view of physical distribution, consistent with the emphasis on supply and channel partnering described in Chapters 7 and 16. Companies now recognize that getting the right items needed for consumption or production to the right place at the right time in the right condition at the right cost is often beyond their individual capabilities and control. Instead, collaboration, coordination, and information sharing among manufacturers, suppliers, and distributors are necessary to create a seamless flow of goods and services to customers. This perspective is represented in the concept of a supply chain and the practice of supply chain management.

A **supply chain** is a sequence of firms that perform activities required to create and deliver a good or service to consumers or industrial users.[5] It differs from a marketing channel in terms of membership. A supply chain includes suppliers who provide raw material inputs to a manufacturer as well as the wholesalers and retailers who deliver finished goods to you. The management process is also different. **Supply chain management** is the integration and organization of information and logistics activities *across firms* in a supply chain for the purpose of creating and delivering goods and services that provide value to consumers. The relation among marketing channels, logistics management, and supply chain management is shown in Figure 17–1. An important feature of supply chain management is its application of electronic commerce technology. Computers, bar coding, point-of-sale scanners, electronic data

FIGURE 17-1
Relating marketing channels, logistics management, and supply chain management

interchange (EDI), Extranets, and electronic funds transfer (EFT) allow companies to share and operate systems for order processing, transportation scheduling, and inventory management.

Sourcing, Assembling, and Delivering a New Car: The Automotive Supply Chain

All companies are members of one or more supply chains. A supply chain is essentially a sequence of linked suppliers and customers in which every customer is, in turn, a supplier to another customer until a finished product reaches the final consumer. Even a simplified supply chain diagram for U.S. car makers shown in Figure 17–2 illustrates how complex a supply chain can be.[6] A U.S. car maker's supplier network includes thousands of firms. They provide items ranging from raw materials such as steel and rubber to components, including transmissions, tires, brakes, and seats, to complex subassemblies and assemblies evident in chassis and suspension systems that make for a smooth, stable ride. Coordinating and scheduling material and component flows for their assembly into actual automobiles by car makers is heavily dependent on logistical activities, including transportation, order processing, inventory control, materials handling, and information technology. For example, suppliers to the U.S. automotive

FIGURE 17-2
The automotive supply chain

WEB LINK

Saturn: Have It Your Way

Supply chain managers are responsible for having the right products at the right place at the right time at the right price for customers. In the automotive industry, this task is complex given the variety of car options available. To appreciate the challenge, visit the Saturn Web site at www.saturn.com, click pricing center, assemble your own Saturn, immediately obtain the manufacturer's suggested retail price (MSRP), and compare *your* assembled Saturn with a friend's Saturn.

This easy task for you represents a sizeable undertaking for a Saturn supply manager. You may not have realized it, but a Saturn comes in some 3,000 versions, including the retailer-installed accessories you might want. A supply of these accessories has to be available at the Saturn retailer for installation when you want to pick up your new car.

industry belong to the Automotive Network Exchange and must be online. A central link is the car maker supply chain manager, who is responsible for translating customer requirements into actual orders and arranging for delivery dates and financial arrangements for automobile dealers. This is not an easy task given different consumer preferences and the amount consumers are willing to pay. To appreciate the challenge facing supply chain managers, visit the Saturn Web site described in the accompanying Web Link, and assemble your own car based on your preferences and price point.

Logistical aspects of the automobile marketing channel are also an integral part of the supply chain. Major responsibilities include transportation [which involves the selection and oversight of external carriers (trucking, airline, railroad, and shipping companies) for cars and parts to dealers], the operation of distribution centers, the management of finished goods inventories, and order processing for sales. Supply chain managers also play an important role in the marketing channel. They work with extensive car dealer networks to ensure that the right mix of automobiles are delivered to different locations. In addition, they make sure that spare and service parts are available so that dealers can meet the car maintenance and repair needs of consumers. All of this is done with the help of Internet and Extranet technology that links the entire automotive supply chain. What does all of this cost? It is estimated that logistics costs represent 25 percent to 30 percent of the retail price of a typical new car.

Supply Chain Management and Marketing Strategy

Recalling your own shopping experiences can show the critical relationship between marketing and supply chains. Consider your disappointment after traveling to a store—in response to an advertised sale—only to find that the items were out of stock or had been lost or damaged in transit. Imagine how a manufacturer such as Compaq Computer reacts upon learning that the product was not on the shelf, after spending huge sums on its extensive promotional campaign. The bottom line is that poor supply chain management practices can do serious damage to an otherwise excellent marketing strategy. To demonstrate the importance of supply chain management to marketing, consider how a supply chain impacts elements of the marketing mix—product factors, pricing factors, promotional factors, and place factors.

Product Factors   The physical characteristics of the product, as well as its raw materials, will often dictate what kinds of transportation can be used, the length of time inventory can be accumulated, and whether markets can be served from one or many locations. One physical characteristic that has important implications is the perishability of the product, or its *shelf life*. For example, the distribution of fresh foods requires timely transportation and low inventories to minimize spoilage. Time-dated food materials must be kept fresh on the store shelves and not allowed to spoil in the warehouse. These products may require specialized transport and storage facilities, such as refrigerated vehicles. Other products have a very short time frame in which to retain their freshness, such as fresh cut flowers, fresh seafoods, or out-of-town newspapers. These require premium transportation, such as air freight, and, in some cases, they can only be distributed to a regional market. For example, newspapers such as *USA Today* and *The New York Times* are printed in a number of cities around the country for regional distribution the same day.

A supply chain manager's nightmare: how to get this dual-pack on a retailer's shelf while balancing logistics and marketing benefits and costs.

One of the most important links between a product's physical characteristics and logistics is the product package. On the one hand, the marketer views the package as an important point-of-purchase promotional device. On the other hand, there are many logistical implications associated with the packaging decision. Does the protective packaging reduce the density of the products so that less product can be loaded into the transport vehicle or warehouse? If so, logistics costs will increase. Does the product's package require it to be placed in an exterior package or carton? In this case, additional handling will be required at the retail level to prepare the product for sale. As described in the accompanying Ethics and Social Responsibility Alert, package features can make handling, stacking, filling, or disposing of the package more difficult, and once again logistics costs will increase.[7]

Pricing Factors   Pricing interacts with a supply chain in several ways. As mentioned in the discussion of geographical pricing adjustments in Chapter 15, price quotations such as FOB origin assign responsibility for arranging and paying for transportation services to the buyer. Logistics costs are also important for determining quantity discounts. According to the Robinson-Patman Act, the "cost justification" defense for discriminatory prices limits discounts to differences in the cost of manufacture, sale, or delivery of various quantities. Although in practice it may be difficult to adequately document differences in selling or manufacturing costs, transportation rate structures make quantity discounts provided by the carrier easy to document for regulators.

Promotional Factors   Promotion interacts with logistics in the areas of advertising, sales promotion, and personal selling. Advertising and promotional campaigns must be planned and coordinated with the logistics system to ensure product availability at the appropriate time. For example, General Motors learned that an eight-week wait was a big turn-off for Floridians thinking about buying a Cadillac, 11 percent of whom then bought a car from a competitor rather than wait for delivery. Cadillac is

ETHICS AND SOCIAL RESPONSIBILITY ALERT

ETHICS

What Are the Social Costs of Packaging?

Some experts believe that the logistic systems of many firms depend too heavily on packaging. While efficient packaging materials allow a firm to use cheaper modes of transportation or less specialized warehouse services, these benefits are offset by costs imposed on society in general. Specifically, what should society do with the excessive packaging that comes with the product? In many cases, the packaging material is difficult to dispose of or is quickly filling landfills. Fur-

ther, the focus on recycled products is a complicated issue and has its own costs and benefits. For example, Procter & Gamble has just introduced a plastic bottle for its Ultra Downy fabric softener that is made of 100 percent recycled plastic. However, because P&G will color the bottle as part of its marketing program, the bottle will be difficult to recycle once it is used.

What are the benefits and costs to society of such packaging trends? What should communities do to counter the trend of overpackaging? What are the responsibilities of global citizens to counteract the trend of overpackaging?

testing the feasibility of customer responsiveness as a competitive differentiator with the objective of delivering popularly configured Cadillacs to customers immediately from dealers' lots, with overnight delivery if the vehicle isn't available on site. For those customers who desire a more custom configuration, Cadillac is taking their orders, assembling and delivering their exact Cadillacs within three weeks under the "Cadillac Custom Rapid Delivery" process.[8] So distribution can and must be synchronized to ensure timely and efficient handling of orders.

Place Factors   It is the responsibility of logistics to get the product to the right place at the right time in usable conditions. Logistics also plays an important part in determining where a firm locates its plants and distribution centers relative to markets. Such decisions must consider transportation costs as well as the ability of the product to be transported long distances and be stored for long periods of time.

Effective logistics can also help gain access to key distribution outlets. In the Nike-Reebok "sneaker war," two critical market segments are teens and Generation X buyers, who are often willing to pay $80, $90, or more for a pair of shoes. These segments are core customers of the Foot Locker chain. Recently, Nike has been winning in Foot Locker sales because—among other things—Reebok needs to overhaul its information-tracking system and fix its distribution snags, which have resulted in limited customer exposure to its lines in Foot Locker outlets.[9]

CONCEPT CHECK

1. What is the principal difference between a marketing channel and a supply chain?

2. How does logistics interact with the product element of the marketing mix?

LOGISTICS MANAGEMENT OBJECTIVE IN A SUPPLY CHAIN

The objective of logistics management in a supply chain is to minimize relevant logistics costs while delivering maximum customer service. Realizing this objective often requires assistance from outside logistics specialists and consultants and highly specialized computer programming and software to track cost and service variables.

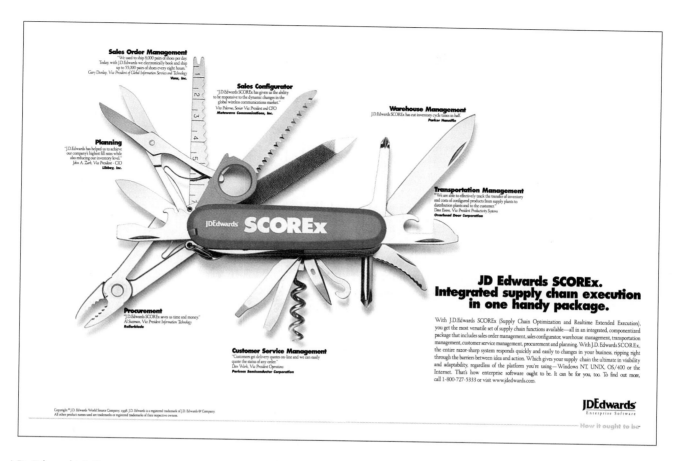

J.D. Edwards & Company is an internationally recognized supply chain management consulting firm.

J.D. Edwards & Company

This becomes apparent in the description of logistics costs and customer service that follows.

Total Logistics Cost Concept

For our purposes **total logistics cost** includes expenses associated with transportation, materials handling and warehousing, inventory, stockouts (being out of inventory), and order processing. A more complete list of decisions that are associated with the flow of product and make up total logistics cost includes the following: [10]

- Transportation.
- Warehousing and storage.
- Packaging.
- Materials handling.
- Inventory control.
- Order processing.
- Customer service level.
- Plant and warehouse site location.
- Return goods handling.

Note that many of these costs are interrelated so that changes in one will impact the others. For example, as the firm attempts to minimize its transportation costs by shipping in larger quantities, it will also experience an increase in inventory levels. Larger inventory levels will not only increase inventory costs but should also reduce stockouts. It is important, therefore, to study the impact on all of the logistics decision areas when considering a change.

FIGURE 17–3
How total logistics cost varies with number of warehouses used

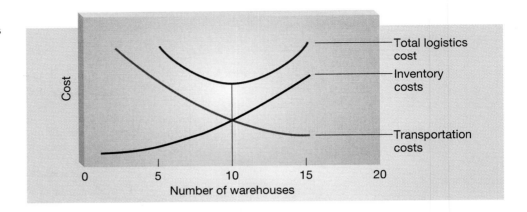

Figure 17–3 provides a graphic example. An oft-used supply chain strategy is for a firm to have a number of warehouses, which receive shipments in large quantities and then redistribute smaller shipments to local customers. As the number of warehouses increases, inventory costs rise and transportation costs fall. That is, more inventory is warehoused, but it is transported in volume closer to customers. The net effect is to minimize the total costs of logistics shown in Figure 17–3 by having 10 warehouses. This means the total cost curve is minimized at a point where neither of the two individual cost elements is at a minimum but the overall system is.

Studying its total logistics cost has had revolutionary consequences for National Semiconductor, which produces computer chips. In two years it cut its standard delivery time 47 percent, reduced distribution costs 2.5 percent, and increased sales 34 percent by shutting down six warehouses around the world and air-freighting its microchips from its huge distribution center in Singapore. It does this even though it has six factories in Israel, Britain, and the United States. National also discovered that a lot of its chips were actually profit-losers, and it cut the number of products it sells by 45 percent, thereby simplifying logistics and increasing profits.[11]

Customer Service Concept

If a supply chain is a *flow,* the end of it—or *output*—is the service delivered to customers. However, service can be expensive. One firm found that to increase on-time delivery from a 95 percent rate to a 100 percent rate tripled total logistics costs. Higher levels of service require tactics such as more inventory to reduce stockouts, more expensive transportation to improve speed and lessen damage, and double or triple checking of orders to ensure correctness. A firm's goal should be to provide adequate customer service while controlling logistics costs. Customer service is now seen not merely as an expense but as a means to increase customer satisfaction and sales. For example, a 3M survey about customer service among 18,000 European customers in 16 countries revealed surprising agreement in all countries about the importance of customer service. Respondents stressed factors such as condition of product delivered, on-time delivery, quick delivery after order placement, and effective handling of problems.[12]

Within the context of a supply chain, **customer service** is the ability of logistics management to satisfy users in terms of time, dependability, communication, and convenience.[13] As suggested by Figure 17–4, a supply chain manager's key task is to balance these four customer service factors against total logistics cost factors.

Time   In a supply chain setting, time refers to **lead time** for an item, which means the lag from ordering an item until it is received and ready for use or sale. This is also referred to as *order cycle time* or *replenishment time* and may be more important to re-

FIGURE 17–4

Logistics managers balance total logistics cost factors against customer service factors

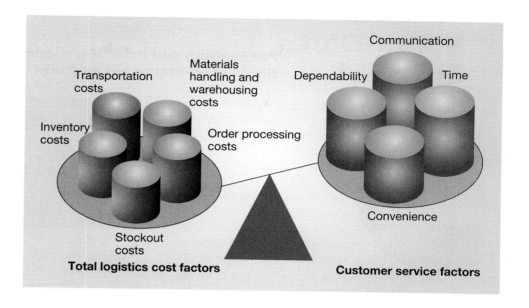

tailers or wholesalers than consumers. The various elements that make up the typical order cycle include recognition of the need to order, order transmittal, order processing, documentation, and transportation. A current emphasis in supply chain management is to reduce lead time so that the inventory levels of customers may be minimized. Another emphasis is to make the process of reordering and receiving products as simple as possible, often through electronic data and inventory systems called **quick response** and **efficient consumer response** delivery systems.[14] These inventory management systems are designed to reduce the retailer's lead time for receiving merchandise, thereby lowering a retailer's inventory investment, improving customer service levels, and reducing logistics expense (see the accompanying Marketing NewsNet).[15] The order processing portion of lead time will be discussed later in this chapter.

Dependability   Dependability is the consistency of replenishment. This is important to all firms in a supply chain and to consumers. It can be broken into three elements: consistent lead time, safe delivery, and complete delivery. Consistent service allows planning (such as appropriate inventory levels), whereas inconsistencies create surprises. Intermediaries may be willing to accept longer lead times if they know about them in advance and can thus make plans. While surprise delays may shut down a production line, early deliveries will be almost as troublesome because of the problems of storing the extra inventory. Dependability is essential for the just-in-time strategies discussed at the end of the chapter.

Communication   Communication is a two-way link between buyer and seller that helps in monitoring service and anticipating future needs. Status reports on orders are a typical example of improved communication between buyer and seller. The increased communication capability of transportation carriers has enhanced the accuracy of such tracing information and improved the ability of buyers to schedule shipments. Note, however, that such information is still reactive and is not a substitute for consistent on-time deliveries. Therefore, some firms have partnered with firms specializing in logistics in an effort to institutionalize a more proactive flow of useful information that, in turn, improves on-time deliveries. Hewlett-Packard (HP), a high-tech computer printer manufacturer, recently turned its inbound raw materials over to a logistics firm, Roadway Logistics. HP lets Roadway manage the warehousing and coordinate parts delivery so that HP can focus on its printer business. In the process, HP estimates it has cut its warehouse operating costs by about 10 percent.[16]

MARKETING NEWSNET

For Fashion and Food Merchandising, Haste Is as Important as Taste

Fashion and food have a lot in common. Both depend a lot on taste and both require timely merchandising. By its nature, fashion dictates that suppliers and retailers be able to adjust to new styles, colors, and different seasons. Fashion retailers need to identify what's hot so it can be ordered quickly and what's not to avoid markdowns. Saks Fifth Avenue has employed a *quick response* delivery system for fashion merchandise since the mid 1990s. Saks' point-of-sale scanner system records each day's sales. When stock falls below a minimum level, the system automatically generates a replenishment order. Vendors of fashion merchandise, such as Donna Karan, receive an electronic order, which is processed within 48 hours.

Food marketers and retailers use the term *efficient consumer response* to describe their replenishment systems. All major food companies, including General Mills, Del Monte, Heinz, Nestlé, and Beatrice Foods, rely on EDI technology to minimize stockouts of popular items and overstocks of slow-moving items. Lowered retailer inventories and efficient logistics practices have been projected to save U.S. grocery shoppers $30 billion a year.

Convenience   The concept of convenience for a supply chain manager means that there should be a minimum of effort on the part of the buyer in doing business with the seller. Is it easy for the customer to order? Are the products available from many outlets? Does the buyer have to buy huge quantities of the product? Will the seller arrange all necessary details, such as transportation? The seller must concentrate on removing unnecessary barriers to customer convenience. This customer service factor has promoted the use of vendor-managed inventory practices discussed later in the chapter.

Customer Service Standards

Firms that operate effective supply chains usually develop a set of written customer service standards. These serve as objectives and provide a benchmark against which results can be measured for control purposes. In developing these standards, information is collected on customers' needs. It is also necessary to know what competitors offer as well as the willingness of customers to pay a bit more for better service. After these and similar questions are answered, realistic standards are set and an ongoing monitoring program is established. Note that the examples in Figure 17–5 suggest that customer service standards will differ by type of firm.

FIGURE 17–5
Examples of customer service standards

TYPE OF FIRM	CUSTOMER SERVICE STANDARD
Wholesaler	At least 98% of orders filled accurately
Manufacturer	Order cycle time of no more than 5 days
Retailer	Returns accepted within 30 days
Airline	At least 90% of arrivals on time
Trucker	A maximum of 5% loss and damage per year
Restaurant	Lunch served within 5 minutes of order

CONCEPT CHECK

1. What is a current strategy adopted by firms attempting to squeeze costs from their logistics system while delivering customer service?

2. In what ways do key customer service factors differ between a manufacturer and a retailer?

3. What is the relationship between transportation costs and volume shipped? What impact does it have on the pricing of the firm?

KEY LOGISTICS FUNCTIONS IN A SUPPLY CHAIN

Penske and Emery Worldwide are two third-party logistics providers that perform most or all of the logistics functions that manufacturers, suppliers, and distributors would normally perform.

Penske
www.penske.com

Emery Worldwide
www.emeryworld.com

The four key logistic functions in a supply chain include (1) transportation, (2) warehousing and materials handling, (3) order processing, and (4) inventory management. These functions have become so complex and interrelated that many companies have outsourced them to third-party logistics providers. **Third-party logistics providers** are firms that perform most or all of the logistics functions that manufacturers, suppliers, and distributors would normally perform themselves.[17] Today, nearly 70 percent of manufacturers listed in the *Fortune* 500 outsource one or more logistics functions, at least on a limited basis. Ryder, UPS Worldwide Logistics, FedEx, Roadway Logistics, Emery Worldwide, Global Logistics, and Penske are just a few of the companies that specialize in handling logistics functions for their clients. For example, UPS Worldwide Logistics manages the distribution of Allied Signal's FRAM, Bendix, and Autolite products made in North America to 10,000 customer locations across the continent. Roadway Logistics Services handles the inbound and outbound shipments of Dell computers. The four major logistics functions and the involvement of third-party logistics providers are described in detail next.

United Airlines Cargo
provides fast, global
delivery—often
utilizing containers.

United Airlines
www.ual.com

is often carried as cargo in the luggage space of scheduled passenger flights. This strategy allows the airline to utilize excess capacity that would otherwise be lost.

Freight Forwarders   **Freight forwarders,** already mentioned a number of times, are firms that accumulate small shipments into larger lots and then hire a carrier to move them, usually at reduced rates. Recall that transportation companies provide rate incentives for larger quantities. Forwarders collect many small shipments consigned to a common destination and pay the carrier the lower rate based on larger volume, so they often convert shipments that are less-than-truckload (LTL) into full truckloads, thereby receiving better shipping rates. The rates charged by the forwarder to the individual shippers, in turn, are somewhat less than the small quantity rate, and the difference is the forwarder's margin. In general, the shipment receives improved service at lower cost. While forwarders may specialize in a particular mode—such as air freight—they are available for all modes of transportation. International freight forwarders play an equally important role in the export/import trades.

Air freight forwarders are an example of specialization in one transportation mode. In some cases, airlines will subcontract excess space to *air freight forwarders* or *express companies,* which are firms that market air express services to the general public. Where markets are large enough, major airlines have responded with pure air freight service between specific airports—often involving international destinations.

Warehousing and Materials Handling

Warehouses may be classified in one of two ways: (1) storage warehouses and (2) distribution centers. In *storage warehouses* the goods are intended to come to rest for some period of time, as in the aging of products or in storing household goods. *Distri-*

bution centers, on the other hand, are designed to facilitate the timely movement of goods and represent a very important part of a supply chain. They represent the second most significant cost in a supply chain after transportation.

Distribution centers not only allow firms to hold their stock in decentralized locations but are also used to facilitate sorting and consolidating products from different plants or different suppliers. Some physical transformation can also take place in distribution centers such as mixing or blending different ingredients, labeling, and repackaging. Paint companies such as Sherwin-Williams and Benjamin Moore use distribution centers for this purpose. In addition, distribution centers may serve as manufacture sales offices, described in Chapter 16, and order processing centers.

Materials handling, which involves moving goods over short distances into, within, and out of warehouses and manufacturing plants, is a key part of warehouse operations. The two major problems with this activity are high labor costs and high rates of loss and damage. Every time an item is handled, there is a chance for loss or damage. Common materials handling equipment includes forklifts, cranes, and conveyors. Recently, materials handling in warehouses has been automated by using computers and robots to reduce the cost of holding, moving, and recording the inventories of stores.

Order Processing

There are several stages in the processing of an order, and a failure at any one of them can cause a problem with the customer. The process starts with transmitting the order by a variety of means such as the Internet, an Extranet, or electronic data interchange (EDI). This is followed by entering the order in the appropriate databases and sending the information to those needing it. For example, a regional warehouse is notified to prepare an order. After checking inventory, a new quantity may need to be reordered from the production line, or purchasing may be requested to reorder from a vendor. If the item is currently out of stock, a "backorder" is created, and the whole process of

Materials handling through automation.

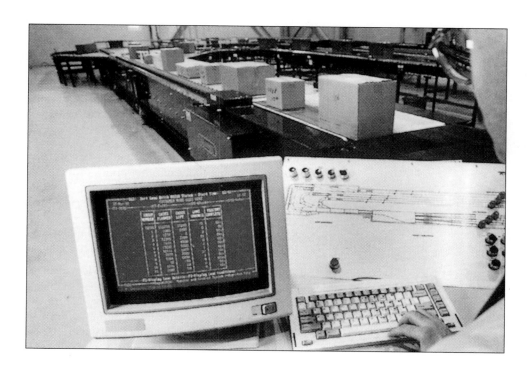

keeping track of a small part of the original order must be managed. In addition, credit may have to be checked for some customers, all documentation associated with the order must be prepared, transportation must be arranged, and a confirmation of the order must be sent. Order processing systems are generally evaluated in terms of speed and accuracy.

Electronic order processing has replaced manual processing for most large companies.[18] For example, IBM expects to be doing business electronically with all of its suppliers, either on the Internet or through EDI by 2000. Kiwi Brands, the Douglassville, Pennsylvania, marketer of Kiwi shoe polish, Endust, Behold, and Ty-D-Bol, receives 75 percent of its retailers' purchase orders via EDI. The company has also implemented financial EDI, sending invoices to retailers and receiving payment order/remittance advice documents and electronic funds transfer (EFT) payments. Shippers as well are linked to the system, allowing Kiwi to receive shipment status messages electronically.

Inventory Management

Inventory management is one of the primary responsibilities of the supply chain manager. The major problem is maintaining the delicate balance between too little and too much. Too little inventory may result in poor service, stockouts, brand switching, and loss of market share; too much leads to higher costs because of the money tied up in inventory and the chance that it may become obsolete. Remember the sting of the bullwhip described at the beginning of the chapter?

Creative inventory management practices can make possible cost savings in the supply chain. For example, IBM has begun closing many of its parts warehouses because Federal Express's reliable overnight delivery (see the Marketing NewsNet box) enables FedEx to inventory high-priced IBM parts at its sorting hubs and deliver them quickly to IBM customers.[19]

Reasons for Inventory   Traditionally, carrying inventory has been justified on several grounds: (1) to offer a buffer against variations in supply and demand, often caused by uncertainty in forecasting demand; (2) to provide better service for those customers who wish to be served on demand; (3) to promote production efficiencies; (4) to provide a hedge against price increases by suppliers; (5) to promote purchasing and transportation discounts; and (6) to protect the firm from contingencies such as strikes and shortages.

Inventory Costs   Specific inventory costs are often hard to detect because they are difficult to measure and occur in many different parts of the firm. A classification of inventory costs includes the following:

- *Capital costs.* The opportunity costs resulting from tying up funds in inventory instead of using them in other, more profitable investments; these are related to interest rates.
- *Inventory service costs.* Items such as insurance and taxes that are present in many states.
- *Storage costs.* Warehousing space and materials handling.
- *Risk costs.* Possible loss, damage, pilferage, perishability, and obsolescence.

Storage costs, risk costs, and some service costs vary according to the characteristics of the item inventoried. For example, perishable products or highly seasonal items have higher risk costs than a commodity type product such as lumber. Capital costs are always present and are proportional to the *values* of the item and prevailing interest rates. The costs of carrying inventory vary with the particular circumstances but quite easily could range from 10 to 35 percent for different firms.

MARKETING NEWSNET

Fly-by-Night Idea + Customer Service + KISS = Federal Express

GLOBAL

Armed with one of his college term papers, which got a C– grade, Frederick W. Smith didn't build a better mousetrap and wait for the world to beat a path to his door. Instead, he set out to show the world that with his simple new innovation *he* could beat a path to everybody else's door.

He gave the name *Federal Express* to his door-to-door parcel service that uses orange, white, and purple jets. And he advertised "absolutely, positively overnight" delivery for his small-parcel service—limited to 70 pounds, the weight one person can carry. "I figured we had to be enormously reliable," says Smith, "since our service is frequently used for expensive spare parts, live organs, or other emergency shipments."

But Federal Express (FedEx) isn't your typical "fly-by-night" outfit. After all, Smith *did* write his term paper at Yale, and he *did* use a family trust of $4 million to get started—and Federal Express *did* lose $27 million in its first 26 months of operation.

What Smith had was a good idea, a good understanding of customer service, and the tenacity and resources to stick with it. First, Smith reasoned, he had to own his own jet aircraft so *all* parcels could be picked

up early in the evening, flown to a single sorting center (Memphis), and rerouted to their final destination before dawn. The KISS (keep it simple, stupid) concept worked to the company's advantage in the early years. Always looking for a better idea, FedEx introduced "FedEx Ship"—a shipping software solution in both Mac and Windows™ versions that lets any customer order pickups, print their shipping labels, and track their express deliveries without touching a telephone. Of course, FedEx benefits, too, by cutting telephone traffic and package pickup costs, and also eliminating paperwork errors that might impact sorting.

Supply Chain Inventory Strategies Conventional wisdom a decade ago was that a firm should protect itself against uncertainty by maintaining a reserve inventory at each of its production and stocking points. This has been described as a "just-in-case" philosophy of inventory management and led to unnecessary high levels of inventory. In contrast is the **just-in-time (JIT) concept,** which is an inventory supply system that operates with very low inventories and requires fast, on-time delivery. When parts are needed for production, they arrive from suppliers "just in time," which means neither before nor after they are needed. Note that JIT is used in situations where demand forecasting is reliable, such as when supplying an automobile production line, and is not suitable for inventories that are to be stored over significant periods of time.

Saturn's manufacturing operation in Spring Hill, Tennessee, uses a sophisticated JIT system. A central computerized system directs trucks to deliver pre-inspected parts at specific times 21 hours a day, six days a week to one of the plant's 56 receiving docks. Incredibly, the JIT system must coordinate Saturn's 339 suppliers located in 39 states, each supplier being an average of 550 miles away from the Spring Hill facility. Does the JIT system work for Saturn? The answer is a resounding yes. The Saturn production line has been shut down only once—for 18 minutes!—because the right part was not delivered at the right place and time.

The key to Saturn's JIT system: a Ryder truck driver downloads a key-shaped floppy disk from an on-board computer to get delivery instructions.

Ryder System, Inc.
www.ryder.com

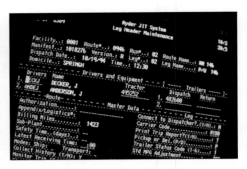

Ryder Integrated Logistics is charged with making Saturn's JIT system work smoothly. Ryder long-haul trucks and their drivers are the most expensive part of the system. The key—very literally—to this JIT system is a computer disk in the form of a plastic key that drivers plug into an on-truck computer. The computer screen then tells the driver where to go, the route to use, and how much time to spend getting there.[20]

Electronic data interchange and electronic messaging technology coupled with the constant pressure for faster response time in replenishing inventory has also changed the way suppliers and customers do business in a supply chain. The approach, called **vendor-managed inventory** (VMI), is an inventory-management system whereby the *supplier* determines the product amount and assortment a customer (such as a retailer) needs and automatically delivers the appropriate items.[21]

Campbell Soup's system illustrates how VMI works.[22] Campbell first establishes EDI links with retailers. Every morning, retailers electronically inform the company of their demand for all Campbell products and the inventory levels in their distribution centers. Campbell uses that information to forecast future demand and determine which products need replenishment based on upper and lower inventory limits previously established with each retailer. Trucks leave the Campbell shipping plant that afternoon and arrive at the retailer's distribution centers with the required replenishments the same day.

Closing the Loop: Reverse Logistics

The flow of goods in a supply chain does not end with the consumer or industrial user. Companies today recognize that a supply chain can work in reverse.[23] **Reverse logistics** is a process of reclaiming recyclable and reusable materials, returns, and reworks from the point of consumption or use for repair, remanufacturing, or disposal. The effect of reverse logistics can be seen in the reduced amount of waste in landfills and lowered operating costs for companies.

Companies such as Eastman Kodak (reusable cameras) and Hewlett-Packard (printer toner cartridges returned for filling) have implemented successful reverse logistics programs. Other firms have enlisted third-party logistics providers to handle this process along with other supply chain functions. GNB Technologies, Inc., a manufacturer of lead-acid batteries for automobiles and boats, has outsourced much of its supply chain activity to UPS Worldwide Logistics (WWL).[24] The company contracts with WWL to manage its shipments between plants, distribution centers, recycling centers, and retailers. This includes movement of both new batteries and used products destined for recycling and covers both truck and railroad shipments. This partnership along with the initiatives of other battery makers has paid economic and ecological dividends. By recycling 90 percent of the lead from used batteries, manufacturers have kept the demand for new lead in check, thereby holding down costs to consumers. Also, solid waste management costs and the environmental impact of lead in landfills is reduced.

CONCEPT CHECK

1. What are the basic trade-offs between the modes of transportation?

2. What types of inventory should use storage warehouses and which type should use distribution centers?

3. What are the strengths and weaknesses of a just-in-time system?

SUMMARY

1   Logistics involves those activities that focus on getting the right amount of the right products to the right place at the right time at the lowest possible cost. Logistics management includes the coordination of the flows of both inbound and outbound goods, an emphasis on making these flows cost-effective, and customer service.

2   A supply chain is a sequence of firms that perform activities required to create and deliver a good or service to consumers or industrial users. Supply chain management is the integration and organization of information and logistics across firms for the purpose of creating value for consumers.

3   Although some marketers may pay little attention to logistics, they do so at their own peril. Logistics directly affects the success of the marketing program and all elements of the marketing mix.

4   The total logistics cost concept suggests that a system of interrelated costs is present such as transportation, materials handling and warehousing, inventory, and stockout costs.

5   Minimizing total logistics cost is irrelevant without specifying an acceptable customer service level that must be maintained. Although key customer service factors depend on the situation, important elements of the customer service program are likely to be time-related dependability, communications, and convenience.

6   Four key logistics in a supply chain include (a) transportation, (b) warehousing and material handling, (c) order processing, and (d) inventory management. Third-party logistics perform most or all of the logistics functions that manufacturers, suppliers, and distributors would normally perform themselves.

7   The modes of transportation (e.g., railroads, motor carriers, air carriers, and trucks) offer shippers different service benefits. Better service often costs more, although it should result in savings in other areas of the logistics system.

8   The function of warehousing and material handling in a supply chain is to facilitate storage and movement of goods. Distribution centers provide flexibility and facilitate sorting and consolidating products from different plants or different suppliers.

9   Inventory management and order processing go hand in hand in a supply chain. Both functions have benefited from the technology of electronic commerce. Two popular supply chain inventory management practices are just-in-time and vendor-managed inventory management systems.

10   Reverse logistics closes the loop in a supply chain. Reverse logistics is the process of reclaiming recyclable and reusable materials, returns, and reworks from the point of consumption or use for repair, remanufacturing, or disposal.

KEY TERMS AND CONCEPTS

logistics p. 444
logistics management p. 444
supply chain p. 444
supply chain management p. 444
total logistics cost p. 449
customer service p. 450
lead time p. 450
quick response p. 451

efficient consumer response p. 451
third-party logistics providers p. 453
intermodal transportation p. 454
freight forwarders p. 456
materials handling p. 457
just-in-time (JIT) concept p. 459
vendor-managed inventory p. 460
reverse logistics p. 460

INTERNET EXERCISE

Third-party logistics providers play an important role in supply chain management. Their numbers continue to increase as marketers look to their expertise and experience in implementing key logistics functions.

The Virtual Logistics Directory (www.logisticdirectory.com) lists many third-party logistics providers and supply chain management consulting firms. Visit the Directory and select the Integrated Logistics category. Go

through the listing with an eye toward answering the following two questions:

1 Which of the four key logistics functions described in the chapter are provided most often and second most often by companies listed in the Directory?
2 What percentage of the listed companies offers services outside North America?

APPLYING MARKETING CONCEPTS AND PERSPECTIVES

1 List several companies to which logistical activities might be unimportant. Also list several whose focus is only on the inbound or outbound side.
2 Give an example of how logistical activities might affect trade promotion strategies.
3 What are some types of businesses in which order processing may be among the paramount success factors?
4 What behavioral problems might arise to negate the logistics concept within the firm?
5 List the customer service factors that would be vital to buyers in the following types of companies: (*a*) manufacturing, (*b*) retailing, (*c*) hospitals, and (*d*) construction.

6 Name some cases when extremely high service levels (e.g., 99 percent) would be warranted.
7 Name the mode of transportation that would be the best for the following products: (*a*) farm machinery, (*b*) cut flowers, (*c*) frozen meat, and (*d*) coal.
8 The auto industry is a heavy user of the just-in-time concept. Why? What other industries would be good candidates for its application? What do they have in common?
9 Look again at Figure 17–3. Explain why as the number of warehouses increases, (*a*) inventory costs rise and (*b*) transportation costs fall.

CASE 17–1 NAVISTAR INTERNATIONAL

How important is supply chain and logistics management in today's business environment? Just ask managers at the Navistar International Corporation, which produces up to 400 customized trucks each day!

THE COMPANY

Navistar International is one of the largest manufacturers of medium and heavy trucks in the world. Much of its success can be attributed to the sophisticated use of micromarketing actions that deliver a customized truck equipped with features designed to improve the productivity of each specific customer. This strategy, however, created a problem—a huge inventory of parts. Tailoring a truck to the unique needs of each buyer requires that Navistar keep 80,000 parts, some of which are needed by only one or just a few customers.

Navistar's success is also the result of superior product quality. The manufacturing department focuses much

of its effort on ensuring that there are few defects in Navistar trucks. This attention to quality, however, slowed the manufacturing process so that Navistar's order cycle time reached 100 days. In fact, one measure of manufacturing efficiency, the percentage of trucks delivered to the customer on time, indicated that 40 percent of Navistar's deliveries were late.

Managers at Navistar realized that to satisfy customer requirements they needed to reduce order cycle time and inventory costs while maintaining high-quality customized products. Logistics management approaches, which balance the needs of the sales, engineering, and manufacturing departments, were an obvious potential solution.

LOGISTICS MANAGEMENT AT NAVISTAR

In response to these issues, Navistar developed an elaborate material requirement planning (MRP) system to manage the purchase of parts and components from its many suppliers. Navistar also developed an electronic data interchange (EDI) with its major suppliers that allowed specifications, quotes, purchase orders, invoices, and even payments to be made electronically. The system was responsible for the elimination of millions of pieces of paper and the errors and inefficiencies caused by the manual processing of thousands of orders. Finally, a just-in-time system (JIT) was added to match deliveries of supplies with its manufacturing requirements.

These systems have helped Navistar begin to integrate the many complex tasks of producing custom-built trucks. In addition, the systems have helped dealers to improve their customer service. Dealers can now submit their orders electronically and receive information about the lead time of the specified components and the probable delivery date of the completed truck. In the future, as Navistar continues to improve its systems, current status of orders, delivery schedule adjustments, and other important information should be available to dealers.

Navistar has set challenging goals for its logistics management systems. First, it hopes to achieve 100 percent on-time delivery ("slot credibility"). Second, managers hope that Navistar can reduce its order cycle time to 30 to 45 days. Finally, the company is determined to minimize inventory. Overall, Navistar believes these changes will represent increased value for its customers and allow Navistar to maintain its dominant position in the truck market.

Questions

1   What factors helped Navistar managers realize that logistics management approaches might help them better satisfy customer requirements?
2   What systems did Navistar develop to improve its production process? How can Navistar measure their impact?
3   Explain how the new systems have improved Navistar's customer service.

Lowest Prices on Earth

HEWLETT®
PACKARD

HP Omnibook XE Celeron-266 4.0GB

EGGHEAD.COM
$1,559 20 *

BUYCOMP.COM
$1,419 95 *

Corel Gallery 1,000,000

BEYOND.COM
$99 95 *

BUYSOFT.COM
$86 95 *

Bella Tuscany by Frances Mayes

AMAZON.COM
$15 00 *

BUYBOOKS.COM
$12 50 *

Rounders *DVD*
©Buena Vista Home Entertainment, Inc. Rated R

REEL.COM
$20 99 *

BUYVIDEOS.COM
$14 99 *

Vigilante 8

EBWORLD.COM
$54 99 *

BUYGAMES.COM
$48 95 *

Will Smith *Big Willie Style*

NEW!

CDNOW.COM
$12 58 *

BUYMUSIC.COM
$9 95 *

BUY.COM
The Internet Superstore

BUYCOMP.COM   BUYSOFT.COM   BUYBOOKS.COM   BUYVIDEOS.COM   BUYGAMES.COM   BUYMUSIC.CO

CHAPTER EIGHTEEN

RETAILING

18

AFTER READING THIS CHAPTER YOU SHOULD BE ABLE TO:

- Identify retailers in terms of the utilities they provide.

- Explain the alternative ways to classify retail outlets.

- Understand the many methods of nonstore retailing.

- Classify retailers in terms of the retail positioning matrix.

- Develop retailing mix strategies over the life cycle of a retail store.

THE LOWEST PRICES ON EARTH!

What would you say to someone who proposed a business that sells dollars for 85 cents? Probably something like "you're crazy" or "that can't work long"! Well, Scott Blum, CEO of Buy.com, has heard both statements many times, but he isn't listening. His online retail business sells consumer products at or below cost. The company's goal is to become the name all consumers associate with low price, and it is emphasized in Buy.com's advertising, which claims to offer "the lowest prices on Earth."

How does Blum do it? First, his software searches competitors' Web sites to make sure that Buy.com's prices are the lowest—even if it means selling at a loss. The second part of his business idea is to make up the deficit by selling advertising space on the Web site. And how is it going? The company currently has more than $15 million in sales each month—a pace likely to make it the fastest growing company in U.S. history. In addition, the company is so optimistic about its growth that it recently purchased more than 2,000 additional domain names that begin with "buy." to allow for expansion into specific product categories.[1]

If you still think it's a crazy idea you may be right. A business based only on price, with little attention to customer service, selection, or other dimensions of the traditional retail experience would be unique. Losing money on every sale is also contrary to the standard notion of selling at a profit. However, if Buy.com succeeds, retailing will truly never be the same, and consumers will have never had it better!

Buy.com is just one example of the dynamic and exciting nature of retailing today. This chapter examines the critical role retailing plays as a component of many distribution channels and the challenging decisions retailers face as they strive to create value for their customers.

What types of products will consumers buy directly through catalogs, the mail, computers, or telephone? In what type of store will consumers look for products they don't buy directly? How important is the location of the store? Will customers expect services such as alterations, delivery, installation, or repair? What price should be charged for each product? These are difficult and important questions that are an integral part of retailing. In the channel of distribution, retailing is where the customer meets the product. It is through retailing that exchange (a central aspect of marketing) occurs. **Retailing** includes all activities involved in selling, renting, and providing goods and services to ultimate customers for personal, family, or household use.

THE VALUE OF RETAILING

Retailing is an important marketing activity. Not only do producers and consumers meet through retailing actions, but retailing also creates customer value and has a significant impact on the economy. To consumers, the value of retailing is in the form of utilities provided. Retailing's economic value is represented by the people employed in retailing as well as by the total amount of money exchanged in retail sales.

Consumer Utilities Offered by Retailing

The utilities provided by retailers create value for consumers. Time, place, possession, and form utilities are offered by most retailers in varying degrees, but one utility is often emphasized more than others. Look at Figure 18–1 to see how well you can match the retailer with the utility being emphasized in the description.

Providing minibanks in supermarkets, as Wells Fargo does, puts the bank's products and services close to the consumer, providing place utility. By providing financing or leasing and taking used cars as trade-ins, Saturn makes the purchase easier and provides possession utility. Form utility—production or alteration of a product—is offered by Levi Strauss & Co. as it creates "Original Spin" jeans to meet each customer's specifications. Finding toy shelves stocked in May is the time utility dreamed

FIGURE 18–1
Which company best represents which utilities?

Wells Fargo www.wellsfargo.com	One of the best-run banks in the United States, Wells Fargo is intensifying its drive to reach retail customers by opening mini-banks in supermarkets. This new form of banking is designed to complement ATMs, which already dispense 75% of the bank's cash.
Saturn www.saturncars.com	Saturn dealers have adopted a one-price strategy that eliminates the need for negotiating. Instead, all customers are offered the same price. Test drives, financing, trade-ins, leasing are all offered to encourage customers to purchase a Saturn.
Levi Strauss www.levi.com	Levi Strauss & Co. now offers the Levi's Original Spin program, which allows customers to create their own jeans by selecting from three models, five leg types, two flys, and many color and fabric options. The jeans are delivered in 2 to 3 weeks for $55.
Toys "Я" Us www.toysrus.com	A distinctive toy store with a backwards R, this company is what every kid dreams about. Walking into a Toys "Я" Us store is like living under a Christmas tree. Unlike most stores, which reduce their space allotted to toys after the holiday season, a huge selection of toys is always available at Toys "Я" Us.

Can You Match Them:

Time	Place	Possession	Form
___	___	___	___

about by every child (and many parents) who enters Toys "Я" Us. Many retailers offer a combination of the four basic utilities. Some supermarkets, for example, offer convenient locations (place utility) and are open 24 hours (time utility). In addition, consumers may seek additional utilities such as entertainment, recreation, or information.[2]

The Global Economic Impact of Retailing

Retailing is also important to the U.S. and global economies. Three of the 25 largest businesses in the United States are retailers (Wal-Mart, Sears, and Kmart).[3] Wal-Mart's $139 billion of sales in 1998 surpassed the gross domestic product of Finland for that same year. Sears, Wal-Mart, and Kmart together have more than 1.5 million employees—more people than live in Austin, Texas, and Spokane, Washington, combined! Many other retailers, including food stores, automobile dealers, and general merchandise outlets, are also significant contributors to the U.S. economy (Figure 18–2).[4]

Outside of the United States, large retailers include Daiei in Japan, Pinault-Printemps in France, Karstadt in Germany, and Marks & Spencer in Britain.[5] In emerging economies such as China and Mexico, a combination of local and global retailers are evolving. Wal-Mart, for example, has 603 stores outside the United States, including joint ventures in China and Korea. The Marketing News-Net on the following page describes the incredible expansion currently under way.[6] In the Arabian Gulf, Dubai is promoting itself as a gateway to the Middle East with the "Dubai Shopping Festival." More than 2,300 retail outlets

FIGURE 18–2
Retail sales, by type of business

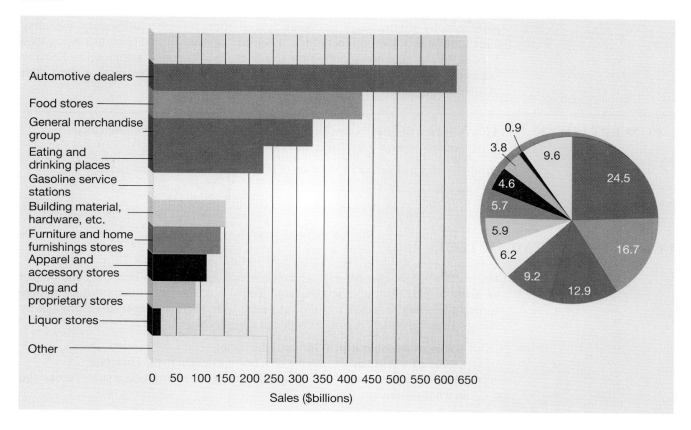

MARKETING NEWSNET

The World Has Become a Shop Window

Around the world, customer tastes are converging, trade restrictions are disappearing, and retailers are responding with frenzied global expansion. Experts estimate that retailers will spend billions during the next two years opening new stores in foreign countries. Wal-Mart, for example, has plans to open 75 to 80 new stores in Argentina, Brazil, Canada, China, Korea, Mexico, and Puerto Rico. Gap plans to add 50 stores to its current international division of 249 stores. Eddie Bauer, Toys "Я" Us, and Home Depot also have expansion plans. Italy's Benetton already has stores in 120 countries, and Britain's Marks & Spencer has grown to 150 stores around the world.

Why are retailers expanding so rapidly? One reason is that the U.S. and European markets are saturated with retailers. Therefore, large merchants are looking for new places to invest. A second reason,

however, is that retailers would like to transform their store names into global brands—a move that will allow them to sell higher-margin private-label goods, avoid price wars, and better negotiate with suppliers. Keith Oates of Marks & Spencer says, "we'll be a global brand in time, like Coca-Cola."

participate by offering sales, discounts, special offers and other promotions, including a high-tech zone called "CyberStreet." Each day the festival also holds a drawing for a $16,000 bar of gold and a raffle for two Lexus GS 300 luxury automobiles. Because the event attracts more than 2 million shoppers retailers are eager to expand their global participation in Dubai and other growing markets.[7]

CONCEPT CHECK

1. When Levi Strauss makes jeans cut to a customer's exact preferences and measurements, what utility is provided?

2. Two measures of the importance of retailing in the global economy are _____ and _____ .

CLASSIFYING RETAIL OUTLETS

For manufacturers, consumers, and the economy, retailing is an important component of marketing that has several variations. Because of the large number of alternative forms of retailing, it is easier to understand the differences among retail institutions by recognizing that outlets can be classified in several ways:

- **Form of ownership.** Who owns the outlet.
- **Level of service.** The degree of service provided to the customer.
- **Merchandise line.** How many different types of products a store carries and in what assortment.

FIGURE 18–3
Classifying retail outlets

METHOD OF CLASSIFICATION	DESCRIPTION OF RETAIL OUTLET
Form of ownership	Independent retailer Corporate chain Contractual system • Retailer-sponsored cooperative • Wholesaler-sponsored voluntary chain • Franchise
Level of service	Self-service Limited-service Full-service
Merchandise line	Depth • Single line • Limited line Breadth • General merchandise • Scrambled merchandising

Within each method of classification there are several alternative types of outlets, as shown in Figure 18–3 and explained in the following pages.

Form of Ownership

Independent Retailer   One of the most common forms of retail ownership is the independent business, owned by an individual. The number of small retailers has grown at a rate of 15 percent to 775,000 companies that dominate employment in hardware, sporting goods, jewelry, and gift stores. They are also popular retailers of auto supplies, books, paint, cameras, and women's accessories. The advantage of this form of ownership for the owner is that he or she can be his or her own boss. For customers, the independent store can offer convenience, quality, personal service, and lifestyle compatibility.[8]

Corporate Chain   A second form of ownership, the corporate chain, involves multiple outlets under common ownership. If you've ever shopped at Dayton's, Hudson's, Marshall Field's, Mervyn's, or Target, you've shopped at a chain outlet owned by the Dayton Hudson Corporation.

In a chain operation, centralization in decision making and purchasing is common. Chain stores have advantages in dealing with manufacturers, particularly as the size of the chain grows. A large chain can bargain with a manufacturer to obtain good service or volume discounts on orders. Kmart's large volume makes it a strong negotiator with manufacturers of most products. The power of chains is seen in the retailing of computers: Small independents buy at 75 percent of list price, but large chains such as Comp USA, Circuit City, and Best Buy may pay only 60 to 65 percent of list price.[9] Consumers also benefit in dealing with chains because there are multiple outlets with similar merchandise and consistent management policies.

Retailing has become a high-tech business for many large chains. Wal-Mart, for example, has developed a sophisticated inventory management and cost control system that allows rapid price changes for each product in every store. Although the technology requires a substantial investment, it is a necessary competitive tool today—a lesson illustrated by Mexico's largest drugstore chain. When Wal-Mart and other discounters opened stores in Mexico, Formacias Benavides used its state-of-the-art computer system to match prices on popular pharmaceutical products that were also available in the new competitors' stores.[10]

Contractual System   Contractual systems involve independently owned stores that band together to act like a chain. The three kinds described in Chapter 16 are retailer-sponsored cooperatives, wholesaler-sponsored voluntary chains, and franchises. One retailer-sponsored cooperative is the Associated Grocers, which consists of neighborhood grocers that all agree with several other independent grocers to buy their meat from the same wholesaler. In this way, members can take advantage of volume discounts commonly available to chains and also give the impression of being a large chain, which may be viewed more favorably by some consumers. Wholesaler-sponsored voluntary chains such as Ace Hardware and Independent Grocers' Alliance (IGA) try to achieve similar benefits.

As noted in Chapter 16, in a franchise system an individual or firm (the franchisee) contracts with a parent company (the franchisor) to set up a business or retail outlet.

McDonald's, Holiday Inn, Midas, and H&R Block all involve some level of franchising. The franchisor usually assists in selecting the store location, setting up the store, advertising, and training personnel. The franchisee pays a one-time franchise fee and an annual royalty, usually tied to the store's sales. Although this might be seen as a relatively new phenomenon, this ownership approach has been used with gas stations since the early 1900s.[11] Franchising is attractive because of the opportunity for people to enter a well-known, established business where managerial advice is provided. Also, the franchise fee may be less than the cost of setting up an independent business. The International Franchise Association recently reported that franchising is one of the strongest segments of the economy, generating close to $800 billion in sales and more than 160,000 new jobs each year.[12]

Franchise fees paid to the franchisor can range from as little as $7,500 for a Radio Shack franchise to $45,000 for a McDonald's restaurant franchise. When the fees are combined with other costs such as real estate and equipment, however, the total investment can be substantial. Figure 18–4 shows some businesses that can be entered through franchise, along with the total costs of becoming a franchisee. By selling franchises, an organization reduces the cost of expansion but loses some control. A good franchisor, however, will maintain strong control of the outlets in terms of delivery and presentation of merchandise and try to enhance recognition of the franchise name.[13]

Level of Service

Even though most customers perceive little variation in retail outlets by form of ownership, differences among retailers are more obvious in terms of level of service. In

FIGURE 18–4
The possibilities and costs of franchising

FRANCHISE	TYPE OF BUSINESS	TOTAL STARTUP COST	NUMBER OF FRANCHISES
McDonald's	Fast-food restaurant	$385,000–$520,000	19,500
Merry Maids	Cleaning service	$27,500–$40,500	700
Jiffy Lube	Automobile fluid service	$208,000–$229,000	667
Mail Boxes Etc.	Postal services	$55,000–$75,000	2,953
Duds'N Suds	Laundry and snack bar	$60,000	80
Radio Shack	Electronic accessories	$67,500	1,934
Barbizon	School of Modeling	$69,500–$124,000	65

some department stores, such as Loehman's, very few services are provided. Some grocery stores, such as the Cub chain, have customers bag the food themselves. Other outlets, such as Neiman Marcus, provide a wide range of customer services from gift wrapping to wardrobe consultation.

Self-Service   Self-service is at the extreme end of the level of service continuum because the customer performs many functions and little is provided by the outlet. Home building supply outlets and gas stations are often self-service. Warehouse stores, usually in buildings several times larger than a conventional store, are self-service with all nonessential customer services eliminated. Several new forms of self-service include Federal Express's placement of hundreds of self-service package shipping stations in retail stores such as Sam's Club and a self-service scanning system called the Portable Personal Shopper now used by some grocery stores in The Netherlands and being considered for testing by Kroger stores in the United States.[14]

Limited Service   Limited-service outlets provide some services, such as credit, and merchandise return, but not others, such as custom-made clothes. General merchandise stores such as Wal-Mart, Kmart, and Target are usually considered limited service outlets. Customers are responsible for most shopping activities, although salespeople are available in departments such as consumer electronics, jewelry, and lawn and garden.

Full-Service   Full-service retailers, which include most specialty stores and department stores, provide many services to their customers. Nordstrom, a Seattle-based retail chain, for example, is legendary for its customer service. The store typically has 50 percent more salespeople on the floor than similar-sized stores. Salespeople often write customers thank-you notes or deliver purchases to customers' homes. In most stores, customers are serenaded by the sounds of a grand piano. These activities are reflected in a biannual industry customer satisfaction survey—the Retail Satisfaction Index—which ranks Nordstrom highest in terms of personalized attention and professional salespeople.[15]

Merchandise Line

Retail outlets also vary by their merchandise lines, the key distinction being the breadth and depth of the items offered to customers (Figure 18–5). **Depth of product line** means that the store carries a large assortment of each item, such as a shoe store that offers running shoes, dress shoes, and children's shoes. **Breadth of product line** refers to the variety of different items a store carries.

FIGURE 18–5
Breadth versus depth of merchandise lines

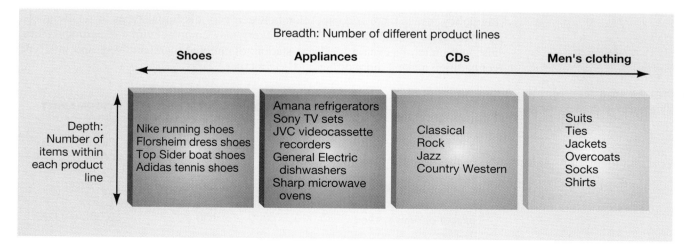

Depth of Line   Stores that carry a considerable assortment (depth) of a related line of items are limited-line stores. Oshman's sporting goods stores carry considerable depth in sports equipment ranging from weight-lifting accessories to running shoes. Stores that carry tremendous depth in one primary line of merchandise are single-line stores. Victoria's Secret, a nationwide chain, carries great depth in women's lingerie. Both limited- and single-line stores are often referred to as *specialty outlets*.

Specialty discount outlets focus on one type of product, such as electronics (Circuit City), business supplies (Office Depot), or books (Barnes and Noble) at very competitive prices. These outlets are referred to in the trade as *category killers* because they often dominate the market. Toys "Я" Us, for example, controls 18 percent of the toy market.[16]

Breadth of Line   Stores that carry a broad product line, with limited depth, are referred to as *general merchandise stores*. For example, large department stores such as Dillard's, Macy's, Marshall Field's, and Neiman Marcus carry a wide range of different types of products but not unusual sizes. The breadth and depth of merchandise lines are important decisions for a retailer. Traditionally, outlets carried related lines of goods. Today, however, **scrambled merchandising,** offering several unrelated product lines in a single store, is common. The modern drugstore carries food, camera equipment, magazines, paper products, toys, small hardware items, and pharmaceuticals. Supermarkets rent video tapes, develop film, and sell flowers.

A form of scrambled merchandising, the **hypermarket,** has been successful in Europe since the late 1960s. These hypermarkets are large stores (more than 200,000 square feet) offering a mix of 40 percent food products and 60 percent general merchandise. Prices are typically 5 to 20 percent below discount stores. The general concept behind the stores is simple: Offer consumers everything in a single outlet, eliminating the need to stop at more than one location.

Despite their success in Europe, hypermarkets have not been popular in the United States. When Wal-Mart opened four Hypermart USA stores and Kmart opened three American Fare stores, they discovered that U.S. shoppers were uncomfortable with the huge size of the stores. In addition, the competitive environment was tough: warehouse stores beat hypermarkets on price, category killers beat them on selection, and discounters beat them on location.

Searching for a better concept, some retailers are trying new stores, called *supercenters*, which combine a typical merchandise store with a full-size grocery. Wal-Mart already operates more than 512 supercenters and has plans to open 150 more, while rival Kmart has close to 100 Super Kmart Centers with plans to open approximately 25 new stores per year in the future.[17] Figure 18–6 shows the differences among discount stores, supercenters, and hypermarkets.[18]

Scrambled merchandising is convenient for consumers because it eliminates the number of stops required in a shopping trip. However, for the retailer this merchandising policy means there is competition between very dissimilar types of retail outlets, or **intertype competition.** A local bakery may compete with a department store, discount outlet, or even a local gas station. Scrambled merchandising and intertype competition make it more difficult to be a retailer.

FIGURE 18–6
Differences in store concepts

	DISCOUNT STORE	SUPERCENTER	HYPERMARKET
Average size (in square feet)	70,000	150,000	230,000
Number of employees	200–300	300–350	400–600
Annual sales ($ millions per store)	$10–$20	$20–$50	$75–$100
Gross margin	18%–19%	15%–16%	7%–8%
Number of items stocked	60,000–80,000	100,000	60,000–70,000

CONCEPT CHECK

1. Centralized decision making and purchasing are an advantage of _____ ownership.

2. What are some examples of new forms of self-service retailers?

3. Would a shop for big men's clothes carrying pants in sizes 40 to 60 have a broad or deep product line?

NONSTORE RETAILING

Most of the retailing examples discussed earlier in the chapter, such as corporate chains, department stores, and limited- and single-line specialty stores, involve store retailing. Many retailing activities today, however, are not limited to sales in a store. Nonstore retailing occurs outside a retail outlet through activities that involve varying levels of customer and retail involvement. Figure 18–7 shows six forms of nonstore retailing: automatic vending, direct mail and catalogs, television home shopping, online retailing, telemarketing, and direct selling.

Automatic Vending

Nonstore retailing includes vending machines, which make it possible to serve customers when and where stores cannot. Maintenance and operating costs are high, so product prices in vending machines tend to be higher than those in stores. Typically, small convenience products are available in vending machines. Of the 3 million vending machines currently in use, more than 1.8 million are soft drink machines. Improved

FIGURE 18–7
Forms of nonstore retailing

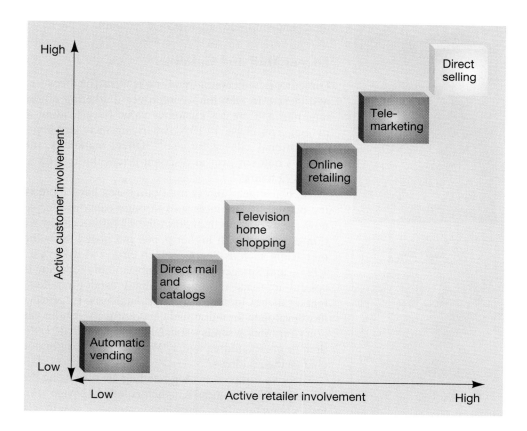

Vending machines serve customers when and where stores cannot.

technology, however, may soon allow vending machines to accept credit cards—a change that will permit more expensive items to be sold through this form of retailing. Some airports, for example, now have vending machines that sell software to commuters with laptop computers. Some fitness centers have vending machines that dispense Joe Boxer underwear, and several supermarkets are testing vending machines that dispense music CDs! Another improvement in vending machines—the use of modems to notify retailers when their machines are empty—is one reason automatic merchandising sales are expected to double in the next five years.[19]

Direct Mail and Catalogs

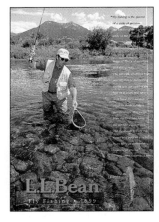

Direct mail and catalog retailing is attractive because it eliminates the cost of a store and clerks. In addition, it improves marketing efficiency through segmentation and targeting and creates customer value by providing a fast and convenient means of making a purchase. In 1998 Americans increased their catalog spending to $87 billion. International sales grew also.[20] Direct marketers, for example, offer rural Japanese farmers outdoor gear at discount prices through direct mail campaigns—and deliver within 72 hours![21]

As consumers' direct mail purchases have increased, the number of catalogs and the number of products sold through catalogs has skyrocketed. A typical household now receives more than 50 of the 12 billion catalogs mailed each year. The competition combined with higher paper and postal costs, however, have hurt large catalog merchants such as Sears—which closed its 100-year-old general catalog business in 1993—and Spiegel—which is substantially reducing the size of its "Big Book." A successful approach now used by many catalog retailers is to send specialty catalogs to market niches identified in their databases. L.L.Bean, a longstanding catalog retailer, has developed an individual catalog for fly fishing enthusiasts. Similarly, Lillian Vernon Corporation sends a specialty catalog called "Lilly's Kids" to customers with children or grandchildren and a "Welcome" catalog of household items to customers who change their address.[22]

Creative forms of catalog retailing are also being developed. Hallmark, for example, offers cards for businesses in their colorful 32-page "Business Expressions" catalog. Victoria's Secret mails as many as 45 catalogs a year to its customers to generate mail-order and 800-number business and to increase traffic in its 600 stores. Many catalog retailers such as the Sharper Image now allow telephone orders, mail orders, and e-mail orders![23]

Television Home Shopping

Television home shopping is possible when consumers watch a shopping channel on which products are displayed; orders are then placed over the telephone. Two popular programs, Home Shopping Network and QVC, reach 60 million households and recently

accounted for combined sales of more than $2 billion. Because these programs have traditionally attracted 40- to 50-year-old women, other programs such as MTV Network's "House of Style," with host Rebecca Romijn-Stamos, is designed to attract a younger audience. A limitation of TV shopping has been the lack of buyer–seller interaction and the inability of consumers to control the items they see. But new technologies will soon allow consumers to choose from as many as 500 channels and interact with the program source.[24]

Online Retailing

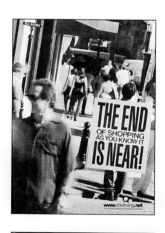

Online retailing allows consumers to search for, evaluate, and order products through the Internet. For many consumers the advantages of this form of retailing are the 24-hour access, the ability to comparison shop, privacy, and variety. The appeal varies among consumer groups, however. Studies of online shoppers have shown that while men and women are equally likely to browse Web sites, men are currently more likely to buy something online. As online retailers improve their Web offerings, though, sales are expected to increase. Forecasts suggest that the current annual sales of $10 billion could reach $100 billion in a few years.[25]

Online retail purchases can be the result of several very different approaches. First, consumers can pay dues to become a member of an online discount service such as CUC International's www.netMarket.com. The service offers more than 1 million items at very low prices to its 2 million subscribers. Another approach to online retailing is to use a shopping "bot" such as www.mysimon.com. This site searches the Web for a product specified by the consumer, and provides a report on the locations of the best prices available. Consumers can also use the Internet to go directly to online malls (www.fashionmall.com), apparel retailers (www.gap.com), book stores (www.amazon.com), computer manufactures (www.dell.com), grocery stores (www.peapod.com), music and video stores (www.cdnow.com), and travel agencies (www.travelocity.com). A final, and quickly growing approach, to online retailing is the online auction, such as www.ebay.com, where consumers bid on more than 1,000 categories of products.[26]

To increase interest in online retailing, many retailers are adding "experiential" or interactive activities to their Web sites. The Web Link on the following page describes how apparel stores use virtual models and virtual dressing rooms to involve consumers in the purchase process and help with product selection.[27] Other changes on the horizon include the availability of very fast Internet connections through satellite services, high-

WEB LINK

Dress (Your Virtual Model) for Success!

Shopping online has many advantages: the convenience of 24-hour access, easy price comparisons, no parking hassles, and trying clothes on in the privacy of your home. That's right, now you can "build" a virtual model that reflects your body type and try on any clothing combination to see how they would look and fit. Want

to try it? Go to www.landsend.com, click on My Personal Model, answer a few questions, and pick out some clothes. Or, go to www.eddiebauer. com, and click on the virtual dressing room. So . . . how do you look?!

speed digital telephone lines, and new-generation cable modems that run 50 to 100 times faster than current telephone lines. The merger of television home shopping and online retailing began with the introduction of WebTV, an Internet access service that uses an "Internet appliance" attached to a television to connect to the Internet. Experts predict the emergence of a new format called Interactive Home Shopping (IHS) as technology increases the interactivity between consumers and retailers. Owning a computer or a television isn't a necessity for online retailing, however, as many "online cafes" now provide guests with access to computer stations linked to the Internet.[28]

Telemarketing

Another form of nonstore retailing, called **telemarketing,** involves using the telephone to interact with and sell directly to consumers. Compared with direct mail, telemarketing is often viewed as a more efficient means of targeting consumers, although the two techniques are often used together. Information Management Network, a Dallas-based company, for example, sends direct mail to 30 million names each year to generate 650,000 responses from people who are then contacted by telemarketers. At Ryder Consumer Truck Rental, well-trained agents talk to 15 prospective customers each hour, while the staff of 24 at Lens Express makes 100,000 calls each month. Telemarketing has grown in popularity as companies search for ways to cut costs but still provide convenient access to their customers. According to the American Telemarketing Association, telemarketing sales exceed $500 billion.[29]

As the use of telemarketing grows, consumer privacy has become a topic of discussion among consumers, Congress, the Federal Trade Commission, and businesses. Issues such as industry standards, ethical guidelines, and new privacy laws are evolving to provide a balance between the varying perspectives. An example is the industry self-regulation program, called Telewatch, which encourages legal, ethical, and professional business conduct among telemarketers.[30]

Direct Selling

Direct selling, sometimes called door-to-door retailing, involves direct sales of goods and services to consumers through personal interactions and demonstrations in their home or office. A variety of companies, including familiar names such as Fuller Brush, Avon, World Book, and Mary Kay Cosmetics, have created an industry with more than $16 billion in sales by providing consumers with personalized service and convenience. In the United States, however, sales have been declining as retail chains such as Wal-Mart begin to carry similar products at discount prices and as the increasing number of dual-career households reduces the number of potential buyers at home.

In response to the changes in the United States, many direct selling retailers are expanding into other markets. Avon, for example, already has 1.3 million sales representatives in 26 countries including Mexico, Poland, Argentina, and China. Similarly, other retailers such as Amway, Herbalife, and Electrolux are rapidly expanding. More than 70 percent of Amway's $7 billion in sales now comes from outside the United States, and sales in Japan alone exceed sales in North America.[31] Direct selling is likely to continue to grow in markets where the lack of effective distribution channels increases the importance of door-to-door convenience and where the lack of consumer knowledge about products and brands will increase the need for a person-to-person approach.[32]

CONCEPT CHECK

1. Successful catalog retailers often send _____ catalogs to _____ markets identified in their databases.

2. How are retailers increasing consumer interest and involvement in online retailing?

3. Where are direct selling retail sales growing? Why?

RETAILING STRATEGY

This section identifies how a retail store positions itself and describes specific actions it can take to develop a retailing strategy.

Positioning a Retail Store

The classification alternatives presented in the previous sections help determine one store's position relative to its competitors.

Retail Positioning Matrix   The **retail positioning matrix** is a matrix developed by the MAC Group, Inc., a management consulting firm.[33] This matrix positions retail outlets on two dimensions: breadth of product line and value added. As defined previously, breadth of product line is the range of products sold through each outlet. The second dimension, *value added*, includes elements such as location (as with 7-Eleven stores), product reliability (as with Holiday Inn or McDonald's), or prestige (as with Saks Fifth Avenue or Brooks Brothers).

FIGURE 18–8
Retail positioning matrix

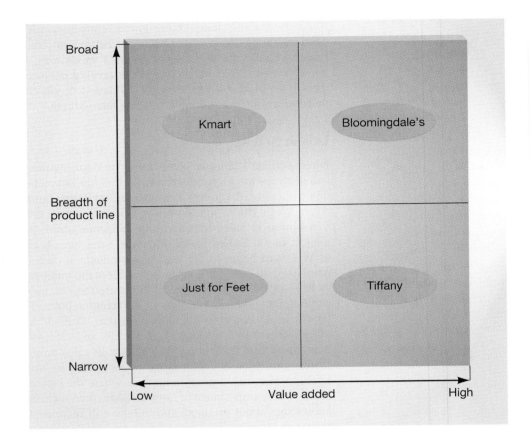

The retail positioning matrix in Figure 18–8 shows four possible positions. An organization can be successful in any position, but unique strategies are required within each quadrant. Consider the four stores shown in the matrix:

1. Bloomingdale's has high value added and a broad product line. Retailers in this quadrant pay great attention to store design and product lines. Merchandise often has a high margin of profit and is of high quality. The stores in this position typically provide high levels of service.
2. Kmart has low value added and a broad line. Kmart and similar firms typically trade a lower price for increased volume in sales. Retailers in this position focus on price with low service levels and an image of being a place for good buys.
3. Tiffany's has high value added and a narrow line. Retailers of this type typically sell a very restricted range of products that are of high status quality. Customers are also provided with high levels of service.
4. Just for Feet has low value added and a narrow line. Such retailers are specialty mass merchandisers. Just for Feet, for example, carries athletic shoes at a discount.[34] These outlets appeal to value-conscious consumers. Economies of scale are achieved through centralized advertising, merchandising, buying, and distribution. Stores are usually the same in design, layout, and merchandise; hence they are often referred to as "cookie-cutter" stores.

Keys to Positioning   To successfully position a store, it must have an identity that has some advantages over the competitors yet is recognized by consumers. A company can have outlets in several positions on the matrix, but this approach is usually done with different store names. Dayton-Hudson, for example, owns Dayton's and Hudson's department stores (with high value added and a broad line) and Target discount stores (low value added and a broad line). Shifting from one box in the retail positioning matrix to another is also possible, but all elements of retailing strategy must be reexamined. For example, JCPenney has modified the visual presentation of its stores and changed the assortment of its merchandise to reposition itself from a mass merchandiser competing with Sears to a contemporary department store competing with stores such as Macy's.[35]

Retailing Mix

In developing retailing strategy, managers work with the **retailing mix,** which includes the (1) goods and services, (2) physical distribution, and (3) communications tactics chosen by a store (Figure 18–9).[36] Decisions relating to the mix focus on the consumer. Each of the areas shown is important, but we will cover only three basic areas: (1) pricing, (2) store location, and (3) image and atmosphere. The communications and promotion components are discussed in Chapter 20 on advertising and Chapter 21 on personal selling.

Retail Pricing   In setting prices for merchandise, retailers must decide on the markup, markdown, and timing for markdowns. As mentioned in the appendix to Chapter 15 (Appendix B), the *markup* refers to how much should be added to the cost

FIGURE 18–9
The retailing mix

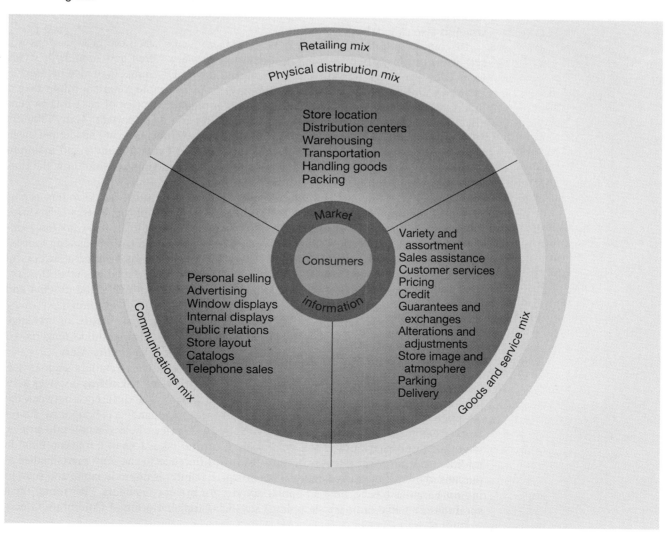

ETHICS AND SOCIAL RESPONSIBILITY ALERT

ETHICS

Who Takes the Five-Finger Discount? You'll Be Surprised

Retailers lose almost 2 percent of their sales to theft each year. To combat the problem many stores attempt to discourage consumers from shoplifting with magnetic detectors, locked cases, and other deterrents. What you may find surprising, though, is that more than 50 percent of the thefts are not made by consumers but by employees! The most popular items to steal are candy from convenience stores, shirts from department stores, batteries from discount stores, and cigarettes from drug stores. When does this happen? The most popular time is between 3 and 6 P.M. Why do you think shoplifting is such a large problem? What recommendations would you make to retailers?

---

the retailer paid for a product to reach the final selling price. Retailers decide on the *original markup,* but by the time the product is sold, they end up with a *maintained markup.* The original markup is the difference between retailer cost and initial selling price. When products do not sell as quickly as anticipated, their price is reduced. The difference between the final selling price and retailer cost is the maintained markup, which is also called the *gross margin.*

Discounting a product, or taking a *markdown,* occurs when the product does not sell at the original price and an adjustment is necessary. Often new models or styles force the price of existing models to be marked down. Discounts may also be used to increase demand for complementary products.[37] For example, retailers might take a markdown on stereos to increase sales of CDs or reduce the price of cake mix to generate frosting purchases. The *timing* of a markdown can be important. Many retailers take a markdown as soon as sales fall off to free up valuable selling space and cash. However, other stores delay markdowns to discourage bargain hunters and maintain an image of quality. There is no clear answer, but retailers must consider how the timing might affect future sales.

Although most retailers plan markdowns, many retailers use price discounts as part of their regular merchandising policy. In March 1989, Sears closed its 824 U.S. stores for 48 hours to lower its shelf prices on 50,000 items and begin an *everyday low pricing* strategy. Although Sears was not successful with its switch, emphasizing consistently low prices and eliminating most markdowns or sales has become a successful strategy for retailers like Wal-Mart and Home Depot.[38] Because consumers often use price as an indicator of product quality, however, the brand name of the product and the image of the store become important decision factors in these situations.[39]

A special issue for retailers trying to keep prices low is **shrinkage,** or breakage and theft of merchandise by customers and employees. Who do you think steals more? For the answer see the accompanying Ethics and Social Responsibility Alert.[40]

Off-price retailing is a retail pricing practice that is used by retailers such as T.J. Maxx, Burlington Coat Factory, and Ross Stores. **Off-price retailing** involves selling brand-name merchandise at lower than regular prices. The difference between the off-price retailer and a discount store is that off-price merchandise is bought by the retailer from manufacturers with excess inventory at prices below wholesale prices, while the discounter buys at full wholesale price (but takes less of a markup than do traditional department stores). Because of this difference in the way merchandise is purchased by the retailer, selection at an off-price retailer is unpredictable, and searching for bargains has become a popular activity for many consumers. "It's more like a sport than it is like ordinary shopping," says Christopher Boring of Columbus, Ohio's

Retail Planning Associates.[41] Savings to the consumer at off-price retailers are reported as high as 70 percent off the prices of a traditional department store.

There are several variations of off-price retailing. One is the warehouse club. These large stores (more than 100,000 square feet) began as rather stark outlets with no elaborate displays, customer service, or home delivery. They require an annual membership fee (usually $25) for the privilege of shopping there. While a typical Kmart stocks 100,000 items, warehouse clubs carry about 3,500 items and usually stock just one brand name of appliance or food product. Service is minimal, and customers usually must pay by cash or check. However, the extremely competitive pricing of merchandise makes warehouse clubs attractive.[42] The major warehouse clubs in the United States include Wal-Mart's Sam's Club, BJ's Wholesale Club, and Costco's Warehouse Club. Sales of these off-price retailers have grown dramatically, reaching $50 billion in 1998 (compared with $4 billion in 1985).[43]

A second variation is the outlet store. Factory outlets, such as Van Heusen Factory Store, Bass Shoe Outlet, and Oneida Factory Store, offer products for 25 to 30 percent off the suggested retail price. Manufacturers use the stores to clear excess merchandise and to reach consumers who focus on value shopping. Retail outlets such as Nordstrom's Rack and Brooks Brothers Outlet Store allow retailers to sell excess merchandise and still maintain an image of offering merchandise at full price in their primary store. The number of factory outlet centers has increased from 183 in 1990 to 312, with sales of $11.2 billion. Some experts expect the next trend to combine the various types of off-price retailers in "value-retail centers."[44]

A third variation of off-price retailing is offered by single-price, or extreme value, retailers such as Family Dollar, Dollar General, and Dollar Tree. These stores average about 6,000 square feet in size and attract customers who want value and a "corner store" environment rather than a large supercenter experience. Some experts predict extraordinary growth of these types of retailers. Dollar General, for example, already has 3,360 stores and plans for 500 new stores in the next year.[45]

Store Location   A second aspect of the retailing mix involves deciding where to locate the store and how many stores to have. Department stores, which started downtown in most cities, have followed customers to the suburbs, and in recent years more stores have been opened in large regional malls. Most stores today are near several others in one of five settings: the central business district, the regional center, the community shopping center, the strip, or the power center.

The **central business district** is the oldest retail setting, the community's downtown area. Until the regional outflow to suburbs, it was the major shopping area, but the suburban population has grown at the expense of the downtown shopping area. Detroit, experiencing a decade of population decline, lost its last major department store in 1982 when Hudson's left the central city.

Regional shopping centers are the suburban malls of today, containing 50 to 150 stores. The typical drawing distance of a regional center is 5 to 10 miles from the mall. These large shopping areas often contain two or three *anchor stores,* which are well-known national or regional stores such as Sears, Saks Fifth Avenue, and Bloomingdale's. The largest variation of a regional center is the West Edmonton Mall in Alberta, Canada. The shopping center is a conglomerate of 600 stores, six amusement centers, 110 restaurants, and a 355-room Fantasyland hotel.[46]

A more limited approach to retail location is the **community shopping center,** which typically has one primary store (usually a department store branch) and often about 20 to 40 smaller outlets. Generally, these centers serve a population of consumers who are within a 10- to 20-minute drive.

Not every suburban store is located in a shopping mall. Many neighborhoods have clusters of stores, referred to as a **strip location,** to serve people who are within a 5- to 10-minute drive. Gas station, hardware, laundry, grocery, and pharmacy outlets are

The Importance of Brands

The use of brands is also changing dramatically. Many retailers have developed their own private-label brands to increase customer loyalty. As a result, many manufacturers have opened their own stores. Single-brand, or company, stores such as the 68,000 square-foot Nike Town in Chicago allow manufacturers to display their entire product line in a controlled "showcase." Other company stores include Speed Authentic Fitness Stores, Original Levi's Stores, OshKosh B'Gosh Stores, and Reebok Concept Stores. Many other manufacturers are showing interest in the concept.

Two of the most successful variations of the company store trend are the Disney and Warner studio stores. The 268 Disney stores and the 67 Warner stores market characters such as Mickey Mouse, Peter Pan, Bugs Bunny, and the Tasmanian Devil directly to the public. While both companies are fortunate to have several characters to promote, they have discovered that preferences vary throughout the world. In British stores, for example, Winnie the Pooh is the top seller, while Bambie and Thumper are preferred in France, and Mickey and Minnie are the first choices in Japan![60]

Most consumers associate strong brand names with specific products such as Coke or Tide, or particular companies such as Microsoft or Motorola. In the future, however, many large merchants will be trying to turn their store names into world brands. The changing role of products, stores, and manufacturers as popular, well-known brands is likely to generate many more changes in the dynamic practice of retailing!

CONCEPT CHECK

1. According to the wheel of retailing, when a new retail form appears, how would you characterize its image?

2. Market share is usually fought out before the _____ stage of the retail life cycle.

3. What is a smart card?

SUMMARY

1 Retailing provides customer value in the form of various utilities: time, place, possession, and form. Economically, retailing is important in terms of the people employed and money exchanged in retail sales.

2 Retailing outlets can be classified along several dimensions: the form of ownership, level of service, or merchandise line.

3 There are several forms of ownership: independent, chain, retailer-sponsored cooperative, wholesaler-sponsored chain or franchise.

4 Stores vary in the level of service they provide. Three levels are self-service, limited service, or full service.

5 Retail outlets vary in terms of the breadth and depth of their merchandise lines. Breadth refers to the number of different items carried, and depth refers to the assortment of each item offered.

6 Nonstore retailing includes automatic vending, direct mail and catalogs, television home shopping, online retailing, telemarketing, and direct selling.

7 A retail store positions itself on two dimensions: breadth of product line and value added, which includes elements such as location, product reliability, and prestige.

8 Retailing strategy is based on the retailing mix, consisting of goods and services, physical distribution, and communication tactics.

9 In retail pricing, retailers must decide on the markup, markdown, and timing for the markdown. Off-price retailers offer brand-name merchandise at lower than regular prices. This retailing form includes warehouse clubs, outlet stores, and single-price retailers.

10 Retail store location is an important retail mix decision. The common alternatives are the central business district, a regional shopping center, a community shopping center, or a strip location. A variation of the strip location is the power center, which is a strip location with multiple national anchor stores and a supermarket.

11 Retail image and atmosphere help retailers create the appropriate buying experience for their target market.

12 New retailing forms are explained by the wheel of retailing. Stores enter as low-status, low-margin outlets. Over time, they add services and raise margins, which allows a new form of low-status, low-margin retailing outlet to enter.

13 Like products, retail outlets have a life cycle consisting of four stages: early growth, accelerated development, maturity, and decline.

14 Technology will change the way consumers pay for purchases in the future. Smart cards may lead to a cashless society.

KEY TERMS AND CONCEPTS

INTERNET EXERCISE

For many consumers comparison shopping is not appealing because of the inconvenience of traveling to multiple locations. Even on the Internet, finding and searching multiple Web sites can be tedious. One solution is a form of software called an "intelligent agent" or "bot" (derived from robot) which automatically searches for the best price. Try each of the following shopping bots—www.mysimon.com, www.jango.com, and www.jahoo.junglee. com— to find the best price for one of the following products:

1 Burton snowboard.
2 Sony TV.
3 Calvin Klein jeans.

How did the three agents differ? What range of prices did you obtain? What shipping and handling charges would apply to each purchase? Why are different recommendation made by the agents?

APPLYING MARKETING CONCEPTS AND PERSPECTIVES

1 Discuss the impact of the growing number of dual-income households on (*a*) nonstore retailing and (*b*) the retail mix.
2 How does value added affect a store's competitive position?
3 In retail pricing, retailers often have a maintained markup. Explain how this maintained markup differs from original markup and why it is so important.
4 What are the similarities and differences between the product and retail life cycles?
5 How would you classify Kmart in terms of its position on the wheel of retailing versus that of an off-price retailer?
6 Develop a chart to highlight the role of each of the three main elements of the retailing mix across the four stages of the retail life cycle.

7 In Figure 18–8 Just for Feet was placed on the retail positioning matrix. What strategies should Just for Feet follow to move itself into the same position as Tiffany?
8 Breadth and depth are two important components in distinguishing among types of retailers. Discuss the breadth and depth implications of the following retailers discussed in this chapter: (*a*) Levi Strauss, (*b*) Wal-Mart, (*c*) L.L.Bean, and (*d*) Circuit City.
9 According to the wheel of retailing and the retail life cycle, what will happen to factory outlet stores?
10 The text discusses the development of online retailing in the United States. How does the development of this retailing form agree with the implications of the retail life cycle?

CASE 18–1   MALL OF AMERICA

"Surely the most mighty and colossal and stupendous shopping and entertainment experience there ever was." In a different era these words might have been attributed to P. T. Barnum; today, however, they describe the Mall of America (www.mallofamerica.com). The mall is the largest, fully enclosed combination retail and family entertainment complex in the United States—a one-stop destination designed to offer extensive guest services, convenience, family entertainment, and fun!

THE IDEA

The idea began with Canada's Ghermezian brothers who had built a similar mall in Edmonton, Alberta. They teamed up with Indianapolis-based Melvin and Herbert Simon, who had built 202 shopping centers in the United States. Together they planned to design and build a mall that would attract people who wanted to shop and to be entertained. In fact, the Simons and Ghermezians hoped they could create a mall that would attract entire families for vacations!

THE MALL

Seven years later the Mall of America opened in Minneapolis, Minnesota, to more than 1 million eager visitors in its first week of operation. The size of the mall—4.2 million square feet—has been difficult for anyone to anticipate. Visitors find anchor stores Bloomingdale's, Macy's, Nordstrom, and Sears and more than 500 specialty stores surrounding a seven-acre entertainment theme park with more than 50 rides.

Other unique aspects of the mall include the following:

- The LEGO Imagination Center—a 6,000-square-foot showplace of LEGO models ranging from clowns to castles to dinosaurs.
- Recycle Now—an in-house recycling plant with displays explaining how recycling can impact the environment.
- Wilderness Theater—a "ranger station" that lets kids and adults learn about birds, mammals, insects, and reptiles through up-close experiences.
- Golf Mountain—a two-level, 18-hole miniature golf course lushly landscaped with seven waterfalls, two streams, trees, and plants.

In addition, the Mall of America has things you would find in other malls—but in larger quantities. For example, the Mall has 12,750 free parking spaces, 17 elevators, 44 escalators, a shuttle bus that runs to the airport every half hour, and 10,000 employees!

THE ISSUES

To ensure that the Mall of America would be a success, managers faced two huge challenges—to find hundreds of retailers to open stores in the mall and to attract more than 40 million visitors each year. Because many retailers were concerned about the uncertainties associated with the new mall, special rent incentives were offered to attract key stores. In addition, small outlets were offered assistance with store layout, lighting, and displays to reduce initial costs for new merchants and ensure that the general decor of the mall would be consistent.

The market for potential visitors was defined in terms of two groups—shoppers and tourists. Shoppers may include the 2.5 million residents of Minneapolis and St. Paul, Minnesota, the 4.8 million people who live within a 150-mile radius, and the 27 million people who live within 400 miles (a day's drive). Tourists were expected from the neighboring 11 states and 2 Canadian provinces.

In addition, more than 2,500 bus tours from across the United States and 90 tour groups from Japan have visited the mall.

Mall of America managers are determined to continue its success by keeping current retailers happy, finding new retailers to open stores in the mall, and maintaining the steady stream of shoppers and tourists. After all what could be more "mighty and colossal and stupendous" than the Mall of America!

Questions

1   What environmental factors suggest that the concept of a mall the size of the Mall of America would be successful? Unsuccessful?

2   What were the primary challenges facing managers as they designed and built the Mall of America?

3   Design a marketing campaign to obtain 40 million visitors to the Mall of America each year.

CHAPTER NINETEEN

INTEGRATED MARKETING COMMUNICATIONS AND DIRECT MARKETING

19

AFTER READING THIS CHAPTER YOU SHOULD BE ABLE TO:

- Explain the communication process and its elements.

- Understand the promotional mix and the uniqueness of each component.

- Select the promotional approach appropriate to a product's life-cycle stage and characteristics.

- Differentiate between the advantages of push and pull strategies.

- Appreciate the value of an integrated marketing communications approach.

- Understand the value of direct marketing for consumers and sellers.

HOW DO MEG AND TOM GET MAIL?

It's Friday night and you are considering taking in a movie. Meg Ryan and Tom Hanks are back together again in a new romantic comedy, so you head for the theater. The name of the movie, *You've Got Mail*, sounds familiar, but it's not until the scenes with Tom and Meg logging on to the Internet and exchanging e-mail that you realize they are using the same online service that you use—American Online. Just a coincidence? Not a chance.

The visibility of American Online in the movie is the result of a promotional agreement between the online service and Warner Bros. movie studios. In exchange for the on-screen exposure, American Online compensated the studio—reportedly between $3 and $6 million. The agreement provided benefits for both partners: Warner Bros. defrayed some of the production and marketing expenses of the movie and added to the realism of the film, and American Online reached an important audience in an extraordinarily long form of communication.

Other movies have also used brand-name products. It was Steven Spielberg's placement of Hershey's Reese's Pieces in *E.T.* that brought a lot of interest to the candy. Similarly, when Tom Cruise wore Bausch and Lomb's Ray-Ban sunglasses in *Risky Business* and its Aviator sunglasses in *Top Gun*—and sales skyrocketed from 100,000 to 7,000,000 pairs in five years—the potential impact of "product placement" was recognized. You might remember that James Bond drove a BMW Z3 roadster in *Goldeneye*, Mel Gibson and Danny Glover ate at Dunkin Donuts in *Lethal Weapon 4*, and Matthew McConaughey and Jenna Elfman used Motorola cell phones in *EdTV*. In *The Horse Whisperer*, the Web site Equisearch.com, which provides information for equestrians, was catapulted from obscurity when the movie showed the page on screen.

It's not just movies, though. Other outlets include music videos, television shows, game shows, and even other companies' commercials. NBC's *Seinfeld* included Junior Mints, Snapple, Colombo frozen yogurt, Rold Gold pretzels, H&H Bagels, and diet Coke in is episodes. The *Seventh Heaven* cast receives Duck Head brand clothes. *Home Improvement* actors have modeled Logo Athletic jackets, and *ER* actors use Compaq computers. Mazda recently placed a Miata in a Chevron ad.[1]

Placement of products in the many media alternatives available today is becoming an important part of marketing and promotion. Applications of the technique demonstrate the importance of creativity in communicating with potential customers. In addition, to ensure that a consistent message is delivered through product placement and all promotional activities, a process that integrates marketing communications is a necessity.

Promotion represents the fourth element in the marketing mix. The promotional element comprises a mix of tools available for the marketer called the *promotional mix*, which consists of advertising, personal selling, sales promotion, public relations, and direct marketing. All of these elements can be used to (1) inform prospective buyers about the benefits of the product, (2) persuade them to try it, and (3) remind them later about the benefits they enjoyed by using the product. This chapter first gives an overview of the communication process and the promotional elements used in marketing and then discusses direct marketing. Chapter 20 covers advertising, sales promotion, and public relations, and Chapter 21 discusses personal selling.

THE COMMUNICATION PROCESS

Communication is the process of conveying a message to others and requires six elements: a source, a message, a channel of communication, a receiver, and the processes of encoding and decoding[2] (Figure 19–1). The **source** may be a company or person who has information to convey. The information sent by a source, such as a description of a new weight reduction drink, forms the **message.** The message is conveyed by means of a **channel of communication** such as a salesperson, advertising media, or public relations tools. Consumers who read, hear, or see the message are the **receivers.**

FIGURE 19–1
The communication process

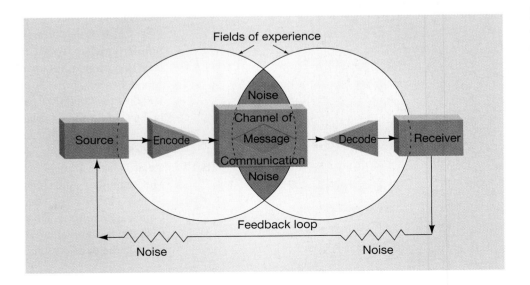

Encoding and Decoding

Encoding and decoding are essential to communication. **Encoding** is the process of having the sender transform an abstract idea into a set of symbols. **Decoding** is the reverse, or the process of having the receiver take a set of symbols, the message, and transform them back to an abstract idea. Look at the accompanying automobile advertisement: Who is the source, and what is the message?

Decoding is performed by the receivers according to their own frame of reference: their attitudes, values, and beliefs.[3] In the ad, Hummer is the source and the message is this advertisement, which appeared in *Wired* magazine (the channel). How would you interpret (decode) this advertisement? The picture and text in the advertisement show that the source's intention is to generate interest in a vehicle in which "it's not a matter of no one else being able to keep up, it's a matter of no one else being able to follow."— a statement the source believes will appeal to the readers of the magazine.

The process of communication is not always a successful one. Errors in communication can happen in several ways. The source may not adequately transform the abstract idea into an effective set of symbols, a properly encoded message may be sent through the wrong channel and never make it to the receiver, the receiver may not properly transform the set of symbols into the correct abstract idea, or finally, feedback may be so delayed or distorted that it is of no use to the sender. Although communication appears easy to perform, truly effective communication can be very difficult.

For the message to be communicated effectively, the sender and receiver must have a mutually shared **field of experience**—similar understanding and knowledge. Figure 19–1 shows two circles representing the fields of experience of the sender and receiver, which overlap in the message. Some of the better-known communication problems have occurred when U.S. companies have taken their messages to cultures with different fields of experience. Many misinterpretations are merely the result of bad translations. For example, General Motors made a mistake when its "Body by Fisher" claim was translated into Flemish as "Corpse by Fisher."[4]

A source and a message.

Hummer
www.hummer.com

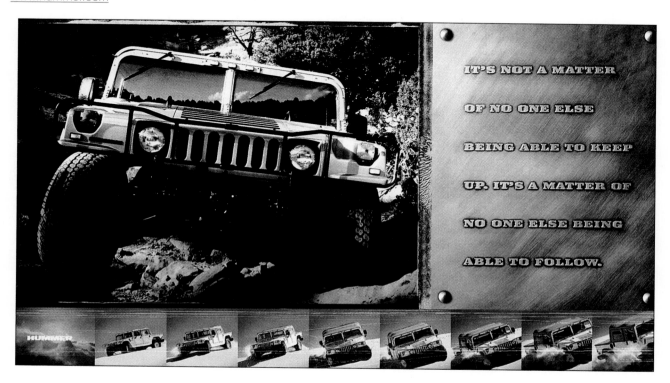

IT'S NOT A MATTER OF NO ONE ELSE BEING ABLE TO KEEP UP. IT'S A MATTER OF NO ONE ELSE BEING ABLE TO FOLLOW.

HUMMER

Feedback

Figure 19–1 shows a line labeled *feedback loop.* **Feedback** is the communication flow from receiver back to sender and indicates whether the message was decoded and understood as intended. Chapter 20 reviews approaches called *pretesting* that ensure that messages are decoded properly.

Noise

Noise includes extraneous factors that can work against effective communication by distorting a message or the feedback received (Figure 19–1). Noise can be a simple error, such as a printing mistake that affects the meaning of a newspaper advertisement, or using words or pictures that fail to communicate the message clearly. Noise can also occur when a salesperson's message is misunderstood by a prospective buyer, such as when a salesperson's accent, use of slang terms, or communication style make hearing and understanding the message difficult.

CONCEPT CHECK

1. What are the six elements required for communication to occur?
2. A difficulty for U.S. companies advertising in international markets is that the audience does not share the same _____ .
3. A misprint in a newspaper ad is an example of _____ .

THE PROMOTIONAL ELEMENTS

To communicate with consumers, a company can use one or more of five promotional alternatives: advertising, personal selling, sales promotion, public relations, and direct marketing. Figure 19–2 summarizes the distinctions among these five elements. Three of these elements—advertising, sales promotion, and public relations—are often said to use

FIGURE 19–2
The promotional mix

PROMOTIONAL ELEMENT	MASS VERSUS CUSTOMIZED	PAYMENT	STRENGTHS	WEAKNESSES
Advertising	Mass	Fees paid for space or time	• Efficient means for reaching large numbers of people	• High absolute costs • Difficult to receive good feedback
Personal selling	Customized	Fees paid to salespeople as either salaries or commissions	• Immediate feedback • Very persuasive • Can select audience • Can give complex information	• Extremely expensive per exposure • Messages may differ between salespeople
Public relations	Mass	No direct payment to media	• Often most credible source in the consumer's mind	• Difficult to get media cooperation
Sales promotion	Mass	Wide range of fees paid, depending on promotion selected	• Effective at changing behavior in short run • Very flexible	• Easily abused • Can lead to promotion wars • Easily duplicated
Direct marketing	Customized	Cost of communication through mail, telephone, or computer	• Messages can be prepared quickly • Facilitates relationship with customer	• Declining customer response • Database management is expensive

mass selling because they are used with groups of prospective buyers. In contrast, personal selling uses *customized interaction* between a seller and a prospective buyer. Personal selling activities include face-to-face, telephone, and interactive electronic communication. Direct marketing also uses messages customized for specific customers.

Advertising

Advertising is any paid form of nonpersonal communication about an organization, good, service, or idea by an identified sponsor. The *paid* aspect of this definition is important because the space for the advertising message normally must be bought. An occasional exception is the public service announcement, where the advertising time or space is donated. A full-page, four-color ad in *Time* magazine, for example, costs $156,000. The *nonpersonal* component of advertising is also important. Advertising involves mass media (such as TV, radio, and magazines), which are nonpersonal and do not have an immediate feedback loop as does personal selling. So before the message is sent, marketing research plays a valuable role; for example, it determines that the message is understood by the target market and that the target market will actually see the medium chosen.

An attention-getting advertisement.

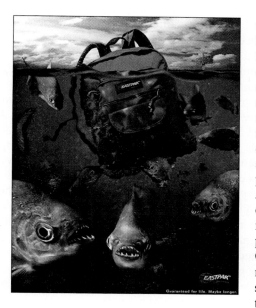

There are several advantages to a firm using advertising in its promotional mix. It can be attention-getting—as with this Eastpak ad—and also communicate specific product benefits to prospective buyers. By paying for the advertising space, a company can control *what* it wants to say and, to some extent, to *whom* the message is sent. If an electronics company wants college students to receive its message about CD players, advertising space is purchased in a college campus newspaper. Advertising also allows the company to decide *when* to send its message (which includes how often). The nonpersonal aspect of advertising also has its advantages. Once the message is created, the same message is sent to all receivers in a market segment. If the message is properly pretested, the company can trust that the same message will be decoded by all receivers in the market segment.

Advertising has some disadvantages. As shown in Figure 19–2 and discussed in depth in Chapter 20, the costs to produce and place a message are significant, and the lack of direct feedback makes it difficult to know how well the message was received.

Personal Selling

The second major promotional alternative is **personal selling,** defined as the two-way flow of communication between a buyer and seller, designed to influence a person's or group's purchase decision. Unlike advertising, personal selling is usually face-to-face communication between the sender and receiver (although telephone and electronic sales are growing). Why do companies use personal selling?

There are important advantages to personal selling, as summarized in Figure 19–2. A salesperson can control to *whom* the presentation is made. Although some control is available in advertising by choosing the medium, some people may read the college newspaper, for example, who are not in the target audience for CD players. For the CD-player manufacturer, those readers outside the target audience are *wasted coverage.*

Wasted coverage can be reduced with personal selling. The personal component of selling has another advantage over advertising in that the seller can see or hear the potential buyer's reaction to the message. If the feedback is unfavorable, the salesperson can modify the message.

The flexibility of personal selling can also be a disadvantage. Different salespeople can change the message so that no consistent communication is given to all customers. The high cost of personal selling is probably its major disadvantage. On a cost-per-contact basis, it is generally the most expensive of the four promotional elements.

Public Relations

Public relations is a form of communication management that seeks to influence the feelings, opinions, or beliefs held by customers, prospective customers, stockholders, suppliers, employees, and other publics about a company and its products or services.[5] Many tools such as special events, lobbying efforts, annual reports, and image management may be used by a public relations department, although publicity often plays the most important role. **Publicity** is a nonpersonal, indirectly paid presentation of an organization, good, or service. It can take the form of a news story, editorial, or product announcement. A difference between publicity and both advertising and personal selling is the "indirectly paid" dimension. With publicity a company does not pay for space in a mass medium (such as television or radio) but attempts to get the medium to run a favorable story on the company. In this sense there is an indirect payment for publicity in that a company must support a public relations staff.

An advantage of publicity is credibility. When you read a favorable story about a company's product (such as a glowing restaurant review), there is a tendency to believe it. Travelers throughout the world have relied on Arthur Frommer's guides such as *Ireland from $50 a Day*. These books outline out-of-the-way, inexpensive restaurants, hotels, inns, and bed-and-breakfast rooms, giving invaluable publicity to these establishments. Such businesses do not (nor can they) buy a mention in the guide, which in recent years has sold millions of copies.

The disadvantages of publicity relate to the lack of the user's control over it. A company can invite a news team to preview its innovative exercise equipment and hope for a favorable mention on the 6 P.M. newscasts. But without buying advertising time, there is no guarantee of any mention of the new equipment or that it will be aired when the target audience is watching. The company representative who calls the station and asks for a replay of the story may be told, "Sorry, it's only news once." With publicity there is little control over what is said, to whom, or when. As a result, publicity is rarely the main component of a promotional campaign.

Sales Promotion

A fourth promotional element is **sales promotion,** a short-term inducement of value offered to arouse interest in buying a good or service. Used in conjunction with advertising or personal selling, sales promotions are offered to intermediaries as well as to ultimate consumers. Coupons, rebates, samples, and sweepstakes are just a few examples of sales promotions discussed later in this chapter.

The advantage of sales promotion is that the short-term nature of these programs (such as a coupon or sweepstakes with an expiration date) often stimulates sales for their duration. Offering value to the consumer in terms of a cents-off coupon or rebate provides an incentive to buy.

Sales promotions cannot be the sole basis for a campaign because gains are often temporary and sales drop off when the deal ends.[6] Advertising support is needed to convert the customer who tried the product because of a sales promotion into a long-term buyer.[7] If sales promotions are conducted continuously, they lose their effectiveness. Customers begin to delay purchase until a coupon is offered, or they question the product's value. Some aspects of sales promotions also are regulated by the federal government. These issues are reviewed in detail later in Chapter 20.

Direct Marketing

Another promotional alternative, **direct marketing**, uses direct communication with consumers to generate a response in the form of an order, a request for further information, or a visit to a retail outlet.[8] The communication can take many forms including face-to-face selling, direct mail, catalogs, telephone solicitations, direct response advertising (on television and radio and in print), and online marketing. Like personal selling, direct marketing often consists of interactive communication. It also has the advantage of being customized to match the needs of specific target markets. Messages can be developed and adapted quickly to facilitate one-to-one relationships with customers.

While direct marketing has been one of the fastest growing forms of promotion, it has several disadvantages. First, most forms of direct marketing require a comprehensive and up-to-date database with information about the target market. Developing and maintaining the database can be expensive and time-consuming. In addition, growing concern about privacy has led to a decline in response rates among some customer groups. Companies with successful direct marketing programs are sensitive to these issues and often use a combination of direct marketing alternatives together, or direct marketing combined with other promotional tools, to increase value for customers.

CONCEPT CHECK

1. Explain the difference between advertising and publicity when both appear on television.

2. Which promotional element should be offered only on a short-term basis?

3. Cost per contact is high with the _____ element of the promotional mix.

INTEGRATED MARKETING COMMUNICATIONS—DEVELOPING THE PROMOTIONAL MIX

A firm's **promotional mix** is the combination of one or more of the promotional elements it chooses to use. In putting together the promotional mix, a marketer must consider several issues. First, the balance of the elements must be determined. Should advertising be emphasized more than personal selling? Should a promotional rebate be offered? Would public relations activities be effective? Several factors affect such decisions: the target audience for the promotion,[9] the stage of the product's life cycle, characteristics of the product, decision stage of the buyer, and even the channel of distribution. Second, because the various promotional elements are often the responsibility of different departments, coordinating a consistent promotional effort is necessary. A promotional planning process designed to ensure integrated marketing communications can facilitate this goal.

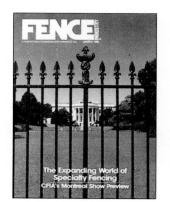

The Target Audience

Promotional programs are directed to the ultimate consumer, to an intermediary (retailer, wholesaler, or industrial distributor), or to both. Promotional programs directed to buyers of consumer products often use mass media because the number of potential buyers is large. Personal selling is used at the place of purchase, generally the retail store. Direct marketing may be used to encourage first-time or repeat purchases.

Advertising directed to industrial buyers is used selectively in trade publications, such as *Fence* magazine for buyers of fencing material. Because industrial buyers often have specialized needs or technical questions, personal selling is particularly important. The salesperson can provide information and the necessary support after sales.

Intermediaries are often the focus of promotional efforts. As with industrial buyers, personal selling is the major promotional ingredient. The salespeople assist intermediaries in making a profit by coordinating promotional campaigns sponsored by the manufacturer and by providing marketing advice and expertise. Intermediaries' questions often pertain to the allowed markup, merchandising support, and return policies.

The Product Life Cycle

All products have a product life cycle (see Chapter 12), and the composition of the promotional mix changes over the four life-cycle stages, as shown for Purina Puppy Chow in Figure 19–3.

Introduction Stage Informing consumers in an effort to increase their level of awareness is the primary promotional objective in the introduction stage of the product life cycle. In general, all the promotional mix elements are used at this time, although the use of specific mix elements during any stage depends on the product and situation. Stories on Purina's new nutritional food are placed in *Dog World* magazine, trial samples are sent to registered dog owners in 10 major cities, advertisements are placed during reruns of the TV show "Lassie," and the salesforce begins to approach supermarkets to get orders. Advertising is particularly important as a means of reaching as many people as possible to build up awareness and interest. Publicity may even begin slightly before the product is commercially available.

Growth Stage The primary promotional objective of the growth stage is to persuade the consumer to buy the product—Purina Puppy Chow—rather than substitutes, so the marketing manager seeks to gain brand preference and solidify distribution. Sales promotion assumes less importance in this stage, and publicity is not a factor because it depends on novelty of the product. The primary promotional element is advertising,

FIGURE 19–3
Promotional tools used over the product life cycle of Purina Puppy Chow

Stage of product life cycle	Introduction	Growth	Maturity	Decline
Promotional objective	To inform	To persuade	To remind	
Promotional activity	• Publicity in veterinary magazines • Advertising • Salesforce calling on intermediaries • Sales promotion in form of free samples	• Personal selling to intermediaries • Advertising to differentiate Puppy Chow attributes from those of competing brands	• Reminder advertising • Sales promotion in form of discounts and coupons • Limited personal selling • Direct mail reminders	• Little money spent on promotion

Purina Puppy Chow: a product in the maturity stage of its life cycle.

IBM

IBM must consider product characteristics such as complexity, risk, and ancillary services when designing its promotional mix.

which stresses brand differences. Personal selling is used to solidify the channel of distribution. For consumer products such as dog food, the salesforce calls on the wholesalers and retailers in hopes of increasing inventory levels and gaining shelf space. For industrial products, the salesforce often tries to get contractual arrangements to be the sole source of supply for the buyer.

Maturity Stage In the maturity stage the need is to maintain existing buyers, and advertising's role is to remind buyers of the product's existence. Sales promotion, in the form of discounts and coupons offered to both ultimate consumers and intermediaries, is important in maintaining loyal buyers. In a test of one mature consumer product, it was found that 80 percent of the product's sales at this stage resulted from sales promotions.[10] Direct marketing actions such as direct mail are used to maintain involvement with existing customers and to encourage repeat purchases. Price cuts and discounts can also significantly increase a mature brand's sales. The salesforce at this stage seeks to satisfy intermediaries. An unsatisfied customer who switches brands is hard to replace.

Decline Stage The decline stage of the product life cycle is usually a period of phaseout for the product, and little money is spent in the promotional mix.

Product Characteristics

The proper blend of elements in the promotional mix also depends on the type of product. Three specific characteristics should be considered: complexity, risk, and ancillary services. *Complexity* refers to the technical sophistication of the product and hence the amount of understanding required to use it. It's hard to provide much information in a

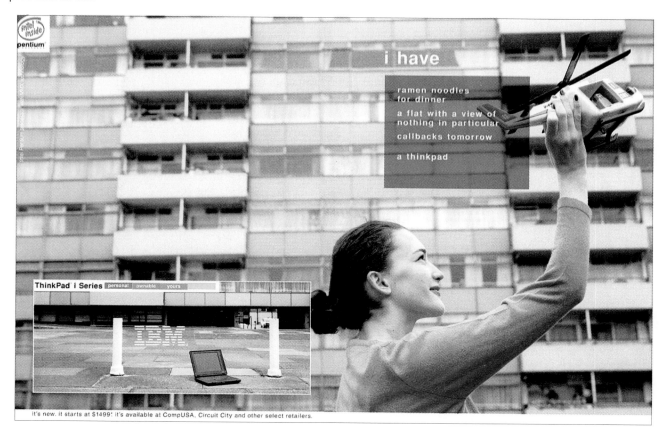

one-page magazine ad or 30-second television ad, so the more complex the product, the greater the emphasis on personal selling.

A second element is the degree of *risk* represented by the product's purchase. Risk for the buyer can be assessed in terms of financial risk, social risk, and physical risk. A hair transplant procedure, for example, might represent all three risks—it may be expensive, people can see and evaluate the purchase, and there may be a chance of physical harm. Although advertising helps, the greater the risk, the greater the need for personal selling.

The level of *ancillary services* required by a product also affects the promotional strategy. Ancillary services pertain to the degree of service or support required after the sale. This characteristic is common to many industrial products and consumer purchases. Who will repair your automobile or VCR? Advertising's role is to establish the seller's reputation. Direct marketing can be used to describe how a product or service can be customized to individual needs. However, personal selling is essential to build buyer confidence and provide evidence of customer service.

Stages of the Buying Decision

Knowing the customer's stage of decision making can also affect the promotional mix. Figure 19–4 shows how the importance of the promotional elements varies with the three stages in a consumer's purchase decision.

Prepurchase Stage   In the prepurchase stage advertising is more helpful than personal selling because advertising informs the potential customer of the existence of the product and the seller. Sales promotion in the form of free samples also can play an important role to gain low-risk trial. When the salesperson calls on the customer after heavy advertising, there is some recognition of what the salesperson represents. This is particularly important in industrial settings in which sampling of the product is usually not possible.

Purchase Stage   At the purchase stage the importance of personal selling is highest, whereas the impact of advertising is lowest. Sales promotion in the form of coupons, deals, point-of-purchase displays, and rebates can be very helpful in encour-

FIGURE 19–4
How the importance of promotional elements varies during the consumer's purchase decision

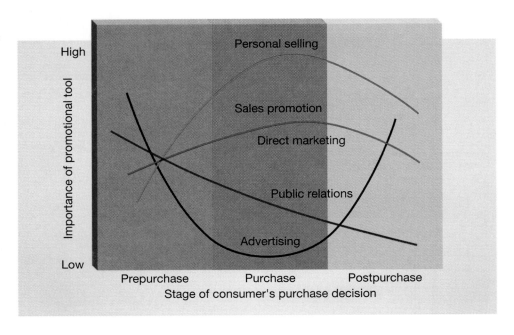

aging demand. In this stage, although advertising is not an active influence on the purchase, it is the means of delivering the coupons, deals, and rebates that are often important.

Postpurchase Stage   In the postpurchase stage the salesperson is still important. In fact, the more personal contact after the sale, the more the buyer is satisfied. Advertising is also important to assure the buyer that the right purchase was made. Advertising and personal selling help reduce the buyer's postpurchase anxiety.[11] Sales promotion in the form of coupons and direct marketing reminders can help encourage repeat purchases from satisfied first-time triers. Public relations plays a small role in the postpurchase stage.

Channel Strategies

Chapter 16 discussed the channel flow from producer to intermediaries to consumer. Achieving control of the channel is often difficult for the manufacturer, and promotional strategies can assist in moving a product through the channel of distribution. This is where a manufacturer has to make an important decision about whether to use a push strategy, pull strategy, or both in its channel of distribution.[12]

Push Strategy   Figure 19–5A shows how a manufacturer uses a **push strategy,** directing the promotional mix to channel members to gain their cooperation in ordering and stocking the product. In this approach, personal selling and sales promotions play major roles. Salespeople call on wholesalers to encourage orders and provide sales assistance. Sales promotions, such as case discount allowances (20 percent off the regular case price), are offered to stimulate demand. By pushing the product through the channel, the goal is to get channel members to push it to their customers.

Anheuser-Busch, for example, spends a significant amount of its marketing resources on maintaining its relationship with its distributors, and through them, with retailers. At a recent meeting of its wholesalers and salespeople, Anheuser-Busch announced that it would provide $250 million of marketing support for its Budweiser

FIGURE 19–5
A comparison of push and pull promotional strategies

brand—an action designed to maintain channel dominance. The company also arranges group discounts on purchase of trucks, insurance, and the computers that wholesalers use to order beer. Even specialized computer software is provided to help retailers maximize the shelf space of Anheuser-Busch products.[13]

Claritin
www.claritin.com

Pull Strategy In some instances manufacturers face resistance from channel members who do not want to order a new product or increase inventory levels of an existing brand. As shown in Figure 19–5B, a manufacturer may then elect to implement a **pull strategy** by directing its promotional mix at ultimate consumers to encourage them to ask the retailer for the product. Seeing demand from ultimate consumers, retailers order the product from wholesalers and thus the item is pulled through the intermediaries. Pharmaceutical companies, for example, historically marketed only to doctors. They now spend more than $1.2 billion annually to advertise prescription drugs directly to consumers. The strategy is designed to encourage consumers to ask their physicians for a specific drug by name—pulling it through the channel. Successful advertising strategies, such as Claritin's "Talk to your doctor . . ." campaign, can have dramatic effects on the sales of a product.[14]

Integrated Marketing Communications

In the past the promotional elements were regarded as separate functions handled by experts in separate departments. The salesforce designed and managed its activities independently of the advertising department, and sales promotion and public relations were often the responsibility of outside agencies or specialists. The result was often an overall communication effort that was uncoordinated and, in some cases, inconsistent. Reebok, for example, had to quickly change its promotion program when a scene involving Cuba Gooding and Reebok products was cut by Sony from its movie *Jerry Maguire*.[15] Today the concept of designing marketing communications programs that coordinate all promotional activities—advertising, personal selling, sales promotion, public relations, and direct marketing—to provide a consistent message across all audiences is referred to as **integrated marketing communications** (IMC).

The key to developing successful IMC programs is to create a process that facilitates their design and use. A tool used to evaluate a company's current process is the IMC audit. The audit analyzes the internal communication network of the company, identifies key audiences, evaluates customer databases, assesses messages in recent ads, public relations releases, packaging, video news releases, signage, sales promotion pieces, and direct mail, and determines managers' knowledge of IMC.[16] While many organizations are interested in improving their IMC process, a recent survey suggests that fewer than one third have been successful at implementing IMC. The reasons include lack of expertise, lack of budget, and lack of management approval.[17]

Once the IMC process is implemented, most organizations want to assess its benefits. The tendency is to try to determine which element of promotion "works" better. In an integrated program, however, media advertising might be used to build awareness, sales promotion to generate an inquiry, direct mail to provide additional information to individual prospects, and a personal sales call to complete the transaction. The tools are used for different reasons, and their combined use creates a synergy that should be the focus of the assessment.[18] The accompanying Marketing NewsNet box describes some of the many promotional activities Taco Bell integrated to become the leading Mexican fast-food restaurant.[19]

MARKETING NEWSNET

Yo Quiero IMC!

Taco Bell's promotional strategy is to attract the fickle 18-to-24-year-old crowd with interactivity, differentiation from other products, challenges, and things that are "cool." Their advertising and promotion budget last year was approximately $250 million and included a variety of integrated communication activities such as

- Advertising campaigns featuring a talking chihuahua, including the campaign introducing Taco Bell's Grande Meal package.
- In-store premiums such as talking Chihuahua dolls. Their lines include "Here lizard, lizard," "Viva Gorditas," "You're Getting Hungry, Very Hungry," and "Yo Quiero Taco Bell!"
- A Web page with nutritional information, restaurant locations, Taco Bell career opportunities, games, and photos from the TV ads, which are available to download.
- A Valentine's Day contest asking consumers to send a video or photo of how they would use a chihuahua toy that says "I Think I'm in Love" in a wedding proposal. The winner receives a $10,000 engagement ring from Taco Bell.

- Licensing agreements to sell backpacks, keychains, hats, and T-shirts, and deals with Target, FAO Schwartz, and Wal-Mart to sell a full-size version of the dog.

The integrated campaign has been a huge success. Sales at Taco Bell now exceed $5 billion, some of the toys are selling on the Internet for as much as $100, and, according to Taco Bell spokesperson Laurie Gannon, "Our customers have asked to see more of the dog." "It appeals to an incredible cross section—young and old, male and female, all across the country. His determination makes him a hero that everybody seems to love."

CONCEPT CHECK

1. For consumer products, why is advertising emphasized more than personal selling?

2. Explain the differences between a push strategy and a pull strategy.

3. Integrated marketing communications programs provide a _____ message across all audiences.

DEVELOPING THE PROMOTION PROGRAM

Because media costs are high, promotion decisions must be made carefully, using a systematic approach. Paralleling the planning, implementation, and control steps described in the strategic marketing process (Chapter 2), the promotion decision process is divided into (1) developing, (2) executing, and (3) evaluating the promotion program (Figure 19–6). Development of the promotion program focuses on the four *W*s:

- *Who* is the target audience?
- *What* are (1) the promotion objectives, (2) the amounts of money that can be budgeted for the promotion program, and (3) the kinds of promotion to use?

FIGURE 19-6
The promotion decision process

• *Where* should the promotion be run?
 • *When* should the promotion be run?

Identifying the Target Audience

The first decision in developing the promotion program is identifying the *target audience,* the group of prospective buyers toward which a promotion program is directed. To the extent that time and money permit, the target audience for the promotion program is the target market for the firm's product, which is identified from marketing research and market segmentation studies. The more a firm knows about its target audience's profile—including their lifestyle, attitudes, and values—the easier it is to develop a promotion program. If a firm wanted to reach you with television and magazine ads, for example, it would need to know what TV shows you watch and what magazines you read.

Specifying Promotion Objectives

After the target audience is identified, a decision must be reached on what the promotion should accomplish. Consumers can be said to respond in terms of a **hierarchy of effects,** which is the sequence of stages a prospective buyer goes through from initial awareness of a product to eventual action (either trial or adoption of the product).[20]

 • *Awareness.* The consumer's ability to recognize and remember the product or brand name.
 • *Interest.* An increase in the consumer's desire to learn about some of the features of the product or brand.
 • *Evaluation.* The consumer's appraisal of the product or brand on important attributes.
 • *Trial.* The consumer's actual first purchase and use of the product or brand.
 • *Adoption.* Through a favorable experience on the first trial, the consumer's repeated purchase and use of the product or brand.

For a totally new product the sequence applies to the entire product category, but for a new brand competing in an established product category it applies to the brand itself. These steps can serve as guidelines for developing promotion objectives.

Although sometimes an objective for a promotion program involves several steps in the hierarchy of effects, it often focuses on a single stage. Regardless of what the specific objective might be, from building awareness to increasing repeat purchases,[21] promotion objectives should possess three important qualities. They should (1) be designed for a well-defined target audience, (2) be measurable, and (3) cover a specified time period.

Setting the Promotion Budget

From Figure 19–7 it is clear that the promotion expenditures needed to reach U.S. households are enormous. Note that 11 companies—General Motors, Procter & Gamble, Philip Morris, Chrysler, Ford, Sears, Walt Disney, PepsiCo, Diageo, McDonald's, and Time Warner—each spend a total of more than $1 billion dollars annually on promotion.

After setting the promotion objectives, a company must decide on how much to spend. Determining the ideal amount for the budget is difficult because there is no precise way to measure the exact results of spending promotion dollars. However, there are several methods used to set the promotion budget.[22]

Percentage of Sales   In the **percentage of sales budgeting** approach, funds are allocated to promotion as a percentage of past or anticipated sales, in terms of either dollars or units sold. A common budgeting method,[23] this approach is often stated in terms such as, "Our promotion budget for this year is 3 percent of last year's gross sales." The advantage of this approach is obvious: it's simple and provides a financial safeguard by tying the promotion budget to sales. However, there is a major fallacy in this approach, which implies that sales cause promotion. Using this method, a company may reduce its promotion budget because of a downturn in past sales or an anticipated downturn in future sales—situations where it may need promotion the most.

Competitive Parity   A second common approach, **competitive parity budgeting**, is matching the competitor's absolute level of spending or the proportion per point of market share. This approach has also been referred to as *matching competitors* or *share of market*. It is important to consider the competition in budgeting.[24] Consumer responses to promotion are affected by competing promotional activities, so if a competitor runs 30 radio ads each week, it may be difficult for a firm to get its message across with only five messages.[25] The competitor's budget level, however, should not be the only determinant in setting a company's budget. The competition might have very different promotional objectives, which require a different level of promotion expenditures.

FIGURE 19–7
Promotion expenditures by companies in 1997

RANK	COMPANY	TOTAL (MILLIONS)	ADVERTISING (MILLIONS)	DIRECT MAIL, SALES PROMOTION, COUPONS, AND OTHER PROMOTIONS (MILLIONS)
1	General Motors	$3,087	$2,262	$ 825
2	Procter & Gamble	2,743	1,690	1,053
3	Philip Morris	2,137	1,319	818
4	Chrysler	1,532	1,302	230
5	Ford	1,281	994	287
6	Sears	1,262	760	502
7	Walt Disney	1,249	749	500
8	PepsiCo	1,244	334	910
9	Diageo	1,206	663	543
10	McDonald's	1,041	580	461
11	Time Warner	1,013	781	232
12	IBM	924	291	633
13	Johnson & Johnson	920	823	97
14	Unilever	909	619	290
15	JCPenney	906	362	544

All You Can Afford   Common to many small businesses is **all-you-can-afford budgeting,** in which money is allocated to promotion only after all other budget items are covered. As one company executive said in reference to this budgeting process, "Why, it's simple. First, I go upstairs to the controller and ask how much they can afford to give us this year. He says a million and a half. Later, the boss comes to me and asks how much we should spend, and I say 'Oh, about a million and a half.' Then we have our promotion appropriation."[26]

Fiscally conservative, this approach has little else to offer. Using this budgeting philosophy, a company acts as though it doesn't know anything about a promotion–sales relationship or what its promotion objectives are.

Objective and Task   The best approach to budgeting is **objective and task budgeting,** whereby the company (1) determines its promotion objectives, (2) outlines the tasks to accomplish these objectives, and (3) determines the promotion cost of performing these tasks.[27]

This method takes into account what the company wants to accomplish and requires that the objectives be specified.[28] Strengths of the other budgeting methods are integrated into this approach because each previous method's strength is tied to the objectives. For example, if the costs are beyond what the company can afford, objectives are reworked and the tasks revised. The difficulty with this method is the judgment required to determine the tasks needed to accomplish objectives. Would two or four insertions in *Time* magazine be needed to achieve a specific awareness level? Figure 19–8 shows a sample media plan with objectives, tasks, and budget outlined. The total amount to be budgeted is $430,000. If the company can only afford $300,000, the objectives must be reworked, tasks redefined, and the total budget recalculated.

Selecting the Right Promotional Tools

Once a budget has been determined, the combination of the five basic IMC tools—advertising, personal selling, sales promotion, public relations, and direct marketing—can be specified. While many factors provide direction for selection of the appropriate mix, the large number of possible combinations of the promotional tools means that many combinations can achieve the same objective. Therefore, an analytical approach and experience are particularly important in this step of the promotion decision process. The specific mix can vary from a simple program using a single tool to a comprehensive program using all forms of promotion. The Olympics have become a very visible example of a comprehensive integrated communication program. Because the Games are repeated every two years, the promotion is almost continuous. Included in the program are advertising campaigns, personal selling efforts by the Olympic committee and organizers, sales promotion activities such as product tie-ins and sponsorships, public relations programs managed by the host cities, and direct marketing

FIGURE 19–8
The objective and task approach

OBJECTIVE	
To increase awareness among college students for a new video game. Awareness at the end of one semester should be 20 percent of all students from the existing 0 percent today.	

TASKS	COSTS
Advertisements once a week for a semester in 500 college papers	$280,000
Direct-mail samples to student leaders on 500 college campuses	50,000
Sponsor a national contest for video-game players	100,000
Total budget	$430,000

efforts targeted at a variety of audiences including governments, organizations, firms, athletes, and individuals.[29] At this stage, it is also important to assess the relative importance of the various tools. While it may be desirable to utilize and integrate several forms of promotion, one may deserve emphasis. The Olympics, for example, place exceptional importance on public relations and publicity.

Designing the Promotion

The central element of a promotion program is the promotion itself. Advertising consists of advertising copy and the artwork that the target audience is intended to see or hear. Personal selling efforts depend on the characteristics and skills of the salesperson. Sales promotion activities consist of the specific details of inducements such as coupons, samples, and sweepstakes. Public relations efforts are readily seen in tangible elements such as news releases, and direct marketing actions depend on written, verbal, and electronic forms of delivery. The design of the promotion will play a primary role in determining the message that is communicated to the audience. This design activity is frequently viewed as the step requiring the most creativity. In addition, successful designs are often the result of insight regarding consumer's interests and purchasing behavior. All of the promotion tools have many design alternatives. Advertising, for example, can utilize fear, humor, or other emotions in its appeal. Similarly, direct marketing can be designed for varying levels of personal or customized appeals. One of the challenges of IMC is to design each promotional activity to communicate the same message.

Scheduling the Promotion

Once the design of each of the promotional program elements is complete, it is important to determine the most effective timing of their use. The promotion schedule describes the order in which each promotional tool is introduced and the frequency of its use during the campaign. The movie *Godzilla*, for example, used an instant-win sweepstakes at Taco Bell to generate interest in the movie months before its release. The sweepstakes was followed by advertising that did not actually show Godzilla. Finally, once the movie was in theaters, product tie-ins and license agreements began.[30] Overall, the scheduling of the various promotions was designed to generate interest, bring consumers into theaters, and then encourage additional purchases after seeing the movie. Several factors such as seasonality and competitive promotion activity can also influence the promotion schedule. Businesses such as ski resorts, airlines, and professional sports teams are likely to reduce their promotional activity during the "off" season. Similarly, restaurants, retail stores, and health clubs are likely to increase their promotional activity when new competitors enter the market.

EXECUTING AND EVALUATING THE PROMOTION PROGRAM

As shown earlier in Figure 19–6, the ideal execution of a promotion program involves pretesting each design before it is actually used to allow for changes and modifications which improve its effectiveness. Similarly, posttests are recommended to evaluate the impact of each promotion and the contribution of the promotion toward achieving the program objectives. The most sophisticated pretest and posttest procedures have been developed for advertising and are discussed in Chapter 20. Testing procedures for sales promotion and direct marketing efforts currently focus on comparisons of different designs or responses of different segments. To fully benefit from IMC programs, companies must create and maintain a test-result database that allows comparisons of the relative impact of the promotional tools, and their execution options, in varying situations. Information from the database will allow informed design and execution decisions and provide support for IMC activities during internal reviews by financial or administrative personnel. The San Diego Padres baseball team, for example, developed a database of information relating attendance to its integrated campaign using a new logo, special events, merchandise sales, and a loyalty program.

Carrying out the promotion program can be expensive and time-consuming. One researcher estimates that "an organization with sales less than $10 million can successfully implement an IMC program in one year, one with sales between $200 million and $500 million will need about three years, and one with sales between $2 billion and $5 billion will need five years." To facilitate the transition there are approximately 200 integrated marketing communications agencies in operation. In addition, some of the largest advertising agencies are adopting approaches that embrace "total communications solutions." J. Walter Thompson USA's Chicago office, for example, now has a 35-person Total Solutions Group that is responsible for designing integrated programs such as the "It's best to be direct" campaign it developed for Dell Computer. While most agencies still have departments dedicated to promotion, direct marketing, and other specialties, the trend today is clearly toward a long-term perspective in which all forms of promotion are integrated.[31]

CONCEPT CHECK	**1.** What are the characteristics of good promotion objectives?
	2. What are the weaknesses of the percentage of sales budgeting approach?
	3. How have advertising agencies changed to facilitate the use of IMC programs?

DIRECT MARKETING

Direct marketing has many forms and utilizes a variety of media. The most popular forms of direct marketing—direct mail and catalogs, television, telemarketing, and direct selling—were discussed as methods of nonstore retailing in Chapter 18. In addition, interactive or online marketing is discussed in detail in Chapter 8. In this section the growth of direct marketing; its benefits; and key global, technological, and ethical issues are discussed.

The Growth of Direct Marketing

The increasing interest in customer relations is reflected in the dramatic growth of direct marketing. The ability to customize communication efforts and create one-to-one interactions is appealing to most marketers, particularly those with IMC programs. While direct marketing methods are not new, the ability to design and use them has increased with the availability of computers and databases. In recent years direct marketing growth—in terms of spending, revenue generated, and employment—has outpaced total economic growth. Figure 19–9 shows the past and projected growth in direct marketing expenditures and revenue between 1993 and 2003. Direct marketing expenditures of $173.7 billion in 1999 are expected to grow 27 percent by 2003. Similarly, 1999 revenues of $1,492.5 billion are expected to grow 38 percent to $2,073.2 billion. Employment has also grown and now numbers more than 13 million employees.[32] The accompanying Web Link describes how to find local direct marketing clubs and associations where employment opportunities may be posted.

Columbia House is one example of the kinds of companies fueling the growth in direct marketing. You may have received the company's letters in the mail offering 12 free music CDs if you agree to buy 4 additional CDs over the next two years. In the past, the CDs were automatically delivered unless the customer tells the company not to send them. Today, through a new program called "Play," customers decide when to

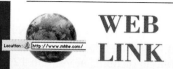

WEB LINK

Is There a Direct Marketing Club Near You?

As one of the fastest growing areas of marketing, there are now a large number of associations and clubs to help marketing students and professionals enhance their direct marketing knowledge and skills. To find out if there is one near you, go to the Direct Marketing Association Web site at www.the-dma.org. Click on "services" and "Local DM Clubs" or "Int'l DM Clubs," and then click on a state or country to find the club or association nearest you! Many of the listings have Web sites where you can obtain information or register to become a member!

order. Columbia House views the change in strategy as an investment in a long-term relationship with their customers. According to Sharon Kuroki, executive vice president of music marketing, "What happens with these members is that they don't buy as much initially, but they stay in the club longer," and "they eventually buy as much" as members did with the old plan.[33]

Another component of the growth in direct marketing is the increasing popularity of the newest direct marketing channel—the Internet. As discussed in Chapter 8, total online expenditures have risen from close to nothing in 1996 to projections approaching 50 billion today. Continued growth in the number of consumers with Internet access and the number of businesses with Web sites and electronic commerce offerings is likely to contribute to the future growth of direct marketing.

FIGURE 19–9
Direct marketing expenditures and sales, 1993–2003

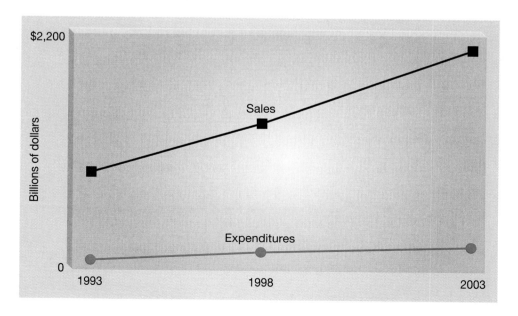

The Value of Direct Marketing

One of the most visible indicators of the value of direct marketing for consumers is the level of use of various forms of direct marketing. For example, 68 percent of the U.S. population has ordered merchandise or services by phone or mail; more than 12 million adults have purchased items from a television offer; the average adult spends more than 30 hours per year accessing online services; and more than 21 percent of all adults make three to five purchases from a catalog each year. Consumers report many benefits, including the following: they don't have to go to a store, they can usually shop 24 hours a day, buying direct saves time, they avoid hassles with salespeople, they can save money, it's fun and entertaining, and direct marketing offers more privacy than in-store shopping. Many consumers also believe that direct marketing provides excellent customer service.[34] Toll-free telephone numbers, customer service representatives with access to information regarding purchasing preferences, overnight delivery services, and unconditional guarantees all help create value for direct marketing customers.

The value of direct marketing for sellers can be described in terms of the responses it generates.[35] **Direct orders** are the result of offers that contain all the information necessary for a prospective buyer to make a decision to purchase and complete the transaction. Club Med, for example, uses direct e-mail offers to sell "last-minute specials" to people in its database. The messages, which are sent midweek, describe rooms and air transportation available at a 30 to 40 percent discount if the customer can make the decision to travel on such short notice.[36] **Lead generation** is the result of an offer designed to generate interest in a product or service and a request for addi-

Mitsubishi Motors
www.mitsubishi-motors.co.ip

Mitsubishi uses a direct-mail offer to generate traffic for dealers.

tional information. Insurance provider Fireman's Fund uses direct mail and direct-response TV ads to generate leads for its agents and brokers. Both offers emphasize possible savings for middle-income, middle-age households and provide an 800 number for prospective customers to call for an insurance quote.[37] Finally, **traffic generation** is the outcome of an offer designed to motivate people to visit a business. Mitsubishi recently mailed a sweepstakes offer to 1 million prospective buyers to encourage them to visit a Mitsubishi dealer and test drive the new Galant. The names of prospects who take test drives were entered in the sweepstakes, which included a Galant, a trip to Hawaii, and large-screen TVs as prizes.[38]

Technological, Global, and Ethical Issues in Direct Marketing

The information technology and databases described in Chapter 9 are key elements in any direct marketing program. Databases are the result of organizations' efforts to collect demographic, media, and consumption profiles of customers so that direct marketing tools—such as catalogs—can be directed at specific customers. For example, Lillian Vernon started her very successful mail-order company four decades ago at her kitchen table by putting all her merchandise in a single catalog: laundry baskets and men's slippers on one page might be followed by toys on the next. But in the last few years Lillian Vernon has shifted to a database approach with the 150 million catalogs she mails annually. There are now home-oriented, children's, and Christmas-ornament catalogs targeted at customers who have purchased these kinds of merchandise from her main catalog in the past.[39]

While most companies try to keep records of their customers' past purchases, many other types of data are needed to use direct marketing to develop one-to-one relationships with customers. Data, however, have little value by themselves. To translate data into information the data must be unbiased, timely, pertinent, accessible, and organized in a way that helps the marketing manager make decisions that lead to direct marketing actions. Some data, such as lifestyles, media use, and consumption behavior, must be collected in consumers' homes. Other types of data can be collected from the businesses where purchases are made. Today, technology such as optical scanners helps collect data with as little intrusion on the customer as possible. Pizza Hut, for example, uses scanners to read bar codes on coupons and track more than 50 million customers currently in its database.[40]

Technology may also prove to be important in the global growth of direct marketing. Compared with the United States, other countries' direct marketing systems are undeveloped. The mail and telephone systems in many countries are likely to improve, however, creating many new direct marketing opportunities. Developments in international marketing research and database management will also facilitate global growth. In Argentina, for example, mail service is very slow, telephone service is poor, and response to some forms of direct marketing such as coupons is negligible. The country is the first, however, to fully deregulate its postal service and expects rapid improvement from the private company, Correo Argentino. In Mexico direct marketing activities are more advanced. Pond's recently mailed 20,000 direct-mail offers within Mexico and was surprised by a 33 percent response.[41] Another issue for global direct marketers is payment. Because fewer consumers have credit cards, alternatives such as C.O.D. and bank deposits are needed.

Global and domestic direct marketers both face challenging ethical issues today. Of course there has been considerable attention given to some annoying direct marketing activities such as telephone solicitations during dinner and evening hours. Recent concerns about privacy, however, have led to various attempts to provide guidelines that balance consumer and business interests. The European Union recently passed a consumer privacy law, called the Data Protection Directive, after several years of discussion with the Federation of European Direct Marketing and the U.K.'s Direct

ETHICS AND SOCIAL RESPONSIBILITY ALERT   **Is Personal Privacy for Sale?**

ETHICS

MasterCard International recently asked 507 people for their views about direct marketing and discovered that 75 percent agreed, "We need to find ways to stop business and government from collecting information about the average person." The Federal Trade Commission has adopted new rules for telemarketers, and more than half of the state legislatures have introduced or enacted legislation likely to affect direct marketing. Some of the key issues and questions include the following:

- *Disclosure*. Should companies be required to disclose to consumers that information about them is being collected?
- *Knowledge*. Should businesses be limited in the types and amount of information collected about individuals?

- *Suppression*. Should consumers be able to remove themselves from databases?

Some experts argue that the First Amendment specifies there should be no restrictions on the collection and use of data. Many businesses advocating self-regulation have adopted privacy principles to guide their marketing practices. The Direct Marketing Association developed the Mail Preference Service as a means for consumers to remove their names from mailing lists. Finally, consumers in the MasterCard survey indicated that they would be more willing to disclose personal information in exchange for an incentive. What were the incentives most preferred by respondents? Better protection against fraud and lower finance charges.

What is your opinion about these privacy issues?

Marketing Association. In the United States, the Federal Trade Commission and many state legislatures have also been concerned about privacy.[42] The accompanying Ethics and Social Responsibility Alert offers some of the details of the debate.[43]

CONCEPT CHECK

1. The ability to design and use direct marketing programs has increased with the availability of _____ and _____ .

2. What are the three types of responses generated by direct marketing activities?

SUMMARY

1 Communication is the process of conveying a message to others and requires a source, a message, a channel of communication, a receiver, and the processes of encoding and decoding.

2 For effective communication to occur, the sender and receiver must have a shared field of experience. Feedback from receiver to sender helps determine whether decoding has occurred or noise has distorted the message.

3 The promotional elements consist of advertising, personal selling, sales promotion, public relations, and direct marketing. These tools vary according to whether they are personal; can be identified with a sponsor; and can be controlled with regard to whom, when, where, and how often the message is sent.

4 In selecting the appropriate promotional mix, marketers must consider the target audience, the stage of the product's

life cycle, characteristics of the product, decision stage of the buyer, and the channel of distribution.

5 The target for promotional programs can be the ultimate consumer, an intermediary, or both. Ultimate consumer programs rely more on advertising, whereas personal selling is more important in reaching industrial buyers and intermediaries.

6 The emphasis on the promotional tools varies with a product's life cycle. In introduction, awareness is important. During growth, creating brand preference is essential. Advertising is more important in the former stage and personal selling in the latter. Sales promotion helps maintain buyers in the maturity stage.

7 The appropriate promotional mix depends on the complexity of the product, the degree of risk associated with its purchase, and the need for ancillary services.

8 In the prepurchase stage of a customer's purchase decision advertising and public relations are emphasized; at the purchase stage personal selling, sales promotion, and direct marketing are most important; and during the postpurchase stage advertising, personal selling, and sales promotion are used to reduce postpurchase anxiety.

9 When a push strategy is used, personal selling and sales promotions directed to intermediaries play major roles. In a pull strategy, advertising and sales promotions directed to ultimate consumers are important.

10 Integrated marketing communications programs coordinate all promotional activities to provide a consistent message across all audiences.

11 The promotion decision process involves developing, executing, and evaluating the promotion program. Developing the promotion program focuses on determining who is the target audience, what to say, where the message should be said, and when to say it.

12 Setting promotion objectives is based on the hierarchy of effects. Objectives should be measurable, have a specified time period, and state the target audience.

13 Budgeting methods often used are percentage of sales, competitive parity, and the all-you-can-afford approaches. The best budgeting approach is based on the objectives set and tasks required.

14 Selecting, designing, and scheduling promotional elements requires experience and creativity because of the large number of possible combinations of the promotion mix.

15 Direct marketing offers consumers convenience, entertainment, privacy, time savings, low prices, and customer service. Sellers benefit from direct orders, lead generation, and traffic generation.

16 Global opportunities for direct marketing will increase as mail and telephone systems improve worldwide. Consumer's concerns about privacy will be a key issue for direct marketers in the future.

KEY TERMS AND CONCEPTS

communication p. 492
source p. 492
message p. 492
channel of communication p. 492
receivers p. 492
encoding p. 493
decoding p. 493
field of experience p. 493
feedback p. 494
noise p. 494
advertising p. 495
personal selling p. 495
public relations p. 496
publicity p. 496

sales promotion p. 496
direct marketing p. 497
promotional mix p. 497
push strategy p. 501
pull strategy p. 502
integrated marketing communications p. 502
hierarchy of effects p. 504
percentage of sales budgeting p. 505
competitive parity budgeting p. 505
all-you-can-afford budgeting p. 506
objective and task budgeting p. 506
direct orders p. 510
lead generation p. 510
traffic generation p. 511

INTERNET EXERCISE

Several large advertising agencies have described shifts in their philosophies to include IMC approaches to communication. In many cases the outcome has been campaigns that utilize a combination of the five promotional elements. Go to J. Walter Thompson's Web site at www.jwt.com, and review its integrated campaigns.

1 Describe the promotional elements of one of the campaigns. Why were these elements selected? How are they integrated?

2 How would you evaluate the effectiveness of each of the promotional elements used? How would you evaluate the effectiveness of the entire campaign?

APPLYING MARKETING CONCEPTS AND PERSPECTIVES

1 After listening to a recent sales presentation, Mary Smith signed up for membership at the local health club. On arriving at the facility, she learned there was an additional fee for racquetball court rentals. "I don't remember that in the sales talk; I thought they said all facilities were included with the membership fee," complained Mary. Describe the problem in terms of the communication process.

2 Develop a matrix to compare the five elements of the promotional mix on three criteria—to *whom* you deliver the message, *what* you say, and *when* you say it.

3 Explain how the promotional tools used by an airline would differ if the target audience were (*a*) consumers who travel for pleasure and (*b*) corporate travel departments that select the airlines to be used by company employees.

4 Suppose you introduced a new consumer food product and invested heavily both in national advertising (pull strategy) and in training and motivating your field salesforce to sell the product to food stores (push strategy). What kinds of feedback would you receive from both the advertising and your salesforce? How could you increase both the quality and quantity of each?

5 Fisher-Price Company, long known as a manufacturer of children's toys, has introduced a line of clothing for children. Outline a promotional plan to get this product introduced in the marketplace.

6 Many insurance companies sell health insurance plans to companies. In these companies the employees pick the plan, but the set of offered plans is determined by the company. Recently Blue Cross–Blue Shield, a health insurance company,

ran a television ad stating, "If your employer doesn't offer you Blue Cross–Blue Shield coverage, ask why." Explain the promotional strategy behind the advertisement.

7 Identify the sales promotion tools that might be useful for (*a*) Tastee Yogurt—a new brand introduction, (*b*) 3M self-sticking Post-it notes, and (*c*) Wrigley's Spearmint Gum.

8 Design an integrated marketing communications program—using each of the five promotional elements—for Music Boulevard, the online music store.

9 BMW recently introduced its first sport-utility vehicle, the X5, to compete with other popular 4X4 vehicles such as the Mercedes-Benz M-class and Jeep Grand Cherokee. Design a direct marketing program to generate (*a*) leads, (*b*) traffic in dealerships, and (*c*) direct orders.

10 Develop a privacy policy for database managers that provides a balance of consumer and seller perspectives. How would you encourage voluntary compliance with your policy? What methods of enforcement would you recommend?

 CASE 19–1   AIRWALK, INC.

"To effectively communicate with the youth audience," observes Sharon Lee, "it is important to earn their respect by knowing what they think and how they think. You must stay one step ahead of them by constantly studying what they are reading, doing, listening to, playing, and watching."

Sharon Lee speaks from experience. She is an account director at Lambesis, the California advertising agency whose integrated marketing communications (IMC) program launched Airwalk shoes into the stratosphere. Lee's job is to be the key link between Airwalk and Lambesis. Her special insights into the youth market have helped make Airwalk's recent success possible. But it wasn't always so easy.

EARLY DAYS: THE STRUGGLE

George Yohn founded the company in 1986—searching for a piece of the fast-growing athletic shoe craze headed by Nike and Reebok. His first efforts marketing an aerobic shoe hit the wall, so he had to find a new product and marketing strategy. Then one of his designers found a sport that other sneaker manufacturers hadn't yet discovered: skateboarding. Yohn watched skateboarders drag their feet to turn and brake, so he developed a special athletic shoe that had extra layers of leather, more rubber in the sole, and double stitching to add longer life. Watching skateboarders do a popular trick of

popping the board into the air, he named his new company "Airwalk."

The colorful skateboard shoes almost jumped off the surf and skate shops stocking them, so Airwalk moved into other freestyle segments like snowboarding and BMX and mountain bike riding. Airwalk sales hit $20 million in 1990, but an anti-snowboarding movement soon closed many slopes to skateboarders and sales fell $8 million in 1992.

REPOSITIONING AIRWALK: TARGETING MAINSTREAM YOUTHS

At this point Yohn got his great insight: if basketball shoes aren't just worn by basketball players, why should skateboarding shoes just be worn by skateboarders? This gave Yohn his new challenge in 1992: reposition Airwalk to bring its hotdogger image to mainstream youths who were looking for stylish shoes but weren't into skateboarding.

While this repositioning looked great on paper, making it actually happen was a big, big order! Although Airwalk was well-known among action-sport enthusiasts, the brand name was almost unknown among mainstream youths. It was at this point that Airwalk introduced its active/casual line of sneakers targeted at these youths, mainly teens.

RESEARCH: FINDING WHAT'S COOL!

Looking back on the early 1990s, it's now possible to find some key elements that have led to Airwalk's success today. One example is the huge effort it puts into "trend spotting" research, discussed earlier in Chapter 9. Dee Gordon, a nationally known expert in trend spotting is on the staff of Lambesis. She authors the *L Report,* published quarterly by Lambesis, that surveys 18,000 trendsetter and mainstream respondents from ages 14 to 30 across the United States and touches on every aspect of their lives. Gordon's research gives other Lambesis employees like Sharon Lee and its clients in-depth insights into what the trendsetters and cool kids are thinking, doing, and buying. Dee Gordon also studies trends around the world as a foundation for global marketing strategies developed by Lambesis clients.

MAKING IT HAPPEN: THE IMC STRATEGY

Airwalk and Lambesis recognized that much of Nike's and Reebok's success is that they recognize their business is no longer simply about selling shoes—it's about creating a cool image for their shoes. Mastering the marketing of the hard-to-define concept known as "cool" was the task that Airwalk dropped in the lap of Lambesis when Airwalk launched its first active/casual footwear line, targeted at the youth market.

The special challenge for Lambesis was to expand the market for Airwalk shoes by reaching the new, broader cool segments for its shoes without diluting their image among the existing core segments. Chad Farmer, the creative director at Lambesis who is charged with coming up with ideas for Airwalk ads, saw an opportunity to position Airwalk to the youth market as the harbinger of style in casual footwear. At the same time, Airwalk's integrated marketing communications program must retain its shoes' reputation for quality and durability while featuring their original designs and colors.

Chad Farmer's IMC program illustrates the diversity of media and strategies available to creative agencies and clients trying to break through the media clutter. This clutter is reflected in today's youths often seeing about 3,000 advertising messages in a typical day. Airwalk's TV commercials and print ads are alive with humor, irreverence, and unrestrained attitude. In many of the 14 countries where Airwalks are sold, youths steal its outdoor posters to hang in their rooms. Airwalk's Web site (www.airwalk.com) not only displays its latest line of shoes, but also provides graphics, animation, and recent TV commercials that can be downloaded.

Airwalk's IMC strategy doesn't stop with conventional media. Airwalk team "riders" include the best competitive skateboarders, snowboarders, mountain bike riders, and surfers who represent the company in major competitions globally. Bands and musicians such as the Beastie Boys, Green Day, Pearl Jam, and R.E.M. wear Airwalks—gaining great visibility for the brand. Lambesis gets product placement everywhere from movies and music videos to skateboard/BMX camps and fashion magazine photos.

What has resulted from all of this? In the mid-1990s, sales increased 400 percent in a single year. Today's sales are more than $300 million. And Teen Research Unlimited, a marketing research group, reports that Airwalk is among the top 20 percent of "coolest" brands and still climbing.

Questions

1   What were Airwalk's promotional objectives when it decided to target mainstream youths with its line of shoes in its IMC program?

2   Airwalk has developed what it calls a "tripod" strategy to stress three simple one-word concepts to communicate to the youth it targets and to stress in its IMC program. From reading the case and from what you know about the youth market, what might these be?

3   Describe how Airwalk and Lambesis might use the following media or promotional elements in their IMC strategy to target the notoriously difficult-to-reach target market of youths: (*a*) TV, (*b*) billboards, (*c*) product placements in movies, (*d*) special events, and (*e*) Web site. Explain your answers.

4   As Airwalk sells its shoes around the world, it has chosen to use a *global* marketing strategy, as defined in Chapter 5. (*a*) What are the advantages and disadvantages for Airwalk of this strategy? (*b*) For example, in print ads how might Airwalk take advantage of this strategy?

CHAPTER TWENTY

ADVERTISING, SALES PROMOTION, AND PUBLIC RELATIONS

20

AFTER READING THIS CHAPTER YOU SHOULD BE ABLE TO:

- Explain the differences between product advertising and institutional advertising and the variations within each type.

- Understand the steps used to develop, execute, and evaluate an advertising program.

- Explain the advantages and disadvantages of alternative advertising media.

- Understand the strengths and weaknesses of consumer-oriented and trade-oriented sales promotions.

- Recognize public relations as an important form of communication.

THE WILD WORLD OF WEB ADVERTISING

If you've been on the Internet you've been exposed to a form of advertising that did not exist only a few years ago. Now advertisers spend more than $500 million on Web advertising each year and, by some estimates, will spend $5 billion in the near future. Why the rapid growth? Of course the growing number of businesses and households on the Internet is appealing to advertisers. Other reasons, however, also contribute to the trend. First, advertising on the Web allows an advertiser to assess the success of the ad. Web technology allows advertisers to count the number of people who see an ad, the number of people who "click through" to the advertiser's own Web page, and, in many cases, the number of people who made a purchase. Such data are appealing because they allow advertisers to design effective ads and to target receptive audiences.

Another reason Web advertising is receiving so much attention is its potential for creating value for customers. By making the ads interactive, advertisers can provide consumers with specific, useful information. For example, you can go to an interactive Claritin ad and find out what the pollen count is in your location. This information may help you decide if and how much Claritin to take. As technology evolves, more interactivity with audio and video elements will be possible. In addition, because Web advertising has the ability to take consumers through the entire purchase process—from creating awareness, to providing information, to placing an order, to customer service—many experts believe it will encourage integrated marketing programs that are consumer friendly.

To facilitate the development of Web advertising, Procter & Gamble (P&G)—one of the world's largest advertisers—recently hosted a "summit" for marketers, Web technology companies, and advertising agencies. The objectives of the summit were to foster collaboration, to discuss common formats for the technological developments, and to improve Web advertising's effectiveness. According to Denis Beausejour, advertising vice president for P&G, a sharp increase in Internet spending "will happen, but not if we don't make some evolutionary and related changes to bring it along." So what does the future hold? According to Beausejour and others, the Net may soon become a mass medium that rivals television![1]

Online advertising is one example of the many exciting changes taking place in the field of advertising today. Chapter 19 described **advertising** as any *paid* form of *nonpersonal* communication about an organization, good, service, or idea, by an identified sponsor. This chapter describes alternative types of advertisements, the advertising decision process, sales promotion, and public relations.

TYPES OF ADVERTISEMENTS

As you look through any magazine, watch television, listen to the radio, or browse on the Web, the variety of advertisements you see or hear may give you the impression that they have few similarities. Advertisements are prepared for different purposes, but they basically consist of two types: product and institutional.

Product Advertisements

Focused on selling a good or service, **product advertisements** take three forms: (1) pioneering (or informational), (2) competitive (or persuasive), and (3) reminder. Look at the ads by Iridium, Tylenol, and Godiva, and determine the type and objective of each ad.

Used in the introductory stage of the life cycle, *pioneering* advertisements tell people what a product is, what it can do, and where it can be found. The key objective of a pioneering ad (such as that for the Iridium global satellite phone) is to inform the target market. Informative ads have been found to be interesting, convincing, and effective.[2]

Advertising that promotes a specific brand's features and benefits is *competitive*. The objective of these messages is to persuade the target market to select the firm's brand rather than that of a competitor. An increasingly common form of competitive

Advertisements serve varying purposes. Which ad would be considered (1) pioneering, which is (2) competitive, and which is used as a (3) reminder?

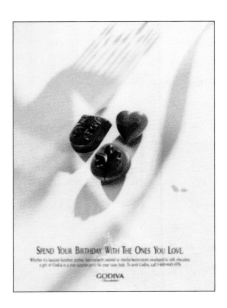

Dial soap uses reinforcement ads to encourage consumers to keep using the product.

GOOD PUBLIC RELATIONS.

Aren't you glad you use Dial.
Don't you wish everybody did?

advertising is *comparative* advertising, which shows one brand's strengths relative to those of competitors.[3] The Barnes and Noble ad, for example, highlights the competitive advantage of Barnes and Noble over its primary competitor, Amazon.com. Studies indicate that comparative ads attract more attention and increase the perceived quality of the advertiser's brand.[4] Firms that use comparative advertising need market research and test results to provide legal support for their claims.[5]

Reminder advertising is used to reinforce previous knowledge of a product. The Godiva ad shown reminds consumers about the association between its product and a special event—in this case, your birthday. Reminder advertising is good for products that have achieved a well-recognized position and are in the mature phase of their product life cycle. Another type of reminder ad, *reinforcement*, is used to assure current users they made the right choice. One example: "Aren't you glad you use Dial? Don't you wish everybody did?"

Institutional Advertisements

The objective of **institutional advertisements** is to build goodwill or an image for an organization, rather than promote a specific good or service. Institutional advertising has been used by companies such as Texaco, Pfizer, and IBM to build confidence in the company name.[6] Often this form of advertising is used to support the public relations plan or counter adverse publicity. Four alternative forms of institutional advertisements are often used:

1. *Advocacy* advertisements state the position of a company on an issue. Miller places ads encouraging the responsible use of alcohol, as shown on the next page.
2. *Pioneering institutional* advertisements, like the pioneering ads for products discussed earlier, are used for announcement about what a company is, what it can do, or where it is located. Recent Bayer ads stating "We cure more headaches than you think" are intended to inform consumers that the company produces many products in addition to aspirin.
3. *Competitive institutional* advertisements promote the advantages of one product class over another and are used in markets where different product classes compete for the same buyers. The State of Florida, Department of Citrus developed the "To Your Health" campaign to show the benefits of orange juice. The goal of these ads is to increase demand for orange juice as it competes against other beverages.
4. *Reminder institutional* advertisements, like the product form, simply bring the company's name to the attention of the target market again.

An advocacy advertisement about the responsible use of alcohol by Miller and a competitive institutional advertisement about the benefits of orange juice by the state of Florida.

CONCEPT CHECK

1. What is the difference between pioneering and competitive ads?

2. What is the purpose of an institutional advertisement?

DEVELOPING THE ADVERTISING PROGRAM

The promotion decision process described in Chapter 19 can be applied to each of the promotional elements. Advertising, for example, can be managed by following the three steps (developing, executing, and evaluating) of the process.

Identifying the Target Audience

To develop an effective advertising program advertisers must identify the target audience. All aspects of an advertising program are likely to be influenced by the characteristics of the prospective consumer. Understanding the lifestyles, attitudes, and demographics of the target market is essential. Mary Quinlan, vice chairman of the MacManus Group advertising agency, suggests that when women are the target it is important that the ad content reflects that women "like to see other women who are diverse, confident, and naturally beautiful," and that "women respond to emotional truth and real-life experience."[7] Similarly, the placement of the ads depends on the audience. When Lincoln Financial Group began its $30 million campaign targeted at households with assets greater than $1 million, it selected *Forbes, Architectural Digest,* and *Travel & Leisure* magazines to carry the ads.[8] Even scheduling can depend on the audience. Rite Aid pharmacies, for example, print targeted information for each consumer only when particular drugs are purchased.[9] To eliminate possible bias that might result from subjective judgments about some population segments, the Federal Communications Commission suggests that advertising program decisions be based on market research about the target audience.[10]

Specifying Advertising Objectives

The guidelines for setting promotion objectives described in Chapter 19 also apply to setting advertising objectives. This step helps advertisers with other choices in the promotion decision process such as selecting media and evaluating a campaign. Advertising with an objective of creating awareness, for example, would be better matched with a magazine than a directory such as the Yellow Pages.[11] The Magazine Publishers of America believe objectives are so important that they offer a $100,000 prize each year to the campaign that best meets its objectives. The last winner, Altoids, won with its "The curiously strong mint" campaign, which helped it achieve the objective of becoming no. 1 in its category.[12] Similarly, the Advertising Research Foundation is collecting information about the effectiveness of advertising, particularly new forms such as online advertising.[13] Experts believe that factors such as product category, brand, and consumer involvement in the purchase decision may change the importance—and, possibly, the sequence—of the stages of the hierarchy of effects. Snickers, for example, knew that its consumers were unlikely to engage in elaborate information processing when it designed a recent campaign. The result was ads with simple humorous messages rather than extensive factual information.[14]

Setting the Advertising Budget

You might not remember who advertised during the 1980 Super Bowl, but it cost the companies $500,000 a minute. By 1999 the cost of one minute during Super Bowl XXXIII was $3.2 million (Figure 20–1). The reason for the escalating cost is the growing number of viewers: 120 million people tune in, approximately 90 percent of them watch the entire game, and 66 percent report total day-after aided recall of the

FIGURE 20–1
Rising media costs: Super Bowl, super dollars

commercials. As a result the Super Bowl attracts new advertisers, such as Hot-jobs.com and Monster.com, and regular advertisers, such as Masterlock, which has advertised on more than 20 Super Bowls![15]

While not all advertising options are as expensive as the Super Bowl, most alternatives still represent substantial financial commitments and require a formal budgeting process. Pepsi and Coca-Cola, for example, have market shares of 31 and 44 percent and advertising budgets of $179 and $254 million, respectively. Using a competitive parity budgeting approach, each company spends exactly $5.77 million for each percent of market share. Using an objective and task approach, Pfizer allocated $90 million to introduce two new drugs, Viagra and an allergy drug, Zyrtec.[16]

Designing the Advertisement

An advertising message usually focuses on the key benefits of the product that are important to a prospective buyer in making trial and adoption decisions. The message depends on the general form or appeal used in the ad and the actual words included in the ad.

Message Content   Most advertising messages are made up of both informational and persuasional elements. These two elements, in fact, are so intertwined that it is sometimes difficult to tell them apart. For example, basic information contained in many ads such as the product name, benefits, features, and price are presented in a way that tries to attract attention and encourage purchase. On the other hand, even the most persuasive advertisements have to contain at least some basic information to be successful.

Information and persuasive content can be combined in the form of an appeal to provide a basic reason for the consumer to act. Although the marketer can use many different types of appeals, common advertising appeals include fear appeals,[17] sex appeals, and humorous appeals.

Fear appeals suggest to the consumer that he or she can avoid some negative experience through the purchase and use of a product or through a change in behavior. Insurance companies often try to show the negative effects of premature death on the relatives of those who don't carry enough life or mortgage insurance. Food producers encourage the purchase of low-fat, high-fiber products as a means of reducing cholesterol levels and the possibility of a heart attack.[18] When using fear appeals, the advertiser must be sure that the appeal is strong enough to get the audience's attention and concern, but not so strong that it will lead them to "tune out" the message. The accompanying Marketing NewsNet suggests some guidelines for developing an ad with a fear appeal.[19]

In contrast, *sex appeals* suggest to the audience that the product will increase the attractiveness of the user. Sex appeals can be found in almost any product category, from automobiles to toothpaste. Victoria's Secret, for example, used this form of advertising on the Super Bowl to generate traffic for a live Web fashion show.[20] Unfortunately, many commercials that use sex appeals are only successful at gaining the attention of the audience; they have little impact on how consumers think, feel, or act. Some advertising experts even argue that such appeals get in the way of successful communication by distracting the audience from the purpose of the ad.

Humorous appeals imply either directly or more subtly that the product is more fun or exciting than competitors' offerings. As with fear and sex appeals, the use of humor is widespread in advertising and can be found in many product categories. Unfortunately for the advertiser, humor tends to wear out quickly, thus boring the consumer. Eveready ads, featuring the Energizer battery bunny, frequently change to avoid this advertising "wearout." Another problem with humorous appeals is that their effectiveness may vary across cultures if used in a global campaign.[21]

MARKETING NEWSNET

Designing Ads That Deal with Negative Issues

Have you ever developed anxiety over a message you've received from an advertisement? If your answer is yes, chances are that your reaction was the result of what advertisers call a *fear appeal*. Examples you may be familiar with include fire or smoke detector ads that depict a family home burning, political candidate endorsements that warn against the rise of other unpopular ideologies, or social cause ads warning of the serious consequences of drug use, alcoholism, or AIDS. This approach is based on three steps—the creation of a fearful situation by giving the audience information about the severity of the threat and the probability of its occurrence, describing the effectiveness of a solution or coping response, and suggesting how the solution can be implemented.

How individuals react to fear appeals, though, varies significantly with their prior knowledge and experience. Indeed, the varying levels of anxiety that result from the ads suggest several ethical concerns for the psychological well-being of consumers. Therefore, advertisers need to consider four guidelines when developing their ads:

1. Whenever possible, use low or moderate (rather than high) levels of fear.
2. Offer more than one alternative as a solution.
3. Avoid deceptive implications (e.g., that a product will completely eliminate a fearful condition).
4. Pretest each ad to ensure a balance between the message and the associated level of anxiety.

Some examples of fear appeal advertisements include the following:

SPONSOR	MEDIUM	THEME
American Express Travelers Checks	Television	A couple on a vacation was shown victimized by a robbery and left in a state of shock and desperation.
Kaiser Permanente	Television, print, radio, and outdoor	A woman is in labor in the delivery room. A voice asks: "What if there are complications?"
American Red Cross	Print	A photo shows a man with a baby. The copy reads: "What if the unthinkable happened? Would you know how to respond?"
Cease Fire	Print	The ads show a gun with a tag describing an accidental shooting of a child. The copy reads: "A gun in the home is much more likely to kill a family member than to kill an intruder."
Prudential Insurance	Television	A man was shown dying on an operating table. The message focused on who will take care of his children.
Partnership for a Drug-Free America	Print and television	Photos of an unbroken egg, a hot pan, and the egg frying in the pan are shown. The copy reads: "This is your brain on drugs."

Creating the Actual Message   The "creative people" in an advertising agency—copywriters and art directors—have the responsibility to turn appeals and features such as quality, style, dependability, economy, and service into attention-getting, believable advertisements.

Advertising agency TBWA Chiat/Day was recently designated as *Advertising Age* magazine's advertising Agency of the Year for "talking with the consumer rather than

A creative advertisement by agency TBWA Chiat/Day for Nissan.

Nissan North America
www.nissan-na.com

at the consumer." One example of the agency's approach is the "Think Different" campaign for Apple Computer. The commercials salute "the crazy ones, the rebels, the trouble makers, and the ones who see things differently." As the ads show personalities such as Albert Einstein, Pablo Picasso, and Jim Hensen, the voice-over claims, "You can disagree with them . . . the only thing you can't do is ignore them. They change things." Other successful campaigns include the Nissan dog-driving-an-armchair ads and the Taco Bell "Yo Quiero" ads.[22]

The use of celebrity spokespersons is a popular form of advertising.

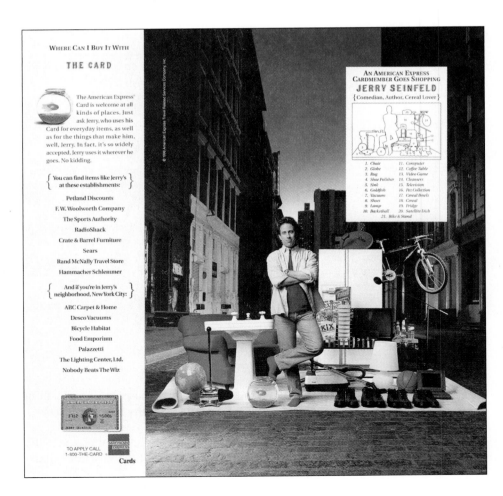

TBWA Chiat/Day's use of well-known personalities in the "Think Different" campaign is an example of a very popular form of advertising today—the use of a celebrity spokesperson. In homes across the United States, sports heros, rock stars, movie stars, and many other celebrities are talking directly to consumers through ads in all of today's many media options. Advertisers who use a celebrity spokesperson believe that the ads are more likely to influence sales. The "Got Milk?" campaign features baseball player Mark McGwire, model Christie Brinkley, cartoon character Garfield (the cat), and many other celebrities in an attempt to reverse the decline in per-capita milk consumption. Similarly, football player Jerry Rice and images of Alfred Hitchcock were part of the "Don't laugh, it works," campaign used to introduce Breathe Right nasal strips. Easy Spirit recently signed Cybil Shepherd to endorse its shoes because "she has a huge awareness [among] our target—women—and lends credibility and style to the brand," according to vice president of marketing Peter Huffine. Long-running campaigns may also encourage consumers to associate a product with a celebrity. For example, when consumers see or hear Bill Cosby, they may think of Jello or Kodak,[23] and when they see or hear Jerry Seinfeld they may think of American Express.

Translating the copywriter's ideas into an actual advertisement is a complex process. Designing quality artwork, layout, and production for the advertisements is costly and time consuming. High-quality TV commercials typically cost about $268,000 to produce a 30-second ad, a task done by about 2,000 small commercial production companies across the United States. High-visibility commercials can be even more expensive: two 15-second Rolaids commercials involved $500,000 and 75 people over a six-month period. About 70 "takes" are necessary, and typical, to get things "right."[24]

CONCEPT CHECK

1. What are characteristics of good advertising objectives?

2. What is the weakness of the percentage of sales budgeting approach?

Selecting the Right Media

Every advertiser must decide where to place its advertisements. The alternatives are the *advertising media*, the means by which the message is communicated to the target audience. Newspapers, magazines, radio, and TV are examples of advertising media. This "media selection" decision is related to the target audience, type of product, nature of the message, campaign objectives, available budget, and the costs of the alternative media. Figure 20–2 on the following page shows the distribution of the $110 billion spent on advertising among the many media alternatives.

Choosing a Medium and a Vehicle within That Medium   In deciding where to place advertisements, a company has several media to choose from and a number of alternatives, or vehicles, within each medium. Often advertisers use a mix of media forms and vehicles to maximize the exposure of the message to the target audience while at the same time minimizing costs. These two conflicting goals of (1) maximizing exposure and (2) minimizing costs are of central importance to media planning.

Basic Terms   Media buyers speak a language of their own, so every advertiser involved in selecting the right media for their campaigns must be familiar with some common terms used in the advertising industry. Figure 20–3 shows the most common terms used in media decisions.

Because advertisers try to maximize the number of individuals in the target market exposed to the message, they must be concerned with reach. **Reach** is the number of

FIGURE 20–2
U.S. advertising expenditures, by category (data in billions of dollars)

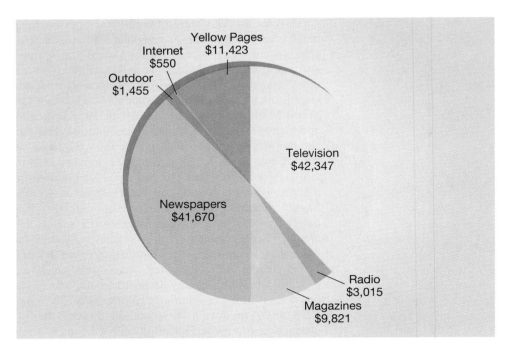

different people or households exposed to an advertisement. The exact definition of reach sometimes varies among alternative media. Newspapers often use reach to describe their total circulation or the number of different households that buy the paper. Television and radio stations, in contrast, describe their reach using the term **rating**— the percentage of households in a market that are tuned to a particular TV show or radio station. In general, advertisers try to maximize reach in their target market at the lowest cost.

Although reach is important, advertisers are also interested in exposing their target audience to a message more than once. This is because consumers often do not pay close attention to advertising messages, some of which contain large amounts of relatively complex information. When advertisers want to reach the same audience more than once, they are concerned with **frequency,** the average number of times a person in the target audience is exposed to a message or advertisement. Like reach, greater frequency is generally viewed as desirable.[25]

FIGURE 20–3
The language of the media buyer

TERM	WHAT IT MEANS
Reach	The number of different people or households exposed to an advertisement.
Rating	The percentage of households in a market that are tuned to a particular TV show or radio station.
Frequency	The average number of times an individual is exposed to an advertisement.
Gross rating points (GRPs)	Reach (expressed as a percentage of the total market) multiplied by frequency.
Cost per thousand (CPM)	The cost of advertising divided by the number of thousands of individuals or households who are exposed.

When reach (expressed as a percentage of the total market) is multiplied by frequency, an advertiser will obtain a commonly used reference number called **gross rating points** (GRPs). To obtain the appropriate number of GRPs to achieve an advertising campaign's objectives, the media planner must balance reach and frequency. The balance will also be influenced by cost. **Cost per thousand** (CPM) refers to the cost of reaching 1,000 individuals or households with the advertising message in a given medium (*M* is the Roman numeral for 1,000).

Different Media Alternatives

Figure 20–4 summarizes the advantages and disadvantages of the important advertising media, which are described in more detail below.

Television   Television is a valuable medium because it communicates with sight, sound, and motion. Print advertisements alone could never give you the sense of a sports car cornering at high speed or communicate Ford's excitement about its new Mustang. In addition, network television is the only medium that can reach 95 percent of the homes in the United States.[26] Recent studies have shown that *out-of-home TV* reaches another 20 million viewers in bars, hotels, offices, and college campuses each week.[27]

Television's major disadvantage is cost: The average price of a prime-time 30-second network spot is now $129,000.[28] Because of these high charges, many advertisers have

FIGURE 20–4
Advantages and disadvantages of major advertising media

MEDIUM	ADVANTAGES	DISADVANTAGES
Television	Reaches extremely large audience; uses picture, print, sound, and motion for effect; can target specific audiences.	High cost to prepare and run ads; short exposure time and perishable message; difficult to convey complex information.
Radio	Low cost; can target specific audiences; ads can be placed quickly; can use sound, humor, and intimacy effectively.	No visual excitement; short exposure time and perishable message; difficult to convey complex information.
Magazines	Can target specific audiences; high-quality color; long life of ad; ads can be clipped and saved; can convey complex information.	Long time needed to place ad; limited control of ad position; relatively high cost; competes for attention with other magazine features.
Newspapers	Excellent coverage of local markets; ads can be placed and changed quickly; ads can be saved; quick consumer response; low cost.	Ads compete for attention with other newspaper features; can't control ad position on page; short life span; can't target specific audiences.
Internet	Video and audio capabilities; animation can capture attention; ads can be interactive and link to advertiser.	Animation and interactivity require large files and more time to "load." Effectiveness is still uncertain.
Outdoor	Low cost; local market focus; high visibility; opportunity for repeat exposures.	Message must be short and simple; low selectivity of audience; criticized as a traffic hazard, eyesore.

Sources: William F. Arens, *Contemporary Advertising*, 7th ed. (New York: McGraw-Hill/Irwin, 1999), pp. 268, R20; and William G. Nickels, James M. McHugh, and Susan M. McHugh, *Understanding Business*, 4th ed. (Homewood, IL: Richard D. Irwin, 1996), p. 495.

reduced the length of their commercials from 30 seconds to 15 seconds. This practice, referred to as *splitting 30s*, reduces costs but severely restricts the amount of informa-

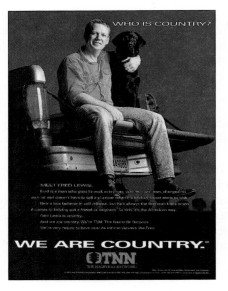

tion and emotion that can be conveyed. Research indicates, however, that two different versions of a 15-second commercial, run back-to-back, will increase recall over long intervals.[29]

Another problem with television is the likelihood of *wasted coverage*—having people outside the market for the product see the advertisement. In recent years the cost and wasted coverage problems of TV have been reduced through the introduction of cable TV. Advertising time is often less expensive on cable channels than on the major networks. In addition, there are currently about 150 cable channels—such as The Nashville Network, MTV, and the Golf Channel—that reach very narrowly defined audiences.[30] Other forms of television may soon change television advertising. Pay-per-episode channels such as DirecTV's Channel 199, pay-per-view movie services, and digital VCRs offer the potential of commercial-free viewing.

A relatively new, and increasingly popular, form of television advertising is the infomercial. **Infomercials** are program-length (30-minute) advertisements that take an educational approach to communication with potential customers. Their use has increased since 1984 when the Federal Communications Commission lifted a restriction on the amount of commercial time television stations could air. Today more than 90 percent of all TV stations air infomercials, and more than 25 percent of all consumers have purchased a product as a result of seeing an infomercial. Volvo, Club Med, General Motors, Bank of America, Mattel, Revlon, Texaco, and many other companies are using infomercials as a means of providing information that is relevant, useful, and entertaining to prospective customers.[31] Volvo's recent infomercial generated 4,000 inquiries for additional information after airing just 13 times during a two-week period.[32]

TV storyboards lead to commercials, which communicate with sight, sound, and motion.

Who is the target audience? In what type of magazine should it be run? What action is it supposed to trigger? For the answers, see the text.

Rolling Stone
www.rollingstone.com

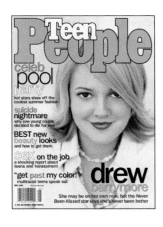

Radio   There are seven times as many radio stations as television stations in the United States. The major advantage of radio is that it is a segmented medium. There are the Farm Radio Network, the Physicians' Network, all-talk shows, and hard rock stations, all listened to by different market segments. The average college student is a surprisingly heavy radio listener and spends more time during the day listening to radio than watching network television—2.2 hours versus 1.6 hours. Thus, advertisers with college students as their target market must consider radio.

The disadvantage of radio is that it has limited use for products that must be seen. Another problem is the ease with which consumers can tune out a commercial by switching stations. Radio is a medium that competes for people's attention as they do other activities such as driving, working, or relaxing. Peak radio listening time is during the drive times (6 to 10 A.M. and 4 to 7 P.M.).

Magazines   Magazines are becoming a very specialized medium, primarily because more than 400 new magazines are launched in the U.S. each year.[33] The marketing advantage of this medium is the great number of special-interest publications that appeal to narrowly defined segments. Runners read *Runner's World*, sailors buy *Sail*, gardeners subscribe to *Organic Gardening*, and teenagers peruse *Teen People*. More than 200 publications cater to the computer industry, and high-tech companies fill about one fourth of the ad pages in *Fortune, Forbes, Business Week,* and *Dun's*.[34] Each magazine's readers often represent a unique profile. Take the *Rolling Stone* reader, who tends to travel, backpack, and ski more than most people—so a manufacturer of ski equipment that places an ad in *Rolling Stone* knows it is reaching the desired target audience. In addition to the distinct audience profiles of magazines, good color production is an advantage that allows magazines to create strong images.[35]

Rolling Stone has had a perception problem: Many prospective advertisers in the magazine saw it as a magazine read only by 1960s-era hippies. To alter this misperception, it developed a series of "Perception–Reality" ads targeted at its prospective advertisers and ran them in magazines such as *Advertising Age*, which media buyers read. The advertising succeeded in describing the diversity of the magazine's readers and increased the number of pages of advertising sold in *Rolling Stone*.

The cost of advertising in national magazines is a disadvantage, but many national publications publish regional and even metro editions, which reduce the absolute cost and wasted coverage. *Time* publishes well over 100 different editions, ranging from a special edition for college students to a version for the area around Austin, Texas. In addition to cost, a limitation to magazines is their infrequency. At best, magazines are printed on a weekly basis, with many specialized publications appearing only monthly or less often.

Newspapers Newspapers are an important local medium with excellent reach potential. Because of the daily publication of most papers, they allow advertisements to focus on specific current events, such as a "24-hour sale." Local retailers often use newspapers as their sole advertising medium.

Newspapers are rarely saved by the purchaser, so companies are generally limited to ads that call for an immediate customer response (although customers can clip and save ads they want). Companies also cannot depend on newspapers for color reproduction as good as that in most magazines.

National advertising campaigns rarely include this medium except in conjunction with local distributors of their products. In these instances both parties often share the advertising costs using a cooperative advertising program, which is described later in this chapter. Another exception is the use of newspapers such as *The Wall Street Journal* and *USA Today*, which have national distribution.

Two trends are influencing newspapers today. The first is a dramatic increase in their cost of paper. In response, many newspapers have attempted to cut costs through hiring freezes, while others have raised prices. The Sunday *New York Times*, for example, recently raised its price by $0.50. The second trend is the rush to deliver online newspapers. More than 60 newspapers, including *The Chicago Tribune*, *The New York Times*, the *Dallas Morning News*, the *San Jose Mercury News*, and the *Washington Post*, are already online, and many others are expected soon.[36]

Internet The Internet represents a relatively new medium for advertisers, although the growth of online advertising has been dramatic and has already attracted a wide variety of industries. Online advertising is similar to print advertising in that it offers a visual message. It has additional advantages, however, because it can also use the audio and video capabilities of the Internet. Movement and sound may simply attract more attention from viewers, or they may provide an element of entertainment to the message. Online advertising also has the unique feature of being interactive. Called *rich media*, these interactive ads have built-in games, drop-down menus, or search engines to engage viewers. Buy.com banner ads, for example, allow selection from a menu and a search for keywords. Online ads also allow viewers to "click-through" to the sponsor's Web site, where additional information or online purchases are available. Online advertising has become increasingly sophisticated in the past few years, and many experts expect the content and style to become similar to television advertising in the near future.[37]

One disadvantage of online advertising is that ads with audio and video elements take time to "load," so a viewer may click to another page before the ad becomes visible. Because the medium is new, there are some difficulties as the industry agrees on technical and administrative standards. The Internet Advertising Bureau and the Coalition for Advertising Supported Information and Entertainment currently provide some guidance for online advertising standards. Finally, another disadvantage of online advertising is the difficulty of measuring traffic. Current measurement techniques lead to very different ratings, which make it difficult for advertisers to know if their expenditures were a good value. According to Norman Lehoullier, managing director of ad agency Grey Interactive Worldwide, "It affects ad spending when you see wide discrepancies in numbers."[38]

Outdoor A very effective medium for reminding consumers about your product is outdoor advertising, such as the scoreboard at San Francisco's 3Com Park. The most common form of outdoor advertising, called *billboards*, often results in good reach and frequency and has been shown to increase purchase rates.[39] The visibility of this medium is good supplemental reinforcement for well-known products, and it is a rela-

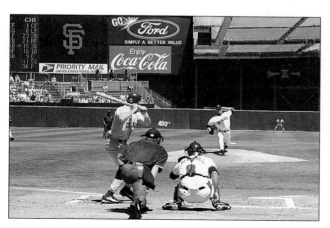

tively low-cost, flexible alternative. A company can buy space just in the desired geographical market. A disadvantage to billboards, however, is that no opportunity exists for lengthy advertising copy. Also, a good billboard site depends on traffic patterns and sight lines. In many areas environmental laws have limited the use of this medium.

If you have ever lived in a metropolitan area, chances are you might have seen another form of outdoor advertising, transit advertising. This medium includes messages on the interior and exterior of buses, subway cars, and taxis. As use of mass transit grows, transit advertising may become increasingly important. Selectivity is available to advertisers, who can buy space by neighborhood or bus route. One disadvantage to this medium is that the heavy travel times, when the audiences are the largest, are not conducive to reading advertising copy. People are standing shoulder to shoulder on the subway, hoping not to miss their stop, and little attention is paid to the advertising.

The outdoor advertising industry has experienced a surge of growth recently. Lower costs, faster technology, and a lot of creativity have attracted large, national advertisers such as Sony, Microsoft, and America Online.[40] Although outdoor advertising expenditures grew to more than $2 billion in 1998, the industry must address environmental concerns through self-regulation or be restricted by legislation. For example, four states have banned billboards, and New York City's Metropolitan Transportation Authority has banned tobacco advertising on buses and subways.[41]

Other Media   As traditional media have become more expensive and cluttered, advertisers have been attracted to a variety of nontraditional advertising options, called *place-based media*. Messages are placed in locations that attract a specific target audience such as airports, doctors' offices, health clubs, theaters (where ads are played on the screen before the movies are shown), even bathrooms of bars, restaurants, and nightclubs![42]

Selection Criteria   Choosing between these alternative media is difficult and depends on several factors. First, knowing the media habits of the target audience is essential to deciding among the alternatives. Second, occasionally product attributes necessitate that certain media be used. For example, if color is a major aspect of product appeal, radio is excluded. Newspapers allow advertising for quick actions to confront competitors, and magazines are more appropriate for complicated messages because the reader can spend more time reading the message. The final factor in selecting a medium is cost. When possible, alternative media are compared using a common denominator that reflects both reach and cost—a measure such as CPM.

Scheduling the Advertising

There is no correct schedule to advertise a product, but three factors must be considered. First is the issue of *buyer turnover*, which is how often new buyers enter the market to buy the product. The higher the buyer turnover, the greater is the amount of advertising required. A second issue in scheduling is the *purchase frequency;* the more frequently the product is purchased, the less repetition is required. Finally, companies must consider the *forgetting rate*, the speed with which buyers forget the brand if advertising is not seen.

Setting schedules requires an understanding of how the market behaves. Most companies tend to follow one of three basic approaches:

1. *Continuous (steady) schedule.* When seasonal factors are unimportant, advertising is run at a continuous or steady schedule throughout the year.
2. *Flighting (intermittent) schedule.* Periods of advertising are scheduled between periods of no advertising to reflect seasonal demand.
3. *Pulse (burst) schedule.* A flighting schedule is combined with a continuous schedule because of increases in demand, heavy periods of promotion, or introduction of a new product.

For example, products such as dry breakfast cereals have a stable demand throughout the year and would typically use a continuous schedule of advertising. In contrast, products such as snow skis and suntan lotions have seasonal demands and receive flighting-schedule advertising during the seasonal demand period. Some products such as toys or automobiles require pulse-schedule advertising to facilitate sales throughout the year and during special periods of increased demand (such as holidays or new car introductions). Some evidence suggests that pulsing schedules are superior to other advertising strategies.[43]

CONCEPT CHECK

1. You see the same ad in *Time* and *Fortune* magazines and on billboards and TV. Is this an example of reach or frequency?

2. Why has the Internet become a popular advertising medium?

3. What factors must be considered when choosing among alternative media?

EXECUTING THE ADVERTISING PROGRAM

Executing the advertising program involves pretesting the advertising copy and actually carrying out the advertising program. John Wanamaker, the founder of Wanamaker's Department Store in Philadelphia, remarked, "I know half my advertising is wasted, but I don't know what half." By evaluating advertising efforts marketers can try to ensure that their advertising expenditures are not wasted.[44] Evaluation is done usually at two separate times: before and after the advertisements are run in the actual campaign. Several methods used in the evaluation process at the stages of idea formulation and copy development are discussed below. Posttesting methods are reviewed in the section on evaluation.

Pretesting the Advertising

To determine whether the advertisement communicates the intended message or to select among alternative versions of the advertisement, **pretests** are conducted before the advertisements are placed in any medium.

Portfolio Tests   Portfolio tests are used to test copy alternatives. The test ad is placed in a portfolio with several other ads and stories, and consumers are asked to read through the portfolio. Afterward subjects are asked for their impressions of the ads on several evaluative scales, such as from "very informative" to "not very informative."

Jury Tests   Jury tests involve showing the ad copy to a panel of consumers and having them rate how they liked it, how much it drew their attention, and how attractive they thought it was. This approach is similar to the portfolio test in that consumer reactions are obtained. However, unlike the portfolio test, a test advertisement is not hidden within other ads.

FIGURE 20–5
Alternative structures of advertising agencies used to carry out the advertising program

TYPE OF AGENCY	SERVICES PROVIDED
Full-service agency	Does research, selects media, develops copy, and produces artwork
Limited-service agency	Specializes in one aspect of creative process; usually provides creative production work; buys previously unpurchased media space
In-house agency	Provides range of services, depending on company needs

Theater Tests   Theater testing is the most sophisticated form of pretesting. Consumers are invited to view new television shows or movies in which test commercials are also shown. Viewers register their feelings about the advertisements either on hand-held electronic recording devices used during the viewing or on questionnaires afterward.

Carrying Out the Advertising Program

The responsibility for actually carrying out the advertising program can be handled in one of three ways, as shown in Figure 20–5. The **full-service agency** provides the most complete range of services, including market research, media selection, copy development, artwork, and production. Agencies that assist a client by both developing and placing advertisements have traditionally charged a commission of 15 percent of media costs. As corporations have reorganized and cut costs, however, new methods of paying agencies have been introduced. About 45 percent of advertisers now pay less than 15 percent, while other pay preset fees. A small but growing number of advertisers pay performance-based fees. Advertising agency Young and Rubicam, Inc., for example, actually earned more than 15 percent from Sears because its "Softer Side of Sears" campaign has been so successful. Wrigley also uses a performance-based system to compensate its agency, BBDO.[45] **Limited-service agencies** specialize in one aspect of the advertising process such as providing creative services to develop the advertising copy or buying previously unpurchased media space. Limited-service agencies that deal in creative work are compensated by a contractual agreement for the services performed. Finally, **in-house agencies** made up of the company's own advertising staff may provide full services or a limited range of services.

EVALUATING THE ADVERTISING PROGRAM

The advertising decision process does not stop with executing the advertising program. The advertisements must be posttested to determine whether they are achieving their intended objectives, and results may indicate that changes must be made in the advertising program.

Posttesting the Advertising

An advertisement may go through **posttests** after it has been shown to the target audience to determine whether it accomplished its intended purpose. Five approaches common in posttesting are discussed here.[46]

Aided Recall (Recognition-Readership)   After being shown an ad, respondents are asked whether their previous exposure to it was through reading, viewing, or listening. The Starch test shown in the accompanying photo uses aided recall to determine the percentage (1) who remember seeing a specific magazine ad (*noted*), (2) who saw or read any part of the ad identifying the product or brand (*seen-associated*), and (3) who read at least half of the ad (*read most*). Elements of the ad are then tagged with the results, as shown in the picture.

Starch scores an advertisement

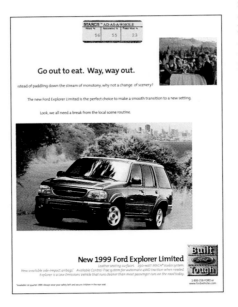

Unaided Recall   A question such as, "What ads do you remember seeing yesterday?" is asked of respondents without any prompting to determine whether they saw or heard advertising messages.

Attitude Tests   Respondents are asked questions to measure changes in their attitudes after an advertising campaign, such as whether they have a more favorable attitude toward the product advertised.[47]

Inquiry Tests   Additional product information, product samples, or premiums are offered to an ad's readers or viewers. Ads generating the most inquiries are presumed to be the most effective.

Sales Tests   Sales tests involve studies such as controlled experiments (e.g., using radio ads in one market and newspaper ads in another and comparing the results) and consumer purchase tests (measuring retail sales that result from a given advertising campaign). The most sophisticated experimental methods today allow a manufacturer, a distributor, or an advertising agency to manipulate an advertising variable (such as schedule or copy) through cable systems and observe subsequent sales effects by monitoring data collected from checkout scanners in supermarkets.[48]

Making Needed Changes

Results of posttesting the advertising copy are used to reach decisions about changes in the advertising program. If the posttest results show that an advertisement is doing poorly in terms of awareness or cost efficiency, it may be dropped and other ads run in its place in the future. On the other hand, sometimes an advertisement may be so successful it is run repeatedly or used as the basis of a larger advertising program, as with Colgate's "White on White" laundry detergent commercials now used in 30 countries.

CONCEPT CHECK

1. Explain the difference between pretesting and posttesting advertising copy.

2. What is the difference between aided and unaided recall posttests?

SALES PROMOTION

The Importance of Sales Promotion

Sales promotion is a supplemental ingredient of the promotional mix and is not as visible as advertising, but more than $200 billion is spent annually on it. As shown in Figure 20–6, during the 1980s there was a major shift of dollars from media advertising to

FIGURE 20–6

Trends in expenditures for media advertising, trade promotion, and consumer promotion

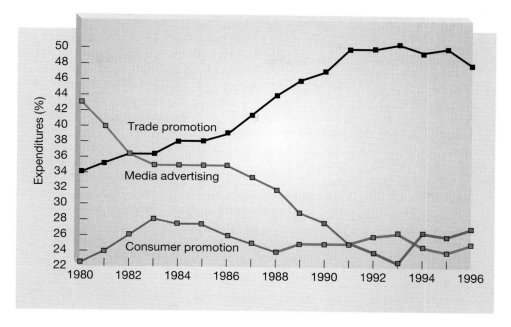

trade and consumer promotion. Today about 75 percent of these expenditures are for trade and consumer promotion.[49] The shift indicates a trend toward integrated promotion programs and the importance of traditional trade promotion. Selection and integration of the many promotion techniques requires a good understanding of the advantages and disadvantages of each kind of promotion.[50]

Consumer-Oriented Sales Promotions

Directed to ultimate consumers, **consumer-oriented sales promotions,** or simply consumer promotions, are sales tools used to support a company's advertising and personal selling. The alternative consumer-oriented sales promotion tools include coupons, deals, premiums, contests, sweepstakes, samples, continuity programs, point-of-purchase displays, rebates, and product placement (see Figure 20–7 on the following page).

Coupons   Coupons are sales promotions that usually offer a discounted price to the consumer, which encourages trial. Approximately 276 billion coupons are distributed in the United States each year. In 1997, the face value of distributed coupons was about $170 billion, and the total value of redeemed coupons was $2.9 billion. The redemption rate for coupons has been declining in recent years, although Internet couponing (see, for example, www.couponsonline.com) represents an opportunity for growth.[51]

Do coupons help increase sales? Studies suggest that market share does increase during the period immediately after coupons are distributed.[52] There are also indications, however, that couponing can reduce gross revenues by lowering the price paid by already-loyal consumers.[53] Therefore, the 9,000 manufacturers who currently use coupons are particularly interested in coupon programs directed at potential first-time buyers. One means of focusing on these potential buyers is through electronic in-store coupon machines that match coupons to your most recent purchases. A recent survey suggests that 81 percent of Americans use coupons when grocery shopping.[54]

Coupons are often far more expensive than the face value of the coupon; a 25 cent coupon can cost three times that after paying for the advertisement to deliver it, dealer handling, clearinghouse costs, and redemption. In addition, misredemption, or paying

KIND OF SALES PROMOTION	OBJECTIVES	ADVANTAGES	DISADVANTAGES
Coupons	Stimulate demand	Encourage retailer support	Consumers delay purchases
Deals	Increase trial; retaliate against competitor's actions	Reduce consumer risk	Consumers delay purchases; reduce perceived product value
Premiums	Build goodwill	Consumers like free or reduced-price merchandise	Consumers buy for premium, not product
Contests	Increase consumer purchases; build business inventory	Encourage consumer involvement with product	Require creative or analytical thinking
Sweepstakes	Encourage present customers to buy more; minimize brand switching	Get customer to use product and store more often	Sales drop after sweepstakes
Samples	Encourage new product trial	Low risk for consumer	High cost for company
Continuity programs	Encourage repeat purchases	Help create loyalty	High cost for company
Point-of-purchase displays	Increase product trial; provide in-store support for other promotions	Provide good product visibility	Hard to get retailer to allocate high-traffic space
Rebates	Encourage customers to purchase; stop sales decline	Effective at stimulating demand	Easily copied; steal sales from future; reduce perceived product value
Product placement	Introduce new products; demonstrate product use	Positive message in a noncommercial setting	Little control over presentation of product

FIGURE 20–7
Sales promotion alternatives

the face value of the coupon even though product was not purchased, should be added to the cost of the coupon. See the accompanying Ethics and Social Responsibility Alert for additional information about misredemption.[55]

Deals   Deals are short-term price reductions, commonly used to increase trial among potential customers or to retaliate against a competitor's actions. For example, if a rival manufacturer introduces a new cake mix, the company responds with a "two packages for the price of one" deal. This short-term price reduction builds up the stock on the kitchen shelves of cake mix buyers and makes the competitor's introduction more difficult.

Premiums   A promotional tool often used with consumers is the premium, which consists of merchandise offered free or at a significant savings over retail. This latter type of premium is called *self-liquidating* because the cost charged to the consumer covers the cost of the item. McDonald's, for example, used both types of premiums in a promotional partnership with Disney/Pixar during the release of the movie *A Bug's Life*. Collectable toys that portrayed movie bug characters were given away free, and clip-on watches featuring movie characters were sold for $1.99 with the purchase of a Happy Meal. Procter & Gamble proved that premiums do not have to be inexpensive when it offered an O-gauge model train set for $79.95 and three proofs of purchase from any of six P&G brands.[56] By offering a premium, companies encourage customers to return frequently or to use more of the product.

Contests   A fourth sales promotion in Figure 20–7, the contest, is where consumers apply their skill or analytical or creative thinking to try to win a prize. For ex-

ETHICS AND SOCIAL RESPONSIBILITY ALERT

Coupon Scams Cost Manufacturers $800 Million Each Year

Coupon fraud has become a serious concern for consumer goods manufacturers. How serious? The Coupon Information Center estimates that companies pay out coupon refunds of more than $800 million a year to retailers and individuals who don't deserve them. That adds a huge cost to promotions designed to help consumers.

The methods used by the cheaters are becoming very sophisticated. For example:

- Some scam artists set up a fake store and send coupons to manufacturers for payment.
- Coupon collectors often sell coupons by the pound to retailers who are paid full face value by manufacturers, even though the products were not sold.

- Retailers increase their refunds by adding extra coupons to those handed in by shoppers.
- Counterfeiters print rebate forms and proofs of purchase to collect big cash rebates without buying the products.

Other methods range from the use of high-tech color copying machines to simply running coupons through the washing machine to give them a handled look.

Some of the steps being taken to reduce coupon and rebate fraud include requiring handwritten redemption requests, printing coupons and forms in at least two colors, keeping expiration dates short, and requiring proof of purchase.

What are your reactions to misredemption? Should action be taken against coupon fraud?

ample, AT&T sponsored a contest called the "AT&T $2 Million Shootout," which was linked to the NBA playoffs. AT&T customers entered to be selected to take five shots worth a total of $2 million at an NBA finals game. AT&T believed that the contest was more appealing to customers than other types of promotion. According to Michael Murphy, AT&T's director of sponsorship and promotions, "In the past, our sports marketing has been about branding, business customer hospitality, and advertising. Now we're totally refocusing our sponsorships to be about adding value to our

Consumer-oriented promotions offering a coupon and a deal to attract prospective customers.

WEB LINK   You're In Luck—Contests Galore!

Location: http://www.mhhe.com/

If you like taking your chances in sweepstakes or if you're a skilled contest participant then this is the place for you! Go to www.playhere.com, and click on "Games and Giveaways." The site lists many contests and sweepstakes designed to attract consumers. Choose one that sounds appealing, and click again. In many cases, you can enter directly over the Internet. Good luck!

customers."[57] If you like contests, read the accompanying Web Link to learn how to enter contests online!

Sweepstakes   *Reader's Digest* and Publisher's Clearing House are two of the better-promoted sweepstakes. These sales promotions require participants to submit some kind of entry form but are purely games of chance requiring no analytical or creative effort by the consumer. The approach is very effective—*Time* magazine obtained 1.4 million new subscribers in one year through sweepstakes promotions.[58] In October 1969 the Federal Trade Commission issued trade rules covering sweepstakes, contests, and games to regulate their fairness, ensure that the chance for winning is represented honestly, and guarantee that the prizes are actually awarded.[59]

Samples   Another common consumer sales promotion is sampling, which is offering the product free or at a greatly reduced price. Often used for new products, sampling puts the product in the consumer's hands. A trial size is generally offered that is smaller than the regular package size. If consumers like the sample, it is hoped they will remember and buy the product. Burger King, for example, recently introduced its new fries by giving away 15 million samples on "Free Fry Day." While samples cost approximately $1 each, Burger King reported that it recouped the money through increased orders of other food that day and increased fry orders in the following months. Overall, companies invest more than $900 million in sampling programs each year.[60]

Continuity Programs   Continuity programs are a sales promotion tool used to encourage and reward repeat purchases by acknowledging each purchase made by a consumer and offering a premium as purchases accumulate. Trading stamps, which were first used by supermarkets and gas stations in the 1960s and 1970s, are an example. More recently airlines and hotels have used frequent-flyer and frequent-traveler programs to reward loyal customers. Chart House Enterprises, a 37-year-old chain of 65 restaurants, recently launched a frequent-diner program that allows members to earn "points" toward dining certificates for every dollar they spend. In addition, members who dine at all 65 Chart House restaurants earn a pair of round-the-world airline tickets.[61] Even GM has a continuity program—a credit card that allows consumers to accumulate up to $3,500 in "points" toward the purchase of a new Chevrolet, Pontiac, Oldsmobile, Buick, or Cadillac.[62]

Point-of-Purchase Displays   In a store aisle, you often encounter a sales promotion called a *point-of-purchase display*. These product displays take the form of advertising signs, which sometimes actually hold or display the product, and are often located in high-traffic areas near the cash register or the end of an aisle. The accompanying picture shows gravity-feed bins that Nabisco uses for its animal crackers; it helps ensure product freshness, provides storage, and captures the consumer's attention as an end-aisle, point-of-purchase display.[63] A recent survey of retailers found that

A gravity-feed bin that doubles as a point-of-purchase display.

87 percent plan to use more point-of-purchase materials in the future, particularly for products that can be purchased on impulse.[64]

Some studies estimate that two thirds of a consumer's buying decisions are made in the store. This means that grocery product manufacturers want to get their message to you at the instant you are next to their brand in your supermarket aisle—perhaps through a point-of-purchase display. At many supermarkets this may be done through Actmedia's in-store marketing network. Supermarket shopping cart displays, video screens in the aisles, and audio messages remind shoppers about products they might consider buying. The advantage of these methods of promotion is that they do not rely on the consumers' ability to remember the message for long periods of time. Other in-store promotions such as interactive kiosks are also becoming popular.[65]

Rebates   Another consumer sales promotion in Figure 20–7, the cash rebate, offers the return of money based on proof of purchase. This tool has been used heavily by car manufacturers facing increased competition. For example, Cadillac increased its sales to maintain its no. 1 position over Lincoln by offering $3,000 rebates.[66] When the rebate is offered on lower-priced items, the time and trouble of mailing in a proof-of-purchase to get the rebate check means that many buyers—attracted by the rebate offer-never take advantage of it. However, this "slippage" is less likely to occur with frequent users of rebate promotions.[67] In fact, a firm now offers a 900 number for consumers to call for information about rebates and for personalized rebate certificates.[68]

Product Placement   A final consumer promotion, **product placement,** involves the use of a brand-name product in a movie, television show, video, or a commercial for another product. Companies are usually eager to gain exposure for their products, and the studios believe that product placements add authenticity to the film or program. The studios also receive fees—between $500 and $20,000—although merchandise may be offered instead of cash. Ford Explorers appeared in *Jurassic Park* because Ford agreed to supply 10 of the vehicles and sell them at wholesale to the production company members after the filming was completed. How are product placements arranged? Many companies simply send brochures and catalogs to the studio resource departments; others are approached by agents who review scripts to find promising scenes where a product might be used.[69]

Trade-Oriented Sales Promotions

Trade-oriented sales promotions, or simply trade promotions, are sales tools used to support a company's advertising and personal selling directed to wholesalers, retailers, or distributors. Some of the sales promotions just reviewed are used for this purpose, but there are three other common approaches targeted uniquely to these intermediaries: (1) allowances and discounts, (2) cooperative advertising, and (3) training of distributors' salesforces.

Allowances and Discounts   Trade promotions often focus on maintaining or increasing inventory levels in the channel of distribution. An effective method for

Point-of-purchase displays reach consumers while they are making many purchase decisions.

encouraging such increased purchases by intermediaries is the use of allowances and discounts. However, overuse of these "price reductions" can lead to retailers changing their ordering patterns in the expectation of such offerings. Although there are many variations that manufacturers can use with discounts and allowances, three common approaches include the merchandise allowance, the case allowance, and the finance allowance.[70]

Reimbursing a retailer for extra in-store support or special featuring of the brand is a *merchandise allowance*. Performance contracts between the manufacturer and trade member usually specify the activity to be performed, such as a picture of the product in a newspaper with a coupon good at only one store. The merchandise allowance then consists of a percentage deduction from the list case price ordered during the promotional period. Allowances are not paid by the manufacturer until it sees proof of performance (such as a copy of the ad placed by the retailer in the local newspaper).

A second common trade promotion, a *case allowance*, is a discount on each case ordered during a specific time period. These allowances are usually deducted from the invoice. A variation of the case allowance is the "free goods" approach, whereby retailers receive some amount of the product free based on the amount ordered, such as 1 case free for every 10 cases ordered.[71]

A final trade promotion, the *finance allowance*, involves paying retailers for financing costs or financial losses associated with consumer sales promotions. This trade promotion is regularly used and has several variations. One type is the floor stock protection program—manufacturers give retailers a case allowance price for products in their warehouse, which prevents shelf stock from running down during the promotional period. Also common are freight allowances, which compensate retailers that transport orders from the manufacturer's warehouse.

Cooperative Advertising   Resellers often perform the important function of promoting the manufacturer's products at the local level. One common sales promotional activity is to encourage both better quality and greater quantity in the local advertising efforts of resellers through **cooperative advertising.** These are programs by which a manufacturer pays a percentage of the retailer's local advertising expense for advertising the manufacturer's products.

Usually the manufacturer pays a percentage, often 50 percent, of the cost of advertising up to a certain dollar limit, which is based on the amount of the purchases the retailer makes of the manufacturer's products. In addition to paying for the advertising, the manufacturer often furnishes the retailer with a selection of different ad executions, sometimes suited for several different media. A manufacturer may provide, for example, several different print layouts as well as a few broadcast ads for the retailer to adapt and use.[72]

Training of Distributors' Salesforces   One of the many functions the intermediaries perform is customer contact and selling for the producers they represent. Both retailers and wholesalers employ and manage their own sales personnel. A manufacturer's success often rests on the ability of the reseller's salesforce to represent its products.

Thus, it is in the best interest of the manufacturer to help train the reseller's salesforce. Because the reseller's salesforce is often less sophisticated and knowledgeable about the products than the manufacturer might like, training can increase their sales performance. Training activities include producing manuals and brochures to educate the reseller's salesforce. The salesforce then uses these aids in selling situations. Other activities include national sales meetings sponsored by the manufacturer and field visits to the reseller's location to inform and motivate the salesperson to sell the products. Manufacturers also develop incentive and recognition programs to motivate reseller's salespeople to sell their products.

CONCEPT CHECK   **1.** Which sales promotional tool is most common for new products?

2. What's the difference between a coupon and a deal?

3. Which trade promotion is used on an ongoing basis?

PUBLIC RELATIONS

As noted in Chapter 19, public relations is a form of communication management that seeks to influence the image of an organization and its products and services. Public relations efforts may utilize a variety of tools and may be directed at many distinct audiences. While public relations personnel usually focus on communicating positive aspects of the business, they may also be called on to minimize the negative impact of a problem or crisis. Intel, for example, had already shipped millions of its Pentium microprocessor chips when it was revealed that the chip had a flaw that caused mathematical errors.[73] Unfortunately, the company initially denied the seriousness of the problem, creating a more difficult situation for the public relations department. The most frequently used public relations tool is publicity.

Publicity Tools

In developing a public relations campaign, several methods of obtaining nonpersonal presentation of an organization, good, or service without direct cost—**publicity tools**—are available to the public relations director. Many companies frequently use the *news release*, consisting of an announcement regarding changes in the company

Cameron Diaz uses publicity to promote her movies.

or the product line. The objective of a news release is to inform a newspaper, radio station, or other medium of an idea for a story. A recent study found that more than 40 percent of all free mentions of a brand name occur during news programs.[74]

A second common publicity tool is the *news conference*. Representatives of the media are all invited to an informational meeting, and advance materials regarding the content are sent. This tool is often used when negative publicity—as in the cases of the Tylenol poisonings, the Audi 5000 acceleration problem, and the Exxon Valdez oil spill—requires a company response.[75]

Nonprofit organizations rely heavily on *PSAs* (*public service announcements*), which are free space or time donated by the media. For example, the charter of the American Red Cross prohibits any local chapter from advertising, so to solicit blood donations local chapters often depend on PSAs on radio or television to announce their needs.

Finally, today many high-visibility individuals are used as publicity tools to create visibility for their companies, their products, and themselves. Michael Eisner uses visibility to promote Disney, Cameron Diaz uses it to promote her movies, and Steve Forbes uses it to promote himself as a political candidate. These publicity efforts are coordinated with news releases, conferences, advertising, donations to charities, volunteer activities, endorsements, and any other activities that may have an impact on public perceptions.[76]

INCREASING THE VALUE OF PROMOTION

Today's customers seek value from companies that provide leading-edge products, hassle-free transactions at competitive prices, and customer intimacy.[77] Promotion practices have changed dramatically to improve transactions and increase customer intimacy by (1) emphasizing long-term relationships, and (2) increasing self-regulation.

Building Long-Term Relationships with Promotion

In 1970, manufacturers offered retailers promotional discounts of approximately 4 percent to encourage special purchases of a product; more recently, as managers have been pressured to produce short-term sales increases, the discounts have averaged about 15 percent. Although this sounds like good news, consumers didn't always receive the discount. The reason: in a practice called *forward buying* supermarkets often purchased more merchandise than they planned to sell during the promotion, only to sell the remaining stock at a regular price later, or the retailer would often "divert" part of the shipment by selling it to a supermarket that had not been offered the manufacturer's discount. In either case, only 30 percent of the discount actually reached the consumer. Over time, retailers began to focus on products offered with discounts, and consumers learned to shop for what was on sale.

In an effort to increase the customer value of trade promotions, consumer goods manufacturers such as P&G are trying to put an end to the discount war. Their first action was to reduce the number of discounts that they offer stores. Second, wholesale prices have been reduced, in some cases by 25 percent. Finally, manufacturers are searching for new promotional activities that may provide more value to consumers.[78] Overall, they hope that these changes will build customer loyalty for the long term—emphasizing a lifetime of purchases rather than a single transaction.

Self-Regulation

Unfortunately, over the years many consumers have been misled—or even deceived—by some promotions. Examples include sweepstakes in which the gifts were not awarded, rebate offers that were a terrible hassle, and advertisements whose promises were great, until the buyer read the small print.

Promotions targeted at special groups such as children and the elderly also raise ethical concerns. For example, providing free samples to children in elementary schools or linking product lines to TV programs and movies have led to questions about the need for restrictions on promotions.[79] Although the Federal Trade Commission does provide some guidelines to protect consumers and special groups from misleading promotions, some observers believe more government regulation is needed.

To rely on formal regulation by federal, state, and local governments of all promotional activities would be very expensive. As a result, there are increasing efforts by advertising agencies, trade associations, and marketing organizations at *self-regulation*.[80] By imposing standards that reflect the values of society on their promotional activities, marketers can (1) facilitate the development of new promotional methods, (2) minimize regulatory constraints and restrictions, and (3) help consumers gain confidence in the communication efforts used to influence their purchases. As organizations strive for effective self-regulation, marketing executives will need to make sound ethical judgments about the use of existing and new promotional practices.

CONCEPT CHECK
   1. What is a news release?

   2. What is the difference between government regulation and self-regulation?

SUMMARY

1 Advertising may be classified as either product or institutional. Product advertising can take three forms: pioneering, competitive, or reminder. Institutional ads are one of these three or advocacy.

2 The promotion decision process described in Chapter 19 can be applied to each of the promotional elements such as advertising.

3 Copywriters and art directors have the responsibility of identifying the key benefits of a product and communicating

them to the target audience with attention-getting advertising. Common appeals include fear, sex, and humor.

4 In selecting the right medium, there are distinct trade-offs among television, radio, magazines, newspapers, direct mail, outdoor, and other media. The decision is based on media habits of the target audience, product characteristics, message requirements, and media costs.

5 In determining advertising schedules, a balance must be made between reach and frequency. Scheduling must take into account buyer turnover, purchase frequency, and the rate at which consumers forget.

6 Advertising is evaluated before and after the ad is run. Pretesting can be done with portfolio, jury, or theater tests. Posttesting is done on the basis of aided recall, unaided recall, attitude tests, inquiry tests, and sales tests.

7 To execute an advertising program, companies can use several types of advertising agencies. These firms can provide a full range of services or specialize in creative or placement activities. Some firms use their own in-house agency.

8 More money is spent on sales promotion than on advertising. Selecting sales promotions requires a good understanding of the advantages and disadvantages of each option.

9 There is a wide range of consumer-oriented sales promotions: coupons, deals, premiums, contests, sweepstakes, samples, continuity programs, point-of-purchase displays, rebates, and product placements.

10 Trade-oriented promotions consist of allowances and discounts, cooperative advertising, and training of distributors' salesforces. These are used at all levels of the channel.

11 The most frequently used public relations tool is publicity—a nonpersonal, indirectly paid presentation of an organization, good, or service conducted through new releases, news conferences, or public service announcements.

12 Efforts to improve the value of promotion include emphasizing long-term relationships and increasing self-regulation.

KEY TERMS AND CONCEPTS

advertising p. 518
product advertisements p. 518
institutional advertisements p. 519
reach p. 525
rating p. 526
frequency p. 526
gross rating points p. 527
cost per thousand p. 527
infomercials p. 528
pretests p. 532

full-service agency p. 533
limited-service agencies p. 533
in-house agencies p. 533
posttests p. 533
consumer-oriented sales promotions p. 535
product placement p. 539
trade-oriented sales promotions p. 539
cooperative advertising p. 541
publicity tools p. 541

Location: http://www.mhhe.com/

INTERNET EXERCISE

Most Web pages accept some form of advertising. If you were to advise your college or university to advertise on the Web, what three Web pages would you recommend? You can use the information at www.adhome.com to help make your recommendation.

1 What is the monthly rate for a full banner ad at each of the Web sites?
2 Describe the profile of the audience for each of the Web sites.
3 Calculate the CPM for each Web site.

WEB SITE	MONTHLY RATE	AUDIENCE PROFILE	CPM
1.			
2.			
3.			

APPLYING MARKETING CONCEPTS AND PERSPECTIVES

1 How does competitive product advertising differ from competitive institutional advertising?

2 Suppose you are the advertising manager for a new line of children's fragrances. Which form of media would you use for this new product?

3 You have recently been promoted to be director of advertising for the Timkin Tool Company. In your first meeting with Mr. Timkin, he says, "Advertising is a waste! We've been advertising for six months now and sales haven't increased. Tell me why we should continue." Give your answer to Mr. Timkin.

4 A large life insurance company has decided to switch from using a strong fear appeal to a humorous approach. What are the strengths and weaknesses of such a change in message strategy?

5 Some national advertisers have found that they can have more impact with their advertising by running a large number of ads for a period and then running no ads at all for a period. Why might such a flighting schedule be more effective than a steady schedule?

6 Which medium has the lowest cost per thousand?

MEDIUM	COST	AUDIENCE
TV show	$5,000	25,000
Magazine	2,200	6,000
Newspaper	4,800	7,200
FM radio	420	1,600

7 Each year managers at Bausch and Lomb evaluate the many advertising media alternatives available to them as they develop their advertising program for contact lenses. What advantages and disadvantages of each alternative should they consider? Which media would you recommend to them?

8 What are two advantages and two disadvantages of the advertising posttests described in the chapter?

9 Federated Banks is interested in consumer-oriented sales promotions that would encourage senior citizens to direct deposit their Social Security checks with the bank. Evaluate the sales promotion options, and recommend two of them to the bank.

10 How can public relations be used by Microsoft, following the antitrust lawsuit filed by the U.S. Justice Department?

11 Describe a self-regulation guideline you believe would improve the value of (*a*) an existing form of promotion and (*b*) a new promotional practice.

 ### CASE 20–1   FALLON McELLIGOTT

"The secret to our success is that we have some core values that are very important to us. They are creativity, insight, and imagination, and it doesn't matter whether you're a copywriter or working in accounts payable. You've got to think creatively and like to think creatively to work here," explains Fred Senn, founding partner at Fallon McElligott.

In the highly competitive world of advertising, Fallon McElligott has consistently ranked among the top three agencies in the world in creative awards. "And it's all due to the people who work there," says Senn. "We hire like-minded souls. People who are very bright and collaborative. People who work here need to be challenged by each other and by ideas all the time. As we grow—we started with 5 employees and we're now at 500—keeping that sense of energy is also important to our success."

HOW AN AD COMES TO LIFE AT FALLON McELLIGOTT

To bring an ad to life, the agency concentrates on creating, reinventing, and reinforcing brands with its adver-

tising. The flow of an ad from start to finish at Fallon McElligott looks something like this:

- "The first part is rather surprising. First we interrogate the brand. We really find out what the brand stands for and we come up with a brand expression, a brand personality," Senn explains.
- Next, the agency develops a creative brief, which outlines exactly what the business problem is, and how it is going to solve the problem with communications. In the context of the brand personality the creative team then goes to work. An art director and copywriter come up with several concepts. The agency gets together with the client at this point and asks for feedback, and then the final concept is developed. That is approved by the client and the production of the creative execution begins.
- The media planning department then decides which media the ads will run in, how often they will run, and exactly when they will run. It also works with the creative team to help define the target audience. "They are charged with making our client's budgets work as hard as they possibly can to effectively reach the members of the target audience that we

define," explains Kathy Spraitz, Director of Human Resources at Fallon.

- Communication with the client occurs at every step of the process. According to Spraitz, "The account management and planning departments are the direct liaisons with the clients and accountable for presenting the voice of the consumer and ensuring the client's business objectives and brand objectives are represented during every step of the ad development process."

A FEATHER IN FALLON'S CAP: THE *TIME* MAGAZINE CAMPAIGN

One of Fallon McElligott's many prestigious clients—which include BMW, Coca-Cola, *Sports Illustrated,* and Miller Beer—is *Time* magazine. *Time* wanted a campaign that would target the loyal readers of the magazine and reinforce the purchase decision that they've made to come to *Time* magazine every week for coverage of local issues, people, and events. Fallon McElligott developed the "Red Border" campaign, which uses the powerful and provocative photography found in *Time* to highlight a topical news story or issue that *Time* has covered that week. A red border is used to frame the portion of the photo the ad's headline speaks to, along with the tagline, "The world's most interesting magazine."

Spraitz, formerly in Account Services for the *Time* account, explains, "Without even talking about the *Time* brand name we've been able to signify that there is something very important and authoritative. There's something you need to know about that topic." This campaign is unique in that each ad is produced in a week's time, which is about two to three times faster

than almost all other print campaigns. But it is intended to accurately reflect *Time*'s primary brand characteristic: timely coverage of topics. "In staying true to the *Time* brand and what *Time* does with such brilliance every week—deliver on immediacy and contemporary topics—we have to move very quickly to reflect these brand attributes," says Spraitz.

The campaign is simple and elegant, something rarely seen in today's cluttered media. Spraitz believes the *Time* campaign attracts attention and lets the reader pause to register the message very quickly without being assaulted. The campaign is well-recognized by the public and has won several awards. It also provides *Time* with communication benefits by reinforcing its primary brand attributes.

WHAT'S IN STORE FOR ADVERTISING AND FALLON?

In the future Spraitz, sees the advertising industry becoming more integrated with other communication media. To provide creative communication solutions for clients, agencies will have to broaden their services, still producing advertising but also including other communication media such as public relations, direct marketing, and interactive electronic media.

As for Fallon McElligott's future, it plans to continue its emphasis on fostering creativity in its employees. "We realize we play a very important role in people's lives and want them to have an enriching cultural experience while they're working. People call us a family. Talent is, after all, what we bring to our clients and what we think makes us successful. And so we invest a lot in our people," says Spraitz. For example, Fallon McElligott provides private conference rooms for people to go and think during the

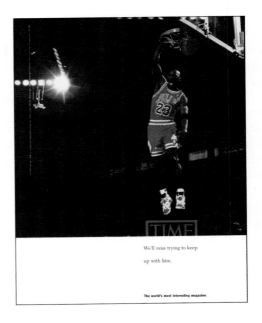

day, places to socialize such as an in-house diner, a continuing learning program with university-modeled curricula, and one of the most technologically advanced workplaces. "We think the environment is crucial not only in inspiring creativity but in respecting the fact that we ask people to work hard to deliver their best product," Spraitz explains.

Questions

1   How do the steps that Fallon uses to develop an ad relate to the elements of the planning stage (developing the ad program) of the promotion decision process?

2   Develop 5 questions that would help you "interrogate the brand" if your client was *Rolling Stone* magazine. What does the brand stand for? What is the brand personality? What are some ways to express that personality creatively in a print advertisement?

3   What appeals does Fallon McElligott use in the *Time* magazine "Red Border" campaign?

4   Scan a recent issue of *Time* magazine. What image would you use for a "Red Border" ad? What media would you place the ad in to reach *Time*'s core loyal readers? How would you evaluate the effectiveness of your ad?

CHAPTER TWENTY-ONE

PERSONAL SELLING AND SALES MANAGEMENT

21

AFTER READING THIS CHAPTER YOU SHOULD BE ABLE TO:

- Recognize different types of personal selling.

- Describe the stages in the personal selling process.

- Specify the functions and tasks in the sales management process.

- Determine whether a firm should use manufacturer's representatives or a company salesforce and the number of people needed in a company's salesforce.

- Understand how firms recruit, select, train, motivate, compensate, and evaluate salespeople.

- Describe recent applications of salesforce automation.

DUN & BRADSTREET: SELLING DATA IN THE INFORMATION AGE

Dun & Bradstreet is a master of database management and marketing. The D&B database of more than 11 million U.S. companies is unrivaled, and its sterling reputation for reliability should make D&B's sales effort easy. If only this were so.

Selling information in the information age is a demanding task. "It's difficult to relay the benefits of our services before customers actually start using them," says Joan Rothman, senior vice president of marketing for D&B's U.S. operations (shown on the opposite page). "Also, our market has become more competitive, especially with the onslaught of the Internet. Customers are able to gather so much raw data for free."

Among D&B's customers are company credit managers, who desire data on the creditworthiness of their customers, and marketing departments that wish to gather information on present and future customers. D&B's 600 field salespeople must demonstrate how much better off credit managers and marketing executives would be had they already been using D&B's information. This sales process is time consuming. It recently took D&B 15 weeks of weekly meetings to sell a new service for the small-business sector to Bank of America—with a seven-person sales and technical support team involved to get the account. "We had to sit down and show Bank of America, step by step, how much more information we had on their small-business customers and prospects than our competitors did," said Mike Archer, D&B's vice president of financial services. The effort paid off. This account now represents a multimillion-dollar business for D&B.[1]

This chapter examines the scope and significance of personal selling and sales management in marketing. It first highlights the many forms of personal selling and outlines the selling process. The functions of sales management are then described, including recent advances in salesforce automation.

SCOPE AND SIGNIFICANCE OF PERSONAL SELLING AND SALES MANAGEMENT

Chapter 19 described personal selling and management of the sales effort as being part of the firm's promotional mix. Although it is important to recognize that personal selling is a useful vehicle for communicating with present and potential buyers, it is much more. Take a moment to answer the questions in the personal selling and sales management quiz in Figure 21–1. As you read on, compare your answers with those in the text.

Nature of Personal Selling and Sales Management

Personal selling involves the two-way flow of communication between a buyer and seller, often in a face-to-face encounter, designed to influence a person's or group's purchase decision. However, with advances in telecommunications, personal selling also takes place over the telephone, through video teleconferencing and interactive computer links between buyers and sellers. For example, customers of Haggar Apparel Company can enter purchase orders into their computer, have it contact Haggar's computer, and find out when the requested products can be shipped.

Personal selling remains a highly human-intensive activity despite the use of technology. Accordingly, the people involved must be managed. **Sales management** involves planning the selling program and implementing and controlling the personal selling effort of the firm. Numerous tasks are involved in managing personal selling, including setting objectives; organizing the salesforce; recruiting, selecting, training, and compensating salespeople; and evaluating the performance of individual salespeople.

Pervasiveness of Selling

"Everyone lives by selling something," wrote author Robert Louis Stevenson a century ago. His observation still holds true today. The Bureau of Labor Statistics reports that almost 16 million people are employed in sales positions in the United States. Included in this number are manufacturing sales personnel, real estate brokers, stockbrokers, and salesclerks who work in retail stores. In reality, however, virtually every occupation that involves customer contact has an element of personal selling. For example, attorneys, accountants, bankers, and company personnel recruiters perform

FIGURE 21–1
Personal selling and sales management quiz

1. What percentage of chief executive officers in the 1,000 largest U.S. corporations have significant sales and marketing experience in their work history? (check one)

   10% _____   30% _____   50% _____
   20% _____   40% _____   60% _____

2. About how much does it cost for a manufacturer's sales representative to make a single personal sales call? (check one)

   $100 _____ $200 _____ $300 _____
   $150 _____ $250 _____ $350 _____

3. "A salesperson's job is finished when a sale is made." True or false? (circle one)

   True   False

4. About what percent of U.S. companies include customer satisfaction as a measure of salesperson performance? (check one)

   10% _____   30% _____   50% _____
   20% _____   40% _____   60% _____

Could this be a salesperson in the operating room? Read the text to find why salespeople visit hospital operating rooms to find better ways to create customer value.

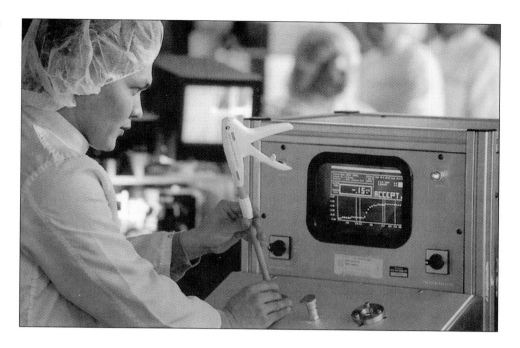

sales-related activities, whether or not they acknowledge it. About 20 percent of the chief executive officers in the 1,000 largest U.S. corporations have significant sales and marketing experience in their work history.[2] (What percentage did you check for question 1 in Figure 21–1?) Thus, selling often serves as a stepping-stone to top management, as well as being a career path in itself.

Personal Selling in Marketing

Personal selling serves three major roles in a firm's overall marketing effort. First, salespeople are the critical link between the firm and its customers. This role requires that salespeople match company interests with customer needs to satisfy both parties in the exchange process. Second, salespeople *are* the company in a consumer's eyes. They represent what a company is or attempts to be and are often the only personal contact a customer has with the company. For example, the "look" projected by salespeople for Avon Products, Inc. is an important factor in communicating the benefits of the company's cosmetic line. Third, personal selling may play a dominant role in a firm's marketing program. This situation typically arises when a firm uses a push marketing strategy, described in Chapter 19. Avon, for example, pays almost 40 percent of its total sales dollars for selling expenses. Pharmaceutical firms and office and educational equipment manufacturers also rely heavily on personal selling in the marketing of their products.

Creating Customer Value through Salespeople: Relationship and Partnership Selling

As the critical link between the firm and its customers, salespeople can create customer value in many ways.[3] For instance, by being close to the customer, salespeople can identify creative solutions to customer problems. Salespeople at U.S. Surgical observe hospital surgical practices and devote hours to questioning surgeons on how surgeries can be improved. One result of this activity was the creation of a new product that makes gallbladder surgery safer, cheaper, and less painful. The product is now used in a majority of gallbladder surgeries in the United States. Salespeople can create value by easing the customer buying process. This happened at AMP, Inc., a producer of electrical products. Salespeople and customers had a difficult time getting product specifications and performance data on AMP's 70,000 products quickly and accurately. The company now records all information on CD-ROM disks that can be scanned instantly by salespeople and customers. Customer value is also created by salespeople who follow through after the sale. At Jefferson Smurfit Corporation, a multibillion dollar supplier of packaging products, one of its salespeople juggled production from three of the company's plants to satisfy an unexpected demand for boxes from General Electric. This person's action led to the company being given GE's "Distinguished Supplier Award."

Customer value creation is made possible by **relationship selling,** the practice of building ties to customers based on a salesperson's attention and commitment to customer needs over time. Relationship selling involves mutual respect and trust among buyers and sellers. It focuses on creating long-term customers, not a one-time sale.[4] A recent survey of 300 senior sales executives revealed that 96 percent consider "building long-term relationships with customers" to be the most important activity affecting sales performance. Companies such as American Express, Electronic Data Systems, Motorola, and Owens-Corning have made relationship building a core focus of their sales effort.[5]

Some companies have taken relationship selling a step further and forged partnerships between buyer and seller organizations. With **partnership selling,** buyers and sellers combine their expertise and resources to create customized solutions; commit to joint planning; and share customer, competitive, and company information for their mutual benefit, and ultimately the customer.[6] As an approach to sales, partnership selling relies on cross-functional business specialists who apply their knowledge and expertise to achieve higher productivity, lower cost, and greater customer value. Partnership selling complements supplier and channel partnering described in Chapters 7, 16, and 17. This practice is embraced by business-to-business marketers such as IBM, DuPont, and Honeywell, which have established partnerships with customers such as American Airlines, Ford, Milliken, and the U.S. government.[7]

CONCEPT CHECK

1. What is personal selling?

2. What is involved in sales management?

THE MANY FORMS OF PERSONAL SELLING

Personal selling assumes many forms based on the amount of selling done and the amount of creativity required to perform the sales task. Broadly speaking, three types of personal selling exist: order taking, order getting, and sales support activities.[8] While some firms use only one of these types of personal selling, others use a combination of all three.

Order Taking

Typically, an **order taker** processes routine orders or reorders for products that were already sold by the company. The primary responsibility of order takers is to preserve an ongoing relationship with existing customers and maintain sales. Two types of order takers exist. *Outside order takers* visit customers and replenish inventory stocks of resellers, such as retailers or wholesalers. For example, Frito-Lay salespeople call on supermarkets, neighborhood grocery stores, and other establishments to ensure that

A Frito-Lay salesperson takes inventory of snacks for the store manager to sign. In this situation, the manager will make a straight rebuy decision.

Frito-Lay, Inc.
www.fritolay.com

the company's line of snack products (such as Lay's and Ruffles potato chips) is in adequate supply. In addition, outside order takers typically provide assistance in arranging displays. *Inside order takers,* also called *order* or *salesclerks,* typically answer simple questions, take orders, and complete transactions with customers. Many retail clerks are inside order takers. Inside order takers are often employed by companies that use *inbound telemarketing,* the use of toll-free telephone numbers that customers can call to obtain information about products or services and make purchases. In industrial settings, order taking arises in straight rebuy situations. Order takers, for the most part, do little selling in a conventional sense and engage in only modest problem solving with customers. They often represent products that have few options, such as confectionary items, magazine subscriptions, and highly standardized industrial products. Inbound telemarketing is also an essential selling activity for more "customer service" driven firms, such as Dell Computer and National Flora in the long-distance floral delivery business. At these companies, order takers undergo extensive training so that they can better assist callers with their purchase decisions.

Order Getting

An **order getter** sells in a conventional sense and identifies prospective customers, provides customers with information, persuades customers to buy, closes sales, and follows up on customers' use of a product or service. Like order takers, order getters can be inside (an automobile salesperson) or outside (a D&B salesperson). Order getting involves a high degree of creativity and customer empathy and is typically required for selling complex or technical products with many options, so considerable product knowledge and sales training are necessary. In modified rebuy or new buy purchase situations in industrial selling, an order getter acts as a problem solver who identifies how a particular product may satisfy a customer's need. Similarly, in the purchase of a service, such as insurance, a Metropolitan Life insurance agent can provide a mix of plans to satisfy a buyer's needs depending on income, stage of the family's life cycle, and investment objectives.

Order getting is not a 40-hour-per-week job. Industry research indicates that outside order getters, or field service representatives, work about 47 hours per week. As

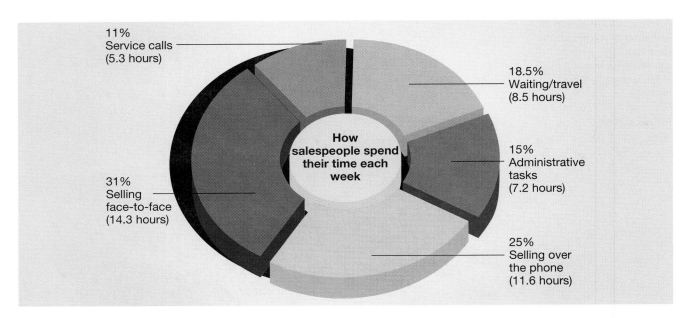

11%
Service calls
(5.3 hours)

18.5%
Waiting/travel
(8.5 hours)

How salespeople spend their time each week

15%
Administrative tasks
(7.2 hours)

31%
Selling face-to-face
(14.3 hours)

25%
Selling over the phone
(11.6 hours)

FIGURE 21–2
How outside order-getting salespeople spend their time each week

shown in Figure 21–2, 56 percent of their time is spent selling and another 11 percent is devoted to customer service calls. The remainder of their work is occupied by getting to customers and performing numerous administrative tasks.[9]

Order getting by outside salespeople is also expensive. It is estimated that the average cost of a single sale by a manufacturer's sales representative is $218.00. The cost is $184.34 in service industries.[10] (What amount did you check for question 2 in Figure 21–1?) These costs illustrate why outbound telemarketing is so popular today. *Outbound telemarketing* is the practice of using the telephone rather than personal visits to contact customers. A significantly lower cost per sales call (in the range of $20 to $25) and little or no field expense accounts for its widespread appeal. Some 40 million outbound telemarketing calls are made each year in the United States![11]

Sales Support Personnel

Sales support personnel augment the selling effort of order getters by performing a variety of services. For example, **missionary salespeople** do not directly solicit orders but rather concentrate on performing promotional activities and introducing new products. They are used extensively in the pharmaceutical industry, where they persuade physicians to prescribe a firm's product. Actual sales are made through wholesalers or directly to pharmacists who fill prescriptions. A **sales engineer** is a salesperson who specializes in identifying, analyzing, and solving customer problems and brings know-how and technical expertise to the selling situation but often does not actually sell products and services. Sales engineers are popular in selling industrial products such as chemicals and heavy equipment.

In many situations firms engage in cross-functional **team selling,** the practice of using an entire team of professionals in selling to and servicing major customers.[12] Team selling is used when specialized knowledge is needed to satisfy the different interests of individuals in a customer's buying center. For example, a selling team might consist of a salesperson, a sales engineer, a service representative, and a financial executive, each of whom would deal with a counterpart in the customer's firm. Selling teams have grown in popularity due to partnering and take different forms. In **conference selling,** a salesperson and other company resource people meet with buyers to discuss problems and opportunities. In **seminar selling,** a company team

MARKETING NEWSNET

Creating and Sustaining Customer Value through Cross-Functional Team Selling

CROSS FUNCTIONAL

The day of the lone salesperson calling on a customer is rapidly becoming history. Many companies today are using cross-functional teams of professionals to work with customers to improve relationships, find better ways of doing things, and, of course, create and sustain value for their customers.

Xerox and IBM pioneered cross-functional team selling, but other firms were quick to follow as they spotted the potential to create and sustain value for their customers. Recognizing that corn growers needed a herbicide they could apply less often, a Du Pont team of chemists, sales and marketing executives, and regulatory specialists created just the right product that recorded sales of $57 million in its first year. Procter & Gamble uses teams of marketing, sales, advertising, computer systems, and distribution personnel to work with its major retailers, such as Wal-Mart, to identify ways to develop, promote, and deliver products. Pitney Bowes, Inc., which produces sophisticated computer systems that weigh, rate, and track packages for firms such as UPS and Federal Express, also uses sales teams to meet customer needs. These teams consist of sales personnel, "carrier management specialists," and engi-

neering and administrative executives who continually find ways to improve the technology of shipping goods across town and around the world.

Efforts to create and sustain customer value through cross-functional team selling will become more popular as customers also seek greater value for their money. According to the vice president for procurement of a Fortune 500 company, "Today, it's not just getting the best price but getting the best value—and there are a lot of pieces to value."

conducts an educational program for a customer's technical staff, describing state-of-the-art developments. IBM and Xerox Corporation pioneered cross-functional team selling in working with prospective buyers. Other firms have embraced this practice and created and sustained value for their customers, as described in the accompanying Marketing NewsNet.[13]

CONCEPT CHECK

1. What is the principal difference between an order taker and an order getter?

2. What is team selling?

THE PERSONAL SELLING PROCESS: BUILDING RELATIONSHIPS

Selling, and particularly order getting, is a complicated activity that involves building buyer–seller relationships. Although the salesperson–customer interaction is essential to personal selling, much of a salesperson's work occurs before this meeting and continues after the sale itself. The **personal selling process** consists of six stages: (1)

prospecting, (2) preapproach, (3) approach, (4) presentation, (5) close, and (6) follow-up (Figure 21–3).

Prospecting

Personal selling begins with *prospecting*—the search for and qualification of potential customers.[14] For some products that are one-time purchases such as encyclopedias, continual prospecting is necessary to maintain sales. There are three types of prospects. A *lead* is the name of a person who may be a possible customer. A *prospect* is a customer who wants or needs the product. If an individual wants the product, can afford to buy it, and is the decision maker, this individual is a *qualified prospect.*

Leads and prospects are generated using several sources. For example, advertising may contain a coupon or a toll-free number to generate leads. Some companies use exhibits at trade shows, professional meetings, and conferences to generate leads or

FIGURE 21–3
Stages and objectives of the personal selling process

Stage	Objective	Comments
1. Prospecting	Search for and qualify prospects	Start of the selling process; prospects produced through advertising, referrals, and cold canvassing.
2. Preapproach	Gather information and decide how to approach the prospect	Information sources include personal observation, other customers, and own salespeople.
3. Approach	Gain prospect's attention, stimulate interest, and make transition to the presentation	First impression is critical; gain attention and interest through reference to common acquaintances, a referral, or product demonstration.
4. Presentation	Begin converting a prospect into a customer by creating a desire for the product or service	Different presentation formats are possible; however, involving the customer in the product or service through attention to particular needs is critical; important to deal professionally and ethically with prospect skepticism, indifference, or objections.
5. Close	Obtain a purchase commitment from the prospect and create a customer	Salesperson asks for the purchase; different approaches include the trial close and assumptive close.
6. Follow-up	Ensure that the customer is satisfied with the product or service	Resolve any problems faced by the customer to ensure customer satisfaction and future sales possibilities.

COMDEX, the largest computer trade show in the world, is viewed as a valuable source of leads and prospects in the computer industry.

COMDEX

www.comdex.com

prospects. Staffed by salespeople, these exhibits are used to attract the attention of prospective buyers and disseminate information. Others use lists and directories. Another approach for generating leads is through *cold canvassing* in person or by telephone. This approach simply means that a salesperson may open a directory, pick a name, and visit or call that individual or business. Although the refusal rate is high with cold canvassing, this approach can be successful. For example, 41 brokers at Lehman Brothers recently identified 18,004 prospects, qualified 1,208 of them, made 659 sales presentations, and opened 40 new accounts in four working days.[15] However, cold canvassing is frowned upon in most Asian and Latin American societies. Personal visits, based on referrals, are expected.[16]

Cold canvassing is often criticized by U.S. consumers and is now regulated. A recent survey reported that 75 percent of U.S. consumers consider this practice an intrusion on their privacy, and 72 percent find it distasteful.[17] The Telephone Consumer Protection Act contains provisions to curb abuses such as early morning or late night calling. Additional federal regulations require more complete disclosure regarding solicitations, include provisions that allow consumers to avoid being called at any time, and impose fines up to $10,000 for violations.[18] Some companies, such as American Express Financial Advisors (AMEX), have banned cold canvassing altogether.

Preapproach

Once a salesperson has identified a qualified prospect, preparation for the sale begins with the preapproach. The *preapproach* stage involves obtaining further information on the prospect and deciding on the best method of approach. Knowing how the prospect prefers to be approached, and what the prospect is looking for in a product or service, is essential regardless of cultural setting. For example, a Merrill Lynch stockbroker will need information on a prospect's discretionary income, investment objectives, and preference for discussing brokerage services over the telephone or in person. For industrial product companies such as Texas Instruments, the preapproach involves identifying the buying role of a prospect (for example, influencer or decision maker), important buying criteria, and the prospect's receptivity to a formal or informal presentation.

Identifying the best time to contact a prospect is also important. For example, Northwestern Mutual Life Insurance Company suggests the best times to call on people in different occupations: dentists before 9:30 A.M., lawyers between 11:00 A.M. and 2:00 P.M., and college professors between 7:00 and 8:00 P.M.

This stage is very important in international selling where customs dictate appropriate protocol. In many South American countries, for example, buyers expect salespeople to be punctual for appointments. However, prospective buyers are routinely 30 minutes late. South Americans take negotiating seriously and prefer straightforward presentations, but a hard-sell approach will not work.[19]

Approach

The *approach* stage involves the initial meeting between the salesperson and prospect, where the objectives are to gain the prospect's attention, stimulate interest, and build the foundation for the sales presentation itself and the basis for a working relationship. The first impression is critical at this stage, and it is common for salespeople to begin the conversation with a reference to common acquaintances, a referral, or even the

product or service itself. Which tactic is taken will depend on the information obtained in the prospecting and preapproach stages.

The approach stage is very important in international settings. In many societies outside the United States, considerable time is devoted to nonbusiness talk designed to establish a rapport between buyers and sellers. For instance, it is common for two or three meetings to occur before business matters are discussed in the Middle East and Asia. Gestures are also very important. The initial meeting between a salesperson and a prospect in the United States customarily begins with a firm handshake. Handshakes also apply in France, but they are gentle, not firm. Forget the handshake in Japan. A bow is appropriate. What about business cards? Business cards should be printed in English on one side and the language of the prospective customer on the other. Knowledgeable U.S. salespeople know that their business cards should be handed to Asian customers using both hands, with the name facing the receiver. In Asia, anything involving names demands respect.[20]

Presentation

The *presentation* is at the core of the order-getting selling process, and its objective is to convert a prospect into a customer by creating a desire for the product or service. Three major presentation formats exist: (1) stimulus-response format, (2) formula selling format, and (3) need-satisfaction format.

Stimulus-Response Format   The **stimulus-response presentation** format assumes that given the appropriate stimulus by a salesperson, the prospect will buy. With this format the salesperson tries one appeal after another, hoping to "hit the right button." A counter clerk at McDonald's is using this approach when he or she asks whether you'd like an order of french fries or a dessert with your meal. The counter clerk is engaging in what is called *suggestive selling.* Although useful in this setting, the stimulus-response format is not always appropriate, and for many products a more formalized format is necessary.

Formula Selling Format   A more formalized presentation, the **formula selling presentation** format, is based on the view that a presentation consists of information that must be provided in an accurate, thorough, and step-by-step manner to inform the prospect. A popular version of this format is the *canned sales presentation,* which is a memorized, standardized message conveyed to every prospect. Used frequently by firms in telephone and door-to-door selling of consumer products (for example, Kirby vacuum cleaners), this approach treats every prospect the same, regardless of differences in needs or preference for certain kinds of information. Canned sales presentations can be advantageous when the differences between prospects are unknown or with novice salespeople who are less knowledgeable about the product and selling process than experienced salespeople. Although it guarantees a thorough presentation, it often lacks flexibility and spontaneity and, more important, does not provide for feedback from the prospective buyer—a critical component in the communication process and the start of a relationship.

Need-Satisfaction Format   The stimulus-response and formula selling formats share a common characteristic: the salesperson dominates the conversation. By comparison, the **need-satisfaction presentation** format emphasizes probing and listening by the salesperson to identify needs and interests of prospective buyers. Once these are identified, the salesperson tailors the presentation to the prospect and highlights product benefits that may be valued by the prospect. The need-satisfaction format, which emphasizes problem solving, is the most consistent with the marketing concept and relationship building. Two selling styles are associated with this format. **Adaptive selling** involves adjusting the presentation to fit the selling situation, such as knowing when to offer solutions and when to ask for more information. **Consultative selling** focuses on problem identification, where the salesperson serves as an expert on problem recognition and resolution.[21] Both styles are used for industrial products such as computers and heavy equipment. Many consumer service firms such as brokerage and insurance firms and consumer product firms like AT&T and Gillette also subscribe to these selling styles.

Handling Objections   A critical concern in the presentation stage is handling objections. *Objections* are excuses for not making a purchase commitment or decision. Some objections are valid and are based on the characteristics of the product or service or price. However, many objections reflect prospect skepticism or indifference. Whether valid or not, experienced salespeople know that objections do not put an end to the presentation. Rather, techniques can be used to deal with objections in a courteous, ethical, and professional manner. The following six techniques are the most common:[22]

1. *Acknowledge and convert the objection.* This technique involves using the objection as a reason for buying. For example, a prospect might say, "The price is too high." The reply: "Yes, the price is high because we use the finest materials. Let me show you . . . ."
2. *Postpone.* The postpone technique is used when the objection will be dealt with later in the presentation: "I'm going to address that point shortly. I think my answer would make better sense then."
3. *Agree and neutralize.* Here a salesperson agrees with the objection, then shows that it is unimportant. A salesperson would say, "That's true and others have said the same. However, they concluded that issue was outweighed by the other benefits."
4. *Accept the objection.* Sometimes the objection is valid. Let the prospect express such views, probe for the reason behind it, and attempt to stimulate further discussion on the objection.
5. *Denial.* When a prospect's objection is based on misinformation and clearly untrue, it is wise to meet the objection head on with a firm denial.
6. *Ignore the objection.* This technique is used when it appears that the objection is a stalling mechanism or is clearly not important to the prospect.

MARKETING NEWSNET

The Subtlety of Saying Yes in East Asia

The economies of East Asia—spanning from Japan to Indonesia—almost equal that of the United States and total about four fifths of the European Union. The marketing opportunities in East Asia are great, but effective selling in these countries requires a keen cultural ear. Seasoned global marketers know that in many Asian societies it is impolite to say *no,* and *yes* has multiple meanings.

Yes in Asian societies can have at least four meanings. It can mean that listeners are simply acknowledging that a speaker is talking to them even though they don't understand what is being said, or it can mean that a speaker's words are understood, but not that they are agreed with. A third

meaning of *yes* conveys that a presentation is understood, but other people must be consulted before any commitment is possible. Finally, *yes* can also mean that a proposal is understood and accepted. However, experienced negotiators also note that this *yes* is subject to change if the situation is changed.

This one example illustrates why savvy salespeople are sensitive to cultural underpinnings when engaged in cross-cultural sales negotiations.

Each of these techniques requires a calm, professional interaction with the prospect and is most effective when objections are anticipated in the preapproach stage. Handling objections is a skill requiring a sense of timing, appreciation for the prospect's state of mind, and adeptness in communication. Objections also should be handled ethically. Lying or misrepresenting product or service features are grossly unethical practices.

Close

The *closing* stage in the selling process involves obtaining a purchase commitment from the prospect. This stage is the most important and the most difficult because the salesperson must determine when the prospect is ready to buy. Telltale signals indicating a readiness to buy include body language (prospect reexamines the product or contract closely), statements ("This equipment should reduce our maintenance costs"), and questions ("When could we expect delivery?"). The close itself can take several forms. Three closing techniques are used when a salesperson believes a buyer is about ready to make a purchase: (1) trial close, (2) assumptive close, and (3) urgency close. A *trial close* involves asking the prospect to make a decision on some aspect of the purchase: "Would you prefer the blue or gray model?" An *assumptive close* entails asking the prospect to consider choices concerning delivery, warranty, or financing terms under the assumption that a sale has been finalized. An *urgency close* is used to commit the prospect quickly by making reference to the timeliness of the purchase: "The low interest financing ends next week," or, "That is the last model we have in stock." Of course, these statements should be used only if they accurately reflect the situation; otherwise, such claims would be unethical. When a prospect is clearly ready to buy, the final close is used, and a salesperson asks for the order.

Knowing when the prospect is ready to buy becomes even more difficult in cross-cultural buyer–seller negotiations where societal customs and language play a large role. Read the accompanying Marketing NewsNet to understand the multiple meanings of *yes* in Japan and other societies in East Asia.[23]

Follow-Up

The selling process does not end with the closing of a sale; rather, professional selling requires customer follow-up. One marketing authority equated the follow-up with courtship and marriage,[24] by observing, ". . . the sale merely consummates the courtship. Then the marriage begins. How good the marriage is depends on how well the relationship is managed." The *follow-up stage* includes making certain the customer's purchase has been properly delivered and installed and difficulties experienced with the use of the item are addressed. Attention to this stage of the selling process solidifies the buyer–seller relationship. Moreover, research shows that the cost and effort to obtain repeat sales from a satisfied customer is roughly half of that necessary to gain a sale from a new customer.[25] In short, today's satisfied customers become tomorrow's qualified prospects or referrals. (What was your answer to question 3 in the quiz?)

CONCEPT CHECK

1. What are the six stages in the personal selling process?

2. What is the distinction between a lead and a qualified prospect?

3. Which presentation format is most consistent with the marketing concept? Why?

THE SALES MANAGEMENT PROCESS

Selling must be managed if it is going to contribute to a firm's overall objectives. Although firms differ in the specifics of how salespeople and the selling effort are managed, the sales management process is similar across firms. Sales management consists of three interrelated functions: (1) sales plan formulation, (2) sales plan implementation, and (3) evaluation and control of the salesforce (Figure 21–4).

Sales Plan Formulation

Formulating the sales plan is the most basic of the three sales management functions. According to the vice president of the Harris Corporation, a global communications company, "If a company hopes to implement its marketing strategy, it really needs a detailed sales planning process."[26] The **sales plan** is a statement describing what is to be achieved and where and how the selling effort of salespeople is to be deployed. Formulating the sales plan involves three tasks: (1) setting objectives, (2) organizing the salesforce, and (3) developing account management policies.

Setting Objectives   Setting objectives is central to sales management because this task specifies what is to be achieved. In practice, objectives are set for the total salesforce and for each salesperson. Selling objectives can be output related and focus on dollar or unit sales volume, number of new customers added, and profit. Alternatively,

FIGURE 21–4
The sales management process

ETHICS AND SOCIAL RESPONSIBILITY ALERT

The Ethics of Asking Customers about Competitors

Salespeople are a valuable source of information about what is happening in the marketplace. By working closely with customers and asking good questions, salespeople often have first-hand knowledge of customer problems and wants. They also are able to spot the activities of competitors. However, should salespeople explicitly ask customers about competitor strategies such as pricing practices, product development efforts, and trade and promotion programs?

Gaining knowledge about competitors by asking customers for information is a ticklish ethical issue. Research indicates that 25 percent of U.S. salespeople engaged in business-to-business selling consider this practice unethical, and their companies have explicit guidelines for this practice. It is also noteworthy that Japanese salespeople consider this practice to be more unethical than do U.S. salespeople.

Do you believe that asking customers about competitor practices is unethical? Why or why not?

they can be input related and emphasize the number of sales calls and selling expenses. Output- and input-related objectives are used for the salesforce as a whole and for each salesperson. A third type of objective that is behaviorally related is typically specific for each salesperson and includes his or her product knowledge, customer service, and selling and communication skills. Increasingly, firms are also emphasizing knowledge of competition as an objective since salespeople are calling on customers and should see what competitors are doing.[27] But should salespeople explicitly ask their customers for information about competitors? Read the accompanying Ethics and Social Responsibility Alert to see how salespeople view this practice.[28]

Whatever objectives are set, they should be precise and measurable and specify the time period over which they are to be achieved. Once established, these objectives serve as performance standards for the evaluation of the salesforce—the third function of sales management.

Organizing the Salesforce   Establishing a selling organization is the second task in formulating the sales plan. Three questions are related to organization. First, should the company use its own salesforce, or should it use independent agents such as manufacturer's representatives? Second, if the decision is made to employ company salespeople, then should they be organized according to geography, customer type, or product or service? Third, how many company salespeople should be employed?

The decision to use company salespeople or independent agents is made infrequently. However, Apple Computer recently switched from using agents to its own salesforce, and Coca-Cola's Food Division replaced its salesforce with independent agents (food brokers). The Optoelectronics Division of Honeywell, Inc. has switched back and forth between agents and its own salesforce over the last 25 years and now uses both. The decision is based on an analysis of economic and behavioral factors. An economic analysis examines the costs of using both types of salespeople and is a form of break-even analysis.

Consider a situation in which independent agents would receive a 5 percent commission on sales, and company salespeople would receive a 3 percent commission, salaries, and benefits. In addition, with company salespeople, sales administration costs would be incurred for a total fixed cost of $500,000 per year. At what sales level would independent or company salespeople be less costly? This question can be an-

FIGURE 21–5

Break-even chart for comparing independent agents and a company salesforce

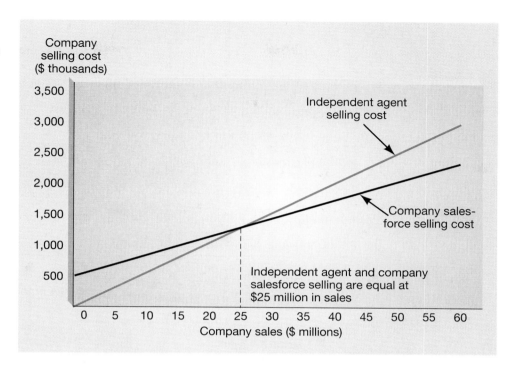

swered by setting the costs of the two options equal to each other and solving for the sales level amount, as shown in the following equation:

$$\frac{\text{Total cost of company salespeople}}{0.03(X) + \$500,000} = \frac{\text{Total cost of independent agents}}{0.05(X)}$$

where X = sales volume. Solving for X, sales volume equals $25 million, indicating that below $25 million in sales independent agents would be cheaper, but above $25 million a company salesforce would be cheaper. This relationship is shown in Figure 21–5.

Economics alone does not answer this question, however. A behavioral analysis is also necessary and should focus on issues related to the control, flexibility, effort, and availability of independent and company salespeople.[29] An individual firm must weigh the pros and cons of the economic and behavioral considerations before making this decision.

If a company elects to employ its own salespeople, then it must choose an organizational structure based on (1) geography, (2) customer, or (3) product (Figure 21–6). A geographical structure is the simplest organization, where the United States, or indeed the globe, is first divided into regions and each region is divided into districts or territories. Salespeople are assigned to each district with defined geographical boundaries and call on all customers and represent all products sold by the company. The principal advantage of this structure is that it can minimize travel time, expenses, and duplication of selling effort. However, if a firm's products or customers require specialized knowledge, then a geographical structure is not suitable.

When different types of buyers have different needs, a customer sales organizational structure is used. In practice this means that a different salesforce calls on each separate type of buyer or marketing channel. For example, Eastman Kodak recently switched from a geographical to a marketing channel structure with different sales teams serving specific retail channels: mass merchandisers, photo specialty outlets, and food and drug stores. The rationale for this approach is that more effective, specialized customer support and knowledge are provided to buyers. However, this structure often leads to higher administrative costs and some duplication of selling effort, because two separate salesforces are used to represent the same products.

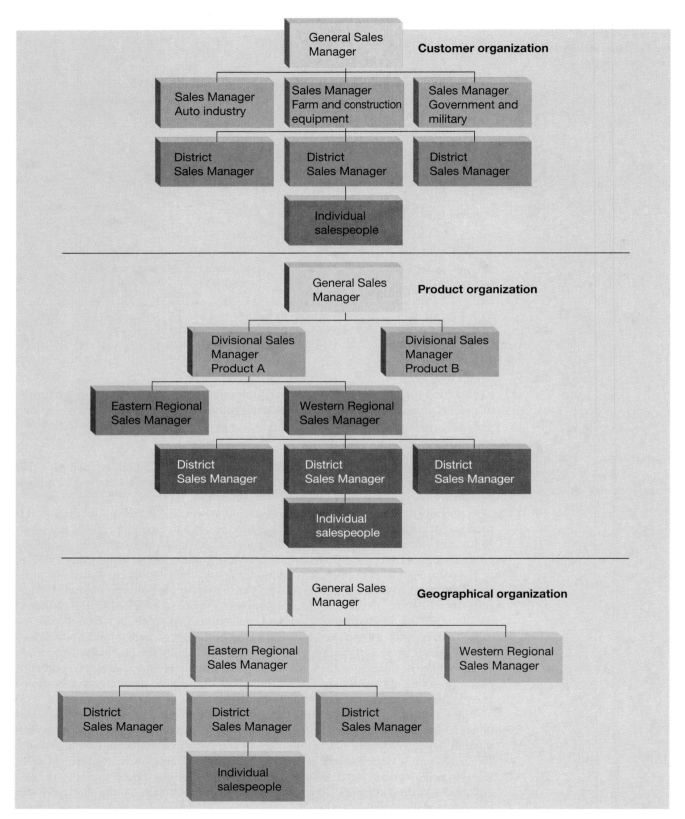

FIGURE 21–6

Organizing the salesforce by customer, product, and geography

A variation of the customer organizational structure is **major account management,** or *key account management,* the practice of using team selling to focus on important customers so as to build mutually beneficial, long-term, cooperative relationships.[30] Major account management involves teams of sales, service, and often technical personnel who work with purchasing, manufacturing, engineering, logistics, and financial executives in customer organizations. This approach, which often assigns company personnel to a customer account, results in "customer specialists" who can provide exceptional service. Procter & Gamble uses this approach with Wal-Mart as does Black & Decker with Home Depot.

When specific knowledge is required to sell certain types of products, then a product sales organization is used. For example, Lone Star Steel has a salesforce that sells drilling pipe to oil companies and another that sells specialty steel products to manufacturers. The primary advantage of this structure is that salespeople can develop expertise with technical characteristics, applications, and selling methods associated with a particular product or family of products. However, this structure also produces high administrative costs and duplication of selling effort because two company salespeople may call on the same customer.

In short, there is no one best sales organization for all companies in all situations. Rather, the organization of the salesforce should reflect the marketing strategy of the firm. Each year about 10 percent of U.S. firms change their sales organizations to implement new marketing strategies.

The third question related to salesforce organization involves determining the size of the salesforce. For example, why does Frito-Lay have about 17,500 salespeople who call on supermarkets, grocery stores, and other establishments to sell snack foods? The answer lies in the number of accounts (customers) served, the frequency of calls on accounts, the length of an average call, and the amount of time a salesperson can devote to selling.

A common approach for determining the size of a salesforce is the **workload method.** This formula-based method integrates the number of customers served, call frequency, call length, and available selling time to arrive at a figure for the salesforce size. For example, Frito-Lay needs about 17,500 salespeople according to the following workload method formula:

$$NS = \frac{NC \times CF \times CL}{AST}$$

where:

NS = Number of salespeople

NC = Number of customers

CF = Call frequency necessary to service a customer each year

CL = Length of an average call

AST = Average amount of selling time available per year

Frito-Lay sells its products to 350,000 supermarkets, grocery stores, and other establishments. Salespeople should call on these accounts at least once a week, or 52 times a year. The average sales call lasts an average of 81 minutes (1.35 hour). An average salesperson works 2,000 hours a year (50 weeks × 40 hours a week), but 12 hours a week are devoted to nonselling activities such as travel and administration, leaving 1,400 hours a year. Using these guidelines, Frito-Lay would need

$$NS = \frac{350,000 \times 52 \times 1.35}{1,400} = 17,550 \text{ salespeople}$$

The value of this formula is apparent in its flexibility; a change in any one of the variables will affect the number of salespeople needed. Changes are determined, in part, by the firm's account management policies.

COMPETITIVE POSITION OF SALES ORGANIZATION

		HIGH	LOW
ACCOUNT OPPORTUNITY	**HIGH**	1 *Attractiveness.* Accounts offer good opportunity because they have high potential and sales organization has a strong position. *Account management policy.* Accounts should receive high level of sales calls and service to retain and possibly build accounts.	3 *Attractiveness.* Accounts may offer good opportunity if sales organization can overcome its weak position. *Account management policy.* Emphasize a heavy sales organization position or shift resources to other accounts if stronger sales organization position impossible.
	LOW	2 *Attractiveness.* Accounts are somewhat attractive because sales organization has a strong position, but future opportunity is limited. *Account management policy.* Accounts should receive moderate level of sales and service to maintain current position of sales organization.	4 *Attractiveness.* Accounts offer little opportunity, and sales organization position is weak. *Account management policy.* Consider replacing personal calls with telephone sales or direct mail to service accounts. Consider dropping account.

FIGURE 21–7
Account management policy grid

Developing Account Management Policies The third task in formulating a sales plan involves developing **account management policies** specifying whom salespeople should contact, what kinds of selling and customer service activities should be engaged in, and how these activities should be carried out. These policies might state which individuals in a buying organization should be contacted, the amount of sales and service effort that different customers should receive, and the kinds of information salespeople should collect before or during a sales call.

An example of an account management policy in Figure 21–7 shows how different accounts or customers can be grouped according to level of opportunity and the firm's competitive sales position.[31] When specific account names are placed in each cell, salespeople clearly see which accounts should be contacted, with what level of selling and service activity, and how to deal with them. Accounts in cells 1 and 2 might have high frequencies of personal sales calls and increased time spent on a call. Cell 3 accounts will have lower call frequencies, and cell 4 accounts might be contacted through telemarketing or direct mail rather than in person. For example, Union Pacific Railroad recently put its 20,000 smallest accounts on a telemarketing program. A subsequent survey of these accounts indicated that 84 percent rated Union Pacific's sales effort "very effective" compared with 67 percent before the switch.[32]

Sales Plan Implementation

The sales plan is put into practice through the tasks associated with sales plan implementation. Whereas sales plan formulation focuses on "doing the right things," implementation emphasizes "doing things right." The three major tasks involved in implementing a sales plan are (1) salesforce recruitment and selection, (2) salesforce training, and (3) salesforce motivation and compensation.

Salesforce Recruitment and Selection Effective recruitment and selection of salespeople is one of the most crucial tasks of sales management. It entails finding people who match the type of sales position required by a firm. Recruitment and selection practices would differ greatly between order-taking and order-getting sales positions, given the differences in the demands of these two jobs. Therefore, recruitment and selection begin with a carefully crafted job analysis and job description followed by a statement of job qualifications.[33]

WEB LINK   What Is Your Emotional Intelligence?

A person's success at work depends on many talents, including intelligence and technical skills. Recent research indicates that an individual's emotional intelligence is also important, if not more important! Emotional intelligence (EI) has five dimensions: (1) self-motivation skills; (2) self-awareness, or knowing one's own emotions; (3) the ability to manage one's emotions and impulses; (4) empathy, or the ability to sense how others are feeling; and (5) social skills, or the ability to handle the emotions of other people.

What is your EI? Visit the Web site at www.utne.com/cgi-bin/eq to find out. Answer the 10 questions to learn what your EI quotient is and obtain additional insights.

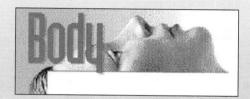

A *job analysis* is a study of a particular sales position, including how the job is to be performed and the tasks that make up the job. Information from a job analysis is used to write a *job description,* a written document that describes job relationships and requirements that characterize each sales position. It explains (1) to whom a salesperson reports, (2) how a salesperson interacts with other company personnel, (3) the customers to be called on, (4) the specific activities to be carried out, (5) the physical and mental demands of the job, and (6) the types of products and services to be sold. The job description is then translated into a statement of job qualifications, including the aptitudes, knowledge, skills, and a variety of behavioral characteristics considered necessary to perform the job successfully. Qualifications for order-getting sales positions often mirror the expectations of buyers: (1) imagination and problem-solving ability, (2) honesty, (3) intimate product knowledge, and (4) attentiveness reflected in responsiveness to buyer needs and customer loyalty and follow-up.[34] Firms use a variety of methods for evaluating prospective salespeople. Personal interviews, reference checks, and background information provided on application forms are the most frequently used methods.

Successful selling also requires a high degree of emotional intelligence. **Emotional intelligence** is the ability to understand one's own emotions and the emotions of people with whom one interacts on a daily basis. These qualities are important for adaptive selling and may spell the difference between effective and ineffective order-getting salespeople.[35] Are you interested in what your emotional intelligence might be? Read the accompanying Web Link and test yourself.

The search for qualified salespeople has produced an increasingly diverse salesforce in the United States. Women now represent half of all professional salespeople, and minority representation is growing. The fastest growth rate is among salespeople of Asian and Hispanic descent (see Figure 21–8).[36]

Salesforce Training   Whereas recruitment and selection of salespeople is a one-time event, salesforce training is an ongoing process that affects both new and seasoned salespeople. For example, Microsoft offers nearly 100 training courses annually for its experienced salespeople alone.[37] Sales training covers much more than selling practices. At U.S. Surgical, discussed earlier, new salespeople must complete an extensive training course with daily exams on medical terminology, human anatomy, surgical scrub technique, and company products. Each year, salespeople must pass a recertification exam.

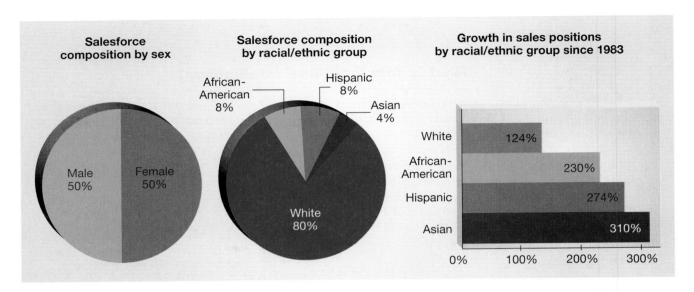

FIGURE 21–8
U.S. salesforce composition and change

Training new salespeople is an expensive process. Almost 5 million U.S. salespeople receive employer-sponsored training annually at a cost of $8 billion per year.[38] On-the-job training is the most popular type of training, followed by individual instruction taught by experienced salespeople. Formal classes and seminars taught by sales trainees are also popular.

Salesforce Motivation and Compensation   A sales plan cannot be successfully implemented without motivated salespeople. Research on salesperson motivation suggests that (1) a clear job description, (2) effective sales management practices, (3) a sense of achievement, and (4) proper compensation, incentives, or rewards will produce a motivated salesperson.[39]

The importance of compensation as a motivating factor means that close attention must be given to how salespeople are financially rewarded for their efforts. Salespeople are paid using one of three plans: (1) straight salary, (2) straight commission, or (3) a combination of salary and commission. Under a *straight salary compensation plan* a salesperson is paid a fixed fee per week, month, or year. With a *straight commission compensation plan* a salesperson's earnings are directly tied to the sales or profit generated. For example, an insurance agent might receive a 2 percent commission of $2,000 for selling a $100,000 life insurance policy. A *combination compensation plan* contains a specified salary plus a commission on sales or profit generated.

Each compensation plan has its advantages and disadvantages. A straight salary plan is easy to administer and gives management a large measure of control over how salespeople allocate their efforts. However, it provides little incentive to expand sales volume. This plan is used when salespeople engage in many nonselling activities, such as account servicing. A straight commission plan provides the maximum amount of selling incentive but can detract salespeople from providing customer service. This plan is common when nonselling activities are minimal. Combination plans are most preferred by salespeople and attempt to build on the advantages of salary and commission plans while reducing potential shortcomings of each.[40] Today, 85 percent of companies use combination plans, 12 percent use straight salary, and 8 percent rely solely on commissions. The popularity of combination plans is evident in the recent decision by Digital Equipment Corporation to convert its computer salespeople from straight salary to a salary plus commission plan.

Nonmonetary rewards are also given to salespeople for meeting or exceeding objectives. These rewards include trips, honor societies, distinguished salesperson awards, and letters of commendation. Some unconventional rewards include the new pink Cadillacs and Pontiacs, fur coats, and jewelry given by Mary Kay Cosmetics to out-standing salespeople. Mary Kay, with 10,000 cars, has the largest fleet of General Motors cars in the world![41]

Mary Kay Cosmetics recognizes a top salesperson at its annual sales meeting.

Mary Kay Cosmetics, Inc.
www.marykay.com

Effective recruitment, se-lection, training, motivation, and compensation programs combine to create a produc-tive salesforce. Ineffective practices often lead to costly salesforce turnover. U.S. firms experience an annual 9.6 percent turnover rate, which means that about 1 of every 10 salespeople are re-placed each year.[42] The expense of replacing and training a new salesperson, including the cost of lost sales, can be high. Moreover, new recruits are often less productive than established salespeople.

Salesforce Evaluation and Control

The final function in the sales management process involves evaluating and control-ling the salesforce. It is at this point that salespeople are assessed as to whether sales objectives were met and account management policies were followed. Both quantita-tive and behavioral measures are used.[43]

Quantitative Assessments   Quantitative assessments, called quotas, are based on input- and output-related objectives set forth in the sales plan. Input-related measures focus on the actual activities performed by salespeople such as those involving sales calls, selling expenses, and account management policies. The number of sales calls made, selling expense related to sales made, and the number of reports submitted to superiors are frequently used input measures.

Output measures focus on the results obtained and include sales produced, accounts generated, profit achieved, and orders produced compared with calls made. Dollar sales volume, last year/current year sales ratio, the number of new accounts, and sales of specific products are frequently used measures when evaluating salesperson output.

Behavioral Evaluation   Behavioral measures are also used to evaluate salespeo-ple. These include assessments of a salesperson's attitude, attention to customers, product knowledge, selling and communication skills, appearance, and professional demeanor. Even though these assessments are sometimes subjective, they are fre-quently considered, and, in fact, inevitable, in salesperson evaluation. Moreover, these factors are often important determinants of quantitative outcomes.

Almost 30 percent of U.S. companies now include customer satisfaction as a be-havioral measure of salesperson performance.[44] (What percentage did you check for question 4 in Figure 21–1?) Indianapolis Power & Light, for example, asks major customers to grade its salespeople from A to F. IBM has been the most aggressive in using this behavioral measure. Forty percent of an IBM salesperson's evaluation is linked to customer satisfaction; the remaining 60 percent is linked to profits achieved. The relentless focus on customer satisfaction by Eastman Chemical Company sales-people contributed to the company being named a recipient of the prestigious Mal-colm Baldrige National Quality Award.[45] Eastman surveys its customers with eight versions of its customer satisfaction questionnaire printed in nine languages. Some

Toshiba America Medical System salespeople have found computer technology to be an effective sales tool and training device.

Toshiba America Medical Systems
ww.toshiba.com

25 performance items are studied, including on-time and correct delivery, product quality, pricing practice, and sharing of market information. The survey is managed by the salesforce, and salespeople review the results with customers. Eastman salespeople know that "the second most important thing they have to do is get their customer satisfaction surveys out to and back from customers," says Eastman's sales training director. "Number one, of course, is getting orders."

Salesforce Automation

Personal selling and sales management are undergoing a technological revolution in the form of salesforce automation. **Salesforce automation** (SFA) is the use of technology designed to make the sales function more effective and efficient. SFA applies to a wide range of activities, including each stage in the personal selling process and management of the salesforce itself. Computer and communication technologies have and will continue to play a central role in salesforce automation.[46]

Salesforce Computerization   Computer technology has become an integral part of field selling through innovations such as laptop, notebook, palmtop, pad, and tablet computers. For example, salespeople for Godiva Chocolates use their laptop computers to process orders, plan time allocations, forecast sales, and communicate with Godiva personnel and customers. While in a department store candy buyer's office, such as Neiman Marcus, a salesperson can calculate the order cost (and discount), transmit the order, and obtain a delivery date within minutes using the buyer's telephone and the computer to communicate with Godiva's order processing department.[47]

Toshiba America Medical System salespeople now use laptop computers with built-in CD-ROM capabilities to provide interactive presentations for their computerized tomography (CT) and magnetic resonance imaging (MRI) scanners. In it the customer sees elaborate three-dimensional animations, high-resolution scans, and video clips of the company's products in operation as well as narrated testimonials from satisfied customers. Toshiba has found this application to be effective both for sales presentations and for training its salespeople.[48]

Salesforce Communication   Technology also has changed the way salespeople communicate with customers, other salespeople and sales support personnel, and management. Facsimile, electronic mail, and voice mail are three common communication technologies used by salespeople today. Cellular (phone) technology, which now allows salespeople to exchange data as well as voice transmissions, is equally popular. Whether traveling or in a customer's office, these technologies provide information at the salesperson's fingertips to answer customer questions and solve problems.

Advances in communication and computer technologies have made possible the mobile sales office. Some salespeople now equip minivans with a fully functional

Computer and communication technologies have made it possible for IBM salespeople to work out of their homes.

IBM
www.ibm.com

desk, swivel chair, light, computer, printer, fax machine, cellular phone, and a satellite dish. Jeff Brown, an agent manager with U.S. Cellular, uses such a mobile office. He says, "If I arrive at a prospect's office and they can't see me right away, then I can go outside to work in my office until they're ready to see me."[49]

Sales Management in the Age of Automation   Salesforce automation represents both an opportunity and a challenge for sales management. Examples of SFA applications include computer hardware and software for account analysis, time management, order processing and follow-up, sales presentations, proposal generation, and product and sales training. But, applications are not free. It is estimated that equipment, software, and training costs for automating a salesforce ranges from $2,500 to $5,000 or more per person. However, companies such as Tandem Computer report that savings from SFA by its 1,700 national and international field salespeople amount to $2 million annually.[50]

Some companies are using SFA to eliminate the need for field sales offices. Compaq Computer Corporation is a case in point. The company recently shifted its entire 224 person U.S. salesforce into home offices, closed three regional sales offices, and saved $10 million in staff salaries and office rent. A fully equipped home office for each salesperson costs the company about $8,000 and includes a notebook computer, fax/copier, cellular phone, two phone lines, and office furniture.[51]

Salesforce automation is clearly changing how selling is done and how salespeople are managed. Its numerous applications promise to boost selling productivity, improve customer service, and decrease selling cost. As applications increase, SFA has the potential to transform selling and sales management in the twenty-first century.

CONCEPT CHECK

1. What are the three types of selling objectives?

2. What three factors are used to structure sales organizations?

3. How does emotional intelligence tie to adaptive selling?

SUMMARY

1 Personal selling involves the two-way flow of communication between a buyer and a seller, often in a face-to-face encounter, designed to influence a person's or group's purchase decision. Sales management involves planning the sales program and implementing and controlling the personal selling effort of the firm.

2 Personal selling is pervasive since virtually every occupation that involves customer contact has an element of selling attached to it.

3 Personal selling plays a major role in a firm's marketing effort. Salespeople occupy a boundary position between buyers and sellers; they *are* the company to many buyers and account for a major cost of marketing in a variety of industries; and they can create value for customers.

4 Three types of personal selling exist: order-taking, order-getting, and sales support activities. Each type differs from the others in terms of actual selling done and the amount of creativity required to perform the job.

5 The personal selling process, particularly for order getters, is a complex activity involving six stages: (1) prospecting, (2)

preapproach, (3) approach, (4) presentation, (5) close, and (6) follow-up.

6 The sales management process consists of three interrelated functions: (1) sales plan formulation, (2) sales plan implementation, and (3) evaluation of the salesforce.

7 A sales plan is a statement describing what is to be achieved and where and how the selling effort of salespeople is to be deployed. Sales planning involves setting objectives, organizing the salesforce, and developing account management policies.

8 Effective salesforce recruitment and selection efforts, sales training that emphasizes selling skills and product knowledge, and motivation and compensation practices are necessary to successfully implement a sales plan.

9 Salespeople are evaluated using quantitative and behavioral measures that are linked to selling objectives and account management policies.

10 Salesforce automation involves the use of technology designed to make the sales function more effective and efficient. It applies to a wide range of activities, including each stage in the personal selling process and management of the salesforce itself.

KEY TERMS AND CONCEPTS

personal selling p. 550
sales management p. 550
relationship selling p. 552
partnership selling p. 552
order taker p. 552
order getter p. 553
missionary salespeople p. 554
sales engineer p. 554
team selling p. 554
conference selling p. 554
seminar selling p. 554
personal selling process p. 555

stimulus-response presentation p. 558
formula selling presentation p. 558
need-satisfaction presentation p. 559
adaptive selling p. 559
consultative selling p. 559
sales plan p. 561
major account management p. 565
workload method p. 565
account management policies p. 566
emotional intelligence p. 567
salesforce automation p. 570

INTERNET EXERCISE

A unique resource for the latest developments in personal selling and sales management is the Sales Marketing Network (SMN) at www.info-now.com. SMN provides highly readable reports on a variety of topics including many discussed in this chapter, such as telemarketing, motivation, sales training, and sales management. These reports contain concise overviews, definitions, statistics, and reviews of critical issues. They also include references to additional information and links to related mate-

rial elsewhere on the SMN site. Registration (at no cost) is required to view some of the reports.

Visit the SMN site and do the following:

1 Select a chapter topic, and update the statistics, for, say, sales training costs or the popularity of different salesforce incentives.

2 Select a topic covered in the chapter such as telemarketing, and summarize the critical issues identified for this practice.

APPLYING MARKETING CONCEPTS AND PERSPECTIVES

1 Jane Dawson is a new sales representative for the Charles Schwab brokerage firm. In searching for clients, Jane purchased a mailing list of subscribers to *The Wall Street Journal* and called them all regarding their interest in discount brokerage services. She asked if they have any stocks and if they have a regular broker. Those people without a regular broker were asked their investment needs. Two days later Jane called back with investment advice and asked if they would like to open an account. Identify each of Jane Dawson's actions in terms of the steps of selling.

2 For the first 50 years of business the Johnson Carpet Company produced carpets for residential use. The salesforce was structured geographically. In the past five years a large percentage of carpet sales has been to industrial users, hospitals, schools, and architects. The company also has broadened its product line to include area rugs, Oriental carpets, and wall-to-wall carpeting. Is the present salesforce structure appropriate, or would you recommend an alternative?

3 Where would you place each of the following sales jobs on the order-taker/order-getter continuum shown below? (*a*) Burger King counter clerk, (*b*) automobile insurance salesperson, (*c*) IBM computer salesperson, (*d*) life insurance salesperson, and (*e*) shoe salesperson.

Order taker   Order getter

4 Listed here are two different firms. Which compensation plan would you recommend for each firm, and what reasons would you give for your recommendations? (*a*) A newly formed company that sells lawn care equipment on a door-to-door basis directly to consumers; and (*b*) the Nabisco Company, which sells heavily advertised products in supermarkets by having the salesforce call on these stores and arrange shelves, set up displays, and make presentations to store buying committees.

5 The TDK tape company services 1,000 audio stores throughout the United States. Each store is called on 12 times a year, and the average sales call lasts 30 minutes. Assuming a salesperson works 40 hours a week, 50 weeks a year, and devotes 75 percent of the time to actual selling, how many salespeople does TDK need?

6 A furniture manufacturer is currently using manufacturer's representatives to sell its line of living room furniture. These representatives receive an 8 percent commission. The company is considering hiring its own salespeople and has estimated that the fixed cost of managing and paying their salaries would be $1 million annually. The salespeople would also receive a 4 percent commission on sales. The company has sales of $25 million dollars, and sales are expected to grow by 15 percent next year. Would you recommend that the company switch to its own salesforce? Why or why not?

7 Suppose someone said to you, "The only real measure of a salesperson is the amount of sales produced." How might you respond?

 CASE 21–1   REEBOK INTERNATIONAL LTD.

"I think face-to-face selling is the most important and exciting part of this whole job. It's not writing the sales reports. It's not analyzing trends and forecasting. It's the two hours that you have to try to sell the buyer your products in a way that's profitable for both you and the retailer," relates Robert McMahon, key account sales representative for Reebok Northeast. As the person in charge of Reebok's largest accounts in New England—including MVP Sports, Modell's, and City Sports in Boston—McMahon's job encompasses a myriad of activities, from supervising other sales representatives to attending companywide computer training sessions to monitoring competitors' activities. But it's the actual selling that is most appealing to McMahon. "That's the challenging, stimulating part of the job. Selling to the buyer is a different challenge every day. Every sales call, as well as you may have preplanned it, can change based on shifts and trends in the market. So you need to be able

to react to those changes and really think on your feet in front of the buyer."

REEBOK—HOT ON NIKE'S HEELS IN THE ATHLETIC SHOE AND APPAREL MARKET

Reebok is the second largest athletic shoe manufacturer behind the market leader, Nike. In addition to its athletic shoes, Reebok also sells Rockport, Greg Norman Collection, and Ralph Lauren Footwear shoes. The Reebok sporting goods line remains the flagship brand, though, and distinguishes itself on the market through the DMX cushioning technology in its footwear. Reebok concentrates its resources on getting its footwear and sporting goods gear into a diversified mix of distribution channels such as athletic footwear specialty stores, department stores, and large sporting goods stores. Reebok is unique in that it emphasizes relationships with the retailers as an integral part of its marketing strategy. As an employee at MVP Sports, one of Reebok's major retailers, puts it, "Reebok is the only company that comes in on a regular basis and gives us information. Nike comes in once in a great while. New Balance comes in every six months. Saucony has come in twice. That's been it. Reebok comes in every month to update us on new information and new products. They tell us about the technology so we can tell the customers." Says Laurie Sipples, "vector" representative for Reebok, "There's a partnership that exists between Reebok and an account like MVP Sports that sets us apart. That relationship is a great asset that Reebok has because the retailer feels more in touch with us than other brands."

THE SELLING PROCESS AT REEBOK

Selling at Reebok includes three elements—building trust between the salesperson and the retailer, providing enough information to the retailer for them to be successful selling Reebok products, and finally supporting the retailer after the sale. Sean Neville, senior vice president and general manager of Reebok North America, explains, "Our goal is not to sell to the retailer, our goal is ultimately to sell to the consumer, and so we use the retailer as a partner. The salespeople are always keeping their eyes open and thinking like the retailer and selling to the consumer."

Reebok sells in teams that consist of the account representatives, who do the actual selling to the retailer, and the "vector" representatives, who spend their time in the stores training the store salespeople and reporting trends back to the account manager. The selling teams are organized geographically so that the salespeople live and work in the area they are selling in. This allows the sales team to understand the consumer intuitively. Neville explains, "If you have someone from New York City fly to L.A. and try to tell someone on the streets of Los Angeles what's happening from a trends standpoint and what products to purchase, it's very difficult."

On average, Reebok salespeople spend 70 percent of their time preparing for a sale and 30 percent of their time actually selling. The sales process at Reebok typically follows the six steps of the personal selling process identified in Figure 21–3: (1) Reebok identifies the outlets it would like to carry its athletic gear; (2) the salesforce prepares for the a presentation by familiarizing themselves with the store and its customers; (3) a Reebok representative approaches the prospect and suggests a meeting and presentation; (4) as the presentation begins, the salesperson summarizes relevant market conditions and consumer trends to demonstrate Reebok's commitment to a partnership with the retailer, states what s/he hopes to get out of the sales meeting, explains how the products work, and reinforces the benefits of Reebok products; (5) the salesperson engages in an action close (gets a signed document or a firm confirmation of the sale); and (6) later, various members of the salesforce frequently visit the retailer to provide assistance and monitor consumer preferences.

THE SALES MANAGEMENT PROCESS AT REEBOK

The sales teams at Reebok are organized based on Reebok's three major distribution channels: athletic specialty stores, sporting goods stores, and department stores. The smaller stores have sales teams assigned to them based on geographical location within the United States (west coast, central, southeast, and northeast). The salesforce is then further broken down into footwear and apparel teams. The salesforce is primarily organized by distribution channel because this is most responsive to customer needs and wants. The salesforce is compensated on both a short-term and long-term basis. In the short-term, salespeople are paid based on sales results and profits for the current quarter as well as forecasting. In the long-term, salespeople are compensated based on their teamwork and teambuilding efforts. As Neville explains, "Money is typically fourth or fifth on the list of pure motivation. Number one is recognition for a job

well done. And that drives people to succeed." Management at Reebok is constantly providing feedback to the salesforce acknowledging their success, not just during annual reviews, and Neville feels this is the key to the high level of motivation, energy, and excitement that exists in the salesforce at Reebok.

WHAT'S NEW ON THE HORIZON FOR THE SALESFORCE AT REEBOK?

Reebok has recently issued laptop computers to its entire salesforce that enable the salespeople to check inventories in the warehouses, make sure orders are being shipped on time, and even enter orders while they're out in the field. Reebok is also focusing more on relationship selling. McMahon describes his relationship with a major buyer as, "one of trust and respect. It's gotten to the point now where we're good friends. We go to a lot of sporting events together, which I think really helps." Another recent innovation is for the salesforce to incentivize the stores sales clerks. For instance, whoever sells the most pairs of Reebok shoes in a month will get tickets to a concert or a football game.

Questions

1   How does Reebok create customer value for its major accounts through relationship selling?

2   How does Reebok utilize team selling to provide the highest level of customer value possible to its major accounts?

3   Is Reebok's salesforce organized based on geography, customer, or product?

4   What are some ways Reebok's selling processes are changing due to technical advancements?

PART FIVE

5

MANAGING THE MARKETING PROCESS

CHAPTER 22
The Strategic Marketing Process

Part Five discusses issues and techniques related to the planning, implementation, and control phases of the strategic marketing process. Chapter 22 explains how marketing executives search for a competitive advantage and allocate the firm's resources to maximize the effects of marketing efforts. Frameworks for improving marketing planning, guidelines for creating an effective marketing plan, and alternatives for organizing a marketing department are also discussed. In addition, General Mills's launch of its Frosted Cheerios breakfast cereal illustrates the planning activities of a successful marketing organization.

THE STRATEGIC MARKETING PROCESS

22

AFTER READING THIS CHAPTER YOU SHOULD BE ABLE TO:

• Explain how marketing managers allocate their limited resources, both in theory and in practice.

• Describe three marketing planning frameworks: Porter's generic strategies, profit enhancement options, and market-product synergies.

• Describe what makes an effective marketing plan and some problems that often exist with them.

• Describe the alternatives for organizing a marketing department and the role of a product manager.

• Schedule a series of tasks to meet a deadline using a Gantt chart.

• Understand how sales and profitability analyses and marketing audits are used to evaluate and control marketing programs.

MARKETING STRATEGY AT GENERAL MILLS: SEGMENTS, SHARES, SPIN-OFFS, SYNERGIES

Assume you are a marketing manager at General Mills responsible for introducing successful new brands of cereal. Here are some facts to tell you how difficult your life is:

• Only one out of five new brands succeeds, "success" here meaning achieving 0.5 percent market share—half of 1 percent—of the $8 billion-a-year U.S. cereal industry.
• A new product launch typically costs up to $40 million.[1]
• Busy Americans on the run are increasingly likely to eat a bagel, muffin, or Pop-Tart for breakfast, causing cold cereal sales to fall by more than $1 billion from 1994 to 1998, so your new cereal must steal sales from existing brands.

Further, today's U.S. ready-to-eat cereal market is seeing smaller competitors introduce "bagged"—really generic—versions of well-known General Mills and Kellogg's brands for about $1 less than their branded counterparts.[2] On the other hand, in your marketing manager position at General Mills you have some good news:

• More young adults are scarfing dry cereal by the handfuls at work or at night a la Jerry Seinfeld; remember Fingo's from Chapter 11?[3]
• The biggest consumers of ready-to-eat cereals are those under 18 and over 44—market segments in the United States that will grow by 4.6 million and 33.6 million, respectively, from 1995 to 2010.[4]
• Because synergies never materialized between General Mills' food and restaurant business and their corporate cultures were far different, it spun off its Red Lobster, Olive Garden, and China Coast chains as Darden, Inc., so you don't have to compete for resources with them.

Following the spin-off of Darden, marketing strategists at General Mills hoped that the company would now be able to focus its marketing efforts to achieve higher growth in sales revenues and profits than in the past. So in your marketing manager position, you'd face touch challenges. We'll visit the launch of one new brand—Frosted Cheerios—in a few pages.

This chapter discusses issues and techniques related to planning, implementation, and control phases of the strategic marketing process, the kind of topics marketing strategists at General Mills face in achieving growth. The individual elements of the strategic marketing process were introduced in Chapter 2.

STRATEGIC MARKETING'S GOAL: EFFECTIVE RESOURCE ALLOCATION

As noted in Chapter 2, corporate and marketing executives search continuously to find a competitive advantage—a unique strength relative to competitors, often based on quality, time, cost, or innovation. Having identified this competitive advantage, they must allocate their firm's resources to exploit it.[5] The timing of product and market actions may also influence the magnitude and duration of a firm's competitive advantage.[6]

Allocating Marketing Resources Using Sales Response Functions

A **sales response function** relates the expense of marketing effort to the marketing results obtained.[7] For simplicity in the examples that follow, only the effects of annual marketing effort on annual sales revenue will be analyzed, but the concept applies to other measures of marketing success—such as profit, units sold, or level of awareness—as well.

Maximizing Incremental Revenue Minus Incremental Cost   Economists give managers a specific guideline for optimal resource allocation: allocate the firm's marketing, production, and financial resources to the markets and products where the excess of incremental revenues over incremental costs is greatest. This parallels the marginal revenue–marginal cost analysis of Chapter 14.

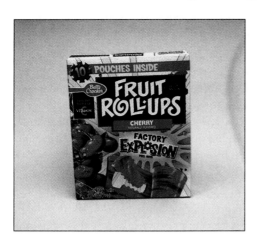

Figure 22–1 illustrates this resource allocation principle. The firm's annual marketing effort, such as sales and advertising expenses, is plotted on the horizontal axis. As this annual marketing effort increases, so does the resulting annual sales revenue. The relationship is assumed to be S-shaped, showing that an additional $1 million of marketing effort results in far greater increases of sales revenue in the mid-range (such as $4 million) than at either end (such as $2 million or $7 million).

A Numerical Example of Resource Allocation   Suppose Figure 22–1 shows the situation for a General Mills product such as Fruit Roll-Ups. Also assume the sales revenue response function doesn't change through time. Point A shows the position of the firm in year 1, and point B shows it three years later in year 4. Marketing effort in the form of advertising and other promotions has increased from $3 million to $6 million a year, while sales revenue has increased from $30 million to $70 million a year.

Let's look at the major resource allocation question: what are the probable increases in sales revenue for Fruit Roll-Ups in years 1 and 4 for an extra $1 million of marketing effort? As Figure 22–1 reveals:

Year 1
Increase in marketing effort from $3 million to $4 million = $1 million
Increase in sales revenue from $30 million to $50 million = $20 million
Ratio of incremental sales revenue to effort = $20,000,000:$1,000,000 = 20:1

FIGURE 22–1
Sales response function showing the situation for two different years

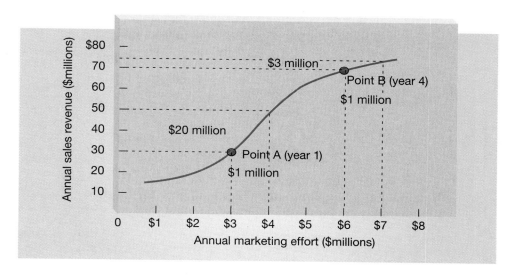

Year 4

Increase in marketing effort from $6 million to $7 million = $1 million

Increase in sales revenue from $70 million to $73 million = $3 million

Ratio of incremental sales revenue to effort = $3,000,000:$1,000,000 = 3:1

Thus, in year 1 a dollar of extra marketing effort returned $20 in sales revenue, whereas in year 4 it returned only $3. If no other expenses are incurred, it might make sense to spend $1 million in year 4 to gain $3 million in incremental sales revenue. However, it may be far wiser for General Mills to invest the money in products in one of its other business units, such as its new Frosted Flakes cereal or its new Betty Crocker Stir 'n Bake desserts, prepared by just adding water.[8] The essence of resource allocation is simple: put incremental resources where the incremental returns are greatest over the foreseeable future.

Allocating Marketing Resources in Practice

General Mills, like many firms in these businesses, does extensive analysis using **share points,** or percentage points of market share, as the common basis of comparison to allocate marketing resources effectively. This allows it to seek answers to the question "How much is it worth to us to try to increase our market share by another 1 (or 2, or 5, or 10) percentage point?"

This also enables higher-level managers to make resource allocation trade-offs among different kinds of business units owned by the company. To make these resource allocation decisions, marketing managers must estimate (1) the market share for the product, (2) the revenues associated with each point of market share (the present-day $72 million for a share point in breakfast cereals may be five times what it is in cake mixes), and (3) the contribution to overhead and profit (or gross margin) of each share point.

The resource allocation process helps General Mills choose wisely from among the many opportunities that exist in its various products and markets.

Resource Allocation and the Strategic Marketing Process

Company resources are allocated effectively in the strategic marketing process by converting marketing information into marketing actions. Figure 22–2 summarizes the strategic marketing process introduced in Chapter 2, along with some details of the marketing actions and information that compose it. Figure 22–2 is really a simplification of the actual strategic marketing process: while the three phases of the strategic marketing process have distinct separations in the figure and the marketing actions are separated from the marketing information, in practice these blend together and interact.

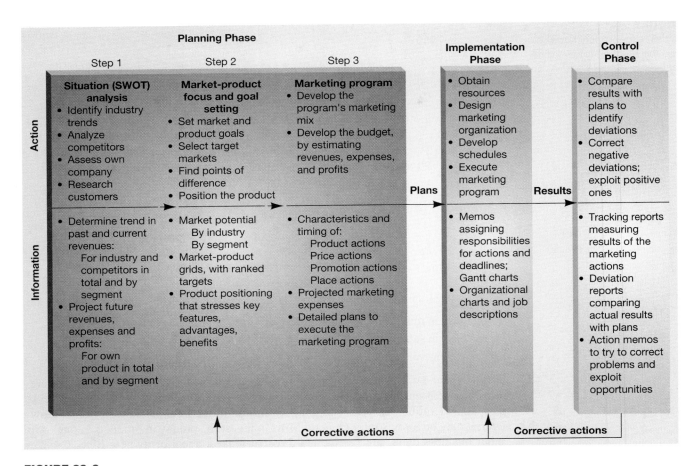

FIGURE 22–2
The strategic marketing process; actions and information

The upper half of each box in Figure 22–2 highlights the actions involved in that part of the strategic marketing process, and the lower half summarizes the information and reports used. Note that each phase has an output report:

PHASE	OUTPUT REPORT
Planning	Marketing plans (or programs) that define goals and the marketing mix strategies to achieve them
Implementation	Results (memos or computer outputs) that describe the outcomes of implementing the plans
Control	Corrective action memos, triggered by comparing results with plans, that (1) suggest solutions to problems and (2) take advantage of opportunities

The corrective action memos become "feedback loops" in Figure 22–2 that help improve decisions and actions in earlier phases of the strategic marketing process.

THE PLANNING PHASE OF THE STRATEGIC MARKETING PROCESS

Three aspects of the strategic marketing process deserve special mention: (1) the varieties of marketing plans, (2) marketing planning frameworks that have proven useful, and (3) some marketing planning and strategy lessons.

The Variety of Marketing Plans

The planning phase of the strategic marketing process usually results in a marketing plan that sets the direction for the marketing activities of an organization. As noted earlier in Appendix A, a marketing plan is the heart of a business plan. Like business plans, marketing plans aren't all from the same mold; they vary with the length of the planning period, the purpose, and the audience. Let's look briefly at three kinds: long-range, annual, and new-product marketing plans.

Long-Range Marketing Plans   Typically, long-range marketing plans cover marketing activities from two to five years into the future. Except for firms in industries such as autos, steel, or forest products, marketing plans rarely go beyond five years into the future because the tremendous number of uncertainties present make the benefits of planning less than the effort expended. Such plans are often directed at top-level executives and the board of directors.

Annual Marketing Plans   Usually developed by a product manager (discussed later in the chapter) in a consumer products firm such as General Mills, annual marketing plans deal with marketing goals and strategies for a product, product line, or entire firm for a single year. Typical steps that firms such as Kellogg's, Coca-Cola, and Johnson & Johnson take in developing their annual marketing plans for their existing products are shown in Figure 22–3.[9] This annual planning cycle typically starts with a detailed marketing research study of current users and ends after 48 weeks with the

FIGURE 22–3
Steps a large consumer package goods firm takes in developing its annual marketing plan

STEPS IN ANNUAL MARKETING PLANNING PROCESS	50	40	30	20	10	0
1. Obtain up-to-date marketing information from marketing research study of product users.	▲					
2. Brainstorm alternatives to consider in next year's plan with own marketing research and outside advertising agency personnel.	◣◢					
3. Meet with internal media specialists to set long-run guidelines in purchase of media.		◣◢				
4. Obtain sales and profit results from last fiscal year, which ended 16 weeks earlier.			◣◢			
5. Identify key issues (problems and opportunities) to address in next year's plan by talks with marketing researchers, advertising agency, and other personnel.			▰▰			
6. Hold key issues meeting with marketing director; form task force of line managers if significant product, package, or size change is considered.				▲		
7. Write and circulate key issues memo; initiate necessary marketing research to reduce uncertainty.				◣◢		
8. Review marketing mix elements and competitors' behavior with key managers, keeping marketing director informed.					▰◢	
9. Draft marketing plan, review with marketing director, and revise as necessary.					◣◢	
10. Present plan to marketing director, advertising agency, division controller, and heads of responsible line departments (product, packaging, sales, etc.) and make necessary changes.						▲
11. Present marketing plan to division general manager for approval, 10 weeks before start of fiscal year.						▲

WEEKS BEFORE APPROVAL OF PLAN

KEY: ▲ Planned period of work, ▲ Planned completion date

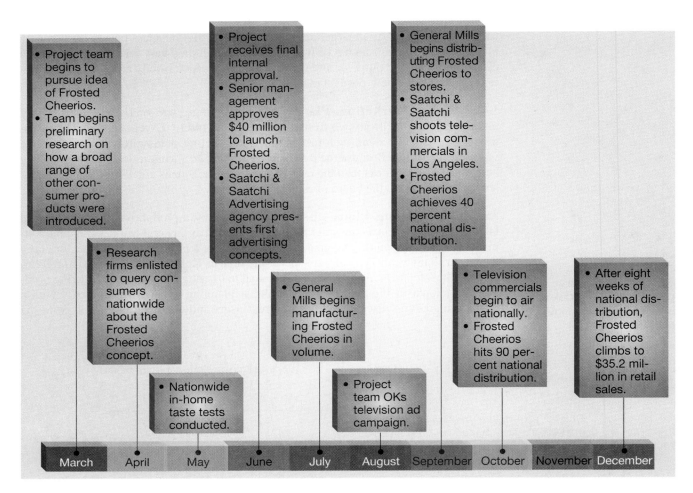

FIGURE 22–4
Frosted Cheerios: from idea to
grocery shelf in six months

approval of the plan by the division general manager—10 weeks before the fiscal year starts. Between these points there are continuing efforts to uncover new ideas through brainstorming and key-issues sessions with specialists both inside and outside the firm. The plan is fine-tuned through a series of often excruciating reviews by several levels of management, which leaves few surprises and little to chance.

Marketing Plans for New-Product Launches: Frosted Cheerios   Planning and implementing the introduction of Frosted Cheerios by a General Mills team shows the interactions of marketing strategy and tactics with the information, actions, and people needed for success. Central to all of this activity is a new-product marketing plan. As noted in Chapter 11, during 1993 and 1994 General Mills introduced a series of breakfast cereals that did poorly in the market. So when Mark Addicks was named director of marketing for new cereal products in March 1995, he knew the company needed a big winner. Figure 22–4 shows a time line of actions in the marketing plan that led to the shipment of Frosted Cheerios to stores in September 1995. The time from the new-product idea in March 1995 to first shipment in September took six months—half the normal new launch time for a new cereal product at General Mills.[10]

Figure 22–4 illustrates many key marketing concepts developed throughout this book:

- *Cross-functional teams.* The first thing Addicks did was recruit a team with a representative from every pertinent department: marketing, sales, research and development (R&D), marketing research, product development, and manufacturing.
- *Corporate goals.* Frosted Cheerios must contribute to General Mills's corporate targets of increasing earnings per share 12 percent annually and growth of unit volume 5 percent annually.

- *Marketing goals.* The new product must not cannibalize sales of the existing brands of Cheerios or hurt their images. Also, as noted earlier, 0.5 percent market share is considered a success.
- *Marketing budget.* Top management allocated $40 million for the launch, the most of any product in its history.
- *Target market.* The target market is kids (60 percent) and baby-boomer adults (40 percent) who do not have the sugared cereals hangup that their parents do.
- *Benchmarking.* The team studied successful product launches of all kinds, including Disney movies and Nickelodeon TV programs, to learn lessons for its cereal launch.
- *Marketing research on consumers.* In April (see Figure 22–4) consumers were asked about the Frosted Cheerios concept; 88 percent of the kids said they would eat them. In-home taste tests in May bore this out and identified the best from among three formulations.
- *Competitive advantages/points of difference.* A big concern was copycat imitations. So Addicks's team targeted these unique elements: complex enough to avoid copying, sweet enough to appeal to the target market, and grainy enough to maintain the Cheerios taste and image.
- *Product strategy.* Manufacturing Frosted Cheerios was a lot more complex than dipping regular Cheerios in sugar. R&D scientists found they had to blend corn flour in with the regular oat flour to give their new product the proper Cheerios "crunch." The final package, shown in Figure 22–5, was selected from seven competing designs. The figure shows the detailed planning needed to position the product favorably in the eyes and minds of consumers.
- *Pricing strategy.* The team set a price consistent with other Cheerios brands and competitive with other sugared cereals, such as Kellogg's Frosted Flakes.
- *Promotion strategy.* Working with the team, its advertising agency shot the TV commercials in September (Figure 22–5), using contemporary and campy characters such as Underdog, rap artist Queen Latifah, and loud-mouth comedian Gilbert Gottfried.[11]
- *Place strategy.* As shown in Figure 22–5, General Mills started shipping to stores in September and had 90 percent distribution the next month.

FIGURE 22–5
The cross-functional team's thinking behind the Frosted Cheerios new package

General Mills, Inc.
www.generalmills.com

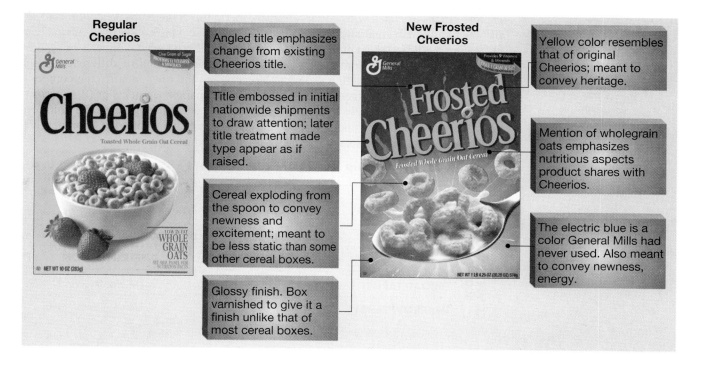

In terms of implementation, Frosted Cheerios was on retailer shelves when the TV ad campaigns started, always a huge concern with new grocery product introductions. Industry analysts have called it the most successful product launch of a ready-to-eat cereal in history.[12] Clearly Frosted Cheerios is a huge success by any standard—a success attributable to a cohesive cross-functional team's attention to detail and deadlines in its new-product marketing plan.

CONCEPT CHECK

1. What is the significance of the S-shape of the sales response function in Figure 22–1?

2. What are the main output reports from each phase of the strategic marketing process?

3. What are three kinds of marketing plans?

Frameworks to Improve Marketing Planning

Marketing planning for a firm with many products competing in many markets—a multiproduct, multimarket firm—is a complex process. Three techniques that are useful in helping corporate and marketing executives in such a firm make important resource allocation decisions are (1) Porter's generic business strategies, (2) profit enhancement options, and (3) market-product synergies. All of these techniques are based on elements introduced in earlier chapters.

Porter's Generic Business Strategies   As shown in Figure 22–6, Michael E. Porter has developed a framework in which he identifies four basic, or "generic," strategies.[13] A **generic business strategy** is one that can be adopted by any firm, regardless of the product or industry involved, to achieve a competitive advantage. Some current research suggests that a firm needs several major competencies, not just one, to sustain its competitive advantage over longer periods;[14] other research suggests that the preferred strategy is to focus on a single discipline—such as operational excellence, product leadership, or customer intimacy.[15]

Although all of the techniques discussed here involve generic strategies, the phrase is most often associated with Porter's framework. In this framework the columns identify the two fundamental alternatives firms can use in seeking competitive advantage: (1) becoming the low-cost producer within the markets in which it competes or (2) differentiating itself from competitors through developing points of difference in its product offerings or marketing programs. In contrast, the rows identify the competitive scope: (1) a broad target by competing in many market segments or (2) a narrow target by competing in only a few segments or even a single segment. The columns and rows result in four business strategies, any one of which can provide a competitive advantage among similar business units in the same industry:

1. A **cost leadership strategy** (cell 1) requires a serious commitment to reducing expenses that, in turn, lowers the price or the items sold in a relatively

---

FIGURE 22–6
Porter's four generic business strategies

	SOURCE OF COMPETITIVE ADVANTAGE	
COMPETITIVE SCOPE	**LOWER COST**	**DIFFERENTIATION**
BROAD TARGET	1. Cost leadership	2. Differentiation
NARROW TARGET	3. Cost focus	4. Differentiation focus

Which of Porter's generic strategies are Delphi Automobile Systems and Volkswagen using? For the answer and a discussion of the strategies, see the text.

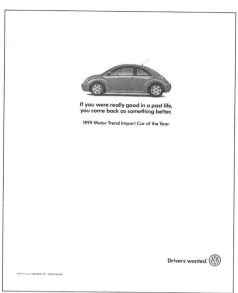

broad array of market segments. Sometimes significant investments in capital equipment may be necessary to improve the production or distribution process to give these low unit costs. The cost leader still must have adequate quality levels. Wal-Mart's sophisticated systems of regional warehouses and electronic data interchange with its suppliers has led to huge cost savings and its cost leadership strategy.

2. A **differentiation strategy** (cell 2) requires innovation and significant points of difference in product offerings, higher quality, advanced technology, or superior service in a relatively broad array of market segments. This allows a price premium. Delphi Automobile Systems has used this strategy to use satellite communications to connect you and your car to 24-hour-a-day emergency services, directions to a destination, and the opportunity to order a movie while on the road.

3. A **cost focus strategy** (cell 3) involves controlling expenses and, in turn, lowering prices, in a narrow range of market segments. Retail chains targeting only a few market segments in a restricted group of products—such as Office Max in office supplies—have used a cost focus strategy successfully. Southwest Airlines has been very successful in offering low fares between very restricted pairs of cities.

4. Finally, a **differentiation focus strategy** (cell 4) utilizes significant points of difference to one or only a few market segments. Volkswagen has achieved spectacular success by targeting the "nostalgia segment," 35- to 55-year-old baby boomers, with its technology-laden New Beetle.[16]

These strategies also form the foundation for Michael Porter's theory about what makes a nation's industries successful, as discussed in Chapter 5.

Profit Enhancement Options   If a business wants to increase, or "enhance," its profits, it can (1) increase revenues, (2) decrease expenses, or (3) do both. Among these "profit enhancement options," let's look first at the strategy options of increasing revenues and then at those for decreasing expenses.

The strategy option of increasing revenues can only be achieved by using one or a combination of four ways to address present or new markets and products (Figure 22–7): (1) market penetration, (2) product development, (3) market development, and (4) diversification (which are described in Chapter 2).

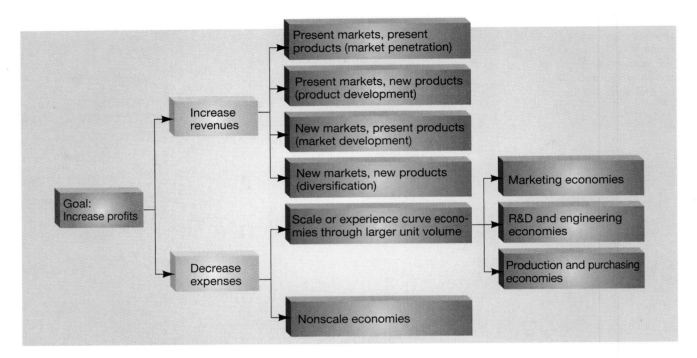

FIGURE 22–7
Profit enhancement options for increasing a firm's profits

Procter & Gamble has followed a successful strategy of market penetration (present markets, present products) by concentrating its effort on becoming the market leader in each of its more than 30 product categories. It is currently first in market share in more than half these product categories. Recent research, however, suggests that while market share may be directly related to profitability in some industries, this is not true for all. Corporate goals such as increasing customer satisfaction may be more successful than simply maximizing market share.[17]

In contrast, Johnson & Johnson has succeeded with a product development strategy—finding new products for its present markets—to complement popular brands such as Tylenol pain reliever and Accuvue contact lenses. To compete with Bristol-Meyers, American Home Products, and other companies, Johnson & Johnson developed Tylenol PM—a combination pain killer and sleeping pill—and Surevue—a long-lasting disposable contact lens.

Walt Disney Co. pursued a market development strategy (new market, present product) following the success of the original Disneyland in Anaheim, California. The first market expansion, of course, was to Orlando, Florida, and more recently Disney built theme parks in Tokyo and Paris.

Finally, Philip Morris, which depended on Marlboro cigarettes for 60 percent of its profits in the late 1980s, has used a diversification strategy (new market, new product) to reduce its dependence on a single brand. In recent years Philip Morris has purchased Seven-Up, Miller Brewing, General Foods, and Kraft to create a portfolio of consumer products.

Strategy options for decreasing expenses fall into two broad categories (Figure 22–7). One is relying on scale economies or experience curve benefits from an increased volume of production to drive unit costs down and gross margins up, the best-known examples being electronic devices such as fax or voice-mail machines whose prices fell by half in a few years. Scale economies may occur in marketing, as well as in R&D, engineering, production, and purchasing.

The other strategy option to decrease expenses is simply finding other ways to reduce costs, such as cutting the number of managers, increasing the effectiveness of

MARKETING NEWSNET

The Strategy Issue of the 1990s: Finding Synergies

Compaq Computer acquires Digital Equipment "to get synergy." Ford buys Volvo "to get synergy." With the current go-go days of giant mergers and acquisitions, the partners in these ventures are looking for synergies that have often proven elusive or impossible to achieve. For example, in 1998 Time Warner's CNN launched its much-ballyhooed "Newstand"—a TV show that was supposed to present news, business, and entertainment in an interesting format. The theory: "Newstand" would benefit from the synergy of CNN's global reach with the popular journalism of its *Time, Fortune,* and *Entertainment Weekly* siblings. The jury is still out about its success.

To try your hand in this multibillion dollar synergy game, let's assume you are vice president of marketing for Great States Corporation, whose product lines are nonpowered lawnmowers and powered walking mowers. A market-product grid for your business is shown at right. You distribute your nonpowered mowers in the three market segments shown and your powered, walking mowers in suburban markets—but you don't yet sell your powered walking mowers in cities or rural areas.

Here are your strategy dilemmas:

1. Where are the marketing synergies (efficiencies)?
2. Where are the R&D and manufacturing synergies (efficiencies)?
3. What would a market-product grid look like for an ideal company for Great States to merge with?

For the answers to these questions, read the text and study Figures 22–8 and 22–9.

the salesforce through more training, or reducing the product rejects by inspectors. Procter & Gamble concluded the world didn't really need 31 varieties of Head & Shoulders shampoo. Cutting the number of packages, sizes, and formulas in hair care alone, P&G has slashed the varieties almost in half—reducing expenses and increasing profits in the bargain.[18]

Market-Product Synergies   Let's use the market-product grid framework introduced in Chapter 10 to extend the profit-enhancement structure in the last section. There are two kinds of synergy that are critical in developing corporate and marketing strategies: (1) marketing synergy and (2) R&D–manufacturing synergy. While the following example involves external synergies through mergers and acquisitions, the concepts apply equally well to internal synergies sought in adding new products or seeking new markets.

A critical step in the external analysis is to assess how these merger and acquisition strategies provide the organization with **synergy,** the increased customer value achieved through performing organizational functions more efficiently. The "increased customer value" can take many forms: more products, improved quality on existing products, lower prices, improved distribution, and so on. But the ultimate criterion is that customers should be better off as a result of the increased synergy. The firm, in turn, should be better off by gaining more satisfied customers.

A market-product grid helps identify important trade-offs in the strategic marketing process. As noted in the Marketing NewsNet, assume you are vice president of

FIGURE 22-8
Market-product grid of
alternative strategies for a
lawnmower manufacturer

marketing for Great States Corporation's line of nonpowered lawnmowers and powered walking mowers sold to the consumer market. You are looking for new product and new market opportunities to increase your revenues and profits.

You conduct a market segmentation study and develop a market-product grid to analyze future opportunities. You identify three major segments in the consumer market based on geography: (1) city, (2) suburban, and (3) rural households. These market segments relate to the size of lawn a consumer must mow. The product clusters are (1) nonpowered, (2) powered walking, and (3) powered riding mowers. Five alternative marketing strategies are shown in the market-product grids in Figure 22–8. As mentioned in Chapter 10, the important marketing efficiencies—or synergies—run horizontally across the rows in Figure 22–8. Conversely, the important R&D and production efficiencies—or synergies—run vertically down the columns. Let's look at the synergy effects for the five combinations in Figure 22–8:

A. *Market-product concentration.* The firm benefits from "focus" on a single product line and market segment, but it loses opportunities for significant synergies in both marketing and R&D–manufacturing.

B. *Market specialization.* The firm gains marketing synergy through providing a complete product line, but R&D–manufacturing have the difficulty of developing and producing two new products.

C. *Product specialization.* The firm gains R&D–manufacturing synergy through production economies of scale, but gaining market distribution in the three different geographic areas will be costly.

D. *Selective specialization.* The firm doesn't get either marketing or R&D–manufacturing synergies because of the uniqueness of the market-product combinations.

E. *Full coverage.* The firm has the maximum potential synergies in both marketing and R&D–manufacturing. The question: Is it spread too thin?

The Marketing NewsNet posed the question of what the ideal partner would be, given the market-product combinations shown in the box. If, as vice president of marketing, you want to follow a full-coverage strategy, then the ideal merger partner is shown in Figure 22–9. This would give the maximum potential synergies—if you are not spreading your merged companies too thin. Marketing gains by having a complete product line in all regions, and R&D–manufacturing gains by having access to new markets that can provide production economies of scale through producing larger volumes of its existing products.

FIGURE 22–9
An ideal merger for Great
States to obtain full market-
product coverage

CONCEPT CHECK

1. Describe Porter's four generic business strategies.

2. What are four alternative ways to increase a firm's profits when considering profit enhancement options strategies?

3. Where do (*a*) marketing synergies and (*b*) R&D–manufacturing synergies appear in a market-product grid framework?

Some Planning and Strategy Lessons

Applying these frameworks is not automatic but requires a great deal of managerial judgment. Commonsense requirements of an effective marketing plan are discussed next, followed by problems that can arise.

Guidelines for an Effective Marketing Plan President Dwight D. Eisenhower, when he commanded Allied armies in World War II, made his classic observation, "Plans are nothing; planning is everything." It is the process of careful planning that focuses an organization's efforts and leads to success. The plans themselves, which change with events, are often secondary. Effective planning and plans are inevitably characterized by identifiable objectives, specific strategies or courses of action, and the means to execute them. Here are some guidelines in developing effective marketing plans:

- *Set measurable, achievable goals.* Ideally, goals should be quantified and measurable in terms of what is to be accomplished and by when. So, "Increase market share from 18 percent to 22 percent by December 31, 2002" is preferable to "Maximize market share given our available resources." Also, to motivate people the goals must be achievable.
- *Use a base of facts and valid assumptions.* The more a marketing plan is based on facts and valid assumptions, rather than guesses, the less uncertainty and risk are associated with executing it. Good marketing research helps.
- *Utilize simple, but clear and specific, plans.* Effective execution of plans requires that people at all levels in the firm understand what, when, and how they are to accomplish their tasks.
- *Have complete and feasible plans.* Marketing plans must incorporate all the key marketing mix factors and be supported by adequate resources.
- *Make plans controllable and flexible.* Marketing plans must enable results to be compared with planned targets, which allows replanning—the flexibility to update the original plans.

"Better ingredients, better pizza"—and better planning and attention to detail: Papa John's!

Papa John's International, Inc.

www.papajohns.com

Problems in Marketing Planning and Strategy   From postmortems on company plans that did work and on those that did not work, a picture emerges of where problems occur in the planning phase of a firm's strategic marketing process. The following list explores these problems:

1. Plans may be based on very poor assumptions about environmental factors, especially changing economic conditions and competitors' actions. A Western Union plan failed because it didn't reflect the impact of deregulation and competitors' actions on business.
2. Planners and their plans may have lost sight of their customers' needs. The "better ingredients, better pizza" slogan makes the hair stand up on the back of the necks of Pizza Hut executives. The reason is that this slogan of Papa John's International pizza chain reflects the firm's obsessive attention to detail, which is stealing market share from five-times-bigger Pizza Hut! Sample detail: If the cheese on the pizza shows a single air bubble or the crust is not golden brown, the offending pizza is not served to the customer![19]
3. Too much time and effort may be spent on data collection and writing the plans. Westinghouse has cut its planning instructions for operating units "that looked like an auto repair manual" to five or six pages.
4. Line operating managers often feel no sense of ownership in implementing the plans. Andy Grove, when he was CEO of Intel, observed, "We had the very ridiculous system . . . of delegating strategic planning to strategic planners. The strategies these [planners] prepared had no bearing on anything we actually did."[20] The solution is to assign more planning activities to line operating managers—the people who actually carry them out.

It is easier to talk about planning than to do it well. Try your hand as a consultant to help Hugo's Ski Shack make some marketing plans, as described in the Web Link box.

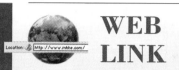

WEB LINK

Marketing 101 Final Exam: Solve the BCG's Hugo Ski Shack Online Case

The Boston Consulting Group, or BCG, is probably best known for its "growth-share" portfolio matrix discussed in Chapter 2. As a very active and respected management consulting organization, BCG maintains a Web site to describe its services. Included in its Web site is an interactive strategy case that asks you to address a dilemma faced by Hugo's Ski Shack,

which rents water skis to vacationers. Should Hugo's expand its water ski rentals based on a possible increase in demand? Access the case at www.bcg.com/case, read the case carefully, solve it within the time limits, and consider becoming a BCG consultant after graduation!

Balancing Value and Values in Strategic Marketing Plans   Two important trends are likely to influence the strategic marketing process in the future. The first, value-based planning, combines marketing planning ideas and financial planning techniques to assess how much a division or strategic business unit (SBU) contributes to the price of a company's stock (or shareholder wealth). Value is created when the financial return of a strategic activity exceeds the cost of the resources allocated to the activity.

The second trend is the increasing interest in value-driven strategies, which incorporate concerns for ethics, integrity, employee health and safety, and environmental safeguards with more common corporate values such as growth, profitability, customer service, and quality. Some experts have observed that although many corporations cite broad corporate values in advertisements, press releases, and company newsletters, they have not yet changed their strategic plans to reflect the stated values.[21]

THE IMPLEMENTATION PHASE OF THE STRATEGIC MARKETING PROCESS

The Monday morning diagnosis of a losing football coach often runs something like "We had an excellent game plan: we just didn't execute it."

Is Planning or Implementation the Problem?

The planning-versus-execution issue applies to the strategic marketing process as well: a difficulty when a marketing plan fails is determining whether the failure is due to a poor plan or poor implementation. Figure 22–10 shows the outcomes of (1) good and bad marketing planning and (2) good and bad marketing implementation.[22] Good

FIGURE 22–10
Results of good and bad marketing planning and implementation

MARKETING PLANNING AND STRATEGY

MARKETING IMPLEMENTATION	GOOD (APPROPRIATE)	BAD (INAPPROPRIATE)
GOOD (EFFECTIVE)	1 *Success:* Marketing program achieves its objectives.	2 *Trouble:* Solution lies in recognizing that only the strategy is at fault and correcting it.
BAD (INEFFECTIVE)	3 *Trouble:* Solution lies in recognizing that only implementation is at fault and correcting it.	4 *Failure:* Marketing program flounders and fails to achieve its objectives.

Swatch watches have
benefited from having both
good marketing planning and
implementation.

planning and good implementation in cell 1 spell success, as with the Swiss firm that
combined a strong product—its Swatch brand watches—with excellent advertising,
distribution, and pricing. NeXT Computer, Inc. fell into the "bad-bad" cell 4 with its
workstation that used a proprietary hardware strategy that discouraged many potential
customers and a salesforce "just too small and strapped for cash to reach many
prospects." NeXT has now closed its computer factory to focus on its software business, which Apple bought in 1997.

Cells 2 and 3 indicate trouble because either the marketing planning *or* marketing
implementation—not both—is bad. A firm or product does not stay permanently in
cell 2 or 3. If the problem is solved, the result can be success (cell 1); if not, it is failure
(cell 4).

Toyota used good implementation on a bad marketing strategy (cell 2) when it applied its superior automobile marketing skills to the introduction of its T100 pickup
truck. Consumer response was well below forecasts because the truck was too big to
compete with smaller "compact" pickups and too small and underpowered to compete
with full-size options. Goodyear Tire and Rubber Co. found itself in cell 3 after it successfully developed all-season radial tires but created problems with the 640 dealer
distribution network by raising wholesale prices. The poor implementation led to a
two-point decline in market share—a drop of 3 million tires.

Increasing Emphasis on Marketing Implementation

In the 1990s, the implementation phase of the strategic marketing process has emerged
as a key factor to success by moving many planning activities away from the duties of
planners to those of line managers.

MARKETING NEWSNET

Implementation in the Organization of Tomorrow

In today's global marketplace, corporations struggle to reduce their response time to windows of opportunity. One of the reasons is that few companies have the complete expertise necessary to quickly launch new products in diverse and changing markets. To excell at implementation of marketing strategies, the organization of tomorrow will emphasize adaptability by taking advantage of information technology and acting, as Peter Drucker suggests, like a symphony orchestra.

Frank Ostroff and Doug Smith at the consulting firm McKinsey & Co. have suggestions for firms making the transition, including:

1. Organize around process, not task.
2. Flatten the hierarchy.
3. Give leaders responsibility for process performance.
4. Link performance to customer satisfaction.
5. Create teams that have managerial and nonmanagerial responsibilities.
6. Reward team performance.

In addition, companies will need to utilize networks of suppliers, customers, and even competitors to create *strategic alliances.*

These developments are described by many terms today, including the *boundaryless company,* the *virtual corporation,* and *capabilities-based competition,* but, regardless of the terminology, you can bet that the future will bring exciting changes in the way marketing plans are implemented. Organizations as diverse as GE, Hallmark Cards, Eastman Kodak, and even the Zoological Society of San Diego are already trying many of these ideas!

GE reorganized to reduce the size of its corporate strategic planning staff from 350 to approximately 20 and also reduced the number of layers of middle managers and pushed decision-making authority lower in the organization. Some experts argue that in the future "boundaryless organizations" in which technology, information, managers, and managerial practices are shared across traditional organizational structures will be necessary.[23] The Marketing NewsNet box describes how implementation activities may occur in tomorrow's organizations.[24]

Improving Implementation of Marketing Programs

No magic formula exists to guarantee effective implementation of marketing plans. In fact, the answer seems to be equal parts of good management skills and practices, from which have come some guidelines for improving program implementation.

Communicate Goals and the Means of Achieving Them   Those called on to implement plans need to understand both the goals sought and how they are to be accomplished. Everyone in Papa John's—from founder John Schnatter to telephone order takers and make-line people—is clear on what the firm's goal is: to deliver better pizzas using better ingredients. The firm's orientation packet for employees lists its six "core values" that executives are expected to memorize. Sample: Core value no. 4 is "PAPA," or "People Are Priority No. 1, Always."[25]

Have a Responsible Program Champion Willing to Act   Successful programs almost always have a **product or program champion** who is able and willing to cut red tape and move the program forward. Such people often have the uncanny ability to move back and forth between big-picture strategy questions and specific details when the situation calls for it. Program champions are notoriously brash in overcoming organizational hurdles. The U.S. Navy's Admiral Grace Murray

Hopper not only gave the world the COBOL computer language but also the word *bug*—meaning any glitch in a computer or computer program. This program champion's famous advice for moving decisions to actions by cutting through an organization's red tape: "Better to ask forgiveness than permission."

Reward Successful Program Implementation   When an individual or a team is rewarded for achieving the organization's goal, they have maximum incentive to see a program implemented successfully because they have personal ownership and a stake in that success. At a General Electric surge protector plant, employees receive a bonus each quarter that the facility meets plantwide performance goals.

Take Action and Avoid "Paralysis by Analysis"   Management experts warn against paralysis by analysis, the tendency to excessively analyze a problem instead of taking action. To overcome this pitfall, they call for a "bias for action" and recommend a "do it, fix it, try it" approach.[26] Conclusion: Perfectionists finish last, so getting 90 percent perfection and letting the marketplace help in the fine tuning makes good sense in implementation.

Lockheed Aircraft's Skunk Works got its name from the comic strip *L'il Abner* and its legendary reputation from achieving superhuman technical feats with a low budget and ridiculously short deadlines by stressing teamwork. Under the leadership of Kelly Johnson, in 35 years the Skunk Works turned out a series of world-class aircraft from the world's fastest (the SR-71 Blackbird) to the nation's most untrackable aircraft (the F-117 Stealth fighter). Two of Kelly Johnson's basic tenets: (1) make decisions promptly and (2) avoid paralysis by analysis. In fact, one U.S. Air Force audit showed that Johnson's Skunk Works could carry out a program on schedule with 126 people, whereas a competitor in a comparable program was behind schedule with 3,750 people.[37] Some of Johnson's other rules for running Skunk Works projects—adapted for managing marketing programs—appear in Figure 22–11.[28]

Foster Open Communication to Surface the Problems   Success often lies in fostering a work environment that is open enough so employees are willing to speak out when they see problems without fear of recrimination. The focus is placed on trying to solve the problem as a group rather than finding someone to blame. Solutions are solicited from anyone who has a creative idea to suggest—from the janitor to the president—without regard to status or rank in the organization.

FIGURE 22–11
Kelly Johnson's rules for managing projects at Lockheed's Skunk Works, adapted for managing marketing programs effectively

1. Delegate the marketing program manager practically complete control of the program—the authority for quick decisions on marketing, financial, or operational matters.
2. Provide strong—but *small*—project offices on both the customer and supplier sides.
3. Restrict project personnel *viciously* to use a *small* number of *good* people.
4. Utilize a very simple planning and reporting system with the flexibility to make schedule recovery in the face of failures.
5. Minimize the number of required reports—but record important work meticulously.
6. Schedule monthly cost reviews covering both (*a*) actual expenditures and commitments and (*b*) projected costs to program conclusions—avoiding cost overrun surprises.
7. Agree on performance specifications in *advance* of contracting.
8. Achieve absolute trust through day-to-day communication and cooperation—thereby minimizing misunderstanding and correspondence.
9. Control access of outsiders to the project and its personnel.
10. Reward good performance by pay—not by number of people supervised—thereby keeping the number of project personnel to a minimum.

For the unusual way General Motors avoided the "NIH syndrome" to help develop the Saturn, see the text.

It's a game of good-natured one-upmanship that has repeated itself since the first Saturn rolled off the line some seven years ago. One that is won by microns and microscopic stress fractures. And one that is played by folks like design engineer Byron Johnson and test engineer Will Bothe.

Byron's job is to make our cars last. Will's job is to tear them apart. (It's as close to a rivalry as you're likely to find around here.)

Which is to say, they don't go at it like Democrats and Republicans. But they still manage, in the most Saturn of ways, to get in their digs. Say a part Byron designed doesn't pass Will's tests. Then let the taunting voice mails begin. And if it does? Then the reverse holds true. Now, this sort of competition isn't limited to Byron and Will; it's repeated by each of the 500 engineers who work here. Each giving a mock insult here, a good-natured jab there. Ultimately ending in some really great cars waiting at your friendly Saturn retailer.

A DIFFERENT KIND OF COMPANY. A DIFFERENT KIND OF CAR.

Two more Kelly Johnson axioms from Lockheed's Skunk Works apply here: (1) When trouble develops, surface the problem immediately, and (2) get help; don't keep the problem to yourself. This latter point is important even if it means getting ideas from competitors.

Saturn is General Motors' attempt to create a new company where participatory management and improved communications lead to a successful product. For example, to encourage discussion of possible cost reductions, each employee receives 100 to 750 hours of training, including balance sheet analysis. To avoid the "NIH syndrome"—the reluctance to accept ideas "not invented here" or not originated inside one's own firm—Saturn engineers bought 70 import cars to study for product design ideas and selected options that would most appeal to their target market.

Schedule Precise Tasks, Responsibilities, and Deadlines   Successful implementation requires that people know the tasks for which they are responsible and the deadline for completing them. To implement the thousands of tasks on an orbiting satellite, Boeing's Aerospace Group typically holds weekly program meetings. The outcome of each of these meetings is an **action item list** that has three columns: (1) the task, (2) the name of the person responsible for accomplishing that task, and (3) the date by which the task is to be finished. Within hours of completing a program meeting, the action item list is circulated to those attending. This then serves as the starting agenda for the next meeting. Meeting minutes are viewed as secondary and backward looking. Action item lists are forward looking, clarify the targets, and put strong pressure on people to achieve their designated tasks by the deadline.

Related to the action item lists are formal *program schedules,* which show the relationships through time of the various program tasks. Scheduling an action program involves (1) identifying the main tasks, (2) determining the time required to complete each, (3) arranging the activities to meet the deadline, and (4) assigning responsibilities to complete each task.

Suppose, for example, that you and two friends are asked to do a term project on the problem, "How can the college increase attendance at its performing arts concerts?"[29] And suppose further that the instructor limits the project in the following ways:

1. The project must involve a mail survey of the attitudes of a sample of students.
2. The term paper with the survey results must be submitted by the end of the 11-week quarter.

FIGURE 22–12

Tasks in complete a term project

Shown below are the tasks you might face as a member of a student team to complete a marketing research study using a mail questionnaire. Elapsed time to complete all the tasks is 15 weeks. How do you finish the project in an 11-week quarter? For an answer, see the text.

TASK	TIME (WEEKS)
1. Construct and test a rough-draft questionnaire for clarity (in person, not by mail) on friends.	2
2. Type and copy a final questionnaire.	2
3. Randomly select the names of 200 students from the school directory.	1
4. Address and stamp envelopes; mail questionnaires.	1
5. Collect returned questionnaires.	3
6. Tabulate and analyze data from returned questionnaires.	2
7. Write final report.	3
8. Type and submit final report.	1
Total time necessary to complete all activities.	15

To begin the assignment, you need to identify all the project tasks and then estimate the time you can reasonably allocate to each one. As shown in Figure 22–12, it would take 15 weeks to complete the project if you did all the tasks sequentially; so to complete it in 11 weeks, your team must work on different parts at the same time, and some activities must be independent enough to overlap. This requires specialization and cooperation. Suppose that of the three of you (A, B, and C), only student C can type. Then you (student A) might assume the task of constructing the questionnaire and selecting samples, and student B might tabulate the data. This division of labor allows each student to concentrate on and become expert in one area, but you should also cooperate. Student C might help A and B in the beginning, and A and B might help C later on.

You must also figure out which activities can be done concurrently to save time. In Figure 22–12 you can see that task 2 must be completed before task 4. However, task 3 might easily be done before, at the same time as, or after task 2. Task 3 is independent of task 2.

Scheduling production and marketing activities—from a term project to a new product rollout to a space shuttle launch—can be done efficiently with Gantt charts. Figure 22–13 shows one variation of a Gantt chart used to schedule the class project, demonstrating how the concurrent work on several tasks enables the students to finish the project on time. Developed by Henry L. Gantt, this method is the basis for the scheduling techniques used today, including elaborate computerized methods. The key to all scheduling techniques is to distinguish tasks that *must* be done sequentially from those that *can* be done concurrently. As in the case of the term project, scheduling tasks concurrently often reduces the total time required for a project.

CONCEPT CHECK

1. Why is it important to include line operating managers in the planning process?

2. What is the meaning and importance of a program champion?

3. Explain the difference between sequential and concurrent tasks in a Gantt chart.

Organizing for Marketing

A marketing organization is needed to implement the firm's marketing plans. Basic issues in today's marketing organizations include understanding (1) how line versus staff positions and divisional groupings interrelate to form a cohesive marketing organization and (2) the role of the product manager.

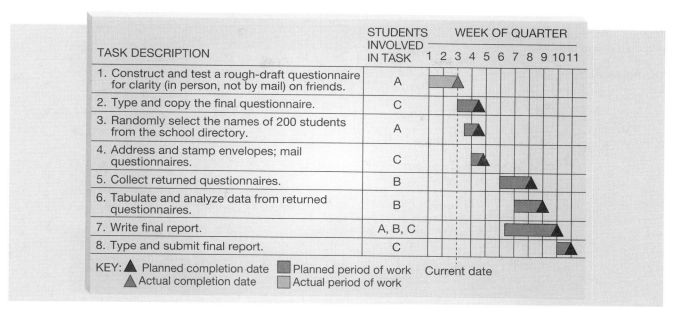

FIGURE 22–13
Gantt chart for scheduling the term project

Line versus Staff and Divisional Groupings   Although simplified, Figure 22–14 shows the organization of Pillsbury's Prepared Dough Products Business Unit in detail and highlights the distinction between line and staff positions in marketing. People in **line positions,** such as group marketing managers, have the authority and responsibility to issue orders to the people who report to them, such as marketing managers. In this organizational chart, line positions are connected with solid lines. Those in **staff positions** (shown by dotted lines) have the authority and responsibility to advise people in line positions but cannot issue direct orders to them.

FIGURE 22–14
Organization of the Pillsbury Company

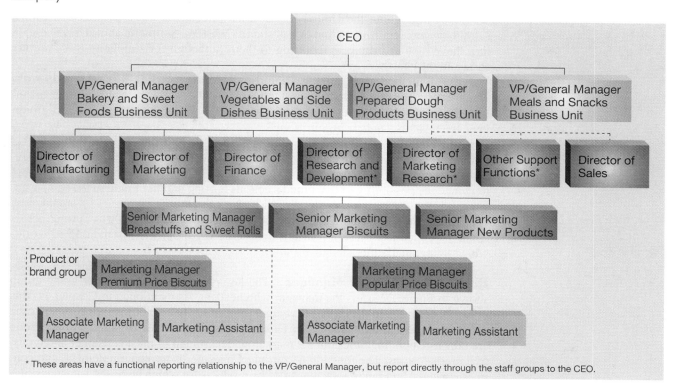

* These areas have a functional reporting relationship to the VP/General Manager, but report directly through the staff groups to the CEO.

Products from Pillsbury's line of
prepared dough products.

The Pillsbury Company
www.pillsbury.com

Most marketing organizations use divisional groupings—such as product line, functional, geographical, and market-based—to implement plans and achieve their organizational objectives. Three of these appear in some form in Pillsbury's organizational chart in Figure 22–14. At the top of its organization, Pillsbury organizes by **product line groupings,** in which a unit is responsible for specific product offerings. For example, Pillsbury has four main product lines: Bakery & Sweet Foods, Vegetables & Side Dishes, Prepared Dough Products, and Meals & Snacks.

The Prepared Dough Products Business Unit is organized by **functional groupings** such as manufacturing, marketing, and finance, which are the different business activities within a firm.

Pillsbury uses **geographical groupings** for its more than 500 field sales representatives throughout the United States. Each director of sales has several regional sales managers reporting to him or her, such as Western, Southern, and so on. These, in turn, have district managers reporting to them (although for simplicity these are not shown in the chart).

A fourth method of organizing a company is to use **market-based groupings,** which utilize specific customer segments, such as the banking, health care, or manufacturing segments. When this method of organizing is combined with product groupings, the result is a *matrix organization.*

A relatively new position in consumer products firms is the *category manager* (senior marketing manager in Figure 22–14). Category managers have profit-and-loss responsibility for an entire product line—all biscuit brands, for example. They attempt to reduce the possibility of one brand's actions hurting another brand in the same category. Procter & Gamble is extending the idea of category managers to organize by "global business units" such as baby care and beauty care by 2001. Cutting across country boundaries, these global business units will implement standardized worldwide pricing, marketing, and distribution.[30]

Role of the Product Manager   The key person in the product or brand group shown in Figure 22–15 is the manager who heads it. As mentioned in Chapter 11, this person is often called the *product manager* or *brand manager,* but in Pillsbury he or she carries the title *marketing manager.* This person and the assistants in the product group are the basic building blocks in the marketing department of most consumer and industrial product firms. The function of a product manager is to plan, implement, and control the annual and long-range plans for the products for which he or she is responsible.

FIGURE 22–15
Units with which the product manager and product group work

There are both benefits and dangers to the product manager system. On the positive side, product managers become strong advocates for the assigned products, cut red tape to work with people in various functions both inside and outside the organization (Figure 22–15), and assume profit-and-loss responsibility for the performance of the product line. On the negative side, even though product managers have major responsibilities, they have relatively little direct authority, so most groups and functions shown in Figure 22–15 must be coordinated to meet the product's goals.[31] To coordinate the many units, product managers must use persuasion rather than orders.

THE CONTROL PHASE OF THE STRATEGIC MARKETING PROCESS

The essence of control, the final phase of the strategic marketing process, is comparing results with planned goals for the marketing program and taking necessary actions.

The Marketing Control Process

FIGURE 22–16
The control phase of the strategic marketing process

Ideally, quantified goals from the marketing plans developed in the planning phase have been accomplished by the marketing actions taken in the implementation phase (Figure 22–16) and measured as results in the control phase. A marketing manager then uses *management by exception,* which means identifying results that deviate from plans to diagnose their causes and take new actions. Often results fall short of plans, and a corrective action is needed. For example, after 50 years of profits Caterpillar accumulated losses of $1 billion. To correct the problem, Caterpillar focused its marketing efforts on core products and reduced its manufacturing costs. At other times the comparison shows that performance is far better than anticipated, in which case the marketing manager tries to identify the reason and move quickly to exploit the unexpected opportunity.

Measuring Results   Without some quantitative goal, no benchmark exists with which to compare actual results. Manufacturers of both consumer and industrial products are increasingly trying to develop marketing programs that have not only specific action programs but also specific procedures for monitoring key measures of performance. Today marketing executives are measuring not only tangible financial targets such as sales revenues and profits, but also less tangible ones such as customer satisfaction, new-product development cycle time, and salesforce motivation.

Taking Marketing Actions   When results deviate significantly from plans, some kind of action is essential. Deviations can be the result of the process used to specify goals or can be due to changes in the marketplace. Beaten badly for years in the U.S. toothpaste market by P&G's Crest, in 1998 Colgate went on the offensive. It took aggressive marketing action to introduce its Total toothpaste, the first "oral pharmaceutical" ever approved by the U.S. Food and Drug Administration. Not only does Total clean teeth, but it helps heal gingivitis, one of the bleeding-gum diseases of increasing concern to aging baby boomers.[32]

Sales Analysis

For controlling marketing programs, **sales analysis**—using the firm's sales records to compare actual results with sales goals and identify areas of strength and weakness—is critical. All the variables that might be used in market segmentation may be used in **sales component analysis** (also called *microsales analysis*), which traces sales revenues to their sources, such as specific products, sales territories, or customers. Common breakdowns include the following:

- Customer characteristics: demographics, NAICS, size, reason for purchase, and type of reseller (retailer or wholesaler).
- Product characteristics: model, package size, and color.
- Geographical region: sales territory, city, state, and region.
- Order size.
- Price or discount class.
- Commission to the sales representative.

Today's computers can easily produce these breakdowns, provided the input data contain these classifications. Therefore, it is critical that marketing managers specify the breakdowns they require from the accounting and information systems departments.

The danger is that marketing managers or chief executive officers get overwhelmed by the volume of computerized reports. To avoid this problem, each Tuesday, Ken Iverson carefully inputs into the computer numbers on the tons of steel each of Nucor's "minimills" produced the previous week. What makes the situation unique is that Iverson is chief executive officer of Nucor. Saving money is *not* the reason he does his own computer analysis. His explanation, "By keying in the numbers, you're forced to look at every figure for every week. That's the value."[33]

Profitability Analysis

To their surprise, marketing managers often discover the 80/20 principle the hard way, on the job. **Profitability analysis** enables the manager to measure the profitability of the firm's products, customer groups, sales territories, channels of distribution, and even order sizes. This leads to decisions to expand, maintain, reduce, or eliminate specific products, customer groups, or channels.

For example, following the 80/20 principle, a marketing manager will try to find the common characteristics among the 20 percent of the customers (or products, brands, sales districts, salespeople, or kinds of orders) that are generating 80 percent (or the bulk) of revenues and profits to find more like them to exploit competitive advantages. Conversely, the 80 percent of customers, products, brands, and so on that are generating few revenues and profits may need to be reduced or even dropped entirely unless a way is found to make them profitable.

The Marketing Audit

Often a broader marketing perspective is needed than is given by sales or profitability analyses, one that covers a longer time horizon and relates the marketing mix factors to environmental variables. This is the role of a **marketing audit,** which is a comprehensive, unbiased, periodic review of the strategic marketing process of a firm or SBU. The purpose of the marketing audit, which serves as both a planning and control technique, is to identify new problems and opportunities that warrant an action plan to improve performance.

Many firms undertaking a marketing audit use a checklist such as that shown in Figure 22–17 as a part of their situation analysis in their strategic marketing process.

FIGURE 22–17
Marketing audit questions

PRODUCTS/SERVICES: THE REASON FOR EXISTENCE

1. Is the product/service free from deadwood?
2. What is the life-cycle stage?
3. How will user demands or trends affect you?
4. Are you a leader in new-product innovation?
5. Are inexpensive methods used to estimate new product potentials before consideration amounts are spent on R&D and market introduction?
6. Do you have different quality levels for different markets?
7. Are packages/brochures effective salespeople for the products/services they present?
8. Do you present products/services in the most appealing colors (formats) for markets being served?
9. Are there features or benefits to exploit?
10. Is the level of customer service adequate?
11. How are quality and reliability viewed by customers?

CUSTOMER: USER PROFILES

1. Who is the current and potential customer?
2. Are there geographic aspects of use: regional, rural, urban?
3. Why do people buy the product/service; what motivates their preferences?
4. Who makes buying decisions; when; where?
5. What is the frequency and quantity of use?

MARKETS: WHERE PRODUCTS/SERVICES ARE SOLD

1. Have you identified and measured major segments?
2. Are small potential market segments overlooked in trying to satisfy the majority?
3. Are the markets for the products/services expanding or declining?
4. Should different segments be developed; are there gaps in penetration?

COMPETITORS: THEIR INFLUENCE

1. Who are the principal competitors, how are they positioned, and where are they headed?
2. What are their market shares?
3. What features of competitors' products/services stand out?
4. Is the market easily entered or dominated?

PRICING: PROFITABILITY PLANNING

1. What are the objectives of current pricing policy: acquiring, defending, or expanding?
2. Are price policies set to produce volume or profit?
3. How does pricing compare with competition in similar levels of quality?
4. Does cost information show profitability of each item?
5. What is the history of price deals, discounts, and promotions?

The checklist used covers factors ranging from the marketing mix factors and customer profiles to markets and competitors.

For a meaningful, comprehensive marketing audit, the individual or team conducting the audit must have a free rein to talk to managers, employees, salespeople, distributors, and customers, as well as have access to all pertinent internal and external reports and memoranda. They need to involve all levels of the organization in the process to ensure that resulting action recommendations have widespread support.

CONCEPT CHECK

1. What is the difference between a line and a staff position in a marketing organization?

2. What are four groupings used within a typical marketing organization?

3. What two components of the strategic marketing process are compared to control a marketing program?

SUMMARY

1 Marketing managers use the strategic marketing process to allocate their resources as effectively as possible. Sales response functions help them assess what the market's response to additional marketing effort will be.

2 The planning phase of the strategic marketing process usually results in a marketing plan that sets the direction for the marketing activities of an organization. Three kinds of marketing plans are long-range, annual, and new-product plans.

3 Three useful frameworks to improve marketing planning are (*a*) Porter's generic business strategies, (*b*) profit enhancement options, and (*c*) market-product synergies.

4 An effective marketing plan has measurable, achievable goals; uses facts and valid assumptions; is simple, clear, and specific; is complete and feasible; and is controllable and flexible.

5 The implementation phase of the strategic marketing process is concerned with executing the marketing program

developed in the planning phase and has achieved increased attention the past decade.

6 Essential to good scheduling is separating tasks that can be done concurrently from those that must be done sequentially. Gantt charts are a simple, effective means of scheduling.

7 Organizing marketing activities necessitates recognition of two different aspects of an organization: (*a*) line and staff positions and (*b*) product line, functional, geographical, and market-based groupings.

8 The product manager performs a vital marketing role in both consumer and industrial product firms, interacting with numerous people and groups both inside and outside the firm.

9 The control phase of the strategic marketing process involves measuring the results of the actions from the implementation phase and comparing them with goals set in the planning phase. Sales analyses, profitability analyses, and marketing audits are used to control marketing programs.

KEY TERMS AND CONCEPTS

sales response function p. 580
share points p. 581
generic business strategy p. 586
cost leadership (generic) strategy p. 586
differentiation (generic) strategy p. 587
cost focus (generic) strategy p. 587
differentiation focus (generic) strategy p. 587
synergy p. 589
product or program champion p. 595
action item list p. 597

line positions p. 599
staff positions p. 599
product line groupings p. 600
functional groupings p. 600
geographical groupings p. 600
market-based groupings p. 600
sales analysis p. 602
sales component analysis p. 602
profitability analysis p. 603
marketing audit p. 603

INTERNET EXERCISE

The Walt Disney Company's main Web site (www.disney. com) is splashy, interactive, and links to other Disney Web sites. These other sites enable the Web user to subscribe to various Disney online services or order other Disney products or services such as movies, theme park reservations, and music. Access the Disney Web site and click on the "Shopping" Web link to go to "The Disney Store Online." To purchase a video, go to the left side of the Web page. Under the "Store Directory," scroll down to the "Video Collection" link. Click on the "New Releases" link. Then, click on a video of your choice (such as *A Bug's Life*). Select either the "DVD" or "VHS" format of the video. Next, select the quantity you want (presumably "1"). Click on the "Add Items to Shopping Basket" button and then click on the "Begin Checkout" button at the top of the page to purchase the video. After you have viewed your order, click on the "Continue to Checkout" button. Enter the personal and credit card information that Disney requires to process your order (be sure to click the button that calculates the shipping and tax) and then click on the "Click Here to Complete Your Purchase" button **ONLY IF** you want to finalize the purchase.

1   Is the process for ordering merchandise from "The Disney Store Online" convenient to you as a consumer?
2   How likely are *you* to make a purchase from any company with an online store now or in the near future? Why or why not? What should companies do to get people to use their online stores instead of retail stores, catalogs, or other distribution outlets for their merchandise or services?

APPLYING MARKETING CONCEPTS AND PERSPECTIVES

1   Assume a firm faces an S-shaped sales response function. What happens to the ratio of incremental sales revenue to incremental marketing effort at the (*a*) bottom, (*b*) middle, and (*c*) top of this curve?
2   What happens to the ratio of incremental sales revenue to incremental marketing effort when the sales response function is an upward-sloping straight line?
3   In 1999 General Mills invested millions of dollars in expanding its cereal and cake mix businesses. To allocate this money between these two businesses, what information would General Mills like to have?
4   Suppose your Great States mower company has the market-product concentration situation shown in Figure 22–8A. What are both the synergies and potential pitfalls of following expansion strategies of (*a*) market specialization and (*b*) product specialization?

5   Are value-driven strategies inconsistent with value-based planning? Give an example that supports your position.
6   The first Domino's Pizza restaurant was near a college campus. What implementation problems are (*a*) similar and (*b*) different for restaurants near a college campus versus a military base?
7   A common theme among managers who succeed repeatedly in program implementation is fostering open communication. Why is this so important?
8   Parts of tasks 6 and 7 in Figure 22–12 are done both concurrently and sequentially. How can this be? How does it help the students meet the term paper deadline?
9   In Pillsbury's organizational chart in Figure 22–14, where do product line, functional, and geographical groupings occur?
10   Why are quantified goals in the planning phase of the strategic marketing process important for the control phase?

CASE 22–1   YOPLAIT USA

"A little bit of constructive restlessness is good," says Chap Colucci, "because you can become too satisfied with your own success, with the status quo. You take your foot off the gas and things begin to stall." Colucci is vice president of marketing and sales of Yoplait USA, a subsidiary of General Mills, Inc., whose experience is in more traditional grocery products like flour, breakfast cereals, and cake mixes.

THE ORIGINAL IDEA

Yoplait's sole product is yogurt, a business far removed from General Mills's regular product lines.

In the late 1970s top management at General Mills asked Steven M. Rothschild to head a team to investigate yogurt as a new business opportunity for the company. In the United States, yogurt had annual sales of $350 million with an annual growth rate of about 18 percent. Rothschild's team discovered that about 95 percent of the yogurt consumed in the United States was mixed with fruit or flavoring, and about 5 percent was plain. About 95 percent was consumed in eight-ounce cups. The team also found the U.S. annual per capita consumption of yogurt was low (5 cups per person) compared with consumption in European countries (27 cups per person a year in France).

Further analysis showed there were four basic types of yogurt:

- Sundae style—fruit on the bottom of the cup.
- Swiss style—fruit blended throughout the cup to keep the fruit from settling on the bottom.
- Western style—fruit on the bottom and flavored syrup on the top.
- Frozen style—ice-cream or soft-custard form.

Other research showed that yogurt was available in 20 different flavors and a wide range of textures. When refrigerated, it had a shelf life of 21 to 60 days, depending on whether preservatives are added.

MEETING CORPORATE NEW PRODUCT GOALS

Rothschild and the team recommended that General Mills enter the yogurt market. In doing so, it committed the yogurt venture to achieve several brand goals set for new products at General Mills:

1 Fit with General Mills's strengths: "high value-added products distributed through supermarkets."

2 Achieve 20 percent share of the yogurt market in five years.
3 Achieve $100 million in sales in five years—double the minimum required by General Mills.
4 Meet internal financial goals of 25 percent ROI in five years.
5 Become a multiproduct business.

A yogurt product also met some other brand goals for a new product at General Mills: (1) a high-turnover branded item that allows a significant profit margin; (2) a product for which the firm's skills in positioning, advertising, packaging, and promotion will provide an advantage over competition; and (3) a business that will capitalize on trends resulting from long-term changes in consumer behavior.

THE COMPANY

Rothschild and his team decided General Mills should buy the rights to market Yoplait yogurt in the United States from Sodima, a large French cooperative. This enabled General Mills to gain Yoplait's technology of producing and distributing a refrigerated product and Yoplait to profit from sales of its product in the United States. It also saved General Mills three years of time in entering the yogurt business.

At that time Yoplait was the best-selling yogurt in France. Marketing research revealed what consumers perceived as Yoplait's key benefits: (1) 100 percent natural yogurt without artificial sweeteners or preservatives, (2) Swiss style, with real fruit mixed throughout, and (3) outstanding taste with a creamy texture. In terms of U.S. competition, there was no national brand of yogurt, but there was a two-tiered group of yogurt producers: (1) premium regional brands such as Dannon and Kraft and (2) private-label brands produced by local dairies.

Yoplait USA moved quickly to gain acceptance for Yoplait as a national brand among American consumers. Yoplait USA positioned its yogurt as the "Yogurt of France" with creative TV commercials featuring personalities like Loretta Swit and Tommy Lasorda eating Yoplait and speaking French.

YOPLAIT TODAY

After its initial success, Yoplait underestimated the competition from national brands (such as Dannon and Kraft). Although number two nationally, Yoplait's market share and profit fell. Its first fruit-on-the-bottom line failed. Chap Colucci, the new vice president of marketing and sales at Yoplait USA, believed that the team had become too satisfied with its early success.

When named to his new job, Chap Colucci conducts a situation analysis in preparation for developing a new marketing strategy for Yoplait USA. His "constructive restlessness" turns up some serious concerns, including:

1 *Retail prices.* Yoplait's price for a six-ounce cup is actually higher on some lines than competitors' eight-ounce cups. For example, the prices on Yoplait's 4 Pack are about 20 percent higher per cup than Dannon's and Kraft's 6 Pack.

2 *Low gross margins.* Margins have declined, at least partly because of high production and overhead costs.

3 *Mix of spending weighted toward trade promotions.* Most is directed at trade (retailers and wholesalers) and only a little at consumers.

4 *Lack of "effective advertising with continuity."* Yoplait has been living off the great Loretta Swit and Tommy Lasorda series of ads that launched the product without a similar creative, follow-up campaign.

5 *Few coupons offered.* In the late 1980s Yoplait cut way back on offering consumer coupons, while its competitors had heavy couponing.

6 *Few new products.* While Yoplait has developed its Lite product-line extension, the remaining new product pipeline is largely empty.

7 *Geographic marketing organization.* Yoplait is organized geographically with three regions—Eastern, Central, and Western. This organization has caused marketing managers to focus on geography, not basic marketing.

Yoplait's performance the previous two years isn't reaching the targets set for it by top management at General Mills. Chap Colucci concludes he must analyze these concerns and take marketing actions.

Questions

1 Without considering Chap Colucci's list of concerns:
 a Compare the situation both today and in 1980 (right after Yoplait appeared nationally in the United States) in terms of:
  (1) Stage of the product life cycle for yogurt in the United States.
  (2) Why Americans might eat yogurt.
 b Describe how these environmental factors might change today's Yoplait USA strategy from what it was in 1980.

2 Now look at Chap Colucci's list of concerns for Yoplait USA. Thinking in terms of the strategic marketing process:
 a Describe the implications for Yoplait USA of each concern.
 b Describe *planning* and *implementation* actions you believe Colucci and Yoplait USA should take to address the concerns.
 c Identify possible objectives that relate to each concern that could serve as a measure of control to determine if the new actions were achieving desired results.

CAREER PLANNING IN MARKETING

GETTING A JOB: THE PROCESS OF MARKETING YOURSELF

Getting a job is usually a lengthy process, and it is exactly that—a *process* that involves careful planning, implementation, and control. You may have everything going for you: a respectable grade point average (GPA), relevant work experience, several extracurricular activities, superior communication skills, and demonstrated leadership qualities. Despite these, you still need to market yourself systematically and aggressively; after all, even the best products lie dormant on the retailer's shelves unless marketed effectively.

The process of getting a job involves the same activities marketing managers use to develop and introduce products into the marketplace.[1] The only difference is that you are marketing yourself, not a product. You need to conduct marketing research by analyzing your personal qualities (performing a self-audit) and by identifying job opportunities. Based on your research results, select a target market—those job opportunities that are compatible with your interests, goals, skills, and abilities—and design a marketing mix around that target market. *You* are the "product"[2]; you must decide how to "position" yourself in the job market. The price component of the marketing mix is the salary range and job benefits (such as health and life insurance, vacation time, and retirement benefits) that you hope to receive. Promotion involves communicating with prospective employers through written correspondence (advertising) and job interviews (personal selling). The place element focuses on how to reach prospective employers—at the campus placement center or job fairs, for example.

This appendix will assist you in career planning by (1) providing information about careers in marketing and (2) outlining a job search process.

CAREERS IN MARKETING

The diversity of marketing opportunities is reflected in the many types of marketing jobs, ranging from purchasing to marketing research to public relations to product manage-

ment. The growing interest in marketing by service and nonprofit organizations—such as hospitals, financial institutions, the performing arts, and government—has added to the numerous opportunities offered by traditional employers such as manufacturers, retailers, consulting firms, and advertising agencies. In addition, as high-tech firms become more consumer-oriented, their demand for employees with marketing skills has soared.[3] Examples of companies that have opportunities for graduates with degrees in marketing include Ford, Cisco, Lucent Technologies, Citibank, Macy's, Hormel, Eddie Bauer, General Electric, and many others.[4] Most of these career opportunities offer the chance to work with interesting people on stimulating and rewarding problems. Comments one product manager, "I love marketing as a career because there are different challenges every day."[5]

Recent studies of career paths and salaries suggest that marketing careers can also provide an excellent opportunity for advancement and substantial pay. For example, a survey of chief executive officers (CEOs) of the nation's 1,000 most valuable publicly held companies revealed that marketing and finance were the most common career paths to their positions.[6] Similarly, reports of average starting salaries of college graduates indicate that salaries in marketing compare favorably with those in many other fields. The average annual starting salary of new marketing undergraduates in 1998 was $29,231, compared with $24,248 for journalism majors and $25,331 for advertising majors.[7] The future is likely to be even better. The National Association of Colleges and Employers reports that the field of marketing, advertising, and public relations is one of the 20 fastest-growing occupations requiring a bachelor's degree. In addition, the Bureau of Labor Statistics suggests that "Increasingly intense domestic and global competition in products and services offered to consumers should require greater marketing, promotional, and public relations efforts through 2006."[8]

Figure C–1 describes marketing occupations in six major categories: product management and physical distribution, advertising, retailing, sales, marketing research, and nonprofit marketing. One of these may be right for you! (Additional sources of marketing career information are provided at the end of this appendix.)

PRODUCT MANAGEMENT AND PHYSICAL DISTRIBUTION

Product manager for consumer goods develops new products that can cost millions of dollars, with advice and consent of management—a job with great responsibility.

Supply chain manager oversees the organization within a company that transports products to consumers and handles customer service.

Operations manager supervises warehousing and other physical distribution functions and often is directly involved in moving goods on the warehouse floor.

Traffic and transportation manager evaluates the costs and benefits of different types of transportation.

Inventory control manager forecasts demand for stockpiled goods, coordinates production with plant managers, and keeps track of current levels of shipments to keep customers supplied.

Administrative analyst performs cost analyses of physical distribution systems.

Customer service manager maintains good relations with customers by coordinating sales staffs, marketing management, and physical distribution management.

Physical distribution specialist is an expert in the transportation and distribution of goods.

SALES

Direct salesperson (door-to-door) calls on consumers in their homes to make sales.

Trade salesperson calls on retailers or wholesalers to sell products for manufacturers.

Industrial or semitechnical salesperson sells supplies and services to businesses.

Complex or professional salesperson sells complicated or custom-designed products to business. This requires understanding of the technology of a product.

NONPROFIT MARKETING

Marketing manager for nonprofit organizations develops and directs mail campaigns, fundraising, and public relations.

ADVERTISING

Account executive maintains contact with clients while coordinating the creative work among artists and copywriters. In full-service ad agencies, account executives are considered partners with the client in promoting the product and helping to develop marketing strategy.

Media buyer deals with media sales representatives in selecting advertising media and analyzes the value of media being purchased.

Copywriter works with art director in conceptualizing advertisements and writes the text of print or radio ads or the storyboards of television ads.

Art director handles the visual component of advertisements.

Sales promotion manager designs promotions for consumer products and works at an ad agency or a sales promotion agency.

Public relations manager develops written or filmed messages for the public and handles contacts with the press.

Specialty advertising manager develops advertising for the sales staff and customers or distributors.

RETAILING

Buyer selects products a store sells, surveys consumer trends, and evaluates the past performance of products and suppliers.

Store manager oversees the staff and services at a store.

MARKETING RESEARCH

Project manager for the supplier coordinates and oversees the market studies for a client.

Account executive for the supplier serves as a liaison between client and market research firm, like an advertising agency account executive.

In-house project director acts as project manager (see above) for the market studies conducted by the firm for which he or she works.

Marketing research specialist for an advertising agency performs or contracts for market studies for agency clients.

Source: David W. Rosenthal and Michael A. Powell, *Careers in Marketing*, ©1984, pp. 352–54. Adapted by permission of Prentice Hall, Englewood Cliffs, NJ.

FIGURE C–1
Twenty-six marketing occupations

Product Management and Physical Distribution

Many organizations assign one manager the responsibility for a particular product. For example, Procter & Gamble (P&G) has separate managers for Tide, Cheer, Gain, and Bold. Product or brand managers are involved in all aspects of a product's marketing program, such as marketing research, sales, sales promotion, advertising, and pricing, as well as manufacturing. Managers of similar products typically report to a category manager and may be part of a *product management team*.[9]

College graduates with bachelor's and master's degrees—often in marketing and business—enter P&G as brand assistants, the only starting position in its product or brand group. Each year students from campuses throughout the United States accept positions with P&G.[10] As brand assistants, their responsibilities consist primarily of selling and sales training.

After one to two years of good performance, the brand assistant is promoted to assistant brand manager and after about the same period to brand (product) manager. These promotions often involve several brand groups. For example, a new employee might start as brand assistant for P&G's soap products, be promoted to assistant brand manager for Crest toothpaste, and subsequently become brand manager for Folger's coffee, Charmin, or Pampers. The reason, as recruiter Henry de Montebello explains, is that "in the future everybody will have strategic alliances with everybody else, and the executives who thrive will be well-rounded."[11]

Several other jobs related to product management (Figure C–1) deal with physical distribution issues such as storing the manufactured product (inventory), moving the product from the firm to the customers (transportation), maintaining good relations with customers (customer service), and engaging in many other aspects of the manufacture and sale of goods. Prospects for these jobs are likely to increase as wholesalers increase their involvement with selling and distribution activities and begin to take advantage of overseas opportunities.[12]

Advertising

Although we may see hundreds of advertisements in a day, what we can't see easily is the fascinating and complex advertising profession. The entry-level advertising positions filled every year include jobs with a variety of firms. Advertising professionals often remark that they find their jobs appealing because the days are not routine and they involve creative activities with many interesting people.

Advertising positions are available in three kinds of organizations: advertisers, media companies, and agencies. Advertisers include manufacturers, retail stores, service firms, and many other types of companies. Often they have an advertising department responsible for preparing and placing their own ads. Advertising careers are also possible with the media: television, radio stations, magazines, and newspapers. Finally, advertising agencies offer job opportunities through their use of account management, research, media, and creative services.

Starting positions with advertisers and advertising agencies are often as assistants to employees with several years of experience. An assistant copywriter facilitates the development of the message, or copy, in an advertisement. An assistant art director participates in the design of visual components of advertisements. Entry-level media positions involve buying the media that will carry the ad or selling air time on radio or television or page space in print media. Advancement to supervisory positions requires planning skills, a broad vision, and an affinity for spotting an effective advertising idea. Students interested in advertising should develop good communication skills and try to gain advertising experience through summer employment opportunities or internships.[13]

Retailing

There are two separate career paths in retailing: merchandise management and store management (Figure C–2). The key position in merchandising is that of a buyer, who is responsible for selecting merchandise, guiding the promotion of the merchandise, setting prices, bargaining with wholesalers, training the salesforce, and monitoring the competitive environment. The buyer must also be able to organize and coordinate many critical activities under severe time constraints. In contrast, store management involves the supervision of personnel in all departments and the general management of all facilities, equipment, and merchandise displays. In addition, store managers are responsible for the financial performance of each department and for the store as a whole. Typical positions beyond the store manager level include district manager, regional manager, and divisional vice president.[14]

FIGURE C–2
Typical retailing career paths

Most starting jobs in retailing are trainee positions. A trainee is usually placed in a management training program and then given a position as an assistant buyer or assistant department manager. Advancement and responsibility can be achieved quickly because there is a shortage of qualified personnel in retailing and because superior performance of an individual is quickly reflected in sales and profits—two visible measures of success.

Sales

College graduates from many disciplines are attracted to sales positions because of the increasingly professional nature of selling jobs and the many opportunities they can provide. A selling career offers benefits that are hard to match in any other field:

(1) the opportunity for rapid advancement (into management or to new territories and accounts); (2) the potential for extremely attractive compensation (the average salary of regional sales managers is $95,000)[15]; (3) the development of personal satisfaction, feelings of accomplishment, and increased self-confidence; and (4) independence—salespeople often have almost complete control over their time and activities. Many companies such as National Semiconductor now offer two sales career paths—one for people who want to go into management, and another for those who want to remain in sales for their entire career.[16]

Employment opportunities in sales occupations are found in a wide variety of organizations, including insurance agencies, retailers, and financial service firms (Figure C–3). In addition, many salespeople work as manufacturer's representatives for organizations that have selling responsibilities for several manufacturers.[17] Activities in sales jobs include *selling duties,* such as prospecting for customers, demonstrating the product, or quoting prices; *sales-support duties,* such as handling complaints and helping solve technical problems; and *nonselling duties,* such as preparing reports, attending sales meetings, and monitoring competitive activities. Salespeople who can deal with these varying activities are critical to a company's success. According to RJR Nabisco, their recruiting priority is "finding quality people who can analyze data from customers, see things from the consumer's eyes,

OCCUPATION	1996 EMPLOYMENT	2006 EMPLOYMENT	PERCENTAGE CHANGE 1996–2006	AVERAGE ANNUAL GROWTH
Insurance agents and brokers	409,000	427,000	+4%	1,800
Retail sales workers	4,522,000	5,021,000	+11	49,900
Securities and financial services sales workers	263,000	363,000	+38	10,000
Real estate agents and brokers	408,000	440,000	+8	3,200
Travel agents	142,000	176,000	+24	3,400
Service sales representatives	694,000	1,087,000	+57	39,300

Source: "The 1996–2006 Job Outlook in Brief," *Occupational Outlook Quarterly* (Spring 1998), p. 22.

FIGURE C–3
Employment opportunities in selected sales occupations (1996 to 2006)

use available sales tools like laptops and syndicated data, and interface with the marketing people at headquarters."[18]

One of the fastest areas of growth in sales positions is in the direct marketing industry. Interest in information technology, relationship marketing, and integrated marketing has increased the demand for contact with customers. Requests for "the most talented people" is "unprecedented," says Hal Crandall, president of New York recruiting firm Crandall Associates. For many firms this means new or additional telemarketing efforts; for other firms it means increasing the amount of time salespeople spend with clients. According to Mutual Life Insurance Company of New York, one of five companies selected by *Sales and Marketing Management* magazine for its Best Sales Force award, successful salespeople "focus on ways to get in front of the client more, by delegating tasks to staff and utilizing technology more effectively."[19]

Marketing Research

Marketing researchers play important roles in many organizations today. They are responsible for obtaining, analyzing, and interpreting data to facilitate making marketing decisions. This means marketing researchers are basically problem solvers. Success in the area requires not only an understanding of statistics and computers but also a broad base of marketing knowledge[20] and an ability to communicate with management. Individuals who are inquisitive, methodical, analytical, and solution oriented find the field particularly rewarding.

The responsibilities of the men and women currently working in the market research industry include defining the marketing problem, designing the questionnaire, selecting the sample, collecting and analyzing the data, and, finally, reporting the results of the research. These jobs are available in three kinds of organizations. *Marketing research consulting firms* contract with large companies to provide research about their products or services.[21] *Advertising agencies* may provide research services to help clients with questions related to advertising and promotional problems. Finally, some companies have an *in-house research staff* to design and execute their research projects. Typical positions would include director, statistician, analyst, field work director, and interviewer.[22]

Although marketing researchers may start as assistants performing routine tasks, they quickly advance to broader responsibilities. Survey design, interviewing, report writing, and all aspects of the research process create a challenging career. In addition, research projects typically deal with such diverse problems as consumer motivation, pricing, forecasting, and competition. A recent survey of research organizations suggested that, to be successful in marketing research positions, students should develop skills in written, oral, and interpersonal communication; statistics and analysis; research design; and logic. The survey also suggested that practical work experience (e.g., internships) provides a useful supplement to classroom education.[23]

International Careers

Many of the careers just described can be found in international settings—in multinational U.S. corporations, small- to medium-size firms with export business, and franchises.

The international public relations firm Burson-Marstellar, for example, has offices in New York, Sydney, Copenhagen, and Bangkok. Similarly, franchises such as Blockbuster Entertainment are expanding in many other markets outside of the United States. The dramatic changes in Europe and the need to rebuild the economies of the former Soviet republics may provide other opportunities. Variations of the permanent international career are also possible—for example, some companies may alternate periods of work at "headquarters" with "field" assignments in foreign countries.[24] Finally, a domestic international career—working for a foreign-owned company with an office in the United States—may be appealing.[25]

Applicants for international positions should first develop a skill that can be applied in an international setting. In addition, however, internationally competent employees will need language and cultural skills. A Conference Board description illustrates the point:

> The successful managers of the future will probably be those who speak both Japanese and English, who have a strong base in Brussels and contacts in the Pacific Rim, and who know the cafes and bars of Singapore.

Further, in many organizations, international experience has become a necessity for promotion and career advancement.[26]

THE JOB SEARCH PROCESS

Activities you should consider during your job search process include assessing yourself, identifying job opportunities, preparing your résumé and related correspondence, and going on job interviews.

Assessing Yourself

You must know your product—you—so that you can market yourself effectively to prospective employers. Consequently, a critical first step in your job search is conducting a self-analysis, which involves critically examining yourself on the following dimensions: interests, abilities, education, experience, personality, desired job environment, and personal goals.[27] The importance of performing this assessment was stressed by a management consultant:[28]

> Many graduates enter the world of work without even understanding the fact that they are specific somebodies, much less knowing the kinds of competencies and motivations with which they have been endowed. . . . The tragedy of not knowing is awesome. Ignorant of who they are, most graduates are doomed to spend too much of their lives in work for which they are poorly suited. . . . Self-knowledge is critical to effectively managing your career.

INTERESTS

How do I like to spend my time?
Do I enjoy being with people?
Do I like working with mechanical things?
Do I enjoy working with numbers?
Am I a member of many organizations?
Do I enjoy physical activities?
Do I like to read?

ABILITIES

Am I adept at working with numbers?
Am I adept at working with computers?
Do I have good verbal and written communication skills?
What special talents do I have?
At which abilities do I wish I were more adept?

EDUCATION

How have my courses and extracurricular activities
   prepared me for a specific job?
Which were my best subjects? My worse? The most fun?
   The least?
Is my GPA an accurate picture of my academic ability?
   Why?
Do I aspire to a graduate degree? Before beginning my
   job?
Why did I choose my major?

PERSONAL GOALS

What are my short-term and long-term goals? Why?
Am I career oriented, or do I have broader interests?
What are my career goals?
What jobs are likely to help me achieve my goals?
What do I hope to be doing in 5 years? In 10 years?
What do I want out of life?

PERSONALITY

What are my good and bad traits?
Am I competitive?
Do I work well with others?
Am I outspoken?
Am I a leader or a follower?
Do I work well under pressure?
Do I work quickly, or am I methodical?
Do I get along well with others?
Am I ambitious?
Do I work well independently of others?

DESIRED JOB ENVIRONMENT

Am I willing to relocate? Why?
Do I have a geographical preference? Why?
Would I mind traveling in my job?
Do I have to work for a large, nationally known firm to be
   satisfied?
Must the job I assume offer rapid promotion
   opportunities?
If I could design my own job, what characteristics would it
   have?
How important is high initial salary to me?

EXPERIENCE

What previous jobs have I held? What were my responsi-
   bilities in each?
What internships or co-op positions have I held? What
   were my responsibilities?
What volunteer positions have I held? What were my
   responsibilities?
Were any of my jobs or positions applicable to positions
   I may be seeking? How?
What did I like the most about my previous jobs? Like the
   least?
Why did I work in the jobs I did?
If I had it to do over again, would I work in these jobs?
   Why?

FIGURE C–4

Questions to ask in your self-analysis

Asking Key Questions   A self-analysis, in part, entails asking yourself some very important and difficult questions (Figure C–4). It is critical that you respond to the questions honestly, because your answers ultimately will be used as a guide in your job selection.[29] A less-than-candid appraisal of yourself might result in a job mismatch.

Identifying Strengths and Weaknesses   After you have addressed the questions posed in Figure C–4, you are ready to identify your strengths and weaknesses. To do so, draw a vertical line down the middle of a sheet of paper and label one side of the paper "strengths" and the other side "weaknesses." Based on your answers to the questions, record your strong and weak points in their respective column. Ideally this cataloging should be done over a few days to give you adequate time to reflect on your attributes. In addition, you might seek input from others who know you well (such as parents, close relatives, friends, professors, or employers) and can offer more objective views. They might even evaluate you on the questions in Figure C–4, and you can compare the results with your own evaluation. A hypothetical list of strengths and weaknesses is shown in Figure C–5.

What skills are most important? The answer, of course, varies by occupation and employer. Recent studies, however, suggest that problem-solving skills, communication skills, interpersonal skills, analytical and computer skills, and leadership skills are

FIGURE C–5
Hypothetical list of job candidate's strengths and weaknesses

STRENGTHS	WEAKNESSES
Enjoy being with people	Am not adept at working with computers
Am an avid reader	Have minimal work experience
Have good communication skills	Have a mediocre GPA
Am involved in many extracurricular activities	Am sometimes impatient
Work well with others	Resent close supervision
Work well independently	Work methodically (slowly)
Am honest and dependable	Will not relocate
Am willing to travel in the job	Anger easily sometimes
Am a good problem solver	Lack of customer orientation
Have a good sense of humor	
Am a self-starter, have drive	

all valued by employers. Personal characteristics employers seek in a job candidate include honesty, integrity, motivation, initiative, self-confidence, flexibility, and enthusiasm. Finally, most employers also look for work experience, internship experience, or co-op experience.[30]

Taking Job-Related Tests   Personality and vocational interest tests, provided by many colleges and universities, can give you other ideas about yourself. After tests have been administered and scored, test takers meet with testing service counselors to discuss the results. Test results generally suggest jobs for which students have an inclination. The most common tests at the college level are the Strong Interest Inventory and the Campbell Interest and Skill Survey. Some counseling centers also administer the Myers-Briggs Type Indicator—a personality measure that helps identify professions you may enjoy.[31] If you have not already done so, you may wish to see whether your school offers such testing services.

Identifying Your Job Opportunities

To identify and analyze the job market, you must conduct some marketing research to determine what industries *and* companies offer promising job opportunities that relate to the results of your self-analysis. Several sources that can help in your search are discussed below.

College Placement Office   Your college placement office is an excellent source of job information. Personnel in that office can (1) inform you about which companies will be recruiting on campus, (2) alert you to unexpected job openings, (3) advise you about short-term and long-term career prospects, (4) offer advice on résumé construction, (5) assess your interviewing strengths and weaknesses, and (6) help you evaluate a job offer. In addition, the office usually contains a variety of written materials focusing on different industries and companies and tips on job hunting. One major publication available in most campus placement offices is the National Association of Colleges and Employers publication *Job Choices*, which contains a list of employers, kinds of job openings for college graduates, and whom to contact about jobs in those firms.

Online Career and Employment Services   Many companies no longer make frequent on-campus visits. Instead, they may use the many online services available to advertise an employment opportunity or to search for candidate information. The National Association of Colleges and Employers, for example, maintains a site on the World Wide Web called JobWeb (www.jobweb.org). Similarly, The Monster Board (www.monster.com) and CareerMosaic (www.fortune.careermosaic.com) are databases of employment ads, candidate resumes, and other career-related information. Some of the information resources include career guidance, a cover letter library, occupational profiles, and résumé templates.[32] Employers may contact students directly when the candidate's qualifications meet their specific job requirements. The advantage of this system for students is that regardless of the size or location of the campus they are attending, many companies have access to their résumé. Your school's career center may also have a "home page" that offers online job search information and links to other World Wide Web sites.

CareerMosaic. We offer more jobs than a month of Sundays.

Over 100,000 fresh jobs to attract today's serious job seekers.

Library   The public or college library can provide you with reference material that, among other things, describes successful firms and their operations, defines the content of various jobs, and forecasts job opportunities. For example, *Fortune* publishes lists of the 1,000 largest U.S. and global companies and their respective sales and profits; Dun & Bradstreet publishes directories of all companies in the United States with a net worth of at least $500,000. *Careers in Marketing*, a publication of the American Marketing Association, presents career opportunities in marketing. The *Occupational Outlook Handbook* is an annual publication of the U.S. Department of Labor that provides projections for specific job prospects, as well as information pertaining to those jobs. A librarian can indicate reference materials that will be most pertinent to *your* job search.

Advertisements   Help-wanted advertisements provide an overview of what is happening in the job market. Local (particularly Sunday editions) and college newspapers, trade press (such as *Marketing News* or *Advertising Age*), and business magazines (such as *Sales and Marketing Management*) contain classified advertisement sections that generally have job opening announcements, often for entry-level positions. Reviewing the want ads can help you identify what kinds of positions are available and their requirements and job titles, which firms offer certain kinds of jobs, and levels of compensation.

Employment Agencies   An employment agency can make you aware of several job opportunities very quickly because of its large number of job listings available through computer databases. Many agencies specialize in a particular field (such as sales and marketing). The advantages of using an agency include that it (1) reduces the cost of a job search by bringing applicants and employers together, (2) often has exclusive job listings available only by working through the agency, (3) performs much of the job search for you, and (4) tries to find a job that is compatible with your qualifications and interests.[33] Employment agencies are much maligned because some engage in questionable business practices, so check with the Better Business Bureau or your business contacts to determine the quality of the various agencies.

Personal Contacts   An important source of job information that students often overlook is their personal contacts. People you know often may know of job opportunities, so you should advise them that you're looking for a job. Relatives and friends might aid your job search. Instructors you know well and business contacts can provide a wealth of information about potential jobs and even help arrange an interview with a prospective employer. They may also help arrange "informational interviews" with employers who do not have immediate openings. These interviews allow you to collect information about an industry or an employer and give you an advantage if a position does become available. It is a good idea to leave your résumé with all your personal contacts so they can pass it along to those who might be in need of your services. Student organizations (such as the student chapter of the American Marketing Association and Pi

Sigma Epsilon, the professional sales fraternity) may be sources of job opportunities, particularly if they are involved with the business community. Local chapters of professional business organizations (such as the American Marketing Association and Sales and Marketing Executives International) also can provide job information; contacting their chapter president is a first step in seeking assistance from these organizations. In the past decade, small employers have provided the greatest growth in employment, and their most common source of new employees is through personal referrals.[34]

State Employment Office   State employment offices have listings of job opportunities in their state and counselors to help arrange a job interview for you. Although state employment offices perform functions similar to employment agencies, they differ in listing only job opportunities in their state and providing their services free.

Direct Contact   Another means of obtaining job information is direct contact—personally communicating to prospective employers (either by mail or in person) that you would be interested in pursuing job opportunities with them. Often you may not even know whether jobs are available in these firms. If you correspond with the companies in writing, a letter of introduction and an attached résumé should serve as your initial form of communication. Your major goal in direct contact is ultimately to arrange a job interview.

Writing Your Résumé

A résumé is a document that communicates to prospective employers who you are. An employer reading a résumé focuses on two key questions: (1) What is the candidate like? and (2) What can the candidate do for me?[35] It is imperative that you design a résumé that addresses these two questions and presents you in a favorable light. Personnel in your campus placement office can provide assistance in designing résumés.

The Résumé Itself   A well-constructed résumé generally contains up to nine major sections: (1) identification (name, address, and telephone number), (2) job or career objective, (3) educational background, (4) extracurricular activities, (5) work experience or history, (6) skills or capabilities (that pertain to a particular kind of job for which you may be interviewing), (7) accomplishments or achievements, (8) personal interests, and (9) personal references.[36] There is no universally accepted format for a résumé, but three are more frequently used: chronological, functional, and targeted. A *chronological* format presents your work experience and education according to the time sequence in which they occurred (i.e., in chronological order). If you have had several jobs or attended several schools, this approach is useful to highlight what you have done. With a *functional* format, you group your experience into skill categories that emphasize your strengths. This option is particularly appropriate if you have no experience or only minimal experience related to your chosen field. A *targeted* format focuses on the capabilities you have for a specific job. This alternative is desirable if you know what job you want and are qualified for it.[37] In any of the formats, if possible, you should include quantitative information about your accomplishments and experience, such as "increased sales revenue by 20 percent" for the year you managed a retail clothing store. A résumé that illustrates the chronological format is shown in Figure C–6.[38]

Technology is creating a need for a new type of résumé—the electronic résumé. While traditional versions of résumés may be easily delivered through fax machines, today most career experts suggest that a second electronic version be available. The reason? Computers read differently than people. To fully utilize online opportunities, an electronic résumé with a popular font and relatively large font size—and without italic text, graphics, shading, underlining or vertical lines—must be available. In addition, because online recruiting starts with a key-word search, it is important to include key words, focus on nouns rather than verbs, and avoid abbreviations.[39]

FIGURE C–6
Chronological résumé

SALLY WINTER

Campus address (until 6/1/2000):
Elm Street Apartments #2B
College Town, Ohio 44042
Phone: (614) 424-1648
swinter@osu.stu.edu

Home address:
123 Front Street
Teaneck, NJ 07666
Phone: (201) 836-4995

EDUCATION
B.S. in Business Administration, Ohio State University, 2000, cum laude—3.3 overall GPA—3.6 GPA in major

WORK EXPERIENCE
Paid for 70 percent of my college expenses through the following part-time and summer jobs:

Legal Secretary, Smith, Lee & Jones, Attorneys at Law, New York, NY—summer 1998
- Took dictation and transcribed tapes of legal proceedings
- Typed contracts and other legal document
- Reorganized client files for easier access
- Answered the phone and screened calls for the partners

Salesclerk, College Varsity Shop, College Town, Ohio—1997–1999 academic years
- Helped customers with buying decisions
- Arranged stock and helped with window displays
- Assisted in year-end inventories
- Took over responsibilities of store manager when she was on vacation or ill

Assistant Manager, Treasure Place Gift Shop, Teaneck, NJ—summers and Christmas vacations—1996–1999
- Supervised two salesclerks
- Helped select merchandise at trade shows
- Handled daily accounting
- Worked comfortably under pressure during busy seasons

CAMPUS ACTIVITIES
- Elected captain of the women's varsity tennis team for two years
- Worked as a reporter and night editor on campus newspaper for two years
- Elected historian for Mortar Board chapter, a senior women's honorary society

COMPUTER SKILLS
- Word, Excel, Microsoft Publisher

PERSONAL INTERESTS
- Collecting antique clocks, listening to jazz, swimming

REFERENCES AVAILABLE ON REQUEST

Letter Accompanying a Résumé   The letter accompanying a résumé, or cover letter, serves as the job candidate's introduction. As a result, it must gain the attention and interest of the reader or it will fail to give the incentive to examine the résumé carefully. In designing a letter to accompany your résumé, address the following issues:[40]

- Address the letter to a specific person.
- Identify the position for which you are applying and how you heard of it.
- Indicate why you are applying for the position.
- Summarize your most significant credentials and qualifications.
- Refer the reader to the enclosed résumé.
- Request a personal interview, and advise the reader when and where you can be reached.

A sample letter comprising these six factors is presented in Figure C–7. Some students have tried creative approaches to making their letter stand out—sending a gift with their letter or using creative packaging, for example. Although these tactics may gain a recruiter's attention, most hiring managers say that a frivolous approach makes for a frivolous employee. As a general rule, nothing works better than an impressive cover letter and good academic credentials.[41]

Interviewing for Your Job

The job interview is a conversation between a prospective employer and a job candidate that focuses on determining whether the employer's needs can be satisfied by the candidate's qualifications. The interview is a "make or break" situation: If the interview goes well, you have increased your chances of receiving a job offer; if it goes poorly, you probably will be eliminated from further consideration.

FIGURE C–7
Sample letter accompanying a résumé

Sally Winter
Elm Street Apartments, #2B
College Town, Ohio 44042
January 31, 2000

Mr. J. B. Jones
Sales Manager
Hilltop Manufacturing Company
Minneapolis, MN 55406

Dear Mr. Jones:

Dr. William Johnson, Professor of Business Administration at the Ohio State University, recently suggested that I write to you concerning your opening and my interest in a sales position. With a B.S. degree in business administration and courses in personal selling and sales management, I am confident that I could make a positive contribution to your firm.

During the past four years I have been a salesclerk in a clothing store and an assistant manager in a gift shop. These two positions required my performing a variety of duties including selling, purchasing, stocking, and supervising. As a result, I have developed an appreciation for the viewpoints of the customer, salesperson, and management. Given my background and high energy level, I feel that I am particularly well qualified to assume a sales position in your company.

My enclosed résumé better highlights my education and experience. My extracurricular activities should strengthen and support my abilities to serve as a sales representative.

I am eager to talk with you because I feel I can demonstrate to you why I am a strong candidate for the position. I have friends in Minneapolis with whom I could stay on weekends, so Fridays or Mondays would be ideal for an appointment. I will call you in a week to see if we can arrange a mutually convenient time for a meeting. I am hopeful that your schedule will allow this.

Thank you for your kind consideration. If you would like some additional information, please feel free to contact me at (614) 424-1648. I look forward to talking with you.

Sincerely,

Sally Winter

enclosure

Preparing for a Job Interview   To be successful in a job interview, you must prepare for it so you can exhibit professionalism and indicate to a prospective employer that you are serious about the job. When preparing for the interview, several critical activities need to be performed.

Before the interview, gather facts about the industry, the prospective employer, and the job. Relevant information might include the general description for the occupation; the firm's products or services; the firm's size, number of employees, and financial and competitive position; the requirements of the position; and the name and personality of the interviewer.[42] Obtaining this information will provide you with additional insight into the firm and help you formulate questions to ask the interviewer. This information might be gleaned, for example, from corporate annual reports, *The Wall Street Journal*, Moody's manuals, Standard & Poor's *Register of Corporations, Directors, and Executives, The Directory of Corporate Affiliations*, selected issues of *Business Week*, or trade publications. If information is not readily available, you could call the company and indicate that you wish to obtain some information about the firm before your interview.

Preparation for the job interview should also involve role playing, or pretending that you are in the "hot seat" being interviewed. Before role playing, anticipate questions interviewers may pose and how you might address them (Figure C–8). Do not memorize your answers, though, because you want to appear spontaneous, yet logical and intelligent. Nonetheless, it is helpful to practice how you might respond to the questions. You should also anticipate a substance abuse screening process—now common among a wide variety of organizations.[43] In addition, develop questions you might ask the interviewer that are important and of concern to you (Figure C–9).

When role playing, you and someone with whom you feel comfortable should engage in a mock interview. Afterward, ask the stand-in interviewer to candidly appraise your interview content and style. You may wish to videotape the mock interview; ask the personnel in your campus placement office where videotaping equipment can be obtained for this purpose.

Before the job interview you should attend to several details. Know the exact time and place of the interview; write them down—do not rely on your memory. Get the full company name straight. Find out what the interviewer's name is and how to pronounce it. Bring a notepad and pen along on the interview, in case you need to record anything. Make certain that your appearance is clean, neat, professional, and conservative. And be punctual; arriving tardy to a job interview gives you an appearance of being unreliable.

Succeeding in Your Job Interview   You have done your homework, and at last the moment arrives and it is time for the interview. Although you may experience

FIGURE C–8
Question frequently asked by interviewers

INTERVIEWER QUESTIONS

1 What can you tell me about yourself?
2 What are your strengths? Weaknesses?
3 What do you consider to be your most significant accomplishment to date?
4 What do you see yourself doing in 5 years? In 10 years?
5 Are you a leader? Explain.
6 What do you really want out of life?
7 How would you describe yourself?
8 Why did you choose your college major?
9 In which extracurricular activities did you participate? Why?
10 What jobs have you enjoyed the most? The least? Why?
11 How has your previous work experience prepared you for a job?
12 Why do you want to work for our company?
13 What qualifications do you think a person needs to be successful in a company like ours?
14 What do you know about our company?
15 What criteria are you using to evaluate the company for which you hope to work?
16 In what kind of city would you prefer to live?
17 What can I tell you about our company?
18 Are you willing to relocate?
19 Are you willing to spend at least six months as a trainee? Why?
20 Why should we hire you?

some apprehension, view the interview as a conversation between the prospective employer and you. Both of you are in the interview to look over the other party, to see whether there might be a good match. You know your subject matter (you); furthermore, because you did not have a job with the firm when you walked into the interview, you really have nothing to lose if you don't get it—so relax.[44]

When you meet the interviewer, greet him or her by name, be cheerful, smile, and maintain good eye contact. Take your lead from the interviewer at the outset. Sit down after the interviewer has offered you a seat. Do not smoke. Sit up straight in your chair, and look alert and interested at all times. Appear relaxed, not tense. Be enthusiastic.

During the interview, be yourself. If you try to behave in a manner that is different from the "real" you, your attempt may be transparent to the interviewer or you may ultimately get the job but discover that you aren't suited for it. In addition to assessing how well your skills match those of the job, the interviewer will probably try to assess your long-term interest in the firm. William Kucker, a recruiter for General Electric, explains, "We're looking for people to make a commitment."[45]

FIGURE C–9
Question frequently asked by interviewees

INTERVIEWEE QUESTIONS

1 Why would a job candidate want to work for your firm?
2 What makes your firm different from its competitors?
3 What is the company's promotion policy?
4 Describe the typical first-year assignment for this job.
5 How is an employee evaluated?
6 What are the opportunities for personal growth?
7 Do you have a training program?
8 What are the company's plans for future growth?
9 What is the retention rate of people in the position for which I am interviewing?
10 How can you use my skills?
11 Does the company have development programs?
12 What kind of image does the firm have in the community?
13 Why do you enjoy working for your firm?
14 How much responsibility would I have in this job?
15 What is the corporate culture in your firm?

As the interview comes to a close, leave it on a positive note. Thank the interviewer for his or her time and the opportunity to discuss employment opportunities. If you are still interested in the job, express this to the interviewer. The interviewer will normally tell you what the employer's next step is. Rarely will a job offer be made at the end of the initial interview. If it is and you want the job, accept the offer; if there is any doubt in your mind about the job, however, ask for time to consider the offer.

Following Up on Your Job Interview   After your interview, send a thank-you note to the interviewer and indicate whether you are still interested in the job. If you want to continue pursuing the job, "polite persistence" may help you get it. According to one expert, "Many job hunters make the mistake of thinking that their career fate is totally in the hands of the interviewer once the job interview is finished."[46] You *can* have an impact on the interviewer *after* the interview is over.

The thank-you note is a gesture of appreciation and a way of maintaining visibility with the interviewer. (Remember the adage, "Out of sight, out of mind.") Even if the interview did not go well, the thank-you note may impress the interviewer so much that his or her opinion of you changes. After you have sent your thank-you note, you may wish to call the prospective employer to determine the status of the hiring decision. If the interviewer told you when you would hear from the employer, make your telephone call *after* this date (assuming, of course, that you have not yet heard from the employer); if the interviewer did not tell you when you would be contacted, make your telephone call a week or so after you have sent your thank-you note.

As you conduct your follow-up, be persistent but polite. If you are too eager, one of two things could happen to prevent you from getting the job: the employer might feel that you are a nuisance and would exhibit such behavior on the job, or the employer may perceive that you are desperate for the job and thus are not a viable candidate.

Handling Rejection   You have put your best efforts into your job search. You developed a well-designed résumé and prepared carefully for the job interview. Even the interview appears to have gone well. Nevertheless, a prospective employer may send you a rejection letter. ("We are sorry that our needs and your superb qualification don't match.") Although you will probably be disappointed, not all interviews lead to a job offer because there normally are more candidates than there are positions available.

If you receive a rejection letter, you should think back through the interview. What appeared to go right? What went wrong? Perhaps personnel from your campus placement office can shed light on the problem, particularly if they are in the custom of having interviewers rate each interviewee. Try to learn lessons to apply in future interviews. Keep interviewing and gaining interview experience; your persistence will eventually pay off.

SELECTED SOURCES OF MARKETING CAREER INFORMATION

The following is a selected list of marketing information sources that you should find useful during your academic studies and professional career.

Business and Marketing Publications

Peter D. Bennett, ed., *Dictionary of Marketing Terms*, 3rd ed. (Lincolnwood, IL: NTC Publishing Group, 1998). This dictionary contains definitions of more than 3,000 marketing terms.

Business Periodicals Index (BPI) (New York: H. W. Wilson Company). This is a monthly (except August) index of almost 400 periodicals from all fields of business and marketing.

Chase Cochrane and Kenneth L. Barasch, *Marketing Problem Solver*, 3rd ed. (Radnor, PA: Chilton Book Company, 1989). A good reference for "how-to" problems, this handbook contains chapters on marketing research, marketing planning, product planning, pricing, advertising, trade shows, sales promotion, legal aspects of marketing, and other topics.

Jill Cousins and Lesley Robinson, eds., *The Online Manual: A Practical Guide to Business Databases*, 2nd ed. (Cambridge, MA: Blackwell Publishers, 1993). This manual is a practical tool to help both the experienced and inexperienced information user select from the thousands of databases now available online.

Encyclopedia of Business Information Sources, 12th ed. (Detroit, MI: Gale Research, Inc, 1998). A bibliographic guide to over 31,000 citations covering more than 1,100 primary subjects of interest to business personnel.

Lorna M. Daniells, *Business Information Sources*, 3rd ed. (Berkeley, CA: University of California Press, 1993). This comprehensive guide to selected business books and reference sources is useful for business students as well as the practicing businessperson.

Jeffrey Heilbrunn, ed., *Marketing Encyclopedia* (Lincolnwood, IL: NTC Business Books, 1995). This book provides a collection of essays by professional and academic marketing experts on issues and trends shaping the future of marketing.

Jerry M. Rosenberg, *Dictionary of Marketing and Advertising* (New York: John Wiley & Sons, 1995). This dictionary contains more than 5,500 concise definitions of marketing and advertising terms.

Jean L. Sears and Marilyn K. Moody, *Using Government Information Sources*, 2nd ed. (Phoenix, AZ: Oryx Press, 1994). An easy-to-use manual arranged by topics such as consumer expenditures, business and industry statistics, economic indicators, and projections. Each chapter contains a search strategy, a checklist of courses, and a narrative description of the sources.

Arlene Fink and Jacqueline B. Kosecoff, *How to Conduct Surveys: A Step by Step Guide*, 2nd ed. (Thousand Oaks, CA: Sage Publications, Inc., 1998). A simple guide to understand how to develop surveys, compare the uses and cost of different survey methods (paper, telephone, Internet, personal interview), analyze the data obtained from surveys, and present the survey results.

Larry Kahaner, *Competitive Intelligence: How to Gather, Analyze, and Use Information to Move Your Business to the Top* (New York: Simon & Schuster, 1998). This book takes readers beyond the Information Age and into the Age of Intelligence, explaining how to turn the raw facts, statistics, and numbers about competitors' activities and market trends into practical guidelines for making the right business decisions. See www.simonsays.com or www.kahaner.com.

Barbara Lewis and Dale Littler, eds., *The Blackwell Encyclopedic Dictionary of Marketing* (Cambridge, MA: Blackwell Publishers, 1997). Part of the 10-volume *Blackwell Encyclopedia of Management*, this book provides clear, concise, up-to-the-minute, and highly informative definitions and explanation of the key concepts and terms in marketing management, consumer behavior, segmentation, organizational marketing, pricing, communications, retailing and distribution, product management, market research and international marketing. See www.blackwellpublishers.co.uk.

Career Planning Publications

Richard N. Bolles, *The 1999 What Color Is Your Parachute?: A Practical Manual for Job-Hunters and Career-Changers*, (Berkeley, CA: Ten Speed Press, 1998). A companion workbook is also available. See www.jobhuntersbible.com.

Karmen Crowther, *Researching Your Way to a Good Job* (New York: John Wiley & Sons, 1993). See www.wiley.com.

Fred E. Jardt and Mary B. Nemnich, *Cyberspace Resume Kit: How to Make and Launch a Snazzy Online Resume* (Indianapolis, IN: JIST Works, Inc., 1998). See www.jist.com.

Margaret Riley, Frances Roehm, and Steve Oserman, *The Guide to Internet Job Searching: 1998–1999 Edition*, (Lincolnwood, IL: NTC Publishing Group, 1998). See www.ntc-cb.com or www.rileypress.com.

The National Business Employment Weekly (New York: Dow Jones and Company, Inc., 1999). See www.nbew.com.

Martin Yate, *Knock 'Em Dead: 1999 Edition; Cover Letters That Knock 'Em Dead; and Resumes That Knock 'Em Dead*, (Holbrook, MA: Adams Media Corporation, 1999). See www.adamsmedia.com or www.knockemdead.com.

Harvard Business School Career Guide for Marketing—1999 (Cambridge, MA: President and Fellows of Harvard College, 1999). See www.hbsp.harvard.edu/hbsp/.com.

Ronald L. Krannich and Caryl Rae Krannich, *The Best Jobs for the 21st Century*, 3rd ed., (1998); *Interview for Success: A Practical Guide to Increasing Job Interviews, Offers, and Salaries*, 7th ed., (1998); *Find a Federal Job Fast*, 4th ed., (1998); *Jobs and Careers with Non Profit Organizations*, (1998); and *The Complete Guide to International Jobs and Careers*, 2nd ed. (1992), (Manassas Park, VA: Impact Publications). See www.impactpublications.com/career.

Gary J. Grappo and Adele B. Lewis, *How to Write Better Résumés*, 5th ed. (Hauppauge, NY: Barron's Educational Series, 1998). See www.barronseduc.com.

Steven Graber, ed., *Job Bank Books* (Holbrook, MA: Adams Media Corporation, 1999). See www.adamsmedia.com.

David W. Rosenthal and Michael A. Powell, *Careers in Marketing* (Englewood Cliffs, NJ: Prentice Hall, 1984).

Anne Wolfinger, *The Quick Internet Guide to Career and College Information* (Indianapolis, IN: JIST Works, Inc., 1998).

Web sites: Resources on jobs searches, résumé writing, interviewing, U.S. and international job postings, etc.

www.ajb.dni.us	www.careermosaic.com
www.careercity.com	www.monster.com
www.careerXroads.com	www.occ.com
www.careers.org	www.jobbankusa.com
www.careerpath.com	www.topjobsusa.com
www.careercentral.com	www.studentcentral.com

Selected Periodicals

Advertising Age, Crain Communications, Inc. (weekly). See www.adage.com (subscription rate: $119)

American Demographics, PRIMEDIA Intertec (monthly). See www.demographics.com (subscription rate: $69)

Barron's, Dow Jones & Co., Inc. (weekly) See www.barrons.com or www.dowjones.com (subscription rates: $145 print; $59)

Brand Week, BPI Communications, Inc. (47 issues). See www.adweek.com. (subscription rate: $140)

Business Horizons, Indiana University c/o JAI Press, Inc. (bimonthly). See www.jaipress.com. (subscription rate: $90)

Business Marketing (w/*Net Marketing*), Crain Communications, Inc. (weekly). See www.businessmarketing.com. (sub. rate: $59)

Business Week, McGraw-Hill Companies (weekly). See www.businessweek.com. (subscription rate: $54.95)

Chain Store Age, Lebhar-Friedman, Inc. (monthly). See www.chainstoreage.com. (subscription rate: $105)

eCommerce Times, eMarketer.com (daily). See www.emarketer/enews.com.

Fortune, Time, Inc. (weekly). See www.businessweek.com. (subscription rate: $119.92)

Harvard Business Review, Harvard University (bimonthly). See www.hbsp.harvard.edu/products/hbr. (subscription rate: $85)

Industrial Marketing Management, Elsevier Science Publishing (bimonthly). See www.elsevier.com. (subscription rate: $468)

Internet Marketing & Technology Report, Internet Marketing Resources (monthly). See www.intermarketing.com. (subscription rate: $337)

Journal of Advertising Research, Advertising Research Foundation (bimonthly). See www.amic.com/arf. (subscription rate: $110)

Journal of Business and Industrial Marketing, MCB University Press (bimonthly). See www.mcb.co.uk. (subscription rate: $629)

Journal of Consumer Marketing, MCB University Press (bimonthly). See www.mcb.co.uk. (subscription rate: $629)

Journal of Consumer Research, University of Chicago Press (quarterly). See www.journals.uchicago.edu/jcr. (subscription rate: nonmembers: $90; members: $45; students: $25)

Journal of Marketing, American Marketing Association (quarterly). See www.ama.org/pubs/jm. (subscription rate: nonmembers: $90; members: $45)

Journal of Marketing Education, University of Colorado (three times per year). Write to: University of Colorado, Graduate School of Business Administration, Campus Box 420, Boulder, CO 80309. (subscription rate: $33)

Journal of Marketing Research, American Marketing Association (quarterly). See www.ama.org/pubs/jmr. (subscription rate: nonmembers: $90; members: $45)

Journal of Personal Selling & Sales Management, CTC press (quarterly). See www.mkt.cba.cmich.edu/jpssm. (subscription rate: $60)

Journal of Retailing, Institute of Retailing Management, JAI Press (quarterly). See www.jaipress.com. (subscription rate: $80)

Journal of the Academy of Marketing Science, Sage Publications, Inc. (quarterly). See www.sagepub.com. (subscription rate: $73)

Marketing Education Review, CTC Press (three times per year). See www.ctcpress.com. (subscription rate: $56)

Marketing Health Services, American Marketing Association (quarterly). Formerly known as the *Journal of Health Care Marketing.* See www.ama.org/pubs/mhs. (subscription rate: nonmembers: $90; members: $45)

Marketing Management, American Marketing Association (quarterly). See www.ama.org/pubs/mr. (subscription rate: nonmembers: $70; members: $45)

Marketing News, American Marketing Association (biweekly). See www.ama.org/pubs/mn. (subscription rate: nonmembers: $75; members: $30)

Marketing Research, American Marketing Association (quarterly). See www.ama.org/pubs/mm. (subscription rate: nonmembers: $70; members: $45)

Media Week, BPI Communications, Inc. (47 issues). See www.adweek.com. (subscription rate: $140)

Sales and Marketing Management, BPI Communications, Inc. (weekly). See www.salesandmarketing.com. (subscription rate: $48)

Stores, National Retail Federation (weekly). See www.nrf.com or stores.org. (subscription rate: $49)

Wall Street Journal Interactive, Dow Jones & Company, Inc. (daily). See www.wsj.com (subscription rates: $175 print; $59 online)

Professional and Trade Associations

American Association of Advertising Agencies
405 Lexington Ave.
New York, NY 10174-1801
(212) 682-2500
www.aaaa.org

American Advertising Federation
1101 Vermont Ave. NW, Suite 500
Washington, DC 20005
(202) 898-0089
www.aaf.org

American Marketing Association
250 S. Wacker Dr., Suite 200
Chicago, IL 60606
(312) 648-0536
www.ama.org

American Society of Transportation and Logistics
216 E. Church St.
Lockhaven, PA 17745
(717) 148-8515
www.astl.org

Association for Interactive Media
1301 Connecticut Ave., NW, 5th Fl.
Washington, DC 20036
(202) 408-0008
www.interactivehq.org

Association of Online Professionals
6096 Franconia Road, Suite D
Alexandria, VA 22310
(703) 924-5800
www.aop.org

Bank Marketing Association
1120 Connecticut Ave. NW
Washington, DC 20036
(202) 663-5268
www.bma.org

Business Marketing Association
150 N. Wacker Dr., Suite 1760
Chicago, IL 60606
(800)B 664-4BMA (4262)
www.marketing.org

Direct Marketing Association
1120 Avenue of the Americas
New York, NY 10036
(212) 768-7277
www.the-dma.org

International Advertising Association
521 Fifth Ave.
New York, NY 10175
(212) 557-1133
www.jaaglobal.org

International Franchise Association
1350 New York Ave. NE, Suite 900
Washington, DC 20005
(202) 628-8000
www.franchise.org

Marketing Research Association
1344 Silas Deane Hwy., Suite 306
Rocky Hill, CT 06067
(860) 257-4008
www.mra-net.org

Marketing Science Institute
1000 Massachusetts Ave.
Cambridge, MA 02138
(617) 491-2060
www.msi.org

National Association of Purchasing Management
2055 E. Centennial Circle
P. O. Box 22160
Tempe, AZ 85285-2160
(602) 752-6276
www.napm.org

National Association of Wholesale-Distributors
1725 K St. NW
Washington, DC 20006
(202) 872-0885

National Retail Federation
325 7th St. NW, Suite 1000
Washington, DC 20004-2802
(202) 783-7971
www.nrf.com

Product Development and Management Association
    401 N. Michigan Ave.
    Chicago, IL 60611
    (312) 527-6644
    www.pdma.org
Public Relations Society of America
    33 Irving Place, 3rd Fl.
    New York, NY 10003
    (212) 995-2230
    www.prsa.org
Sales and Marketing Executives International
    Staler Office Tower, #977
    Cleveland, OH 44115
    (770) 661-8500
    www.smei.org

Society for Marketing Professional Services
    99 Canal Center Plaza, Suite 250
    Alexandria, VA 22314
    (703) 549-6117
    www.smps.org
Women in Advertising and Marketing
    4200 Wisconsin Ave. NW
    Suite 106-238
    Washington, DC 20016
    (301) 369-7400
    www.wamdc.org

ALTERNATE CASES

CASE D–1   BURTON SNOWBOARDS

THE COMPANY

At the age of 23, Jack Burton Carpenter quit a well-paid financial position to pursue his passion for snowboarding. He founded Burton Snowboards with a $20,000 inheritance in Manchester, Vermont, in 1977.

Carpenter first became interested in snowboarding when he received a Snurfer for Christmas in the late 1960s. The Snurfer was essentially two skis bound together with a rope for steering. Although the Snurfer was never a commercial success, Carpenter never forgot the product, and it became the basis for the Burton snowboard. The early years were rough. He sold fewer than 1,500 boards in his first three years in business. The big break came in 1983 when Vermont's Stratton Mountain became the first ski resort to allow snowboarding. Burton (he dropped the Carpenter to avoid confusion) sent employees out to more than 300 ski resorts to lobby to allow boarders on the hills. Burton Snowboarding has grown to be the leading snowboard maker in the world with offices in Japan, Austria, and Vermont. Estimated 1997 sales were $150 million.

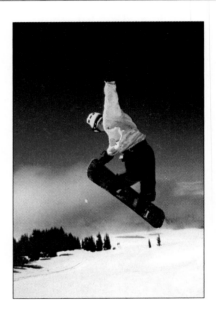

THE INDUSTRY

Snowboarding is a wintertime sport that resembles surfing on a ski hill. The modern snowboard industry began around 20 years ago. Snowboarding is currently considered one of the hottest sports around. With an annual growth rate of 30 percent, there are more than 4.2 million snowboarders in the United States, according to the Sporting Manufacturing Association. Snowboarders represent more than 25 percent of all ski passes and are the fastest growing part of the ski industry. The number of snowboarders is expected to exceed the number of skiers by 2010.

Snowboarding is achieving worldwide attention and acceptance. The International Olympic Committee and the International Ski Federation first accepted snowboarding as a medal sport in the 1998 Winter Olympics, held in Nagano, Japan.

THE COMPETITION

Estimates are that there are 300 snowboarding companies. Barriers to entry are relatively low, so new entrants can be expected. Industry giants such as Burton, Sims, and Nitro account for the bulk of the market, but Solomon and Forum are becoming very popular.

Burton is not only the pioneer but has also been the trendsetter for snowboarding. Burton has the product line with the greatest depth and breadth with racing, free riding, park, and pipe boards. Burton's line appeals to novice as well as professional boarders. Prices range from $300 to $800. In addition to boards, Burton offers helmets (through its wholly owned subsidiary, Red), bags, bindings, and boots. For information on Burton's product line, visit them at www.burton.com.

THE ISSUES

Burton uses print advertisements in such magazines as *Snowboarder* and *transworld SNOWboarding*. The ads are often tied in with reader service cards at the back of the magazine so that additional information can be requested. Burton also sponsors riders—a very important promotional tool and vital to the sport's success. These team members are often role models for young boarders. Among Burton's celebrity riders are Terje Haakonsen, Jim Rippey, Shannon Dunn, and Johan Olafsson. Even well-known celebrity boarders couldn't survive financially without such sponsorship. Burton also sponsors snowboarding events such as the 1999 U.S. Open. Other promotional items include posters and stickers.

Snowboard design is constantly changing. Currently boards are becoming longer (for better landings), are trending toward unidirectional styles (rather than the blunt nosed boards that can ride in both directions), and now have more sidecuts and narrower stances than in the past.

Burton has been very loyal to the distributors that have helped them build the business. While Burton tends to be distributed primarily in specialty shops, there may be increasing pressure to offer the boards at national chains.[1]

Questions

1   What are the environmental forces influencing the snowboarding industry?

2   What are the differences in marketing goals for Burton Snowboarding in (*a*) its early years while developing the industry and (*b*) today with growing competition?

3   Identify the elements of the marketing mix for Burton currently. What marketing mix would you recommend for Burton, given the changes occurring in the snowboarding marketplace?

CASE D–2   GIRL SCOUTS OF AMERICA

Be Prepared. The motto of the Girl Scouts of America (GSA) has been the same since Mrs. Juliette Gordon Low founded the organization in 1912 with money from an inheritance and a divorce settlement. However, Girl Scout membership has declined from an all-time high of 3.9 million in 1969 to 2.6 million girls in 1998. It is still the world's largest organization for girls. Had the principles underlying GSA become obsolete, or were there other forces operating that could explain declining membership? Furthermore, would recent changes adopted by GSA lead to success?

When Low founded the GSA, she wanted young girls to be self-reliant and independent and to uphold the highest standards of citizenship and moral character. The many activities of the GSA focused on young girls developing into wives and mothers, and merit badges were awarded for accomplishments such as dressmaking, homemaking, and being a hostess. The GSA also had focused on traditional family life and increasingly found itself following population migration to the suburbs and away from the cities. This meant that the GSA recruited many scouts from white, middle-class families.

However, the environment has changed in recent years. Divorce has fractured the traditional family, opportunities for women to work outside the home have expanded, more married women are working, fewer children are being born, and the technology affecting everyday living has become more complex. The racial and ethnic composition in the United States also has changed, with a growing number of African-Americans, Hispanics, and Asian-Americans.

In addition to fewer girls becoming scouts, the GSA observed that girls who had become Girl Scouts as youngsters did not continue as they grew older. Many girls who had progressed from Brownies (the youngest group of 6- to 8-year-olds) to Juniors (ages 9 to 11) had dropped out before attaining the rank of Cadette at age 12, and thus never achieved the highest rank of Senior (ages 14 to 17). It seemed that the scout troop organizational structure had contributed to the loss of scouts as they grew older. The troop format required frequent meetings and was believed to be too confining as teenagers became involved in a wider range of activities. Another disadvantage of the troop format was that it demanded considerable time from the adult troop leader.

To counteract the forces in the environment, the GSA has adopted different approaches for attracting and retaining young people. For example, the GSA has focused attention on recruiting young girls, particularly African-Americans and Hispanics, in cities as well as the suburbs. Emphasis has been placed on recruiting lower-income and delinquent girls as well. The GSA has reached out to pregnant teenagers with a program dealing with career opportunities. GSA activities also have changed, as evidenced by the new merit badges. Today they are awarded in categories such as "Aerospace," "Business-Wise," "Computer Fun," and "Ms. Fix-it," which recognizes skill in home repairs. An increasing emphasis on careers is also evident. The troop concept and requirement has been relaxed. Girls can now become scouts without joining a troop, provided they attend one official event per year. Once members, they are invited to participate in special-interest projects that include field trips, guest speakers, and conferences.

These efforts were detailed in a print, radio, and television public service campaign titled "Brainstorm," aimed at encouraging girls to become scouts and stay in the program even after they entered high school. The campaign included a 30-second TV message that covered sights and sounds related to ocean liners and travel, tap dancing, piano playing, airplanes, filmmaking, a space capsule taking off, and meeting young men. To learn more about the Girl Scouts, visit their Web site: www.gsusa.org.

Questions

1 Did the business definition of GSA change?
2 How did the market-product grid for the GSA change, given environmental trends?
3 What is your prognosis for the GSA, given its response to the environment?

CASE D–3 JAMBA JUICE

What were you doing in 10th grade? Waiting to get your driver's license? Kirk Perron was thinking about his future and putting together a deal that would help launch the successful Jamba Juice chain. It sounds incredible, but Kirk Perron bought the real estate for the first juice bar when he was in 10th grade. He borrowed money from a high school counselor, the librarian, and his school bus driver to put together the $12,000 down payment.

THE COMPANY

Kirk Perron opened up his first operation as The Juice Club in 1990 in San Luis Obispo, California. He hit on the idea for a convenient, delicious, healthful food store on a long weekend bike ride. An avid cyclist with a life-long interest in health and nutrition, he wanted to offer an alternative to typical fast-food fare. The idea was a hit and quickly spread. In 1995, the company changed its name from The Juice Club to Jamba Juice. Today Jamba Juice has more than 100 stores offering a wide variety of healthy drinks and snacks.

THE IDEA

Jamba Juice is all about healthy food. This is captured in "jambaisms" such as: "Your body is a temple, littering is strictly prohibited." (Jambaism # 1) and "Eternal youth does not come from a fountain. It comes from a four-speed blender." (Jambaism #6). Walk into a Jamba Juice store and customers can choose from a wide variety of Jamba Juice specialties, including 16 types of smoothies, fresh-squeezed fruit and vegetable juices, and healthy snacks. Jamba has recently introduced Souprimos—freshly prepared, healthy soups. Souprimos have the recommended "5-a-Day" servings of vegetables in each cup and are low in fat and calories. Jambolas are another new product—low-fat, low-calorie breads that are high in protein and nutrients. Jambolas are served hot and toasted and can be teamed up with a Souprimo or a smoothie for a power meal.

Smoothies are the bulk of the Jamba Juice's business. They are made with juice and fruit and often yogurt, sherbet, or ice milk. A typical smoothie gets most of its calories from carbohydrates and protein, providing a low- or no-fat, nutritious meal. Jamba smoothies and soups are designed to meet "heart-healthy" FDA requirements. Nutritional supplements called "boosts," such as "energy juice boost" with ginseng and gingko biloba and "immunity juice boost" with echinacea and antioxidants, are available at 50 cents per boost for smoothies and soups. Learn more about Jamba at www.jambajuice.com/home.html.

As you sit at the counter in a Juice Club, you can watch friendly, well-schooled Juice Club employees whip, beat, and blend your smoothie right before your eyes. Stores also feature nutrition centers called "Learn Jamba," where customers can get a complete nutritional breakdown for each product. Outlets also feature a merchandising area called "Shop Jamba," which has Jamba Juice juicers, mugs, hats, and T-shirts.

And now Jamba Juice outlets have a new look. The newly designed stores feature tropical louvered menu boards, slowly rotating fan blades, and Jamba colors and aromas that create an image of a lazy Caribbean day.

THE COMPETITION

Juice bars are one of the hottest trends. Juice bar chains, particularly in the South and West, have ambitious plans for hundreds of new locations in the coming months. Barriers to entry are fairly low. Single store outlets or small chains within a city or region are common. Jamba has had to fight to maintain its trademark in a competitive market. A San Francisco juice bar called Jamm'n Juice was forced to change its name after Jamba complained that Jamm'n Juice and its animated fruit and vegetables were too close to the Jamba trademark and logo.

THE MARKET

Juice bars have existed for decades, often in health food stores and gyms, and were associated with what was a small group of intensely health-conscious customers. That small demographic group has boomed in recent years, fueling the market for fat-free foods and fitness equipment and apparel. Industry analysts wonder what the long-run potential for juice bars actually is. For example, they doubt whether a significant number of men will substitute a healthful smoothie for a fat-laden fast-food lunch.

However, Jamba Juice is optimistic about the opportunities for expanding the market. About two thirds of Juice Club's customers are between the ages of 15 and 25—not exactly the same demographic group as the traditional health-conscious baby boomer. Age and education level are important selection criteria for opening new Jamba Juice outlets. Kirk Perron believes that the more highly educated potential customers are, the more likely they will be to stop in for a nutritious smoothie. In fact, many of the current and planned Jamba outlets are in college towns, and partnerships have been formed to open outlets in universities and airports. Jamba also has agreements with Barnes & Noble and Whole Foods Markets, two partners that share Jamba's values and commitment to healthy living.

THE ISSUES

Purists insist that the best drinks come from completely fresh products. Fresh produce can be hard to work with to provide consistent tasting drinks. Also, the price of fresh produce can change drastically throughout the year.

As a response to this problem Michael Owings developed the California Juice Oasis concept that utilizes bag-in-the-box "mother juices," such as apple, cranberry, and nonpulp orange and frozen fruit to create bases for the various mixed drinks. Bar guns dispense the mother juices in four different ounce-based measures for convenience and portion-size control.

With fairly limited menus, juice bars are considered great as an add-on rather than a stand-alone retail establishment since they are usually not strong enough to draw customer traffic on their own. Personnel are important to the success of a juice bar—described as "bartenders," they have to be able to put on a good show for the customer.[2]

Questions

1 Conduct an environmental scan for the Juice Club as it considers opening a new juice bar near your university. Identify factors that you feel have an impact on the juice bar market, and indicate whether these factors would tend to enhance opportunities or represent threats.
2 Given your environmental analysis, which environmental force do you feel is most critical for Jamba Juice, and why?
3 Examine the competitive environment for juice bars. Consider the likelihood of new entrants, barriers to entry, existing competitors, and substitutes. How would you summarize the current competitive environment?

CASE D–4   H. B. FULLER

In January 1996, H. B. Fuller was sued in U.S. District Court for allegedly causing the 1993 death of Joel Linares, a 16-year-old Guatemalan boy. The lawsuit claimed that Fuller's toxic glue product, Resistol, caused severe physical and neurological injuries to the boy, who had inhaled it, which led to his death.

THE COMPANY AND PRODUCT

H. B. Fuller is a long-time manufacturer of glues and inks, competing in many international markets. It has a tradition of social responsibility. Like only a handful of other American companies, it contributes 5 percent of its earnings to charitable causes. H. B. Fuller takes pride in its research center designed to be environmentally sensitive and energy efficient. *Fortune* magazine has named H. B. Fuller one of the best U.S. firms for which an employee can work. To learn more about H. B. Fuller, visit the company Web site at www.hbfuller.com.

Through its research H. B. Fuller developed Resistol, a glue used in shoe manufacture and repair, leather work, and carpentry. Its advantages over water-based glues include rapid setup time, better adhesion, and superior water resistance. In the early 1980s Resistol was sold in Central America in small packages affordable by firms that used the product for legitimate purposes. Many of the firms using Resistol were small businesses and could not afford to buy or store large containers of the product. Fuller's profits from selling Resistol in Central America are less than $500,000 annually. Resistol was sold in Central America by a wholly owned, but autonomous, subsidiary of H. B. Fuller. This subsidiary is one of the 500 largest firms in Latin America. This firm's management also stressed its ethical obligations.

THE "RESISTOLEROS"

In 1985, Fuller's product Resistol was publicized because of its use by Honduran street children seeking a cheap "high." Inhaling the product dulled their hunger pangs and sensitivity to the cold, but it caused addiction and irreversible brain damage. While children throughout Central and South America abuse a variety of chemical substances, the name "Resistoleros" became synonymous with Latin American street children, whether they used inhalants or not.

Central American countries are very poor, have high infant mortality rates, and have short life expectancies among their citizens. Primary exports are agricultural products such as bananas and coffee. Surplus rural workers migrate to overcrowded cities in search of work. In the cities, they find high rates of unemployment and low wages. Children work to help support their families. It is these city children that have been given the Resistoleros name.

In the 1980s H. B. Fuller's Latin American subsidiary responded to reports of abuse of Resistol by children by pointing out that Resistol was not the only product abused by street children; glue-sniffing was a social, not a corporate concern, and Resistolero should not be used as a term synonymous with drug addict. Social activists asked the subsidiary to add mustard oil to the glue. H. B. Fuller's researchers found that mustard oil is carcinogenic and causes short-term damage to the respiratory tract, eyes, and skin of any workers who come into contact with even minute quantities of this oil. It induces nausea in anyone who sniffs the glue. The oil has a shelf-life of only six months, greatly complicating distribution.

THE 1992 DECISIONS

In 1992 Fuller announced it would stop sales of Resistol in Central America "wherever it is being misused." As a result, Fuller said it was removing the product from retail sales in Central American countries such as Guatemala and Honduras. After extensive study the company also concluded the following:

1. It would fund social, educational, and drug treatment programs to try to help Central American street children.
2. It would not add mustard oil to its adhesives because adding another toxic ingredient would harm legitimate users such as shoemakers.
3. It would put labels warning against the product's misuse on large containers—unaffordable by street children—in which it shipped Resistol from its U.S. production site to Central America.
4. It would continue research to try to find a water-based, nontoxic replacement glue for toluene, the chemical that gives Resistol its glue-sniffing "high."

These decisions—particularly the first one—caused children's advocates to laud the company for its position that inhalant abuse should be attacked on a broader scale.

THE ISSUES IN 1996

The 1996 lawsuit alleged that H. B. Fuller was negligent in that it knew that its glue was dangerous when inhaled but did not issue adequate warnings of this fact. The Texas attorney who filed the suit on behalf of the boy's family said that he will try to convert this lawsuit into a class action on behalf of all children in Central America who have sniffed glue. H. B. Fuller replied that it put warning labels on the containers in which it shipped the glue to Central America, but that its subsidiary repackaged the product into smaller containers that did not have warning labels. It also observed that most of the street children who abuse the product are illiterate, so warning labels on small containers would have no effect. The lawsuit also claimed that tighter controls on distribution would have prevented Fuller's products from "falling into the hands of children such as Joel Linares."

This U.S. District Court suit is a product-liability action. Product-liability law embodies the expectations held by some segments of American society about the high level of safety they expect to be built into consumer products. However, achieving safety is not free. Furthermore, it may be impossible to produce absolutely safe products or to foresee all situations or uses of the products that might cause harm to its users or to bystanders.[3]

Questions

1 Do you see H. B. Fuller's position today as ethical but illegal, ethical and legal, unethical but legal, or unethical and illegal? Why?

2 (*a*) Who are the primary stakeholders affected by the decision about whether to continue producing and marketing Resistol, and (*b*) how is each affected positively or negatively?

3 Should H. B. Fuller be held liable for the physical effects on Central American children or their possible deaths? Explain.

4 What are the implications of your answer to question 3 (*a*) for the employees of manufacturers producing products that might be misused? (*b*) for the distributors? (*c*) for consumers?

5 What should H. B. Fuller do now about its production and marketing of Resistol to Central American customers?

CASE D–5   CALLAWAY GOLF

The popularity of golf in the 1990s has skyrocketed for a number of reasons—aging baby boomers looking for a quality way to enjoy precious leisure time, the Tiger Woods phenomenon, and probably, to some degree the increased wealth of the middle class during an extended period of unprecedented economic growth. This economic prosperity, the Bull Market Factor, might also explain the increased practice of business entertainment and conferencing on and around the golf course. Technological improvements in golf clubs, components, and equipment have made the game easier and more enjoyable to play. Also, the construction of more golf courses in the United States and worldwide has increased the opportunity for many people to play golf.

THE COMPANY

Callaway Golf Company was formed in 1982 in Carlsbad, California, when Ely Callaway, a former president of Burlington Industries, purchased a hickory-shafted golf club company. Originally named Callaway Hickory Stick USA, Inc., the company was renamed Callaway Golf, and the seeds were planted for one of the golf industry's greatest stories. Callaway Golf struggled as a small equipment company in an extremely competitive arena against such giants as Wilson, Titleist, Spalding, Ping, McGregor, Taylor Made, and others that had dominated the club market for years. Taylor Made golf clubs were fast becoming popular as they had recently introduced, with much success, the first metal wood or driver. Callaway's club sales took off in 1991 with the introduction of the first popular oversized driver, the Big Bertha.

Focusing on the use of high technology and aerospace materials, the Big Bertha driver, named after a WWI German cannon, quickly became popular with golfers of all abilities. The Big Bertha driver provided a larger sweet spot for an increased effective hitting area. This large sweet spot, through design and material technology, made the Big Bertha driver one of the most forgiving clubs manufactured to date. It became extremely popular, and Callaway experienced phenomenal sales growth shortly after its introduction. Sales at Callaway more than doubled from 1990 to 1991 from $22 million to $55 million. As word spread among golfers, sales for 1992 to 1993 more than doubled again from $55 million to $132 million.

Callaway quickly followed up its Big Bertha driver introduction with a full line of metal fairway woods that also proved to be very well designed, very forgiving, and easier to hit than long irons for many men and women golfers. These clubs were given cute and clever names such as The Deuce, Heaven Wood, and Divine Nine, which also became popular with the average golfer. Sales continued to explode at Callaway Golf. In 1993 sales increased to $255 million, and in 1994 sales hit $449 million. With the huge success of the Big Bertha oversized driver and the equally popular and cleverly marketed fairway woods, Callaway planted the seeds or ideas for other new startup companies to enter the market.

Most golfers, pros and amateurs alike, probably experiment more with new drivers, fairway woods, and putters than any other clubs. In fact many top professionals and amateurs choose to play with their old favorite irons for years and years before changing. Callaway Golf was smart to enter the club market the way it did and then follow it up with specialty clubs that golfers enjoy to tinker with more than irons. Callaway sales continued to increase, reaching $843 million in 1997, following the introduction of its most popular titanium club, the Great Big Bertha driver. Metal woods and drivers make up 64 percent of Callaway Golf's total product sales. Its entry into the market with high-quality, premium-priced metal woods and drivers allowed Callaway to expand into putter and iron sales. However, Callaway's bread and butter was market entry via premium-quality fairway woods and drivers of superior design and technology. To learn more about Callaway and its products, visit the company Web site at www.callawaygolf.com.

THE GLOBAL GOLF INDUSTRY

The golf industry has a strong worldwide appeal and, in many respects, has links across the globe. Golf is extremely popular in many countries around the world, including Scotland (golf's birth place), England, Sweden, Spain, South Africa, Australia, New Zealand, and Japan, where golf enthusiasm rises to unheard-of levels. Many countries and continents from around the world are represented both professionally and at the amateur level in local and world-wide competitions. The professional golf tours from around the world have done much to link golf as a global sport. The Ryder Cup and the Solheim Cup competitions for years have matched the European and U.S. PGA and LPGA tour players. The Walker cup and others have done the same for amateur men and women. The recently formed Presidents Cup matches the best of the PGA tour against the best inter-national players from outside of Europe. The most recent international golf competition is the newly formed World Golf Championships, which pit the best players from around the world in match play and stroke play competi-tions. The five world professional golf tours—the PGA, the European PGA, the Japan PGA, the Austrailasian PGA, and the South African PGA—are all represented in the newly formed World Golf Championships.

Golf enthusiasts around the world follow the sport through televised tournaments, golf magazines, cover-age in newspapers and sports reports, as well as through Internet Web sites. Many of the golf-related Web sites are very popular, and their prevalence on the Internet continues to grow.

Golf is truly a global sport. Courses and competition are held in many countries and on almost every conti-nent—except Antarctica. Professional and amateur play-ers from around the world compete and interact with a high degree of etiquette and sportsmanship. Professional players represent equipment manufacturers from around the world. Japanese players may use and represent American golf equipment manufacturers, while Ameri-can players may choose to endorse and represent Japan-ese equipment manufactures. The same goes for players and equipment companies from Europe and other coun-tries. Golfers, at both the professional and amateur lev-els, share ideas and experiences from the game they play. When it comes to the equipment they use, golfers for the most part choose the clubs and equipment that works for them. For any equipment manufacturer, the world is the market, and the market is the world.

CALLAWAY'S INTERNATIONAL MARKETING

For Callaway Golf, one of the largest American golf club equipment manufacturers, the world market is a very big part of its total market for clubs. About 35 percent of the company's 1997 sales came from outside the United States. Sales from Japan alone represented 10 percent of all 1997 product sales. International golf professionals, from England's Colin Montgomerie to Sweden's Annika Sorenstam, represent Callaway Golf. At the same time, Callaway claims hundreds of pros and more than 7 mil-lion amateurs worldwide as players and representatives of their clubs. For Callaway Golf, golf is truly a global sport, and the market is truly a global market.

THE GOLF EQUIPMENT MARKET

The golf equipment market is highly congested and very competitive. Many players exist, large and small, and the field is constantly changing with new startups, mergers, and acquisitions. Major players include Fortune Brands (Titleist), Adams Golf, Karsten (Ping), Taylor Made Golf, Orlimar Golf, Spalding Holdings, Mizuno, and many others.

Two of these club manufacturers in particular have re-cently followed the Callaway plan to the marketplace. Adams Golf and Orlimar Golf have successfully launched and captured a significant share of the fairway wood and specialty club market. Both companies offer unique tech-nological innovations and premium products that deliver, and both companies make claims to be the No. 1 fairway wood on one pro tour or another. Other club manufactur-ers followed Callaway's "bigger is better" philosophy. Taylor Made Golf, Titleist, Ping, and many others have designed popular oversized drivers. Many oversized pre-mium golf clubs exist today, offering technical innova-tion, forgiveness, power, distance, and accuracy that golfers look for in a driver. The club market is crowded, and Callaway's market share is under attack, but Callaway Golf still claims to be the No. 1 club manufacturer and one of the most popular golf clubs in use today.

ISSUES

In sports, it is often said that getting to the top is easier than staying there. Callaway Golf is faced with this chal-lenge. Callaway Golf became so big so fast, rising from nowhere in 1990 to becoming one of the largest golf club equipment manufacturers at the end of the decade, that in many respects, it is challenged with sustaining its phe-nomenal growth and protecting its market share. Now it seems every competitor, new and old, is after a piece of the Callaway's pie because Callaway has the largest piece to share.

For Callaway Golf, one of the largest current issues is the status of global economic prosperity. As countries from Japan to Europe experience struggling economies, golf—an expensive leisure luxury—becomes an activ-ity people partake of less or learn to enjoy with the equipment at hand. Golf equipment can last for many years. If times are tough, people can still play, but they'll probably play with the equipment they already own. Other issues for Callaway include the fast followers, Orlimar and Adams. Both companies have developed products that cut into Callaway's bread and butter—the fairway wood and specialty wood market. The Adams Tight Lies fairway woods and the Orlimar Tri-metal woods are both popular clubs with pros and amateurs. Both companies have also launched High-Tech drivers that could capture some of Callaway's driver market share. The other Big Players in the equipment business are also after Callaway's market share and may pose a greater threat to Callaway's business. These companies are large and strong enough to survive any market slump and also have the resources to buy up smaller successful companies that may provide them

with popular products and technology. Finally, Callaway's biggest problem might be coming up with new products that are as popular as the ones that took them to the top in the early 1990s.[4]

Questions

1 What are the pros and cons of a global versus a multidomestic approach to marketing golf clubs for Callaway? Which approach do you feel would have more merit and why?
2 What are some of the significant environmental factors that could have a *major* impact on the marketing of golf clubs internationally? Describe each factor and the nature of its possible effect.
3 What marketing mix recommendations would you have for Callaway as they attempt to increase international market share?

CASE D–6   THE JOHNSONS BUY A FOOD PROCESSOR

At 4:52 P.M. on Friday, January 15, 1999, Brock and Alisha Johnson bought a food processor. There was no doubt about it. Any observer would agree that the purchase took place at precisely that time. Or did it?

When questioned after the transaction, neither Brock nor Alisha could remember which of them at first noticed or suggested the idea of getting a food processor. They do recall that in the summer of 1997 they attended a dinner party given by a friend who specialized in French and Chinese cooking. The meal was delicious, and their friend Brad was very proud of the Cuisinart food processor he had used to make many of the dishes. The item was expensive, however—about $200.

The following summer, Alisha noticed a comparison study of food processors in *Better Homes and Gardens*. The performance of four different brands was compared. At about the same time, Brock noticed that *Consumer Reports* also compared a number of brands of food processors. In both instances, the Cuisinart brand came out on top.

Later that fall, new models of the Cuisinart were introduced, and the old standard model went on sale in department stores at $140. The Johnsons searched occasionally for Cuisinarts in discount houses or in wholesale showroom catalogs, even searching the Internet, hoping to find a lower price for the product. They were simply not offered there.

For Christmas 1998, the Johnsons traveled from Atlanta to the family home in Michigan. While there, the Johnsons received a gift of a Sunbeam Deluxe Mixer from a grandmother. While the mixer was beautiful, Alisha immediately thought how much more versatile a

food processor would be. One private sentence to that effect brought immediate agreement from Brock. The box was (discreetly) not opened, although many thanks were expressed. The box remained unopened the entire time the Johnsons kept the item.

Back home in Atlanta in January, Alisha again saw the $140 Cuisinart advertised by Rich's, one of the two major full-service department stores in Atlanta. Brock and Alisha visited a branch location on a Saturday afternoon and saw the item. The salesperson, however, was not knowledgeable about its features and not very helpful in explaining its attributes. The Johnsons left, disappointed.

Two days later, Alisha called the downtown location, where she talked to Ms. Evans, a seemingly knowledgeable salesperson who claimed to own and love exactly the model the Johnsons had in mind. Furthermore, Ms. Evans said that they did carry Sunbeam mixers and would make an exchange of the mixer, which had been received as a gift and for which no receipt was available.

On the following Friday morning, Brock put the mixer in his car trunk when he left for work downtown. That afternoon, Alisha and 6-month-old Brock, Jr., rode the bus downtown to meet Brock and make the transaction. After meeting downtown, they drove through heavy rainy-day traffic to Rich's to meet Ms. Evans, whom they liked as much in person as they did on the telephone. After a brief, dry-run demonstration of the use and operation of the attachments for all of the models, the Johnsons confirmed their initial decision to take the $140 basic item. They then asked about exchanging the Sunbeam mixer that they had brought with them. "No problem," said Ms. Evans.

After making a quick phone call, Ms. Evans returned with bad news. Rich's had not carried that particular model of mixer. This model mixer (i.e., I-73) was a single-color model that is usually carried at discount houses, catalog sales houses, and jewelry stores. The one carried by the better department stores, such as Rich's, was a two-tone model. Ms. Evans was sorry she could not make the exchange, but suggested that other stores such as Davison's, Richway Discount, or American Jewelers might carry the item. She even offered to allow the Johnsons to use her phone to verify the availability of the item. The Johnsons did exactly that.

Alisha dialed several of the suggested stores, looking for a retailer who carried both the Cuisinart and the Sunbeam Model I-73, but she quickly learned that they were distributed through different types of retail stores. The young man who answered the phone at American Jewelers, however, seemed friendly and helpful, and Alisha was able to obtain his agreement to take the item as a return if she could get there that afternoon.

American Jewelers was about 1/2 mile away. Brock volunteered to babysit for Brock, Jr., at Rich's while Al-isha returned the mixer. She took the downtown shoppers' bus to American Jewelers with the still unopened mixer box under her arm.

About an hour later, Alisha returned, cold and wet, with a $57 refund. Brock, having run out of ways to entertain a 6-month-old, was very happy to see her. Together they bought the Cuisinart at 4:52 P.M. and proudly took it home.[5]

Questions

1 Which of the Johnsons decided to buy a food processor? The Cuisinart?
2 When was the decision to buy made?
3 What were the important attributes in the evaluation of the Cuisinart brand?
4 Would you characterize the Johnsons' purchase decision process as routine problem solving, limited problem solving, or extended problem solving? Why?

CASE D–7 HONEYWELL, INC.: OPTOELECTRONICS DIVISION

After several years of developing fiber-optic technology for U.S. Department of Defense projects, executives in the Optoelectronics Division of Honeywell, Inc. decided to pursue commercial applications for their products and technology. The task would not be easy because fiber optics was a new technology that many firms would find unfamiliar. Fiber optics is the technology of transmitting light through long, thin, flexible fibers of glass, plastic, or other transparent materials. When it is used in a commercial application, a light source emits infrared light flashes corresponding to data. Millions of light flashes per second send streams through a transparent fiber. A light sensor at the other end of the fiber "reads" the data transmitted. It is estimated that sales of fiber-optic technology could exceed $3 billion in 1997. Almost half the dollar sales volume would come from telecommunications, about 25 percent from government or military purchases, and about 25 percent from commercial applications in computers, robotics, cable TV, and other products.

Interest in adapting fiber-optic technology and products for commercial applications had prompted Honeywell executives to carefully review buying behavior associated with the adoption of a new technology. The buying process appeared to contain at least six phases: (1) need recognition, (2) identification of available products, (3) comparison with existing technology, (4) vendor or seller evaluation, (5) the decision itself, and (6) follow-up on technology performance. Moreover, there appeared to be several people within the buying organization who would play a role in the adoption of a new technology. For example, top management (such as the president and executive vice presidents) would certainly be involved. Engineering and operations management (e.g., vice presidents of engineering and manufacturing) and design engineers (e.g., persons who develop specifications for new products) would also play a major role. Purchasing personnel would have a say in such a decision and particularly in the vendor-evaluation process. The role played by each person in the buying organization was still unclear to Honeywell. It seemed that engineering management personnel could slow the adoption of fiber optics if they did not feel it was appropriate for the products made by the company. Design engineers, who would actually apply fiber optics in product design, might be favorably or unfavorably disposed to the technology depending on whether they knew how to use it. Top management personnel would participate in any final decisions to use fiber optics and could generate interest in the technology if stimulated to do so.

This review of buying behavior led to questions about how to penetrate a company's buying organization and have fiber optics used in the company's products. Although Honeywell was a large, well-known company with annual sales exceeding $8 billion, its fiber-optic technology capability was much less familiar. Therefore the executives thought it was necessary to establish Honeywell's credibility in fiber optics. This was done, in part, through an advertising image campaign that featured Honeywell Optoelectronics as a leader in fiber optics. For more information about Honeywell and its fiber-optics products, visit the company Web site at www.honeywell.com.

Questions

1 What type of buying situation is involved in the purchase of fiber optics, and what will be important buying criteria used by companies considering using fiber optics in their products?
2 Describe the purchase decision process for adopting fiber optics, and state how members in the buying center for this technology might play a part in this process.
3 What effect will perceived risk have on a company's decision of whether to use fiber optics in its products?
4 What role does the image advertising campaign play in Honeywell Optoelectronics' efforts to market fiber optics?

CASE D–8   XOOM.COM

Xoom.com, Inc. is a leading Internet-based direct electronic commerce company that attracts members to its site by offering them a variety of free Web-based services including Web page hosting, chat rooms, message boards, e-mail, and online greeting cards. The company gets its revenue from two main streams—electronic commerce (selling products to its member database) and advertising (charging other companies to place banners and links on its often-visited site).

Xoom.com, based in San Francisco, was started in September 1996. The company had 1998 sales of $8.3 million, with a phenomenal one-year growth rate of 937.5 percent. Its Web properties reached almost one out of every three people on the Web during December 1998 (29.5 percent unduplicated Web site reach) and, according to Media Metrix, is adding new members at a rate of approximately 23,000 per day.

Xoom.com competes with Web portals such as Yahoo! and Lycos for advertising customers and firms such as GeoCities for both advertisers and members.

THE IDEA

Xoom.com offers a variety of free services to attract Web surfers to its site. To become a member, you must register and provide Xoom.com with your e-mail address and other demographic information and agree to receive product offers from the company via e-mail. This database of users is one of Xoom.com's most valuable assets. Not only does it allow Xoom.com to expose its users to targeted advertising on site, but it also allows the company to send customized retail offers and newsletters to its members on a regular basis. Xoom.com members can purchase such products as computer modems, DVD players, digital cameras, and collectibles. Because the free services that attracted members to Xoom.com are Web-based services such as Web page hosting and chat rooms, these members tend to be more receptive to buying on the Internet. Users are obviously using the Internet for more than just work. Members are fairly evenly divided between male and female (52.6 percent male versus 47.4 percent female) but more than 70 percent have at least some college. Less than 2 percent of members classified their occupation as being "factory worker or laborer," while administrative/clerical, technical, and professional profession accounted for almost 35 percent of members.

Xoom.com's Buyer's Club Partner Program is a turnkey direct marketing platform for firms with Web sites to sell products directly to Xoom.com visitors and customers. Companies that are just developing a customer database can benefit from participation in the Xoom.com Buyer's Club Partner Program as it provides an opportunity to learn not only how to sell direct but also what types of products and services are desired. Xoom.com has a number of co-branded Web sites with firms such as Phillips Publishing, *USA Today*, ZD Net, eBay, GoTo.com, and BUYDIRECT.COM, among others.

By partnering with other companies, Xoom.com can benefit consumers by targeting product offers to the particular needs of the members. Partnering companies also benefit from this access to a carefully targeted group of consumers who are most likely to be interested in their product. By creating a model that outsources the functions of physical fulfillment, inventory, and customer service, Xoom.com is moving its business closer to a "zero gravity" model of electronic commerce.

Xoom.com's Internet-based direct marketing model is also based on speed. Sending product offers to targeted consumers via e-mail not only eliminates mailing and printing costs but also allows for rapid testing. Using the Internet, Xoom.com can achieve campaign results with lower working capital and greater profitability with lower response rates.

THE ISSUES

The challenge for Xoom.com is to develop and hold a loyal group of subscribers in the face of an ever-increasing number of competitors. This will be critical for attracting and holding advertisers and partners. Some users also tire of the regular e-mail solicitations. However, Xoom.com continuously upgrades its free services to provide members with a reason to stay loyal. Xoom.com also uses very advanced modeling systems and market testing to estimate member responses to various special offers. For example, it may send out a "test mailing" of an offer at several different price points to decide on the optimal price point for an offer. Responses are also tracked by the minute to forecast sales on an ongoing basis. Because of the low cost of mailings, Xoom.com can afford to send their "test" mailing to sev-

eral hundred thousand members, which allows for accurate forecasting of final campaign results.

The fact that Xoom.com's electronic commerce model is based exclusively on the Internet and their resulting expertise in the domain has given it a decided edge as companies take advantage of the international reach of the Internet. In March 1999, Xoom.com announced the launch of Xoom Italy at www.Xoom.com.it with localized content and local partners. This is just a first step in its aggressive expansion into Europe and then the rest of the world.[6]

Questions

1 How does Xoom.com create customer value (*a*) for its advertisers and partners and (*b*) for consumers?
2 Xoom.com has two revenue streams—electronic commerce and advertising. What is the relationship between these two revenue streams? What kind of marketing environment does the company face for each of these streams?
3 What iVALS consumer profiles most likely fit the Xoom.com subscriber? Why do you think these particular consumer profiles are more likely to be Xoom.com subscribers?
4 What are the problems and issues electronic commerce companies such as Xoom.com face as they take full advantage of the global reach of the Internet?

CASE D–9   BOOKWORMS, INC.

Late one August morning, Nancy Klein, co-owner of Bookworms, Inc., sat at her desk near the back wall of a cluttered office. With some irritation, she had just concluded that her nearby calculator could help no more. "What we still need," she thought to herself, "are estimates of demand and market share . . . but at least we have two weeks to get them."

Klein's office was located in the rear of Bookworms, Inc., an 1,800-square-foot bookstore specializing in quality paperbacks. The store carries more than 10,000 titles and sold more than $520,000 worth of books in 1995. Titles were stocked in 18 categories, ranging from art, biography, and cooking to religion, sports, and travel.

Bookworms, Inc. was located in a small business district across the street from the boundary of Verdoon University (VU). VU currently enrolled about 12,000 undergraduate and graduate students majoring in the liberal arts, the sciences, and the professions. Despite national trends in enrollment, the VU admissions office predicted that the number of entering students would grow at about 1 percent per year through the 1990s. The

surrounding community, a city of about 350,000, was projected to grow at about twice that rate.

Bookworms, Inc. carried no texts, even though many of its customers were VU students. Both Klein and her partner, Susan Berman, felt that the VU bookstore had simply too firm a grip on the textbook market in terms of price, location, and reputation. Bookworms also carries no classical records, as of two months ago. Klein recalled with discomfort the $15,000 or so they had lost on the venture. "Another mistake like that and the bank will be running Bookworms," she thought. "And, despite what Susan thinks, the copy service could just be that final mistake."

The idea for a copy service came from Susan Berman. She saw the candy store next door to Bookworms (under the same roof) go out of business in July. She immediately asked the building's owner, Ed Anderson, about the future of the 800-square-foot space. Upon learning it was available, she met with Klein to discuss her idea for the copy service. She spoke excitedly about the opportunity: "It can't help but make money. I could work there part-time and the rest of the time we could hire students. We could call it 'Copycats' and even use a sign with the same kind of letters as we do in 'Bookworms.' I'm sure we could get Ed to knock the wall out between the two stores, if you think it would be a good idea. Probably we could rent most of the copying equipment, so there's not much risk."

Klein was not so sure. A conversation yesterday with Anderson disclosed his desire for a five-year lease (with an option to renew) at $1,000 per month. He promised to hold the offer open for two weeks before attempting to lease the space to anyone else. Representatives from copying-equipment firms estimated that charges would run between $200 and $2,000 per month, depending on equipment, service, and whether the equipment was bought or leased. The copy service would also have other fixed costs in terms of utility expenses, interest, insurance, and the inventory (and perhaps equipment). Klein concluded that the service would begin to make a profit at about 20,000 copies per month under the best-case assumptions, and at about 60,000 copies per month under the worst-case assumptions.

Further informal investigation identified two major competitors. One was the copy center located in the Krismann Library on the west side of the campus, a mile away. The other was a private firm, Kinko's, located on the south side of the campus, also one mile away. Both offered service while you wait, on several machines. The library's price was about cent per copy higher than Kinko's. Both offered collating, binding, color copying, and other services, all on a seven-days-a-week schedule.

Actually, investigation discovered that a third major "competitor" consisted of the VU departmental machines scattered throughout the campus. Most faculty and administrative copying was done on these machines, but students were allowed the use of some, at cost. In addition, at least 20 self-service machines could be found in the library and in nearby drugstores, grocery stores, and banks.

Moving aside a stack of books on her desk, Nancy Klein picked up the telephone and dialed her partner.

When Berman answered, Klein asked, "Susan, have you any idea how many copies a student might make in a semester? I mean, according to my figures, we would break even somewhere between 20,000 and 60,000 copies per month. I don't know if this is half the market or what."

"You know, I have no idea," Berman answered. "I suppose when I was going to school I probably made 10 copies a month—for articles, class notes, old tests, and so on."

"Same here," Klein said. "But some graduate students must have done that many each week. You know, I think we ought to do some marketing research before we go much further on this. What do you think?"

"Sure. Only it can't take much time or money. What do you have in mind, Nancy?"

"Well, we could easily interview our customers as they leave the store and ask them how many copies they've made in the past week or so. Of course, we'd have to make sure they were students."

"What about a telephone survey?" Berman asked. "That way we can have a random sample. We would still ask about the number of copies, but now we would know for sure they would be students."

"Or what about interviewing students in the union cafeteria? There's always a good-sized line there around noon, as I remember, and this might be even quicker."

"Boy, I just don't know. Why don't I come in this afternoon and we can talk about it some more?"

"Good idea," Klein responded. "Between the two of us, we should be able to come up with something."[7]

Questions

1 What sources of information should Klein and Berman use?

2 How should Klein and Berman gather primary data about their potential customers?

3 What questions should they ask?

4 How should they sample?

CASE D–10   THE HUMMER

What in the world is a Hummer? The Hummer was originally designed for the U.S. Army as a jeep. This rugged vehicle is constructed of corrosion-proof aircraft aluminum. The chassis is made of massive, hollow girders, and hundreds of rivets cover the exterior and interior surface. At 6 feet 3 inches in height, 15 feet 4 inches long, with giant front tires, and at twice the diameter of a passenger car, the Hummer can splash through water 30 inches deep. It can climb 45-degree inclines, hills, and mountains. It is virtually unstoppable. Not surprisingly, it gets a whopping 11.5 miles to the gallon.

THE COMPANY

The Hummer is produced by AM General of South Bend, Indiana. AM General and its predecessor companies have been a leader in the design and manufacture of light- and medium-duty trucks for the military for more than 50 years.

AM General has been bought, sold, and renamed numerous times over its history. AM General's history is traced to the Standard Wheel Company, a bicycle manufacturer, in Terre Haute, Indiana. In 1903, Standard Wheel made the decision to diversify into automobile manufacturing and introduced its first product, the Overland Runabout through the newly formed Overland Automotive Division. Acquisition of Overland created the Willys-Overland company in 1908, and the new company began producing the Willys-Knight series of vehicles. In 1953, the company was again purchased and renamed Willys Motors, Inc., later changed to Kaiser-Jeep Corporation following the company's acquisition of a contract to manufacture military trucks from the defunct Studebaker Corporation. American Motors purchased the company in 1970, renaming it Jeep Corporation. Two divisions were created—the Commercial Products Division and the General Products Division. The General Products Division was spun off as a wholly owned subsidiary of American Motors in 1971 under its current name, AM General Corporation. In 1983 AM General was acquired by LTV Corporation, and most recently was purchased by its current owner, the Renco Group, in 1992.

AM General's 1998 sales were down more than $75 million from the previous year to $392.8 million. Declining military demand and falling sales over the past 3 years have led AM General to consider closing plants and laying off workers.

THE PRODUCT

The Hummer's history is much shorter than that of AM General. In 1979 AM General entered competition for the development of a high-mobility multipurpose wheeled vehicle (HMMWV) to meet the demanding standards of the U.S. Army.

The Army created a list of objectives for the vehicle. For instance, the Army wanted a vehicle that could climb a 60-degree grade without bogging down as well as traverse a 40-degree side slope with stability while carrying a 2-ton payload. The Army's requirements were for a new kind of vehicle, one that would be versatile, reliable, and easy to maintain. AM General engineers were not told *how* to reach these objectives but rather what was desired in the vehicle. AM General engineers then found unique design solutions to solve the problems created by the performance objectives.

The prototype Hummer went to test in the Nevada desert in July 1980, less than 1 year after initial designs were drawn. After extensive testing, the Army awarded 3 contracts for test vehicles to General Dynamics, Tele-

dyne, and AM General. Within 10 months, AM General delivered its Hummer prototypes to the Army. After 5 months of testing, the AM General Hummer was judged the superior product, and AM General was given an initial production contract of 55,000 vehicles over a 5-year period.

Since production began in 1983, AM General has sold 110,000 Humvees, or Hummers as it was affectionately nicknamed, to the military. The Hummer replaced several vehicles in the U.S. Army's fleet, including the Jeep. More than 20,000 Hummers were used in the 1991 Gulf War alone, where they were transformed into everything from ambulances to missile launchers.

The Hummer has many unique design features. Independent suspension for all four wheels avoids ground clearance limits of most conventional four-wheel-drive vehicles. The truck's wide track and well-distributed weight keep the center of gravity low, preventing the truck from tipping over. Tire pressure can be adjusted on the go, from 15 psi in soft sand to 30 psi on asphalt, to obtain the best traction and handling on changing terrain.

THE CONSUMER MARKET

The development of the Hummer illustrates collaboration between one type of customer, the military, and AM General. The development of a new market for the Hummer—the consumer market—was the result of close interaction with selected consumers or perhaps one key consumer.

Believe it or not, Arnold Schwarzenegger is reportedly responsible for AM General's entry into the consumer market. Shortly after the Gulf War began, AM General's president, James Armour, received a call from Arnold Schwarzenegger. Armour thought his secretary was joking when she said, "Arnold is on the phone." Armour recounts the conversation this way: "This is Arnold. I want to see you." Armour told Schwarzenegger that he wouldn't sell Arnold the Hummer unless they were able to sell them to everyone. Arnold's response, "What do I have to do to get you to sell them to the public?" From this, the development of the consumer version of the Hummer emerged. For more information about Hummer, visit its Web site at <u>www.hummer.com</u>.

Arnold became the first civilian customer for the Hummer. But there have been many more. First sold in 1992, there are currently 4 different 1998 civilian models available at Hummer dealerships around the country. Prices range from $56,500 for a 2-passenger hard top to more than $72,000 for a 4-passenger wagon. Standard equipment includes auxiliary fuel tank, halogen headlights, power door locks, power steering, high-back bucket seats, and more. Options include your choice of diesel, gas, or turbo diesel engine (diesel is standard); a 12,000-pound winch; power windows; power mirrors; even a CD player. However, even the largest Hummer only has room for four passengers with narrow, airplane-style seats: two in front, two in back.

The typical Hummer household consumers make $200,000 to $300,000 per year, and are almost all men. Most buyers have two or three other cars already. Reportedly, doctors buy Hummers, but attorneys do not. Hummers sell well on the East Coast and West Coast but not in mid-America. Entrepreneurs, not corporate conformists, tend to buy the Hummer. Let's face it. This is not a vehicle to own if you want to be inconspicuous. The Hummer is not a product for everyone, even if the product is now available to you, the U.S. Army, and Arnold Schwarzenegger.

AM General has little experience in consumer marketing but has signed a number of licensing agreements for the use of the Hummer name—with Converse to market rugged footwear and with Timex to produce a "Hummer" watch.[8]

Questions

1 What types of market segments exist for the Hummer (*a*) in the consumer market and (*b*) in the business-to-business market?

2 What are the pros and cons of the market segments that you identified? Which market segments should AM General target given the falloff in demand from the government segment?

3 How would AM General's marketing mix and positioning differ for its consumer market segments and a business-to-business segment such as targeting the Hummer to logging companies?

CASE D–11   THE APPLE iMAC

TIME Digital called it the 1998 Machine of the Year—Apple's revolution in a box. It has been touted as a design and technology breakthrough. Andy Grove, chairman of Intel, has said of the iMac, "Not for the first time something Apple is doing is electrifying the entire industry."

THE PRODUCT/IDEA

"Is it a landmark work of industrial design or a bizarre curiosity that looks like a 1960s vintage TV set?" Steve Jobs, one of the original founders of Apple and interim CEO, wanted the company to develop a computer "like the Jetsons would use." British designer, Jonathon Ive, Apple's 31-year-old vice president of design, and his largely international design team were responsible for translating Jobs' vision into a computer people could relate to.

The product is the Apple iMac. The "i" in iMac stands for Internet, and the iMac is designed to be a Web cruiser. It is described as a "very nice, fast computer for a decent price." The iMac has built-in stereo speakers, a CD-ROM drive conveniently located below the screen, and a mouse that is round rather than elongated. Like the original Macintosh, the iMac combines the computer and monitor in one unit. Unlike the original Macintosh, the iMac has a curvy, translucent appearance. The iMac takes up less space and is very simple to set up. Originally the iMac was offered in Bondi blue—funky blue-green and off-white two-tone. The iMac is now available in different "flavors" including blueberry, grape, tangerine, lime, and strawberry. Perhaps most compelling is the iMac's tactile appeal. Customers want to touch the machine and feel a connection with it.

Apple has been criticized for abandoning old technology too soon. The biggest perceived drawbacks to the iMac are that it doesn't have a built-in floppy disk drive and it depends on next-generation plugs for peripherals such as printers. These shortcomings can be overcome easily but will raise the price. Other best-selling computers in 1998 included the Hewlett-Packard 6355 and Compaq's three Presario computer models. While these machines have many of the same functions, they don't deliver the speed and style of the iMac.

MARKETING OF THE IMAC

Apple launched the iMac with a $100 million marketing blitz in television and print advertising. Apple's tagline "Think Different" was used across all Apple products as well as for the iMac.

Apple's iMac computer was the number-one-selling PC through retail and mail-order channels during the 1998 holiday season. Since its introduction in mid-August 1998, it has been the number-one-selling PC, capturing 6 percent of total unit sales in addition to leading overall sales in the fourth quarter, according to Stephen Baker, senior hardware analyst at PC Data. Sales of the iMac also helped Apple boost its overall share from retail and mail-order channels from 6.7 percent to 9.6 percent in 6 months. Overall unit sales growth for first quarter of 1999 were up 49 percent over the previous year to date. All this comes on the heels of 3 years of losses at Apple.

The iMac is primarily aimed at the educational and consumer markets. Apple claims that about 30 percent of iMac sales are from "newbies," first-time computer buyers, and 12 percent are converts from Windows.[9]

Check out the latest on Apple and the iMac at www. apple.com.

Questions

1 From a consumer's standpoint, what type of innovation is the iMac? Would this be any different for consumers who already own other Apple products?
2 What are the different types of consumers that Apple is trying to target with the iMac? Discuss the implication for Apple as it markets the iMac in terms of the other marketing mix elements of channel, price, and promotion.
3 Evaluate Apple's iMac on the following five factors that are common reasons for new product failure: (*a*) size of market, (*b*) significant points of difference, (*c*) product quality, (*d*) access to consumers, and (*e*) timing.

CASE D-12   GOLDEN VALLEY MICROWAVE FOODS, INC.

"Do you know how to identify the pioneers?" asks Jim Watkins. "They're the ones face down in the mud with arrows in their backs," he answers very descriptively. Watkins should know. As one of the food industry's foremost entrepreneurs, he has been responsible for improving microwave popcorn, developing nutritious microwave breakfasts, and introducing the first brown-and-crisp microwave french fries.

THE IDEA

After working at Pillsbury from 1971 to 1978 on a research team developing microwave foods, Jim Watkins hit a roadblock. Pillsbury executives were not enthusiastic about the team's new product ideas because less than 15 percent of U.S. households had microwave ovens and they felt consumers preferred conventional ovens.

So Watkins started his own firm—Golden Valley Microwave Foods, Inc. (GVMF). Watkins believed that the convenience of microwave cooking would appeal to consumers. He also knew, however, that a small, startup company would have difficulty competing in an industry dominated by large, well-established corporations. Watkins's solution was to focus on high-quality microwave-only foods that required significant technological input. He says: "We had the conviction that by combining low-cost production and aggressive marketing skills with high-quality products developed expressly for the microwave oven, our company, could not only survive but prevail."

THE COMPANY

Golden Valley initially focused its efforts on microwave popcorn—a product that has grown from a junk food to a health food (low calorie, high fiber). After years of testing, GVMF researchers developed an innovative packaging technology for popcorn. It used a laminated paper that focused microwave energy and allowed more complete popping of the corn. This was important because consumers had expressed concern about unpopped kernels in competitive products, and it gave the Golden Valley product an important advantage over competing popcorns—or a "point of difference." In addition, the new technology allowed the use of low-power microwave ovens (about 50 percent of all microwaves) and, therefore, increased the size of the potential market.

Distribution was critical for a product such as popcorn. Unfortunately, GVMF had no other products to offer supermarkets, which preferred dealing with large manufacturers. GVMF distributed the popcorn through vending machines and discount stores and had 50 percent of the nongrocery popcorn market. Today nearly 90 percent of American homes have microwave ovens. This means interest in microwave foods has increased but so has competition from firms such as Orville Redenbacher and Pillsbury.

To continue its growth GVMF needed additional products. Golden Valley introduced microwave pancakes as its second product and began development of microwave french fries. Again Watkins was determined to address consumers' needs, and, if possible, exceed their expectations. He hired Dr. Sara Risch as director of advanced technologies to help design the product. According to Dr. Risch, the "target in developing the microwave french fry was to try to get what consumers consider the gold standard for french fries, and that is something that comes out of a deep-fat fryer—a shoe-string potato that is crisp and lightly brown." The result is a unique package that will crisp and brown each french fry individually, and that, Watkins believes, can unlock a much larger market by offering a restaurant-quality product.

In the microwaveable french fries market, Golden Valley faces two sizable competitors: J. R. Simplot, a privately-held Idaho potato processor, and the Ore-Ida division of Heinz. To have the financial resources to compete in this market, Golden Valley formed a joint venture with ConAgra, a large U.S. food company. For more information on Golden Valley and ConAgra, visit its Web site at www.gvmf.com.

THE ISSUES

Watkins knows that if Golden Valley is to build a reputation as a leader in microwave foods, it must continue to develop new products, market them effectively, and in-

crease its distribution. Because GVMF's popcorn and french fries are at different stages of their product life cycles, somewhat different marketing strategies are needed.

Finally, with sales in 30 countries, GVMF has begun to follow the penetration of microwave ovens around the world. Microwave ovens are currently found in approximately 40 percent of Japanese homes and 30 percent of home kitchens in the United Kingdom. Throughout Western Europe the increasing demand for microwave ovens makes them the single fastest-growing home appliance. Some countries, however, present special problems. The United Kingdom, for example, thinks of popcorn as a candy or child's food rather than the salty snack it is in the United States. Germans and French consumers sprinkle sugar on their popcorn, and Swedes like theirs very buttery. Many Mexicans like jalapeno-flavored popcorn.

Questions

1 What points of difference should GVMF offer its customers with (*a*) popcorn and (*b*) french fries?

2 What criteria should GVMF use to select new products?

3 Looking at GVMF's product line in the accompanying photo, (*a*) what kind of branding strategy does it use, and (*b*) what benefits and dangers does the strategy pose?

4 What functions does GVMF's packaging perform for its popcorn and french fries?

5 (*a*) At what stage of their product life cycles are GVMF's popcorn and french fries? (*b*) What marketing strategies seem appropriate for each?

6 What unique marketing issues does GVMF face as it pursues growth in international markets?

CASE D–13   MEMORIAL HOSPITAL MEDICAL EMERGENCY CLINIC

"We've been open for 11 months and have yet to break even in any one month," mulled Heather Waite as she scanned last month's revenue and expense summary for the Medical Emergency Clinic (MEC) operated by Memorial Hospital. As the administrator for MEC, Waite knows that something has to change. Even though Memorial is a nonprofit hospital, the charter for MEC stipulates that it has to be self-supporting in its second year of operation.

MEC was established to serve the health care needs of people who work in the central business district. The specific services offered by MEC included (1) preventive health care (such as physical examinations), (2) minor emergencies, (3) specialized employer services (such as preemployment examinations and workers' compensation injuries), and (4) primary health care services (for personal illnesses). A breakdown of average monthly service usage and the average charge for each service is as follows:

SERVICE	PERCENTAGE OF VISITS	AVERAGE CHARGE
Personal illness	39%	$25
Physical examinations	14	25
Workers' compensation	25	39
Employment or insurance examinations	19	47
Emergency	3	67

The weighted average charge per visit is $33.94, and the weighted average variable cost per visit is $5.67. Fixed costs per month average $17,500. The average number of visits per month is 590.

Since its opening, MEC has surveyed patients to find out how it might better serve their needs. Patient concerns fell into two categories: service hours and waiting time. To date, MEC has been open from 8 A.M. to 5 P.M., Monday through Friday. However, patients have requested extended hours, with an opening time of 7 A.M. and a closing time at 7 P.M. A second concern is waiting time, particularly during lunch hours (11 A.M. to 2 P.M.). A check of MEC records indicate that 70 percent of patient visits occur during this period, and most of these visits are for personal illnesses and examinations for various reasons. Further checking revealed that people actually left MEC because of congestion and did not return at a later date. Waite believes these concerns could be dealt with if MEC increased its personnel. Her plan is to add

another physician and support personnel to create two staffs. One staff could work from 7 A.M. to 3 P.M., and a second staff could work from 11 A.M. to 7 P.M. By using paramedical personnel and part-time medical assistants, she estimates that average monthly fixed costs will increase by only 25 percent, even with a raise in personnel salaries next year. The staff overlap at lunchtime will alleviate some of the congestion.

Still, Waite feels that something has to be done about the uneven demand for MEC's services during operating hours. She knows that personal physical examinations and employment and insurance examinations can be handled by appointment. Moreover, these services might be provided before or after normal working hours (before 8 A.M. or after 5 P.M.). Her interviews with employers and insurance companies revealed that they will schedule employment and insurance examinations during this period. Based on her interviews, she estimates that MEC could significantly modify its visit mix and number of patients in an average month. Specifically, she believes MEC will have an average of 749 patient visits per month if the hours were expanded. Almost all the additional visits will be for employment and insurance examinations. In addition, Waite received approval to increase the prices of MEC's major services. The new prices, which will become effective at the beginning of the second year of operation, and the forecast mix of patient visits are as follows:

SERVICE	PERCENTAGE OF VISITS	AVERAGE CHARGE
Personal illness	31%	$27
Physical examinations	11	37
Workers' compensation	20	41
Employment or insurance examinations	36	50
Emergency	2	70

Waite believes that the average variable cost per patient visit will be $6 next year, regardless of the mix of patient visits.

As she prepared her recommendation to the Memorial Hospital administrator, she identified at least two options to enable MEC to break even. She could simply institute the price increase, or she could increase prices, expand hours, and incur higher fixed costs. Whatever she recommends, she knows has to support her argument from both a profit and service perspective.

Questions

1 How many visits below the break-even point is MEC at the present time?

2 Can MEC break even when the price increases are put into effect, assuming fixed costs remain unchanged, the visit mix is the same, but variable costs become $6 per visit?

3 Can MEC expand its hours, thereby increasing fixed cost, and break even given a price increase, the increased variable cost per visit, and the new patient visit mix expected by Waite?

CASE D–14 HEALTH CRUISES, INC.

Health Cruises, Inc. packages cruises to Caribbean islands such as Martinique and the Bahamas. Like conventional cruises, the packages are designed to be fun. But the cruise is structured to help participants become healthier by breaking old habits, such as smoking or overeating. The Miami-based firm was conceived by Susan Isom, 30, a self-styled innovator and entrepreneur. Prior to this venture, she had spent several years in North Carolina promoting a behavior-modification clinic.

Isom determined that many people were very concerned about developing good health habits, yet they seemed unable to break away from their old habits because of the pressures of day-to-day living. She reasoned that they might have a chance for much greater success in a pleasant and socially supportive environment, where good health habits were fostered. Accordingly, she established Health Cruises, Inc., hired 10 consulting psychologists and health specialists to develop a program, and chartered a ship. DeForrest Young, a Miami management consultant, became the chairperson of Health Cruises. Seven of Isom's business associates contributed an initial capital outlay totaling more than $250,000. Of this amount, $65,000 went for the initial advertising budget, $10,000 for other administrative expenses, and $220,000 for the ship rental and crew.

Mary Porter, an overweight Denver schoolteacher, has signed up to sail on a two-week cruise to Nassau, departing December 19. She and her shipmates will be paying an average of $1,500 for the voyage. The most desirable staterooms cost $2,200.

Mary learned of the cruise by reading the travel section of her Sunday newspaper on October 16. On that date, the Pittsford and LaRue Advertising Agency placed promotional notices for the cruise in several major metropolitan newspapers. Mary was fascinated by the idea of combining therapy sessions with swimming, movies, and an elegant atmosphere.

Pittsford and LaRue account executive Carolyn Sukhan originally estimated that 300 people would sign up for the cruise after reading the October 16 ads. But as of November 14, only 200 had done so. Isom and Health Cruises, Inc. faced an important decision.

"Here's the situation as I see it," explained a disturbed Ms. Isom at the Health Cruises board meeting. "We've already paid out more than a quarter of a million to get this cruise rolling. It's going to cost us roughly $200 per passenger for the two weeks, mostly for food. Pittsford and LaRue predicted that 300 people would respond to the advertising campaign, but we've only got 200.

"I see three basic options: (1) we cancel the cruise and take our losses; (2) we run the cruise with the 200 and a few more that will trickle in over the next month; or (3) we shell out some more money on advertising and hope that we can pull in more people.

"My recommendation to this board is that we try to recruit more passengers. There are simply too many empty rooms on that ship. Each one costs us a bundle."

At this point, Carolyn Sukhan addressed the board: "I've worked out two possible advertising campaigns for the November 20 papers. The first, the limited campaign, will cost $6,000. I estimate that it will bring in some 20 passengers. The more ambitious campaign, which I personally recommend, would cost $15,000. I believe this campaign will bring in a minimum of 40 passengers.

"I realize that our first attempt was somewhat disappointing. But we're dealing here with a new concept, and a follow-up ad might work with many newspaper readers who were curious and interested when they read our first notice.

"One thing is absolutely certain," Sukhan emphasized. "We must act immediately if there's any hope of getting more people on board. The deadline for the Sunday papers is in less than 48 hours. And if our ads don't appear by this weekend, you can forget it. No one signs up in early December for a December 18 sailing date."

Isom interrupted, shaking her head. "I just don't know what to say. I've looked over Carolyn's proposals, and they're excellent. Absolutely first-rate. But our problem, to be blunt, is money. Our funds are tight, and our investors are already nervous. I get more calls each day, asking me where the 300 passengers are. It won't be easy to squeeze another $6,000 out of these people. And to ask them for $15,000—well, I just don't know how we're going to be able to justify it."[10]

Questions

1 What is the minimum number of passengers that Health Cruises must sign up by November 20 to break even with the cruises? (Show your calculations.)

2 Should Health Cruises go ahead with the cruise, since 200 passengers had signed up as of November 14?
3 Would it be worthwhile for Health Cruises to spend either $6,000 or $15,000 for advertising on November 20? If so, which figure would you recommend?
4 How realistic are Carolyn Sukhan's estimates of 20 more passengers for the $6,000 advertising campaign and 40 more passengers for the $15,000 campaign?
5 Should Health Cruises consider cutting its prices for this maiden voyage health cruise?

CASE D–15   THE EASY EMBERS™ CHARCOAL STARTER

"I know barbecuers are going to love Easy Embers™, as long as we price it right so they'll give it a try," said Julie Brighton to herself, as she pondered recent market data regarding consumer buying and behavioral trends in the barbecue industry. According to the Barbecue Industry Association, consumers spend $4.35 billion annually on all barbecue-related items. This greatly excited Brighton because Alma Products, Inc., her new business venture, intended to enter the barbecue market with its newly created charcoal starter.

This latest demand information (see Exhibit 1) was an important consideration for Brighton before making a final pricing decision for her company's first product (see illustration). With this industry and census data, Brighton had as much information as she could get before determining the manufacturer's suggested retail price and the wholesale price retailers would pay for Easy Embers™.

EASY EMBERS™ PRODUCT BENEFITS

For the moment, Alma Products planned to market a single product, the Easy Embers™ Charcoal Starter. Easy Embers™, with its brightly colored label, was intended for sale through hardware stores, home centers, and discount department stores. The charcoal starter was a metal cylinder, approximately 1 foot high and tapered toward the top, with an attached wooden handle and a heat shield. Inside, a metal grate was located 2 inches from the bottom to support charcoal. Instructions for use were quite simple. Two sheets of newspaper were crumpled and stuffed underneath the grate; then the charcoal starter was set inside the barbecue. Charcoal was poured into the top, and the newspaper lit from holes along the bottom rim of the device. Once the coals were hot, they were ready to be dumped into the barbecue. The Easy Embers™ starter held up to $4\frac{1}{2}$ pounds of charcoal bri-

quettes, and Brighton's tests showed that it was twice as fast as using lighter fluid (10 to 12 minutes to start a typical 4-pound batch of charcoal, compared with 20 to 25 minutes for lighter fluid), which was the most prevalent method of starting barbecue charcoal. The tapered design concentrated the rising heat around each briquette, allowing an even burn and a hotter fire.

Brighton designed the product after having seen some campers light charcoal using a crude device made of a 3-

EXHIBIT 1   Barbecue industry market data

UNIT SALES: BARBECUE GRILLS

YEAR	CHARCOAL	GAS	ELECTRIC	TOTAL
1993	7,504,000	3,472,000	224,000	11,200,000
1995	7,068,000	4,218,000	114,000	11,400,000
1997	6,380,000	4,988,000	232,000	11,600,000

CHARCOAL BRIQUETTE SALES

YEAR	TONS	PERCENT CHANGE FROM PREVIOUS 2-YEAR PERIOD
1993	809,000	—
1995	824,000	1.85
1997	884,000	7.28

SELECTED BARBECUE INDUSTRY DATA

	1985	1995	1997
Households owning BBQ grills	79%	83%	84%
Households owning charcoal grills	73	62	54
Households owning LP gas grills	15	54	57
Households owning natural gas grills	NA	NA	8
Households owning electric grills	NA	NA	3

CENSUS DATA

	1995	1996	1998
Number of households—United States	94,312,000	98,751,000	102,528,000
Number of households—California	10,381,000	11,101,000	—

FREQUENCY OF BARBECUE OCCASIONS AMONG HOUSEHOLDS OWNING GRILLS

	PERCENT OF HOUSEHOLDS
More than 16 times/year	20%
12–15 times/year	45
6–11 times/year	25
Less than 6 times/year	10

pound coffee can with holes punched around the bottom and coat hanger wire. She thought she could have some fun and make some money building a business around this simple but ingenious idea.

COSTS

Brighton negotiated an arrangement with a local sheet metal fabricator, Santa Fe Engineering, Inc., to manufacture the Easy Embers™ in lots of 1,000 units at a cost of $3.00 each to Alma Products, which included all packaging, labor, and materials. Santa Fe was also charging a one-time tooling cost of $10,000 to make the dies with which the metal parts would be stamped. Furthermore, because Alma did not own a warehouse facility, Santa Fe agreed to ship finished products directly to Alma's customers using shipping labels and packing lists provided by Alma. The product would be shipped in a display car-

ton of 12. Brighton estimated that freight charges to ship the products to Alma's retailers would average $6.00 per case for small orders and about $3.00 per case when 10 or more cases were shipped.

Another variable cost associated with the products included sales commissions to be paid to a manufacturer's representative agency retained a month ago. Davis & Davis Associates, whose other clients included well-known manufacturers of barbecue grills and other summer seasonal products, had agreed to a 10 percent commission on all sales made to retail stores and exclusive coverage of retail accounts in California. Brighton hired the agency, in part, because it was easily more affordable than hiring an internal salesforce. Alma would simply pay the commission to the agency, which, in turn, was responsible for providing the salary, benefit, travel, individual commission, and overhead expenses for each of its reps. Aside from being more cost effective, Davis & Davis also had well-established contacts with the retail buyers in the barbecue industry, contacts that could take years for Alma to form on its own.

Fixed costs associated with running Alma were expected to be minimal. Brighton, living off consulting income and savings from her career as a retailing executive, planned to forego any salary for the first year of business. Using Brighton's home as an office for the company would save monthly rent expense, and for now, only a part-time secretary would be needed to help handle orders. Therefore, total monthly office expenses, including the phone and the secretary's salary, were expected to be around $500.

TARGET MARKET

In its first year of business, Alma planned to target retail stores located in California. Home centers, hardware stores, and mass merchandisers sold most barbecue grills and seemed (to Brighton) to be the best retail distribution channels for her product. Brighton's knowledge of retailing and discussions with her manufacturer's representative indicated that these retail chains would require a 40 percent gross margin on their selling price on an item like Easy Embers™.

COMPETITION

In its home state of California, Alma found a few local retailers that sold a similar item, the Adamson QuickFire, for $9.95. However, this item was also new, and the manufacturer, Adamson, Inc., did not appear to have established distribution with any large retail chains. Brighton looked in the stores of large chain retailers and found the QuickFire in none of them. The only stores that carried the QuickFire seemed to be small, individually owned hardware stores. A clerk in one of the small stores told Brighton that the store bought the QuickFires from "some guy from Berkeley." Brighton was able to find no telephone listing for Adamson, Inc. in Berkeley or its surrounding area.

Broader competition included manufacturers of electric charcoal starters, which sold for about $5.95 in most stores, and companies marketing charcoal lighter fluid. Lighter fluid still dominated the market for starting barbecue charcoal. A quart can of lighter fluid sold for about $2.00 in most stores and contained enough fluid to start 8 to 12 barbecue fires.

BRIGHTON'S PRICING DECISION

Brighton knew that by Friday she needed to have suggested retail and wholesale prices determined. She was not yet sure whether a skimming or a penetration pricing strategy made more sense. She did know, however, that her decisions must include her intended prices to the consumer (even though she could not really control the retailers' pricing) as well as the prices she would charge the retailers. Brighton had no expectations of making much money her first year in business, but she did want to be certain to at least break even on a cash basis.[11]

Questions

1 Based on the data in Exhibit 1, how many charcoal starters do you estimate that the company will sell in California in its first year?

2 Does a skimming or penetration pricing strategy make more sense in this situation. Why?

3 What price should Brighton charge the retailers for Easy Embers™, and what should the suggested retail selling price be for the product?

4 How many Easy Embers™ units must be sold for Alma Products to break even on a cash basis in its first 12 months of operation?

CASE D–16   STARBUCKS COFFEE

What'll you have? Skinny latte, espresso, almond truffle mocha? Increasingly Americans are turning to Starbucks to quench a growing thirst for specialty coffee.

THE COMPANY

Starbucks Coffee has been hugely successful. Net sales have grown from $65,309,000 in 1991 to $465,213,000 in 1995. Starbucks got its start in 1971 as a gourmet coffee bean store in Seattle. In 1987, Starbucks' current chief executive, Howard Schultz, opened the first stylish Starbucks coffee bar. The focus then and now has been on high-end gourmet coffees. Customers can buy fresh roasted beans from around the world, gift packs, Starbucks coffee cups and sweets, as well as freshly brewed coffees. All coffee beans are roasted in-house to maintain quality. The company prides itself on buying top-quality beans, vacuum packs the beans 2 hours after roasting, and donates to charity any beans that go unsold 7 days after opening the bag.

Starbucks employees are recruited from college campuses and community groups and given more than 24 hours of coffee-making training and lore. Starbucks maintains designers and architects in-house to develop, maintain, and update the hip, upscale image of the stores. All of this has led to the high-quality service that has built Starbucks' brand loyalty.

Citing concern about maintaining quality, Starbucks has turned down lucrative franchising agreements. All stores are company owned. Starbucks had more than 1,900 stores in place in early 1999. The company purposely opens stores near one another, even if it involves some cannibalization, to ensure intensive distribution coverage.

Airports, hotels, and malls are all locations for Starbucks coffee bars. Another unique approach to distributing the product is developing special coffee blends for others. For example, Barnes and Noble bookstores have their own coffee bars in many locations, and these coffee bars exclusively sell the Starbucks "Barnes and Noble Coffee Blend." United Airlines is running advertising touting the fact that it now serves Starbucks coffee in every class on every flight worldwide.

Research also is a key part of Starbucks' success. A sophisticated point-of-sale systems allows the company to track store and regional buying trends. The Starbucks real estate division sifts through data on potential markets and market characteristics for at least 9 months prior to a store opening.

THE COFFEE MARKET

The coffee market wasn't always perking along. As recently as 10 years ago, the National Coffee Association was concerned about declining coffee consumption among younger adults. However, the growth of specialty coffees has not only boosted coffee consumption (nationally, 47 percent of Americans consider themselves coffee drinkers today) but has repositioned a product category that had little differentiation. Coffee was coffee, almost a generic product.

There are still concerns about the long-term trend in coffee consumption. While specialty brews have increased, Americans now drink an average of 1.87 cups a day, a decline from the early 1960s when the average per-capita consumption was more than 3 cups per day.

THE COMPETITION

Today, Starbucks faces competition from a number of national, regional, and even local coffee bars and houses. Starbucks is credited with helping to educate the public about specialty coffee, creating the opening for large and small competitors. New World Coffee and Bagels is the largest coffee franchisor in the United States with 1997 revenues of $15.9 million. Chock Full O-Nuts has developed drive-through coffee outlets called Quickava. Even fast-food outlets such as Dunkin Donuts are improving their coffee offerings.

Starbucks' CEO Schultz views supermarkets as Starbucks' main competition. Supermarkets sell about 70 percent of all coffee and are increasingly going upscale, selling whole beans to be ground in the store. Starbucks has turned down opportunities to distribute its coffee through supermarkets until recently. In 1998 Starbucks began test sales of ground and whole bean coffee in Chicago area supermarkets. Kraft Foods has entered into a licensing agreement with Starbucks to place coffee in grocery stores across the country.

THE ISSUES

A major issue for Starbucks is the price of coffee, which can fluctuate wildly. Frost in Brazil, the world's largest coffee producer, can damage coffee plants for years. New bushes can take 5 years to mature. Commodity coffee prices doubled while specialty premium coffees briefly tripled in price as recently as the mid-1990s.

With increasing domestic competition, Starbucks has expanded to Europe and Asia. Starbucks has retail

We're about to give airplane coffee a good name.

United is now serving Starbucks® coffee in every class, on every flight worldwide. An improvement that makes perfect sense, coming from the more than 50,000 employees who own United. After all, we don't just work here. We drink the coffee, too. Come fly our friendly skies.

UNITED AIRLINES

locations in Japan, Singapore, the Philippines, Taiwan, Thailand, the United Kingdom, New Zealand, and Malaysia. Starbucks opened its first store in Beijing, China, in 1999, partnering with Beijing Mei Da Coffee Co. Ltd., its distributor for wholesale operations in Beijing since 1994. Starbucks also opened its first outlet in the Middle East in Kuwait.

Frappucino, a blended coffee and milk drink served chilled or over ice, is a product developed by Starbucks in conjunction with PepsiCo. In spite of the fact that few Americans drank cold coffee prior to Frappucino's introduction as well as General Foods' market failure with a cold cappucino product called Cappio, Frappucino appears to be gaining acceptance. Pepsi's venture with Lipton Tea Company produced the number one product in the ready-made iced tea category. Starbucks' has also developed Starbucks' coffee-flavored ice cream in partnership with Dryer's Grand Ice Cream, Inc. These products have made Starbucks a more significant brand within the grocery store channel. Starbucks also sells coffee and products such as espresso machines, coffee presses, music, and books through its coffee bars and its Web site at www.starbucks.com.[12]

Questions

1 What type of distribution strategy is Starbucks employing? How does this distribution strategy fit in with Starbucks' product and positioning?

2 What is Starbucks' competitive advantage? Discuss whether you feel this is a sustainable competitive advantage.

3 Starbucks' current distribution system can be described as a corporate vertical marketing system (VMS) for its coffee bars. In addition, Starbucks uses channel partnerships for some of its ventures (such as its relationships with Barnes and Noble and with Dryer's Grand Ice Cream). Starbucks has turned down lucrative franchising agreements that would create a contractual VMS. What are the pros and cons of continuing the present distribution system versus a contractual (franchising) VMS as Starbucks continues to grow and expand? What recommendations would you make to Starbucks concerning changes in its distribution strategy given its growth objectives?

CASE D-17   DELL COMPUTER CORPORATION

THE COMPANY

Dell is the largest direct seller of computers in the world and one of the top global PC manufacturers. Dell had more than $12.3 billion in sales in 1998, a 58.9 percent annual increase in sales. Dell offers PCs, notebooks, network servers, peripherals, and software. More than 90 percent of Dell's sales are to businesses and governmental customers. Dell's success is attributed in large part to its effective use of supply chain management.

SUPPLY CHAIN MANAGEMENT AT DELL

"Supply chain management is what it's all about. It's velocity," according to Tom Meredith, chief financial officer of Dell Computer Corporation. "The customer is interested in speed when it comes to innovation, pricing, configuration, delivery, and support."

Dell has closely aligned its suppliers with its direct channel strategy, resulting in dramatic improvements in inventory management and control. Inventories are down from 45 days worth of supply for production and operations to less than 11 days worth of supplies from 5 years ago. The newest Dell manufacturing plant is running with 7 hours worth of inventory! This is important in an industry where component costs can decline 30 percent to 35 percent per year. This helps Dell take advantage of lower anticipated inventory costs in the future as well as minimizing the risk of holding obsolete parts in inventory. Meredith states that Dell "went negative in our cash conversion cycle for the last several quarters. In other words, we get paid faster than we pay."

No less significant have been Dell's efforts to work with vendors to reduce vendor cycle times—the time that elapses from Dell placing an order to receiving that order in a Dell manufacturing facility. Dell has reduced its supplier base from more than 300 suppliers to well under 100 over the last 5 years. Dell communicates with its suppliers and supply chain partners through "platinum supplier" Web pages. These pages provide each vendor with information on Dell's forecasted demand for the vendor's products, share production schedules, and allow for e-mail communication to make adjustments and changes.

The Dell web site (www.dell.com) allows customers to shop online. Different online "stores" are available for different types of customers such as education, government, home/home office, and businesses. Shoppers can select the items they want and place them in their shopping basket. Once the order has been submitted, the Web site has the capability to check delivery dates and even to monitor the status of the order with its online tracking system. Meredith states that Dell sees more than $3 million in sales per day over the Internet.

Dell works closely with its customers. Dell achieves customer intimacy with daily contact, and because of these relationships and customer input, the company is able to develop products on schedules that anticipate customer demand. Currently, Dell's more than 9,000 "elite customers" have personalized Web pages, and the top 40 corporate customers that represent about $1 billion in sales have "premier pages" for communication and information exchange.

Dell uses an architectural approach called G2 to integrate all its electronic commerce and communication systems. Dell's G2 uses browser and Internet/Intranet technology as the interface for all applications. This makes it possible for every PC in the world to interact with Dell.

Dell utilizes decision support applications for modeling and simulating materials and factory scheduling to improve supply chain efficiency. For example, Dell can look out hours or days in advance, match this up with materials flow, and, based on this information, optimize a manufacturing plan to execute in the factory.

What does this all mean for the customer? Better services and lower costs—value that gives Dell an edge in the marketplace.[13]

Questions

1 Explain how Dell's approach to supply chain management satisfies the logistical objectives of minimizing logistics costs while maximizing customer service.
2 What are the supply chain management implications for Dell's competitors that primarily utilize an indirect channel strategy? What supply chain and marketing recommendations do you suggest for Dell, given the competitive environment?
3 How does supply chain management relate to the marketing concept at Dell?

CASE D–18   NORDSTROM, INC.

Company lore says that John Nordstrom founded the department store that bears his name today using his stake from the Alaska gold rush. Whether the story is fact or fiction, the philosophy behind the company has made its success one of the real gold nuggets in U.S. retailing.

THE COMPANY

Started in Seattle in 1901 as a shoe store by Swedish immigrant John Nordstrom and a partner, Carl F. Wallin, the business prospered. In 1928, John Nordstrom sold his stake in the company to his three sons: Everett, Elmer, and Lloyd. Wallin sold his stake the following year. By 1959, Nordstrom was the largest independently owned shoe store in the United States. Nordstrom operated 27 stores in 1963. That same year Nordstrom acquired Best's Apparel, a decision that moved Nordstrom beyond shoes and launched it into women's fashions.

The third family generation took over Nordstrom management in 1970. At that point Nordstrom not only offered shoes but apparel and accessories for the entire family. Although Nordstrom went public as Nordstrom, Inc. in 1971, the Nordstrom family still retains controlling interest in the company. The fourth generation of the family now manages the company.

Nordstrom has grown from a single shoe store to more than 99 stores, including 68 full-line fashion special stores in more than 22 states with reported 1997 annual sales of more than $4.9 billion. Expansion has moved it from the West Coast and Seattle area, where Nordstrom has had a major presence, to strategic locations throughout the country. New stores planned to open in the year 2000 include locations such as the Mall of Georgia in Atlanta, downtown Chicago, Boca Raton

Towne Center in Florida, and University Mall in Orem, Utah. Nordstrom stores are generally located in major or regional malls and feature a wide selection of apparel and shoes for men, women, and children. Nordstrom stores may include a gift department and often a small restaurant. Nordstrom does not carry furniture, linens, housewares, or electronics—items often found in department stores.

THE IDEA

The hallmark of Nordstrom is service. The initial philosophy of the two founders, still guiding Nordstrom today, was to offer the *very best* service, selection, quality, and value to the customer. This commitment to exceptional customer service has been combined with an environment that encourages and supports entrepreneurial spirit among employees to react to customer needs.

Extraordinary tales are told of sales associates that went the extra mile to satisfy the customer. Reportedly a customer fell in love with a pair of Donna Karan slacks that had just gone on sale at the Nordstrom store in downtown Seattle. The salesperson, unable to track down the slacks at any of the other five Seattle area stores, secured some petty cash from her department manager, ran across the street to the Frederick and Nelson department store where she bought the slacks at full price, and returned triumphantly to Nordstrom to sell them to the customer at the Nordstrom sale price.

Another fabled story is of a loyal Nordstrom customer who died with her Nordstrom account $1,000 in arrears. Nordstrom not only settled her account but also sent flowers to the funeral.

Nordstrom salespeople make the customer feel special. You won't find Nordstrom customers running to another part of the store to find a gift box (gift boxes are provided, complete with gift card and complimentary bow, in the department in which you make your purchase). One surprised father found that the Nordstrom's men's room had a changing table with complimentary diapers when he went inside to change his young son.

It is not unusual for a customer to receive a thank-you note from his or her Nordstrom salesperson or a phone call or note concerning new merchandise of particular interest to them. Salespeople keep customer books listing customer information such as likes and dislikes, sizes, and past purchases. This allows the salesperson to notify customers when merchandise arrives that could be of interest. One salesperson had the challenge of selling different "looks" to 40 different partners within the same 120-attorney office. It simply wouldn't do for the attorneys to show up in the office with the same suit!

Nordstrom is known not only for its salespeople but also for its generous guarantee return policy and wel-coming, comfortable, and hassle-free store designs. One pleased spouse of a devoted Nordstrom customer wrote: "Of all the stores, Nordstrom was best. They gave a husband a place to rest."

THE ISSUES

In an increasingly competitive environment, Nordstrom's emphasis on building customer loyalty and retaining customers provides an advantage. While Nordstrom provides customers with what they consider an unsurpassed commitment to quality and value, increasing price competition and price-conscious consumers may be a threat.

Primary competition for Nordstrom could come from popular specialty stores such as Talbots or Ann Taylor for women's clothing; Brooks Brothers for men's clothing; Joseph Banks, Abercrombie and Fitch, and J. Crew for both men and women; and Kids Talbot and Gymboree for children. In addition, Nordstrom recognizes The Gap and Banana Republic as competitors. Because apparel specialty stores focus on more narrow product lines such as professional apparel, sportswear, or casualwear, or on type of customer, the competition can be quite diverse. In addition, traditional department stores such as Dayton-Hudson, Bloomingdale's, and Nieman Marcus are primary competitors. Department store competitors and specialty store competitors vary, depending on the particular market and geographic location, because many are regional rather than national in scope. It is worth noting that Nordstrom will experience competition not only from specialty stores for particular product lines (e.g., shoes) but also from stores offering broader lines, such as traditional department stores. Continued geographic expansion can provide Nordstrom with additional opportunities for growth but also exposes it to new competitors that may attempt to imitate Nordstrom's famous service and quality.

Nordstrom is looking to the future with investments in online catalogs (www.nordstrom.com), banking, and electronic commerce. For example, Nordstrom has made a significant investment in Streamline, a pioneer in offering direct consumer services (www.streamline.com). Streamline provides services for busy families such as groceries, prepared meals, dry cleaning, Blockbuster Video, Kodak Premium Processing, UPS package pickup, and bottle and can redemption. Streamline customers place orders online, by fax, or by phone for delivery to a patented service box—refrigerator/freezer and dry storage unit in the customer's garage and accessed by a keypad entry system. These and other investments in electronic commerce may provide access and know-how for Nordstrom products and services as the company leverages its strong brand name and reputation for advantages in the years to come.[14]

Questions

1 How would Nordstrom be classified as a retail outlet in terms of form of ownership, level of service, and merchandise line?
2 What type of retail position does Nordstrom occupy? Who do you see as its primary competitors, given this position?

3 How do you reconcile Nordstrom's growth and success with the fact that department stores as a category are in the maturity stage of the retail life cycle? What implications are there for Nordstrom, given the maturity of the category as well as the wheel of retailing concept?

CASE D–19   THE NEW VOLKSWAGEN BEETLE

"Hug it? Drive it? Hug it? Drive it?" It's new, it's old. It's nostalgia. It's cutting edge. It's the New Volkswagen Beetle, reintroduced to the North American market after a 19-year absence. Consumer reaction has been overwhelming. People stop to look at the car, honk at the driver, and give a "thumbs up." People can't help but smile when they see one. It's the renewal of an automobile love affair that has resulted in astonishing success for the New Beetle as well as for other VW products such as the Cabriolet, Jetta, Golf, and Passat. The automotive industry has taken note and attempted to take advantage of "retro" designs in other new cars such as the Ford Thunderbird in 2000.

THE PRODUCT AND MARKET

Volkswagen originally designed the Beetle in pre–World War II Germany as a people's car—*volks* (people) *wagen* (car). It provided dependable, reliable, and economical transportation. The car was first sold in the United States in 1949 with a list price of $800. The car was a commercial success around the world with more than 21 million built, more than any other car in history. However, VW all but discontinued manufacturing the car by 1986. The original Bug was last sold in the United States in 1979. In Brazil the product was discontinued in 1986, but there was such an emotional outpouring of support and cries for the return of the *Fusca* (Portuguese for "beetle") that the company reintroduced the Bug in 1993. No less than the president of Brazil called for the return of the Beetle. His name was the first on a waiting list of more than 18,000 Brazilians waiting to buy the car. Mexico was the only market where the original Beetle continued to be produced without interruption. *Vocho*, the pet name for the Bug in Mexico, is the most popular car in the country—and the most affordable at about $8,000.

"The original Volkswagen Beetle was the biggest-selling and best-loved car in American history," according to *Adweek*. Why then did Volkswagen discontinue the product? Why not reintroduce the original product to the North American market? Why redesign a New Bee-

tle? There are a number of theories. The vintage Beetle probably would not meet government-mandated safety standards for new automobiles in the United States. In addition, VW seemingly attempted to reposition the company and its newer products as more upscale than the unpretentious Beetle. The New Beetle has a water-cooled engine in the front of the car, more horsepower, dual front- and side-impact airbags, and new features that even include a bud vase within the familiar Beetle silhouette.

Research conducted by Volkswagen's advertising agency, Arnold Communications, showed that the car appealed to a broad audience. Instead of targeting a market segment based on demographics such as age and income, Arnold targeted a psychographic profile. Customers for the New Beetle were confident, unique, and not afraid of being the center of attention.

THE PROMOTIONAL LAUNCH

The New Beetle promotional campaign was designed around very simple silhouettes of the car against stark backgrounds with short, witty tag lines. Some examples include

> "If you were really good in a past life (photo of the original Beetle), you can come back as something better" (photo of the New Beetle).
>
> "If you sold your soul in the '80s, here's your chance to buy it back."
>
> "The engine's in the front, but its heart's in the same place."
>
> "Less flower, more power."
>
> "A work of art with side-impact airbags, and a bud vase."

Print advertising; television advertising on such shows as "X-Files," "The Practice," and "Ally McBeal"; and point-of-purchase brochures all conveyed the same designs and appeal. Volkswagen's Web page carries information about the New Beetle as well as other Volkswagen products at www.vw.com. The "Drivers wanted" tag line used across all VW products is also included in Beetle advertising. Publicity came from stories in the media written about the car, about the advertising awards won by Arnold Communications for its work on the campaign, as well as from unanticipated sources. Matt Drudge, Internet gossip hound, reported that Chelsea Clinton had a new black Beetle. The White House has denied that there is a "First Beetle." Although VW doesn't seem to need the publicity, it is hardly stopping the rumors.

The results of the promotional campaign were impressive. There was up to 3-month-long waiting lists for the New Beetle. Buyers were paying full price for the car, and then some. In Southern California, the region's 34 dealers pre-sold about 400 cars.[15]

Questions

1 What are the primary promotional objectives for the launch of the New Beetle? How do you expect these objectives to change after the New Beetle has been on the market for 5 years?

2 How did Volkswagen use integrated marketing communications to launch the New Beetle? What are the strengths and weaknesses of each element of the promotional mix, and how do they correspond to Volkswagen's promotional objectives for the New Beetle?

3 Volkswagen's launch of the New Beetle program heavily emphasized a pull promotional strategy versus a push promotional strategy. Why? Is this emphasis likely to change over time?

CASE D–20 TIMEX: CHANGING AN IMAGE

"Takes a licking and keeps on ticking." For years this is the image that has been associated with Timex watches—dependable, reliable, almost indestructible. Timex's advertising was closely associated with the Timex image. The advertising campaign featured different attempts to destroy Timex watches that failed to stop the Timex from ticking. One memorable ad showed a Timex watch strapped to the propeller of a motor boat before being driven across the lake. The dripping watch was proudly displayed as the second hand swept past the face of the watch.

THE COMPANY

Timex has been the industry leader since 1960. In fact, Timex's share of the of the U.S. watch market was 50 percent by the late 1960s and as much as 20 percent worldwide. However, Timex missed several important environmental trends that changed the industry. For one thing, Timex stuck to analog technology, losing money and market share to competitors that adopted digital technology in the 1970s. By the time Timex caught on to the importance of the electronic watch, competitors had already developed and marketed far-superior products. Timex employees dubbed the first Timex electronic watches "quarter pounders" because of their clumsy, clunky appearance. In 1982, a Swiss company approached Timex and asked it to do the worldwide marketing for a new product. Timex turned down the offer, believing the garish plastic watches would be a flop. It was a major blunder for Timex. The Swatches that Timex turned down became a fashion success around the globe. By 1983, U.S. market share for Timex had fallen to about 17 percent, with operating losses approaching $100 million.

THE MARKET

Times changed and so did consumer needs and wants for watches. Timex's biggest mistake was failing to keep up with the watch's evolution from a functional object to a fashion accessory. Coordinating watches with clothing, changing watch bands for different occasions, and wearing designer watches that convey status and prestige are increasingly important to consumers. According to the Jewelers of America, the average consumer today owns 5 watches compared with 1.5 about 30 years ago. Timex was left behind as the rest of the industry moved from watches as a functional tool to watches as fashion statements.

THE PRODUCT

Timex appears to have learned from its mistakes. Fashion consultants now visit twice a year from New York and Paris to provide insight to Timex on trends and interests that can translate into new watch styles. Timex executives travel to retailers and other trade shows to spot fashion trends. Timex took advantage of consumer interest in sport watches to develop the Indiglo watch. Indiglo patented technology uses energy from the watch battery to excite electrons in the watch face. Unlike other watches that require exposure to the sun or lamp, the Timex Indiglo does not need to be "charged" to emit light.

Timex was also very successful advertising the Indiglo watches when the technology was introduced in 1992. Its introductory commercial effectively conveyed the simple message about the glowing watch face while hinting at the "takes a licking and keeps on ticking" theme. In the background, Sinatra sings "strangers in the night . . ." as a smitten firefly hovers over the glowing watch dial. Smack! A huge hand suddenly swats at the infatuated firefly but misses, hitting the watch. *Time* magazine called this campaign "the best television campaign of 1992." The 1992 Gallup Watch Brand Survey found that 98 percent of consumers knew the Timex brand, followed by Seiko (87 percent).

Recognizing that simply introducing a unique product with a patented technology is insufficient to gain market share, Timex boosted its ad budget significantly in the mid-1990s. Timex also faced increasing competition from major competitors. Hearing that Seiko, Armitron, and Citizen planned to add watches to their lines with a lighting technology similar to Indiglo, Timex initially responded with advertising blitzes, especially at the holiday season. Additionally, Timex has made a major change in its advertising strategy. Watch companies traditionally focused their advertising campaigns in the spring and fall. In what industry executives call a first, Timex Corporation began advertising continuously throughout the year. Given its success, it is not surprising that Timex put almost its entire advertising budget into campaigns for Indiglo in the mid-1990s. Timex was fortunate enough to get some impressive testimonials from customers that rolled in along with sales. These stories provided some fascinating material for potential ad campaigns. Consider the following:

- A man led a group of people down 34 unlit flights of stairs in the bombed World Trade Center in New York City by the light of an Indiglo.
- A Los Angeles couple lit their way to safety after an earthquake with an Indiglo watch.
- Four people clung to a capsized fishing boat overnight, comforted by the reassuring blue beam of a Timex Indiglo.

The Indiglo technology is "making ho-hum Timex kind of hip." In fact, earlier attempts to upscale the product line and develop more fashionable products were hampered by perceptions that the products have "got a $12.95 name on them." In fact, Timex was named the top fashion brand by the Fairchild 100—the fashion industry's version of the *Fortune* 100. Timex was named the number one brand in jewelry and watches category, surpassing Swatch, a distant second.

Currently more than 65 percent of Timex watches are equipped with Indiglo technology, part of a product line that includes 1,500 styles, up from 300 in 1970. Indiglo technology has been improved and refined, making it available on both analog and digital watches. All Day Indiglo technology, using holographic film, now makes it easier to read your Timex in low light conditions when the night light is not activated.

THE COMPETITION

Competitors are taking two positions with respect to the popularity of the Timex Indiglo. Some are attempting to imitate the technology. For example, Seiko's LumiBrite watch has dials coated with a nonradioactive compound that absorbs light during the day and re-emits it for up to 5 hours in the dark. Others suggest that the light-up dial is a novelty that will not appeal to the masses. Bulova's marketing vice president, Philip Shaw, does not feel that night-lighting technology will become a watch standard, unlike water resistance. Shaw states, "People buy our watches for style."

THE ISSUES TODAY

Industry observers expect the next big technological trend in watches will be two-way voice communication timepieces—Dick Tracy style. Prototypes have been too large and do not easily fit on the wrist. However, early test models of the Indiglo were too large as well. The next best thing right now may be Beepwear, a Timex partnership with Motorola to combine pager and watch technology.

Timex also scored a critical hit with its high-tech Data-Link watch. The Data-Link watches allowed users to download a variety of information from their personal computers, such as phone numbers, appointments, birthdays, etc., to their Timex watches simply by pointing the face of their watches to a flashing PC screen. These products are targeted toward business executives, professionals, managers, salespeople, and students.

Timex has also launched new products such as the Humvee watch line based on a licensing agreement between Timex and AM General, the manufacturer of the Humvee and Hummer. Timex has also been very successful with its Disney licensing agreement. The Pooh and Pooh Adult watches are among its most popular, including models that have a three-dimensional effect making it appear that a swarm of bees or leaves rotate around the dial and one model that plays the "Winnie the Pooh" theme song with the touch of a button. The Timex Pulse Timing Watch for medical personnel was developed based on customer requests. The Timex Ironman Triathalon, the best selling watch for 11 years running, has been given a total make-over. Timex also has finger watches and 12 unique watch styles inspired by ancient civilizations. To learn more about the latest from Timex, visit it at www.timex.com.[16]

Questions

1   How did Timex change its image through advertising? What role did new product development play in this image change?

2   What advertising objectives should Timex have for the Indiglo today? How do objectives for the Indiglo affect advertising objectives for other Timex products?

3   Discuss what sort of promotional message should be emphasized in Timex ads. (Emphasize the technology, the styling, and competitive advantages.)

4   What type of advertisements, media, and scheduling would you recommend for Timex?

CASE D–21   FIELD FURNITURE ENTERPRISES

Edward Meadows, president of Field Furniture Enterprises, met with representatives of Kelly, Astor, & Peters Advertising (KAP) and Andrew Reed, Field's vice president of marketing and sales, to discuss the company's advertising program for 1999. The KAP representatives recommended that Field Furniture increase its advertising in shelter magazines (such as *Good Housekeeping* and *Better Homes and Gardens*, which feature home improvement ideas and new ideas in home decorating) by $250,000 and maintain the expenditures for other promotional efforts at a constant level during 1999. The rationale given for the increase in advertising was that Field Furniture had low name recognition among prospective buyers of furniture, and it intended to introduce new styles of living and dining room furniture. Reed, however, had a different opinion as to how Field Furniture should spend the $250,000. He thought it was necessary to (1) hire additional salespeople to call on the 30 new retail stores to be added by the company in 1999, (2) increase the funds devoted to cooperative advertising, and (3) improve the selling aids given to retail stores and salespeople.

THE COMPANY

Field Furniture is a medium-sized manufacturer of medium- to high-priced living and dining room furniture. Sales in 1998 were $50 million. The company sells its furniture through 1,000 furniture specialty stores nationwide, but not all stores carry the company's entire line. This fact bothered Meadows because, in his words, "If they ain't got it, they can't sell it!" The company employs 10 full-time salespeople, who receive a $40,000 base salary annually and a small commission on sales. A company salesforce is atypical in the furniture industry because most furniture manufacturers use selling agents or manufacturer's representatives who carry a wide assortment of noncompeting furniture lines and receive a commission on sales. "Having our own sales group is a

policy my father established 30 years ago," noted Meadows, "and we've been quite successful having people who are committed to our company. Our people don't just take furniture orders. They are expected to motivate retail salespeople to sell our line, assist in setting up displays in stores, coordinate cooperative advertising plans, and give advice on a variety of matters to our retailers and their salespeople."

In 1998, Field spent $2.45 million for total promotional expenditures, excluding the salary of the vice president of marketing and sales. Promotional expenditures were categorized into four groups: (1) sales expense and administration, (2) cooperative advertising programs with retailers, (3) trade promotions, and (4) consumer advertising. Cooperative advertising allowances are usually spent on newspaper advertising in a retailer's city and are matched by the retailer's funds on a dollar-for-dollar basis. Trade promotion is directed toward retailers and takes the form of catalogs, trade magazine advertisements, booklets for consumers, and point-of-purchase materials such as displays for use in retail stores. Also included in this category is the expense of trade shows. Field Furniture is represented at two trade shows a year. Consumer advertising is directed to potential consumers through shelter magazines. The typical format used in consumer advertising is to highlight new furniture and different living and dining room arrangements. Dollar allocation for each program in 1998 was as follows:

PROMOTIONAL PROGRAM	EXPEDITURE
Sales expense and administration	$ 612,500
Cooperative advertising	1,102,500
Trade advertising	306,250
Consumer advertising	428,750
Total	$2,450,000

THE INDUSTRY

The household wooden furniture industry is composed of more than 5,000 firms. Industry sales at manufacturers' prices were $10 billion. California, North Carolina, Virginia, New York, Tennessee, Pennsylvania, Illinois, and Indiana are the major U.S. furniture-producing areas. Although Ethan Allen, Bassett, Henredon, and Kroehler are the major furniture manufacturers, no one firm captured more than 3 percent of the total household wooden furniture market.

The buying and selling of furniture to retail outlets centers around manufacturers' expositions at selected times and places around the country. At these marts, as they are called in the furniture industry, retail buyers view manufacturers' lines and often make buying commitments for their stores. However, Field's experience has shown that sales efforts in the retail store by company representatives account for as much as half the company's sales in a given year. The major manufacturer expositions are held in High Point, North Carolina, in October and April. Regional expositions are also scheduled in June through August in locations such as Dallas, Los Angeles, New York, and Boston.

Company research on consumer furniture-buying behavior indicated that people visit several stores when shopping for furniture, and the final decision is made jointly by a husband and wife in about 90 percent of furniture purchases. Other noteworthy findings are as follows:

- Eighty-four percent of buyers believe "the higher the price, the higher the quality" when buying home furnishings.
- Seventy-two percent of buyers browse or window shop in furniture stores even if they don't need furniture.
- Eighty-five percent read furniture ads before they actually need furniture.
- Ninety-nine percent agreed with the statement, "When shopping for furniture and home furnish-

ings, I like the salesperson to show me what alternatives are available, answer my questions, and let me alone so I can think about it and maybe browse around."
- Ninety-five percent get redecorating ideas from shelter magazines.
- Forty-one percent have written off for a manufacturer's booklet.
- Sixty-three percent feel they need decorating advice for "putting it all together."

BUDGETARY ISSUES

After the KAP Advertising representatives made their presentation, Reed again emphasized that the incremental $250,000 should not be spent for consumer advertising. He noted that Field Furniture had set as an objective that each salesperson would make 6 calls per year at each store and spend at least 4 hours at each store on every call. "Given that our salespeople work a 40-hour week, 48 weeks per year, and devote only 80 percent of their time to selling due to travel time between stores, we already aren't doing the sales job," Reed added. Meadows agreed but reminded Reed that the $250,000 increment in the promotional budget was a maximum the company could spend, given other cost increases.

Questions

1 How might you describe furniture buying using the purchase decision process described in Chapter 6?
2 How might each of the elements of the promotional program influence each stage in the purchase decision process?
3 What should Field's promotional objectives be?
4 How many salespeople does Field need to adequately service its accounts?
5 Should Field Furniture emphasize a push or pull promotional strategy? Why?

CASE D-22   AT&T'S a2b music

Today many Web sites—not just the hills—are alive with the sound of music. These Web sites are at the leading edge of "digital distribution," such as downloading music directly from the Internet to the computer in a college student's dorm room. That this is revolutionizing music distribution is clear. What isn't at all clear is where all this will end!

THE COMPANY

In 1995 Larry Miller joined the management consulting practice of AT&T Solutions, focusing on clients in the media, entertainment, and communications industries. Working on a project with Bell Labs and the U.S. Federal Communications Commission to test new standards of digital broadcasting, Miller and his colleagues held the pieces of a technological jigsaw puzzle to make digital distribution of music by the Internet possible.

Miller and AT&T Solution then undertook a consulting project with all the major record companies to study the feasibility of such music distribution. Miller got a call at home from a group of executives from different labels, acting together. What they said, Miller relates, was "Larry, we really like the idea of what you're doing, but what we *don't* want is a consulting study, and what we *do* want is a business with AT&T." In meetings over the next 3 months with representatives from the labels and several units of AT&T, a strategy gradually emerged: AT&T would continue to study business opportunities in digital music delivery through the Internet, with the record labels interested in becoming customers. Miller helped launch AT&T's a2b music (www.a2bmusic.com) in November 1997 and serves today as its chief operating officer.

THE PRODUCT AND TECHNOLOGY

The first-time end-user must download the a2b music player program from the Web site, then close and re-open the browser application before reentering the site. The end-user may then download from the player on the site a 30-second excerpt of a song (approximately 3 minutes to download with a standard 28.8-baud modem) or the entire song (anywhere from 10 to 30 minutes to download), receiving the music in CD-quality sound fidelity.

a2b music employs a proprietary version of the MPEG-AAC audio compression technology. This compresses the memory taken up by 1 minute of audio from 10 kilobytes to less than 1 kilobyte, which, in turn, allows more audio files to be downloaded more quickly without adversely affecting sound quality. Improvements in broadband and compression technology are currently proceeding at such a rate that digital distribution of entire albums is likely to be possible by 2002.

The PolicyMaker software of a2b music is designed to safeguard soundfiles from unauthorized duplication. The software package's three components are (1) the content, or musical selection/soundfile (the intellectual property of the artists and their record companies); (2) the "digital key," which opens the content according to the license from the record company; and (3) the license itself, which sets the terms and boundaries of the digital key in tracking the extent to which the limited number of downloads has been reached—thereby protecting the revenue stream that should rightfully accrue to the artist and record company. The digital key also automatically collects marketing research information about users with the aim of building loyalty to the site.

THE STRATEGY: SEARCHING FOR A WIN-WIN-WIN RESULT!

In this complex world, a2b music promises to take the digital revolution a day at a time and make a lot of friends in the process. "We can talk all we want about the future and bandwidth and what's going to happen with digital distribution," says the company's chief technical officer, Howard Singer, "but right now the industry is about selling CDs. And right now our platform and approach is to serve that industry as it exists today." The company is currently using its compression technology to help both online and traditional "brick and mortar" retail outlets sell CDs by offering CD-quality, downloadable promotional singles.

The November 1997 launch of a2b music's Web site illustrates how the company wants a win-win-win strategy for the recording artist, the recording label company, and the retail music stores. a2b music partnered with the BMG record studio to offer a free—otherwise unreleased—live version of the Verve Pipe's "Reverend Girl." Users could download the free a2b music player, along with a 96K (15:1 compression) or 128K (11:1 compression) copy of the song. The visitor was registered for new download music and e-mailed a coupon entitling the bearer to buy "Villains"—the new Verve Pipe album—for a special price of $12.99 online at Music Boulevard or "on foot" at any Trans World Entertainment record store (Coconut's, Record Town, F.Y.E., Waxie Maxies, etc.). The "Reverend Girl" promotion was unique by being the first to integrate online and offline channels for a single CD sales promotion.

This a2b music launch was a far cry from the traditional "this-is-war" relationship online retailers and physical retailers have had in the past. Capitol Records and Liquid Audio, another Internet music distributor, discovered this lesson the hard way. In September 1997 they announced that a direct download of the first single—"Electric Barbarella"—from Duran Duran's latest full-length release would be available on the Internet before it was shipped to traditional retail outlets. This so outraged these retailers that many brick-and-mortar outlets boycotted the release altogether.

Currently, a2b music is not a record company, distributor, or retailer. Rather, its business mission is to work with record companies and artists that want to offer downloadable music. The company targets two segments: (1) music-related businesses (record companies, retail outlets) and (2) the actual end-users (music fans, Internet-savvy consumers). a2b music's revenue stream derives from licensing its platform and production tools to any business that seeks to encode and encrypt music. Web site visits and end-user deployment of the a2b music player exert an additional influence on a2b music's revenues through the relationships it can develop with users through its emerging customer data base.[17]

Suggestion: Before answering the questions below, go to a2bmusic's Web site (www.a2bmusic.com) and (1) first download the a2bmusic player for your type of PC by following the installation instruction carefully, and (2) then download the music. Warning: Technology and mergers are changing this industry so quickly that the Web site and marketing information may be out of date by the time you read this.

Questions

1 (*a*) What are the major consumer segments for recorded music? (*b*) Which segments should be targeted by a2b music?

2 Considering your answers to question 1, (*a*) at which retail (offline) outlets do consumers purchase recorded music today, and (*b*) what are the advantages and disadvantages of using a2bmusic compared with the offline outlets mentioned?

3 What strategies should a2b music use to obtain further cooperation with (*a*) current record companies and (*b*) individual artists?

4 Suggest a creative 4 P's marketing program that a2b music might use to most effectively reach the segment(s) you identified in question 1*b*.

GLOSSARY

80/20 rule The principle that 80 percent of sales (and costs) are generated by 20 percent of the items or customers, and vice versa, thus suggesting priorities.

above-, at-, or below-market pricing Pricing based on what the market price is.

accelerated development The second stage of the retail life cycle, characterized by rapid increases in market share and profitability.

account management policies Policies that specify whom salespeople should contact, what kinds of selling and customer service activities should be engaged in, and how these activities should be carried out; in advertising agency, refers to policies used by an account executive in dealing with clients.

action item list An aid to implementing a market plan, consisting of three columns: (1) the task, (2) the name of the person responsible for completing the task, and (3) the date by which the task is to be finished.

adaptive selling A need-satisfaction sales presentation involving adjusting the presentation to fit the selling situation.

advertising Any paid form of nonpersonal communication about an organization, good, service, or idea by an identified sponsor.

advocacy advertisements Institutional advertisements that state the position of a company on an issue.

all-you-can-afford budgeting Allocating funds to advertising only after all other budget items are covered.

anchor stores Well-known national or regional stores that are located in regional shopping centers.

approach stage In the personal selling process, the initial meeting between the salesperson and prospect where the objectives are to gain the prospect's attention, stimulate interest, and build the foundation for the sales presentation.

aseptic packaging Germfree packaging that allows products to be sealed in paper containers and stored for extended periods of time without refrigeration.

atmosphere A store's ambiance or setting.

attitudes Learned predispositions to respond to an object or class of objects in a consistent manner.

average revenue The average amount of money received for selling one unit of a product.

baby boomers The generation of children born between 1946 and 1964.

baby boomlet The generation of Americans born after 1976. Also described as Generation Y, or the Net Generation.

back translation The practice of retranslating a word or phrase into the original language by a different interpreter to catch errors.

bait-and-switch advertising An advertising practice in which a company shows a product that it has no intention of selling to lure the customer into the store and sell him a higher-priced item.

balance of trade The difference between the monetary value of a nation's exports and imports.

banner ads Strip ads in online advertising that usually contain a company or product name or some kind of promotional offer.

barriers to entry Business practices or conditions that make it difficult for a new firm to enter the market.

barter The practice of exchanging goods and services for other goods and services rather than for money.

basing-point pricing Selecting one or more geographic locations (basing point) from which the list price for products plus freight expenses are charged to buyers.

beliefs A consumer's subjective perception of how well a product or brand performs on different attributes; these are based on personal experience, advertising, and discussions with other people.

benchmarking Discovering how other organizations do something better than yours so your firm can imitate or leapfrog competition.

bidder's list A list of firms believed to be qualified to supply a given item.

blended family Two families from prior marriages merged into a single household as spouses remarry.

bots Electronic shopping agents or robots that comb Web sites to compare prices and product or service features.

brand equity The added value a given brand name provides a product.

brand extension The practice of using a current brand name to enter a completely different product class.

brand loyalty A favorable attitude toward and consistent purchase of a single brand over time.

brand manager (see product manager)

brand name Any word or device (design, shape, sound, or color) that is used to distinguish one company's products from a competitor's.

brand personality A set of human characteristics associated with a brand name.

branding Activity in which an organization uses a name, phrase, design, or symbol, or a combination of these, to identify its products and distinguish them from those of a competitor.

breadth of product line The variety of different items a store or wholesaler carries.

break-even analysis An analysis of the relationship between total revenue and total cost to determine profitability at various levels of output.

break-even chart A graphic presentation of a break-even analysis.

break-even point (BEP) Quantity at which total revenue and total cost are equal and beyond which profit occurs.

brokers Channel intermediaries that do not take title to merchandise and make their profits from commissions and fees by negotiating contracts or deals between buyers and sellers.

buildup forecast Summing the sales forecasts of each of the components to arrive at a total forecast.

bundle pricing The marketing of two or more products in a single "package" price.

business analysis Involves specifying the features of the product and the marketing strategy needed to commercialize it and making necessary financial projections.

business analysis stage Step 4 of the new-product process, which involves specifying the product features and marketing strategy and making necessary financial projections to commercialize a product.

business culture Comprises the effective rules of the game, the boundaries between competitive and unethical behavior, and the codes of conduct in business dealings.

business firm A privately owned organization that serves its customers in order to earn a profit.

business marketing The marketing of goods and services to commercial enterprises, governments, and other profit and not-for-profit organizations for use in the creation of goods and services that they then produce and market to other business customers as well as individuals and ultimate consumers.

business plan A roadmap for the entire organization for a specific future period of time, such as one year or five years.

business portfolio analysis Analysis of a firm's strategic business units (SBUs) as though they were a collection of separate investments.

business unit Element of a firm that markets a set of related products to a clearly defined group of customers.

business unit competencies Special capabilities resulting from the business unit's personnel, resources, or functional units.

business unit goal A performance target the business unit seeks to reach to achieve its mission.

business unit level Level at which business unit managers set directions for their products and markets.

business unit mission A statement specifying the markets and product lines in which a business unit will compete.

buy classes Groups of three specific buying situations organizations face: new buy, straight rebuy, and modified rebuy.

buyer turnover The frequency with which new buyers enter the market to buy a product.

buying center The group of persons within an organization who participate in the buying process and share common goals, risks, and knowledge important to that process.

buying criteria The factors buying organizations use when evaluating a potential supplier and what it wants to sell.

capacity management Managing the demand for a service so that it is available to consumers.

case allowance A trade-oriented sales promotion in which retailers receive a discount on each case ordered during a specific time period.

cash and carry wholesaler A limited-service merchant wholesaler that takes title to merchandise but sells only to buyers who call on it and pay cash for and transport their own merchandise.

category killers Specialty discount outlets that focus on one product category such as electronics or business supplies at very competitive prices.

cause-related marketing Tying the charitable contributions of a firm directly to the customer revenues produced through the promotion of one of its products.

caveat emptor A Latin term that means "let the buyer beware."

cease and desist order An action by the Federal Trade Commission (FTC) ordering a company to stop practices it considers unfair.

cells Boxes in a table or cross tabulation.

central business district The oldest retail setting; the community's downtown area.

channel captain A marketing channel member that coordinates, directs, and supports other channel members; may be a manufacturer, wholesaler, or retailer.

channel of communication The means (e.g., a salesperson, advertising media, or public relations tools) of conveying a message to a receiver.

channel partnership Agreements and procedures among channel members for ordering and physically distributing a producer's product through the channel to the ultimate consumer.

Clayton Act (1914) A law that forbids certain actions that lessen competition, like tie-in sales, exclusive dealing arrangements, and acquisitions whose effect might be to lessen competition or help create a monopoly.

closed-end question (see fixed alternative question)

closing stage The stage in the personal selling process that involves getting a purchase commitment from a prospect.

co-branding The pairing of two brand names of two manufacturers on a single product.

code of ethics A formal statement of ethical principles and rules of conduct.

cognitive dissonance The feeling of postpurchase psychological tension or anxiety a consumer often experiences.

combination compensation plan A compensation plan whereby a salesperson is paid a specified salary plus a commission based on sales or profit.

commercialization The final phase of the new-product process in which the product is positioned and launched into full-scale production and sale.

commercial online services Companies that provide electronic information and marketing services to subscribers who are charged a monthly fee.

communication The process of conveying a message to others. Six elements—a source, a message, a channel of communication, a receiver, and the processes of encoding and decoding—are required for communication to occur.

community shopping center A retail location that typically has one primary store (usually a department store branch) and 20 to 40 smaller outlets and serves a population base of about 100,000.

company forecast (see sales forecast)

comparative advertisements Advertisements that show one brand's strengths relative to those of competitors.

competition The set of alternative firms that could provide a product to satisfy a specific market's needs.

competitive advantage A unique strength relative to competitors, often based on quality, time, cost, or innovation.

competitive advertisements Advertisements that promote a specific brand's features and benefits.

competitive institutional advertisements Institutional advertisements that promote the advantages of one product class over another and are used in markets where different product classes compete for the same buyer.

competitive parity budgeting   Matching the competitors' absolute level of spending or the proportion per point of market share.

computer-assisted retailing   A retailing method whereby customers order products over computer linkups from their home after viewing items on the TV or on their computer monitor.

computer-mediated buying   The use of Internet technology to seek information, evaluate alternatives, and make purchase decisions.

concept tests   External evaluations of a product idea that consist of preliminary testing of the new product idea (rather than the actual product) with consumers.

conference selling   A form of team selling where a salesperson and other company resource people meet with buyers to discuss problems and opportunities.

consolidated metropolitan statistical area (CMSA)   The largest designation in terms of geographical area and market size, made up of several primary metropolitan statistical areas (PMSAs).

constraints   The restrictions, such as time and money, placed on potential solutions by the nature and importance of the problem.

consultative selling   A need-satisfaction sales presentation where the salesperson focuses on problem definition and serves as an expert on problem recognition.

consumer behavior   Actions of a person to purchase and use products and services, including the mental and social processes that precede and follow these actions.

Consumer Bill of Rights   The rights of consumers in the exchange process, including the right to safety, to be informed, to choose, and to be heard.

consumer ethnocentrism   The tendency to believe that it is inappropriate, indeed immoral, to purchase foreign-made products.

consumer goods   Products purchased by the ultimate consumer.

consumer-oriented sales promotion   Sales tools used to support a company's advertising and personal selling efforts directed to ultimate consumers; examples include coupons, sweepstakes, and trading stamps.

Consumer Product Safety Act (1972)   A law that established the Consumer Product Safety Commission to monitor product safety and establish uniform product safety standards.

consumer socialization   The process by which people acquire the skills, knowledge, and attitudes necessary to function as consumers.

consumerism   A movement to increase the influence, power, and rights of consumers in dealing with institutions.

contest   A sales promotion in which consumers apply their analytical or creative thinking to win a prize.

continuity programs   Sales promotions used to encourage and reward repeat purchases by acknowledging each purchase made by a consumer and offering a premium as purchases accumulate.

continuous innovations   New products that require no new learning to use.

continuous schedule   A scheduling approach in which advertising is run at a continuous schedule throughout the year; sometimes called "steady" scheduling.

contracting   A strategy used during the decline stage of the product life cycle in which a company contracts the manufacturing or marketing of a product to another firm.

contractual vertical marketing system   A channel arrangement whereby independent production and distribution firms integrate their efforts on a contractual basis to obtain greater economies and marketing impact.

control group   A group not exposed to the experimental variable in an experiment.

controlled distribution minimarkets   Test markets run in smaller test areas that electronically monitor product purchases at checkout counters for more careful testing at reduced costs.

convenience goods   Items that the consumer purchases frequently and with a minimum of shopping effort.

cookies   Computer files that a marketer can download onto the computer of an online shopper who visits the marketer's Web site.

cooperative advertising   Advertising programs in which a manufacturer pays a percentage of the retailer's local advertising expense for advertising the manufacturer's products.

corporate chain   A type of retail ownership in which a single firm owns multiple outlets.

corporate culture   A system of shared attitudes and behaviors held by the employees that distinguish an organization from others.

corporate goals   Strategic performance targets that the entire organization must reach to pursue its vision.

corporate level   Level at which top management directs overall strategy for the entire organization.

corporate philosophy   The values and "rules of conduct" for running an organization.

corporate takeover   The purchase of a firm by outsiders.

corporate vertical marketing system   A channel arrangement whereby successive stages of production and distribution are combined under a single owner.

corporate vision   A clear word picture of the organization's future, often with an inspirational theme.

corporate Web site   A Web site designed to accommodate interactive communication initiated by a company's employees, investors, suppliers, and customers.

corrective advertising   FTC action requiring a company to spend money on advertising to correct prior misleading ads.

cost focus strategy   Involves controlling expenses and, in turn, lowering prices, in a narrow range of market segments.

cost leadership strategy   Using a serious commitment to reducing expenses that, in turn, lowers the price of the items sold in a wide range of market segments.

cost of goods sold   Total value of the products sold during a specified time period.

cost per thousand (CPM)   The cost of reaching 1,000 individuals or households with an advertising message in a given medium. (M is the Roman numeral for 1,000.)

cost plus fixed-fee pricing   A pricing method where a supplier is reimbursed for all costs, regardless of what they may be, plus a fixed fee allowed as profit that is independent of the final cost of the project.

cost plus percentage-of-cost pricing   Setting the price of a product or service by adding a fixed percentage to the production or construction costs.

cost-plus pricing   The practice of summing the total unit cost of providing a product or service and adding a specific amount to the cost to arrive at a price.

countertrade Using barter rather than money in making international sales.

coupons Sales promotions that usually offer a discounted price to consumers.

cross-cultural analysis The study of similarities and differences between consumers in two or more nations or societies.

cross-functional teams A small number of people from different departments in an organization who are mutually accountable to a common set of performance goals.

cross-tabulation Method of presenting and relating data on two or more variables to display summary data and discover relationships in the data.

cue A stimulus or symbol perceived by the consumer.

cultural ethnocentricity The belief that aspects of one's culture are superior to another's.

cultural symbols Things that represent ideas and concepts.

culture The sets of values, ideas, and attitudes of a homogeneous group of people that are transmitted from one generation to the next.

cumulative quantity discounts The discount given to a buyer based on the accumulation of purchases of a product over a given time period, typically a year.

currency exchange rate The price of one country's currency expressed in terms of another country's currency.

customary pricing A method of pricing based on a product's tradition, standardized channel of distribution, or other competitive factors.

customer contact audit A flow chart of the points of interaction between a consumer and a service provider.

customer service The ability of a logistics system to satisfy users in terms of time, dependability, communications, and convenience.

customer value The unique combination of benefits received by targeted buyers that includes quality, price, convenience, on-time delivery, and both before-sale and after-sale service.

customs Norms and expectations about the way people do things in a specific country.

data The facts and figures pertinent to the problem, composed of primary and secondary data.

deal A sales promotion that offers a short-term price reduction.

deceptive pricing A practice by which prices are artificially inflated and then marked down under the guise of a sale.

decision A conscious choice from among two or more alternatives.

decision making The act of consciously choosing from alternatives.

decision-making unit (DMU) The people in a household or an organization's buying center who are involved in the decision to buy a product.

decline stage The fourth and last stage of the product life cycle when sales and profitability decline.

decoding The process of having the receiver take a set of symbols, the message, and transform them back to an abstract idea.

deletion A strategy of dropping a product from the product line, usually in the decline stage of the product life cycle.

delivered pricing A pricing method where the price the seller quotes includes all transportation costs.

demand curve The summation of points representing the maximum quantity of a product consumers will buy at different price levels.

demand factors Factors that determine the strength of consumers' willingness and ability to pay for goods and services.

demographics A description of the population according to selected characteristics such as age, sex, ethnicity, income, and occupation.

depth of product line The assortment of each item a store or wholesaler carries.

derived demand Sales of a product (typically industrial) that result from the sales of another item (often consumer).

desk jobber (see drop shipper)

development Phase of the new product process in which the idea on paper is turned into a prototype; includes manufacturing and laboratory and consumer tests.

dichotomous question A fixed alternative question that allows only a "yes" or "no" response.

differentiation focus strategy Using significant points of difference in the firm's offerings to reach one or only a few market segments.

differentiation positioning Positioning a product in a smaller market niche that is less competitive.

differentiation strategy Using innovation and significant points of difference in product offerings, higher quality, advanced technology, or superior service in a wide range of market segments.

diffusion of innovation The process by which people receive new information and accept new ideas and products.

direct channel A marketing channel where a producer and ultimate consumer interact directly with each other.

direct exporting A firm selling its domestically produced goods in a foreign country without intermediaries.

direct forecast An estimate of the value to be forecast without the use of intervening steps.

direct investment In global marketing, a domestic firm actually investing in and owning a foreign subsidiary or division.

direct marketing A promotional alternative that uses direct communication with consumers to generate a response in the form of an order, a request for further information, or a visit to a retail outlet.

direct marketing channels Allow consumers to buy products by interacting with various advertising media without a face-to-face meeting with a salesperson.

direct orders The result of direct marketing offers that contain all the information necessary for a prospective buyer to make a decision to purchase and complete the transaction.

discontinuous innovations New products that require totally new consumption patterns.

discounts Reductions from list price that a seller gives a buyer as a reward for some buyer activity favorable to the seller.

discretionary income The money that remains after taxes and necessities have been paid for.

disintermediation The practice whereby a channel member bypasses another member and sells or buys products direct.

disposable income The money a consumer has left after taxes to use for food, shelter, and clothing.

diversification A strategy of developing new products and selling them in new markets.

downsizing   The practice of reducing the content of package without changing package size and maintaining or increasing the package price.

drive   A stimulus that moves an individual to action.

drop shipper   A merchant wholesaler that owns the merchandise it sells but does not physically handle, stock, or deliver; also called a desk jobber.

dual distribution   An arrangement by which a firm reaches buyers by employing two or more different types of channels for the same basic product.

dumping   When a firm sells a product in a foreign country below its domestic price.

durable good   An item that lasts over an extended number of uses.

dynamically continuous innovations   Products that disrupt the consumer's normal routine but do not require learning totally new behaviors.

early adopters   The 13.5 percent of the population who are leaders in their social setting and act as an information source on new products for other people.

early growth   The first stage of the retail life cycle, when a new outlet emerges as a sharp departure from competitive forms.

early majority   The 34 percent of the population who are deliberate and rely on personal sources for information on new products.

Economic Espionage Act   A law that makes the theft of trade secrets a federal crime in the United States.

economic infrastructure   A country's communication, transportation, financial, and distribution systems.

economy   The income, expenditures, and resources that affect the cost of running a business and household.

efficient consumer response   (see quick response)

elastic demand   A situation where a percentage decrease in price produces a larger percentage increase in quantity demanded, thereby actually increasing sales revenue.

electronic commerce   Any activity that uses some form of electronic communication in the inventory, exchange, advertisement, distribution, and payment of goods and services.

electronic data interchange (EDI)   Proprietary computer and telecommunication technologies that exchange electronic invoices, payments, and information between businesses, such as suppliers, manufacturers, and retailers.

elements of the marketing mix   (see marketing mix)

emotional intelligence   The ability to understand one's own emotions and the emotions of people with whom one interacts on a daily basis.

encoding   The process of having the sender transform an abstract idea into a set of symbols.

environmental factors   The uncontrollable factors involving social, economic, technological, competitive, and regulatory forces.

environmental scanning   The process of acquiring information on events occurring outside the company and interpreting potential trends.

ethics   The moral principles and values that govern the actions and decisions of an individual or group.

euro-branding   The strategy of using the same brand name for the same product across all countries in the European Community.

Eurostyle   A no frills, monochrome, geometric look to product design.

evaluative criteria   Both the objective and subjective attributes of a brand important to consumers when evaluating different brands or products.

everyday low pricing   The practice of replacing promotional allowances given to retailers with lower manufacturer list prices.

evoked set   The group of brands a consumer would consider acceptable out of the set of brands in the product class of which he or she is aware.

exchange   The trade of things of value between buyer and seller so that each is better off after the trade.

exclusive dealing   An arrangement a manufacturer makes with a reseller to handle only its products and not those of competitors.

exclusive distribution   A distribution strategy whereby a producer sells its products or services in only one retail outlet in a specific geographical area.

exclusive territorial distributorship   A manufacturer grants a reseller sole rights to sell a product in a specific geographic area.

experience curve pricing   A method of pricing where price often falls following the reduction of costs associated with the firm's experience in producing or selling a product.

experiment   Obtaining data by manipulating factors under highly controlled conditions to test cause and effect.

experimental group   A group exposed to the experimental variable in an experiment.

exporting   Producing goods in one country and selling them in another country.

express warranties   Written statements of a manufacturer's liabilities for product deficiencies.

external secondary data   Published data from outside the firm or organization.

Extranet   An Internet/Web-based network that permits private business-to-business communications between a company and its suppliers, distributors, and other partners.

exurbs   The remote suburbs to which the population began to shift in the 1990s.

facilitators   Intermediaries that assist in the physical distribution channel by moving, storing, financing, or insuring products.

fad   A product whose life cycle has two stages consisting of rapid introduction and equally quick decline.

failure fees   A penalty payment made to retailers by manufacturers if a new product does not reach predetermined sales levels.

Fair Packaging and Labeling Act (1966)   A law that requires manufacturers to state on the package the ingredients, volume, and identity of the manufacturer.

family branding   (see multiproduct branding)

family life cycle   The concept that each family progresses through a number of distinct phases, each of which is associated with identifiable purchasing behaviors.

Farm Bill (1990)   Legislation that sets the standards for organic foods and products that use the term "organic."

fashion product   A product whose life-cycle curve may decline, then return through another life cycle.

feedback   The communication flow from receiver back to sender; indicates whether the message was decoded and understood as intended.

field experiment A test of marketing variables in actual store or buying settings.

field of experience A person's understanding and knowledge; to communicate effectively, a sender and a receiver must have a mutually shared field of experience.

field warehouse A specialized public warehouse that takes possession of a firm's goods and issues a receipt that can be used as collateral for a loan.

finance allowance A trade-oriented sales promotion in which retailers are paid for financing costs or financial losses associated with consumer sales promotions.

fixed alternative question A question in which the respondent merely checks an answer from predetermined choices.

fixed cost An expense of the firm that is stable and does not change with the quantity of product that is produced and sold.

flexible-price policy Offering the same product and quantities to similar customers, but at different prices.

flighting schedule A scheduling approach in which periods of advertising are scheduled between periods of no advertising to reflect seasonal demand.

FOB (free on board) Refers to the point at which the seller stops paying transportation costs.

FOB origin pricing A method of pricing where the title of goods passes to the buyer at the point of loading.

FOB with freight-allowed pricing A method of pricing that allows the buyer to deduct freight expenses from the list price of the product sold; also called freight absorption pricing.

focus group An informal session of 6 to 10 current or potential users of a product in which a discussion leader seeks their opinions on the firm's or a competitor's products.

follow-up stage The phase of the personal selling process that entails making certain that the customer's purchase has been properly delivered and installed and that any difficulties in using the product are promptly and satisfactorily addressed.

Food, Drug, and Cosmetic Act (1938) A law that prevents the adulteration or misbranding of these three categories of products.

forced distribution markets (see selected controlled markets)

Foreign Corrupt Practices Act A law that makes it a crime for U.S. corporations to bribe an official of a foreign government or political party to obtain or retain business in a foreign country.

forgetting rate The speed with which buyers forget a brand if advertising is not seen.

form of ownership Who owns a retail outlet. Alternatives are independent, corporate chain, cooperative, or franchise.

form utility The value to consumers that comes from production or alteration of a good or service.

formula selling presentation The selling format that consists of providing information in an accurate, thorough, and step-by-step manner to persuade the prospect to buy.

forward buying A response to discounts offered by manufacturers in which supermarkets purchase more merchandise than they plan to sell during the promotion. The remaining stock is sold at regular price later, or diverted to another store.

four I's of service Four unique elements to services: intangibility, inconsistency, inseparability, and inventory.

four P's (see marketing mix)

franchising The contractual agreement between a parent company and an individual or firm that allows the franchisee to operate a certain type of business under an established name and according to specific rules.

freight consolidators (see freight forwarders)

freight forwarders Firms that accumulate small shipments into larger lots and then hire a carrier to move them, usually at reduced rates.

frequency The average number of times a person in the target audience is exposed to a message or advertisement.

FTC Act (1914) A law that established the Federal Trade Commission (FTC) to monitor deceptive or misleading advertising and unfair business practices.

full warranty A statement of liability by a manufacturer that has no limits of noncoverage.

full-service agency An advertising agency providing a complete range of services, including market research, media selection, copy development, artwork, and production.

full-service retailer A retailer that provides a complete list of services to cater to its customers.

functional groupings Organizational groupings in which a unit is subdivided according to the different business activities within a firm, such as manufacturing, marketing, and finance.

functional level Level at which groups of specialists create value for the organization.

gap analysis An evaluation tool that compares expectations about a particular service to the actual experience a consumer has with the service.

General Agreement on Tariffs and Trade (GATT) An international treaty intended to limit trade barriers and promote world trade through the reduction of tariffs.

general merchandise stores General merchandise stores carry a broad product line with limited depth.

general merchandise wholesaler A full-service merchant wholesaler that carries a broad assortment of merchandise and performs all channel functions.

Generation X The 17 percent of the population born between 1965 and 1976.

generational marketing The use of marketing programs designed for the distinct attitudes and consumer behavior of the cohorts, or generations, that make up the marketplace.

generic brand A branding strategy that lists no product name, only a description of contents.

generic business strategy Strategy that can be adapted by any firm, regardless of the product or industry involved, to achieve a competitive advantage.

geographic information systems (GIS) Technology that represents different layers of data on one map.

geographical groupings Organization groupings in which a unit is subdivided according to geographical location.

global competition A competitive situation that exists when firms originate, produce, and market their products and services worldwide.

global consumers Customer groups living in many countries or regions of the world who have similar needs or seek similar features and benefits from products and services.

global marketing strategy The practice of standardizing marketing activities when there are cultural similarities and adapting them when cultures differ.

goal A targeted level of performance set in advance of work.

government units   The federal, state, and local agencies that buy goods and services for the constituents they serve.

gray market   A situation in which products are sold through unauthorized channels of distribution; also called parallel importing.

green marketing   Marketing efforts to produce, promote, and reclaim environmentally sensitive products.

gross domestic product   The monetary value of all goods and services produced in a country during one year.

gross income   The total amount of money earned in one year by a person, family, or household.

gross margin   Net sales minus cost of goods sold.

gross rating points (GRPs)   A reference number for advertisers, created by multiplying reach (expressed as a percentage) by frequency.

growth stage   The second stage of the product life cycle characterized by rapid increases in sales and by the appearance of competitors.

harvesting   A strategy used during the decline stage of the product life cycle in which a company continues to offer a product but reduces support costs.

head-to-head positioning   Competing directly with competitors on similar product attributes in the same target market.

hierarchy of effects   The sequence of stages a prospective buyer goes through from initial awareness of a product to eventual action (either trial or adoption of the product). The stages include awareness, interest, evaluation, trial, and adoption.

high learning product   A product that has a long introductory phase to its life cycle because significant education is required for consumers to use the item or appreciate its benefits.

horizontal conflict   Disagreements between intermediaries at the same level in a marketing channel.

horizontal price fixing   The practice whereby two or more competitors explicitly or implicitly collaborate to set prices.

hypermarket   A large store (over 200,000 square feet) offering a mix of food products and general merchandise.

hypothesis   A conjecture or idea about the relationship of two or more factors or what might happen in the future.

hypothesis evaluation   Research to test ideas discovered in the hypothesis generation stage to assist in making recommendations for marketing actions.

hypothesis generation   A search for ideas that can be evaluated in later research.

idea generation   A phase of the new product process, in which a firm develops a pool of concepts as candidates for new products.

idle production capacity   A situation where a service provider is available but there is no demand.

implied warranties   Warranties assigning responsibility for product deficiencies to a manufacturer even though the item was sold by a retailer.

inbound telemarketing   The use of toll-free telephone numbers that customers can call to obtain information about products or services and make purchases.

inconsistency   A unique element of services; variation in service quality because services are delivered by people with varying capabilities.

independent retailer   A retail outlet for which there is an individual owner.

indirect channel   A marketing channel where intermediaries are situated between the producer and consumers.

indirect exporting   A firm selling its domestically produced goods in a foreign country through an intermediary.

individual interviews   A situation where a single researcher asks questions of one respondent.

industrial distributor   A specific type of intermediary between producers and consumers that generally sells, stocks, and delivers a full product assortment.

industrial espionage   The clandestine collection of trade secrets or proprietary information about a company's competitors.

industrial firm   An organizational buyer that in some way reprocesses a good or service it buys before selling it again.

industrial goods   Products used in the production of other items for ultimate consumers.

industry   A group of firms offering products that are close substitutes for each other.

industry potential   (see market potential)

inelastic demand   A situation where a small percentage decrease in price produces a smaller percentage increase in quantity demanded.

information technology   Involves designing and managing computer and communication networks to provide an information system to satisfy an organization's needs for data storage, processing, and access.

infomercials   Program length advertisements, often 30 minutes long, that take an educational approach to communicating with potential customers.

in-house agency   A company's own advertising staff, which may provide full services or a limited range of services.

innovators   The 2.5 percent of the population who are venturesome and highly educated, use multiple information sources, and are the first to adopt a new product.

inseparability   A unique element of services; the fact that a service cannot be separated from the deliverer of the service or the setting in which the service occurs.

institutional advertisement   Advertisements designed to build goodwill or an image for an organization, rather than promote a specific good or service.

intangibility   A unique element of services; the fact that services cannot be held, touched, or seen before the purchase decision.

integrated marketing communications   The concept of designing marketing communications programs that coordinate all promotional activities—advertising, personal selling, sales promotion, public relations, and direct marketing—to provide a consistent message across all audiences.

intensive distribution   A distribution strategy whereby a producer sells products or services in as many outlets as possible in a geographic area.

interactive marketing   Buyer–seller electronic communications in a computer-mediated environment in which the buyer controls the kind and amount of information received from the seller.

intermodel transportation   Combining different transportation modes in order to get the best features of each.

internal marketing   The notion that a service organization must focus on its employees, or internal market, before successful programs can be directed at customers.

internal secondary data   Data that have already been collected and exist inside a business firm or organization.

Internet   An integrated global network of computers that gives users access to information and documents.

Internet marketing channels   Channels that employ the Internet to make goods and services available for consumption or use by consumers or industrial buyers.

intertype competition   Competition between dissimilar types of retail outlets brought about by scrambled merchandising.

Intranet   An Internet/Web-based network used within the boundaries of an organization.

introductory phase   The first stage of the product life cycle in which sales grow slowly and profit is low.

inventory   (1) Physical material purchased from suppliers, which may or may not be reworked and is available for sale to customers. (2) A unique element of services; the need for and cost of having a service provider available.

involvement   The personal, social, and economic significance of the purchase to the consumer.

ISO 14000   Worldwide standards for environmental quality and green marketing practices.

ISO 9000   International standards for registration and certification of a manufacturer's quality management and quality assurance system.

job analysis   A written description of what a salesperson is expected to do.

job description   Written document that describes job relationships and requirements that characterize each sales position.

joint venture   In international trade, an arrangement in which a foreign company and a local firm invest together to create a local business.

jury of executive opinion forecast   Asking knowledgeable executives inside the firm about likely sales during a coming period.

jury test   A pretest in which a panel of customers is shown an advertisement and asked to rate its attractiveness, how much they like it, and how much it draws their attention.

just-in-time (JIT) concept   An inventory supply system that operates with very low inventories and requires fast, on-time delivery.

laboratory experiment   A simulation of marketing-related activity in a highly controlled setting.

laggards   The 16 percent of the market who have fear of debt, use friends for information sources, and accept ideas and products only after they have been long established in the market.

Lanham Act (1946)   A law that allows a company to register a trademark (symbol or word) for its exclusive use.

late majority   The 34 percent of the population who are skeptical, below average in social status, and rely less on advertising and personal selling for information than do innovators or early adopters.

laws   Society's values and standards that are enforceable in the courts.

lead generation   The result of a direct marketing offer designed to generate interest in a product or a service, and a request for additional information.

lead time   Lag from ordering an item until it is received and ready for use.

learning   Those behaviors that result from (1) repeated experience and (2) thinking.

level of service   The degree of service provided to the customer by the retailer: self, limited, or full.

licensing   A contractual agreement whereby a company allows another firm to use its brand name, patent, trade secret, or other property for a royalty or fee.

lifestyle   A mode of living that is identified by how people spend their time and resources (activities), what they consider important in their environment (interests), and what they think of themselves and the world around them (opinions).

Likert scale   A fixed alternative question in which the respondent indicates the extent to which he agrees or disagrees with a statement.

limited-coverage warranty   A manufacturer's statement indicating the bounds of coverage and noncoverage for any product deficiencies.

limited-line store   A retail outlet, such as a sporting goods store, that offers considerable assortment, or depth, of a related line of items.

limited-service agency   An agency that specializes in one aspect of the advertising process such as providing creative services to develop the advertising copy or buying previously unpurchased media space.

limited-service retailer   A retailer that provides selected services such as credit or merchandise return to customers.

line extension   The practice of using a current brand name to enter a new market segment in its product class.

line positions   People in line positions, such as group marketing managers, have the authority and responsibility to issue orders to the people who report to them, such as marketing managers.

logistics management   The practice of organizing the cost-effective flow of raw materials, in-process inventory, finished goods, and related information from point-of-origin to point-of-consumption to satisfy customer requirements.

loss-leader pricing   Deliberately pricing a product below its customary price to attract attention to it.

lost-horse forecast   Starting with the last known value of the item being forecast, listing the factors that could affect the forecast, assessing whether they have a positive or negative impact, and making the final forecast.

low-learning product   A product that has an immediate gain in sales in the introductory phase because the benefits are easily observed by consumers and little education is required to use it.

macromarketing   The study of the aggregate flow of a nation's goods and services to benefit society.

Magnuson-Moss Warranty/FTC Improvement Act (1975)   An act that regulates the content of consumer warranties and also has strengthened consumer rights with regard to warranties through class action suits.

mail-order retailer   A retailing operation in which merchandise is offered to customers by mail.

maintained markup   The difference between the final selling price and retailer cost; also called gross margin.

major account management   The practice of using team selling to focus on important customers to build mutually beneficial long-term, cooperative relationships.

make-buy decision   An evaluation of whether a product or its parts will be purchased from outside suppliers or built by the firm.

management by exception   A tool used by a marketing manager that involves identifying results that deviate from plans, diagnosing their cause, making appropriate new plans, and taking new actions.

manufacturer branding   A branding strategy in which the brand name for a product is designated by the producer, using either a multiproduct or multibranding approach.

manufacturer's agents   Individuals or firms that work for several producers and carry noncompetitive, complementary merchandise in an exclusive territory; also called manufacturer's representatives.

manufacturer's branch office   A wholly owned extension of a producer that performs channel functions, including carrying inventory, generally performed by a full-service merchant wholesaler.

marginal analysis   Principle of allocating resources that balances incremental revenues of an action against incremental costs.

marginal cost   The change in total cost that results from producing and marketing one additional unit.

marginal revenue   The change in total revenue obtained by selling one additional unit.

markdown   Reduction in retail price usually expressed as a percentage equal to the amount reduced, divided by the original price and multiplied by 100.

market   People with the desire and ability to buy a specific product.

market-based groupings   Organizational groupings that assign responsibility for a specific type of customer to a unit.

market development   Selling existing products to new markets.

market growth rate   The annual rate of growth of the specific market or industry in which a firm or SBU is competing; often used as the vertical axis in business portfolio analysis.

market modification   Attempts to increase product usage by creating new-use situations or finding new customers.

market orientation   Focusing organizational efforts on (1) continuously collecting information about customers' needs and competitors' capabilities, (2) sharing this information across departments, and (3) using the information to create customer value.

market penetration   A strategy of increasing sales of present products in their existing markets.

market potential   Maximum total sales of a product by all firms to a segment under specified environmental conditions and marketing efforts of the firms (also called industry potential).

market-product grid   Framework for relating market segments to products offered or potential marketing actions by a firm.

market segmentation   Aggregating prospective buyers into groups, or segments, that (1) have common needs and (2) will respond similarly to a marketing action.

market segments   The groups that result from the process of market segmentation; these groups ideally (1) have common needs and (2) will respond similarly to a marketing action.

market share   The ratio of sales revenue of the firm to the total sales revenue of all firms in the industry, including the firm itself.

market testing   A phase of the new product process, in which prospective consumers are exposed to actual products under realistic purchase conditions to see if they will buy.

marketing   The process of planning and executing the conception, pricing, promotion, and distribution of ideas, goods, and services to create exchanges that satisfy individual and organizational objectives.

marketing audit   A comprehensive, unbiased, periodic review of the strategic marketing process of a firm or a strategic business unit (SBU).

marketing channel   People and firms involved in the process of making a product or service available for use or consumption by consumers or industrial users.

marketing concept   The idea that an organization should (1) strive to satisfy the needs of consumers (2) while also trying to achieve the organization's goals.

marketing decision support system (MDSS)   A computerized method of providing timely, accurate information to improve marketing decisions.

marketing mix   The marketing manager's controllable factors of product, price, promotion, and place he or she can take to solve a marketing problem.

marketing orientation   When an organization focuses its efforts on (1) continuously collecting information about customers' needs and competitors' capabilities, (2) sharing this information across departments, and (3) using the information to create customer value.

marketing plan   A roadmap for the marketing activities of an organization for a specified future period of time, such as one year or five years.

marketing program   A plan that integrates the marketing mix to provide a good, service, or idea to prospective consumers.

marketing research   The process of defining a marketing problem and opportunity, systematically collecting and analyzing information, and recommending actions to improve an organization's marketing activities.

marketing strategy   The means by which a marketing goal is to be achieved, characterized by (1) a specified target market and (2) a marketing program to reach it.

marketing tactics   The detailed day-to-day operational decisions essential to the overall success of marketing strategies.

marketing Web site   A Web site designed to engage consumers in interactive communication or dialogue that will result in the sale of a company's product or service or move the consumer closer to a purchase.

marketspace   An information- and communication-based electronic exchange environment mostly occupied by sophisticated computer and telecommunication technologies and digitized offerings.

markup   The amount added to the cost of goods sold to arrive at a selling price, expressed in dollar or percentage terms.

mass customization   Tailoring goods or services to the tastes of individual customers in high volumes at a relatively low cost.

materials handling   Moving goods over short distances into, within, and out of warehouses and manufacturing plants.

mature households   Households headed by people over age 50.

maturity phase   The third stage of the product or retail life cycle in which market share levels off and profitability declines.

measures of success   Criteria or standards used in evaluating proposed solutions to the problem.

Meat Inspection Act (1906)   An act that regulated that meat products be wholesome, unadulterated, and properly labeled.

mechanical observational data Data collected by electronic or other impersonal means, such as meters connected to television sets in viewers' homes.

merchandise allowance A trade-oriented sales promotion in which a retailer is reimbursed for extra in-store support or special featuring of the brand.

merchandise line The number of different types of products and the assortment a store carries.

message The information sent by a source to a receiver in the communication process.

methods The approaches that can be used to solve all or part of a problem.

metropolitan statistical area (MSA) An area within (1) a city having a population of at least 50,000 or (2) an urbanized area with a population in excess of 50,000 with a total population of at least 100,000.

micromarketing How an organization directs its marketing activities and allocates its resources to benefit its customers.

missionary salespeople Sales support personnel who do not directly solicit orders but rather concentrate on performing promotional activities and introducing new products.

mixed branding A branding strategy in which the company may market products under their own name and that of a reseller.

modified rebuy A buying situation in which the users, influencers, or deciders change the product specifications, price, delivery schedule, or supplier.

monopolistic competition A competitive setting in which a large number of sellers offer unique but substitutable products.

monopoly A competitive setting in which there is a single seller of a good or service.

moral idealism A personal moral philosophy that considers certain individual rights or duties as universal regardless of the outcome.

motivation Motivation is the energizing force that causes behavior that satisfies a need.

multibranding A manufacturer's branding strategy in which a distinct name is given to each of its products.

multidomestic marketing strategy A firm's worldwide marketing strategy that offers as many different product variations, brand names, and advertising programs as countries in which it does business.

multiple-zone pricing Pricing products the same when delivered within one of several specified zones or geographical areas, but with different prices for each zone depending on demand, competition, and distance: also called zone-delivered pricing.

multiproduct branding A branding strategy in which a company uses one name for all products; also called blanket or family branding.

national character A distinct set of personality characteristics common among people of a country or society.

need That which occurs when a person feels deprived of food, clothing, or shelter.

need-satisfaction presentation A selling format that emphasizes probing and listening by the salesperson to identify needs and interests of perspective buyers.

new buy The first-time purchase of a product or service, characterized by greater potential risk.

new-product concept A tentative description of a product or service a firm might offer for sale.

new-product process The sequence of activities a firm uses to identify business opportunities and convert them to a saleable good or service. There are seven steps: new-product strategy, idea generation, screening and evaluation, business analysis, development, testing, and commercialization.

new-product strategy development The phase of the new-product process in which a firm defines the role of new products in terms of overall corporate objectives.

news conference A publicity tool consisting of an informational meeting with representatives of the media who received advanced materials on the meeting content.

news release A publicity tool consisting of an announcement regarding changes in the company or product line.

noise Extraneous factors that work against effective communication by distorting a message or the feedback received.

noncumulative quantity discounts Price reductions based on the size of an individual purchase order.

nondurable good An item consumed in one or a few uses.

nonprobability sampling Using arbitrary judgments to select the sample so that the chance of selecting a particular element may be unknown or zero.

nonprofit organization A nongovernmental organization that serves its customers but does not have profit as an organizational goal.

nonrepetitive decisions Those decisions unique to a particular time and situation.

North American Industry Classification System (NAICS) A system for classifying organizations on the basis of major activity or the major good or service provided used by the three NAFTA countries—Canada, Mexico, and the United States.

objective and task budgeting A budgeting approach whereby the company (1) determines its advertising objectives, (2) outlines the tasks to accomplish the objectives, and (3) determines the advertising cost of performing these tasks.

objectives Specific, measurable performance targets and deadlines.

observational data Facts and figures obtained by watching, either mechanically or in person, how people actually behave.

odd-even pricing Setting prices a few dollars or cents under an even number, such as $19.95.

off-peak pricing Charging different prices during different times of the day or days of the week to reflect variations in demand for the service.

off-price retailing Selling brand name merchandise at lower than regular prices.

oligopoly A competitive setting in which a few large companies control a large amount of an industry's sales.

one-price policy Setting the same price for similar customers who buy the same product and quantities under the same conditions.

one-price stores A form of off-price retailing in which all items in a store are sold at one low price.

open-end question A question that a respondent can answer in his or her own words.

opinion leaders Individuals who exert direct or indirect social influence over others.

order getter   A salesperson who sells in a conventional sense and engages in identifying prospective customers, providing customers with information, persuading customers to buy, closing sales, and following on customer experience with product or service.

order taker   A salesperson who processes routine orders and reorders for products that have already been sold by the company.

organizational buyers   Units such as manufacturers, retailers, or government agencies that buy goods and services for their own use or for resale.

organizational buying behavior   The decision-making process that organizations use to establish the need for products and identify, evaluate, and choose among alternative brands and suppliers.

organizational buying criteria   The objective attributes of the supplier's products and services and the capabilities of the supplier itself.

organizational goals   Specific objectives a business or nonprofit unit seeks to achieve and by which it can measure its performance.

original markup   The difference between retailer cost and initial selling price.

outbound telemarketing   Use of the telephone rather than personal visits to contact customers.

Pacific Rim   The area of the world consisting of countries in Asia and Australia.

packaging   The container in which a product is offered for sale and on which information is communicated.

panel   A sample of consumers or stores from which researchers take a series of measurements.

parallel development   An approach to new product development that involves the simultaneous development of the product and production process.

partnership selling   The practice whereby buyers and sellers combine their expertise and resources to create customized solutions, commit to joint planning, and share customer, competitive, and company information for their mutual benefit, and ultimately the customer.

patent   Exclusive rights to the manufacture of a product or related technology granted to a company for 17 years.

penetration pricing   Pricing a product low in order to discourage competition from entering the market.

penturbia   The small towns to which the population began to shift in the 1990s.

per se illegality   An action that by itself is illegal.

perceived risk   The anxieties felt because the consumer cannot anticipate the outcome but sees that there might be negative consequences.

percent of sales budgeting   Allocating funds to advertising as a percentage of past or anticipated sales, in terms of either dollars or units sold.

perception   The process by which an individual selects, organizes, and interprets information to create a meaningful picture of the world.

perceptual map   A graph displaying consumers' perceptions of product attributes across two or more dimensions.

personal selling   The two-way flow of communication between a buyer and seller, often in a face-to-face encounter, designed to influence a person's or group's purchase decision.

personal selling process   Sales activities occurring before and after the sale itself, consisting of six stages: (1) prospecting, (2) preapproach, (3) approach, (4) presentation, (5) close, and (6) follow-up.

personality   A person's consistent behaviors or responses to recurring situations.

piggyback franchising   A variation of franchising in which stores operated by one chain sell the products or services of another franchised firm.

pioneering advertisements   Advertisements that tell what a product is, what it can do, and where it can be found.

pioneering institutional advertisements   Institutional advertisements about what a company is or can do or where it is located.

place-based media   Advertising media alternative that places messages in locations that attract a specific target audience such as airports, doctor's offices, and health clubs.

place utility   The value to consumers of having a good or service available where needed.

point-of-purchase displays   Displays located in high-traffic areas in retail stores, often next to checkout counters.

points of difference   Those characteristics of a product that make it superior to competitive substitutes.

population   The universe of all people, stores, or salespeople about which researchers wish to generalize.

portals   Electronic gateways to the World Wide Web that supply a broad array of news and entertainment, information resources and shopping services.

portfolio test   A pretest in which a test ad is placed in a portfolio with other ads and consumers are questioned on their impressions of the ads.

possession utility   The value of making an item easy to purchase through the provision of credit cards or financial arrangements.

posttests   Tests conducted after an advertisement has been shown to the target audience to determine whether it has accomplished its intended purpose.

power center   Large strip malls with multiple anchor (or national stores), a convenient location, and a supermarket.

preapproach stage   The stage of the personal selling process that involves obtaining further information about a prospect and deciding on the best method of approach.

precycling   Efforts by manufacturers to reduce waste by decreasing the amount of packaging they use on products.

predatory pricing   Selling products at a low price to injure or eliminate a competitor.

premium   A sales promotion that consists of offering merchandise free or at significant savings over retail.

presentation stage   The core of the personal selling process in which the salesperson tries to convert the prospect into a customer by creating a desire for the product or service.

prestige pricing   Setting a high price so that status-conscious consumers will be attracted to the product.

pretests   Tests conducted before an advertisement is placed to determine whether it communicates the intended message or to select between alternative versions of an advertisement.

price   The money or other considerations exchanged for the purchase or use of the product, idea, or service.

price discrimination   The practice of charging different prices to different buyers for goods of like trade and quality; the

Clayton Act as amended by the Robinson-Patman Act prohibits this action.

price elasticity of demand The percentage change in quantity demanded relative to a percentage change in price.

price fixing A conspiracy among firms to set prices for a product.

price lining Setting the price of a line of products at a number of different specific pricing points.

pricing constraints Factors that limit a firm's latitude in the price it may set.

pricing objectives Goals that specify the role of price in an organization's marketing and strategic plans.

primary data Facts and figures that are newly collected for the project.

primary demand Desire for a product class rather than for a specific brand.

primary metropolitan statistical area (PMSA) An area that is part of a larger consolidated statistical metropolitan area with a total population of 1 million or more.

prime rate The rate of interest banks charge their largest customers.

private branding When a company manufactures products that are sold under the name of a wholesaler or retailer.

proactive strategies New product strategies that involve an aggressive allocation of resources to identify opportunities for product development.

probability sampling Using precise rules to select the sample such that each element of the population has a specific known chance of being selected.

product A good, service, or idea consisting of a bundle of tangible and intangible attributes that satisfies consumers and is received in exchange for money or other unit of value.

product advertisements Advertisements that focus on selling a good or service and take three forms: (1) pioneering (or informational), (2) competitive (or persuasive), and (3) reminder.

product (program) champion A person who is able and willing to cut red tape and move a product or program forward.

product class An entire product category or industry.

product counterfeiting Low-cost copies of a popular brand, not manufactured by the original producer.

product development A strategy of selling a new product to existing markets.

product differentiation A strategy having different but related meanings; it involves a firm's using different marketing mix activities, such as product featuring and advertising, to help consumers perceive the product as being different and better than other products.

product form Variations of a product within a product class.

product item A specific product noted by a unique brand, size, and price.

product life cycle The life of a product over four stages: introduction, growth, maturity, and decline.

product line A group of products closely related because they satisfy a class of needs, are used together, are sold to the same customer group, are distributed through the same outlets, or fall within a given price range.

product line groupings Organizational groupings in which a unit is responsible for specific product offerings.

product line pricing The setting of prices for all items in a product line.

product manager A person who plans, implements, and controls the annual and long-range plans for the products for which he or she is responsible.

product mix The number of product lines offered by a company.

product modifications Strategies of altering a product characteristic, such as quality, performance, or appearance.

product placement Advertising media alternative in which the manufacturer pays for the privilege of having a brand name product used in a movie.

product positioning The place an offering occupies in a consumer's mind with regard to important attributes relative to competitive offerings.

production goods Products used in the manufacturing of other items that become part of the final product.

profit A business firm's reward for the risk it undertakes in offering a product for sale; the money left over after a firm's total expenses are subtracted from its total revenues.

profit equation Profit = Total revenue − Total cost.

profit responsibility The view that companies have a single obligation, which is to maximize profits for its owners or stockholders.

profitability analysis A means of measuring the profitability of the firm's products, customer groups, sales territories, channels of distribution, and order sizes.

program schedule A formal time-line chart showing the relationships through time of the various program tasks.

promotional allowance The cash payment or extra amount of "free goods" awarded sellers in the channel of distribution for undertaking certain advertising or selling activities to promote a product.

promotional mix The combination of one or more of the promotional elements a firm uses to communicate with consumers. The promotional elements include: advertising, personal selling, sales promotion, and publicity.

prospecting stage In the personal selling process, the search for and qualification of potential customers.

protectionism The practice of shielding one or more sectors of a country's economy from foreign competition through the use of tariffs, or quotas.

protocol In the new product development process, an early statement that identifies a well-defined target market; specifies customers' needs, wants, and preferences; and states what the product will be and do.

psychographics Characteristics represented by personality and lifestyle traits (activities, interests, and opinions).

public relations A form of communication management that seeks to influence the feelings, opinions, or beliefs held by customers, stockholders, suppliers, employees, and other publics about a company and its products or services.

public service announcement (PSA) A publicity tool that uses free space or time donated by the media.

publicity A nonpersonal, indirectly paid presentation of an organization, good, or service.

publicity tools Methods of obtaining nonpersonal presentation of an organization, good, or service without direct cost. Examples include news releases, news conferences, and public service announcements.

pull strategy Directing the promotional mix at ultimate consumers to encourage them to ask the retailer for the product.

pulse schedule The combination of a steady schedule and a flighting schedule because of increases in demand, heavy periods of promotion, or introduction of a new product.

purchase decision process Steps or stages a buyer passes through in making choices about which products to buy.

purchase frequency The frequency of purchase of a specific product.

pure competition A competitive setting in which a large number of sellers compete with similar products.

push strategy Directing the promotional mix to channel members or intermediaries to gain their cooperation in ordering and stocking a product.

quality Those features and characteristics of a product that influence its ability to satisfy customer needs.

quantity discounts Reductions in unit costs for a larger order quantity.

questionnaire data Facts and figures obtained by asking people about their attitudes, awareness, intentions, and behaviors.

quick response An inventory management system designed to reduce the retailer's lead time for receiving merchandise.

quota In international marketing, a restriction placed on the amount of a product allowed to enter or leave a country.

rack jobber A merchant wholesaler that furnishes racks or shelves to display merchandise in retail stores, performs all channel functions, and sells on consignment.

rating (TV or ratio) The percentage of households in a market that are tuned to a particular TV show or radio station.

reach The number of different people or households exposed to an advertisement.

reactive strategies New product strategies that are defensive approaches in response to competitors' new items by developing new products.

rebate A sales promotion in which money is returned to the consumer based on proof of purchase.

receivers The consumers who read, hear, or see the message sent by a source in the communication process.

reciprocity An industrial buying practice in which two organizations agree to purchase products from each other.

recycling The use of technological developments to allow products to go through the manufacturing cycle several times.

reference group People to whom a person turns as a standard of self-appraisal or source of personal standards.

regional marketing A form of geographical segmentation that develops marketing plans to reflect specific area differences in taste preferences, perceived needs, or interests.

regional rollouts Introducing a new product sequentially into geographical areas to allow production levels and marketing activities to build up gradually.

regional shopping centers Suburban malls with up to 100 stores that typically draw customers from a 5- to 10-mile radius, usually containing one or two anchor stores.

regulation The laws placed on business with regard to the conduct of its activities.

reinforcement A reward that tends to strengthen a response.

relationship marketing Linking the organization to its individual customers, employees, suppliers, and other partners for their mutual long-term benefits.

relationship selling The practice of building ties to customers based on a salesperson's attention and commitment to customer needs over time.

relative market share The sales of a firm or SBU divided by the sales of the largest firm in the industry; often used as a horizontal axis in business portfolio analysis.

reminder advertisements Advertisements used to reinforce previous knowledge of a product.

reminder institutional advertisements Institutional advertisements that bring a company's name to the attention of the target market.

repeat purchasers People who tried the product, were satisfied, and buy again.

repetitive decisions Decisions repeated at standard intervals during the work year.

repositioning Changing the place an offering occupies in a consumer's mind relative to competitive products.

requirements contract A contract that requires a buyer to meet all or part of its needs for a product from one seller for a period of time.

reseller A wholesaler or retailer that buys physical products and resells them again without any processing.

restructuring (reengineering or streamlining) Striving for more efficient corporations that can compete globally by reducing duplicate efforts in multiple company locations, closing or changing unprofitable plants and offices, and laying off employees.

retail life cycle A concept that describes a retail operation over four stages: early growth, accelerated development, maturity, and decline.

retail positioning matrix A framework for positioning retail outlets in terms of breadth of product line and value added.

retailer-sponsored cooperative chain A contractual system involving independently owned stores that bind together to act like a chain.

retailing All the activities that are involved in selling, renting, and providing goods and services to ultimate consumers for personal, family, or household use.

retailing mix The strategic components that a retailer manages, including goods and services, physical distribution, and communication tactics.

return on investment (ROI) The ratio of after-tax net profit to the investment used to earn that profit.

returns Refunds or credit granted a customer for an item returned to the seller.

reverse logistics The process of reclaiming recyclable and reusable materials, returns, and reworks from the point-of-consumption or use for repair, remanufacturing, or disposal.

reverse marketing The effort by organizational buyers to build relationships that shape suppliers' products, services, and capabilities to fit a buyer's needs and those of its customers.

rich media Online promotion, such as banner advertising, that utilizes the audio, video, and interactive capabilities of the Internet to attract more attention from viewers and to provide an element of entertainment to the message.

Robinson-Patman Act (1936) A regulation that makes it unlawful to discriminate in prices charged to different purchasers of the same product where the result is to substantially lessen competition or help create a monopoly.

sales analysis   A tool for controlling marketing programs where sales records are used to compare actual results with sales goals and to identify strengths and weaknesses.

sales component analysis   A tool for controlling marketing programs that traces sales revenues to their sources such as specific products, sales territories, or customers.

sales engineer   A salesperson who specializes in identifying, analyzing, and solving customer problems and who brings technological expertise to the selling situations, but does not actually sell goods and services.

salesforce automation   The use of technology designed to make the sales function more effective and efficient.

salesforce survey forecast   Asking the firm's salespeople to estimate sales during a coming period.

sales forecast   What one firm expects to sell under specified conditions for the uncontrollable and controllable factors that affect the forecast.

sales management   Planning, implementing, and controlling the personal selling effort of the firm.

sales plan   A statement describing what is to be achieved and where and how the selling effort of salespeople is to be deployed.

sales promotion   A short-term inducement of value offered to arouse interest in buying a good or service.

sales response function   The relationship between the expense of marketing effort and the marketing results obtained. Measures of marketing results include sales revenue, profit, units sold, and level of awareness.

samples   (1) Some elements taken from the population or universe, or (2) a sales promotion consisting of offering a product free or at a greatly reduced price.

sampling   (1) the process of selecting elements from a population, or (2) the process manufacturers use of giving away free samples to introduce a new product.

scrambled merchandising   Offering several unrelated product lines in a single retail store.

screening and evaluation   The phase of the new product process in which a firm uses internal and external evaluations to eliminate ideas that warrant no further development effort.

seasonal discounts   Price reductions granted buyers for purchasing products and stocking them at a time when they are not wanted by customers.

secondary data   Facts and figures that have already been recorded before the project at hand.

selected controlled markets   These sites, also referred to as forced distribution markets, are where a market test for a new product is conducted by an outside agency and retailers are paid to display the new product.

selective comprehension   Interpreting information to make it consistent with one's attitude and beliefs.

selective demand   Demand for a specific brand within a product class.

selective distribution   A distribution strategy whereby a producer sells its products in a few retail outlets in a specific geographical area.

selective exposure   The tendency to seek out and pay attention to messages consistent with one's attitudes and beliefs and to ignore messages inconsistent with them.

selective perception   The tendency for humans to filter or choose information from a complex environment so they can make sense of the world.

selective retention   The tendency to remember only part of all the information one sees, hears, or reads.

self-concept   The way people see themselves and the way they believe others see them.

self-liquidating premium   A sales promotion offering merchandise at a significant cost savings to the customer, its price covering the cost of the premium for the company.

self-regulation   An industry policing itself rather than relying on government controls.

selling agent   A person or firm that represents a single producer and is responsible for all marketing functions of that producer.

semantic differential scale   A seven-point scale in which the opposite ends have one- or two-word adjectives with opposite meanings.

seminar selling   A form of team selling where a company team conducts an educational program for a customer's technical staff describing state-of-the-art developments.

semiotics   The field of study that examines the correspondence between symbols and their role in the assignment of meaning for people.

sensitivity analysis   Asking "What if . . ." questions to determine how changes in a factor like pricing or advertising affect marketing results like sales revenue or profits.

service continuum   A range from the tangible to the intangible or good-dominant to service-dominant offerings available in the marketplace.

services   Intangible items such as airline trips, financial advice, or telephone calls that an organization provides to consumers in exchange for money or something else of value.

share points   Percentage points of market share; often used as the common basis of comparison to allocate marketing resources effectively.

shelf life   The time a product can be stored before it spoils.

Sherman Anti-Trust Act (1890)   A law that forbids (1) contracts, combinations, or conspiracies in restraint of trade and (2) actual monopolies or attempts to monopolize any part of trade or commerce.

shopping goods   Products for which the consumer will compare several alternatives on various criteria.

shrinkage   A term used by retailers to describe breakage and theft of merchandise by customers and employees.

single-line store   A store that offers tremendous depth in one primary line of merchandise; for example, a running shoe store.

single-source data   Information provided by a single firm on household demographics and lifestyle, purchases, TV viewing behavior, and responses to promotions like coupons and free samples.

single-zone pricing   Pricing policy in which all buyers pay the same delivered product price, regardless of their distance from the seller; also known as uniform delivered pricing or postage stamp pricing.

situation analysis   Taking stock of where the firm or product has been recently, where it is now, and where it is headed in terms of the organization's plans and the external factors and trends affecting it.

situational influences   A situation's effect on the nature and scope of the decision process. These include (1) the purchase task, (2) social surroundings, (3) physical surroundings, (4) temporal effects, and (5) antecedent states.

skimming pricing   A high initial price attached to a product to help a company recover the cost of development.

slotting fees   Payment by a manufacturer to place a new product on a retailer's shelf.

social audit   A systematic assessment of a firm's objectives, strategies, and performance in the domain of social responsibility.

social classes   The relatively permanent and homogeneous divisions in a society of people or families sharing similar values, lifestyles, interests, and behavior.

social forces   The demographic characteristics of the population and its values in a particular environment.

social responsibility   The idea that organizations are part of a larger society and are accountable to society for their actions.

societal marketing concept   The view that an organization should discover and satisfy the needs of its customers in a way that also provides for society's well-being.

societal responsibility   The view that firms have obligations to preserve the ecological environment and benefit the general public.

solution   The best alternative that has been identified to solve the problem.

source   A company or person who has information to convey.

specialty merchandise wholesaler   A full-service merchant wholesaler that offers a relatively narrow range of products but has an extensive assortment within the products carried.

specialty outlet   Retailers that offer large selections in a narrow range of products.

specialty goods   Products that a consumer will make a special effort to search out and buy.

splitting 30s   Reducing the length of a standard commercial from 30 seconds to 15 seconds.

staff positions   People in staff positions have the authority and responsibility to advise people in the line positions but cannot issue direct orders to them.

stakeholder responsibility   The view that an organization has an obligation only to those constituencies that can affect achievement of its objectives.

standard markets   Sites where companies test market a product through normal distribution channels and monitor the results.

standard markup pricing   Setting prices by adding a fixed percentage to the cost of all items in a specific product class.

Starch test   A posttest that assesses the extent of consumers' recognition of an advertisement appearing in a magazine they have read.

statistical inference   Drawing conclusions about a population from a sample taken from that population.

stimulus discrimination   The ability to perceive differences in stimuli.

stimulus generalization   When a response elicited by one stimulus (cue) is generalized to another stimulus.

stimulus-response presentation   A selling format that assumes the prospect will buy if given the appropriate stimulus by a salesperson.

stock keeping unit (SKU)   A distinct ordering number to identify a product item.

store audits   Measurements of the sales of the product in stores and the number of cases ordered by a store from the wholesaler.

straight commission compensation plan   A compensation plan where the salesperson's earnings are directly tied to his sales or profit generated.

straight rebuy   The reordering of an existing product or service from the list of acceptable suppliers, generally without checking with the various users or influencers.

straight salary compensation plan   A compensation plan where the salesperson is paid a fixed amount per week, month, or year.

strategic alliances   Agreements between two or more independent firms to cooperate for the purpose of achieving common goals.

strategic business unit (SBU)   A decentralized profit center of a large firm that is treated as though it were a separate, independent business.

strategic business unit (SBU)   (see business unit)

strategic channel alliances   A practice whereby one firm's marketing channel is used to sell another firm's products.

strategic marketing process   The activities whereby an organization allocates its marketing mix resources to reach its target markets.

strip location   A cluster of stores that serves people who live within a 5- to 10-minute drive in a population base of under 30,000.

subcultures   Subgroups within the larger or national culture with unique values, ideas, and attitudes.

subliminal perception   Means that a person sees or hears messages without being aware of them.

supply chain   A sequence of firms that perform activities required to create and deliver a good or service to consumers or industrial users.

supply chain management   The integration and organization of information and logistic activities across firms in a supply chain for the purpose of creating and delivering goods and services that provide value to customers.

supply partnerships   A relationship between an organizational buyer and its supplier created to adopt mutually beneficial efforts to lower the cost and/or increase value delivered to the ultimate consumer.

support goods   Items used to assist in the production of other goods.

survey of buyers' intentions forecast   A method of forecasting sales that involves asking prospective customers whether they are likely to buy the product or service during some future time period.

survey of experts forecast   Asking experts on a topic to make a judgment about some future event.

sustainable competitive advantage   A strength, relative to competitors, in the markets served and the products offered.

sustainable development   The practice of conducting business in a way that protects the natural environment while making economic progress.

sweepstakes   Sales promotions consisting of a game of chance requiring no analytical or creative effort to win a prize.

SWOT analysis   An acronym describing an organization's appraisal of its internal strengths and weaknesses and its external opportunities and threats.

synergy   The increased customer value achieved through performing organizational functions more efficiently.

target market One or more specific groups of potential consumers toward which an organization directs its marketing program.

target pricing The practice of deliberately adjusting the composition and features of a product to achieve the target price to consumers.

target profit pricing Setting a price based on an annual specific dollar target volume of profit.

target return-on-investment pricing Setting a price to achieve a return-on-investment target.

target return-on-sales pricing Setting a price to achieve a profit that is a specified percentage of the sales volume.

tariff In international marketing, a government tax on goods or services entering a country.

team selling Using a group of professionals in selling to and servicing major customers.

technology An environmental force that includes inventions or innovations from applied science or engineering research.

telemarketing Involves the use of the telephone to interact with and sell directly to consumers.

television home shopping (see telemarketing)

test marketing The process of offering a product for sale on a limited basis in a defined area to gain consumer reaction to the actual product and to examine its commercial viability and the marketing program.

theater test A pretest in which consumers view test ads in new television shows or movies and report their feelings on electronic recording devices or questionnaires.

third-party logistics providers Firms that perform most or all of the logistics functions that manufacturers, suppliers, and distributors would normally perform themselves.

TIGER (Topologically Integrated Geographic Encoding and Reference) A landmark project in demography by the U.S. Census Bureau that will provide a minutely detailed computerized map of the entire United States that can be combined with a company's own data.

time utility The value to consumers of having a good or service available when needed.

timing The issue of deciding when to discount the price of merchandise.

top-down forecast Subdividing an aggregate forecast into its principal components.

total cost The total expense a firm incurs in producing and marketing a product, which includes fixed cost and variable cost; in physical distribution decisions, the sum of all applicable costs for logistical activities.

total logistics cost Expenses associated with transportation, materials handling and warehousing, inventory, stockouts, and order processing.

total revenue The total amount of money received from the sale of a product.

trade (functional) discounts Price reductions granted to wholesalers or retailers on the basis of future marketing functions they will perform for the manufacturer.

trade feedback effect A country's imports affect its exports and exports affect imports.

trade name The commercial name under which a company does business.

trade-oriented sales promotions Sales tools used to support a company's advertising and personal selling efforts directed to wholesalers, distributors, or retailers. Three common approaches are allowances, cooperative advertising, and salesforce training.

trademark Legal identification of a company's exclusive rights to use a brand name or trade name.

Trademark Law Revision Act (1988) A legislative change to the Lanham Act by which a company can secure the rights to a name before actual use by declaring intent to use the name.

trading down Reducing the number of features, quality, or price of a product.

trading up Adding value to a product by including more features or higher quality materials.

traffic generation The outcome of a direct marketing offer designed to motivate people to visit a business.

trend extrapolation Extending a pattern observed in past data into the future.

trial The initial purchase of a product by the consumer.

truck jobber Small merchant wholesalers that usually handle limited assortments of fast-moving or perishable items that are sold directly from trucks for cash.

tying arrangement A seller's requirement that the purchaser of one product also buy another product in the line.

ultimate consumers People who use the goods and services purchased for a household; sometimes also called ultimate users.

uncontrollable factors (see environmental factors)

uniform delivered pricing A geographical pricing practice where the price the seller quotes includes all transportation costs.

unit train A train that is dedicated to one commodity, is loaded and unloaded with sophisticated equipment, and runs from origin to destination at high speed.

unit variable cost Variable cost expressed on a per unit basis.

unitary demand elasticity A situation where the percentage change in price is identical to the percentage change in quantity demanded.

universal product code (UPC) A number assigned to identify each product, represented by a series of bars of varying widths for scanning by optical readers.

unsought goods Products that the consumer does not know about or knows about and does not initially want.

usage rate Refers to quantity consumed or patronage during a specific period, and varies significantly among different customer groups.

utilitarianism A personal moral philosophy that focuses on the "greatest good for the greatest number" by assessing the costs and benefits of the consequences of ethical behavior.

utility The benefits or customer value received by users of the product.

value Specifically, value can be defined as the ratio of perceived quality to price (Value = Perceived benefits/Price).

value added In retail strategy decisions, a dimension of the retail positioning matrix that refers to the service level and method of operation of the retailer.

value analysis A systematic appraisal of the design, quality, and performance requirements of a product to reduce purchasing costs.

value consciousness Consumer concern for obtaining the best quality, features, and performance of a product or service for a given price.

value pricing   The practice of simultaneously increasing service and product benefits and decreasing price.

values   The beliefs of a person or culture; when applied to pricing, the ratio of perceived quality to price (Value = Perceived benefits/Price).

variable cost   An expense of the firm that varies directly with the quantity of product produced and sold.

vending machines   A retailing operation in which products are stored in and sold from machines.

vendor-managed inventory   An inventory management system whereby the supplier determines the product amount and assortment a customer (such as a retailer) needs and automatically delivers the appropriate items.

venture teams   Multidisciplinary groups of marketing, manufacturing, and R&D personnel who stay with a new product from conception to production.

vertical conflict   Disagreement between different levels in a marketing channel.

vertical marketing systems   Professionally managed and centrally coordinated marketing channels designed to achieve channel economies and maximum marketing impact.

vertical price fixing   The practice whereby sellers are required to not sell products below a minimum retail price, sometimes called resale price maintenance.

want   A need that is shaped by a person's knowledge, culture, and individual characteristics.

warehouse   A location, often decentralized, that a firm uses to store, consolidate, age, or mix stock; house product-recall programs; or ease tax burdens.

warehouse clubs   Large retail stores (over 100,000 square feet) that require a yearly fee to shop at the store.

warranty   A statement indicating the liability of the manufacturer for product deficiencies.

wasted coverage   People outside a company's target audience who see, hear, or read the company's advertisement.

webcasting   The practice of pushing out corporate and marketing Web site information to online consumers rather than waiting for them to find the site on their own.

Web communities   Web sites that cater to a particular group of individuals who share a common interest.

weighted-point system   A method of establishing screening criteria, assigning them weights, and using them to evaluate new product ideas.

wheel of retailing   A concept that describes how new retail outlets enter the market as low-status, low-margin stores and change gradually in terms of status and margin.

whistleblowers   Employees who report unethical or illegal actions of their employers.

wholesaler-sponsored voluntary chain   A contractual system involving independently owned wholesalers who band together to act like a chain.

word of mouth   People influencing each other during their face-to-face conversations.

workload method   A formula-based method for determining the size of a salesforce that integrates the number of customers served, call frequency, call length, and available time to arrive at a salesforce size.

World Trade Organization   An institution that sets rules governing trade among its members through a panel of experts.

World Wide Web   A part of the Internet that supports a retrieval system that formats information and documents into Web pages.

yield management pricing   The charging of different prices to maximize revenue for a set amount of capacity at a given time.

CHAPTER NOTES

CHAPTER 1

1. Personal interview with David Samuels, February 1999.
2. Web site for the U.S. Patent and Trademark Office.
3. Steven A. Meyerowitz, "Surviving Assaults on Trademarks," *Marketing Management* (no. 1, 1994), pp. 44–46; and Carrie Goerne, "Rollerblade Reminds Everyone That Its Success Is Not Generic," *Marketing News* (March 2, 1992), pp. 1–2.
4. Peter D. Bennett, *Dictionary of Marketing Terms,* 2nd ed. (Lincolnwood, IL: NTC Publishing Group, 1995), p. 166.
5. Frederick E. Webster, Jr., "The Changing Role of Marketing in the Corporation," *Journal of Marketing,* (October 1992), pp. 1–17; and Jagdish N. Sheth and Rajendra S. Sisodia, "Feeling the Heat," *Marketing Management* (Fall 1995), pp. 9–23.
6. Richard P. Bagozzi, "Marketing as Exchange," *Journal of Marketing* (October 1975), pp. 32–39; and Gregory T. Gundlach and Patrick E. Murphy, "Ethical and Legal Foundations of Relational Marketing Exchanges," *Journal of Marketing* (October 1993), pp. 35–46.
7. E. Jerome McCarthy, *Basic Marketing: A Managerial Approach* (Homewood, IL: Richard D. Irwin, 1960); and Walter van Waterschoot and Christophe Van den Bulte. "The 4P Classification of the Marketing Mix Revisited," *Journal of Marketing* (October 1992), pp. 83–93.
8. James Surowiecki, "The Return of Michael Porter," *Fortune* (February, 1999), pp. 135–38; and Kathleen M. Eisenhardt and Shona L. Brown, "Time Pacing: Competing in Markets That Won't Stand Still," *Harvard Business Review* (March–April 1998), pp. 59–69.
9. Rahul Jacob, "The Struggle to Create an Organization for the 21st Century," *Fortune* (April 3, 1995), pp. 90–99; and "Putting a Price on Customer Loyalty," *Dallas Morning News* (June 26, 1994), p. 2H. See also "What's a Loyal Customer Worth?" *Fortune* (December 11, 1995), p. 182.
10. Michael Treacy and Fred D. Wiersema, *The Discipline of Market Leaders* (Reading, MA: Addison-Wesley, 1995); Michael Treacy and Fred Wiersema, "How Market Leaders Keep Their Edge," *Fortune* (February 6, 1995), pp. 88–98; and Michael Treacy, "You Need a Value Discipline—But Which One?" *Fortune* (April 17, 1995), p. 195.
11. "Faded Blues: Levi Struggles to Fit in Again," *Star Tribune* (February 23, 1999), pp. A1, A6.
12. Susan Fournier, Susan Dobseha, and David Glen Mick, "Preventing the Premature Death of Relationship Marketing," *Harvard Business Review* (January–February 1998), pp. 42–51.
13. The material on Rollerblade's current marketing strategy is based on a personal interview with David Samuels, information from the Rollerblade Web site, and Rollerblade sales materials.
14. Joseph Pereira, "Your Inner Skateboard: 'Grinding Shoes,'" *The Wall Street Journal* (November 9, 1998), pp. B1, B4.
15. Robert F. Keith, "The Marketing Revolution," *Journal of Marketing* (January 1960), pp. 35–38.
16. *1952 Annual Report* (New York: General Electric Company, 1952), p. 21.
17. John C. Narver, Stanley F. Slater, and Brian Tietje, "Creating a Market Orientation," *Journal of Market Focused Management* (no. 2, 1998), pp. 241–55; Stanley F. Slater and John C. Narver, "Market Orientation and the Learning Organization," *Journal of Marketing* (July 1995), pp. 63–74; and George S. Day, "The Capabilities of Market-Driven Organizations," *Journal of Marketing* (October 1994), pp. 37–52.
18. Minnette E. Drumwright, "Socially Responsible Organizational Buying: Environmental Concern as a Noneconomic Buying Criterion," *Journal of Marketing* (July 1994), pp. 1–19; Michael E. Porter and Claas van er Linde, "Green and Competitive Ending the Stalemate," *Harvard Business Review* (September–October 1995), pp. 120–34; Jacquelyn Ottman, "Edison Winners Show Smart Environmental Marketing," *Marketing News* (July 17, 1995), pp. 16, 19; and Jacquelyn Ottman, "Mandate for the '90s: Green Corporate Image," *Marketing News* (September 11, 1995), p. 8
19. Shelby D. Hunt and John J. Burnett. "The Macromarketing/Micromarketing Dichotomy: A Taxonomical Model," *Journal of Marketing* (Summer 1982), pp. 9–26.
20. Philip Kotler and Sidney J. Levy, "Broadening the Concept of Marketing," *Journal of Marketing* (January 1969), pp. 10–15.
21. C. K. Prahalad and Kenneth Lieberthal, "The End of Corporate Imperialism," *Harvard Business Review* (July–August 1998), pp. 69–79.

Rollerblade, Inc.: This case was written by Giana Eckhardt of the University of Minnesota.

CHAPTER 2

1. *1997 Annual Report of Ben & Jerry's Homemade, Inc.* (South Burlington, VT: Ben & Jerry's, 1998).
2. Blair S. Walker, "Good-Humored Activist Back to the Fray," *USA Today* (December 8, 1992), pp. 1B–2B.
3. Jim Castelli, "Finding the Right Fit: Are You Weird Enough?" *HR Magazine* (September 1990), pp. 38–39.
4. *1997 Annual Report of Ben & Jerry's.*
5. Roger A. Kerin, Vijay Mahajan, and P. Rajan Varadarajan, *Contemporary Perspectives on Strategic Marketing Planning* (Boston: Allyn & Bacon, 1990), Chapter 1; and Orville C. Walker, Jr., Harper W. Boyd, Jr., and Jean-Claude Larreche, *Marketing Strategy* (Burr Ridge, IL: Richard D. Irwin, 1992), Chapters 1 and 2.
6. Charles W. L. Hill and Gareth R. Jones, *Strategies Management: An Integrated Approach* 4th ed. (Boston: Houghton-Mifflin, 1998).
7. Gary Hamel and C. K. Prahalad, "Strategic Intent," *Harvard Business Review* (May–June 1989), pp. 63–76.
8. Theodore Levitt, "Marketing Myopia," *Harvard Business Review* (July–August 1960), pp. 45–56.
9. James C. Cullins and Jerry I. Porras, "Building Your Company's Vision," *Harvard Business Review* (September–October 1996), pp. 66–77.
10. William McDonough, "Wiser Decisions Could Ensure a Sustainable Future," *Star Tribune* (April 4, 1998), p. A19; Joan Magretta, "Growth

through Global Sustainability," *Harvard Business Review* (January–February 1997), pp. 79–88; and Stuart L. Hart, "Beyond Greening: Strategies for a Sustainable World," *Harvard Business Review* (January–February, 1997), pp. 66–76.

11. W. Edwards Deming, *Out of the Crisis* (Cambridge, MA: MIT Center for Advanced Engineering Study, 1986).

12. Jeffrey Abrahams, *The Mission Statement Book* (Berkeley, CA: Ten Speed Press, 1995), p. 41.

13. Matt Siegel, "The Perils of Culture Conflict," *Fortune* (November 9, 1998), pp. 257–62.

14. Christopher K. Bart, "Sex, Lies, and Mission Statements," *Business Horizons* (November–December 1997), pp. 9–18.

15. *1997 Sears Annual Report* (Chicago: Sears, 1998).

16. *Moody's Industrial Manual,* vol. 2 (New York: Moody's Investors Service, 1997), pp. 4142–4155.

17. Robert S. Kaplan and David P. Norton, "The Balanced Scoreboard Measures That Drive Performance," *Harvard Business Review* (January–February 1992), pp. 71–79.

18. Adapted from "The Experience Curve Reviewed, IV. The Growth Share Matrix of the Product Portfolio" (Boston: The Boston Consulting Group, 1973).

19. Kerin, Mahajan, and Vardarajan, p. 52.

20. Strengths and weaknesses of the BCG technique are based largely on Derek F. Abell and John S. Hammond, *Strategic Market Planning: Problem and Analytic Approaches* (Englewood Cliffs, NJ: Prentice Hall, 1979); and Yoram Wind, Vijay Mahajan, and Donald Swire, "An Empirical Comparison of Standardized Portfolio Models," *Journal of Marketing* (Spring 1983), pp. 89–99.

21. Rich Brown, "Making the Product Portfolio a Basis for Action," *Long Range Planning* (February 1991), pp. 102–10.

22. J. Scott Armstrong and Roderick J. Brodie, "Effects of Portfolio Planning Methods on Decision Making: Experimental Results," *International Journal of Research in Marketing* (Winter 1994), pp. 73–84.

23. George Stalk, Phillip Evans, and Lawrence E. Shulman, "Competing on Capabilities: The New Rules of Corporate Strategy," *Harvard Business Review* (March–April 1992), pp. 57–69.

24. Roger A. Kerin and Robert A. Peterson, *Strategic Marketing Problems: Cases and Comments.* 8th ed. (Englewood Cliffs, NJ: Prentice Hall, 1997), pp. 2–3; and Derek F. Abell, *Defining the Business* (Englewood Cliffs, NJ: Prentice Hall, 1980), p. 18.

25. Christopher Meyer, *East Cycle Time* (New York: Free Press, 1993); and Michael E. Porter, *Competitive Advantage* (New York: Free Press, 1985).

26. Loyd Eskildson, "TQM's Role in Corporate Success: Analyzing the Evidence," *National Productivity Review* (Autumn 1995), pp. 25–38.

27. Roger O. Crockett and Peter Elstrom, "How Motorola Lost Its Way," *Business Week* (May 4, 1998), pp. 140–48; and Daniel Roth, "Burying Motorola," *Fortune* (July 6, 1998), pp. 28–29.

28. Peter Nulty, "Kodak Grabs for Growth Again," *Fortune* (May 16, 1994), pp. 76–78.

29. Ibid.

30. Mark Maremont, "Kodak's New Focus," *Business Week* (January 30, 1995), pp. 63–68.

31. Claudia H. Deutsch, "There's Gold in These Old Photos in the Attic," *The New York Times* (June 30, 1998), p. C6.

32. Michael J. Himowitz, "Kodak's Cool Digital Pix Site," *Fortune* (September 28, 1998), p. 285; The ads were provided by Ogilvy & Mather, Atlanta, GA.

33. Laura Johannes, "Kodak Looks for Another Moment with Film for Pros," *The Wall Street Journal* (March 13, 1998), pp. B1, B6.

34. Emily Nelson, "For Kodak's Advantix, Double Exposure as Company Relaunches Camera System," *The Wall Street Journal* (April 23, 1998), pp. B1, B11; and Linda Grant, "Why Kodak Still Isn't Fixed," *Fortune* (May 11, 1998), pp. 179–81.

35. Tony Walker, "Kodak Focuses on China for Enlarged Growth," *Financial Times* (May 21, 1998), p. 16.

Specialized Bicycle Components, Inc.: This case was written by Giana Eckardt of the University of Minnesota.

APPENDIX A

1. Personal interview with Arthur R. Kydd, St. Croix Venture Partners.

2. Examples of guides to writing marketing plans include: William A. Cohen, *The Marketing Plan* (New York: John Wiley & Sons, Inc., 1995); Mark Nolan, *The Instant Marketing Plan* (Santa Maria, CA: Puma Publishing Company, 1995); and Roman G. Hiebing, Jr., and Scott W. Cooper, *The Successful Marketing Plan,* 2nd ed. (Lincolnwood, IL: NTC Business Books, 1997).

3. Examples of guides to writing business plans include the following: Rhonda M. Abrahms, *The Successful Business Plan: Secrets & Strategies,* 2nd ed. (Grants Pass, OR: The Oasis Press/PSI Research, 1993); Joseph A. Covello and Brian J. Hazelgren, *The Complete Book of Business Plans* (Naperville, IL: Sourcebooks, Inc., 1995); Joseph A. Covello and Brian J. Hazelgren, *Your First Business Plan,* 3rd ed. (Naperville, IL: Sourcebooks, Inc., 1998); and Angela Shupe, ed., *Business Plans Handbook,* vols. 1–4 (Detroit: Gale Research, 1997).

4. Abrahms, *The Successful Business Plan,* p. 30.

5. Some of these points are adapted from Abrahms, pp. 30–38; others are adapted from William Rudelius, *Guidelines for Technical Report Writing* (Minneapolis, MN: University of Minnesota, undated).

6. The authors are indebted to Randall F. Peters and Leah Peters for being allowed to adapt elements of a business plan for Paradise Kitchens, Inc. for the sample marketing plan and for their help and suggestions.

CHAPTER 3

1. Don Tapscott, *Growing Up Digital* (New York: McGraw-Hill, 1998); Melinda Beck, "Generation Y: Next Population Bulge Shows Its Might," *The Wall Street Journal* (February 3, 1997), p. B1; and Faye Rice, "Making Generational Marketing Come of Age," *Fortune* (June 26, 1995), pp. 110–14.

2. "U.S. Consumption of Coffee Drops to Record Low," *Food and Drink Weekly* (April 20, 1998); and "Gourmet Coffee Craze Bucks National Decline in Coffee Consumption," *PR Newswire* (September 29, 1998); Shannon Dortch, "Coffee at Home," *American Demographics* (August 1995), pp. 4–6; and Marcia Mogelonsky, "Instant's Last Drop," *American Demographics* (August 1995), p. 10.

3. Seanna Browder and Emily Thornton, "Reheating Starbucks," *Business Week* (September 28, 1998), pp. 66, 70.

4. "American Marketing Association Special Report on Trends and Forces Shaping the Future of Marketing," (Chicago: American Marketing Association), May 19, 1998; James Heckman, Maricris G. Briones, and Michelle Wirth Fellman, "Outlook 99: A Look at What the Year Ahead Will Bring," *Marketing News* (December 7, 1998); p. 1; Brent Schlender, "Peter Drucker Takes the Long View," *Fortune* (September 28, 1998), pp. 162–73; Michael J. Mandel, "The 21st Century Economy," *Business Week* (August 31, 1998), pp. 58–67; Annetta Miller, "The Millennial Mind-set," *American Demographics* (January 1999); pp. 60–65; Nina Munk, "The New Organization Man," *Fortune* (March 16, 1998), pp. 63–74; and Harry S. Dent, Jr., *The Roaring 2000s* (New York: Simon and Schuster, 1998).

5. U.S. Bureau of the Census, "Current Population Report, Residential Population Projections" (March 1996).

6. Jennifer Cheeseman Day, "Population Projections of the United States by Age, Sex, Race, and Hispanic Origin: 1995–2050," in U.S. Bureau of the Census, "Current Population Reports" (March 1996), p. 25.

7. D. Allan Kerr, "Where There's Gray There's Green," *Marketing News* (June 22, 1998), p. 2.

8. Patricia Braus, "The Baby Boom at Mid-Decade," *American Demographics* (April 1995), pp. 40–45; and Cheryl Russell, "On the Baby-Boom Bandwagon," *American Demographics* (May 1991), pp. 24–31.

9. Marcy Magiera and Pat Sloan, "Levis, Lee Loosen Up for Baby Boomers," *Advertising Age* (August 3, 1992), p. 9.

10. Toddi Gutner, "Generation X: To Be Young, Thrifty, and in the Black," *Business Week* (July 21, 1997), p. 76; Howard Gleckman, "Generation $ Is More Like It," *Business Week* (November 3, 1997), p. 44; Karen Ritchie, "Marketing to Generation X," *American Demographics* (April 1995), pp. 34–39; and Diane Crispell," Generations to 2025," *American Demographics* (January 1995), p. 4.

11. Beck, "Generation Y: Next Population Bulge Shows Its Might"; and Susan Mitchell, "The Next Baby Boom," *American Demographics* (October 1995), pp. 22–31.

12. J. Walker Smith and Ann Clurman, *Rocking the Ages,* (New York: HarperCollins Publishers, Inc., 1997); Kevin T. Higgins, "Generational Marketing," *Marketing Management* (Fall, 1998) pp. 6–9; and Geoffrey Meredith and Charles Schewe, "The Power of Cohorts," *American Demographics* (December 1994), pp. 22–31.

13. Ken Bryson and Lynne M. Casper, "Household and Family Characteristics: March 1997," U.S. Department of Commerce (April 1998); U.S. Bureau of the Census, "Current Population Survey" (March 1998); and Peter Francese, "America at Mid-Decade," *American Demographics* (February 1995), pp. 23–29.

14. Diane Crispell, "Duel-Earner Diversity," *American Demographics* (July 1995), pp. 32–37; and Jan Larson, "Understanding Stepfamilies," *American Demographics* (July 1992), pp. 36–40.

15. Paul Campbell, "Population Projections: States, 1995–2025," Current Population Report, U.S. Department of Commerce (May 1997).

16. Harry S. Dent, Jr., *The Roaring 2000s,* (New York: Simon and Schuster, 1998), p. 211.

17. This discussion is based on Francèse, "America at Mid-Decade"; Maria Shad, Christopher Power, and Laura Zinn, "Suddenly, Asian-Americans Are a Marketer's Dream," *Business Week* (June 17, 1991), pp. 54–55; and Joe Schwartz and Thomas Exter, "All Our Children," *American Demographics* (May 1989), pp. 34–37.

18. "Resident Population of the United States: Estimates by Sex, Race, and Hispanic Origin, with Median Age," U.S. Bureau of the Census (December 28, 1998).

19. Zachary Schiller, "Stalking the New Consumer," *Business Week* (August 28, 1989), pp. 54–62.

20. Christine Dugas, Mark N. Vamos, and Jonathon B. Levine, "Marketing's New Look," *Business Week* (January 26, 1987), pp. 64–69; see also Shawn McKenna, *The Complete Guide to Regional Marketing* (Homewood, IL: Business One Irwin, 1992).

21. William Frey, "The Diversity Myth," *American Demographics* (June 1998), pp. 39–43; and Jeffery D. Zbar, "In Diverse Hispanic World, Image Counts," *Advertising Age* (April 3, 1995), pp. 518–19.

22. Christopher J. Farrell, "The Labor Pool Is Deeper Than It Looks," *Business Week* (November 24, 1997), p. 39; Howard V. Hayghe, "Developments in Women's Labor Force Participation," *Monthly Labor Review* (September 1997), pp. 41–46; and "Labor Force Statistics from the Current Population Survey," Bureau of Labor Statistics (January 1999).

23. Patricia Sellers, "The 50 Most Powerful Women in American Business," *Fortune* (October 12, 1998), pp. 76–98.

24. Julie Ralston, "Chevy Targets Women," *Advertising Age* (August 7, 1995), p. 24; Tim Triplett, "Women and Cigars," *Marketing News* (December 4, 1995), pp. 1, 5; and Chad Rubel, "Parents Magazines Make Room for Daddy," *Marketing News* (February 27, 1995), pp. 1, 5, 14.

25. Jill Smolowe, "Do You Still Know Me?" *Time* (September 12, 1994), p. 60; and Judann Dagnoli, "Value Strategy to Battle Recession," *Advertising Age* (January 7, 1991), pp. 1, 44.

26. Peter Brimelow, "The Education Paradox," *Forbes* (July 6, 1998), pp. 178–79.

27. Michael Mandel, "Yes, Virginia, There Will Be Recessions," *Business Week* (August 31, 1998), p. 64.

28. "The Index of Consumer Sentiment," Survey Research Center, University of Michigan (1998); and Blayne Cutler, "The Feel-Good Index," *American Demographics* (September 1992), pp. 56–60.

29. Bureau of Labor Statistics and the Bureau of the Census, "Annual Demographic Survey" (March 1998), Table H-1.

30. Owen Ullmann, "Forget Saving, America. Your Job Is to Spend," *Business Week* (December 28, 1998), p. 54; Gene Koretz, "Savings' Death Is Exaggerated," *Business Week* (September 14, 1998), p. 26; and Marcia Mogelonsky, "No More Food, Thanks," *American Demographics* (August 1998), p. 59.

31. Berna Miller, "Fun Money," *American Demographics* (March 1997), p. 33.

32. Robert D. Hof, Gary McWilliams, and Gabrielle Saveri, "The 'Click Here' Economy," *Business Week* (June 22, 1998), pp. 122–28; Rochelle Garner, "The Ecommerce Connection," *Sales and Marketing Management* (January 1999), pp. 40–46; Clint Willis, "25 Cool Things You Wish You Had and Will," *Forbes ASAP* (June 1, 1998), pp. 49–60; and Rebecca Piirto, "Cable TV," *American Demographics* (June 1995), pp. 40–43.

33. Neil Gross, Peter Coy, and Otis Post, "The Technology Paradox," *Business Week* (March 6, 1995), pp. 76–84.

34. Leon Jaroff, "Smart's the Word in Detroit," *Time* (February 6, 1995), pp. 50–52.

35. Clint Willis, "25 Cool Things You Wish You Had and Will," *Forbes ASAP* (June 1, 1998), pp. 49–60.

36. Stephanie Anderson, "There's Gold in Those Hills of Soda Bottles," *Business Week* (September 11, 1995), p. 48; Maxine Wilkie, "Asking Americans to Use Less Stuff," *American Demographics* (December 1994), pp. 11–12; and Jacquelyn Ottman, "New and Improved Won't Do," *Marketing News* (January 30, 1995), p. 9.

37. Don Peppers, Martha Rogers, and Bob Dorf, "Is Your Company Ready for One-to-One Marketing?" *Harvard Business Review* (January–February 1999), pp. 151–60; and Peter Burrows, "Instant Info Is Not Enough," *Business Week* (June 22, 1998), p. 144.

38. Eugene Carlson, "Business Maps Plans for the Use of TIGER Geographic Files," *The Wall Street Journal* (June 8, 1990), p. B2; and Ruth Hamel "AAA Goes GIS," *American Demographics* (September 1992), p. 53.

39. Henry Goldblatt, "The End of the Long Distance Club," *Fortune* (May 26, 1997), p. 30; and "Wheel of Fortune," *The Economist* (November 21, 1998), p. 53.

40. DeAnn Weimer, "Don't Be Shocked by Surges in the Price of Power," *Business Week* (July 27, 1998), p. 33

41. Steve Hamm, Amy Cortese, and Susan B. Garland, "Microsoft's Future," *Business Week* (January 19, 1998), pp. 59–68.

42. Michael Porter, *Competitive Advantage* (New York: Free Press, 1985); and Michael Porter, *Competitive Strategy* (New York: Free Press, 1980).

43. Catherine Arnst, "For Lucent, a Shining Moment," *Business Week* (April 21, 1997), p. 126.

44. Cary Hamel and Jeff Sampler, "The E-Corporation," *Fortune* (December 7, 1998), pp. 80–92; Shikhar Ghosh, "Making Business Sense of the Internet," *Harvard Business Review* (March–April 1998), pp. 127–35; Ramon J. Peypoch, "The Case for Electronic Business Communities," *Business Horizons* (September–October 1998), pp. 17–20; Harry S. Dent, Jr., *The Roaring 2000s,* p. 137; and Erick Schonfeld, "Schwab Puts It All Online," *Fortune* (December 7, 1998), pp. 94–100.

45. James B. Treece, Kathleen Kerwin, and Heidi Dawley, "Ford," *Business Week* (April 3, 1995), pp. 94–104; and Keith Hammonds, Kevin Kelly, and Karen Thurston, "The New World of Work," *Business Week* (October 17, 1994), pp. 76–87.

46. Geoffrey Colvin," The Year of the Megamerger," *Fortune* (January 11, 1999), pp. 62–64; and Gene G. Marcial, "That Was Just the Warm-up," *Business Week* (December 28, 1998), p. 151.

47. Michael Mandel, Christopher Farrell, and Catherine Yang, "Land of the Giants," *Business Week* (September 11, 1995), pp. 34–35; and Howard Chua-Eoan, "Too Big or Not Too Big?" *Time* (October 2, 1995), pp. 32–33.

48. "A New Copyright Law?" *Business Week* (August 3, 1998), p. 45.

49. James Heckman, "Laws That Take Effect—and Some Likely to Return—in 1999 Mean Marketers Must Change Some Policies," *Marketing News* (December 7, 1998), pp. 1, 16.

50. "Washington Outlook," *Business Week* (July 5, 1993), p. 43; "Soft on 'Green' Crime?" *Business Week* (August 10, 1992), p. 40; "Execs Get Little Sympathy for Crimes against Nature," *The Wall Street Journal* (March 11, 1992), p. B1; and "Poll: Execs as Green as Public," *Advertising Age* (May 25, 1992), p. 18.

51. Dorothy Cohen, "Trademark Strategy Revisited," *Journal of Marketing* (July 1991), pp. 46–59.

52. Paul Barrett, "High Court Sees Color as Basis for Trademarks," *The Wall Street Journal* (March 29, 1995), p. A6; Paul Barrett, "Color in the Court," *The Wall Street Journal* (January 5, 1995), p. A1; and David Kelly, "Rainbow of Ideas to Trademark Color," *Advertising Age* (April 24, 1995), pp. 20, 22.

53. Paul M. Eng and Marsh Johnston, "Get Your Hands Off My .Com," *Business Week* (July 28, 1997), p. 88; and John R. Wilke, "Who Owns the Name 'Internet Explorer'? (Hint: Not Microsoft)," *The Wall Street Journal* (June 26, 1998), p. A1.

54. Dick Mercer, "Tempest in a Soup Can," *Advertising Age* (October 17, 1994), pp. 25–29.

55. Mark McFadden, "The BBB on the WWW," *HP Professional* (September 1997), p. 36.

CHAPTER 4

1. *Fighting Alcohol Abuse through Awareness & Education* and *Anheuser-Busch Environmental Profile* (St. Louis: Anheuser-Busch Companies, 1998).

2. For a discussion of the definition of ethics, see Eugene R. Lazniak and Patrick E. Murphy, *Ethical Marketing Decisions: The Higher Road* (Boston: Allyn & Bacon, 1993), chapter 1.

3. Verne E. Henderson, "The Ethical Side of Enterprise," *Sloan Management Review* (Spring 1982), pp. 37–47. See also, Joseph L. Badaracco, Jr., *Defining Moments: When Managers Must Choose between Right and Right* (Boston: Harvard Business School Press, 1997).

4. "Just How Honest Are You?" *Inc.* (February 1995), p. 104.

5. "In Hong Kong, Tobacco Promotes Away," *The Wall Street Journal* (June 30, 1998), p. B8; "Exporting Death," *Time* (April 13, 1998), p. 63; Ray O. Werner, "Marketing and the Supreme Court in Transition, 1982–1984," *Journal of Marketing* (Summer 1985), pp. 97–105; and Jane Bryant Quinn, "Computer Program Deceives Consumers," *Dallas Morning News* (March 2, 1998), p. B3.

6. "Embracing Ethics," *Dallas Morning News* (June 10, 1998), pp. 1D, 10D; *U.S. Employee Perceptions of Ethics in Organizations* (Indianapolis, IN: Walker Information, 1998); "Who's Trusted, Who's Not?" *American Demographics* (June 1995), p. 55; and James Krohe, Jr., "Ethics Are Nice, But Business Is Business," *Across the Board* (April 1997), pp. 16–22.

7. See, for example, Lawrence B. Chonko, *Ethical Decision Making in Marketing* (Thousand Oaks, CA: Sage, 1995).

8. Thomas Donaldson, "Values in Tension: Ethics Away from Home," *Harvard Business Review* (September–October 1996), pp. 48–62.

9. "Levi Only Comfortable Dealing with Countries That Fit Its Image," *Dallas Morning News* (January 9, 1995), p. D2. See also William Beaver, "Levi's Is Leaving China," *Business Horizons* (March–April 1995), pp. 35–40.

10. Barry R. Shapiro, "Economic Espionage," *Marketing Management* (Spring 1998), pp. 56–58; and Damon Darlin, "Where Trademarks Are Up for Grabs," *The Wall Street Journal* (December 5, 1989), pp. B1, B4.

11. "Borrowing Software," *Brandweek* (March 2, 1998), p. 20; and "Piracy Losses Top $12 Billion," *Dallas Morning News* (February 17, 1999), p. 2D.

12. Vern Terpstra and Kenneth David, *The Cultural Environment of International Business,* 3rd ed. (Cincinnati: South-Western Publishing Co., 1991), p. 12.

13. "Carnivore in the Cabbage Patch," *U.S. News and World Report* (January 20, 1997), p. 69.

14. "Three Ad Agencies Settle FTC Charges of Deceptive Car-Leasing Commercials," *The Wall Street Journal* (January 21, 1998), p. B2.

15. "A Little Privacy, Please," *Business Week* (March 6, 1998), pp. 98–102; "Is Nothing Private?" *U.S. News & World Report* (June 15, 1998), p. 59; and "On-Line Groups Are Offering Up Private Plans," *The Wall Street Journal* (June 22, 1998), pp. B1, B3.

16. Lois Therrion, "Want Shelf Space at Supermarkets? Ante Up," *Business Week* (August 7, 1989), pp. 60–61.

17. "In Crackdown on Fraud, FTC Moves to Regulate Telemarketing Practices," *The Wall Street Journal* (February 10, 1995), p. B12. See also, "Special Report: Fighting Phone Fraud," *AARP Bulletin* (December 1997), pp. 9–12.

18. William J. Holstein, "Corporate Spy Wars," *U.S. News & World Report* (February 23, 1998), pp. 46–52; and "More Spies Targeting U.S. Firms," *Dallas Morning News* (January 12, 1998), pp. 1D, 4D.

19. "P&G Expected to Get about $120 Million in Settlement of Chewy-Cookie Lawsuit," *The Wall Street Journal* (September 11, 1989), p. B10.

20. Shapiro, "Economic Espionage."

21. "Honda Is Expected to Pay $316 Million in Kickback Suit," *Dallas Morning News* (July 29, 1998), p. 2D; and Andy Pasztor, *When the Pentagon Was for Sale: Inside America's Biggest Defense Scandal* (New York: Scribner, 1995).

22. "Bye-Bye to Bribes," *U.S. News & World Report* (December 22, 1997), pp. 39–44.

23. "Six Deadly Sins," *The Economist* (March 7, 1998), pp. 12–13.

24. "Good Grief," *The Economist* (April 8, 1995), p. 57. See also James Krohe, Jr., "The Big Business of Business Ethics," *Across the Board* (May 1997), pp. 23–29.

25. "Good Grief."

26. Savior L. S. Nwachukwu and Scott J. Vitell, Jr., "The Influence of Corporate Culture on Managerial Ethical Judgments," *Journal of Business Ethics,* vol. 17 (1997), pp. 757–76; and Ismael R. Akaah and Daultram Lund, "The Influence of Personal Values and Organizational Values on Marketing Professionals' Ethical Behavior," *Journal of Business Ethics,* vol. 13 (1994), pp. 417–30.

27. J. Badaracco, Jr., and A. Webb, "Business Ethics: A View from the Trenches," *California Management Review* (Winter 1995), pp. 8–28; "Workers Who Blow the Whistle on Bosses Often Pay a High Price," *The Wall Street Journal* (July 18, 1995), p. B1; and Randi L. Sims and John P. Keenan, "Predictors of External Whistleblowing: Organizational and Intrapersonal Variables," *Journal of Business Ethics* (March 1998), pp. 411–21.

28. For an extensive discussion on these moral philosophies, see R. Eric Reidenbach and Donald P. Robin, *Ethics and Profits* (Englewood Cliffs, NJ: Prentice Hall, 1989); Chonko, *Ethical Decision Making;* and Lazniak and Murphy, *Ethical Marketing Decisions.*

29. "Bad Apple for Baby," *Financial World* (June 27, 1989), p. 48; and "What Led Beech-Nut Down the road to Disgrace," *Business Week* (February 22, 1988), pp. 124–27.

30. James Q. Wilson, "Adam Smith on Business Ethics," *California Management Review* (Fall 1989), pp. 59–72; Edward W. Coker, "Smith's Concept of the Social System," *Journal of Business Ethics,* vol. 9 (1990), pp. 139–42; and George M.Zinkhan, Michael Bisesi, and Mary Jane Saxton, "MBAs: Changing Attitudes Toward Marketing Dilemmas," *Journal of Business Ethics,* vol. 8 (1989), pp. 963–74.

31. Alix M. Freedman, "Bad Reaction: Nestlé's Bid to Crash Baby-Formula Market Ache U.S. Stirs a Row," *The Wall Street Journal* (February

16, 1989), pp. A1, A6; and Alix Freedman, "Nestlé to Drop Claim on Label of Its Formula," *The Wall Street Journal* (March 13, 1989), p. B5.

32. Robert B. Reich, "The New Meaning of Corporate Social Responsibility," *California Management Review* (Winter 1998), pp. 8–17.

33. Milton Friedman, "A Friedman Doctrine: The Social Responsibility of Business Is to Increase Profits," *New York Times Magazine* (September 13, 1970), p. 126.

34. "Beating the Odds in Biotech," *Newsweek* (October 12, 1992), p. 63.

35. "Can Perrier Purify Its Reputation?" *Business Week* (February 26, 1990), p. 45; and "Perrier Expands North American Recall to Rest of Globe," *The Wall Street Journal* (February 15, 1990), pp. B1, B4.

36. "Environment Winners Show Sustainable Strategies," *Marketing News* (April 27, 1998), p. 6; and Bennett Davis, "Whole Earth Commerce," *Ambassador Magazine* (May 1998), pp. 36–41. See also, Ajay Menon and Anil Menon, "Environpreneurial Marketing Strategy: The Emergence of Corporate Environmentalism as Market Strategy," *Journal of Marketing* (January 1997), pp. 51–67; and Cathy L. Hartman and Edwin R. Stafford, "Crafting 'Environpreneurial' Value Chain Strategies through Green Alliances," *Business Horizons* (March–April 1998), pp. 62–72.

37. See Olivier Boiral and Jean-Marie Sala, "Environmental Management: Should Industry Adapt ISO 14001?" *Business Horizons* (January–February 1998), pp. 57–64.

38. For an extended discussion on this topic, see P. Rajan Varadarajan and Anil Menon, "Cause-Related Marketing: A Coalignment of Marketing Strategy and Corporate Philanthropy," *Journal of Marketing* (July, 1988), pp. 58–74. The examples given are found in this article and Daniel Kadlec, "The New World of Giving," *Time* (May 5, 1997), pp. 62–63; and "Companies Trumpet Virtues of Causes in Selling Products," *Dallas Morning News* (February 15, 1998), pp. 1J, 11J.

39. "Reinventing Cause Marketing," *Brandweek* (October 27, 1997), p. 17; "A Market For Charity," *Dallas Morning News* (February 15, 1998), pp. 1J, 11J; "Switching for a Cause," *American Demographics* (April 1997), pp. 26–27; and Kadlec, "The New World of Giving."

40. These steps are adapted from J. J. Carson and G. A. Steiner, *Measuring Business Social Performance: The Corporate Social Audit* (New York: Committee for Economic Development, 1974). See also, Sandra A. Waddock and Samuel B. Graves, "The Corporate Social Performance–Financial Performance Link," *Strategic Management Journal,* vol. 18 (1997), pp. 303–19.

41. D. A. Rondinelli and G. Vastag, "International Standards and Corporate Policies: An Integrated Framework," *California Management Review* (Fall 1996), pp. 106–22.

42. "Santa's Sweatshop," *U.S. News & World Report* (December 16, 1996), pp. 50–60.

43. Cyndee Miller, "Marketers Weight Effects of Sweatshop Crackdown," *Marketing News* (May 12, 1997), pp. 1, 19. See also, "Nike Battles Backlash from Overseas Sweatshops," *Marketing News* (November 9, 1998), p. 14.

44. Paul Bernstein, "Cheating: The New National Pastime?" *Business* (October–December 1995), pp. 24–33; "Video Vice: 1 in 10 Copy Videotapes Illegally," *USA Weekend* (February 9–11, 1996), p. 18; and "Trade Tripwires," *The Economist* (August 27, 1994), p. 61.

45. See, for example, "Consumers Lean Toward Green," *Marketing News* (August 31, 1998), p. 2; and Tibbett L. Speer, "Growing the Green Market," *American Demographics* (August 1997), pp. 45–49.

46. Speer, "Growing the Green Market."

47. "FTC Stands by Regs for 'Green' Ad Claims," *Advertising Age* (October 7, 1996), p. 61.

Pricing in the Pharmaceutical Industry: Sources: "U.S. Has Developed an Expensive Habit; Now, How to Pay for It?" *The Wall Street Journal* November 16, 1998), pp. A1, A10; "Drug Costs Can Leave Elderly a Grim Choice: Pills or Other Needs," *The Wall Street Journal* (November 17, 1998), pp. A1, A15; and "Why Generic Drugs Often Can't Compete Against Brand Names," *The Wall Street Journal* (November 18, 1998), pp. A1, A10; and "Who's Really Raising Drug Prices?" *Time* (March 8, 1999), pp. 46–48.

CHAPTER 5

1. Personal interview with Dr. Daniel E. Cohen, Chief Executive Officer of CNS, Inc., June 1998.

2. These estimates are based on statistics from *Direction of Trade Statistics Yearbook, 1998* (Washington, DC: International Monetary Fund, 1998), and trend projections by the authors. Trade statistics reported in this chapter also come from these sources, unless otherwise indicated.

3. "American Trade Policy," *The Economist* (January 30, 1999), pp. 63–65.

4. "Bartering Gains Currency in Hard-Hit Southeast Asia," *The Wall Street Journal* (April 6, 1998), p. A10; and Beatrice B. Lund, "Corporate Barter as a Marketing Strategy," *Marketing News* (March 3, 1997), p. 8.

5. Dennis R. Appleyard and Alfred J. Field, Jr., *International Economies,* 3rd ed. (Burr Ridge, IL: Irwin/McGraw-Hill, 1998), pp. 10–11.

6. Appleyard and Field, *International Economies.*

7. Michael E. Porter, *The Competitive Advantage of Nations* (New York: The Free Press, 1990), pp. 577–615; and Michael E. Porter, "Why Nations Triumph," *Fortune* (March 12, 1990), pp. 94–108. For another view, see David S. Landes, *The Wealth and Poverty of Nations* (New York: W. W. Norton & Company, 1998).

8. "Rougher Sailing Across the Atlantic," *Business Week* (July 27, 1998), p. 29; "Japan's Price of Protection," *Fortune* (March 6, 1995), p. 48; and "New World Trade Chief Fears Economic Nationalism," *Dallas Morning News* (March 22, 1995), p. 11D.

9. "Trade Winds," *The Economist* (November 8, 1997), pp. 85–86.

10. "The Beef Over Bananas," *The Economist* (March 6, 1999), pp. 65–66; Gary C. Hufbauer and Kimberly A. Elliott, *Measuring the Cost of Protection in the United States* (Washington D.C.: Institute for International Economies, 1994).

11. "It Ain't Just Peanuts," *Business Week* (December 18, 1995), p. 30.

12. "The WTO Crunch," *The Economist* (April 4, 1998), pp. 78–79; Paul Magrusson, "Why the WTO Needs an Overhaul," *Business Week* (June 29, 1998), p. 35.

13. "Industrial Evolution," *Business Week* (April 27, 1998), pp. 100–101; for a comprehensive report on marketing strategy for the European Union, see Colin Egan and Peter McKiernan, *Inside Fortress Europe: Strategies for the Single Market* (Reading, MA: Addison-Wesley, 1994).

14. "Special Report: The Euro," *Business Week* (April 27, 1998), pp. 90–108.

15. Joachim Bamrud, "Setting the Agenda: From Miami to Brazil," *Latin Trade* (June 1998), pp. 3A–12A.

16. "Special Report: East Asian Economies," *The Economist* (March 7, 1998); and "Will East Asia Slam the Door?" *The Economist* (September 12, 1998), p. 88.

17. "Juniper's New-Router Shipments Kick Off Race in Internet Devices," *The Wall Street Journal* (September 16, 1998), p. 86; and General Mills, Inc., *Annual Report,* 1998.

18. For an excellent overview of different types of global companies and marketing strategies, see Warren J. Keegan, *Global Marketing Management,* 6th ed. (Upper Saddle River, NJ: Prentice Hall, Inc., 1998), pp. 43–54.

19. "Global Companies Don't Work; Multinationals Do," *Advertising Age* (April 18, 1994), p. 23.

20. For an extensive discussion on identifying global consumers, see Jean-Pierre Jeannet and H. David Hennessey, *Global Marketing Strategies,* 4th ed. (Boston: Houghton Mifflin Company, 1998).

21. "Ready to Shop Until They Drop," *Business Week* (June 22, 1998), pp. 104 ff; Chip Walker, "Can TV Save the Planet?" *American Demographics* (May 1996), pp. 21–29; *Global Teenager Is a Myth, But Asian Teenagers Are Going Global* (New York: McCann-Erickson, 1997); "Teens Seen as the First Truly Global Consumers," *Marketing*

News (March 27, 1995), p. 9; Shawn Tully, "Teens: The Most Global Market of All," *Fortune* (May 16, 1994), pp. 90–97; and Dan S. Acuff, *What Kids Buy and Why* (New York: The Free Press, 1997).

22. For comprehensive references on cross-cultural aspects of marketing, see Paul A. Herbig, *Handbook of Cross-Cultural Marketing* (New York: The Halworth Press, 1998); and Jean-Claude Usunier, *Marketing Across Cultures*, 2nd ed. (London: Prentice Hall Europe, 1996). Unless otherwise indicated, examples found in this section appear in these excellent references.

23. "McDonald's Adapts Mac Attack to Foreign Tastes with Expansion," *Dallas Morning News* (December 7, 1997), p. 3H; and "Taking Credit," *The Economist* (November 2, 1996), p. 75.

24. "Clash of Cultures," *Brandweek* (May 4, 1998), p. 28. See also, R. L. Tung, *Business Negotiations with the Japanese* (Lexington, MA: Lexington Books, 1993).

25. These examples appear in Del I. Hawkins, Roger J. Best, and Kenneth A. Coney, *Consumer Behavior*, 7th ed. (Burr Ridge, IL: Irwin/Mc-Graw-Hill, 1998), Chap. 2.

26. "Greeks Protest Coke's Use of Parthenon," *Dallas Morning News* (August 17, 1992), p. D4.

27. "Buying American," *American Demographics* (March 1998), pp. 32–38; and Poly LaBarre, "Quality's Silent Partner," *Industry Week* (April 18, 1994), pp. 47–48.

28. "Geo Gaffes," *Brandweek* (February 23, 1998), p. 20.

29. The following examples appear in "Global Thinking Paces Computer Biz," *Advertising Age* (March 6, 1995), p. 10; and "U.S. Firms Sometimes Lose It in the Translation," *Dallas Morning News* (August 17, 1992), pp. D1, D4.

30. Terrence A. Shimp and Subhash Sharma, "Consumer Ethnocentrism: Construction and Validation of the CETSCALE," *Journal of Marketing Research* (August 1987), pp. 280–89.

31. Subhash Sharma, Terrence Shimp, and Jeongshin Shin, "Consumer Ethnocentrism: A Test of Antecedents and Moderators," *Journal of the Academy of Marketing Science* (Winter 1995), pp. 26–37; Joel Herche, "A Note on the Predictive Validity of the CETSCALE," *Journal of the Academy of Marketing Science* (Summer 1992), pp. 261–64; Richard G. Netemeyer, Srinivas Durvasula, and Donald R. Lichtenstein, "A Cross-National Assessment of the Reliability and Validity of the CETSCALE," *Journal of Marketing Research* (August 1991), pp. 320–27; Jill Gabrielle Klein, Richard Ettenson, and Marlene D. Morris, "The Animosity Model of Foreign Product Purchase: An Empirical Test in the People's Republic of China," *Journal of Marketing* (January 1998), pp. 89–100; and Shimp and Sharma, "Consumer Ethnocentrism."

32. This example is based on "Global Coffee Market Share Comparisons," *Advertising Age* (December 10, 1995), p. 47; Carla Rapoport, "Nestlé's Brand Building Machine," *Fortune* (September 19, 1995), pp. 147–56; and Nestlé Corporation, *Annual Report*, 1997.

33. "Selling in Russia: The March on Moscow," *The Economist*, March 18, 1995, pp. 65–66.

34. "Rubles? Who Needs Rubles?" *Business Week* (April 13, 1998), pp. 45–46.

35. "Russia and Central-Eastern Europe: World's Apart," *Brandweek* (May 4, 1998), pp. 30–31; "We Will Bury You . . . With a Snickers Bar," *U.S. News & World Report* (January 26, 1998), pp. 50–51; and "Selling in Russia."

36. Chip Walker, "The Global Middle Class," *American Demographics* (September 1995), pp. 40–47.

37. "Consumer Abroad: Developing Shopaholics," *U.S. News & World Report* (February 10, 1997), p. 55.

38. "Mattel Plans to Double Sales Abroad," *The Wall Street Journal* (February 11, 1998), pp. A3, A11.

39. Philip R. Cateora and John L. Graham, *International Marketing*, 10th ed. (Burr Ridge, IL: Irwin/McGraw-Hill, 1999), p. 560.

40. This discussion is based on Jean-Louis Mucchielli, Peter J. Buckley, and Victor V. Cordell, *Globalization and Regionalization: Strategies,*

Policies, and Economic Environments (New York: The Halworth Press, 1998); "European Union: Europe's Mid-Life Crisis," *The Economist* (May 31, 1997), pp. 38–42; and "East Asian Economies."

41. "Small Firms Flock to Quality System," *Nation's Business* (March 1998), pp. 65–67.

42. For an extensive examination of these market entry options, see, for example, Masaaki Kotake and Kristiaan Helsen, *Global Marketing Management* (New York: John Wiley & Sons, 1998); Johny K. Johansson, *Global Marketing* (Chicago: Richard D. Irwin, 1997); Vern Terpstra and Ravi Sarathy, *International Marketing*, 7th ed. (Fort Worth, TX: The Dryden Press, 1997); Sak Onkuisit and John J. Shaw, *International Marketing*, 3rd ed. (Upper Saddle River, NJ: Prentice Hall, 1997); Keegan, *Global Marketing Management;* and Cateora and Graham, *International Marketing.*

43. Harley Davidson, *Annual Report and 10-K Report*, 1997.

44. U.S. Department of Commerce, *Survey of Current Business* (April 1998).

45. McDonald's *Annual Report*, 1997; and "Globalization: Get Rich Quick," *Time* (April 13, 1998), pp. 204–5.

46. Avraham Shama, "Entry Strategies of U.S. Firms to the Newly Independent States, Baltic States, and Eastern European Countries," *California Management Review* (Spring 1995), pp. 90–109.

47. Michael Hirsh, "The New China: Tricks of the Trade," *Newsweek* (June 29, 1998), pp. 40–42.

48. Masaaki Kotake and Maria Cecilia Coutinho de Arruda, "South America's Free Trade Gambit," *Marketing Management* (Spring 1998), pp. 39–46; "Going It Alone," *The Economist* (April 19, 1997), pp. 64–65; and "Mercedes: Made in Alabama," *Fortune* (July 7, 1997), pp. 150 ff.

49. Shama, "Entry Strategies of U.S. Firms."

50. The examples are found in "It's Goo, Goo, Goo, Goo Vibrations at the Gerber Lab," *The Wall Street Journal* (December 4, 1996), pp. A1, A6; Donald R. Graber, "How to Manage a Global Product Development Process," *Industrial Marketing Management* (November 1996), pp. 483–489; and Usunier, *Marketing Across Cultures.*

51. This discussion is based on John Fahy and Fuyuki Taguchi, "Reassessing the Japanese Distribution System," *Sloan Management Review* (Winter 1995), pp. 49–61.

52. Edward Tse, "The Right Way to Achieve Profitable Growth in the Chinese Consumer Market," *Strategy & Business* (Second Quarter 1998), pp. 10–21.

53. "Rotten Apples," *Dallas Morning News* (April 7, 1998), p. 14A.

54. "Copyright Scope Limited for Some Firms," *The Wall Street Journal* (March 10, 1998), p. B10; "Parallel Imports: A Grey Area," *The Economist* (June 13, 1998), pp. 61–62; and "When Grey Is Good," *The Economist* (August 22, 1998), p. 17.

CNS, Inc., and 3M: Breathe Right® Nasal Strips: This case was prepared by Giana Eckardt. Sources: *CNS, Inc., 1997 Annual Report* (Minneapolis, MN: CNS, Inc., 1998); personal interview with Dr. Daniel E. Cohen, Chief Executive Officer of CNS (June 1998).

CHAPTER 6

1. Elena Scotti, "Born to be Mild, or Wild?" *BRANDWEEK* (March 16, 1998), pp. 22–23; Jon Berry, "Consumers Keep the Upper Hand," *American Demographics* (September 1998), pp. 20–22; "GM Taps Harris to Help Lure Women," *Advertising Age* (February 17, 1997), pp. 1, 37; "Dealer Dilemma," *BRANDWEEK* (March 16, 1998), p. 22; and "Elle Launches Guide for Women Car Buyers," *Advertising Age* (April 6, 1998), p. 34.

2. James F. Engel, Roger D. Blackwell, and Paul Miniard, *Consumer Behavior*, 9th ed. (Fort Worth, TX: Dryden Press, 1998). See also, Gordon C. Bruner III and Richard J. Pomazal, "Problem Recognition: The Crucial First Stage of the Consumer Decision Process," *Journal of Consumer Marketing* (Winter 1988), pp. 53–63.

3. For thorough descriptions of consumer experience and expertise, see Stephen J. Hoch and John Deighton, "Managing What Consumers

Learn from Experience," *Journal of Marketing* (April 1989), pp. 1–20; and Joseph W. Alba and J. Wesley Hutchinson, "Dimensions of Consumer Expertise," *Journal of Consumer Research* (March 1987), pp. 411–54.

4. For in-depth studies on external information search patterns, see Sridhar Moorthy, Brian T. Ratchford, and Debabrata Tulukdar, "Consumer Information Search Revisited: Theory and Empirical Analysis," *Journal of Consumer Research* (March 1997), pp. 263–77; Joel E. Urbany, Peter R. Dickson, and William L. Wilkie, "Buyer Uncertainty and Information Search," *Journal of Consumer Research* (March 1992), pp. 452–63; and Sharon E. Beatty and Scott M. Smith, "External Search Effort: An Investigation Across Several Product Categories," *Journal of Consumer Research* (June 1987), pp. 83–95.

5. For an extended discussion on evaluative criteria, see Del J. Hawkins, Roger J. Best, and Kenneth A. Coney, *Consumer Behavior,* 7th ed. (New York: Irwin/McGraw-Hill, 1998), pp. 550–67.

6. John A. Howard, *Buyer Behavior in Marketing Strategy,* 2nd ed. (Englewood Cliffs, NJ: Prentice Hall, 1994), pp. 101, 128–89. For an extended discussion on consumer choice sets, see Allan D. Shocker, Moshe Ben-Akiva, Bruno Boccara, and Prakesh Nedungadi, "Consideration Set Influences on Consumer Decision-Making and Choice: Issues, Models, and Suggestions," *Marketing Letters* (August 1991), pp. 181–98.

7. William J. McDonald, "Time Use in Shopping: The Role of Personal Characteristics," *Journal of Retailing* (Winter 1994), pp. 345–66; Robert J. Donovan, John R. Rossiter, Gillian Marcoolyn, and Andrew Nesdale, "Store Atmosphere and Purchasing Behavior,"*Journal of Retailing* (Fall 1994), pp. 283–94; and Eric A. Greenleaf and Donald R. Lehman, "Reasons for Substantial Delay in Consumer Decision Making," *Journal of Consumer Research* (September 1995), pp. 186–99.

8. For a review of how computer-mediated buying can influence the consumer decision process, see Russell S. Winer et al., "Choice in Computer-Mediated Environments," *Marketing Letters,* vol. 8, no. 3 (1997), pp. 287–96.

9. "Future Shop," *Forbes ASAP* (April 6, 1998), pp. 37–52; "General Motors' to Take Nationwide Test Drive on Web," *The Wall Street Journal* (September 28, 1998), p. B4.

10. Ruth N. Bolton and James H. Drew, "A Multistage Model of Customers' Assessment of Service Quality and Value," *Journal of Consumer Research* (March 1991), pp. 376–84.

11. Jagdish N. Sheth, Banwari Mitral, and Bruce Newman, *Consumer Behavior* (Fort Worth, TX: Dryden Press, 1999), p. 22.

12. Rahul Jacob, "The Struggle to Create an Organization for the 21st Century," *Fortune* (April 3, 1995), pp. 90–99.

13. "Customers, 800-Lines May Not Connect," *The Wall Street Journal* (November 20, 1990), p. B1.

14. For an overview of research on involvement, see John C. Mowen and Michael Minor, *Consumer Behavior,* 5th ed. (Upper Saddle River, NJ: Prentice Hall 1998), pp. 64–68; and Frank R. Kardes, *Consumer Behavior* (Reading, MA: Addison-Wesley, 1999), pp. 256–58.

15. For an overview on the three problem-solving variations, see Hawkins, Best, and Coney, *Consumer Behavior,* pp. 498–501; Howard, *Buyer Behavior,* pp. 69–162.

16. Russell Belk, "Situational Variables and Consumer Behavior," *Journal of Consumer Research* (December 1975), pp. 157–63. Representative recent studies on situational influences are discussed in Mowen and Minor, *Consumer Behavior,* pp. 451–75.

17. A. H. Maslow, *Motivation and Personality* (New York: Harper & Row, 1970). Also see Richard Yalch and Frederic Brunel, "Need Hierarchies in Consumer Judgments of Product Designs: Is It Time to Reconsider Maslow's Hierarchy?" in Kim Corfman and John Lynch, eds., *Advances in Consumer Research* (Provo, UT: Association for Consumer Research, 1996), pp. 405–10.

18. Arthur Koponen, "The Personality Characteristics of Purchasers," *Journal of Advertising Research* (September 1960), pp. 89–92; Joel B.

Cohen, "An Interpersonal Orientation to the Study of Consumer Behavior," *Journal of Marketing Research* (August 1967), pp. 270–78; and Rena Bartos, *Marketing to Women Around the World* (Cambridge, MA: Harvard Business School, 1989).

19. Terry Clark, "International Marketing and National Character: A Review and Proposal for an Integrative Theory," *Journal of Marketing* (October 1990), pp. 66–79.

20. For an interesting analysis of self-concept, see Russell W. Belk, "Possessions and the Extended Self," *Journal of Consumer Research* (September 1988), pp. 139–68.

21. Myron Magnet, "Let's Go for Growth," *Fortune* (March 7, 1994), p. 70.

22. This example provided in Michael R. Solomon, *Consumer Behavior,* 4th ed. (Upper Saddle River, NJ: Prentice Hall, 1999), p. 59.

23. For further reading on subliminal perception, see Anthony G. Greenwald, Sean C. Draine, and Richard L. Abrams, "Three Cognitive Markers of Unconscious Semantic Activation," *Science* (September 1996), pp. 1699–1701; Joel Saegert, "Why Marketing Should Quit Giving Subliminal Advertising the Benefit of the Doubt," *Psychology & Marketing* (Summer 1987), pp. 107–20; Dennis L. Rosen and Surendra N. Singh, "An Investigation of Subliminal Embed Effect on Multiple Measures of Advertising Effectiveness," *Psychology & Marketing* (March/April 1992), pp. 157–173; and Kathryn T. Theus, "Subliminal Advertising and the Psychology of Processing Unconscious Stimuli: A Review of Research," *Psychology & Marketing* (May/June 1994), pp. 271–90.

24. "I Will Love This Story," *U.S. News & World Report* (May 12, 1997), p. 12; "Dr. Feelgood Goes Subliminal," *Business Week* (November 6, 1995), p.6; and "Firm Gets Message Out Subliminally," *Dallas Morning News* (February 2, 1997), pp. 1H, 6H.

25. "Customer Loyalty: Going, Going . . . ," *American Demographics* (September 1997), pp. 20–23; *Brand-Driven Marketers Are Beating Themselves in the War Against Price-Based and Private Label Competition* (New York: Bates USA, 1994).

26. Martin Fishbein and I. Aizen, *Belief, Attitude, Intention and Behavior: An Introduction to Theory and Research* (Reading, MA: Addison Wesley Publishing, 1975), p. 6.

27. Richard J. Lutz, "Changing Brand Attitudes through Modification of Cognitive Structure," *Journal of Consumer Research* (March 1975), pp. 49–59. See also, Mowen and Minor, *Consumer Behavior,* pp. 287–88.

28. "Pepsi's Gamble Hits Freshness Dating Jackpot," *Advertising Age* (September 19, 1994), p. 50.

29. "The Marketing 100: Colgate Total," *Advertising Age* (June 29, 1998), p. 544.

30. "The Frontiers of Psychographics," *American Demographics* (July 1996), pp. 38–43; http://future.sri.com. See also, "You Can Buy A Thrill: Chasing the Ultimate Rush," *American Demographics* (June 1997), pp. 47–51.

31. See, for example, Lawrence F. Feick and Linda Price, "The Market Maven: A Diffuser of Marketplace Information," *Journal of Marketing* (January 1987), pp. 83–97; and Peter H. Block, "The Product Enthusiast: Implications for Marketing Strategy," *Journal of Consumer Marketing* (Summer 1986), pp. 51–61.

32. "Survey: If You Must Know, Just Ask One of These Men," *Marketing News* (October 25, 1992), p. 13.

33. "Maximizing the Market with Influentials," *American Demographics* (July 1995), p. 42.

34. "Put People Behind the Wheel," *Advertising Age* (March 22, 1993), p. S-28.

35. "Importance of Image," *The Wall Street Journal* (August 12, 1985), p. 19; and "What Soviets Think: A Gallup Poll," *Advertising Age* (February 28, 1990), p. 46.

36. Representative recent work on positive and negative word of mouth can be found in Robert E. Smith and Christine A. Vogt, "The Effects of Integrating Advertising and Negative Word-of-Mouth Communications on Message Processing and Response," *Journal of Consumer*

Psychology, 4 (1995), pp. 133–51; Paula Bone, "Word-of-Mouth Effects on Short-Term and Long-Term Product Judgments," *Journal of Business Research,* 32 (1995), pp. 213–23; Chip Walker, "Word of Mouth," *American Demographics* (July 1995), pp. 38–45; and Dale F. Duhan, Scott D. Johnson, James B. Wilcox, and Gilbert D. Harrell, "Influences on Consumer Use of Word-of-Mouth Recommendation Sources," *Journal of the Academy of Marketing Science* (Fall 1997), pp. 283–95.

37. "We Will Bury You . . . With a Snickers Bar," *U.S. News and World Report* (January 26, 1998), p. 50ff; "A Beer Tampering Scare in China Shows Peril of Global Marketing," *The Wall Street Journal* (November 3, 1995), p. B1; and "Pork Rumors Vex Indonesia," *Advertising Age* (February 16, 1989), p. 36.

38. For an extended discussion on reference groups, see Wayne D. Hoyer and Deborah J. MacInnis, *Consumer Behavior* (Boston: Houghton Mifflin Co., 1997), Chapter 15.

39. For an extended discussion on consumer socialization, see George P. Moschis, *Consumer Socialization* (Lexington, MA: Lexington Books, 1987).

40. "Get 'em While They're Young," *Marketing News* (November 10, 1997), p. 2.

41. This discussion is based on J. Paul Peter and Jerry C. Olson, *Consumer Behavior and Marketing Strategy,* 5th ed. (New York: Irwin/McGraw-Hill 1999), pp. 341–43; Robert E. Wilkes, "Household Life-Cycle Stages, Transitions, and Product Expenditures," *Journal of Consumer Research* (June 1995), pp. 27–42; and Jan Larson, "The New Face of Homemakers," *American Demographics* (September 1997), pp. 45–50.

42. Diane Crispell, "Dual-Earner Diversity," *American Demographics* (July 1995), pp. 32–37.

43. "Wearing the Pants," *BRANDWEEK* (October 20, 1997), pp. 20, 22; and "Look Who's Shopping," *Progressive Grocer* (January 1998), p. 18.

44. "Marketing," *BRANDWEEK* (May 18, 1998), pp. 46–52; and "Teen Green," *American Demographics* (February 1998), p. 39. See also, James V. McNeal, "Tapping the Three Kids' Markets," *American Demographics* (April 1998), pp. 37–41; and "Hey Kid, Buy This," *Business Week* (June 30, 1997), pp. 62–69.

45. For a recent description of social class structure in the United States, see Kenneth Labich, "Class in America," *Fortune* (February 7, 1994), pp. 114–26. For research on social classes in other countries, see "Gallup Offers New Take on Latin America," *Advertising Age* (November 13, 1995), p. 21; Sarah O'Brien and Rosemary Ford," Can We at Last Say Goodbye to Social Class?" *Journal of the Market Research Society* (July 1988), pp. 289–331; and Donald W. Hendon, Emelda L. Williams, and Douglas E. Huffman, "Social Class System Revisited," *Journal of Business Research,* vol. 17 (1988), pp. 259–70.

46. "Minority Marketing," *LUXE* (Summer 1998), p. 82; and "Defining the 'New America,'" *Advertising Age* (October 5, 1998), p. 22.

47. For a summary of representative research on African-American consumers, see Solomon, *Consumer Behavior,* pp. 444–45; Mowen and Minor, *Consumer Behavior,* pp. 597–98. See also, "Black Surfing," *BRANDWEEK* (November 17, 1997), p. 36.

48. This observation is based on a series of articles in H. P. McAdoo, ed., *Black Families* (Newbury Park, CA: Sage Publications, 1988).

49. "A Little Latin Logic," *BRANDWEEK* (July 20, 1998), p. 12; and "Marketing to Hispanics," *Advertising Age* (August 24, 1998), pp. S1–S27.

50. "Hispanics Don't Exist," *U.S. News & World Report* (May 11, 1998), pp. 26–32.

51. "Now You Know," *BRANDWEEK* (June 1, 1998), p. 22; and "A Yen for Brands," *BRANDWEEK* (January 5, 1998), p. 17. See also, "The Diversity Myth," *American Demographics* (June 1998), pp. 39–43.

CHAPTER 7

1. Interview with Gary Null, Honeywell, MICRO SWITCH Division, August 25, 1998.

2. Peter LaPlaca, "From the Editor," *Journal of Business and Industrial Marketing* (Summer 1992), p. 3.

3. Based on *Statistical Abstract of the United States,* 118th ed. (Washington, DC: U.S. Department of Commerce, 1998).

4. "FAA Announces Contract for New Workstations," *Dallas Morning News* (April 30, 1997), p. 16H.

5. *1997 North American Industry Classification System* (Washington, DC: Office of Management and Budget, 1998).

6. An argument that consumer buying and organizational buying do not have important differences is found in Edward F. Fern and James R. Brown, "The Industrial/Consumer Marketing Dichotomy: A Case of Insufficient Justification," *Journal of Marketing* (Spring 1984), pp. 68–77. However, most writers on the subject do draw distinctions between the two types of buying. See, for example, Michael D. Hutt and Thomas W. Speh, *Business Marketing Management,* 6th ed. (Fort Worth, TX: Dryden Press, 1998); and H. Michael Hayes, Per V. Jenster, and Nils-Erik Aaby, *Business Marketing: A Global Perspective* (Chicago: Richard D. Irwin, 1996).

7. This listing and portions of the following discussion are based on Edward G. Brierty, Robert W. Eckles, and Robert R. Reeder, *Business Marketing,* 3rd ed. (Upper Saddle River, NJ: Prentice Hall, 1998); Frank G. Bingham, Jr., *Business Marketing Management* (Lincolnwood, IL: NTC, 1998); and Hutt and Speh, *Business Marketing Management.*

8. "Silicon Valley's Stamina," *Business Week* (August 31, 1998), pp. 88–93; "The I-Way Will Be Paved with Silicon," *Business Week* (January 9, 1995), p. 77; and "TI Introduces Smaller, Faster DSPs," *Dallas Morning News* (September 29, 1998), p. 4D.

9. "Latin Trade Connection," *Latin Trade* (June 1997), p.72.

10. "Diversity: A Busines Imperative," *Forbes* (April 20, 1998), Special Section, pp. 1–3.

11. "Sears, Roebuck and Co.: Minority Suppliers Energize Growth and the Bottom Line," *Forbes* (April 20, 1998), Special Section, p. 14.

12. For a study of buying criteria used by industrial firms, see Daniel H. McQuiston and Rockney G. Walters, "The Evaluative Criteria of Industrial Buyers: Implications for Sales Training," *Journal of Business & Industrial Marketing* (Summer/Fall 1989), pp. 65–75. See also, "What Buyers Look For," *Sales & Marketing Management* (August 1995), p. 31.

13. "Small Firms Flock to Quality System," *Nation's Business* (March 1998), pp. 66–67.

14. David L. Blenkhorn and Peter M. Banting, "How Reverse Marketing Changes Buyer-Seller Roles," *Industrial Marketing Management* (August 1991), pp. 185–90; and Michael R. Leenders and David L. Blenkhorn, *Reverse Marketing: The New Buyer-Supplier Relationship* (New York: Free Press, 1996).

15. "Chrysler's Neon," *Business Week* (May 3, 1993), p. 119.

16. For an up-to-date discussion on JIT, see Douglas M. Lambert, James R. Stock, and Lisa M. Ellram, *Fundamentals of Logistics Management* (New York: Irwin/McGraw-Hill, 1998).

17. "$35 Million Machine: Wires Not Included," *Newsweek* (April 15, 1995), p. 25.

18. This discussion is based on N. Craig Smith and John A. Quelch, *Ethics in Marketing* (Homewood, IL: Richard D. Irwin, 1993), p. 796; Nathaniel Gilbert, "The Case for Countertrade," *Across the Board* (May 1992), pp. 43–45; and Alan J. Dubinsky, Marvin A. Jolson, Masaaki Kotobe, and Che Un Lim, "A Cross-National Investigation of Industrial Salespeople's Ethical Perceptions," *Journal of International Business Studies* (Fourth Quarter 1991), pp. 651–70.

19. Pratibha A. Dabholkar, Wesley J. Johnston, and Amy S. Cathey, "The Dynamics of Long-Term Business-to-Business Exchange Relation-

ships," *Journal of Academy of Marketing Science,* vol. 22, 2 (1994), pp. 130–45.

20. "Boeing Receives a Key Order for Airlines," *The Wall Street Journal* (March 15, 1996), pp. A3, A10.

21. This discussion is based on James C. Anderson and James A. Narus, *Business Market Management* (Upper Saddle River, NJ: Prentice Hall, 1999); Robert D. Buzzell and Gwen Ortmeyer, "Channel Partnerships Streamline Distribution," *Sloan Management Review* (Spring 1995), pp. 85–96; and Neil Rackham, Lawrence Friedman, and Richard Ruff, *Getting Partnering Right* (New York: McGraw-Hill, 1996).

22. "Log On, Link Up, Save Big," *Business Week* (June 22, 1998), pp. 132–38; and "Finally, Europeans Are Storming the Net," *Business Week* (May 11, 1998), pp. 48–49. See also, Earl D. Honeycutt, Jr., Theresa B. Flaherty, and Ken Benassi, "Marketing Industrial Products on the Internet," *Industrial Marketing Management* (January 1998), pp. 63–72.

23. These examples appear in "The 'Click Here' Economy," *Business Week* (June 22, 1998), pp. 122–28; "Bringing Electronic Commerce Into Reach," *Industrial Distribution* (September 1998), pp. T12–T15; and "Log On, Link Up, Save Big," *Business Week.*

24. "To Byte the Hand That Feeds," *The Economist* (January 17, 1998), pp. 61–62; and "The 'Click Here' Economy," *Business Week.*

25. Thomas V. Bonoma, "Major Sales: Who Really Does the Buying?" *Harvard Business Review* (May–June 1982), pp. 11–19. For recent research on buying centers, see Morry Ghinghold and David T. Wilson, "Buying Center Research and Business Marketing Practices: Meeting the Challenge of Dynamic Marketing," *Journal of Business & Industrial Marketing,* vol. 13, no. 2 (1998), pp. 96–108; and Philip L. Dawes, Don Y. Lee, and Grahame R. Dowling, "Information Control and Influence in Emerging Buying Centers," *Journal of Marketing* (July 1998), pp. 55–68.

26. Paul A. Herbig, *Handbook of Cross-Cultural Marketing* (New York: The Halworth Press, 1998).

27. Jule M. Bristor, "Influence Strategies in Organizational Buying: The Importance of Connections to the Right People in the Right Places," *Journal of Business-to-Business Marketing,* vol. 1 (1993), pp. 63–98.

28. These definitions are adapted from Frederick E. Webster, Jr., and Yoram Wind, *Organizational Buying Behavior* (Englewood Cliffs, NJ: Prentice Hall, 1972), p. 6.

29. For an extensive description of 18 industrial purchases, see Arch G. Woodside and Nyren Vyas, *Industrial Purchasing Strategies: Recommendations for Purchasing and Marketing Managers* (Lexington, MA: Lexington Books, 1987). See also, Joseph A. Bellizzi, "Business-to-Business Selling and the Organizatonal Buying Process," in Sidney J. Levy, George R. Frerichs, and Howard L. Gordon, eds., *Marketing Managers Handbook* Chicago: The Dartnell Corporation, 1994).

30. Patrick J. Robinson, Charles W. Faris, and Yoram Wind, *Industrial Buying and Creative Marketing* (Boston: Allyn & Bacon, 1967).

31. Representative studies on the buy-class framework that document its usefulness include Erin Adnerson, Wujin Chu, and Barton Weitz, "Industrial Purchasing: An Empirical Exploration of the Buy-Class Framework," *Journal of Marketing* (July 1987), pp. 71–86; Morry Ghingold, "Testing the 'Buy-Grid' Buying Process Model," *Journal of Purchasing and Materials Management* (Winter 1986), pp. 30–36; P. Matthyssens and W. Faes, "OEM Buying Process for New Components: Purchasing and Marketing Implications," *Industrial Marketing Management* (August 1985), pp. 145–57; and Thomas W. Leigh and Arno J. Ethans, "A Script-Theoretic Analysis of Industrial Purchasing Behavior," *Journal of Marketing* (Fall 1984), pp. 22–32. Studies not supporting the buy-class framework include Joseph A. Bellizi and Philip McVey, "How Valid Is the Buy-Grid Model?" *Industrial Marketing Management* (February 1983), pp. 57–62; and Donald W. Jackson, Janet E. Keith, and Richard K. Burdick, "Purchasing Agents'

Perceptions of Industrial Buying Center Influences: A Situational Approach," *Journal of Marketing* (Fall 1984), pp. 75–83.

32. See, for example, R. Vekatesh, Ajay Kohli, and Gerald Zaltman, "Influence Strategies in Buying Centers," *Journal of Marketing* (October 1995), pp. 61–72; Gary L. Lilien and Anthony Wong, "An Exploratory Investigation of the Structure of the Buying Center in the Metal Working Industry," *Journal of Marketing Research* (February 1984), pp. 1–11; and Wesley J. Johnston and Thomas V. Bonoma, "The Buying Center: Structure and Interaction Patterns," *Journal of Marketing* (Summer 1981), pp. 143–56. See also, Christopher P. Puto, Wesley E. Patton III, and Ronald H. King, "Risk Handling Strategies in Industrial Vendor Selection Decisions," *Journal of Marketing* (Winter 1985), pp. 89–98.

CHAPTER 8

1. George Anders, "The Race for 'Sticky' Web Sites," *The Wall Street Journal* (February 11, 1999), p. B1; Russ Mitchell, "Why AOL Really Clicks," *U.S. News & World Report* (December 7, 1998), pp. 52–53; and "America Online—The Leader in Online Shopping—Kicks Off 1998 Online Shopping Season," *American Online News Release* (November 18, 1998); and "AOL Hits $1.3B in Revenue," *USA Today* (April 28, 1999), p. B1.

2. International Trade Administration definition reported in A. J. Campbell, "Ten Reasons Why Your Company Should Use Electronic Commerce," *Business America* (May 1998), p. 12.

3. Unless otherwise indicated, this discussion is based on "Latest Headcount: 148 Million Online," www.cyberatlas.com, downloaded February 18, 1999; Andrew Urbaczewski, Leonard M. Jessup, and Bradley C. Wheeler, "A Manager's Primer on Electronic Commerce," *Business Horizons* (September–October 1998), pp. 5–16; Ravi Kalakota and Andrew B. Whinston, *Electronic Commerce: A Manager's Guide* (Reading, MA: Addison-Wesley 1997); Tim McCullum, "The Net Result of Computer Links," *Nation's Business* (March 1998), pp. 55–57; and "Online Population to Quadruple," www.cyberatlas.com, downloaded February 17, 1999.

4. Michael Krantz, "Click Till You Drop," *Time* (July 20, 1998), pp. 34–39. See also Paul Foley and David Sutton, "Boom Time for Electronic Commerce—Rhetoric or Reality," *Business Horizons* (September–October 1998), pp. 21–30; and "When the Bubble Bursts," *The Economist* (January 30, 1999), pp. 23–25.

5. "International Data Corporation: 133 Million Intranet Users By 2001," *Nua Internet Surveys* (www.nua.ie/surveys), downloaded January 27, 1999.

6. See "An R_x for Communication, ELVIS Saves Eli Lilly Time, Money," *PC Today Processor* (www.pctoday.com), downloaded January 28, 1999.

7. Raymond S. Bamford and Robert A. Burgelman, "Internet-Based Electronic Commerce in 1997: A Primer" (Graduate School of Business, Stanford University, 1997).

8. Shawn Tully, "How Cisco Mastered the Net," *Fortune* (August 17, 1998), pp. 207–10.

9. David Kirkpatrick, "The E-Ware War," *Fortune* (December 7, 1998), pp. 102–12; and Eryn Brown, "VF Corp. Changes Its Underware," *Fortune* (December 7, 1998), pp. 115–18.

10. Heather Green and Seanna Growder, "Cyberspace Winners: How They Did It," *Business Week* (June 22, 1998), pp. 154–60.

11. Amy Cortese, "A Census in Cyberspace," *Business Week* (May 5, 1997), p. 84.

12. This discussion is based on "Online with the Operator," *American Demographics* (February 1999), pp. 36–38; Paul Judge, "How Safe Is the Net?" *Business Week* (June 22, 1998), pp. 148–52; "Nielsen Media: Online Purchasing Doubles," *Nua Internet Surveys* (www.nua.ie/surveys), downloaded January 27, 1999; Joel Kotkin, "The Mother of All Malls," *Forbes ASAP* (April 6, 1998), pp. 60–64; and "More

Firms See the Net as Tool for Selling Cars," *The Wall Street Journal* (February 8, 1999), p. B7D.

13. The source for iVALS descriptions is found at the SRI International Web site: http://future.sri.com:80/vals/ivals.index.html, downloaded February 1, 1999.

14. Russell S. Winer et al., "Choice in Computer-Mediated Environments," *Marketing Letters* (vol. 8, no. 3, 1997), pp. 287–96; and Joseph Alba et al., "Interactive Home Shopping: Consumer, Retailer, and Manufacturer Incentives to Participate in the Electronic Marketplace," *Journal of Marketing* (July 1997), pp. 38–53.

15. "Future Shop," *Forbes ASAP* (April 6, 1998), pp. 37–5; and Foley and Sutton, "Boom Time for Electronic Commerce."

16. "The E-commerce Cometh," *Brandweek* (September 21, 1998), p. 10.

17. The breakdown shown in this figure consolidate several estimates, principally from Juniper Communications and Forrester Research. See, for example, "Online Shopping Revenues by Type: 1996–2002," *Advertising Age* (October 26, 1998), p. S14.

18. "A Cybershopper's Best Friend," *Business Week* (May 4, 1998), p. 84.

19. "It's a Woman's Web," *Brandweek* (September 7, 1998), pp. 46–47.

20. Erick Schonfeld, "The Customized, Digitized, Have-It-Your-Way Economy," *Fortune* (September 28, 1998), pp. 115–21.

21. 'Now It's Your Web," *Business Week* (October 5, 1998), pp. 164–74.

22. Matt Lake, "The New Megasites: All-in-One Web Supersites," *PC World Online*, www.pcworld.com, downloaded February 9, 1999; and "Portals Rethink Retail Strategies, Shopping Agents," *Advertising Age* (February 1, 1999), pp. 28, 32.

23. "Branding on the Net," *Business Week* (November 9, 1998), pp. 78–86.

24. "Is Public Concern about Privacy Holding up Commerce on the Internet?" *American Demographics* (February 1999), p. 35; Judge, "How Safe Is the Net?"; Paulette Thomas, "Clicking Coupons Online Has a Cost: Privacy," *The Wall Street Journal* (June 19, 1998), p. B1; Varun Grover, Liz Hall, and Scott Rosenberg, "The Web of Privacy: Business in the Information Age," *Business Horizons* (July–August 1998), pp. 5–11; and "Special Report: Privacy," *Business Week* (April 5, 1999), pp. 84–90.

25. "Cookies," *PC Webopaedia Definition and Links,* www.webopedia.com, downloaded February 10, 1999.

26. Clay Hathorn, "Online Business: Trying to Turn Cookies into Dough," *Microsoft Internet Magazine Archive,* www.microsoft.com, downloaded February 15, 1999.

27. For an early, but still relevant, description of how the new marketspace will influence marketing, see Jeffrey F. Rayport and John J. Sviokla, "Managing in the Marketspace," *Harvard Business Review* (November–December 1994), pp. 141–53; Jeffrey F. Rayport and John J. Sviokla, "Exploiting the Virtual Value Chain," *Harvard Business Review* (November–December 1995), pp. 75–85; and Donna L. Hoffman and Thomas P. Novak, "Marketing in a Hypermedia Computer-Mediated Environment: Conceptual Foundations," *Journal of Marketing* (July 1996), pp. 50-68. See also Robert A. Peterson, Sridhar Balasubramanian, and Bart J. Bronnenberg, "Exploring the Implications of the Internet for Consumer Marketing," *Journal of the Academy of Marketing Science,* (Fall 1997), pp. 329–46.

28. This discussion is based on John Deighton, "Note on Marketing and the World Wide Web," *Harvard Business School Note #9-597-037* (Boston: Harvard Business School Publishing, 1997). Also see John Deighton, "The Future of Interactive Marketing," *Harvard Business Review* (November–December 1996), pp. 151–62.

29. "Random Access: Dell's Sell," *Forbes ASAP* (February 22, 1999), p. 16; and "Online with the Operator," *American Demographics.*

30. "The Corporation of the Future," *Business Week* (August 31, 1998), pp. 102–6; "Net Sales," *Sales & Marketing Management* (April 1998), pp. 90–91; and www.cisco.com, downloaded February 10, 1999.

31. Procter & Gamble, Inc., www.pg.com, downloaded February 10, 1999.

32. These examples are found in "Met Life Backs Local Agents with Sidewalk Sponsorship," *Marketing News* (January 18, 1999), p. 38; and "Branding on the Net," *Business Week.*

33. Deighton, "Note on Marketing and the World Wide Web."

34. George E. Belch and Michael A. Belch, *Advertising and Promotion: An Integrated Marketing Communications Approach,* 4th ed. (New York: Irwin/McGraw-Hill, 1998). For extensive coverage of the different forms of online advertising, see William F. Arens, *Contemporary Advertising,* 7th ed. (New York: Irwin/McGraw-Hill, 1999), pp. 515–24.

35. "A Shameless Bribe," *Online Media Strategies for Advertising: A Supplement to Advertising Age* (Spring 1998), p. 60A.

36. "IAB: Internet Advertising Will Near $2 Bil for 1998," *Advertising Age* (February 15, 1999), p. 34.

37. Nelson Wang, "Sponsorships Popular with Web Advertisers," *Internet World,* www.internetworld.com, downloaded February 17, 1999.

38. "Berkeley Systems Finds Interstitials Beat Other Ads," *Advertising Age* (August 12, 1998), p. 3.

39. "Intermercials, Sponsorships Will Emerge as New Online Ad Models," *Advertising Age* (June 27, 1997), p. 24.

40. For an extensive discussion of webcasting, see *Webcasting and Push Technology Strategies* (Charleston, SC: Computer Technology Research Corp., 1999).

41. Point Cast, Inc., www.pointcast.com, downloaded February 15, 1999.

42. Amy Cortese, "It's Called Webcasting, and It Promises to Deliver the Info You Want, Straight to Your PC," *Business Week* (February 24, 1997), pp. 95–104.

43. Bob Donath, "Managing the Workhorses of the Web," *Marketing News* (January 18, 1999), p. 6.

44. Krantz, "Click Till You Drop."

45. Scott Woolley, "I Got It Cheaper Than You," *Forbes* (November 2, 1998), pp. 82, 84.

46. For useful reading on the challenges of interactive marketing, see Don Peppers, Martha Rogers, and Bob Dorf, "Is Your Company Ready for One-to-One Marketing?" *Harvard Business Review* (January–February 1999), pp. 151–60; and Larry Downes and Chunka Mui, *Unleashing the Killer App: Digital Strategies for Market Dominance* (Boston, MA: Harvard Business School Press, 1998).

47. Mary Beth Grover, "Lost in Cyberspace," *Forbes* (March 8, 1999), pp. 124–28.

America Online, Inc.: This case was written by Michael Vessey.

CHAPTER 9

1. John Horn, "Studios Play Name Game," *Star Tribune* (August 10, 1997), p. F11.

2. Peter Passell, "As Cost of Movie Making Rises, Hollywood Bets It All on Openings," *Star Tribune* (December 29, 1997), pp. D1, D4.

3. Thomas R. King, "How Big Will Disney's 'Pocahontas' Be?" *The Wall Street Journal* (May 15, 1995), pp. B1, B8.

4. Richard Turner and John R. Emshwiller, "Movie-Research Czar Is Said by Some to Sell Manipulated Findings," *The Wall Street Journal* (December 17, 1993), p. A1.

5. Helene Diamond, "Lights, Camera . . . Research!" *Marketing News* (September 11, 1989), pp. 10–11; and "Killer!" *Time* (November 16, 1987), pp. 72–79.

6. Jeff Strickler, "Titanic Director Was Floating on Air after Local Test," *Star Tribune* (December 26, 1997), pp. D1, D2.

7. Bruce Orwall, "'Primary Colors' Had So Much Going for It, and Then It Just Sank," *The Wall Street Journal* (April 15, 1998), pp. A1, A10.

8. "The Business of Blockbusters," *Wharton Alumni Magazine* (Fall, 1997), pp. 8–12.

9. "New Marketing Research Definition Approved," *Marketing News* (January 2, 1987), pp. 72–79.

10. John Cloud, "How the Furby Flies," *Time* (November 30, 1998), pp. 84–85; Joseph Pereira, "To These Youngsters, Trying Out Toys Is Hardly Kids' Play," *The Wall Street Journal* (December 17, 1997), pp.

A1, A11; and "Toy of the Year Awards, 1998," *Family Fun* (November 1998), pp. 125–57.

11. Lawrence D. Gibson, "Defining Marketing Problems," *Marketing Research* (Spring 1998), pp. 4–12.

12. Laurence N. Gold, "High Technology Data Collection for Measurement and Testing," *Marketing Research* (March 1992), pp. 29–38.

13. Joe Schwartz, "Back to the Source," *American Demographics* (January 1989), pp. 22–26; and Felix Kessler, "High-Tech Shocks in Ad Research," *Fortune* (July 7, 1986), pp. 58–62.

14. Michelle Wirth Fellman, "A SMART Move: 'Boutique' Firm Breaks Out in TV Ratings Game," *Marketing News* (September 14, 1998), pp. 1, 7, 43; and Kyle Pope, "Networks to Launch a Rival to Nielsen Service," *The Wall Street Journal* (August 3, 1998), pp. B1, B3.

15. Mark Maremont, "New Toothbrush is Big-Ticket Item," *The Wall Street Journal* (October 27, 1998), pp. B1, B6.

16. Susan Feyder, "It Took Tinkering by Twin Cities Firms to Save Some Sure Bets," *Minneapolis Star Tribune* (June 9, 1982), p. 11A.

17. Constance Gustke, "Built to Last," *Sales and Marketing Management* (August 1997), pp. 78–83.

18. Michael J. McCarthy, "Ford Companies Hunt for a 'Next Big Thing' but Few Can Find One," *The Wall Street Journal* (May 6, 1997), pp. A1, A6.

19. "Focus on Consumers," *General Mills Midyear Report* (Minneapolis, MN: January 8, 1998), pp. 2–3.

20. Bruce Stanley, "Redesigning Heinz Ketchup Label Is a Kid's Job," *Marketing News* (June 9, 1997), p. 5.

21. Michael J. McCarthy, "Stalking the Elusive Teenage Trendsetter," *The Wall Street Journal* (November 19, 1998), pp. B1, B10.

22. Roy Furchgott, "For Cool Hunters, Tomorrow's Trend Is the Trophy," *The New York Times* (June 28, 1998), p. 10; and Emily Nelson, "The Hunt for Hip: A Trend Scout's Trail," *The Wall Street Journal* (December 9, 1998), pp. B1, B6.

23. Wendy Zellner, "Look Out, Supermarkets—Wal-Mart Is Hungry," *Business Week* (September 14, 1998), pp. 98–100.

24. John A. Byrne, "Virtual Management," *Business Week* (September 21, 1998), pp. 80–82.

25. Steve Alexander, "Data Mining," *Star Tribune* (August 17, 1997), pp. D1, D5.

26. James H. Gilmore and B. Joseph Pine II, "The Four Faces of Mass Customization," *Harvard Business Review* (January–February 1997), pp. 91–101; Susan Phinney, "Lenses, Levis Lead the Way in Products Made to Individual Order," *Star Tribune* (May 14, 1997), p. B2; and Erick Schonfeld, "The Customized, Digitized, Have-It-Your-Way Economy," *Fortune* (September 28, 1998), pp. 115–24.

27. Joseph Pereira, "Unknown Fruit Takes on Unfamiliar Markets," *The Wall Street Journal* (September 9, 1995), pp. B1, B5.

28. Kevin P. Lonnie, "Researchers Must *Show* Their Findings to Clients," *Marketing News* (May 11, 1998), p. 4.

29. Mark A. Moon, John T. Mentzer, Carlo D. Smith, and Michael S. Garver, "Seven Keys to Better Forecasting," *Business Horizons* (September–October 1998), pp. 44–52.

Envirosell: This case was prepared by Linda Rochford of the University of Minnesota–Duluth.

CHAPTER 10

1. Joseph Pereira, "Board-Riding Youths Take Sneaker Maker on a Fast Ride Uphill," *The Wall Street Journal* (April 16, 1998), pp. A1, A8; and Joseph Pereira, "Sneaker Company Tops Out-of-Breath Baby Boomers," *The Wall Street Journal* (January 16, 1998), pp. B1, B2.

2. James Champy, "Ending Your Company's Slump," *Sales & Marketing Management* (May, 1998), p. 26; and Bill Saporito, "Can Nike Get Unstuck," *Time* (March 30, 1998), pp. 48–53.

3. Steven Greenhouse, "Groups Reach Agreement for Curtailing Sweatshops; Approve Monitoring and a Code of Conduct," *The New York Times* (November 5, 1998), p. A20.

4. Kenneth Labich, "Nike vs. Reebok: A Battle for Hearts, Minds, and Feet," *Fortune* (September 18, 1995), pp. 90–106.

5. Robert Lohrer, "Reebok in Tailored Clothing Business; Greg Norman Collection Adds Blazers, Dress Slacks," *Daily News Record* (January 29, 1997), p. 1; and "Reebok DMX Trac Golf Shoe Is Giving Retailers a Profitable Playing Partner," *PR Newswire* (July 22, 1998), p. 7.

6. Jeff Jensen, "Reebok Backs New Shoe with Anti-Nike Stance," *Advertising Age* (May 25, 1998), p. 4; and "Air Apparent," *Time* (March 2, 1998), p. 20.

7. David Leohnardt, "Two-Tier Marketing," *Business Week* (March 17, 1997), pp. 82–90.

8. Erick Schonfeld, "The Customized, Digitized, Have-It-Your-Way Economy," *Fortune* (September 28, 1998), pp. 115–24; and James H. Gilmore and B. Joseph Pine III, "The Four Faces of Mass Customization," *Harvard Business Review* (January–February 1997), pp. 91–101.

9. Issues in using marketing segmentation studies are described in William Rudelius, John R. Walton, and James C. Cross, "Improving the Managerial Relevance of Market Segmentation Studies," in Michael J. Houston, ed., *1987 Review of Marketing* (Chicago: American Marketing Association, 1987), pp. 385–404.

10. "Will the U.S. Chicken Out on Russia," *Fortune* (November 23, 1998), pp. 52–53.

11. Laura Zinn, "Real Men Buy Paper Towels Too," *Business Week* (November 9, 1997), pp. 75–76.

12. Jean C. Darian and Judy Cohen, "Segmenting by Consumer Time Shortage," *Journal of Consumer Marketing* vol. 12 (1995), pp. 32–44; Bill Saporito, "What's for Dinner?" *Fortune* (May 15, 1995), pp. 50–64; and Susan Chandler, "The Grocery Cart in Your PC," *Business Week* (September 11, 1995), pp. 61–64.

13. *Choices System: Fast Food Restaurants* (New York: Copyright Simmons Market Research Bureau, Inc., Spring 1998).

14. Ibid., p. 0003, Summary Appendix.

15. The discussion of Apple's segmentation strategies through the years is based on information from its Web site: www.apple-history.com/history.html.

16. Jim Carlton, "Apple to Post Profit Again on Sales Gains," *The Wall Street Journal* (January 6, 1999), pp. A3, A8.

17. Craig S. Smith and Rebecca Blumenstein, "In China, GM Bets Billions on a Market Strewn with Casualties," *The Wall Street Journal* (February 11, 1998), pp. A1, A11; and Rebecca Blumenstein, "GM Is Building Plants in Developing Nations to Wow New Markets," *The Wall Street Journal* (August 4, 1997), pp. A1, A4.

18. Gregory L. White, "GM to Crunch Five Marketing Divisions into One," *The Wall Street Journal* (August 5, 1998), p. A3, A6; and "GM Aims to Cut Time to Market with $1.5 Billion Modernization," *Star Tribune* (November 11, 1998), p. D7.

19. Angelo B. Henderson, "U-Turn on Caddy Truck Detours GM Strategy," *The Wall Street Journal* (March 26, 1998), pp. B1, B9.

20. Alex Taylor III, "Is Jack Smith the Man to Fix GM?" *Fortune* (August 3, 1998), pp. 86–92; and Bill Vlasic, "Too Many Models, Too Little Focus," *Business Week* (December 1, 1997), p. 148.

21. Kathleen Kerwin, "Why Didn't GM Do More for Saturn?" *Business Week* (March 16, 1998), p. 62.

Paisley Park Records: This case was prepared by Tom Davies from a personal interview with Alan Leeds.

CHAPTER 11

1. Personal interview with Todd DiMartini, 3M, 1998.

2. Ibid.

3. Bob Kearney, "Joining Forces: 3M Puts Stock in Bonding," *3M Today* (January 1995), pp. 2–5.

4. Definitions within this section are from Committee on Definitions, *Marketing Definitions: A Glossary of Marketing Terms* (Chicago: American Marketing Association, 1960).

5. Frank Gibney, Jr., "A New World at Sony," *Time* (November 17, 1997), pp. 56–64; and Frank Gibney, Jr., and Sebastian Moffett, "Sony's Vision Factory," *Time Digital* (March 10, 1997), pp. 30–34.

6. Neil Gross and Paul C. Judge, "Let's Talk!" *Business Week* (February 23, 1998), pp. 61–72.

7. Greg A. Stevens and James Burley, "3,000 Raw Ideas = 1 Commercial Success!" *Research-Technology Management* (May–June 1997), pp. 16–27.

8. R. G. Cooper and E. J. Kleinschmidt, "New Products—What Separates Winners from Losers?" *Journal of Product Innovation Management* (September 1987), pp. 169–84. Copyright © 1987 by Elsevier Science Publishing Co., Inc.; and Robert G. Cooper, *Winning at New Products*, 2nd ed. (Reading, MA: Addison-Wesley Publishing, 1993), pp. 49–66.

9. An example is the Stanford Innovation Project studies of the U.S. electronics industry, whose results are reported in B. J. Zirger and M. A. Maidique, "A Model of New Product Development: An Empirical Test," *Management Science* (July 1990), pp. 867–83.

10. Greg Burns, "Has General Mills Had Its Wheaties?" *Business Week* (May 8, 1995), pp. 68–69.

11. Marcia Mogelonsky, "Product Overload?" *American Demographics* (August 1998), pp. 5–12.

12. John Gilbert, "To Sell Cars in Japan, U.S. Needs to Offer More Right-Drive Models," *Star Tribune* (May 27, 1995), p. M1.

13. Dan Morse, "High-Tech Bat Swings for Fences," *The Wall Street Journal* (July 9, 1998), pp. B1–B7.

14. Magelonsky, "Product Overload?" p. 5.

15. Larry Armstrong, "Channel-Surfing's Next Wave," *Business Week* (July 31, 1995), pp. 90–91.

16. "They're Still Talkin' about 'Team Talk'," *3M Stemwinder* (May 17, 1995), pp. 1, 4.

17. Constance Gustke, "Built to Last," *Sales and Marketing Management* (August 1997), pp. 78–83.

18. Gibney, and Moffett, "Sony's Vision Factory."

19. Otis Port, "Xerox Won't Duplicate Past Errors," *Business Week* (September 29, 1998), pp. 98–101.

20. Larry Armstrong, "Video: Eye-Popping TV—But It Will Cost You," *Business Week* (February 23, 1998), pp. 118–20; Janet Moore, "Television's Digital Future?" *Star Tribune* (August 8, 1998), pp. D1–D3; and Chris O'Malley, "HDTV Is Here! So What?" *Time* (October 5, 1998), p. 52.

21. William M. Bulkeley, "Scientists Try to Make Broccoli 'Fun'," *The Wall Street Journal* (July 17, 1995), pp. B1, B3.

22. Dennis Berman, "Now, Tennis Balls Are Chasing Dogs," *Business Week* (July 23, 1998), pp. 138.

23. Cynthia Clark, "We're Stuck On Magnetic Poetry," *Publisher's Weekly* (September 28, 1998), p. 27.

24. Bill Vlasic, "When Air Bags Aren't Enough," *Business Week* (June 8, 1998), pp. 84–86; and Arthur J. Cummins, "Detroit Faces Crunch Time: Designing Gentler SUV's," *The Wall Street Journal* (February 25, 1998), pp. B1, B9.

25. William M. Carley, "Engine Troubles Put GE Behind in Race to Power New 777s," *The Wall Street Journal* (July 12, 1995), pp. A1, A6.

26. Michael White, "California Dreamin' Is the Theme for Auto Designers," *Star Tribune* (June 6, 1998), p. M1.

Palm Computing, Inc.: This case was written by Michael Vessey.

CHAPTER 12

1. "Stirring Things Up at Quaker Oats," *Business Week* (March 20, 1998), p. 42; "Gatorade Frost: Sue Wellington, "*Advertising Age* (June 29, 1998), p. SB; "Gatorade Re-Ups with NFL at $130M," *BRANDWEEK* (June 8, 1998), p. 4; *The Quaker Oats Company 1997 Annual Report* (Chicago: The Quaker Oats Company, 1998); and "Gatorade Gets Fierce with Next Sub-Brand," *BRANDWEEK* (October 19, 1998), p. 6.

2. For an extended discussion of the generalized product life-cycle curve, see David M. Gardner, "Product Life Cycle: A Critical Look at the Literature," in Michael Houston, ed., *Review of Marketing 1987* (Chicago: American Marketing Association, 1987), pp. 162–94.

3. "The Sun Chip Also Rises," *Advertising Age* (April 27, 1992), pp. S2, S6; and "How Gillette Brought Its MACH3 to Market," *The Wall Street Journal* (April 15, 1998), pp. B1, B8.

4. Orville C. Walker, Jr., Harper W. Boyd, Jr., and Jean-Claude Larréché, *Marketing Strategy*, 3rd ed. (New York: Irwin/McGraw Hill, 1999), p. 231.

5. Portions of the discussion on the fax machine industry are based on "Atlas Electronics Corporation," in Roger A. Kerin and Robert A. Peterson, *Strategic Marketing Problems: Cases and Comments*, 8th ed. (Upper Saddle River, NJ: Prentice Hall, 1998), pp. 494–506; "Think It's New? Think Again!" *Popular Mechanics* (December 1997), p. 32; "The Facts on Faxes," *Dallas Morning News* (May 12, 1997), p. 20; and "The Technology that Won't Die," *Forbes* (April 5, 1999), p. 56.

6. "E-Mail, IP Transmission Will Imitate, Not Replace, Fax Machines," *News Release* (San Jose, CA: Dataquest, June 1, 1998); and "Old Champions, New Contenders," *The Economist* (October 11, 1997), pp. 78–79.

7. Glenn Rifkin, "Mach 3: Anatomy of Gillette's Latest Global Launch," *Strategy & Business* (Second Quarter 1999), pp. 34–41.

8. For more on fads, see "The Theory of Fads," *Fortune* (October 14, 1996), pp. 49, 52.

9. Based on "The Games Sony Plays," *Business Week* (June 15, 1998), pp. 128–30; "Giants of Video-Game Industry Rallying for Rebound," *The Wall Street Journal* (May 31, 1996), p. B3; "Zap, Kaboom! Video Games Sizzle for Holidays," (November 13, 1997), pp. B1, B15; "Looking for a Sonic Boom," *BRANDWEEK* (March 2, 1998), pp. 26–29; and "U.S. Retail Sales of Video Games Up 32% for Year," *The Wall Street Journal* (November 6, 1998), p. B10.

10. "Sonic Strikes Back," *BRANDWEEK* (February 16, 1998), pp. 1, 6 and "Sony Unveils 128-bit PlayStation," *Dallas Morning News* (March 3, 1999), p. 20.

11. Everett M. Rogers, *Diffusion of Innovations*, 4th ed. (New York: The Free Press, 1995).

12. S. Ram and Jagdish N. Sheth, "Consumer Resistance to Innovation: The Marketing Problem and Its Solution," *Journal of Consumer Marketing* (Spring 1989), pp. 5–14.

13. Allison Wellner, "Try It—You'll Like It!" *American Demographics* (August 1998), pp. 42, 44.

14. For an historical perspective on the product/brand manager system, see George S. Low and Ronald A. Fullerton, "Brands, Brand Management, and the Brand Manager System: A Critical-Historical Evaluation," *Journal of Marketing Research* (May 1994), pp. 173–90.

15. "Haggar, Farah, Levi's Iron Out the Wrinkles," *Advertising Age* (March 6, 1995), p. 12; and "Modified Screwdrivers May Prevent Slips," *The Wall Street Journal* (March 1, 1990), p. B1.

16. "E-Z Rider," *BRANDWEEK* (August 18, 1997), pp. 24–28; and "Sony and Nintendo Battle for Kids Under 13," *The Wall Street Journal* (September 24, 1998), p. B4.

17. "P&G's Soap Opera: New Ivory Bar Hits the Bottom of a Tub," *The Wall Street Journal* (October 23, 1992), p. B11.

18. "Will the British Warm Up to Iced Tea? Some Big Marketers Are Counting on It," *The Wall Street Journal* (August 22, 1994), p. B1; and "Sneaker Company Tags Out-of-Breath Baby Boomers," *The Wall Street Journal* (January 16, 1998), pp. B1, B2.

19. "Food for What Ails You," *BRANDWEEK* (May 4, 1998), pp. 37–42; and "Nutri-Grain Targets Kids with Enhanced Calcium," *BRANDWEEK* (April 5, 1998), p. 6.

20. "Marketers Try to Ease Sting of Price Increases," *Marketing News* (October 9, 1995), pp. 5–6; "It's the Pits," *Consumer Reports* (February 1992), p. 203; and John G. Hinge, "Critics Call Cuts in Package Size Deceptive Move," *The Wall Street Journal* (February 5, 1991), pp. B1, B8.

21. This discussion is based on Kevin Lane Keller, *Strategic Brand Management* (Upper Saddle River, NJ: Prentice Hall, 1998); and Jennifer L. Aaker, "Dimensions of Brand Personality," *Journal of Marketing Research* (August 1997), pp. 347–56. See also, Susan Fournier, "Consumers and Their Brands: Developing Relationship Theory in Consumer Research," *Journal of Consumer Research* (March 1998), pp. 343–73.

22. For an extended treatment of brand equity, see David A. Aaker, *Building Strong Brands* (New York: The Free Press, 1996); and Tom Duncan and Sandra Moriarity, *Driving Brand Value* (New York: McGraw-Hill, 1997).

23. "License to Sell," *BRANDWEEK* (June 8, 1998), pp. 37–42.

24. "Losing the Name Game," *Newsweek* (June 8, 1998), p. 44.

25. "A Good Name Should Live Forever," *Forbes* (November 16, 1998), p. 88.

26. Rob Osler, "The Name Game: Tips on How to Get It Right," *Marketing News* (September 14, 1998), p. 50; and Keller, *Strategic Brand Management*. See also, "Pamela W. Henderson and Joseph A. Cote, "Guidelines for Selecting or Modifying Logos," *Journal of Marketing* (April 1998), pp. 14–30.

27. "Buying the Ranch on Brand Equity," *BRANDWEEK* (October 25, 1992), p. 6; and "Kellogg Changes Name of Controversial Cereal," *Marketing News* (August 19, 1991), p. 22.

28. "A Survey of Multinationals," *The Economist* (June 24, 1995), p. 8.

29. For an overview of brand equity and brand extensions, see Vicki R. Lane, "Brand Leverage Power: The Critical Role of Brand Balance," *Business Horizons* (January–February 1998), pp. 25–84.

30. "When Brand Extension Becomes Brand Abuse," *BRANDWEEK* (October 26, 1998), pp. 20, 22.

31. Stephanie Thompson, "Brand Buddies," *BRANDWEEK* (February 23, 1998), pp. 22–23ff. For an in-depth discussion on co-branding, see Akshay R. Rao and Robert W. Ruekert, "Brand Alliances as Signals of Product Quality," *Sloan Management Review* (Fall 1994), pp. 87–97.

32. "Brands Fight Back Against Private Labels," *Marketing News* (January 16, 1995), pp. 8–9.

33. "Kodak Pursues a Greater Market Share in Japan with New Private-Label Film," *The Wall Street Journal* (March 7, 1995), p. B11.

34. "The National Peztime," *The Dallas Morning News* (October 9, 1995), pp. 1C, 2C; David Welch, *Collecting Pez* (Murphysboro, IL: Bubba Scrubba Publications, 1995); and "Pez: Dispense with Idea It's Just for Kids," *BRANDWEEK* (September 26, 1996), p. 10.

35. "Coca-Cola Finds Success Trading New for the Old," *The Wall Street Journal* (March 24, 1995), p. B5.

36. "Which Hue Is Best? Test Your Color I.Q.," *Advertising Age* (September 14, 1987), pp. 18, 20; and "Supreme Court to Rule on Colors as Trademarks," *Marketing News* (January 2, 1995), p. 28.

37. This discussion is based, in part, on Barry N. Rosen and George B. Sloane III, "Environmental Product Standards, Trade and European Consumer Goods Marketing," *Columbia Journal of World Business* (Spring 1995), pp. 74–86; "Life Ever After," *The Economist* (October 9, 1993), p. 77; and "How to Make Lots of Money, and Save the Planet Too," *The Economist* (June 3, 1995); pp. 57–58. See also, Stuart L. Hart, "Beyond Greening: Strategies for a Sustainable World," *Harvard Business Review* (January–February 1997), pp. 66–77; and Ajay Menon and Anil Menon, "Enviropreneurial Marketing Strategy: The Emergence of Corporate Environmentalism as Market Strategy," *Journal of Marketing* (January 1997), pp. 51–67.

38. Paula Mergenbagen, "Product Liability: Who Sues?" *American Demographics* (June 1995), pp. 48–54; and "Bottled Up," *The Economist* (December 17, 1994), p. 69.

39. For representative research on warranties, see Joydeep Srivastava and Anusree Mitra, "Warranty as a Signal of Quality: The Moderating Effect of Consumer Knowledge on Quality Evaluations," *Marketing Letters* (November 1998), pp. 327–36; Melvyn A. Menezes and John A. Quelch, "Leverage Your Warranty Program," *Sloan Management*

Review (Summer 1990), pp. 69–80; and "Broken? No Problem," *U.S. News & World Report* (January 11, 1999), pp. 68–69.

BMW: This case was written by Giana Eckardt.

CHAPTER 13

1. Margaret Loftus, "Bargain Prices On the Slopes," *U.S. News and World Report* (November 23, 1998), p. 84; Catherine Arnst, "Rocky Mountain High Tech," *Business Week* (April 7, 1997), p. 80; Catherine Arnst, "A Cold Shoulder On the Slopes," *Business Week* (February 9, 1998), p. 70; Candyce H. Stapen, "Summer Prices Friendly for Guests at Winter Resorts," *Washington Times* (July 20, 1997), p. E3; Debra Rosenberg, "All Aboard," *Newsweek* (February 9, 1998), p. 72; Sandra Dalas and Gary McWilliams, "Going to Extremes—To Lure the Hot Dogs Back," *Business Week* (March 13, 1995), p. 100; and Roy Furchgott, "Downhill Biker: Cycling the Ski Slopes," *Business Week* (July 10, 1995), p. 132.

2. Survey of Current Business (Washington, DC: U.S. Department of Commerce, 1998); and John Greenwald, "The New Service Class," *Time* (November 14, 1994), pp. 72–73.

3. Marc Ballon, "Concierge Makes Hay in Corporate Fields," *Inc.* (September 1998), p. 23; "The Top Entrepreneurs," *Business Week* (January 11, 1999), pp. 82–84; "Techwatch," *Time* (January 12, 1998), p. 28; and "A Branch In All But Name," *U.S. Banker* (May 1998), p. 18.

4. Janet R. McColl-Kennedy and Tina White, "Service Provider Training Programs at Odds with Customer Requirements in Five Star Hotels," *Journal of Services Marketing* vol. 11, no. 4 (1997), pp. 249–64; Ellyn A. McColgan, "How Fidelity Invests in Service Professionals," *Harvard Business Review* (January–February 1997), pp. 137–43; and Frederick F. Reichheld and W. Earl Sasser, Jr., "Zero Defections: Quality Comes to Services," *Harvard Business Review* (September–October 1990), pp. 105–11.

5. Christopher H. Lovelock and George S. Yip, "Developing Global Strategies for Service Businesses," *California Management Review* (Winter 1996), pp. 64–86.

6. Ibid.

7. Tim Taylor," Audience Info the Key to Sports Marketers," *Marketing News* (January 18, 1999), p. 10; Subir Bandyopadhyay and Mario Bottone, "Playing to Win," *Marketing Management* (Spring 1997), p. 9–19; Aviv Shoham, Gregory M. Rose, and Lynn R. Kahle, "Marketing of Risky Sports: From Intention to Action," *Journal of the Academy of Marketing Science* (Fall 1998), pp. 307–21; Roger O. Crockett, David Leonhardt, Richard A. Melcher, Mark Hyman, Ronald Grover, Linda Himelstein, and Richard Siklos, "Yikes! Mike Takes a Hike," *Business Week* (January 25, 1999), pp. 74–76; and Allen St. John, "Who's on Deck?" *American Demographics* (October 1998), pp. 60–71.

8. Howard Schlossberg, "Electric Utilities Finally Discover Marketing," *Marketing News* (November 20, 1989), pp. 1, 2.

9. Paul Magnusson, "It's Open Season on Nonprofits," *Business Week* (July 3, 1995), p. 31.

10. Ani Hadjian, "Follow the Leader," *Fortune* (November 27, 1995), p. 96; and John A. Byrne, "Profiting from the Nonprofits," *Business Week* (March 26, 1990), pp. 66–74.

11. William Dowell, Chandrani Ghosh, and Bruce van Voorst, "Zapping the Post Office," *Time* (January 19, 1998), pp. 46–47; and Anne Faircloth, "The World Takes on the USPS," *Fortune* (July 24, 1995), p. 28.

12. Keith B. Murray, "A Test of Services Marketing Theory: Consumer Information Acquisition Activities," *Journal of Marketing* (January 1991), pp. 10–25.

13. Dawn Iacobucci, "An Empirical Examination of Some Basic Tenets in Services: Goods-Services Continua," Teresa Swartz, David E. Bowen, and Stephen W. Brown, eds., in *Advances in Services Marketing and Management* vol. 1 (Greenwich, CT: JAI Press), pp. 23–52; and Valerie A. Zeithaml, "How Consumer Evaluation Processes Differ Between Goods and Services," in James H. Donnelly and William R.

George, eds., *Marketing of Services* (Chicago: American Marketing Association, 1981).

14. Murray, "A Test of Services Marketing Theory."

15. John Ozment and Edward Morash, "The Augmented Service Offering for Perceived and Actual Service Quality," *Journal of the Academy of Marketing Science* (Fall 1994), pp. 352–63.

16. A. Parasuraman, Valerie A. Zeithaml, and Leonard L. Berry, "Reassessment of Expectations as a Comparison Standard in Measuring Service Quality: Implications for Further Research," *Journal of Marketing* (January 1994), pp. 111–24; and Leonard L. Berry, *On Great Service* (New York: Free Press, 1995).

17. Valerie A. Zeithaml, A. Parasuraman, and Leonard L. Berry, *Delivering Quality Service* (New York: Free Press, 1990); and Stephen W. Brown and Teresa Swartz, "A Gap Analysis of Professional Service Quality," *Journal of Marketing* (April 1989), pp. 92–98.

18. Amy Ostrom and Dawn Iacobucci, "Consumer Trade-Offs and the Evaluation of Services," *Journal of Marketing* (January 1995), pp. 17–28; and J. Joseph Cronin, Jr., and Steven A. Taylor, "Measuring Service Quality: A Reexamination and Extension," *Journal of Marketing* (July 1992), pp. 55–68.

19. Stephen S. Tax and Stephen W. Brown, "Recovering and Learning from Service Failure," *Sloan Management Review* (Fall 1998), pp. 75–88; Stephen S. Tax, Stephen W. Brown, and Murali Chandrashekaran, "Customer Evaluations of Service Complaint Experiences: Implications for Relationship Marketing," *Journal of Marketing* (April 1998), pp. 60–76; Stephen W. Brown, "Service Recovery Through IT," *Marketing Management* (Fall 1997), pp. 25–27; and Leonard L. Berry and A. Parasuraman, "Listening to the Customer—The Concept of a Service-Quality Information System," *Sloan Management Review* (Spring 1997), pp. 65–76.

20. Vicki Clift, "Everyone Needs Service Flow Charting," *Marketing News* (October 23, 1995), pp. 41, 43; Mary Jo Bitner, Bernard H. Booms, and Mary Stanfield Tetreault, "The Service Encounter: Diagnosing Favorable and Unfavorable Incidents," *Journal of Marketing* (January 1990), pp. 71–84; Eberhard Scheuing, "Conducting Customer Service Audits," *Journal of Consumer Marketing* (Summer 1989), pp. 35–41; and W. Earl Susser, R. Paul Olsen, and D. Daryl Wyckoff, *Management of Service Operations* (Boston: Allyn & Bacon, 1978).

21. Leonard L. Berry, "Relationship Marketing of Services—Growing Interest, Emerging Perspectives," *Journal of the Academy of Marketing Science* (Fall 1995), pp. 236–45; Mary Jo Bitner, "Building Service Relationships: It's All About Promises," *Journal of the Academy of Marketing Science* (Fall 1995), pp. 246–51; Kevin P. Gwinner, Dwayne D. Gremler, and Mary Jo Bitner, "Relational Benefits in Services Industries: The Customer's Perspective," *Journal of the Academy of Marketing Science* (Spring 1998), pp. 101–14; Susan Fournier, Susan Dobscha, and David Glen Mick, "Preventing the Premature Death of Relationship Marketing," *Harvard Business Review* (January–February 1998), pp. 42–51; and John V. Petrof, "Relationship Marketing: The Wheel Reinvented?" *Business Horizons* (November–December 1997), pp. 26–31.

22. Thomas S. Gruca, "Defending Service Markets," *Marketing Management* (1994), no. 1, pp. 31–38; and Leonard L. Berry, Jeffrey S. Conant, and A. Parasuraman, "A Framework for Conducting a Services Marketing Audit," *Journal of the Academy of Marketing Science* (Summer 1991), pp. 255–68.

23. Patriya Tansuhaj, Donna Randall, and Jim McCullough, "A Services Marketing Management Model: Integrating Internal and External Marketing Functions," *Journal of Sciences Marketing* (Winter 1998), pp. 31–38.

24. Christian Gronroos, "Internal Marketing Theory and Practice," in Time Bloch, G. D. Upah, and V. A. Zeithaml, eds., *Services Marketing in an Changing Environment* (Chicago: American Marketing Association, 1984).

25. Ibid.

26. March C. Gilly and Mary Wolfinbarger, "Advertising's Internal Audience," *Journal of Marketing* (January 1998), pp. 69–88.

27. Dan R. E. Thomas, "Strategy Is Different in Service Businesses," *Harvard Business Review* (July–August 1978), pp. 158–65.

28. Haim Oren, "Branding Financial Services Helps Consumers Find Order in Chaos," *Marketing News* (March 29, 1993), p. 6; and Leonard L. Berry, Edwin F. Lefkowith, and Terry Clark, "In Services, What's in a Name?" *Harvard Business Review* (September–October 1988), pp. 28–30.

29. Frederick H. deB. Harris and Peter Peacock, "Hold My Place, Please," *Marketing Management* (Fall 1995), pp. 34–46.

30. Christopher Lovelock, *Services Marketing* (Englewood Cliffs, NJ: Prentice Hall, 1991), pp. 122–27.

31. Kent B. Monroe, "Buyer's Subjective Perceptions of Price," *Journal of Marketing Research* (Feubary 1973), pp. 70–80; and Jerry Olson, "Price as an Informational Cue: Effects on Product Evaluation," in A. G. Woodside, J. N. Sheth, and P. D. Bennett, eds., *Consumer and Industrial Buying Behavior* (New York: Elsevier North-Holland, 1977), pp. 267–86.

32. Kirk Johnson, "A Flip Side to E-Z Pass: East River Tolls and Rush-Hour Prices," *The New York Times* (August 2, 1997), p. 21.

33. Robert E. Hite, Cynthia Fraser, and Joseph A. Bellizzi, "Professional Service Advertising: The Effects of Price Inclusion, Justification, and Level of Risk," *Journal of Advertising Research,* vol. 30 (August/September 1990), pp. 23–31; William R. George and Leonard L. Berry, "Guidelines for the Advertising of Services," *Business Horizons* (July–August 1981), pp. 52–56; and Eugene M. Johnson, Eberhard E. Scheuing, and Kathleen A. Gaida, *Profitable Service Marketing* (Homewood, IL: Dow Jones-Irwin, 1986).

34. Sak Onkvisit and John J. Shaw, "Service Marketing: Image, Branding, and Competition," *Business Horizons* (January–February 1989), pp. 13–18.

35. *Bates and O'Sheen v. State of Arizona,* 433 U.S. 350, pp. 351–95 (1977); and "Supreme Court Opens Way for Lawyers to Advertise Prices for Routine Services," *The Wall Street Journal* (June 28, 1977), p. 4.

36. "Blond Ambition." *ABA Journal* (January 1996), p. 12.

37. Joe Adams, "Why Public Service Advertising Doesn't Work," *Ad Week* (November 17, 1980), p. 72.

38. Thomas A. Stewart, "A New 500 for the New Economy," *Fortune* (May 15, 1995), pp. 166–78; Philip Elmer-Dewitt, "Mine, All Mine," *Time* (June 5, 1995), pp. 46–54; and James Brian Quinn and Penny C. Paquette," "Technology in Services: Creating Organizational Revolutions," *Sloan Management Review* (Winter 1990), pp. 67–78.

39. Ann B. Fisher, "What Consumers Want in the 1990s," *Fortune* (January 29, 1990), pp. 108–12.

LearningByte International: This case was written by Giana Eckardt.

CHAPTER 14

1. Frederic M. Biddle and John Helyar, "Behind Boeing's Woes: Clunky Assembly Line, Price War with Airbus," *The Wall Street Journal* (April 24, 1998), pp. 1A, 16A.

2. Aaron Bernstein, Andy Reinhardt, and Seanna Browder, "Lost in Space at Boeing," *Business Week* (April 27, 1998), pp. 42, 44; Seanna Browder, "Course Change at Boeing," *Business Week* (July 27, 1998), p. 14; and "The Jumbo Stumbles," *The Economist* (October 11, 1997), p. 74.

3. Frederic M. Biddle, "Boeing Plans $350 Million Pretax Charge," *The Wall Street Journal* (April 10, 1998), p. 3A.

4. Frederic M. Biddle, "Boeing Is Placing Its Bets on Smaller, Cheaper Airlines," *The Wall Street Journal* (July 6, 1998), p. 22A.

5. Andy Reinhardt and Seanna Browder, "Fly, Damn It, Fly," *Business Week* (November 9, 1998), pp.150–56; and Frederic M. Biddle and Andy Paztor, "Boeing to Cut Output, Jobs Due to Asia," *The Wall Street Journal* (December 2, 1998), pp. A3, A4.

6. Alex Taylor III, "Boeing: Sleepy in Seattle," *Fortune* (August 7, 1995), pp. 92–98; and Alison L. Sprout, "How to Sit Pretty in the Boeing 777," *Fortune* (August 7, 1995), p. 29.

7. www.http://lamborghini.itg.net/main/diablo; and www.kelleybluebook.com.

8. Adapted from Kent B. Monroe, *Pricing: Making Profitable Decisions,* 2nd ed. (New York: McGraw-Hill, 1990), chapter 4. See also David J. Curry, "Measuring Price and Quality Competition," *Journal of Marketing* (Spring 1985), pp. 106–17.

9. Numerous studies have examined the price-quality-value relationship. See, for example, Jacob Jacoby and Jerry C. Olsen, eds., *Perceived Quality* (Lexington, MA: Lexington Books, 1985); Kent B. Monroe and William B. Dodds, "A Research Program for Establishing the Validity of the Price-Quality Relationship," *Journal of the Academy of Marketing Science* (Spring 1988), pp. 151–68; Akshay R. Rao and Kent B. Monroe, "The Effect of Price, Brand Name, and Store Name on Buyers' Perceptions of Product Quality: An Integrative Review," *Journal of Marketing Research* (August 1989), pp. 351–57; William D. Dodds, Kent B. Monroe, and Dhruv Grewal, "Effects of Price, Brand, and Store Information on Buyers' Product Evaluations," *Journal of Marketing Research* (August 1991), pp. 307–19; and Roger A. Kerin, Ambuj Jain, and Daniel J. Howard, "Store Shopping Experience and Consumer Price-Quality-Value Perceptions," *Journal of Retailing* (Winter 1992), pp. 235–45. For a thorough review of the price-quality-value relationship, see Valerie A. Ziethaml, "Consumer Perceptions of Price, Quality, and Value," *Journal of Marketing* (July 1988), pp. 2–22. Also see Jerry Wind, "Getting a Read on Market-Defined 'Value'," *Journal of Pricing Management* (Winter 1990), pp. 5–14.

10. These examples are from Roger A. Kerin and Robert A. Peterson, "Carrington Furniture (A)," *Strategic Marketing Problems: Cases and Comments,* 8th ed. (Englewood Clifs, NJ: Prentice Hall, 1998), pp. 307–17; and "Software Economics 101," *Forbes* (January 28, 1985), p. 88.

11. Julie Chao, "Is Kona Coffee Good to the Last Drop? That's All You Get," *The Wall Street Journal* (August 24, 1995), pp. A1, A6.

12. Carol VinZant, "Electronic Books Are Coming at Last," *Fortune* (July 6, 1998), pp. 119–24.

13. J. C. Conklin, "Don't Throw Out Those Old Sneakers, They're a Gold Mine," *The Wall Street Journal,* (September 21, 1998), pp. A1, A20; Richard Gibson, "Bean Market? Some Worry That Beanies Are Ripe for a Fall," *The Wall Street Journal* (September 25, 1998), pp. A1, A11; and Ken Bensinger, "Racing for Mint-Condition Toys," *The Wall Street Journal* (September 25, 1998), p. W10.

14. Daniel Levy, Mark Bergen, Shautanu Dutta, and Robert Venable, "The Magnitude of Menu Costs: Direct Evidence from Large U.S. Supermarket Chains," *The Quarterly Journal of Economics* (August, 1997), pp. 791–825.

15. David Wessel, "The Price Is Wrong, and Economics Are in an Uproar," *The Wall Street Journal* (January 2, 1991), pp. B1, B6.

16. Ron Winslow, "How a Breakthrough Quickly Broke Down for Johnson & Johnson," *The Wall Street Journal* (September 18, 1998), pp. A1, A5.

17. Bruce Orwall, "Theater Consolidation Jolts Hollywood Power Structure," *The Wall Street Journal* (January 21, 1998), pp. B1, B2.

18. "Price War Is Raging in Europe," *Business Week* (July 6, 1992), pp. 44–45.

19. Michael Garry, "Dollar Strength: Publishers Confront the New Economic Realities," *Folio: The Magazine for Magazine Management* (February 1989), pp. 88–93; Cara S. Trager, "Right Price Reflects a Magazine's Health Goals," *Advertising Age* (March 9, 1987), pp. 5–8ff; and Frank Bruni, "Price of Newsweek? It Depends," *Dallas Times Herald* (August 14, 1986), pp. S1, S20.

20. Vanessa O'Connell, "How Campbell Saw a Breakthrough Menu Turn into Leftovers," *The Wall Street Journal* (October 6, 1998), pp. A1, A12.

21. For an overview of price elasticity studies, see Ruth N. Bolton, "The Robustness of Retail-Level Elasticity Estimates," *Journal of Retailing* (Summer 1989), pp. 193–219; and Gerald J. Tellis, "The Price Elasticity of Selective Demand: A Meta-analysis of Econometric Models of Sales," *Journal of Marketing Research* (November 1988), pp. 331–41.

22. See, for example, Susan L. Holak and Srinivas K. Reddy, "Effects of a Television and Radio Advertising Ban: A Study of the Cigarette Industry," *Journal of Marketing* (October 1986), pp. 219–27; and Rick Andrews and George R. Franke, "Time-Varying Elasticities of U.S. Cigarette Demand, 1933–1987," *AMA Educators' Conference Proceedings* (Chicago: American Marketing Association, 1990), p. 393.

23. Andrew E. Serwer, "Head to Head with Giants—and Winning," *Fortune* (June 13, 1994), p. 154.

24. Kent B. Monroe, *Pricing: Making Profitable Decisions,* 2nd ed. (New York: McGraw-Hill, 1990), pp. 24–26.

25. Gregory L. White, "General Motors to Take Nationwide Test Drive on Web," *The Wall Street Journal* (September 28, 1998), p. B4.

CHAPTER 15

1. Mark Moremont, "How Gillette Brought Its MACH 3 to Market," *The Wall Street Journal* (April 15, 1998), pp. B1, B8; "Taking It on the Chin," *The Economist* (April 18, 1998), pp. 60–61; and "Gillette's Edge," *Business Week* (January 19, 1998), pp. 70–77.

2. "New Gillette MACH 3 Shaving System Begins Shipping to Stores Across North America," *The Gillette Company New Release* (June 26, 1998).

3. "Sony Prices Its Advanced Game Player at $299, Near Low End of Expectations," *The Wall Street Journal* (May 12, 1995), p. B4.

4. "Sony Slashes the Price of Play Station Game by More Than 25%," *The Wall Street Journal* (March 5, 1997), p. B6.

5. For the classic description of skimming and penetration pricing, see Joel Dean, "Pricing Policies for New Products," *Harvard Business Review* (November–December 1976), pp. 141–53. See also, Reed K. Holden and Thomas T. Nagle, "Kamikaze Pricing," *Marketing Management* (Summer 1998), pp. 31–39.

6. Jean-Noel Kapferer, "Managing Luxury Brands," *The Journal of Brand Management* (July 1997), pp. 251–60.

7. "Luxury Steals Back," *Fortune* (January 16, 1995), pp. 112–19. See also, "Buying Time," *Fortune* (September 8, 1997), p. 192.

8. See, for example, V. Kumar and Robert P. Leone, "Measuring the Effects of Retail Store Promotions on Brand and Store Substitution," *Journal of Marketing Research* (May 1998), pp. 178–85; and "AT&T Simplifies Price Tiers," *Dallas Morning News* (November 5, 1997), p. 10.1D.

9. Robert M. Schindler and Thomas M. Kibarian, "Increased Consumer Sales Response Through Use of 99-Ending Prices," *Journal of Retailing* (Summer 1996), pp. 187–99. For further reading on odd-even pricing, see Mark Stiving and Russell S. Winer, "An Empirical Analysis of Price Endings with Scanner Data," *Journal of Consumer Research* (June 1997), pp. 57–67; and Robert M. Schindler, "Patterns of Rightmost Digits Used in Advertised Prices: Implications for Nine-Ending Effects," *Journal of Consumer Research* (September 1997), pp. 192–201.

10. "PCs: The Battle for the Home Front," *Business Week* (September 25, 1995), pp. 110–14; David Kirkpatrick, "The Revolution at Compaq Computer," *Fortune* (December 14, 1992), pp. 80–82ff; and "Compaq Worldwide PC Leadership Expands in Third Quarter," *Compaq News Release* (October 26, 1998).

11. Thomas T. Nagle and Reed K. Holder, *The Strategy and Tactics of Pricing,* 2nd ed. (Englewood Cliffs, NJ: Prentice Hall, 1995), pp. 225–28.

12. Kent B. Monroe, *Pricing: Making Profitable Decisions,* 2nd ed. (New York: McGraw-Hill, 1990), pp. 326–27.

13. Robert J. Dolan and Hermann Simon, *Power Pricing: How Managing Price Transforms the Bottom Line* (New York: The Free Press, 1996), p. 249.

14. "Lawyers Start to Stop the Clock," *Business Week* (August 17, 1995), p. 108.

15. George E. Belch and Michael A. Belch, *Introduction to Advertising and Promotion,* 4th ed. (New York: Irwin/McGraw-Hill, 1998), p. 85.

16. For a comprehensive discussion on the experience curve, see Roger A. Kerin, Vijay Mahajan, and P. Rajan Varadarajan, *Contemporary Perspectives on Strategic Market Planning* (Boston: Allyn and Bacon, 1990), chapter 4.

17. "HDTV SETS: Too Pricey, Too Late?" *The Wall Street Journal* (January 7, 1998), pp. B1, B11.

18. "Gillette Co. Sees Strong Early Sales for Its New Razor," *The Wall Street Journal* (July 17, 1998), p. B3.

19. Aimee L. Stern, "The Pricing Quandry," *Across the Board* (May 1997), pp. 16–22.

20. "Hewlett-Packard Cuts Office-PC Prices in Wake of Moves by Compaq and IBM," *The Wall Street Journal* (August 22, 1995), p. B11.

21. "Retailers Using Cut-Rate Videos as Lures," *Dallas Morning News* (October 4, 1995), p. 5H.

22. Ann Faircloth, "Value Retailers Go Dollar for Dollar," *Fortune* (July 6, 1998), pp. 164–66.

23. Ian Ayres and Peter Siegelman, "Race and Gender Discrimination in Bargaining for a New Car," *The American Economic Review* (June 1995), pp. 304–21; "Saturn's Uniform Pricing Extended to Used Cars," *Dallas Morning News* (August 14, 1995), p. 4D; and "Goodbye to Haggling," *U.S. News & World Report* (October 20, 1997), p. 57.

24. Jeffrey A. Trachtenberg, "Sony Sells 100,000 Video-Game Units on First Weekend," *The Wall Street Journal* (September 12, 1995), p. A12.

25. Monroe, *Pricing*, p. 304.

26. Timothy Smith, "Why Air Travel Doesn't Work," *Fortune* (April 3, 1995), pp. 42–56; and David R. Henderson, "What Are Price Wars Good For? Absolutely Nothing," *Fortune* (May 12, 1997), p. 156.

27. For an extensive discussion on discounts, see Monroe, *Pricing,* chapters 14 and 15.

28. Kenneth C. Manning, William O. Bearden, and Randall L. Rose, "Development of a Theory of Retailer Response to Manufacturers' Everyday Low Cost Programs," *Journal of Retailing* (Spring 1998), pp. 107–37; "Everyday Low Profits," *Harvard Business Review* (March–April 1994), p. 13; Stephen J. Hoch, Xavier Dreze, and Mary E. Purk, "EDLP, Hi-Lo, and Margin Arithmetic," *Journal of Marketing* (October 1994), pp. 16–27; and Tibbett Speer, "Do Low Prices Bore Shoppers?" *American Demographics* (January 1994), pp. 11–13. See also, Philip Zerillo and Dawn Iacobucci, "Trade Promotions: A Call for a More Rational Approach," *Business Horizons* (July–August 1995), pp. 69–76; and Barbara E. Kahn and Leigh McAlister, *The Grocery Revolution: The New Focus on the Consumer* (Reading, MA: Addison-Wesley Educational Publishers, 1996).

29. Dorothy Cohen, *Legal Issues in Marketing Decision Making* (Cincinnati, OH: South-Western, 1995).

30. "Vitamin Firms to Pay U.S. $725 Million," *The Wall Street Journal* (May 21, 1999), pp. A3, A6.

31. "Reebok and FTC Settle Price-Fixing Charges," *The Wall Street Journal* (May 5, 1995), pp. B1, B8.

32. "Price Fixation," *U.S. News & World Report* (November 17, 1997), p. 79.

33. For a discussion on predatory pricing, see "Does Predatory Pricing Make Microsoft a Predator?" *Business Week* (November 23, 1998), pp.130, 132.

My Own Meals: Sources: Personal interview with Mary Anne Jackson; Mike Duff, "New Children's Meals: Not Just Kids Stuff," *Supermarket Business* (May 1990), p. 93; Heidi Parson, "MOM, Incorporated," *Poultry Processing* (August–September 1989); Lisa R. Van Wagner, "Kids Meals: The Market Grows Up," *Food Business* (May 20, 1991); Mary Ellen Kuhn, "Women to Watch in the 90's," *Food Business* (September 10, 1990); and Arlene Vigoda, "Small Fry Microwave Meals Become Big Business," *USA Today* (June 4, 1990).

CHAPTER 16

1. Alan Goldstein, "Off-Line Opportunity," *Dallas Morning News* (December 9, 1998), pp. 1D, 11D; "About Gateway," www.gateway.com, December 9, 1998; "Gateway to Use Its Stores to Lure Small Businesses," *The Wall Street Journal* (April 8, 1999), pp. B1, B4.

2. See, Peter D. Bennett, ed., *Dictionary of Marketing Terms,* 2nd ed. (Chicago: American Marketing Association, 1995).

3. Based on Frederick E. Webster, Jr., *Industrial Marketing Strategy,* 2nd ed. (New York: John Wiley & Sons, 1998).

4. PepsiCo, Inc., *Annual Report,* 1997.

5. "Compaq Computer Picks Dealers to Finish Assembling Its Pcs," *The Wall Street Journal* (July 7, 1997), p. B6.

6. Donald V. Fites, "Make Your Dealers Your Partners," *Harvard Business Review* (March–April 1996), pp. 84–95.

7. This discussion is based on Bert Rosenbloom, *Marketing Channels: A Management View,* 6th ed. (Fort Worth, TX: Dryden Press, 1999), pp. 452–58.

8. *Economic Impact: U.S. Direct Marketing Today* (New York: The Direct Marketing Association, 1998).

9. For a discussion on strategic channel alliances, see P. Rajan Varadarajan and Margaret H. Cunningham, "Strategic Alliances: A Synthesis of Conceptual Foundations," *Journal of the Academy of Marketing Science* (Fall 1995), pp. 282–96; and Johny K. Johansson, "International Alliances: Why Now?" *Journal of the Academy of Marketing Science* (Fall 1995), pp. 301–4. The examples appear in "Pepsi, Ocean Spray Renew Deal; Fruitworks Expands," *BRANDWEEK* (April 6, 1998), p. 14; and "GM Pondering Consolidations in Field Marketing," *Advertising Age* (May 11, 1998), p. 4.

10. General Mills, Inc., *Annual Report,* 1998; and "Spoon-to-Spoon Combat Overseas," *The New York Times* (January 1, 1995), p. 17.

11. For an extensive discussion of wholesaling, see Louis W. Stern, Adel I. El-Ansary, and Anne T. Coughlan, *Marketing Channels,* 5th ed. (Upper Saddle River, NJ: Prentice Hall, 1996), chapter 3.

12. For an overview of vertical marketing systems, see Lou Peltson, David Strutton, and James R. Lumpkin, *Marketing Channels* (Chicago: Richard D. Irwin, 1997), chapter 14.

13. Statistics provided by the International Franchise Association. Also see, "Franchising the American Dream," *Time* (November 7, 1998), p. 178.

14. For a review of channel partnering, see Robert D. Bussell and Gwen Ortmeyer, "Channel Partnerships Streamline Distribution," *Sloan Management Review* (Spring 1995), pp. 85–96. See also, Jakki J. Mohr and Robert E. Spekman, "Perfecting Partnerships," *Marketing Management*(Winter/Spring 1996), pp. 35–43.

15. Edwin R. Rigsbee, *The Art of Partnering* (Dubuque, IA: Kendall/Hunt Publishing Co., 1994), pp. 82–83.

16. Kroger, Inc., *Annual Report,* 1998.

17. "Future Shop," *Forbes ASAP* (April 6, 1998), pp. 37–53.

18. "General Motors to Take Nationwide Test Drive on Web," *The Wall Street Journal* (September 28, 1998), p. B4.

19. "Radio Shack to Sell Only Compaq PCs," *Dallas Morning News* (January 29, 1998), p. 2D.

20. "Gillette Tries to Nick Schick in Japan," *The Wall Street Journal* (February 4, 1991), pp. B3, B4.

21. This discussion is based on John Fahy and Fuyuki Taguchi, "Reassessing the Japanese Distribution System," *Sloan Management Review* (Winter 1995), pp. 49–61; Michael R. Czinkota and Jon Woronoff, *Unlocking Japanese Markets* (Chicago: Probus Publishing Co., 1991), pp. 92–97; and "Japan Keeping U.S. Products Out of Asia; Intricate Network Known as 'Keiretsu' Excludes Outsiders," *The Baltimore Sun* (November 9, 1997), p. 6F.

22. Based on an interview with Pamela Viglielmo, Director of International Marketing, Fran Wilson Cosmetics; "U.S. Firm Gives Lip (Coloring) Service to Japan," *Marketing News* (March 16, 1992), p. 6; and "At Last, a Product That Makes Japan's Subways Safe for Men," *Advertising Age* (January 16, 1995), p. I-24.

23. "Black Pearls Recast for Spring," *Advertising Age* (November 13, 1995), p. 49.

24. Studies that explore the dimensions and use of power and influence in marketing channels include the following: Gul Butaney and Lawrence H. Wortzel, "Distributor Power versus Manufacturer Power: The Cus-

tomer Role," *Journal of Marketing* (January 1988), pp. 52–63; Kenneth A. Hunt, John T. Mentzer, and Jeffrey E. Danes, "The Effect of Power Sources on Compliance in a Channel of Distribution: A Causal Model," *Journal of Business Research* (October 1987), pp. 377–98; John F. Gaski, "Interrelations Among a Channel Entity's Power Sources: Impact of the Exercise of Reward and Coercion on Expert, Referent, and Legitimate Power Sources," *Journal of Marketing Research* (February 1986), pp. 62–67; Gary Frazier and John O. Summers, "Interfirm Influence Strategies and Their Application within Distribution Channels," *Journal of Marketing* (Summer 1984), pp. 43–55; Sudhir Kale, "Dealer Perceptions of Manufacturer Power and Influence Strategies in a Developing Country," *Journal of Marketing Research* (November 1986), pp. 387–93; George H. Lucas and Larry G. Gresham, "Power, Conflict, Control, and the Application of Contingency Theory in Channels of Distribution," *Journal of the Academy of Marketing Science* (Summer 1985), pp. 27–37; and F. Robert Dwyer and Julie Gassenheimer, "Relational Roles and Triangle Dramas: Effects on Power Play and Sentiments in Industrial Channels," *Marketing Letters,* vol. 3 (1992), pp. 187–200.

25. For an overview of how costly slotting allowances have become in the grocery industry, see Nancy Millman, "Grocers' Aisles the Arena in the Battle for Shelf Space," *Chicago Tribune* (July 29, 1996), p. NW1.

26. For a comprehensive treatment of legal issues pertaining to marketing channels, see Dorothy Cohen, *Legal Issues in Marketing* (Cincinnati, OH: South-Western, 1995), chapters 12 and 13.

CHAPTER 17

1. David Bovet and Yossi Sheffi, "The Brave New World of Supply Chain Management," *Supply Chain Management Review* (Spring 1998), pp. 14–23; and H. Lee, V. Padmanabhan, and S. Whang, "The Bullwhip Effect in Supply Chains," *Sloan Management Review* (Spring 1997), pp. 93–102.

2. These estimates are based on "U.S. Logistics Closing on Trillion Dollar Mark," *Business Week* (December 28, 1998), p. 78.

3. *What's It All About?* (Oakbrook, IL: Council of Logistics Management, 1993).

4. Ken Cottrill, "Reforging the Supply Chain," *Journal of Business Strategy* (November/December 1997), pp. 35–39.

5. This discussion is based on Robert B. Handfield and Earnest Z. Nichols, *Introduction to Supply Chain Management* (Upper Saddle River, NJ: Prentice Hall 1998), chapter 1.

6. This description is based on Robert M. Monczka and Jim Morgan, "Supply Chain Management Strategies," *Purchasing* (January 15, 1998), pp. 78–85; "Survey of Manufacturing," *The Economist* (June 20, 1998), Special Report; "Restructure of Dealer Networks Will Change Retailing," *Marketing News* (October 26, 1998), p. 10; and Handfield and Nichols, *Introduction to Supply Chain Management.*

7. John Holusha, "P&G Downy Bottles Use Recycled Plastic," *The New York Times* (January 14, 1993), p. C5; and Bruce Van Voorst, "The Recycling Bottleneck," *Time* (September 14, 1992), p. 52.

8. Bovet and Sheffi, "The Brave New World of Supply Chain Management."

9. Joseph Pereira, "In Reebok-Nike War, Big Woolworth Chain Is a Major Battlefield," *The Wall Street Journal* (September 22, 1995), pp. A1, A5.

10. For an extensive description of total logistics costs, see Douglas M. Lambert, James R. Stock, and Lisa M. Ellram, *Fundamentals of Logistics Management* (New York: Irwin/McGraw-Hill, 1998), pp. 15–24.

11. Ronald Henkoff, "Delivering the Goods," *Fortune* (November 28, 1994), pp. 64–78.

12. Toby B. Gooley, "How Logistics Drive Customer Service," *Traffic Management* (January 1996), p. 46.

13. For an overview of how customer service has been viewed and defined, see "A Compendium of Research in Customer Service," *International Journal of Physical Distribution and Logistics Management,* 24, no. 4 (1994), pp. 1–68.

14. Michael Levy and Barton A. Weitz, *Retailing Management,* 3rd ed. (New York: Irwin/McGraw Hill, 1998), p. 331.

15. Ibid, p. 332; and Handfield and Nichols, *Introduction to Supply Chain Management,* p. 18.

16. Jon Bigness, "In Today's Economy, There Is Big Money to Be Made in Logistics," *The Wall Street Journal* (September 6, 1995), pp. A1, A9.

17. Robert C. Lieb and Arnold Maltz, "What's the Future for Third-Party Logistics?" *Supply Chain Management Review* (Spring 1998), pp. 71–79.

18. "IBM Moves Procurement to the Web-Big Time," *Purchasing* (December 10, 1998), p. S13; and Sherree DeCovny, "Electronic Commerce Comes of Age," *Journal of Business Strategy* (November/December 1998), pp. 38–44.

19. Scott Leibs, "Using IT to Grow," *Industry Week* (December 21, 1998), pp. 56–59; Christina Duff and Bob Ortega, "Watch Out for Flying Packages," *Business Week* (November 14, 1995), p. 40; Roy Rowan, "Business Triumphs of the Seventies," *Fortune* (December 1979), p. 34; and Lieb and Maltz, "What's the Future for Third-Party Logistics?"

20. Henkoff, "Delivering the Goods."

21. Cottrill, "Reforging the Supply Chain."

22. Marshall L. Fisher, "What Is the Right Supply Chain for Your Product?" *Harvard Business Review* (March–April 1997), pp. 105–16.

23. For an excellent overview on reverse logistics, see Edward J. Marien, "Reverse Logistics as Competitive Strategy," *Supply Chain Management Review* (Spring 1998), pp. 43–53.

24. Doug Bartholomew, "IT Delivers for UPS," *Industry Week* (December 21, 1998), pp. 60–63.

CHAPTER 18

1. J. William Gurley, "Buy.com May Fail, but If It Succeeds, Retailing May Never Be the Same," *Fortune* (January 11, 1999), pp. 150–52.

2. Kenneth Cline, "The Devil in the Details," *Banking Strategies* (November/December 1997), p. 24; and Roger Trap, "Design Your Own Jeans," *The Independent* (October 18, 1998), p. 22.

3. "The Fortune 500," *Fortune* (April 26, 1999), p. F-60.

4. *Statistical Abstract of the United States,* 118th ed. (Washington, DC: U.S. Department of Commerce, Bureau of the Census, October 1998).

5. "The Fortune Global 500," *Fortune* (August 3, 1998), p. F-20.

6. Lorrie Grant, "Global Reach Rings Up Earnings Boost for U.S. Retailers," *USA Today* (March 23, 1998), p. 7B; "Retailers Rush to Capture New Markets," *Financial Times* (March 13, 1998), p. 2; Carla Rapoport and Justin Martin, "Retailers Go Global," *Fortune* (February 20, 1995), pp. 102–8; William Symonds, "Invasion of the Retail Snatchers," *Business Week* (May 9, 1994), pp. 72–73; and Eugene Fram and Riad Ajami, "Globalization of Markets and Shopping Stress: Cross-Country Comparisons," *Business Horizons* (January–February 1994), pp. 17–23.

7. Jo Foley, "To Buy or Not to Buy in Dubai," *The Times* (March 7, 1998); and "Fly, Buy a Bigger Dubai," *The Hindu* (March 15, 1998).

8. Gene Koretz, "Those Plucky Corner Stores," *Business Week* (December 5, 1994), p. 26.

9. Alison L. Sprout, "Packard Bell Sells More PCs in the US than Anyone," *Fortune* (June 12, 1995), pp. 82–88; Marcia Berss, "We Will Not Be in a National Chain," *Forbes* (March 27, 1995), p. 50; and Steve Kichen, "Pick a Channel," *Forbes* (March 2, 1992), pp. 108, 110.

10. Christopher Palmeri, "Who's Afraid of Wal-Mart?" *Forbes* (July 31, 1995), p. 81.

11. Richard C. Hoffman and John F. Preble, "Franchising into the Twenty-First Century," *Business Horizons* (November–December 1993), pp. 35–43.

12. Allen Whitehead, "Trouble in Franchise Nation," *Fortune* (March 6, 1995), pp. 115–29; and Jennifer S. Stack and Joseph E. McKendrick, "Franchise Market Expands as Rest of Economy Slumps," *Marketing News* (July 6, 1992), p. 11.

13. LaVerne L. Ludden, *Franchise Opportunities Handbook* (Indianapolis, IN: JIST Works, Inc., 1999); and Scott Shane and Chester Spell, "Factors for New Franchise Success," *Sloan Management Review* (Spring 1998), pp. 43–50.

14. Marc Rice, "Competition Fierce in Complex Business of Delivering Packages," *Marketing News* (May 22, 1995), p. 5; Tim Triplett, "Scanning Wand Makes Checkout Lines Disappear," *Marketing News* (July 4, 1994), p. 6; and Tara Parker-Pope," New Devices Add Up Bill, Measure Shoppers' Honesty," *The Wall Street Journal* (June 6, 1995), pp. B1, 13.

15. Cyndee Miller, "Nordstrom Is Tops in Survey," *Marketing News* (February 15, 1993), p. 12; "Daytons Is Top Retailer in Customer Satisfaction Survey," *Marketing News* (June 6, 1994), p. 8; and Richard Stevenson, "Watch Out, Macy's, Here Comes Nordstrom," *New York Times Magazine* (August 27, 1989), p. 40.

16. Hank Kim and Andrew McMains, "Games A Foot at Toys 'Я' Us," *ADWEEK* (January 11, 1999), p. 2.

17. Wendy Zellner, "A Grand Reopening for Wal-Mart," *Business Week* (February 9, 1998), pp. 86–88; and Elliot Zwiebach, "With Renewed Financial Resources Kmart Is Starting on a Journey of Growth," *Supermarket News* (November 16, 1998), p. 1.

18. Laurie M. Grossman, "Hypermarkets: A Sure-Fire Hit Bombs," *The Wall Street Journal* (June 25, 1992), p. B1.

19. Steve Scrupski, "Tiny 'Brains' Seen for Vending Machines," *Electronic Design* (December 1, 1998), p. 64F; Dan Alaimo, "Two Stores Are Recording a Hit with CD Vending Machine," *Supermarket News* (June 15, 1998), p. 65; "Scoop," *Seventeen* (January 1999), p. 28; "Vending Machine Software," *Marketing News* (May 8, 1995), p. 1; and "Coke Machine Modems Send Distress Signals," *Marketing News* (October 9, 1995), p. 2.

20. Anne D'Innocenzio, "Getting Booked: Coping with Catalog Crunch," *WWD* (December 9, 1998), p. 8.

21. Edward Nash, "The Roots of Direct Marketing," *Direct Marketing* (February 1995), pp. 38–40; and Edith Hipp Updike and Mary Kurtz, "Japan Is Dialing 1 800 BUYAMERICA," *Business Week* (June 12, 1995), pp. 61–64.

22. Susan Chandler and Therese Palmer, "Can Spiegel Pull Out of the Spiral?" *Business Week* (August 28, 1995), p. 80; Gary McWilliams, Susan Chandler, and Julie Tilsner, "Strategies for the New Mail Order," *Business Week* (December 19, 1994), pp. 82–85; and Annetta Miller, "Up to the Chin in Catalogs," *Newsweek* (November 20, 1989), pp. 27–58.

23. Christopher Palmeri, "Victoria's Little Secret," *Forbes* (August 24, 1998), p. 58; Robert Lenzner and Philippe Mao, "Banking Pops Up in the Strangest Places," *Forbes* (April 10, 1995), pp. 72–76; and Dyan Machan, "Sharing Victoria's Secrets," *Forbes* (June 5, 1995), pp. 132–33.

24. Gail DeGeorge and Lori Bongiorno, "Polishing Up the Cubic Zirconia," *Business Week* (July 31, 1995), pp. 83–84; Chad Rubel, "Home Shopping Network Targets Young Audience," *Marketing News* (July 17, 1995), pp. 13, 26; and Kathy Haley, "Keys Are Interactive TV and Channel Expansion," *Advertising Age* (February 22, 1993), p. C16.

25. Raymond R. Burke, "Do You See What I See? The Future of Virtual Shopping," *Journal of the Academy of Marketing Science* (Fall 1997), pp. 352–60; Ellen Neuborne and Stephanie Anderson Forest, "Retailing," *Business Week* (January 12, 1998), p. 116; and Maricris G. Briones, "On-line Retailers Seek Ways to Close Shopping Gender Gap," *Marketing News* (September 14, 1998), pp. 2, 10.

26. Mary J. Cronin, "Business Secrets of the Billion-Dollar Website," *Fortune* (February 2, 1998), p. 142; Robert D. Hof, Ellen Neuborne, and Heather Green, "Amazon.com: The Wild World of E-Commerce," *Business Week* (December 14, 1998), pp. 106–19; "Future Shop," *Forbes ASAP* (April 6, 1998), pp. 37–52; Chris Taylor, "Cybershop," *Time* (November 23, 1998), p. 142; Stephen H. Wildstrom, "'Bots' Don't Make Great Shoppers," *Business Week* (December 7, 1998), p.

27. Steve Casimiro, "Shop Till You Crash," *Fortune* (December 21, 1998), pp. 267–70; De'Ann Weimer, "Can I Try (Click) That Blouse (Drag) in Blue?" *Business Week* (November 9, 1998), p. 86.

28. Chris O'Malley, "No Waiting on the Web," *Time* (November 16, 1998), p. 76; B. G. Yovovich, "Webbed Feat," *Marketing News* (January 19, 1998), p. 1, 18; Joseph Alba, John Lynch, Barton Weitz, Chris Janiszewski, Richard Lutz, Alan Sawyer, and Stacy Wood, "Interactive Home Shopping: Consumer, Retailer, and Manufacturer Incentives to Participate in Electronic Marketplace," *Journal of Marketing* (July 1997), pp. 38–53.

29. Donna Bursey, "Targeting Small Businesses for Telemarketing and Mail Order Sales," *Direct Marketing* (September 1995), pp. 18–20; "Inbound, Outbound Telemarketing Keeps Ryder Sales in Fast Lane," *Direct Marketing* (July 1995), pp. 34–36; "Despite Hangups, Telemarketing a Success," *Marketing News* (March 27, 1995), p. 19; Kelly Shermach, "Outsourcing Seen as a Way to Cut Costs, Retain Service," *Marketing News* (June 19, 1995), pp. 5, 8; and Greg Gattuso, "Marketing Vision," *Direct Marketing*, (February 1994), pp. 24–26.

30. "TeleWatch to Help Control Unethical Telemarketing," *Telemarketing & Call Center Solutions* (April 1998), p. 28.

31. Bill Vlasic and Mary Beth Regan, "Amway II: The Kids Take Over," *Business Week* (February 1, 1998), pp. 60–70.

32. Mathew Schifrin, "Okay, Big Mouth," *Forbes* (October 9, 1995), pp. 47–48; Veronica Byrd and Wendy Zellner, "The Avon Lady of the Amazon," *Business Week* (October 24, 1994), pp. 93–96; and Ann Marsh "Avon Is Calling on Eastern Europe," *Advertising Age* (June 20, 1994), p. 116.

33. The following discussion is adapted from William T. Gregor and Eileen M. Friars, *Money Merchandizing: Retail Revolution in Consumer Financial Services* (Cambridge, MA: Management Analysis Center, Inc., 1982).

34. Nicole Harris, "Just For Feet Is Making Tracks," *Business Week* (July 20, 1998), pp. 70–72.

35. Gail Tom, Michelle Dragics, and Christi Holdregger, "Using Visual Presentation to Assess Store Positioning: A Case Study of JCPenney," *Marketing Research* (September 1991), pp. 48–52.

36. William Lazer and Eugene J. Kelley, "The Retailing Mix: Planning and Management," *Journal of Retailing* (Spring 1961), pp. 34–41.

37. Francis J. Mulhern and Robert P. Leon, "Implicit Price Bundling of Retail Products: A Multiproduct Approach to Maximizing Store Profitability," *Journal of Marketing* (October 1991), pp. 63–76.

38. Gwen Ortmeyer, John A. Quelch, and Walter Salmon, "Restoring Credibility to Retail Pricing," *Sloan Management Review* (Fall 1991), pp. 55–66.

39. William B. Dodds, "In Search of Value: How Price and Store Name Information Influence Buyers' Product Perceptions," *Journal of Consumer Marketing* (Spring 1991), pp. 15–24.

40. "A Time To Steal," *Brandweek* (February 16, 1999), p. 24.

41. Rita Koselka, "The Schottenstein Factor," *Forbes* (September 28, 1992), p. 104, 106.

42. Rice, "Competition Fierce"; and Gary Strauss, "Warehouse Clubs Heat Up Retail Climate," *USA Today* (September 7, 1990), pp. 1B, 2B.

43. "Warehouse Clubs Fine-tune Units," *Chain Drug Review* (June 29, 1998), p. 38; James M. Degen, "Warehouse Clubs Move from Revolution to Evolution," *Marketing News* (August 3, 1992), p. 8; Dori Jones Yang, "Bargains by the Forklift," *Business Week* (July 15, 1991), p. 152; and "Fewer Rings on the Cash Register," *Business Week* (January 14, 1991), p. 85.

44. Ira P. Schneiderman, "Value Keeps Factory Outlets Viable," *Daily News Record* (July 20, 1998), p. 10; Stephanie Anderson Forest, "I Can Get It for You Retail," *Business Week* (September 18, 1995), pp. 84–8; and Adrienne Ward, "New Breed of Mall Knows: Everybody Loves a Bargain," *Advertising Age* (January 27, 1992), p. 55.

45. Anne Faircloth, "Value Retailers Go Dollar For Dollar," *Fortune* (July 6, 1998), pp. 164–66.

46. Barry Brown, "Edmonton Makes Size Pay Off in Down Market," *Advertising Age* (January 27, 1992), pp. 4–5.

47. James R. Lowry, "The Life Cycle of Shopping Centers," *Business Horizons* (January–February 1997), pp. 77–86; Eric Peterson, "Power Centers! Now!" *Stores* (March 1989), pp. 61–66; and "Power Centers Flex Their Muscle," *Chain Store Age Executive* (February 1989), pp. 3A, 4A.

48. Pierre Martineau, "The Personality of the Retail Store," *Harvard Business Review* (January–February 1958), p. 47.

49. Julie Baker, Dhruv Grewal, and A. Parasuraman, "The Influence of Store Environment on Quality Inferences and Store Image," *Journal of the Academy of Marketing Science* (Fall 1994), pp. 328–39; Howard Barich and Philip Kotler, "A Framework for Marketing Image Management," *Sloan Management Review* (Winter 1991), pp. 94–104; Susan M. Keaveney and Kenneth A. Hunt, "Conceptualization and Operationalization of Retail Store Image: A Case of Rival Middle-Level Theories," *Journal of the Academy of Marketing Science* (Spring 1992), pp. 165–75; James C. Ward, Mary Jo Bitner, and John Barnes, "Measuring the Prototypicality and Meaning of Retail Environments," *Journal of Retailing* (Summer 1992), p. 194; and Dhruv Grewal, R. Krishnan, Julie Baker, and Norm Burin, "The Effect of Store Name, Brand Name and Price Discounts on Consumers' Evaluations and Purchase Intentions," *Journal of Retailing* (Fall 1998), pp. 331–52. For a review of the store image literature, see Mary R. Zimmer and Linda L. Golden, "Impressions of Retail Stores: A Content Analysis of Consumer Images," *Journal of Retailing* (Fall 1988), pp. 265–93.

50. Mary Jo Bitner, "Servicescapes: The Impact of Physical Surroundings on Customers and Employees," *Journal of Marketing* (April 1992), pp. 57–71.

51. Jans-Benedict Steenkamp and Michel Wedel, "Segmenting Retail Markets on Store Image Using a Consumer-Based Methodology," *Journal of Retailing* (Fall 1991), p. 300; and Philip Kotler, "Atmospherics as a Marketing Tool," *Journal of Retailing*, vol. 49 (Winter 1973–74), p. 61.

52. De'Ann Weimer, "The Softest Side of Sears," *Business Week* (December 28, 1998), pp. 60–62; Susan Chandler, "Drill Bits, Paint Thinner, Eyeliner," *Business Week* (September 25, 1995), pp. 83–84.

53. The wheel of retailing theory was originally proposed by Malcolm P. McNair, "Significant Trends and Development in the Postwar Period," in A. B. Smith, ed., *Competitive Distribution in a Free, High-Level Economy and Its Implications for the University* (Pittsburgh: University of Pittsburgh Press, 1958), pp. 1–25; see also Stephen Brown, "The Wheel of Retailing—Past and Future," *Journal of Retailing* (Summer 1990), pp. 143–49; and Malcolm P. McNair and Eleanor May, "The Next Revolution of the Retailing Wheel," *Harvard Business Review* (September–October 1978), pp. 81–91.

54. Andrew E. Serwer, "McDonald's Conquers the World," *Fortune* (October 17, 1995), pp. 103–16; Lois Therrien, "McRisky," *Business Week* (October 21, 1991), pp. 114–22; and Gail DeGeorge, "Someone Woke the Elephants," *Business Week* (April 4, 1994), p. 52.

55. Bill Saporito, "What's for Dinner?" *Fortune* (May 15, 1995), pp. 51–64.

56. William R. Davidson, Albert D. Bates, and Stephen J. Bass, "Retail Life Cycle," *Harvard Business Review* (November–December 1976), pp. 89–96.

57. Gretchen Morgenson, "Here Come the Cross-Shoppers," *Forbes* (December 7, 1992), pp. 90–101.

58. Michael Krantz, "The First Bank of Redmond," *Time* (April 27, 1998), p. 52; Russell Mitchell, "The Smart Money Is on Smart Cards," *Business Week* (August 14, 1995), p. 68; Thomas McCarroll, "No Checks. No Cash. No Fuss," *Time* (May 9, 1994), pp. 60–62; and Robert Shaw, "How the Smart Card Is Changing Retailing," *Long Range Planning* (February 1991), pp. 111–14.

59. Mary Kuntz, Lori Bongiorno, Keith Naughton, Gail DeGeorge, and Stephanie Anderson Forest, "Reinventing the Store," *Business Week* (November 27, 1995), pp. 84–96; and David Fischer, "The New Meal Deals," *U.S. News & World Report* (October 30, 1995), p. 66.

60. Mary Kuntz, "These Ads Have Windows and Walls," *Business Week* (February 27, 1995), p. 74; and Richard Corliss, "What's Hot, Doc? Retail!" *Time* (May 9, 1994), pp. 64–66.

Mall of America: This case was prepared by Patrick Hetzel.

CHAPTER 19

1. Dale Buss, "You Ought to Be in Pictures," *Business Week* (June 22, 1998), p. ENT 16; Julia Fein Azoulay, "Getting Product Placed in Film and TV," *ASAP* (October 21, 1998), p. 46; T. L. Stanley and Karen Benezra, "Hollywood Creative Types Getting in on Corporate Partner Development," *BRANDWEEK* (May 19, 1998); Shinan Govani, "Product Placement in Movies—Is It Really So Bad?" *The Christian Science Monitor* (February 10, 1999), p. 11; and Blair R. Fischer, "Making Your Product the Star Attraction," *PROMO* (January 1996), pp. 42–47, 88.

2. Wilbur Schramm, "How Communication Works," in Wilbur Schramm, ed., *The Process and Effects of Mass Communication* (Urbana, IL: University of Illinois Press, 1955), pp. 3–26.

3. E. Cooper and M. Jahoda, "The Evasion of Propaganda," *Journal of Psychology*, vol. 22 (1947), pp. 15–25; H. Hyman and P. Sheatsley, "Some Reasons Why Information Campaigns Fail," *Public Opinion Quarterly*, vol. 11 (1947), pp. 412–23; and J. T. Klapper, *The Effects of Mass Communication* (New York: Free Press, 1960), chapter VII.

4. David A. Ricks, Jeffrey S. Arpan, and Marilyn Y. Fu, "Pitfalls in Advertising Overseas," *Journal of Advertising Research*, vol. 14 (December 1974), pp. 47–51.

5. Adapted from *Dictionary of Marketing Terms*, 2nd ed., Peter D. Bennett, ed. (Chicago: American Marketing Association, 1995), p. 231.

6. B. C. Cotton and Emerson M. Babb, "Consumer Response to Promotional Deals," *Journal of Marketing*, vol. 42 (July 1978), pp. 109–13.

7. Robert George Brown, "Sales Response to Promotions and Advertising," *Journal of Advertising Research*, vol. 14 (August 1974), pp. 33–40.

8. Adapted from *Economic Impact: U.S. Direct Marketing Today* (New York: Direct Marketing Association, 1998), p. 25.

9. Siva K. Balasubramanian and V. Kumar, "Analyzing Variations in Advertising and Promotional Expenditures: Key Correlates in Consumer, Industrial, and Service Markets," *Journal of Marketing* (April 1990), pp. 57–68.

10. Dunn Sunnoo and Lynn Y. S. Lin, "Sales Effects of Promotion and Advertising," *Journal of Advertising Research*, vol. 18 (October 1978), pp. 37–42.

11. J. Ronald Carey, Stephen A. Clique, Barbara A. Leighton, and Frank Milton, "A Test of Positive Reinforcement of Customers," *Journal of Marketing*, vol. 40 (October 1976), pp. 98–100.

12. James M. Olver and Paul W. Farris, "Push and Pull: A One-Two Punch for Packages Products," *Sloan Management Review* (Fall 1989), pp. 53–61.

13. Julia Flynn and Michael Oneal, "A Tall Order for the Prince of Beers," *Business Week* (March 23, 1992), pp. 66–68; and Patricia Sellers, "How Busch Wins in a Doggy Market," *Fortune*, (June 22, 1987), pp. 99–111.

14. Joseph Weber, "Drug Ads: A Prescription for Controversy," *Business Week* (January 18, 1993), pp. 58–60.

15. T. L. Stanley, "The Big Biz: Place Based Media," *BRANDWEEK* (May 11, 1998).

16. Tom Duncan, "Is Your Marketing Communications Integrated?" *Advertising Age* (January 24, 1994), p. 26.

17. Kim Cleland, "Few Wed Marketing, Communications," *Advertising Age* (February 27, 1995), p. 10.

18. Don Schultz, "Objectives Drive Tactics in IMC Approach," *Marketing News* (May 9, 1994), pp. 14, 18; and Neil Brown, "Redefine Integrated Marketing Communications," *Marketing News* (March 29, 1993), pp. 4–5.

19. Betsy Spethmann, "The Nation's Top Promoted Brands," *PROMO* (December 1998), p. 50; Theresa Howard, "Taco Bell Stakes $75M on Buying Dinner," *BRANDWEEK* (February 22, 1999); T. L. Stanley and Becky Ebenkamp, "Against the Force," *BRANDWEEK* (February 15, 1999); and Theresa Howard, "Taco Bell Aims to Inspire Holiday Feeding Frenzy with Plush Chihuahuas," *BRANDWEEK* (September 14, 1998).

20. Robert J. Lavidge and Gary A. Steiner, "A Model for Predictive Measurement of Advertising Effectiveness," *Journal of Marketing* (October 1961), p. 61.

21. Brian Wansink and Michael Ray, "Advertising Strategies to Increase Usage Frequency," *Journal of Marketing* (January 1996), pp. 31–46.

22. Don E. Schultz and Anders Gronstedt, "Making Marcom an Investment," *Marketing Management* (Fall 1997), pp. 41–49; and J. Enrique Bigne, "Advertising Budget Practices: A Review," *Journal of Current Issues and Research in Advertising* (Fall 1995), pp. 17–31.

23. John Philip Jones, "Ad Spending: Maintaining Market Share," *Harvard Business Review* (January–February 1990), pp. 38–42; and Charles H. Patti and Vincent Blanko, "Budgeting Practices of Big Advertisers," *Journal of Advertising Research*, vol. 21 (December 1981), pp. 23–30.

24. James A. Schroer, "Ad Spending: Growing Market Share," *Harvard Business Review* (January–February 1990), pp. 44–48.

25. Jeffrey A. Lowenhar and John L. Stanton, "Forecasting Competitive Advertising Expenditures," *Journal of Advertising Research*, vol. 16, no. 2 (April 1976), pp. 37–44.

26. Daniel Seligman, "How Much for Advertising?" *Fortune* (December 1956), p. 123.

27. James E. Lynch and Graham J. Hooley, "Increasing Sophistication in Advertising Budget Setting," *Journal of Advertising Research*, vol. 30 (February/March 1990), pp. 67–75.

28. Jimmy D. Barnes, Brenda J. Muscove, and Javad Rassouli, "An Objective and Task Media Selection Decision Model and Advertising Cost Formula to Determine International Advertising Budgets," *Journal of Advertising*, vol. 11, no. 4 (1982), pp. 68–75.

29. Don E. Schultz, "Olympics Get the Gold Medal in Integrating Marketing Event," *Marketing News* (April 27, 1998), pp. 5, 10.

30. Betsy Spethmann, "The Nation's Top Promoted Brands," *PROMO* (December 1998), p. 50; and Wayne Friedman, "Saying Goodbye to Hollywood," *Advertising Age* (January 11, 1999), p. 12.

31. Kate Fitzgerald, "Beyond Advertising," *Advertising Age* (August 3, 1998), pp. 1, 14; Curtis P. Johnson, "Follow the Money: Sell CFO on Integrated Marketing's Merits," *Marketing News* (May 11, 1998), p. 10; and Laura Schneider, "Agencies Show That IMC Can Be Good for Bottom Line," *Marketing News* (May 11, 1998), p. 11.

32. *Economic Impact: U.S. Direct Marketing Today* (New York: Direct Marketing Association, 1998), pp. 30, 32.

33. Carol Krol, "Columbia House Looks Down the Road for Gains from Play," *Advertising Age* (March 1, 1999), p. 20.

34. *Statistical Fact Book '98* (New York: The Direct Marketing Association, 1998).

35. Adapted from *Economic Impact: U.S. Direct Marketing Today* (New York: Direct Marketing Association, 1998), pp. 25–26.

36. Carol Krol, "Club Med Uses E-mail to Pitch Unsold, Discounted Packages," *Advertising Age* (December 14, 1998), p. 40.

37. Carol Krol, "Insurer Fireman's Fund Sees Direct as 'Channel of the Future,'" *Advertising Age* (February 15, 1999), p. 18.

38. Jean Halliday, "Taking Direct Route," *Advertising Age* (September 7, 1998), p. 17.

39. Julie Tilsner, "Lillian Vernon: Creating a Host of Spin-offs from Its Core Catalog," *Business Week* (December 19, 1994), p. 85; and Lisa Coleman, "I Went Out and Did It," *Forbes* (August 17, 1992), pp. 102–4.

40. Carol Krol, "Pizza Hut's Database Makes Its Couponing More Efficient," *Advertising Age* (November 30, 1998), p. 27.

41. Alan K. Gorenstein, "Direct Marketing's Growth Will Be Global," *Marketing News* (December 7, 1998), p. 15; Don E. Schultz, "Integrated Global Marketing Will Be the Name of the Game," *Marketing News* (October 26, 1998), p. 5; and Mary Sutter and Andrea Mandel-Campbell, "Customers Are Eager, Infrastructure Lags," *Advertising Age International* (October 5, 1998), p. 12.

42. Juliana Koranten, "European Privacy Rules Go into Effect in 15 EU States," *Advertising Age* (October 26, 1998), p. S31; and Rashi Glazer, "The Illusion of Privacy and Competition for Attention," *Journal of Interactive Marketing* (Summer 1998), pp. 2–4.

43. Laura Loro, "Downside for Public Is Privacy Issue," *Advertising Age* (October 2, 1995), p. 32; Cyndee Miller, "Concern Raised over Privacy on Infohighway," *Marketing News* (January 2, 1995), pp. 1, 7; "Telemarketing Rules OK'd," *Marketing News* (September 11, 1995), p. 1; Judithe Waldrop, "The Business of Privacy," *American Demographics* (October 1994), pp. 46–55; and Mag Gottlieb, "Telemarketing and the Law," *Direct Marketing* (February 1994), pp. 22–23.

CHAPTER 20

1. Maricris G. Briones, "Plotting a Course for Internet Ads," *Marketing News* (September 28, 1998), pp. 1, 12; Kate Maddox, "P&G's Plan: Jump-Start Web as Viable Ad Medium," *Advertising Age* (August 17, 1998), pp. 1, 14; and Jane Hodges, "P&G Tries to Push Online Advertising," *Fortune* (September 28, 1998), p. 280.

2. David A. Aaker and Donald Norris, "Characteristics of TV Commercials Perceived as Informative," *Journal of Advertising Research*, vol. 22, no. 2 (April–May 1982), pp. 61–70.

3. Larry D. Compeau and Dhruv Grewal, "Comparative Price Advertising: An Integrative Review," *Journal of Public Policy & Marketing* (Fall 1998), pp. 257–73; and William Wilkie and Paul W. Farris, "Comparison Advertising: Problems and Potentials," *Journal of Marketing* (October 1975), pp. 7–15.

4. Jennifer Lawrence, "P&G Ads Get Competitive," *Advertising Age* (February 1, 1993), p. 14; Jerry Gotlieb and Dan Sorel, "The Influence of Type of Advertisement, Price, and Source Credibility on Perceived Quality," *Journal of the Academy of Marketing Science* (Summer 1992), pp. 253–60; and Cornelia Pechman and David Stewart, "The Effects of Comparative Advertising on Attention, Memory, and Purchase Intentions," *Journal of Consumer Research* (September 1990), pp. 180–92.

5. Bruce Buchanan and Doron Goldman, "Us vs. Them: The Minefield of Comparative Ads," *Harvard Business Review* (May–June 1989), pp. 38–50; Dorothy Cohen, "The FTC's Advertising Substantiation Program," *Journal of Marketing* (Winter 1980), pp. 26–35; and Michael Etger and Stephen A. Goodwin, "Planning for Comparative Advertising Requires Special Attention," *Journal of Advertising*, vol. 8, no. 1 (Winter 1979), pp. 26–32.

6. Lewis C. Winters, "Does It Pay to Advertise to Hostile Audiences with Corporate Advertising?" *Journal of Advertising Research* (June/July 1988), pp. 11–18; and Robert Selwitz, "The Selling of an Image," *Madison Avenue* (February 1985), pp. 61–69.

7. Mary Lou Quinlan, "Women: We've Come a Long Way, Maybe," *Advertising Age* (February 22, 1999), p. 46.

8. Beth Snyder, "Lincoln Financial Aims Ad Effort at Superrich in U.S.," *Advertising Age* (March 15, 1999), p. 26.

9. Carol Krol, "Database Marketing Proves Rx Value," *Advertising Age* (March 15, 1999), p. S-18.

10. Ira Teinowitz, "Self-regulation Urged to Prevent Bias in Ad Buying," *Advertising Age* (January 18, 1999), p. 4.

11. Bob Donath, "Match Your Media Choice and Ad Copy Objective," *Marketing News* (June 8, 1998), p. 6.

12. Bradley Johnson, "Burnett Dominates Kellys with Altoids Magazine Ads: TBWA, Martin Also Take Prizes at MPA Affair," *Advertising Age* (April 27, 1998), p. 67.

13. Kate Maddox, "ARF Forum Examines Internet Research Effectiveness," *Advertising Age* (January 11, 1999), p. 28.

14. Demetrios Vakratsas and Tim Ambler, "How Advertising Works: What Do We Really Know?" *Journal of Marketing* (January 1999), pp. 26–43.

15. Wayne Friedman, "Fox Boasts $150 Mil Super Bowl Sunday Record," *Advertising Age* (January 18, 1999), pp. 1, 46; Ellen Neuborne and Roger Crockett, "More Bang for the Super Bowl Bucks," *Business Week* (January 2, 1998), p. 70; Jeff Jensen, "Oscar Mayer Scores Super Bowl Halftime," *Advertising Age* (January 8, 1996), pp. 1, 32; and Bob Garfield, "Wieners and Losers," *Advertising Age* (January 29, 1996), pp. 1, 37.

16. Louise Kramer, "Cola War May Get Ferocious between Coke, Pepsi," *Advertising Age* (October 5, 1998), pp. S-6, 10; and Michael Wilke, "Drug Companies Shift DTC Work to Single Managers," *Advertising Age* (October 5, 1998), p. S-14.

17. Michael S. LaTour and Herbert J. Rotfeld, "There Are Threats and (Maybe) Fear-Caused Arousal: Theory and Confusions of Appeals to Fear and Fear Arousal Itself," *Journal of Advertising* (Fall 1997), pp. 45–59.

18. Bob Garfield, "Allstate Ads Bring Home Point about Mortgage Insurance," *Advertising Age* (September 11, 1989), p. 120; and Judann Dagnoli, "'Buy or Die' Mentality Toned Down in Ads," *Advertising Age* (May 7, 1990), p. S-12.

19. Hank Kim and Scott Hume, "Positioning: Blue Cross, Kaiser Permanente Ads Play Big on HMO Trust Factor," *BRANDWEEK* (September 14, 1998); Jeffrey D. Zbar, "Fear!" *Advertising Age* (November 14, 1994), pp. 18–19; John F. Tanner, Jr., James B. Hunt, and David R. Eppright, "The Protection Motivation Model: A Normative Model of Fear Appeals," *Journal of Marketing* (July 1991), pp. 36-45; Michael S. LaTour and Shaker A. Zahra, "Fear Appeals as Advertising Strategy: Should They Be Used?" *The Journal of Consumer Marketing* (Spring 1989), pp. 61–70; and Joshua Levine, "Don't Fry Your Brain," *Forbes* (February 4, 1991), pp. 116–17.

20. Bob Garfield, "Chauvinist Pigskin," *Advertising Age* (February 1, 1999), pp. 1, 45.

21. Dana L. Alden, Wayne D. Hoyer, and Chol Lee, "Identifying Global and Culture-Specific Dimensions of Humor in Advertising: A Multinational Analysis," *Journal of Marketing* (April 1993), pp. 64–75; and Johny K. Johansson, "The Sense of 'Nonsense': Japanese TV Advertising," *Journal of Advertising* (March 1994), pp. 17–26.

22. Alice Z. Cuneo and Laura Petrecca, "The Best Agencies: Different Thinking and Business Wins Make TBWA Chiat/Day Agency of the Year," *Advertising Age* (March 30, 1998), pp. S-1, 4.

23. Paul Lukas, "Got Milk? Got Books? Got a Clue?" *Fortune* (September 7, 1998), p. 40; "Easy Spirit Signs Cybil," *Footwear News* (December 7, 1998), p. 13; Brian D. Till and Terence A. Shimp, "Endorsers in Advertising: The Case of Negative Celebrity Information," *Journal of Advertising* (March 22, 1998), pp. 67; and Alan R. Miciak and William L. Shanklin, "Choosing Celebrity Endorsers," *Marketing Management* (vol. 3, no. 3), pp. 51–59.

24. Kim Cleland, "More Advertisers Put Infomercials into Their Plans," *Advertising Age* (September 18, 1995), p. 50; and John Pfeiffer, "Six Months and a Half a Million Dollars, All for 15 Seconds," *Smithsonian* (October 1987), pp. 134–35.

25. Giles D'Souza and Ram C. Rao, "Can Repeating an Advertisement More Frequently than the Competition Affect Brand Preference in a Mature Market?" *Journal of Marketing* (April 1995), pp. 32–42.

26. Katherine Barrett, "Taking a Closer Look," *Madison Avenue* (August 1984), pp. 106–9.

27. Joe Mandese, "Out-of-Home TV: Does It Count?" *Advertising Age* (January 18, 1993), p. 53.

28. "How Much a 30-Second Spot Costs in Fall's Prime-Time Schedule," *Advertising Age* (September 7, 1992), p. 36.

29. Surendra N. Singh, Denise Linville, and Ajay Sukhdial, "Enhancing the Efficacy of Split Thirty-Second Television Commercials: An Encoding Variability Application," *Journal of Advertising* (Fall 1995), pp. 13–23; Scott Ward, Terence A. Oliva, and David J. Reibstein, "Effectiveness of Brand-Related 15-Second Commercials," *Journal of Consumer Marketing*, no. 2 (1994), pp. 38–44; and Surendra N. Singh and Catherine Cole, "The Effects of Length, Content, and Repetition on Television Commercial Effectiveness," *Journal of Marketing Research* (February 1993), pp. 91–104.

30. J. William Gurley, "How the Web Will Warp Advertising," *Fortune* (November 9, 1998), pp. 119–20; and Joe Mandese, "In New Growth Phase, Cable Feeding on Itself," *Advertising Age* (March 27, 1995), pp. S-1, 2, 10.

31. Jacqueline M. Graves, "The Fortune 500 Opt for Infomercials," *Fortune* (March 6, 1995), p. 20; and William McCall, "Infomercial Pioneer Becomes Industry Leader," *Marketing News* (June 19, 1995), p. 14.

32. Jean Halliday, "Volvo Ready to Act on Leads after Infomercial Success," *Advertising Age* (January 25, 1999), p. 61.

33. George R. Milne, "A Magazine Taxonomy Based on Customer Overlap," *Journal of the Academy of Marketing Science* (Spring 1994), pp. 170–79.

34. "Clutter Bucks," *Fortune* (October 29, 1984), pp. 78–79.

35. Julia Collins, "Image and Advertising," *Harvard Business Review* (January–February 1989), pp. 93–97.

36. Kim Cleland, "Online Soon to Snare 100-plus Newspapers," *Advertising Age* (April 24, 1995), p. S-6.

37. Judy Strauss and Raymond Frost, *Marketing on the Internet: Principles of Online Marketing* (Englewood Cliffs, NJ: Prentice Hall, 1999), pp. 196–249; and Maricris G. Briones, "Rich Media May Be Too Rich for Your Blood," *Marketing News* (March 29, 1999), p. 4.

38. Strauss and Frost, *Marketing on the Internet;* and Heather Green, "The New Ratings Game," *Business Week* (April 27, 1998), pp. 73–78.

39. Arch G. Woodside, "Outdoor Advertising as Experiments," *Journal of the Academy of Marketing Science*, 18 (Summer 1990), pp. 229–37.

40. Ronald Grover, "Billboards Aren't Boring Anymore," *Business Week* (September 21, 1998), pp. 86–90; and Marc Gunther, "The Great Outdoors," *Fortune* (March 1, 1999), p. 150–57.

41. Charles R. Taylor and Weih Chang, "The History of Outdoor Advertising Regulation in the United States," *Journal of Macromarketing* (Spring 1995), pp. 47–59; Cyndee Miller, "Outdoor Advertising Weathers Repeated Attempts to Kill It," *Marketing News* (March 16, 1992), pp. 1, 9; Ricardo Davis, "Outdoor Ad Giants Trim Pay to Agencies," *Advertising Age* (January 18, 1993), p. 54; and Patricia Winters, "Outdoor Builds New Areas to Replace Tobacco and Liquor," *Advertising Age* (October 12, 1992), pp. 5–24.

42. Ed Brown, "Advertisers Skip to the Loo," *Fortune* (October 26, 1998), p. 64; John Cortex, "Growing Pains Can't Stop the New Kid on the Ad Block," *Advertising Age* (October 12, 1992), pp. 5–28; Allen Banks, "How to Assess New Place-Based Media," *Advertising Age* (November 30, 1992), p. 36; and John Cortex, "Media Pioneers Try to Corral On-the-Go Consumers," *Advertising Age* (August 17, 1992), p. 25.

43. Sehoon Park and Minhi Hahn, "Pulsing in a Discrete Model of Advertising Competition," *Journal of Marketing Research* (November 1991), pp. 397–405.

44. Rob Norton, "How Uninformative Advertising Tells Consumers Quite a Bit," *Fortune* (December 26, 1994), p. 37; and "Professor Claims Corporations Waste Billions on Advertising," *Marketing News* (July 6, 1992), p. 5.

45. Pat Sloan and Judann Pollack, "Wrigley to Compensate BBDO on Performance: Gum Marketer Exec Says Plan in Works for U.S. Advertising," *Advertising Age* (April 14, 1997), p. 4; and Mary Kuntz,

"Now Mad Ave Really Has to Sing for Its Supper," *Business Week* (December 18, 1995), p. 43.

46. The discussion of posttesting is based on William F. Arens, *Contemporary Advertising*, 6th ed. (Burr Ridge, IL: Richard D. Irwin, 1996), pp. 181–82.

47. David A. Aaker and Douglas M. Stayman, "Measuring Audience Perceptions of Commercials and Relating Them to Ad Impact," *Journal of Advertising Research*, vol. 30 (August/September 1990), pp. 7–17; and Ernest Dichter, "A Psychological View of Advertising Effectiveness," *Marketing Management*, vol. 1, no. 3 (1992), pp. 60–62.

48. David Kruegel, "Television Advertising Effectiveness and Research Innovation," *Journal of Consumer Marketing* (Summer 1988), pp. 43–51; and Laurence N. Gold, "The Evolution of Television Advertising-Sales Measurement: Past, Present, and Future," *Journal of Advertising Research* (June/July 1988), pp. 19–24.

49. *Cox Direct 19th Annual Survey of Promotional Practices* (1997); and "Promotion Expenditures Shift," *Promo* (August 1995), pp. 1, 9.

50. Magid M. Abraham and Leonard M. Lodish, "Getting the Most Out of Advertising and Promotion," *Harvard Business Review* (May–June 1990), pp. 50–60; Steven W. Hartley and James Cross, "How Sales Promotion Can Work for and against You," *Journal of Consumer Marketing* (Summer 1988), pp. 35–42; Robert D. Buzzell, John A. Quelch, and Walter J. Salmon, "The Costly Bargain of Trade Promotion," *Harvard Business Review* (March–April 1990), pp. 141–49; and Mary L. Nicastro, "Break-Even Analysis Determines Success of Sales Promotions," *Marketing News* (March 5, 1990), p. 11.

51. "The 1998 Annual Report on the Promotion Industry," *Promo* (July 1998), p. S14; "Competing with Coupons," *Marketing News* (March 15, 1999), p. 2.

52. Kapil Bawa and Robert W. Shoemaker, "Analyzing Incremental Sales from a Direct-Mail Coupon Promotion," *Journal of Marketing* (July 1898), pp. 66–78.

53. Roger A. Strang, "Sales Promotion—Fast Growth, Faulty Management," *Harvard Business Review*, vol. 54 (July–August 1976), pp. 115–24; and Ronald W. Ward and James E. Davis, "Coupon Redemption," *Journal of Advertising Research*, vol. 18 (August 1978), pp. 51–58. Similar results on favorable mail-distributed coupons were reported by Alvin Schwartz, "The Influence of Media Characteristics on Coupon Redemption," *Journal of Marketing*, vol. 30 (January 1966), pp. 41–46.

54. "Competing with Coupons," *Marketing News* (March 15, 1999), p. 2; and Larry Armstrong, "Coupon Clippers, Save Your Scissors," *Business Week* (June 20, 1994), pp. 164–66.

55. "Nine Steps to a Fraud-Proof Rebate Form," *Promo* (December 1994), p. 16; Kerry Smith, "The Promotion Gravy Train," *Promo* (August 1995), pp. 50–52; Christopher Power, "Coupon Scams Are Clipping Companies," *Business Week* (June 15, 1992), pp. 110–11; and Kerry J. Smith, "Coupon Scam Uncovered in Detroit," *Promo* (December 1992), pp. 1, 45.

56. "McDonald's Starts 'Buzzing' with Holiday Promotion to Celebrate Disney/Pixar's 'A Bug's Life' Movie," *PR Newswire* (November 11, 1998); and Blair Fischer, "The Top 10 Premium Promotions of the Past Ten Years," *Promo* (May 1995), pp. P17–21.

57. Jeff Jensen, "AT&T Shifts Its Focus for NBA Promo: Contest Tied to League Brings 'Value to Customers,'" *Advertising Age* (April 13, 1998), p. 41.

58. Lorraine Woellert, "The Sweepstakes Biz Isn't Feeling Lucky," *Business Week* (March 22, 1999), p. 80.

59. Fred C. Allvine, Richard D. Teach, and John Connelly, Jr., "The Demise of Promotional Games," *Journal of Advertising Research*, vol. 16 (October 1976), pp. 79–84.

60. "Sampling Continues to Stretch Out," *Promo* (July 1998), pp. S29–30.

61. Kerry Smith, "Building a Winning Frequency Program—The Hard Way," *Promo* (December 1995), pp. 36–38.

62. Gary McWilliams and Mark Maremont, "Forget the Green Stamps—Give Me a Ticket to Miami," *Business Week* (February 24, 1992), pp.

70–71; Glenn Heitsmith, "Credit Cards Form Hub of Loyalty Programs," *Promo* (October 1992), p. 30, 56; and Howard Schlossberg, "Frequency Programs Work Best when Data Are Leveraged Properly," *Marketing News* (November 9, 1992), pp. 3, 5.

63. "New Handy Snack Display Is Dandy," *Marketing News* (October 9, 1987), p. 15.

64. Cyndee Miller, "P-O-P Gains Followers as 'Era of Retailing' Dawns," *Marketing News* (May 14, 1990), p. 2.

65. Kathleen Deveny, "Displays Pay Off for Grocery Marketers," *The Wall Street Journal* (October 15, 1992), pp. B1, B5; "VideOcart Is Rolling Again," *Promo* (August 1991), pp. 1, 36; and Bradley Johnson, "Retailers Check Out In-Store," *Advertising Age* (December 16, 1991), p. 23.

66. Bradley Johnson, "How Rebates Saved Cadillac," *Advertising Age* (January 11, 1999), p. 8.

67. Marvin A. Jolson, Joshua L. Wiener, and Richard B. Rosecky, "Correlates of Rebate Proneness," *Journal of Advertising Research* (February–March 1987), pp. 33–43.

68. Alison Fahey, "Rebate Program Rings Wright Bell," *Advertising Age* (May 21, 1990), p. 44.

69. Danon Darlin, "Junior Mints, I'm Going to Make You a Star," *Forbes* (November 6, 1995), pp. 90–94.

70. This discussion is drawn particularly from John A. Quelch, *Trade Promotions by Grocery Manufacturers: A Management Perspective* (Cambridge, MA: Marketing Science Institute, August 1982).

71. Michael Chevalier and Ronald C. Curhan, "Retail Promotions as a Function of Trade Promotions: A Descriptive Analysis," *Sloan Management Review*, vol. 18 (Fall 1976), pp. 19–32.

72. G. A. Marken, "Firms Can Maintain Control over Creative Co-op Programs," *Marketing News* (September 28, 1992), pp. 7, 9.

73. Leon Reinstein, "Intel's Pentium: A Study in Flawed Public Relations," *Business Week* (January 23, 1995), p. 13; and David Kirkpatrick, "Intel's Tainted Tylenol?" *Fortune* (December 26, 1994), pp. 23–24.

74. Scott Hue, "Free 'Plugs' Supply Ad Power," *Advertising Age* (January 29, 1990), p. 6.

75. Marc Weinberger, Jean Romeo, and Azhar Piracha, "Negative Product Safety News: Coverage, Responses, and Effects," *Business Horizons* (May–June 1991), pp. 23–31.

76. Irving Rein, Philip Kotler, and Martin Stoller, *High Visibility* (New York: Dodd, Mead & Co., 1987); and Steven Colford, "Ross Perot: A Winner after All," *Advertising Age* (December 21, 1992), pp. 4, 18.

77. Michael Treacy and Fred Wiersema, "Customer Intimacy and Other Value Disciplines," *Harvard Business Review* (January–February 1993), pp. 84–93.

78. Scott Hume and Ricardo Davis, "Successful Promos Stress Value-Added," *Advertising Age* (September 21, 1992), p. 35; Zachary Schiller, "Not Everyone Loves a Supermarket Deal," *Business Week* (February 17, 1992), pp. 64–68; and Patricia Sellers, "The Dumbest Marketing Ploy," *Fortune* (October 5, 1992), pp. 88–94.

79. "Kid Stuff," *Promos*, vol. 4 (January 1991), pp. 25, 42; Steven W. Colford, "Fine-Tuning Kids' TV," *Advertising Age* (February 11, 1991), p. 35; and Kate Fitzgerald, "Toys Star-Struck for Movie Tie-Ins," *Advertising Age* (February 18, 1991), p. 3, 45.

80. Herbert J. Rotfeld, Avery M. Abernathy, and Patrick R. Parsons, "Self-Regulation and Television Advertising," *Journal of Advertising*, 19, no. 4 (1990), pp. 18–26.

Fallon McElligott: This case was prepared by Giana Eckhardt of the University of Minnesota.

CHAPTER 21

1. This discussion is based on Geoffrey Brewer, "Selling an Intangible," *Sales & Marketing Management* (January 1998), pp. 52–58; and Dun & Bradstreet, *www.dnb.com*.

2. "A Portrait of the Boss," *Business Week* (November 25, 1991), p. 180.

3. Jaclyn Fierman, "The Death and Rebirth of the Salesman," *Fortune* (July 25, 1994), pp. 80–91; "Teaming Up," *Sales & Marketing Management* (October 1993), pp. 98–104; "Getting Hot Ideas from Customers," *Business Week* (May 18, 1992), pp. 86–87; and Brian Tracy, "Stop Talking and Start Asking Questions," *Sales & Marketing Management* (February 1995), pp. 79–87.

4. For recent research and commentary on relationship selling, see John R. DeVincentis and Neil Rackham, "Breadth of a Salesman," *The McKinsey Quarterly,* no. 4 (1998), pp. 32–43; Michael J. Swenson and Greg Link, "Relationship Selling: New Challenges for Today's Salesperson," and Kenneth R. Evans, David Good, and Theodore W. Hellman, "Relationship Selling: New Challenges for Today's Sales Manager," in Gerald J. Bauer et al., eds., *Emerging Trends in Sales Thought and Practice* (Westport, CT: Quorum Books, 1998); and Marvin A. Jolson, "Broadening the Scope of Relationship Selling," *Journal of Personal Selling & Sales Management* (Fall 1997), pp. 75–88; and Barton A. Weitz and Kevin D. Bradford, "Personal Selling and Sales Management: A Relationship Marketing Perspective," *Journal of the Academy of Marketing Science* (Spring 1999), pp. 241–254.

5. David W. Cravens, "The Changing Role of the Sales Force," *Marketing Management* (Fall 1995), pp. 49–57.

6. F. Robert Dwyer and John F. Tanner, Jr., *Business Marketing* (New York: Irwin/McGraw-Hill 1999), p. 376.

7. Douglas J. Dalrymple and William L. Cron, *Sales Management*, 6th ed. (New York: John Wiley & Sons, Inc., 1998), p. 45.

8. For a perspective on types of selling, see Thomas R. Wotruba, "The Evolution of Personal Selling," *Journal of Personal Selling & Sales Management* (Summer 1991), pp. 1–12. See also, René Y. Darmon, "A Conceptual Scheme and Procedure for Classifying Sales Positions," *Journal of Personal Selling & Sales Management* (Summer 1998), pp. 31–46.

9. Christen Heide, *Dartnell's 29th Salesforce Compensation Survey 1996–1997* (Chicago: The Dartnell Corporation, 1996), p. 117. See also, "Give Me Two Weeks and We'll Give You a New Salesforce," *Sales & Marketing Management* (December 1998), pp. 31–43.

10. "What a Sales Call Cost," *Sales & Marketing Management* (December 1998), pp. 42–43.

11. "Critical Issues in Research Must Be Faced Now," *Marketing News* (June 8, 1998), p. 15.

12. For recent research and commentary on team selling, see Keith A. Chrzanowski and Thomas W. Leigh, "Customer Relationship Strategy and Customer-Focused Teams," in Gerald J. Bauer et al. *Emerging Tends;* Mark A. Moon and Susan Forquer Gupta, "Examining the Formation of Selling Centers: A Conceptual Framework," *Journal of Personal Selling & Sales Management* (Spring 1997), pp. 31–41.

13. Neil Rackham, Lawrence Friedman, and Richard Ruff, *Getting Partnering Right* (New York: McGraw-Hill, 1996), pp. 47–48; and "The Selling Game," *The Wall Street Journal* (March 29, 1994), p. A1.

14. For an interesting overview on prospecting, see "Give Us Leads! Give Us Leads!" *Sales & Marketing Management* (July 1997), pp. 67–72; and "The Best Way to Prospect," *Sales & Marketing Management* (January 1998), p. 80.

15. Carol J. Loomis, "Have You Been Cold-Called?" *Fortune* (December 16, 1991), pp. 109–15.

16. "Corporate Cultures: Clearing Customs," *SKY Magazine* (July 1995), pp. 35–40.

17. These results are reported in Irma Zandl and Richard Leonard, *Targeting the Trendsetting Consumer* (Homewood, IL: Business One Irwin, 1992), p. 141.

18. "Out of the Cold: Banned from Cold Calling, Amex Financial Reps Have to Warm Up to Referrals," *Selling* (May 1996), pp. 22–24.

19. Paul A. Herbing, *Handbook of Cross-Cultural Marketing* (New York: The Holworth Press, 1998).

20. "French Connections," *Dallas Morning News* (December 28, 1998), p. 2D.

21. For an extensive treatment of adaptive and consultative selling, see Bart A. Weitz, Stephen B. Castleberry, and John F. Tanner, *Selling: Building Relationships* (New York: Irwin/McGraw-Hill, 1998), chapter 6.

22. For an extensive discussion of objections, see Charles M. Futrell, *Fundamentals of Selling* (New York: Irwin/McGraw-HIll, 1999), chapter 10.

23. Philip R. Cateora and John L. Graham, *International Marketing,* 10th ed. (New York: Irwin/McGraw-Hall, 1999), p. 128, 131; and Herbing, *Handbook of Cross-Cultural Marketing,* p. 60.

24. Theodore Levitt, *The Marketing Imagination* (New York: Free Press, 1983), p. 111.

25. "Leading Edge," *Sales & Marketing Management* (July 1995), p. 13. See also, "Focus on the Customer," *Fortune* (September 7, 1998), Special Advertising Section.

26. *Management Briefing: Sales and Marketing* (New York: The Conference Board, October 1996), pp. 3–4.

27. "Why It Pays to Be Curious," *Sales & Marketing Management* (August 1998), p. 76.

28. Alan J. Dubinsky, Marvin A. Jolson, Ronald E. Michaels, Masaaki Katobe, and Chae Un Lim, "Ethical Perceptions of Field Sales Personnel: An Empirical Assessment," *Journal of Personal Selling & Sales Management* (Fall 1992), pp. 9–21; and Alan J. Dubinsky, Marvin A. Jolson, Masaaki Katobe, and Chae Un Lim, "A Cross-National Investigation of Industrial Salespeople's Ethical Perceptions," *Journal of International Business Studies* (Fourth Quarter 1991), pp. 651–70.

29. See Gilbert A. Churchill, Neil M. Ford, and Orville C. Walker, J., *Sales Force Management,* 5th ed. (New York: Irwin/McGraw-Hall 1997), pp. 112–13.

30. Dalrymple and Cron, *Sales Management,* p. 44. See also, Arun Sharma, "Who Prefers Key Account Management Programs? An Investigation of Business Buying Behavior and Buying Firm Characteristics," *Journal of Personal Selling & Sales Management* (Fall 1997), pp. 27–39; Dan C. Weilbaker and William A. Weeks, "The Evolution of National Account Management: A Literature Perspective," *Journal of Personal Selling & Management* (Fall 1997), pp. 49–50; and Paul Dishman and Philip S. Nitse, "National Accounts Revisited," *Industrial Marketing Management* (January 1998), pp. 1–9.

31. Several variations of the account management policy grid exists. See, for example, Dalrymple and Cron, *Sales Management,* pp. 183–89; Churchill, Ford, and Walker, *Sales Force Management,* pp. 203–8.

32. Patricia Sellers, "How to Remake Your Sales Force," *Fortune* (May 4, 1992), p. 103. See also, "Look Who's Calling," *Sales & Marketing Management* (May 1998), pp. 43–46.

33. This discussion is based on Dalrymple and Cron, *Sales Management,* pp. 332–36.

34. See, for example, "What Buyers Look For," *Sales & Marketing Management* (August 1995), p. 31; and "The Best Sales Reps Will Take on Their Bosses for You," *Purchasing* (November 7, 1996), p. 81.

35. Weitz, Castleberry, and Tanner, *Selling,* p. 22. For further reading see, Daniel Goleman, "What Makes a Leader?" *Harvard Business Review* (November–December 1998), pp. 93–102; and A. Fisher, "Success Secret: A High Emotional IQ," *Fortune* (October 26, 1998), pp. 293–98.

36. *Statistical Abstract of the United States,* 118th ed. (Washington, DC: U.S. Department of Commerce, 1998). See also, Lucette B. Comer, J.A.F. Nicholls, and Leslie J. Vermillion, "Diversity in the Sales Force: Problems and Challenges," *Journal of Personal Selling & Marketing* (Fall 1998), pp. 1–20; and *Occupation Outlook Quarterly* (Washington, DC: U.S. Department of Labor, Fall 1998).

37. "Is There a Payoff?" *Sales & Marketing Management* (June 1995), pp. 64–71.

38. "Training #9010: Overview and Statistics," *Sales Marketing Network,* www.info-now.com, downloaded January 5, 1999.

39. See, for example, Melanie Berger, "When Their Ship Comes In," *Sales & Marketing Management* (April 1997), pp. 60–65; William L. Cron, Alan J. Dubinsky, and Ronald E. Michaels, "The Influence of Career Stages on Components of Salesperson Motivation," *Journal of Marketing* (January 1988), pp. 78–82; Pradeep K. Tyagi, "Relative Importance of Key Job Dimensions and Leadership Behaviors in Motivating Salesperson Work Performance," *Journal of Marketing* (Summer 1985), pp. 76–86; Richard C. Beckerer, Fred Morgan, and Lawrence Richard, "The Job Characteristics of Industrial Salespersons: Relationship of Motivation and Satisfaction," *Journal of Marketing* (Fall 1982), pp. 125–35; and Walter Kiechel III, "How to Manage Salespeople," *Fortune* (March 14, 1988), pp. 179–80.

40. Churchill, Ford, and Walker, *Sales Force Management,* p. 508.

41. "Mary Kay's Off-Road Bonus," *Business Week* (April 6, 1998), p. 8.

42. Michele Marchetti, "Effective Recruiting Means Cloning Your Sales Force's Heavyweights," *Sales & Marketing Management* (December 1998), p. 32.

43. For further reading, see Goutam N. Challagolla and Tassadduq A. Shervani, "A Measurement Model of the Dimensions and Types of Output and Behavior Control: An Empirical Test in the Salesforce Context," *Journal of Business Research* (July 1997), pp. 159–72.

44. "More Companies Link Sales Pay to Customer Satisfaction," *The Wall Street Journal* (March 29, 1994), p. A1; and "IBM Leans on Its Sales Force," *Business Week* (February 7, 1994), p. 110. For further reading on this topic, see Arun Sharma and Dan Sarrel, "The Impact of Customer Satisfaction Based Incentive Systems on Salespeople's Customer Service Response," *Journal of Personal Selling & Sales Management* (Summer 1995), pp. 17–29.

45. Melissa Campanelli, "Eastman Chemical: A Formula for Quality," *Sales & Marketing Management* (October 1994), p. 88; William Keenan, Jr., "What's Sales Got to Do with It?" *Sales & Marketing Management* (March 1994), pp. 66–70; and Cravens, "The Changing Role of the Sales Force."

46. Ginger Conlon, "Automating Your Sales Force," *Sales & Marketing Management* (December 1998), pp. 63–71. See also, George W. Colombo, *Sales Force Automation* (New York: McGraw-Hill, 1994). For additional insight into the adoption and implementation, see two articles in *The Journal of Business & Industrial Marketing,* vol. 12, number 3/4, 1997: Madhavan Parthasarathy and Ravipreet S. Sohgi, "Salesforce Automation and the Adoption of Technological Innovations by Salespeople: Theory and Implications"; and Bruce D. Keillor, R. Edward Bashaw, and Charles E. Pettijohn, "Salesforce Automation Issues Prior to Implementation: The Relationship between Attitudes toward Technology, Experience, and Productivity."

47. Cravens, "The Changing Role of the Sales Force."

48. Robert L. Lindstrom, "Training Hits the Road," *Sales & Marketing Management,* part 2 (June 1995), pp. 10–14.

49. "Going Mobile, Part 2," *Sales & Marketing Management* (June 1994), p. 5.

50. Cravens, "The Changing Role of the Sales Force."

51. "Supercharged Sell," *Inc. Tech* (November 1998), pp. 42–50.

Reebok International Ltd.: This case was written by Giana Eckardt.

CHAPTER 22

1. Richard Gibson, "A Cereal Maker's Quest for the Next Grape-Nuts," *The Wall Street Journal* (January 23, 1997), pp. B1, B7.

2. David Leonhardt, "Cereal-Box Killers Are on the Loose," *Business Week* (October 12, 1998), pp. 74–77.

3. Ellen Neuborne, "MMM! Cereal for Dinner," *Business Week* (November 24, 1997), pp. 105–106.

4. *1997 General Mills Annual Report* (Minneapolis: General Mills, Inc., 1997), p. 5.

5. Pankaj Ghemawat, "Sustainable Advantage," *Harvard Business Review* (September–October 1986), pp. 53–58.

6. Roger A. Kerin, P. Rajan Varadarajan, and Robert A. Peterson, "First-Mover Advantage: A Synthesis, Conceptual Framework, and Research Propositions," *Journal of Marketing* (October 1992), pp. 33–52.

7. Murali K. Mantrala, Prabhakant Sirha, and Andris A. Zoltners, "Impact of Resource Allocation Rules on Marketing Investment-Level Decisions and Profitability," *Journal of Marketing Research* (May 1992), pp. 162–75.

8. *1998 General Mills Annual Report* (Minneapolis: General Mills, Inc., 1998), p. 7.

9. This discussion and Figure 22–3 are adapted from Stanley F. Stasch and Patricia Longtree, "Can Your Marketing Planning Procedures Be Improved?" *Journal of Marketing* (Summer 1980), p. 82; by permission of the American Marketing Association.

10. Terry Fledler, "Soul of a New Cheerios," *Star Tribune* (January 28, 1996), pp. D1, D4; and Tony Kennedy, "New Cheerios about to Sweeten Cereal Market," *Star Tribune* (July 25, 1995), pp. 1D, /2/d.

11. Ibid.

12. Fledler, "Soul of a New Cheerios," p. 1D.

13. Adapted with permission of The Free Press, a Division of Macmillan, Inc., from *Competitive Advantage: Creating and Sustaining Superior Performance* by Michael E. Porter. Copyright 1985 by Michael E. Porter.

14. William B. Wertner, Jr., and Jeffrey L. Kerr, "The Shifting Sands of Competitive Advantage," *Business Horizons* (May–June, 1995), pp. 11–17.

15. Michael Treacy and Fred Wiersema, "How Market Leaders Keep Their Edge," *Fortune* (February 6, 1995), pp. 88–89.

16. Keith Naughton and Bill Vlasic, "The Nostalgia Boom," *Business Week* (March 23, 1998), pp. 58–64; and David Woodruff and Keith Naughton, "Hard Driving Boss," *Business Week* (October 5, 1998), pp. 82–90.

17. J. Martin Fraering and Michael S. Minor, "The Industry-Specific Basis of the Market Share-Profitability Relationship," *Journal of Consumer Marketing,* vol. 11, no. 1 (1994), pp. 27–37.

18. Zachary Schiller, Greg Burns, and Karen Lowry Miller, "Make It Simple," *Business Week* (September 9, 1996), pp. 96–104.

19. John Greenwald, "Slice, Dice, and Devour," *Time* (October 26, 1998), pp. 64–66.

20. Stratford Sherman, "How Intel Makes Spending Pay Off," *Fortune* (February 22, 1993), pp. 57–61.

21. Lee Ginsburg and Neil Miller, "Value-Driven Management," *Business Horizons* (May–June 1992), pp. 23–27; Richard L. Osborn, "Core Value Statements: The Corporate Compass," *Business Horizons* (September–October 1991), pp. 28–34; and Charles E. Watson, "Managing with Integrity: Social Responsibilities of Business as Seen by America's CEOs," *Business Horizons* (July–August 1991), pp. 99–109.

22. Reprinted by permission of the *Harvard Business Review.* An exhibit from "Making Your Marketing Strategy Work" by Thomas V. Bonoma (March/April 1984). Copyright ©1984 by the President and Fellows of Harvard College; all rights reserved.

23. Larry Hirschhorn and Thomas Gilmore, "The New Boundaries of the 'Boundaryless' Company," *Harvard Business Review* (May–June 1992), pp. 104–15.

24. Hans Hinterhuber and Wolfgang Popp, "Are You a Strategist or Just a Manager?" *Harvard Business Review* (January–February 1992), pp. 105–13; Thomas Steward, "The Search for the Organization of Tomorrow," *Fortune* (May 18, 1992), pp. 92–98; George Stalf, Philip Evans, and Lawrence Shulman, "Competing on Capabilities: The New Rules of Corporate Strategy," *Harvard Business Review* (March–April 1992), pp. 57–69; and Jon Katzenbach and Douglas Smith, *The Wisdom of Teams* (Boston: Harvard Business School Press, 1992).

25. Daniel Roth, "This Ain't No Pizza Party," *Fortune* (November 9, 1998), pp. 158–64.

26. Thomas J. Peters and Robert H. Waterman, Jr., *In Search of Excellence: Lessons from America's Best-Run Companies* (New York: Harper & Row, 1982).

27. Ralph Vartabedian, "Built for the Future," *Minneapolis Star Tribune* (April 7, 1992), pp. 1D, 7D; Roy J. Harris, Jr., "The Skunk Works: Hush-Hush Projects Often Emerge There," *The Wall Street Journal* (October 13, 1980), p. 1; and Tom Peters, "Winners Do Hundreds of Percent over Norm," *Minneapolis Star Tribune* (January 8, 1985), p. 5B.

28. Ben Rich and Leo Janos, *Skunk Works* (Boston: Little Brown and Company, 1994), pp. 51–53.

29. The scheduling example is adapted from William Rudelius and W. Bruce Erickson, *An Introduction to Contemporary Business,* 4th ed. (New York: Harcourt Brace Jovanovich, 1985), pp. 94–95.

30. Peter Galuska, Ellen Neuborne, and Wendy Zellner, "P&G's Hottest New Product: P&G," *Business Week* (October 5, 1998), pp. 92–96.

31. Robert W. Ruekert and Orville W. Walker, Jr., "Marketing's Interaction with Other Functional Units: A Conceptual Framework and Empirical Evidence," *Journal of Consumer Marketing* (Spring 1987), pp. 1–19; and Steven Lysonski, Alan Singer, and David Wilemone, "Coping with Environmental Uncertainty and Boundary Spanning in the Product Manager's Role," *Journal of Consumer Marketing* (Spring 1989), pp. 33–43.

32. Linda Grant, "Outmarketing P&G," *Fortune* (January 12, 1998), pp. 150–52.

33. John Grossman, "Ken Iverson: Simply the Best," *American Way* (August 1, 1987), pp. 23–25; Thomas Moore, "Goodbye, Corporate Staff," *Fortune* (December 21, 1987), pp. 65–76; and Michael Schroeder and Walecia Konrad, "Nucor: Rolling Right into Steel's Big Time," *Business Week* (November 19, 1990), pp. 76–81.

Yoplait USA: Sources: Personal interviews with Chap Colucci and Steven M. Rothschild.

APPENDIX C

1. Denny E. McCorkle, Joe F. Alexander, and Memo F. Diriker, "Developing Self-Marketing Skills for Student Career Success," *Journal of Marketing Education* (Spring 1992), pp. 57–67.

2. James McBride, "Job-Search Strategies to Begin the Next Millennium," *Planning Job Choices: 1999,* 42nd ed. (Bethlehem, PA: National Association of Colleges and Employers, 1998), pp. 14–18.

3. James Heckman, "Marketers Making $$$ in High Tech," *Marketing News* (November 23, 1998), pp. 1, 20; and Michael J. Mandel and Toddi Gutner, "Your Next Job," *Business Week* (October 13, 1997), pp. 64–70.

4. *Job Choices in Business,* 42nd ed. (Bethlehem, PA: National Association of Colleges and Employers, 1998).

5. Nicholas Basta, "The Wide World of Marketing," *Business Week's Guide to Careers* (February–March 1984), pp. 70–72.

6. "The Corporate Elite," *Business Week* (October 12, 1992), pp. 119–46.

7. "Average Yearly Salary Offers," *Salary Survey* (Bethlehem, PA: National Association of Colleges and Employers, September 1998), p. 4.

8. *Occupational Outlook Handbook* (Indianapolis, IN: JIST Works, Inc., 1998), pp. 4, 70.

9. Linda M. Gorchels, "Traditional Product Management Evolves," *Marketing News* (January 30, 1995), p. 4; "Focus on Five Stages of Category Management," *Marketing News* (September 28, 1992), pp. 17, 19; and Sandy Gillis, "On the Job: Product Manager," *Business Week's Guide to Careers* (April–May 1988), pp. 63–66.

10. Phil Moss, "What It's Like to Work for Procter & Gamble," *Business Week's Guide to Careers* (March–April 1987), pp. 18–20.

11. David Kirkpatrick, "Is Your Career on Track?" *Fortune* (July 2, 1990), pp. 38–48.

12. Robin T. Peterson, "Wholesaling: A Neglected Job Opportunity for Marketing Majors," *Marketing News* (January 15, 1996), p. 4.

13. "Advertising," *Career Guide to America's Top Industries* (Indianapolis, IN: JIST Works, 1994), pp. 142–45.

14. "The Climb to the Top," *Careers in Retailing* (January 1995), p. 18.

15. Justin Martin, "How Does Your Pay Really Stack Up?" *Fortune* (June 26, 1995), pp. 79–86.

16. Milan Moravec, Marshall Collins, and Clinton Tripoli, "Don't Want to Manage? Here's Another Path," *Sales and Marketing Management* (June 1990), pp. 62–75.

17. Robin T. Peterson, "Startup Careers through Rep Firms," *Marketing News* (August 4, 1997), p. 8.

18. William Keenan, Jr., "America's Best Sales Forces: Six at the Summit," *Sales and Marketing Management* (June 1990), pp. 62–72.

19. Perri Capell, "Direct-Marketing Pros Enjoy Surging Demand," *National Business Employment Weekly* (January 1–January 7, 1995), pp. 23–24; and "1995 Best Sales Force Awards," *Sales and Marketing Management* (October 1995), pp. 52–63.

20. Michael R. Wukitsch, "Should Research Know More about Marketing?" *Marketing Research* (Winter 1993), p. 50.

21. "Market Research Analyst," in Les Krantz, ed., *Jobs Rated Almanac,* 3rd ed., (New York: John Wiley & Sons, 1995).

22. Cyndee Miller, "Marketing Research Salaries Up a Bit, But Layoffs Take Toll," *Marketing News* (June 19, 1995), pp. 1, 3.

23. Joby John and Mark Needel, "Entry-Level Marketing Research Recruits: What Do Recruiters Need?" *Journal of Marketing Education* (Spring 1989), pp. 68–73.

24. Susan B. Larsen, "International Careers: Reality, Not Fantasy," *CPC Annual: A Guide to Employment Opportunities for College Graduates,* 36th ed. (Bethlehem, PA: College Placement Council, Inc., 1992), pp. 78–85; and Hal Lancaster, "Global Managers Need Boundless Sensitivity, Rugged Constitutions," *The Wall Street Journal* (October 13, 1998), p. B1.

25. John W. Buckner, "Working Abroad at Home," *Managing Your Career* (Spring 1992), pp. 16–17.

26. Kathryn Petras and Ross Petras, *Jobs 95* (New York: Fireside, 1994), pp. 100–18.

27. "Your Job Search Starts with You," *Job Choices: 1996,* 39th ed. (Bethlehem, PA: National Association of Colleges and Employers, 1995), pp. 6–9; Hugh E. Kramer, "Applying Marketing Strategy and Personal Value Analysis to Career Planning: An Experiential Approach," *Journal of Marketing Education* (Fall 1988), pp. 69–73; Alan Deutschman, "What 25-Year-Olds Want," *Fortune* (August 27, 1990), pp. 42–50; and Dawn Richerson, "Personality and Your Career," *Career Woman* (Winter 1993), pp. 46–47.

28. Arthur F. Miller, "Discover Your Design," in *CPC Annual,* vol. 1 (Bethlehem, PA: College Placement Council, Inc., 1984), p. 2.

29. Robin T. Peterson and J. Stuart Devlin, "Perspectives on Entry-Level Positions by Graduating Marketing Seniors," *Marketing Education Review* (Summer 1994), pp. 2–5.

30. Callum J. Floyd and Mary Ellen Gordon, "What Skills Are Most Important? A Comparison of Employer, Student, and Staff Perceptions," *Journal of Marketing Education* (August, 1998), pp. 103–9; "What Employers Want," *Job Outlook '98* (Bethlehem, PA: National Association of Colleges and Employers); and Andrew Marlatt, "Demand for Diverse Skills Is On Upswing," *Internet World* (January 4, 1999).

31. Diane Goldner, "Fill in the Blank," *The Wall Street Journal* (February 27, 1995), pp. R5, R11.

32. Karen Epper Hoffman, "Recruitment Sites Changing Their Focus," *Internet World* (March 15, 1999); Pamela Mendels, "Now That's Casting a Wide Net," *Business Week* (May 25, 1998); and James C. Gonyea, *The Online Job Search Companion* (New York: McGraw-Hill, 1995).

33. Ronald B. Marks, *Personal Selling* (Boston: Allyn & Bacon, 1985), pp. 451–62.

34. Constance J. Pritchard, "Small Employers—How, When & Who They Hire," *Job Choices: 1996,* 39th ed. (Bethlehem, PA; National Association of Colleges and Employers, 1995), pp. 66–69.

35. John L. Munschauer, "How to Find a Customer for Your Capabilities," in 1984–1985 *CPC Annual*, vol. 1 (Bethlehem, PA: College Placement Council, Inc., 1984), p. 24.

36. C. Randall Powell, "Secrets of Selling a Résumé," in Peggy Schmidt, ed., *The Honda How to Get a Job Guide* (New York: McGraw-Hill, 1984), pp. 4–9.

37. Ibid., p. 4.

38. Adapted from Ibid., pp. 4–9.

39. Joyce Lain Kennedy, "Computer-Friendly Resume Tips," *Planning Job Choices: 1999*, 42nd ed. (Bethlehem, PA: National Association of Colleges and Employers, 1998), p. 49; and Joyce Lain Kennedy and Thomas J. Morrow, *Electronic Resume Revolution* (New York: John Wiley & Sons, 1994).

40. Arthur G. Sharp, "The Art of the Cover Letter," *Career Futures*, vol. 4, no. 1 (1992), pp. 50–51.

41. Perri Capell, "Unconventional Job Search Tactics," *Managing Your Career* (Spring 1991), pp. 31, 35.

42. Julie Griffin Levitt, *Your Career: How to Make It Happen* (Cincinnati: South-Western Publishing Co., 1985).

43. Deborah Vendy, "Drug Screening and Your Career," *CPC Annual* (Bethlehem, PA: College Placement Council, 1992), pp. 61–62.

44. Marks, *Personal Selling*, p. 469.

45. Terence P. Pare, "The Uncommitted Class of 1989," *Fortune* (June 5, 1989), pp. 199–210.

46. Bob Weinstein, "What Employers Look For," in Peggy Schmidt, ed., *The Honda How to Get a Job Guide* (New York: McGraw-Hill, 1985), p. 10.

APPENDIX D

1. This case was prepared by Linda Rochford from the following sources: Burton Web site at www.burton.com; www.hoovers.com/capsules/51732.html; Burton Snowboards, Hoover's Online Profile, 1999; 1998 State of the Industry Report, Sporting Goods Manufacturers Association (SGMA); www.sportlink.com/research/1998research/industry/98soti.html; Sports Participation Trends Report 1997; www.sporlink.com/research.1998r...ch/industry/98participationtrends.html; and interview with Ben Gustafson, snowboarding competitor and enthusiast.

2. This case was prepared by Linda Rochford from the following sources: Nancy Rivera Brooks, "How to Get a Business Loan," *Los Angeles Times* (May 16, 1993); David Eddy, "Juice Club: Smoothin' Its Way to Success," *San Luis Obispo County Telegram-Tribune* (April 23, 1993); Kinney Littlefield, "Slurp to Heart's Content at Juice Club," *The Orange County Register* (April 23, 1993); Beth Lorenzini, "Turn Up the Juice," *Restaurants and Institutions*, vol. 105, no. 3 (February 1, 1995), p. 113; Louis Trager, "Get Ready for Juice Bars, at a Corner Nearby Soon," *San Francisco Examiner* (1995); and Jamba Juice Web site at www.jambajuice.com.

3. This case was adapted by Mark Weber from a case originally written by Norman Bowie and Stefanie Ann Lenway and from additional sources, including Paul McEnroe and Susan E. Peterson, "H.B. Fuller Sued in Teen's Death," *Minneapolis Star Tribune* (January 4, 1996), pp. D1, D2.

4. This case was prepared by Paul H. Sandholm and Linda Rochford from the following sources:
www.hoovers.com/capsules/15521.html;
wysiwyg://9/http://www.hoovers.com/annuals/15521af.html;
wysiwyg://4/http:www.hoovers.com/capsules/15521af.html; and
http:www.golfweek.com.

5. This case was prepared by Roy D. Adler, professor of marketing at Pepperdine University–Malibu, as a basis for class discussion. Copyright by Roy D. Adler. Reproduced with permission.

6. This case was prepared by Linda Rochford and Rajiv Vaidyanathan, University of Minnesota–Duluth, from the following sources: www.xoom.com; www.hoovers.com/capsules/57391.html; and personal interviews with Xoom.com executives.

7. This case was prepared by Professor James E. Nelson, University of Colorado, at Boulder. Used with permission.

8. This case was prepared by Linda Rochford from the following sources: Stuart F. Brown, "Quest for the Boojum," *Popular Science* (July 1995), pp. 77–81; Brian O'Reilly, "What's a Hummer? Aah! Thought You'd Never Ask," *Fortune* (October 2, 1995), p. 146; "His Summer in a Hummer," *Fortune* (October 2, 1995), pp. 154–55; AM General press package 1996; www.hoovers.com/capsules54364.html; and "Converse and Hummer Team Up to Produce Unrivaled, Rugged Footwear," *Business Wire* (January 5, 1999).

9. This case was prepared by Linda Rochford from the following sources: Alan Goldstein, "The iMac: Funny Look, Serious PC," *Dallas Morning News* (August 25, 1998), Personal Technology Section, p. 1F; "Apple's Revolution in a Box," *TIME Digital*, cgi.pathfinder.com/time/digital/feature/0,2955,18248,00.html (January 1999) pp. 1–5; "iMac Tops Fourth Quarter US Retail/Mail Order PC Sales," *PRNewsletter* www.prnewswire.com/cgi-bin/stories.pl?ACCT=104&STORY=/www/story/01-21-1999/0000850728& (January 21, 1999); "Apple Reports Fiscal First Quarter Profits of $152 Million," www.apple.com/pr/library/199/jan/13earnings.html (January 13, 1999); and "The Mac: Then and Now" www.cnet.com/Content/Reports/Special/ Mac/ (1999).

10. This case was prepared by Professors Maurice Mandell and Larry J. Rosenberg. Reprinted by permission of Prentice Hall, Inc.

11. This case was prepared by Professor John W. Mullins and Christina L. Grippi, University of Denver. Copyright © by the *Case Research Journal*.

12. This case was prepared by Linda Rochford from the following sources: John Welbes, "Coffee Connoisseurs," *Duluth News Tribune* (September 25, 1995), pp. 1B, 3B, 5B; Dori Jones Yang, "The Starbucks Enterprise Shifts into Warp Speed," *Business Week*, (October 24, 1994), pp. 76–77; Rhonda Brammer, "Grounds for Caution," *Barrons*, (August 15, 1994), p. 20; www.hoovers.com/capsules/15745.html; and www.starbucks.com.

13. This case was prepared by Linda Rochford from the following sources: David E. Kalish, "Secret of Success: Enterpreneur Michael Dell Had a Better Idea and Decided to Stick With It," *Chicago Tribune, Business News* (August 30, 1998); www.dell.com; www.hoovers.com/capsules/13193.html; and "Supply Chain Management Is Velocity: The Manufacturer's View," www.sun.com/products-n-solutions/manufacturing/pubs/om-3/.

14. This case was prepared by Linda Rochford from the following sources: Brian Silverman, "Shopping for Loyal Customers," *Sales and Marketing Management* (March 1995), pp. 96–97; Nordstrom Employment Opportunities, publication P3003, Rev. 5/94; Robert Spector and Patrick D. McCarthy, *The Nordstrom War: The Inside Story of America's #1 Customer Service Company* (New York: John Wiley and Sons, 1994); and Nordstrom Web site at www.nordstrom.com.

15. This case was prepared by Linda Rochford from the following sources: "New VW Beetle Ads to Bow This Week," *Ad Week*, vol. 9, no. 10 (1998), p. 76; "Snyder's Arnold Communications Awarded Top International Advertising Honors," *Business Wire* (July 10, 1998); "Beetlemania," *Ad Week*, vol. 39, no. 28 (July 13, 1998), p. 24; Paul Dean, "The New Beetle: 23 Smiles Per Gallon," *Los Angeles Times* (February 19, 1998), Life & Style, Part E, p. 1; Alison Fahey and Eleftheria Parpis, "Lion Roars for Arnold, VW Hub Shop Wins Top Print Prize at International Fete," *Ad Week* (June 29, 1998); Debra Goldman, "Bug Redux: the New Volkswagen Beetle," *Ad Age*, vol. 39, no. 12 (March 23, 1998), p. 38; Janice L. Jones, "Meet the Beetles: How Volkswagen's New Beetle Compares with the Legendary One," *Los Angeles Times* (February 26, 1998), Business section, Part D, p. 1; David Kiley, "The Point: A Rolls by Any Other Name," *Brandweek* (April 6, 1998); John O'Dell, "VW's New Version of 'Bug' Off' to a Fast Start in the U.S.," *Los Angeles Times* (February 26, 1998), Business section, Part D, p. 1; Owen Ullmann and Bill Vlasic, "Was This

White House Bug All Buzz?" *Business Week,* no. 3585 (July 6, 1998), p. 4; Judy Warner, "Arnold Unveils New Beetle TV Spots for Volkswagen of America," *Ad Week,* vol. 39, no. 11 (March 16, 1998), p. 5; and Craig Wilson, "VW's New Beetle Becomes a National Obsession," *USA Today* (April 22, 1998), pp. 1A–2A, 76.

16. This case was prepared by Linda Rochford and Rajiv Vaidyanathan, University of Minnesota–Duluth, from the following sources: "Image-conscious Consumers Wear Social Ambitions on Wrist," *Duluth News Tribune* (August 2, 1995), p. 6; "Timex Plans $10M Push in 4th Quarter," *Advertising Age* (September 6, 1993), p. 23; "Timex Swatch Campaigns Set for Battle," *The Wall Street Journal* (May 31, 1995), p. B9; "The Best Advertising of 1992," *Time* (January 4, 1993), p. 70; Riccardo A. Davis, "More Ads to Watch," *Advertising Age* (February 7, 1994), p. 50; Elaine Underwood, "Indiglo Watch Lights Up, Better Times for Timex," *Brandweek,* (April 25, 1994), pp. 30–32; Neal McGrath, "Timex, After a Licking, They're Back Ticking," *Asian Business* (December 1994), pp. 18, 20; Chris Roush, "At Timex, They're Positively Glowing," *Business Week,* (July 12, 1993), p. 141; Swatch Web site at www.swatch.com; Seiko Web site www.SeikoUSA.com; and Timex Web site www.timex.com.

17. This case was prepared by Jay Krasnow, University of Minnesota. It is based on information and assistance provided by a2bmusic.

CREDITS

CHAPTER 1

p. 2, Courtesy of Rollerblade, Inc.; p. 4, Courtesy Rollerblade, Inc.; p. 11, New Product Showcase and Learning Center, Inc., photograph by Robert Haller; p. 13 (left), Courtesy Wal-Mart Stores, Inc.; p. 13 (right), Reprinted with permission of Lands' End, Inc.; p. 17, Courtesy of Rollerblade, Inc.; p. 18, All photos courtesy of Rollerblade, Inc.; p. 19, All photos courtesy of Rollerblade, Inc.; p. 23 (top right), Courtesy Hellenic National Tourism Organization; p. 23 (bottom), Courtesy Compuware Corporation.

CHAPTER 2

p. 28, Used with permission of Ben & Jerry's Homemade Holdings, Inc.; p. 33, DILBERT reprinted by permission of United Features Syndicate, Inc.; p. 36, Reprinted courtesy of Sears, Roebuck and Co.; p. 37, Figure 2–3: Moody's Industrial Manual; p. 38 (left), Reproduced by permission of Intel Corporation, Copyright 1998 Intel Corporation; p. 38 (right), Duncan Hines ad: Courtesy of Aurora Foods; p. 39, Courtesy of Nokia Americas; p. 43, Used with permission of Ben & Jerry's Homemade Holdings, Inc.; p. 46, ©1996 Paradise Kitchens, Inc. Reprinted with permission; p. 49, Courtesy of Eastman Kodak Co.: agency: Ogilvy & Mather/Atlanta; p. 53, Courtesy of Specialized Bicycles.

APPENDIX A

pp. 57, 59, 63, 65, 67, 68, ©1996 Paradise Kitchens Inc. All photos and ads reprinted with permission.

CHAPTER 3

p. 72, Courtesy Microsoft Corporation; p. 76, Figure 3–3: U.S. Bureau of the Census; p. 77, Courtesy of Club Med Sales, Inc.; p. 81, Courtesy of Saturn Corporation; p. 82, Figure 3–5: *Surveys of Consumers,* Survey Research Center, The University of Michigan; p. 83, Courtesy CACI Marketing Systems; p. 84, Courtesy Westin Hotels & Resorts, agency: Cole & Weber, Seattle, photographers: Kathleen Norris Cook and Tim Bieber/Image Bank Northwest and Tony Stone Images; p. 85 (left), Courtesy IBM; p. 85 (center), Courtesy Diamond Multimedia Systems, Inc.; p. 85 (right), Courtesy of USSB; p. 86 (left), Courtesy Young & Rubicam/Frankfurt; p. 86 (right), Courtesy of Lever Brothers Company; p. 87, Graphic image supplied courtesy of Environmental Systems Research Institute, Inc.(ESRI); p. 88, Courtesy IBM; p. 92, Sharon Hoogstraten; p. 93, Reprinted with permission of the Council of Better Business Bureaus, Inc., copyright 1999.

Council of Better Business Bureaus, Inc., 4200 Wilson Boulevard, Arlington, VA 22203. World Wide Web http://www.bbb.org; p.96, Both courtesy of Imagination Pilots Entertainment; p. 97, Courtesy of Imagination Pilots Entertainment.

CHAPTER 4

p. 98, Courtesy of Anheuser-Busch Companies, Inc.; p. 103, Rex USA Ltd.; p. 104, Charlie Archambault, U.S. News & World Report; p. 105, Courtesy Transparency International; p. 110 (top), Tony Stone Images; p. 110 (bottom), Courtesy Irwin Professional Publishing; p. 111, Courtesy McDonald's Corporation; p. 112, Courtesy Reebok International Ltd.

CHAPTER 5

p. 118, Courtesy CNS, Inc.; p. 123 (left), Courtesy of Sony Electronics, Inc.; p. 123 (right), Courtesy of Bruno Magli; p. 128, Courtesy ALMAP/BBDO, Sao Paulo; p. 129, Levi ad: Courtesy Harrod & Mirlin/FCB, Toronto; p. 131, Travelpix/FPG International; p. 132, Courtesy Nestlé S.A.; p. 133, Sharon Hoogstraten; p. 134, Reprinted with permission of Reader's Digest/photograph by Richard Hong; p. 135, Courtesy of The Coca-Cola Company; p. 136, Figure 5–5: American Demographics Magazine, ©1995. Reprinted with permission; p. 137, Courtesy The PRS Group; p. 139, James Schnepf; p. 140, Courtesy of McDonald's Corporation; p. 141, Figure 5–7: Reprinted by permission of Prentice Hall, Inc. Upper Saddle River, NJ.; p. 142, Courtesy, The Gillette Company; p. 146 (top), Copyright ©1997 Universal Press Syndicate. All rights reserved; p. 146 (bottom), Courtesy CNS, Inc.

CHAPTER 6

p. 148, Courtesy Campbell Ewald, Warren, MI; p. 151, Figure 6–2: *Consumer Reports Buying Guide,* 1998, pp. 70–71; p. 152, Courtesy Grey Advertising; p. 153, Courtesy of Eddie Bauer, Inc.; p. 158, Courtesy inscape for Time Warner Interactive; p. 159 (left), ©1998 National Fluid Milk Processor Promotion Board; agency: Bozell Worldwide/New York; p. 159 (right), Photograph by Greg Wolff; p. 161 (left), Courtesy of Colgate-Palmolive Company; p. 161 (right), The Bayer Company; p. 162, Figure 6–6: VALS2, SRI International, Menlo Park, CA; p. 163, VALS™ is a trademark of SRI International; p. 164 (left), Courtesy, The Gillette Company; p. 164 (right), Courtesy Omega U.S./Bide Quervain; p. 165, Les Stone/Sygma; p. 166, The *Sports Illustrated for Kids* cover is reprinted courtesy of *Sports Illustrated for Kids* December

1998 issue. Copyright ©1998, Time, Inc. All rights reserved; p. 167, Figure 6–7: Patrick G. Murphy and William A. Staples, "A Modernized Family Life Cycle," *Journal of Consumer Research,* January 1979, p. 17; p. 168, Courtesy of Haggar Clothing Co. ©1997 Haggar Clothing Co.; p. 169, Courtesy of The Black World Today; p. 170, Courtesy The Pepsi Cola Company; p. 171, Courtesy of Pacific Bell; pp. 173, 174, All courtesy of Ken Davis Products, Inc.

CHAPTER 7

p. 176, ©1999 Endacott Ltd.; p. 178, Figure 7–1: Based on *Statistical Abstract of the United States,* 115th ed. (Washington, DC: U.S. Department of Commerce, 1995); p. 180, Reprinted with permission of the Census Bureau; p. 183, Courtesy of SGS-Thomson Microelectronics; p. 184, Courtesy of Sylvania/GTE Products Corporation; p. 185, Courtesy Anthony Mark Hankins™; p. 186, Courtesy of Chrysler Corporation; p. 188, Reproduced by permission of Intel Corporation, Copyright 1998 Intel Corporation; p. 189, Courtesy of GE Information Services; p. 190, Dan Bosler/Tony Stone Images; p. 193, Courtesy of Allen-Bradley Company, Inc.; p. 194, Courtesy of American Harvest, Inc.

CHAPTER 8

p. 202, Courtesy of AOL; p. 204 (top), Michael J. Hruby; p. 204 (bottom), Courtesy Toys "Я" Us; p. 209, Figure 8-4: iVALS Internet User Segments, SRI Consulting.; p. 210, Courtesy SRI Consulting; p. 213, ©Matt Mahurin Inc.; p. 215, Courtesy Cisco Systems, Inc.; p. 216 (left), Advertising created for Onsale, Inc. by USWEB/CKS; p. 216 (right), Courtesy Women.Com Networks, Inc.; p. 217, Courtesy of Praco, Ltd.; p. 218, Reprinted with permission of The Gap; pp. 221, 222, Courtesy of America Online.

CHAPTER 9

p. 224, Shooting Star; p. 227, Courtesy Fisher-Price; p. 229, Courtesy Fisher-Price; p. 231, Michael J. Hruby; p. 235 (left), Courtesy, The Gillette Company; p. 235 (center), Courtesy 3M; p. 235 (right), Courtesy of Skechers USA, p. 235 (bottom), Shooting Star; p. 236, Figure 9–4: Nielsen Media Research; p. 237, Courtesy of Teen Research Unlimited; p. 239, Courtesy Wendy's International Inc.; p. 244, Both ads courtesy of Ocean Spray; p. 247, Figure 9–8: *Sales & Marketing Management,* "1998 Survey of Buying Power."

CHAPTER 10

p. 254, Brent Jones; p. 256 (top), Courtesy New Balance Athletic Shoe, Inc.; p. 256 (bottom), Courtesy Vans, Inc.; p. 260, Courtesy of Street & Smith's Annuals; p. 262, DILBERT reprinted by permission of United Features Syndicate, Inc.; p. 264, Courtesy of Microfridge, Inc.; p. 265, Photos by John Abbott; p. 265, Figure 10–5: Simmons 1993 Study of Media and Markets: Restaurants, Stores, and Grocery Shopping, P-10 (New York: Simmons Market Research Bureau, Inc., 1993), pp. 0001, 0026 Summary Appendix; p. 266, Figure 10–6: Simmons 1993 Study of Media and Markets: Restaurants, Stores, and Grocery Shopping, P-10 (New York: Simmons Market Research Bureau, Inc., 1993), pp. 0003 Summary Appendix; p. 267, Courtesy of Genova & Partners; p. 270, Courtesy of Wendy's International, Inc.; p. 272, Courtesy of Apple Computer, Inc.; p. 277 (left), Courtesy of Buick Motor Division.; p. 277 (right), Courtesy of Oldsmobile; agency: Leo Burnett.

CHAPTER 11

p. 284, Courtesy of 3M Company; p. 287, Courtesy of Nike, Inc.; p. 288, Courtesy Rolex Watch USA, Inc.; p. 291 (top), Courtesy Sony Computer Entertainment America Inc.; p. 291 (bottom), Breathe Right™ nasal strips are manufactured by CNS, Inc., Minneapolis, MN/Advertising agency: Seitsema, Engeland Partners, Minneapolis, MN; p. 294 (left), New Product Showcase and Learning Center, Inc./Photograph by Robert Haller; p. 294 (right), Courtesy of the Original Pet Drink Co., Inc.; p. 296, Sharon Hoogstraten; p. 298, Courtesy of 3M Company; p. 299 (left), Copyright Nissan 1998. Infiniti, QX4 and the Infiniti logo are registered trademarks of Nissan; p. 299 (right), Copyright (1998) Mazda North America Operations. Used by permission; p. 301 (top), Courtesy Penn Racquet Sports; Agency: Veritas Advertising, Inc.; p. 301 (bottom), Courtesy of Frito-Lay, Inc.; p. 303 (top), Jose Azel/Aurora; p. 303 (bottom), John Madere/The Stock Market; p. 305, Figure 11–7, *Sales & Marketing Management,* "The Nation's Most Popular Test Markets," pp. 65–69; p. 306, Churchill & Klehr/Tony Stone Images; p. 307, Courtesy of Hewlett-Packard Company; p. 310, 3Com, the 3Com logo, and Palm Computing are registered trademarks, and Palm V and the Palm V logo are trademarks of Palm Computing, Inc., 3Com Corporation, or its subsidiaries.

CHAPTER 12

p. 312, Foote Cone & Belding, Chicago, IL; photographer: Steve Bonini; client: Gatorade; p. 317 (left), Courtesy American Honda Motor Company, Inc.; agency: Rubin Postaer and Associates; p. 317 (right), Courtesy of Canon USA, Inc.; p. 323, Courtesy of the National Fluid Milk Processor Promotion Board; agency: Bozell, Chicago; p. 327, Courtesy of Elite Foods, Inc.; p. 330, Courtesy Louis Vuitton; p. 331 (left),

Courtesy of Black & Decker (U.S.), Inc.; p. 331 (right), Courtesy of DeWalt Industrial Tool Company; p. 332, Courtesy of Pez Candy, Inc.; p. 333, Courtesy of The Coca-Cola Company; p. 334, ©The Procter & Gamble Company. Used with permission; p. 338, ©1999 BMW of North America, Inc. Used with permission. The BMW name and logo are registered trademarks; p. 339, ©1999 BMW of North America, Inc. Used with permission. The BMW name and logo are registered trademarks.

CHAPTER 13

p. 340, Chris Noble/Tony Stone Images; p. 343 (top left), Courtesy British Airways; p. 343 (top right), Courtesy Korean Air Lines; p. 343 (bottom), Courtesy of American Express Co.; p. 344, Courtesy of Hyatt Hotels Corporation; p. 346, Courtesy Patagonia, Inc.; p. 347, Figure 13–4: Reprinted by permission of Harvard Business Review. An exhibit from "Strategy Is Different in Service Businesses," by Dan R. E. Thomas, July-August, 1978. Copyright (1978 by the President and Fellows of Harvard College, all rights reserved.; p. 348 (top left), Courtesy The Salvation Army; p. 348 (top right), Courtesy ©1999 Outward Bound USA; p. 348 (bottom), Reprinted with permission of the United States Postal Service; p. 350, Figure 13–6: ON GREAT SERVICE, p. 79. Reprinted with permission of The Free Press, a division of Simon & Schuster from ON GREAT SERVICE: A Framework for Action by Leonard L. Berry.; p. 350, Figure 13–7: Adapted from W. Earl Sasser, R. Paul Olsen, and D. Daryl Wyckoff, *Management of Service Operations: Text, Cases, and Readings* (Boston: Allyn & Bacon, 1978).; p. 351, Courtesy of the Sears, Roebuck & Co.; p. 353 (left), Courtesy of McDonald's Corporation; p. 353 (center), Courtesy of Sprint; p. 353 (right), Courtesy of American Red Cross; p. 355 (top), Courtesy of Hartej S. Sood, DDS; p. 355 (bottom left), Courtesy Andersen Consulting; p. 355 (bottom right), Courtesy Kelly Services.

CHAPTER 14

p. 360, Matthew McVay/Tony Stone Images; p. 362, Courtesy Boeing; p. 364, ©Kohler Company; p. 366 (left), Michael J. Hruby; p. 366 (right), Courtesy of Nike, Inc.; p. 368, Michael J. Hruby; p. 370, Courtesy of Fiat USA, Inc.; p. 371, Sharon Hoogstraten; p. 375, Courtesy of Luigines, Inc.

CHAPTER 15

p. 384, Courtesy, The Gillette Company; p. 389, Courtesy Compaq Computer Corporation; p. 390, Courtesy of Rock & Roll Hall of Fame and Museum; p. 391, Courtesy Grey Advertising; p. 393, Courtesy, The Gillette Company; p. 395, Andrew Garn; p. 397, Sharon Hoogstraten; p. 400, Courtesy of The Toro Company; p. 402, Photograph by Monci Jo Williams, FORTUNE, ©1983 Time Inc. All rights reserved.

APPENDIX B

pp. 413, 416, Both photos courtesy of The Caplow Company.

CHAPTER 16

p. 418, Courtesy Gateway 2000; p. 420, Figure 16–1: Reprinted by permission of the publisher from *Dictionary of Marketing Terms,* Peter D. Bennett, Editor, (1996 by the American Marketing Association; p. 426, Courtesy Nestlé S.A.; p. 431, Courtesy of the Kroger Company; p. 432, Courtesy FAO Schwartz; p. 433, Courtesy VISA; p. 434, Courtesy of Dai-Ichi Kikaku Co., Ltd. and Warner Lambert; p. 435, Courtesy of Sanyu Boh Co., Ltd.

CHAPTER 17

p. 442, Reprinted with permission of *Business-Week;* illustration by David Cale; p. 446, Courtesy Saturn Corporation; p. 447, Sharon Hoogstraten; p. 449, Courtesy of J.D. Edwards World Solutions Company; p. 452, Mark Richards/PhotoEdit; p. 453 (left), Courtesy of Penske Truck Leasing Co. ©1997; p. 453 (right), Courtesy Emery Worldwide; p. 455, Courtesy of Maersk, Inc.; p. 456, Ads courtesy of United Airlines; p. 457, Courtesy of Rapistan Demag Corporation; p. 459, Courtesy of Federal Express Corporation; p. 460, Both photos Fritz Hoffmann/Imageworks.

CHAPTER 18

p. 464, Courtesy Buy.Dot.Com; p. 466, Courtesy of Levi Strauss & Co.; p. 467, Wide World Photo; p. 468, Corbis/Bettmann; p. 470, Reprinted with permission of Tandy Corporation; p. 474 (top), Paul Chesley/Tony Stone Images; p. 474 (middle), Courtesy of L.L. Bean, Inc.; p. 474 (bottom), Courtesy of Lillian Vernon Corporation; p. 475 (top), Courtesy of QVC Network, Inc.; p. 475 (middle), Courtesy of Shabang; p. 475 (bottom), Courtesy of amazon.com; p. 476 (top), Reprinted with permission of Lands' End, Inc.; p. 476 (bottom), Courtesy of Cybersmith, Cambridge, MA.; p. 483, Courtesy Taco Bell; p. 486, Courtesy of Nike, Inc.; p. 488, Both photos courtesy of Mall of America.

CHAPTER 19

p. 490, Shooting Star; p. 493, Courtesy of Pyro; p. 495, Courtesy of East Pak; p. 496, Reprinted with permission of Macmillan General References USA, a division of Ahsuog, Inc. from *Frommer's Ireland from $50 a Day,* by Mark Meagher, Elizabeth Neave, Susan fro Poole, Robert Emmet Meagher. Copyright ©1998 by Simon & Schuster, Inc.; p. 497, Courtesy Fence Magazine; p. 499 (top), Photography by Greg Wolff; p. 499 (bottom), Courtesy IBM; p. 502, Courtesy The Quantum Group; p. 503, Courtesy Taco Bell; p. 505, Figure 19–7: "100 Leading National Advertisers," *Advertising Age*

(September 28, 1998), p. 54; p. 509, Courtesy the Direct Marketing Association; p. 510, ©Mitsubishi Motors Corporation: agency: Direct Partners/Los Angeles; photographers: ©Vincent Dente, ©Bob Stevens, and ©Tim Baur; p. 515, Courtesy of Items International, Inc.

CHAPTER 20

p. 516 (top), Courtesy Yahoo!; p. 516 (bottom), Courtesy ESPN Internet Ventures, Inc.; p. 518 (left), Courtesy Iridium North America; agency: Ammirati Puris Lintas; p. 518 (center), Courtesy banrnesandnoble.com; p. 518 (right), Courtesy of Godiva Chocolatier; p. 519, Courtesy of DDB Needham Worldwide and The Dial Corporation; p. 520 (left), Courtesy of Miller Brewing Company; p. 520 (right), Courtesy of Florida Department of Citrus; p. 521, Figure 20–1 (top photo), Courtesy of Master Lock Company and (bottom photo), Courtesy hotjobs.com; p. 524, Copyright, Nissan 1997; Nissan, Frontier, and the Nissan logo are registered trademarks of Nissan; p. 525, Courtesy American Express; p. 526, "National Ad Spending by Media," *Advertising Age* (September 28, 1998), p. 55.; p. 528 (top), Courtesy of Group W. Satellite Communications; p. 528 (bottom), Courtesy of Ford Motor Company; p. 529 (top), By Fallon McElligott/Rolling Stone Magazine. By Straight Arrow Publishers Company, L.P. All Rights Reserved. Reprinted by Permission; p. 529 (bottom), People Magazine Syndication; p. 531, Otto Greule/Allsport; p. 534, Courtesy Ford Motor Company; p. 537 (left), Courtesy Sara Lee Corporation; p. 537 (right), Courtesy Elizabeth Arden; photographer: Jonathan Kanto; p. 538, Courtesy of GM Credit Card Operations; p. 539, Ray Marklin; p. 540,

Courtesy News America Marketing; p. 542, NBC Photo by Margaret Norton, Courtesy of "The Tonight Show With Jay Leno."; p. 546 (left), ©1999 Time, Inc.; photo by Wide World Photo; p. 546 (right), ©1999 Time, Inc.; photo by Sports Illustrated Picture Sales.

CHAPTER 21

p. 548, ©Arnold Adler; p. 551, ©John Madere; p. 553, ©Jay Brousseau; p. 555, Courtesy Xerox Corporation; p. 557, Courtesy ZD Events; p. 558, CB Productions/The Stock Market; p. 560, Ken Ross/FPG International; p. 567, Courtesy UTNE Reader; p. 569, Courtesy of Mary Kay; p. 570, Courtesy of Toshiba America Medical Systems and Interactive Media; p. 571, Jose Pelaez/The Stock Market; p. 574, Courtesy Reebok International Ltd.

CHAPTER 22

p. 578, Michael J. Hruby; p. 580, Michael J. Hruby; p. 586, Figure 22–6: Reprinted with permission from The Free Press, a division of Simon & Schuster, from Competitive Advantage: Creating and Sustaining Superior Performance by Michael E. Porter. Copyright ©1985 by Michael E. Porter; p. 587 (left), Courtesy Delphi Automotive Systems; p. 587 (right), Courtesy Volkswagen of America, Inc. and Arnold Communications, Inc.; p. 592, Courtesy of Papa John's International; p. 593, Figure 22–10: Reprinted by permission of Harvard Business Review. An exhibit from "Making Your Marketing Strategy Work," by Thomas V. Bonoma, March–April 1984. Copyright ©1984 by the President and Fellows of Harvard

College, all rights reserved; p. 594, Courtesy Swatch Group (U.S.) Inc.; p. 596, Courtesy of Lockheed Advanced Development Company; p. 597, Courtesy of Saturn Corporation; p. 598, Figure 22–12: Figure from *An Introduction to Contemporary Business,* Fourth Edition by William Rudelius and W. Bruce Erickson, copyright ©1985 by Harcourt Brace & Co., reproduced by permission of the publisher; p. 599, Figure 22–13: Figure from *An Introduction to Contemporary Business,* Fourth Edition by William Rudelius and W. Bruce Erickson, copyright ©1985 by Harcourt Brace & Co., reproduced by permission of the publisher; p. 600, Sharon Hoogstraten.

APPENDIX C

p. 610, Paul Elledge; p. 611, Courtesy AT&T; p. 613, Courtesy of Dell Computer Corporation; p. 616, Courtesy Career Mosaic; p. 615, Reprinted from JobWeb (www.jobweb.org), with permission of the National Association of Colleges and Employers, copyright holder; p. 620, Thatch cartoon by Jeff Shesol/Reprinted with permission of Vintage books; p. 622, Julie Houck/Tony Stone Images.

APPENDIX D

p. 626, Courtesy of Kingpin Snowboarding; p. 638, Courtesy of AM General Corporation; p. 641, Courtesy of Golden Valley; p. 644, Courtesy of Easy Embers; p. 645, Exhibit 1: Barbecue Industry Association, *Statistical Abstract of the United States,* Alma Products, Inc.; p. 647, Courtesy of United Airlines; p. 649, Courtesy of Nordstrom.

NAME INDEX

COMPANY/PRODUCT INDEX

SUBJECT INDEX

THE PLAYING FIELD IS NOW LEVEL.

"The Equalizer." "The A-Maker." "The Turbo Tutorial." Call it what you will. Just be sure to use this CD-ROM as you read the textbook. A digital version of the text and video clips bring greater mastery of key concepts. And Concept Checks and Practice Quizzes ensure that you remember what you've read. In short, with this CD-ROM you don't just study for exams, you eat them for breakfast.

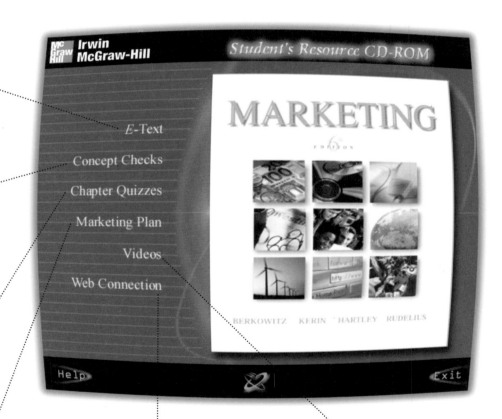

E-Text
With the whole textbook on the CD-ROM (graphics and all) reviewing for a test becomes an exercise in simplicity.

Concept Checks
These "checkpoints" test your understanding of a portion of the chapter before continuing to the next section.

Chapter Quizzes
These multiple-choice questions are great for review. Answer correctly, you move on. Answer incorrectly and you're referred to pages in the text where you need further review.

Marketing Plan
Build a marketing plan by answering a series of narrated questions. The narrator explains the different parts of the marketing plan and its significance. Need help? A click of the mouse lets you see and hear how an actual company developed its marketing strategy.

Web Connection
The textbook is peppered with examples of actual businesses. Click on their Web site address to learn more about the company and see examples of their marketing efforts.

Videos
Sometimes the best way to understand concepts is to see them in action. Click on a video clip to see how companies like BMW and AOL apply concepts introduced in the text.